ANNOTATED TEACHER'S EDITION

Western World

An Introduction to World Studies

HOLT, RINEHART AND WINSTON
A Harcourt Education Company
Orlando • Austin • New York • San Diego • Toronto • London

THE AUTHORS

Prof. David M. Helgren is Director of the Center for Geographic Education at San Jose State University in California, where he is also Chair of the Department of Geography. Prof. Helgren received his Ph.D. in geography from the University of Chicago. He is the coauthor of several geography textbooks and has written many articles on the geography of Africa. Awards from the National Geographic Society, the National Science Foundation, and the L. S. B. Leakey Foundation have supported his many field research projects. Prof. Helgren is a former president of the California Geographical Society and a founder of the Northern California Geographic Alliance.

Prof. Robert J. Sager is Chair of Earth Sciences at Pierce College in Lakewood, Washington. Prof. Sager received his B.S. in geology and geography and M.S. in geography from the University of Wisconsin and holds a J.D. in international law from Western State University College of Law. He is the coauthor of several geography and earth science textbooks and has written many articles and educational media programs on the geography of the Pacific. Prof. Sager has received several National Science Foundation study grants and has twice been a recipient of the University of Texas NISOD National Teaching Excellence Award. He is a founding member of the Southern California Geographic Alliance and former president of the Association of Washington Geographers.

Prof. Alison S. Brooks is Professor of Anthropology at George Washington University and a Research Associate in Anthropology at the Smithsonian Institution. She received her A.B., M.A., and Ph.D. in Anthropology from Harvard University. Since 1964, she has carried out ethnological and archaeological research in Africa, Europe, and Asia and is the author of more than 300 scholarly and popular publications. She has served as a consultant to Smithsonian exhibits and to National Geographic, Public Broadcasting, the Discovery Channel, and other public media. In addition, she is a founder and editor of *Anthro Notes: The National Museum of Natural History Bulletin for Teachers* and has received numerous grants and awards to develop and lead in-service training institutes for teachers in grades 5–12. She served as the American Anthropological Association's representative to the NCSS task force on developing Scope and Sequence guidelines for Social Studies Education in grade K–12.

While the details of the young people's stories in the chapter openers are real, their identities have been changed to protect their privacy.

Cover and Title Page Photo Credits: (child image) AlaskaStock Images; (bkgd) Image Copyright © 2003 PhotoDisc, Inc./HRW

Copyright © 2005 by Holt, Rinehart and Winston

All rights reserved. No part of this publication may be reproduced or transmitted in any form or by any means, electronic or mechanical, including photocopy, recording, or any information storage and retrieval system, without permission in writing from the publisher.

Requests for permission to make copies of any part of the work should be mailed to the following address: Permissions Department, Holt, Rinehart and Winston, 10801 N. MoPac Expressway, Building 3, Austin, Texas 78759.

For acknowledgments, see page R38, which is an extension of the copyright page.

CNN is a registered trademark and **CNN STUDENT NEWS** is a trademark of Cable News Network LP, LLLP, a Time Warner Company.

Printed in the United States of America

ISBN 0-03-037647-5

2 3 4 5 6 7 8 9 032 07 06 05 04

CONTENT REVIEWERS

Robin Datel
*Instructor in Geography
California State University,
Sacramento*

David Dickason
*Professor of Geography
Western Michigan University*

Dennis Dingemans
*Professor of Geography
University of California, Davis*

Robert Gabler
*Professor of Geography
Western Illinois University*

Jeffrey Gritzner
*Professor of Geography
University of Montana*

W. A. Douglas Jackson
*Professor of Geography, Emeritus
University of Washington*

Robert B. Kent
*Professor of Geography
and Planning
University of Akron*

Kwadwo Konadu-Agyemang
*Professor of Geography
and Planning
University of Akron*

Nancy Lewis
*Professor of Geography
University of Hawaii*

Bill Takizawa
*Professor of Geography
San Jose State University*

EDUCATIONAL REVIEWERS

Patricia Britt
*Durant Middle School
Durant, Oklahoma*

Marcia Caldwell
*Lamar Middle School
Austin, Texas*

Marcia Clevenger
*Roosevelt Junior High School
Charleston, West Virginia*

James Corley
*Durant Middle School
Durant, Oklahoma*

Maureen Dempsey
*Spring Creek Middle School
Spring Creek, Nevada*

Jean Eldredge
*Teague Middle School
Altamonte, Florida*

Cindy Herring
*Old Town Elementary School
Round Rock, Texas*

Lois Jordan
*Pearl/Cohn Comprehensive
High School
Nashville, Tennessee*

Kay A. Knowles
*Montross Middle School
Montross, Virginia*

Wendy Mason
*Corbett Junior High School
Schertz, Texas*

Rebecca Minnear
*Burkholder Middle School
Las Vegas, Nevada*

Jane Palmer
*District Supervisor for
Social Studies
Sanford, Florida*

Sandra Rojas
*Adams City Middle School
Commerce City, Colorado*

JoAnn Sadler
*Curriculum Supervisor
Buffalo City Schools
Buffalo, New York*

Celeste Smith
*Crockett High School
Austin, Texas*

Frank Thomas
*Crockett High School
Austin, Texas*

Susan Walker
*Beaufort County School District
Beaufort, South Carolina*

Field Test Teachers

Ricky A. Blackman
*Rawlinson Road Middle School
Rock Hill, South Carolina*

Lisa Klien
*Daniels Middle School
Raleigh, North Carolina*

Deborah D. Larry
*Garland V. Stewart Middle School
Tampa, Florida*

Linda P. Moore
*Cramerton Middle School
Cramerton, North Carolina*

Earl F. Sease
*Portage Area School District
Portage, Pennsylvania*

Christi Sherrill
*Grier Middle School
Gastonia, North Carolina*

John W. Watkins, Jr.
*Clark Middle School
East St. Louis, Illinois*

It's All About

INTERVIEWS with young people from around the world begin each chapter, making real world peer connections for your students. Plus students can read the interviews in their entirety on our Web site.

The first step to success in the social studies classroom is capturing and sustaining the interest of your students. **HOLT PEOPLE, PLACES, AND CHANGE** is designed to be open and friendly to all students, so that they develop an enthusiasm for learning and an appreciation for their world.

HOLT PEOPLE, PLACES, AND CHANGE offers
- Built-in Reading Support
- Technology with Instructional Value
- Standardized Testing Strategies and Skill Building
- The Best Teacher's Management System in the Industry

RELEVANCE

CNNStudentNews.com is designed to give students in grades 6–12 access to the news about people, places, and environments around the globe while offering "real-world" articles, career and college resources, and online activities.

In-Text Features that Put Geography into Perspective

- Case Study
- Connecting to Art
- Connecting to History
- Connecting to Literature
- Connecting to Math
- Connecting to Science
- Connecting to Technology
- Daily Life
- Focus on Culture
- Focus on Economy
- Focus on Environment
- Focus on Government
- Focus on Regions
- Geo Skills
- Hands On Geography
- Our Amazing Planet
- Why It Matters

M1

Reading for

At Holt, we don't assume that students know how or have any desire to make sense of what they're reading, and we develop our programs based on that assumption. We don't just ask students questions about content, we give them strategies to get to that content. Through design, research, and the help of experts like Dr. Judith Irvin, we make sure students' reading needs are covered with our programs.

Helping Students Make Sense of What They're Reading

An Essay by Dr. Judith Irvin, Ph.D.

Who in middle and high schools helps students become more successful at reading and writing informational text? When I ask this question of a school faculty, the Language Arts/English teachers point to the social studies and science teachers because they are the ones with this type of textbook. The social studies and science teachers point to the Language Arts/English teachers because they are the ones that "do" words.

I advocate teachers taking an active role in helping students learn how to use text structure and context to understand what they read. Through consistent and systematic instruction that includes modeling of effective reading behavior, teachers can assist students in becoming better readers while at the same time helping them learn more content material.

The strategies in this book are designed to assist students with getting started, maintaining focus with reading, and organizing information for later retrieval. They engage students in learning material, provide the vehicle for them to organize and reorganize concepts, and extend their understanding through writing.

When teachers combine the teaching of reading and the teaching of content together into meaningful, systematic, and corrected instruction, students can apply what they have learned to understanding increasingly more difficult and complex texts as they progress through the school years.

READING STRATEGIES FOR THE SOCIAL STUDIES CLASSROOM

by Dr. Judith Irvin, Ph.D., Reading Education

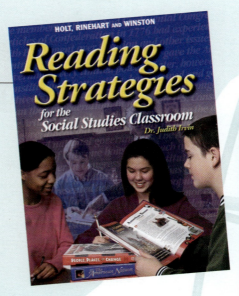

Additional Reading Support

- Graphic Organizer Activities
- Guided Reading Strategies
- Main Idea Activities for English Language Learners and Special-Needs Students
- Audio CD Program

MEANING

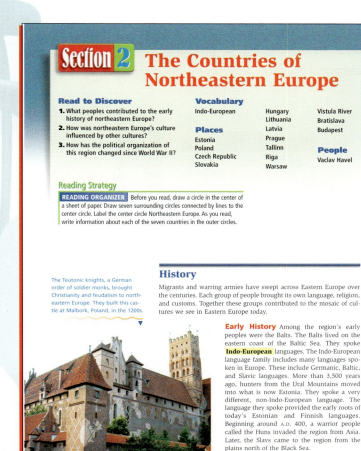

Successful Readers must have:

1 AN ENGAGING NARRATIVE

Great care is taken in selecting and presenting content in a way that students will find motivating and engaging. Features such as **Youth Interviews** help students connect their own lives to the lives and cultures of other students around the world.

2 TIPS ON READING THE TEXT—THE WHY AND HOW

Read to Discover questions give students insight into the content they will cover in the coming section. **Reading Strategies** provide various methods, including **FoldNotes**, for approching new text.

3 VOCABULARY DEFINED IN CONTEXT

Important new terms are identified at the beginning of every section and are defined in context so students will develop an understanding of the contextual meaning of all terms.

4 STRATEGIES FOR UNDERSTANDING WHAT THEY READ

Through the design of the text, students are led through the content using built-in reading strategies. For example, **Reading Checks** in the text are used as a comprehension tool. The checks remind students to stop and engage with what they have read, functioning as a "Tutor in the Text."

M3

Get Your Students

Your students love activities that get them involved with the content. That's why Holt offers active-learning resources that link directly to program content and provide a multitude of different lessons for large-group, small-group, and individual projects.

CREATIVE TEACHING STRATEGIES

These innovative teaching strategies can be utilized at various points in your lesson. The wide range of cooperative-learning activities, including learning stations and simulations, motivate your students and help them develop critical-thinking skills.

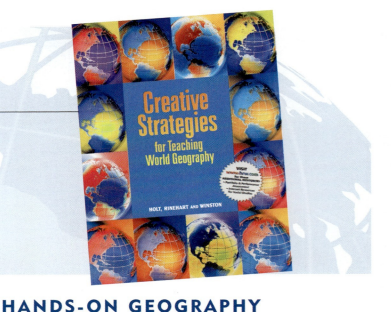

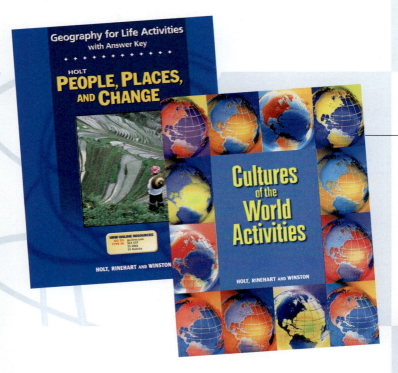

HANDS-ON GEOGRAPHY ACTIVITIES

From hands-on study of world cultures to hands-on practice with skill building, the following booklets cover it all. *Cultures of the World Activities* is a stand-alone booklet containing recipes, games, and craft activities. *Geography for Life Activities with Answer Key* contains a a problem-solving activity for each chapter, reflecting the skills and knowledge called for in the **National Geography Standards.**

GEOGRAPHY APPLICATIONS

For use in geography as well as earth science courses, here are two stand-alone booklets that organize applications with special relevance. *Environmental and Global Issues Activities* contains activities related to current environmental and global issues. *Lab Activities for Geography and Earth Science* contains laboratory activities related to physical geography and earth science.

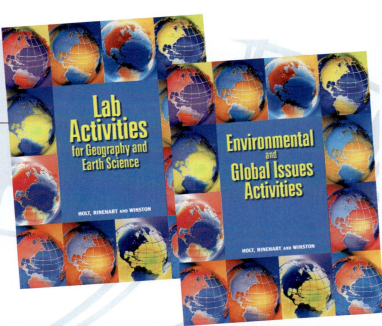

Involved in Learning

Resources for Active Lessons

- Block Scheduling Handbook
- Creative Strategies for Teaching World Geography
- Critical Thinking Activities
- Cultures of the World Activities
- Environmental and Global Issues Activities
- Geography and Cultures Visual Resources with Teaching Activities
- Geography for Life Activities
- Interdisciplinary Activities for the Middle Grades
- Lab Activities for Geography and Earth Science
- Map Activities
- Regions of the World Map Posters
- World and Regional Outline Maps
- World History and Geography Document-Based Questions Activities

Joining Forces

CNN® Presents

Geography: Yesterday and Today
- Mapping Change
- Birth of an Island
- Global Warming
- Farming with Saltwater
- World Population—Hitting Six Billion
- What's Cooking for the Holidays?
- Do Aspen Trees Hold the Key?
- Tradition and Change—The James Bay Project
- Baseball, Mexican Style
- Preserving Heritage
- The Power of Poetry
- Destination Brazil
- Harnessing Nature
- The Fishing Life
- Europe's Immigration Challenge
- The Mountain People of Yo
- Castles for Sale
- Lake Baykal
- Cossacks Return to Power
- Dateline Kazakhstan
- Jordan's Water Crisis
- Kuwait—Restoring the Environment
- Cairo—Selling the Suburbs
- The Women of Nigeria
- The Nairobi National Park
- The Medicine Tree
- Mining in South Africa the Traditional Way
- The Yangtze (Chang) River Dam
- The Tokyo Grave Crisis
- The Highway to Prosperity
- The Borobudur Temple of Indonesia
- Indian Pop Music
- The Tengboche Monastery
- The Great Barrier Reef
- Dateline Antarctica

World Cultures: Yesterday and Today
- The Kennewick Man
- Restoring the Sphinx
- The Sacred Ganges
- Treasures from China
- Crete: Past and Present
- The Ancient Theaters of Epidaurus
- In the Shadow of Mt. Vesuvius
- The Silk Road
- Pilgrimage to Mecca
- Mother Teresa: A Devoted Life
- The Bells of Agnone
- Buddhism in Mongolia
- The Inca's Frozen Past
- Da Vinci for Sale
- Worlds Meet in the Americas
- Restoring St. Petersburg
- The New Globe Theater
- A Key to the Bastille
- Hong Kong: Past and Present
- Riverboats Return
- Endangered Edison
- Honoring Women's Suffrage
- Fabergé: The Czar's Jeweler
- The Farms of Zimbabwe
- Recovering Russia's Royalty
- The Killer Flu of 1918
- The Great Depression
- Japan's Royal Family
- Rosie the Riveter
- NATO at 50
- North Korea Turns 50
- A Kenyan Reggae Festival
- Dateline Iraq
- Mexico's Jewish Community
- The History of Haiti
- The Walls That Divide
- Mission to Mars

to Enrich Your Classroom

CNNStudentNews.com

At **CNNStudentNews.com**, students will love exploring news stories written by experienced journalists as well as student bureau reporters. Stories link to homework help and lesson plans.

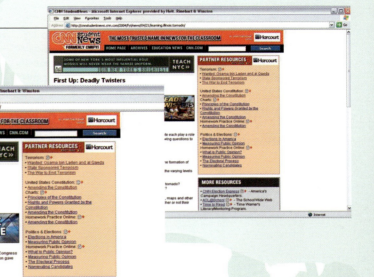

CNN PRESENTS VIDEO LIBRARY

The **CNN PRESENTS** video collection tackles the issue of making content relevant to students head on. Real-world news stories enable students to see the connections between classroom curriculum and today's issues and events around the nation and the world.

CNN PRESENTS...

- **America: Yesterday and Today, Beginnings to 1914**
- **America: Yesterday and Today, 1850 to Present**
- **America: Yesterday and Today, Modern Times**
- **Geography: Yesterday and Today**
- **World Cultures: Yesterday and Today**
- **American Government**
- **Economics**
- **September 11, 2001, Part One**
- **September 11, 2001, Part Two**

Holt is proud to team up with **CNN/TURNER LEARNING®** to provide you and your students with exceptional current and historical news videos and online resources that add depth and relevance to your daily instruction. This information collection takes your classroom to the far corners of the globe without students ever leaving their desks!

Your Multitalented Classroom

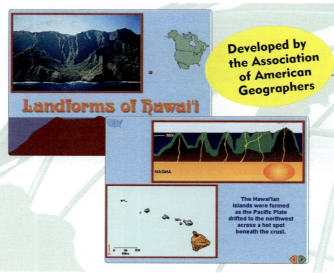

Developed by the Association of American Geographers

ACTIVITIES AND READINGS IN THE GEOGRAPHY OF THE WORLD

Integrate real geography into the topic you're studying with **Activities and Readings in the Geography of the World (ARGWorld).** This CD-ROM features world geography case studies with a multitude of activities that focus around geographical themes, population geography, economic geography, political geography, and environmental issues. Case studies will help teachers address the National Geography Standards.

HOLT RESEARCHER ONLINE: WORLD HISTORY AND CULTURES

New and online—students can access this outstanding research tool at www.hrw.com. A fully searchable database provides biographies, nation profiles and statistics, a glossary, and powerful graphic capabilities.

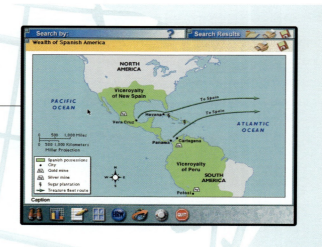

GLOBAL SKILL BUILDER CD-ROM

This CD-ROM is a comprehensive program containing interactive lessons that motivate your students to strengthen their map, graph, and computer skills. A handy **User's Guide and Teacher's Manual** provides student project sheets for each lesson along with optional suggestions for using the Internet to help complete the activity.

needs Multimedia Tools

THE WORLD TODAY VIDEODISC PROGRAM

This unique resource offers a stimulating outlook on world geography by showing your students the different ways geographers organize the world, and challenging them to contemplate and discuss significant world issues. Compelling video segments with in-depth content cover contemporary culture in every major world region.

PEOPLE, PLACES, AND CHANGE AUDIO CD PROGRAM

The **Audio CD Program** provides in-depth audio section summaries and self-check activity sheets to help those students who respond to auditory learning. Available in English and Spanish.

Audio CD Program

Other Multimedia Products

- CNN Presents Geography: Yesterday and Today
- CNN Presents World Cultures: Yesterday and Today
- Holt Researcher Online: World History and Cultures

Technology with

go.hrw.com FOR TEACHERS

Throughout the *Annotated Teacher's Edition*, you'll find **Internet Connect** boxes that take you to specific chapter activities, links, current events, and more that correlate directly to the section you are teaching. Through **go.hrw.com** you'll find a wealth of teaching resources at your fingertips for fun, interactive lessons.

- DIRECT LAUNCH TO CHAPTER ACTIVITIES
- GUIDED ONLINE ACTIVITIES
- LINKS FOR EVERY SECTION
- MAPS AND CHARTS
- INTERACTIVE PRACTICE AND REVIEW
- RUBRICS FOR SUBJECTIVE GRADING
- UP-TO-DATE INFORMATION
- CLASSROOM PRESENTATION SUPPORT
- PRACTICE FOR READING SUCCESS
- WEB RESOURCES FOR CURRENT ISSUES

Instructional Value

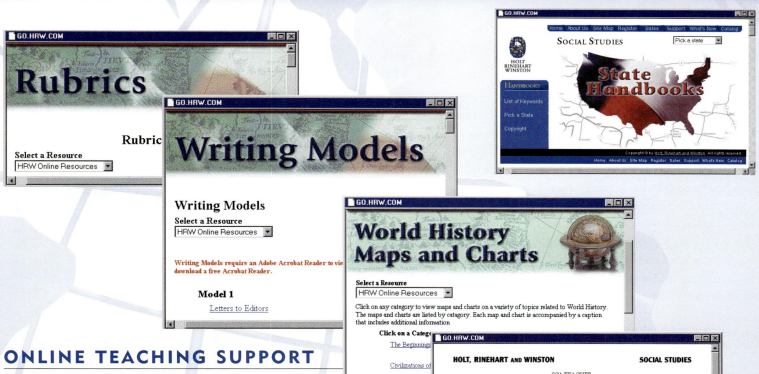

ONLINE TEACHING SUPPORT

Teacher materials on **go.hrw.com** offer you multiple resources for keeping content current. From **World History Maps and Charts** to **State Handbooks,** we've got it all.

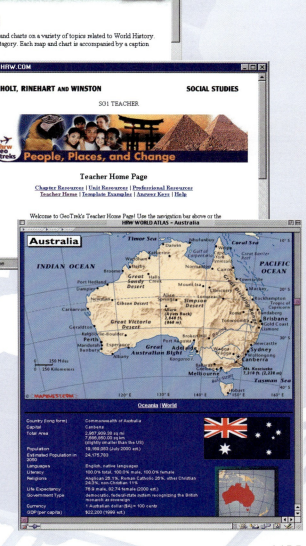

CLASSROOM PRESENTATION SUPPORT

Lecture notes and animated graphic organizers help add visual support to your classroom presentations.

M11

Technology that

go.hrw.com FOR STUDENTS

Your students can access interactive activities, homework help, up-to-date maps, and more when they visit **go.hrw.com** and type in the keywords they find in their text.

ONLINE WORLD TRAVEL

When you log on to **go.hrw.com**, you and your students gain passage to **GeoTreks**—a site with guided Internet activities that integrate program content, spark imaginations, and promote online research skills. You'll find:

- **Interactive templates** for creating newspapers, postcards, travel brochures, guided research reports, and more
- **GeoMaps**—Interactive satellite maps of the world's regions for content review
- **Drag-and-drop exercises** to review chapter content in short, fun activities
- **Chapter Web Links** for prescreened, age-appropriate Web sites and current events

HOMEWORK PRACTICE

This helpful tool allows students to practice and review content by chapter anywhere there is a computer.

HRW ONLINE ATLAS AND HISTORICAL MAPS

The helpful online atlas contains over 300 well-rendered and clearly labeled country and state maps. Available in English and Spanish, these maps are continually updated so you can rest assured that you and your students have the latest and most accurate geographical content.

Online historical maps provide fascinating visual "snapshots" of the past. Students will relish the chance to explore medieval European trade routes, explorers' routes, ancient African kingdoms, and more.

M12

Delivers Content

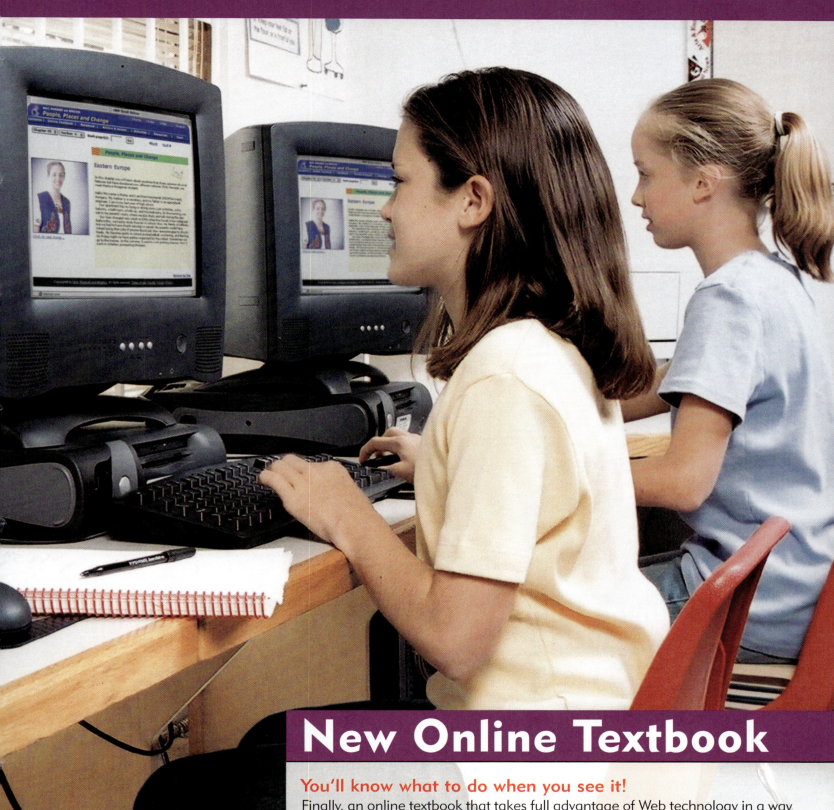

New Online Textbook

You'll know what to do when you see it!
Finally, an online textbook that takes full advantage of Web technology in a way that makes sense—***HOLT PEOPLE, PLACES, AND CHANGE ONLINE EDITION.***

- **Entire student edition online, formatted to match printed text**
- **User-friendly navigation**
- **Hot links to interactive activities, practice, and assessment**
- **Student Notebook for online responses**

Unique Teacher's

In-Text Chapter Planning

TEACHER TO TEACHER

These strategies are offered in the columns of your *Annotated Teacher's Edition* and provide you with valuable, classroom-tested ideas and activities that have been developed and successfully applied by your peers.

OBJECTIVE-BASED LESSON CYCLE

With lively activities and presentation strategies such as **Bellringer, Building Vocabulary,** and **Graphic Organizers,** your step-by-step lesson cycle makes planning your lessons easy and productive.

Side-Column Annotations that Spark Curiosity

- Across the Curriculum: Art
- Across the Curriculum: History
- Across the Curriculum: Literature
- Across the Curriculum: Math
- Across the Curriculum: Science
- Across the Curriculum: Technology
- Cooperative Learning
- Cultural Kaleidoscope
- Daily Life
- Eye on Earth
- Geography sidelight
- Global Perspectives
- Historical Geography
- Linking Past to Present
- National Geography Standards
- People in the Profile
- Using Illustrations

M14

Management System

Everything you need is on one disc!

ONE-STOP PLANNER® CD–ROM WITH TEST GENERATOR

Holt brings you the most user-friendly management system in the industry with the **One-Stop Planner CD–ROM with Test Generator.** Plan and manage your lessons from this single disc containing all the teaching resources for **Holt People, Places, and Change,** valuable planning and assessment tools, and more.

- **Editable lesson plans**
- **Classroom Lecture Notes and Animated Graphic Organizers**
- **Easy-to-use test generator**
- **Previews of all teaching and video resources**
- **Easy printing feature**
- **Direct launch to go.hrw.com**

BLOCK SCHEDULING HANDBOOK

This is more than a pacing guide—it provides daily lesson plans that suggest practical ways to cover more than one textbook section in an extended class period and ways to make interdisciplinary connections.

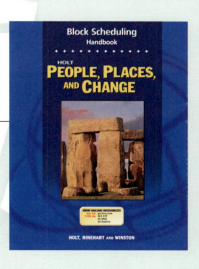

PRESENTATIONS THAT BENEFIT LEARNING

Classroom presentations and lecture notes can be accessed with ease when you use Holt's **Presentation** tool found on the **One-Stop Planner CD–ROM**. This resource helps you spice up your presentations and gives you ideas to build on. You'll find Microsoft® PowerPoint® presentations that include lecture notes and animated graphic organizers for each chapter and section of your text.

M15

Assessment for

INTERACTIVE PRACTICE ACTIVITIES FOR EACH SECTION

CRITICAL-THINKING REINFORCEMENT

Chapter 21 Review and Practice

Define and Identify
Identify each of the following:
1. nature reserves
2. Mongols
3. serfs
4. Cossacks
5. soviet
6. homogeneous
7. agrarian

Review the Main Ideas
8. Where are this region's highest and lowest points?
9. What part of Ukraine has a Mediterranean climate?
10. What is Ukraine's greatest natural resource?
11. How did Vikings and Byzantine missionaries affect Ukraine?
12. Why were Ukraine and Belarus so valuable to the Soviet Union?
13. How did Soviet rule affect Ukraine and Belarus?
14. What happened at Chernobyl in 1986? How did this event affect Belarus?
15. What groups of people have ruled the Caucasus region?
16. What happened to the Armenians during World War I?
17. What happened in Georgia in 2003?
18. What natural disaster occured in Armenia in 1988?
19. What kind of society does Azerbaijan have?
20. What is Azerbaijan's main industry?

Think Critically
21. **Drawing Inferences and Conclusions** How might ethnic diversity affect relations among the countries in this chapter?
22. **Summarizing** What is the history of the serfs in Ukraine and Belarus?
23. **Analyzing Information** Of the countries covered in this chapter, which do you think was the most important to the former Soviet Union? Why do you think this was so?
24. **Summarizing** Why did the countries of the Caucasus develop so differently from Russia, Ukraine, and Belarus?
25. **Finding the Main Idea** Why are the economies of each of the Caucasus countries so different from one another?

Map Activity
26. On a separate sheet of paper, match the letters on the map with their correct labels.
    - Caucasus Mountains
    - Pripyat Marshes
    - Carpathian Mountains
    - Crimean Peninsula
    - Mount Elbrus
    - Donets Basin
    - Chernobyl

492 • Chapter 21

THE SUPERIOR TEST GENERATOR THAT REALLY WORKS!

GEOGRAPHY SKILLS PRACTICE

M16

Every Student

ACCESS ONLINE RUBRICS FOR GRADING PROJECTS AND PORTFOLIO ASSIGNMENTS

WORLD HISTORY AND GEOGRAPHY DOCUMENT-BASED QUESTIONS ACTIVITIES

This resource provides a wide variety of primary sources and thought-provoking questions to help students develop intelligent, well-formed opinions. Important historical and geographical themes are grouped together, allowing for scaffolded instruction.

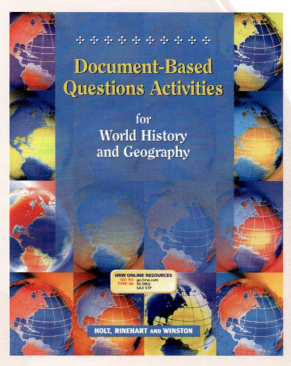

Writing Activity

ose one of the countries covered in this chapter to arch. Write a report about your chosen country's strug- to establish stability since 1991. Include information ut the country's government and economic reforms. cribe the social, political, and economic problems the ntry has faced. Be sure to use standard grammar, sen- e structure, spelling, and punctuation.

internet connect

Internet Activity: go.hrw.com
KEYWORD: SJ5 G21

Choose a topic to explore about Ukraine, Belarus, and the Caucasus.
- Trek through the Caucasus Mountains.
- Design Ukrainian Easter eggs.
- Investigate the Chernobyl disaster.

Social Studies Skills Practice

Interpreting Maps

y the following map of Azerbaijan. Then answer the stions.

rce: Central Intelligence Agency, *The World Factbook 2003*

How may Baku's location have affected the city's economic development?

Note the part of Azerbaijan named Naxçivan. How is its connection to the rest of the country indicated?

How may the location of Naxçivan lead to political problems?

Compare this map to the physical-political map at the beginning of the chapter. What is unusual about the area labeled Kur-Araz Ovaligi?

Analyzing Primary Sources

Read the following passage from *Chernobyl Legacy*, by Paul Fusco. Then answer the questions.

"The Chernobyl disaster revealed that the world community was not ready to face global disasters. Today, due to the grievous [painful] experience gained from Chernobyl, people are better prepared to combat possible catastrophes protecting life and health of themselves and those of their children. Chernobyl resulted in a worldwide realization of the fact that the Earth is our common home . . . having become so fragile in the hands of man who harnessed atomic power."

1. According to the passage, what truth did the disaster reveal?
2. What does the author think has been gained from the Chernobyl disaster?
3. Do you think the author is hopeful about the future? Why or why not?
4. In the last sentence, what does the word *fragile* mean?

Ukraine, Belarus, and the Caucasus • 493

SOCIAL STUDIES SKILLS REVIEW

Additional Print and Technology Assessment Resources

- **Daily Quizzes**
- **Chapter Tutorials for Students, Parents, Mentors, and Peers**
- **Chapter and Unit Tests**
- **Chapter and Unit Tests for English Language Learners and Special-Needs Students**
- **Alternative Assessment Handbook**
- **Test Generator (located on the One-Stop Planner)**

M17

HOLT
PEOPLE, PLACES, AND CHANGE
Western World

Atlas **A1**
Geography and Map Skills Handbook **S1**

- Mapping the Earth
- Mapmaking
- Map Essentials
- Working with Maps
- Using Graphs, Diagrams, Charts, and Tables
- Reading a Time-Zone Map
- Geographic Dictionary

UNIT 1 — An Introduction to World Geography and Cultures 1

Notes from the Field

PLANNING GUIDE	1A
1 A Geographer's World	**2**
1 Developing a Geographic Eye	3
2 Themes and Essential Elements of Geography	6
3 Being a Geographer	11
Connecting to Technology: Computer Mapping	12
Case Study: How Geographers Track Hurricanes	14
PLANNING GUIDE	17A
2 Planet Earth	**18**
1 The Land	19
Reading a Topographic Map	23
2 Water and Air	25
3 Climate, Weather, and Vegetation	32
4 Natural Resources	38

PLANNING GUIDE **45A**

3 The World's People **46**
  1 What is Culture? 47
  2 Economics and Population 53
  3 Global Connections 60

Focus on Regions: What Is a Region? 66
Building Skills for Life: Drawing Mental Maps 68
Hands On Geography: Making a Map from Memory 69

UNIT 2 United States and Canada 70
Notes from the Field

Unit 2 Atlas: The World in Spatial Terms 72
Fast Facts: The United States and Canada 78

PLANNING GUIDE **81A**

4 The Geography and History of the United States **80**
  1 Physical Geography 81
  2 Early Peoples of North America 86
  3 From Colonies to an Independent Country 90
  4 The United States Becomes a World Power 96
    Connecting to Art: Art and Memories 104

Contents • v

	PLANNING GUIDE	**107A**
5	**The Regions of the United States**	**108**
	1 The Northeast	109
	2 The South	114
	Focus on Culture: Tasting Local Culture	116
	3 The Midwest	118
	Connecting to Technology: The Great Lakes and the St. Lawrence Seaway	120
	4 The Interior West	122
	5 The Pacific States	127
	PLANNING GUIDE	**133A**
6	**Canada**	**134**
	1 Physical Geography	135
	2 History and Culture	138
	3 Canada Today	143
	Connecting to Literature: Anne of Green Gables	145

Could You Survive? The Canadian Arctic 150

Building Skills for Life: Analyzing Changing Landscapes 152

Hands On Geography: Urban Growth in Las Vegas, Nevada 153

UNIT 3 Middle and South America 154

Notes from the Field

Unit 3 Atlas: The World in Spatial Terms 156

Fast Facts: Middle and South America 162

PLANNING GUIDE 165A

7 History of Middle and South America 166
  1 The Maya and Aztec 167
     History Close-Up: Aztec Daily Life 172
  2 The Inca 174
     Connecting to History: Inca Mummies 177
  3 Spanish Colonies and Independence 180

PLANNING GUIDE	185A
8 Mexico	**186**
1 Physical Geography	187
2 History and Culture	191
Connecting to History: Tenochtitlán	193
Case Study: Maquiladoras *along the U.S.-Mexico Border*	196
3 Mexico Today	198

PLANNING GUIDE	203A
9 Central America and the Caribbean Islands	**204**
1 Physical Geography	205
2 Central America	208
Connecting to Math: Maya Calendar	210
3 The Caribbean Islands	213
Focus on Culture: Ice Cream Houses of Curaçao	216

PLANNING GUIDE	219A
10 Caribbean South America	**220**
1 Physical Geography	221
2 Colombia	224
Connecting to Science: Fighting Malaria	226
3 Venezuela	228
4 The Guianas	231

	PLANNING GUIDE **235A**
11	**Atlantic South America** **236**
	1 Physical Geography 237
	2 Brazil 241
	3 Argentina 245
	Connecting to Literature: *The Gaucho Martín Fierro* 247
	4 Uruguay and Paraguay 249

	PLANNING GUIDE **253A**
12	**Pacific South America** **254**
	1 Physical Geography 255
	2 History and Culture 259
	Connecting to Technology: Inca Roads 261
	3 Pacific South America Today 264

Could You Survive? *The Amazon* 270

Building Skills for Life: Understanding Migration Patterns 272

Hands On Geography: Looking at Migration 273

UNIT 4 Europe ... 274

Notes from the Field

Unit 4 Atlas: The World in Spatial Terms ... 276

Fast Facts: Europe ... 282

PLANNING GUIDE ... 285A

13 The Early History of Europe ... 286

1. Early Greek Civilizations ... 287
   Focus on Culture: Greek Myths ... 289
2. The Glory of Greece ... 292
   Connecting to Literature: History of the Peloponnesian War ... 294
3. The Roman Republic ... 297
   History Close-Up: The Roman Forum ... 299
4. The Roman Empire ... 302
   Connecting to Technology: The Roman Arch ... 306
5. The Middle Ages ... 308

PLANNING GUIDE ... 315A

14 Europe in Transition ... 316

1. The Renaissance and Reformation ... 317
   Connecting to Technology: The Printing Press ... 319
2. Exploration and Conquest ... 323
3. Enlightenment and Revolution ... 330
4. Industrial Revolution and Reform ... 337

	PLANNING GUIDE	**345A**
15	**Modern Europe**	**346**
	1 World War I	347
	2 The Great Depression and the Rise of Dictators	352
	3 World War II	356
	4 Europe Since 1945	361
	PLANNING GUIDE	**367A**
16	**Southern Europe**	**368**
	1 Physical Geography	369
	2 Greece	372
	Connecting to Math: Greek Math and Science	374
	3 Italy	376
	4 Spain and Portugal	380
	Focus on Culture: Party Time!	382
	PLANNING GUIDE	**385A**
17	**West-Central Europe**	**386**
	1 Physical Geography	387
	2 France	390
	3 Germany	394
	4 The Benelux Countries	398
	Connecting to Technology: Dutch Polders	399
	5 The Alpine Countries	401

	PLANNING GUIDE **405A**
18	**Northern Europe** **406**
	1 Physical Geography 407
	Could You Survive?: *Iceland* 410
	2 The United Kingdom 412
	3 The Republic of Ireland 416
	4 Scandinavia 419
	Connecting to Art: *Stave Churches* 421
	PLANNING GUIDE **425A**
19	**Eastern Europe** **426**
	1 Physical Geography 427
	2 The Countries of Northeastern Europe 430
	Connecting to Literature: *Robot Robota* 433
	3 The Countries of Southeastern Europe 436
	Focus on Culture: *Roma Women in a Changing World* 440

Focus on Economics: The European Union 444

Building Skills for Life: Analyzing Settlement Patterns 446

Hands On Geography: Planning a City 447

xii • Contents

UNIT 5 Russia and Its Western Neighbors 448

Notes from the Field

Unit 5 Atlas: The World in Spatial Terms 450

Fast Facts: Russia and Its Western Neighbors 456

PLANNING GUIDE 457A

20 Russia 458
1 Physical Geography 459
   Focus on Culture: A Wooden World 461
2 History and Culture 463
   Connecting to Literature: Aunt Rimma's Treat 466
3 The Russian Heartland 469
4 Siberia 472
5 The Russian Far East 475

PLANNING GUIDE	**479A**
21 Ukraine, Belarus, and the Caucasus	**480**
1 Physical Geography	481
2 Ukraine and Belarus	484
Connecting to Science: Wheat: From Field to Consumer	487
3 The Caucasus	489
Focus on Culture: Changing Perceptions of Russia's Southern Neighbors	494
Building Skills for Life: Addressing Environmental Problems	496
Hands On Geography: Looking at Chelyabinsk's Environment	497

REFERENCE SECTION

FoldNotes Appendix	R0
Gazetteer	R4
Glossary	R12
Spanish Glossary	R19
Index	R26
Acknowledgments	R38

FEATURES

Biographies
George Washington 94
Abraham Lincoln 98
Samuel de Champlain 139
Simón Bolívar 182
Benito Juárez 194
Eva Perón 246
Pericles 291
Julius Caesar 301
Christopher Columbus 325
Winston Churchill 358
Anne Frank 359
Melina Mercouri 375
Ludwig van Beethoven 396
Mary Robinson 417
Vaclav Havel 434
Mikhail Gorbachev 465

Connecting to Art
Art and Memories 104
Stave Churches 421

Connecting to History
Inca Mummies 177
Tenochtitlán 193

Connecting to Literature
Anne of Green Gables 145
The Gaucho Martín Fierro 247
History of the Peloponnesian War 294
Robot Robota 433
Aunt Rimma's Treat 466

Connecting to Math
Maya Calendar 210
Greek Math and Science 374

Connecting to Science
Fighting Malaria 226
Wheat: From Field to
  Consumer 487

Connecting to Technology
Computer Mapping 12
The Great Lakes and
St. Lawrence Seaway 120
Inca Roads 261
The Roman Arch 306
The Printing Press 319
Dutch Polders 399

CASE STUDY
How Geographers Track Hurricanes 14
Maquiladoras along the
  U.S.-Mexico Border 196

COULD YOU SURVIVE?
The Canadian Arctic 150
The Amazon 270
Iceland 410

FEATURES

Focus On

Regions: What Is a Region? 66
Culture: Tasting Local Culture 116
Culture: Ice Cream Houses of Curaçao . . . 216
Culture: Greek Myths 289
Culture: Party Time! 382
Culture: Roma Women in a
  Changing World 440
Economics: The European Union 444
Culture: A Wooden World 461
Culture: Changing Perceptions of
  Russia's Southern Neighbors 494

History Close-Up

Aztec Daily Life 172
The Roman Forum 299

Geo Skills

Drawing Mental Maps 68
Analyzing Changing Landscapes 152
Understanding Migration Patterns 272
Analyzing Settlement Patterns 446
Addressing Environmental Problems 496

Hands On Geography

Making a Map from Memory 69
Urban Growth in Las Vegas,
  Nevada 153
Looking at Migration 273
Planning a City 447
Looking at Chelyabinsk's
  Environment 497

MAPS

Atlas A1–A22
Path of Hurricane Fran, 1996 14
California 17
Plate Tectonics 19
Topographic Map of Austin, Texas 23
Reading a Weather Map 34
World Climate Regions 37
World Religions 48
World Population Density 58
Major World Regions 67
The United States and Canada:
  Comparing Sizes 72
The United States and Canada: Physical 73
The United States and Canada: Political 74
The United States and Canada: Climate 75
The United States and Canada: Population . . 76
The United States and Canada: Land Use
  and Resources 77
The United States: Physical-Political 81
Physical Regions of the United States
  and Canada 83
Peoples of North America,
  2550 B.C.–A.D. 1550 87
The 13 Colonies 92
The Triangular Trade 107
Northeastern United States:
  Physical-Political 109
Southern United States:
  Physical-Political 114
Midwestern United States:
  Physical-Political 118
The Great Lakes and
  St. Lawrence Seaway 120
Interior West: Physical-Political 122
Pacific States: Physical-Political 127
Highway Map of Southern Florida 133
Canada: Physical-Political 135
Size Comparison—Canada to the
  United States 135
Languages in Canada 149
The United States and Middle and
  South America: Comparing Sizes 156
Middle and South America: Physical 157
Middle and South America: Political 158
Middle and South America: Climate 159
Middle and South America: Population 160

FEATURES

Middle and South America: Land Use and Resources	161
Mesoamerican Civilizations	170
The Inca Empire	175
Mexico: Physical-Political	187
Size Comparison—Mexico to the United States	187
The States of Mexico	189
U.S.-Mexico Border Region	197
Central America and the Caribbean Islands: Physical-Political	205
Size Comparison—Central America and the Caribbean Islands to the United States	205
Caribbean South America: Physical-Political	221
Size Comparison—Caribbean South America to the United States	221
Atlantic South America: Physical-Political	237
Size Comparison—Atlantic South America to the United States	237
Pacific South America: Physical-Political	255
Size Comparison—Pacific South America to the United States	255
Inca Lands of Southern Peru	269
Damaged and Threatened Areas of the Amazon Rain Forest	271
The United States and Europe: Comparing Sizes	276
Europe: Physical	277
Europe: Political	278
Europe: Climate	279
Europe: Population	280
Europe: Land Use and Resources	281
Early Greece	287
The Roman Empire	303
Spread of the Black Death	315
European Explorations, 1492–1535	324
Cabral's Route, April 1500	345
Europe at the Beginning of World War I	348
Europe in the Cold War	363
Southern Europe: Physical-Political	369
Size Comparison—Southern Europe to the United States	369
The Re-conquest of Spain	385
West-Central Europe: Physical-Political	387
Size Comparison—West-Central Europe to the United States	387
Germany after World War II	405
Northern Europe: Physical-Political	407
Size Comparison—Northern Europe to the United States	407
Volcanoes and Fissures of Iceland	411
Eastern Europe: Physical-Political	427
Size Comparison—Eastern Europe to the United States	427
The European Union	445
The United States and Russia and Its Western Neighbors: Comparing Sizes	450
Russia and Its Western Neighbors: Physical	451
Russia and Its Western Neighbors: Political	452
Russia and Its Western Neighbors: Climate	453
Russia and Its Western Neighbors: Population	454
Russia and Its Western Neighbors: Land Use and Resources	455
Russia: Physical-Political	459
Size Comparison—Russia to the United States	459
History of Russian Expansion	464
Ukraine, Belarus, and the Caucasus: Physical-Political	481
Size Comparison—Ukraine, Belarus, and the Caucasus to the United States	481
Azerbaijan	493
Language Groups of Southwest and Central Asia	495

DIAGRAMS, CHARTS, and TABLES

Saffir-Simpson Scale	14
Hurricane Mitch, 1998: Position and Strength	15
The Water Cycle	27
Some Sources of Water Pollution from a Home	29
The Greenhouse Effect	31
The Seasons	33
Reading a Weather Map	34
Landforms and Precipitation	35
World Climate Regions	36
Energy Consumption in the United States, 2002	45

DIAGRAMS, CHARTS, and TABLES *continued*

Four Types of Economic Activities 54
Comparing Developed
 and Developing Countries 55
The United States and Canada:
 Elevation Profile 72
The Northeast 110
Corn: From Field to Consumer 119
Moving through a Canal Lock 120
Canada 141
Middle and South America:
 Elevation Profile 156
Growth in *Maquiladora* Plants 196
Mexico 198
Vehicles in Mexico City 203
Central America 212
Caribbean Islands 214
Population Densities of Selected
 Caribbean Islands 219
Elevation Zones in the Andes 222
Colombia 225
Venezuela 229
The Guianas 232
Age Structure of the Guianas and the
 United States 235
Brazil 243
Major Producers of Coffee 244
Uruguay and Paraguay 250
The Argentine Economy 253

Pacific South America 265
Europe: Elevation Profile 276
European Explorers 326
Military Losses in World War I 350
Losses of the Major Wartime
 Powers in World War II 360
Imports and Exports of Southern Europe ... 370
Italy 379
Spain and Portugal 382
Germany 397
The Alpine Countries 403
Some of Iceland's Major Volcanoes 410
The United Kingdom 414
Religion: A Divided Island 415
Ireland 418
Health Spending Per Person
 in Scandinavia 425
Northeastern Europe 432
Southeastern Europe 441
Religious Practice in Bosnia
 and Herzegovina 443
Russia and Its Western Neighbors:
 Elevation Profile 450
Russia 467
Republics of the Russian Federation 468
Wheat: From Field to Consumer 487
Belarus and Ukraine 488

ATLAS CONTENTS

World: Physical **A2**
World: Political **A4**
The United States of America: Physical **A6**
The United States of America: Political **A8**
North America: Physical **A10**
North America: Political **A11**
South America: Physical **A12**
South America: Political **A13**
Europe: Physical **A14**
Europe: Political **A15**
Asia: Physical **A16**
Asia: Political **A17**
Africa: Physical **A18**
Africa: Political **A19**
Australia and New Zealand **A20**
Pacific Islands **A21**
North Pole and South Pole **A22**

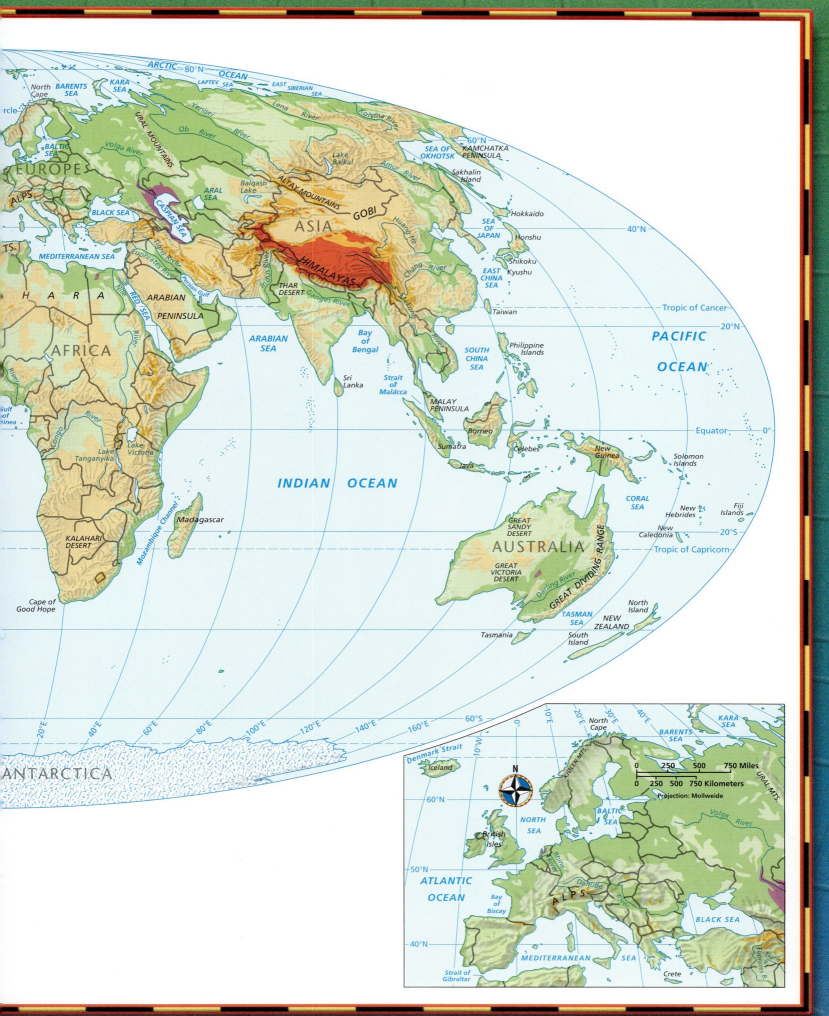

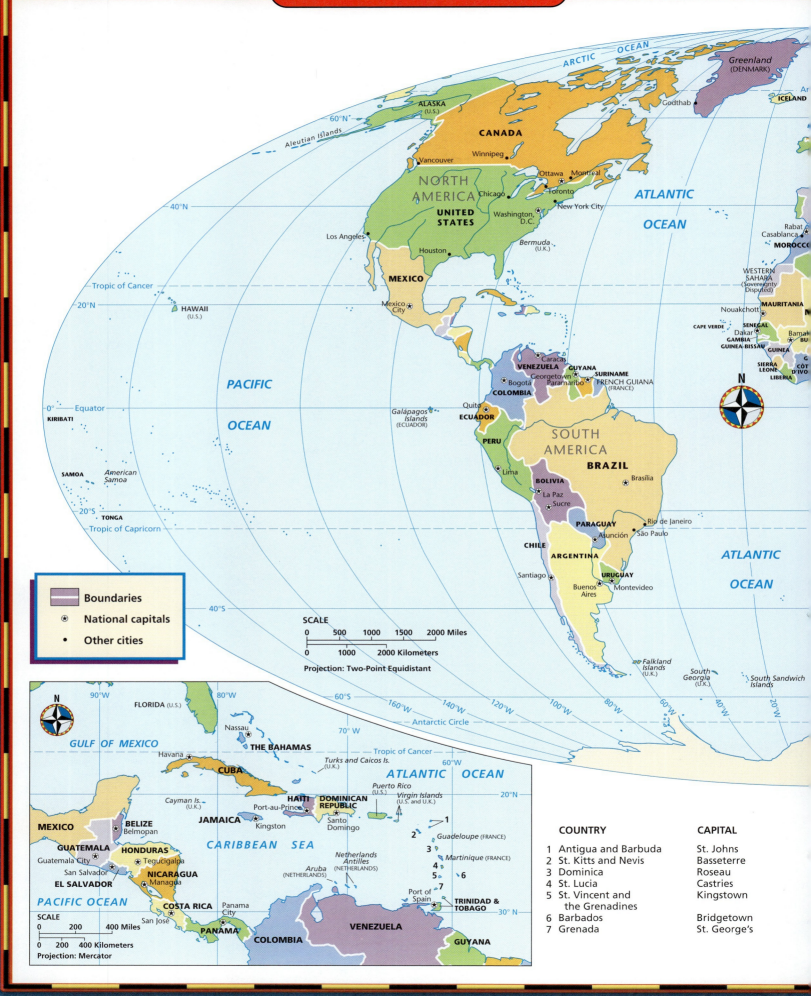

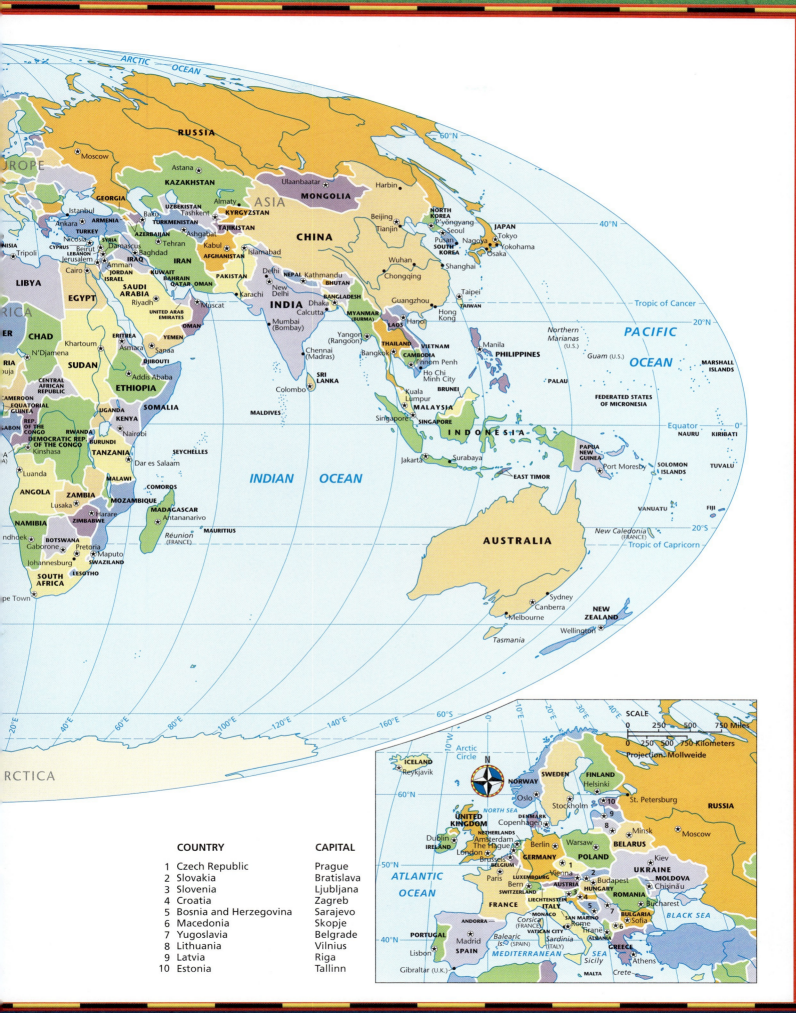

EUROPE: POLITICAL

Legend:
- Boundaries
- ✪ National capitals
- • Other cities

Scale: 0, 250, 500 Miles / 0, 250, 500 Kilometers
Projection: Azimuthal Equal Area

Atlas • A15

ASIA: PHYSICAL

ELEVATION

FEET	METERS
13,120	4,000
6,560	2,000
1,640	500
656	200
0 (Sea level)	0 (Sea level)
Below sea level	Below sea level

Ice cap

ASIA: POLITICAL

Atlas • A17

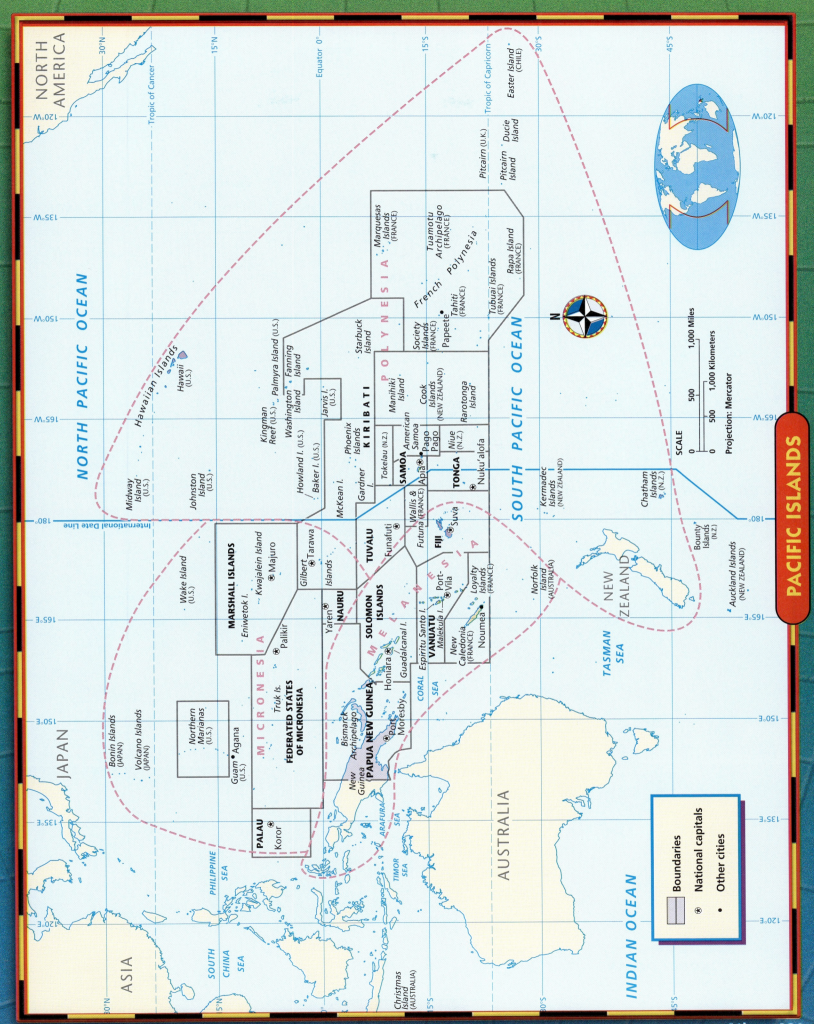

GEOGRAPHY & MAP SKILLS HANDBOOK

Studying geography requires the ability to understand and use various tools. This Skills Handbook explains how to use maps, charts, and other graphics to help you learn about geography and the various regions of the world. Throughout this textbook, you will have the opportunity to improve these skills and build upon them.

CONTENTS

MAPPING THE EARTH	S2
MAPMAKING	S4
MAP ESSENTIALS	S6
WORKING WITH MAPS	S8
USING GRAPHS, DIAGRAMS, CHARTS, AND TABLES	S10
READING A TIME-ZONE MAP	S14
GEOGRAPHIC DICTIONARY	S16

GEOGRAPHIC
Vocabulary

- globe
- grid
- latitude
- equator
- parallels
- degrees
- minutes
- longitude
- prime meridian
- meridians
- hemispheres
- continents
- islands
- ocean
- map
- map projections
- compass rose
- scale
- legend

SKILLS HANDBOOK

Global Skill Builder CD–ROM

You might wish to use **Mapping the Earth** from the interactive Global Skill Builder CD–ROM to reinforce students' understanding of maps and globes.

MAPPING THE EARTH

The Globe

A **globe** is a scale model of Earth. It is useful for looking at the entire Earth or at large areas of Earth's surface.

The pattern of lines that circle the globe in east-west and north-south directions is called a **grid**. The intersection of these imaginary lines helps us find places on Earth.

The east-west lines in the grid are lines of **latitude**. These imaginary lines measure distance north and south of the **equator**. The equator is an imaginary line that circles the globe halfway between the North and South Poles. Lines of latitude are called **parallels** because they are always parallel to the equator. Parallels measure distance from the equator in **degrees**. The symbol for degrees is °. Degrees are further divided into **minutes**. The symbol for minutes is ′. There are 60 minutes in a degree. Parallels north of the equator are labeled with an N. Those south of the equator are labeled with an S.

The north-south lines are lines of **longitude**. These imaginary lines pass through the Poles. They measure distance east and west of the **prime meridian**. The prime meridian is an imaginary line that runs through Greenwich, England. It represents 0° longitude. Lines of longitude are called **meridians**.

Lines of latitude range from 0°, for locations on the equator, to 90°N or 90°S, for locations at the Poles. See **Figure 1**. Lines of longitude range from 0° on the prime meridian to 180° on a meridian in the mid-Pacific Ocean. Meridians west of the prime meridian to 180° are labeled with a W. Those east of the prime meridian to 180° are labeled with an E. See **Figure 2**.

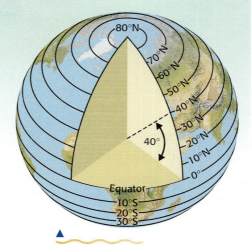

Figure 1: The east-west lines in the grid are lines of latitude.

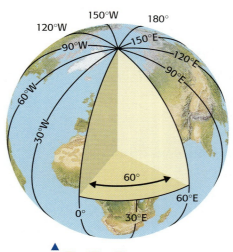

Figure 2: The north-south lines are lines of longitude.

S2 • Skills Handbook

NORTHERN HEMISPHERE

SOUTHERN HEMISPHERE

Figure 3: The hemispheres

The equator divides the globe into two halves, called **hemispheres**. See **Figure 3**. The half north of the equator is the Northern Hemisphere. The southern half is the Southern Hemisphere. The prime meridian and the 180° meridian divide the world into the Eastern Hemisphere and the Western Hemisphere. The prime meridian separates parts of Europe and Africa into two different hemispheres. To prevent this, some mapmakers divide the Eastern and Western hemispheres at 20° W. This places all of Europe and Africa in the Eastern Hemisphere.

Our planet's land surface is organized into seven large landmasses, called **continents**. They are identified in **Figure 3**. Landmasses smaller than continents and completely surrounded by water are called **islands**. Geographers also organize Earth's water surface into parts. The largest is the world **ocean**. Geographers divide the world ocean into the Pacific Ocean, the Atlantic Ocean, the Indian Ocean, and the Arctic Ocean. Lakes and seas are smaller bodies of water.

EASTERN HEMISPHERE

WESTERN HEMISPHERE

YOUR TURN

1. Look at the Student Atlas map on page A4. What islands are located near the intersection of latitude 20° N and longitude 160° W?
2. Name the four hemispheres. In which hemispheres is the United States located?
3. Name the continents of the world.
4. Name the oceans of the world.

SKILLS HANDBOOK

SKILL SIDELIGHT

Point out to students that phrases such as "Western influences," "Western world," and "Western society" do not refer to the Western Hemisphere. Rather, these phrases refer to ideas and ways of life associated with western Europe and North America.

Your Turn

Answers
1. The Hawaiian Islands
2. The United States is located in the Northern and Western Hemispheres. The other two hemispheres are the Southern and Eastern.
3. North America, South America, Africa, Europe, Asia, Australia, Antarctica
4. Pacific, Atlantic, Indian, Arctic

SKILLS HANDBOOK

SKILL SIDELIGHT

Although most maps are oriented with north being "up," maps can also be oriented with the South Pole at the top. Lead a discussion about how the two different map orientations might give different impressions of the world.

Global Skill Builder CD–ROM

You might wish to use **Understanding Map Projections** from the interactive Global Skill Builder CD–ROM to reinforce students' understanding of mapmaking.

MAPMAKING

A **map** is a flat diagram of all or part of Earth's surface. Mapmakers have different ways of showing our round Earth on flat maps. These different ways are called **map projections**. Because our planet is round, all flat maps lose some accuracy. Mapmakers must choose the type of map projection that is best for their purposes. Many map projections are one of three kinds: cylindrical, conic, or flat-plane.

Figure 4: If you remove the peel from the orange and flatten the peel, it will stretch and tear. The larger the piece of peel, the more its shape is distorted as it is flattened. Also distorted are the distances between points on the peel.

Figure 5A: Paper cylinder

Cylindrical projections are designed from a cylinder wrapped around the globe. See **Figure 5A**. The cylinder touches the globe only at the equator. The meridians are pulled apart and are parallel to each other instead of meeting at the Poles. This causes landmasses near the Poles to appear larger than they really are. **Figure 5B** is a Mercator projection, one type of cylindrical projection. The Mercator projection is useful for navigators because it shows true direction and shape. The Mercator projection for world maps, however, emphasizes the Northern Hemisphere. Africa and South America appear smaller than they really are.

Figure 5B: A Mercator projection, although accurate near the equator, distorts distances between regions of land. This projection also distorts the sizes of areas near the poles.

Conic projections are designed from a cone placed over the globe. See **Figure 6A**. A conic projection is most accurate along the lines of latitude where it touches the globe. It retains almost true shape and size. Conic projections are most useful for areas that have long east-west dimensions, such as the United States. See the map in **Figure 6B**.

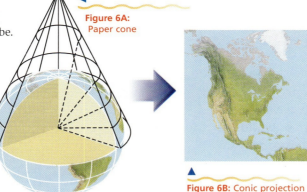

Figure 6A: Paper cone

Figure 6B: Conic projection

Flat-plane projections are designed from a plane touching the globe at one point, such as at the North Pole or South Pole. See **Figures 7A** and **7B**. A flat-plane projection is useful for showing true direction for airplane pilots and ship navigators. It also shows true area. However, it distorts true shape.

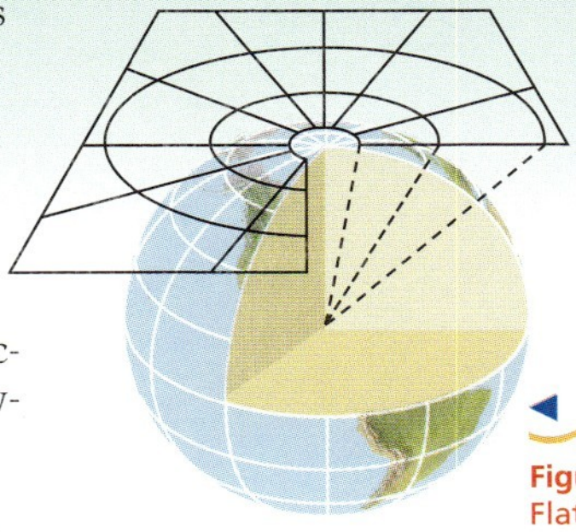

Figure 7A: Flat plane

Figure 7B: Flat-plane projection

The Robinson projection is a compromise between size and shape distortions. It often is used for world maps, such as the map on page 76. The minor distortions in size at high latitudes on Robinson projections are balanced by realistic shapes at the middle and low latitudes.

YOUR TURN

1. What are three major kinds of map projections?
2. Why is a Robinson projection often used for world maps?
3. What kind of projection is a Mercator map?
4. When would a mapmaker choose to use a conic projection?

SKILLS HANDBOOK

Your Turn

Answers
1. cylindrical, conic, flat-plane
2. The minor distortions in size at high latitudes are balanced by realistic shapes at the middle and low latitudes.
3. cylindrical
4. when mapping areas that have long east-west dimensions, such as the United States

SKILLS HANDBOOK

SKILL SIDELIGHT

Most compass roses in this textbook are placed along lines of longitude. Directions that are true north and true south follow the longitude lines, which are curved on many map projections.

Global Skill Builder CD–ROM

You might wish to use **Map Legends and Symbols** from the interactive Global Skill Builder CD–ROM to reinforce students' understanding of map essentials.

MAP ESSENTIALS

In some ways, maps are like messages sent out in code. Mapmakers provide certain elements that help us translate these codes. These elements help us understand the message they are presenting about a particular part of the world. Of these elements, almost all maps have directional indicators, scales, and legends, or keys. **Figure 8**, a map of East Asia, has all three elements.

Figure 8: East and Southeast Asia—Physical

A directional indicator shows which directions are north, south, east, and west. Some mapmakers use a "north arrow," which points toward the North Pole. Remember, "north" is not always at the top of a map. The way a map is drawn and the location of directions on that map depend on the perspective of the mapmaker. Maps in this textbook indicate direction by using a **compass rose** ①. A compass rose has arrows that point to all four principal directions, as shown in **Figure 8**.

Mapmakers use scales to represent distances between points on a map. Scales may appear on maps in several different forms. The maps in this textbook provide a line **scale** ②. Scales give distances in miles and kilometers (km).

To find the distance between two points on the map in **Figure 8**, place a piece of paper so that the edge connects the two points. Mark the location of each point on the paper with a line or dot. Then, compare the distance between the two dots with the map's line scale. The number on the top of the scale gives the distance in miles. The number on the bottom gives the distance in kilometers. Because the distances are given in intervals, you will have to approximate the actual distance on the scale.

S6 • Skills Handbook

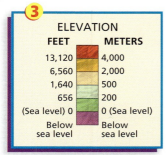

The **legend** ③, or key, explains what the symbols on the map represent. Point symbols are used to specify the location of things, such as cities, that do not take up much space on a large-scale map. Some legends, such as the one in **Figure 8**, show which colors represent certain elevations. Other maps might have legends with symbols or colors that represent things such as roads. Legends can also show economic resources, land use, population density, and climate.

Physical maps at the beginning of each unit have size comparison maps ④. An outline of the mainland United States (not including Alaska and Hawaii) is compared to the area under study in that chapter. These size comparison maps help you understand the size of the areas you are studying in relation to the size of the United States.

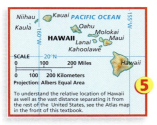

Inset maps are sometimes used to show a small part of a larger map. Mapmakers also use inset maps to show areas that are far away from the areas shown on the main map. Maps of the United States, for example, often include inset maps of Alaska and Hawaii ⑤. Those two states are too far from the other 48 states to accurately represent the true distance on the main map. Subject areas in inset maps can be drawn to a scale different from the scale used on the main map.

YOUR TURN

Look at the Student Atlas map on pages A4 and A5.

1. Locate the compass rose. What country is directly west of Madagascar in Africa?
2. What island country is located southeast of India?
3. Locate the distance scale. Using the inset map, find the approximate distance in miles and kilometers from Oslo, Norway, to Stockholm, Sweden.
4. What is the capital of Brazil? What other cities are shown in Brazil?

SKILLS HANDBOOK

Your Turn

Answers
1. Mozambique
2. Sri Lanka
3. less than 500 miles (800 km)
4. Brasília is the capital. Rio de Janeiro and São Paulo are also shown.

SKILLS HANDBOOK

Global Skill Builder CD-ROM

You might wish to use **Using Different Types of Maps** and **Comparing Maps** from the interactive Global Skill Builder CD–ROM to reinforce students' work with different kinds of maps.

WORKING WITH MAPS

The Atlas at the front of this textbook includes two kinds of maps: physical and political. At the beginning of most units in this textbook, you will find five kinds of maps. These physical, political, climate, population, and land use and resources maps provide different kinds of information about the region you will study in that unit. These maps are accompanied by questions. Some questions ask you to show how the information on each of the maps might be related.

Mapmakers often combine physical and political features into one map. Physical maps, such as the one in **Figure 8** on page S6, show important physical features in a region, including major mountains and mountain ranges, rivers, oceans and other bodies of water, deserts, and plains. Physical-political maps also show important political features, such as national borders, state and provincial boundaries, and capitals and other important cities. You will find a physical-political map at the beginning of most chapters.

Figure 9: East and Southeast Asia—Climate

Mapmakers use climate maps to show the most important weather patterns in certain areas. Climate maps throughout this textbook use color to show the various climate regions of the world. See **Figure 9**. Colors that identify climate types are found in a legend with each map. Boundaries between climate regions do not indicate an immediate change in the main weather conditions between two climate regions. Instead, boundaries show the general areas of gradual change between climate regions.

Skills Handbook

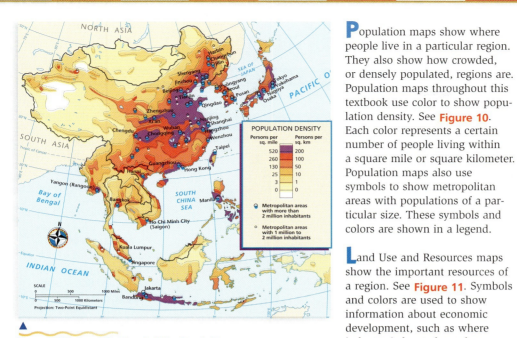

Figure 10: East and Southeast Asia—Population

Population maps show where people live in a particular region. They also show how crowded, or densely populated, regions are. Population maps throughout this textbook use color to show population density. See **Figure 10**. Each color represents a certain number of people living within a square mile or square kilometer. Population maps also use symbols to show metropolitan areas with populations of a particular size. These symbols and colors are shown in a legend.

Land Use and Resources maps show the important resources of a region. See **Figure 11**. Symbols and colors are used to show information about economic development, such as where industry is located or where farming is most common. The meanings of each symbol and color are shown in a legend.

Figure 11: East and Southeast Asia—Land Use and Resources

SKILLS HANDBOOK

Your Turn

Answers

1. to show the most important weather patterns in certain areas
2. more than 520 persons per square mile (200 per sq km)
3. oil

YOUR TURN

1. What is the purpose of a climate map?
2. Look at the population map. What is the population density of the area around Qingdao in northern China?
3. What energy resource is found near Ho Chi Minh City?

SKILLS HANDBOOK

Global Skill Builder CD–ROM

You might wish to use **Reading Graphs** and **Presenting Data Graphically** from the interactive Global Skill Builder CD–ROM to reinforce students' understanding of graphics and their uses.

USING GRAPHS, DIAGRAMS, CHARTS, AND TABLES

Bar graphs are a visual way to present information. The bar graph in **Figure 12** shows the imports and exports of the countries of southern Europe. The amount of imports and exports in billions of dollars is listed on the left side of the graph. Along the bottom of the graph are the names of the countries of southern Europe. Above each country or group of countries is a vertical bar. The top of the bar corresponds to a number along the left side of the graph. For example, Italy imports $200 billion worth of goods.

▲ Figure 12: Reading a bar graph

Often, line graphs are used to show such things as trends, comparisons, and size. The line graph in **Figure 13** shows the population growth of the world over time. The information on the left shows the number of people in billions. The years being studied are listed along the bottom. Lines connect points that show the population in billions at each year under study. This line graph projects population growth into the future.

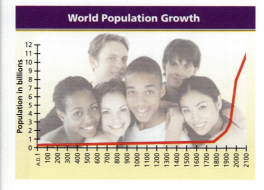

◀ Figure 13: Reading a line graph

A pie graph shows how a whole is divided into parts. In this kind of graph, a circle represents the whole. The wedges represent the parts. Bigger wedges represent larger parts of the whole. The pie graph in **Figure 14** shows the percentages of the world's coffee beans produced by various groups of countries. Brazil is the largest grower. It grows 25 percent of the world's coffee beans.

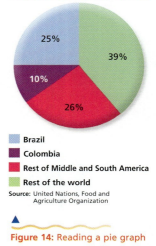

▲ Figure 14: Reading a pie graph

S10 • Skills Handbook

Age structure diagrams show the number of males and females by age group. These diagrams are split into two sides, one for male and one for female. Along the bottom are numbers that show the number of males or females in the age groups. The age groups are listed on the side of the diagram. The wider the base of a country's diagram, the younger the population of that country. The wider the top of a country's diagram, the older the population.

Some countries have so many younger people that their age structure diagrams are shaped like pyramids. For this reason, these diagrams are sometimes called population pyramids. However, in some countries the population is more evenly distributed by age group. For example, see the age structure diagram for Germany in **Figure 15**. Germany's population is older. It is not growing as fast as countries with younger populations.

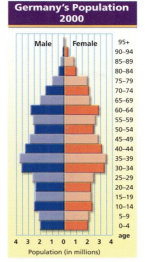

Figure 15: Reading an age structure diagram

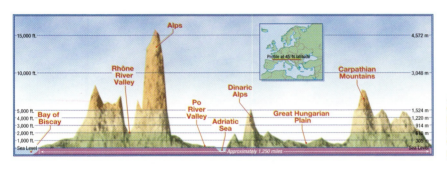

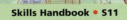

Figure 16: Reading an elevation profile

Each unit atlas includes an elevation profile. See **Figure 16**. It is a side view, or profile, of a region along a line drawn between two points.

Vertical and horizontal distances are figured differently on elevation profiles. The vertical distance (the height of a mountain, for example) is exaggerated when compared to the horizontal distance between the two points. This technique is called vertical exaggeration. If the vertical scale were not exaggerated, even tall mountains would appear as small bumps on an elevation profile.

SKILLS HANDBOOK

SKILL SIDELIGHT

Direct students' attention to the statistical chart on this page. Point out that most chapters contain statistical charts that provide information about the populations of countries within a region. Each statistical chart also includes information for the United States. The U.S. statistical information is provided for comparison.

Global Skill Builder CD–ROM

You might wish to use **Using Time Lines, Reading Graphs, Presenting Data Graphically,** and **Creating Graphic Organizers** from the interactive Global Skill Builder CD–ROM to reinforce students' understanding of charts, tables, and diagrams.

In each unit and chapter on the various regions of the world, you will find tables that provide basic information about the countries under study.

The countries of Spain and Portugal are listed on the left in the table in **Figure 17**. You can match statistical information on the right with the name of each country listed on the left. The categories of information are listed across the top of the table.

Graphic organizers can help you understand certain ideas and concepts. For example, the diagram in **Figure 18** helps you think about the uses of water. In this diagram, one water use goes in each oval. Graphic organizers can help you focus on key facts in your study of geography.

Time lines provide highlights of important events over a period of time. The time line in **Figure 19** begins at the left with 5000 B.C., when rice was first cultivated in present-day China. The time line highlights important events that have shaped the human and political geography of China.

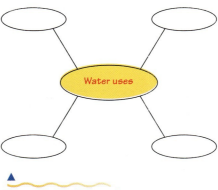

Spain and Portugal

Country	Population/ Growth Rate	Life Expectancy	Literacy Rate	Per Capita GDP
Portugal	10,102,022 0.1%	72, male 80, female	93%	$18,000
Spain	40,217,413 0.1%	75, male 82, female	97%	$20,700
United States	290,342,554 0.9%	74, male 80, female	97%	$37,600

Source: Central Intelligence Agency, *The World Factbook 2003*

▲ **Figure 17:** Reading a table

▲ **Figure 18:** Graphic organizer

Historic China: A Time Line

▲ **Figure 19:** Reading a time line

Corn: From Field to Consumer

A Corn can be processed in a variety of ways. Some corn is cooked and then canned.

B Corn is ground and used for livestock feed.

C Corn also might be wet-milled or dry-milled. Then grain parts are used to make different products.

D Corn by-products, such as cornstarch and corn syrup, are used to make breads, breakfast cereals, puddings, and snack foods. Corn oil is used for cooking.

▲ **Figure 20:** Reading a flowchart

Flowcharts are visual guides that explain different processes. They lead the reader from one step to the next, sometimes providing both illustrations and text. The flowchart in **Figure 20** shows the different steps involved in harvesting corn and preparing it for use by consumers. The flowchart takes you through the steps of harvesting and processing corn. Captions guide you through flowcharts.

YOUR TURN

1. Look at the statistical table for Spain and Portugal in Figure 17. Which countries have the highest literacy rate?
2. Look at the China time line in Figure 19. Name two important events in China's history between 1200 and 1400.
3. Look at Figure 20. What are three corn products?

SKILLS HANDBOOK

Your Turn

Answers

1. Spain and the United States
2. Mongols invade China, rise of Ming dynasty
3. Students should name three of the following products: livestock feed, candy, glue, corn oil, cornstarch, tortillas, cornmeal, corn flour

SKILLS HANDBOOK

SKILL SIDELIGHT

Point out that worldwide time zones were established in 1884. That same year, the United States was divided into four time zones. Prior to 1884, time was set locally. In addition, railroad companies set railroad times along their routes. About 100 such railroad times existed by 1883. There are six time zones in the United States today.

Global Skill Builder CD–ROM

You might wish to use **Understanding Time Zones** from the interactive Global Skill Builder CD–ROM to reinforce students' understanding of time-zone maps.

READING A TIME-ZONE MAP

The sun is not directly overhead everywhere on Earth at the same time. Clocks are set to reflect the difference in the sun's position. Our planet rotates on its axis once every 24 hours. In other words, in one hour, it makes one twenty-fourth of a complete rotation. Since there are 360 degrees in a circle, we know that the planet turns 15 degrees of longitude each hour. (360° ÷ 24 = 15°) We also know that the planet turns in a west-to-east direction. Therefore, if a place on Earth has the sun directly overhead at this moment (noon), then a place 15 degrees to the west will have the sun directly overhead one hour from now. During that hour the planet will have rotated 15 degrees. As a result, Earth is divided into 24 time zones. Thus, time is an hour earlier for each 15 degrees you move westward on Earth. Time is an hour later for each 15 degrees you move eastward on Earth.

By international agreement, longitude is measured from the prime meridian. This meridian passes through the Royal Observatory in Greenwich, England. Time also is measured from Greenwich and is called Greenwich mean time (GMT). For each time zone east of the prime meridian, clocks must be set one hour ahead of GMT. For each time zone west of Greenwich, clocks are set back one hour from GMT. When it is noon in London, it is 1:00 P.M. in Oslo, Norway, one time zone east. However, it is 7 A.M. in New York City, five time zones west.

WORLD TIME ZONES

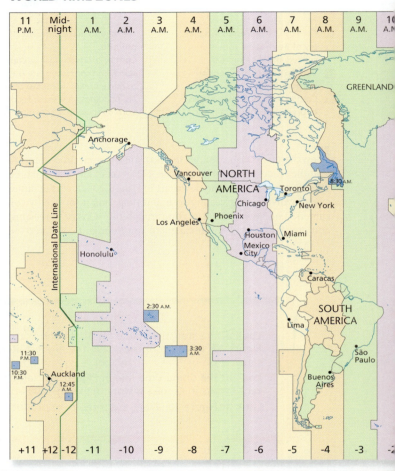

As you can see by looking at the map below, time zones do not follow meridians exactly. Political boundaries are often used to draw time-zone lines. In Europe and Africa, for example, time zones follow national boundaries. The mainland United States, meanwhile, is divided into four major time zones: Eastern, Central, Mountain, and Pacific. Alaska and Hawaii are in separate time zones to the west of the mainland.

Some countries have made changes in their time zones. For example, most of the United States has daylight savings time in the summer in order to have more evening hours of daylight.

The international date line is a north-south line that runs through the Pacific Ocean. It is located at 180°, although it sometimes varies from that meridian to avoid dividing countries.

At 180°, the time is 12 hours from Greenwich time. There is a time difference of 24 hours between the two sides of the 180° meridian. The 180° meridian is called the international date line because when you cross it, the date and day change. As you cross the date line from the west to the east, you gain a day. If you travel from east to west, you lose a day.

SKILLS HANDBOOK

Your Turn

Answers

1. Answers will vary. If students are in the Eastern time zone, the time is the same as New York's. The time is one hour behind New York for each time zone moving westward.
2. four
3. five (includes Seychelles and Mauritius)
4. 9 A.M. The two locations are in the same time zone. The wide north-south distance between the locations makes no difference in time.

YOUR TURN

1. In which time zone do you live? Check your time now. What time is it in New York?
2. How many hours behind New York is Anchorage, Alaska?
3. How many time zones are there in Africa?
4. If it is 9 A.M. in the middle of Greenland, what time is it in São Paulo?

Skills Handbook • S15

SKILLS HANDBOOK

GEOGRAPHIC DICTIONARY

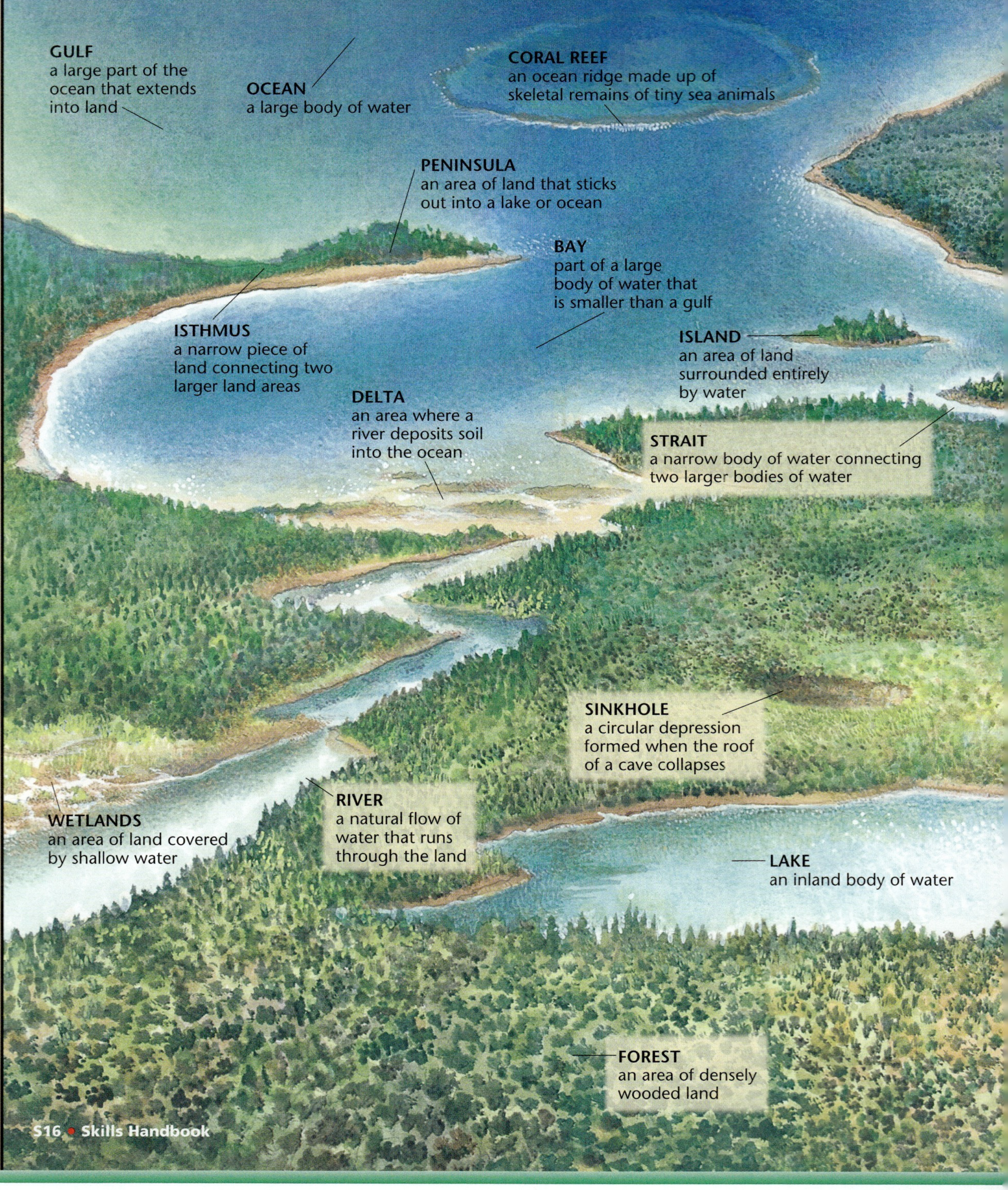

GULF a large part of the ocean that extends into land

OCEAN a large body of water

CORAL REEF an ocean ridge made up of skeletal remains of tiny sea animals

PENINSULA an area of land that sticks out into a lake or ocean

BAY part of a large body of water that is smaller than a gulf

ISTHMUS a narrow piece of land connecting two larger land areas

ISLAND an area of land surrounded entirely by water

DELTA an area where a river deposits soil into the ocean

STRAIT a narrow body of water connecting two larger bodies of water

SINKHOLE a circular depression formed when the roof of a cave collapses

WETLANDS an area of land covered by shallow water

RIVER a natural flow of water that runs through the land

LAKE an inland body of water

FOREST an area of densely wooded land

UNIT 1

UNIT OBJECTIVES

1. Introduce geography as a field of study.
2. Explain the formation of the shapes on Earth's surface.
3. Analyze the interrelationships of wind, climate, and natural environments.
4. Identify major resources and how people use them.
5. Describe the development of cultures and the results of population expansion.
6. Learn to draw sketch maps and use them as geographic tools.

Your Classroom Time Line

To help you create a time line to display in your classroom, the most important dates and time periods discussed in each unit's chapters are compiled for you. Some additional dates have been inserted for clarity and continuity. Note that many dates, particularly those in the distant past, are approximate. In each unit, the lists begin in the sidebar on the page with the political map. You may want to have students use colored markers to differentiate among political, scientific, religious, and artistic events or achievements. You might also want to create your own categories.

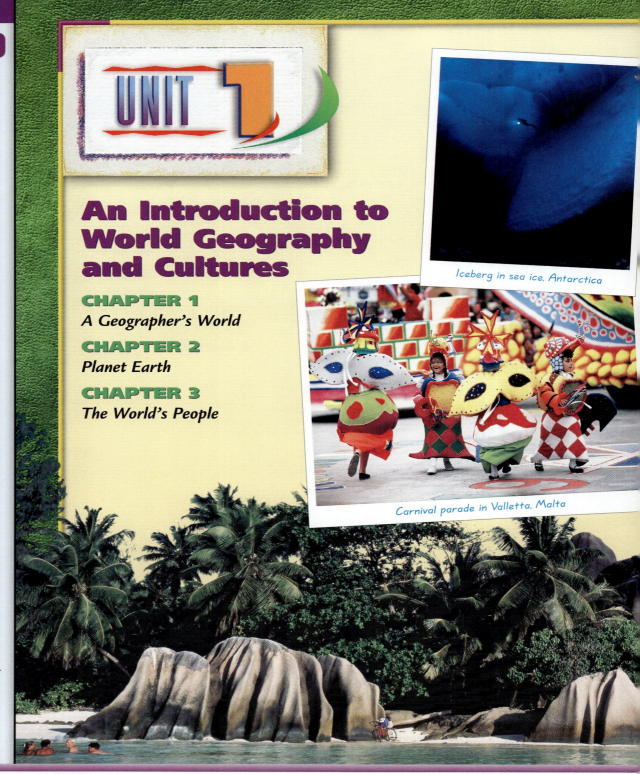

UNIT 1

An Introduction to World Geography and Cultures

CHAPTER 1
A Geographer's World

CHAPTER 2
Planet Earth

CHAPTER 3
The World's People

Iceberg in sea ice, Antarctica

Carnival parade in Valletta, Malta

USING THE ILLUSTRATIONS

Direct students' attention to the photographs on these pages. Point out that in this unit students will learn there are two major branches of geography. One is physical geography, which deals with land, water, climate, and similar topics; the other is human geography, which involves people. Ask students which photos may relate more closely to physical geography **(rosettes, tropical landscape, iceberg)** and which relate more to human geography **(Carnival scene).**

Ask which photo shows a cold climate **(iceberg),** and which shows a warm climate **(La Digue Island).** On what familiar images or clues do we depend for the answers? **(Possible answers: ice, lush vegetation, palm trees)** Ask why the photo of the rosette plants does not give us much information about how warm or cold the climate may be. **(Because the plant is not familiar to most of us, we do not know where it grows.)**

You may want to invite students to speculate about the construction or meaning of the costumes in the Carnival photo. Lead a discussion about what kinds of parades are held in your community and what costumes the participants wear.

UNIT 1

Notes from the Field

A Physical Geographer in Mountain Environments

Professor Francisco Pérez studies tropical mountain environments. He is interested in the natural processes, plants, and environments of mountains. **WHAT DO YOU THINK?** *What faraway places would you like to study?*

I became attracted to mountains when I was a child. While crossing the Atlantic Ocean in a ship, I saw snow-capped Teide Peak in the Canary Islands rising from the water. It was an amazing sight.

As a physical geographer, I am interested in the unique environments of high mountain areas. This includes geological history, climate, and soils. The unusual conditions of high mountain environments have influenced plant evolution. Plants and animals that live on separate mountains sometimes end up looking similar. This happens because they react to their environments in similar ways. For example, several types of tall, weird-looking plants called giant rosettes grow in the Andes, Hawaii, East Africa, and the Canary Islands. Giant rosettes look like the top of a pineapple at the end of a tall stem.

I have found other strange plants, such as rolling mosses. Mosses normally grow on rocks. However, if a moss plant falls to the ground, ice crystals on the soil surface lift the moss. This allows it to "roll" downhill while it continues to grow in a ball shape!

I like doing research in mountains. They are some of the least explored regions of our planet. Like most geographers, I cannot resist the attraction of strange landscapes in remote places.

Rosette plants, Ecuador

La Digue Island, Seychelles

Sturgeonfish

Understanding Primary Sources

1. What are three parts of the environment that Francisco Pérez studies?
2. Why do some plants that live on separate mountains look similar?

More from the Field

Living things that are not related sometimes develop similar physical traits because they live in similar environments. This process is called convergent evolution. For example, tuna (fish) and dolphins (mammals) both have streamlined bodies and fins for living in the water.

For a land-based example, compare the serval of Africa, a cat, and the maned wolf of South America, a dog. Both have long necks, long legs, and large ears. They hunt small animals in grassy plains areas. Their long legs and necks elevate their ears above the grass. As a result, they can hear the slightest sound made by their prey.

Understanding Primary Sources
Answers
1. geological history, climate, soils
2. because they react to their environments in similar ways

An Introduction to World Geography and Cultures • 1

CHAPTERS

1 A Geographer's World
introduces the study of geography, its six essential elements, and its two main branches: human geography and physical geography.

2 Planet Earth
explores the importance of landforms, the geological forces that shape the land, water, air, climate, weather, and vegetation.

3 The World's People
introduces human geography, culture, economics and population, and global issues.

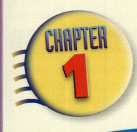

Chapter 1: A Geographer's World
Chapter Resource Manager

Objectives	Pacing Guide	Reproducible Resources
SECTION 1 **Developing a Geographic Eye** (pp. 3–5) 1. Explain the role perspective plays in the study of geography. 2. Describe some issues and topics that geographers study. 3. Identify the three levels geographers use to view the world.	**Regular** 1 day Lecture Notes, Section 1 **Block Scheduling** .5 day Block Scheduling Handbook, Chapter 1	**RS** Know It Notes S1 **E** Geography for Life Activity 1 **ELL** Main Idea Activity S1
SECTION 2 **Themes and Essential Elements of Geography** (pp. 6–10) 1. Identify the tools geographers use to study the world. 2. Identify what shapes Earth's features. 3. Examine how humans shape the world. 4. Explain how studying geography helps us understand the world.	**Regular** 1 day Lecture Notes, Section 2 **Block Scheduling** .5 day Block Scheduling Handbook, Chapter 1	**RS** Know It Notes S2 **RS** Graphic Organizer 1 **SM** Map Activity 1 **E** Creative Strategies for Teaching World Geography, Lessons 1–3 **E** Lab Activities for Geography and Earth Science, Hands-On 2 **ELL** Main Idea Activity S2
SECTION 3 **Being a Geographer** (pp. 11–13) 1. Explain the study of human geography. 2. Describe the study of physical geography. 3. Investigate the types of work that geographers do.	**Regular** 1 day Lecture Notes, Section 3 **Block Scheduling** .5 day Block Scheduling Handbook, Chapter 1	**RS** Know It Notes S3 **E** Lab Activities for Geography and Earth Science, Hands-On 1 **E** Biography Activity: John Snow **ELL** Main Idea Activity S3

Chapter Resource Key

- **RS** Reading Support
- **IC** Interdisciplinary Connections
- **E** Enrichment
- **SM** Skills Mastery
- **A** Assessment
- **REV** Review
- **ELL** Reinforcement and English Language Learners and English for Speakers of Other Languages (ESOL)
- Internet
-  Holt Presentation Maker Using Microsoft® PowerPoint®
- Transparencies
- CD–ROM
- Music
- Video

 One-Stop Planner CD–ROM

See the *One-Stop Planner* for a complete list of additional resources for students and teachers.

One-Stop Planner CD–ROM

It's easy to plan lessons, select resources, and print out materials for your students when you use the *One-Stop Planner CD–ROM with Test Generator.*

internet connect

HRW ONLINE RESOURCES

GO TO: go.hrw.com
Then type in a keyword.

TEACHER HOME PAGE
KEYWORD: SJ5 TEACHER

CHAPTER INTERNET ACTIVITIES
KEYWORD: SJ5 GT1

Choose an activity to:
• learn to use online maps.
• be a virtual geographer for a day.
• compare regions around the world.

CHAPTER ENRICHMENT LINKS
KEYWORD: SJ5 CH1

CHAPTER MAPS
KEYWORDS: SJ5 MAPS1

ONLINE ASSESSMENT
Homework Practice
KEYWORD: SJ5 HP1
Standardized Test Prep Online
KEYWORD: SJ5 STP1
Rubrics
KEYWORD: SS Rubrics

COUNTRY INFORMATION
KEYWORD: SJ5 Almanac

CONTENT UPDATES
KEYWORD: SS Content Updates

HOLT PRESENTATION MAKER
KEYWORD: SJ5 PPT1

ONLINE READING SUPPORT
KEYWORD: SS Strategies

CURRENT EVENTS
KEYWORD: S5 Current Events

Technology Resources

- One-Stop Planner CD-ROM, Lesson 1.1
- Global Skill Builder CD-ROM, Project 1
- *ARGWorld* CD–ROM
- Homework Practice Online
- HRW Go site

- One-Stop Planner CD-ROM, Lesson
- *ARGWorld* CD–ROM
- Homework Practice Online
- HRW Go site

- One-Stop Planner CD-ROM, Lesson
- *ARGWorld* CD–ROM
- Homework Practice Online
- HRW Go site

Review, Reinforcement, and Assessment Resources

ELL	Main Idea Activity S1
REV	Section 1 Review
A	Daily Quiz 1.1
REV	Chapter Summaries and Review
ELL	English Audio Summary 1.1
ELL	Spanish Audio Summary 1.1

ELL	Main Idea Activity S2
REV	Section 2 Review
A	Daily Quiz 1.2
REV	Chapter Summaries and Review
ELL	English Audio Summary 1.2
ELL	Spanish Audio Summary 1.2

ELL	Main Idea Activity S3
REV	Section 3 Review
A	Daily Quiz 1.3
REV	Chapter Summaries and Review
ELL	English Audio Summary 1.3
ELL	Spanish Audio Summary 1.3

Meeting Individual Needs

Ability Levels

Level 1 Basic-level activities designed for all students encountering new material

Level 2 Intermediate-level activities designed for average students

Level 3 Challenging activities designed for honors and gifted-and-talented students

ESOL Activities that address the needs of students with Limited English Proficiency

Chapter Review and Assessment

SM	Critical Thinking Activity 1
REV	Chapter 1 Review and Practice
REV	Chapter Summaries and Review
ELL	Vocabulary Activity 1
A	Chapter 1 Test
A	Chapter 1 Test Generator (on the One-Stop Planner)
	Audio CD program, Chapter 1
A	Chapter 1 Test for English Language learners and Special Needs Students
	HRW Go site

CHAPTER 1

A Geographer's World
Previewing Chapter Resources

Holt Online Learning

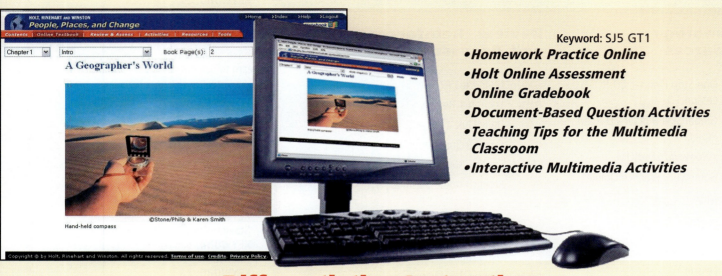

Keyword: SJ5 GT1
- Homework Practice Online
- Holt Online Assessment
- Online Gradebook
- Document-Based Question Activities
- Teaching Tips for the Multimedia Classroom
- Interactive Multimedia Activities

Differentiating Instruction

Reading and Writing Support
◄ Graphic Organizer Activity
- Vocabulary Activity
- Chapter Summary and Review
- Know It Notes S1–3
- Audio CD

Active Learning
◄ Block Scheduling Handbook
- Cultures of the World Activity
- Interdisciplinary Activity
- Map Activity
- Critical Thinking Activity 1

Primary Sources and Advanced Learners
- Geography for Life Activity: Spatial Perspective
◄ Map Activity: Absolute and Relative Location
- Readings in World Geography, History and Culture:
  - 1 Ancient Geographers
  - 2 Mapping Earth from Space

Assessment Program
◄ Daily Quizzes S1–3
- Chapter Test
- Chapter Test for English Language Learners and Special-Needs Students

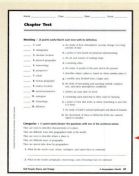

Spanish and ESOL
- Vocabulary Activity
- Main Idea Activities for English Language Learners and Special-Needs Students
- Chapter Summary and Review
- Spanish Audio Summary
- Know It Notes S1–3
◄ Chapter Test for English Language Learners and Special-Needs Students

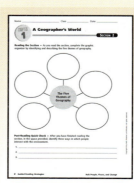

Special Education Modifications
Your **I.D.E.A. Works! CD-ROM** will provide modified versions of the following teaching materials:
◄ Guided Reading Strategies S1–3
- Vocabulary Activity
- Main Idea Activities S1–3
- Daily Quizzes S1–3
- Chapter 1 Test
- Flash cards of chapter vocabulary terms

Teacher Resources

Books for Teachers

Gould, Peter. *Becoming a Geographer.* Syracuse University Press, 1999.

Lippard, Lucy R. *The Lure of the Local: Senses of Place in a Multicentered Society.* New Press, 1997.

Sack, Robert David. *Homo Geographicus: A Framework for Action, Awareness, and Moral Concern.* Johns Hopkins University Press, 1997.

Schama, Simon. *Landscape and Memory.* Knopf, 1995.

Books for Students

Baicker-McKee, Carol. *Mapped Out!: The Search for Snookums.* Gibbs Smith, 1997. Interactive mystery teaches map-reading and problem-solving skills.
SHELTERED ENGLISH

Dunn, Margery G., ed. *Exploring Your World: The Adventure of Geography.* National Geographic Society, 1993. Presents more than 300 topics in physical and human geography.

Geography on File. Facts On File, 1999. Overview of physical and human geography from global and regional perspectives.

Multimedia Materials

Compton's Interactive World Atlas (Classic). CD–ROM. The Learning Company.

Eartha Global Explorer. CD–ROM. DeLorme.

My City. CD–ROM. Glencoe.

Videos and CDs

Videos
- **CNN** Presents Geography: Yesterday and Today, Segment 1 Mapping Change
- ARG World

Holt Researcher
http://researcher.hrw.com
- Rural and Urban Populations in the United States, 1900-1990
- World
- Vital Statistics of Selected Countries, 2000
- Communications Technologies in Selected Countries
- Total GDP for Selected Countries

Transparency Packages

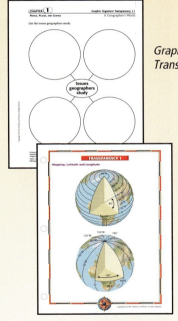

Graphic Organizer Transparencies 1.1–3

Geography and Cultures Visual Resources Transparencies
1 Latitude and Longitude
2 Earth's Hemispheres
3 Mercator Projection
4 Comic Projection
5 Flat-Plane Projections
6 Reading a Time Zone Map

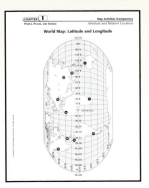

Map Activities Transparency 01 Absolute and Relative Location

CHAPTER 1

WHY IT MATTERS

You may want to share with your students the following reasons for gaining a basic understanding of geography as a field of study:

- Knowing the fundamentals of geography will help students learn more about all aspects of their world.
- Getting an overview from Chapter 1 will make it easier to grasp details in later chapters.
- Throughout the book, connections are made to the five themes and six essential elements of geography. These ideas are explained fully in Chapter 1.
- Geography is an expanding field that includes a wide range of specializations. Students may want to consider geography as a career.

CHAPTER 1

A Geographer's World

Hand-held compass

Chart of the Mediterranean and Europe, 1559

GPS (global positioning satellite) receiver

CHAPTER PROJECT

Different cultures use different methods for showing directions and locations. For example, long ago Polynesians developed shell maps to help them navigate in the vast Pacific Ocean. Have students work in groups to devise new ways to record information about a region familiar to them. Ask them to include a standard map of the area along with the new map. They should also write a legend or key for the new map.

STARTING THE CHAPTER

Ask students to name a country they would like to visit and to give a reason why they want to travel to that particular country. (Examples: France, for the food; China, to see the Great Wall) Point out that their interests could probably be the subject of serious study by a geographer. (Examples: A geographer may study patterns in food preferences among French people or the regional use of ingredients and cooking techniques. Another may use satellite technology to find forgotten sections of the Great Wall.) Use several of the students' suggestions to show geography's wide range. Then ask students to create "geographic studies" based on their classmates' chosen destinations.

Section 1
Developing a Geographic Eye

Read to Discover
1. What role does perspective play in the study of geography?
2. What are some issues or topics that geographers study?
3. At what three levels can geographers view the world?

Vocabulary
- perspective
- spatial perspective
- geography
- urban
- rural

Reading Strategy
VISUALIZING INFORMATION Look at the photographs in this section. What do you see in the photographs that would tell you about some of the topics geographers study? Write your answers on a sheet of paper.

Perspectives

People look at the world in different ways. Their experiences shape the way they understand the world. This personal understanding is called **perspective**. Your perspective is your point of view. A geographer's point of view looks at where something is and why it is there. This point of view is known as **spatial perspective**. Geographers apply this perspective when they study the arrangement of towns in a state. They might also use this perspective to examine the movement of cars and trucks on busy roads.

Geographers also work to understand how things are connected. Some connections are easy to see, like highways that link cities. Other connections are harder to see. For example, a dry winter in Colorado could mean that farms as far away as northern Mexico will not have enough water.

Geography is a science. It describes the physical and cultural features of Earth. Studying geography is important. Geographically informed people can see meaning in the arrangement of things on Earth. They know how people and places are related. Above all, they can apply a spatial perspective to real life. In other words, people familiar with geography can understand the world around them.

This fish-eye view of a large city shows highway patterns.

✓ **READING CHECK:** *The World in Spatial Terms* What role does perspective play in the study of geography? Geographers use perspective when they study where something is and why it is there.

A Geographer's World • 3

CHAPTER 1, Section 1

SECTION 1 RESOURCES
Reproducible
- Lecture Notes, Section 1
- Block Scheduling Handbook, Chapter 1
- Know It Notes S1
- Geography for Life Activity 1

Technology
- One-Stop Planner CD–ROM, Lesson 1.1
- Homework Practice Online
- Global Skill Builder CD–ROM, Project 1
- HRW Go site

Reinforcement, Review, and Assessment
- Section 1 Review
- Daily Quiz 1.1
- Main Idea Activity S1
- Chapter Summaries and Review
- English Audio Summary 1.1
- Spanish Audio Summary 1.1

Objectives
1. Explain the role perspective plays in the study of geography.
2. Describe some issues or topics that geographers study.
3. Identify the three levels geographers use to view the world.

FOCUS
 Bellringer

Select several photographs of scenes from around the world and display them in the classroom. Copy the following instructions on the chalkboard: *Choose one of the photographs and write down three questions you would like to ask about the place in the picture.* Call on students to read their questions aloud, and use their questions as the basis for a discussion about the issues that professional geographers study. Tell students that in Section 1 they will learn more about developing a geographic eye.

Building Vocabulary
Write the vocabulary terms on the chalkboard. Tell students that **perspective** is based on a word meaning "to look" and that **spatial** is based on a word meaning "space." Then, as a class, decide on a definition for **spatial perspective**. Compare this definition to the one in Section 1. Then, point out that **geography** is based on two Greek roots: *geō-*, which means "Earth," and *graphein*, which means "to write." Ask students to compare the meaning of the root words to the textbook's definition and explain the relationship. Finally, have students read the definitions for **urban** and **rural** and then provide examples of urban and rural areas in their region.

A Geographer's World **3**

CHAPTER 1, Section 1

PHYSICAL SYSTEMS

Islanders and Their Tiny Island Geographers study how people all around the world react to Earth's processes. Tristan da Cunha is one of a group of small islands in the South Atlantic Ocean about midway between Africa and South America. It is a British territory.

A volcano 6,760 feet (2,060 m) high dominates the island. Its peak is often shrouded in clouds. Lava flows have continually shaped the island's landscape. A volcanic eruption in 1961 forced the evacuation of the island's residents. After the danger passed, most of the Tristanians returned to their isolated island.

Critical Thinking: How have Earth's physical processes affected Tristanians?

Answer: They were forced to evacuate their homeland because of a volcano.

Visual Record Answer

Answers will vary, but students may mention possible political instability, a negative or fearful atmosphere, or fewer people to fill jobs.

The movement of people is one issue that geographers study. For example, political and economic troubles led many Albanians to leave their country in 1991. Many packed onto freighters like this one for the trip. Geographers want to know how this movement affects the environment and other people.

Interpreting the Visual Record
Movement How do you think Albania has been affected by so many people leaving the country?

GO TO: go.hrw.com
KEYWORD: SK5 CH1
FOR: Web sites about the geographer's world

4 • Chapter 1

Geographic Issues

Issues geographers study include Earth's processes and their impact on people. Geographers study the relationship between people and environment in different places. For example, geographers study tornadoes to find ways to reduce loss of life and property damage. They ask how people prepare for tornadoes. Do they prepare differently in different places? When a tornado strikes, how do people react?

Geographers also study how governments change and how those changes affect people. Czechoslovakia, for example, split into Slovakia and the Czech Republic in 1993. These types of political events affect geographic boundaries. People react differently to these changes. Some people are forced to move. Others welcome the change.

Other issues geographers study include religions, diet (or food), **urban** areas, and **rural** areas. Urban areas contain cities. Rural areas contain open land that is often used for farming.

✓ **READING CHECK:** *The Uses of Geography* What issues or topics do geographers study? Earth's processes, the relationship between people and environment, changes of government, religions, diet, urban areas, and rural areas

Local, Regional, and Global Geographic Studies

With any topic, geographers must decide how large an area to study. They can focus their study at a local, regional, or global level.

Local Studying your community at the local, or close-up, level will help you learn geography. You know where homes and stores are located. You know how to find parks, ball fields, and other fun places. Over time, you see your community change. New buildings are constructed. People move in and out of your neighborhood. New stores open their doors, and others go out of business.

TEACH

Teaching Objective 1

ALL LEVELS: (Suggested time: 10 min.) Discuss geographers' use of spatial perspective. Then have students examine the aerial photograph on the previous page and suggest why the highways are located where they are. **ESOL,** **LS** VISUAL-SPATIAL

Teaching Objectives 2–3

ALL LEVELS: (Suggested time: 20 min.) Copy the following graphic organizer onto the chalkboard, omitting the blue answers. Use it to help students understand the issues geographers study and the level at which they view the world. **ESOL,** **LS** VISUAL-SPATIAL

STUDY OF GEOGRAPHY	
Issues/Topics	Levels
Earth's processes	local
relationships between people and environment	regional
governments	global
religion and food	local, regional
urban and rural areas	local, regional

4 Chapter 1

Region The southwest is a region within the United States. One well-known place that characterizes the landscape of the southwest is the Grand Canyon. The Grand Canyon is shown in the photo at left and in the satellite image at right.

Regional Regional geographers organize the world into convenient parts for study. For example, this book separates the world into big areas like Africa and Europe. Regional studies cover larger areas than local studies. Some regional studies might look at connections like highways and rivers. Others might examine the regional customs.

Global Geographers also work to understand global issues and the connections between events. For example, many countries depend on oil from Southwest Asia. If those oil supplies are threatened, some countries might rush to secure oil from other areas. Oil all over the world could then become much more expensive.

✓ **READING CHECK:** *The World in Spatial Terms* What levels do geographers use to focus their study of an issue or topic? **local, regional, or global**

Section Review 1

Define and explain: perspective, spatial perspective, geography, urban, rural

Reading for the Main Idea
1. How can a spatial perspective be used to study the world?
2. Why is it important to study geography?

Critical Thinking
3. **Drawing Inferences and Conclusions** How do threatening weather patterns affect people, and why do geographers study these patterns?
4. **Drawing Inferences and Conclusions** Why is it important to view geography on a global level?

Organizing What You Know
5. **Finding the Main Idea** Copy the following graphic organizer. Use it to examine the issues geographers study. Write a paragraph on one of these issues.

Section 1 Review

Answers to Section 1 Review

Define For definitions, see the glossary.

Reading for the Main Idea
1. to understand how things are connected (NGS 3)
2. to see meaning in the arrangement of things on Earth and to understand the world (NGS 17, 18)

Critical Thinking
3. They can cause loss of life or property damage; to help people protect themselves from dangerous weather situations (NGS 15)
4. Answers will vary but might include to gain an understanding of how events in one region can affect other regions.

Organizing What You Know
5. Answers will vary but should be issues geographers study.

CLOSE

Ask students to imagine that they are geographers from the planet Geog who have landed on Earth. Have students list what human activities they would study first and what sources they would use in their research.

Have students complete Main Idea Activity S1. Then have them illustrate one of the section's topics. Ask students to explain their illustrations. **ESOL, LS VISUAL-SPATIAL**

REVIEW, ASSESS, RETEACH

Have students complete the Section Review. Then have students work in groups to create short quizzes based on the section's material. Have groups exchange quizzes and complete another group's quiz. Then have students complete Daily Quiz 1.1. **COOPERATIVE LEARNING**

EXTEND

Have interested students conduct research on the history of the field of geography and its influence on society. They may want to concentrate on ancient Greek or Arabic achievements. Ask them to create illustrated charts showing their research. **BLOCK SCHEDULING**

CHAPTER 1, Section 2

SECTION 2 RESOURCES

Reproducible
- Lecture Notes, Section 2
- Know It Notes S2
- Graphic Organizer 1
- Map Activity 1
- Creative Strategies for Teaching World Geography, Lessons 1–3
- Lab Activities for Geography and Earth Science, Hands-On 2

Technology
- One-Stop Planner CD–ROM, Lesson 1.2
- Homework Practice Online
- HRW Go site

Reinforcement, Review, and Assessment
- Section 2 Review
- Daily Quiz 1.2
- Main Idea Activity S2
- Chapter Summaries and Review
- English Audio Summary 1.2
- Spanish Audio Summary 1.2

Visual Record Answer ▶

in northern Egypt, near the pyramids

Section 2: Themes and Essential Elements of Geography

Read to Discover
1. What tools do geographers use to study the world?
2. What shapes Earth's features?
3. How do humans shape the world?
4. How does studying geography help us understand the world?

Vocabulary
- absolute location
- relative location
- place
- region
- movement
- diffusion
- human-environment interaction

Reading Strategy

TAKING NOTES Taking notes while you read will help you understand and remember the information in this section. Write down the headings in the section. As you read, fill in notes under each heading. Underline the most important details you find.

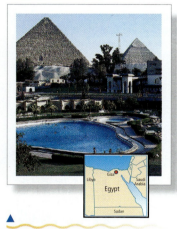

▲ The location of a place can be described in many ways.

Interpreting the Visual Record

Location Looking at the photo of this hotel in Giza, Egypt, and at the map, how would you describe Giza's location?

Learning Geography

The study of geography has long been organized according to five important themes, or topics of study. One theme, location, deals with the exact or relative spot of something on Earth. Place includes the physical and human features of a location. Human-environment interaction covers the ways people and environments affect each other. Movement involves how people change locations and how goods are traded as well as the effects of these movements. For example, when people move they may bring animals, diseases, and their own culture to a new place. Region organizes Earth into geographic areas with one or more shared characteristics.

Another way to look at geography, however, is to study its essential elements, or most important parts. In 1994, several geographers and teachers created national geography standards called *Geography For Life*. The six essential elements they created to organize the study of geography are The World in Spatial Terms, Places and Regions, Physical Systems, Human Systems, Environment and Society, and The Uses of Geography. Because the six essential elements and the five themes share many of the same properties, both will be used throughout this textbook. Look for labels on questions, photographs, maps, graphs, and charts that show which geography theme or essential element is the main focus. In this section we discuss several topics related to the geography themes and essential elements. Here you will discover the relationship between these two ways of learning about our world.

✓ **READING CHECK:** *The Uses of Geography* What are the five themes of geography? What are the six essential elements? **location, place, human-environment interaction, movement, region; the world in spatial terms, places and regions, physical systems, human systems, environment and society, the uses of geography**

6 • Chapter 1

Section 2

Objectives
1. Identify tools geographers use to study the world.
2. Identify what shapes Earth's features.
3. Examine how humans shape the world.
4. Explain how studying geography helps us understand the world.

FOCUS

Bellringer

Write the following question on the chalkboard: *Where is your favorite shopping mall or movie theater located?* Have students respond to the question. If a student names the actual address for the building, explain that he or she has provided its absolute location. Tell students that in Section 1 they will learn about the difference between absolute and relative location and other topics of geography.

Building Vocabulary

Write the vocabulary terms on the chalkboard. Ask what we mean when we say "It's all relative" and "Absolutely!" Ask students for suggestions on how those phrases could relate to **absolute location** and **relative location**. Have students look up the remaining vocabulary terms in the text or glossary and write sentences using them.

The World in Spatial Terms

This element focuses on geography's spatial perspective. As you learned in Section 1, geographers apply spatial perspective when they look at the location of something and why it is there.

Location The term location can be used in two ways. **Absolute location** defines an exact spot on Earth. For example, the address of the Smithsonian American Art Museum is an absolute location. The address is at 8th and G Streets, N.W., in Washington, D.C. City streets often form a grid. This system tells anyone looking for an address where to go. The grid formed by latitude and longitude lines also pinpoints absolute location. Suppose you asked a pilot to take you to 52° north latitude by 175° west longitude. You would land at a location on Alaska's Aleutian Islands.

Relative location describes the position of a place in relation to another place. Measurements of direction, distance, or time can define relative location. For example, the following sentences give relative location. "The hospital is one mile north of our school." "Canada's border is about an hour's drive from Great Falls, Montana."

A geographer must be able to use maps and other geographic tools and technologies to determine spatial perspective. A geographer must also know how to organize and analyze information about people, places, and environments using geographic tools.

✓ **READING CHECK:** *The World in Spatial Terms* What two ways describe location? **absolute location and relative location**

PLACES AND REGIONS

Channeled Scablands
Geographers study not just the unique features of places and regions, but also how those features came to be. For example, geographers think that large Ice Age floods originating in western Montana created the Channeled Scablands in eastern Washington state. A glacier blocked a river and created a glacial lake near Missoula in present-day Montana. When this ice dam broke, a wall of water perhaps 2,000 feet (610 m) high crashed through the region, carving out unusual landforms such as the Channeled Scablands—an area marked by channels, cliffs, and steep-sided canyons. Scientists suspect that water poured from the lake at 60 or more miles per hour and that the glacial lake near Missoula may have filled and emptied dozens of times.

Places and Regions

To help explain why many areas of the world are similar to or different from one another, geographers organize Earth's surface into different places and regions. The Places and Regions essential element deals with how people have created regions based on Earth's features and how culture and other factors affect how we see places and regions.

Place Our world has a vast number of unique places and regions. A **place** can be described both by its physical location and by its physical and human features. Physical features include coastlines and landforms. They can also include lakes, rivers, or soil types. For example, Colorado is flat in the east but mountainous in the west. This is an example of a place being described in terms of its landforms. A place can also be described by its climate. For example, Greenland has long, cold winters. Florida has mild winters and hot, humid summers.

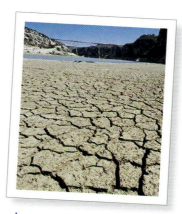

Place Places can be described by what they do not have. This photo shows the result of a long period without rain.

TEACH

Teaching Objectives 1–2
ALL LEVELS: (Suggested time: 20 min.) Pair students and have each pair create a geography fact sheet for the school. Fact sheets should include the school's absolute and relative location as well as several of its physical or human characteristics. Ask volunteers to read their fact sheets to the class. Then discuss why pairs may have chosen different identifying features. **ESOL, COOPERATIVE LEARNING**

Teaching Objectives 3–4
ALL LEVELS: (Suggested time: 30 min.) Have students draw maps of their neighborhoods, including homes, stores, streets, and other landmarks. Then have them locate their neighborhoods on a map of their town, city, or county. Tell students to label items on their maps that represent the relationship between environment and society. (such as dams, recycling plants, airports, train stations, and highways) Ask volunteers to share their maps with the class. **ESOL, LS VISUAL-SPATIAL**

CHAPTER 1, Section 2

PHYSICAL SYSTEMS

Permafrost Some of the factors in a physical system aren't immediately apparent. Some, for example, lie far underground. Permafrost lies under some 20 to 25 percent of the world's land surface. It occurs in more than 50 percent of Russia and Canada and more than 80 percent of Alaska.

Permafrost gives scientists a window into the plant and animal life of the past. The various layers of permafrost contain plant and animal remains from different periods of Earth's history. Some of these layers are more than 30,000 years old.

Scientists also use permafrost to assess the rate of global warming. By studying ground temperatures and preserved plant and animal life, scientists can understand past climatic conditions and current temperature change.

Critical Thinking: What may the presence of oak tree remains in a layer of permafrost indicate about past temperatures in a region near the North Pole?

Answer: that long ago the region was warmer

Visual Record Answer ▶

It represents a human adaptation to Egypt's environment.

Movement People travel from place to place on miles of new roadway.

Men in rural Egypt wear a long shirt called a *galabia*. This loose-fitting garment is ideal for people living in Egypt's hot desert climate. In addition, the galabia is made from cotton, an important agricultural product of Egypt.

Interpreting the Visual Record
Human-Environment Interaction How does the *galabia* show how people have adapted to their environment?

8 • Chapter 1

Region A **region** is an area of Earth's surface with one or more shared characteristics. Many of the characteristics that describe places can also be used to describe regions. Regions vary in size. Some are very large, like North America. Others are much smaller, like the Florida Keys. Regions are also different from the surrounding areas. For example, Silicon Valley is a region in California that is known for its many computer companies and engineers.

What defines a region? Some regions have boundaries that are easy to define. For example, natural vegetation regions have similar plants. Deserts, forests, and grasslands are examples of natural regions with fairly clear boundaries. A region can also be described as cultural, economic, or political.

✓ **READING CHECK:** *Places and Regions* What features can you use to describe a place? **physical and human features**

Physical Systems

Physical systems shape Earth's features. Geographers study earthquakes, mountains, rivers, volcanoes, weather patterns, and similar topics and how these physical systems have affected Earth's characteristics. For example, geographers might study how volcanic eruptions in the Hawaiian Islands spread lava, causing landforms to change. They might note that southern California's shoreline changes yearly, as winter and summer waves move beach sand.

Geographers also study how plants and animals relate to these nonliving physical systems. For example, deserts are places with cactus and other plants, as well as rattlesnakes and other reptiles, that can live in very dry conditions. Geographers also study how different types of plants, animals, and physical systems are distributed on Earth.

✓ **READING CHECK:** *Physical Systems* What types of physical systems do geographers study? **earthquakes, mountains, rivers, volcanoes, weather patterns, plants and animals, and similar topics**

Teaching Objective 4

ALL LEVELS: (Suggested time: 30 min.) Copy the following graphic organizer onto the chalkboard, omitting the blue answers. Use it to help students illustrate how regions and subregions help geographers understand our world. Using the United States as an example, tell students to identify regions (such as the East or the Midwest) and subregions (such as their state). Remind students that regions and subregions may vary in size and can be categorized as cultural, economic, or political. Then have students identify subregions of one subregion and classify each into one of these three categories. **ESOL**

REGIONS AND SUBREGIONS

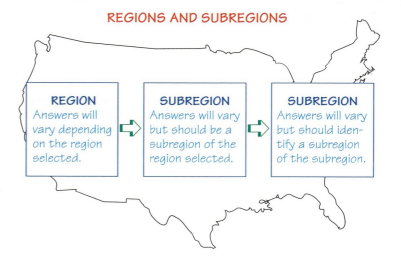

REGION	SUBREGION	SUBREGION
Answers will vary depending on the region selected.	Answers will vary but should be a subregion of the region selected.	Answers will vary but should identify a subregion of the subregion.

8 Chapter 1

Human Systems

People are central to geography. Geographers study human systems, or the human activities, movements, and settlements that shape Earth's surface. Human systems also include peoples' customs, history, languages, and religions.

Movement Geographers study the **movement** of people and ideas. When people move, they may go to live in other countries or move within a country. Geographers want to know how and why people move from place to place.

People move for many reasons. Some move to start a new job. Some move to attend special schools. Others might move to be closer to family. People move either when they are pushed out of a place or when they are pulled toward another place. In the Dust Bowl, for example, crop failures pushed people out of Oklahoma in the 1930s. Many were pulled to California by their belief that they would find work there.

Geographers also want to know how ideas or behaviors move from one region to another. The movement of ideas occurs through communication. There are many ways to communicate. People visit with each other in person or on the phone. New technology allows people to communicate by e-mail. Ideas are also spread through films, magazines, newspapers, radio, and television. The movement of ideas or behaviors from one region to another is known as **diffusion**.

The things we produce and trade are also part of the study of human systems. Geographers study trading patterns and how countries depend on each other for certain goods. In addition, geographers look at the causes and results of conflicts between peoples. The study of governments we set up and the features of cities and other settlements we live in are also part of this study.

✓ **READING CHECK:** *Human Systems* What are some reasons why people move? *start a new job, attend schools, be closer to family, to find work*

▲ A satellite dish brings different images and ideas to people in a remote area of Brazil.
Interpreting the Visual Record How might resources have affected the use of technology here?

▲ This woman at a railway station in Russian Siberia sells some goods that were once unavailable in her country.

Environment and Society

Human actions, such as using oil or water, affect the environment. At the same time, Earth's physical systems, such as climate or natural hazards, affect human activities. Our survival depends on what Earth provides. Many geographers consider the relationship between people and the environment a central focus of geography.

Human-Environment Interaction Geographers study how people and their surroundings affect each other. This relationship between people and the environment, or **human-environment interaction**, can be examined in three ways. First, geographers study

---

CHAPTER 1, Section 2

HUMAN SYSTEMS

Megamalls At more than 5 million square feet (465,000 sq m), West Edmonton Mall in Alberta, Canada, is the largest indoor shopping and entertainment complex in the world. The Mall of America, near Minneapolis, Minnesota, is the largest mall in the United States. These malls combine hundreds of stores, full-scale amusement parks, and other attractions. They have become the top tourist destination in their regions and attract people from as far away as Asia and Europe.

Activity: Have students conduct research on sales at West Edmonton Mall and the Mall of America. Ask students to compare the sales at these malls, explain their differences, and identify what role these malls play in the movement of goods.

▲ **Visual Record Answer**

People in the region value the ability to obtain information from other parts of the world and have invested their apparently scant resources in costly technology.

TEACHER TO TEACHER

Rebecca Minnear of Las Vegas, Nevada, suggests the following activity to help students understand the six essential elements of geography. Prior to class, draw an outline map of your community on six transparencies. Organize the class into six groups and assign one element to each group. Give each group a transparency sheet and a marker. Each group should draw on the transparency ways its element relates to the community. For example, the "places and regions" group might draw features of the local landscape. The "environment and society" group might draw waterways, streets, airports, and so on. Groups should draw the parts of the community in their proper place so that when the transparencies are placed on top of each other there will be an overlap.

▶**ASSIGNMENT:** Have students recall the most beautiful, interesting, or exciting place they have ever visited. Then have them write words or phrases that describe that place in terms of landforms, climate, animal life, plant life, language spoken, common religion, history, customs, or other physical or human characteristics. Ask students to consult primary or secondary sources for additional information. Then have students write a description of their chosen locale's relative location and find its absolute location by calculating latitude and longitude. You may also want to have students interpret the place in terms of the five themes of geography.

Section 2 Review

Answers to Section 2 Review

Define For definitions, see the glossary.

Reading for the Main Idea
1. with maps and other geographic tools (NGS 1)
2. physical systems such as earthquakes, mountains, rivers, volcanoes, weather patterns (NGS 7)

Critical Thinking
3. through their activities, movements, settlements, modifications
4. provides clues to the past and helps geographers plan for the future
5. The World in Spatial Terms—using maps and other geographic tools to look at the world with a spatial perspective; Places and Regions—studying the physical and human features of a place; Physical Systems—systems that have shaped Earth's features; Human Systems—how people have shaped Earth's surface; Environment and Society—how people and their surroundings affect each other; The Uses of Geography—how geography helps us understand relationships among people, places, and the environment over time

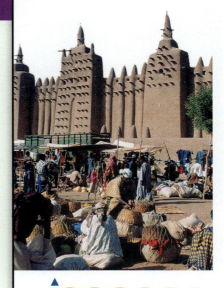

▲ Open-air markets like this one in Mali provide opportunities for farmers to sell their goods.

how humans depend on their physical environment to survive. Human life requires certain living and nonliving resources, such as freshwater and fertile soil for farming.

Geographers also study how humans change their behavior to be better suited to an environment. These changes or adaptations include the kinds of clothing, food, and shelter that people create. These changes help people live in harsh climates.

Finally, humans change the environment. For example, farmers who irrigate their fields can grow fruit in Arizona's dry climate. People in Louisiana have built levees, or large walls, to protect themselves when the Mississippi River floods.

✓ **READING CHECK:** *Environment and Society* How might people change to live in certain environments? **by changing the kinds of clothing, food, and shelter they create**

The Uses of Geography

Geography helps us understand the relationships among people, places, and the environment over time. Understanding how a relationship has developed can help in making plans for the future. For example, geographers can study how human use of the soil in a farming region has affected that region over time. Such knowledge can help them determine what changes have been made to the soil and whether any corrective measures need to be taken.

✓ **READING CHECK:** *The Uses of Geography* How can studying geography help plan for the future? **by helping us understand the relationships among people, places, and environments over time**

Homework Practice Online
Keyword: SK5 HP1

Section Review 2

Define and explain: absolute location, relative location, place, region, movement, diffusion, human-environment interaction

Reading for the Main Idea
1. *The World in Spatial Terms* How do geographers study the world?
2. *Physical Systems* What shapes Earth's features? Give examples.

Critical Thinking
3. **Finding the Main Idea** How do humans shape the world in which they live?
4. **Analyzing Information** What benefits can studying geography provide?

Organizing What You Know
5. **Summarizing** Copy the following graphic organizer. Use it to identify and describe all aspects of each of the six essential elements.

Element	Description

10 • Chapter 1

CLOSE

Display a picture of a well-known local landmark. Call on students to suggest how the themes and essential elements of geography relate to it.

REVIEW, ASSESS, RETEACH

Have students complete the Section Review. Then organize students into groups of four or five. Assign each group a city that appears on one of the Atlas maps in the textbook. Have students create a travel guide that describes the region in which the city is located. Then have students complete Daily Quiz 1.2. **COOPERATIVE LEARNING**

Have students complete Main Idea Activity S2. Then organize students into groups and assign each group one of the six essential elements. Ask members of each group to write a paragraph describing their element in relation to your school. **ESOL**, **LS VISUAL-LINGUISTIC**

EXTEND

Ask interested students to imagine that they have been hired to submit a building plan for a recreation center in their community. Tell them to use the themes and essential elements of geography to determine the center's location and construction features. Ask students to include a drawing of the building and a map showing its location. **BLOCK SCHEDULING**

Section 3: Being a Geographer

Read to Discover
1. What is included in the study of human geography?
2. What is included in the study of physical geography?
3. What types of work do geographers do?

Vocabulary
human geography
physical geography
cartography
meteorology
climatology

Reading Strategy

READING ORGANIZER Before you read this section, create a three column chart. Title the columns Human Geography, Physical Geography, and Working as a Geographer. As you read, write information that you learn about each topic on your chart.

Human Geography

The study of people, past or present, is the focus of **human geography**. People's location and distribution over Earth, their activities, and their differences are studied. For example, people living in different countries create different kinds of governments. Political geographers study those differences. Economic geographers study the exchange of goods and services across Earth. Cultural geography, population geography, and urban geography are some other examples of human geography. A professional geographer might specialize in any of these branches.

✓ **READING CHECK:** *Human Systems* How is human geography defined? *as the study of people, past or present*

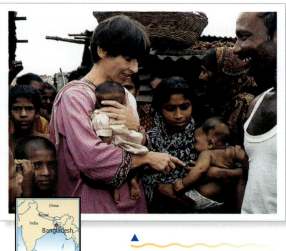

A volunteer visits a poor area of Bangladesh. Geographers study economic conditions in regions to help them understand human geography.

Physical Geography

The study of Earth's natural landscapes and physical systems, including the atmosphere, is the focus of **physical geography**. The world is full of different landforms such as deserts, mountains, and plains. Climates affect these landscapes. Knowledge of physical systems helps geographers understand how a landscape developed and how it might change.

A Geographer's World • 11

Section 3

Objectives
1. Explain the study of human geography.
2. Describe the study of physical geography.
3. Investigate the types of work that geographers do.

FOCUS

 **Bellringer**

Ask students what they would do if they were lost in an unfamiliar part of town. Then have them work in pairs to list ways to find their way home. (asking for directions or consulting a map) Ask them to describe the advantages or disadvantages of these options. Have them choose one of these solutions and create a map or written directions for a place with which they are both familiar. Tell them to evaluate the effectiveness of the solution by presenting their work to another pair.

Building Vocabulary

Tell students that the word **cartography** contains the common suffix *-graphy*, which means "writing or representation." Ask students what other words they know that contain the suffix. Point out that the prefix *cart-* indicates maps, so the complete word means writing or representing maps. Divide **meteorology** also: *meteor-*, from a Greek word meaning "high in the air"; and *-logy*, meaning "a branch of learning." Then ask students to use what they just learned to define **climatology**.

CHAPTER 1, Section 3

FOOD FESTIVAL

The Geography of Food
Have students bring food items to class and use them to discuss human and physical geography. For example, a student may bring a can of green beans and note that certain soil, sunlight, and climate conditions must be present to grow the beans. Or a student may use the can to discuss how people in different parts of the country prepare green beans, or how farms and canneries affect local economies.

Connecting to Technology
Answers
1. It can help planners build roads, dams, or other structures.
2. greater knowledge about population, profitable economic activities, or change to the environment

Connecting to Technology

A mapmaker creates a digital map.

Maps are tools that can display a wide range of information. Traditionally, maps were drawn on paper and could not be changed to suit the user. However, computers have revolutionized the art of mapmaking.

Today, mapmakers use computers to create and modify maps for different uses. They do this by using a geographic information system, or GIS. A GIS is a computer system that combines maps and satellite photographs with other kinds of spatial data—information about places on the planet. This information might include soil types, population figures, or voting patterns.

Using a GIS, mapmakers can create maps that show geographic features and relationships. For example, a map showing rainfall patterns in a particular region might be combined with data on soil types or human settlement to show areas of possible soil erosion.

The flexibility of a GIS allows people to seek answers to specific questions. Where should a new road be built to ease traffic congestion? How are changes in natural habitat affecting wildlife? These and many other questions can be answered with the help of computer mapping.

Computer Mapping

Understanding What You Read
1. How could a GIS help people change their environment?
2. What social, environmental, or economic consequences might future advances in GIS technology have?

Knowledge of physical and human geography will help you understand the world's different regions and peoples. In your study of the major world regions, you will see how physical and human geography connect to each other.

✓ **READING CHECK:** *Physical Systems* What is included in the study of physical geography? *Earth's natural landscapes and physical systems, including the atmosphere*

Working as a Geographer

Geography plays a role in almost every occupation. Wherever you live and work, you should know local geography. School board members know where children live. Taxi drivers are familiar with city streets. Grocery store managers know which foods sell well in certain areas.

TEACH

Teaching Objectives 1–3
ALL LEVELS: (Suggested time: 20 min.) Copy the following graphic organizer onto the chalkboard, omitting the blue answers. Use it to help students distinguish between the study of human geography and the study of physical geography and to identify the types of work geographers do. **ESOL**, **LS** VISUAL-SPATIAL

Geography helps us understand the world.

Physical Geography	Types of work	Human Geography
the study of	include	the study of
• Earth's natural landscapes and physical systems	• cartography • meteorology • climatology	• people, past or present • politics, economy, and culture
• different landforms		

They also know where they can obtain these products throughout the year. Local newspaper reporters are familiar with town meetings and local politicians. Reporters also know how faraway places can affect their communities. Doctors must know if their towns have poisonous snakes or plants. City managers know whether nearby rivers might flood. Emergency workers in mountain towns check snow depth so they can give avalanche warnings. Local weather forecasters watch for powerful storms and track their routes on special maps.

Some specially trained geographers practice in the field of **cartography**. Cartography is the art and science of mapmaking. Today, most mapmakers do their work on computers. Geographers also work as weather forecasters. The field of forecasting and reporting rainfall, temperature, and other atmospheric conditions is called **meteorology**. A related field is **climatology**. These geographers, known as climatologists, track Earth's larger atmospheric systems. Climatologists want to know how these systems change over long periods of time. They also study how people might be affected by changes in climate.

Governments and a variety of organizations hire geographers to study the environment. These geographers might explore such topics as pollution, endangered plants and animals, or rain forests. Some geographers who are interested in education become teachers and writers. They help people of all ages learn more about the world. Modern technology allows people all over the world to communicate instantly. Therefore, it is more important than ever to be familiar with the geographer's world.

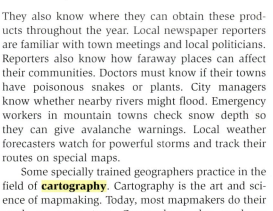

Experts examine snow to help forecast avalanches. They study the type of snow, weather conditions, and landforms.

✓ **READING CHECK:** (The Uses of Geography) What types of work do geographers perform? They make maps, work as weather forecasters, track atmospheric systems, or work as teachers or writers.

Homework Practice Online
Keyword: SK5 HP1

Section Review 3

Define and explain: human geography, physical geography, cartography, meteorology, climatology

Reading for the Main Idea
1. (Human Systems) What topics are included in the study of human geography?
2. (The Uses of Geography) How do people who study the weather use geography?

Critical Thinking
3. **Finding the Main Idea** Why is it important to study physical geography?
4. **Making Generalizations and Predictions** How might future discoveries in the field of geography affect societies, world economies, or the environment?

Organizing What You Know
5. **Categorizing** Copy the following graphic organizer. Use it to list geographers' professions and their job responsibilities.

Cartographer		
–makes maps		
–studies maps		

A Geographer's World • 13

Section 3 Review

Answers to Section 3 Review

Define For definitions, see the glossary.

Reading for the Main Idea
1. Topics are the study of people, their location and distribution, their activities, and their differences. **(NGS 9)**
2. by tracking Earth's larger atmospheric systems **(NGS 18)**

Critical Thinking
3. to learn how a landscape developed and how it might change
4. by helping resolve problems regarding population, pollution, endangered plants and animals, or through increased economic activities **(NGS 18)**

Organizing What You Know
5. meteorologist—tracks weather and atmospheric conditions; climatologist—tracks atmospheric systems

---

CLOSE

Write the following statement on the chalkboard: *A cartographer's work is never done.* Ask students why might this be true. (Possible answers: changes required by physical processes, new roads and suburbs, and political boundary changes)

Have students complete Main Idea Activity S3. Then have them complete the following sentence: "I used my knowledge of geography today when I . . . " Ask volunteers to read their sentences to the class. **ESOL, LS INTERPERSONAL**

REVIEW, ASSESS, RETEACH

Have students complete the Section Review. Then pair students and have each pair locate newspaper or magazine articles that relate to some aspect of human or physical geography. Have pairs write a few sentences explaining the connection between the articles and human or physical geography. Then have students complete Daily Quiz 1.3. **COOPERATIVE LEARNING**

EXTEND

Have interested students conduct research on the history of cartography in an area that has been mapped since antiquity. Have them use copies of ancient maps to investigate how maps of that region have evolved over time and then present their findings to the class. **BLOCK SCHEDULING**

A Geographer's World 13

CHAPTER 1

HISTORICAL GEOGRAPHY

Hurricanes and typhoons—as these large storms are called when they occur in the Pacific Ocean—have changed history. Here are just three examples.

In 1281 the Mongol ruler Kublai Khan was ready to invade Japan, but a typhoon scattered his huge fleet of ships. A second storm, dubbed the Great Hurricane, ravaged the Caribbean in October 1780. It killed approximately 22,000 people and may be the deadliest hurricane on record. British and French fleets involved in the American Revolutionary War were both ravaged. Finally, in December 1944, during World War II, a sudden typhoon east of the Philippines caught the U.S. Third Fleet by surprise. Three destroyers, 146 aircraft, and several hundred men were lost.

Critical Thinking: How could early storm warning technology have changed world history?

Answer: Answers will vary but students might mention a successful invasion by Kublai Khan, fewer deaths in the Caribbean, and fewer ships and lives lost during the Revolutionary War and World War II.

➤ This Case Study feature addresses National Geography Standards 4, 15, and 17.

CASE STUDY

HOW GEOGRAPHERS TRACK HURRICANES

As you learned in Chapter 1, geographers called climatologists study Earth's atmosphere. Sometimes large circulating storms called hurricanes develop in the atmosphere above tropical oceans. Hurricanes often move over land and into populated areas. When a hurricane approaches land, it brings strong winds, heavy rains, and large ocean waves.

Climatologists try to predict where these storms will travel. They want to be able to warn people in the hurricane's path. Early warnings can help people be better prepared for the deadly winds and rain. It is a difficult job because hurricanes can change course suddenly. Hurricanes are one of the most dangerous natural hazards.

The map below shows the path of Hurricane Fran in 1996. Notice how Fran moved to the west and became stronger until it reached land. It began as a tropical depression and became a powerful hurricane as it passed over warm ocean waters.

One way of determining a hurricane's strength is by measuring the atmospheric pressure inside it. The lower the pressure, the stronger the storm. Hurricanes are rated on a scale of one to five. Study Table 1 to see how wind speed and air pressure are used to help determine the strength of a hurricane.

Hurricane Mitch formed in October 1998. The National Weather Service (NWS) recorded Mitch's position and strength. They learned that Mitch's pressure was one of the lowest ever recorded. The

Table 1: Saffir-Simpson Scale

HURRICANE TYPE	WIND SPEED MPH	AIR PRESSURE MB (INCHES)
Category 1	74–95	more than 980 (28.94)
Category 2	96–110	965–979 (28.50–28.91)
Category 3	111–130	945–964 (27.91–28.47)
Category 4	131–155	920–944 (27.17–27.88)
Category 5	more than 155	less than 920 (27.17)

Source: Florida State University, <http://www.met.fsu.edu/explores/tropical.html>

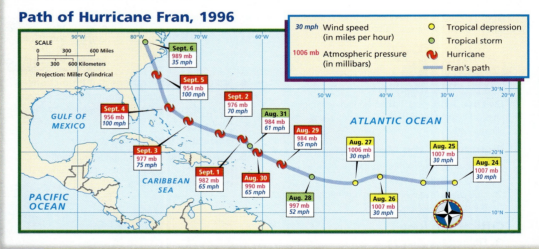

Path of Hurricane Fran, 1996

Setting the Scene

Every year, hurricanes torment residents of the Caribbean islands, the coastlands bordering the Gulf of Mexico, and the East Coast of the United States. Because hurricanes get their strength from warm water, hurricane season lasts through summer and into fall. These storms carry tremendous energy. In one day an average hurricane releases at least 8,000 times the daily electrical power output of the United States. Severe hurricanes can cause billions of dollars of damage. Fewer lives are lost now than in years past, however, because early warning systems help predict the storms' paths and power. Coastal towns and cities evacuate people before the storms arrive. Satellites provide much of the information used to make storm predictions.

Building a Case

Have students read "Hurricane: Tracking a Natural Hazard" and follow the instructions in You Be the Geographer. Ask on what date the atmospheric pressure was lowest. (10/27) How did Mitch register on the Saffir-Simpson Scale that day? (category 5) Compare Hurricane Mitch with the hurricane that struck Galveston on September 8, 1900.

The storm headed for Galveston was first observed on August 30. The Weather Bureau placed Galveston under a storm warning on September 7. September 8 dawned rainy and gusty. Though the storm worsened, few residents left the city. At 6:30 P.M. a storm surge flooded the city. The lowest barometer reading was 27.91. Windspeed was estimated at more than 120 mph. By 10:00 P.M. much of the city was wrecked. As many as 8,000 city residents died.

Table 2: Hurricane Mitch, 1998 Position and Strength

Date	Latitude (degrees)	Longitude (degrees)	Wind Speed (mph)	Pressure (millibars)	Storm Type
10/22	12 N	78 W	30	1002	Tropical depression
10/24	15 N	78 W	90	980	Category 2
10/26	16 N	81 W	130	923	Category 4
10/27	17 N	84 W	150	910	Category 5
10/31	15 N	88 W	40	1000	Tropical storm
11/01	15 N	90 W	30	1002	Tropical depression
11/03	20 N	91 W	40	997	Tropical storm
11/05	26 N	83 W	50	990	Tropical storm

Source: <http://www.met.fsu.edu/explores/tropical.html>

NWS estimated that Mitch's maximum sustained surface winds reached 180 miles per hour.

Hurricanes like Mitch cause very heavy rains in short periods of time. These heavy rains are particularly dangerous. The ground becomes saturated, and mud can flow almost like water. The flooding and mudslides caused by Mitch killed an estimated 10,000 people in four countries. Many people predicted that the region would not recover without help from other countries.

In the southeastern United States, many places have emergency preparedness units. The people assigned to these groups organize their communities. They provide food, shelter, and clothing for those who must evacuate their homes.

You Be the Geographer

1. Trace a map of the Caribbean. Be sure to include latitude and longitude lines.
2. Use the data about Hurricane Mitch in Table 2 to plot its path. Make a key with symbols to show Mitch's strength at each location.
3. What happened to Mitch when it reached land?

This satellite image shows the intensity of Hurricane Mitch. With advanced technology, hurricane tracking is helping to save lives.

CHAPTER 1

You Be the Geographer

1. Students may trace the map on the previous page. Or, provide an outline map to students.
2. On student maps, from its first position Hurricane Mitch should progress north-northwest toward Cuba, swing southwest toward Nicaragua, then back northeast across the Yucatán Peninsula on its way to the open Atlantic Ocean.
3. When it reached land, Mitch's strength weakened.

internet connect
GO TO: go.hrw.com
KEYWORD: SG5 CH1
FOR: Web sites about hurricanes

A Geographer's World • 15

Drawing Conclusions

Lead a discussion comparing the two storms. According to wind speed and air pressure, what level storm was the Galveston hurricane? **(3)** Which was the stronger storm? **(Mitch)** Which hurricane lasted longer? **(Mitch)** Why did the 1900 storm kill so many people in such a short time? **(They had not evacuated the city.)** If there had been no warning system, how might Hurricane Mitch have affected the Caribbean region? **(It might have killed even more people.)**

What might have happened if Galveston had been warned earlier? Have students prepare and present an alternate newscast for the morning of September 9, 1900, based on this possibility.

Going Further: Thinking Critically

Locate detailed maps of the Gulf of Mexico or Atlantic coasts of the United States. Use maps of different areas or concentrate on one region. Have students work in groups to answer some or all of these questions:

- What cities and towns might be threatened by a hurricane? Can students estimate how many people live in the area?
- What routes could residents use to evacuate? What factors might slow evacuation? If they could travel about 30 mph **(48 km/h)**, how far could people travel in one day? two days?
- What would happen if residents were warned just a few hours before a hurricane? What effect might an early warning system have on this region?

A Geographer's World 15

CHAPTER 1 REVIEW

Define and Identify
For definitions and identifications, see the glossary and index.

Review the Main Ideas

18. a science that describes the physical and cultural features of Earth
19. cities; open land that is often used for farming (NGS 12)
20. local, regional, or global; answers will vary
21. a street address; where it is relative to known landmarks (NGS 1)
22. both by its physical location and by its physical and human features
23. in terms of vegetation; also cultural, economic, or political (NGS 5)
24. to start a new job, attend schools, be closer to family, find work (NGS 9)
25. by changing kinds of clothing, food, and shelter (NGS 15)
26. possible answers: because accurate maps can help businesses, can help people enjoy travel, and even save lives (NGS 3)
27. possible answers: study pollution, endangered plants and animals, or rain forests; teach or write

Think Critically

28. Answers will vary, but students might mention that a geographer identifies where things are so that connections can be made.
29. when—daily; how—answers will vary; examples might include building dams and irrigating fields
30. Students might mention the movement of people, trade networks, or the diffusion of ideas between groups.
31. both human and physical characteristics
32. by helping us see meaning in the arrangement of things on Earth

Map Activity
33. A. Europe
    B. North America
    C. Antarctica
    D. South America
    E. Asia
    F. Australia
    G. Africa

CHAPTER 1 Review and Practice

Define and Identify
Identify each of the following:

1. perspective
2. spatial perspective
3. geography
4. urban
5. rural
6. absolute location
7. relative location
8. place
9. region
10. movement
11. diffusion
12. human-environment interaction
13. human geography
14. physical geography
15. cartography
16. meteorology
17. climatology

Review the Main Ideas

18. What is geography?
19. What do urban areas contain? What do rural areas contain?
20. What are three ways to study geography? Give an example of when each type could be used.
21. What kind of directions would you give to indicate a place's absolute location? Its relative location?
22. How can a place be described?
23. What are some ways to define a region?
24. What are some reasons why people move?
25. How do some people adapt to better suit their environment?
26. Why is cartography important?
27. What types of jobs do geographers do?

Think Critically

28. **Analyzing Information** How can a geographer use spatial perspective to explain how things in our world are connected?
29. **Drawing Inferences and Conclusions** When and how do humans relate to the environment? Provide some examples of this relationship.
30. **Summarizing** How are patterns created by the movement of goods, ideas, and people?
31. **Finding the Main Idea** How are places and regions defined?
32. **Finding the Main Idea** How does studying geography help us understand the world?

Map Activity

33. On a separate sheet of paper, match the letters on the map with their correct labels.

    Africa   Europe
    Antarctica   North America
    Asia   South America
    Australia

16 • Chapter 1

Writing Activity

Write a letter persuading another student to enroll in a geography class. Include examples of professions that use geography and relate that information to the everyday life of a student. Be sure to use standard grammar, spelling, sentence structure, and punctuation.

internet connect

Internet Activity: go.hrw.com
KEYWORD: SJ5 GT1

Choose a topic to explore online:
- Learn to use online maps.
- Be a virtual geographer for a day.
- Compare regions around the world.

Social Studies Skills Practice

Interpreting Maps

Study the following map of the state of California. Use what you know about location to answer the questions.

1. How would you describe the relative location of Los Angeles?
2. If you were in San Francisco, how would you describe the relative location of Yosemite National Park?
3. What would you use on this map to find the absolute location of places?
4. What is the absolute location of Los Angeles?

Analyzing Primary Sources

Read the following quote from geographer Dr. Reginald G. Golledge. Then answer the questions.

"As I was growing up in Australia, my family moved frequently, largely from one small town to another . . . The small-town environment and the surrounding countryside favored the development of a state of mind that constantly asked, 'What's over the next hill? How far is it to the river? Where are the wild berries and fruits located?'"

Source: *Geographical Voices: Fourteen Autobiographical Essays*

1. Did Dr. Golledge grow up in a rural area or an urban area?
2. How do you think Dr. Golledge's childhood experiences led him to become a geographer?
3. As a child, was Golledge interested more in human geography or physical geography?
4. Which two of the five geography themes best describes the questions Dr. Golledge asks?

A Geographer's World • 17

CHAPTER 1 REVIEW

Writing Activity

Letters will vary, but should include various professions that use geography. Letters should also relate the use of geography to the everyday life of a student. Use Rubric 25, Personal Letters, to evaluate student work.

Interpreting Maps

1. on the southern coast of California
2. east of San Francisco, in the Sierra Nevada
3. lines of latitude and longitude
4. 118°W, 34°N

Analyzing Primary Sources

1. rural
2. by stimulating his curiosity about his surroundings
3. physical geography
4. possible answer: location and place

REVIEW AND ASSESSMENT RESOURCES

Reproducible
- Readings in World Geography, History, and Culture 1, 2
- Critical Thinking Activity 1
- Vocabulary Activity 1

Technology
- Chapter 1 Test Generator (on the One-Stop Planner)
- Audio CD Program, Chapter 1
- HRW Go site

Reinforcement, Review, and Assessment
- Chapter 1 Review and Practice
- Chapter Summaries and Review
- Chapter 1 Test
- Chapter 1 Test for English Language Learners and Special-Needs Students

internet connect

GO TO: go.hrw.com
KEYWORD: SJ5 Teacher
FOR: a guide to using the Internet in your classroom

CHAPTER 2: Planet Earth
Chapter Resource Manager

Objectives	Pacing Guide	Reproducible Resources
SECTION 1 **The Land** (pp. 19–24) 1. Describe the processes that build up the land. 2. Describe the processes that shape Earth's surface. 3. Show how topography has affected human history and culture.	**Regular** 1.5 day Lecture Notes, Section 1 **Block Scheduling** 1 day Block Scheduling Handbook, Chapter 2	**RS** Know It Notes S1 **RS** Graphic Organizer 2 **SM** Critical Thinking Activity 2 **E** Environmental and Global Issues Activity 3 **E** Lab Activities for Geography and Earth Science, Hands-On 5, Demonstrations 3–10 **E** Readings in World Geography, History, and Culture, Reading 3 **E** Biography Activity: Louis Agassiz **ELL** Main Idea Activity S1
SECTION 2 **Water and Air** (pp. 25–31) 1. Identify where water is found on Earth. 2. Analyze the water cycle. 3. Explore how people and water affect each other. 4. Explain the short-term and long-term results of air pollution.	**Regular** 1.5 day Lecture Notes, Section 2 **Block Scheduling** 1 day Block Scheduling Handbook, Chapter 2	**RS** Know It Notes S2 **IC** Lab Activities for Geography and Earth Science, Demonstration 1 **ELL** Main Idea Activity S2
SECTION 3 **Climate, Weather and Vegetation** (pp. 32–37) 1. Identify the factors that create climate and weather. 2. Describe how climate, plants, and animal life are related.	**Regular** 1.5 day Lecture Notes, Section 3 **Block Scheduling** 1 day Block Scheduling Handbook, Chapter 2	**RS** Know It Notes S3 **IC** Environmental and Global Issues Activities 1, 2 **SM** Map Activity 3 **E** Lab Activities for Geography and Earth Science, Hands-On 1, Demonstrations 11, 12 **E** Geography for Life Activities 2–4 **E** Creative Strategies for Teaching World Geography, Lesson 13 **ELL** Main Idea Activity S3
SECTION 4 **Natural Resources** (pp. 38–43) 1. Identify the most important renewable resources. 2. Explain how the main energy resources differ. 3. Explore how we use mineral resources. 4. Discover how resources affect people.	**Regular** 1.5 day Lecture Notes, Section 4 **Block Scheduling** 1 day Block Scheduling Handbook, Chapter 2	**RS** Know It Notes S4 **IC** Environmental and Global Issues Activities 1, 2, 4–8 **IC** Lab Activities for Geography and Earth Science, Hands-On 3, Demonstration 8 **E** Geography for Life Activity 4 **E** Readings in World Geography, History, and Culture, Readings 5, 7, 8 **SM** Map Activity 4 **E** Creative Strategies for Teaching World Geography, Lesson 8 **ELL** Main Idea Activity S4

Chapter Resource Key

- **RS** Reading Support
- **IC** Interdisciplinary Connections
- **E** Enrichment
- **SM** Skills Mastery
- **A** Assessment
- **REV** Review
- **ELL** Reinforcement and English Language Learners and English for Speakers of Other Languages (ESOL)
- Transparencies
- CD–ROM
- Music
- Video
- Internet go.hrw.com
- Holt Presentation Maker Using Microsoft® PowerPoint®

One-Stop Planner CD–ROM

See the *One-Stop Planner* for a complete list of additional resources for students and teachers.

One-Stop Planner CD-ROM

It's easy to plan lessons, select resources, and print out materials for your students when you use the *One-Stop Planner CD–ROM with Test Generator.*

Technology Resources

- One-Stop Planner CD-ROM, Lesson 2.1
- *ARGWorld* CD–ROM
- Homework Practice Online
- HRW Go site

Review, Reinforcement, and Assessment Resources

- **ELL** Main Idea Activity S1
- **REV** Section 1 Review
- **A** Daily Quiz 2.1
- **REV** Chapter Summaries and Review
- **ELL** English Audio Summary 2.1
- **ELL** Spanish Audio Summary 2.1

- One-Stop Planner CD-ROM, Lesson 2.2
- Geography and Cultures Visual Resources 13
- *ARGWorld* CD–ROM
- Homework Practice Online
- HRW Go site

- **ELL** Main Idea Activity S2
- **REV** Section 2 Review
- **A** Daily Quiz 2.2
- **REV** Chapter Summaries and Review
- **ELL** English Audio Summary 2.2
- **ELL** Spanish Audio Summary 2.2

- One-Stop Planner CD-ROM, Lesson 2.3
- *ARGWorld* CD–ROM
- Homework Practice Online
- HRW Go site

- **ELL** Main Idea Activity S3
- **REV** Section 3 Review
- **A** Daily Quiz 2.3
- **REV** Chapter Summaries and Review
- **ELL** English Audio Summary 2.3
- **ELL** Spanish Audio Summary 2.3

- One-Stop Planner CD-ROM, Lesson 2.4
- *ARGWorld* CD–ROM
- Homework Practice Online
- HRW Go site

- **ELL** Main Idea Activity S4
- **REV** Section 4 Review
- **A** Daily Quiz 2.4
- **REV** Chapter Summaries and Review
- **ELL** English Audio Summary 2.4
- **ELL** Spanish Audio Summary 2.4

---

internet connect

HRW ONLINE RESOURCES

GO TO: go.hrw.com
Then type in a keyword.

TEACHER HOME PAGE
KEYWORD: SJ5 TEACHER

CHAPTER INTERNET ACTIVITIES
KEYWORD: SJ5 GT2

Choose an activity to:
- learn more about using weather maps.
- discover facts about Earth's water.
- investigate earthquakes.

CHAPTER ENRICHMENT LINKS
KEYWORD: SJ5 CH2

CHAPTER MAPS
KEYWORD: SJ5 MAPS2

ONLINE ASSESSMENT
Homework Practice
KEYWORD: SJ5 HP2
Standardized Test Prep Online
KEYWORD: SJ5 STP2
Rubrics
KEYWORD: SS Rubrics

COUNTRY INFORMATION
KEYWORD: SJ5 Almanac

CONTENT UPDATES
KEYWORD: SS Content Updates

HOLT PRESENTATION MAKER
KEYWORD: SJ5 PPT2

ONLINE READING SUPPORT
KEYWORD: SS Strategies

CURRENT EVENTS
KEYWORD: S5 Current Events

Meeting Individual Needs

Ability Levels

Level 1 Basic-level activities designed for all students encountering new material

Level 2 Intermediate-level activities designed for average students

Level 3 Challenging activities designed for honors and gifted-and-talented students

ESOL Activities that address the needs of students with Limited English Proficiency

---

Chapter Review and Assessment

- **E** Readings in World Geography, History, and Culture 5–8
- **SM** Critical Thinking Activity 2
- **REV** Chapter 2 Review and Practice
- **REV** Chapter Summaries and Review
- **ELL** Vocabulary Activity 2
- **A** Chapter 2 Test
- **A** Chapter 2 Test Generator (on the One-Stop Planner)
- Audio CD program, Chapter 2
- **A** Chapter 2 Test for English Language learners and Special Needs Students
- HRW Go site

Chapter 2: Planet Earth
Previewing Chapter Resources

Holt Online Learning

Keyword: SJ5 GT2

- Homework Practice Online
- Holt Online Assessment
- Online Gradebook
- Document-Based Question Activities
- Teaching Tips for the Multimedia Classroom
- Interactive Multimedia Activities

Differentiating Instruction

Reading and Writing Support
- Graphic Organizer Activity
- Vocabulary Activity
- Chapter Summary and Review
- Know It Notes
- Audio CD

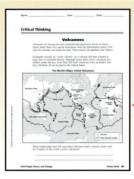

Active Learning
- Block Scheduling Handbook
- Cultures of the World Activity
- Interdisciplinary Activity
- Map Activity
- Critical Thinking Activity: Volcanoes

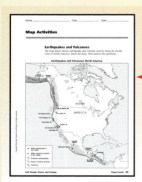

Primary Sources and Advanced Learners
- Geography for Life Activity: Hurricane Season
- Map Activity: Earthquakes and Volcanoes
- Readings in World Geography, History and Culture:
  - 3 Preparing for the Big One
  - 4 Earth's Rotation in Our Daily Lives

Assessment Program
- Daily Quizzes S1–4
- Chapter Test
- Chapter Test for English Language Learners and Special-Needs Students

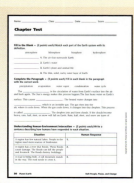

Spanish and ESOL
- Vocabulary Activity
- Main Idea Activities for English Language Learners and Special-Needs Students
- Chapter Summary and Review
- Spanish Audio Summary
- Know It Notes S1–4
- Chapter Test for English Language Learners and Special-Needs Students

Special Education Modifications
Your **I.D.E.A. Works! CD-ROM** will provide modified versions of the following teaching materials:
- Guided Reading Strategies S1–4
- Vocabulary Activity
- Main Idea Activities S1–4
- Daily Quizzes S1–4
- Chapter 2 Test
- Flash cards of chapter vocabulary terms

Teacher Resources

Books for Teachers
Jones, William Barrie. *Discovering the Solar System.* John Wiley & Sons, 1999.

Munsart, Craig A. *American History through Earth Science.* Teacher Ideas Press, 1997.

Windley, Brian F. *The Evolving Continents.* John Wiley & Sons, 1995.

Books for Students
Farndon, John. *How the Earth Works.* Reader's Digest, 1992. Descriptions, illustrations, and experiments about Earth. **SHELTERED ENGLISH**

Lauber, Patricia. *Volcano: The Eruption and Healing of Mount St. Helens.* Aladdin Paperbacks, 1993. Why it erupted, the destruction it caused, and the return of life to the mountain.

Redfern, Martin. *The Kingfisher Young People's Book of Space.* Kingfisher, 1998. Definitions of black holes, galaxies, the solar system, the Milky Way, and more.

Singh, Madanjeet, and UNESCO. *The Timeless Energy of the Sun.* Sierra Club Books, 1999. Explores the potential for integrating the latest solar technologies into traditional cultures.

Multimedia Materials
Earth Quest. CD–ROM. DK Family Learning.

Interactive Earth. CD–ROM. Worldlink.

On the Edge of the World. Video, 60 min. Films for the Humanities and Sciences.

Videos and CDs

Videos
- **CNN.** *Presents Geography: Yesterday and Today, Segment 2 Birth of an Island; Segment 3 Global Warming*
- *ARG World*

Holt Researcher
http://researcher.hrw.com
- *Global Problem of Acid Rain*
- *Clean Air Act of 1970*
- *Clean Water Act (Federal Water Pollution Control Act Amendments)*
- *Water Quality Improvement Act*
- *World*

Transparency Packages

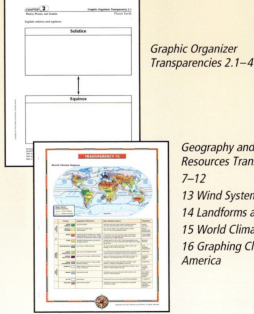

Graphic Organizer Transparencies 2.1–4

Geography and Cultures Visual Resources Transparencies
7–12
13 Wind Systems
14 Landforms and Precipitation
15 World Climate Regions
16 Graphing Climate in South America

Map Activities Transparency 02 Earthquakes and Volcanoes

17D

CHAPTER 2

WHY IT MATTERS

These are among the reasons why students should take an interest in this chapter's topics:

- By learning more about how land is formed and changed, we can save lives threatened by earthquakes, volcanoes, and other hazards.
- To protect our supplies of clean water and clean air, we should know more about these precious resources.
- We can plan daily activities better if we understand the weather and how it changes.
- We make decisions about using resources every day. We need to be informed to make good decisions.

CHAPTER 2

Planet Earth

Diver, coral, and fish, Fiji Islands

Quartz crystals

Erupting volcano

Tornado in Saskatoon, Canada

18 • Chapter 2

CHAPTER PROJECT

Have students research the origin of local or nearby landforms. (Possible origins include glacial action, volcanic action, and sedimentation.) To present their findings, have students label landforms on a topographic map according to how they were formed. You may want to have students design models that show the formation processes. Photograph the models and place the pictures in student portfolios.

STARTING THE CHAPTER

Write *air, earth, fire,* and *water* on the chalkboard. Tell students that long ago, people thought that these four were elements and that everything was made from them. Ask students to identify different forms of these "elements." Write their responses under the appropriate categories on the chalkboard. (Examples: air—wind, tornadoes, ozone; earth—dirt, landslides, mountains; fire—volcanoes, forest fires; water—rain, oceans, rivers, water from pipes and faucets) Tell students that although we now know that air, earth, fire, and water are not elements, understanding their characteristics and relationships helps us understand geography and life on Earth.

Section 1 The Land

Read to Discover
1. What processes build up the land?
2. What processes shape Earth's surfaces?
3. How has topography affected human history and culture?

Vocabulary
- landforms
- topography
- plate tectonics
- subduction
- earthquakes
- lava
- fault
- weathering
- erosion
- plain
- alluvial fan
- floodplain
- delta
- glaciers
- terraces

Reading Strategy

TAKING NOTES Taking notes while you read will help you understand and remember the information in this section. Write down the headings in the section. As you read, fill in notes under each heading. Underline the most important details you find.

Building Up the Land

Landforms are shapes on Earth's surface. The shape, height, and arrangement of landforms in a certain place is called **topography**. The theory of **plate tectonics** helps explain how Earth's topography formed and how it changes. According to this theory, Earth's surface is divided into several large plates, or pieces. There are also a number of smaller plates. These plates move very slowly—just inches per year.

Plate Tectonics

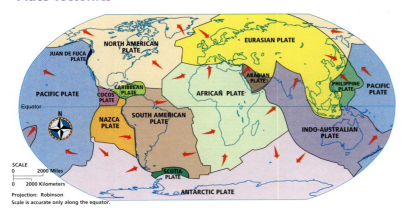

The plates that make up Earth's crust are moving, usually a few inches per year. This map shows the plates and the direction of their movement.

CHAPTER 2, Section 1

SECTION 1 RESOURCES
Reproducible
- Lecture Notes, Section 1
- Know It Notes S1
- Environmental and Global Issues Activity 3
- Lab Activities for Geography and Earth Science, Hands-On 5, Demonstrations 3–10
- Geography for Life Activity 4
- Readings in World Geography, History, and Culture, Reading 3
- Map Activity 2
- Critical Thinking Activity 2
- Main Idea Activity S1
- Biography Activity: Louis Agassiz

Technology
- One-Stop Planner CD-ROM, Lesson 2.1
- Homework Practice Online
- Geography and Cultures Visual Resources 11–13
- HRW Go Site

Reinforcement, Review, and Assessment
- Section 1 Review
- Daily Quiz 2.1
- Main Idea Activity S1
- Chapter Summaries and Review
- English Audio Summary 2.1
- Spanish Audio Summary 2.1

Planet Earth • 19

Section 1

Objectives
1. Describe the processes that build up the land.
2. Describe the processes that shape Earth's surface.
3. Show how topography has affected human history and culture.

FOCUS

 Bellringer
Write the following question on the chalkboard: *What do we mean when we say "solid as a rock," "mountain of strength," or "older than dirt"?* Use student responses to conduct a class discussion. Then ask students what the phrases suggest about Earth *(that it is unchangeable and permanent)*. Tell students that in Section 1 they will learn that Earth is actually in motion and changes both slowly and quickly.

Building Vocabulary
Write the vocabulary words on slips of paper and have each student draw one from a hat. You will probably need to have duplicates of some terms. Ask students to find the definitions in the text and read them to the class. Then write *shapes on Earth's surface*, *slow movement*, and *fast change* on the chalkboard. Have the students determine the appropriate category for each term.

CHAPTER 2, Section 1

Linking Past to Present
Lava and Ice

According to some historical accounts, Iceland has experienced about 60 gigantic floods since the Vikings arrived in the A.D. 800s. Scientists had doubted the accuracy of these accounts. However, events in November 1996 showed how these floods could have occurred.

Water that had been melted by a volcanic eruption broke out from under the Vatnajökull ice cap. Ash and steam gushed up through the ice, melting a huge hole in it. The runoff carved a canyon in the ice—a canyon 500 feet deep and more than two miles long. Magma melted more of the ice cap's bottom layers. Billions of gallons of water drained into an ice-covered crater. The water raised the crater's thick lid of ice and then flowed downhill underneath the ice cap. Finally, the water burst out from under the ice. Blocks of ice as large as buildings ripped loose. When the flood crashed into a bridge it was flowing at 1.6 million cubic feet per second.

Visual Record Answer

The mountains have been thrust up by the force of colliding plates.

Colliding Plates Some of the plates collide as they move, and one plate may move underneath the other. This process is called **subduction**. In subduction zones, volcanoes and **earthquakes** are common. An earthquake is a sudden, violent movement along a break within the outer layers of Earth's crust.

Look at the Plate Tectonics map on the previous page and find the Pacific plate. Where the Pacific plate moves against neighboring plates, volcanoes and earthquakes are common. In fact, the edge of the Pacific plate is called the Ring of Fire because it is rimmed by active volcanoes. The region's earthquakes and volcanoes have killed thousands of people and caused terrible destruction. Several major earthquakes have hit California in recent years. Local authorities along the West Coast are constantly preparing for future earthquakes. Scientists predict that one of the strongest earthquakes in U.S. history may occur in the San Francisco Bay area within the next 30 years.

In some places, colliding plates have other results. Instead of sinking, one of the plates may crumple up and form a mountain range. The Andes in South America and the Himalayas in Asia formed in this way.

Other Plate Movements In other parts of the world, plates move away from each other. From the gap, hot **lava**, or melted rock from deep in the Earth, may emerge. The lava may build up, forming a mountain range. This process is happening in the Atlantic Ocean where the Eurasian plate and the North American plate are moving away from each other.

Tectonic plates can also slide past each other. Earthquakes occur from these sudden changes in Earth's crust. In California the Pacific plate is sliding northwestward along the edge of the North American plate. This movement has created the San Andreas Fault zone. A **fault** is a fractured surface in Earth's crust where a mass of rock is in motion.

These steep peaks in Chile are part of the Andes. **Interpreting the Visual Record** *Place* How do these mountains show the effects of colliding plates?

✓ **READING CHECK:** *Physical Systems* What are three ways that tectonic plates move? *collide, move away from each other, slide past each other*

20 • Chapter 2

TEACH

Teaching Objective 1

LEVEL 1: (Suggested time: 45 min.) Provide students with nature and tourism magazines. Have them find and cut out photographs of different types of topography and use the Geographic Dictionary at the front of this book to label them. Call on volunteers to display their labeled photos.

Then lead a class discussion about which photos may show landforms built up by tectonic action. **ESOL, LS KINESTHETIC**

LEVELS 2 AND 3: Provide extra time and additional resources for this activity. Have each student create a three-panel brochure titled "When Plates Collide." Each panel should contain a description of a landform created by colliding tectonic plates, a diagram of the process involved in creating the landform, and an example of a place where that process is occurring. Display brochures in the classroom. **LS VISUAL-SPATIAL**

20 Chapter 2

Shaping Earth's Surface

The forces of plate tectonics build up the land. At the same time, water, wind, and ice constantly break down rock and move rocky material. This process of breaking down landforms and creating new ones is called **weathering**.

Heat, Water, and Chemical Action Weathering breaks rocks into smaller pieces in several ways. Heat can cause rocks to crack. Water may then get into the cracks. If the water freezes, the ice expands with a force great enough to break the rock. Water can also work its way underground and slowly dissolve minerals such as limestone. This process sometimes carves out caves. In some areas small plants called lichens attach to bare rock. Chemicals in the lichens gradually break down the stone. All these processes eventually break rock down into sediment, in the form of gravel, sand, silt, or clay. Then water, ice, or wind can move the sediment and create new topography with it. This process of moving rocky material or sediment to another place is called **erosion**.

Moving water is the most common force that erodes the land. Flowing water carries sediment. This sediment eventually forms different kinds of landforms depending on where it is deposited. For example, a river flowing from a mountain range onto a flat area, or **plain**, may deposit sediment there. The sediment sometimes builds up into a fan-shaped form called an **alluvial fan**. A **floodplain** is created when rivers flood their banks and deposit sediment. A **delta** forms where a river carries sediment all the way to the ocean. The sediment settles to the bottom where the river meets the ocean. The Nile and Mississippi Rivers have two of the world's largest deltas.

Waves in the ocean or lakes also shape the land they touch. Waves can shape beaches into great dunes, such as on the shore of Long Island. Oregon's jagged coastline also shows how waves can erode land.

Erosion wears away Earth's surface at an island beach off the Florida coast. **Interpreting the Visual Record**
(Place) What physical process is causing erosion on this beach?

Ocean water turns muddy as the Mississippi River pushes sediment out of its delta.

CHAPTER 2, Section 1

EYE ON EARTH

A Rapid Change Weathering and erosion are slow processes. Sometimes, however, landforms can break down very quickly.

For example, many years ago miners in Switzerland carved slate from the base of a mountain cliff, creating a huge overhang. Big cracks appeared in the cliff. Finally, on September 11, 1881, millions of cubic yards of rock fell. The avalanche of rocks didn't stop when it hit the valley floor. Instead, the broken rock continued up the valley's other side. More than 100 people were killed. This type of event is called a debris avalanche.

Critical Thinking: In what other ways do humans change their environment that may create conditions for debris avalanches?

Answer: cutting through mountains to build highways, constructing buildings on hillsides, cutting down trees, and other disturbances of steep slopes

▲ **Visual Record Answer**
wave action

TEACH

Teaching Objective 2

ALL LEVELS: (Suggested time: 45 min.) Organize students into teams and have them explore the school grounds or a nearby park to find examples of weathering and erosion. Ask them to collect rocks and try to figure out how they have been weathered. Also have students try to determine if and why any of the forces of weathering or erosion are not present in their region. Discuss results as a class. (Examples: Students in warm regions may state that ice is not a factor there. Inland areas are not subject to wave action.)
ESOL, **LS** **KINESTHETIC**

CHAPTER 2, Section 1

National Geography Standard 7

Creating Soil We can put aside concerns about soil erosion briefly to learn more about how soil is formed in the first place.

The next time you see a fallen tree in the forest, don't think of it as just a dead log. It's a soil factory! As the tree decays and crumbles, it adds nutrients to the forest soil. The fallen tree doesn't do its work alone, however.

When a tree falls, weevils, bark beetles, carpenter ants, termites, and other insects bore into the wood and start to break it down. Bacteria and other microorganisms invade the wood contribute to the process. In this way, fallen trees provide as much as one third of the organic matter in forest soil.

Visual Record Answer ▶

by building terraces

Ice and Wind Action In high mountain settings and in the coldest places on Earth one finds **glaciers**. These large, slow-moving rivers of ice can move tons of rock.

Glaciers covered most of Canada and the United States during the last ice age—or period of extreme cold. As they advanced, the glaciers carved out gashes in Earth's surface. Glaciers dug the Great Lakes. As the ice melted and retreated, tons of rock and sediment were left behind.

Wind also shapes the land. Strong winds can lift soil into the air and carry it far away. On beaches and in deserts, wind drops sand, which piles up into dunes. In addition, blowing sand can wear away rock. The sand acts like sandpaper to polish jagged edges and rough surfaces.

Erosion and Soil These processes of breaking down Earth's surface create deposits of soil. People need soil to grow food. Erosion, however, can also remove soil from farmers' fields. Heavy rainfall can wash away soil. Strong winds can blow it away.

Over the centuries, however, people have developed ways to conserve our precious soil. Some farmers plant rows of trees to block the wind. Others who farm on steep hillsides build **terraces** into the slope. Terraces are horizontal ridges like stair steps. By slowing the downhill rush of water the terraces keep the soil in place. They also provide more space for growing crops.

✓ **READING CHECK:** (Physical Systems) What forces cause erosion? water, ice, and wind

Rice paddies like these in Indonesia are common throughout island Southeast Asia.
Interpreting the Visual Record
(Human-Environment Interaction)
How have farmers limited erosion in the rice paddies pictured below?

22 • Chapter 2

Teaching Objectives 1–2

LEVEL 2: (Suggested time: 20 min.) Copy the following graphic organizer onto the chalkboard, omitting the blue answers. Use it to help students describe the differences between landforms created by tectonic plate movement and those shaped by weathering and erosion. **ESOL**

Landforms created by tectonic plate movement	Landforms shaped by weathering and erosion
• created by subduction, colliding plates, or plates moving apart	• shaped by the actions of water, wind, and ice
• masses of rock raised by volcanic eruptions	• include alluvial fans, floodplains, and deltas
• include mountains on land and under the oceans	

22 Chapter 2

People and Topography

Topography has quite a bit to do with human history and culture. Those effects are so big, however, that we may not see them easily.

Landforms and Life Why do you live where you live? Perhaps your parents moved to your city to take jobs in the tourist industry. Do tourists visit your area partly because of its landforms, such as mountains? Or maybe your town grew up on a river delta. People could farm the delta's fertile soil. They could also use either the river or the sea for trade and travel. What are some more ways that your area's topography may have influenced its growth?

Reading a Topographic Map

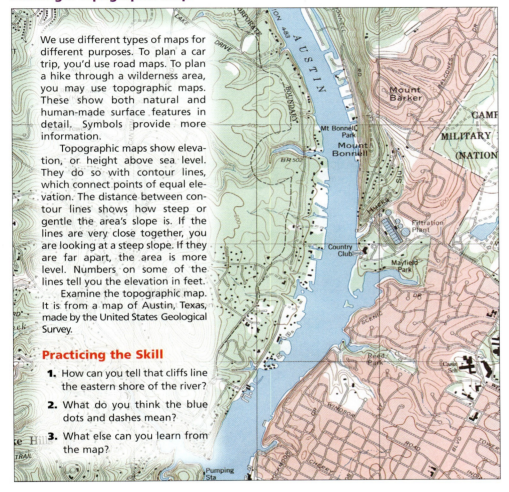

We use different types of maps for different purposes. To plan a car trip, you'd use road maps. To plan a hike through a wilderness area, you may use topographic maps. These show both natural and human-made surface features in detail. Symbols provide more information.

Topographic maps show elevation, or height above sea level. They do so with contour lines, which connect points of equal elevation. The distance between contour lines shows how steep or gentle the area's slope is. If the lines are very close together, you are looking at a steep slope. If they are far apart, the area is more level. Numbers on some of the lines tell you the elevation in feet.

Examine the topographic map. It is from a map of Austin, Texas, made by the United States Geological Survey.

Practicing the Skill

1. How can you tell that cliffs line the eastern shore of the river?
2. What do you think the blue dots and dashes mean?
3. What else can you learn from the map?

CHAPTER 2, Section 1

Cultural Kaleidoscope

Topography and Legends According to Irish legend, a giant named Finn Mac Cool built the Giant's Causeway, a formation of about 40,000 stone columns on the coast of Northern Ireland. By one account, Mac Cool drove the columns into place so he could walk to Scotland to fight a fellow giant. Later, his enemy broke the causeway so that Mac Cool couldn't reach him.

The basalt columns were actually formed 50 to 60 million years ago when lava cooled as it reached the sea. Pressure shaped the rock into columns with three to seven sides. The columns average 330 feet high.

Activity: Have students identify an unusual landform in your state and find out how it was formed. Then have them write and act out legends that describe the feature's origin.

Practicing the Skill Answers

1. The contour lines are very close together.
2. creekbeds that may or may not have water in them
3. locations of roads, river, individual houses, radio towers, pumping station, vegetation, built-up areas, corporate boundaries, names of major streets, and other features

Planet Earth • 23

TEACHER TO TEACHER

Kay A. Knowles, of Montross, Virginia, suggests the following activity to help students identify landforms and predict where certain landforms may be found. Display a wall map and have students point out examples of these landforms: continent, isthmus, peninsula, plain, and plateau. Also, ask students to identify places where they would expect to find these landforms: alluvial fan, floodplain, and delta.

Teaching Objective 3

LEVEL 2: (Suggested time: 45 min.) Begin by asking students to name historical events with which they are familiar. From the suggestions, choose one that occurred where topography seems to have played a role in the event's outcome. (Examples may include a battle, invasion, or natural disaster.) Then lead a class discussion about how topography affected the event. Challenge students to confirm their suggestions by checking historical resources. Call on volunteers to find the place where the event happened in an atlas and relate its topography to its history.

LS INTERPERSONAL

Planet Earth 23

Section 1 Review

Answers to Section 1 Review

Define For definitions, see the glossary.

Reading for the Main Idea
1. volcanoes and earthquakes (NGS 7)
2. by depositing sediment (NGS 7)

Critical Thinking
3. weathering—breaks down rock; erosion—moves rocky material or sediment
4. Ways of making a living, leisure activities, threats from natural hazards, ease of travel and communication, and other factors may all be different.

Organizing What You Know
5. heat—cracks rock; cold—ice cracks rock; water moving through limestone—dissolves minerals; chemicals in lichens—break down stone; waves—build up dunes or erode beaches; glaciers—carve and dig, leave rock and sediment as they melt; wind—carries soil away, deposits soil and sand, wears away rock if blown

Visual Record Answer

mountains

▲ In 1914 an enormous canal was completed across the Isthmus of Panama, linking the Pacific and Atlantic Oceans. Workers used millions of pounds of explosives and steam-powered shovels to cut through much of the landscape.

Interpreting the Visual Record

Human-Environment Interaction

Through what landforms did the Panama Canal workers have to dig?

Landforms affect the history of entire countries. For one example, start by looking at a map of India. You will see that the Ganges River crosses a broad plain before emptying into the Bay of Bengal. This river has brought sediment down from the Himalayas for countless centuries. It dropped the sediment on the plain, forming a vast area of excellent farmland. Many invaders have attacked India, trying to win this rich plain for themselves.

Here is an example of how landforms affected language. Find the island of New Guinea on a map of Southeast Asia. Notice how mountainous it is. These mountains have isolated New Guinea's peoples so much that many languages developed. In fact, more than 700 different languages are spoken on the island today.

Changing Landforms For thousands of years, people have changed Earth's surface to suit their needs. They have dug canals for irrigation ditches and carved terraces for farms. They have created artificial hills on which to build temples. People have even held back the sea to claim more dry land. Today, engineers build dams to control river flooding. They drill tunnels through mountains instead of laying roads over the mountains. Thus, while earthquakes, volcanoes, weathering, and erosion change Earth's surface, people do so also.

✓ **READING CHECK:** *Environment and Society* What are some landforms that could affect human history and culture? mountains, hills, plains, deltas, others

Homework Practice Online
Keyword: SK5 HP2

Section Review 1

Define and explain: landforms, topography, plate tectonics, subduction, earthquakes, lava, fault, weathering, erosion, plain, alluvial fan, floodplain, delta, glaciers, terraces

Reading for the Main Idea
1. (*Physical Systems*) What events are common where tectonic plates collide?
2. (*Physical Systems*) How do rivers create new landforms?

Critical Thinking
3. **Comparing and Contrasting** How are weathering and erosion different?
4. **Making Predictions** How may the lives of people who live in the mountains or on plains be different?

Organizing What You Know
5. **Categorizing** Copy the following graphic organizer. Use it to describe the results of each force of erosion or weathering.

heat ⇨
cold ⇨
water moving through limestone ⇨
chemicals in lichens ⇨
waves ⇨
glaciers ⇨
wind ⇨

24 • Chapter 2

CLOSE

Focus students' attention on the map on this section's first page. Point out that the shapes of South America and Africa provided an early clue in the development of the plate tectonics theory. Ask students what other kinds of evidence might indicate that now-distant continents were once joined. **(Possible answers: corresponding fossils and mineral deposits)**

REVIEW, ASSESS, RETEACH

Have students complete the Section Review. Then pair students and instruct pairs to write sentences that illustrate the connection between two of the vocabulary terms. **(Example: Erosion can form an alluvial fan.)** Call on volunteers to read their sentences to the class. Continue until all major points have been covered. Then have students complete this section's Daily Quiz.

Have students complete Main Idea Activity S1. Then pair students and have them create brief descriptions of each main idea in the section. Have students consult atlases, globes, or encyclopedias to locate two examples of each feature or main idea. **ESOL**

EXTEND

Have interested students conduct research in newspapers, magazines, and online sources on how recent changes in Earth's surface have affected cities. Examples include volcanic eruptions, earthquakes, and landslides. **BLOCK SCHEDULING**

Section 2 Water and Air

CHAPTER 2, Section 2

Read to Discover
1. Where is water found on Earth?
2. What is the water cycle?
3. How do people and water affect each other?
4. What are short-term and long-term results of air pollution?

Vocabulary
tributary
groundwater
aquifers
water cycle
evaporation
water vapor
condensation
precipitation
acid rain
ozone layer
global warming
greenhouse effect

Reading Strategy
READING ORGANIZER Before you read this section, create a spider map. Label the circle Water and Air. Create a leg for each of these topics: Geographic Distribution of Water, The Water Cycle, Water and People, and The Air We Breathe. As you read the section, fill in the map with details about each topic.

Section 2 Resources

Reproducible
- Know It Notes S2
- Lab Activities for Geography and Earth Science, Demonstration 1
- Main Idea Activity S2

Technology
- One-Stop Planner CD-ROM, Lesson 2.2
- Homework Practice Online
- Geography and Cultures Visual Resources 13, 16
- HRW Go Site

Reinforcement, Review, and Assessment
- Section 2 Review
- Daily Quiz 2.2
- Main Idea Activity S2
- Chapter Summaries and Review
- English Audio Summary 2.2
- Spanish Audio Summary 2.2

▲ **Visual Record Answer**

being overturned by waves caused by calving glacier

Geographic Distribution of Water

Water is essential for life. The presence or absence of water in a place affects whether people can live there. Water, therefore, is part of both physical and human geography. Throughout this book, you will see how water or its lack determines what life is like around the world.

The oceans contain about 97 percent of Earth's water. Another 2 percent is locked in the ice of Earth's polar regions and glaciers. Only about 1 percent is freshwater in lakes, streams, rivers, and below Earth's surface.

Earth's freshwater resources are not evenly distributed. Some places are extremely dry. Dry states such as Nevada have few natural lakes. Others have many lakes and rivers. For example, in the United States, Minnesota has more than 11,000 lakes. Some areas have too much water. Floods can make survival difficult in places where rainfall is very heavy or where rivers burst their banks.

Mountain glaciers like this one can move slowly downhill. This photo shows the face of a glacier. Here chunks may break off, or calve, and form icebergs.

Interpreting the Visual Record What dangers may these kayakers face?

Planet Earth • 25

Objectives
1. Identify where water is found on Earth.
2. Analyze the water cycle.
3. Explore how people and water affect each other.
4. Explain the short-term and long-term results of air pollution.

Focus

Bellringer
Write the following instructions on the chalkboard: *Draw as many quick sketches as you can, in two minutes, of the ways you use water throughout the day.* Discuss completed drawings. Then ask students to write a summary sentence beneath their drawings. **(Possible answers: We can't live without water. We use water every day in many ways.)** Display sketches around the classroom. Tell students that in this section they will learn more about the role of water and air on Earth.

Building Vocabulary
Explain that adding -*tion* to a root verb usually turns the verb into a noun. Point out that verbs from which the words *evaporation, condensation,* and *precipitation* are formed **(evaporate, condense, precipitate)**. Have students use these vocabulary words in sentences relating the words to bodies of water in their region. Students should use the U.S. map in the textbook's Atlas for help. **(Example: Precipitation that falls in Illinois may end up in the Mississippi River.)**

Planet Earth **25**

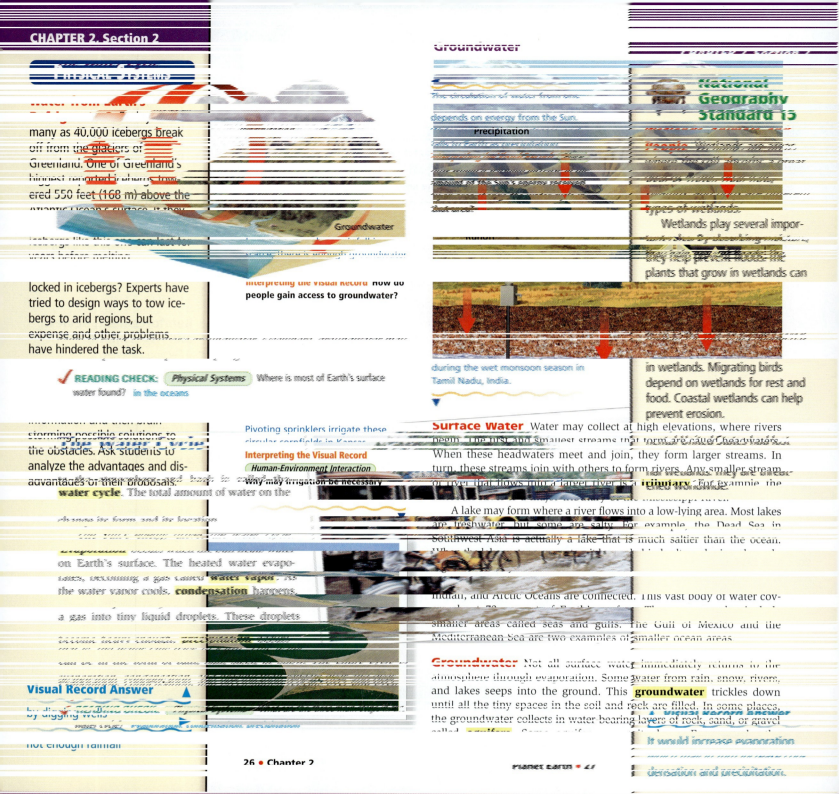

CHAPTER 2, Section 2

GLOBAL PERSPECTIVES

Dams: Pro and Con One way that people have conserved water is by building dams. They have been doing so for at least 5,000 years. More than 800,000 dams have been constructed around the world.

Dams and the reservoirs that form behind them can provide a steady water supply, hydroelectricity, protection from floods, and increased fish yields. However, they can also displace people, submerge farmland and cultural sites, disrupt animal migration patterns, and even increase the risk of certain diseases. Malaria, for example, is spread by mosquitoes that can breed in the standing water of reservoirs. For these and other reasons, dam construction has slowed in recent years.

Activity: Have students search news media for information on dams in your state. Students should concentrate on these questions: What controversies have arisen? What possible solutions have been suggested to address these controversies?

Visual Record Answer

uses no electricity, wastes less water than some modern methods that spray water into the air over a large area

Davenport, Iowa, located on the Mississippi River, suffered severe flooding when heavy rains caused the river to rise above its banks.

An Omani man collects water from a local *falaj*, or aqueduct. These channels are dug to carry water from desert springs to farms and villages. **Interpreting the Visual Record**
Human-Environment Interaction How does this method of irrigation differ from modern methods?

28 • Chapter 2

Water and People

Water plays a vital role in our survival. As a result, you will often see events and problems related to water in the news. Some of those events are natural disasters. Some of them are issues that people create.

Water Hazards Water can be extremely destructive. Thunderstorms, especially when accompanied by hail or tornadoes, can damage buildings and ruin crops. Heavy rains can cause floods, the world's deadliest natural hazard. Of every ten people who die from natural disasters, four die in floods. Some floods occur in usually dry places when a large amount of rain falls in a short amount of time. Then the water collects on the surface instead of soaking into the hard, dry ground. Normally dry creekbeds can suddenly gush with rushing water. People and livestock are sometimes caught in these flash floods.

Floods also happen in low-lying places next to rivers and on coastlines. Too much rain or snowmelt entering a river can push the water over the river's banks. Powerful storms, especially hurricanes, can cause ocean waters to surge into coastal areas. Is your region ever threatened by floods? What causes floods where you live?

Water Conservation In those places where there isn't enough water, however, many people try to use as little as possible. Scientists have developed new water management methods for saving the precious liquid. Many modern factories now recycle water. Farmers can irrigate their crops more efficiently. Cities build water treatment plants to purify water that might otherwise be wasted. Some people in dry regions use desert plants instead of grass for landscaping. As a result, they use less water in their yards.

Teaching Objective 3

ALL LEVELS: (Suggested time: 20 min.) Copy the following graphic organizer onto the chalkboard, omitting the blue answers. Use it to help students explore how water affects people and how people affect water. Have students copy the organizer into their notebooks and complete it. Challenge students to add other topics, especially topics that have local significance. **ESOL,** **LS VISUAL-SPATIAL**

WATER AND PEOPLE

- damage from thunderstorms
- floods
- recycling
- efficient irrigation
- changes in gardening
- use of aquifers
- pollution of water by agriculture and industry
- pollution of water from other sources
- costs of pollution control
- spread of pollution

28 Chapter 2

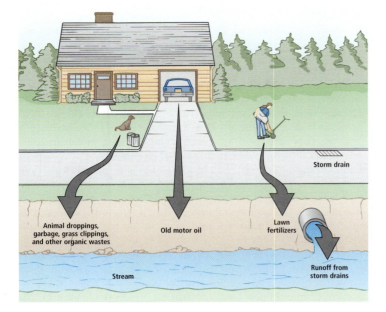

Most of the water that goes down drains, or wastewater, flows through pipes to a wastewater treatment plant. There the polluted water is treated before being returned to a river or a lake. Most of the wastewater from homes is easy to purify. However, industrial wastewater and storm runoff from streets and fields contain toxic substances that are difficult to purify.

Interpreting the Diagram What are some sources of pollution created by this single home?

Water management is often a local environmental issue. Growing cities may want to pump more groundwater from an aquifer, while farmers say they need that water for their crops. In dry areas, businesses that use large amounts of water, such as golf courses or fish farms, may draw criticism. What are the water management issues in your community?

Water Pollution Even where water is plentiful, it may not be clean enough to use. Polluted water can carry disease-causing bacteria or substances that harm people and animals.

Water pollution has many causes. Agriculture and industry are two main ones. When farmers use too many chemical fertilizers and pesticides, these chemicals ooze into local streams. Industrial waste may drain poisons or metals into the water supply. Heavy rain can wash motor oil from parking lots into groundwater. In addition, some poor communities don't have quality sewer systems for household wastes. Although most countries try to keep their water clean, sometimes the cost of doing so is higher than they can afford.

Pollution may spread far from its source. Rivers carry chemicals from distant factories to the oceans. There, pollution can sicken or kill fish and shellfish. People who eat these foods from polluted waters can get sick.

✓ **READING CHECK:** *Environment and Society* What are some causes of water pollution? **agriculture, industry, motor oil, household wastes**

CHAPTER 2, Section 2

ENVIRONMENT AND SOCIETY

Dangerous Water In some places, dangerous substances found in water didn't come from factories or other common sources of pollution. Bangladesh, a small country in South Asia, faces such a problem. Because Bangladesh experiences heavy flooding, which can ruin surface water supplies, the government has dug deep wells. Much of the groundwater, however, contains naturally occurring arsenic. Arsenic is a poison that causes serious health problems and, in large amounts, death.

The arsenic was first detected in 1993. Recent surveys report that about 75 million people are at risk for arsenic poisoning. The World Bank has committed $30 million to solve the problem, but Bangladesh will need much more money and time to provide totally clean drinking water.

▲ **Diagram Answer**

animal droppings, garbage, grass clippings, other organic wastes, motor oil, lawn fertilizers

---

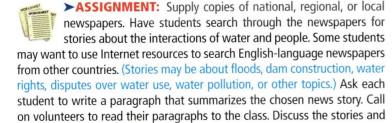

▶**ASSIGNMENT:** Supply copies of national, regional, or local newspapers. Have students search through the newspapers for stories about the interactions of water and people. Some students may want to use Internet resources to search English-language newspapers from other countries. (Stories may be about floods, dam construction, water rights, disputes over water use, water pollution, or other topics.) Ask each student to write a paragraph that summarizes the chosen news story. Call on volunteers to read their paragraphs to the class. Discuss the stories and the issues they raise.

CHAPTER 2, Section 2

COOPERATIVE LEARNING

Air and Borders Natural phenomena regularly cross international boundaries. For examples, wind, rain, and migrating animals pay no attention to borders. Similarly, pollution created in one country can contaminate the air of another country. Organize students into groups to study this process. Have each group select a major international border and report on pollution issues regarding that border. Instruct groups to identify the economic reasons why the controversy exists.

Visual Record Answer

eye irritation, lung diseases, accumulation on buildings and other surfaces, acid rain

The Air We Breathe

Like water, air is necessary for survival. Just as human activities can pollute our water, they can also pollute our air.

Air Pollution Air pollution comes from several sources. Burning fuels for heating and running factories releases chemicals into the air. A major cause of air pollution is exhaust from the hundreds of millions of motor vehicles on the planet. Particularly in big cities, all these chemicals build up in the air. They create a mixture called smog.

Some cities have special problems with smog. Denver, Los Angeles, and Mexico City, for example, lie in bowl-shaped valleys that trap air pollution. On some days, the air in these cities gets so thick with smog that officials urge residents to stay indoors to protect their health.

When air pollution combines with moisture in the air, it can form an acid similar in strength to vinegar. When it falls to the ground, this liquid is called **acid rain**. It can damage or kill trees. Acid rain can even kill fish.

Many countries have laws to limit pollution. However, pollution is an international problem. Winds can blow polluted air away, but just to another place. Pollution can easily blow from one country to another. It can even pass across continents. As a result, countries that keep their own air clean can still suffer from other countries' pollution.

Pollution and Climate Change Smog and acid rain are short-term effects of air pollution. Air pollution may also have long-term effects by changing Earth's atmosphere. Certain kinds of pollution damage the **ozone layer** in the upper atmosphere. This ozone layer protects living things by absorbing harmful ultraviolet light from the Sun. Damage to Earth's ozone layer may cause human health problems such as skin cancer.

Another issue of growing concern is **global warming**—a slow increase in Earth's average temperature. The Sun constantly warms Earth's surface. The gases and water vapor in the atmosphere trap some of the heat. This process helps keep Earth warm. Without the atmosphere, heat would escape into space, and we would freeze. The process is called the **greenhouse effect**. In a greenhouse the Sun's heat passes through the glass roof but is then trapped inside. Evidence suggests that pollution causes the atmosphere to trap more heat. As a result, Earth would get warmer.

Heavy smog clouds the Los Angeles skyline. *Interpreting the Visual Record* **Human-Environment Interaction** What problems do you think smog would create in everyday life?

30 • Chapter 2

Teaching Objective 4

ALL LEVELS: (Suggested time: 20 min.) First, lead a class discussion about the causes of air pollution. (Causes include burning fuels, running factories, and operating motor vehicles.) Then copy the following graphic organizer onto the chalkboard, omitting the blue answers. Have students complete it to learn the short- and long-term effects of air pollution.

Results of Air Pollution	
Short-term results	Long-term results
• smog	• damage to the ozone layer
• acid rain	• global warming

The Greenhouse Effect

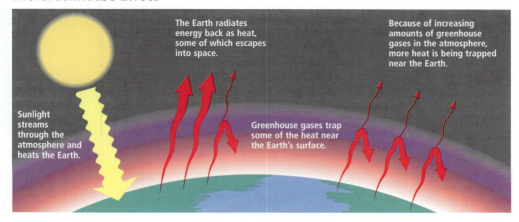

▲ The Earth's atmosphere acts like the glass in a greenhouse. Sunlight passes through the atmosphere and heats the Earth. As heat radiates up from the Earth, some heat escapes into space. The rest of the heat is trapped by gases in the atmosphere.

Interpreting the Diagram What is one result of an increase in greenhouse gases in the atmosphere?

Scientists agree that Earth's climate has warmed during the last century. Not all agree, however, on the explanation. Most scientists say that air pollution caused by people has made temperatures rise. Burning fuels such as oil and coal is listed as the main culprit. Other scientists think warmer temperatures have resulted from natural causes. There is also disagreement about what has caused the thinning of the ozone layer.

✓ **READING CHECK:** *Environment and Society* How may air pollution affect Earth's climate? **may lead to global warming**

Define and explain: tributary, groundwater, aquifers, water cycle, evaporation, water vapor, condensation, precipitation, acid rain, ozone layer, global warming, greenhouse effect

Reading for the Main Idea

1. *Environment and Society* What are some hazards that water can create?
2. *Environment and Society* What are the main causes of air pollution?

Keyword: SK5 HP2

Critical Thinking

3. **Analyzing Information** Why would protecting groundwater from pollution be important?
4. **Making Generalizations and Predictions** What may happen if air pollution continues to increase?

Organizing What You Know

5. **Sequencing** Copy the following graphic organizer. Use it to describe the steps in the water cycle.

Planet Earth • 31

Section 2 Review

Answers to Section 2 Review

Define For definitions, see the glossary.

Reading for the Main Idea

1. damage from thunderstorms, floods (NGS 7)
2. burning fuels, running factories, operating motor vehicles (NGS 14)

Critical Thinking

3. Unless pollutants can be removed, polluted groundwater is no longer safe for human or animal consumption.
4. Health problems may increase due to loss of the ozone layer and increased irritants in the air, and global warming may increase.

Organizing What You Know

5. Graphic organizers should reflect the diagram of the water cycle in this section.

▲ **Diagram Answer**

global warming

CLOSE

Lead a class discussion about how students would cope if suddenly your community's water supply became too polluted for human use.

REVIEW, ASSESS, RETEACH

Have students complete the Section Review. Then have each student write a paragraph about how individuals can reduce water and air pollution. Then have students complete Daily Quiz 2.2. **LS INTRAPERSONAL**

Have students complete Main Idea Activity S2. Then have students describe the content of the section's photos and diagrams and relate the content to the section's text. **LS VISUAL-SPATIAL**

EXTEND

Have interested students conduct research on a significant flood that occurred in the past 10 years. Tell students to provide a map of the areas hurt by the flood as well as information on how the flood affected the area's people, plants, animals, and economy. Students should also note the long-term effects of the flood. **BLOCK SCHEDULING**

CHAPTER 2, Section 3

SECTION 3 RESOURCES

Reproducible
- Know It Notes S3
- Environmental and Global Issues Activities 1, 2
- Lab Activities for Geography and Earth Science, Hands-On 1, Demonstrations 11, 12
- Geography for Life Activities 2–4
- Map Activity 3
- Creative Strategies for Teaching World Geography, Lesson 13
- Main Idea Activity S3

Technology
- One-Stop Planner CD-ROM, Lesson 2.3
- Homework Practice Online
- Geography and Cultures Visual Resources 14, 15, 17
- HRW Go Site

Reinforcement, Review, and Assessment
- Section 3 Review
- Daily Quiz 2.3
- Main Idea Activity S3
- Chapter Summaries and Review
- English Audio Summary 2.3
- Spanish Audio Summary 2.3

Visual Record Answer
High elevations keep temperatures low.

Section 3 Climate, Weather, and Vegetation

Read to Discover
1. What factors create climate and weather?
2. How are climate, plants, and animal life related?

Vocabulary
weather
climate
prevailing winds
currents
rain shadow

Reading Strategy

FOLDNOTES: TRI-FOLD Create a **Tri-Fold** FoldNote as described in the Appendix. Label the columns "Know," "Want," and "Learn." Use the main ideas to write down what you know about weather and climate. Then write down what you want to know. After you study the section, write down what you learned.

Wildlife eat the summer vegetation in the Alaskan tundra.
Interpreting the Visual Record Why is there snow on the mountain peaks during summer?

Factors Affecting Climate and Weather

Weather is the condition of the atmosphere at a certain time and place. **Climate** refers to the weather conditions in an area over a long period of time. Weather and climate then help determine what kind of plants grow in a certain place.

Several factors determine a region's climate. Some of the forces that affect whether it will be sunny or rainy today are related to what is happening on the other side of the planet. Other forces are local.

The Sun Solar heat, or heat from the Sun, makes life possible on Earth. It also affects our weather and climate. The Sun doesn't heat Earth evenly, however. Because Earth is a sphere, areas closest to the North Pole and the South Pole don't receive direct rays from the Sun. Also, because Earth is tilted on its axis, areas away from the Sun receive less heat. Regions closer to the equator receive more heat. Therefore, the higher a place's latitude, the less solar heat it gets and the colder its climate.

32 • Chapter 2

Objectives
1. Identify the factors that create climate and weather.
2. Describe how climate, plants, and animal life are related.

FOCUS

Bellringer
Copy the following instructions onto the chalkboard: *Write down three words or phrases you use to describe the climate or weather events in our area* (Possible answers include muggy, bone-chilling, gully-washer, nor'easter, raining cats and dogs.) Point out that having so many terms for our weather indicates that weather is very important to us. Tell students that in Section 3 they will also learn that climate and weather affect what plants and animals live in an area.

Building Vocabulary
Write the vocabulary terms on the chalkboard. Call on volunteers to find and read aloud the definitions from the text or glossary. Discuss the word *prevail* ("to be or become effective") as the root word for **prevailing winds**. You may want to introduce *orographic effect* as the term for what causes a **rain shadow**.

Each year is divided into periods of time called seasons. Each season is known for a certain type of weather, based on temperature and amount of precipitation. Winter, spring, summer, and fall are examples of seasons that are described by their average temperature. "Wet" and "dry" seasons are described by their precipitation. The seasons change as Earth orbits the Sun. As this happens, the amount of solar energy received in any given location changes.

Winds Solar heat doesn't stay in one place. It moves around the planet. Otherwise, some places would be much hotter and others much colder than they are now. Winds, created by changes in air pressure, move the heat.

You may think of air as weightless, but it isn't. Cold air weighs more than warm air. When air warms, it gets lighter and rises. Colder air then moves in to replace the rising air. Wind is the result of this process.

Winds blow in great streams of air around the planet. Winds that blow in the same direction over large areas of Earth are called **prevailing winds**. These winds then make a region warmer or colder, drier or wetter, depending on from where they blow.

Some regions on Earth, particularly in the tropics, have seasons tied to precipitation rather than temperature. Shifting wind patterns are one cause of seasonal change. For example, in January winds from the north bring dry air to India. By June the winds have shifted, coming from the southwest and bringing moisture from the Indian Ocean.

As Earth revolves around the Sun, the tilt of the poles toward and away from the Sun causes the seasons to change. The day when the Sun's vertical rays are farthest from the equator is called a solstice. Solstices occur twice a year—about June 21 and about December 22. The days when the Sun's rays strike the equator directly are called equinoxes. These days mark the beginning of spring and fall.

Interpreting the Diagram At what point is the North Pole tilted toward the Sun?

The Seasons

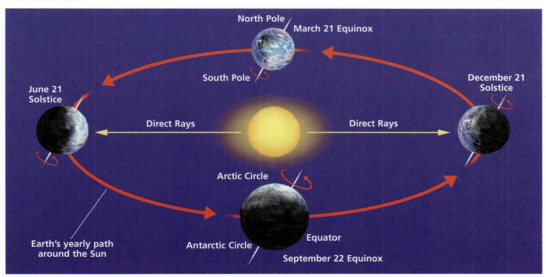

CHAPTER 2, Section 3

Across the Curriculum
SCIENCE

The Sun Burps Heat doesn't always flow from the Sun at a steady rate. During a solar storm called a coronal mass ejection (CME), the Sun spews up to 10 billion tons of hot, electrically charged gas into space. The gas cloud travels at speeds reaching 1,250 miles per second. If a really strong CME reaches Earth, it can damage satellites, interrupt communication systems, and cause power blackouts. For example, in 1989 a CME left about 6 million people in Canada's Quebec province without electricity.

Technicians can prevent potential damage if they know when a CME is about to happen. Scientists have discovered that a gigantic "S" shape on the Sun's surface seems to indicate that the Sun may launch a CME soon. The "S" shapes are areas where the Sun's magnetic field has twisted back on itself.

◄**Diagram Answer**

on December 21, the winter solstice

Teaching Objective 1

LEVEL 1: (Suggested time: 30 min.) Pair students and have each pair create an informational brochure titled "The Study of Weather." In their brochures, students should identify and create a symbol for each of the factors that influence climate and weather. (Brochures should identify the Sun, winds, oceans and currents, and elevation and mountain effects.) Call on volunteers to display and discuss their brochures.
COOPERATIVE LEARNING, LS **VISUAL-SPATIAL**

►**ASSIGNMENT:** Ask students to watch a weather forecast on television or listen to one on the radio. Have then write down any unfamiliar terms (examples: dew point, dry line, lake effect) in the forecast. In class, provide resource materials for students to research these terms and relate them to the text material.

CHAPTER 2, Section 3

EYE ON EARTH

Weird Waves We think of ocean waves as racing across miles of open water within hours. However, an odd type of waves called Rossby waves can take years to travel across the ocean. These waves may be only a few inches high, but they can be many miles long. Because they move slowly, Rossby waves can carry a "memory" of storms or other oceanic events that happened years earlier. For example, oceanographers mapped a Rossby wave in 1994 that seemed to show evidence of a 1982–83 El Niño. Understanding Rossby waves helps meteorologists predict the weather because the waves may push powerful ocean currents away from their usual paths.

Visual Record Answer

the Southwest, from Arizona through West Texas

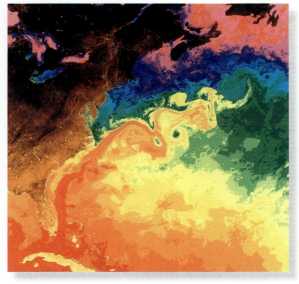

This infrared satellite image shows the Gulf Stream moving warm water from lower latitudes to higher latitudes. The dark red shape alongside Florida's east coast is the Gulf Stream.

Weather maps show atmospheric conditions as they currently exist or as they are forecast for a particular time period. Most weather maps have legends that explain what the symbols on the map mean. This map shows a cold front sweeping through the central United States. A low-pressure system is at the center of a storm bringing rain and snow to the Midwest. Notice that temperatures behind the cold front are considerably cooler than those ahead of the front.

You Be the Geographer According to this map, what region is experiencing the highest temperatures?

Oceans and Currents Winds move ocean water in the same general directions as the air above it moves. Warm ocean water from near the equator moves in giant streams, or **currents**, to colder areas. Cold water flows from the polar regions to the tropics. So, just as wind moves heat between places, so do ocean currents.

The Gulf Stream is an important ocean current. It moves warm water north from the Gulf of Mexico to the east coast of the United States. It then moves across the Atlantic Ocean toward Europe. The warm air that moves with it keeps winters mild. As a result, much of western Europe has warmer winters than areas in Canada that are just as far north.

Distance from the ocean also affects a region's climate. Water heats and cools more slowly than land. Therefore, coastal areas don't have the wide differences in temperature that areas in the middle of continents have. For example, Kansas City has colder winters and hotter summers than San Francisco. The cities are at about the same latitude, but Kansas City is in the continent's interior. In contrast, San Francisco lies on the Pacific Ocean.

Reading a Weather Map

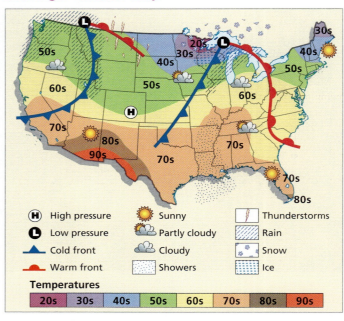

34 • Chapter 2

LEVEL 2: (Suggested time: 30 min.) In advance, prepare photocopies of the local weather map from your daily newspaper or the U.S. weather map in a national paper. Review the "Reading a Weather Map" feature on this page. Have students circle and label the information on their maps that illustrates the conditions that affect weather. **LS KINESTHETIC**

LEVEL 3: (Suggested time: 30 min.) Have students look through this textbook for photographs that show or imply specific weather conditions. Challenge students to find the approximate location of the place in the photo in the appropriate unit's physical and climate maps and to speculate about what causes climate and weather conditions in that place. **ESOL**

Landforms and Precipitation

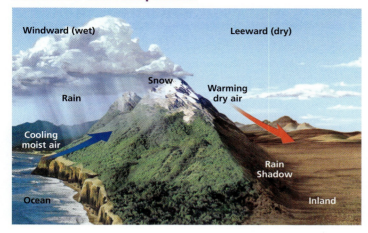

Moist air from the ocean cools as it moves up the windward side of a mountain. The water vapor in the air condenses and falls in the form of rain or snow. The drier air then moves down the leeward side of a mountain. This drier air brings very little precipitation to areas in the rain shadow.

Pictured in the bottom photo are mountains in the western part of the Sierra Nevada in Sequoia National Park. The top photo shows part of the eastern slope of the same range near Bishop, California.

Place How does the vegetation of these places differ? What causes the difference?

Elevation and Mountain Effects

Have you seen photos of Kilimanjaro, a mountain in East Africa? The mountain has snow on it all year although it is only about 250 miles from the equator. How can this be?

An increase in elevation—height on Earth's surface above sea level—causes a drop in temperature. This happens because the air is less dense at higher elevations. Thus the base of a mountain may be hot while the top is covered with ice.

Elevation has another effect on weather and climate. Warm, moist air blowing against a mountainside will rise. As it rises, it cools and forms clouds. Precipitation falls from the clouds. The side of the mountain facing the wind often gets heavy rain. By the time the air reaches the other side of the mountain it has lost most of its moisture. This can create a dry area called a **rain shadow**. Compare some of the physical maps and climate maps in the unit atlases to find examples of this effect.

✓ **READING CHECK:** *Physical Systems* What are the main factors affecting climate and weather? **the Sun, winds, oceans and currents, elevation and mountain effects**

CHAPTER 2, Section 3

Cultural Kaleidoscope
Religion and Weather Cultural and religious explanations of climate and weather have influenced people's understanding of the physical world. In the American Southwest, the Hopi rain dance reveals that culture's attitude toward nature. By dancing and making offerings, the Hopi show respect to the kachinas, or spirits of ancestors, that they believe control the natural world. The Hopi believe the kachinas will return the favor by sending rain. Many other cultures have ceremonies designed to affect the weather.

Activity: Have students conduct research on ways that weather has been incorporated into other cultures' religious beliefs or folklore and analyze the similarities and differences. Have students present their findings to the class.

◀ **Visual Record Answer**
The area in the top photo is drier because it is in a rain shadow caused by the Sierra Nevada. It thus has less vegetation than the area in the bottom photo.

Teaching Objective 2

ALL LEVELS: (Suggested time: 10 min.) Tell students to use the World Climate, Plant, and Animal Regions map on the following pages to locate the region where they live. Have them refer to the chart to identify the state's climate region. Then tell them to read the description of the weather patterns for their climate region. Ask whether the description corresponds to their observations of weather patterns in the area. **ESOL**

LEVEL 2: (Suggested time: 30 min.) Have students write trivia questions about each of the climate types. (At this point, they don't have to know the answers.) Tell students to refer to the world climate regions map on page 37 and the text atlas to help them write questions. (Examples of questions: What is the coldest temperature ever recorded at the South Pole? What is the hottest desert? What is the approximate temperature of the oval-shaped current in the North Atlantic Ocean?) Then have students consult reference materials to find the answers to their questions.
LS VERBAL-LINGUISTIC

CHAPTER 2, Section 3

Linking Past to Present

Changing Climates
Just because today an area has a certain climate—and the plants and animals that are typical of that climate—doesn't mean that it's always been that way. For example, the Sahara was once a vast grassland. Researchers recently concluded that the Sahara's transformation into a desert was triggered by changes in Earth's orbit and the tilt of its axis. These changes occurred in two phases, with the first happening some 6,700 to 5,500 years ago and the second 4,000 to 3,600 years ago.

The orbital changes caused fairly sudden changes in North Africa's climate. Rains stopped coming to the Sahara and regional temperatures rose. Within a few hundred years the moist Sahara became a desert scrubland. Researchers think that ancient civilizations in the Sahara may have moved to the Nile River valley in response to the climate changes.

Discussion: What ancient civilization with which the students may already be familiar developed as a result of the changing climate of North Africa? *(Egyptian civilization)*

Climate Regions, Plants, and Animals

The chart below describes the 12 main climate types in terms of weather. Climate affects what kind of plants, or vegetation, can grow in a certain area. For example, if your region has a tundra climate, you won't be able to grow palm trees in your yard. Palm trees need a much warmer climate.

In turn, vegetation helps determine what animals are present. If you live in a desert, you won't see tree-dwelling monkeys, except in a zoo! What plants and animals live in your area?

World Climate, Plant, and Animal Regions

Climate	Major Weather Patterns	Vegetation	Animals You May See in the Climate Region (Animals Vary by Region.)
HUMID TROPICAL	warm and rainy all year	rain forest	bats, tree frogs, monkeys, jaguars, tigers, snakes, parrots
TROPICAL SAVANNA	warm all year, with rainy and dry seasons	grassland with scattered trees	anacondas, lions, elephants, gazelles, ostriches, hyenas, rhinoceroses, zebras
DESERT	dry and sunny	a few hardy plants such as cacti	lizards, scorpions, snakes, bats, bobcats, coyotes
STEPPE	semiarid, hot summers with cooler winters	grassland and a few trees	antelope, wild horses, kangaroos, coyotes, camels
MEDITERRANEAN	dry, sunny, warm winters and mild, wetter winters	scrub woodland and grassland	deer, elk, mountain lions, wolves
HUMID SUBTROPICAL	hot, humid summers and mild, humid winters; rain all year	mixed forest	alligators, deer, bears, squirrels, foxes, snakes, many species of birds
MARINE WEST COAST	cloudy, mild summers and cool, rainy winters	evergreen forest	wild boars, deer, bears, seals
HUMID CONTINENTAL	four distinct seasons; long, cold winters and short, warm summers	mixed forest	wolverines, wild boars, deer, badgers, beavers, ducks
SUBARCTIC	long, cold winters and short, warm summers; low	evergreen forest	rabbits, moose, elk, wolves, lynxes, bears
TUNDRA	cold all year, little precipitation	moss, lichens, low shrubs, marshes during the summer	rabbits, reindeer, wolves, foxes
ICE CAP	freezing cold all year	no vegetation	animals that depend on the sea, such as polar bears, seals, and penguins
HIGHLAND	wide range of temperatures and precipitation amounts, depending on elevation	forest to tundra vegetation, depending on location and elevation	wide range of animals, depending on location, elevation, and vegetation

36 • Chapter 2

▶**ASSIGNMENT:** Prepare a list of 10 to 20 major world cities. Include cities in all climate zones except for the ice cap zone. Give students copies of the list and have them locate the cities in the text's atlas. Then have them write down each city's climate type and temperatures, moisture, vegetation, sunlight levels, and storms that would be common there.

TEACHER TO TEACHER

Maureen Dempsey of Spring Creek, Nevada, suggests the following activity to help students summarize climate types: Organize students into small groups. Then have each group fold and staple 12 sheets of white paper together to create booklets entitled **Climates of the World**. Students should describe the climate on one page and illustrate it on the opposite page. They may draw pictures, cut them from magazines, or download images from the Internet. Each student's book should include a table of contents and a cover illustration.

World Climate Regions

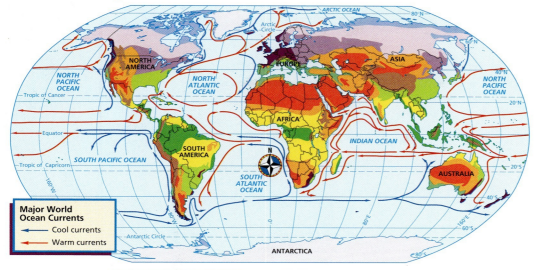

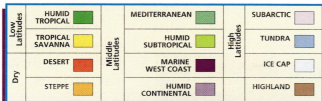

Section Review 3

Define and explain: weather, climate, prevailing winds, currents, rain shadow

Reading for the Main Idea

1. **(Physical Systems)** How does the Sun's heat affect temperature and winds?
2. **(Physical Systems)** What effect does the Gulf Stream have on Europe's climates?

Critical Thinking

3. **Drawing Inferences** From looking at the map, why do you think central Asia is very cold in winter and often hot in the summer?
4. **Finding the Main Idea** Why may a mountaintop and a nearby valley have wide differences in temperature?

Organizing What You Know

5. **Summarizing** Copy the following graphic organizer. Use it to summarize the 12 climate types.

Climate	Weather	Vegetation	Animals

Homework Practice Online Keyword: SK5 HP2

Section 3 Review

Answers to Section 3 Review

Define For definitions, see the glossary.

Reading for the Main Idea

1. The higher a place's latitude, the less heat it receives from the Sun. The Sun's heat makes air get lighter and rise, causing wind. **(NGS 7)**
2. keeps Europe relatively warm **(NGS 7)**

Critical Thinking

3. The region is far from the ocean, which would otherwise moderate its climate.
4. because elevation keeps temperatures lower

Organizing What You Know

5. For climate types, latitudes, and characteristics, see the table in this section.

CLOSE

People live in almost every climate on Earth, including extreme climates. Have students suggest ways that people have adapted to them.

REVIEW, ASSESS, RETEACH

Have each student choose a climate type and write five adjectives to describe it. Have students read their adjectives to the class, and other students guess which climate type is being described. Then have students complete Daily Quiz 2.3. **LS INTERPERSONAL**

Have students complete Main Idea Activity S3. Then have them choose specific locations and write postcards from that place describing the weather there. **ESOL**

EXTEND

Have interested students perform a simple experiment to illustrate dew point—the temperature at which water vapor begins to condense. Put water into a coffee can, and gradually add ice cubes while stirring with a thermometer. Record the temperature at the moment when condensation forms on the outside of the coffee can. This temperature is the dew point. Have students conduct research on the relationship between relative humidity and dew point to explain the results of their experiment. Students may also want to investigate places in the world where very little rain falls and where dew sustains plants and animals. **BLOCK SCHEDULING**

CHAPTER 2, Section 4

SECTION 4 RESOURCES
Reproducible
- Know It Notes S4
- Environmental and Global Issues Activities 1, 2, 4–8
- Lab Activities for Geography and Earth Science, Hands-On 3, Demonstration 8
- Geography for Life Activity 4
- Readings in World Geography, History, and Culture, Readings 5, 7, 8
- Map Activity 4
- Critical Thinking Activity 4
- Creative Strategies for Teaching World Geography, Lesson 8
- Main Idea Activity S4

Technology
- One-Stop Planner CD-ROM, Lesson 2.4
- Homework Practice Online
- HRW Go Site

Reinforcement, Review, and Assessment
- Section 4 Review
- Daily Quiz 2.4
- Main Idea Activity S4
- Chapter Summaries and Review
- English Audio Summary 2.4
- Spanish Audio Summary 2.4

Visual Record Answer ▶
They may reduce wind erosion.

Section 4 Natural Resources

Read to Discover
1. What are the most important renewable resources?
2. How do the main energy resources differ?
3. How do we use mineral resources?
4. How do resources affect people?

Vocabulary
renewable resources
nonrenewable resources
deforestation
reforestation
fossil fuels
petroleum
hydroelectric power
geothermal energy
solar power

Reading Strategy
TAKING NOTES As you read this section, list the natural resources mentioned in the text. Beside each resource, write R if the resource is renewable and N if the resource is nonrenewable.

▲ A row of poplar trees divides farmland near Aix-en-Provence, France.
Human-Environment Interaction What effect will these trees have on erosion?

Using Renewable Resources

The landforms, water, climate, and weather of a place all affect the people who live there. Another factor that affects daily life is the resources available to them. A resource is any material that is part of Earth and that people need and value.

Some of Earth's resources are renewable, while others are nonrenewable. **Renewable resources**, such as soil and forests, are those that natural processes continuously replace. **Nonrenewable resources** are those that can't be replaced naturally after they have been used. Once they've been used, they're gone forever!

You read in Section 1 about the need to preserve soil, since it is essential to survival. Soil qualifies as a renewable resource because natural processes create more of it. For example, when a tree dies and falls to the forest floor, the tree decays and adds valuable nutrients to the soil. Bacteria and other organisms break down the wood and turn it into humus. However, these processes are very slow. Soil that required hundreds of years to build up can be washed away in a few seconds.

38 • Chapter 2

Section 4

Objectives
1. Identify the most important renewable resources.
2. Explain how the main energy resources differ.
3. Explore how we use mineral resources.
4. Discover how resources affect people.

FOCUS

Bellringer
Copy the following riddle onto the chalkboard and ask students to solve it.
   It lies all around us.
   We don't give it a thought,
   It puts food on the table.
   What it gives can't be bought.
(The riddle refers to soil.) Tell students that in Section 4 they will learn more about the importance of soil and the other resources on which we depend.

Building Vocabulary
Write the vocabulary terms on the chalkboard. Point out that the prefix *re-* often means "again." So, **renewable resources** are those that can be new again. **Reforestation** indicates that a forest can grow again in the same place. Ask students what they already know about fossils and relate their knowledge to the term **fossil fuels**.

38 Chapter 2

Forests Forests are renewable resources because we can plant new trees. People use trees for many products. Wood products include lumber for buildings and furniture. Plastics and some fabrics use wood in the manufacturing process. Cooking oils, medicines, nuts, and rubber are among the many products that trees supply. In addition, trees and other plants release oxygen into the atmosphere. We enjoy forests for hiking and camping. Wildlife depends on forests for food and shelter.

Like soil, forests can be destroyed much faster than they can grow. In some places, forests are not being replaced as quickly as they are cut down. This loss of forest areas is called **deforestation**. People can reverse the trend by planting new trees. This practice, called **reforestation**, is important for both people and wildlife.

Resources and Land Management The preservation of renewable resources is often part of larger land management issues. For example, suburbs spring up on what was valuable farmland. Fertile soil there can no longer grow food. Or, a developer may want to build a shopping mall in a forested area. Residents may prefer to preserve the trees within a park. These and similar local environmental issues are debated across the United States as towns and cities grow.

✓ **READING CHECK:** *Environment and Society* How can people help preserve forest resources? **by planting new trees and by using wise resource and land management procedures**

Human-Environment Interaction
Villagers work on a reforestation project in Cameroon.

Human-Environment Interaction
Development at the edge of Danville, California, is replacing farmland and rangeland.

CHAPTER 2, Section 4

Linking Past to Present

Ancient Deforestation Although they didn't have access to modern technology, ancient peoples often dramatically affected natural landscapes. Some archaeologists think that during the Neolithic era—beginning about 8,000 years ago—people may have deforested large areas of central and western Europe. They chopped down trees to clear land for farming. They also used timber for fuel and building. For example, a single fort in the British Isles could use up several thousand trees.

Activity: Have students conduct research on ancient and recent deforestation. Challenge students to compare the deforestation of the two time periods in terms of causes, methods, and results.

internet connect
GO TO: go.hrw.com
KEYWORD: SJ5 CH2
FOR: Web sites about deforestation

Teaching Objective 1

ALL LEVELS: (Suggested time: 15 min.) Copy the following graphic organizer onto the chalkboard, omitting the blue answers. Use it to help students understand the importance of preserving soil and forests. Call on students to supply the main ideas from this subsection on these resources. Then lead a class discussion about the question in the bottom rectangle. You may want to provide local newspapers to help students explore the issues. **ESOL**, **LS INTERPERSONAL**

Soil and Forests: Important Renewable Resources

Soil	Forests
• essential for our survival	• wood used in many products
• created by natural processes	• produce oxygen
• from decayed plant materials	• important for recreation, wildlife
• can easily be washed away	• importance of reforestation

Resources and Land Management

What are the resources and land management issues in your community?

CHAPTER 2, Section 4

Across the Curriculum
SCIENCE

Energy from the Ocean Floor? There is a strange form of ice on the ocean floor called methane hydrate. A methane hydrate crystal consists of a natural gas molecule surrounded by water molecules. Methane hydrates resemble regular ice, but unlike ice they can burn! The compounds are abundant on the ocean floor and may provide new sources of energy. In fact, the amount of carbon locked in methane hydrates may be twice as big as the total amount of carbon in all other fossil fuels.

However, because they are formed under pressure, hydrates can disintegrate when removed from the ocean. Furthermore, in terms of its potential effect on global warming, methane as a greenhouse gas is 10 times worse than carbon dioxide, which is released in the burning of traditional fossil fuels.

Visual Record Answer ▶
People have taken advantage of a windy location by using turbines to generate power.

Human-Environment Interaction Deep underground, a miner digs coal in a narrow tunnel.

Wind turbines are just one source of electricity. **Interpreting the Visual Record** **Human-Environment Interaction** How does this photo show human adaptation to the environment?

Energy Resources

Most of the energy we use comes from the three **fossil fuels**: coal, petroleum, and natural gas. Fossil fuels were formed from the remains of ancient plants and animals. These remains gradually decayed and were covered with sediment. Over long periods of time, pressure and heat changed these materials. They became completely different solids, liquids, or gases. All fossil fuels are nonrenewable resources.

For thousands of years, people have burned coal for heat. Burning coal pollutes the air, however. Modern ways of burning coal produce less pollution, but cost more money. **Petroleum** may be the fossil fuel with which you are most familiar. When it is first pumped out of the ground, petroleum is a dark oily liquid called crude oil. It is then processed into gasoline, diesel and jet fuels, and heating oil. Burning these fuels also creates air pollution. The cleanest-burning fossil fuel is natural gas, which is usually found near petroleum deposits.

Renewable Energy Resources Energy sources besides fossil fuels exist. Their big advantage is they are cleaner, in general. Renewable energy sources aren't available everywhere, however. They may also cost more money. Some of these energy sources have other drawbacks too.

40 • Chapter 2

Teaching Objective 2

LEVEL 1: (Suggested time: 45 min.) Organize the class into three groups and assign each group one of these topics: fossil fuels, clean energy sources, and nuclear power. Within each group, have students discuss the advantages and disadvantages of each type and then summarize their discussions for the class. **COOPERATIVE LEARNING**

LEVELS 2 AND 3: In advance, gather resource materials about various energy resources. Using the same groups as in the Level 1 activity, challenge students to locate statistical information on the assigned energy source. For example, the fossil fuel group may locate figures on how many tons of coal are mined and burned in the United States each year and how many tons of carbon dioxide are released into the atmosphere as a result. Or, students may calculate how these figures average out to consumption per person. **LS LOGICAL-MATHEMATICAL**

Water pours through Owen Falls Dam in Uganda. More than 99 percent of Uganda's electricity comes from hydroelectric power.
Interpreting the Visual Record What body of water is used to produce hydroelectric power?

France has 59 nuclear reactors like this one and depends on nuclear power for about 77 percent of its energy.

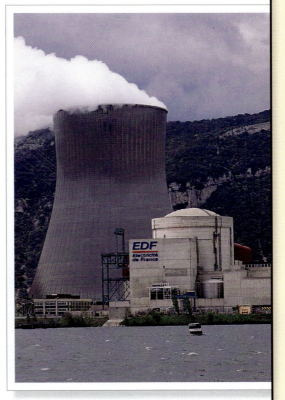

Clean Energy Sources The most commonly used renewable energy source is **hydroelectric power**—the production of electricity by waterpower. Dams harness the energy of falling water from rivers to run generators that produce electricity. Although hydroelectric power doesn't pollute the air, it does affect the environment. The lakes that form when dams block rivers may drown farmland and forests. Fish and wildlife habitats are also affected.

Wind has powered sailing ships and windmills for centuries. Now wind has a new use. It can create electricity by turning a system of fan blades called a turbine. "Wind farms" with hundreds of wind turbines have been built in windy places. The heat of Earth's interior—**geothermal energy**—is another clean source of power. People can use the energy directly to heat water, or they can generate electricity with it. **Solar power**—heat and light from the Sun—can heat water or homes. Special solar panels also absorb solar energy to make electricity.

Nuclear Power The last major renewable energy resource is nuclear power. Although operating a nuclear power plant doesn't release pollution into the air, it does produce waste materials that will be deadly for many centuries. Management of these wastes is a serious problem. In addition, some nuclear power plants have had serious accidents. A nuclear accident in Chernobyl in Ukraine killed people, caused cancer in survivors, and poisoned farmland.

✓ **READING CHECK:** *Environment and Society* What are the main advantages of using renewable energy sources? **They don't pollute and they are based on resources that won't run out.**

CHAPTER 2, Section 4

ENVIRONMENT AND SOCIETY

Hot Times in Idaho
Geothermal energy is becoming a useful alternative energy source in some places in the United States. Idaho began harnessing geothermal power in 1892. The state has already developed 70 direct-use geothermal sites. Idaho uses geothermal energy for fish farms, greenhouses, heated swimming pools, and for other applications. In addition, the Idaho State Capitol is the only U.S. capitol building heated with hot water from deep in the Earth.

Other states also are developing geothermal potential. California generates the most geothermal energy in the country, followed by Nevada, Utah, and Hawaii. As our energy needs increase, we may find a renewable resource right under our feet.

▲ **Visual Record Answer**
a lake

Teaching Objective 3

ALL LEVELS: (Suggested time: 10 min.) First, discuss with students the guessing game of "animal, vegetable, or mineral," in which players describe unnamed common objects as belonging to one of these categories. Ask what the word *mineral* means in this context. (Possible answers: rocks, something that is not alive and never has been alive, or materials dug from the ground.) Using students' definitions, ask the class to list minerals and products made from minerals that they see or use in daily life.
LS INTERPERSONAL

LEVEL 2: (Suggested time: 10 min.) Quiz the class on what they may already know about recycling in your community. Then have students write letters to the editor of your local newspaper urging the community to begin or expand a recycling program. **LS VERBAL-LINGUISTIC**

CHAPTER 2, Section 4

FOOD FESTIVAL

The Mineral on Your French Fries One of the most widely used minerals is salt. It is plentiful, cheap, and essential to good health. We are most familiar with salt as an ingredient in foods, but it is also used in many other products and processes.

Salt removes unwanted minerals from the water supply. Farm animals and poultry consume salt. Food processors such as pickle makers use tons of the mineral. Salt makes dyes colorfast in fabric. Film companies use salt in chemical solutions. Health spas offer salt baths and rubs. Salt producers have claimed that salt has 14,000 uses.

Have students examine labels of common packaged foods to find salt as an ingredient. You may also want to have them bring samples of different types of salt to class, such as rock salt, kosher salt, sea salt, or gourmet flavored salts.

Visual Record Answer ▶
for easier access for repairs

Human-Environment Interaction A mine employee shows the reddish ore of an iron mine located deep in the forest of northern Brazil.

Stretching from north to south across Alaska, a pipeline carries oil to the port of Sitka. **Interpreting the Visual Record** *Human-Environment Interaction* Why do you think the pipeline is above ground?

Mineral Resources

Energy resources are not the only nonrenewable resources that come out of the ground. We also use solid substances called minerals. Examples include metals, rocks, and salt.

Minerals fulfill many needs. Look around you to see just a few of the ways we use minerals. Your school is probably built on steel girders made from iron. The outside walls may be granite, limestone, or other types of rock. Window glass is made from quartz, a mineral found in sand. The "lead" in your pencil is actually graphite, another mineral. Metals are everywhere—from the staples through your homework papers to the coins in your wallet and the watch on your wrist.

Because they are nonrenewable, we need to conserve mineral resources. Recycling common items, such as aluminum cans, will make the supply of these resources last longer. It also reduces the amount of energy that factories use to convert metal into useful objects.

✓ **READING CHECK:** *Environment and Society* How can people conserve mineral resources? **by recycling**

Resources and People

Why does it matter what resources an area has, or how much it has of a resource? Actually, resources affect culture, history, and current events.

Resources and Wealth As you read this book, you will find that some places are rich in resources of many kinds. For example, the United States has fertile soil, forests, oil, metals, and many other resources. These riches have allowed our country to develop its economy. Our resources provide raw materials for various industries, from building houses to making cars. We also grow huge amounts of food. Partly because the United States has such a powerful economy, we also have great power in world affairs.

In contrast, some other countries are poor in resources. There, few industries grow, and people don't have many choices about how to earn a living. Some countries

---

Teaching Objective 4

ALL LEVELS: (Suggested time: 20 min.) Have students flip through this textbook looking for photographs that show or imply the relationship of people to the resources available to them. Then ask students to skim the text about that place for more information on how the resources in that place affect the people who live there. They may need to use the index to find information in other chapters. (Example: The lower photo on this page shows the Alaska pipeline. In the material on the United States, students will learn that oil provides significant income to that state.) After a discussion of their findings, ask students to write down a conclusion that they have drawn about people and resources. (Example: People with many available resources have many options about how to make a living.)

have large amounts of some resources but not of others. For example, Saudi Arabia is rich in oil but lacks water for growing food. Saudi Arabia pays other countries for food with the profit it earns on oil.

Resources and Daily Life The resources available to people affect how they live. In this country we have many resources. We can choose among many different ways to dress, build our homes, eat, travel, and entertain ourselves. People of other cultures may have fewer choices because they have fewer resources. Or, their environments may offer resources that we don't use.

Consider people who live in a rain forest, far from any city or factory. These people depend on the resources in their environment for all their needs. They may craft containers by weaving plant fibers together or canoes by hollowing out tree trunks. Their musical instruments are not electric guitars, but perhaps flutes made from bamboo. What kinds of songs would they sing? These forest people would be more likely to sing about finding food than about new cars.

✓ READING CHECK:
 How does the lack of resources affect people? **affects the choices they have for many aspects of daily life**

This Brazilian rain forest is being cleared by burning.
Human-Environment Interaction
How do you think the loss of land affects people who live in the rain forest?

Define and explain: renewable resources, nonrenewable resources, deforestation, reforestation, fossil fuels, petroleum, hydroelectric power, geothermal energy, solar power

Reading for the Main Idea
1. (Environment and Society) What are fossil fuels, and how are they used?
2. (Environment and Society) What are the main renewable energy sources?

Critical Thinking
3. **Analyzing Information** How are preserving soil and forest resources related to resource and land management?
4. **Making Generalizations and Predictions** How may a country that has only one or two valuable resources develop its economy?

Organizing What You Know
5. **Categorizing** Copy the following graphic organizer. Use it to describe the mineral resources that may be used in a typical home.

Homework Practice Online
Keyword: SK5 HP2

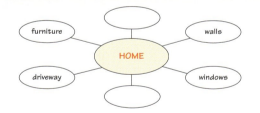

Planet Earth • 43

Section 4 Review

Answers to Section 4 Review

Define For definitions, see the glossary.

Reading for the Main Idea
1. fuels formed from the remains of ancient plants and animals; used in the form of coal, oil, or natural gas (NGS 16)
2. hydroelectric power, wind, geothermal energy, solar power (NGS 16)

Critical Thinking
3. Careful resource and land management can help preserve soil and forests. (NGS 16)
4. Possible answer: using profits from the sale or development of a resource to diversify the country's economy

Organizing What You Know
5. Answers will vary, but students should note a wide range of resources.

▲ **Visual Record Answer**
destroys plant life and the habitat of animals on which they depend

---

CLOSE

Ask students to suggest advertising slogans or logos for companies that harness and sell hydroelectric power, wind energy, geothermal energy, or solar energy.

REVIEW, ASSESS, RETEACH

Have students complete the Section Review. You may also have them prepare an outline of the section. Then have students complete Daily Quiz 2.4.

Have students complete Main Idea Activity S4. Then have them create crossword puzzles using the section's vocabulary terms. Ask students to exchange and solve another classmate's puzzle.
ESOL, LS VERBAL-LINGUISTIC

EXTEND

Have interested students conduct research on the Arctic National Wildlife Refuge (often abbreviated as ANWAR) and the controversy surrounding oil development there. **BLOCK SCHEDULING**

Planet Earth 43

CHAPTER 2 REVIEW

Define and Identify
For definitions, see the glossary.

Review the Main Ideas
11. It explains how Earth's topography formed and changes; Earth's surface is divided into plates which move very slowly. (NGS 7)
12. Hot lava may emerge and build up to form a mountain range. (NGS 7)
13. Ice cracks rocks; water dissolves underground minerals; water and ice move sediment; water waves shape beaches and coastlines. (NGS 7)
14. Rows of trees are planted to block wind; terraces are built into slopes of hillsides.
15. 1%; the Pacific, Atlantic, Indian, and Arctic Oceans, which are connected (NGS 7)
16. evaporation, condensation, and precipitation; the Sun's energy (NGS 7)
17. agriculture and industry
18. Wind blows polluted air from one place to another.
19. regions closer to the equator; because they receive the most direct rays from the Sun (NGS 7)
20. changes in air pressure as light, warm air rises and heavy, cold air moves in (NGS 7)
21. Distance from the ocean affects a region's climate, because water heats and cools more slowly than land. Because Kansas City is far from the ocean, its weather is not moderated by the ocean. (NGS 7)
22. An increase in elevation causes a drop in temperature because the air is less dense. (NGS 7)
23. The processes of renewal can take many years, while these resources can be used or destroyed within seconds.
24. They are nonrenewable resources, and they create air pollution.

Chapter 2 Review and Practice

Define and Identify
Identify each of the following:
1. topography
2. plate tectonics
3. erosion
4. tributary
5. water cycle
6. global warming
7. climate
8. rain shadow
9. nonrenewable resources
10. geothermal energy

Review the Main Idea
11. What is the theory of plate tectonics and how does it work?
12. What may occur when tectonic plates move away from each other?
13. How is water involved in erosion?
14. What methods are used to protect soil from erosion?
15. What percentage of Earth's water is freshwater? What covers 70% of Earth's surface?
16. What are the three phases of the water cycle? What drives the water cycle?
17. What are the two main causes of water pollution?
18. Why may one country suffer from another country's air pollution?
19. What parts of the Earth receive the most solar heat? Why?
20. What makes wind?
21. Explain why Kansas City has more extreme seasons than San Francisco.
22. Why may the base of a mountain be hot while the top is covered in ice?
23. Why is it important to preserve renewable resources such as soil and forests?
24. What problems are associated with fossil fuels?
25. What are some examples of renewable energy resources?
26. What are minerals used for?

Think Critically
27. **Drawing Inferences and Conclusions** Why are we developing alternative energy sources?
28. **Finding the Main Idea** How are the Earth's land, water, and atmosphere related?
29. **Understanding Cause and Effect** How may a dam affect a river and its surrounding areas?
30. **Drawing Inferences and Conclusions** How do the laws that govern and restrict pollution both help and hurt people?
31. **Making Generalizations and Predictions** Why is pollution a global concern?

Map Activity
32. Match the letters on the map with their correct labels.
    - Humid subtropical
    - Steppe climate
    - Marine west coast climate
    - Mediterranean climate
    - Desert
    - Humid tropical
    - Tropical savanna

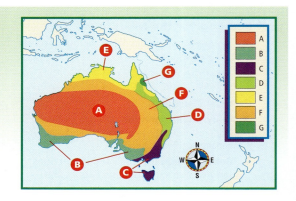

25. hydroelectric power, wind, geothermal energy, solar power, nuclear power (NGS 16)
26. Answers may vary but may include: salt; metals and rocks are used for building; glass is made from the mineral quartz; pencils; staples; coins; jewelry; aluminum and tin cans; cars (NGS 16)

Think Critically
27. Because fossil fuels are nonrenewable, they will eventually run out. Also, alternative energy resources may help to reduce air pollution.
28. Answers will vary but should include: water, wind, and ice break down land forms; weathering and erosion occur; winds lift and carry soil and wear down rocks; the water cycle moves water from Earth to the atmosphere and back to Earth.
29. A dam changes the flow of a river, which alters the river's ecosystem and that of its coastal areas. Land upstream from the dam will have more water, land downstream from the dam will have less water.
30. Limiting pollution keeps the air and ground cleaner and healthier for people. These limitations sometimes inhibit business and industry, which can hurt the economy.
31. Air and water pollution have no boundaries. All countries must address these issues in order to make a difference.

CHAPTER 2 REVIEW

Writing Activity

Imagine you are writing a report about your region of the United States for students around the world. Use your textbook, the library, and the Internet to research the landforms, climate, resources, and history of your region. Then write a few paragraphs highlighting what you discover.

internet connect
Internet Activity: go.hrw.com
KEYWORD: SK5 GT2

Choose a topic to explore online:
- Learn more about using weather maps.
- Discover facts about Earth's water.
- Investigate earthquakes.

Map Activity
32. A. Desert climate
    B. Mediterranean climate
    C. Marine west coast climate
    D. Humid subtropical
    E. Tropical savanna
    F. Steppe climate
    G. Humid tropical

Writing Activity

Reports will vary but should include accurate information on the region's landforms, climate, resources, and history. Use Rubric 40, Writing to Describe, to evaluate student work.

Interpreting Graphs

1. 6%
2. petroleum
3. hydroelectric, solar, and wind power
4. Possible answer: The high cost of harnessing these resources limits their use.

Analyzing Primary Sources

1. No, the earthquake occurred without warning.
2. Chunks of plaster fell from the ceilings, and many items were broken.
3. Windows were broken, and buildings were demolished.
4. Builders can avoid fault lines and build earthquake-resistant structures. Communities prone to earthquakes can develop emergency response systems.

Social Studies Skills Practice

Interpreting Graphs

The United States uses different resources to meet its energy needs. Study the following graph and answer the questions.

Energy Consumption in the United States, 2002

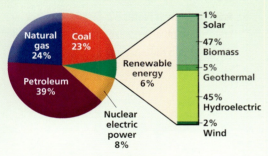

Natural gas 24%, Coal 23%, Petroleum 39%, Nuclear electric power 8%, Renewable energy 6%
Renewable energy breakdown: 1% Solar, 47% Biomass, 5% Geothermal, 45% Hydroelectric, 2% Wind

Source: Energy Information Administration

1. What percentage of the nation's energy consumption is renewable?
2. Which fossil fuel is used the most?
3. Based on what you have learned in this chapter, which renewable resources provide the cleanest energy?
4. Why do you think solar, wind, and geothermal energy are not commonly used resources?

Analyzing Primary Sources

In 1906, San Francisco experienced the most powerful earthquake recorded in the United States. Read the following account of the disaster from Peter Bacigalupi, one of San Francisco's shop owners. Then answer the questions.

"I was awakened from a sound slumber by a terrific trembling, which acted in the same manner as would a bucking broncho . . . My bed was going up and down in all four directions at once, while all about me I heard screams, wails, and crashing of breaking china-ware and nick-nacks. A great portion of plaster right over the head of my bed fell all around me, and caused a cloud of dust, which was very hard to breathe through . . . I started to walk downtown, and arriving within eight blocks of the business section, noted that there were hardly any panes of glass left in any of the show windows . . . Buildings were tumbled over on their sides, others looked as though they had been cut off short with a cleaver."

1. Was there any warning that the earthquake was about to occur?
2. What effect did the earthquake have on Mr. Bacigalupi's house?
3. What did he witness when he walked around the city?
4. How do you think communities can prepare for earthquakes such as this one?

Planet Earth • 45

CHAPTER 2

REVIEW AND ASSESSMENT RESOURCES

Reproducible
- Readings in World Geography, History, and Culture 5–8
- Critical Thinking Activity 2
- Vocabulary Activity 2

Technology
- Chapter 2 Test Generator (on the One-Stop Planner)
- HRW Go site
- Audio CD Program, Chapter 2

Reinforcement, Review, and Assessment
- Chapter 2 Review and Practice
- Chapter Summaries and Review
- Chapter 2 Test
- Chapter 2 Test for English Language Learners and Special-Needs Students

internet connect
GO TO: go.hrw.com
KEYWORD: SJ5 Teacher
FOR: a guide to using the Internet in your classroom

CHAPTER 3: The World's People
Chapter Resource Manager

Objectives	Pacing Guide	Reproducible Resources
SECTION 1		
What is Culture? (pp. 47–52) 1. Define culture. 2. Identify the importance of cultural symbols. 3. Trace how cultures develop. 4. Explain how agriculture affected culture.	**Regular** 1 day Lecture Notes, Section 1 **Block Scheduling** .5 day Block Scheduling Handbook, Chapter 3	RS Know It Notes S1 SM Map Activity 3 E Creative Strategies for Teaching World Geography, Lessons 4, 5 E Lab Activity for Geography and Earth Science, Hands-On 4 E Biography Activity: Ruth Benedict ELL Main Idea Activity S1
SECTION 2		
Economics and Population (pp. 53–59) 1. Define economics. 2. Compare how industrialized countries are different from developing countries. 3. Identify the different types of economic systems. 4. Explain where most people on Earth live.	**Regular** 1 day Lecture Notes, Section 2 **Block Scheduling** .5 day Block Scheduling Handbook, Chapter 3	RS Know It Notes S2 RS Graphic Organizer 3 ELL Main Idea Activity S2
SECTION 3		
Global Connections (pp. 60–63) 1. Define globalization and describe how people around the world are connected. 2. Explore refugees as a global problem, famine, and how people in need get help.	**Regular** 1 day Lecture Notes, Section 3 **Block Scheduling** .5 day Block Scheduling Handbook, Chapter 3	RS Know It Notes S3 E Environmental and Global Issues Activity 8 ELL Main Idea Activity S3

Chapter Resource Key

- **RS** Reading Support
- **IC** Interdisciplinary Connections
- **E** Enrichment
- **SM** Skills Mastery
- **A** Assessment
- **REV** Review
- **ELL** Reinforcement and English Language Learners and English for Speakers of Other Languages (ESOL)

 Transparencies

 CD–ROM

Music

  Video

 Internet

Holt Presentation Maker Using Microsoft® PowerPoint®

 **One-Stop** Planner CD–ROM

See the *One-Stop Planner* for a complete list of additional resources for students and teachers.

One-Stop Planner CD–ROM

It's easy to plan lessons, select resources, and print out materials for your students when you use the *One-Stop Planner CD–ROM with Test Generator.*

internet connect

HRW ONLINE RESOURCES

GO TO: go.hrw.com
Then type in a keyword.

TEACHER HOME PAGE
KEYWORD: SJ5 TEACHER

CHAPTER INTERNET ACTIVITIES
KEYWORD: SJ5 GT3

Choose an activity to:
- visit famous buildings and monuments around the world.
- compare facts about life in different countries.
- examine world population growth.

CHAPTER ENRICHMENT LINKS
KEYWORD: SJ5 CH3

CHAPTER MAPS
KEYWORDS: SJ5 MAPS3

ONLINE ASSESSMENT
Homework Practice
KEYWORD: SJ5 HP3
Standardized Test Prep Online
KEYWORD: SJ5 STP3
Rubrics
KEYWORD: SS Rubrics

COUNTRY INFORMATION
KEYWORD: SJ5 Almanac

CONTENT UPDATES
KEYWORD: SS Content Updates

HOLT PRESENTATION MAKER
KEYWORD: SJ5 PPT3

ONLINE READING SUPPORT
KEYWORD: SS Strategies

CURRENT EVENTS
KEYWORD: S5 Current Events

Technology Resources

Review, Reinforcement, and Assessment Resources

 One-Stop Planner CD-ROM, Lesson 3.1
 ARGWorld CD–ROM
 Homework Practice Online
HRW Go site

ELL	Main Idea Activity S1
REV	Section 1 Review
A	Daily Quiz 3.1
REV	Chapter Summaries and Review
ELL	English Audio Summary 3.1
ELL	Spanish Audio Summary 3.1

 One-Stop Planner CD-ROM, Lesson 3.2
 ARGWorld CD–ROM
 Homework Practice Online
HRW Go site

ELL	Main Idea Activity S2
REV	Section 2 Review
A	Daily Quiz 3.2
REV	Chapter Summaries and Review
ELL	English Audio Summary 3.2
ELL	Spanish Audio Summary 3.2

 One-Stop Planner CD-ROM, Lesson 3.3
 Yourtown CD-ROM
 ARGWorld CD–ROM
 Homework Practice Online
 HRW Go site

ELL	Main Idea Activity S3
REV	Section 3 Review
A	Daily Quiz 3.3
REV	Chapter Summaries and Review
ELL	English Audio Summary 3.3
ELL	Spanish Audio Summary 3.3

Meeting Individual Needs

Ability Levels

Level 1 Basic-level activities designed for all students encountering new material

Level 2 Intermediate-level activities designed for average students

Level 3 Challenging activities designed for honors and gifted-and-talented students

ESOL Activities that address the needs of students with Limited English Proficiency

Chapter Review and Assessment

SM	Critical Thinking Activity 3
REV	Chapter 3 Review and Practice
REV	Chapter Summaries and Review
ELL	Vocabulary Activity 3
A	Chapter 3 Test
A	Chapter 3 Test Generator (on the One-Stop Planner)
	Audio CD program, Chapter 3
A	Chapter 3 Test for English Language Learners and Special-Needs Students
	HRW Go site

45B

CHAPTER 3: The World's People
Previewing Chapter Resources

Holt Online Learning

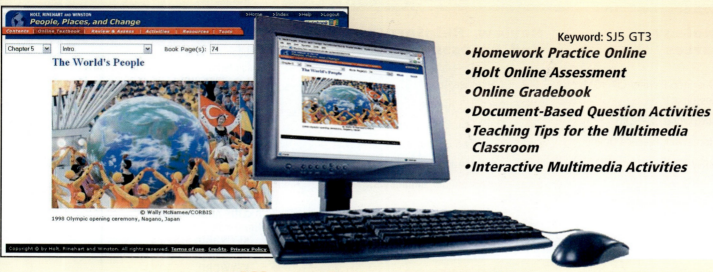

Keyword: SJ5 GT3

- Homework Practice Online
- Holt Online Assessment
- Online Gradebook
- Document-Based Question Activities
- Teaching Tips for the Multimedia Classroom
- Interactive Multimedia Activities

Differentiating Instruction

Reading and Writing Support
- ◀ Graphic Organizer Activity
- Vocabulary Activity
- Chapter Summary and Review
- Know It Notes
- Audio CD

Active Learning
- Block Scheduling Handbook
- Cultures of the World Activity
- Interdisciplinary Activity
- Map Activity
- Critical Thinking Activity: Wheat and the World

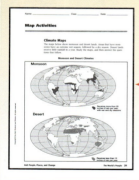

Primary Sources and Advanced Learners
- Geography for Life Activity: What Region Do You Live In?
- ◀ Map Activity: Languages of Europe
- Readings in World Geography, History and Culture:
  - 9 How Many Is Too Many?
  - 10 People and Migration

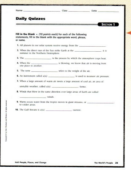

Assessment Program
- ◀ Daily Quizzes S1–3
- Chapter Test
- Chapter Test for English Language Learners and Special-Needs Students

Spanish and ESOL
- Vocabulary Activity
- ◀ Main Idea Activities for English Language Learners and Special-Needs Students
- Chapter Summary and Review
- Spanish Audio Summary
- Know It Notes S1–3
- Chapter Test for English Language Learners and Special-Needs Students

Special Education Modifications
Your **I.D.E.A. Works! CD-ROM** will provide modified versions of the following teaching materials:

- ◀ Guided Reading Strategies S1–3
- Vocabulary Activity
- Main Idea Activities S1–3
- Daily Quizzes S1–3
- Chapter 3 Test
- Flash cards of chapter vocabulary terms

Teacher Resources

Books for Teachers

Gallant, Roy A. *The Peopling of Planet Earth: Human Population Growth Through the Ages.* Macmillan Publishing Company, 1990.

Hirschman, Charles, Josh Dewind, and Philip Kasintz, eds. *The Handbook of International Migration.* Russell Sage Foundation, 1999.

Johnston, R.J., and David M. Smith, ed. *Dictionary of Human Geography.* Blackwell Publishing, 1994.

Books for Students

Ajerma, Maya, and Anna Rhesa Versola (contributor). *Children from Australia to Zimbabwe.* Charlebridge Publishing, 1997. Photographs of children at work, play, and worship showing the differences and similarities among civilizations. **SHELTERED ENGLISH**

Ellwood, Robert, ed. *The Encyclopedia of World Religions.* Facts on File, 1998. Maps, charts, and chronologies of major religions and related world events.

Pollack, Steve. *The Atlas of Endangered Peoples.* Facts on File, 1995. Human-made and natural problems threatening human life around the world and proposed solutions.

Roundtree, Lester. *Diversity amid Globalization.* Prentice Hall, 2000. Interconnections among the regions of the world.

Multimedia Materials

Folktales of Peace, Vol. I. Video, 22 min. The Video Project.

6.4 Billion: Will the Earth Drown in People? Video and Teacher's Guide, 60 min. Agency for Instructional Technology.

The World and Its People. Videodisc, 60 min. Glencoe.

Videos and CDs

Videos
- CNN Presents Geography: Yesterday and Today, Segment 5 World Population—**Hitting Six Billion**
- ARG World

Holt Researcher

http://researcher.hrw.com

- *Natural Increase in Population*
- *Population and Population Projections—Asia*
- *Total GDP for Selected Countries*
- *Immigrants to The United States by Region*
- *U.S. Trade with Selected Countries, 2000*
- *Major Religions of the World*

Transparency Packages

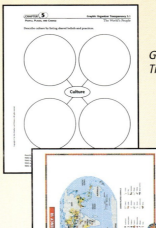

Graphic Organizer Transparencies 3.1–3

Geography and Cultures Visual Resources Transparencies
18 World Domestication
19 Age Structure Diagrams
20 Population Growth in the Americas

Map Activities Transparency
03 Languages of Europe

CHAPTER 3

WHY IT MATTERS

State these points to emphasize the importance of learning the basics of human geography.

- In order to understand individual cultures, we need to understand basic concepts of culture.
- Cultural differences affect world events and our daily lives. We should understand why cultures are different.
- We will participate more effectively in our own culture if we know how it developed.
- Population issues affect food production, international conflicts, and environmental questions—all of which can affect Americans directly.
- Modern technology connects people around the world like never before.

CHAPTER 3
The World's People

The Colosseum, Rome, Italy

1998 Olympic opening ceremony, Nagano, Japan

Easter Island, Chile

CHAPTER PROJECT

Have students collect symbols and logos—on signs, clothing, and food and beverage labels, for example—that are part of American culture. They may need to photograph or draw some symbols. Ask students how they would interpret the images if they lived in another culture. Have them write brief explanations of the symbols' meaning. Include descriptions in portfolios.

STARTING THE CHAPTER

Display a news-story photo that shows elements of physical and human geography. (Examples: natural disaster, new medicine discovered in rain forest) Ask students to list the physical and human elements shown or implied in the photo. (For example, for a hurricane: physical—rain, mud slides, beach erosion, high tides; human—people forced from homes, businesses hurt) Point out to students that their interpretation of the photo would be incomplete if they left out either the physical or human issues. Similarly, the study of geography must include the human element. Tell students they will learn more about the human element of geography in this chapter.

Section 1: What Is Culture?

CHAPTER 3, Section 1

Read to Discover
1. What is culture?
2. Why are cultural symbols important?
3. What influences how cultures develop?
4. How did agriculture affect the development of culture?

Vocabulary
- culture
- culture region
- culture traits
- ethnic groups
- multicultural
- race
- acculturation
- symbol
- ethnocentrism
- domestication
- subsistence agriculture
- commercial agriculture
- civilization

Reading Strategy
READING ORGANIZER Before you read, create a chart with columns titled Term, Definition, Example. Write each of the terms above in the left column. As you read write the definition and give an example in the other two columns.

Section 1 Resources
Reproducible
- Lecture Notes, Section 1
- Block Scheduling Handbook, Chapter 3
- Know It Notes S1
- Creative Strategies for Teaching World Geography, Lessons 4, 5
- Map Activity 3
- Lab Activity for Geography and Earth Science, Hands-On 4
- Biography Activity: Ruth Benedict

Technology
- One-Stop Planner CD–ROM, Lesson 3.1
- Homework Practice Online
- HRW Go site

Reinforcement, Review, and Assessment
- Section 1 Review
- Daily Quiz 3.1
- Main Idea Activity S1
- Chapter Summaries and Review
- English Audio Summary 3.1
- Spanish Audio Summary 3.1

Aspects of Culture

The people of the world's approximately 200 countries speak hundreds of different languages. They may dress in different ways and eat different foods. However, all societies share certain basic institutions, including a government, an educational system, an economic system, and religious institutions. These vary from society to society and are often based on that society's **culture**. Culture is a learned system of shared beliefs and ways of doing things that guides a person's daily behavior. Most people around the world have a national culture shared with people of their own country. They may also have religious practices, beliefs, and language in common with people from other countries. Sometimes a culture dominates a particular region. This is known as a **culture region**. In a culture region, people may share certain **culture traits**, or elements of culture, such as dress, food, or religious beliefs. West Africa is an example of a culture region. Culture can also be based on a person's job or age. People can belong to more than one culture and can choose which to emphasize.

Dance is an example of a culture trait. Dancers from central Texas perform a traditional Czech dance.

Race and Ethnic Groups Cultural groups share beliefs and practices learned from parents, grandparents, and ancestors. These groups are sometimes called **ethnic groups**. An ethnic group's shared culture may include its religion, history, language, holiday traditions, and special foods.

When people from different cultures live in the same country, the country is described as **multicultural** or multiethnic. Many countries

The World's People • 47

Objectives
1. Define culture.
2. Identify the importance of cultural symbols.
3. Trace how cultures develop.
4. Explain how agriculture affected culture.

Focus

Bellringer
Copy the following question onto the chalkboard: *What are some organized events that occur regularly in our community?* Discuss responses. (Possible answers: parades, festivals, garage sales, sports tournaments, concerts) Point out that the events they listed are part of the community's culture. Ask if students know of similar events elsewhere. If so, compare those events with the students' lists to note ways in which other communities have different cultures. Tell students that in Section 1 they will learn more about culture.

Building Vocabulary
Write the vocabulary terms on the chalkboard. Underline the prefixes *multi-* and *sub-*. Explain that they mean, respectively, "many" and "below" or "almost." Ask students to find the terms' definitions in the text or glossary and to relate the prefix meanings to **multicultural** and **subsistence agriculture**. Call on students to read the remaining definitions. Ask each student to choose a vocabulary term and write a sentence to define it. Call on students to read their sentences. Continue until all of the terms have been covered.

The World's People 47

CHAPTER 3, Section 1

DAILY LIFE

Mancala! Peoples of many races and ethnic groups often enjoy the same entertainments. For example, a board game called *mancala* is popular in many parts of the world. *Mancala* is possibly the oldest board game in the world. Egyptians played this counting and strategy game before 1400 B.C. It is popular across Africa, among all ages and social classes.

Mancala is played on boards of different sizes and shapes or simply with shallow holes in the ground. Counters can be anything from seashells to seeds. Versions of *mancala* can be found thousands of miles from Africa, in Southeast Asia. The game's actual origin is not known, however.

Activity: Have students conduct research on the rules for playing *mancala*. Ask them to determine similarities and differences in rules from different countries. Then have them construct *mancala* boards from egg cartons. Hold a *mancala* tournament in your classroom.

internet connect
GO TO: go.hrw.com
KEYWORD: SG5 CH3
FOR: Web sites about mancala

World Religions

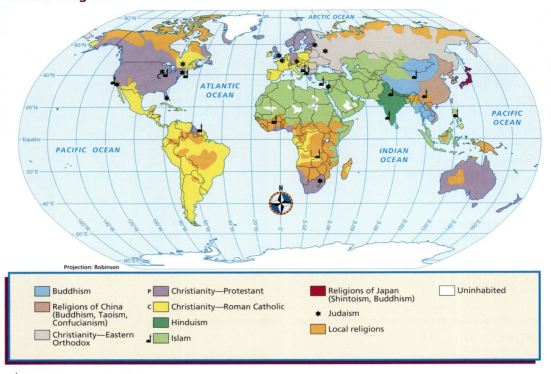

Legend:
- Buddhism
- Religions of China (Buddhism, Taoism, Confucianism)
- Christianity—Eastern Orthodox
- Christianity—Protestant
- Christianity—Roman Catholic
- Hinduism
- Islam
- Religions of Japan (Shintoism, Buddhism)
- Judaism
- Local religions
- Uninhabited

Projection: Robinson

▲ Religion is one aspect of culture.

A disc jockey plays Cuban music for the large Cuban ethnic group of Miami, Florida.

are multicultural. In some countries, such as Belgium, different ethnic groups have cooperated to form a united country. In other cases, such as in French-speaking Quebec, Canada, ethnic groups have frequently been in conflict. Sometimes, people from one ethnic group are spread over two or more countries. For example, Germans live in different European countries: Germany, Austria, and the Czech Republic. The Kurds, who are a people with no country of their own, live mostly in Syria, Iran, Iraq, and Turkey.

Race is based on inherited physical or biological traits. It is sometimes confused with ethnic group. For example, the Hispanic ethnic group in the United States includes people who look quite different from each other. However, they share a common Spanish or Latin American heritage. As you know, people vary in physical appearance. Some of these differences have developed in response to climate factors like cold and sunlight. Because people have moved from region to region throughout history, these differences are not clear-cut. Each culture defines race in its own way, emphasizing particular biological and ethnic characteristics. An example can be seen in Rwanda, a country in East Africa. In this country, the Hutu and the Tutsi have carried on a bitter civil war. Although both are East African, each one

48 • Chapter 3

TEACH

Teaching Objectives 1 and 3
ALL LEVELS: (Suggested time: 30 min.) Ask students to write on a slip of paper three of the cultures or culture regions to which they belong. Collect the suggestions. (Responses may include ethnic groups, sports teams, state or regional affiliations, or many other possibilities.) On the chalkboard, draw three columns. Label them *Culture, History,* and *Environment.* Choose a range of the student suggestions. As you record each group on the chart, lead a discussion on how it fulfills the definition of culture and how history and environment helped shape that culture. **ESOL**

Teaching Objective 2
ALL LEVELS: Point out that gestures are symbols and that they vary among cultures. Call on volunteers to demonstrate how they would show appreciation after a school play or choir concert (polite applause) and after the home team's winning goal at a sports event (cheers, high fives). Then have students conduct research on how people in other countries display approval in similar situations. Ask them to speculate how history and the environment have shaped the customs. Tell them to consider the effect of having a culture region divided by political boundaries. How might gestures or symbols in general change? You may need to extend this activity to another class period so that students can use other sources. **ESOL**

considers itself different from the other. Their definition of race involves height and facial features. Around the world, people tend to identify races based on obvious physical traits. However, these definitions of race are based primarily on attitudes, not actual biological differences.

Cultural Change Cultures change over time. Humans invent new ways of doing things and spread these new ways to others. The spread of one culture's ways or beliefs to another culture is called diffusion. Diffusion may occur when people move from one place to another. The English language was once confined to England and parts of Scotland. It is now one of the world's most widely spoken languages. English originally spread because people from England founded colonies in other regions. More recently, as communication among cultures has increased, English has spread through English-language films and television programs. English has also become an international language of science and technology.

People sometimes may borrow aspects of another culture as the result of long-term contact with another society. This process is called **acculturation**. For example, people in one culture may adopt the religion of another. As a result, they might change other cultural practices to conform to the new religion. For example, farmers who become Muslim may quit raising pigs because Islam forbids eating pork.

✓ **READING CHECK:** (Human Systems) What is the definition of culture? a learned system of shared beliefs and ways of doing things that guides a person's daily behavior

Cultural Differences

A **symbol** is a sign that stands for something else. A symbol can be many things such as a word, a shape, a color, or a flag. People learn symbols from their culture. The sets of sounds of a language are symbols. These symbols have meaning for the people who speak that language. The same sound may mean something different to people who speak another language. The word bad means "evil" in English, "cool" to teenagers, and "bath" in German.

If you traveled to another country, you might notice immediately that people behave differently. Some people, however, may see the differences in other cultures as inferior to their own. This view is called **ethnocentrism**. Many people may even have an ethnocentric view toward the foods some cultures eat. For example, they may think it is disgusting that the Inuit of Canada eat whale blubber. To the Inuit, however, eating blubber is perfectly normal.

✓ **READING CHECK:** (Human Systems) How do symbols reflect differences among societies and cultures? They show the societies' particular cultural expressions or belief systems.

▲ Movement Some immigrants from China settle in New York City's Chinatown.

Fans cheer for the U.S. Olympic soccer team.
Interpreting the Visual Record Why do you think symbols such as flags create strong emotions?

The World's People • 49

CHAPTER 3, Section 1

National Geography Standard 10

Lost and Found Diffusion has carried elements of modern cultures into the far corners of the world, from vast deserts to rain forests.

In 1972, newspapers reported that a "lost" culture had been found in the Philippines. The Tasaday supposedly led an isolated existence and had never before encountered other cultures. However, in 1986 the story was revealed as a hoax. The Tasaday were well aware of modern cultures.

Discussion: Lead a discussion on these questions: Do isolated peoples have the right to be left alone? What may be the consequences of improved communication between these cultures and modern cultures?

◀ **Visual Record Answer**

because they can evoke strong feelings of national pride

Teaching Objective 4

LEVEL 1: (Suggested time: 30 min.) Copy the following graphic organizer onto the chalkboard, omitting the blue answers. Use it to help students describe how agriculture affected culture. Call on students to fill in the boxes. Then have them choose a step and illustrate it. Display the illustrated diagrams. **ESOL,** **LS** VISUAL-SPATIAL

LEVELS 2 AND 3: (Suggested time: 45 min.) Organize students into groups. Have each group create a scenario that describes what human life would be like today if the progression from hunting and gathering to civilization had been interrupted. Instruct students to create feasible scenarios. You may want to have students act out their ideas. Have group members summarize in a paragraph the reasoning they used.
COOPERATIVE LEARNING, **LS** KINESTHETIC

AGRICULTURE AND CIVILIZATION

The World's People 49

CHAPTER 3, Section 1

Linking Past to Present
Nile River

Cultures Without the Nile River, the civilization whose people built the pyramids and the Sphinx could never have existed. The thousands of workers who labored on these and other monumental projects could be fed only because the river made intensive agriculture possible. The Nile Valley and Delta have been densely populated for thousands of years. Hunter-gatherers may have started to move into the Nile Valley by 12,000 B.C. By about 3,000 B.C. a great civilization flourished.

Alexandria, Egypt, was built next to the Nile Delta. During the 200s B.C. Alexandria may have been the largest metropolis in the world. Cleopatra's palace was there. During the 1980s, archaeologists began excavating the ruins of the city, which is now under water. They mapped the Royal Quarter, where Cleopatra had lived. Today, Alexandria is Egypt's second-largest city, with more than 4 million inhabitants.

Visual Record Answer

possible answers: streets narrower and appear to be laid out in a random pattern, houses closer together and with flat roofs

▲ A couple prepares for a wedding ceremony in Kazakhstan.

The layout of Marrakech, Morocco, is typical of many North African cities.
Interpreting the Visual Record (Place)
How are the streets and houses of Marrakech different from those in your community?
▼

Development of a Culture

All people have the same basic needs for food, water, clothing, and shelter. People everywhere live in families and mark important family changes together. They usually have rituals or traditions that go with the birth of a baby, the wedding of a couple, or the death of a grandparent. All human societies need to deal with natural disasters. They must also deal with people who break the rules of behavior. However, people in different places meet these needs in unique ways. They eat different foods, build different kinds of houses, and form families in different ways. They have different rules of behavior. Two important factors that influence the way people meet basic needs are their history and environment.

History Culture is shaped by history. A region's people may have been conquered by the same outsiders. They may have adopted the same religion. They may have come from the same area and may share a common language. However, historical events may have affected some parts of a region but not others. For example, in North America French colonists brought their culture to Louisiana and Canada. However, they did not have a major influence on the Middle Atlantic region of the United States.

Cultures also shape history by influencing the way people respond to the same historical forces. Nigeria, India, and Australia were all colonized by the British. Today each nation still uses elements of the British legal system, but with important differences.

Environment The environment of a region can influence the development of culture. For example, in Egypt the Nile River is central to people's lives. The ancient Egyptians saw the fertile soils brought by the flooding of the Nile as the work of the gods. Beliefs in mountain spirits were important in many mountainous regions of the world. These areas include Tibet, Japan, and the Andes of South America.

▶**ASSIGNMENT:** Tell students that the cultures to which we belong affect practically all aspects of our daily lives—what we wear, how we talk, what we do at school, our choices in friends, how we relate to our families, what we do for fun, and so on. Have students write either a paragraph or a list of ways in which culture influences what they do throughout the day. For each event, ask students to speculate how someone in another culture may perform that action. You may want to have students discuss what factors would affect that choice. For example, we may eat store-bought cereal for breakfast. In another culture, a Chinese teen would eat boiled rice instead because his or her family members raise rice on their farm.

TEACHER TO TEACHER

Lois Jordan of Nashville, Tennessee, suggests this research project to help students explore how minority groups can affect a country's development and culture. Organize the class into teams. Assign one country per team. Have each team use primary and secondary sources to research the country's minority groups and the geographical or historical reasons why the groups are there. Students should try to answer questions such as these: Are members of the minority groups spread throughout the country or concentrated in one area? In what ways are the minority cultures different from the majority culture? How do the majority and minority cultures relate to each other politically and socially? Have the students share their findings in a panel discussion.

Culture also determines how people use and shape their landscape. For example, city plans are cultural. Cities in Spain and its former colonies are organized around a central plaza, or square, with a church and a courthouse. On the other hand, Chinese cities are oriented to the four compass points. American cities often follow a rectangular grid plan. Many French city streets radiate out from a central core.

✓ **READING CHECK:** *Human Systems* What are some ways in which culture traits spread? **through historical events such as conquest by outsiders or colonization**

Development of Agriculture

For most of human history people ate only wild plants and animals. When the food ran out in one place, they migrated, or moved to another place. Very few people still live this way today. Thousands of years ago, humans began to help their favorite wild plant foods to grow. They probably cleared the land around their campsites and dumped seeds or fruits in piles of refuse. Plants took root and grew. People may also have dug water holes to encourage wild cattle to come and drink. People began cultivating the largest plants and breeding the tamest animals. Gradually, the wild plants and animals changed. They became dependent on people. This process is called **domestication**. A domesticated species has changed its form and behavior so much that it depends on people to survive. Domestic sheep can no longer leap from rock to rock like their wild ancestors. However, the wool of domestic sheep is more useful to humans. It can be combed and twisted into yarn.

Domestication happened in many parts of the world. In Peru llamas and potatoes were domesticated. People in ancient Mexico and Central America domesticated corn, beans, squash, tomatoes, and hot peppers. None of these foods was grown in Europe, Asia, or Africa before the time of Christopher Columbus's voyages to the Americas. Meanwhile, Africans had domesticated sorghum and a kind of rice. Cattle, sheep, and goats were probably first raised in Southwest Asia. Wheat and rye were first domesticated in Central Asia. The horse was also domesticated there. These domesticated plants and animals were unknown in the Americas before the time of Columbus.

▲ This ancient Egyptian wall painting shows domesticated cattle.
Interpreting the Visual Record Can you name other kinds of domesticated animals?

CHAPTER 3, Section 1

ENVIRONMENT AND SOCIETY

The Animals around Us
We know cats, dogs, cattle, horses, sheep, and other familiar animals have served or been dependent on humans for many centuries. Creatures we think of as living only in the wild have also been tamed.

Cheetahs were tamed perhaps 5,000 years ago. Ancient Egyptians and early rulers of India kept them as pets and trained them to hunt. Hunting with falcons and hawks has been known since before 700 B.C. Elephants have served as beasts of burden and have been used to drag heavy equipment over difficult terrain. As early as the 200s B.C. and as late as the 1940s elephants have been used in warfare.

Activity: What other examples of tamed animals can students find in books and nature television programs? To depict their findings, have them paint a mural in the style of a cave painting.

◀ **Visual Record Answer**

possible answers: cats, chickens, dogs, ducks, geese, goats, horses, pigs, sheep, turkeys

The World's People • 51

CLOSE

Call on students to suggest foods that are typical of a local culture. (Possible answers: pierogi, quesadillas, dim sum, gumbo, grits) Ask them to speculate how the popularity of that dish spread to the region. (Possible answers: television ads, families moving to new regions, national restaurant franchises) Point out how food is related to the main topics of the section.

REVIEW, ASSESS, RETEACH

Have students complete the Section Review. Then have them work in pairs to draw flow charts or other graphic organizers of the section material. Then have students complete Daily Quiz 3.1 **COOPERATIVE LEARNING**

Have students complete Main Idea Activity S1. Then have them work in groups to invent a previously unknown culture. Have them write sentences describing the features and development of their culture by using the vocabulary terms. Discuss the invented cultures to check on students' understanding of key concepts. **ESOL, COOPERATIVE LEARNING**

Section 1 Review

Answers to Section 1 Review

Define For definitions, see the glossary.

Reading for the Main Idea

1. People may belong to cultures based on where they live, their job, religious practices, beliefs, or age. **(NGS 10)**
2. Government, education, an economic system, religious institutions are basic to all. **(NGS 10)**

Critical Thinking

3. history—conquered by the same outsiders, have same religion or language; environment—affects religion, land use and planning; French colonists brought their culture to Louisiana; Nile River's influence on Egyptians

4. People built permanent settlements; surplus of food developed; population grew; civilizations formed.

Organizing What You Know

5. possible answers: religion, age, job, race, where we live, language and other cultural symbols

---

Thousands of years ago, domesticated dogs came with humans across the Bering Strait into North America. A breed called the Carolina dog may be descended almost unchanged from those dogs. The reddish yellow, short-haired breed also appears to be closely related to Australian dingoes.

Agriculture and Environment Agriculture changed the landscape. To make room for growing food, people cut down forests. They also built fences, dug irrigation canals, and terraced hillsides. Governments were created to direct the labor needed for these large projects. Governments also defended against outsiders and helped people resolve problems. People could now grow enough food for a whole year. Therefore, they stopped migrating and built permanent settlements.

Types of Agriculture Some farmers grow just enough food to provide for themselves and their own families. This type of farming is called **subsistence agriculture**. In the wealthier countries of the world, a small number of farmers can produce food for everyone. Each farm is large and may grow only one product. This type of farming is called **commercial agriculture**. In this system companies rather than individuals or families may own the farms.

Agriculture and Civilization Agriculture enabled farmers to produce a surplus of food—more than they could eat themselves. A few people could make things like pottery jars instead of farming. They traded or sold their products for food. With more food a family could feed more children. As a result, populations began to grow. More people became involved in trading and manufacturing. Traders and craftspeople began to live in central market towns. Some towns grew into cities, where many people lived and carried out even more specialized tasks. For example, cities often supported priests and religious officials. They were responsible for organizing and carrying out religious ceremonies. When a culture becomes highly complex, we sometimes call it a **civilization**.

✓ **READING CHECK:** *Environment and Society* In what ways did agriculture affect culture? Permanent settlements developed; a surplus of food developed; the population grew; civilizations developed.

Define and explain: culture, culture region, culture trait, ethnic groups, multicultural, race, acculturation, symbol, ethnocentrism, domestication, subsistence agriculture, commercial agriculture, civilization

Reading for the Main Idea

1. *Human Systems* How can an individual belong to more than one cultural group?
2. *Human Systems* What institutions are basic to all societies?

Critical Thinking

3. **Drawing Inferences and Conclusions** In what ways do history and environment influence or shape a culture? What examples can you find in the text that explain this relationship?
4. **Analyzing Information** What is the relationship between the development of agriculture and culture?

Organizing What You Know

5. **Summarizing** Copy the following graphic organizer. Use it to describe culture by listing shared beliefs and practices.

EXTEND

Have interested students use primary and secondary sources to research how archaeology has shed light on when and where various plants and animals were domesticated for use as food. Then challenge them to choose a certain time period and region and write recipes appropriate to the available foods. Students may want to prepare an "ancient" meal for the class. Substitutions will be necessary. **BLOCK SCHEDULING**

Section 2: Economics and Population

CHAPTER 3, Section 2

Read to Discover
1. What is economics?
2. How are industrialized countries different from developing countries?
3. What are the different types of economic systems?
4. Where do most people on Earth live?

Vocabulary
- gross national product
- gross domestic product
- industrialized countries
- literacy rate
- developing countries
- third-world countries
- free enterprise
- market economy
- command economy
- tradition-based economy
- mixed economy
- one-crop economy
- exports
- imports
- interdependence
- birthrate
- death rate
- population density
- overpopulation
- migration
- emigrant
- immigrant

Section 2 Resources

Reproducible
- Lecture Notes, Section 2
- Know It Notes S2
- Graphic Organizer 3

Technology
- One-Stop Planner CD–ROM, Lesson 3.2
- Homework Practice Online
- HRW Go site

Reinforcement, Review, and Assessment
- Section 2 Review
- Daily Quiz 3.2
- Main Idea Activity S2
- Chapter Summaries and Review
- English Audio Summary 3.2
- Spanish Audio Summary 3.2

Reading Strategy

FOLDNOTES: FOUR-CORNER FOLD Create a **Four-Corner Fold** described in the Appendix. Title the flaps The Economy, Developed and Undeveloped Countries, Types of Economies, and Population. As you read, write what you learn about each topic beneath its flap.

The Economy

All of the activities that people do to earn a living are part of a system called the economy. This includes people going to work, making things, selling things, buying things, and trading services. Economics is the study of the production, distribution, and use of goods and services.

Economic Indicators A common means of measuring a country's economy is the **gross national product** (GNP). The GNP is the value of all goods and services that a country produces in one year. It includes goods and services made by factories owned by that country's citizens but located in foreign countries. Most economists use **gross domestic product** (GDP) instead of GNP. GDP includes only those goods and services produced within a country. GDP divided by the country's population is called per capita GDP. This figure shows individual purchasing power and is useful for comparing levels of economic development.

Economic Activities Economists divide economic activities into four industries—primary, secondary, tertiary, and quaternary (see chart on the next page). A country's economy is usually based on one or more of these activities.

Shoppers crowd a street in Tokyo, Japan.

The World's People • 53

Section 2

Objectives
1. Define economics.
2. Compare how industrialized countries are different from developing countries.
3. Identify the different types of economic systems.
4. Explain where most people on Earth live.

Focus

Bellringer

Write these instructions on the chalkboard: *Everyone except those on the first row should move to the back third of the room. I will explain soon.* Then tell students the crowded area represents a densely populated country, such as India, and the front of the room a thinly populated one, such as Mongolia. Discuss with students the advantages and disadvantages they would experience as citizens of these countries, based on their population density. Tell students that in Section 2 they will learn more about population issues and economics.

Building Vocabulary

Write the vocabulary terms on the chalkboard. Call on volunteers to read the definitions aloud. Then label some of them according to these categories: Ways to Measure Economic Development (**gross national product, gross domestic product, industrialized countries,** and **developing countries**); Economic Systems (**free enterprise, market, command, tradition-based economy**); and Concepts Related to Population (**population density, overpopulation, migration, emigrant,** and **immigrant**).

The World's People 53

CHAPTER 3, Section 2

HUMAN SYSTEMS

Development in India India provides a good example of a country that has industries but is still usually considered a developing country. One factor that keeps India from reaching its development goals is its huge and growing population. The population surpassed 1 billion in the year 2000 and may surpass the population of China by 2050. For most of these people, the standard of living is still low. Many villages lack any telephone service. Industrial growth is hampered by lack of sufficient energy, transportation, and communication resources.

Economic Activities

ECONOMIC INDUSTRIES	DESCRIPTION	TYPES OF ACTIVITIES	EXAMPLE
Primary industry	Involves natural resources or raw materials	Farming, fishing, mining, forestry	Dairy farmer feeds his cows.
Secondary industry	Makes finished products using natural resources or raw materials	Manufacturing and construction	Factories make cheese.
Tertiary industry	Handles goods that are ready for sale	Trucking, restaurants, grocery stores	Grocery stores sell cheese.
Quaternary industry	Collects information	Research and management	A technician inspects dairy products in a lab.

Interpreting the Chart Which economic industry involves selling goods?

A monorail in Sydney, Australia takes passengers throughout the city's central business district.
Interpreting the Visual Record *Place* What in this photo suggests that this is a city in an industrialized country?

Chart Answer
tertiary

Visual Record Answer
tall buildings, advanced transportation system, recreational facilities

The World's Rich and Poor

Economists divide the countries of the world into two groups. They use various measures including GNP, GDP, per capita GDP, life expectancy, and literacy to determine a country's stage of development. Developed countries like the United States, Canada, Japan, and most European countries are the world's wealthiest. They are called **industrialized countries**.

Industrialization occurs when a country relies more on manufacturing and less on agriculture. In industrialized countries, many people work in manufacturing, service, and information industries. These countries have strong secondary, tertiary, and quaternary industries. They have good health care systems. Industrialized countries also have good systems of education. The **literacy rate**, or the percentage of people, who can read and write is high.

Most people in industrialized countries live in cities and have access to telecommunications systems—systems that allow long-distance communication. The level of technology in most countries is usually measured by how many telephones, televisions, or computers are in use.

54 • Chapter 3

TEACH

Teaching Objective 1

LEVEL 1: (Suggested time: 20 min.) Organize the class into groups. Have each group examine a common object (examples—dish, book, sock, eyeglasses) and discuss among themselves what role primary, secondary, tertiary, and quaternary industries have played in the object's "history." Then have students in each group create a flow chart to display their ideas. **ESOL, COOPERATIVE LEARNING**

LEVELS 2 AND 3: (Suggested time: 20 min.) Point out that students may play different roles in economies at different times—sometimes a consumer and sometimes a producer. Discuss these concepts. Then have each student write a brief essay titled "How I Participate in the Economy." Encourage students to consider not just the local economy, but the state, regional, national, and global economies. **LS INTRAPERSONAL**

Developing countries make up the second group. They are in different stages of moving toward development. About two thirds of the world's people live in developing countries. These countries are poor. People often work in farming or other primary industries earning low wages. Cities in developing countries are often very crowded. Many people move to cities to find work. Most people are not educated. They usually have little access to health care or telecommunications.

Some developing countries have made economic progress in recent decades. South Korea and Mexico are good examples. These countries are experiencing strong growth in manufacturing and trade. However, some of the world's poorest countries are developing slowly or not at all.

One Planet, Four Worlds Some people also refer to developing countries as **third-world countries**. These countries lack the economic opportunities of most industrialized countries. Some industrialized countries are called first-world and second-world countires. First-world countries include the United States, Canada, Western Europe, Japan and Australia. Second-world countries include Russia, the former Soviet republics, China, and Eastern Europe.

Third-world countries in Latin America, however, experience some economic growth. Countries like Haiti, however, show no economic growth. They are known as fourth-world countries.

✓ **READING CHECK:** What are some of the differences between industrialized and developing countries? *differences in income; reliance on industry or agriculture; access to health care, education, and telecommunications*

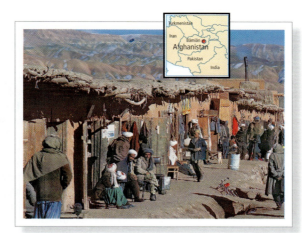

This photo shows daily life in a village in eastern Afghanistan.
Interpreting the Visual Record *Place* What in this photo suggests that this village is in a developing country?

Interpreting the Chart Which countries have the highest literacy rates?

Comparing Developed and Developing Countries

Country	Population	Population Growth Rate	Per Capita GDP	Life Expectancy	Literacy Rate	Telephone Lines
United States	290.3 million	0.9%	$ 37,600	77	97%	194 million
France	60.1 million	0.4%	$ 26,000	79	99%	35 million
South Korea	48.2 million	0.7%	$ 19,600	75	98%	24 million
Mexico	104.9 million	1.4%	$ 8,900	72	92%	9.6 million
Poland	38.6 million	0.0%	$ 9,700	73	99%	8 million
Brazil	182.1 million	1.1%	$ 7,600	71	86%	17 million
Egypt	74.7 million	1.8%	$ 4,000	70	57%	3.9 million
Myanmar	42 million	0.5%	$ 1,700	55	83%	250,000
Mali	11.6 million	2.8%	$ 900	45	46%	23,000

Source: Central Intelligence Agency, *The World Factbook 2003*

CHAPTER 3, Section 2

GLOBAL PERSPECTIVES

Population and Policy
Beliefs and events can influence population issues. For example, in 1967 Iran became one of the first developing countries to institute a policy to slow population growth. The government declared family planning a human right and promoted it as a policy.

After Iran's 1979 Islamic Revolution, earlier efforts to limit family size were criticized as pro-West. The population growth rate climbed to more than 3 percent per year. However, a long war with Iraq badly damaged Iran. The leaders decided that it would be hard to rebuild their country while the population continued to expand so rapidly. As a result, the policy changed back to favoring small families.

Discussion: Lead a discussion on the relationship among religion, philosophical ideas, and Iranian culture with regard to population growth.

◄**Visual Record Answer**
dirt streets, poor clothing, houses in need of repair

◄**Chart Answer**
United States, France, South Korea, Poland

Teaching Objective 2

LEVEL 1: (Suggested time: 20 min.) Copy the following graphic organizer onto the chalkboard, omitting the blue answers. Use it to help students learn the characteristics of industrialized and developing countries. **ESOL,** **LS** VISUAL-SPATIAL

COMPARING COUNTRIES

Industrialized Countries	Developing Countries
• relies more on manufacturing • strong secondary, tertiary, quaternary industries • good health care and education systems • high literacy rates • most people in cities, have access to telecommunications	• relies more on agriculture • most people in primary industries • people looking for work in crowded cities • low levels of education • little access to health care or telecommunications

LEVELS 2 AND 3: (Suggested time: 20 min.) Organize the class into two groups. Using the characteristics noted in the section, have one half write a what-I-did-today journal entry for a youngster in an imaginary developed country and the other half do the same for an imaginary developing country. Call on volunteers to read their entries. Lead a discussion on how the journal entries compare to the characteristics mentioned in the section. **COOPERATIVE LEARNING,** **LS** VERBAL-LINGUISTIC

CHAPTER 3, Section 2

Across the Curriculum
MATH

Per Capita GDP A country's gross domestic product (GDP) indicates the total size of its economy. However, it may not be a clear indication of an average citizen's wealth. For that purpose per capita GDP is more useful.

For example, China's GDP for 1998 was estimated at $4.4 trillion, making China a major economic power. However, China's per capita GDP was only $3,600, because the GDP figure was divided among China's immense population of more than 1 billion. In contrast, Chile's GDP the same year was about $184.6 billion. With a population of about 15 million, Chile's per capita GDP was $12,500. This comparison indicates that an average citizen in Chile is probably better off financially than an average citizen in China.

Activity: Use an almanac to provide students with GDP and population figures for several countries. Have each student choose a country and divide its gross GDP by its population to calculate its per capita GDP. Ask them to write a brief paragraph describing the information they found.

Making a Living

Countries organize their economies in different ways. Most developed countries have an economic system called **free enterprise**. This system is organized around the production and distribution of goods and services. The United States operates under a free enterprise system. There are many benefits of this system. Companies are free to make whatever goods they wish. Employees can seek the highest wages for their work. People, rather than the government, control the factors of production. Factors of production are the things that determine what goods are produced in an economy. They include the natural resources that are available for making goods for sale. They also include the capital, or money, needed to pay for production and the labor needed to manufacture goods. The work of entrepreneurs is another factor of production. Entrepreneurs are people who start businesses in a free enterprise system.

Business owners in a free enterprise system sell their goods in a **market economy**. In such an economy, business owners and customers make decisions about what to make, sell, and buy. In contrast, the governments of some countries control the factors of production. The government decides what, and how much, will be produced. It also sets the prices of goods to be sold. This is called a **command economy**.

Some countries with a command economy are communist. Communism is a political system where the government owns almost all the factors of production. Only five countries in the world are communist today—China, Cuba, Laos, North Korea, and Vietnam.

The third type of economy is called a **tradition-based economy**. This type of economy is based on customs and tradition. Economic activities are based on laws, rituals, religious beliefs, or habits developed by the society long ago. The Mbuti people of the Democratic Republic of the Congo practice a tradition-based economy.

Large shopping malls, such as this one in New York City's Trump Tower, are common in countries that have market economies and a free enterprise system. Shoppers here can find a wide range of stores and goods concentrated in one area.

Teaching Objectives 3 and 4

ALL LEVELS: (Suggested time: 15 min.) Copy the following graphic organizer onto the chalkboard, omitting the blue answers. Use it to help students understand the connection between economics and politics. Point out that many countries do not follow the chart's model exactly but are a mixture of economic and political systems. **ESOL**

LEVELS 2 AND 3: (Suggested time: 20 min.) Have students formulate and write hypotheses to explain why developed countries are usually based on free enterprise and democracy and why the economies of developing countries are often controlled by the government. **LS VERBAL-LINGUISTIC**

ECONOMICS AND POLITICS

	Developed Countries	Developing Countries
Economy	free enterprise	government control, communism
Political System	democracy	communism

▲ At a plantation in Costa Rica, workers wash bananas before shipping them around the world.

Interpreting the Visual Record

(Movement) Why may having a one-crop economy cause problems for a country?

Another economic system is called a **mixed economy**. Most countries have this type of economy. Their economy is based on at least two of the economic systems you've learned about. For example, the United States has a market economy but certain things are regulated by the government.

Finally, some countries in tropical and subtropical regions have a **one-crop economy**. Their economy is based on a single crop, such as bananas, sugarcane, or cacao.

Buying and Selling International trade plays a large role in a country's economy. A country's **exports** include products sold to other countries. On the other hand, a country's **imports** include products a country buys from other countries. Imported products are usually things that aren't produced or available in the country that is buying the item. For example, Japan must import many agricultural products from other countries. Because Japan is a relatively small island, it does not have enough land suitable for crop growing.

Getting the Goods In international trade a condition known as **interdependence** occurs between countries when they depend on each other for resources or goods and services. An industrialized country may depend on the raw materials of a developing country. However, the developing country depends on the finished goods and technology of the industrialized country. For example, Mexico exports crude oil to the United States. In return, the United States exports computer equipment to Mexico.

✓ **READING CHECK:** (Human Systems) What are the four types of economies? market, command, tradition-based, mixed, one-crop

CHAPTER 3, Section 2

COOPERATIVE LEARNING

Negotiating for a Factory
Organize the class into small groups. Tell students to imagine that an automobile company wants to build a factory in a developing country.

Have some members of each group play the role of automobile executives and have others be officials of the developing country's government. Assign one member of each group to conduct research on (or invent) characteristics that describe the country (location, labor force, resources, environment, type of government). Ask students to address these questions and others while they negotiate the business deal: How much control will government officials have over the factory? Who will decide which designs to use? What will happen if the factory pollutes the air or water? What will happen if car buyers have complaints? Then set negotiations into motion. Challenge students to draw conclusions about the relationships between economics and politics.

◄ **Visual Record Answer**

If drought, war, or other problems caused a bad harvest, the country's entire economy could be damaged.

The World's People • 57

Teaching Objective 4

LEVEL 1: (Suggested time: 15 min.) Lead a class discussion on why people live where they do in your state. Encourage students to consider issues such as climate, availability of jobs, cultural and educational opportunities, and proximity to transportation facilities. Then call on volunteers to suggest how state population patterns can be compared to entire countries. (People have the same basic needs and wants everywhere. More people live where their wants can be fulfilled most easily.) **ESOL**

LEVELS 2 AND 3: (Suggested time: 30 min.) In advance, prepare names of countries on slips of paper. Include densely populated nations (United Kingdom, Bangladesh, Japan) and sparsely populated ones (Mongolia, Australia, Canada). Have students pick a country and find population data on that country in the text or in other secondary sources. They should also look for information on the country's resources and climate. Then have students write a paragraph describing the influences on that country's population density. Ask students to use the Fast Facts features or a world almanac to calculate the population density for their chosen country.

CHAPTER 3, Section 2

Linking Past to Present

Population Density and Disease In order to sustain themselves, many organisms that cause infectious diseases require large, dense populations like those found in cities.

In Rome, for example, about one-third of the population died of smallpox in A.D. 165, and measles caused 5000 deaths a day there in A.D. 251. In the 1300s the Black Death swept through densely populated cities from China to Europe. This disease–borne by flea-infested rodents–killed up to one-quarter of Europe's population between 1346 and 1352. The influenza epidemic of 1918–19 killed 21 million people worldwide–more than twice the number killed in World War I.

Today's jet travel provides rapid transit for contagious diseases. Some scientists warn that overuse of antibiotics and the immunity that can result have made our crowded cities vulnerable to another serious epidemic.

Six Billion and Counting

In 1960, the world's population hit three billion. Since then the world's population has grown to over six billion. More than 90 percent of this population growth was in the developing countries of Africa, Latin America, and Asia. More than a quarter of the world's six billion people are between the ages of 10 and 24. About 86 percent of these young people live in developing countries.

World of People Some countries are very crowded. Others are only thinly populated. People who study these differences in the world's population are called demographers. They collect information, or demographics, which include population size, and the ages and gender of the population. They also determine **population density**, or how many people live closely together. Population density is calculated by dividing a country's population by its area—stated in either square miles or square kilometers. When a country has an extremely high population density, it may be suffering from **overpopulation**. An overpopulated country usually cannot support its people without outside help.

People are spread unevenly across Earth. Some places are crowded with people, while others are empty. Where do most of the world's people live? Asia is the world's most populated region. China and India both have more than a billion people! In addition, Indonesia, Pakistan, Japan, and Bangladesh each have over 100 million people.

The regions on this map that are shaded dark purple have a high population density.
Interpreting the Map How do you think the patterns on this map will change over the next 100 years? Why?

World Population Density

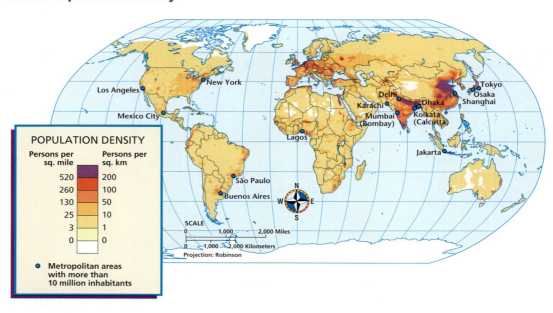

58 • Chapter 3

CLOSE

To illustrate the meaning of 6 billion, the approximate total world population, challenge students to calculate how long it would take for 6 billion seconds to go by (approximately 190 years).

REVIEW, ASSESS, RETEACH

Have students complete the Section Review. Then refer them to the list of vocabulary terms. Call on students to create a sentence that relates the first term to the second, then the second to the third, and so on. Then have students complete Daily Quiz 3.2.

Have students complete Main Idea Activity S2. Then have students work in pairs to create web diagrams to illustrate the section's main points.
ESOL, COOPERATIVE LEARNING

58 Chapter 3

Growing Pains Births add to a country's population. Deaths subtract from it. The number of births per 1,000 people in a year is called the **birthrate**. Similarly, the **death rate** is the annual number of deaths per 1,000 people. The birthrate minus the death rate equals the rate of natural population increase. This number is expressed as a percentage. The birthrate in developing countries is more than double that of industrialized countries. For example, the birthrates of Niger and Bulgaria are very different. Niger has the world's highest birthrate. Most women in Niger have about seven children. On the other hand, Bulgaria has the world's lowest birthrate. Most Bulgarian women only have one child.

On the Move Throughout history, people have moved from place to place looking for better opportunities. People are constantly moving within their own country or across international borders. This movement of people is called **migration**. One person or a group migrate either for a short period of time or permanently. There are several different types of migration. Someone who leaves one place for another is called an **emigrant**.

On the other hand, an **immigrant** is someone arriving from another country. A migrant worker is someone looking for work by regularly moving from place to place. Some people move to other countries for opportunities they don't have in their homeland. Most people emigrate for economic reasons.

✓ **READING CHECK:** *Human Systems* What region of the world has the most people? **Asia**

Section Review 2

Define and explain: gross national product, gross domestic product, industrialized countries, literacy rate, developing countries, third-world countries, free enterprise, market economy, command economy, tradition-based economy, mixed economy, one-crop economy, exports, imports, interdependence, birthrate, death rate, population density, overpopulation, migration, emigrant, immigrant

Reading for the Main Idea
1. *Environment and Society* What geographic features influence population density?
2. *Human Systems* What characteristics do developed nations share?

Critical Thinking
3. **Finding the Main Idea** What are the different economic systems? Describe each.
4. **Drawing Inferences and Conclusions** What causes overpopulation and how can it be prevented?

Organizing What You Know
5. **Summarizing** Copy the following graphic organizer. Use it to study your local community and classify the businesses in your area.

Primary Industries	Secondary Industries	Tertiary Industries	Quaternary Industries
•	•	•	•
•	•	•	•

Homework Practice Online Keyword: SK5 HP3

Section 2 Review

Answers to Section 2 Review

Define For definitions, see the glossary.

Reading for the Main Idea
1. good soil, water, jobs (NGS 15)
2. free enterprise, democracy, high per capita GDP, high life expectancy and literacy (NGS 14)

Critical Thinking
3. market—business owners and customers decide what to sell and buy; command—government makes decisions; tradition-based—based on custom (NGS 14)
4. inability of a country to support its population without outside help; perhaps by reducing the birthrate and/or immigration

Organizing What You Know
5. Answers will vary according to the community.

◀ **Map Answer**

Possible answer: Purple, red, and orange areas will expand because populations continue to grow.

EXTEND

No longer does one have to live in a large city to be employed by a large company. Have interested students conduct research on the effects of telecommuting—using an electronic linkup with a central office to work out of one's home—on population densities in the United States. Students may want to concentrate on one of your state's major cities and the towns nearby. Have students report their findings in a bar graph.
BLOCK SCHEDULING

CHAPTER 3, Section 3

SECTION 3 RESOURCES

Reproducible
- Lecture Notes, Section 3
- Know It Notes S3
- Environmental and Global Issues Activity 8

Technology
- One-Stop Planner CD–ROM, Lesson 3.3
- Yourtown CD–ROM
- Homework Practice Online
- HRW Go site

Reinforcement, Review, and Assessment
- Section 3 Review
- Daily Quiz 3.3
- Main Idea Activity S3
- Chapter Summaries and Review
- English Audio Summary 3.3
- Spanish Audio Summary 3.3

Section 3 Global Connections

Read to Discover
1. What is globalization? How are people around the world connected?
2. Why are refugees a global problem? What causes famine? How do people in need get help?

Vocabulary
globalization
popular culture
refugees
famine
humanitarian aid
drought

Reading Strategy
READING ORGANIZER Before you read, create a spider map. Label the center oval Global Connections. Draw seven legs and label them Technology, Cities, Travel, Trade, Sports, Refugees, and Assistance. As you read, write what you learn about these topics beneath each of the legs.

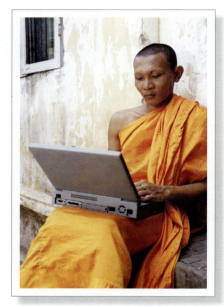

▲ A Buddhist monk in Cambodia may use this laptop computer to log on to the Internet.

Living in a Small World

In just seconds an e-mail message sent by a teenager in India beams all the way to a friend in the United States. A businesswoman in Singapore takes a call from her cell phone from an investor in New York. With just a few taps on a computer's keyboard, anyone in the world can also immediately access the Internet. These are all examples of how small our world has become with the use of cell phones, e-mail, the Internet, and satellite television.

Global Tech Thanks to these technologies, people around the world communicate and do business with each other faster than anyone ever thought possible. **Globalization** is the term most often used to describe how time and distance in the world seem to be shrinking. Globalization is also used to describe how countries are increasingly linked through **popular culture** and a global economy. Popular culture includes things people across the world share such as movies, literature, music, clothing, and food. For example, you can find the American restaurant, McDonald's, in almost every major world city today. Kids throughout the world exchange Pokemon trading cards from Japan. Millions read Harry Potter.

60 • Chapter 3

Objectives
1. Define globalization and describe how people around the world are connected.
2. Explore refugees as a global problem, famine, and how people in need get help.

FOCUS

Bellringer
Write the following questions on the chalkboard: *How many different brands can you write down that are for products made outside the United States? What kinds of products are they?* (Students will probably list many brands of electronic equipment, cars, and athletic shoes.) Discuss responses. Point out that these products illustrate one way in which countries are connected today—through trade. Tell students that in Section 3 they will learn more about these and other connections.

Building Vocabulary
Write the vocabulary terms on the chalkboard and have students find the definitions in the text. Point out that **globalization** and **popular culture** may be connected in some cases. For example, a singer or sports star from another country represents globalization and is a leading figure in the world of popular culture.

60 Chapter 3

Speaking Globally Almost 6,000 languages are spoken today. English, however, is the language of globalization. As a result, a quarter of the world's population speaks English for global business, communications, higher education, diplomacy, aviation, the Internet, science, popular music, entertainment and international travel. American news channels and movies are seen everywhere. For example, CNN uses satellites to broadcast in English to millions of TV sets around the world.

Cultural Centers Even with fast communication, globalization wouldn't be possible without major cities. As transportation and cultural centers, cities provide the perfect place for different people to exchange goods and ideas. For example, Miami is sometimes called the "Gateway to Latin America." As an international port and multicultural city, many companies that operate in Latin America are headquartered in Miami. Many other global cities also depend on their geographical location for international business. Seattle and San Francisco have economic ties to major Asian cities located across the Pacific Ocean, such as Tokyo and Hong Kong.

This restaurant in Ecuador provides visitors with Internet access.

Ships dock in Miami, Florida.
Interpreting the Visual Record
(Movement) What in this photo suggests that Miami is a major international city?

CHAPTER 3, Section 3

USING ILLUSTRATIONS

E-Travel Focus students' attention on the photo of the Internet café on this page. Point out that modern telecommunications have made international travel much easier than it was a few decades ago. Ask students why this may be so. Remind them of advertisements or commercials related to the travel industry that they have seen. (Possible answers: Tourists can buy tickets, make hotel reservations, and get information about destinations online. Upon arrival, they can use ATM machines for cash instead of traveler's checks. Internet cafés or the tourist's own laptop can provide instant connections to friends, family, and coworkers back home.) Lead a discussion about how "e-travel" may affect students' interest in international travel.

◀ **Visual Record Answer**

commercial and cruise ships, extensive dock facilities

TEACH

Teaching Objective 1
LEVEL 1: (Suggested time: 30 min.) Provide several copies of national newspapers or the main section of your local newspaper. Have students work in pairs to find examples of globalization in the newspapers. **ESOL, COOPERATIVE LEARNING**

LEVEL 2: You will need extra time for this activity. Point out that increased globalization has some critics. Provide research materials so students can conduct research on the criticism. (Critics charge that globalization is responsible for the eradication of native cultures, child labor abuses, and environmental damage, among other problems.) When students have completed their research, stage a debate about the benefits and costs of globalization. Ask each student to write a paragraph summarizing the arguments presented in the debate. **LS LOGICAL-MATHEMATICAL**

LEVEL 3: (Suggested time: 30 min.) Have students use what they have learned from the Level 2 activity to draw editorial cartoons about globalization. **LS VISUAL-SPATIAL**

The World's People

CHAPTER 3, Section 3

FOOD FESTIVAL

Gobbling Up Globalization
The shrinkage of our world is evident in the expansion of our supermarkets. All kinds of foods from around the world—fresh, frozen, dried, canned, and packaged—flow into U.S. grocery stores. Shoppers in communities lacking big supermarkets can order many exotic foodstuffs from online suppliers.

Without telling students the purpose of their choice, have each student select a different country. Then challenge students to find a food product from that country in the local supermarket or from an online supplier. If circumstances permit, encourage students to bring their foods to class. Or, students may simply bring to class printed information about the products from the Internet.

Visual Record Answer ▶

because it combines both English and Japanese and celebrates a Japanese athlete playing for a U.S. team

---

Travel Ills There's a downside, however, to life in a well-connected world. You can board a plane at any major airport today and travel to just about anywhere in the world. Some people, however, carry more than just their luggage on to these flights. They can also carry diseases. For example, in 2003, one woman who didn't realize she was infected with the contagious disease called SARS, traveled from China to Toronto, Canada. As she made contact with several people in Toronto, they too came down with the disease. However, steps are now taken to prevent people with contagious diseases from boarding international flights.

Quick Trades Globalization not only links the world's people, it also connects businesses and countries. For centuries, people have traded. But, never as fast as today. Through the use of the Internet it is quick and simple to order goods from anywhere in the world. For example, a shoe retailer in Chicago can find a Web site that links them to someone in China who makes the sneakers they need. The order is then flown to Chicago the following day. That afternoon the sneakers are sold to customers.

Fans of Hideki Matsui—a professional baseball player from Japan—show their support as they watch him play for the New York Yankees.
Interpreting the Visual Record
Movement How is this sign an example of globalization?

Made in the USA? Check the label on your shoes, other clothing, or book bag to see where it's made. It probably doesn't say the United States. Why? Most clothing and a lot of electronic equipment are imported to the United States from other countries. Many international companies build their factories in places where workers will work for less money than American workers. By hiring cheap labor, these companies lower their manufacturing costs. As a result, these products usually have a lower price tag than products made in the United States.

World Sports You've already learned that money, ideas, and goods are traded in the global economy. But, did you also know that people could be exchanged as well? For example, more and more baseball players from Latin America and Asia are now playing professionally in the United States. In addition, many American and European soccer teams frequently trade players across the Atlantic.

✓ **READING CHECK:**
Human Systems What are some examples of globalization?
spread of English language, use of telecommunications, spread of popular culture, growth of international cities, global trade, global trade in athletes

---

Teaching Objective 2

ALL LEVELS: (Suggested time: 45 min.) Pair students and have students re-read the "Helping People in Need" subsection aloud to each other. Then have them design book covers for an imaginary book of the same title. Pairs should include both text and pictures in their designs. **ESOL,** **LS VISUAL-SPATIAL**

ALL LEVELS: (Suggested time: 15 min.) Lead a class discussion about whether individuals in the United States can help refugees and victims of other problems in foreign countries and, if so, how to do so. Continue with a discussion of how nonprofit organizations can pool the efforts and funds of individuals, making the aid more effective. **LS INTERPERSONAL**

Helping People in Need

In a smaller world, global problems also connect the world's people. What happens in one part of the world affects the entire planet. Millions of people today suffer without life's necessities. In response to these problems, the global community tries to help as many people as possible.

Searching for Home One of the major global problems today are the 14 million people who seek refuge in other countries. These **refugees** require food, shelter, and help with finding jobs. Many international agencies help refugees start new lives. Unlike immigrants, however, refugees flee their countries because of persecution, war, or economic reasons. Some refugees even eventually become citizens in the country they settle in. For example, many Cuban refugees and their families are now United States citizens.

Hungry Planet A great shortage of food, or **famine**, affects millions of people throughout the world. International relief agencies provide **humanitarian aid** to famine areas. This aid includes medicine and millions of pounds of grain and other foods. These efforts, however, sometimes are not enough to relieve the problem. Today in Ethiopia more than 12 million people are at risk for starvation. The lack of rain, or **drought**, has prevented farmers from growing enough food to feed their country's population.

✓ **READING CHECK:** *Human Systems* What are some reasons why refugees flee their homeland? persecution, war, or economic reasons

Movement In the late 1990s unrest in Kosovo, Yugoslavia, disrupted the lives of hundreds of thousands of ethnic Albanians. Many people were forced from their homes. Here, refugees in neighboring Macedonia wait to be transported to nearby transition camps.

Section Review 3

Homework Practice Online
Keyword: SK5 HP3

Define and explain: globalization, popular culture, refugees, famine, humanitarian aid, drought

Reading for the Main Idea
1. *Human Systems* What are some effects of globalization?
2. *Human Systems* How does humanitarian aid help people?

Critical Thinking
3. **Drawing Conclusions** How has globalization made the world smaller?
4. **Making Predictions** What will happen if the number of refugees continues to grow?

Organizing What You Know
5. **Contrasting** Copy the following graphic organizer. Use it to discuss two arguments about globalization.

Good results of globalization	Bad results of globalization

The World's People • 63

Section 3 Review

Answers to Section 3 Review

Define For definitions, see the glossary.

Reading for the Main Idea
1. increased communication, shared popular culture, spread of English language, growth of major cities, spread of disease, increased trade, decrease in U.S.-made products, more movement of people from country to country
2. provides medicine, millions of pounds of grain and other foods

Critical Thinking
3. Possible answer: by reducing barriers to trade, travel, and communication
4. Possible answer: many deaths from starvation or violence, political chaos in the countries affected (NGS 9)

Organizing What You Know
5. good—increased communication and availability of products and ideas; bad—increased risk of disease, low pay for foreign workers

---

CLOSE
Ask students how decisions they make now and in the future may reflect or affect globalization.

REVIEW, ASSESS, RETEACH
Have students complete the Section Review. Then have students work in groups to use the spider maps referenced in the Reading Strategy at the beginning of this section to review its main concepts. Then have students complete Daily Quiz 3.3. **COOPERATIVE LEARNING**

Have students complete Main Idea Activity S3. Then have students write one sentence per paragraph to summarize that paragraph.
LS VERBAL-LINGUISTIC

EXTEND
Some of the cheap foreign-made products we buy are made by children. Have interested students conduct research on Iqbal Masih, a Pakistani youngster who, from his own experiences as an exploited child worker, spoke out against child labor practices. Iqbal was killed to silence him. This tragic story inspired a Canadian boy named Craig Kielburger to found Free the Children, an organization that tries to help the millions of children who work long hours under miserable conditions. Ask students to report on the current state of child labor to the class. **BLOCK SCHEDULING**

The World's People 63

CHAPTER 3 REVIEW

Define and Identify
For definitions, see the glossary.

Review the Main Ideas

20. People study culture, which is a learned system of shared beliefs, to understand the different ways in which people live all over the world. (NGS 10)

21. People move from one place to another and bring their ways or beliefs to another culture.

22. history and environment

23. subsistence agriculture—produces only enough food to feed the farmer's family; commercial agriculture—large farms, often run by companies, produce food for many people

24. GNP—measures all goods and services a nation produces, even those manufactured in foreign countries; GDP—measures goods and services produced in a country

25. third-world countries—developing nations with some economic growth; fourth-world countries—those with no economic growth

26. to acquire things that aren't produced or available in the country importing the items

27. More and more people speak English, the language of globalization. They also use electronic technologies such as the Internet to communicate around the world.

28. Refugees flee their countries because of persecution, war, economic problems or other troubles; immigrants move of their own choice in search of economic opportunity.

Think Critically

29. People may use someone's appearance, which is more closely connected to his or her race, to define the person's ethnic group.

Chapter 3 Review and Practice

Define and Identify
Identify each of the following:

1. culture
2. ethnic groups
3. ethnocentrism
4. domestication
5. subsistence agriculture
6. civilization
7. gross national product
8. literacy rate
9. third-world countries
10. mixed economy
11. imports
12. birthrate
13. population density
14. migration
15. immigrant
16. globalization
17. popular culture
18. refugees
19. humanitarian aid

Review the Main Ideas

20. What is culture, and why should people study it?
21. How does diffusion occur?
22. What are two important factors that influence the way people meet basic needs?
23. What is the difference between subsistence and commercial agriculture?
24. How does gross national product differ from gross domestic product?
25. How do third-world countries differ from fourth-world nations?
26. Why do countries import products?
27. How has globalization affected how people communicate?
28. How do refugees differ from immigrants?

Think Critically

29. Drawing Inferences and Conclusions Why are ethnic groups sometimes confused with races?
30. Identifying Cause and Effect How did the development of agriculture affect the global population?
31. Comparing and Contrasting How do industrialized countries differ from developing countries?
32. Summarizing How have new technologies helped to create a global culture?
33. Finding the Main Idea How has globalization changed how countries trade with each other?

Map Activity

34. On a separate sheet of paper, match the letters on the map with their correct labels.
- Buddhism
- Christianity—Eastern Orthodox
- Christianity—Protestant
- Christianity—Roman Catholic
- Hinduism
- Islam

64 • Chapter 3

---

30. After the development of agriculture, the global population increased as the food supply increased.

31. industrialized countries—rely on industry, have educated populace, access to health care and communications; developing countries—agriculture or primary industries, poorly educated populace, little access to health and telecommunications

32. Technologies such as e-mail, the Internet, and satellite television have made it easier for people to share popular culture all over the globe.

33. Trade is faster, and some goods are available at lower prices.

Map Activity
34. A. Christianity—Eastern Orthodox
B. Hinduism
C. Islam
D. Christianity—Roman Catholic
E. Buddhism
F. Christianity—Protestant

Writing Activity

Research the economy of your community. Has the economy grown or declined in the last 10 years? Why? What goods are exported from your community? What goods are imported to your community? Write about what you learn from your research. Then write about how you think your community might change in the future.

internet connect

Internet Activity: go.hrw.com
KEYWORD: SJ5 GT3

Choose a topic to explore online:
- Visit famous buildings and monuments around the world.
- Compare facts about life in different countries.
- Examine world population growth.

Social Studies Skills Practice

Interpreting Cartoons

Study the following cartoon. Then answer the questions.

1. What is the main idea of this cartoon?
2. Why is the Earth in the middle of a maze?
3. Does the cartoonist believe it is difficult or easy to connect with people around the world by using the Internet? Why?
4. How is this cartoon an example of globalization?

Analyzing Primary Sources

Read the following quote from French-American film director Jean-Marc Barr. Then answer the questions.

"We believe Europe is going to exist because the English language allows it to culturally. Never on this continent has there been a language that all the classes can speak, from a Polish man to a Spaniard to an Icelandic. My biggest and most rewarding events in my life have been because I have been able to speak English with people all over the world."

1. What advantage does Barr see for Europe as English is used more?
2. Why would a film director such as Barr be especially interested in language?
3. Based on your knowledge of culture, why might some Europeans resist the use of English?
4. How do you think Barr feels about globalization?

The World's People • 65

CHAPTER 3 REVIEW

Writing Activity

Answers will vary, but the information included should be consistent with text material. Students' predictions should be supported by logical arguments. Use Rubric 37, Writing Assignments, to evaluate student work.

Interpreting Cartoons

1. Once you find your way in the Internet you can find anything in the world.
2. Reaching the information may be difficult, but gaining the whole world makes it worthwhile.
3. By drawing a maze, the cartoonist shows that it may be hard to find what you are looking for on the Internet.
4. It shows how anyone can make global connections by using the Internet.

Analyzing Primary Sources

1. English provides a common language for all Europeans, no matter what their first language may be.
2. If more people can understand the language used in a movie, the potential audience will be much greater.
3. They may see English as replacing their native language and, in the process, destroying their native cultures.
4. He seems to feel that globalization is a good thing because it increases communication.

internet connect

GO TO: go.hrw.com
KEYWORD: SJ5 Teacher
FOR: a guide to using the Internet in your classroom

CHAPTER 3 — REVIEW AND ASSESSMENT RESOURCES

Reproducible
- Readings in World Geography, History, and Culture 9 and 10
- Critical Thinking Activity 3
- Vocabulary Activity 3

Technology
- Chapter 3 Test Generator (on the One-Stop Planner)
- HRW Go site
- Audio CD Program, Chapter 3

Reinforcement, Review, and Assessment
- Chapter 3 Review and Practice
- Chapter Summaries and Review
- Chapter 3 Test
- Chapter 3 Test for English Language Learners and Special-Needs Students

The World's People 65

UNIT 1

GEOGRAPHY SIDELIGHT

Physical, political, economic, and cultural changes can affect the way we define regions and draw their boundaries.

Physical changes are often slow to occur, but they are important. Beaches erode. Rivers run dry. Forests grow up on abandoned farmland. Political changes also bring regional redefinitions. For example, one large country may break up into several smaller ones, or small countries may unite to form a larger country.

Economic changes occur as different resources or economic activities decline or increase in importance. For example, a community once known for its manufacturing industries may now be part of an area that focuses on services. Finally, changing cultural characteristics can reshape regions as people of various language, religious, or ethnic groups move across regional boundaries.

Critical Thinking: What factors affect how we define regions?

Answer: physical, political, economic, and cultural changes

➤ This Focus On Regions feature addresses National Geography Standards 5 and 6.

Focus on REGIONS

What is a Region?

Think about where you live, where you go to school, and where you shop. These places are all part of your neighborhood. In geographic terms, your neighborhood is a region. A region is an area that has common features that make it different from surrounding areas.

What regions do you live in? You live on a continent, in a country, and in a state. These are all regions that can be mapped.

Regions can be divided into smaller regions called subregions. For example, Africa is a major world region. Africa's subregions include North Africa, West Africa, East Africa, central Africa, and southern Africa. Each subregion can be divided into even smaller subregions.

Regional Characteristics Regions can be based on physical, political, economic, or cultural characteristics. Physical regions are based on Earth's natural features, such as continents, landforms, and climates. Political regions are based on countries and their subregions, such as states, provinces, and cities. Economic regions are based on money-making activities such as agriculture or industries. Cultural regions are based on features such as language, religion, or ethnicity.

▲ East Africa is a subregion of Africa. It is an area of plateaus, rolling hills, and savanna grasslands.

66 • Unit 1

FOCUS ON REGIONS

Identifying Local Regions

Ask students to write down regions in which they live, go to school, shop, and pursue other daily activities. Call on volunteers for their responses. Record them on the chalkboard, placing the largest regions (continent, country) at the top and placing smaller regions (neighborhoods, boroughs, blocks) at the bottom. Note at what point descriptions of regions where students live differ from each other (probably at the town or neighborhood level). Draw a line separating these smaller divisions from the larger ones. Have students work in small groups to draw large maps showing these local regions and their relationships.

Major World Regions

Regional Boundaries All regions have boundaries, or borders. Boundaries are where the features of one region meet the features of a different region. Some boundaries, such as coastlines or country borders, can be shown as lines on a map. Other regional boundaries are less clear.

Transition zones are areas where the features of one region change gradually to the features of a different region. For example, when a city's suburbs expand into rural areas, a transition zone forms. In the transition zone, it may be hard to find the boundary between rural and urban areas.

Types of Regions There are three basic types of regions. The first is a formal region. Formal regions are based on one or more common features. For example, Japan is a formal region. Its people share a common government, language, and culture.

The second type of region is a functional region. Functional regions are based on movement and activities that connect different places. For example, Paris, France, is a functional region. It is based on the goods, services, and people that move throughout the city. A shopping center or an airport might also be a functional region.

The international border between Kenya and Tanzania is a clearly defined regional boundary.

The third type of region is a perceived region. Perceived regions are based on people's shared feelings and beliefs. For example, the neighborhood where you live may be a perceived region.

The three basic types of regions overlap to form complex world regions. The world can be divided into nine major world regions (see map above). Each has general features that make it different from the other major world regions. These differences include physical, cultural, economic, historical, and political features.

Understanding What You Read

1. Regions can be based on what types of characteristics?
2. What are the three basic types of regions?

Focus on Regions • 67

UNIT 1

Understanding What You Read

Answers
1. Regions can be based on physical, political, economic, or cultural characteristics.
2. The three basic types of regions are: formal, functional, and perceived.

Going Further: Thinking Critically

Have students compare their maps. Note areas where regions overlap and ask students how they might describe these areas (transition zones). Also have them look at how maps of the same regions have different boundaries. Point out that these are perceived regions. The word *perceived* has to do with getting information from one's senses. Therefore, perceived regions differ according to how one "sees" the region. Ask students how they decided on the boundaries that they drew. Use their responses to illustrate the differences in perceived regions. Finally, review formal and functional regions and ask whether any regions shown on the maps fulfill the definitions.

UNIT 1

PRACTICING THE SKILL

1. The prime meridian extends through western Europe (England, western France, northeastern Spain) and western Africa (Algeria, Mali, Burkina Faso, Togo, Ghana).

2. Students' sketch maps should show the equator, Tropic of Cancer, Tropic of Capricorn, prime meridian, and continents in their approximate locations.

3. Answers will vary. Students might notice that the international date line does not cross any major landmasses, the Southern Hemisphere has much more water than land, South America extends farther south than Africa, or other similar facts.

▶ This GeoSkills feature addresses National Geography Standards 1, 2, and 3.

GeoSKILLS

Building Skills for Life: Drawing Mental Maps

We create maps in our heads of all kinds of places—our homes, schools, communities, country, and the world. Some of these places we know well. Others we have only heard about. These images we carry in our heads are shaped by what we see and experience. They are also influenced by what we learn from news reports or other sources. Geographers call the maps that we carry around in our heads mental maps.

We use mental maps to organize spatial information about people and places. For example, our mental maps help us move from classroom to classroom at school or get to a friend's home. A mental map of the United States helps us list the states we would pass through driving from New York City to Miami.

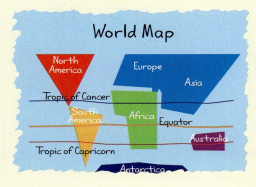

We use our mental maps of places when we draw sketch maps. A sketch map showing the relationship between places and the relative size of places can be drawn using very simple shapes. For example, triangles and rectangles could be used to sketch a map of the world. This quickly drawn map would show the relative size and position of the continents.

Think about some simple ways we could make our map of the world more detailed. Adding the equator, Tropic of Cancer, and Tropic of Capricorn would be one way. Look at a map of the world in your textbook's Atlas. Note that the bulge in the continent of Africa is north of the equator. Also note that all of Asia is north of the equator. Next note that the Indian subcontinent extends south from the Tropic of Cancer. About half of Australia is located north of the Tropic of Capricorn. As your knowledge of the world increases, your mental map will become even more detailed.

PRACTICING THE SKILL

1. Look at the maps in your textbook's Atlas. Where does the prime meridian fall in relation to the continents?

2. On a separate sheet of paper, sketch a simple map of the world from memory. First draw the equator, Tropic of Cancer, Tropic of Capricorn, and prime meridian. Then sketch in the continents. You can use circles, rectangles, and triangles.

3. Draw a second map of the world from memory. This time, draw the international date line in the center of your map. Add the equator, Tropic of Cancer, and Tropic of Capricorn. Now sketch in the continents. What do you notice?

GeoSkills

Going Further: Thinking Critically

Prepare two sets of words on slips of paper. One set should consist of action words, such as *go, fly, run, skip, dig, walk, swim, climb,* and *drive*. The other set should consist of nouns having to do with places, such as *tree, house, cliff, beach, road, river, mountain, church, rock, cave, highway,* and *ocean*. Students will draw at least one word of each type from a hat. Using their chosen words at least once, students should write travel or adventure stories set in familiar places. You may want to require that the stories be a certain length or that the students mention a certain number of places in their stories. Tell students that when they finish they should be able to draw maps of the settings through which the characters travel. When all the students have completed their stories, have them exchange papers to draw maps of each other's story settings.

HANDS on GEOGRAPHY

Mental maps are personal. They change as we learn more about the world and the places in it. For example, they can include details about places that are of interest only to you.

What is your mental map of your neighborhood like? Sketch your mental map of your neighborhood. Include the features that you think are important and that help you find your way around. These guidelines will help you get started.

1. Decide what your map will show. Choose boundaries so that you do not sketch more than you need to.
2. Determine how much space you will need for your map. Things that are the same size in reality should be about the same size on your map.
3. Decide on and note the orientation of your map. Most maps use a directional indicator. On most maps, north is at the top.
4. Label reference points so that others who look at your map can quickly and easily figure out what they are looking at. For example, a major street or your school might be a reference point.
5. Decide how much detail your map will show. The larger the area you want to represent, the less detail you will need.
6. Use circles, rectangles, and triangles if you do not know the exact shape of an area.
7. As you think of them, fill in more details, such as names of places or major land features.

Lab Report

1. What are the most important features on your map? Why did you include them?
2. Compare your sketch map to a published map of the area. How does it differ?
3. At the bottom, list three ways that you could make your sketch map more complete.

Lab Report
Answers

1. Important features on student maps will probably be their own homes, friends' homes, major streets, schools, restaurants, stores or malls, and recreation facilities.
2. Students' maps will probably omit secondary streets, boundaries of political divisions, elevation figures, contour lines, and similar details. They may record more labeled individual buildings or natural features than the published maps.
3. Answers will vary. Students might suggest that their maps include more streets, features be more to scale, or other changes be made.

UNIT 2

Unit Objectives

1. Describe the landforms, climates, and resources found in the United States and Canada.
2. Examine the geography, history, and cultures of the United States.
3. Identify the similarities and differences that exist between various regions of the United States.
4. Examine the historical and cultural geography of Canada.
5. Interpret special-purpose maps, graphs, and charts to better understand the interrelationships of each country's physical and human geography.

UNIT 2

United States and Canada

CHAPTER 4
The Geography and History of the United States

CHAPTER 5
The Regions of the United States

CHAPTER 6
Canada

Canadian Rocky Mountains

CN Tower and SkyDome, Toronto, Canada

Using the Illustrations

Direct students' attention to the photographs on these pages. Ask them to cover the captions and to determine which of the smaller photos was most likely taken in the United States. **(people standing near the American flag and Statue of Liberty replica).** How can they tell? **(Possible answer: because the flag and Statue of Liberty are symbols of the United States)** Remind students that a symbol is a sign that stands for something else. Ask what the Statue of Liberty stands for. **(Possible answers: freedom, a new life for immigrants)** Ask which other images on the pages may serve as symbols **(CN Tower, buffalo)** and what they may symbolize. **(Possible answers: modern Canada, the American West)** You may want to point out that although the buffalo is sometimes used as a symbol for the United States, the largest unrestricted buffalo herd is in Canada.

Then point out that the mountain and lake scene, although in Canada, looks like many places in the United States because the Rocky Mountains extend through both countries. in fact, the two countries share several landforms, such as the Great Plains. The United States and Canada share all but one of the Great Lakes.

UNIT 2

An Englishman in Texas

Jon Hall grew up in the London suburbs. He studied Greek and Latin as a student in Texas. Here he contrasts what he sees as the British and Texan attitudes toward personal space and sports. **WHAT DO YOU THINK?** How do you think people in your community feel about these topics?

As an Englishman, the absence in Texas of fences and walls and clearly marked boundaries made me rather nervous at first. In London, with thousands of people in a small space, everyone is uptight about fencing off *their* little bit of land. In Texas, front yards and parks and parking lots sprawl casually without boundaries. And Texans really are more open and friendly than others. On the street, in a store, in a restaurant, greeting strangers is just the thing to do.

Brits and Texans support sports differently. In Britain, the spectators tend to be males between 15 and 45 years old—definitely not a family atmosphere. But at Texas football games, you'll see grandparents with their grandkids and guys and gals on dates. At the high school level too, there is much wider participation: the band, cheerleaders, parents, fans. I played soccer for my high school and most Saturdays we'd have a crowd of about seven.

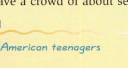
American teenagers

Street scene in Austin, Texas

Understanding Primary Sources

1. Why does Jon Hall think the people of London are more concerned about boundaries than Texans?
2. According to Jon Hall, what gives Texas football games a "family atmosphere"?

American buffalo

MORE FROM THE FIELD

Although the Texas plains may appear to be wide-open, fences now divide the land.

Early settlers in eastern Texas used ditches, mud fences, and hedges of the thorny bois d'arc tree, also known as the Osage orange, to fence off their property. Bois d'arc fences were said to be "pig tight, horse high, and bull strong." Dry western Texas had fewer fencing materials available, however, and westward expansion slowed as a result. In the 1870s barbed wire, consisting of thornlike barbs wrapped around smooth wires, was introduced. The invention was reportedly advertised as being "light as air, stronger than whiskey, and cheap as dirt."

Activity: Ask students to imagine that they are the first ranchers or farmers to settle in their area. What materials would they use if they wanted to build fences or mark their property?

Understanding Primary Sources
Answers
1. because so many people are crowded into a small space
2. families, people on dates, wider participation, better attendance

CHAPTERS

4 **The Geography and History of the United States**
explores the physical, historical, economic, and cultural geography of the United States.

5 **The Regions of the United States**
examines the physical features, climate, and economy of each region in the United States.

6 **Canada**
focuses on the significant characteristics of Canada.

UNIT 2 ATLAS

PEOPLE IN THE PROFILE

Note that the elevation profile crosses southeastern Pennsylvania. This farming region is known for its large Amish population.

The Amish, a conservative Christian group related to the Mennonites, were one of the many groups that left Europe for the Americas for religious freedom. The first large group of Amish to settle in Lancaster County, Pennsylvania, arrived in the early 1700s. Amish clothing styles echo the same era—dark colors, hooks and eyes instead of buttons, long skirts and bonnets for women, wide-brimmed black hats for men. The Amish do not use telephones, electric lights, or cars. They use horse-drawn farm machinery and buggies.

There are special customs for Amish weddings, which are held in November and December. Instead of an engagement ring, the young man gives his fiancée china or a clock. The bride's simple blue wedding dress will later serve as her Sunday church attire. On the wedding day, several hundred guests gather at the bride's home. After a three-hour service everyone sits down to a big dinner.

Activity: Have students research Amish culture and then lead a class discussion on some of the characteristics of Amish culture.

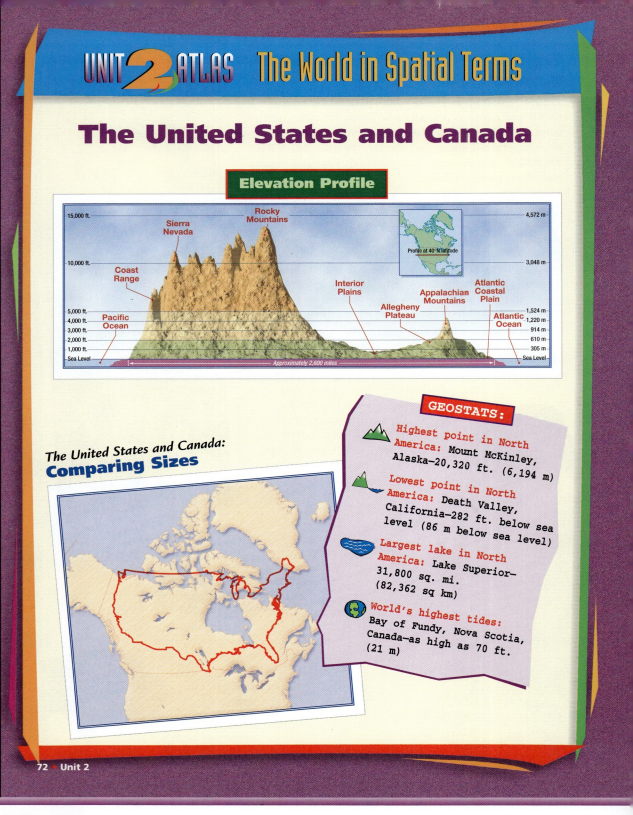

UNIT 2 ATLAS   The World in Spatial Terms

The United States and Canada

Elevation Profile

The United States and Canada: Comparing Sizes

GEOSTATS:

- **Highest point in North America:** Mount McKinley, Alaska—20,320 ft. (6,194 m)
- **Lowest point in North America:** Death Valley, California—282 ft. below sea level (86 m below sea level)
- **Largest lake in North America:** Lake Superior—31,800 sq. mi. (82,362 sq km)
- **World's highest tides:** Bay of Fundy, Nova Scotia, Canada—as high as 70 ft. (21 m)

OVERVIEW

In this unit, students will learn about the tremendous geographical differences within the United States and Canada.

The landscape of the United States is immensely varied, from high mountains to flat coastal plains. There are also many climates represented. The diverse population reflects the many cultures that have played a role in the country's history. Although agriculture in the United States is highly productive, few people live on farms. Most of the population lives in cities and towns. Workers in the United States are part of the most technologically advanced economy in the world. The country's wealth is based on its many natural resources, free enterprise economy, and democratic government.

Many landforms extend from the United States into Canada, the second-largest country in the world. Our northern neighbor has a colder climate and a much smaller population. Most Canadians also enjoy a high standard of living. France and Great Britain influenced Canada's culture. Asians form another important immigrant group. The Inuit have recently gained greater control over their traditional homelands.

United States and Canada: Physical

UNIT 2 ATLAS

UNIT 2 ATLAS

internet connect

ONLINE ATLAS
GO TO: go.hrw.com
KEYWORD: SJ5 MapsU2
FOR: Web links to online maps of the region

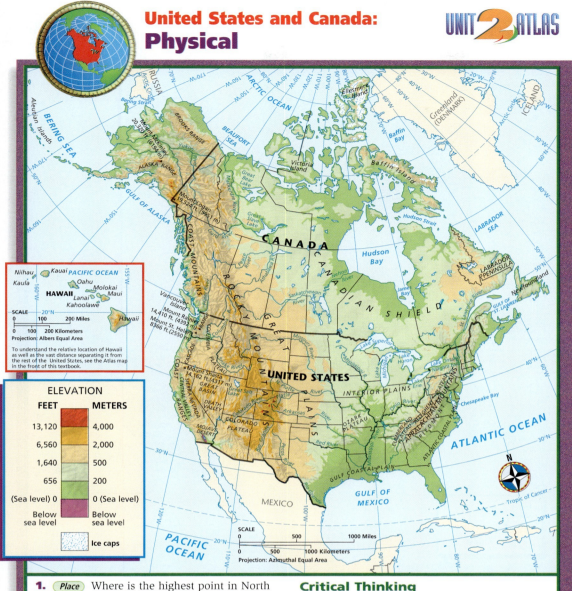

1. **Place** Where is the highest point in North America? Which southwestern desert includes an area below sea level?
2. **Region** Which two large lakes are entirely within Canada?
3. **Region** What are four tributaries of the Mississippi River?

Critical Thinking

4. **Human-Environment Interaction** Compare this map to the **population map** of the region. What is one physical feature that many of the largest cities have in common? What is the connection between the cities' locations and these physical features?

Physical Map
Answers
1. Mount McKinley in Alaska; Mojave Desert
2. Great Bear Lake, Great Slave Lake
3. Red River, Arkansas River, Missouri River, Ohio River

Critical Thinking
4. located on bodies of water; aids trade, transportation, industry, communication

United States and Canada • 73

USING THE PHYSICAL MAP

Focus students' attention on the **physical map** on this page. Have each student write a sentence that describes a physical feature in terms of its relative location. (Examples: The Labrador Peninsula is in eastern Canada, between Hudson Bay and the Labrador Sea. The Rocky Mountains are in western North America. The Great Plains are east of the Rocky Mountains.) Call on volunteers to read their sentences. Continue until all the major physical features have been located.

United States and Canada **73**

UNIT 2 ATLAS

Your Classroom Time Line

These are the major dates and time periods for this unit. Have students enter them on the time line. You may want to watch for these dates as students progress through the unit.

c.* 18,000 B.C. People first cross into North America.

c. A.D. 700 Anasazi develop irrigation system.

c. 1000 The first Europeans to attempt settlement in Canada arrive.

late 1400s European exploration of the North Atlantic coast of North America resumes.

1500s Europeans begin settling in North America.

*c. stands for *circa* and means "about."

internet connect
ONLINE ATLAS
GO TO: go.hrw.com
KEYWORD: SJ5 MapsU2

Political Map
Answers
1. Rio Grande

Critical Thinking
2. Canadian; because much of the Mexican border runs through a desert
3. Nunavut; Quebec; because Nunavut includes many islands

United States and Canada: Political

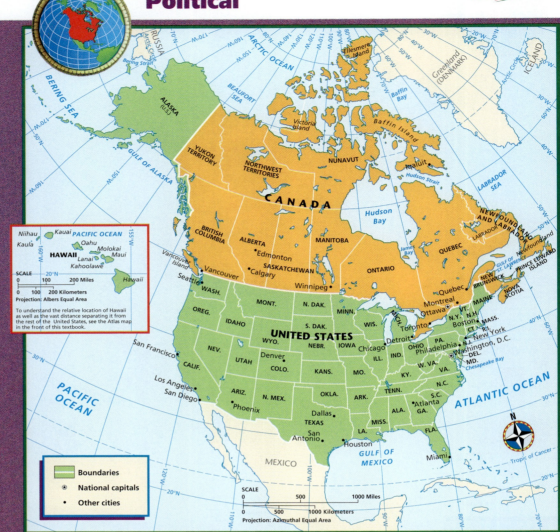

1. **Place** Compare this map to the **physical map** of the region. What physical feature forms part of the border between the United States and Mexico?

Critical Thinking

2. **Movement** Compare this map to the **climate** and **population maps**. Which U.S. border—the Canadian or Mexican—has a denser population? Why?

3. **Region** Which Canadian province or territory appears to be the largest? the second largest? Why is it hard to compare their sizes?

74 • Unit 2

USING THE POLITICAL MAP

Have students use the **political map** on this page to locate their home state. Ask them to compare it to the **physical map** to identify their state's landforms, rivers, lakes, and seacoasts.

Ask students to name the capitals of the United States (Washington, D.C.) and Canada (Ottawa).

United States and Canada: Climate

UNIT 2 ATLAS

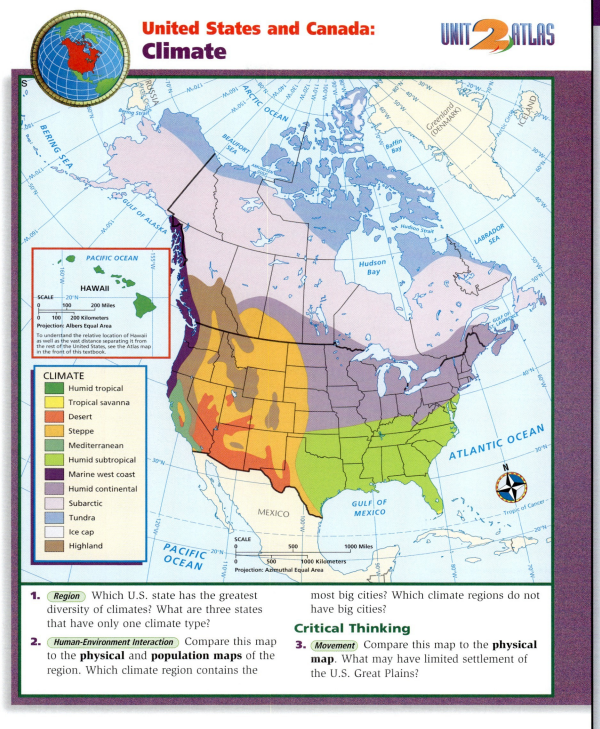

1. **Region** Which U.S. state has the greatest diversity of climates? What are three states that have only one climate type?
2. **Human-Environment Interaction** Compare this map to the **physical** and **population maps** of the region. Which climate region contains the most big cities? Which climate regions do not have big cities?

Critical Thinking
3. **Movement** Compare this map to the **physical map**. What may have limited settlement of the U.S. Great Plains?

UNIT 2 ATLAS

Your Classroom Time Line (continued)

1600s The first enslaved Africans are brought to English colonies in North America.

1608 Quebec City is founded.

1756–63 The Seven Years' War, known in North America as the French and Indian War, is fought.

1776 The 13 American colonies declare independence from Great Britain.

1867 The United States buys Alaska from Russia.

1867 The British Parliament creates the Dominion of Canada.

1870 Manitoba becomes a province.

1885 The Canadian Pacific Railroad is completed.

Climate Map
Answers
1. California; any of the states that are one solid color
2. humid continental; ice cap, tundra, subarctic

Critical Thinking
3. lack of water

United States and Canada • 75

USING THE CLIMATE MAP

Direct students' attention to the **climate map** of the United States and Canada on this page. Ask students what climate type covers most of Canada's territory **(subarctic)** and what climate regions of the United States are not found in Canada **(humid subtropical, Mediterranean, tropical savanna, desert, humid tropical)**.

Have students compare this map to the **population map** on the next page. Call on volunteers to identify major cities and the climate regions in which they are located. **(Examples: Dallas—humid subtropical; Los Angeles—Mediterranean; Phoenix—desert; Toronto—humid continental; Vancouver—marine west coast)**

United States and Canada **75**

UNIT 2 ATLAS

Your Classroom Time Line (continued)

1898 The United States annexes Hawaii.

1905 Alberta and Saskatchewan become provinces.

1917–18 The United States fights in World War I.

1941 Japan bombs Pearl Harbor, Hawaii. The United States enters World War II.

1945 World War II ends.

1949 Newfoundland becomes Canada's 10th province.

1963 President John F. Kennedy is assassinated.

1990 The Cold War ends.

Population Map
Answers

1. United States
2. Toronto, Montreal
3. northeast coast; because it has the densest population

Critical Thinking

4. Seattle lies on the Pacific coast and has a mild climate because water heats and cools more slowly than land. Montreal is inland and does not benefit from the ocean's moderating effect on climate.

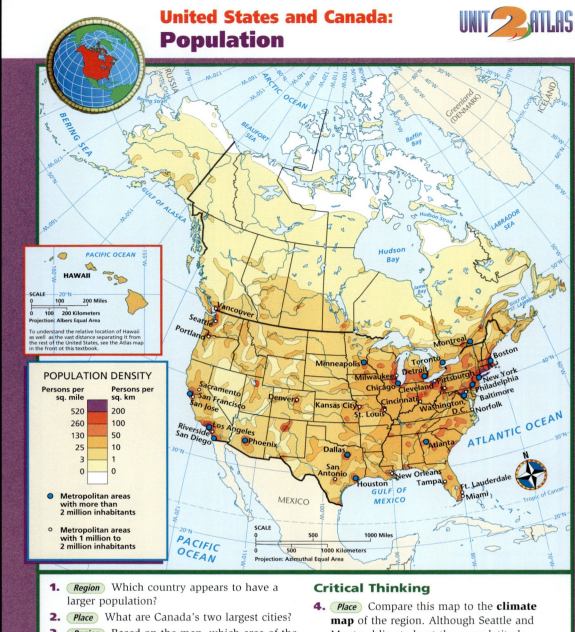

United States and Canada: Population

1. **Region** Which country appears to have a larger population?
2. **Place** What are Canada's two largest cities?
3. **Region** Based on the map, which area of the United States do you think was settled first? Why?

Critical Thinking

4. **Place** Compare this map to the **climate map** of the region. Although Seattle and Montreal lie at about the same latitude, Montreal has a colder climate. What may account for this difference?

76 • Unit 2

USING THE POPULATION MAP

 While students examine the **population map** on this page, ask them to locate cities they have lived in, visited, or heard about from movies, television, or sports events. You might ask them to tell what they know about those cities.

Ask students which country has the largest area where practically no one lives (Canada). Have students compare this map to the **political map** to determine which of the U.S. states appear to have the lowest overall population densities (Alaska and Nevada).

internet connect

ONLINE ATLAS
GO TO: go.hrw.com
KEYWORD: SJ5 MapsU2

United States and Canada: Land Use and Resources

UNIT 2 ATLAS

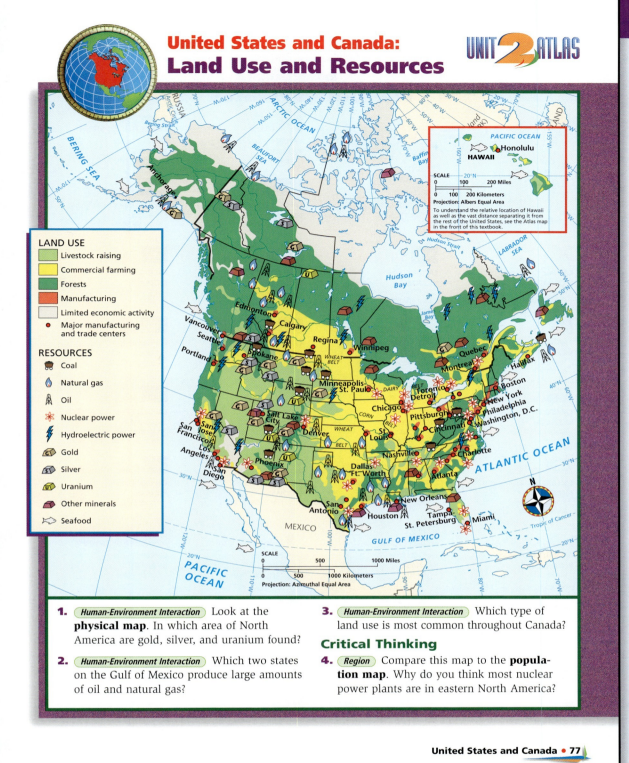

LAND USE
- Livestock raising
- Commercial farming
- Forests
- Manufacturing
- Limited economic activity
- ● Major manufacturing and trade centers

RESOURCES
- Coal
- Natural gas
- Oil
- Nuclear power
- Hydroelectric power
- Gold
- Silver
- Uranium
- Other minerals
- Seafood

1. **Human-Environment Interaction** Look at the **physical map**. In which area of North America are gold, silver, and uranium found?

2. **Human-Environment Interaction** Which two states on the Gulf of Mexico produce large amounts of oil and natural gas?

3. **Human-Environment Interaction** Which type of land use is most common throughout Canada?

Critical Thinking

4. **Region** Compare this map to the **population map**. Why do you think most nuclear power plants are in eastern North America?

UNIT 2 ATLAS

Your Classroom Time Line (continued)

1992 The U.S. Congress approves NAFTA.

1995 Canadian referendum on independence for Quebec is defeated by slim margin.

2001 Terrorists strike the United States on September 11. U.S. forces strike Taliban targets in Afghanistan.

2003 U.S. forces lead campaign to topple regime of Saddam Hussein.

2003 Power blackout strikes the northeastern United States, Toronto, Ottawa, and other parts of Ontario.

Land Use and Resources Map
Answers
1. in the west, concentrated in the Rocky Mountains
2. Texas and Louisiana
3. forests

Critical Thinking
4. Dense populations and manufacturing centers require large amounts of power.

United States and Canada • 77

USING THE LAND USE AND RESOURCES MAP

Have students locate the state in which they live on the **land use and resources map**. Tell them to identify the economic activities and resources that are found in their state. Ask students to use the map to identify economic patterns in the United States and Canada. Have each student write a sentence to summarize these patterns. Have students use other maps to help them write their sentences. (Examples: There are more nuclear power plants in the eastern United States than in the western part of the country. Large parts of Canada have limited economic activity. Coal mining is common in the Appalachian Mountains.)

FAST FACTS

Fast Facts Activities

LEVEL 1: (Suggested time: 30 min.) Call students' attention to the population figures for the United States and Canada. Have them calculate how many times larger the U.S. population is than Canada's. (Divide the U.S. population total by Canada's population total. The result is about 9.)

Tell students the United States has about 78 people per square mile and Canada about 8 people per square mile. Then review the climate map at the beginning of this unit with students. Have them identify the main climate types in Canada (subarctic and tundra). Ask students why Canada has a lower population density than the United States. (Areas with subarctic and tundra climates are unsuitable for large permanent settlements.)

LEVEL 2: (Suggested time: 30 min.) Organize the class into small groups. Draw students' attention to the nicknames listed under each state. Ask the groups to identify three states whose nicknames refer to historical events (such as Alaska, Connecticut, Delaware), to physical characteristics (such as Illinois, Michigan, South Dakota), and to climatic and economic conditions (such as California, Florida, Maine).

Challenge each group to create nicknames for the Canadian provinces. Nicknames should be based on characteristics similar to those that inspired the nicknames of the U.S. states. Have students use this unit's atlas for help. *(Example: British Columbia could be nicknamed The Pacific Province.)*

LEVEL 3: (Suggested time: 45 min.) Have students imagine that they work for the Canadian travel bureau. It is their job to create materials that tell travelers about the provinces and entice tourists to vacation there. Assign each student a province or territory. Have each student create an illustrated travel poster for their province. Ask them to highlight the capital city and include a nickname for the province. Have students use this unit's atlas for information. *(Example: British Columbia—the Pacific Province. Come climb our mountains, camp our forests, and sail along the lovely Fraser River. Explore Vancouver, our capital city!)*

CHAPTER 4: The Geography and History of the United States

Chapter Resource Manager

Objectives	Pacing Guide	Reproducible Resources
SECTION 1		
Physical Geography (pp. 81–85) 1. Describe the major physical features of the United States. 2. Examine the climate regions found in the United States. 3. Identify the natural resources of the United States.	**Regular** 1 day *Lecture Notes, Section 1* **Block Scheduling** .5 day *Block Scheduling Handbook, Chapter 4*	**RS** Know It Notes S1 **RS** Graphic Organizer 4 **IC** Interdisciplinary Activity for Middle Grades 6 **ELL** Main Idea Activity S1
SECTION 2		
Early Peoples of North America (pp. 86–89) 1. Explain how people first came to the Americas. 2. Describe some ways in which the first cultures of the Americas adapted to their environments.	**Regular** 1 day *Lecture Notes, Section 2* **Block Scheduling** .5 day *Block Scheduling Handbook, Chapter 4*	**RS** Know It Notes S2 **E** Cultures of the World Activities, Region 1 **ELL** Main Idea Activity S2
SECTION 3		
From Colonies to an Independent Country (pp. 90–95) 1. Describe the roles that people of various cultures and occupations played in the American colonies. 2. Explain why the American colonists fought the Revolutionary War. 3. Analyze the effects of American Independence.	**Regular** 3 days *Lecture Notes, Section 3* **Block Scheduling** 1.5 days *Block Scheduling Handbook, Chapter 4*	**RS** Know It Notes S3 **SM** Map Activity **E** Biography Activity: Thomas Jefferson **ELL** Main Idea Activity S3
SECTION 4		
The United States Becomes a World Power (pp. 96–103) 1. Identify who took part in westward expansion and explain what drew these people west. 2. Summarize the main causes and results of the Civil War. 3. Identify the events that marked the 1900s. 4. Describe some of the challenges that face the United States in the 2000s.	**Regular** 3 days *Lecture Notes, Section 4* **Block Scheduling** 1.5 days *Block Scheduling Handbook, Chapter 4*	**RS** Know It Notes S4 **E** Readings in World Geography, History, and Culture: Reading 12 **E** Biography Activity: Martin Luther King Jr. **ELL** Main Idea Activity S4

Chapter Resource Key

- **RS** Reading Support
- **IC** Interdisciplinary Connections
- **E** Enrichment
- **SM** Skills Mastery
- **A** Assessment
- **REV** Review
- **ELL** Reinforcement and English Language Learners and English for Speakers of Other Languages (ESOL)
- Internet
- Holt Presentation Maker Using Microsoft® PowerPoint®
- Transparencies
- CD–ROM
- Music
- Video

One-Stop Planner CD–ROM

See the *One-Stop Planner* for a complete list of additional resources for students and teachers.

One-Stop Planner CD–ROM

It's easy to plan lessons, select resources, and print out materials for your students when you use the *One-Stop Planner CD–ROM with Test Generator.*

internet connect

HRW ONLINE RESOURCES
GO TO: go.hrw.com
Then type in a keyword.

TEACHER HOMEPAGE
KEYWORD: **SJ5 TEACHER**

CHAPTER INTERNET ACTIVITIES
KEYWORD: **SJ5 GT4**

Choose an activity to:
- experience life in the early colonies.
- search letters and journal entries written by soldiers in the Civil War.
- explore the advance of civil rights in the United States.

CHAPTER ENRICHMENT LINKS
KEYWORD: **SJ5 CH4**

CHAPTER MAPS
KEYWORDS: **SJ5 MAPS4**

ONLINE ASSESSMENT
Homework Practice
   KEYWORD: **SJ5 HP4**
Standardized Test Prep Online
   KEYWORD: **SJ5 STP4**
Rubrics
   KEYWORD: **SS Rubrics**

COUNTRY INFORMATION
KEYWORD: **SJ5 Almanac**

CONTENT UPDATES
KEYWORD: **SS Contents Updates**

HOLT PRESENTATION MAKER
KEYWORD: **SJ5 PPT4**

ONLINE READING SUPPORT
KEYWORD: **SS Strategies**

CURRENT EVENTS
KEYWORD: **SS Current Events**

Technology Resources

Review, Reinforcement, and Assessment Resources

	Technology		Review
	One-Stop Planner CD-ROM, Lesson 4.1	ELL	Main Idea Activity S1
	Geography and Cultures Visual Resource 26	REV	Section 1 Review
	ARGWorld CD-ROM	A	Daily Quiz 4.1
	Homework Practice Online	REV	Chapter Summaries and Review
	HRW Go Site	ELL	English Audio Summary 4.1
		ELL	Spanish Audio Summary 4.1
	One-Stop Planner CD-ROM, Lesson 4.2	ELL	Main Idea Activity S2
	Geography and Cultures Visual Resource 26	REV	Section 2 Review
	ARGWorld CD-ROM	A	Daily Quiz 4.2
	Homework Practice Online	REV	Chapter Summaries and Review
	HRW Go site	ELL	English Audio Summary 4.2
		ELL	Spanish Audio Summary 4.2
	One-Stop Planner CD-ROM, Lesson 4.3	ELL	Main Idea Activity S3
	Geography and Cultures Visual Resource 26	REV	Section 3 Review
	ARGWorld CD–ROM	A	Daily Quiz 4.3
	Homework Practice Online	REV	Chapter Summaries and Review
	HRW Go site	ELL	English Audio Summary 4.3
		ELL	Spanish Audio Summary 4.3
	One-Stop Planner CD-ROM, Lesson 4.4	ELL	Main Idea Activity S4
	Geography and Cultures Visual Resources 26, 30	REV	Section 4 Review
	ARGWorld CD–ROM	A	Daily Quiz 4.4
	Homework Practice Online	REV	Chapter Summaries and Review
	HRW Go site	ELL	English Audio Summary 4.4
		ELL	Spanish Audio Summary 4.4

Meeting Individual Needs

Ability Levels

Level 1 Basic-level activities designed for all students encountering new material

Level 2 Intermediate-level activities designed for average students

Level 3 Challenging activities designed for honors and gifted-and-talented students

ESOL Activities that address the needs of students with Limited English Proficiency

Chapter Review and Assessment

E	Readings in World Geography, History, and Culture 12
SM	Critical Thinking Activity 4
REV	Chapter 4 Review and Practice
REV	Chapter Summaries and Review
ELL	Vocabulary Activity 4
A	Chapter 4 Test
A	Chapter 4 Test Generator (on the One-Stop Planner)
	Audio CD Program, Chapter 4
A	Chapter 4 Test for English Language Learners and Special-Needs Students
	HRW Go site

79B

CHAPTER 4

The Geography and History of the

Previewing Chapter Resources

Holt Online Learning

Keyword: SJ5 GT4

- Homework Practice Online
- Holt Online Assessment
- Online Gradebook
- Document-Based Question Activities
- Teaching Tips for the Multimedia Classroom
- Interactive Multimedia Activities

Differentiating Instruction

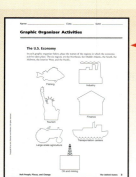

Reading and Writing Support
- ◄ Graphic Organizer Activity
- Vocabulary Activity
- Chapter Summaries and Review
- Know It Notes
- Audio CD

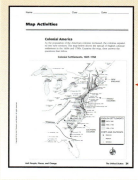

Active Learning
- Block Scheduling Handbook
- Cultures of the World Activity
- Interdisciplinary Activity
- ◄ Map Activity
- Critical Thinking Activity 6
- Music of the World Audio CD Program: Dixieland Jazz

Primary Sources and Advanced Learners
- ◄ Geography for Life Activity: Shopping Rules!
- Map Activity: Colonial America
- Readings in World Geography, History and Culture:
  - 11 The Expanse of Texas
  - 12 Change Comes to the Hudson River Valley

Assessment Program
- Daily Quizzes S1–4
- ◄ Chapter Test
- Chapter Test for English Language Learners and Special-Needs Students

Spanish and ESOL
- Vocabulary Activity
- ◄ Main Idea Activities for English Language Learners and Special-Needs Students
- Chapter Summary and Review
- Spanish Audio Summary
- Know It Notes S1–4
- Chapter Test for English Language Learners and Special-Needs Students

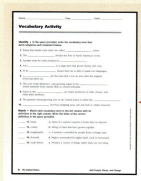

Special Education Modifications
Your I.D.E.A. Works! CD-ROM will provide modified versions of the following teaching materials:
- Know It Notes S1–4
- ◄ Vocabulary Activity
- Main Idea Activities S1–4
- Daily Quizzes S1–4
- Chapter 4 Test
- Flash cards of chapter vocabulary terms

the United States
Teacher Resources

Books for Teachers
Corner, James S., and Alex S. MacLean. *Taking Measures Across the American Landscape.* Yale University Press, 1996.

Dean, Cornelia. *Against the Tide: The Battle for America's Beaches.* Columbia University Press, 1999.

Donahue, Brian. *Reclaiming the Commons: Community Farms and Forests in a New England Town.* Yale University Press, 1999.

Hoobler, Dorothy, and Thomas Hoobler. *The American Family Albums.* Oxford University Press, 1994–96.

Books for Students
Budhos, Marina. *Remix: Conversations with Immigrant Teenagers.* Holt, 1999. Twenty teens—from countries including Ethiopia, Bangladesh, and Ukraine—discuss their experiences in the United States.

Gordon, Patricia, and Reed C. Snow. *Learn America!: Bringing Geography to Life with People, Places, and History.* Williamson Publishing, 1999. Combines history, culture, geography, and natural sciences.

Krull, Kathleen. *Wish You Were Here: Emily's Guide to the United States.* Bantam Books, 1997. Combination atlas and travel diary with geographical and tourist information on each state. **SHELTERED ENGLISH**

Multimedia Materials
A Day in the Life of America. Video, 18 min. AIMS Media.

Latino Art and Culture in the United States. Video, 30 min. Alarion Press.

On Common Ground. CD–ROM. Columbia University Press.

Videos and CDs

Videos
- CNN. *Presents Geography: Yesterday and Today,* Segments 6 and 7
- CNN. *Presents World Cultures: Yesterday and Today,* Segments 20, 21, 22 and 29
- ARG World

Holt Researcher
http://researcher.hrw.com
- U.S. Constitution
- United States
- Births, Deaths, Marriages, and Divorces in The United States
- Immigrants to The United States by Region
- United States Commission on Civil Rights

Transparency Packages

Graphic Organizer Transparencies 4.1–3

Geography and Cultures Visual Resources Transparencies
21 US and Canada: Physical
22 US and Canada: Political
23 US and Canada: Climate
24 US and Canada: Population
25 US and Canada: Land Use and Resources
26 US: Physical-Political
30 US Freeway Mural in Los Angeles

Map Activities Transparency 04 Colonial America

CHAPTER 4

WHY IT MATTERS

Use these points to emphasize the importance of knowing more about the geography and history of the United States:

- Economic development and population movement are both affected by geographical features.
- Some of the issues that led to the founding of this country, such as the proper role of government, are still being debated today.
- Many of the trends and patterns that have appeared throughout the history of the United States are still evident in our country today.
- We can be more effective citizens if we understand the physical and human geography of our country.

CHAPTER 4

The Geography and History of the United States

Our country's history includes many exciting stories. Some of the stories tell about deeds performed by young people. Here we meet a brave girl who lived in the 1770s.

Dr. Martin Luther King Jr. in Washington, D.C., in 1963

Think back to what you already know about the American Revolution. You probably remember Paul Revere's ride and his warning that British redcoats, or soldiers, were coming. What if a teenage girl had ridden twice as far as Paul Revere to awaken her neighbors to danger? That's the story of Sybil Ludington.

Sybil's father led a group of colonists who wanted independence. One day, a messenger brought word to him that the British were coming. They were marching toward where the group's supplies were stored. However, the messenger and his horse were too tired to go on, and Colonel Ludington had to organize his fighters. So Sybil spread the alarm. She covered nearly 40 miles of unfamiliar roads before returning home.

An American girl of the mid-1700s

New York City scene, late 1800s

CHAPTER PROJECT

Have students make relief maps of the United States from papier maché, clay, or flour-salt dough. Models should show the gradual rise in elevation of the United States from east to west, the Great Plains, the Rocky Mountains, and the Appalachians. Students can paint their maps with different colors to show varying elevations and provide a color key. Have students write a paragraph explaining what they did. Display projects in the classroom or a public area of the school.

STARTING THE CHAPTER

Provide a small group of volunteers with the lyrics to "America the Beautiful," and ask them to sing the first verse. As students sing, write key phrases such as *amber waves of grain, purple mountain majesties, fruited plain* on the chalkboard. Ask students what these phrases mean and what they tell us about our country. (Possible answer: The United States has fertile farmlands and high mountains.) Tell students they will learn more about our country's physical features and history in this chapter.

80 Chapter 4

Section 1: Physical Geography

CHAPTER 4, Section 1

Read to Discover
1. What are the major physical features of the United States?
2. What climate regions are found in the United States?
3. What natural resources does the United States have?

Vocabulary
contiguous
Continental Divide
basins

Places
Coastal Plain
Appalachian Mountains
Interior Plains
Rocky Mountains
Great Lakes
Mississippi River
Great Plains
Columbia River
Great Basin
Colorado Plateau
Sierra Nevada
Cascade Range
Aleutian Islands

Reading Strategy
VISUALIZING INFORMATION Previewing the images in this section will help you understand the written information. What are some things that the map below and the pictures in this section tell you about the physical geography of the United States? Write down your answers. As you read, add more information.

Section 1 Resources

Reproducibles
- Lecture Notes, Section 1
- Block Scheduling Handbook, Chapter 4
- Know It Notes S1
- Interdisciplinary Activity for Middle Grades 6

Technology
- One-Stop Planner CD-ROM, Lesson 4.1
- Geography and Cultures Visual Resource 26
- Homework Practice Online
- HRW Go Site

Review, Reinforcement, and Assessment Resources
- Section 1 Review
- Daily Quiz 4.1
- Main Idea Activity S1
- Chapter Summaries and Review
- English Audio Summary 4.1
- Spanish Audio Summary 4.1

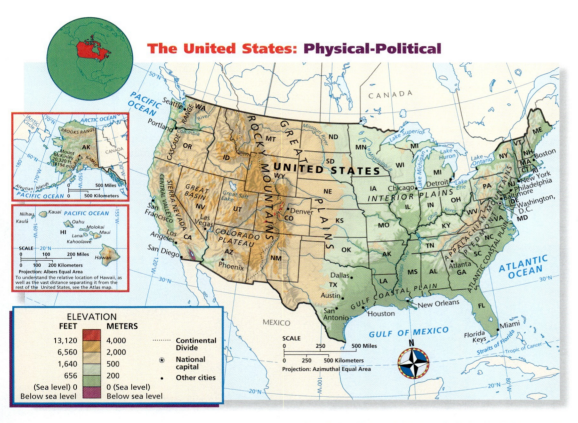

The United States: Physical-Political

The Geography and History of the United States • 81

Section 1

Objectives
1. Describe the major physical features of the United States.
2. Examine the climate regions found in the United States.
3. Identify the natural resources of the United States.

Focus

 Bellringer
Copy the following questions onto the chalkboard: *How would you describe the land and climate of your hometown? Is it flat, hilly, or mountainous? Is the climate cold, hot, dry, or rainy?* Ask students to respond in writing and discuss their responses. Tell students that in Section 1 they will learn about the physical geography of the United States.

Using the Physical-Political Map
Have students examine the map on this page. Ask volunteers to identify the principal landforms and bodies of water. Have students locate the areas where they live and name other areas they have visited. Then have students compare the physical and political features of the areas mentioned.

The Geography and History of the United States 81

CHAPTER 4, Section 1

National Geography Standard 15

Shaky Plains Although most people associate earthquakes with California, several significant earthquakes have shaken the Interior Plains. On December 16, 1811, the first of three magnitude 8 earthquakes to rock the central Mississippi River valley awakened the residents of New Madrid, in the Missouri Territory. No recorded earthquake has ever exceeded a value of 9 on the Richter scale. Thousands of aftershocks followed during the winter of 1811–12. The greatest quake was felt as far away as Chicago, New Orleans, Boston, and even parts of Canada. Although the land heaved, buckled, and cracked, few people were killed because the region was sparsely populated.

Today, that region is home to millions of people. Some scientists worry that the next big earthquake may occur there.

GO TO: go.hrw.com
KEYWORD: SJ5 CH4
For: Web sites about earthquakes

Visual Record Answer ▶

Students might note the smooth, gentle slopes, which appear to be heavily eroded.

internet connect
GO TO: go.hrw.com
KEYWORD: SJ5 CH4
FOR: Web sites about the United States

Physical Features

The 48 **contiguous** American states and the District of Columbia lie between the Atlantic and Pacific Oceans. Contiguous states are those that border each other. Two states are not contiguous: Alaska, to the northwest of Canada, and Hawaii, in the Pacific Ocean. The United States also has territories in the Pacific Ocean and the Caribbean Sea. We will now look at the physical features of the 50 states. You can use the map on the next page to follow along.

The East The eastern United States rises from the Coastal Plain to the Appalachian Mountains. The Coastal Plain is a low region that lies close to sea level. It rises gradually inland. The Coastal Plain stretches from New York to Mexico along the Atlantic and Gulf of Mexico coasts.

The Appalachians include mountain ranges and river valleys from Maine to Alabama. The mountains are very old. Erosion has lowered and smoothed the peaks for more than 300 million years. The highest mountain in the Appalachians rises to just 6,684 feet (2,037 m).

At the foot of the Appalachians, between the mountains and the Coastal Plain, is the Piedmont. The Piedmont is a region of rolling plains. It begins in New Jersey and extends as far south as Alabama.

The Interior Plains Vast plains make up most of the United States west of the Appalachians. This region is called the Interior Plains. The Interior Plains stretch westward to the Rocky Mountains.

After the last ice age, glaciers shrank. They left rolling hills, lakes, and major river systems in the northern Interior Plains. The Great Lakes were created by these retreating ice sheets. From west to east, the Great Lakes are Lake Superior, Lake Michigan, Lake Huron, Lake Erie, and Lake Ontario.

The Mississippi River and its tributaries drain the Interior Plains. Along the way, they deposit rich soils that produce fertile farmlands. A tributary is a stream or river that flows into a larger stream or river. Tributaries of the Mississippi include the Missouri and Ohio Rivers.

The Great Smoky Mountains of Tennessee are a range of the Appalachian Mountains.
Interpreting the Visual Record *Place*
What clues from this photograph might tell you that these mountains are very old?

TEACH

Teaching Objective 1

LEVEL 1: (Suggested time: 15 min.) Ask students to identify types of landforms. (Possible answers: mountains, plains, and rivers) Write these types on the chalkboard and then have volunteers list—under each landform category—specific examples of these physical features that can be found in the United States. Tell students to write a paragraph summarizing the information in their notebooks. **ESOL,** **LS VERBAL-LINGUISTIC**

LEVELS 2 AND 3: (Suggested time: 30 min.) Pair students and have each pair sketch an elevation profile of the United States from New York to San Francisco. You may want to have some students sketch other elevation profiles such as along specific lines of latitude. Students should label the mountain ranges, rivers, lakes, plains, and other major physical features on their elevation profiles. **COOPERATIVE LEARNING,** **LS VISUAL-SPATIAL**

Physical Regions of the United States and Canada

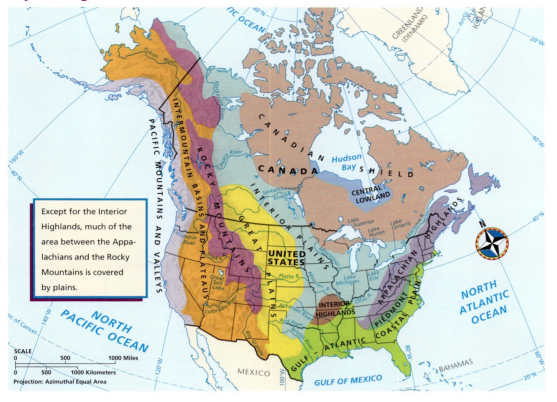

Except for the Interior Highlands, much of the area between the Appalachians and the Rocky Mountains is covered by plains.

In some places on its way to the Gulf of Mexico, the great Mississippi River is 1.5 miles (2.4 km) wide!

The flattest part of the Interior Plains is the Great Plains region. It lies closest to the Rocky Mountains. The region has a higher elevation than the rest of the Interior Plains. The Great Plains extend from Mexico in the south into Canada in the north.

The West As we continue westward, we reach the Rocky Mountains. The Rockies include a series of mountain ranges separated by high plains and valleys. They extend from Mexico to the cold Arctic. Many Rocky Mountain peaks reach more than 14,000 feet (4,267 m).

Running along the crest of the Rockies is the **Continental Divide**. It divides the flow of North America's rivers. Rivers east of the divide, such as the Missouri, flow eastward. Rivers west of the divide, such as the Columbia, flow westward.

West of the Rockies is a region of plateaus and **basins**. A basin is a region surrounded by higher land, such as mountains. The Great Basin in Nevada and Utah, for example, is surrounded by high mountains. Southeast of the Great Basin is the

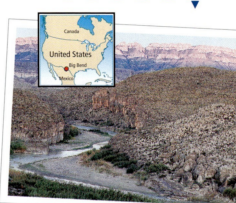

The Rio Grande cuts through Big Bend National Park.
Interpreting the Visual Record *Place*
What landforms appear in this area?

CHAPTER 4, Section 1

ENVIRONMENT AND SOCIETY

River on a Rampage In 1993 heavy rains caused the upper sections of the Mississippi River to flood surrounding lands. These floods affected about 20 million acres (8 million hectares) and caused at least $17 billion in damages. The town of Valmeyer, Illinois, was completely devastated. More than 90 percent of the town was underwater, and residents were forced to leave.

When floodwaters receded, the residents had to decide whether to rebuild in the same place or to relocate. The Federal Emergency Management Administration helped the town's residents obtain funding to rebuild their town in a new location several miles north of the old one. The new Valmeyer occupies a bluff that had been a cornfield.

Activity: Have students examine your community's physical geography to determine what flood threats exist and where citizens might rebuild if a disastrous flood were to occur.

◄ **Visual Record Answer**

canyons, mountains, and a narrow floodplain

Teaching Objective 2

LEVELS 1 AND 2: (Suggested time: 20 min.) Copy the following graphic organizer onto the chalkboard, omitting the blue answers. Use it to help students examine climate regions in the United States. Have students supply words and phrases describing the climate regions and use their descriptions to complete the organizer. Students should copy the chart into their notebooks. **ESOL,** **LS** **VISUAL-SPATIAL**

LEVEL 3: (Suggested time: 30 min.) Pair students and tell each pair to prepare a weather forecast for a television station in one of the following cities: Buffalo, New York; Chicago, Illinois; Denver, Colorado; Fairbanks, Alaska; Los Angeles, California; Miami, Florida; Phoenix, Arizona; or Seattle, Washington. Have pairs present their forecasts to the class, using props, maps, and graphics. **COOPERATIVE LEARNING** **LS** **INTERPERSONAL**

Climate Regions in the United States

The East	The Interior	The West	Hawaii	Alaska
humid continental, humid subtropical	humid continental, humid subtropical, steppe	steppe, highland, desert, marine west coast, Mediterranean	tropical, tropical savanna	subarctic, tundra

CHAPTER 4, Section 1

EYE ON EARTH

A Watery Treasure One of the most remarkable physical features of the United States is the Everglades. The Everglades, a marshland, once covered almost 9 million acres (3.6 million hectares) in southern Florida. During the last 100 years much of the land has been drained and used for residential development and farming. The Everglades National Park includes about one sixth of the original marshland.

The Everglades ecosystem depends on a huge supply of freshwater. Excess rainwater used to overflow the southern rim of Lake Okeechobee in south-central Florida and then travel in a broad, shallow sheet of water through the Everglades to the Gulf of Mexico. Much of the water is now redirected to the large farms and population centers of South Florida. As a result, the ecosystem has suffered. Of the species that live in the Everglades, more than 50 are endangered or threatened. These include the American crocodile and the Florida panther. A plan proposed in 1999 to restore a supply of freshwater to the Everglades may take decades to implement and cost more than $7 billion.

Colorado Plateau. The Colorado Plateau lies in Utah, Colorado, New Mexico, and Arizona. West of the Great Basin lie the Sierra Nevada, the Coast Ranges, and many valleys. The Cascade Range in the Pacific Northwest was formed by volcanic eruptions. Volcanic eruptions and earthquakes are a danger in the Pacific states. In this area, the North American plate is colliding with the Pacific plate.

Hawaii and Alaska Farther west, Hawaii and Alaska also experience tectonic activity. The Hawaiian Islands were formed by large volcanoes that have risen from the floor of the Pacific Ocean. Alaska's Aleutian (uh-LOO-shuhn) Islands also have volcanic origins.

Southeastern and south-central Alaska are very mountainous. The highest mountain in North America is Mount McKinley, in the Alaska Range. The American Indian name for Mount McKinley is Denali. It soars to a height of 20,320 feet (6,194 m).

✓ **READING CHECK:** *Places and Regions* What are the major physical features of the United States? plains, mountain ranges, rivers, river valleys, lakes, Continental Divide, plateaus, basins

Climate

The climates of the United States are varied. The country has 11 climate types—the greatest variety of climates of any country.

The East Most of the eastern United States is divided into two climate regions. In the north is a humid continental climate with snowy winters and warm, humid summers. Southerners experience the milder winters and warm, humid summers of a humid subtropical climate. Coastal areas often experience tropical storms. Southern Florida, with a tropical savanna climate, is warm all year.

The Interior Plains Humid continental, humid subtropical, and steppe climates meet in the interior states. People there sometimes experience violent weather, such as hail and tornadoes. The steppe climate of the Great Plains supports wide grasslands. Summers are hot, and droughts can be a problem. Blinding snowstorms called blizzards sometimes occur during winters, which can be very cold.

Ⓐ Winter in Massachusetts
Ⓑ Spring in California
Ⓒ Summer in Florida
Ⓓ Fall in Colorado

The West Climates in the West are mostly dry. Steppe and varied highland climates dominate much of the Rocky Mountain region. Temperatures and the amount of rain and snow vary.

84 • Chapter 4

Teaching Objective 3

ALL LEVELS: (Suggested time: 30 min.) Tell students to imagine that they are economists who are representing the United States at a foreign trade conference. They must give a presentation on the natural resources of the United States. (Presentations should discuss farmlands and their products, coal and other minerals, forests, and natural beauty.) Students' presentations should also discuss how these natural resources contribute to the U.S. economy. Reintroduce the concepts of primary, secondary, tertiary, and quaternary industries to students and ask them to refer to these concepts and give examples of them in their presentations.
ESOL, **LS** **VERBAL-LINGUISTIC**

CLOSE

Have a volunteer point to random places on a wall map of the United States. Ask the class to describe the physical features, climate(s), and natural resources of those locations. Ask students how these factors would affect the daily lives and economic activities of people living there.

Much of the Southwest has a desert climate. The West Coast has two climate types. The forested north has a wet and mild marine west coast climate. A drier Mediterranean climate is found in the south.

Except in the southeast, most of Alaska has very cold subarctic and tundra climates. Hawaii is the only state within the tropics. Northeasterly trade winds bring rain to eastern sides of the islands. Hawaii's western slopes have a drier tropical savanna climate.

✓ **READING CHECK:** *The World in Spatial Terms* What climate regions are found in the United States? humid continental, humid subtropical, tropical savanna, steppe, varied highland, desert, marine west coast, Mediterranean, subarctic, tundra, tropical, tropical savanna

Natural Resources

The United States has many resources. Some of the most productive farmlands in the world are found in the Interior Plains. Ranches and farms produce beef, wheat, corn, and soybeans. California, Florida, Texas, and other areas grow fruit, vegetables, and cotton.

Alaska, California, Texas, and other states supply oil and natural gas. Coal and other minerals are found in Appalachian and western states. Gold and silver mines also operate in some western states.

Forests, especially in the Northwest and the Southeast, are important sources of lumber. The Atlantic Ocean, Gulf of Mexico, and Pacific Ocean are rich sources of fish and other seafood. The natural beauty of the country is also a valuable resource for tourism. All these resources help support industry and other economic activities.

✓ **READING CHECK:** *Places and Regions* What natural resources does the United States have? productive farm and ranch land, oil and natural gas, minerals, precious metals, forests, seafood

Redwoods, the tallest trees in the world, grow in California and Oregon. They can grow well over 300 feet (90 m) high with trunks 20 feet (6 m) in diameter. Some redwood trees are more than 1,500 years old!

Homework Practice Online
Keyword: SJ5 HP4

Section Review 1

Define and explain: contiguous, Continental Divide, basins

Working with Sketch Maps On a map of the United States that you draw or that your teacher provides, label the following: Coastal Plain, Appalachian Mountains, Interior Plains, Rocky Mountains, Great Lakes, Mississippi River, Great Plains, Columbia River, Great Basin, Colorado Plateau, Sierra Nevada, Cascade Range, and Aleutian Islands.

Reading for the Main Idea

1. *Places and Regions* What are the two major mountain regions in the United States? What major landform region lies between them?
2. *Places and Regions* What resources are found in the country? Why are they important for the economy?
3. *Places and Regions* What parts of the United States have particularly rich farmlands?

Critical Thinking

4. **Drawing Inferences and Conclusions** The Rockies are higher than the Appalachians. How is this fact a clue to the relative age of the two mountain systems?

Organizing What You Know

5. **Categorizing** Copy the following graphic organizer. Use it to categorize the major physical features and climates of the East, Interior Plains, and West.

	Physical Features	Climates
East		
Interior Plains		
West (including Alaska and Hawaii)		

Section 1 Review

Answers to Section 1 Review

Define For definitions see the glossary and index.

Working with Sketch Maps Listed places should be labeled accurately.

Reading for the Main Idea

1. the Rocky and Appalachian Mountains; the Interior Plains
2. resources—farmland, oil, natural gas, coal, minerals, forests, seafood, natural beauty; importance—pump money into the U.S. economy
3. the Interior Plains (NGS 5)

Critical Thinking

4. The Rockies are younger because they have not been eroded as much as the Appalachians. (NGS 7)

Organizing What You Know (NGS 5),

5. East—physical features: mountain ranges, river valleys, and rolling plains; climates: humid continental, humid subtropical, and tropical savanna; Interior Plains—physical features: plains, hills, lakes, and major river systems; climates: humid continental, humid subtropical, and steppe; West—physical features: mountain ranges, plateaus, basins, valleys, plains, and hills; climates: steppe, varied highlands, desert, marine west coast, Mediterranean, subarctic, tundra, and tropical

---

REVIEW, ASSESS, RETEACH

Have students complete the Section Review. Then have each student create a crossword puzzle using 10 terms. The terms and their clues should cover the main ideas of the section. Pair students and have partners solve each other's puzzles. Then have students complete Daily Quiz 4.1.

Have students complete Main Idea Activity S1. Then organize students into three groups. Assign each group one of the following aspects of the United States: physical features, climates, or natural resources. Have groups produce skits or infomercials on their topics. Groups should write a script and provide some visual resources. Have the groups present their skits or infomercials to the class. **ESOL, COOPERATIVE LEARNING**

EXTEND

Have interested students conduct research on the landforms, rivers, climates, and unique attractions of a national park. Ask students to imagine that they are park rangers and have them create a brief orientation on the park's attractions to present to a group of tourists. **BLOCK SCHEDULING**

CHAPTER 4, Section 2

SECTION 2 RESOURCES

Reproducibles
- Lecture Notes, Section 2
- Block Scheduling Handbook, Chapter 4
- Know It Notes S2
- Cultures of the World Activities, Region 1

Technology
- One-Stop Planner CD-ROM, Lesson 4.2
- Geography and Cultures Visual Resource 26
- Homework Practice Online
- HRW Go Site

Review, Reinforcement, and Assessment Resources
- Section 2 Review
- Daily Quiz 4.2
- Main Idea Activity S2
- Chapter Summaries and Review
- English Audio Summary 4.2
- Spanish Audio Summary 4.2

Section 2: Early Peoples of North America

Read to Discover
1. How did people first come to the Americas?
2. What are some ways in which the first cultures of the Americas adapted to their environments?

Vocabulary
migrate
tepees
adobe
kiva
Iroquois League

People
Hohokam
Anasazi

Reading Strategy

READING ORGANIZER Before you read, draw a large circle on a sheet of paper. Draw two lines through the circle to divide it into quarters. Label the quarters Northwest, Great Plains, Southwest, and Eastern Woodlands. As you read, write or draw pictures to describe how people in these regions adapted to their environments.

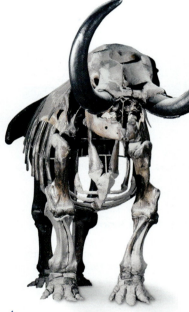

▲ Early North American peoples hunted mammoths like the one whose skeleton is shown here.

The First Americans

The first Americans probably came from northeastern Asia. However, the stormy Bering Sea separates Asia from North America. How did people get here? For the answer, we must go back thousands of years.

From Asia to America In an earlier chapter you read about the ice ages. Long ago, huge ice sheets covered much of the Earth. So much water was frozen that sea level dropped many feet. As a result, what is now the Bering Sea was once dry land.

People used this "land bridge" to **migrate**, or move, out of northeastern Asia. This process probably began about 18,000 years ago. These early people were nomads who collected plants, hunted, and fished for their food. They may have followed herds of animals that moved into the Americas. Over many years, some of these people migrated to the central and eastern parts of North America. Others traveled all the way to the tip of South America.

Later Migrations The last ice age ended about 10,000 years ago. As the ice melted, the sea level rose. The land bridge disappeared beneath the waves. Still, more people came from Asia to the Americas. These people, however, probably came in small boats.

86 • Chapter 4

Section 2

Objectives
1. Explain how people first came to the Americas.
2. Describe some ways in which the first cultures of the Americas adapted to their environments.

FOCUS

Bellringer

Write these instructions on the chalkboard: *Look at the photographs in this section and read the captions. Select one image and write two more things that you would like to know about the image.* (mammoth—how early Americans hunted and killed mammoths or how dangerous the creatures were; Anasazi cliff dwelling—why the Anasazi lived there; snake mound—why the mound is in the image of a snake, how it was made) Tell students that in this section they will learn more about the America's first peoples.

Building Vocabulary

Write the vocabulary terms on the chalkboard. Call on volunteers to locate the definitions and read them aloud. Then ask students to write sentences that each use at least two of the terms. (Example: Tepees and adobe cliff dwellings are two types of American Indian dwellings.) Call on students to share their sentences with the class.

Scientists have made many discoveries in recent years about humans in the Americas. Scholars have combined clues from archaeological sites with DNA evidence to draw conclusions. Research continues, though. As they learn more, scientists may develop new theories about the migration of people to the Americas.

✓ **READING CHECK:** *Human Systems* How did the first migration of people to the Americas differ from later migrations? **first—over a land bridge from northeastern Asia; later—probably in small boats**

Early Cultures of North America

The Americas stretch north to south for more than 11,000 miles. Almost every climate, landform, or resource can be found somewhere on either North America or South America. Because environment affects how people live, cultures developed differently throughout the two continents.

You will read about peoples who settled in modern Canada in another chapter. Here we will start with the Pacific coast of what is now the United States.

Peoples of North America

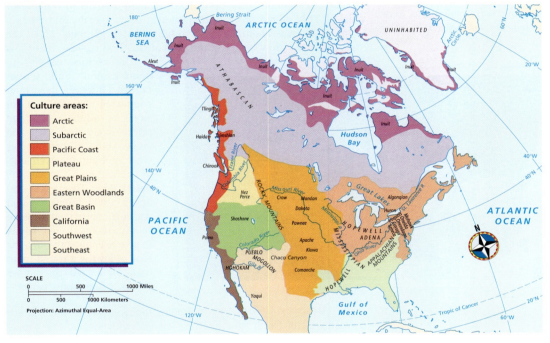

Various groups of people settled across the North American continent, adapting to geographic conditions from the frozen Arctic to the desert Southwest.
Interpreting the Map Which peoples lived in your state?

CHAPTER 4, Section 2

Cultural Kaleidoscope
Jicarilla Apache

The Jicarilla Apache belong to the larger native group called the Apache. Traditionally, the Jicarilla Apache lived in the American Southwest, including parts of Arizona, Colorado, New Mexico, and Texas, as well as the northern Mexican states of Chihuahua and Sonora. Today several thousand Jicarilla Apache live in the United States. The total number of American Indians and Alaskan natives in the United States today is about 2.5 million.

Activity: Have students identify some of the major American Indian groups living in the United States today and plot the groups' traditional homelands on a map. Tell students that many but not all American Indians now live on reservations.

◀ **Map Answer**
Students' answers should accurately identify the American Indian groups that lived in the area of their state.

TEACH

Teaching Objective 1

LEVELS 1 AND 2: (Suggested time: 30 min.) Point out to students the location of the Bering Strait on a wall map. Ask students to speculate about what sort of landscape awaited the migrants who crossed the Bering "land bridge" to America. **(Students will probably suggest a frozen, white wasteland with cold temperatures and harsh living conditions.)** Then have each student create a map showing the migration of the first people to America. Students' maps should include arrows illustrating the gradual movement of these people over the land bridge and throughout the Americas. In addition, students should include a map annotation or caption that indicates approximately when the migration occurred. **ESOL,** **VISUAL-SPATIAL**

LEVEL 3: (Suggested time: 45 min.) Ask students to imagine that they are descendents of the first people who came to America. The oral history of how their people came to where they now live has been passed down from generation to generation. The time has come for them to tell the story to the next generation. Have students use their historical imaginations to write a probable oral history based on the information in the section. Then call on one or two volunteers to tell their oral histories to the class.
VERBAL-LINGUISTIC

CHAPTER 4, Section 2

Linking Past to Present

The American Buffalo At one time, as many as 50 million buffalo roamed the American Great Plains. As railroads extended into the West, most of these buffalo were rapidly killed off. By 1889, fewer than 1,000 buffalo remained in the United States. Actions to save the buffalo have helped them survive, however. Today, American buffalo number several hundred thousand. Many of these buffalo live on government preserves. Some ranchers raise buffalo as well.

The Northwest People who settled along the cool Pacific coast lived near the sea. Thus they depended largely on fish for food. The region's tall forests provided lumber. Woodworking was a valued skill among Pacific Coast peoples. They carved great totem poles for signposts, grave markers, property markers, and other purposes. They also made canoes from trees that could hold 60 people.

The Great Plains The region that stretches from southern Canada to Texas, the Great Plains, was once covered with grass. Millions of buffalo roamed over the grassland. Peoples of the Great Plains hunted the buffalo. Because there were no horses in North America at this time, the hunters had to chase their prey on foot. To make their hunts more successful, sometimes they drove entire herds of buffalo over high cliffs. At other times, they built pens into which they drove the buffalo.

The hunters used nearly every part of the buffalo in some way. They ate the meat and made tools from the bones. Buffalo hides were made into clothing and for tents called **tepees**. The buffalo was so important that some people considered it sacred. Hunters may have held ceremonies before a hunt and given thanks afterwards.

The Southwest The southwestern part of North America has a hot and dry climate. The **Hohokam** and **Anasazi** (ah-nuh-SAH-zee) people who lived there found ways to survive in this harsh environment. For example, they developed irrigation systems to water their fields. They stored precious rainwater in dams, canals, and ditches. The water was channeled to carefully tended gardens. Thus, the people could grow beans, corn, and cotton. Because few trees grow in the region, early residents couldn't build timber houses. Instead, they built connected houses out of stone or **adobe**—sun-dried bricks made from clay and straw. Some of these homes were built into the overhangs of cliffs, high above the desert floor. The largest had up to 1,000 rooms. Within Anasazi settlements were special rooms called **kivas** that were entered through the roof. A kiva is a round room used for sacred ceremonies and as a community center.

Anasazi homes were built of stone and sun-dried clay bricks. They were built in openings in high cliffs.

The Eastern Woodlands Unlike the Southwest, the Eastern Woodlands of North America were covered with forests. The people who settled there hunted forest animals. They also gathered wild plants and later learned how to farm.

88 • Chapter 4

Teaching Objective 2

ALL LEVELS: (Suggested time: 20 min.) To help students describe some ways in which the first cultures of the Americas adapted to their environments, copy the following graphic organizer onto the chalkboard, omitting the blue answers. Have students complete the organizer by describing the environment of each region and then explaining the ways in which cultures in each region adapted to their environment. **LS VISUAL-SPATIAL**

Region	Environment	How adapted to environment
Northwest	cool; seacoast; tall forests	• depended on fish for food • used wood from forests to create canoes for transportation, totem poles for various uses
Great Plains	grasslands; buffalo herds	• depended on the buffalo for food, clothing, materials for tepees, tools, and other items • sometimes used cliffs to aid buffalo hunts
Southwest	hot, dry, harsh	• farmed • developed irrigation systems to water crops • stored rainwater in dams, canals, and ditches • made dwellings from adobe or stone because few trees for wood • set dwellings into cliff overhangs for protection
Eastern Woodlands	covered with forests	• hunted forest animals; fished (Iroquois) • gathered wild plants; later farmed • built large earthen mounds for various uses • traded for resources not available locally

Some of the Eastern Woodlands peoples lived in large settlements. One of these early cultures, the Hopewell, thrived in the Ohio Valley region between about 300 B.C. and A.D. 400. The Hopewell built large earthen mounds—some shaped like animals. These people built mounds for burials, ceremonial sites, and perhaps for defense. They also traded over long distances. Bear teeth from present-day Wyoming and shark teeth from the Gulf Coast are among the items found in Hopewell graves.

Another people, the Mississippians, built the largest ceremonial center in North America. Between A.D. 1050 and 1250 Cahokia, near present-day East St. Louis, was home for up to 20,000 people. Chiefs of Cahokia traded for copper, shells, and a mineral called mica.

In what is today New York State and the surrounding region, the Iroquois (IR-uh-kwoy) hunted, fished, and farmed. The Iroquois fought with other peoples over hunting grounds. They also fought among themselves. Finally, war threatened to destroy everyone in the region. In response, the Iroquois formed the **Iroquois League**. Members of the league agreed to keep the peace among themselves. Conflict with other peoples continued, though. Warfare became more common as Europeans and their descendants moved into the region.

✓ **READING CHECK:** Human Systems What are some of the different ways in which early American peoples adapted to their environments? depended on fish or buffalo, developed irrigation and water-storage systems, used adobe as building material, learned how to farm

Eastern Woodlands people created this snake-shaped mound in present-day Ohio. It is more than 400 yards long. Mounds like this one may have been used for burials.

Section Review 2

Define and explain: migrate, tepees, adobe, Anasazi, kiva, Cahokia, Iroquois League

Reading for the Main Idea
1. *Environment and Society* What did climate have to do with people coming to the Americas?
2. *Environment and Society* Why did early peoples of North America develop different ways of life?

Critical Thinking
3. **Making Predictions** How might drought have affected the Anasazi?
4. **Analyzing Information** What can the great earthen mounds of the Eastern Woodlands tell us about the societies that built them?

Homework Practice Online
Keyword: SJ5 HP4

Organizing What You Know
5. **Categorizing** Copy the following graphic organizer. Use it to list some culture features of the peoples who lived in each region.

Region	Culture Features
Northwest	
Great Plains	
Southwest	
Eastern Woodlands	

Section 2 Review

Answers to Section 2 Review

Define or identify For definitions and identifications, see the glossary and index.

Reading for the Main Idea
1. The cold climate of the ice ages caused huge ice sheets to form, which lowered the sea level, exposed dry land connecting Asia to North America, and enabled people from Asia to cross to America.
2. because North America has a variety of different environments, and environment affects how people live

Critical Thinking
3. may have led them to ration water, may have decreased harvests as a result of less water for irrigation, may have led to illness and death from lack of water or food, may have led them to move away (NGS 15)
4. To build such mounds, these societies must have been large, organized, and have good food supplies, tools, and some knowledge of engineering, surveying, and mathematics.

Organizing What You Know
5. Use the section content under Early Cultures of North America for answers.

CLOSE

Have students discuss which early culture of North America they would have wanted to live in, if given the choice. Students should use information from the text to explain their choices.

REVIEW, ASSESS, RETEACH

Have students complete the Section Review. Then have students work in pairs to review the early North American cultures described in this section. Partners should take turns telling each other about each culture. Then have students complete Daily Quiz 4.2.

Have students complete Main Idea Activity S2. Then ask students to create flashcards for the section's vocabulary terms and main ideas. **ESOL**

EXTEND

Organize students into small groups. Give each group a description of a hypothetical location. The description should provide information about the location's climate, landforms, vegetation, wildlife, and natural resources. Have the groups create descriptions of cultures that might develop in the locations. **BLOCK SCHEDULING**

CHAPTER 4, Section 3

SECTION 3 RESOURCES

Reproducibles
- Lecture Notes, Section 3
- Block Scheduling Handbook, Chapter 4
- Know It Notes S3
- Map Activity
- Biography Activity: Thomas Jefferson

Technology
- One-Stop Planner CD-ROM, Lesson 4.3
- Geography and Cultures Visual Resource 26
- HRW Go Site

Review, Reinforcement, and Assessment Resources
- Daily Quiz 4.3
- Main Idea Activity S3
- Chapter Summaries and Review
- English Audio Summary 4.3
- Spanish Audio Summary 4.3

Section 3: From Colonies to an Independent Country

Read to Discover
1. What roles did people of various cultures and occupations play in the American colonies?
2. Why did the American colonists fight the Revolutionary War?
3. What were the effects of American independence?

Vocabulary
colony
triangular trade
plantation
frontier
popular sovereignty
alliance
federal

People
Thomas Jefferson
George Washington

Reading Strategy

READING ORGANIZER As you read this section, make a flowchart of the steps that changed the American colonies into an independent country. Illustrate the flowchart when you have finished reading the section.

The American Colonies

Our history has been made by people from many different cultures. It begins with the first Americans you have just read about—the people who came to be known as Indians. Our country's history is filled with both earth-shattering and ordinary events. It is a story of great discoveries, courageous journeys, and sweeping political movements. However, war and suffering are also part of the story.

Puritan colonists from England built their first settlement in New England.

The New Colonists Beginning in the late 1400s Europeans from Spain, France, the Netherlands, and other countries started traveling to the Americas. During the late 1500s England also began claiming lands and establishing colonies. A **colony** is a territory controlled by people from a foreign land. In 1607 England established Jamestown, Virginia. In 1620, settlers founded Plymouth, Massachusetts. Sometimes the settlers and local Indians became friends. More often Indians and settlers fought.

Section 3

Objectives
1. Describe the roles that people of various cultures and occupations played in the American colonies.
2. Explain why the American colonists fought the Revolutionary War.
3. Analyze the effects of American Independence.

FOCUS

Bellringer

Write the following on the chalkboard: *Name five events that you think were important in early American history.* Discuss students' responses. As students name events, write them on the chalkboard. Keep a list of these events to refer to at the end of the section. Tell students that in Section 3 they will learn more about the people, events, and issues that helped shape the United States from its colonization to its emergence as an independent nation.

Building Vocabulary

Write the vocabulary terms on the chalkboard. Have students define each term. Next, ask students to group related terms into two to three categories. Students should provide a descriptive label for each category. Then ask volunteers to explain some of their categories to the class.

The Slave Trade Starting in 1619, enslaved Africans were brought to North America. Many others went to South America and the West Indies. The brutal traffic in human beings was part of a network called the **triangular trade**. Included in the network were England, West Africa, and England's American colonies. Raw materials flowed from North America and the West Indies to England, which sent manufactured goods to Africa. There traders exchanged the English products for slaves. When they arrived in the colonies, most of the Africans faced a very harsh life.

Most slaves worked in the southern colonies on plantations. A **plantation** is a large farm that grows mainly one crop to sell. Plantations were common in the southern colonies because of the area's rich soils and mild climates. Cotton and tobacco were the main plantation crops.

Life in the Colonies By the mid-1700s many British subjects lived in 13 colonies along the Atlantic coast. Some came in search of wealth. Others came seeking religious freedom. Settlers had also come from Scotland, Ireland, Germany, France, Sweden, and other countries. Many families worked small farms. The northern colonies—the New England and Middle colonies—became centers for trade, shipbuilding, and fishing. Boston and New York were major seaports.

Craftworkers such as blacksmiths also contributed to the economy. They produced a variety of goods. As the economies grew, colonists didn't need to import as many products from Great Britain.

Most of the people who came to America settled along the coast. As these areas became more crowded, people moved to the **frontier**. The frontier referred to land west of the colonies that wasn't yet settled by Europeans. These lands, however, were not empty. They were Indian lands.

The British weren't the only ones to take over Indian lands. The French and Spanish also claimed lands that had long been home to American Indians. The French had established a fur-trading business with some Indians. Many Indian tribes remained French allies for years.

▲ Enslaved Africans were brought to colonial Jamestown and other settlements. The trip across the Atlantic was filled with misery and hardship. Many Africans died on board the ships.

◄ This painting shows a southern plantation as a small community. **Interpreting the Visual Record** How do you think products from this plantation were sent to markets?

CHAPTER 4, Section 3

Across the Curriculum
LITERATURE

Gullah Folktales The coastal Islands of Georgia and South Carolina are home to a unique dialect and culture known as Gullah. This culture originated among enslaved West Africans who were brought to the coastal islands. The Gullah dialect is a combination of English and nearly 6,000 African words.

Gullah folktales are best known through the writing of Joel Chandler Harris and his "Uncle Remus" stories. Like Aesop's fables, many of these stories feature "critters" such as Brer Rabbit, who is a trickster. Unlike Aesop's fables, Uncle Remus tales were meant to entertain not to teach lessons. In the stories, Uncle Remus often cautions his listeners that the animals' conduct should not be taken as a model for how humans should behave.

Activity: Have students find and read a Gullah folktale and then summarize it for the class. If possible, find and play an audio recording of the Gullah dialect for the class as well.

◄ **Visual Record Answer**

based on the image, students might suggest by ship and wagon

TEACH

Teaching Objective 1

ALL LEVELS: (suggested time: 25 minutes) Have students identify the main European countries that established colonies in North America starting in the late 1400s (England, France, the Netherlands, and Spain). Next, ask students what other groups lived in the American colonies and surrounding areas (American Indians, enslaved Africans, and other Europeans). Have students examine the map on p. 92. Ask them to identify the 13 colonies and describe some differences between the southern colonies and the New England and Middle colonies.

Then ask students to imagine that their families have settled in one of the southern, New England, or Middle colonies. Have students write letters to friends in England that describes life in their region. The letter should include information about why people are coming to the colonies, the various groups who live in the region, and some of the main occupations of people in the colonies. **LS VERBAL/LINGUISTIC**

►**ASSIGNMENT:** Have each student write a few sentences describing the point of view of someone from each of the following groups toward European colonization in North America: American Indian living near the colonies, enslaved African brought to the colonies, French fur trader, and an English colonist.

CHAPTER 4, Section 3

Across the Curriculum
GOVERNMENT

Growing Colonial Resentment Until the Seven Years' War, Great Britain had intervened very little in the affairs of its American colonies. Only colonial governors and officials in charge of enforcing the Navigation Acts had any control in the colonies. Rather, the colonial assemblies set internal policies for the colonies and also determined the salaries of the colonies' British-appointed governors.

Critical Thinking: Ask students how the colonists' political experience was a factor in the outbreak of the American Revolution.

Answer: Many colonists, because of their political independence and government structures, resented Britain decreasing their independence and getting more involved in colonial government.

Map Answer

The need for access to the sea for trade and transportation determined the location of the colonies along the Atlantic coast. The Appalachian Mountains formed a barrier to further colonial expansion westward.

Visual Record Answer

with outrage and a growing call for independence from Great Britain

---

The Thirteen Colonies

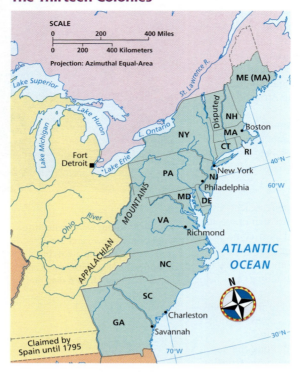

Interpreting the Map How did physical geography seem to affect the location and size of the 13 colonies?

This painting shows a scene of the Boston Massacre, March 5, 1770. British troops in Boston opened fire on an angry crowd, killing several.
Interpreting the Visual Record How do you think the people of Boston reacted to the Boston Massacre?

92 • Chapter 4

Trouble Brewing At the same time, British colonists were moving onto lands claimed by France. Britain and France had already been fighting wars in Europe for years. In 1754 their rivalry led to conflict in North America in what was called the French and Indian War. The British colonists fought not only French forces but also their Indian allies.

By 1763 Great Britain had won the war. However, it cost a great deal of money. To raise cash, the British Parliament placed new restrictions on the colonists and created new taxes. Many colonists protested, saying that Parliament had no right to tax them without the consent of their own colonial assemblies. They called the British policies "taxation without representation." Some colonists refused to buy British products.

A worried Parliament sent British soldiers to Boston to control the protests. However, each new British act only made the colonists angrier and more determined to work together. Slowly the 13 colonies were becoming united.

✓ **READING CHECK:** *Human Systems* What groups of people took part in the American colonies' development? *settlers from Spain, France, Netherlands, England, other countries; slaves from Africa; farmers, craftworkers, traders*

The American Revolution

The British colonists had developed new ways of life and a new relationship with their home country. Each colony held its own elections and made its own laws. The colonists were still British subjects, though.

Teaching Objective 2

LEVEL 1: (Suggested time: 15 min.) To help students explain why the American colonists fought the Revolutionary War, copy the following graphic organizer onto the chalkboard, omitting the blue answers. Have students complete the organizer by listing each of the factors that led to the outbreak of the American Revolution. **LS VISUAL-SPATIAL**

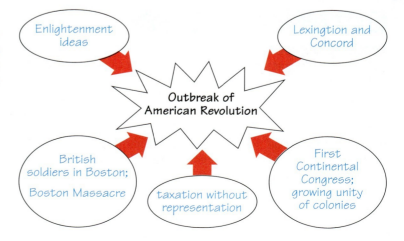

92 Chapter 4

At the same time, new ideas were developing among American and European thinkers. These philosophers proposed greater freedom and equality for the common people—ideas central to a movement called the Enlightenment. Enlightenment ideas helped inspire the American colonists to resist the British Parliament and the British king.

The Growing Conflict As their unhappiness increased, the colonists united against British rule. In 1774, 12 colonies sent representatives to the First Continental Congress. The Congress pledged to stop trade with Britain until the colonies gained representation in Parliament. The next year, however, British troops tried to seize guns and gunpowder from the colonists. At Lexington and Concord, near Boston, the British met armed resistance from the colonists. British soldiers and Americans died in the fighting.

Colonists who called themselves Patriots wanted full independence. They made up about one third of the population. The Loyalists, who made up another third, wanted to remain loyal to Britain. The rest were undecided.

The Declaration of Independence In July 1776, the Continental Congress adopted the Declaration of Independence. Thomas Jefferson was the Declaration's main author. The Declaration clearly showed the influence of Enlightenment thinkers. The document stated that "all men are created equal" and have the right to "life, liberty, and the pursuit of happiness." The ideal of individual liberty excluded women and slaves. Nevertheless, the Declaration was a great step toward equality and justice.

Enlightenment ideas about **popular sovereignty** were included in the Declaration. The phrase means that all powers of government come from the people. The Declaration said that no government can exist without the consent of those it governed and that government is created to protect individual rights. In addition, it stated that if a government fails to protect these rights, the people may change it and set up a new government—by force if necessary.

◀
This painting shows the Second Continental Congress in session. The congress not only adopted the Declaration of Independence, but also served as the new nation's first governing body. It issued currency, borrowed money, created a postal service, and started a navy.

CHAPTER 4, Section 3

Linking Past to Present

A Rich Man's War? Many historians note that the American Revolution was primarily a struggle for power among members of the upper class. Many of the colonial leaders who were at the forefront of the revolt belonged to the wealthy ruling class. George Washington, for instance, was the richest man in the thirteen colonies at the time. Yet, the majority of colonists who fought in the Revolutionary War were poor men. Several factors contributed to this situation. Wealthier men could avoid being drafted into the army by paying for substitutes, an option the less wealthy did not have. In addition, military service offered poorer men the potential to gain money, rank, and social status.

Critical Thinking: Ask students what current issues in American society and politics tend to be split between wealthier and poorer voters.

Answer: Students might mention issues such as school funding, tax rates and the capital gains tax, social security, and welfare.

LEVEL 2: (Suggested time: 20 min.) Ask students to imagine that they are one of the colonists calling for independence from Great Britain. Their fellow Patriots have asked them to create a broadside that clearly and briefly lists the colonists' complaints against Great Britain and urges the colonists to revolt. The broadside should include at least one image.
VERBAL-LINGUISTIC

LEVEL 3: (Suggested time: 30 min.) Ask students to imagine that they are one of the colonists calling for independence from Great Britain. Their fellow Patriots have asked them to give a speech urging other colonists to rise up against Great Britain and fight for independence. Have each student write a speech that outlines the colonists' complaints against Great Britain, explains why the colonists should revolt, and uses persuasive techniques to urge them to do so. Ask one or two volunteers to deliver their speeches to the class. **VERBAL-LINGUISTIC**

▶**ASSIGNMENT:** Have each student create a time line of the main events of the American Revolution, based on the information in the text. In addition, you might have students do research to provide information beyond that in the text. (Students' time lines should include the following: July 1776: Declaration of Independence; 1778: French ally with American Patriots; 1781: American forces defeat the main British army and win the war; 1783: Treaty of Paris.)

CHAPTER 4, Section 3

Across the Curriculum
GOVERNMENT

The U.S. Congress At the 1787 Constitutional Convention, delegates from the large states wanted representation in Congress to be based on population. Delegates from the small states objected, fearing they would have too little power in Congress. Instead, these delegates wanted all states to have the same representation. Eventually, the delegates reached an agreement called the Great Compromise. It called for a Congress with two parts, or houses—the House of Representatives and the Senate. In the House of Representatives, population would determine the number of each state's representatives. In the Senate, each state would have the same number of representatives.

Activity: Have students conduct research to identify the names of the U.S. senators and representatives from your state. Then have students contrast the number of their representatives with those from other states.

Biography Answer ▲

By serving as a citizen, Washington helped lead the United States during its fight for independence and early nationhood.

Visual Record Answer ▶

his sword, symbolic of surrender

BIOGRAPHY
George Washington
(1732–99)

Character Trait: Citizenship

As the first president of the United States, George Washington is known as the Father of His Country. Washington was also the commander in chief of the Continental Army during the Revolutionary War. Washington was admired for his heroism and honesty as a general. Representatives at the Constitutional Convention chose him to preside over their meetings. Washington was then unanimously elected president in 1789. After serving two terms as president, Washington died only three years into his retirement at his Mount Vernon estate in Virginia. **How did George Washington demonstrate the value of citizenship?**

▶ British General John Burgoyne surrendered his army to American Patriot General Horatio Gates at Saratoga, New York, on October 17, 1777.
Interpreting the Visual Record In the painting, what is Burgoyne handing over to the Americans?

War and Peace When the Declaration of Independence was written, the colonies were already at war with Great Britain. At first, the British forces seemed unbeatable. Then in 1778 the French formed an **alliance** with the Americans. An alliance is an agreement made to help both partners. By aiding the United States, France hoped to weaken its enemy Britain.

In 1781 American forces under General George Washington and their French allies defeated the main British army. The Americans had won the Revolutionary War. Peace terms were settled in the Treaty of Paris in 1783. Britain recognized the independence of the United States. All British land east of the Mississippi was granted to the new nation.

✓ **READING CHECK:** *Human Systems* How did the Enlightenment influence the American Revolution? *proposed greater freedom and equality for the common people*

Effects of American Independence

In 1777, the Americans adopted a plan of government called the Articles of Confederation. The Articles set up a central government, but it was weak on purpose. Many Americans didn't trust a central government to protect the individual rights and liberties they had fought for in the Revolution. Thus Congress could not raise taxes or coin money. It could not regulate trade. Within 10 years, however, it was clear that the lack of a strong central government kept the country from working as a whole.

In May 1787, delegates from all the states met at a convention in Philadelphia to revise the Articles. The delegates soon realized that making changes in the Articles would not be enough. They decided instead to write a new constitution.

After the delegates chose George Washington to preside over the convention, they went to work. The new Constitution they

Teaching Objective 3

ALL LEVELS: (suggested time: 20 min.) Have each student fold a piece of paper horizontally in thirds. Tell students to unfold the paper and draw a line separating the bottom third of the paper from the top two thirds. Then have students draw a line down the middle of the top section to divide it in half vertically. In the top left section, have students describe the Articles of Confederation. In the top right section, have students describe the U.S. Constitution. Students' descriptions might include words, phrases, symbols, and images. When students have finished the activity, have the class compare and contrast the Articles of Confederation and the U.S. Constitution. Then have each student summarize the effects of American independence in the bottom section. **ESOL,** **LS** **VISUAL-SPATIAL**

CLOSE

Ask students to name the two to three events covered in this section that they think were the most significant in American history. Have students compare this list to the list that they compiled at the start of the section and discuss reasons or explanations for differences between the two.

wrote set up a **federal** system of government. This is a system in which power is divided between a central government and individual states. The central government was given several basic powers. It can raise taxes, declare war, raise armies, make treaties, coin money, and regulate trade with other countries. The states and the people keep most other powers. The federal government has three branches. Each branch acts as a check on the power of the others. The legislative branch makes the laws. The executive branch enforces the laws. The judicial branch interprets the laws.

Some states wouldn't ratify, or approve, the new Constitution until it guaranteed several individual freedoms. These were included in the first 10 amendments, or changes, to the Constitution. Among them are freedom of religion, freedom of speech, and freedom of the press. As a group, the amendments are known as the Bill of Rights. The Constitution was approved in 1789.

The American Revolution and the writing of the U.S. Constitution were major events in world history. Enlightenment ideas had actually been put into practice. The success of the American nation also encouraged people elsewhere to fight for political freedoms. Of course, American democracy in 1789 wasn't perfect. Women had few rights, and slavery was legal. Still, the world now had a new country that inspired the loyalty of most of its citizens.

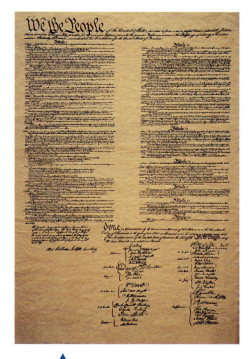

"We the People" begins this signed copy of the U.S. Constitution.

✓ **READING CHECK:** *Human Systems* How was the new Constitution different from the old Articles of Confederation? **set up a stronger central government, included a Bill of Rights**

Define or identify: colony, triangular trade, plantation, frontier, Thomas Jefferson, popular sovereignty, alliance, George Washington, federal

Reading for the Main Idea
1. *Environment and Society* How did the physical geography of the northern and southern colonies affect ways of life?
2. *Human Systems* Why did the American colonists demand better treatment from Parliament?
3. *Human Systems* How did the American Revolution and the writing of the U.S. Constitution affect other countries?

Critical Thinking
4. **Finding the Main Idea** What were the basic ideas stated in the Declaration of Independence?

Organizing What You Know
5. **Summarizing** Copy the time line below into your notebook. Use it to list some important dates, periods, and events that occurred from the 1490s to 1789.

1490s ——————————————————— 1789

Section 3 Review

Answers to Section 3 Review

Define or identify For definitions or identifications, see the glossary and index.

Reading for the Main Idea physical geography affect ways of life
1. southern colonies—farming main way of life because of the area's rich soils and mild climates; northern colonies—centers for trade, shipbuilding, and fishing because of the area's seaports and colder climates
2. because Parliament had placed new restrictions and taxes on the colonists without the consent of their colonial assemblies
3. encouraged people elsewhere to fight for political freedoms

Critical Thinking
4. Enlightenment ideas of equality, individual rights, and popular sovereignty

Organizing What You Know
5. Use section content to find events of the late 1400s, late 1500s, 1607, 1619, 1620, mid-1700s, 1754–63, late 1760s–1770s, 1774, 1775–83, 1776, 1777, 1781, 1783, 1787, and 1789.

REVIEW, ASSESS, RETEACH

Have students complete the Section Review. Then have each student list on separate slips of paper significant events discussed in this section. Collect the slips and have students take turns drawing two of the slips of paper and telling which event occurred first. Then have students complete Daily Quiz 4.3.

Have students complete Main Idea Activity S3. Then write the following headings on the chalkboard: *The New Colonists, The Slave Trade, Life in the Colonies, Trouble Brewing, The Growing Conflict, The Declaration of Independence, War and Peace,* and *Effects of American Independence.* Call on students to supply a short summary of the material under each heading.

EXTEND

Have students use the library and other resources to research a major figure, battle, or event of the American Revolution. Then ask students to imagine that they worked for a Patriot newspaper during the war. Have each student either write an editorial or draw a political cartoon from the colonial viewpoint about the person, battle, or event that they researched.
BLOCK SCHEDULING

CHAPTER 4, Section 4

SECTION 4 RESOURCES

Reproducibles
- Lecture Notes, Section 4
- Block Scheduling Handbook, Chapter 4
- Know It Notes S4
- Readings in World Geography, History, and Culture, Reading 12
- Biography Activity: Martin Luther King, Jr.

Technology
- One-Stop Planner CD-ROM, Lesson 4.4
- Geography and Cultures Visual Resources 26, 30
- Homework Practice Online
- HRW Go Site

Review, Reinforcement, and Assessment Resources
- Section 4 Review
- Daily Quiz 4.4
- Main Idea Activity S4
- Chapter Summaries and Review
- English Audio Summary 4.4
- Spanish Audio Summary 4.4

Section 4: The United States Becomes a World Power

Read to Discover
1. Who took part in westward expansion, and what drew these people west?
2. What were the main causes and results of the Civil War?
3. What events marked the 1900s?
4. What are some of the challenges that face the United States in the 2000s?

Vocabulary

pioneers
seceded
Emancipation Proclamation
tenements
Roaring Twenties
Great Depression
New Deal
Allied Powers
United Nations
Cold War

Reading Strategy

FOLDNOTES: FOUR-CORNER FOLD   Create the FoldNote titled **Four-Corner Fold** described in the Appendix. Before you read, write each of the headings in this section on a flap. As you read, write down details on the paper under each flap.

This painting by American artist Albert Bierstadt (1830–1902) shows a group of pioneers heading west across the Great Plains.

Albert Bierstadt, *Emigrants Crossing the Plains*, 1867, oil on canvas, AO1.IT: The National Cowboy Hall of Fame and Western Heritage Center, Oklahoma City, OK

Westward Expansion

While Great Britain still ruled the 13 Colonies, the British had tried to keep Americans east of the Appalachian Mountains. After the Revolution, however, rich farmland between the mountains and the Mississippi River attracted American farmers. As a result, during the 1790s and 1800s Americans began to cross the Appalachians in large numbers.

These new settlers were called **pioneers**. They were people who were leading the way into new areas. Settlement spread westward as the boundaries of the United States shifted. By the 1820s, pioneers had crossed the Mississippi River and settled as far south as Texas. By the mid-1800s, the country stretched from the Atlantic to the Pacific coast.

Section 4

Objectives
1. Identify who took part in westward expansion and explain what drew these people west.
2. Summarize the main causes and results of the Civil War.
3. Identify the events that marked the 1900s.
4. Describe some of the challenges that face the U.S. in the 2000s.

FOCUS

 Bellringer

Write the following on the chalkboard: *What do you think are some major challenges facing the United States today? List at least two.* Discuss students' responses. Make a list of the challenges. Tell students that in Section 4 they will learn more about the history of the United States during the 1800s and 1900s and up to the present.

Building Vocabulary

Write the vocabulary terms **Emancipation Procla-Proclamation, Roaring Twenties, Great Depression, New Deal, United Nations,** and **Cold War** on the chalkboard. Have students define each term. Then ask students to organize the terms along a time line.

The government sold land cheaply or gave it away to encourage people to settle in new areas. Many people arrived on the Pacific coast after gold was discovered in California in 1848. However, few people settled in the deserts and mountains of the western United States or in the Great Plains. This area was called the Great American Desert by those who thought it was too dry to support farming.

As pioneers moved westward they began to have bitter conflicts with American Indians. Many American Indians did not own land as individuals. Instead, they considered land a shared resource. As settlers occupied and divided up the land, they pushed American Indians farther west or, later, onto reservations. Many died from warfare or from diseases carried by settlers.

Migration from Other Areas People from places besides the original 13 colonies also played a role in the country's growth. Spaniards had arrived in the south and southwest starting in the 1500s. In fact, Saint Augustine, Florida, is North America's oldest European settlement. By the 1700s, California, New Mexico, Arizona, and Texas had Spanish missions and settlers. French colonists lived in Louisiana. From across the Bering Strait, Russians established outposts as far south as California and as far north as Alaska. Of course, immigrants continued to arrive in the Atlantic ports also.

✓ READING CHECK: **Environment and Society** What drew pioneers across the Appalachian Mountains? *rich farmland sold cheaply or given away, discovery of gold in California*

The Civil War and After

By 1830, factories were sprouting across the northeastern United States. Industries and railroads spread. In the South, however, the economy was based on slave labor, tobacco, and cotton. The North, with its factories and large cities, had less use for slave labor. Economic differences between the North and South, and the South's insistence on maintaining slavery, eventually led to war.

The Slavery Issue Pioneers pushed farther west. New states were organized. As states entered the Union, bitter arguments raged over whether they would allow slavery. The Missouri Compromise of 1820 let Missouri enter the Union as a slave state. It also prohibited slavery in parts of U.S. territory in the West. Many people, however, wanted to abolish slavery completely. As the election of 1860 approached, the issue of slavery threatened to rip the country apart.

This painting shows a typical textile mill. Water turned wheels that powered the factory's machinery.
Interpreting the Visual Record How do you think textile mills affected life in towns like the one shown?

CHAPTER 4, Section 4

GLOBAL PERSPECTIVES

Civil War in World History
The American Civil War, in which the one part of the nation fought for independence from the other, illustrates one kind of civil war. Another more common type of civil war is the kind that occurs when factions, or groups, within a country struggle for control of the nation. For example, in the English Civil War, fought in the 1640s and 1650s, Parliament established supremacy over the monarchy, which remains the situation today. In recent times, the secession of Bosnia from Yugoslavia in 1992, and the struggle between the Tutsis and Hutus for control in Rwanda in 1994, both led to civil wars.

◀ **Visual Record Answer**
provided jobs, improved the economy, perhaps increased pollution

---

TEACH

Teaching Objective 1

LEVEL 1: (Suggested time: 15 min.) Pair students and have each pair create a cause-and-effect chart for westward expansion before the Civil War. *(causes—rich farmland between the Appalachians and the Mississippi River attracted farmers; cheap or free land; discovery of gold in California in 1848; expansion of French, Spanish, and Russian settlement; effects—frontier and U.S. boundaries gradually moved west until the United States stretched from the Atlantic to the Pacific coast; American Indians pushed further west and eventually onto reservations; many American Indians died from warfare or from diseases).*
COOPERATIVE LEARNING, **LS** VISUAL-SPATIAL

LEVELS 2 AND 3: (Suggested time: 30 min.) Lead students in a discussion of who took part in westward expansion and what drew these people west. Then have students create print advertisements urging people to go west. Students should create one advertisement for each of the causes of western expansion. *(See the Level 1 activity on this page.)* Encourage students to include one or more images in their advertisements. Have volunteers share their ads with the class.

CHAPTER 4, Section 4

DAILY LIFE

Juneteenth: Celebrating Slavery's End On June 19, 1865, nearly one month after the Civil War had ended, the news finally spread to enslaved African Americans in Texas that they were free. As slaves learned the news, celebrations broke out. In Texas, the date of June 19 became known as Juneteenth. Texas African Americans celebrated Juneteenth with parades, picnics, dances, blues festivals, and other events. In 1980, Juneteenth became an official Texas state holiday. Some other states have begun celebrating Juneteenth as well.

Activity: Have students find out if Juneteenth is observed in their state or community. If so, have them write a brief report on the activities that are part of the holiday. If not, have them consider starting a Juneteenth celebration in their school or community.

Visual Record Answer

Union point of view, because the painting shows Union soldiers charging, fighting, and dying heroically, while two American flags remind the viewer of the reason for the war—to protect the Union

Biography Answer

by being tolerant to criticism, open-minded to other points of view, and working with others despite personal differences or disagreements

▲
During the Civil War soldiers on each side were often ordered to attack well-defended positions. This led to many casualties.
Interpreting the Visual Record Whose point of view do you think the artist is trying to portray? Why?

In 1860, Abraham Lincoln was elected president. Lincoln thought that slavery was evil and unjust. He opposed its spread. In response, South Carolina **seceded**, or withdrew from, the United States. Other southern states soon followed. They formed the Confederate States of America.

Lincoln argued that states had no right under the U.S. Constitution to secede. He said that the government must put down the rebellion. In 1861, the long, bloody Civil War began. As fighting started, both sides had advantages. The North had more money, soldiers, and railways. The South, however, had many skilled officers and was fighting a defensive war. Both sides suffered terribly, though, as hundreds of thousands of people died, families were divided, and property was destroyed. The Civil War finally ended in 1865 when the Confederacy surrendered. Bitter feelings about the war lasted, however, far into the next century.

During the war, Lincoln issued the **Emancipation Proclamation**. This document freed slaves in the states that were in rebellion. After the war, amendments to the Constitution were approved that ended slavery and guaranteed the former slaves' rights. However, for many former slaves, life didn't get much better.

Abraham Lincoln (1809–1865) **Character Trait: Fairness**

President Abraham Lincoln was known for his fairness toward others. Lincoln not only tolerated strong criticism from the press and political opponents, but he also stayed open-minded about differing points of view. For instance, some members of his cabinet were former Republican rivals. Lincoln had a talent for smoothing over personal differences and remaining loyal to those with whom he disagreed. His speeches embodied this spirit in his famous words "with malice toward none, with charity for all."
In what ways did Abraham Lincoln show fairness?

Teach Objective 2

LEVEL 1: (Suggested time: 15 min.) To help students identify the main causes and effects of the Civil War, copy the following graphic organizer onto the chalkboard, omitting the blue answers. Have students complete the organizer by listing each of the war's main causes and effects. Review the answers as a class. **LS VISUAL-SPATIAL**

CAUSES
• slavery issue and abolition movement
• growing division between North and South
• 1860 election of Abraham Lincoln as president
• secession of South Carolina, other southern states

⬇

EFFECTS
• loss of thousands of lives
• many families divided
• destruction and devastation, especially in the South
• end of slavery
• remaining bitterness between North and South

Growth and Expansion after the War Most of the Civil War had been fought in the South. It took a long time for the South to recover and rebuild. In the meantime, the rest of the country changed rapidly.

Immigrants continued to pour into the United States. During the mid-1800s, revolution or hunger troubled parts of Europe. Millions of people fled to the United States for a better life. Ireland and Germany were the main sources of immigrants. For example, more than 1.5 million people left Ireland for the United States within a seven-year period. These Europeans were desperate for work.

They found jobs in the country's growing industries, especially in the northeastern cities. Life was hard, though, for the immigrants. Most spoke no English. Many lived in crowded, dark, dirty apartment houses called **tenements**. Some suffered discrimination and violence. Still they came, making the United States the most diverse country in the world.

Technology and the West The first transcontinental railroad was completed in 1869. It linked the east and west coasts. Railroads made it much easier to move goods and people across the country. They also allowed major cities to develop far from navigable rivers.

With new agricultural machinery, farms required fewer workers but could produce more food than before. Irrigation and better plows allowed farmers to grow crops in the country's dry interior. As a result, people began to settle in the Great Plains too.

✓ **READING CHECK:** *The Uses of Geography* Why did many immigrants come to American cities during the 1800s? **looking for jobs, fleeing revolution or hunger**

▲ The development of steamships during the second half of the 1800s allowed a great increase in immigration to the United States. In this image from the late 1800s, immigrants land at Ellis Island, New York.

Interpreting the Visual Record How can you tell that the voyage was difficult for the immigrants in the painting?

◀ On May 10, 1869, the Union Pacific and Central Pacific railroads met at Promontory Point, Utah, joining East Coast to West.

CHAPTER 4, Section 4

HUMAN SYSTEMS

Ellis Island In 1875 the U.S. government built facilities for "processing" immigrants on Ellis Island. This tiny Island is located in New York Harbor and named for Sam Ellis, a merchant who lived during the American Revolution. The first immigrant to enter the United States through Ellis Island was 15-year-old Annie Moore of County Cork, Ireland. She arrived on January 1892.

In all, more than 12 million immigrants entered the United States through Ellis Island before the facilities closed in 1954. Some 40 percent of U.S. citizens can now trace their ancestry to someone who came through Ellis Island. Today the facilities are a museum where visitors can search an immigration database to look for ancestors.

▲ **Visual Record Answer**
because of the immigrants' tired, haggard faces and many burdens

---

ALL LEVELS: (Suggested time: 45 min.) Lead students in a discussion of the Civil War. As part of the discussion, have students identify and explain the war's main causes and effects (causes—slavery issue, sectionalism, abolition movement, Lincoln's election, secession of southern states; effects—loss of thousands of lives; many families divided; property destruction, particularly in the South; end of slavery; long time for the South to rebuild and recover; remaining bitterness between the South and the North). Then have each student either draw a picture or write a poem or lyrics to the tune of an existing song from the point of view of a former slave celebrating his or her freedom. **LS VERBAL-LINGUISTIC, VISUAL-SPATIAL**

TEACHER TO TEACHER

Brian Callahan of Patterson, New York, suggests this activity to help students learn more about the issues that led to the Civil War. Have students conduct research on John Brown's raid and then hold a mock trial of John Brown. Assign students the roles of Brown, defense attorneys, prosecutors, and jury members. If needed, other students can act as newspaper reporters covering the trial. As in a real trial, all evidence discovered by the prosecution must be shared with the defense team. In addition, remind prosecutors and defense attorneys to base their arguments on logic and the facts. Ask a teacher from another class to act as the judge for the trial.
COOPERATIVE LEARNING, LS LOGICAL-MATHEMATICAL

CHAPTER 4, Section 4

HUMAN SYSTEMS

The Crash of '29 The stock market crash of 1929 set in motion a chain of events that let to the Great Depression. After the crash, many investors panicked and sold their stocks. Soon, Americans began rushing to banks to withdraw their savings, only to find the banks did not have enough cash on hand to give everyone their money. Banks began demanding that borrowers repay their loans, but many borrowers did not have the money to do so. Soon, the entire U.S. economy was in crisis.

African American soldiers fought during World War I. The French government awarded these men the Croix de Guerre (krwah-di-GER), or "Cross of war," for their bravery.

These photos show the misery of the Great Depression. On the left, a man sells apples to earn a little money. The photo on the right shows the struggles many farm families faced.

The 1900s

In the 1900s, the United States experienced big social, economic, political, and technological changes. Some of those changes were painful. The twentieth century's first major crisis began in 1914, when several European countries went to war. At first this conflict was called The Great War. Later it became known as World War I.

War and Depression The United States joined the fighting in 1917, on the side of Britain and France. The main enemy was Germany, which was finally defeated in 1918. U.S. losses were low compared to Europe's. In the peace treaty that ended the war, the European victors punished Germany. They felt Germany had started the war and should pay for it.

During the 1920s, business boomed in the United States. Many Americans enjoyed wealth and good times. In fact, the decade was called the **Roaring Twenties**. The fun didn't last, however, because it was based in part on risky business practices. In 1929 the stock market crashed. This event marked the beginning of the **Great Depression**. Eventually, millions of Americans were out of work. Others lost their life savings, their farms, or their homes. Because countries' economies had become connected, the Depression became a worldwide event.

Franklin D. Roosevelt became president during the Depression. He began government-funded jobs programs to put Americans back to work. Roosevelt called his plan for ending the Depression the **New Deal**. By the end of the 1930s, the economy was recovering. However, the Depression didn't end in the United States until World War II began.

Teach Objective 3

ALL LEVELS: (Suggested time: 20 min.) Have students choose an event or discovery of the 1900s that they think most changed people's lives in the United States. Then have them draw pictures to illustrate the event and its effects on American society. Call on volunteers to share and explain their choices. **ESOL,** LS **VISUAL-SPATIAL**

LEVEL 2: (Suggested time: 35 min.) Have students write a series of newspaper headlines for each of the main events that marked the 1900s. You might want to review with students proper headline style and model the activity for one event. Then have each student select the headline for one of the most significant events of the century and write a newspaper article to go with the headline. Encourage students to conduct research to learn more about the event. LS **VERBAL-LINGUISTIC**

◀ The quiet of a Sunday morning was shattered when about 360 Japanese planes attacked Pearl Harbor. The U.S. military suffered more than 2,300 people killed, more than 188 aircraft destroyed, and 19 naval vessels sunk or damaged.
Interpreting the Visual Record How do you think most American citizens reacted to news of the attack?

World War II Germany suffered terribly during the Depression. Many Germans also wanted revenge for the harsh treatment their country received in the World War I peace treaty. The Nazi Party took advantage of these emotions. Under their leader, Adolf Hitler, the Nazis pushed Germany into war. World War II began September 1, 1939, when Germany invaded Poland. Great Britain and France—the **Allied Powers**—stood against Germany and its allies Italy and Japan. The Soviet Union joined the Allies later.

The Nazis had other targets also. They killed about 6 million Jews. People with mental illness, gypsies, and political opponents were among the Nazis' other victims.

Meanwhile, Japan wanted to create an empire in Asia. On December 7, 1941, Japan attacked a U.S. naval base at Pearl Harbor, in Hawaii. The United States promptly declared war on the side of the Allied Powers, or Allies. U.S. forces fought both in Europe and in the Pacific. In June of 1944 the Allies launched an invasion of German-held territory in Europe. After another year of fierce combat, Germany surrendered. War in the Pacific continued, however. In August 1945, the United States dropped atomic bombs on two Japanese cities. Japan surrendered soon after.

World War II was a human disaster. Although no one knows the exact number, probably about 50 million people lost their lives. Many of those were civilians. Millions more were left homeless. In an effort to prevent future wars, 51 countries formed a new organization—the **United Nations**. The UN was created to keep the peace among nations and to punish aggressors.

CHAPTER 4, Section 4

COOPERATIVE LEARNING

Pearl Harbor Focus students' attention on the photo on this page and discuss what it would have been like to experience this horrific event. Then organize the class into groups to conduct further research on Pearl Harbor. Here are some possibilities for groups' topics: warnings about the attack, heroic actions of Americans under attack, assessments of damage done, the affect on Americans' sentiments, and the site today. Ask each group to present an illustrated report.

◀ **Visual Record Answer**

with horror, grief, and outrage, and calls for war against Japan

---

LEVEL 3: (Suggested time: 35 min.) Organize students into small groups. Have each group make a list of the main events that marked the 1900s. Then tell each group to discuss the event that they think was the most significant and prepare logical arguments to support their choice. Tell students to prepare to defend their arguments as well. Have each group present its choice and arguments to the class. Encourage other students to question the group and force it to defend its arguments.
COOPERATIVE LEARNING, **LS** **LOGICAL-MATHEMATICAL**

▶**ASSIGNMENT:** Have each student interview a parent, grandparent, or other adult to learn which event of the 1900s the adult thinks was the most significant. Tell students they should ask why the adult feels this way. Students might want to tape record or videotape their interviews, if the interviewee agrees. Have students share their findings with the class.

CHAPTER 4, Section 4

FOOD FESTIVAL

Changing Food Fashions
Have students interview parents or other adults to find how food fashions and cooking methods have changed over time. (Examples: convenience foods, TV dinners, fast food, the fondue craze, and so on.) Invite students to bring samples to share with the class. Interested students may also conduct research on how kitchens have changed over time (electric and gas stoves replacing wood burners; refrigerators replacing ice boxes).

Challenge students to identify connections between changes in eating and cooking habits and changes in society. (Example: Convenience foods became popular when women began to work outside of the home.)

Magazine covers illustrate 20th-century events. The top two relate to the civil rights movement. The bottom one refers to an unsuccessful U.S.-sponsored invasion of Communist Cuba.

The Postwar World Unlike much of the world, North America had not been a battlefield. U.S. supplies and troops had played big roles in winning the war. In addition, the U.S. economy was intact. As a result, after World War II the United States was the most powerful country in the world.

A new war threatened, though—the **Cold War**. The United States and the Soviet Union, which had a communist government, became rivals for power and influence. Both countries built up huge military forces and developed nuclear weapons. The two countries never actually went to war against each other. However, they supported different sides in conflicts around the world. The Cold War would end decades later when the Soviet Union collapsed.

The 1950s and 1960s saw the rise of the civil rights movement. One of its most important leaders was the Reverend Martin Luther King Jr., who fought discrimination with nonviolent means. The government ended many forms of segregation and discrimination. Hispanics, American Indians, and women also fought for and won gains in the fight for equal treatment and equal opportunity.

✓ **READING CHECK:** (Human Systems) What role did the United States play in the wars of the 1900s?
played large role in victories of World Wars I and II

Into the 2000s

In the late 1900s, daily life changed in many ways. Air travel became commonplace, making the world a "global village." Personal computers became available to millions of Americans. The Internet and cellular phones linked people instantly. These technologies created huge new industries. Still, industrial growth and international influence have brought problems with them into the twenty-first century. As the United States moves further into the 2000s, it confronts several issues.

Political Issues at Home U.S. citizens enjoy a high standard of living. More than ever, most Americans can look forward to the future. Still, problems remain to be solved. Discrimination limits the lives of some people. Poverty, unemployment, and access to health care are still serious issues.

102 • Chapter 4

Teach Objective 4

ALL LEVELS: (Suggested time: 30 min.) Students will need old magazines, newspapers, and poster boards to complete this activity. On the chalkboard, draw a three-column chart and label the columns *Political Issues at Home, Environmental Issues,* and *Global Political Issues.* Ask students to identify some of the challenges that face the United States in the 2000s. As students identify the challenges, list them in their appropriate category. Then have each student create a triptych collage that visually represents the information in the chart. **ESOL,** **LS** **VISUAL-SPATIAL**

LEVELS 2 AND 3: Students will need to conduct research to complete this activity. Organize students into small groups and assign each group one of the challenges that faces the United States in the 2000s, based on the text. Have each group conduct research on its challenge and then prepare a bulletin board or large triptych providing information about it. Groups should assign members specific roles and tasks. Set up the groups' completed work in the classroom and have students tour the material. **COOPERATIVE LEARNING,** **LS** **INTERPERSONAL**

102 Chapter 4

Environmental Issues More industry, more cars, more people—along with benefits come drawbacks, including environmental damage. Americans are asking serious questions about the environment. Can U.S. prosperity be maintained if we don't conserve our natural resources? Will we lose our quality of life if we don't keep our air and water clean and preserve our wilderness for future generations?

Global Political Issues At the beginning of the twenty-first century, terrorism became a major threat to world peace. In 2003, U.S. military forces invaded Iraq. They were sent to prevent Iraq from using chemical and biological weapons. The initial invasion deposed Saddam Hussein, Iraq's brutal ruler. However, some Iraqis and terrorists from other countries continued to target American soldiers. The U.S. government's responses to the threat of terrorism have raised other questions. Arguments over personal freedoms and the role of government concern many Americans.

As the most powerful country in the world, the United States has often been involved in conflicts abroad. In some of those events deadly opposition has plagued U.S. forces. At other times the United States has protected innocent civilians or helped bring peace to a war-torn region.

✓ **READING CHECK:** *The Uses of Geography* What are some problems the United States faces as it moves further into the 2000s? *political issues at home, environmental issues, global political issues, especially terrorism*

▲ Firefighters played a key role in the search and recovery efforts at the site of the September 11, 2001, terrorist attacks on the World Trade Center in New York.

Homework Practice Online
Keyword: SJ5 HP4

Section Review 4

Define and explain: pioneers, seceded, Emancipation Proclamation, tenements, Roaring Twenties, Great Depression, New Deal, Allied Powers, United Nations, Cold War

Reading for the Main Idea
1. *Places and Regions* Why did pioneers push westward across North America?
2. *The Uses of Geography* What basic differences between North and South caused the Civil War?
3. *Human Systems* What was life like for European immigrants to the northeastern cities?

Critical Thinking
4. **Supporting a Point of View** Which challenges of the 2000s do you think are the most serious? Why?

Organizing What You Know
5. **Sequencing** Copy the step diagram below into your notebook. Use it to place in order and describe important events of the 1900s. Add more boxes as needed.

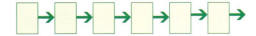

Section 4 Review

Answers to Section 4 Review

Define or identify For definitions or identifications, see the glossary and index.

Reading for the Main Idea
1. rich farmland available at cheap prices or for free; 1848 discovery of gold in California
2. North—more industrialized economy, little need for slave labor; South—agricultural economy based on slave labor; insistence on maintaining slavery
3. hard because few immigrants spoke English; many lived in crowded, dark, dirty tenements; and some suffered discrimination and violence

Critical Thinking
4. Answers will vary, but challenges include poverty, unemployment, access to health care, pollution and environmental damage, terrorism, government restrictions on personal freedoms, and conflicts abroad. LA.2.3.1

Organizing What You Know
5. Students should list and describe the following events: World War I, Roaring Twenties, Great Depression, Roosevelt's New Deal, World War II, creation of the United Nations, the Cold War, and the civil rights movement.

CLOSE
Have students discuss challenges not mentioned in the text that they think the United States faces today. Encourage students to discuss how the challenges affect them and ways to address the challenges.

REVIEW, ASSESS, RETEACH
Have students complete the Section Review. Then pair students and have each pair create an outline based on the material covered in this section. Have partners take turns using the outline to give an oral summary of the information. Then have students complete Daily Quiz 4.4.

Have students complete Main Idea Activity S4. Then ask each student to compile two multiple-choice questions for each of this section's Read to Discover question. Remind students to provide the answer to each question as well.

EXTEND
Have interested students conduct further research on daily life in a particular decade of American history that is covered in this section. Direct students to focus their attention on changes or developments that occurred during their chosen decade. Have students create posters, dioramas, triptychs, or multimedia displays to present their findings. **BLOCK SCHEDULING**

CHAPTER 4

COOPERATIVE LEARNING

Memorial Art Around the World After the class has read "Art and Memories," call on a volunteer to reread the first paragraph to the class. You may want to ask students if they have seen such statues in their own communities or in places they have visited. Then organize the class into small groups to study memorial statues in other countries. The following are three famous memorial statues that you might want to suggest: a concrete statue more than 170 feet tall of Mother Russia in Volgograd, Russia; a bronze statue in London of Queen Boudicca, who led a revolt against the Romans in A.D. 60; and a statue of the Burghers of Calais in Calais, France. The burghers were local leaders who offered their lives to save the rest of the town in the 1300s. Students may locate other examples.

Have each group conduct research on their selected statue's creator and subject matter. Groups should also find out more about the statue's construction and other interesting details. Have each group report its findings to the class.

Connecting to Art

Art and Memories

Throughout history, people have created statues to help them remember past events. Some of these monuments remind us of tragedies and of the sacrifices made by our fellow citizens. For hundreds, even thousands of years, most of these memorial works of art have been fairly realistic statues of people. For example, the ancient Greeks and Romans carved statues of soldiers who died in battle. Your city may have a similar monument—perhaps a bronze statue dedicated to local citizens who served in World War II.

In Washington, D.C., the Vietnam Veterans Memorial honors the men and women who gave their lives during the Vietnam War. A college student named Maya Lin designed the main feature of the memorial—a wall made of two black granite panels. Each panel is more than 246 feet long. Etched into the dark rock are the names of the 58,226 Americans who died in Vietnam. The monument was controversial at first because it was very different from the traditional style for memorials. Since then, millions of Americans have come to appreciate the new design. In fact, they have made it their own by leaving mementos at the wall. Among the thousands of items that have been left there are children's toys, family photographs, birthday cards, and battered combat boots.

On April 19, 1995, 168 Americans died in a terrorist attack on the Murrah Building in Oklahoma City, Oklahoma. Like the Vietnam wall, the design for the Oklahoma City National Memorial didn't follow traditional styles. Instead, nine rows of chairs, one for each of the victims, are silent

Memorial Day and Veterans Day draw many visitors to the Vietnam Veterans Memorial.

104 • Chapter 4

LEVEL 1: (Suggested time: 15 min.) Lead a class discussion to find out what students already know about the Vietnam War, the Oklahoma City bombing, and the September 11, 2001 attack on the World Trade Center. Then ask students how well they think the memorials reflect those events.
ESOL, LS VISUAL-SPATIAL

LEVEL 2: (Suggested time: 30 min.) Point out that in many museums visitors rent earphones through which they can hear speeches, news broadcasts, or music related to the museum's displays. Challenge students to write song lyrics for music that visitors to the three memorials discussed here could hear while viewing them. **LS AUDITORY-MUSICAL**

The empty chairs of the Oklahoma City National Memorial symbolize the loss felt by the victims' families and friends. Each bronze, stone, and glass chair bears the name of one of the Murrah Building victims.

This picture shows what designers and architects have planned for the World Trade Center site in New York City. The view is from the southeast.

reminders of the horror. To commemorate the children who died in the tragedy, 19 of the chairs are smaller than the others.

The United States experienced another tragedy with the terrorist attacks on the World Trade Center in New York City on September 11, 2001. Soon after that terrible day, visitors began leaving candles, notes, flowers, and other tributes on a nearby fence. To create a permanent memorial, thousands of people would also participate. Artists around the world submitted designs for the memorial to the lives lost. In 2004, a panel of experts that included Maya Lin announced the winner from over 5,200 entries.

The winning design, called *Reflecting Absence*, will be built on the site where the World Trade Center Twin Towers once stood. The memorial includes two reflecting pools and the names of those who died in the attack.

Understanding What You Read

1. How do memorial designs of recent years differ from traditional designs?
2. How have Americans shown their respect for the people who lost their lives in the Vietnam War and the terrorist attacks?

CHAPTER 4

Understanding What You Read

1. They are not realistic statues of people, but include other design elements. The three examples listed also include the names of all the people whom the statue commemorates. In addition, a wide range of people propose designs.
2. Americans have left mementoes at the memorials.

ALL LEVELS: (Suggested time: 45 min.) Have students work in groups to design a memorial to people who died in a tragedy, whether recent or from the distant past. Possibilities include wars, civil rights demonstrations, natural disasters, and industrial accidents. Each group should create a sketch of its design and provide information about the event the statue design commemorates. Have groups present their work to the class.
ESOL, COOPERATIVE LEARNING, LS VISUAL-SPATIAL

ALL LEVELS: (Suggested time: 30 min.) This activity is based on the previous one. Ask each group to explain the elements of its design. How are the design elements related to the event being memorialized? Are some aspects of the event emphasized more than others? In addition, have each group explain how members reached their design decisions. Did group members agree on whether the design should be traditional or more similar to the memorials discussed in the feature? How did group members come to a consensus? **ESOL, COOPERATIVE LEARNING, LS INTERPERSONAL**

CHAPTER 4 REVIEW

Define and Identify
For definitions and identifications, see the glossary and index.

Review the Main Ideas
13. Appalachian Mountains (older) and the Rocky Mountains (NGS 4)
14. from Asia across the Bering "land bridge," which was exposed during an ice age
15. by using locally available plants, animals, and resources for their food, clothing, dwellings, and tools
16. because Britain had begun placing new restrictions and taxes on the colonists without the consent of their colonial assemblies, and sending British soldiers to stop the colonists from protesting
17. the independence of the United States, a new U.S. government under first the Articles of Confederation and then the U.S. Constitution, encouraged people elsewhere to fight for political freedoms
18. slave labor, tobacco, and cotton (NGS 17)
19. loss of thousands of lives; many families divided; property destruction, particularly in the South; end of slavery; long time for the South to rebuild and recover; remaining bitterness between the South and the North
20. Spanish—South and Southwest; French—Louisiana; Russian—along the Pacific coast from Alaska to California
21. Few immigrants spoke English; many lived in crowded, dark, dirty tenements; and some suffered discrimination and violence.
22. U.S. forces fought both in Europe and in the Pacific, and dropped atomic bombs on Japan, which helped lead to Japan's surrender.

CHAPTER 4 Review and Practice

Define and Identify
Identify the following:
1. contiguous
2. Continental Divide
3. tepees
4. Anasazi
5. colony
6. triangular trade
7. federal
8. George Washington
9. Emancipation Proclamation
10. Great Depression
11. United Nations
12. Cold War

Review the Main Ideas
13. What are the two major mountain regions of the United States? Which is older?
14. From where did the first Americans migrate? How did they get here?
15. How did some early peoples adapt to their environments in North America?
16. Why did the Patriots want independence from Great Britain?
17. What were the effects of the American Revolution?
18. On what three things was the South's economy based?
19. How did the Civil War affect both North and South?
20. Where were the main Spanish, French, and Russian settlements?
21. What problems faced immigrants to large U.S. cities?
22. What was the role of the United States in World War II?

Think Critically
23. **Contrasting** Why were the east and west coasts of the country settled before much of the interior?
24. **Summarizing** What are some of the main ideas of the Declaration of Independence?
25. **Analyzing Information** How did the slave trade affect U.S. history?
26. **Understanding Cause and Effect** Why was the United States the most powerful country in the world after World War II?
27. **Analyzing Information** How did new technologies affect the settling of the American frontier?
28. **Supporting a Point of View** Which of the challenges facing the United States do you think is the most serious? Why?

Map Activity
29. Identify the places marked on the map.
    Atlantic Ocean   Great Lakes
    Pacific Ocean   New York City
    Alaska   Los Angeles
    Hawaii   Miami
    Gulf of Mexico   Chicago

106 • Chapter 4

Think Critically
23. before the coasts were where people first arrived, these regions provided sea access and fertile farmland, because of interior mountain barriers, and because the interior plains were long believed to be a dry, infertile desert
24. Enlightenment ideas of equality, individual rights, and popular sovereignty
25. led to the enslavement of many African Americans, the development of a southern economy based on slave labor, a growing split between the North and the South and eventually civil war, death and destruction as a result of the war, remaining bitterness between the North and the South, and remaining hardship and discrimination for African Americans even after slavery ended
26. because while much of Europe had suffered property destruction and economic ruin, the United States had not been a battleground, and the U.S. economy was in tact
27. railroads—made it easier to move goods and people across the country, which led to increased westward settlement and city growth; agricultural machinery—made farming possible in the dry interior plains, which drew people to the region
28. poverty, unemployment, access to health care, pollution and environmental damage, terrorism, gov-

Writing Activity

You may be familiar with the song "America the Beautiful." It reminds the listener of the physical beauty of the United States—"from sea to shining sea." Write a short poem, song, or rap describing the physical geography of the eastern, interior, or western United States. To prepare, first review the lyrics for "America the Beautiful." You may also need to review this chapter's information on the country's physical geography. Then decide what aspects of the United States on which to focus and start writing.

internet connect

Internet Activity: go.hrw.com
KEYWORD: SJ5 GT4

Choose a topic to explore about the United States:
- Experience life in the early colonies.
- Search letters and journal entries written by soldiers in the Civil War.
- Explore the advance of civil rights in the United States

Social Studies Skills Practice

Interpreting Maps

Examine the map of the triangular trade that connected Europe, Africa, and North America. Then answer the questions.

1. What goods were exported from North America to Europe? from Europe to Africa?
2. Which area manufactured more finished products at the time? How can you tell?
3. What part of Africa did the slaves imported to the Americas come from?
4. How does the map indicate that many different ports were involved at each stage of the triangular trade?

Analyzing Primary Sources

As explorers pushed west, they encountered the raw beauty of North America. Read the following excerpt from the journal of John Ordway, member of the Corps of Discovery led by Captains Lewis and Clark, written on July 4, 1804. Then answer the questions.

"We passed a Creek on the south side . . . and as it has no name & as it is the 4th Of July, Capts. name it Independence Creek. We fired our bow piece [a big gun] this morning & one in the evening for Independence of the U. S. We saw a number of Goslings [young geese] half grown today. We camped in the plains, one of the most beautiful places I ever Saw in my life, open and beautifully Diversified with hills & valleys all presenting themselves to the River."

1. How did the explorers observe Independence Day?
2. What animal life did they see on July 4?
3. How did the landscape compare to other places that Ordway had seen? What were the various elements of the landscape?
4. Do you think Ordway was enjoying the trip? Why or why not?

The Geography and History of the United States • 107

REVIEW AND ASSESSMENT RESOURCES

Reproducible
- Readings in World Geography, History, and Culture 12
- Critical Thinking Activity 4
- Vocabulary Activity 4

Technology
- Chapter 4 Test Generator (on the One-Stop Planner)
- HRW Go site
- Audio CD Program, Chapter 4

Reinforcement, Review, and Assessment
- Chapter 4 Review and Practice
- Chapter Summaries and Review
- Chapter 4 Test
- Chapter 4 Test for English Language Learners and Special-Needs Students

---

CHAPTER 4 REVIEW

ernment restrictions on personal freedoms, and conflicts abroad

Map Activity

29. A. Atlantic Ocean
    B. Great Lakes
    C. Hawaii
    D. Los Angeles
    E. Gulf of Mexico
    F. Alaska
    G. Chicago
    H. Miami
    I. Pacific Ocean
    J. New York City

Writing Activity

Poems, songs, or raps will vary but should accurately describe some of the selected region's physical geography. Use Rubric 40, Writing to Describe, to evaluate student work.

Interpreting Maps

1. North America to Europe—sugar, cotton, molasses, rum, tobacco; Europe to Africa—pots and pans, cloth, guns, alcohol
2. Europe, because goods shipped to Africa were manufactured products instead of raw materials
3. West Africa
4. the breadth of the arrows

Analyzing Primary Sources

1. by naming a creek Independence Creek and firing a big gun
2. goslings, or young geese
3. He felt it was one of the most beautiful places he had ever seen; plains, hills, valleys, and a river were all visible.
4. enjoying it; writes only neutral facts or glowing descriptions.

The Geography and History of the United States

CHAPTER 5: The Regions of the United States
Chapter Resource Manager

Objectives	Pacing Guide	Reproducible Resources
SECTION 1		
The Northeast (pp. 109–13) 1. Describe the features of the Northeast. 2. Describe the landforms and climates found in New England and the Middle Atlantic states. 3. Explain how physical features affect the economies of New England and the Middle Atlantic states.	**Regular** 1 day Lecture Notes, Section 1 **Block Scheduling** .5 day Block Scheduling Handbook, Chapter 5	**RS** Know It Notes S1 **RS** Graphic Organizer 5 **E** Creative Strategies for Teaching World Geography, Lesson 7 **E** Cultures of the World Activity 1 **IC** Interdisciplinary Activity for the Middle Grades 7, 8 **ELL** Main Idea Activity S1
SECTION 2		
The South (pp. 114–17) 1. Describe the landforms found in the South. 2. Describe the climates of the South. 3. Identify the resources and industries important to the economy of the South.	**Regular** .5 day Lecture Notes, Section 2 **Block Scheduling** .5 day Block Scheduling Handbook, Chapter 5	**RS** Know It Notes S2 **E** Biography Activity: Sojourner Truth **ELL** Main Idea Activity S2
SECTION 3		
The Midwest (pp. 118–21) 1. Describe the landform regions of the Midwest. 2. Identify some agricultural products of the Midwest. 3. Describe the main industries of the Midwest.	**Regular** .5 day Lecture Notes, Section 3 **Block Scheduling** .5 day Block Scheduling Handbook, Chapter 5	**RS** Know It Notes S3 **E** Biography Activity: Henry Ford **ELL** Main Idea Activity S3
SECTION 4		
The Interior West (pp. 122–26) 1. Identify major landform regions of the Interior West. 2. Describe the climates of the Interior West. 3. List some economic activities of the Interior West.	**Regular** 1 day Lecture Notes, Section 4 **Block Scheduling** .5 day Block Scheduling Handbook, Chapter 5	**RS** Know It Notes S4 **ELL** Main Idea Activity S4
SECTION 5		
The Pacific States (pp. 127–31) 1. Identify the types of landforms found in the Pacific states. 2. Explain how the climates of the Pacific states differ. 3. Explain how the Pacific states contribute to the economy of the United States.	**Regular** 1 day Lecture Notes, Section 5 **Block Scheduling** .5 day Block Scheduling Handbook, Chapter 5	**RS** Know It Notes S5 **SM** Map Activity 5 **ELL** Main Idea Activity S5

Chapter Resource Key

RS Reading Support **IC** Interdisciplinary Connections **E** Enrichment **SM** Skills Mastery **A** Assessment **REV** Review	**ELL** Reinforcement and English Language Learners and English for Speakers of Other Languages (ESOL) Transparencies CD-ROM Music	Video Internet Holt Presentation Maker Using Microsoft® PowerPoint®	**One-Stop Planner CD-ROM** See the *One-Stop Planner* for a complete list of additional resources for students and teachers.	

One-Stop Planner CD–ROM

It's easy to plan lessons, select resources, and print out materials for your students when you use the *One-Stop Planner CD–ROM with Test Generator*.

Technology Resources

- One-Stop Planner CD–ROM, Lesson 5.1
- *ARGWorld* CD–ROM
- Homework Practice Online
- HRW Go site

- One-Stop Planner CD–ROM, Lesson 5.2
- *ARGWorld* CD–ROM
- Music of the World Audio CD Program, Selection 1
- Homework Practice Online
- HRW Go site

- One-Stop Planner CD–ROM, Lesson 5.3
- *ARGWorld* CD–ROM
- Homework Practice Online
- HRW Go site

- One-Stop Planner CD–ROM, Lesson 5.4
- *ARGWorld* CD–ROM
- Homework Practice Online
- HRW Go site

- One-Stop Planner CD–ROM, Lesson 5.5
- *ARGWorld* CD–ROM
- Homework Practice Online
- HRW Go site

Review, Reinforcement, and Assessment Resources

ELL	Main Idea Activity S1
REV	Section 1 Review
A	Daily Quiz 5.1
REV	Chapter Summaries and Review
ELL	English Audio Summary 5.1
ELL	Spanish Audio Summary 5.1

ELL	Main Idea Activity S2
REV	Section 2 Review
A	Daily Quiz 5.2
REV	Chapter Summaries and Review
ELL	English Audio Summary 5.2
ELL	Spanish Audio Summary 5.2

ELL	Main Idea Activity S3
REV	Section 3 Review
A	Daily Quiz 5.3
REV	Chapter Summaries and Review
ELL	English Audio Summary 5.3
ELL	Spanish Audio Summary 5.3

ELL	Main Idea Activity S4
REV	Section 4 Review
A	Daily Quiz 5.4
REV	Chapter Summaries and Review
ELL	English Audio Summary 5.4
ELL	Spanish Audio Summary 5.4

ELL	Main Idea Activity S5
REV	Section 4 Review
A	Daily Quiz 5.5
REV	Chapter Summaries and Review
ELL	English Audio Summary 5.5
ELL	Spanish Audio Summary 5.5

internet connect

HRW ONLINE RESOURCES

GO TO: go.hrw.com
Then type in a keyword.

TEACHER HOME PAGE
KEYWORD: SJ5 TEACHER

CHAPTER INTERNET ACTIVITIES
KEYWORD: SJ5 GT5

Choose an activity to:
- examine growth and development along the Great Lakes and St. Lawrence River.
- create a brochure on Hawaii's environment.
- create a newspaper article on the Gulf Coast of Texas.

CHAPTER ENRICHMENT LINKS
KEYWORD: SJ5 CH5

CHAPTER MAPS
KEYWORD: SJ5 MAPS5

ONLINE ASSESSMENT
Homework Practice
KEYWORD: SJ5 HP5
Standardized Test Prep Online
KEYWORD: SJ5 STP5
Rubrics
KEYWORD: SS Rubrics

COUNTRY INFORMATION
KEYWORD: SJ5 Almanac

CONTENT UPDATES
KEYWORD: SS Content Updates

HOLT PRESENTATION MAKER
KEYWORD: SJ5 PPT5

ONLINE READING SUPPORT
KEYWORD: SS Strategies

CURRENT EVENTS
KEYWORD: S5 Current Events

Chapter Review and Assessment

SM	Critical Thinking Activity 5		Chapter 5 Test Generator (on the One-Stop Planner)
REV	Chapter 5 Review and Practice		Audio CD Program, Chapter 5
REV	Chapter Summaries and Review	**A**	Chapter 5 Test for English Language Learners and Special-Needs Students
ELL	Vocabulary Activity 5		
A	Chapter 5 Test		
A	Unit 3 Test	**A**	Unit 3 Test for English Language Learners and Special-Needs Students

Meeting Individual Needs

Ability Levels

Level 1 Basic-level activities designed for all students encountering new material

Level 2 Intermediate-level activities designed for average students

Level 3 Challenging activities designed for honors and gifted-and-talented students

ESOL Activities that address the needs of students with Limited English Proficiency

CHAPTER 5

The Regions of the United States
Previewing Chapter Resources

Holt Online Learning

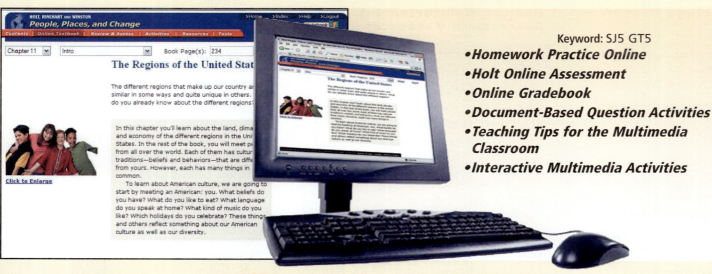

Keyword: SJ5 GT5

- Homework Practice Online
- Holt Online Assessment
- Online Gradebook
- Document-Based Question Activities
- Teaching Tips for the Multimedia Classroom
- Interactive Multimedia Activities

Differentiating Instruction

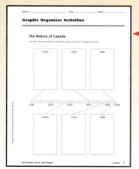

Reading and Writing Support
◀ Graphic Organizer Activity
- Vocabulary Activity
- Chapter Summary and Review
- Know It Notes
- Audio CD

Active Learning
◀ Block Scheduling Handbook
- Cultures of the World Activity
- Interdisciplinary Activity
- Map Activity
- Critical Thinking Activity 7
- Music of the World Audio CD: Traditional Music of Vancouver Island

Primary Sources and Advanced Learners
- Geography for Life Activity: The Changing Geography of Ice Hockey
◀ Map Activity: The Growth of Canada
- Readings in World Geography, History and Culture:
  - 13 Cruising to School
  - 14 Nunavut: Canada's Newest Territory

Assessment Program
◀ Daily Quizzes S1–3
- Chapter Test
- Chapter Test for English Language Learners and Special-Needs Students

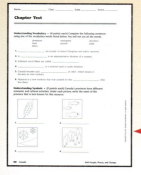

Spanish and ESOL
- Vocabulary Activity
- Main Idea Activities for English Language Learners and Special-Needs Students
- Chapter Summary and Review
- Spanish Audio Summary
- Know It Notes S1–3
◀ Chapter Test for English Language Learners and Special-Needs Students

Special Education Modifications
Your **I.D.E.A. Works! CD-ROM** will provide modified versions of the following teaching materials:

- Guided Reading Strategies S1–3
- Vocabulary Activity
◀ Main Idea Activities S1–3
- Daily Quizzes S1–3
- Chapter 5 Test
- Flash cards of chapter vocabulary terms

107C

Teacher Resources

Books for Teachers

Houston, James. *Confessions of an Igloo Dweller.* Houghton Mifflin, 1996.

Malcolm, Andrew H. *The Canadians.* St. Martin's Press, 1992.

Riendeau, Roger E. *A Brief History of Canada.* Facts on File, 1999.

Wilson, Ian and Sally Wilson. *Arctic Adventures: Exploring Canada's North by Canoe and Dog Team.* Gordon Soules Publishing, 1997.

Books for Students

Barlas, Robert, Norm Thompsett, and Susan McKay. *Canada.* (Festivals of the World). Gareth Stevens, 1997. How Canada's culture is reflected in its festivals. **SHELTERED ENGLISH**

Durbin, William. *The Broken Blade.* Delacorte Press, 1997. Set in 1800, follows 13-year-old Pierre on a rigorous 2,000-mile canoe trip through the Canadian wilderness. Fiction.

Durbin, William. *Wintering.* Delacorte Press, 1999. Sequel follows 13-year-old Pierre's first full winter in the Canadian backwoods to the Great Lakes. Fiction.

Van Stockum, Hilda. *Canadian Summer.* The Hilda Van Stockum Family Collection. Bethlehem Books, 1997.

Multimedia Materials

Anyplace Wild III: Adventuring in Canada. Video, 60 min. PBS.

The Canadian Way of Life. The Way of Life Series. Video, 21 min. AIMS Media.

ZipZapMap! Canada. Software Game. National Geographic Society.

Videos and CDs

Videos
- CNN Presents Geography: Yesterday and Today, Segment 8 Tradition and Change—**The James Bay Project**
- ARG World

Holt Researcher

http://researcher.hrw.com

- Canada
- North American Free Trade Agreement (NAFTA)
- Group of Seven (G-7)
- French and Indian War
- Early European Settlements

Transparency Packages

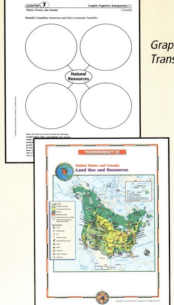

Graphic Organizer Transparencies 5.1–3

Geography and Cultures Visual Resources Transparencies
21 US and Canada: Physical
22 US and Canada: Political
23 US and Canada: Climate
24 US and Canada: Population
25 US and Canada: Land Use and Resources
27 Physical Regions of the US and Canada
31 Canada: Physical-Political

Map Activities Transparency
05 The Growth of Canada

CHAPTER 5

WHY IT MATTERS

You may want to share with your students the following reasons for learning more about the regions of the United States:

- We can better understand our country as a whole by understanding the similarities and differences among the regions.
- Each region has a unique history that contributes to the history of our country.
- The United States is a wealthy and beautiful country. We need to learn how to appreciate and protect the many advantages our country enjoys.
- Learning about the geography of the United States might help us decide where we would like to visit or live someday.

CHAPTER 5

The Regions of the United States

The different regions that make up our country are similar in some ways and quite unique in others. What do you already know about the different regions?

In this chapter you'll learn about the land, climate, and economy of the different regions in the United States. In the rest of the book, you will meet people from all over the world. Each of them has cultural traditions—beliefs and behaviors—that are different from yours. However, each has many things in common.

To learn about American culture, we are going to start by meeting an American: you. What beliefs do you have? What do you like to eat? What language do you speak at home? What kind of music do you like? Which holidays do you celebrate? These things and others reflect something about our American culture as well as our diversity.

CHAPTER PROJECT

Literature that uses local color incorporates characteristics—such as speech patterns, specific locations, or regional occupations—of a particular place. Have students write short stories using local color about their own area or another within the United States. Ask them to underline words that identify the characteristics of the location.

STARTING THE CHAPTER

Ask students the following question: *How many different ways can you think of to identify the part of the United States in which we live?* Discuss student responses. Point out that people often use many different names to refer to a single part of the country. For example, the phrases *New England* and *the Northeast* can be used to identify the same area. Texas is sometimes considered part of the South, sometimes part of the West, and sometimes part of the Southwest. Tell students that they will learn about one system for dividing the United States into regions in this chapter.

Section 1: The Northeast

CHAPTER 5, Section 1

Read to Discover
1. What are some features of the Northeast?
2. What kinds of landforms and climates are found in New England and the Middle Atlantic states?
3. How do physical features affect the economies of New England and the Middle Atlantic states?

Vocabulary
megalopolis
moraine
second-growth forests
estuary

Places
White Mountains
Green Mountains
Longfellow Mountains
Berkshire Hills
Cape Cod
Nantucket
Martha's Vineyard
Chesapeake Bay
Susquehanna River
Washington, D.C.
Philadelphia
Baltimore

Reading Strategy
USING PRIOR KNOWLEDGE Write down some facts that you already know about the Northeastern United States on the left side of a sheet of paper. As you read, write down new facts from this section on the right side of the paper.

Section 1 Resources
Reproducible
- Lecture Notes, Section 1
- Block Scheduling Handbook, Chapter 5
- Know It Notes S1
- Graphic Organizer 5
- Creative Strategies for Teaching World Geography, Lesson 7
- Cultures of the World Activity 1
- Interdisciplinary Activities for Middle Grades 7, 8

Technology
- One-Stop Planner CD–ROM, Lesson 5.1
- Homework Practice Online
- HRW Go site

Reinforcement, Review, and Assessment
- Main Idea Activity S1
- Section 1 Review
- Daily Quiz 5.1
- Chapter Summaries and Review
- English Audio Summary 5.1
- Spanish Audio Summary 5.1

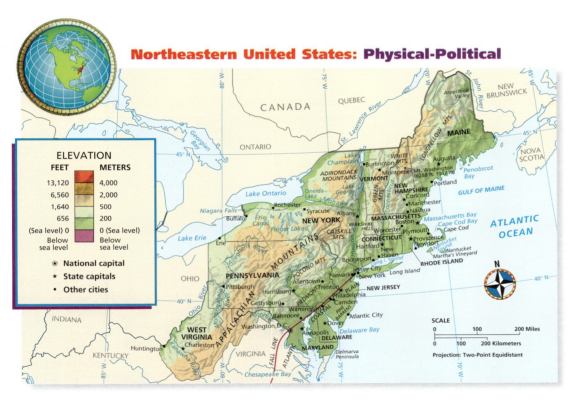

Northeastern United States: Physical-Political

The Regions of the United States • 109

Section 1

Objectives
1. Describe the features of the Northeast.
2. Describe the landforms and climates found in New England and the Middle Atlantic states.
3. Explain how physical features affect the economies of New England and the Middle Atlantic states.

Focus

Bellringer
Copy the following instructions onto the board: *What is life like in a big city? Write down your ideas.* Discuss student responses. Point out that most people in the Northeast live in cities and that many cities in the region are very large. Identify some of the major cities of the Northeast on a wall map, including Baltimore, Boston, New York, Philadelphia, and Washington, D.C. Tell students that they will learn more about life in this largely urban area in Section 1.

Using the Physical-Political Map
Have students examine the map on this page. Ask them to describe the region's physical geography (mostly plains along the coast, with higher elevations to the west). Tell students that many cities in the Northeast are ports. Ask them to identify some of the bodies of water on which these cities lie (Atlantic Ocean, Gulf of Maine, Massachusetts Bay, Cape Cod Bay, Delaware Bay, Chesapeake Bay, Lake Erie, Long Island Sound).

The Regions of the United States 109

CHAPTER 5, Section 1

COOPERATIVE LEARNING

Business Boosters
Organize the class into small groups and assign each group one of the cities of the megalopolis. Tell students that each group represents the chamber of commerce of its assigned city and that each group should create a brochure designed to attract businesses to its city.

Provide research materials and art supplies. Each group will need to discuss its assigned city's attributes, particularly features that make it a desirable location for business. The brochures should describe established industries and businesses, transportation systems, educational facilities, cultural activities, and so on. Remind students that their brochures should also include pictures and have them create drawings or cut pictures from magazines to illustrate their work. Call on groups to share their brochures with the class.

Visual Record Answer
Location on rivers and a harbor allowed trade to prosper and the city to grow.

The Northeast

NEW ENGLAND STATES
Connecticut
Maine
Massachusetts
New Hampshire
Rhode Island
Vermont

MIDDLE ATLANTIC STATES
Delaware
Maryland
New Jersey
New York
Pennsylvania
West Virginia

New York's skyscrapers tower over the Hudson River.
Interpreting the Visual Record
Movement How may the city's location have affected its growth?

A View of the Northeast

Although the Northeast is the smallest region in the United States, it has the most people. It has the country's greatest concentration of cities, factories, banks, universities, and transportation centers. The region includes New York City, the country's largest city, and Washington, D.C., its capital.

The states of the Northeast are grouped into two subregions. The New England states are located in the northeastern portion of the country. The Middle Atlantic states stretch from the Appalachians to the Atlantic coast. There are six states in each subregion.

Megalopolis Overlapping the two subregions of the Northeast is a huge densely populated urban area. This area is called a **megalopolis**. A megalopolis is a string of cities that have grown together. This urban area stretches along the Atlantic coast from Boston to Washington, D.C. Major cities that are part of the megalopolis include New York City, Philadelphia, and Baltimore. At least 40 million people live in this area.

Except for Washington, D.C., all of these cities were founded during the colonial era. They grew because they were important seaports. Today they are major industrial and financial centers as well. These cities are connected by roads, railroads, and airline routes. Many of the world's largest companies have home offices in these cities. Washington, D.C. is the country's capital and the center of government offices. D.C. stands for District of Columbia.

✓ **READING CHECK:** *Places and Regions* Into what areas is the Northeastern region divided? two sub-regions, each with six states and overlapping string of cities known as megalopolis

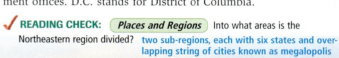

110 • Chapter 5

TEACH

Teaching Objectives 1

LEVEL 1: (Suggested time: 35 min.) Provide art supplies and old magazines to the class and have students create collages that illustrate some features of the Northeast. Direct students to draw images and to cut out photographs from the magazines to use in their collages. Ask volunteers to present their collages to the class and describe the features they depict. **ESOL, LS VISUAL-SPATIAL**

LEVELS 2 AND 3: (Suggested time: 30 min.) Pair students and provide them with an assortment of newspapers. Have students look through the newspapers for articles with datelines from the cities of the megalopolis or other cities from the Northeast. Have each pair select one article and explain to the class what it says about the city in which it was written. Lead a class discussion about the cities of the Northeast and their significance to the rest of the country. **COOPERATIVE LEARNING, LS VERBAL-LINGUISTIC**

110 Chapter 5

New England

The New England states are famous for their scenic beauty and varied landforms. The subregion has also been the site of many important events in American history. The Pilgrims landed here in 1620 and were soon followed by other colonists. In the late 1700s, New England was the center of the American Revolution.

Landforms The Appalachian Mountains cross much of northern New England. The Appalachian system is actually made up of many small ranges. In New England, these include New Hampshire's White Mountains, Vermont's Green Mountains, and Maine's Longfellow Mountains. At 6,288 feet (1,917 m), Mount Washington in the White Mountains is the highest peak. Because of glacial erosion, northern New England has thousands of lakes.

Southern New England mainly is a hilly region. As glaciers pushed to the Atlantic coast, they left rock material in the form of hundreds of hills. The Berkshires of western Massachusetts are the highest hilly region. The only plains in New England are along the Atlantic coast and in the Connecticut River valley.

New England's coastline varies greatly from north to south. In the north, the scenic coast of Maine is made of granite. Granite is a hard, speckled rock. Maine's coast is rugged and rocky with many narrow inlets, bays, peninsulas, and islands.

Glaciers are responsible for the features of the southern New England coast. Cape Cod and the islands of Nantucket and Martha's Vineyard are glacial **moraine** materials. A moraine is a ridge of rocks, gravel, and sand piled up by the huge ice sheets.

Climate New England has a humid continental climate. Each autumn the region's brightly colored leaves attract tourists. Winter sports fans like its snowy winters. In the summer, fog is common along the coast. Very rarely during the summer, a hurricane may strike the coast of southern New England. More common are winter storms from the North Atlantic called northeasters. These storms bring cold, snowy weather with strong winds and high ocean waves.

Economy Dairy farming is the region's most important agricultural activity. Other important crops are cranberries and potatoes. However, a short growing season and rocky terrain limit farming in New England. As a result, most farms in this region are small. Some are now used as second homes or retirement retreats.

Cool, shallow waters off the coast are good fishing areas. Cod and shellfish are the most valuable seafood. The U.S. government has set rules to prevent overfishing in some areas.

Small towns and beautiful scenery can be found throughout Vermont and the rest of New England.

CHAPTER 5, Section 1

PLACES AND REGIONS

License Plate Geography
In designing license plates for automobiles, state governments typically select an aspect of the state's geography, economy, history, or tourist attractions to highlight. The lobster appearing on Maine's license plates, for example, refers to the state's physical and economic geography.

Activity: Invite students to create license-plate designs for the other New England states. Have students suggest symbols representing the physical geography of the states or tourist attractions associated with landforms and climate. Encourage students to consult almanacs and encyclopedias for additional information about each state.

The Regions of the United States • 111

Teaching Objective 2

LEVEL 1: (Suggested time: 20 min.) Have each student write three questions about the landforms and climates of New England and the Middle Atlantic states. (Examples: What kind of landform dominates much of northern New England? What is a northeaster? What process shaped many of the landforms of the Northeast?) Direct students to write each question on one side of an index card and to write its answer on the other side. Then have volunteers ask their questions in front of the class and have classmates answer them. **ESOL, INTERPERSONAL**

LEVELS 2 AND 3: (Suggested time: 30 min.) Have pairs of students consult the text, map, and images in this section to prepare an itinerary for a scenic tour of New England. Tell students to identify towns, states, and major landforms along their planned routes. Ask them to choose a season for travel and to describe the typical weather conditions they may encounter at that time of year. **COOPERATIVE LEARNING**

CHAPTER 5, Section 1

Across the Curriculum
MATH

The Appalachian Trail The Appalachian Trail is a footpath that extends from Maine to northern Georgia. The 2,167 mile (3,488 km) trail closely follows the ridge line of the Appalachian Mountains. It passes through 14 states and eight national forests. More than 4 million people use some part of the trail annually. Most are short-term hikers, but each year several thousand people try to hike the entire trail in one continuous journey. Most of these so-called thru-hikers start in the South in early spring and hike the entire trail in five to six months.

Activity: Have students calculate how far hikers must travel each day in order to complete the entire trail in five months (approximately 14 miles a day).

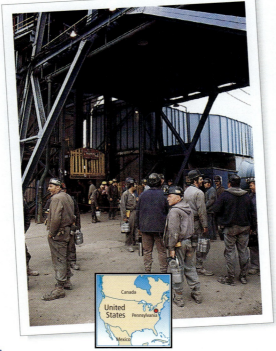

▲ These Pennsylvania miners are waiting to enter one of the many coal mines in the Middle Atlantic states.

Shipbuilding was a major industry in colonial New England. Builders used wood from the region's forests. Nearly all of New England's forests today are **second-growth forests**. These are the trees that cover an area after the original, or old-growth, forest has been cut.

New England was the country's first industrial area. Textile mills and shoe factories were built along rivers and swift streams. The water was a handy power source for factories. Today, many banks, investment houses, and insurance companies are based in the region. In addition, the area has many respected colleges and universities. These schools include Harvard, Yale, and the Massachusetts Institute of Technology.

✓ **READING CHECK:** *Places and Regions* Why was New England better suited for industrial growth than for agriculture? *agriculture limited by terrain and climate; rivers and streams as close and available power source*

Middle Atlantic States

About one fifth of the U.S. population lives in the Middle Atlantic states subregion. It is one of the world's most industrialized and urbanized areas.

Landforms Three landform regions cross the Middle Atlantic states. They are the Coastal Plain, the Piedmont, and the Appalachian Mountains. The Coastal Plain stretches across all of the Middle Atlantic states except West Virginia. This flat plain does not rise much above sea level. Long Island and Chesapeake Bay are both part of the Coastal Plain.

Chesapeake Bay is fed by the Susquehanna River. It is the largest **estuary** on the Atlantic coast. An estuary is a body of water where salty seawater and freshwater mix. As Ice Age glaciers melted along this coast, the sea level rose. The rising sea filled low river valleys and formed the bay.

Inland from the Coastal Plain is the Piedmont. This region slopes down from the Appalachians to the Coastal Plain. Where these regions meet, rivers plunge over rapids and waterfalls. These rivers supplied waterpower for the early towns and cities.

The northern part of the Appalachian Mountains crosses the Middle Atlantic states. Several major rivers cut through the Appalachians here on their way to the Atlantic Ocean. These include the Potomac, Susquehanna, Delaware, and Hudson rivers.

Climates The Middle Atlantic states have two major climate types. The north has a humid continental climate, while the south has a humid subtropical climate. Summers in both climate regions can be

Teaching Objective 3
ALL LEVELS: (Suggested time: 30 min.) Copy the following graphic organizer onto the board, omitting the blue answers. Have students complete the chart to describe the relationships between the physical features and the economies of New England and the Middle Atlantic states. Call on volunteers to share their organizers with classmates. Then lead a class discussion about the economic activities of the Northeast. **ESOL**

Region	Physical Features	Economic Activities
New England	• rocky terrain • coastal waters • seaport • scenic natural sites	• little farming • seafood industry • shipping industry • tourist industry
Middle Atlantic States	• good soil • coal • seaport	• good farming • mining industry • shipping industry • tourist industry

very hot and humid. Winds passing over the warm Gulf Stream and the Gulf of Mexico bring hot humid air inland.

During winter, arctic air from the north sometimes enters the region. Winters are colder away from the coast, particularly in the north. Snowfall can be heavy in some areas, especially in the Appalachians and upstate New York. Like the New England coast, the Middle Atlantic coast may experience hurricanes and northeasters.

Economy Soils are better for farming in the Middle Atlantic states than in New England. However, the region's expanding cities have taken over most of the available farmland.

Major coal-mining areas are found in the Appalachians, particularly in West Virginia and Pennsylvania. Coal is used in steelmaking. The steel industry helped make Pittsburgh, in western Pennsylvania, the largest industrial city in the Appalachians.

Today nearly every kind of manufacturing and service industry can be found in the Middle Atlantic states. Major seaports allow farmers and companies to ship their products to markets around the world. In addition, tourists visit natural and historical sites. These include Niagara Falls between New York and Canada and Gettysburg, a major Civil War battleground in Pennsylvania.

✓ **READING CHECK:** *Physical Systems* How are the climates of the Middle Atlantic states similar to those of New England? **humid, continental climates**

Place Developments like Camden Yards baseball stadium and a new harbor have strengthened the economy of Baltimore, Maryland.

Define and explain: megalopolis, moraine, second-growth forests, estuary

Working with Sketch Maps On a map of the United States that you draw or that your teacher provides, label the region's 12 states and the following: White Mountains; Green Mountains; Longfellow Mountains; Berkshire Hills; Cape Cod; Nantucket; Martha's Vineyard; Chesapeake Bay; Susquehanna River; Washington, D.C.; Philadelphia; Baltimore.

Reading for the Main Idea

1. *Human Systems* What are some characteristics of the Northeast?
2. *Human Systems* In what way is New York, New York, unique?
3. *Human Systems* How do landforms and climate affect the economies of New England and the Middle Atlantic states?

Critical Thinking

4. **Drawing Conclusions** What kinds of environmental challenges might threaten the cities of the megalopolis? Why do you think this?

Organizing What You Know

5. **Categorizing** Copy the following graphic organizer. Use it to categorize the major landforms and climates of the Northeast.

Homework Practice Online
Keyword: SJ5 HP5

	Landforms	Climates
New England		
Middle Atlantic states		

The Regions of the United States • 113

Section 1 Review

Answers to Section 1 Review

Define For definitions, see the glossary.

Working with Sketch Maps Maps will vary, but listed places should be labeled in their approximate locations.

Reading for the Main Idea

1. heavily populated; many cities, factories, universities, banks, transportation centers (NGS 4)
2. It is the country's largest city. (NGS 4)
3. good farmland in Middle Atlantic; good fishing areas and seaports; coal deposits; tourist sites (NGS 4)

Critical Thinking

4. Possible answers: overcrowding, pollution; reasons will vary. (NGS 18)

Organizing What You Know

5. New England—Appalachians, glacial hills, plains, granite coastline, moraine islands; humid continental; Middle Atlantic—Coastal Plain, Piedmont, Appalachians; humid continental, humid subtropical

---

CLOSE

Ask students to name factors that make the Northeast important to the country as a whole. (Possible answers: its industrial and financial centers, government offices, universities, factories, natural resources, scenic beauty, historic sites)

REVIEW, ASSESS, RETEACH

Have students complete the Section Review. Then pair students. Have each pair create an outline based on the material discussed in this section. Have partners take turns using the outline to give an oral summary of the information. Then have students complete Daily Quiz 5.1.
COOPERATIVE LEARNING

Have students complete Main Idea Activity S1. Then arrange students in three groups to create storyboards for documentary films about the Northeast. One group should focus on the megalopolis, one on landforms and climates, and the third on economic activities.
ESOL, COOPERATIVE LEARNING, **VISUAL-SPATIAL**

EXTEND

Have interested students conduct research on the use of coal in the United States. Ask them to draw a line graph showing its use over the past 50 years and to draw conclusions from their graphs. **BLOCK SCHEDULING**

The Regions of the United States

CHAPTER 5, Section 2

SECTION 2 RESOURCES

Reproducible
- Lecture Notes, Section 2
- Know It Notes S2

Technology
- One-Stop Planner CD–ROM, Lesson 5.2
- Music of the World Audio CD Program, Selection 1
- Homework Practice Online
- HRW Go site

Reinforcement, Review, and Assessment
- Main Idea Activity S2
- Section 2 Review
- Daily Quiz 5.2
- Chapter Summaries and Review
- English Audio Summary 5.2
- Spanish Audio Summary 5.2

Section 2 The South

Read to Discover
1. What landform regions are found in the South?
2. What are the characteristics of climates in the South?
3. What resources and industries are important to the economy of the South?

Vocabulary
barrier islands
wetlands
sediment
diversify

Places
Everglades
Okefenokee Swamp
Mississippi Delta
Blue Ridge Mountains
Great Smoky Mountains
Cumberland Plateau
Ozark Plateau
Interior Plains
Atlanta
Houston
New Orleans
Miami
Dallas

Reading Strategy

TAKING NOTES As you read this section, use the headings to create an outline. Beneath the headings write down the information you learn about each main idea.

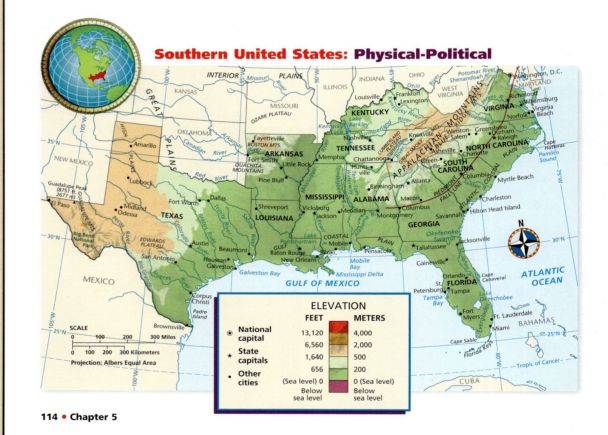

114 • Chapter 5

Section 2

Objectives
1. Describe the landform regions found in the South.
2. Describe the climates of the South.
3. Identify the resources and industries important to the economy of the South.

FOCUS

Bellringer
Copy the following passage onto the chalkboard: *Think about the following list of terms: bayous, citrus fruit, hurricanes, petroleum, plantations, swamps, thunderstorms, and tourism. What do these words all have in common?* (They are all associated with the South.) Tell students that they will learn more about the land, climate, and economy of the South in this section.

Building Vocabulary
Write the vocabulary terms on the chalkboard. Have students find the definitions in the textbook or glossary. Ask students to suggest a variety of crops that southern farmers who **diversify** might produce. Help students use the map on this page to find examples of **barrier islands** (Hilton Head Island, Padre Island), **wetlands** (Okefenokee Swamp, Everglades), and an area formed by **sediment** (Mississippi Delta).

114 Chapter 5

Landforms

The South stretches in a great arc from Virginia to Texas. The 12 states of this region are Virginia, North Carolina, South Carolina, Georgia, Florida, Alabama, Mississippi, Tennessee, Kentucky, Arkansas, Louisiana, and Texas. Texas, the largest state in the region, shares a long border with Mexico.

The Coastal Plain is the major landform region of the South. It stretches inland from the Atlantic Ocean and the Gulf of Mexico. **Barrier islands** line most of the shore along this low area. A barrier island is a long, narrow, sandy island separated from the mainland. Many coastal areas of the South are covered by **wetlands**. Wetlands are land areas that are flooded for at least part of the year.

Two of the largest wetlands areas found along the Coastal Plain are the Everglades in Florida and the Okefenokee Swamp in Georgia. In Louisiana, hundreds of coastal marsh areas can be seen on the Mississippi River Delta. The Mississippi is one of the largest rivers in the world. It carries small bits of mud, sand, or gravel called **sediment** that collects at the river's mouth. This sediment has built up to form the large Mississippi Delta—a low, swampy area cut by small streams.

Inland from the Coastal Plain lies the Piedmont, an upland region. Its rolling hills cover much of Virginia, the Carolinas, and Georgia. Farther from the coast are the southern Appalachian Mountains. Landforms in this region include the Blue Ridge and Great Smoky Mountains and the Cumberland Plateau. The Appalachians cross parts of Virginia, the Carolinas, Kentucky, Tennessee, Georgia, and Alabama.

Another landform of the South is the Ozark Plateau. This ancient plateau lies mainly in Arkansas but extends into Oklahoma and Missouri as well. It is a rugged, hilly region. The Arkansas River runs between the Ozark Plateau and another upland area, the Ouachita (WASH-i-taw) Mountains. Although they are called mountains, the Ouachitas are really rugged hills.

To the east and west of the Ozarks are the rolling hills of the Interior Plains. These plains cover most of central Kentucky and Tennessee. Eastern Texas is also part of the Interior Plains region. Most of central and western Texas is part of the Great Plains. In some places the land rises between 2,000 and 5,000 feet (600 and 1,500 m). While eastern Texas is low and hilly, southwest Texas is a region of mountain ranges and desert basins.

✓ **READING CHECK:** *Places and Regions* What landform regions are found in the South? Coastal Plain, Piedmont, Appalachian Mountains, Ozark Plateau, Interior Plains

The Florida Everglades is a rich habitat for plants and wildlife.
Interpreting the Visual Record
Human-Environment Interaction What happens to natural habitats when developers drain wetlands?

CHAPTER 5, Section 2

Linking Past to Present

The Galveston Hurricane In terms of loss of life, the worst natural disaster in U.S. history was a hurricane that struck Galveston Island in Texas on September 8, 1900. Storm warnings had been issued, but fallen wires kept the news from spreading. Many people ignored the warnings that did reach the island. Consequently, few people had evacuated when all the bridges to the mainland collapsed.

Wind gusts estimated at 130 miles per hour (209 kmh) drove huge waves onto the shore. Seawater poured into the city of Galveston, flooding some streets to a depth of 15 feet (4.6 m). As many as 8,000 people died in the city, and perhaps 4,000 more on the rest of the island. Contemporary estimates of property damage range as high as $30 million. This figure is equivalent to a much higher number today.

▲ **Visual Record Answer**

Possible answer: Habitats can be destroyed, resulting in loss of plants and wildlife.

TEACH

Teaching Objective 1
ALL LEVELS: (Suggested time: 20 min.) Copy the following graphic organizer onto the chalkboard, omitting the blue answers. Use it to help students identify and describe the various landform regions of the South. Pair students and have each pair find material in the text to complete the chart. Then lead a class discussion about the physical geography of the South.
ESOL, COOPERATIVE LEARNING

Landform Region	Coastal Plain	Piedmont	Ozark Plateau	Interior Plains
Description	low, wetlands, barrier islands	upland region, rolling hills	rugged, hilly, Arkansas River	some places low and hilly; mountains, basins
Location	along Atlantic Ocean and Gulf of Mexico	Virginia, Carolinas, Georgia; inland from Coastal Plain	mostly in Arkansas	east and west of Ozarks; Kentucky, Tennessee, Texas

CHAPTER 5, Section 2

GLOBAL PERSPECTIVES

The South and the Sky
In addition to its many aerospace-related industries, the South hosts some of the major U.S. space exploration and launching facilities, including the John F. Kennedy Space Center in Cape Canaveral, Florida, and the Lyndon B. Johnson Space Center in Houston, Texas. The space shuttles are launched from Cape Canaveral. During flight, however, they are controlled by teams in Houston.

The shuttles put satellites into place and maintain them, thus playing an important role in global communications and in monitoring Earth's weather and environment. The shuttles also carry experiments and projects for other countries.

Discussion: Lead a discussion based on the following question: What benefits may international cooperation in the exploration of space bring to participating nations?

Focus on Culture Answer ▶
Answers will vary according to region and crops.

FOCUS ON CULTURE

Tasting Local Culture

The agricultural heritage of the South is celebrated in many of the region's towns. For example, Luling, Texas, holds the Watermelon Thump every summer. Several Georgia towns put on peach festivals in tribute to that state's popular crop. Shenandoah Valley Apple Day happens in Virginia. Crowley, Louisiana, celebrates the state's huge rice crop. Homestead, Florida, honors its strawberries. Other Florida towns hold annual citrus events.

Parades, beauty pageants, cooking contests, and armadillo races are among the many events that entertain visitors to these lively festivals.

Place What festivals related to local crops are held in your community or region?

Climate

Most people who live in the South, particularly along the Coastal Plain, are used to a humid subtropical climate. Winters are mild, and summers are long, hot, and humid. Not all of the South, however, has a subtropical climate. In higher areas such as the Appalachians and Ozarks, temperatures are cooler. Because it is so big, Texas has several climate regions, from humid subtropical to desert.

Most of the South receives between 40 and 60 inches (100 and 150 cm) of rainfall per year. Thunderstorms, which often create dangerous lightning and tornadoes, bring much of this rain to the region. Some areas of the Appalachians may experience occasional winter snowstorms. During late summer and early fall, hurricanes may strike coastal areas.

✓ **READING CHECK:** *Places and Regions* What types of storms are common in the South?
Thunderstorms, tornadoes, snowstorms, hurricanes

Economy

Historically, the South was mainly rural and agricultural. In recent decades, however, the region has attracted many new industries. As the economy has grown, so have many cities. Houston is now the fourth-largest city in the country. Dallas-Fort Worth, Atlanta, Miami, and New Orleans have also grown to be major cities and commercial centers.

Agriculture Although agriculture is no longer the South's major economic activity, many small towns and farming areas stretch across the region. The region has long been a major producer of cotton, tobacco, and citrus fruit. In recent years, some farmers have decided to **diversify**. This means that farmers are producing a variety of crops instead of just one.

Resources The coastal waters of the Gulf of Mexico and the Atlantic are rich in ocean life. Though all the southern coastal states have fishing industries, Louisiana and Texas are the leaders. The shallow waters around the Mississippi Delta produce great quantities of oysters, shrimp, and other seafood. The major mineral and energy resources of the region include coal, sulfur, salt, phosphates, oil, and natural gas. Oil is found in Texas and Louisiana. These two states also lead the country in the production of sulfur. Florida has the country's largest phosphate-mining industry, for making fertilizer. Much of it is exported to Japan.

Industry Today many textile factories operate in the Piedmont areas of Georgia, the Carolinas, and Virginia. The Texas Gulf Coast and the

---

Teaching Objective 2
ALL LEVELS: (Suggested time: 30 min.) Direct students to create a climate map of the South. Ask them to create symbols for the different types of weather common to this region and to draw the symbols in appropriate locations on a map. Remind students to include keys with their maps.
ESOL, **LS** VISUAL-SPATIAL

Teaching Objective 3
ALL LEVELS: (Suggested time: 45 min.) Organize the class into five groups: citrus farmers, oil workers, fishers and shrimpers, textile manufacturers, and high-tech industries. Have each group write a script for a television commercial that highlights its industry's importance to the South and to the rest of United States. Have groups present their commercials to the class. **COOPERATIVE LEARNING,** **LS** AUDITORY-MUSICAL

A Louisiana shrimper clears the day's catch. The Gulf Coast is the richest shrimp-producing region in the United States.

Interpreting the Visual Record

Human-Environment Interaction How do you think oil spills could affect Louisiana's economy?

lower Mississippi River area have huge oil refineries. Houston, New Orleans, and other major seaports ship the oil. Some cities such as Austin, Texas, also have computer, software, and publishing companies.

Warm weather and beautiful beaches draw many vacationers to resorts in the South. People vacation in eastern Virginia, Florida, and the coastal islands of the Carolinas and Texas. Tourist attractions in cities like New Orleans, San Antonio, and Nashville also attract many visitors.

Many cities in the South have important links with countries in Central and South America. Miami is an important travel connection with Caribbean countries, Mexico, and South America. Atlanta, Houston, and Dallas also are major transportation centers.

✓ **READING CHECK:** *Places and Regions* How does geography affect the economic resources of the South? *Supports agriculture, industry, and the transportation of goods.*

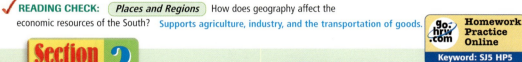

Section Review 2

Define and explain: barrier islands, wetlands, sediment, diversify

Working with Sketch Maps On the map that you created in Section 1, label the 12 states of the South. Then label the following: Everglades, Okefenokee Swamp, Mississippi Delta, Blue Ridge Mountains, Great Smoky Mountains, Cumberland Plateau, Ozark Plateau, Interior Plains, Atlanta, Houston, New Orleans, Miami, Dallas

Reading for the Main Idea

1. *Places and Regions* What areas of the South are wetlands?
2. *Places and Regions* Which southern state has many climates? What are two of these climates?
3. *Places and Regions* How has the economy of the South changed in recent years?

Critical Thinking

4. **Supporting a Point of View** Use what you learned in this section, and what you know to support this statement: Industry should continue to grow in the South.

Organizing What You Know

5. **Summarizing** Copy the following graphic organizer. Use it to describe the resources and industries that contribute to the economy of the South.

Homework Practice Online
Keyword: SJ5 HP5

The Regions of the United States • 117

Section 2 Review

Answers to Section 2 Review

Define For definitions, see the glossary.

Working with Sketch Maps Maps will vary, but listed places should be labeled in their approximate locations.

Reading for the Main Idea
1. Everglades, Okefenokee Swamp, Mississippi Delta, coastal marsh areas (NGS 4)
2. Texas; humid subtropical, desert (NGS 4)
3. It has become more urban and industrial.

Critical Thinking
4. Answers will vary, but students should note that the South's climate and geography attract business and workers.

Organizing What You Know
5. farming, fishing, textile workers, tourism, oil refineries, computer/software companies, publishing companies

▲ **Visual Record Answer**
pollute beaches that attract vacationers, driving them away and hurting the tourist industry

---

CLOSE

Ask students to name cities or other locations in the South that they would like to visit. Call on volunteers to explain their choices to the class.

REVIEW, ASSESS, RETEACH

Have students complete the Section Review. Have students work in pairs to create graphic organizers about one of the section's topics. Then have students complete Daily Quiz 5.2. **COOPERATIVE LEARNING**

Have students complete Main Idea Activity S2. Then assign each of three groups one of the following topics: landforms, climates, or resources and industries. Have each group create a poster related to its topic.
ESOL, COOPERATIVE LEARNING

EXTEND

Tell students that the South has been the birthplace of many musical styles. Have interested students conduct research on southern music. Styles include bluegrass, *conjunto*, country/western, jazz, Cajun, and zydeco. Students may want to play for the class brief examples of the music.
BLOCK SCHEDULING

The Regions of the United States 117

CHAPTER 5, Section 3

SECTION 3 RESOURCES

Reproducible
- Lecture Notes, Section 3
- Know It Notes S3

Technology
- One-Stop Planner CD–ROM, Lesson 5.3
- Homework Practice Online
- HRW Go site

Reinforcement, Review, and Assessment
- Main Idea Activity S3
- Section 3 Review
- Daily Quiz 5.3
- Chapter Summaries and Review
- English Audio Summary 5.3
- Spanish Audio Summary 5.3

Section 3 The Midwest

Read to Discover
1. What types of landforms and climates are found in the Midwest?
2. What are some agricultural products grown in the region?
3. What are the main industries of the Midwest?

Vocabulary
droughts
Corn Belt
Dairy Belt

Places
Chicago
Detroit

Reading Strategy

READING ORGANIZER Before you read this section, draw a concept map by drawing a circle with rays that attach smaller circles. In the large circle write Economy of the Midwest. As you read, write in the smaller circles the information you learn about economic activities in this region.

Midwestern United States: Physical-Political

Section 3

Objectives
1. Describe the landform regions of the Midwest.
2. Identify some agricultural products of the Midwest.
3. Describe the industries of the Midwest.

FOCUS

Bellringer

Copy the following instructions and questions onto the chalkboard: *Find the Great Lakes on the section map. Which lake is largest? Which is smallest? Which border Canada?* Discuss responses. Challenge students to make a word using the first letter in the name of each lake. Point out that many people use the word *HOMES* to help them remember the lakes' names. Then tell students that in Section 3 they will learn more about the importance of the Great Lakes to the Midwest.

Building Vocabulary

Write the vocabulary terms on the board and have students locate and read the definitions in the text or in the glossary. Ask students to think of problems that may be caused by **droughts**. (Possible answers: Farmers could not grow crops; rivers may dry up; fires could start in dry areas.) Then call on students to point out on a wall map the locations of the **Corn Belt** and the **Dairy Belt**.

118 • Chapter 5

Landforms and Climate

The Midwest includes eight states: Ohio, Michigan, Indiana, Illinois, Wisconsin, Minnesota, Iowa, and Missouri. All but Iowa and Missouri have shorelines on the Great Lakes, the largest freshwater lake system in the world.

Most of the Midwest lies within the Interior Plains, a region of flat plains and low hills. The most rugged areas are in the Ozark Plateau, which stretches into southern Missouri. During the Ice Age the northern part of the region was eroded by glaciers. These glaciers created the Great Lakes. They also left behind thin soils and many thousands of smaller lakes.

The entire Midwest has a humid continental climate with four distinct seasons. The whole region experiences cold arctic air and snow in winter. The region is subject to thunderstorms, tornadoes, and occasional summer **droughts**. Droughts are periods when little rain falls and crops are damaged.

✓ **READING CHECK:** *Places and Regions* In which landform and climate regions are the Midwest located? **Interior Plains; humid continental**

The northern part of the Midwest has thousands of lakes. Minnesota alone has more than 10,000 lakes.

Economy

Agriculture Good soils and flat land have helped make the Midwest one of the world's great farming regions. Farmers produce corn, dairy products, and soybeans and raise cattle. The core of the Midwest's corn-growing region is the **Corn Belt**. It stretches from central Ohio to central Nebraska. Much of the corn is used to feed livestock, such as beef cattle and hogs.

States in the **Dairy Belt** are major producers of milk, cheese, and other dairy products. Most of the Dairy Belt is pasture. Located north of the Corn Belt, the area includes Wisconsin and most of Minnesota and Michigan.

Corn: From Field to Consumer

Ⓐ Corn can be processed in a variety of ways. Some corn is cooked and then canned.
Ⓑ Corn is ground and used for livestock feed.
Ⓒ Corn also might be wet-milled or dry-milled. Then grain parts are used to make different products.
Ⓓ Corn by-products, such as cornstarch and corn syrup, are used to make breads, breakfast cereals, and snack foods.

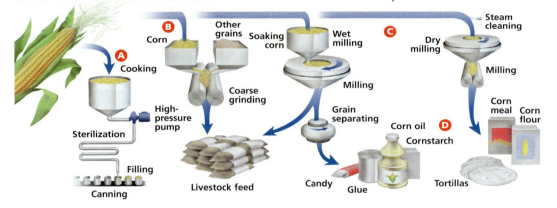

CHAPTER 5, Section 3

ENVIRONMENT AND SOCIETY

Super Soybeans The Corn Belt could easily be called the Soy Belt instead. Soybeans go into many food products and into animal feed. They also improve soil quality. The plant was introduced into the midwest at the beginning of the 1800s. A visitor to China smuggled a few soybean seeds out of that country, where the plant had been domesticated for about 5,000 years, and brought them to the United States.

Farmers often rotate soybeans with corn, a process that reduces insect infestations and disease. In addition, soybeans, which are legumes, fix nitrogen in the soil. Corn needs nitrogen-rich soil to thrive. The beans themselves are consumed by humans and livestock and are made into numerous products.

Critical Thinking: Why may more farmers in the Midwest be switching to soybeans?

Answer: In recent years, unprocessed soybeans have been recognized as a nutritious food for humans.

The Regions of the United States • 119

TEACH

Teaching Objective 1

ALL LEVELS: (Suggested time: 30 min.) Copy the following graphic organizer onto the board, omitting the blue names and check marks. Ask students to copy the table into their notebooks. Pair students and have each pair fill in the names of the Midwestern states in the first column. Then have them identify the physical features of the states by placing check marks in the boxes below features located in or lakes that border each state.
ESOL, COOPERATIVE LEARNING

PHYSICAL FEATURES OF THE MIDWEST					
State	Interior Plains	Lake Superior	Lake Michigan	Lake Huron	Lake Erie
Ohio	√				√
Michigan	√	√	√	√	√
Indiana	√		√		
Illinois	√		√		
Wisconsin	√	√	√		
Minnesota	√	√			
Iowa	√				
Missouri	√				

CHAPTER 5, Section 3

EYE ON EARTH

Great Lakes Legends

Long before ships sailed on the Great Lakes, the Algonquin and Iroquois knew that crossing the lakes in the fall was dangerous. Legends told of a Mighty Serpent of the Lakes whose wrath caused great gusts of wind and walls of water to drown travelers. Sailors today speak of the Witch of November, who is said to stir up gale-force winds and gigantic waves. There is no witch, of course, but November storms on the lakes can be fierce.

Meteorologists suggest that the jet stream in the area pulls down cold Arctic air. When it meets warm, humid air from the Gulf of Mexico, violent storms can result.

Activity: Have students explore the basis of legends related to other locations. Have them report their findings in paragraphs.

Connecting to Technology
Answers
1. Duluth, Sault Ste. Marie, Green Bay, Milwaukee, Chicago, Gary, Detroit, Toledo, Cleveland, Erie, Buffalo; were near water and easy shipping
2. Lake Superior; Lake Ontario

Connecting to Technology

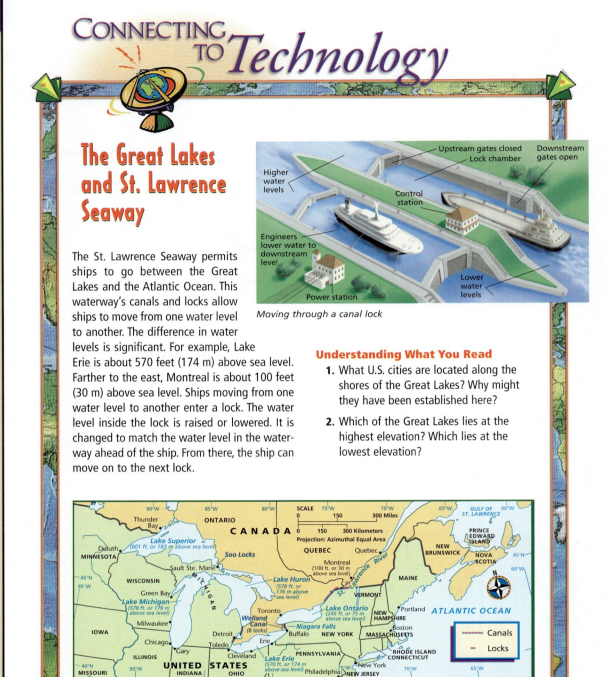

The Great Lakes and St. Lawrence Seaway

The St. Lawrence Seaway permits ships to go between the Great Lakes and the Atlantic Ocean. This waterway's canals and locks allow ships to move from one water level to another. The difference in water levels is significant. For example, Lake Erie is about 570 feet (174 m) above sea level. Farther to the east, Montreal is about 100 feet (30 m) above sea level. Ships moving from one water level to another enter a lock. The water level inside the lock is raised or lowered. It is changed to match the water level in the waterway ahead of the ship. From there, the ship can move on to the next lock.

Moving through a canal lock

Understanding What You Read
1. What U.S. cities are located along the shores of the Great Lakes? Why might they have been established here?
2. Which of the Great Lakes lies at the highest elevation? Which lies at the lowest elevation?

120 • Chapter 5

Teaching Objectives 1–2

ALL LEVELS: (Suggested time: 45 min.) Organize students into four or five groups. Have the groups meet to discuss where they would choose to live and what jobs they would want to pursue if they lived in the Midwest. Ask students if they would prefer to live in the Corn Belt or the Dairy Belt and be involved in agriculture, or live in one of the Midwest's big cities, such as Chicago, St. Louis, or Detroit, where they might work in business or manufacturing. Ask students to be specific in their answers. For example, they should name the crops they might grow as farmers or the industry in which they might work in a city. Have the groups create balance sheets on which they record the advantages and disadvantages of each lifestyle. Allow groups to compare their charts. **ESOL, COOPERATIVE LEARNING**

▶**ASSIGNMENT:** Provide students with a copy of Carl Sandburg's poem "Chicago." Ask them to read it and then write a poem about another important Midwestern city in a style that, like Sandburg's, describes the city as if it were a person. Ask volunteers to read their poems to the class. **LS VERBAL-LINGUISTIC**

Many of the Midwest's products are shipped to markets by water. One route is along the Mississippi River to the Gulf of Mexico. The other is through the Great Lakes.

Industry Chicago, Illinois, is one of the busiest shipping ports on the Great Lakes and has one of the world's busiest airports. Chicago is linked to the rest of the region by highways and railroads. In the late 1800s, its industries attracted many immigrants. They worked in steel mills, meat-packing plants, and other businesses. Today, Chicago is the third-largest city in the United States.

Other Midwest cities such as Cleveland, Detroit, and Milwaukee were also founded on important transportation routes, either on the Great Lakes or on major rivers. The locations of these cities gave industries access to nearby farm products, coal, and iron ore. Those resources have supported thriving industries such as food processing, iron, steel, machinery, and automobile manufacturing. Detroit, Michigan, has been the nation's leading automobile producer since the early 1900s.

On the upper Mississippi River, Minneapolis and St. Paul are major distribution centers for agricultural and industrial products from the upper Midwest. On the western bank of the Mississippi River is St. Louis. About two hundred years ago, it became the center for pioneers heading west and the nation's leading riverboat port.

The Midwest's traditional industries declined in the late 1900s. In addition, industrial pollution threatened the Great Lakes and surrounding areas. In response, companies have modernized their plants and factories. The region has also attracted new industries. Many produce high-technology products. The Midwest is again a prosperous region. Stricter pollution laws have made many rivers and the Great Lakes much cleaner.

✓ **READING CHECK:** *Places and Regions* What are the major economic activities of the Midwest? agriculture, industry, transportation

The Sears Tower (at left) in downtown Chicago is one of the world's tallest buildings.

Section Review 3

Define and explain: droughts, Corn Belt, Dairy Belt

Working with Sketch Maps On the map that you created in Section 2, label the eight states of the Midwest. Then label Chicago, Detroit, and St. Louis.

Reading for the Main Idea
1. *Places and Regions* Which Midwestern states are in the Corn Belt? Which are in the Dairy Belt?
2. *Places and Regions* Why are Chicago and Detroit important Midwestern cities?
3. *Human Systems* How do farm and industrial products from the Midwest get to markets elsewhere?

Critical Thinking
4. **Drawing Inferences and Conclusions** How might the physical geography of the Midwest be different if the Ice Age had not occurred?

Organizing What You Know
5. **Cause and Effect** Copy the following graphic organizer. Use it to show how location on important transportation routes helped the economy of Midwest cities to grow.

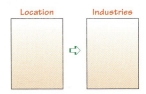

Section 3 Review

Answers to Section 3 Review

Define For definitions, see the glossary.

Working with Sketch Maps Maps will vary, but listed places should be labeled in their approximate locations.

Reading for the Main Idea
1. Corn Belt—Ohio, Indiana, Illinois, Iowa, Missouri; Dairy Belt—Wisconsin, Minnesota, Michigan (NGS 4)
2. Chicago—busy transportation center with airports, highways, railroads, Great Lakes port; Detroit—nation's leading auto producer (NGS 12)
3. many shipped by water on the Mississippi River or through the Great Lakes (NGS 11)

Critical Thinking
4. fewer lakes and rivers; soils less fertile

Organizing What You Know
5. Location—ports on Great Lakes, major rivers; Industries—food processing, iron, steel, machinery, automobiles, high-technology products

Close

Have students take turns naming Midwestern states. Have each student point out the state on a wall map of the United States and relate a fact about its landforms, agricultural products, or industries.

Review, Assess, Reteach

Have students complete the Section Review. Then have each student create a crossword puzzle based on the material in Section 3. Tell students to include clues for 10 terms. Pair students and invite them to solve each other's puzzles. Then ask students to complete Daily Quiz 5.3.
COOPERATIVE LEARNING, LS VERBAL-LINGUISTIC

Have students complete Main Idea Activity S3. Organize the class into four groups to plan state pavilions for a Midwest Fair. Assign two states to each group and have members design displays to educate visitors about the landforms, agriculture, and industry of their states. **ESOL**

Extend

Have interested students choose a Midwestern state and compile a fact sheet on that state. Students should include information such as population, area, state capital, state bird, state flower, nickname, and state motto. They may provide additional facts such as how the state got its name and famous people born in the state. **BLOCK SCHEDULING**

CHAPTER 5, Section 4

SECTION 4 RESOURCES

Reproducible
- Lecture Notes, Section 4
- Know It Notes S4

Technology
- One-Stop Planner CD–ROM, Lesson 5.4
- Homework Practice Online
- HRW Go site

Reinforcement, Review, and Assessment
- Main Idea Activity S4
- Section 4 Review
- Daily Quiz 5.4
- Chapter Summaries and Review
- English Audio Summary 5.4
- Spanish Audio Summary 5.4

Section 4: The Interior West

Read to Discover
1. What are the major landform regions of the Interior West?
2. What are the characteristics of the Interior West's climates?
3. What economic activities are important in the Interior West?

Vocabulary
badlands
chinooks
Wheat Belt
center-point irrigation
strip mining
national parks

Places
Phoenix
Las Vegas
Denver

Reading Strategy

FOLDNOTES: FOUR-CORNER FOLD — Create the FoldNote titled **Four-Corner Fold** described in the Appendix. Title the flaps Region, Land Description, Climate, and How Land Is Used. As you read, fill in information you learn about each topic beneath its flap.

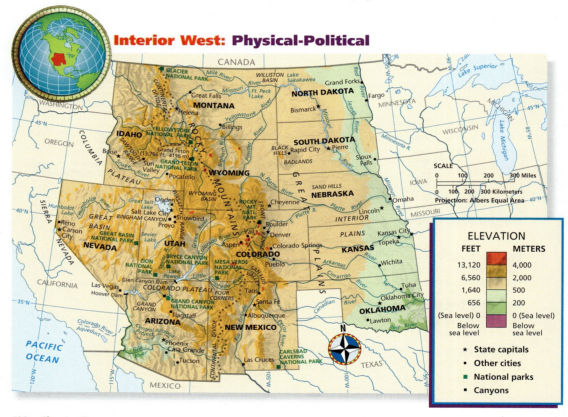

Interior West: Physical-Political

122 • Chapter 5

Section 4

Objectives
1. Identify the major landform regions of the Interior West.
2. Describe the climates of the Interior West.
3. List some economic activities of the Interior West.

Focus

Bellringer

Copy the following question onto the chalkboard: *What images come to mind when you think of the Great Plains?* Have students write down their answers. Discuss responses. (Students may mention large, flat areas covered by prairie grasses.) Point out that the region also has a variety of other landforms, including hills, mountains, and sand dunes. Tell students they will learn more about the Great Plains and other features of the Interior West in Section 4.

Building Vocabulary

Write the vocabulary terms on the chalkboard and have students read their definitions from the glossary or text. Ask students which words relate to landforms (**badlands**), climate (**chinooks**), agriculture (**Wheat Belt, center-point irrigation**), mining **strip mining**, and tourism (**national parks**).

122 Chapter 5

Landforms

The Interior West includes the states of North Dakota, South Dakota, Nebraska, Kansas, Oklahoma, Montana, Wyoming, Colorado, Idaho, Utah, Nevada, New Mexico, and Arizona. These states occupy three landform regions: the Great Plains, the Rocky Mountains, and the Intermountain West.

The Great Plains were formed over millions of years by the depositing of sediment from mountains. Rivers carried this sediment onto the plains, slowly increasing their elevation. The plains are known for their flat, sweeping horizons. A few areas, however, feature more varied landforms. The Sand Hills of Nebraska are ancient, grass-covered sand dunes. In the Dakotas, rugged areas of soft rock called **badlands** are found. Badlands are areas that have been eroded by wind and water into small gullies. They have little vegetation or soil.

West of the Great Plains are the Rocky Mountains. They stretch from the Arctic through Idaho, Montana, Wyoming, Utah, Colorado, and New Mexico. The Rockies are actually a series of mountain ranges, passes, and valleys.

Two other major landforms, the Great Basin and the Colorado Plateau, are located west of the Rockies. They are both part of the Intermountain West region. The rivers of the Great Basin do not reach the sea. Instead they flow into low basins and dry up. There they leave behind dry lake beds or salt flats. The Colorado Plateau is known for its deep canyons. The largest of these is the Grand Canyon.

✓ **READING CHECK:** *Places and Regions* What kinds of landforms are found in the Interior West? **flat plains, sand dunes, mountain ranges, passes, valleys, basins, canyons**

▲ Storms like this one are common on the Great Plains of Wyoming.

◄ **Region** The Rocky Mountains create beautiful views in much of Colorado. The highest mountain peaks reach elevations where trees cannot grow.

CHAPTER 5, Section 4

PLACES AND REGIONS

Mighty Mount Rushmore
One of the most recognizable symbols of the United States is Mount Rushmore in Keystone, South Dakota. This monument is a symbol of the birth and development of the country, personified in the 60-foot (18 m) busts of Presidents George Washington, Thomas Jefferson, Abraham Lincoln, and Theodore Roosevelt. Between 1927 and 1941, artist Gutzon Borglum and 400 workers carved the likenesses of these presidents into the Black Hills.

Discussion: Lead a class discussion about why these four presidents where chosen for Mount Rushmore. (*Possible answers: Washington represents the country's founding, Jefferson embodies its political philosophy, Lincoln signifies preservation, and Roosevelt stands for expansion and conservation.*)

The Regions of the United States • 123

TEACH

Teaching Objective 1

LEVEL 1: (Suggested time: 40 min.) Have students imagine they are landscape artists who recently visited the Interior West. Ask them to sketch four of the landforms they saw there. Display the drawings. Then lead a class discussion about the physical features of the Interior West.
ESOL, **LS** **VISUAL-SPATIAL**

LEVELS 2 AND 3: (Suggested time: 30 min.) Have each student write a list of six terms that are related to the landforms of the Interior West. Then have each student exchange lists with a partner and write a paragraph or two describing the landforms of the Interior West. Tell students that they should use all of the terms they have received in their descriptions. Call on volunteers to share their work with the class.
COOPERATIVE LEARNING, **LS** **VERBAL-LINGUISTIC**

The Regions of the United States   123

CHAPTER 5, Section 4

COOPERATIVE LEARNING

A Very Grand Canyon
Tell students that the Grand Canyon is among North America's most spectacular physical features. Rock layers hundreds of millions of years old are visible in the colorful sides of the canyon. Rocks at the bottom of the canyon are several billion years old. Point out that this scenic area is a national park.

Organize the class into groups of four or five. Direct each group to conduct research and write a brief report on Grand Canyon National Park. The report should note when the park was established and what attractions it offers. Students should also note steps the government is taking to correct problems caused by overcrowding in the park. Have students share their reports.

internet connect
GO TO: go.hrw.com
KEYWORD: SJ5 CH5
FOR: Web sites about Grand Canyon National Park

Visual Record Answer
erosion caused by flowing water

▲ These cacti are native to the desert climate of Arizona. The short plant is a teddy bear cholla (CHOY-yuh). The tall cactus is a saguaro (suh-WAHR-uh).

▶ The Colorado River flows through Marble Canyon in Arizona.
Interpreting the Visual Record How do you think this canyon was formed?

124 • Chapter 5

Climate

Most of the Great Plains region has a steppe climate. The plains are semiarid and become drier toward the west. Temperatures can vary greatly. Winter temperatures in some areas can drop to -40°F (-40°C), while summer temperatures might rise above 110°F (43°C). Droughts are a major climate hazard in this region. During drought periods, dust storms may cover huge areas. In addition, strong, dry winds blow from the Rocky Mountains onto the Great Plains. These winds are called **chinooks**.

The highland climates of the Rocky Mountain region vary, depending on elevation. Semiarid grasslands usually are found at the foot of the mountains. Most of the slopes, on the other hand, are forested. The forests capture the winter snowfall and form the source for the rivers that flow across the Great Plains. Climates in the Great Basin and the Colorado Plateau also vary. Arizona, New Mexico, and Nevada have mostly desert climates. Utah and southern Idaho have mainly steppe climates. Some parts of this region lie in the rain shadow created by the Rocky Mountains. These areas receive almost no rain at all. This is particularly true in low-lying areas of the Great Basin.

Because the region's climate is so varied, many types of vegetation grow in the Interior West. The Great Plains were once covered with grasses, shrubs, and sagebrush. Most of the native vegetation, however, has been cut to allow farming and ranching. The drier desert areas of the Southwest have less vegetation. Bushes and cacti are the most common plants in the region.

✓ **READING CHECK:** *Places and Regions* Why do the Rockies have several different types of climate? **different elevations**

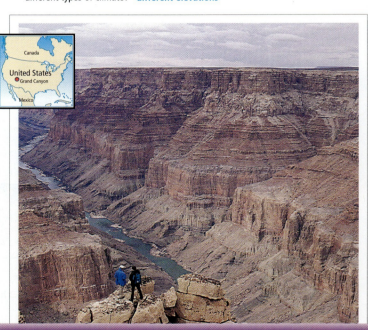

Teaching Objective 2
ALL LEVELS: (Suggested time: 20 min.) Copy the following graphic organizer onto the chalkboard, omitting the blue answers. Ask students to copy the organizer into their notebooks. Have students complete the chart with words that describe the climates of the three Interior West subregions. Discuss the completed charts. **ESOL**

CLIMATES OF THE INTERIOR WEST		
Great Plains	**Rocky Mountains**	**Intermountain West**
• steppe climate • dust storms • droughts • chinooks	• highland climate • semiarid grasslands • snowy winter slopes	• desert climate • steppe climate • almost no rain in some areas

Economy

Ranching became important in the Interior West in the 1800s. Great herds of cattle and flocks of sheep roamed the Great Plains. Today, both ranching and wheat farming are common. The greatest wheat-growing area is known as the **Wheat Belt**. It stretches across the Dakotas, Montana, Nebraska, Kansas, Oklahoma, Colorado, and Texas.

Irrigation Because this region receives relatively little rainfall, farmers depend on irrigation to water their crops. Much of the farmland in the Interior West must be irrigated. One method of irrigation uses long sprinkler systems mounted on wheels. The wheels rotate slowly. In this way, the sprinkler irrigates the area within a circle. This is called **center-point irrigation**.

Historically most of the water used to irrigate fields in the Interior West was drawn from underground aquifers. Overuse of this water, however, has drained much of the water from these aquifers. As a result, some farmers have begun to seek new sources for water. They want to preserve some of the region's valuable groundwater.

Movement Wheat from the Great Plains is shipped to other countries.

Place Workers have dug this pit to mine coal near Sheridan, Wyoming. Wyoming has the largest coal deposits in the Interior West.

CHAPTER 5, Section 4

Linking Past to Present

The Comstock Lode In the late 1850s prospectors discovered gold in western Nevada. Miners near the small community of Virginia City complained that the small deposits of gold they found had to be dug out of a sticky blue-gray mud that clung to their picks and shovels. This troublesome mud, however, was soon identified as the richest deposit of silver ore ever found in the United States. It became known as the Comstock Lode.

Silver mining was the most important activity in Nevada for many years, but the metal began to decline in value in the 1870s. The Comstock Lode, stripped of its gold and silver, was abandoned by 1900. Tourism has become Virginia City's primary industry.

Critical Thinking: How did the Comstock Lode help settlements in Nevada grow?

Answer: Many prospectors were lured to the area by the potential to get rich.

Teaching Objective 3
LEVEL 1: (Suggesting time: 20 min.) Organize the class into three groups representing ranchers, farmers, and miners. Have each student write down one or two facts from the textbook about his or her assigned economic group. Call on students in each group to state a different fact until all the information has been covered. Then lead a discussion about the economies of the states of the Interior West. **COOPERATIVE LEARNING**

LEVELS 2 AND 3: (Suggesting time: 45 min.) Arrange the class into two groups to prepare a debate. Ask one group to prepare arguments supporting agriculture as the most important economic feature of the Interior West. The other group should argue that mining is more important to the region. Encourage students to conduct additional research for more information. Stage the debate. **COOPERATIVE LEARNING, INTERPERSONAL**

Section 4 Review

Answers to Section 4 Review

Define For definitions, see the glossary.

Working with Sketch Maps Maps will vary, but listed places should be labeled in their approximate locations.

Reading for the Main Idea
1. Great Plains, Rocky Mountains, Great Basin, Colorado Plateau; steppe, highland, desert **(NGS 4)**
2. has plains suitable for ranching and wheat farming, deposits of minerals for mining, and scenic areas for tourism **(NGS 11)**

Critical Thinking
3. possible answer: to preserve natural beauty, environment
4. probably not; without it people might not tolerate hot climate

Organizing What You Know
5. Badlands—gullies, no plants or soil; wind and water erosion; Great Basin—dry lake beds, salt flats; rivers flowing into low basins and drying up; Grand Canyon—deep gorges; carved by Colorado River

---

Yellowstone is the country's oldest national park, dating back to 1872. Yellowstone National Park has about 200 geysers—including the famous Old Faithful—and 10,000 hot springs.

Mining and Industry Mining is a key economic activity in the Rocky Mountains. Early prospectors struck large veins of gold and silver there. Today Arizona, New Mexico, and Utah are leading copper-producing states. Nevada is a leading gold-mining state. Lead and many other ores are also found in the Interior West.

However, mining can cause problems. For example, coal miners in parts of the Great Plains strip away soil and rock. This process is called **strip mining**. This kind of mining leads to soil erosion and other problems. Today, laws require miners to restore damaged areas.

One of the Interior West's greatest resources is its natural beauty. The U.S. government has set aside large scenic areas known as **national parks**. Among these are Yellowstone, Grand Teton, Rocky Mountain, and Glacier National Parks. Tourists are also drawn to other areas of the Rocky Mountains. Ski resorts like Aspen and Vail in Colorado and Taos in New Mexico attract many people to the region. Another popular attraction is Mount Rushmore. In the early 1900s, sculptors carved the faces of four presidents into one of the Black Hills of South Dakota. Las Vegas, Nevada, is likewise one of the country's most popular tourist destinations.

Interior West cities like Phoenix, Arizona, and Denver, Colorado, are growing rapidly. The population of Phoenix, for example, has doubled since 1980. Many retirement communities have sprung up in the desert. After World War II, the federal government built dams, military bases, and major highways in the area. The widespread use of air conditioning has made the Phoenix area even more attractive.

✓ **READING CHECK:** *Places and Regions* What makes agriculture possible in the climate of the Great Plains? *irrigation*

Keyword: SJ5 HP5

Define and explain: badlands, chinooks, Wheat Belt, center-point irrigation, strip mining, national parks

Working with Sketch Maps On the map that you created for Section 3, label the 13 Interior West states. Then label Phoenix and Las Vegas.

Reading for the Main Idea
1. *Places and Regions* What landform regions and climates are found in the Interior West?
2. *Human Systems* How does geography contribute to the economy of the Interior West?

Critical Thinking
3. **Drawing Inferences** Why has the U.S. government created national parks in this region?
4. **Drawing Inferences and Conclusions** Would cities such as Phoenix be experiencing such rapid growth if air conditioning had not been invented? Why or why not?

Organizing What You Know
5. **Identifying Cause and Effect** Copy the following graphic organizer. Use it to describe landforms of the Interior West and what created them.

Landform	Description	Formation
Badlands		
Great Basin		
Grand Canyon		

126 • Chapter 5

CLOSE

Ask students to make up descriptive mottoes for each subregion of the Interior West. Encourage student to mention landforms, climates, or economic activities in their mottoes.

REVIEW, ASSESS, RETEACH

Have students complete the Section Review. Then have each student make four flash cards. On one side of three cards, tell students to write the name of an Interior West subregion. They should label the fourth card Challenges. On the back of each card have students should write three questions. Pair students and have them quiz each other. Then have students complete Daily Quiz 5.4.

Have students complete Main Idea Activity S4. Then organize students into three groups to construct mobiles. One group's mobile should depict landforms of the Interior West, the second should show climates, and the third resources and industries. **ESOL, COOPERATIVE LEARNING**

EXTEND

Have interested students conduct research on the Dust Bowl of the 1930s and its effects on farming in the Interior West. Have each student present his or her findings in a brief oral report. Encourage students to provide visual aids to accompany their reports. **BLOCK SCHEDULING**

Section 5: The Pacific States

Read to Discover
1. What types of landforms do the different Pacific states share?
2. How do the climates of the Pacific states differ?
3. How do the Pacific states contribute to the economy of the United States?

Vocabulary
caldera

Places
Coast Ranges
Sierra Nevada
Death Valley
Willamette Valley
Cascades
Los Angeles
Seattle

Reading Strategy

COMPARING AND CONTRASTING INFORMATION Before you read, draw three overlapping ovals on a sheet of paper. Label them California, Oregon and Washington, and Alaska and Hawaii. As you read the section, write characteristics about each area in an oval. Write shared characteristics where the ovals overlap.

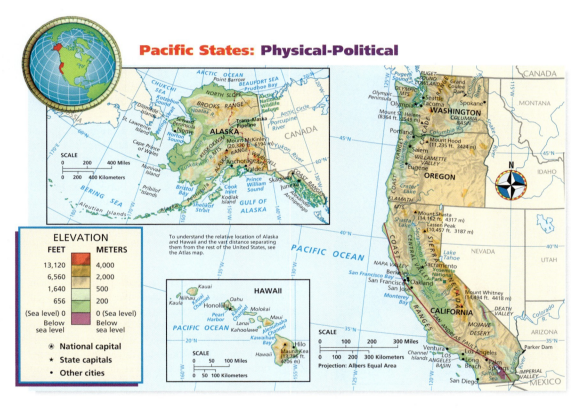

Pacific States: Physical-Political

CHAPTER 5, Section 5

SECTION 5 RESOURCES

Reproducible
- Lecture Notes, Section 5
- Know It Notes S5
- Map Activity 11

Technology
- One-Stop Planner CD–ROM, Lesson 5.5
- Homework Practice Online
- HRW Go site

Reinforcement, Review, and Assessment
- Main Idea Activity S5
- Section 5 Review
- Daily Quiz 5.5
- Chapter Summaries and Review
- English Audio Summary 5.5
- Spanish Audio Summary 5.5

Objectives
1. Identify the types of landforms found in the Pacific states.
2. Explain how the climates of the Pacific states differ.
3. Explain how the Pacific states contribute to the economy of the United States.

Focus

Bellringer
Copy the following questions onto the chalkboard: *What are some things you associate with Alaska? What do you associate with Hawaii? Do you have similar associations with California, Oregon, or Washington?* Discuss responses. Point out that although these five states are very different, they can be viewed together as a single region. Tell students that they will learn more about the Pacific states in this section.

Building Vocabulary
Write **contiguous** and **caldera** on the chalkboard and have students read their definitions from the glossary. Point out that there are 48 contiguous states in the United States. Ask students which two are the exceptions (Alaska, Hawaii). Then tell students that *caldera* comes from the Latin *calidaria*, the same root as *cauldron*. Ask students what a cauldron is (a large pot or vessel) and how the two words are related. (A caldera and a cauldron have similar shapes.)

The Regions of the United States 127

CHAPTER 5, Section 5

ENVIRONMENT AND SOCIETY

Earthquakes and Building Construction Los Angeles lies west of the San Andreas Fault, and it also sprawls across 40 smaller faults. The construction codes that restricted building heights until the 1950s were written because of fears about earthquake damage. Today, advances in engineering techniques have allowed the construction of skyscrapers of 50 stories or more that should withstand earthquakes.

Activity: Have students conduct research on California building codes. Ask students to construct a scale model or draw a diagram of a building or other kind of structure showing the special measures taken to help make it "earthquake-proof."

GO TO: go.hrw.com
KEYWORD: SJ5 CH5
FOR: Web sites about earthquakes

A View of the Pacific States

If you looked at a map, you might wonder why California, Oregon, Washington, Alaska, and Hawaii are grouped together as a region. Alaska and Hawaii are separated from each other and from the 48 contiguous states. Contiguous states are those that border each other. Yet these states share a physical environment characterized by mountains, volcanoes, and earthquakes. They share cultural, political, and economic similarities as well. In addition, each of the states is working to protect fragile wilderness areas, fertile agricultural lands, and valuable natural resources. In many cases, these features are what first attracted people to the region.

Landforms

California California can be divided into four major landform areas. They are the Coast Ranges, the Sierra Nevada, the Central Valley, and the desert basins and ranges. The Coast Ranges form a rugged coastline along the Pacific.

The Sierra Nevada range lies east of the Coast Ranges. It is one of the longest and highest mountain ranges in the United States. Mount Whitney, the highest peak in the 48 contiguous states, rises above the Sierra Nevada.

Between the Sierra Nevada and the Coast Ranges is a narrow plain known as the Central Valley. This plain stretches more than 400 miles (644 km). The Central Valley is irrigated by rivers that flow from the Sierra Nevada.

To the east of the Sierra Nevada are desert basins and mountain ranges. Included in this region is Death Valley, the lowest point in all of North America.

Earthquakes are common in California due to the San Andreas Fault system. This fault was formed where the Pacific and North American plates meet. The Pacific plate is slowly moving northward along the San Andreas Fault, past the North American plate. The shock waves caused by this activity can create severe earthquakes.

Oregon and Washington Four landform regions dominate Oregon and Washington. As in California the Coast Ranges form the scenic Pacific Northwest coastline. Just east of these mountains are two lowlands areas. The Puget Sound Lowland is in Washington, and the Willamette Valley lies in Oregon. These rich farmlands contain most of the population of each state.

The San Andreas Fault caused a severe earthquake in Los Angeles in 1994. Scientists warn that future severe earthquakes threaten California.

128 • Chapter 5

TEACH

Teaching Objective 1

LEVEL 1: (Suggested time: 20 min.) Show students pictures of some landforms that might be found in the Pacific states. Some examples might include steep mountains, rocky coastlines, volcanoes, deserts, river and valleys. Then call on students to point out on a large wall map where in the region they might see such scenes. **ESOL, LS VISUAL-SPATIAL**

LEVEL 2: (Suggested time: 30 min.) Point out that many television game shows are produced in California. Have students prepare questions about California's physical geography that could be used for a game show. Have students take turns acting as the host of the show, asking questions of the other members of the class. **COOPERATIVE LEARNING**

◀ Crater Lake is what remains of a volcanic mountain that erupted more than 6,000 years ago.

The Cascades are a volcanic mountain range stretching across both states into northern California. The range includes Oregon's Crater Lake, the deepest lake in the United States. Crater Lake fills a huge **caldera**. A caldera is a large depression formed after a major eruption and collapse of a volcanic mountain.

East of the Cascades is a region of dry basins and mountains. Much of this area is known as the Columbia Basin. It is drained by the Columbia River.

Alaska and Hawaii Alaska occupies a huge peninsula that juts out from the northwestern part of North America. The volcanic Aleutian Islands form an arc to the southwest. The mountain ranges of Alaska are some of the most rugged in the world. The state has more than 3 million lakes. Ice fields and glaciers cover 4 percent of the state.

The Hawaiian Islands are a chain of eight major islands and more than 100 smaller islands. Although the islands are volcanic in origin, only one has active volcanoes. This is Hawaii, the largest of the islands. The Hawaiian Islands have scenic coasts with coral reefs that erode into fine, white beach sand.

Sunlight reflects off the rugged cliffs of Kalau Valley on the Hawaiian island of Kauai.
Interpreting the Visual Record Why do you suppose few roads have been built in some parts of Kauai?

✓ **READING CHECK:**
Identifying Cause and Effect
What causes severe earthquakes in California? shock waves created by the movement of the Pacific plate northward along the San Andreas Fault, past the North American plate

CHAPTER 5, Section 5

Across the Curriculum
MUSIC
Slack Key Guitar Spanish and Mexican vaqueros, or cowboys, probably brought the first guitars to Hawaii. In the 1830s, King Kamehameha III hired vaqueros to control the wild cattle population on the islands. Some Hawaiians began playing these guitars and adapting them to suit Hawaiian musical rhythms. By loosening the instrument's strings, the musicians created a rich, full sound. They also used traditional drum and dance rhythms. The Hawaiian guitar style is called *ki ho'alu*, or "slack key."

Activity: Play a recording of Hawaiian slack key guitar music and a recording of American folk guitar music. Ask students to listen for and to describe the differences between the two recordings. Have students discuss why they think this style became popular.

◀ **Visual Record Answer**
The steep, rugged cliffs would make road building impossible.

The Regions of the United States • 129

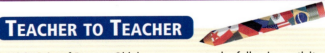

LEVEL 3: (Suggested time: 15 min.) List the following Pacific states on the chalkboard: Oregon, Washington, Alaska, Hawaii. Ask students to identify the physical features of these states that are related to water in some way. (Possible answers: Oregon—Willamette Valley, Crater Lake; Washington—Puget Sound, Columbia Basin; Alaska—Aleutian Islands, lakes, ice fields, glaciers; Hawaii—Hawaiian Islands, coral reefs) Then ask students to name some landforms created by tectonic activity. (Possible answers: calderas, Hawaiian islands) Call on volunteers to explain how these landforms are similar to those found in California.

TEACHER TO TEACHER
Patricia Britt of Durant, Oklahoma, suggests the following activity to help students understand the five Pacific states. After students have read this section, have each student plan a trip to one of the states. Provide students with itinerary forms, atlases, and travel guides. Students should plan where they will stay, what they will see, and about how much the trip might cost. They should also write journal entries describing the landforms, bodies of water, climates, and vegetation they might see on their trip. Students might also discuss regional foods they might enjoy and with which they are familiar.

The Regions of the United States **129**

CHAPTER 5, Section 5

FOOD FESTIVAL

Eating Your Way across the U.S.A. Each region of the United States contributes to the country's food supply. Have each student create a dinner menu that includes foods from each region. Tell students to choose items that are specialties of the regions. Students may wish to look in cookbooks to learn ways that regional foods are prepared. Invite students to decorate the their menus and, if possible, to bring samples of some recipes to class.

Only animals that can survive cold harsh climates, like the polar bear, live in northern Alaska.

Our Amazing Planet

Part of the island of Kauai in Hawaii is considered the wettest place in the world.

Climate

The climates of the Pacific states vary. Seven different climates can be found within this region. They range from tropical to tundra climates.

California The northern coast of California has a marine west coast climate. Along the southern coast and in central California, the climate is Mediterranean. Temperatures are warm all year, even in winter. Summers are dry with hot winds. The basins of eastern California experience desert and steppe climates. Summer temperatures in Death Valley often reach 120° F (49° C).

Oregon and Washington The Cascades divide Oregon and Washington into two climate regions. To the west, the climate is marine west coast. Temperatures are mild year-round, with cloudy, rainy winters and warm, sunny summers. To the east of the Cascades are drier desert and steppe climates.

Alaska and Hawaii A marine west coast climate is found along the southeast coast of Alaska. Most of the state, especially the interior, has a subarctic climate. Summers are short, while winters are long and severe. Most precipitation is in the form of snow. The northern area of Alaska along the Arctic Ocean has a tundra climate.

Hawaii has little daily or seasonal temperature change. During Honolulu's coldest month, the temperature averages 72° F (22° C). It averages 81° F (27° C) during the warmest month. The climate of the eastern slopes of the islands is humid tropical with heavy rainfall.

✓ **READING CHECK:** *Supporting a Point of View* Which climate of the Pacific states would you prefer? Why? Answers will vary, but should be supported by details about a particular climate found in the Pacific states.

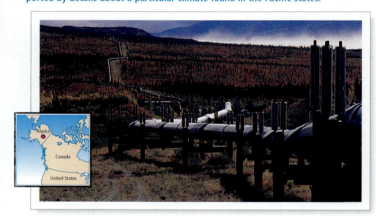

The Trans-Alaska Pipeline snakes across mountain ranges and tundra.

130 • Chapter 5

Teaching Objective 2
ALL LEVELS: (Suggested time: 30 min.) Organize the class into several groups and provide each group with a large piece of butcher paper. Have each group draw a large freehand map of the Pacific West states and mark various climates found in the Pacific states. **ESOL**, **LS** VISUAL-SPATIAL

Teaching Objective 3
ALL LEVELS: (Suggested time: 15 min.) Copy the following graphic organizer onto the chalkboard, omitting the blue answers. Have students fill in the space below each state's name with some of the economic activities found there.

ECONOMIC CHARACTERISTICS OF THE PACIFIC WEST STATES				
California	Oregon	Washington	Alaska	Hawaii
agriculture	forests	forests	oil	tourism
aerospace	fish	fish	forests	agriculture
construction		software	fish	
computers				
software				
entertainment				
tourism				

130 Chapter 5

Economy

Each of the Pacific states contributes to the economy of the United States. California is the leading agricultural producer and leading industrial state. Crops include cotton, nuts, vegetables, and fruit. Aerospace, construction, entertainment, computers, software, and tourism are important industries in the state.

Forests and fish are two of the most important resources in Oregon and Washington. Seattle, Washington, is home to many important industries, including a major computer software company.

Alaska's economy is largely based on oil, forests, and fish. Hawaii's natural beauty, mild climate, and fertile soils are its most important resources. Hawaii's volcanic soils and climate are ideal for growing sugarcane, pineapples, and coffee. Millions of tourists visit the islands each year. Both states lack diverse agriculture and industry. As a result most goods must be imported from other states.

READING CHECK: *Drawing Conclusions* What can you conclude about how Hawaii contributes to the U.S. economy as a result of having a mild climate and fertile soils? Answers will vary, but should include that Hawaii contributes as an agricultural producer.

Timber harvesting in Washington's Olympic National Forest has left irregular patterns in the forest.

Interpreting the Visual Record
Human-Environment Interaction How may cutting down too many trees change these landforms over time?

Section Review 5

Define and explain: caldera

Working with Sketch Maps On the map that you created for Section 4, label the five Pacific states. Then label the following places: Coast Ranges, Sierra Nevada, Death Valley, Willamette Valley, Cascades, Los Angeles, Seattle.

Reading for the Main Idea

1. *Places and Regions* What are five physical features of the Pacific states?
2. *Places and Regions* What are the seven climates of the Pacific states?
3. *Human Systems* What resources, agricultural products, and industries are important to the economy of the Pacific states?

Critical Thinking

4. **Analyzing** How might severe hurricane damage affect Hawaii's economy?

Organizing What You Know

5. **Categorizing** Copy the following graphic organizer. Use it to categorize the different landform areas in each of the Pacific states.

State	Landform Areas
California	
Oregon	
Washington	
Alaska	
Hawaii	

Section 5 Review

Answers to Section 5 Review

Define For definitions, see the glossary.

Working with Sketch Maps Maps will vary, but listed places should be labeled in their approximate locations.

Reading for the Main Idea

1. mountains, valleys, basins, lowland, islands (NGS 4)
2. marine west coast, Mediterranean, desert, steppe, subarctic, tundra, humid tropical (NGS 4)
3. forests, fish, oil; nuts, fruit, vegetables; software, tourism, aerospace (NGS 11)

Critical Thinking

4. might make natural areas less inviting and hurt tourism

Organizing What You Know

5. California—Coast Ranges, Sierra Nevada, Central Valley, desert basins; Oregon—Coast Ranges, Willamette Valley, Cascades, Columbia Basin; Washington—Coast Ranges, Puget Sound Lowland, Cascades; Alaska—mountains, ice fields, glaciers; Hawaii—mountains, islands, beaches

▲ **Visual Record Answer**

Removing the trees could lead to increased erosion, which would change the landforms.

CLOSE

Ask students to choose a Pacific state and tell what characteristics of the state appeal to them and which do not. Have students explain their answers.

REVIEW, ASSESS, RETEACH

Have students complete the Section Review. Then begin an outline on the chalkboard titled *Geography of the Pacific States*. Write three headings under the title: *Landforms, Climates,* and *Economy.* Have students work in pairs to complete the outline. Then have students complete Daily Quiz 5.5.

Have students complete Main Idea Activity S5. Then have them work in groups to make cards. Give each group ten index cards. On each of five cards, have students write the name of a Pacific state. On each remaining card, have them name or draw an important physical feature from each state. Have groups match each other's cards. **ESOL, COOPERATIVE LEARNING**

EXTEND

Have students conduct research on the oil resources of Alaska. Ask them to focus their research on the following questions: How important is oil to the economy of Alaska and our country? What debates have taken place over Alaska's oil resources? **BLOCK SCHEDULING**

CHAPTER 5 REVIEW

Define and Identify
For definitions, see the glossary and index.

Review the Main Ideas
16. The cities are important seaports and are connected by roads, railroads, and airline routes. (NGS 5)
17. The Appalachians, particularly in West Virginia and Pennsylvania
18. the Everglades in Florida and the Okefenokee Swamp in Georgia
19. has become more industrialized
20. good soils, flat land (NGS 4)
21. steel mills, meat-packing plants, and other businesses
22. thunderstorms, tornadoes, droughts (NGS 15)
23. soil and rock being stripped away by mining (NGS 5)
24. San Andreas Fault system (NGS 7)
25. Oregon, Washington, and Alaska

Think Critically
26. No, regions are defined also by common landforms, climates, and economies.
27. Possible answers: glaciers; waves and tides; river rapids; waterfalls; earthquakes; volcanoes; wind; storms
28. because they are isolated from the other 48 states, and many products have to be imported, driving up costs
29. Answers will vary.
30. They are great source of income for a region. Students most likely will predict that these industries will grow even larger because technology keeps advancing.

132 Chapter 5

Chapter 5 Review and Practice

Define and Identify
Identify each of the following:
1. megalopolis
2. moraine
3. estuary
4. barrier islands
5. wetlands
6. sediment
7. diversify
8. droughts
9. Corn Belt
10. Dairy Belt
11. badlands
12. chinooks
13. Wheat Belt
14. strip mining
15. caldera

Review the Main Ideas
16. What helped the megalopolis in the Northeast become a major industrial and financial center?
17. What are the main coal-mining areas of the Middle Atlantic states?
18. Where are the South's major wetlands?
19. How is the South's economy changing?
20. What factors have helped make the Midwest a great farming region?
21. What industries drew immigrants to Chicago during the 1800s?
22. What climate and weather hazards sometimes threaten the Interior West?
23. Why has mining caused problems in the Interior West?
24. What landform feature causes earthquakes in California?
25. In which three Pacific states are forests and fish important resources?

Think Critically
26. **Evaluating** Are regions defined solely on the basis of location? Explain your answer.
27. **Analyzing** What natural forces have contributed to shaping the landforms in the regions of the United States?
28. **Understanding Cause and Effect** Why may some goods be more expensive in Alaska and Hawaii than in other states?
29. **Supporting a Point of View** In which region or state in particular would you most like to live in the future? Explain your answer.
30. **Making Generalizations and Predictions** Why have most regions developed high-technology industries? What do you think will happen in the future to these industries?

Map Activity
31. On a separate sheet of paper, match the letters on the map with their correct labels.

Aleutian Islands   Detroit
Arctic Ocean   Hawaii
Cape Cod   New Orleans
Chesapeake Bay   Phoenix
Crater Lake   Seattle

132 • Chapter 5

Map Activity
31.
A. New Orleans
B. Cape Cod
C. Arctic Ocean
D. Seattle
E. Hawaii
F. Chesapeake Bay
G. Detroit
H. Aleutian Islands
I. Phoenix
J. Crater Lake

Writing Activity

Each region of the United States welcomes tourists. Pleasant climates, natural sites, and historic sites attract visitors. Write a short travel ad for a magazine describing the attractions of one region. Be sure to use standard grammar, spelling, sentence structure, and punctuation.

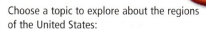

Internet Activity: go.hrw.com
KEYWORD: SJ5 GT5

Choose a topic to explore about the regions of the United States:
- Examine growth and development along the Great Lakes and St. Lawrence River.
- Create a brochure on Hawaii's environment.
- Create a newspaper article on the Gulf Coast of Texas.

CHAPTER 5 REVIEW

Writing Activity
Answers will vary, but the information included should be consistent with text material. Use Rubric 2, Advertisements, and Rubric 40, Writing to Describe, to evaluate student work.

Interpreting Highway Maps
1. Interstates have red, white, and blue signs; other highways have black and white signs of a different design.
2. about 9 miles or 15 kilometers
3. A small white box indicates interchanges where drivers can enter the highway.
4. possible answers: Highway 826, going north; or north on unnamed road to Highway 27 and then northwest

Interpreting Primary Sources
1. presence of standing dead trees and rotting logs
2. provide good cover for amphibians
3. Outdoor recreation compacts the soil, damaging the forest.
4. They may see it as messy, as a place where undesirable plants and animals may live, or better used as a source of timber.

Social Studies Skills Practice

Interpreting Highway Maps
Study this highway map of southern Florida. Then answer the questions.

1. How can you tell the interstates from other national and state highways?
2. About how far is it between the Highway 27 and Highway 41 intersections on Florida's Turnpike?
3. What symbol indicates that drivers can enter the highways only at certain points?
4. What is the most direct route from South Miami to Hialeah? In what general direction would you be traveling?

Interpreting Primary Sources
Read the following excerpt from a letter written by Al Wurth of the Sierra Club about an old-growth forest in Pennsylvania. Then answer the questions.

"The presence of . . . standing dead trees . . . with ample numbers of rotting logs indicates this forest has not been logged for many decades. This abundance [large amount] of decaying wood on the forest floor provides good cover for amphibians. . . . Some of the greatest concentrations of native wildflowers in the Lehigh Valley can be found in areas of this forest where outdoor recreation has not compacted its soil."

1. What are some signs that this forest has not been disturbed for a long time?
2. What use do the dead trees and decaying material serve?
3. What is the connection between outdoor recreation and damage to the forest?
4. Why do you think some people may not enjoy the old-growth forest that Wurth describes?

The Regions of the United States • 133

REVIEW AND ASSESSMENT RESOURCES

Reproducible
- Critical Thinking Activity 5
- Vocabulary Activity 5

Technology
- Chapter 5 Test Generator (on the One-Stop Planner)
- Audio CD Program, Chapter 5
- HRW Go site

Reinforcement, Review, and Assessment
- Chapter 5 Review and Practice
- Chapter Summaries and Review
- Chapter 5 Test
- Chapter 5 Test for English Language Learners and Special-Needs Students

GO TO: go.hrw.com
KEYWORD: SJ5 Teacher
FOR: a guide to using the Internet in your classroom

Chapter 6: Canada
Chapter Resource Manager

Objectives	Pacing Guide	Reproducible Resources
SECTION 1 **Physical Geography** (pp. 135–37) 1. Identify Canada's major landforms, rivers, and lakes. 2. Identify the major climate types and natural resources of Canada.	**Regular** 1 day Lecture Notes, Section 1 **Block Scheduling** .5 day Block Scheduling Handbook, Chapter 6	**RS** Know It Notes S1 **IC** Interdisciplinary Activity for the Middle Grades 6 **ELL** Main Idea Activity S1
SECTION 2 **History and Culture** (pp. 138–42) 1. Describe how France and Britain affected Canada's history. 2. Explain how immigrants have influenced Canadian culture.	**Regular** 1.5 days Lecture Notes, Section 2 **Block Scheduling** .5 day Block Scheduling Handbook, Chapter 6	**RS** Know It Notes S2 **RS** Graphic Organizer 6 **E** Cultures of the World Activity 1 **E** Biography Activity: Glenn Gould **ELL** Main Idea Activity S2
SECTION 3 **Canada Today** (pp. 143–47) 1. Describe how regionalism has affected Canada. 2. Identify the major areas and provinces into which Canada is divided.	**Regular** .5 day Lecture Notes, Section 3 **Block Scheduling** .5 day Block Scheduling Handbook, Chapter 6	**RS** Know It Notes S3 **SM** Map Activity 6 **SM** Geography for Life Activity 7 **ELL** Main Idea Activity S3

Chapter Resource Key

- **RS** Reading Support
- **IC** Interdisciplinary Connections
- **E** Enrichment
- **SM** Skills Mastery
- **A** Assessment
- **REV** Review
- **ELL** Reinforcement and English Language Learners and English for Speakers of Other Languages (ESOL)
- Transparencies
- CD–ROM
- Music
- Video
- Internet
- Holt Presentation Maker Using Microsoft® PowerPoint®

One-Stop Planner CD-ROM

See the *One-Stop Planner* for a complete list of additional resources for students and teachers.

One-Stop Planner CD–ROM

It's easy to plan lessons, select resources, and print out materials for your students when you use the *One-Stop Planner CD–ROM with Test Generator.*

internet connect

HRW ONLINE RESOURCES

GO TO: go.hrw.com
Then type in a keyword.

TEACHER HOME PAGE
KEYWORD: **SJ5 TEACHER**

CHAPTER INTERNET ACTIVITIES
KEYWORD: **SJ5 GT6**

Choose an activity to:
- take a trip to the Yukon Territory.
- learn about Canada's First Nations.
- meet the people of Quebec.

CHAPTER ENRICHMENT LINKS
KEYWORD: **SJ5 CH6**

CHAPTER MAPS
KEYWORD: **SJ5 MAPS6**

ONLINE ASSESSMENT
Homework Practice
KEYWORD: **SJ5 HP6**
Standardized Test Prep Online
KEYWORD: **SJ5 STP6**
Rubrics
KEYWORD: **SS Rubrics**

COUNTRY INFORMATION
KEYWORD: **SJ5 Almanac**

CONTENT UPDATES
KEYWORD: **SS Content Updates**

HOLT PRESENTATION MAKER
KEYWORD: **SJ5 PPT6**

ONLINE READING SUPPORT
KEYWORD: **SS Strategies**

CURRENT EVENTS
KEYWORD: **S5 Current Events**

Technology Resources

 One-Stop Planner CD–ROM, Lesson 6.1
 Geography and Cultures Visual Resources with Teaching Activities 11–16
 ARGWorld CD–ROM
 Homework Practice Online
HRW Go site

 One-Stop Planner CD–ROM, Lesson 6.2
 ARGWorld CD–ROM
 Music of the World Audio CD Program, Selection 2
 Homework Practice Online
HRW Go site

 One-Stop Planner CD–ROM, Lesson 6.3
 ARGWorld CD–ROM
Homework Practice Online
HRW Go site

Review, Reinforcement, and Assessment Resources

ELL	Main Idea Activity S1
REV	Section 1 Review
A	Daily Quiz 6.1
REV	Chapter Summaries and Review
ELL	English Audio Summary 6.1
ELL	Spanish Audio Summary 6.1
ELL	Main Idea Activity S2
REV	Section 2 Review
A	Daily Quiz 6.2
REV	Chapter Summaries and Review
ELL	English Audio Summary 6.2
ELL	Spanish Audio Summary 6.2
ELL	Main Idea Activity S3
REV	Section 3 Review
A	Daily Quiz 6.3
REV	Chapter Summaries and Review
ELL	English Audio Summary 6.3
ELL	Spanish Audio Summary 6.3

Meeting Individual Needs

Ability Levels

Level 1 Basic-level activities designed for all students encountering new material

Level 2 Intermediate-level activities designed for average students

Level 3 Challenging activities designed for honors and gifted-and-talented students

ESOL Activities that address the needs of students with Limited English Proficiency

Chapter Review and Assessment

E	Readings in World Geography, History, and Culture 13 and 14
SM	Critical Thinking Activity 6
REV	Chapter 6 Review and Practice
REV	Chapter Summaries and Review
ELL	Vocabulary Activity 6
A	Chapter 6 Test
A	Unit 2 Test
	Chapter 6 Test Generator (on the One-Stop Planner)
	Audio CD Program, Chapter 6
A	Chapter 6 Test for English Language Learners and Special-Needs Students
A	Unit 2 Test for English Language Learners and Special-Needs Students
	HRW Go site

133B

CHAPTER 6

Canada
Previewing Chapter Resources

Holt Online Learning

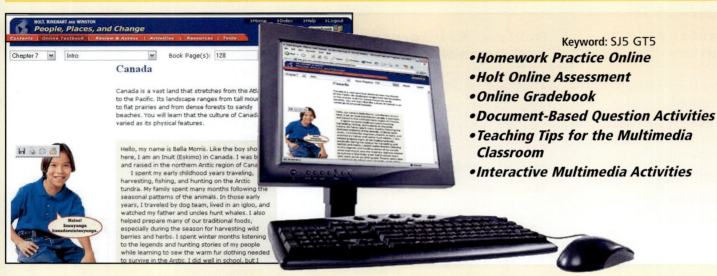

Keyword: SJ5 GT5

- Homework Practice Online
- Holt Online Assessment
- Online Gradebook
- Document-Based Question Activities
- Teaching Tips for the Multimedia Classroom
- Interactive Multimedia Activities

Differentiating Instruction

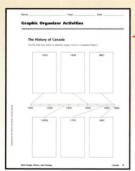

Reading and Writing Support
◄ Graphic Organizer Activity
- Vocabulary Activity
- Chapter Summary and Review
- Know It Notes
- Audio CD

Active Learning
◄ Block Scheduling Handbook
- Cultures of the World Activity
- Interdisciplinary Activity
- Map Activity
- Critical Thinking Activity 7
- Music of the World Audio CD: Traditional Music of Vancouver Island

Primary Sources and Advanced Learners
- Geography for Life Activity: The Changing Geography of Ice Hockey
◄ Map Activity: The Growth of Canada
- Readings in World Geography, History and Culture:
  - 13 Cruising to School
  - 14 Nunavut: Canada's Newest Territory

Assessment Program
◄ Daily Quizzes S1–3
- Chapter Test
- Chapter Test for English Language Learners and Special-Needs Students

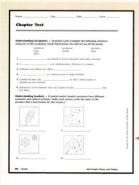

Spanish and ESOL
- Vocabulary Activity
- Main Idea Activities for English Language Learners and Special-Needs Students
- Chapter Summary and Review
- Spanish Audio Summary
- Know It Notes S1–3
◄ Chapter Test for English Language Learners and Special-Needs Students

Special Education Modifications
Your **I.D.E.A. Works! CD-ROM** will provide modified versions of the following teaching materials:
- Guided Reading Strategies S1–3
- Vocabulary Activity
◄ Main Idea Activities S1–3
- Daily Quizzes S1–3
- Chapter 6 Test
- Flash cards of chapter vocabulary terms

133C

Teacher Resources

Books for Teachers

Houston, James. *Confessions of an Igloo Dweller.* Houghton Mifflin, 1996.

Malcolm, Andrew H. *The Canadians.* St. Martin's Press, 1992.

Riendeau, Roger E. *A Brief History of Canada.* Facts on File, 1999.

Wilson, Ian and Sally Wilson. *Arctic Adventures: Exploring Canada's North by Canoe and Dog Team.* Gordon Soules Publishing, 1997.

Books for Students

Barlas, Robert, Norm Thompsett, and Susan McKay. *Canada.* (Festivals of the World). Gareth Stevens, 1997. How Canada's culture is reflected in its festivals. **SHELTERED ENGLISH**

Durbin, William. *The Broken Blade.* Delacorte Press, 1997. Set in 1800, follows 13-year-old Pierre on a rigorous 2,000-mile canoe trip through the Canadian wilderness. Fiction.

Durbin, William. *Wintering.* Delacorte Press, 1999. Sequel follows 13-year-old Pierre's first full winter in the Canadian backwoods to the Great Lakes. Fiction.

Van Stockum, Hilda. *Canadian Summer.* The Hilda Van Stockum Family Collection. Bethlehem Books, 1997.

Multimedia Materials

Anyplace Wild III: Adventuring in Canada. Video, 60 min. PBS.

The Canadian Way of Life. The Way of Life Series. Video, 21 min. AIMS Media.

ZipZapMap! Canada. Software Game. National Geographic Society.

Videos and CDs

Videos
- CNN Presents Geography: Yesterday and Today, Segment 8 Tradition and Change—**The James Bay Project**
- ARG World

Holt Researcher
http://researcher.hrw.com
- Canada
- North American Free Trade Agreement (NAFTA)
- Group of Seven (G-7)
- French and Indian War
- Early European Settlements

Transparency Packages

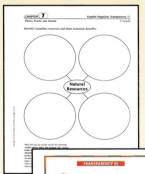

Graphic Organizer Transparencies 6.1–3

Geography and Cultures Visual Resources Transparencies
21 US and Canada: Physical
22 US and Canada: Political
23 US and Canada: Climate
24 US and Canada: Population
25 US and Canada: Land Use and Resources
27 Physical Regions of the US and Canada
31 Canada: Physical-Political

Map Activities Transparency 06 The Growth of Canada

133D

CHAPTER 6

WHY IT MATTERS

You may want to emphasize the importance of learning about Canada by sharing these reasons with your students:

▶ Canada and the United States share the longest unguarded boundary in the world. We are also allies.

▶ Each country is the other's most important trading partner. Changes in either country's government can affect that relationship.

▶ We share a language, some aspects of history, and many cultural traditions.

▶ Canada is a beautiful country to visit!

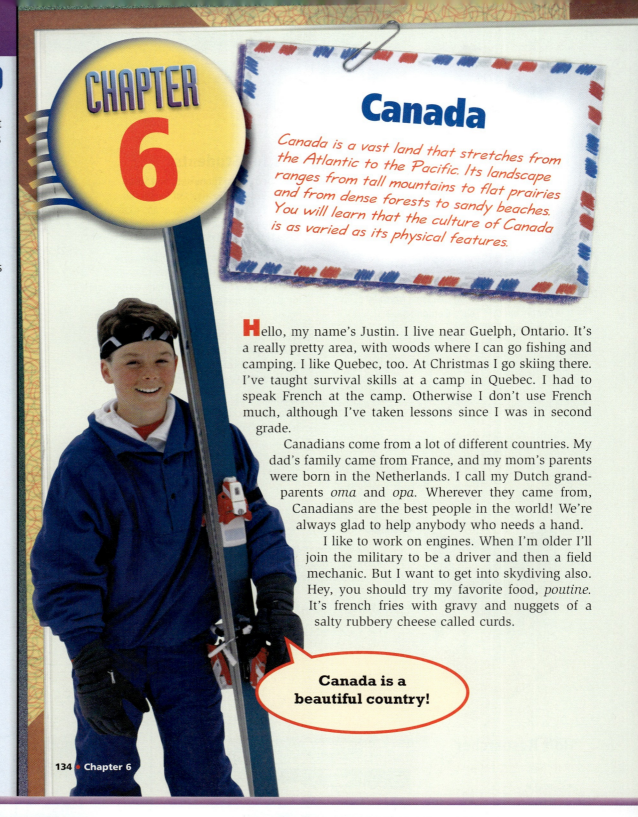

CHAPTER 6

Canada

Canada is a vast land that stretches from the Atlantic to the Pacific. Its landscape ranges from tall mountains to flat prairies and from dense forests to sandy beaches. You will learn that the culture of Canada is as varied as its physical features.

Hello, my name's Justin. I live near Guelph, Ontario. It's a really pretty area, with woods where I can go fishing and camping. I like Quebec, too. At Christmas I go skiing there. I've taught survival skills at a camp in Quebec. I had to speak French at the camp. Otherwise I don't use French much, although I've taken lessons since I was in second grade.

Canadians come from a lot of different countries. My dad's family came from France, and my mom's parents were born in the Netherlands. I call my Dutch grandparents *oma* and *opa*. Wherever they came from, Canadians are the best people in the world! We're always glad to help anybody who needs a hand.

I like to work on engines. When I'm older I'll join the military to be a driver and then a field mechanic. But I want to get into skydiving also. Hey, you should try my favorite food, *poutine*. It's french fries with gravy and nuggets of a salty rubbery cheese called curds.

Canada is a beautiful country!

134 • Chapter 6

CHAPTER PROJECT

Organize the class into small groups. Each group will serve as a planning committee to host an international geographers' tour of Canada. Each committee should prepare a detailed, illustrated itinerary that includes as much variety as possible. Have students place copies of the tour package in their portfolios, along with a description of their own contributions to the project.

STARTING THE CHAPTER

Ask students what images or impressions of Canada and Canadians they have received from movies and television. (Students may mention hockey, snow, lumberjacks, Royal Canadian Mounted Police, or other images.) Ask which they think are true, which are false, and which are exaggerations. Tell them they will learn to distinguish between some facts and fiction about Canada in this chapter. You may want to ask students what impressions they think Canadians may have about citizens of the United States. Which of those do students think are true and which false?

134 Chapter 6

Section 1: Physical Geography

Read to Discover
1. What are Canada's major landforms, rivers, and lakes?
2. What are the major climate types and natural resources of Canada?

Vocabulary
- potash
- pulp
- newsprint

Places
- Rocky Mountains
- Appalachian Mountains
- Canadian Shield
- Hudson Bay
- Great Lakes
- St. Lawrence River
- Great Bear Lake
- Great Slave Lake

Reading Strategy

READING ORGANIZER Before you read, create four boxes on a sheet of paper by drawing a line down the center and a line across the middle of the page. Label the boxes Land, Water, Climate, and Resources. As you read the section, write down what you learn.

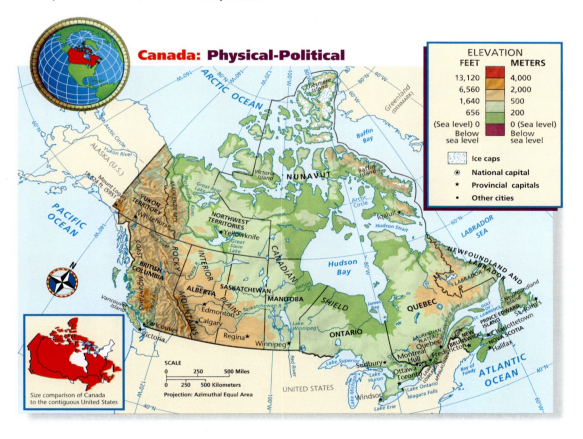

Canada: Physical-Political

Size comparison of Canada to the contiguous United States

CHAPTER 6, Section 1

SECTION 1 RESOURCES

Reproducible
- Lecture Notes, Section 1
- Block Scheduling Handbook, Chapter 6
- Know It Notes S1
- Interdisciplinary Activity for the Middle Grades 6

Technology
- One-Stop Planner CD–ROM, Lesson 6.1
- Homework Practice Online
- Geography and Cultures Visual Resources with Teaching Activities 21–31
- HRW Go site

Reinforcement, Review, and Assessment
- Section 1 Review
- Daily Quiz 6.1
- Main Idea Activity S1
- Chapter Summaries and Review
- English Audio Summary 6.1
- Spanish Audio Summary 6.1

Section 1

Objectives
1. Describe Canada's major landforms, rivers, and lakes.
2. Identify Canada's major climate types and natural resources.

FOCUS

Bellringer

Copy the following instructions onto the chalkboard: *During frontier days in the United States, people went west to find wealth and adventure. Why do you think Canadians might go north today? Discuss the question with a partner.* Allow students time to talk with their partners. Discuss student responses. (Northern Canada is undeveloped and sparsely populated, but its natural resources and beauty offer great opportunities.) Tell students they will learn more about Canada's physical features and resources in Section 1.

Using the Physical-Political Map

Have students examine the map on this page. Call on volunteers to name the bodies of water that surround Canada (Pacific Ocean, Atlantic Ocean, Arctic Ocean, Baffin Bay, and Labrador Sea) and to describe the land boundary that separates it from the United States (straight line for most of its length). Ask students to compare the countries' sizes and to find the largest and smallest of Canada's provinces and territories. Ask how their sizes appear to compare to the largest and smallest states in the United States.

CHAPTER 6, Section 1

EYE ON EARTH

Islands of Life The harsh climate of Canada's western mountains makes life there difficult but not impossible.

Nunataks are small, isolated mountaintops that poke through ice fields, such as those in the Yukon's St. Elias Mountains. These microenvironments, most no bigger than a few acres, shelter tiny flower meadows, lichens, mosses, and rare insects and spiders.

Small rabbitlike animals called pikas are the only year-round mammal residents of the nunataks. They supplement their diet of plants with the bodies of dead birds that wander too far into the ice fields. How the pikas find enough mates to maintain their populations, since they usually venture only a few yards in any direction, is still unknown.

Activity: Have students conduct research on nunataks and other microenvironments around the world. Ask them to construct scale models to show the interrelationships of the microenvironments' plants and animals.

Visual Record Answer

highland, subarctic

---

internet connect
GO TO: go.hrw.com
KEYWORD: SJ5 CH6
FOR: Web sites about Canada

Physical Features

The physical geography of Canada has much in common with that of the United States. Both countries share some major physical regions. For example, the Coast Mountains and the Rocky Mountains extend into western Canada. Broad plains stretch across the interiors of both countries. Also, the Appalachian Mountains extend into southeastern Canada.

The Canadian Shield, a region of rocky uplands, borders Hudson Bay. To the south are some of Canada's most fertile soils, in the St. Lawrence River Valley and the Great Lakes region. The Great Lakes are Lake Erie, Lake Huron, Lake Michigan, Lake Ontario, and Lake Superior.

Canada has thousands of lakes and rivers. Many of Canada's lakes were carved out by Ice Age glaciers. The Great Bear and Great Slave are two of Canada's larger lakes. The most important river is the St. Lawrence. The St. Lawrence River links the Great Lakes to the Atlantic Ocean.

✓ **READING CHECK:** *Places and Regions* What are the major physical features of Canada? Mountains, Canadian Shield, fertile soil in the St Lawrence River Valley and Great Lakes region, Great Lakes, Great Bear, Great Slave, and St. Lawrence River

Climate

The central and eastern parts of southern Canada have a humid continental climate. The mildest area of Canada is in the southwest. This region has a marine west coast climate. Here, winters are rainy and heavy snow falls in the mountains. Much of central and northern Canada has a subarctic climate. The far north has tundra and ice-cap climates. Permafrost underlies about half of Canada.

✓ **READING CHECK:** *Places and Regions* What are Canada's climates? Humid continental, marine west coast, subarctic, tundra, and ice cap

Banff National Park is Canada's oldest and most famous national park. The park has spectacular views of Canada's Rocky Mountains.
Interpreting the Visual Record *Place*
What types of climate would you expect to find here?

136 • Chapter 6

TEACH

Teaching Objectives 1–2
ALL LEVELS: (Suggested time: 30 min.) Copy the following graphic organizer onto the chalkboard, omitting the blue answers. Use it to help students describe Canada's major landforms, rivers and lakes, climates, and resources. Have students copy the chart into their notebooks and complete it. **ESOL,** **LS** **VISUAL-SPATIAL**

CANADA'S PHYSICAL GEOGRAPHY

Landforms	Lakes and Rivers	Climates	Resources
• Coast Mountains and Rocky Mountains • Canadian Shield • fertile farmland in St. Lawrence River valley and Great Lakes region	• Great Lakes • thousands of lakes and rivers, many carved by glaciers • St. Lawrence River links Great Lakes to Atlantic Ocean	• central and eastern—humid continental • southwest—marine west coast • central and north—subarctic • far north—tundra, ice cap	• rich fishing areas • tourism • fertile soil • minerals—nickel, zinc, uranium, lead, copper, gold, silver, coal, potash • oil and natural gas • forests

136 Chapter 6

Resources

Canada's Atlantic and Pacific coastal waters are among the world's richest fishing areas. Canada's many lakes and streams provide freshwater fish and attract tourists as well. Wheat farmers and cattle producers benefit from Canada's fertile soil.

Minerals are the most valuable of Canada's natural resources. The Canadian Shield contains many mineral deposits. Canada is a leading source of the world's nickel, zinc, and uranium. Lead, copper, gold, silver, and coal are also present. Saskatchewan has the world's largest deposits of **potash**, a mineral used to make fertilizer. Alberta produces most of Canada's oil and natural gas.

A belt of coniferous forests stretches across Canada from Labrador to the Pacific coast. These trees provide lumber and **pulp**. Pulp—softened wood fibers—is used to make paper. The United States, the United Kingdom, and Japan get much of their **newsprint** from Canada. Newsprint is cheap paper used mainly for newspapers.

✓ **READING CHECK:** *Environment and Society* How do Canada's major resources affect its economy? *Coastal waters, lakes, streams provide fish, attract tourists; fertile soil is good for farming, ranching; minerals, oil, natural gas are most valuable economic resources; forests provide lumber pulp.*

Canada's resources can be shipped to markets through Vancouver.

Logs are floated down British Columbia's rivers to sawmills. Timber is a major resource.

Homework Practice Online
Keyword: SJ5 HP6

Section Review 1

Define and explain: potash, pulp, newsprint

Working with Sketch Maps On a map of Canada that you draw or that your teacher provides, label the following: Rocky Mountains, Appalachian Mountains, Canadian Shield, Hudson Bay, Great Lakes, St. Lawrence River, Great Bear Lake, and Great Slave Lake.

Reading for the Main Idea

1. *Places and Regions* What are Canada's major landforms?
2. *Places and Regions* What river links the Great Lakes to the Atlantic Ocean?

Critical Thinking

3. **Drawing Inferences and Conclusions** Why do you think there are so many lakes in Canada?
4. **Drawing Inferences and Conclusions** Where would you expect to find Canada's mildest climate? Why?

Organizing What You Know

5. **Finding the Main Idea** Use the following graphic organizer to identify Canadian resources and their economic benefits.

Section 1 Review

Answers to Section 1 Review

Define For definitions, see the glossary.

Working with Sketch Maps Maps will vary, but listed places should be labeled in their approximate locations.

Reading for the Main Idea
1. Rocky Mountains, Coast Mountains, interior plains, Appalachian Mountains, Canadian Shield, and St. Lawrence River valley (NGS 4)
2. St. Lawrence River (NGS 4)

Critical Thinking
3. glacial action, humid climate (NGS 7)
4. southern part of Pacific coast; marine west coast climate influenced by nearby Pacific Ocean (NGS 4)

Organizing What You Know
5. Webs will vary but should include the following: coastal waters, lakes, and streams—fish, tourism; fertile soil—farms, ranching; minerals—nickel, zinc, uranium, lead, copper, gold, silver, coal; potash—fertilizer; oil and gas—fuel; trees—lumber, pulp.

CLOSE

Tell students this detail about Canada's great outdoors: Wood Buffalo National Park, in Alberta and the Northwest Territories, contains the largest herd of free-roaming bison in the world.

REVIEW, ASSESS, RETEACH

Have students complete the Section Review. Then assign each student landforms, rivers and lakes, climate, or resources. Ask each student to write a fill-in-the-blank question, with answer, on his or her topic. Then collect students' questions and use them to quiz the class. Then have students complete Daily Quiz 6.1.

Have students complete Main Idea Activity S1. Then focus students' attention on the Section 1 illustrations. Have the students write new captions for them that include information on the section's main topics. **ESOL**

EXTEND

Have students investigate acid rain's effect on Canada. Some members of Canada's government believe that pollution from U.S. industries causes much of the acid rain in the country. Ask students to write mock correspondence between Canadian and U.S. environmental officials that reflects the students' findings. **BLOCK SCHEDULING**

CHAPTER 6, Section 2

SECTION 2 RESOURCES

Reproducible
- Lecture Notes, Section 2
- Know It Notes S2
- Graphic Organizer 6
- Cultures of the World Activity 1
- Biography Activity: Glenn Gould

Technology
- One-Stop Planner CD–ROM, Lesson 6.2
- Music of the World Audio CD Program, Selection 2
- Homework Practice Online
- HRW Go site

Reinforcement, Review, and Assessment
- Section 2 Review
- Daily Quiz 6.2
- Main Idea Activity S2
- Chapter Summaries and Review
- English Audio Summary 6.2
- Spanish Audio Summary 6.2

Section 2 History and Culture

Read to Discover
1. How did France and Britain affect Canada's history?
2. How have immigrants influenced Canadian culture?

Vocabulary
provinces
dominion
Métis

People
Samuel de Champlain

Places
Quebec
Ontario
Nova Scotia
New Brunswick
Newfoundland
Prince Edward Island
British Columbia
Manitoba
Alberta
Saskatchewan

Reading Strategy

TAKING NOTES As you read, create an outline by using the headings in this section. Fill in notes beneath each heading. Include dates of important events in your notes.

▲ A French artist shows an early expedition in Canada led by French explorer Jacques Cartier. Cartier explored the St. Lawrence River area up to present-day Montreal in the 1500s.

History

As the ice sheets of the ice ages melted, people moved into all areas of what is now Canada. As they did elsewhere in the Americas, Native Canadians adapted to the physical environment.

Over the years, these first Canadians divided into groups known as the First Nations. Cree, Déné, Mohawk, Ojibwa, Oneida, and Kwakiutl are a few of their names. In the far north the Inuit adapted to the region's extreme cold, where farming was impossible. By hunting seals, whales, walruses, and other animals, the Inuit could feed, clothe, and house themselves.

European Settlement The first Europeans in Canada were the Vikings, or Norse. They landed on Newfoundland Island in about A.D. 1000. Norse settlement either failed or was abandoned. European exploration began again in the late 1400s. Explorers and fishers from western Europe began crossing the Atlantic.

Europeans valued the furs that Native Canadians supplied. The Canadians wanted European metal goods like kettles and axes. Both groups began to adopt aspects of each other's culture, including foods, clothing, and travel methods.

138 • Chapter 6

Section 2

Objectives
1. Discuss the effect France and Britain had on Canada's history.
2. Describe how immigrants have influenced Canadian culture.

FOCUS

Bellringer

Copy the following instructions onto the chalkboard: *Look at the painting at the beginning of Section 2. Can you find the area shown in the painting on a map of Canada?* You may want to refer students to more detailed maps in atlases or other sources. Offer a hint for finding the area: turn the painting upside down. It shows the Gulf of St. Lawrence. Then lead a discussion about why the artist chose this view and what other elements the painting contains.

Building Vocabulary

Have students find the vocabulary terms' definitions in the text or glossary. All of the terms come from Latin words. Provincia means the same as *province*. Add an *s* for the plural form, **provinces**. Dominus, from which we get **dominion**, means "master." You may want to introduce and relate the word *dominate* if it is unfamiliar to students. **Métis** comes from *mixticius*, meaning "mixed."

138 Chapter 6

The French built the Fortress of Louisbourg in Nova Scotia. The British captured the fortress in 1758.

CHAPTER 6, Section 2

Culture and Music
First Nations

Cultures The Haida are among Canada's First Nations, or native peoples. Their homeland is a group of islands off the British Columbia coast.

For centuries, Haida artists have decorated jewelry, bowls, totem poles, and other objects with vivid symmetrical designs, often heavily outlined in black and red. Most of the patterns are based on animal and bird forms, especially animal faces. Often these forms combine to portray a Haida supernatural being—Konankada, the Chief of the Undersea World. Today, Haida artists use the traditional style to create new objects of great beauty.

Activity: Have students conduct research to find examples of art made by Haida or other First Nations peoples. One of these was the Ditidaht of Vancouver Island. For a song from the Ditidaht, play Selection 2 on the Music of the World Audio CD Program. Use the text and questions in the Teacher's Guide.

New France France was the first European country to successfully settle parts of what would become Canada. Quebec City was founded in 1608. The French called their new territories in North America New France. At its height, New France included much of eastern Canada and the central United States. New France was important for several reasons. It was part of the French Empire. It was a base that could be used to spread France's religion and culture. It was also an important commercial area for France's empire.

France and Britain were rival colonial powers. Part of their competition included building and defending their empires around the world. The French built trade and diplomatic relations with the First Nations people. The French did this to increase their power and influence on the continent. Furs, fish, and other products were traded between New France and other parts of the French Empire. Manufactured goods from France and other countries in Europe became the main imports to New France. French missionaries tried to convert native people to Christianity. Some did become Christians, while others held to their traditional beliefs.

New France lasted a century and a half before it was conquered by the British. During that time, it shaped the geography of Canada in important ways. The descendants of French settlers form one of Canada's major ethnic groups today. Almost a quarter of present-day Canadians are of French ancestry. This has deeply affected Canada's culture and politics.

British Conquest and American Revolution The Seven Years' War (1756–63) was mainly fought in Europe. This same period of conflict in the American colonies was called the French and Indian War. As a result of that war the British took control of New France. A

BIOGRAPHY

Samuel de Champlain
(1567–1635)

Character Trait: Pursuit of Excellence

Known as the Father of New France, Samuel de Champlain established the first permanent French colony in North America in 1604 in Nova Scotia. He later moved the colony to Quebec City. In 1629, English forces captured Quebec and put Champlain in prison. When France regained control of Quebec, Champlain returned to New France to serve as governor.

How did Champlain pursue excellence?

◀ **Biography**
He continued to serve his country, even after being imprisoned.

TEACH

Teaching Objectives 1–2

ALL LEVELS: (Suggested time: 20 min.) Copy the following graphic organizer onto the chalkboard, omitting the blue answers. Use it to help students trace major events in Canadian history as the country steps into the 2000s. Lead a discussion about the most important aspects of each step and the effect that France and Britain have had on Canada's history. **ESOL**, **LS** VISUAL-SPATIAL

Canada's First Nations — A.D. 1000–Vikings arrive — 1400s–European explorers and fishers — 1608–New France founded — mid-1700s–British control — 1867–Dominion of Canada — Growth and Immigration — Canada Today

CHAPTER 6, Section 2

Cultural Kaleidoscope

Acadians and Cajuns The term *Acadian* refers to French immigrants who settled in Nova Scotia and nearby areas in the 1600s. Great Britain won these lands from France in 1713. In 1755 British authorities ordered the Acadians to leave. Some fled to nearby Quebec, while others were scattered far and wide. Many families were separated. This episode inspired Henry Wadsworth Longfellow's poem "Evangeline." Some Acadians settled in Louisiana, which was then a French colony, where they became known as Cajuns.

GO TO: go.hrw.com
KEYWORD: SJ5 CH12
FOR: Web sites about Nova Scotia

small number of French went back to France. However, the great majority of the *habitants* (inhabitants) stayed. For most of them, few changes occurred in their daily activities. They farmed the same land, prayed in the same churches, and continued to speak French. Few English-speaking settlers came to what is now called Quebec.

The American Revolution pushed new groups of people into other areas of British North America. Many United Empire Loyalists—Americans who remained loyal to the king of England—fled north. Most Loyalists either could not stay in the new United States or were too afraid to remain. For some, their political views may have led them to move to British-controlled territories. For many others, it was the desire to get free land. This movement of people was part of a larger westward migration of pioneers.

After the American Revolution, the borders of British North America were redrawn. Quebec was divided into two colonies. Lower Canada was mostly French-speaking, and Upper Canada was mostly English-speaking. The boundary between Upper and Lower Canada forms part of the border between the **provinces** of Quebec and Ontario today. Provinces are administrative divisions of a country. To the east, Nova Scotia (noh-vuh skoh-shuh) was also divided. A new province called New Brunswick was created where many of the British Loyalists lived.

Creation of Canada For two generations these colonies developed separately. The British also maintained colonies in Newfoundland, Prince Edward Island, the western plains, and the Pacific coast. The colonies viewed themselves as different from other parts of the British Empire. Therefore, the British Parliament created the Dominion of Canada in 1867. A **dominion** is a territory or area of influence. For Canadians, the creation of the Dominion was a statement of independence. They saw a future separate from that of the United States. The motto of the new Dominion was "from sea to sea."

The British flag flies alongside the provincial flag at government buildings in Victoria, British Columbia. Canada is a member of the British Commonwealth of Nations. In fact, the British monarch also is Canada's.

Teaching Objective 2
LEVEL 2: (Suggested time: 30 min.) Pair students. Give each pair a yard of adding-machine tape or several pages of accordion-folded computer paper. Point out that Canada developed like a ribbon unrolling from east to west along its southern border. Instruct each pair to arrange and label its paper with East Coast on the right end and West Coast on the left. Have them place Viking explorers, fur traders, railroad builders, ranchers, farmers, and other groups on the paper according to where and when they settled.
COOPERATIVE LEARNING, **LS KINESTHETIC**

▶**ASSIGNMENT:** In advance, write the names of places in Canada on slips of paper. Be sure the places you choose appear on either the chapter or unit map. Have students draw the slips from a hat. Then have them imagine that they are exchange students living in the places they drew. Ask them to write letters home to their families, describing their physical surroundings and the regional history. You may want to have students research and report on a local festival that reflects the heritage of their Canadian home away from home. Students might also illustrate their letters.

However, it included only New Brunswick, Nova Scotia, and the southern parts of Ontario and Quebec.

How would Canadians create a nation from sea to sea? With railroads. The Canadian heartland in Ontario and Quebec was already well served by railroads. From the heartland the Intercolonial Railway would run east to the Atlantic Ocean. The Canadian Pacific Railroad would be the first of three transcontinental railroads running west to the Pacific Ocean. It was completed in 1885. Both British Columbia and Prince Edward Island were quickly added to the Dominion.

Canada also acquired vast lands between the original provinces and British Columbia. It also expanded to the north. Much of this land was bought from the Hudson's Bay Company, a British fur-trading business. Most of the people in this area were Canadian Indians and **Métis** (may-TEES). Métis, people of mixed European and native ancestry, considered themselves a separate group. With the building of the railroads and the signing of treaties with Native Canadians, the way was opened for settlement of the area. Manitoba became a province in 1870. Alberta and Saskatchewan followed in 1905.

Government Canada is a federation today. It has a central government led by a prime minister. Its 10 provincial governments are each led by a premier. Canada's central government is similar to our federal government. Its provincial governments are much like our state governments. A federal system lets people keep their feelings of loyalty to their own province. At the same time they remain part of a larger national identity.

✓ **READING CHECK:** Human Systems How is Canada's government similar to that of the United States?

It has a central government like our federal government and provincial governments like our state governments.

Culture

A history of colonial rule and waves of immigration have shaped Canada today. The country is home to a variety of ethnic groups and cultures. They have combined to form a single country and Canadian identity.

Immigration During the late 1800s and early 1900s, many immigrants from Europe came to Canada. Many farmed, but others worked in mines, forests, and factories. British Columbia became the first Canadian province to have a substantial Asian minority. Many Chinese Canadians helped build the railroads.

These immigrants played an important part in the economic boom that Canada experienced in the early 1900s. Quebec, New Brunswick,

This train follows the Bow River in Alberta.

Interpreting the Visual Record
Human-Environment Interaction How did railroad technology help people change their environment?

Canada

Country	Population/ Growth Rate	Life Expectancy	Literacy Rate	Per Capita GDP
Canada	32,207,113 0.94%	76, male 83, female	97%	$29,400
United States	290,342,554 0.9%	74, male 80, female	97%	$37,600

Source: Central Intelligence Agency, *The World Factbook 2003*

Interpreting the Chart Which country has the greater growth rate?

Canada • 141

CHAPTER 6, Section 2

Linking Past to Present
Lighthouses

European immigrants to Canada faced a difficult voyage across the North Atlantic Ocean. Even when they were within sight of their goal, the dangers were not over, for ships could easily be wrecked on the rocky coast.

Newfoundland lighthouses helped sailors find their way to safety. The region's first lighthouse was set up in 1813 to mark the narrow channel that connects St. John's harbor to the ocean.

In the 1800s and early 1900s, many European ships bound for North America set their course for the Cape Race Lighthouse on the southeastern tip of Newfoundland Island. Millions of European immigrants first set foot in North America at Cape Race.

Modern technology has made the old lighthouses obsolete. Most have been automated and no longer require human operators.

Activity: Have students write a lighthouse-keeper's log for several days in the 1800s.

▲ **Visual Record Answer**

It allowed them to settle more of Canada and reach more remote locations.

◄ **Chart Answer**

Canada

TEACHER TO TEACHER

Susan Walker of Beaufort, South Carolina, suggests this activity to introduce students to the French heritage of Canada. Tell them about Mi-Carême, a mid-Lent festival still held in a few Canadian villages. It is held on the third Thursday of the 40 days before Easter. During Mi-Carême people disguise themselves in masks and costumes, visit their friends and relatives, and challenge their hosts to identify them. Music and food are part of the fun. Mi-Carême is also the name of a Santa Claus–like female figure who was said to leave treats in good children's socks or hats and to punish disobedient children. Have students make masks and costumes that represent French influence in Canada.

CLOSE

Lead a discussion on how the histories of Canada and the United States are similar in some ways but very different in others. (examples of similarities: European settlement, British influence, large immigrant population; examples of differences: Canada did not revolt against Britain, French influence remains strong)

Canada 141

Section 2 Review

Answers to Section 2 Review

Define or identify For definitions and identifications, see the glossary and index.

Working with Sketch Maps All of the provinces and territories except New Brunswick, Prince Edward Island, and Nova Scotia use lines of latitude for boundaries.

Reading for the Main Idea
1. Colonization influenced language, government, customs, other aspects of culture. (NGS 9)
2. through their work—on farms and railroads, in mines, forests, and in factories—contributed to economic boom of the early 1900s (NGS 9)

Critical Thinking
3. brought metal goods, disease, traded with Native Canadians
4. created by British Parliament as a dominion because the colonies viewed themselves as different from other parts of British Empire

Organizing What You Know
5. Subsequent boxes should be labeled New Brunswick, Nova Scotia, Manitoba, British Columbia, Prince Edward Island, Alberta, and Saskatchewan.

Visitors enjoy the sights and sounds of a children's festival in Vancouver. Vancouver and other Canadian cities are home to large and increasingly diverse populations.

and Ontario produced wheat, pulp, and paper. British Columbia and Ontario supplied minerals and hydroelectricity. By the 1940s Canadians enjoyed one of the highest standards of living in the world.

Movement to Cities In recent years Canadians have moved from farms to the cities. Some settlements in Newfoundland—which became Canada's 10th province in 1949—and rural Saskatchewan disappeared because the people left. Many Canadians have moved to Ontario to find jobs. Others moved to British Columbia for its mild climate. Resources such as oil, gas, potash, and uranium have changed the economies of the western provinces. The economic center of power remains in the cities of southern Ontario and southwestern Quebec. Toronto is now Canada's largest city. Many Canadian businesses have their main offices there.

After World War II, another wave of immigrants from Europe came to Canada. They were joined by other people from Africa, the Caribbean, Latin America, and particularly Asia. Asian businesspeople have brought a great deal of wealth to Canada's economy. Most immigrants have settled in Canada's large cities. Toronto has become one of the most culturally diverse cities in the world. Many Canadians now enjoy Thai, Vietnamese, and other Asian foods. Chinese New Year parades and other colorful festivals attract tourists.

✓ **READING CHECK:** *Human Systems* How has immigration changed Canada? *It has given Canada a significant Asian population, helped create an economic boom, and added to the wealth of Canada's economy and to the cultural diversity of the country.*

Define or identify: Samuel de Champlain, provinces, dominion, Métis

Working with Sketch Maps On the map you created in Section 1, label Quebec, Ontario, Nova Scotia, New Brunswick, Newfoundland, Prince Edward Island, British Columbia, Manitoba, Alberta, and Saskatchewan. Which provinces seem to use lines of latitude as boundaries?

Reading for the Main Idea
1. *Human Systems* How did French and British colonization influence Canada's history?
2. *Human Systems* How did immigrants contribute to Canada?

142 • Chapter 6

Keyword: SJ5 HP6

Critical Thinking
3. **Identifying Cause and Effect** Why did Europeans come to Canada? What was the effect of the arrival of Europeans on the First Nations?
4. **Summarizing** How and why was the country of Canada created?

Organizing What You Know
5. **Sequencing** Copy the following graphic organizer. Use it to explain how the Dominion of Canada developed. Add boxes as needed.

REVIEW, ASSESS, RETEACH

Have students complete the Section Review. Then organize the class into three teams, for the French, British, and other major Canadian culture groups. Give each team a large sheet of butcher paper and have them create flowcharts to show the history of their culture group in Canada. Have some team members concentrate on displaying basic facts while others add details with webs or other graphics. Then have the teams meet to fill in any gaps and display connections among the facts they have recorded. (For example, add the Vikings before the French arrival. Connect Asian immigrants with French and British influences by means of business, foods, and festivals.) Then have students complete Daily Quiz 6.2.
COOPERATIVE LEARNING

EXTEND

Canada's national anthem is "O Canada." Have students explain the lyrics to the anthem and then write a new national anthem for Canada, using information in the text as a basis. You may want to let students use a tune with which they are already familiar and simply write new lyrics.
BLOCK SCHEDULING, **LS** AUDITORY-MUSICAL

Section 3: Canada Today

Read to Discover
1. How has regionalism affected Canada?
2. Into what major areas and provinces is Canada divided?

Vocabulary
regionalism
maritime
Inuit

Places
Gulf of St. Lawrence
Labrador
Halifax
Windsor
Quebec City
Montreal
Toronto
Ottawa
Edmonton
Calgary
Winnipeg
Vancouver
Yukon Territory
Northwest Territories
Nunavut

Reading Strategy
MNEMONIC DEVICE Use the chapter map or skim the section to find the names of Canada's provinces. Write down the names. As you read, create a mnemonic device, or memory game, that helps you remember an important fact about each province.

Regionalism

English is the main language in most of Canada. In Quebec, however, French is the dominant language. The cultural differences between English and French Canada have created problems. When Canadians from different regions discuss important issues, they are often influenced by **regionalism**. Regionalism refers to the strong connection that people feel toward their region. Sometimes, this connection is stronger than their connection to their country as a whole.

Regionalism was very important in America during the 1800s. At that time the United States split into the North and the South as its citizens fought the Civil War. The country was divided over issues such as slavery. People supported whichever group shared their beliefs. In Canada many residents of Quebec, or Quebecois (kay-buh-kwah), believe their province should be given a special status. Quebecois argue that this status would recognize the cultural differences between their province and the rest of Canada. Some even want Quebec to become independent.

On the other hand, many English-speaking Canadians think Quebec already has too many privileges. Others, especially in western Canada, want the provinces to have more freedom from national control. Most Canadians, however, still support a united Canada. Strong feelings of regionalism will continue to be an important issue in Canada's future.

Residents of Quebec demonstrate for independence. The sign reads "Yes, it becomes possible."

✓ **READING CHECK:** *Human Systems* Why do some people in Quebec want independence from the rest of Canada?
Because of the cultural differences between English and French Canadians

---

Section 3

Objectives
1. Analyze how regionalism has affected Canada.
2. Identify Canada's major areas and provinces.

Focus

Bellringer
Copy the following instructions onto the chalkboard: *Without opening your textbook, write three statements about Canada.* Allow students time to write their answers. Then tell students to work with a partner to decide if the statements are facts or opinions. Discuss the results to confirm the facts, and ask for arguments to back up any opinions. Tell students that in Section 3 they will learn more about Canada today.

Building Vocabulary
Tell students that when *-ism* appears at the end of a word, it means the root word has sometimes been turned into a noun. Call on a volunteer to define "regional" and another to propose a definition for **regionalism**. Point out that **maritime** relates to the Latin word *mare*, or "sea." Ask if the students know other words that contain the same root. (examples: marine, marina) Explain that **Inuit** is preferred to *Eskimo* because it is what the people call themselves. Call on volunteers to read the text definitions aloud.

CHAPTER 6, Section 3

GLOBAL PERSPECTIVES

Canada on TV Most residents of Canada's eastern provinces and the country's heartland live close to the United States, both physically and culturally.

Modern technology has increased communications between the two countries. U.S. companies control much of Canada's film, video, recording, and book publishing industries. As a result, Canadians are bombarded with American music, movies, and other examples of U.S. popular culture. This disturbs Canadians who want to maintain their own cultural identity.

In response, the Canadian government has passed rules that require that a certain percentage of all television and musical radio programming be written or performed by Canadians.

Discussion: Ask how students would feel if only Canadian performers appeared on MTV or if their local theater showed only Canadian movies. Then ask if they support the Canadian government's efforts to protect Canadian popular culture. Why or why not?

Visual Record Answer
because the many fish in the waters surrounding the peninsula are the basis of the region's economy

▲
The harbor at Avalon Peninsula is home to many fishing boats.
Interpreting the Visual Record Place
Why do you think most people in the Maritime Provinces live in coastal cities?

Canada's Bay of Fundy has some of the highest tides in the world—up to 70 feet (21 m). The tide brings water from the North Atlantic into the narrow bay. The bore, or leading wave of the incoming water, can roar like a big truck as the tide rushes in.

The Eastern Provinces

New Brunswick, Nova Scotia, and Prince Edward Island are often called the Maritime Provinces. **Maritime** means "on or near the sea." Each of these provinces is located near the ocean. Prince Edward Island is a small island, and Nova Scotia occupies a peninsula. New Brunswick has coasts on the Gulf of St. Lawrence and on the Bay of Fundy. Newfoundland and Labrador is usually not considered one of the Maritime Provinces. It includes the island of Newfoundland and a large region of the mainland called Labrador.

A short growing season and poor soils make farming difficult in the eastern provinces. Most of the region's economy is related to forestry and fishing.

Many people in the eastern provinces are descendants of families that emigrated from the British Isles. In addition, many French-speaking families have moved from Quebec to New Brunswick. Most of the region's people live in coastal cities. The cities have industrial plants and serve as fishing and shipping ports. Halifax, Nova Scotia, is the region's largest city.

✓ **READING CHECK:** Places and Regions Why are most of the eastern provinces called the Maritime Provinces? Because they are located near the sea

The Heartland

Inland from the eastern provinces are Quebec and Ontario. More than half of all Canadians live in these heartland provinces. In fact, the chain of cities that extends from Windsor, Ontario, to the city of Quebec is the country's most urbanized region.

144 • Chapter 6

TEACH

Teaching Objective 1
ALL LEVELS: (Suggested time: 20 min.) Copy the following graphic organizer onto the chalkboard, omitting the blue answers. Use it to help students understand how regionalism has caused conflict in Canada. Call on students to suggest phrases to fill in the ovals. You may want to extend the activity by challenging students to draw editorial cartoons to illustrate the issues. **ESOL**, **LS VISUAL-SPATIAL**

- Quebecois believe Quebec should have special status.
- Some Quebecois want independence for Quebec.
- **Regionalism in Canada**
- English-speaking Canadians believe there are too many privileges already for Quebec.
- Other provinces, particularly in western Canada, want more freedom from national control.

144 Chapter 6

Connecting to Literature

Anne of Green Gables
by Lucy Maud Montgomery

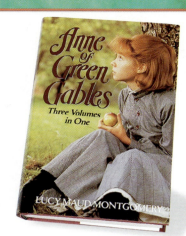

Canada's smallest province, Prince Edward Island, was the birthplace (in 1874) of one of the country's best-loved writers. Lucy Maud Montgomery based her *Anne of Green Gables* series on the island she loved. She created characters and situations that lived in the minds of readers. Since its publication in 1908, *Anne of Green Gables* put the tiny island on the map, inspiring tours and festivals. It has even drawn tourists from as far away as Japan. They come to capture the spirit of the brave orphan. In this passage, young Anne is being driven to Green Gables by her new guardian, Matthew. He is kind but hardly imaginative!

Anne says, "When I don't like the name of a place or a person I always imagine a new one and always think of them so. There was a girl at the asylum [orphanage] whose name was Hepzibah Jenkins, but I always imagined her as Rosalia DeVere." . . .

They had driven over the crest of a hill. Below them was a pond. . . . A bridge spanned it midway and from there to its lower end, where an amber-hued belt of sand hills shut it in from the dark-blue gulf beyond, the water was a glory of many shifting hues. . . .

"That's Barry's pond," said Matthew.

"Oh, I don't like that name, either. I shall call it—let me see—the Lake of Shining Waters. Yes, that is the right name for it. I know because of the thrill. When I hit on a name that suits exactly it gives me a thrill. Do things ever give you a thrill?"

Matthew ruminated.[1] "Well now, yes. It always kind of gives me a thrill to see them ugly white grubs[2] that spade up in the cucumber beds. I hate the look of them."

"Oh, I don't think that can be exactly the same kind of thrill. Do you think it can? There doesn't seem to be much connection between grubs and lakes of shining waters, does there? But why do other people call it Barry's pond?"

"I reckon because Mr. Barry lives up there in that house."

Analyzing Primary Sources
1. Why is *Anne of Green Gables* popular outside of Prince Edward Island?
2. How does imagination affect a person's view of the world?

Definitions [1]ruminate: to think over in the mind slowly [2]grubs: wormlike insect larvae

---

CHAPTER 6, Section 3

HUMAN SYSTEMS

From Canada to Japan
Lucy Maud Montgomery's *Anne of Green Gables* series is popular around the world, particularly in Japan. Japanese tourists flock to Prince Edward Island to see the places associated with Anne. Every year several Japanese couples marry in the same room where the author was wed.

Many reasons have been proposed for the connection Japanese readers feel with the spunky orphan. When the book first appeared in Japan in 1952, there were many orphans in the war-torn country. Some of them read the Anne books in school and were inspired by her example. Another reason may be Anne's devotion to her studies and her efforts to win a scholarship, since education is highly valued in Japan.

Activity: Have students read various selections from the *Anne of Green Gables* series and discuss how people of different cultures might respond to the passages.

Connecting to Literature Answers
1. Answers will vary but should mention Anne's bravery in the face of hardship.
2. possible answer: makes one's view of the world more interesting or fun

Canada • 145

Teaching Objective 2

LEVEL 1: (Suggested time: 45 min.) Explain that Canada's independence day is called Canada Day and occurs on July 1. Organize students into 13 groups or pairs—one for each province or territory. Have each group create a banner for a Canada Day parade to represent its part of the country. You may also want to have the groups write slogans for their provinces or territories. Have students use this unit's atlas and material in Sections 1 and 2 when creating their banners. **ESOL, COOPERATIVE LEARNING**

LEVELS 2 AND 3: (Suggested time: 30 min.) Have students work in pairs to create acronym sentences to help them remember Canada's provinces and territories in clockwise order, starting with Newfoundland. Ask students to write one or two sentences comprised of words that begin with *n, p, n, n, q, o, m, s, a, b, y, n,* and *n*. Sentences may be humorous or serious. (Example: Noisy penguins never need quiet old motorcycles. Strong astronauts become your nearest neighbors.) Ask a student to read the sentence(s) while his or her partner tells for which province or territory each word stands. Then ask other students to provide a fact for each province or territory. **COOPERATIVE LEARNING,** **VERBAL-LINGUISTIC**

Canada 145

CHAPTER 6, Section 3

FOOD FESTIVAL

Canadian Teatime Many Canadians enjoy afternoon tea—snacks or a light meal with a cup of hot tea. Have students research and bring teatime foods that represent the many peoples who have influenced Canadian culture. For example, cucumber sandwiches and small, thick pancakes called crumpets could represent the British. Crusty bread and cheese could stand for French immigrants. Students representing Asians could bring steamed dumplings or egg rolls. Be sure to include Canada's First Nations and the Inuit.

Day draws to a close in Toronto, Ontario. The city is located at the site of a trading post from the 1600s. Today Toronto is one of North America's major cities.

Canada's Prairie Provinces are home to productive farms like this one near Brandon, Manitoba.
Interpreting the Visual Record *Place* What can you tell about the physical geography of this region of Canada?

Visual Record Answer
flat, with fertile soil

Quebec The city of Quebec is the capital of the province. The city's older section has narrow streets, stone walls, and French-style architecture. Montreal is Canada's second-largest city and one of the largest French-speaking cities in the world. About 3.5 million people live in the Montreal metropolitan area. It is the financial and industrial center of the province. Winters in Montreal are very cold. People in the city center use underground passages and overhead tunnels to move between buildings.

Ontario Ontario is Canada's leading manufacturing province. It is also Canada's most populous province. About 4.7 million people live in the metropolitan area of Toronto, Ontario's capital. Toronto is a major center for industry, finance, education, and culture. Toronto's residents have come from many different regions, including China, Europe, and India. Between Toronto and Montreal lies Ottawa, Canada's capital. In Ottawa many people speak both English and French. It has grand government buildings, parks, and several universities.

✓ **READING CHECK:** *Places and Regions* What are the major cities of Canada's heartland? Quebec, Montreal, Toronto, Ottawa

The Western Provinces

Farther to the west are the major farming regions of Manitoba, Saskatchewan, and Alberta. These three provinces are called the Prairie Provinces. Along the Pacific coast is British Columbia.

CLOSE

Lead a class discussion on the advantages and disadvantages Canadians may face because they live in a huge country with a relatively small population. (possible answers for advantages: many opportunities for economic growth, minimal crowding, fewer problems with pollution or traffic; possible answers for disadvantages: inconveniently long distances for pleasure or business travel, lack of unity, many people cut off from educational or cultural opportunities)

REVIEW, ASSESS, RETEACH

Have students complete the Section Review. Then call on a volunteer to describe a place in Canada by starting a sentence with "I am thinking of a place where...." The student should list physical, economic, or cultural details without revealing the location. That student then calls on another to tell which place was described. Continue until all the provinces, territories, and major cities have been discussed.

Have students complete Main Idea Activity S3. Then have students work in pairs to create a third column for the graphic organizer in the Section 3 Review. Title the third column "What I should remember about this province or territory." Discuss student responses. **ESOL**

The Prairie Provinces More people live in Quebec than in all of the Prairie Provinces combined. The southern grasslands of these provinces are part of a rich wheat belt. Farms here produce far more wheat than Canadians need. The extra wheat is exported. Oil and natural gas production also are important in Alberta. Rocky Mountain resorts in western Alberta attract many tourists. The major cities of the Prairie Provinces are Edmonton, Calgary, and Winnipeg.

British Columbia British Columbia is Canada's westernmost province. This mountainous province has rich natural resources, including forests, salmon, and important minerals. Almost 4 million people live in British Columbia. Nearly half of them are in the coastal city of Vancouver. Vancouver is a multicultural city with large Chinese and Indian populations. It also is a major trade center.

✓ **READING CHECK:** *Environment and Society* How does geography affect the location of economic activities in the Prairie Provinces?
Grasslands good for growing wheat; oil and natural gas reserves also add to the economy

The Canadian North

Canada's vast northern lands include the Yukon Territory, the Northwest Territories, and Nunavut (noo-nah-vuht). Nunavut is a new territory created for the **Inuit** (Eskimos) who live there. *Nunavut* means "Our Land" in the Inuit language. Nunavut is part of Canada, but the people have their own local government. The three territories cover more than one third of Canada but are home to only about 100,000 people. Boreal forests, tundra, and frozen Arctic ocean waters separate isolated towns and villages.

✓ **READING CHECK:** Who lives in Nunavut? The Inuit

In the St. Elias Mountains in the Yukon Territory is the world's largest nonpolar ice field. The field covers an area of 15,822 square miles (40,570 sq km) and stretches into Alaska.

First Nations people of British Columbia created this totem pole.

Homework Practice Online
Keyword: SJ5 HP6

Define and explain: regionalism, maritime, Inuit

Working with Sketch Maps On the map that you created in Section 2, locate and label the major cities of Canada's provinces and territories. Where are most of these major cities located? What may have led to their growth?

Reading for the Main Idea
1. *Places and Regions* How does regionalism affect Canada's culture?
2. *The World in Spatial Terms* Into which provincial groups is Canada divided?

Critical Thinking
3. **Drawing Inferences and Conclusions** What makes the heartland a good area in which to settle?
4. **Finding the Main Idea** Why was Nunavut created?

Organizing What You Know
5. **Categorizing** Use the following graphic organizer to identify Canada's regions and provinces.

Region	Provinces

Canada • 147

Section 3 Review

Answers to Section 3 Review

Define For definitions, see the glossary.

Working with Sketch Maps Places should be labeled in approximate locations; most in southeast or on Pacific coast; both regions have waterways for trade, travel

Reading for the Main Idea
1. divisions between English, French speakers and between western, eastern provinces (NGS 6)
2. eastern; heartland; western (prairie and British Columbia); north (NGS 3)

Critical Thinking
3. financial, industrial, governmental, educational, and cultural center
4. created for native Inuit

Organizing What You Know
5. eastern—New Brunswick, Nova Scotia, Prince Edward Island, Newfoundland; heartland—Quebec, Ontario; western—Manitoba, Saskatchewan, Alberta, British Columbia; north—Yukon and Northwest Territories, Nunavut (NGS 4)

EXTEND

Have students report on the life and achievements of Adrienne Clarkson, who in 1999 became the first Asian Canadian to be appointed governor general, the personal representative of Queen Elizabeth II to Canada. Madame Clarkson, born Adrienne Poy, came to Canada in 1942 from Hong Kong. **BLOCK SCHEDULING**

CHAPTER 6 REVIEW

Define and Identify
For definitions and identifications, see the glossary and index.

Review the Main Ideas
11. some major physical regions in common, such as the Rocky Mountains and plains in the interiors (NGS 4)
12. Ice Age glaciers (NGS 7)
13. southwest (NGS 9)
14. fish, nickel, zinc, uranium, lead, copper, gold, silver, coal, potash, oil, natural gas; Prairie Provinces (NGS 16)
15. Cree, Déné, Mohawk, Ojibwa, Oneida, Kwakiutl (NGS 10)
16. seals, whales, walruses, and other animals (NGS 10)
17. Newfoundland Island; what is now Quebec City, eastern Canada (NGS 9)
18. furs, fish, manufactured goods (NGS 16)
19. conquered by British during the Seven Years' War
20. pushed Loyalists into Canada (NGS 9)
21. opened settlement to other parts of the country (NGS 9)
22. federation led by a prime minister; 10 provincial governments each led by a premier
23. regionalism, desire by some Quebecois for special status (NGS 13)
24. Prince Edward Island, Nova Scotia, New Brunswick; Quebec and Ontario; Manitoba, Saskatchewan, Alberta, British Columbia
25. chain of cities that extends from Windsor, Ontario, to Quebec (NGS 9)
26. Halifax, Quebec, Montreal, Toronto, Ottawa, Edmonton, Calgary, Winnipeg, Vancouver

Think Critically
27. federation; central and provincial governments similar to central U.S. government and states

148 Chapter 6

Chapter 6 Review and Practice

Define and Identify
Identify each of the following:
1. potash
2. pulp
3. newsprint
4. Samuel Champlain
5. provinces
6. dominion
7. Métis
8. regionalism
9. maritime
10. Inuit

Review the Main Ideas
11. How is the physical geography of Canada similar to that of the United States?
12. What created many of Canada's lakes?
13. What part of Canada has the mildest climate?
14. What natural resources does Canada have? Where is Canada's major wheat-farming area?
15. What are some of the First Nations called?
16. On what animals did the Inuit depend?
17. Where did the Vikings settle? Where did French colonists settle?
18. What products did the First Nations people and the French trade?
19. How did Canada come under British control?
20. How did the American Revolution affect Canada?
21. How did the railroad change Canada?
22. What kind of government does Canada have?
23. What issue causes conflict in Quebec?
24. What are the Maritime, Heartland, and Western Provinces?
25. Where is Canada's most densely populated area?
26. What are Canada's main cities?

Think Critically
27. **Comparing** How is Canada's government similar to that of the United States?
28. **Finding the Main Idea** How has immigration changed Canada?
29. **Drawing Inferences and Conclusions** How have past events shaped current conflicts in Canada?
30. **Drawing Inferences and Conclusions** If fishing and lumber are the primary industries of the Maritime Provinces, what are some likely secondary industries? List three industries.
31. **Summarizing** What geographic factors are responsible for economic activities in the Canadian provinces?

Map Activity
32. On a separate sheet of paper, match the letters on the map with their correct labels.
    - Great Slave Lake
    - Great Bear Lake
    - Newfoundland and Labrador
    - Prince Edward Island
    - Manitoba
    - Alberta
    - Toronto
    - Calgary
    - Vancouver
    - Nunavut

148 • Chapter 6

28. possible answer: has created ethnic and cultural diversity
29. 150 years of French colonization created a strong French-speaking population that currently is in conflict with the English-speaking population.
30. possible answers: shipping, shipbuilding, seafood processing, lumber processing, furniture manufacturing
31. Maritime Provinces—good fishing waters; heartland provinces—urban centers of finance and industry; Prairie Provinces—good farmland; British Columbia—prime location for Pacific trade

Map Activity
32. A. Toronto
    B. Manitoba
    C. Vancouver
    D. Alberta
    E. Nunavut
    F. Calgary
    G. Great Slave Lake
    H. Newfoundland
    I. Great Bear Lake
    J. Prince Edward Island

Writing Activity

Write three paragraphs explaining where in Canada you might like to live and why. Name a province and describe the geographic, climatic, political, and cultural features that make it attractive to you. Would you want to live in one of that province's cities? If so, which one, and why? Be sure to use standard grammar, sentence structure, spelling, and punctuation.

Internet Activity: go.hrw.com
KEYWORD: SJ5 GT6

Choose a topic to explore about Canada:
- Take a trip to the Yukon Territory.
- Learn about Canada's First Nations.
- Meet the people of Quebec.

CHAPTER 6 REVIEW

Writing Activity
Answers will vary, but information included should be consistent with text material. Check to see that students have written about geographic, climatic, political, and cultural features. Use Rubric 37, Writing Assignments, to evaluate each student's work.

Interpreting Maps
1. concentrations of English- and French-speaking Canadians
2. eastern and southeastern Canada
3. They are thinly populated, or neither language dominates.
4. the Inuit language, languages of First Nations peoples, Chinese, or languages of other major immigrant groups

Analyzing Primary Sources
1. families sleeping in shifts, effect of sleeplessness on absenteeism and school performance, health problems, employment problems
2. caused respiratory difficulties and communicable diseases
3. made it difficult to fill jobs that don't include housing
4. affected school performance

Social Studies Skills Practice

Interpreting Maps
Study the map and answer the questions below.

Languages in Canada

Concentrations of English-speaking Canadians
Concentrations of French-speaking Canadians

Source: Thomas M. Poulsen, "Nations and States: A Geographic Background to World Affairs"

1. What information does this map offer?
2. Where do most French-speaking Canadians live?
3. Why do you think large areas of the map are blank?
4. Based on your knowledge of Canada, what additional languages might be added to this map?

Analyzing Primary Sources
Read the following quote about housing problems in Nunavut. Then answer the questions.

"... we heard ... reports of families sleeping in shifts because there is insufficient [not enough] room for all members to sleep at once. The lack of sleep has in turn affected employee absenteeism and children's performance in school. Crowded housing conditions ... have contributed to health problems such as respiratory [breathing] difficulties and communicable [spreadable] diseases. The shortage has also affected the economy by making it difficult to recruit employees. Quite often a job without available housing is a job unfilled. At the same time, an individual may be reluctant to change employers if it means losing their home."

1. What evidence does the report use to prove that a housing crisis exists?
2. How has the crisis affected the health of Nunavut's citizens?
3. How has the housing shortage affected the economy?
4. What effects has the housing problem had on children?

CHAPTER 6 — REVIEW AND ASSESSMENT RESOURCES

Reproducible
- Readings in World Geography, History, and Culture 13 and 14
- Critical Thinking Activity 6
- Vocabulary Activity 6

Technology
- Chapter 6 Test Generator (on the One-Stop Planner)
- Audio CD Program, Chapter 6
- HRW Go site

Reinforcement, Review, and Assessment
- Chapter 6 Review
- Chapter Summaries and Review
- Chapter 6 Test
- Chapter 6 Test for English Language Learners and Special-Needs Students
- Unit 2 Test
- Unit 2 Test for English Language Learners and Special-Needs Students

GO TO: go.hrw.com
KEYWORD: SJ5 Teacher
FOR: a guide to using the Internet in your classroom

CHAPTER 6

GEOGRAPHY SIDELIGHT

The Arctic Supermarket Do you think that starvation is a constant threat to the Inuit? If you said "yes," you'd be wrong!

In general, the traditional Inuit diet—called country foods—has kept the Inuit well fed and healthy. All basic nutrients, including vitamins, are provided. In fact, many non-Inuit who have moved into the Canadian Arctic and tried to maintain their own traditional diets have suffered. Scurvy was a particular problem among area whalers who didn't change their diets. Country foods are also much cheaper than imported foods. For example, the cost of imported pork can be more than 41 times the cost of harvesting caribou.

Now some country foods are threatened with contamination. Dangerous chemicals are making their way into the foods from industrial, agricultural, and military sources far away.

Activity: Have students conduct research on the concentration of chemicals and metals such as mercury in fish.

GO TO: go.hrw.com
KEYWORD: SJ5 CH6
FOR: more information on the Canadian Arctic.

COULD YOU SURVIVE THE CANADIAN ARCTIC?

ON-LINE EXPEDITIONS
GO TO: go.hrw.com
KEYWORD: SJ5 CH6

A Land of Ice and Snow

Northeastern Canada is no place for the timid. It's cold! Average winter temperatures are way below zero. Ice and snow then cover the land. Even in summer the temperature seldom rises above freezing. Few plants besides mosses and lichens can survive the cold. Yet the Inuit have survived here for thousands of years. How?

SURVIVAL CHALLENGE

Now imagine that you are an explorer of the 1800s. You have bought the map pictured here from a mysterious old fellow. He told you the X marks the location of a pile of silver left long ago by Vikings. You can't wait to go in search of the treasure! However, because you don't want any competition for the loot, you don't want to draw attention to yourself by packing in lots of supplies. You decide to live off the land. What should you take with you that will help you do so? What natural resources can you use in this harsh environment? Keep in mind that almost nothing from your regular environment is available. There are no plants to eat. What would you do to replace torn or worn-out clothes? What if you needed a tool you didn't have with you?

Along with the map, the old man sold you the two diagrams shown. The information on them came from the Inuit. What do the diagrams mean? Could they help you survive?

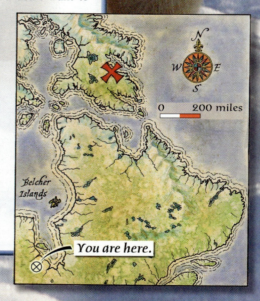

150 • Unit 2

Survival Challenge Activity

First, emphasize that the Inuit have lived in the region for thousands of years. Ask: Of the materials that we call natural resources, which may be lacking in this environment? (Soil, coal, building stone, iron, gold, and other minerals are buried under the ice. There is practically no wood.)

Then draw students' attention to the top diagram. What may "longest day" at the top mean? When is the longest day in the year? (summer solstice, about June 22) If this diagram indicates a certain day, and it's divided into 12 sections, what may it actually be? (Each section represents a month, so the diagram is a circular calendar.) Then point out the correspondence between the two diagrams. (Each gives the names of animals in Inuktitut, the Inuit language of eastern Canada.) Now what does the calendar mean? (The arrows show during which months the animals named can be successfully hunted.) You may want to quiz students about the availability of various animals throughout the year. For example, when should one hunt walrus (*aiviq*)? (early September to late October) When are polar bears available? (January through March) During which month may survival be most difficult? (April) What may the other lines on the calendar mean? (times for hunting other animals) Then let students quiz each other about what animals are useful for various needs—food, clothing, shelter, lamp oil, needles, and so on—and when they can be harvested. Finally, ask: What are the main natural resources in the Inuit environment? On what, therefore, must our treasure hunter rely? (animals)

CHAPTER 6

Learning the Land

As part of the planning for your trip, you must decide the best way to reach the treasure. If you start at the southern edge of the area shown on the map, what route should you take to the X? How would your route affect the natural resources on which you can rely?

If you reach the treasure, you will have learned an important lesson about natural resources. What do you think it is?

Polar bears prowl the ice at the edge of Canada's Hudson Bay.

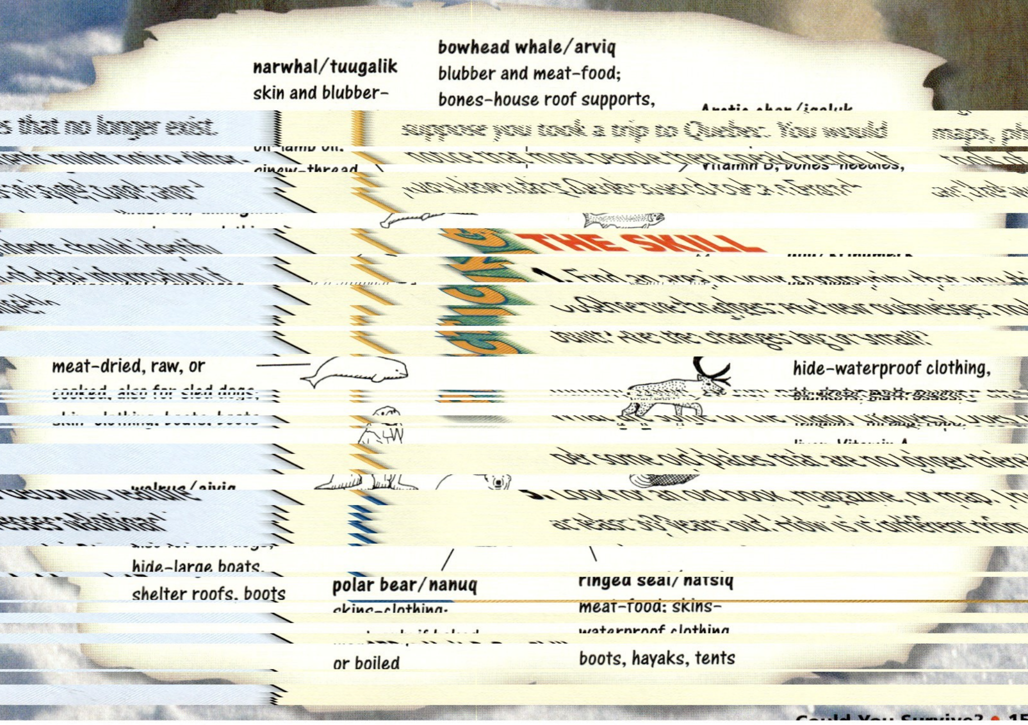

Seasonal foods of...

Source: Voices from the Bay: Traditional Ecological Knowledge of Environmental Changes in Hudson and James Bays, Part I.

- **narwhal/tuugalik** — skin and blubber-
- **bowhead whale/arviq** — blubber and meat-food; bones-house roof supports,
- **meat-dried, raw, or cooked, also for sled dogs**
- **hide-waterproof clothing,**
- **walrus/aiviq**
- **hide-large boats, shelter roofs, boots**
- **polar bear/nanuq** — skins-clothing;
- **ringed seal/natsiq** — meat-food; skins-waterproof clothing, boots, kayaks, tents

...or boiled

Going Further: Thinking Critically

the only indigenous people who harvest healthy foods from a difficult environment.

Organize the class into two groups. Have one group conduct research on the San of the Kalahari in Africa. The San live in parts of Botswana, Namibia, and South Africa. Have the other group research the Aborigines of Australia. Ask each group to concentrate on the diets of the assigned people. How do they

What are the sources of vitamins and minerals? Ask the students also to compare San and Aborigine knowledge of the natural resources in their environments to the Inuit's knowledge.

Geography Standards 3, 15, and 15

GeoSkills

Going Further: Thinking Critically

Have students collect old photos of buildings, roads, parks, factories, farms,

Refer again to the diagrams. Point out that the Inuit have learned a great deal about the behavior of the animals, where they live, and how they migrate. As one can infer from the diagram, the Belcher Islands Inuit have tracked animals' movements carefully.

Refer back to the treasure map. Now that we know the treasure hunter must rely on animals and that they are not all available in all places at all times, what area would provide the greatest variety of animal resources? How does the lower diagram help answer this question? **(Many of the animals live in the sea or on the coast. The treasure hunter would be wise to stay near the coast.)** You may want to refer students to that would allow the treasure-hunter the best chance for survival. **(Possible answer: north along the western coast of Quebec on the coast of Hudson Bay)**

Now return to the last question under "Learning the Land." What is the

Have students work individually or in pairs to study the photo-map collection.

Could You Survive 151

HANDS on GEOGRAPHY

You can analyze changing landscapes by comparing old photographs of a place to new ones. Important changes might be easy to see. For example, new buildings and new roads often stand out on the more recent photographs.

Look at the two photographs below. They show a small section of Las Vegas, Nevada. The photograph on the left was taken in 1963. The photograph on the right was taken 35 years later in 1998. Now compare the two photographs. What do you notice?

◄ Las Vegas, 1963

▲ Las Vegas, 1998

Lab Report

1. How do you know these two photographs show the same place? What evidence do you see?
2. How did this section of Las Vegas change between 1963 and 1998? Do you think these are big changes or small ones?
3. Find a street map of Las Vegas and try to figure out exactly what part of the city the photographs show. Then compare the map with the 1998 photograph. What information does the map give about this section of the city?

Lab Report

Answers

1. The same street layouts are visible in each photograph.
2. Students should notice an increase in the number of buildings and a decrease in the amount of open space. They may also note changes such as new roads and parking lots. Students should conclude that these are big changes.
3. Students might suggest names of streets and highways, elevations, names of public buildings, or other features.

UNIT 3

UNIT OBJECTIVES

1. Describe the landforms, bodies of water, climates, and resources of Middle and South America.
2. Analyze the influence of ancient American civilizations, European colonialism, and recent events on societies in Middle and South America.
3. Identify the political, economic, social, cultural, and environmental challenges facing the region's countries.
4. Interpret special-purpose diagrams to better understand human-environment interaction in Middle and South America.

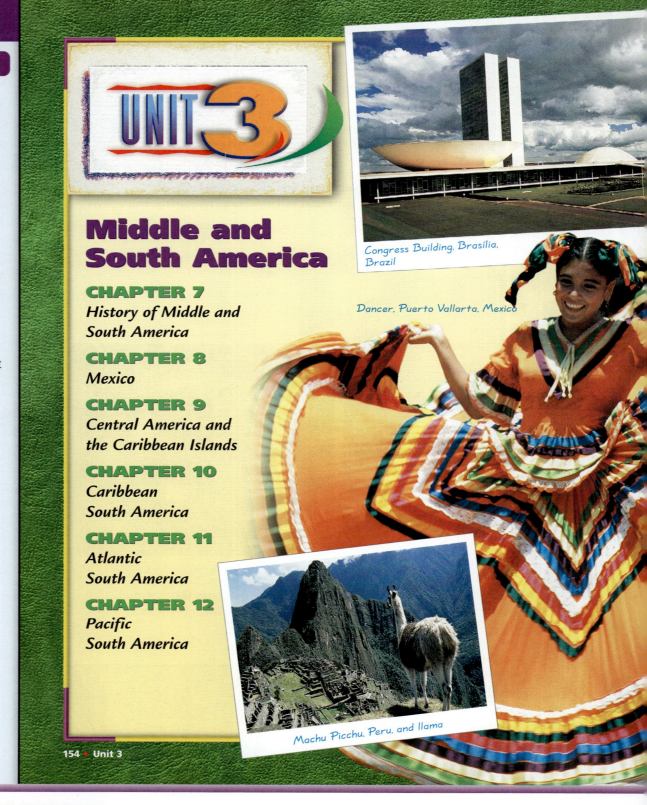

UNIT 3

Middle and South America

CHAPTER 7
History of Middle and South America

CHAPTER 8
Mexico

CHAPTER 9
Central America and the Caribbean Islands

CHAPTER 10
Caribbean South America

CHAPTER 11
Atlantic South America

CHAPTER 12
Pacific South America

Congress Building, Brasília, Brazil

Dancer, Puerto Vallarta, Mexico

Machu Picchu, Peru, and llama

154 ◆ Unit 3

USING THE ILLUSTRATIONS

Direct students' attention to the photographs on these pages. Remind students that animals have adapted in many ways so they can survive in the ecosystems where they live. Focus attention on the frog and butterfly. Point out that the frog's skin secretes a deadly poison. Ask how the creatures' distinctive appearance may help them survive. (Possible answers: Attackers may not see the butterfly because they can see through its wings. The frog's color may attract mates or warn attackers.)

Tell students that the buildings in the photos are separated by about 1,660 miles (2,671 km) and that one was built hundreds of years before the other. Yet the two building sites have at least two qualities in common. Ask what they might be. (Possible answers: apparently built of durable materials, use many straight lines)

Finally, focus attention on the dancer in the center of the page. You may want to have students try to estimate how many yards of fabric and ribbon were required to make her costume.

UNIT 3

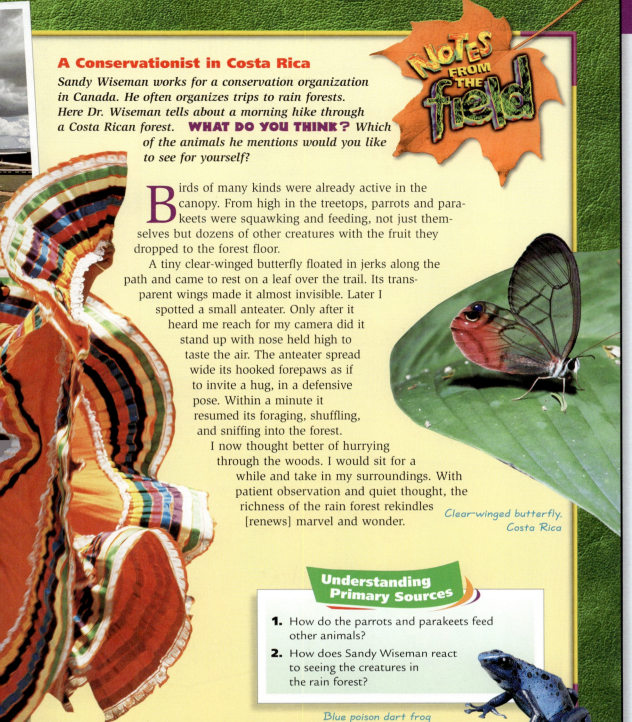

Notes from the Field

A Conservationist in Costa Rica

Sandy Wiseman works for a conservation organization in Canada. He often organizes trips to rain forests. Here Dr. Wiseman tells about a morning hike through a Costa Rican forest. **WHAT DO YOU THINK?** Which of the animals he mentions would you like to see for yourself?

Birds of many kinds were already active in the canopy. From high in the treetops, parrots and parakeets were squawking and feeding, not just themselves but dozens of other creatures with the fruit they dropped to the forest floor.

A tiny clear-winged butterfly floated in jerks along the path and came to rest on a leaf over the trail. Its transparent wings made it almost invisible. Later I spotted a small anteater. Only after it heard me reach for my camera did it stand up with nose held high to taste the air. The anteater spread wide its hooked forepaws as if to invite a hug, in a defensive pose. Within a minute it resumed its foraging, shuffling, and sniffing into the forest.

I now thought better of hurrying through the woods. I would sit for a while and take in my surroundings. With patient observation and quiet thought, the richness of the rain forest rekindles [renews] marvel and wonder.

Clear-winged butterfly, Costa Rica

Understanding Primary Sources

1. How do the parrots and parakeets feed other animals?
2. How does Sandy Wiseman react to seeing the creatures in the rain forest?

Blue poison dart frog

MORE FROM THE FIELD

Costa Rica, with its incredible biodiversity, is an ecotourism success story. A recent study found that more than 66 percent of all tourists traveling to Costa Rica had visited a natural protected area.

Nature preserves can protect animals while welcoming tourists. For example, many visitors to Costa Rica's Monteverde Cloud Forest Preserve want to see magnificent birds called quetzals. While the female quetzals are building nests, trails in their nesting areas are closed. The trails open again while the birds incubate their eggs and tolerate visitors more easily.

Activity: Have students conduct research on one of the animals mentioned in Notes from the Field. Ask them to speculate on the accommodations visitors to the animal's habitat may need to make.

Understanding Primary Sources
Answers
1. by dropping fruit to the forest floor
2. sits down and takes in his surroundings

CHAPTERS

7 History of Middle and South America
introduces the region's ancient cultures and traces its history through the independence movements.

8 Mexico
focuses on the physical geography, economy, and regions of Mexico.

9 Central America and the Caribbean Islands
describes the countries of Central America and the Caribbean islands.

10 Caribbean South America
features Colombia, Venezuela, and the Guianas: Guyana, Suriname, and French Guiana.

11 Atlantic South America
explores the countries of eastern South America, including Brazil and Argentina.

12 Pacific South America
describes the landforms, climate regions, economies, and political situations of Ecuador, Peru, Bolivia, and Chile.

UNIT 3 ATLAS

PEOPLE IN THE PROFILE

Note that the elevation profile crosses the Brazilian Highlands, which includes the state of Bahia. Today, Salvador, the state capital, is perhaps the largest center of African culture in the Americas.

Many Africans were brought to Bahia as slaves. Their influence is readily seen in spicy foods, music, crafts, and a unique folk dance called *capoeira*.

There are several theories about the origins of *capoeira*, which evolved from an Angolan martial art into a dance. The most widely accepted theory suggests that *capoeira* was created in the 1600s by escaped slaves who had fled to the forests and formed independent villages called *quilombos*. These people defended their villages with *capoeira*, a fighting style that they had developed in secret.

In 1974 *capoeira* was recognized as the national sport of Brazil. As practiced today, *capoeira* combines dancing, fighting, acrobatics, and music.

Critical Thinking: How does *capoeira* reflect Africans' resistance to slavery?

Answer: It was developed as a secret fighting style by escaped slaves to protect their villages.

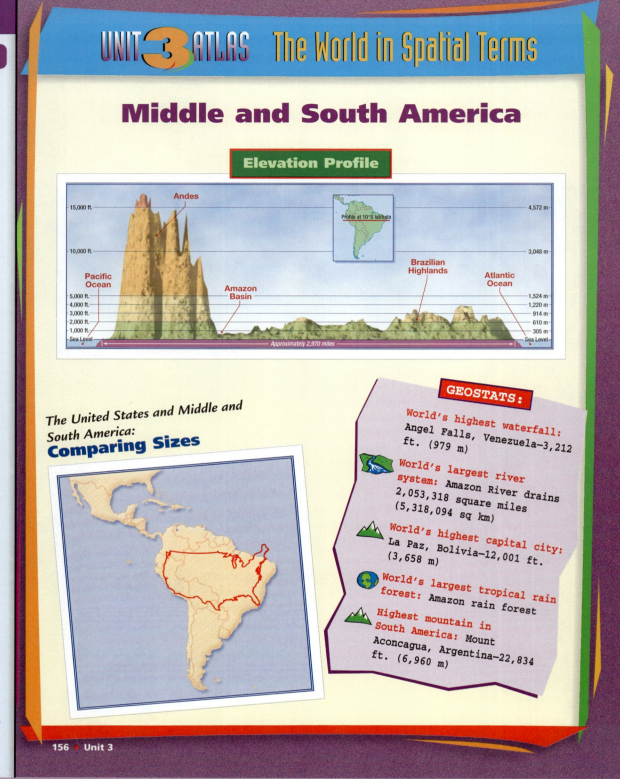

UNIT 3 ATLAS: The World in Spatial Terms

Middle and South America

Elevation Profile

Andes — 15,000 ft. / 4,572 m
Profile at 10°S latitude
Pacific Ocean
Amazon Basin
Brazilian Highlands
Atlantic Ocean
10,000 ft. / 3,048 m
5,000 ft. / 1,524 m
4,000 ft. / 1,220 m
3,000 ft. / 914 m
2,000 ft. / 610 m
1,000 ft. / 305 m
Sea Level
Approximately 2,970 miles

The United States and Middle and South America: Comparing Sizes

GEOSTATS:

- **World's highest waterfall:** Angel Falls, Venezuela—3,212 ft. (979 m)
- **World's largest river system:** Amazon River drains 2,053,318 square miles (5,318,094 sq km)
- **World's highest capital city:** La Paz, Bolivia—12,001 ft. (3,658 m)
- **World's largest tropical rain forest:** Amazon rain forest
- **Highest mountain in South America:** Mount Aconcagua, Argentina—22,834 ft. (6,960 m)

OVERVIEW

In this unit, students will learn about the physical geography and cultures of Middle and South America.

Much of the region is within the tropics; tropical and savanna climates predominate. Mountainous areas have highland climates. Although subsistence and commercial agriculture are widespread, large areas are undeveloped and almost completely uninhabited. Cities are concentrated along coasts and in highland areas. Industrial growth draws people to the rapidly expanding cities.

The region's cultures reflect its history of colonization by Spain, Portugal, and other European countries. In most countries people of mixed heritage are in the majority, with European and indigenous peoples in the minority.

The countries of Middle and South America face many challenges, such as improving standards of living, increasing personal freedoms, and protecting fragile ecosystems.

Middle and South America: Physical

UNIT 3 ATLAS

ONLINE ATLAS
GO TO: go.hrw.com
KEYWORD: SJ5 MapsU3
FOR: Web links to online maps of the region

1. **Region** Which country has two highland regions and a large plateau?
2. **Region** Which country has two large peninsulas that extend into different oceans?
3. **Region** Which island groups separate the Caribbean Sea from the Gulf of Mexico and the Atlantic Ocean?

Critical Thinking

4. **Movement** Find central Mexico on the map. Why do you think east-west travel might be difficult in this area? What physical feature do you think would make travel easier in northern Brazil?

Physical Map
Answers
1. Brazil
2. Mexico
3. Greater Antilles and Lesser Antilles

Critical Thinking
4. presence of two mountain ranges—the Sierra Madre Occidental and the Sierra Madre Oriental; Amazon River

USING THE PHYSICAL MAP

As students examine the map on this page, call their attention to the physical features they will study in this unit. Ask them to name the major landforms of South America (Amazon Basin, Andes). You may want to review the meaning of *basin* and relate the word to the elevation patterns of Brazil. Ask students where the mountains are concentrated (along the western edge of the landmass). Then ask students to name other countries whose highest mountains are in the west (United States, Canada).

Call on volunteers to identify the major rivers of South America and the countries through which they flow. Point out that Middle America has few major rivers.

Middle and South America 157

UNIT 3 ATLAS

Your Classroom Time Line

These are the major dates and time periods for this unit. Have students enter them on the time line you created earlier. You may want to watch for these dates as students progress through the unit.

c.* 1500 B.C. Small farming villages are established in Mesoamerica.

c. 900 B.C. Peru's first advanced civilization reaches its height.

C. A.D. 800 Maya civilization begins to collapse.

c. 1300 The Aztec establish Tenochtitlán.

1492 Christopher Columbus sails into the Caribbean.

1500s Spain and Portugal establish colonies in the Americas.

*c. stands for *circa* and means "about."

Political Map
Answers
1. Panama
2. Mexico; Brazil

Critical Thinking
3. Río Negro, Orinoco, Paraguay, Paraná, and Uruguay Rivers
4. located in dense rain forest

Middle and South America: Political

1. **Location** Which country connects Middle America and South America?
2. **Region** What is the largest country in Middle America? in South America?

Critical Thinking

3. **Human-Environment Interaction** Compare this map to the **physical map** of the region. What are some rivers that mark the borders between different countries in South America?
4. **Human-Environment Interaction** Compare this map to the **land use and resources** and **physical maps** of the region. Why would it be difficult to mark the boundaries where Colombia, Brazil, and Peru meet?

158 • Unit 3

USING THE POLITICAL MAP

 Focus students' attention on the capital cities on the **political map** of Middle and South America on this page. Ask students to name some of the capital cities that are located on or very near a seacoast **(Havana, Panama City, Caracas, Lima, Buenos Aires, Montevideo, Georgetown, Paramaribo)** and to name one reason why so many capitals are located on seacoasts **(for trade and communication with other regions)**. Then ask which capitals are located closer to the countries' center **(Mexico City, Bogotá, Quito, Santiago, Brasília)** and what might be the advantage of these more centrally located capitals **(more accessible to all parts of the country)**. Finally, ask which country has two capital cities **(Bolivia)**.

internet connect

ONLINE ATLAS
GO TO: go.hrw.com
KEYWORD: SJ5 MapsU3

158 Unit 3

Middle and South America: Climate

1. **Region** Which two climate types cover the largest area?
2. **Place** Which countries have coastal areas with cool damp climates?
3. **Region** Compare this map to the **physical map** of the region. What type of climate does most of the Amazon Basin have?

Critical Thinking

4. **Region** Compare this map to the **population map**. How might climate affect the distribution of Brazil's population?

Middle and South America • 159

UNIT 3 ATLAS

Your Classroom Time Line (continued)

1521 Hernán Cortés conquers the Aztec.

1535 Inca Empire ends.

1600s–1700s The English, French, Dutch, and Danish establish Caribbean colonies.

1800s Many Central and South American countries gain their independence.

1804 Haiti wins its independence from France.

1810 Miguel Hidalgo y Costilla begins the Mexican revolt against the Spanish.

1830 Venezuela becomes independent.

1846 The Mexican War begins.

1898 The United States takes Cuba from Spain in the Spanish-American War.

Climate Map
Answers
1. humid tropical and tropical savanna
2. Chile, Argentina, Brazil
3. humid tropical

Critical Thinking

4. population distribution apparently affected by humid tropical climate

USING THE CLIMATE MAP

Direct students' attention to the **climate map** of Middle and South America on this page. Point out the wide variety of climate types in the region. Ask students to compare this map to the **physical map** of the region. You might have them write sentences to describe the relative locations of the main climate regions of South America. (Examples: The highland climate runs the length of the Andes. A humid tropical climate exists in the Amazon Basin.) Ask students to study the map legend and to choose the climate that is not found on the mainland of the region (subarctic).

Middle and South America 159

UNIT 3 ATLAS

Your Classroom Time Line (continued)

1902 Cuba gains its independence.

1910 The Mexican Revolution begins.

1914 The United States finishes the Panama Canal.

1920 The Mexican Revolution ends.

1959 Fidel Castro seizes power in Cuba.

1960s The United States begins ban on trade with Cuba and restrictions on travel by U.S. citizens to Cuba.

1973–74 Juan Perón serves his second term as president of Argentina.

1979 The Sandinistas overthrow a dictator in Nicaragua.

internet connect
ONLINE ATLAS
GO TO: go.hrw.com
KEYWORD: SJ5 MapsU3

Population Map
Answers
1. French Guiana
2. Cuba, Hispaniola

Critical Thinking
3. Manaus is located where the Río Negro joins the Amazon River, making it a good place for trade.
4. Lake Nicaragua, Lake Titicaca

Middle and South America: Population

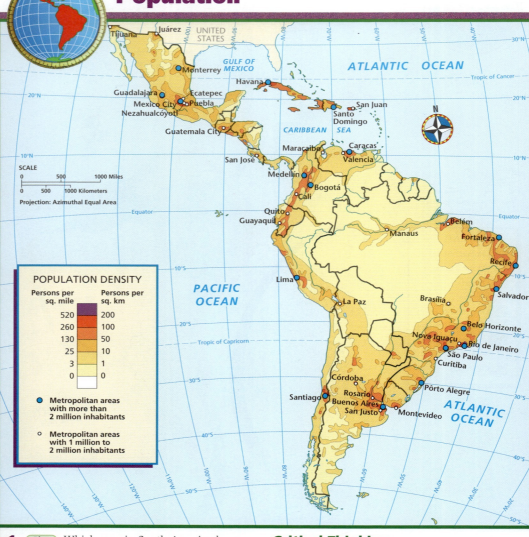

1. **Place** Which area in South America has no place with more than three people per square mile?

2. **Place** Compare this map to the **physical map** of the region. Which two islands have cities with populations of more than 2 million?

Critical Thinking

3. **Movement** Compare this map to the **physical map**. Why might a major city be located deep in the rain forest?

4. **Human-Environment Interaction** Compare this map to the **physical map**. Which lakes seem to affect population density?

160 • Unit 3

USING THE POPULATION MAP

Have students examine the **population map** on this page. Ask them to describe the general pattern of population distribution in South America. (Possible answers: Most people live near the coast or in highland regions; the interior is very sparsely populated.) Then ask students to suggest reasons why the population is distributed in this way. (Possible answers: The coasts are more accessible than the interior. The highlands have a more temperate climate than lower elevations.)

160 Unit 3

Middle and South America: Land Use and Resources

UNIT 3 ATLAS

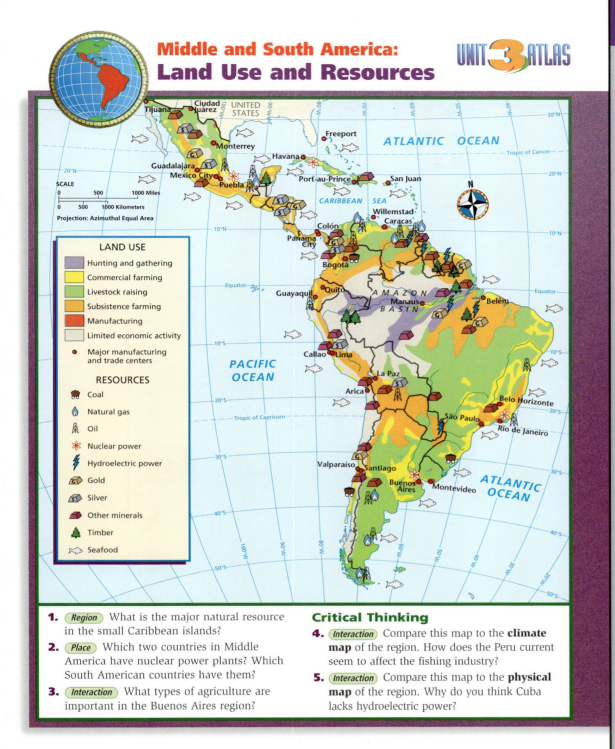

1. **Region** What is the major natural resource in the small Caribbean islands?
2. **Place** Which two countries in Middle America have nuclear power plants? Which South American countries have them?
3. **Interaction** What types of agriculture are important in the Buenos Aires region?

Critical Thinking
4. **Interaction** Compare this map to the **climate map** of the region. How does the Peru current seem to affect the fishing industry?
5. **Interaction** Compare this map to the **physical map** of the region. Why do you think Cuba lacks hydroelectric power?

Middle and South America • 161

UNIT 3 ATLAS
Your Classroom Time Line (continued)

1980s Civil war in El Salvador begins.
1983 Argentina's defeat in the Falklands War leads to governmental reforms.
1990s Volcanic eruptions cause great damage on the island of Montserrat.
1990s The collapse of the Soviet Union hurts Cuba's economy.
1990s The Children's Movement of Colombia is nominated for the Nobel Peace Prize.
1990s Chile becomes a democracy.
1990s Civil wars in Central America decline.
1994 NAFTA takes effect.
1999 The United States gives up control of the Panama Canal to Panama.
2000 Vicente Fox is sworn in as Mexico's president.
2002 Argentina's economy falls into chaos.

Land Use and Resources Map
Answers
1. seafood
2. Mexico, Cuba; Brazil, Argentina
3. livestock raising and commercial farming

Critical Thinking
4. seems to provide nutrients for good fishintg in the area
5. no major rivers

USING THE LAND USE AND RESOURCES MAP

Have students examine the map on this page. Call on volunteers to name the countries that have oil or natural gas reserves (Mexico, Venezuela, Colombia, Ecuador, Bolivia, Chile, Argentina, Brazil). Ask students to identify areas in South America where hydroelectric power has been developed (on rivers in the northeast and southeast). Then ask how the availability of oil, natural gas, or hydroelectric power might affect the industrial development of individual countries. (Possible answer: Because factories use large amounts of power, industrial development could probably increase if these energy resources were available.)

FAST FACTS

UNITED STATES OF AMERICA

CAPITAL: Washington, D.C.
AREA: 3,717,792 sq. mi. (9,629,091 sq km)
POPULATION: 290,342,554
MONEY: U.S. dollar
LANGUAGES: English, Spanish (spoken by a large minority)
CHILDREN BORN/WOMAN: 2.07

Fast Facts — Middle and South America

ANTIGUA AND BARBUDA
CAPITAL: Saint John's
AREA: 171 sq. mi. (442 sq km)
POPULATION: 67,897
MONEY: East Caribbean dollar
LANGUAGES: English
CHILDREN BORN/WOMAN: 2.3

BELIZE
CAPITAL: Belmopan
AREA: 8,867 sq. mi. (22,966 sq km)
POPULATION: 266,440
MONEY: Belizean dollar
LANGUAGES: English (official), Spanish, Mayan, Garifuna (Carib)
CHILDREN BORN/WOMAN: 3.9

ARGENTINA
CAPITAL: Buenos Aires
AREA: 1,068,296 sq. mi. (2,766,890 sq km)
POPULATION: 38,740,807
MONEY: Argentine peso
LANGUAGES: Spanish (official), English, Italian, German, French
CHILDREN BORN/WOMAN: 2.3

BOLIVIA
CAPITAL: La Paz, Sucre
AREA: 424,162 sq. mi. (1,098,580 sq km)
POPULATION: 8,586,443
MONEY: boliviano
LANGUAGES: Spanish, Quechua, Aymara (all official)
CHILDREN BORN/WOMAN: 3.2

BAHAMAS
CAPITAL: Nassau
AREA: 5,382 sq. mi. (13,940 sq km)
POPULATION: 297,477
MONEY: Bahamian dollar
LANGUAGES: English, Creole (among Haitian immigrants)
CHILDREN BORN/WOMAN: 2.2

BRAZIL
CAPITAL: Brasília
AREA: 3,286,470 sq. mi. (8,511,965 sq km)
POPULATION: 182,032,604
MONEY: real
LANGUAGES: Portuguese (official), Spanish, English, French
CHILDREN BORN/WOMAN: 2.0

BARBADOS
CAPITAL: Bridgetown
AREA: 166 sq. mi. (430 sq km)
POPULATION: 277,264
MONEY: Barbadian dollar
LANGUAGES: English
CHILDREN BORN/WOMAN: 1.6

CHILE
CAPITAL: Santiago
AREA: 292,258 sq. mi. (756,950 sq km)
POPULATION: 15,665,216
MONEY: Chilean peso
LANGUAGES: Spanish
CHILDREN BORN/WOMAN: 2.1

Countries not drawn to scale.

162 • Unit 3

FAST FACTS ACTIVITIES

LEVEL 1: (Suggested time: 30 min.) Have students examine the figures that describe the number of children born per woman. Students may notice that many of the figures contain decimals. Invite students to suggest how to interpret "less than one" child. *(The decimals are the result of calculating an average. For example, consider a group of 10 women. If one woman had one child, another had seven, five had three each, and the rest had none, the average number of children per woman would be 2.3. If the group of women were considered a country, that country would report that an average of 2.3 children were born per woman.)*

Have students list the six countries with the highest number of children per woman *(Belize, Bolivia, Guatemala, Haiti, Honduras, and Paraguay).* Then have students identify the six countries with the lowest number of children per woman *(Barbados, Cuba, Dominica, Puerto Rico, and St. Vincent and the Grenadines, Trinidad and Tobago).*

LEVEL 2: (Suggested time: 45 min.) Have students create a chart with four columns labeled Country, Children Born per Woman, Literacy Rate, and Percent of Population below the Poverty Level. Ask them to fill in their charts with the six countries with the highest number of children born per woman and the countries with the lowest number. Countries should be listed from the highest to the lowest figure.

162 Unit 3

Provide a copy of the table on the next pages to students. Ask them to suggest how literacy rates and poverty relate to the children per woman figures. (Answers will vary.) Have students add the relevant literacy and poverty figures to their charts.

Explain that high birthrates are generally associated with low education and low income, while low birthrates are generally linked with high education and high income. Have students refer to their charts to determine whether the figures they have gathered tend to support this statement. Then have students write a paragraph explaining the possible reasoning behind this statement, and whether they feel the data support it. (Countries with the lowest children per woman figures also had high literacy rates. No conclusion can be drawn regarding poverty level as these figures were not available for all the countries. Every country with a large number of children born per woman, with the exception of Paraguay, had a low literacy rate and a large percentage of its population living below poverty level. Because there are countries with high literacy rates that also have a large number of children born per woman—Grenada, for example—this statement should only be taken as a generalization.)

FAST FACTS

GUATEMALA
CAPITAL: Guatemala City
AREA: 42,042 sq. mi. (108,890 sq km)
POPULATION: 13,909,384
MONEY: quetzal
LANGUAGES: Spanish, Quiche, Cakchiquel, Kekchi
CHILDREN BORN/WOMAN: 4.6

MEXICO
CAPITAL: Mexico City
AREA: 761,602 sq. mi. (1,972,550 sq km)
POPULATION: 104,907,991
MONEY: Mexican peso
LANGUAGES: Spanish, Mayan, Nahuatl, ethnic languages
CHILDREN BORN/WOMAN: 2.5

GUYANA
CAPITAL: Georgetown
AREA: 83,000 sq. mi. (214,970 sq km)
POPULATION: 702,100
MONEY: Guyanese dollar
LANGUAGES: English, ethnic dialects
CHILDREN BORN/WOMAN: 2.1

NICARAGUA
CAPITAL: Managua
AREA: 49,998 sq. mi. (129,494 sq km)
POPULATION: 5,128,517
MONEY: gold cordoba
LANGUAGES: Spanish (official), English, ethnic languages
CHILDREN BORN/WOMAN: 3.0

HAITI
CAPITAL: Port-au-Prince
AREA: 10,714 sq. mi. (27,750 sq km)
POPULATION: 7,527,817
MONEY: gourde
LANGUAGES: French (official), Creole
CHILDREN BORN/WOMAN: 4.9

PANAMA
CAPITAL: Panama City
AREA: 30,193 sq. mi. (78,200 sq km)
POPULATION: 2,960,784
MONEY: balboa
LANGUAGES: Spanish (official), English
CHILDREN BORN/WOMAN: 2.5

HONDURAS
CAPITAL: Tegucigalpa
AREA: 43,278 sq. mi. (112,090 sq km)
POPULATION: 6,669,789
MONEY: lempira
LANGUAGES: Spanish, ethnic languages
CHILDREN BORN/WOMAN: 4.1

PARAGUAY
CAPITAL: Asunción
AREA: 157,046 sq. mi. (406,750 sq km)
POPULATION: 6,036,900
MONEY: guarani
LANGUAGES: Spanish (official), Guarani
CHILDREN BORN/WOMAN: 4.0

JAMAICA
CAPITAL: Kingston
AREA: 4,243 sq. mi. (10,990 sq km)
POPULATION: 2,695,867
MONEY: Jamaican dollar
LANGUAGES: English, Creole
CHILDREN BORN/WOMAN: 2.0

PERU
CAPITAL: Lima
AREA: 496,223 sq. mi. (1,285,220 sq km)
POPULATION: 28,409,897
MONEY: nuevo sol
LANGUAGES: Spanish (official), Quechua (official), Aymara
CHILDREN BORN/WOMAN: 2.8

Countries not drawn to scale.

Literacy and Poverty in Middle and South America

Country	Literacy Rate (Percent)	People below Poverty Level (Percent)
Antigua and Barbuda	89	*
Argentina	97	37
Bahamas	97	*
Barbados	97	*
Belize	94	33
Bolivia	87	70
Brazil	86	22
Chile	96	21
Colombia	93	55
Costa Rica	96	20.6
Cuba	97	*
Dominica	94	30
Dominican Republic	85	25
Ecuador	93	70
El Salvador	80	48
French Guiana	83	*
Grenada	98	32
Guatemala	71	75
Guyana	99	*
Haiti	53	80
Honduras	76	53
Jamaica	88	34.2
Mexico	92	40
Nicaragua	68	50
Panama	93	37
Paraguay	94	36
Peru	91	50
Puerto Rico	94	*

*data not available

UNIT 3 ATLAS — FAST FACTS

PUERTO RICO (U.S. Commonwealth)
CAPITAL: San Juan
AREA: 3,515 sq. mi. (9,104 sq km)
POPULATION: 3,937,316
MONEY: U.S. dollar
LANGUAGES: Spanish, English
CHILDREN BORN/WOMAN: 1.9

SAINT KITTS AND NEVIS
CAPITAL: Basseterre
AREA: 101 sq. mi. (261 sq km)
POPULATION: 38,763
MONEY: East Caribbean dollar
LANGUAGES: English
CHILDREN BORN/WOMAN: 2.4

SAINT LUCIA
CAPITAL: Castries
AREA: 239 sq. mi. (620 sq km)
POPULATION: 162,157
MONEY: East Caribbean dollar
LANGUAGES: English (official), French patois
CHILDREN BORN/WOMAN: 2.3

SAINT VINCENT AND THE GRENADINES
CAPITAL: Kingstown
AREA: 150 sq. mi. (389 sq km)
POPULATION: 116,812
MONEY: East Caribbean dollar
LANGUAGES: English, French patois
CHILDREN BORN/WOMAN: 2.0

SURINAME
CAPITAL: Paramaribo
AREA: 63,039 sq. mi. (163,270 sq km)
POPULATION: 433,998
MONEY: Surinamese guilder
LANGUAGES: Dutch (official), English, Sranang Tongo
CHILDREN BORN/WOMAN: 2.5

TRINIDAD AND TOBAGO
CAPITAL: Port-of-Spain
AREA: 1,980 sq. mi. (5,128 sq km)
POPULATION: 1,104,209
MONEY: Trinidad and Tobago dollar
LANGUAGES: English, Hindi, French, Spanish
CHILDREN BORN/WOMAN: 1.8

URUGUAY
CAPITAL: Montevideo
AREA: 68,039 sq. mi. (176,220 sq km)
POPULATION: 3,413,329
MONEY: Uruguayan peso
LANGUAGES: Spanish, Portunol
CHILDREN BORN/WOMAN: 2.4

VENEZUELA
CAPITAL: Caracas
AREA: 352,143 sq. mi. (912,050 sq km)
POPULATION: 24,654,694
MONEY: bolivar
LANGUAGES: Spanish (official), many ethnic languages
CHILDREN BORN/WOMAN: 2.4

internet connect
COUNTRY STATISTICS
GO TO: go.hrw.com
KEYWORD: SJ5 FactsU3
FOR: more facts about Middle and South America

Literacy and Poverty in Middle and South America

Country	Literacy Rate (Percent)	People below Poverty Level (Percent)
St. Kitts and Nevis	97	*
St. Lucia	67	*
St. Vincent and the Grenadines	96	*
Suriname	93	70
Trinidad and Tobago	99	21
Uruguay	98	6
Venezuela	93	47
United States	97	12.7

*data not available

LEVEL 3: (Suggested time: 40 min.) Have students compose an essay discussing some of the issues that adults in the United States take into account when making decisions about family size. In addition, have students tell how the issues may differ in a Middle or South American country. Students should refer to this unit's Fast Facts feature to support the statements they make in their essay. (Essays should address economic, social, and educational issues.)

CHAPTER 7
History of Middle and South America
Chapter Resource Manager

Objectives	Pacing Guide	Reproducible Resources
SECTION 1 **The Maya and Aztec** (pp. 167–173) 1. Describe the early civilizations that developed in Mexico and Central America. 2. Explain some achievements of the Maya. 3. Explore what Aztec civilization was like, and tell what weakened it.	**Regular** 2 days *Lecture Notes, Section 1* **Block Scheduling** 1 day *Block Scheduling Handbook, Chapter 7*	**RS** Know It Notes S1 **RS** Graphic Organizer 7 **SM** Map Activity 8 **E** Readings in World Geography, History, and Culture: Reading 17 **ELL** Main Idea Activity S1
SECTION 2 **The Inca** (pp. 174–179) 1. Analyze some achievements of South America's early cultures. 2. Describe some features of Inca culture.	**Regular** 1 day *Lecture Notes, Section 2* **Block Scheduling** .5 day *Block Scheduling Handbook, Chapter 7*	**RS** Know It Notes S2 **SM** Map Activity 12 **ELL** Main Idea Activity S2
SECTION 3 **Spanish Colonies and Independence** (pp. 180–183) 1. Trace how the Spaniards conquered civilizations in Middle and South America. 2. Analyze how the region changed after the Spanish conquest.	**Regular** 2 days *Lecture Notes, Section 3* **Block Scheduling** 1 day *Block Scheduling Handbook, Chapter 7*	**RS** Know It Notes S3 **E** Biography Activities: Miguel Hidalgo y Costilla, Simón Bolivar **SM** Critical Thinking Activity 10 **ELL** Main Idea Activity S3

Chapter Resource Key

- **RS** Reading Support
- **IC** Interdisciplinary Connections
- **E** Enrichment
- **SM** Skills Mastery
- **A** Assessment
- **REV** Review
- **ELL** Reinforcement and English Language Learners and English for Speakers of Other Languages (ESOL)
- Transparencies
- CD–ROM
- Music
- Video
- Internet
- Holt Presentation Maker Using Microsoft® PowerPoint®

 One-Stop Planner CD–ROM

See the *One-Stop Planner* for a complete list of additional resources for students and teachers.

One-Stop Planner CD–ROM

It's easy to plan lessons, select resources, and print out materials for your students when you use the *One-Stop Planner CD–ROM with Test Generator.*

internet connect

HRW ONLINE RESOURCES

GO TO: go.hrw.com
Then type in a keyword.

TEACHER HOME PAGE
KEYWORD: **SJ5 TEACHER**

CHAPTER INTERNET ACTIVITIES
KEYWORD: **SJ5 GT7**

Choose an activity to:
- dive into a sacred Maya well.
- explore Aztec ruins in the heart of Mexico City.
- learn more about struggles for independence in South America.

CHAPTER ENRICHMENT LINKS
KEYWORD: **SJ5 CH7**

CHAPTER MAPS
KEYWORDS: **SJ5 MAPS7**

ONLINE ASSESSMENT
Homework Practice
KEYWORD: **SJ5 HP7**
Standardized Test Prep Online
KEYWORD: **SJ5 STP7**
Rubrics
KEYWORD: **SS Rubrics**

COUNTRY INFORMATION
KEYWORD: **SJ5 Almanac**

CONTENT UPDATES
KEYWORD: **SS Content Updates**

HOLT PRESENTATION MAKER
KEYWORD: **SJ5 PPT7**

ONLINE READING SUPPORT
KEYWORD: **SS Strategies**

CURRENT EVENTS
KEYWORD: **S5 Current Events**

Technology Resources

- One-Stop Planner CD-ROM, Lesson 7.1
- Geography and Cultures Visual Resources 37, 38
- *ARGWorld* CD–ROM
- Homework Practice Online
- HRW Go site

- One-Stop Planner CD-ROM, Lesson 7.2
- Geography and Cultures Visual Resources 42, 43
- Music of the World Audio CD Program, Selection 5
- *ARGWorld* CD–ROM
- Homework Practice Online
- HRW Go site

- One-Stop Planner CD-ROM, Lesson 7.3
- Geography and Cultures Visual Resources 37–42
- Music of the World Audio CD Program, Selections 3–5
- *ARGWorld* CD–ROM
- Homework Practice Online
- HRW Go site

Review, Reinforcement, and Assessment Resources

ELL	Main Idea Activity S1
REV	Section 1 Review
A	Daily Quiz 7.1
REV	Chapter Summaries and Review
ELL	English Audio Summary 7.1
ELL	Spanish Audio Summary 7.1

ELL	Main Idea Activity S2
REV	Section 2 Review
A	Daily Quiz 7.2
REV	Chapter Summaries and Review
ELL	English Audio Summary 7.2
ELL	Spanish Audio Summary 7.2

ELL	Main Idea Activity S3
REV	Section 3 Review
A	Daily Quiz 7.3
REV	Chapter Summaries and Review
ELL	English Audio Summary 7.3
ELL	Spanish Audio Summary 7.3

Meeting Individual Needs

Ability Levels

Level 1 Basic-level activities designed for all students encountering new material

Level 2 Intermediate-level activities designed for average students

Level 3 Challenging activities designed for honors and gifted-and-talented students

ESOL Activities that address the needs of students with Limited English Proficiency

Chapter Review and Assessment

E	Readings in World Geography, History, and Culture 17
SM	Critical Thinking Activity 7
REV	Chapter 7 Review and Practice
REV	Chapter Summaries and Review
ELL	Vocabulary Activity 7
A	Chapter 7 Test
A	Chapter 7 Test Generator (on the One-Stop Planner)
	Audio CD Program, Chapter 7
A	Chapter 7 Test for English Language Learners and Special-Needs Students
	HRW Go site

Chapter 7: History of Middle and South America

Previewing Chapter Resources

Holt Online Learning

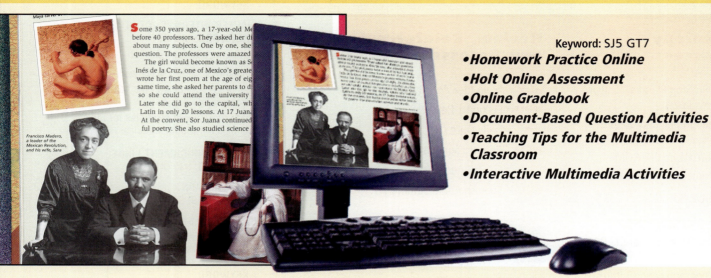

Keyword: SJ5 GT7

- Homework Practice Online
- Holt Online Assessment
- Online Gradebook
- Document-Based Question Activities
- Teaching Tips for the Multimedia Classroom
- Interactive Multimedia Activities

Differentiating Instruction

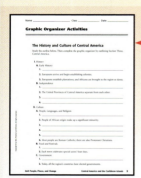

Reading and Writing Support
- ◀ Graphic Organizer Activity
- Vocabulary Activity
- Chapter Summaries and Review
- Know-It Notes S1–3
- Audio CD

Active Learning
- Block Scheduling Handbook
- Cultures of the World Activity
- Interdisciplinary Activity
- Map Activity
- ◀ Critical Thinking Activity 10

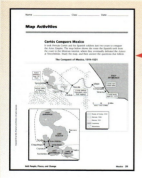

Primary Sources and Advanced Learners
- ◀ Map Activity: Cortés Conquers Mexico
- Readings in World Geography, History and Culture:
  - 23 Paraguay's Bumpy Ride

Assessment Program
- ◀ Daily Quizzes S1–3
- Chapter Test
- Chapter Test for English Language Learners and Special-Needs Students

Spanish and ESOL
- Vocabulary Activity
- Main Idea Activities for English Language Learners and Special-Needs Students
- Chapter Summaries and Review
- Spanish Audio Summary
- ◀ Know-It Notes S1–3
- Chapter Test for English Language Learners and Special-Needs Students

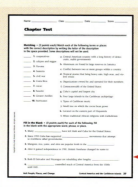

Special Education Modifications
Your **I.D.E.A. Works! CD-ROM** will provide modified versions of the following teaching materials:
- Know It Notes S1–3
- Vocabulary Activity
- Main Idea Activities S1–3
- Daily Quizzes S1–3
- ◀ Chapter 7 Test
- Flash cards of chapter vocabulary terms

Teacher Resources

Books for Teachers

Freidel, David and Linda Schele. *A Forest of Kings: The Untold Story of the Ancient Maya.* Quill, 1992.

Coe, Michael D. and Rex Kootnz. *Mexico: From the Olmecs to the Aztecs.* Thames & Hudson, 2002.

Malpass, Michael A. *Daily Life In The Inca Empire.* Greenwood Press, 1996.

Chasteen, John Charles. *Born in Blood and Fire:* A Concise History of Latin America. W.W. Norton & Company, 2000.

Books for Students

Day, Nancy. *Your Travel Guide to Ancient Mayan Civilization.* Information on Maya culture, geography, economy, recipes, games, and time lines. Runestone Press, 2000.

Rhoads, Dorothy. *The Corn Grows Ripe.* Puffin, 1993. A 12-year-old Maya boy must learn to plant and harvest corn after his father is injured. Fiction.

Steele, Philip. *Aztec News.* Candlewick Press, 2000. Presents Aztec culture, sports, politics, and religion in a newspaper-style format with full-color illustrations.

Reinhard, Johan. *Discovering the Inca Ice Maiden.* National Geographic, 1998. Anthropologist tells story of finding a mummified Inca maiden in the Peruvian Andes.

Lee, Claudia M. ed., *Messengers of Rain: And Other Poems of Latin America.* Illustrated collection of poetry from 19 Middle and South American countries. Groundwood Books, 2002.

Multimedia Materials

Lost Kingdoms of the Maya. Video, National Geographic.

Aztec Empire. Video, A & E Entertainment.

Fall of the Aztec and Maya Empires. Video, Questar Inc.

NOVA: Secrets of Lost Empires: Inca. Video, WGBH Boston

Videos and CDs

Videos
- 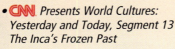 Presents World Cultures: Yesterday and Today, Segment 13 The Inca's Frozen Past
- ARG World

Holt Researcher
http://researcher.hrw.com

- *Montezuma II*
- *Empires in the Americas*
- *Empires of the Americas*
- *Aztec and Inca*
- *Columbus and the Taino*

Transparency Packages

Geography and Cultures Visual Resources Transparencies
32 Middle and South America: Physical

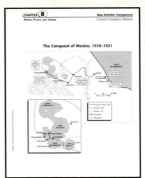

Map Activities Transparency
Cortés Conquers Mexico

CHAPTER 7

Why It Matters

Use these points to emphasize the importance of knowing more about the history of Middle and South America:

- The present-day cultures of the region vividly reflect some aspects of ancient cultures.
- Issues of land ownership and class distinctions that began hundreds of years ago still affect politics in the region.
- Archaeologists are still making dramatic discoveries about the civilizations that flourished there.
- We will better understand the region today if we learn about its past.

CHAPTER 7

History of Middle and South America

Civilizations combined in this region to create new cultures. Let's begin by studying some of the earliest civilizations.

20th-century painting of a Maya carver at work

Some 350 years ago, a 17-year-old Mexican girl stood before 40 professors. They asked her difficult questions about many subjects. One by one, she answered every question. The professors were amazed by her learning.

The girl would become known as Sor (Sister) Juana Inés de la Cruz, one of Mexico's greatest writers. Juana wrote her first poem at the age of eight. At about the same time, she asked her parents to dress her as a boy so she could attend the university in Mexico City. Later she did go to the capital, where she learned Latin in only 20 lessons. At 17 Juana became a nun. At the convent, Sor Juana continued to write beautiful poetry. She also studied science and music.

Francisco Madero, a leader of the Mexican Revolution, and his wife, Sara

Sor Juana Inés de la Cruz

Chapter Project

Ask students to imagine that they are Spanish or Portuguese adventurers of the early 1500s who want to explore Middle or South America. Have students work in groups to write skits about the stages in the trip. Skits may include petitioning monarchs to finance the voyage, scenes on board the ship, exploration through harsh environments, encounters with the native peoples, or the establishment of settlements. Assign one stage to each group. However, groups should coordinate their efforts in order to maintain continuity. Place scripts in student portfolios.

Starting the Chapter

Call on a volunteer to read aloud the information above about Sor Juana Inés de la Cruz. Lead a discussion about how her thirst for education may compare to the interest some of today's students take in learning. Then point out that the illustrations on the page represent three important eras in the region's history—pre-Columbian times (the Maya carver), the colonial period (Sor Juana), and the modern era (Francisco and Sara Madero). Tell students they will learn more about all of these time periods in this chapter.

Section 1: The Maya and Aztec

Read to Discover
1. What early civilizations developed in Mexico and Central America?
2. What were some achievements of the Maya?
3. What was Aztec civilization like, and what weakened it?

Vocabulary
glyphs
pok-a-tok
obsidian
chinampas

Places
Mesoamerica
Yucatán Peninsula
Teotihuacán
Tenochtitlán

People
Olmec
Pacal
Maya
Aztec

Reading Strategy

FOLDNOTES: PYRAMID   Create the FoldNote titled **Pyramid** described in the Appendix. As you read, write down information about the Early Cities and Empires on one triangle, information about the Maya on another triangle, and information about the Aztec on the third triangle. Use tape or glue to attach one of the flaps on top of the blank flap.

Early Cities and Empires

While cultures were developing in North America, other peoples were building civilizations to the south. As early as 2000 B.C., villages thrived in the areas now known as Mexico and Central America. This area is also known as Mesoamerica. (Meso means "in the middle.")

Like other ancient peoples, early residents of the region learned to grow food and raise animals. In time these villages began to trade with each other. As trading centers were created, cities grew. The cities competed for trade and territory. Some of the cities disappeared. Other Mesoamerican cities, however, grew into great empires. For example, empires with complex religious beliefs emerged in the valley of central Mexico and in the rain forests of the Yucatán Peninsula.

The Olmec The Olmec developed the earliest known civilization in Mexico. This culture was located along the Gulf of Mexico's southern coast. Appearing by about 1500 B.C., Olmec civilization lasted for some 1,000 years.

This gigantic head from the Olmec civilization is about six feet tall and five feet across.

Interpreting the Visual Record What does the statue appear to be wearing on its head?

History of Middle and South America • 167

CHAPTER 7, Section 1

SECTION 1 RESOURCES
Reproducibles
◆ Lecture Notes, Section 1
◆ Block Scheduling Handbook, Chapter 7
◆ Know It Notes S1
◆ Readings in World Geography, History, and Culture, Reading 17
◆ Map Activity 8

Technology
◆ One-Stop Planner CD-ROM, Lesson 7.1
◆ Geography and Cultures Visual Resources 37, 38
◆ Homework Practice Online
◆ HRW Go Site

Review, Reinforcement, and Assessment Resources
◆ Section 1 Review
◆ Daily Quiz 7.1
◆ Main Idea Activity S1
◆ Chapter Summaries and Review
◆ English Audio Summary 7.1
◆ Spanish Audio Summary 7.1

◀ **Visual Record Answer**

a helmet

Section 1

Objectives
1. Describe the early civilizations that developed in Mexico and Central America.
2. Explain some achievements of the Maya.
3. Explore what Aztec civilization was like, and tell what weakened it.

Focus

 Bellringer

Write these instructions on the board: *Look at the photograph on the first page of Section 1. What are two more things that you would like to know about this statue?* (Students may want to know who the Olmec were, how much the statue weighs, or where it was found. The Olmec were a people who lived along Mexico's southern coast, where the stone was found, from about 1500 B.C. to 500 B.C. Some of the heads weigh 40 tons.) Students will learn more about the Olmec, Maya, and Aztec in this section.

Building Vocabulary

Write the vocabulary terms on the chalkboard and ask: Which one sounds like it could be a ball game? (pok-a-tok) Which one may have something to do with writing? (glyphs) Which word may have come to us through Spaniards who wrote about what they saw? (*chinampas*) Which is the word for a type of natural glass that forms as a result of volcanic action? (obsidian) Discuss the complete definitions.

History of Middle and South America 167

CHAPTER 7, Section 1

Linking Past to Present

La Venta The gigantic head pictured on the previous page is from an Olmec settlement now called La Venta. The site dates from between 800 B.C. and 400 B.C. It is located near the border of Tabasco and Veracruz, states of present-day Mexico. The orientations of the major structures have led scientists to propose that the buildings were aligned with a certain star or constellation. The site also contains a 100-foot clay cone-shaped mound, a ceremonial enclosure containing a number of tombs, and mosaic pavements of jaguar masks.

Activity: Have students conduct research to find pictures of structures left behind by the Olmec, particularly those found at La Venta. Then have some students create replicas of Olmec structures and display them for the class. Ask other students to write tourist guides for La Venta.

Visual Record Answer ▶

steps or stairs; allowed priests or other officials to climb the pyramid to perform ceremonies at the top

Archaeologists have found objects that suggest the Olmec had an advanced society. For example, the Olmec carved huge heads out of stone. These heads weigh as much as 40 tons. The stone from which they were carved came from a quarry nearly 50 miles away from where the stones now rest! No one knows how the Olmec moved the stone.

Teotihuacán By about A.D. 500 as many as 200,000 people may have lived in Teotihuacán (tay-oh-tee-wah-KAHN), a city in south-central Mexico. There is no special name for these people—just the people of Teotihuacán. At the time, it was one of the world's largest cities. Its people grew rich from trade. Their wealth helped them gain control over the surrounding region.

Teotihuacán contained many plazas and a broad marketplace. It also had apartment buildings, residential neighborhoods, and hundreds of pyramids. An enormous Pyramid of the Sun dominated the city. The pyramid was built over a natural cave. The people of Teotihuacán may have believed their ancestors emerged from the Earth through this cave.

Teotihuacán quickly declined after A.D. 700. Archaeologists think that farmers may have worn out the land. This problem, combined with drought or other natural disasters, would have ruined the city's food supply.

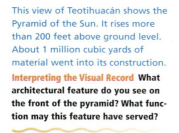

This view of Teotihuacán shows the Pyramid of the Sun. It rises more than 200 feet above ground level. About 1 million cubic yards of material went into its construction.
Interpreting the Visual Record What architectural feature do you see on the front of the pyramid? What function may this feature have served?

✓ **READING CHECK:** (Analyzing) What were the main features of early Mesoamerican civilizations? *agriculture, trade, complex religions, cities, pyramids*

TEACH

Teaching Objective 1

LEVEL 1: (Suggested time: 15 min.) Copy the following graphic organizer onto the chalkboard, omitting the blue answers. Point out that the oval resembles the giant head statues that the Olmec carved, and the flat-topped pyramid represents the Pyramid of the Sun built by the people of Teotihuacán. Have students fill in the first shape with background information about early civilizations of Mexico and Central America, the oval with details about the Olmec, and the pyramid with information on Teotihuacán.
ESOL, **LS** **VISUAL-SPATIAL**

Early Cities and Empires of Mesoamerica

Background
- villages thriving as early as 2000 B.C.
- farming, raising animals, trading with each other
- empires in valley of Mexico and Yucatán Peninsula

Olmec
- earliest known civilization in Mexico
- located along southern coast
- from about 1500 B.C., lasted 1,000 years
- advanced society
- carved huge stone heads

Teotihuacán
- by about A.D. 500 had population of 200,000
- south-central Mexico
- one of the world's largest cities
- wealthy from trade
- plazas, marketplace, apartments, pyramids
- Pyramid of the Sun
- declined after 700, perhaps because land was worn out

Murals in Bonampak, Mexico, display Maya battles, rituals, and processions.

The Maya

At about the same time that Teotihuacán was extending its influence across central Mexico, the Maya were growing in power. The Maya lived farther to the south and east in southern Mexico and the Yucatán Peninsula. They also lived in what are today Belize, Guatemala, and Honduras. Some historians say the Maya were the most technologically advanced early civilization in the Americas. Maya culture reached its height between A.D. 300 and A.D. 900.

Ruins of beautiful Maya cities still stand in the region's forests. These ruins show that the Maya were skilled architects and engineers. They were also fascinated by astronomy. To study the skies they built huge pyramids and tall round buildings we call observatories. Careful observation of the heavens helped the Maya develop an accurate 365-day calendar.

Maya Writing The Maya also created the only complete writing system in the ancient Americas. This system was based on a type of picture writing called hieroglyphics. Written characters, or **glyphs**, represented both objects and sounds. By carving glyphs onto stone monuments, the Maya left behind a record of their history. Modern scholars can now read most Maya glyphs. Among the inscriptions that scholars have deciphered are lists of kings.

These are just a few of the Maya glyphs that scholars can now read.

Across the Curriculum
SCIENCE
Maya Astronomy

The ancient Maya considered stars and planets to be gods, so they watched the heavens to predict how their gods would control events on Earth. Because they wanted the predictions to be correct, the Maya made many accurate astronomical observations.

Through observation, the Maya developed a 365-day calendar. They also realized that the moon has a 29- or 30-day cycle. The Maya paid particular attention to the planet Venus. They determined that Venus took 584 days to reappear at the same point on the horizon. All these conclusions were made without sophisticated instruments. Instead, the Maya relied on careful observation of the night sky. Most Maya observatories were high enough to allow a clear view of the horizon.

History of Middle and South America • 169

LEVEL 2: (Suggested time: 30 min.) When students have completed the Level 1 graphic organizer, ask them to write diary entries as if they were either Olmec stone carvers or construction workers in Teotihuacán. Challenge students to answer the question "Why do I do what I do?" in their diary entries. **LS INTRAPERSONAL**

Teaching Objective 2
LEVEL 1: (Suggested time: 20 min.) Organize the class into pairs. Have each pair compile a list of facts about the Maya. Then ask each pair to compose sentences that answer these questions: "Which features of this civilization would make you want to go back in time and visit? Which features would not make you want to visit the Maya?"
ESOL, COOPERATIVE LEARNING

CHAPTER 7, Section 1

EYE ON EARTH

Sacrifices and Sinkholes
The northern part of the Yucatán Peninsula has a dry climate. Therefore, very little surface water was available to the Maya who lived there. However, the Maya could reach plentiful water through deep natural wells called *cenotes*. A *cenote* would form when the roof of a limestone cavern collapsed. These features are also known as sinkholes. Ordinarily, a cenote's water level is far below sheer limestone walls.

The Maya associated the *cenotes* with their rain gods, called Chacs. Sometimes the Maya made sacrifices to the Chacs by throwing humans, usually children, into the *cenotes*. Precious gold and jade objects were also tossed into the water. This practice was most common at Chichén Itzá. Archaeologists have discovered many skeletons and beautiful objects in a *cenote* at this important Maya site.

Map Answer

Aztec and Maya

Pacal's tomb lay within the Temple of Inscriptions. On a carved portrait found there Pacal is shown wearing an elaborate headdress.

Interpreting the Map Which civilizations stretched from the Gulf of Mexico to the Pacific Ocean?

One of the most important Maya kings was Pacal, whose tomb lies in a place called Palenque. Pacal ruled for 68 years, starting in A.D. 615. Pacal was only 12 years old when he inherited the throne from his mother. One of Pacal's accomplishments was the construction of a building now called the Temple of Inscriptions. On the temple's walls is writing that lists the past kings of Palenque. This detailed record of royal ancestry shows the importance of history to the Maya.

Maya Games Another interesting feature of Maya civilization was a ball game called **pok-a-tok**. Some cities had large stone courts where crowds could gather to watch games. To win, players had to move a hard, heavy ball through a stone ring high above their heads. Playing this game required great skill. Players could only bounce the ball off their hips, shoulders, or arms. They couldn't throw or kick the ball. Winners of the game won gold, clothes, or even houses. The losers sometimes lost their lives as human sacrifices.

Sacrifices Maya kings offered human and other sacrifices to their gods. The Maya believed that the gods needed blood or the world would fall apart. For sacrifices, the Maya usually used enemy prisoners. In this ritual, the victim's still-beating heart was cut out of his chest. The Maya also held ceremonies to give up their own blood. Royal blood was especially prized. For example, a stone carving shows a queen, Lady Xoc, drawing a cord studded with thorns through her pierced tongue.

Mesoamerican Civilizations

170 • Chapter 7

LEVEL 2: (Suggested time: 30 min.) Have students work in pairs to write dialogues between the people pictured in the Bonampak mural and Pacal. Dialogues should display knowledge of Maya civilization.
LS VERBAL-LINGUISTIC

LEVEL 3: You will need to provide extra time and research materials for this activity. Organize the class into small groups. Have groups conduct research to locate meanings for Maya glyphs. Ask each group to convert key phrases about the Maya into glyphs and to provide a key to aid in translation. Then have groups exchange their phrases and challenge each other to read their glyphs.
COOPERATIVE LEARNING, LS LOGICAL-MATHEMATICAL

Trade The Maya traded with peoples throughout Mesoamerica. For example, the Maya traded the brilliant green, blue, and red feathers of the sacred quetzal bird. In return, the Maya received black **obsidian** from Teotihuacán. Obsidian is a form of natural glass that forms when volcanic lava cools quickly. A skilled craftworker could chip flakes off a piece of obsidian to shape an extremely sharp knife. Other products traded throughout Mesoamerica included salt, jade, ceramics, shells, turquoise, and cacao for making chocolate.

Maya civilization had largely declined by A.D. 800. The great cities were abandoned or destroyed by war. However, the Maya did not die out. Millions of people of Maya descent live in Mexico and Central America today. Many of them speak languages related to those of their Maya ancestors.

✓ **READING CHECK:** *Summarizing* What are some achievements of the Maya?

The Aztec

Sometime around A.D. 1200, a people from the north called the Aztec began moving into central Mexico. They founded their capital, Tenochtitlán (tay-nawch-teet-LAHN), on an island in the middle of Lake Texcoco. As the capital grew, its population reached about 200,000.

Aztec Life and Society In Tenochtitlán ordinary citizens lived in clans. Each clan had its own school and temple. Families built garden plots that floated on Lake Texcoco's surface. On these plots, called **chinampas** (chee-NAHM-pahs), families grew corn, beans, and peppers. Since pigs and cattle had not yet been brought to the Americas, sources of meat were limited. Common people ate dog meat on special occasions. However, only rich people regularly ate meat or drank chocolate.

Run by the military, Aztec society was dominated by warriors. These powerful men gained glory and wealth. The fierce Aztec quickly conquered many groups who lived in the surrounding areas. The Aztec then learned skills from the peoples they conquered. They learned metalworking, pottery, and weaving. Calendars and mathematics were also part of Aztec life.

This Aztec Calendar Stone was used in ceremonies honoring the sun god. The god's face can be seen in the center of the stone.

CHAPTER 7, Section 1

Linking Past to Present

A Fungus among Us? Before the arrival of the Spaniards in the Americas, Mexican Indians ate protein-rich moth larvae, grasshoppers, locusts, ant larvae, and live worms. Now these and other exotic pre-conquest foods are popular in some Mexican restaurants.

Among the foods eaten by the Aztec was a grayish fungus called *cuitlacoche* (weet-lah-KOH-chay), known in the United States as corn smut. American farmers once considered the fungus a problem. Now, however, some cultivate it because the fungus has become a popular gourmet item. *Cuitlacoche* is sold canned or frozen in gourmet markets and can be used much like cooked mushrooms.

Critical Thinking: Why may a farmer switch from fighting the fungus to cultivating it?

Answer: The farmer can probably make more profit on the gourmet item than on corn.

▶**ASSIGNMENT:** First, tell students about the Maya numbering system. The Maya didn't use digits as we do. Instead, they used a system of dots and bars. One dot stood for the number 1, and one bar stood for the number 5. The Maya created other numbers by combining dots and bars. For example, one bar with two dots above it stood for the number 7, and three bars with three dots above them stood for 18. The Maya system also included a symbol for zero. It looked like the outline of a football. The zero is a useful concept because it works as a placeholder. Ask students to write their telephone numbers by using the Maya numbering system.

Teaching Objective 3
LEVEL 1: (Suggested time: 15 min.) Organize the class into pairs. Have each pair create a graphic organizer that describes the Aztec civilization within these three categories: the Aztec at the height of their power, the Aztec in decline, and remains of Aztec culture today. Call on volunteers to write their graphic organizers on the chalkboard or a transparency for the overhead projector. **ESOL, COOPERATIVE LEARNING**

CHAPTER 7, Section 1

USING ILLUSTRATIONS

Mexico City Then and Now
Point out how tall and impressive the temples in this illustration must have been to the people of Tenochtitlán during the height of Aztec rule. One may think that the pyramids would have towered over settlement in all the centuries since then. This assumption, however, would be incorrect.

After Hernán Cortés captured Tenochtitlán in 1521, he tore down much of the Aztec city. To build Mexico City, the Spaniards built new palaces and churches on top of the ruins. They even used stone from the Aztec buildings in the new construction. The temple to Huitzilopochtli and Tlaloc disappeared beneath the rubble. Centuries later, in 1978, workers excavating for the electrical utility company discovered a statue of the Aztec goddess Coyolxauhqui. Scholars knew that the sculpture was once part of the pyramid site. Archaeologists carefully excavated the ruins. Although the pyramids have been much reduced, the Templo Mayor, or Great Temple, again rises above the pavement of central Mexico City.

LEVELS 2 AND 3: (Suggested time: 30 min.) Organize the class into pairs. Provide each pair with a small stack of sticky notes. Ask them to create speech balloons for people in the History Close-Up feature in the style of a comic book and attach them in the right places. Call on volunteers to read their characters' comments. **COOPERATIVE LEARNING,** **KINESTHETIC**

Teaching Objectives 1–3
ALL LEVELS: Duplicate and photocopy a map of Mesoamerica. Have students work in pairs or groups to illustrate the map with pictures that provide information about the Olmec, people of Teotihuacán, Maya, and Aztec. Display the maps in the classroom. **ESOL, COOPERATIVE LEARNING, VISUAL-SPATIAL**

History Close-Up

Aztec Daily Life Hundreds of temples rose within the city of Tenochtitlán. The most important one, shown in the background of the painting, was dedicated to Huitzilopochtli (WEE-tsee-loh-POHCH-tlee), the Aztec god of war, and Tlaloc (tlah-LOHK), the rain god. In the painting's foreground, farmers grow vegetables on *chinampas*. In the center, shoppers crowd a market. **How do you think Tenochtitlán's physical geography affected commerce?**

Like the Maya, the Aztec believed the gods kept them from danger and gave them good luck. In addition, they believed that each night the sun god had to fight the forces of darkness. A new day wouldn't dawn if the god failed. To give the sun god strength to fight, the Aztec offered human sacrifices.

The Aztec forced the conquered peoples to pay taxes and provide captives for sacrifices. As a result, many of them came to resent the Aztec. Eventually, these bad feelings would weaken the Aztec Empire.

Aztec culture is part of modern Mexican culture. For example, what we call tortillas are modern versions of Aztec cornmeal pancakes. At least a million Mexicans speak Nahuatl, a form of the Aztec language. Place-names across central Mexico reflect Aztec roots. You can find them on a detailed map of Mexico. Netzahualcóyotl and Xochihuehuetlán are just two of the many cities or towns with tongue-twisting Nahuatl names.

✓ **READING CHECK:** What are some achievements of Aztec civilization?
chinampas, calendar, mathematics, pyramids, and temples

Define or identify: Olmec, Maya, glyphs, Pacal, pok-a-tok, obsidian, Aztec, *chinampas*

Reading for the Main Idea
1. **Human Systems** What was the Olmec's greatest artistic achievement?
2. **Human Systems** What are some features of Maya writing? What have we learned from Maya writing?

Critical Thinking
3. **Finding the Main Idea** What aspects of Aztec civilization are still part of Mexican culture?
4. **Identifying Cause and Effect** What are some things a civilization needs in order to grow? How did these needs affect the Maya and Aztec?

Organizing What You Know
5. **Categorizing** Copy the following graphic organizer. Use it to describe the Maya and Aztec civilizations. Fill in the ovals with features of each culture. In the center, list features they had in common.

Section 1 Review

Answers to Section 1 Review

Define or identify For definitions and identifications, see the glossary and index.

Reading for the Main Idea
1. huge heads carved out of stone
2. used written characters, or glyphs, to represent both objects and sounds; Maya history, lists of kings

Critical Thinking
3. tortillas, Nahuatl, place-names
4. Possible answer: mathematics, calendars, arts and crafts, laws; Maya and Aztec advanced in these areas

Organizing What You Know
5. Maya—southern and eastern Mexico, architects and engineers, astronomy, writing system, pok-a-tok, trade; Aztec—central Mexico, Tenochtitlán, farmed *chinampas,* dominated by warriors, conquered other peoples; both—developed calendars, sacrifices

◄ **Visual Record Answer**

Tenochtitlán's physical geography probably stimulated commerce because merchants and buyers could use the canals to get to the markets quickly and easily. In addition, using the *chinampas* provided fresh food.

CLOSE

Challenge students to pronounce the two Nahuatl place-names in the section's last paragraph. Approximate pronunciations are: ne-tsah-wahl-KOH-yohtl and hoh-chee-hwe-hwe-TLAHN. If you have a large atlas in your classroom, you may want to let volunteers search for similar Nahuatl place-names on the map of Mexico.

REVIEW, ASSESS, RETEACH

Have students complete the Section Review. Then have students work in pairs to review the map in this section, telling each other about each culture that is noted on the map. Then have students complete Daily Quiz 7.1.

Have students complete Main Idea Activity S1. Then ask students to make a chart about features of the civilizations discussed in this section.

EXTEND

Have interested students conduct research on specific Maya or Aztec archaeological sites and report their findings to the class as a travelogue.
BLOCK SCHEDULING

CHAPTER 7, Section 2

SECTION 2 RESOURCES

Reproducibles
- Lecture Notes, Section 2
- Block Scheduling Handbook, Chapter 7
- Know It Notes S2
- Map Activity 12

Technology
- One-Stop Planner CD-ROM, Lesson 7.2
- Geography and Cultures Visual Resources 42, 43
- Music of the World Audio CD Program, Selection 5
- Homework Practice Online
- HRW Go Site

Review, Reinforcement, and Assessment Resources
- Section 2 Review
- Daily Quiz 7.2
- Main Idea Activity S2
- Chapter Summaries and Review
- English Audio Summary 7.2
- Spanish Audio Summary 7.2

Section 2 — The Inca

Read to Discover
1. What were some achievements of South America's early cultures?
2. What were some features of Inca culture?

Vocabulary
Quechua
quipu

Places
Andes
Peru
Cuzco
Lake Titicaca

People
Chavín
Moche
Nazca
Pachacutec
Atahualpa

Reading Strategy

TAKING NOTES Before you read, look at the headings and subheadings in the section. Write them down on the left side of a piece of paper. As you read, write what you learn related to those headings on the right side of your paper.

Early Cultures of South America

Some scholars think that people lived in western South America as early at 12,500 B.C. These early peoples survived through farming. They planted beans and potatoes on terraces cut into the steep mountainsides of the Andes. People who lived along the Pacific Ocean fished. Domesticated animals included the llama (LAH-muh) and alpaca (al-PA-kuh). Andean peoples wove the wool from these animals into colorful patterned cloth.

Peruvian women pose with their llamas before an ancient wall. For centuries, people of South America have raised llamas for their wool, hides, and meat. Llamas can also carry heavy loads.

174 • Chapter 7

Section 2 Objectives

1. Analyze some achievements of South America's early cultures.
2. Describe some features of Inca culture.

Focus

Bellringer

Write the following questions on the chalkboard: *How well do you think a civilization that had neither a writing system nor use of wheels could develop? What might that civilization be like?* Discuss responses. Point out that although the Inca had neither an actual writing system nor the wheel, they developed a technologically advanced civilization, about which they will learn more in this section.

Building Vocabulary

Call on volunteers to locate and read the definitions of **Quechua** and **quipu**. Point out that some people of South America still speak Quechua, the language of the Inca. Here are a few words in Quechua: *alqo* ("dog"), *k'upa chukcha* ("curly hair"), *p'acha* ("clothing"), and *lanlaku* ("athlete"). The word *quipu* is also Quechuan.

174 Chapter 7

Peru's first advanced civilization, now called the Chavín (chah-VEEN), reached its height between about 900 B.C. and 200 B.C. The Chavín built a town of large stone structures in an Andean valley. Carved jaguars, crocodiles, and snakes decorated the town's temples. A people along the Pacific coast, the Moche (MOH-chay), developed a sophisticated irrigation system. They built canals to channel and store water, control flooding, and nourish their crops. The Moche also built pyramids about 100 feet (30 m) high.

Another people, the Nazca, scratched outlines of animals and other shapes into the surface of the Peruvian desert. These images are known today as the Nazca lines. Some of the marks are straight lines hundreds of feet long. Others show outlines of plants and animals. The designs include a monkey 360 feet long and a hummingbird that extends 165 feet across the bare ground. Because the designs are so large, they can be seen clearly only from the air. No one knows for sure why the Nazca drew these lines. Some scholars, however, believe the lines were used as sacred paths for use during religious ceremonies.

The Nazca people cut this picture of a hummingbird into the desert floor.

✓ **READING CHECK:** (Human Systems) What were some achievements of South America's early cultures? *stone structures and pyramids; sophisticated irrigation system; large images of animals and other shapes in the desert*

Rulers of the Andes

Historians say that the Inca Empire officially began in A.D. 1438. This date marks when a prince named Pachacutec (pah-chah-KOO-tek) defeated invaders who had attacked and destroyed the city of Cuzco. After his great victory Pachacutec rebuilt the city. He then sent his armies to take control of the farmland around Lake Titicaca.

By the early 1500s, the Inca Empire was well established in the shadows of the towering Andes. It included about 12 million people. The Inca controlled an area of South America reaching from what is now southern Colombia to central Chile. Some people who live there today still speak **Quechua** (KE-chuh-wuh), the language of the Inca.

Religion People worshipped Pachacutec as a god and called him "The Inca." Over time *Inca* began to refer to both the emperor and to the people he ruled.

In addition to their emperor, the Inca had many other gods. The supreme god who created the Sun and the Moon was called Viracocha. According to Inca belief, men were descended from the Sun and women from the Moon. The Inca emperor was known as the Son of the Sun. He led the worship of the Sun. The Inca queen was known as the Daughter of the Moon, and she led its worship. When the emperor was away at war, the queen ruled from Cuzco. She had her own palace with shrines, gardens, and baths. She was pampered and wore the finest clothes.

Inca Empire

▲ **Interpreting the Map** Why might communication have been a challenge for the Inca?

CHAPTER 7, Section 2

COOPERATIVE LEARNING

Mysteries of the Nazca Lines Organize the class into two groups. Assign one group the task of conducting research on theories about the purpose and creation of the Nazca lines. (One particularly intriguing theory involves the use of hot-air balloons.) Have the other group demonstrate the creation of the Nazca lines by layering light and dark sand or gravel in shallow pans. Students should then duplicate some of the designs by scratching away the darker material. Ask both groups to present their work to the class.

◄ **Map Answer**

because their empire covered a huge north-to-south distance and included parts of the rugged Andes

History of Middle and South America • 175

TEACH

Teaching Objective 1

ALL LEVELS: (Suggested time: 10 min.) First, call on a volunteer to read the introductory paragraph on the previous page aloud. Then copy the following graphic organizer onto the chalkboard, omitting the blue answers. Have students suggest details about the cultures and fill them in as they speak. **ESOL,** **LS** **VISUAL-SPATIAL**

Early Cultures of South America

Chavín	Moche	Nazca
at height between 200 B.C. and 900 B.C., built town in Andean valley of large stone structures with carved animals on the temples	lived along the Pacific coast, developed sophisticated irrigation system, built pyramids	scratched outlines of animals and other shapes into surface of Peruvian desert that can only be seen well from the air

History of Middle and South America **175**

CHAPTER 7, Section 2

National Geography Standard 13

Division and Control under the Inca The Inca maintained order by relocating conquered peoples when they thought it necessary. The rulers moved people because new agricultural projects required more labor than was available locally or because they thought a certain group of people was causing trouble. By moving people from one part of the empire to another the Inca found that they could meet their labor needs and maintain political control over distant areas.

Critical Thinking: Ask students what this practice of relocation suggests about the amount of control the Inca exercised over subject peoples.

Answer: The Inca seem to have had almost complete power over conquered peoples.

Visual Record Answer

The zigzag design of the walls allowed defenders to see a wide area while remaining protected. It may also have made the walls stronger.

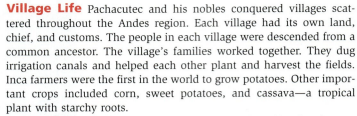

The Inca built the fortress of Sacsahuamán (sahk-sah-wah-MAHN) near Cuzco. Some of the stones weigh hundreds of tons. The stones were moved to the site without wheeled vehicles and are fitted closely together without mortar.
Interpreting the Visual Record How would the design of these walls aid in defense?

Village Life Pachacutec and his nobles conquered villages scattered throughout the Andes region. Each village had its own land, chief, and customs. The people in each village were descended from a common ancestor. The village's families worked together. They dug irrigation canals and helped each other plant and harvest the fields. Inca farmers were the first in the world to grow potatoes. Other important crops included corn, sweet potatoes, and cassava—a tropical plant with starchy roots.

The village chief resolved conflicts. He distributed land and water to each family. He made sure that planting and harvesting began at proper times. The villagers believed that the chief spoke with the gods on their behalf. In return, village families worked for the chief.

Each village had its own sacred place and its own sacred objects. When the Inca rulers added new regions to their empire, they often allowed local chiefs to stay in power. In return, however, each village had to bring a sacred object to the great temple in Cuzco. The rulers believed that fear of losing the sacred object would keep a village from rebelling. Cuzco was also where nobles had to send their sons to school. There they learned the empire's laws.

Government Pachacutec replaced the Inca chiefdom with a centralized state. The Inca organized the conquered villages into groups. An imperial official headed each group. Each family in the empire had to pay taxes to the official. These taxes usually took the form of goods and labor. Women paid with cloth. Men paid by laboring in work gangs.

Teaching Objective 2

ALL LEVELS: You may need to allow extra time for this activity. Organize the class into groups—either one group per subhead under "Rulers of the Andes" or reapportioned according to the amount of information and the number of students. Provide butcher paper and art supplies. Have groups work together to create a mural titled "Rulers of the Andes," in which they portray the basic facts about the Inca. Display the mural in the classroom.
ESOL, COOPERATIVE LEARNING, **LS** VISUAL-SPATIAL

LEVEL 2: (Suggested time: 45 min.) Have students write outlines for the script of a television news story titled "Against the Odds: No Wheels, No Writing, No Horses, No Problem" about the Inca. You may want groups to develop some scenes for performance. **LS** AUDITORY-MUSICAL

Connecting to History

This young woman may have been put to death to stop a nearby volcano from erupting.

To the Inca, the highest peaks of the Andes were gods. As a special offering to them, the Inca sacrificed their own people. These sacrifices, however, were made only when people were seriously threatened by starvation or a similar disaster. Children were usually sacrificed because they were thought to be purer than adults. The Inca honored those that were sacrificed, believing they would live with the gods forever.

Elaborate ceremonies and a procession led up to these mountain sacrifices. As priests and the victim climbed the mountain, they suffered from lack of oxygen, due to the high elevation, and extreme cold. When they reached the sacrifice site, the victims were most likely drugged. Some of the children received a blow to the head to knock them out. So, the children were probably unconscious when they were placed, still alive, in holes on the mountainside. The children probably froze to death.

In 1999 on a peak in Argentina archaeologists discovered three Inca children who had been sacrificed 500 years before. These perfectly preserved bodies were of two girls and a boy. They had died between the ages of 8 and 15. The frozen bodies were found wrapped tightly in cloth, lying in a small grave. After centuries of exposure to the cold and dry mountain air, the bodies had dried to become mummies. In 2004, archaeologists found 26 more Inca tombs, perhaps containing dozens of mummies, on the outskirts of Lima, Peru.

INCA MUMMIES

We now know a great deal about the Inca from studying these mummies and the objects buried with them. Artifacts found in the graves include human and llama figurines, sandals, and shell necklaces. Archaeologists assume the human figurines were to be companions for the children in an afterlife. These figurines are fully dressed in colorful cloth. Some have feather headdresses. The children wore similar clothing that was actually too big for them. The Inca may have believed these children would grow into larger clothes as they made their way through the afterlife.

Understanding What You Read
1. Why did the Inca sacrifice children on top of mountains?
2. What was the purpose of burying the mummies with various objects?

CHAPTER 7, Section 2

Across the Curriculum
SCIENCE
Ancient Mummies, Modern Tools Scientists use the most modern methods of forensic medicine to decipher the lives—and deaths—of the Inca mummies. DNA analysis can shed light on their ethnicity, perhaps even linking them with living relatives. Examining stomach contents can tell more about diet. X-rays provide clues about general health.

Other scientists can make other contributions to the study of the mummies. For example, an ornithologist can tell more about the birds from whose feathers a headdress was made. A botanist can decipher what plants grew nearby from pollen remains and other clues. Many other specialists may become involved before the mummies give up all their secrets.

Connecting to History Answers
1. They thought the highest peaks of the Andes were gods, so the Inca sacrificed children to them in times of starvation or similar disaster.
2. for companionship and use in an afterlife

LEVEL 3: (Suggested time: 30 min.) Lead a discussion about the Ice Mummies feature. Point out that a procession accompanied the children to the sacrifice site. Then ask interested students to write lyrics for songs that the priests may have sung as they trudged up the mountain.
LS **AUDITORY-MUSICAL**

Teacher to Teacher

Celeste Smith of Austin, Texas, suggests this activity for familiarizing students with ancient cultures of South America. Have students work in groups to make a large salt-dough map of the continent. They should stick toothpicks in the dough at the locations of important archaeological sites and attach paper flags to the toothpicks on which details of the sites are described.

CHAPTER 7, Section 2

DAILY LIFE

Inca Textiles The Inca wove exquisite textiles, or cloth, from the wool of their animals. In fact, cloth made up part of the pay of Inca soldiers, who would rebel if they didn't receive the expected amount. One cloth manufacturing center was said to have employed a thousand male workers. There were also special buildings where women would weave cloth in seclusion. These weavers were called Chosen Women. The first Spanish observers of Inca civilization wrote with great wonder about storehouses packed with finely woven cloth.

Museums throughout the world may contain hundreds of examples of Inca textiles.

Critical Thinking: Why may Inca textiles have survived long enough to be collected by museums?

Answer: Climatic conditions may have allowed the preservation of the textiles.

Visual Record Answer

The first step would probably have been to get a cable across the canyon. Perhaps it was thrown with a weight on the other end, or a strong swimmer took it across. Discuss all possibilities.

The Inca spanned Andean canyons with braided rope bridges. People of Peru can still cross rivers on some of the Inca bridges.
Interpreting the Visual Record What do you think were the first steps in this bridge's construction?

Inca artisans crafted this sheet of gold in the shape of a shirt.

Skilled Artisans The Inca learned many skills from the peoples they ruled. For example, the Inca learned how to build irrigation systems and roads from the Chimú. The Inca, however, improved upon the Chimú's building skills. Instead of using adobe mud to construct their buildings, the Inca used large stone blocks. The blocks fit so tightly together that cement was not even needed. Because of their strong stone construction, Inca buildings in the city of Cuzco have even survived earthquakes.

The Inca were also creative artists. Metalworkers made spectacular gold and silver objects. Some were decorated with emeralds. In a temple courtyard, workers created a garden of gold plants with silver stems.

Inca Roads Another great Inca achievement was their road system. Thousands of miles of stone-paved roads connected the Inca Empire. This network crossed high mountains, tropical rain forests, and deserts. Rope bridges spanned valleys and rivers.

178 • Chapter 7

 ASSIGNMENT: Have students write a paragraph titled "What I Saw as I Walked to the Market" as if it were written by an Inca teen.

CLOSE

Tell students that the Inca were also very skilled in medicine. They treated malaria with quinine, which is still a useful treatment for the disease. Inca surgeons used anesthetics when they operated. They even performed operations on the brain!

A road stretching more than 1,500 miles (2,414 km) linked the capitals of Cuzco and Quito. Along the roadway were rest houses, temples, and storerooms full of food. Among the foodstuffs they stored were potatoes that had been freeze-dried in the cold mountain air.

For communicating across their vast empire, the Inca used teams of runners to carry messages. A message passed between many runners could travel up to 150 miles (241 km) in one day. However, because Quechua was not a written language, the messengers didn't carry letters.

Instead of written words, the Inca used a device called a **quipu** (KEE-poo). Quipus are sets of colored strings with knots. Different colors represented different people or items. The knots represented numbers. Information about important events, populations, animals, and food supplies were all recorded on quipus. Specially trained Inca officials created and interpreted them.

Civil War In about A.D. 1500 the Inca Empire began to suffer serious problems. When Inca armies entered the Amazon rain forest, the local people fought back. The Inca lost thousands of troops in battle and to fever. In A.D. 1525, the emperor Huayna Capac, grandson of Pachacutec, died. Two of his sons, Huáscar (WAHS-kahr) and Atahualpa (ah-tah-WAHL-pah), fought over who would assume the empire's throne. Huáscar became the new emperor.

Huáscar upset the nobility when he announced that their lands would be taken over by the royal family. In protest, the Inca nobles turned to Huáscar's brother, Atahualpa, to lead a revolt. Although he was successful, Atahualpa couldn't celebrate his victory for long. His empire would soon fall to a new threat—one that came from far away.

✓ **READING CHECK:** *Human Systems* What were some achievements of the Inca? *stone structures, highly skilled metalwork, road system, quipus*

Homework Practice Online
Keyword: SJ5 HP7

Section Review 2

Define or Identify: Chavín, Moche, Nazca, Pachacutec, Quechua, quipu, Atahualpa

Reading for the Main Idea
1. *Human Systems* How did the Inca communicate across great distances?
2. *Human Systems* What were some of the skills at which the Inca excelled?

Critical Thinking
3. **Analyzing Information** How were Inca villages organized?
4. **Summarizing** How did the Chavín and the Moche alter their environments?

Organizing What You Know
5. **Identifying Cause and Effect** Copy the following graphic organizer. Use it to develop a cause-and-effect chart to identify events related to the Inca Empire. This chart is started for you. Add more lines as needed.

Cause	Effect
Pachacutec came to power in Cuzco →	

History of Middle and South America • 179

Section 2 Review

Answers to Section 2 Review

Define or identify For definitions and identifications, see the glossary and index.

Reading for the Main Idea
1. teams of runners, excellent road system, quipus
2. organizing a large empire, building irrigation systems and roads, stone construction, metalwork, building bridges, using quipus

Critical Thinking
3. Chief distributed water and goods to families and organized planting and harvesting. Conquered villages were organized into group headed by an imperial official who collected taxes.
4. Chavín—built town of large stone structures; Moche—built canals and pyramids

Organizing What You Know
5. Pachacutec in power in Cuzco. → He rebuilt the city, conquered more land. Pachacutec replaced the Inca chiefdom with a centralized state. → Villagers paid taxes to officials. Inca armies entered the rain forest. → Troops lost to battle and fever. Huayna Capac died → Sons fought. Huáscar upset nobility. → Atahualpa led a revolt.

REVIEW, ASSESS, RETEACH

Have students complete the Section Review. The organize students into groups and assign one of the early cultures of South America to each group. Have groups compose two questions about the assigned culture and then quiz each other. Then have students complete Daily Quiz 7.2.

Have students complete Main Idea Activity S2. Then have students work in pairs to create posters with captions to summarize the section's main points. **ESOL, COOPERATIVE LEARNING,** LS **VISUAL-SPATIAL**

EXTEND

Have interested students conduct research on Inca crafts such as weaving and metalworking. Encourage them to use what they have learned to draw their own designs for objects similar to those the Inca created. **BLOCK SCHEDULING**

CHAPTER 7, Section 3

Section 3 Resources

Reproducibles
- Lecture Notes, Section 3
- Block Scheduling Handbook, Chapter 7
- Know It Notes S3
- Critical Thinking Activity 10
- Biography Activities: Miguel Hidalgo y Costilla, Simón Bolivar

Technology
- One-Stop Planner CD-ROM, Lesson 7.3
- Geography and Cultures Visual Resources 37–42
- Music of the World Audio CD Program, Selections 3–5
- Homework Practice Online
- HRW Go Site

Review, Reinforcement, and Assessment Resources
- Daily Quiz 7.3
- Main Idea Activity S3
- Chapter Summaries and Review
- English Audio Summary 7.3
- Spanish Audio Summary 7.3

Visual Record Answer
metal armor

Section 3: Spanish Colonies and Independence

Read to Discover
1. How did Spaniards conquer civilizations in Middle and South America?
2. How did the region change after the Spanish conquest?

Vocabulary
conquistadores
epidemic
nationalist

People
Hernán Cortés
Moctezuma II
Francisco Pizarro
Tupac Amarú
Simón Bolívar

Reading Strategy
READING ORGANIZER As you read this section, create a chain-of-events chart on which you write down important events from the Spanish conquest through independence.

Explorer Hernán Cortés conquered the mighty Aztec civilization and claimed Mexico for Spain. Cortés is pictured here capturing the Aztec ruler Moctezuma.
Interpreting the Visual Record
According to this picture, what is one advantage the Spaniards had over the Aztec?

Spanish Conquests in the Americas

The search for gold and silver drew explorers from Spain to Middle and South America. These Spaniards hoped they would become wealthy and famous if they conquered new lands for Spain.

Cortés Conquers the Aztec In 1519, Spanish explorer Hernán Cortés arrived in Mexico with about 600 soldiers. The Aztec ruler Moctezuma II (mawk-tay-SOO-mah) greeted these Spanish **conquistadores** (kahn-kees-tuh-DAWR-eez), or conquerers. At first, Moctezuma thought the Spaniards were like gods. The Aztec had never seen anything like these pale, armor-wearing men. Nor had they seen the four-legged animals on which the strangers rode. At first, they thought a man on horseback was one creature.

The Aztec had also never been exposed to diseases that the Spaniards unknowingly brought with them. In 1520, the first **epidemic**, or widespread outbreak, of smallpox struck Mexico. Thousands died from the disease. This loss of life weakened the Aztec's power. Partly on account of this weakness, Cortés was able to conquer the Aztec and other peoples of southern Mexico.

After the conquest, the Spanish destroyed much of Tenochtitlán. They built their own capital on its ruins. We know the new city as Mexico City. As the

---

Section 3

Objectives
1. Trace how the Spaniards conquered civilizations in Middle and South America.
2. Analyze how the region changed after the Spanish conquest.

FOCUS

Bellringer
Write the following passage on the chalkboard: *Look at the picture at the beginning of Section 3. If you were the man on the right, and you had never seen people like the man on the left, what kind of impression would this person make on you?* (Students may reply that they would think the man had metal skin. Reactions may range from curiosity to fear to admiration.) Tell students that in this section they will learn more about what did happen when these two people met.

Building Vocabulary
Write the vocabulary terms on the board and have students read their definitions aloud. Point out that **nationalist** is a complicated idea. Some nationalists are concentrated on gaining independence for an oppressed people. However, nationalists may also live in an independent country but care only about their own country's interests, even when it hurts other people or other countries. The first definition applies in this case.

Spaniards took over most of present-day Mexico, they used the region as a base for further conquests. To the north, the Spaniards claimed much of what is now the western United States. To the south, they pushed into Central America. Some Spaniards heard about another rich civilization located farther south in the Andes. There they discovered the Inca Empire.

Pizarro Conquers the Inca In 1532, while on his way to Cuzco to be crowned, Atahualpa met Spanish explorer Francisco Pizarro. Pizarro's small group of men and horses had recently landed on the Pacific shore. Pizarro was in search of gold and silver.

Pizarro captured Atahualpa, who ordered his people to fill a room with gold and silver. These riches were supposed to buy the ruler's freedom. However, Pizarro ordered the Inca emperor killed. After Atahualpa's death, the Spaniards continued to conquer Inca lands. By 1535, the Inca Empire no longer existed.

Spanish Colonialism Spanish colonial rulers treated the native peoples of Middle and South America poorly. Indians worked in gold and silver mines and on the Spaniards' plantations. Thanks to the Indians' labor, rich supplies of precious metals and agricultural products were shipped to Europe. Most of the workers had no land rights and received none of the wealth that their labor created. In addition, the Spaniards tore down Aztec and Inca temples to make way for their own churches and houses. A viceroy, or governor, strictly enforced Spanish laws and customs.

✓ **READING CHECK:** *Movement* How did Spanish explorers affect Middle and South America? carried smallpox, which killed thousands; forced native people to work in mines and on plantations

In this picture from the 1500s, Atahualpa is executed by a Spanish soldier.

Examples of colonial architecture survive in a park outside Mexico City.

CHAPTER 7, Section 3

National Geography Standard 16

Inca Resources Francisco Pizarro's navigator, Bartolomé Ruiz, was the first European to have contact with the magnificent Inca society. He described coming upon one of their rafts loaded down with goods: "They were carrying many pieces of silver and gold as personal ornaments...including crowns and diadems, belts and bracelets... they were carrying many wool and cotton mantles and Moorish tunics... and many other pieces of clothing colored with cochineal, crimson, blue, yellow and all other colors, and worked with different types of ornate embroidery....They were taking all this to trade for fish shells from which they make counters, colored scarlet and white."

Critical Thinking Which part of Ruiz' description may have been particularly interesting to the conquistadors?

Answer: The silver and gold objects probably would have caught the attention of Pizzaro and his men, since the precious metals would have suggested that the Inca civilization was wealthy.

TEACH

Teaching Objective 1

ALL LEVELS: (Suggested time: 45 min.) Organize the students into pairs. Have half of the pairs prepare broadcasts for a news anchor and on-the-scene reporter to relate about the Spanish conquest of the Aztec. Have the other pairs do the same for the conquest of the Inca. Call on volunteers to present their broadcasts. Then lead a discussion about what an expert analyst of the time may have predicted about the nature of Spanish colonialism. **ESOL, COOPERATIVE LEARNING, LS AUDITORY-MUSICAL**

LEVEL 2: (Suggested time: 10 min.) Have students complete the All Levels activity. Then ask each student to write a memo that he or she would have sent to any of the participants right before the Spanish conquests of the Aztec and Inca. (Students may warn Atahualpa not to trust Pizarro to keep his side of the bargain, or similar memos.) **LS VERBAL-LINGUISTIC**

Although many colonial churches were beautifully decorated with gold, most of the riches from Spanish and Portuguese colonies in the Americas were taken to Europe. This is the interior of a church built during the mid-1600s in Oaxaca, Mexico.

The Changing Face of the Region

Life in Middle and South America changed greatly in the 1500s after the European conquest. Portugal controlled Brazil. The much larger Spanish territory stretched from what is now Kansas all the way to the southern tip of South America.

Even though most native peoples were powerless, they sometimes rebelled against their European rulers. In 1780 and 1781, an Indian of Inca descent named Tupac Amarú (too-PAHK ahm-AHR-oo) led a revolt. This revolt spread from Peru to Bolivia and Argentina, but it was put down quickly and brutally by Spanish forces.

Over time, colonists in Middle and South America no longer thought of themselves as Europeans. Each colony had developed its own way of life and wanted to control its own government. Colonists didn't want to pay taxes to a distant country that was taking such rich resources from them without giving back much in return. Nationalist movements began to gather strength. These were movements driven by a desire for independence.

Central America Spanish settlers in Central America had established colonies with towns and large farm estates. As in Mexico, a few rich people owned the land. Although these colonies won independence from Spain, not much changed after Spanish officials left. Foreign countries such as the United States and Great Britain built railroads and made business investments. Most local people remained poor.

South America The demand for self-rule spread to other parts of the Americas. One of the most famous South American revolutionaries was Simón Bolívar. Called "the Liberator," Bolívar led a revolt against Spain that lasted several years. By the early 1830s, almost all the colonies in South America ruled themselves.

Simón Bolívar (1783–1830) Character Trait: Integrity
Known as the "George Washington of South America," Simón Bolívar was a revolutionary general. In the early 1800s, he liberated several South American countries from Spanish rule.
In 1811, Bolívar first freed his native Venezuela. He was president of Gran Colombia (present-day Venezuela, Colombia, Panama, and Ecuador) and then Peru. He was also the first president of Bolivia, which is named in his honor. People across South America admire Bolívar for his determination in achieving independence for the former Spanish colonies. Today in both Venezuela and Bolivia, Bolívar's birthday is a national holiday. *As a leader, how did Bolívar show integrity?*

Mexico In 1810 the Mexican people revolted against Spain. After a struggle that lasted until 1821, Mexico finally won its independence. American and European investments helped Mexico grow economically, but most Mexicans were still poor. Although Mexico was independent, political unrest would continue over the next 100 years.

During the 1820s and early 1830s, many Americans moved from the United States to a part of northern Mexico now known as Texas. Eventually, the Texans broke away from Mexico. In 1845 Texas became part of the United States. This event helped trigger a war between the United States and Mexico.

Unrest in Mexico increased in the early 1900s. The government was under the dictatorship of Porfirio Díaz. Once again, the rich people became richer and controlled much of the country's land. Most people, however, were poor and had no land of their own. In 1911 a revolution began. The Mexican Revolution continued for about ten years and claimed at least a million lives.

Land reform was one of the revolution's main goals. Over time, large farms were broken up and given to villages. At the same time, the Mexican government became more involved in the national economy. Many foreign-owned businesses were forced out of Mexico.

✓ **READING CHECK:** *Human Systems* Why did the people of Middle and South America revolt against Spain? *After years of mistreatment, they wanted independence.*

Artist Jose Clemente Orozco portrayed Father Miguel Hidalgo, a hero of Mexico's revolt against Spain, on a mural in Guadalajara, Mexico.

Define and explain: Hernán Cortés, Moctezuma II, conquistadores, epidemic, Francisco Pizarro, Tupac Amarú, nationalist, Simón Bolívar

Reading for the Main Idea
1. *Human Systems* What role did disease play in the Spanish conquests in the Americas?
2. *Human Systems* What was life like for the common people in Spain's American colonies?

Critical Thinking
3. **Drawing Conclusions** What advantages did Cortés have in his conquest of the Aztec?

Keyword: SJ5 HP7

4. **Finding the Main Idea** Why did people rebel against Spanish rule?

Organizing What You Know
5. **Sequencing** Copy the following graphic organizer. Use it to show important events in Mexico's history. Add more boxes as needed.

Section 3 Review

Answers to Section 3 Review

Define or identify For definitions and identifications, see the glossary and index.

Reading for the Main Idea
1. a large part, because disease killed thousands of the Aztec, weakening the Aztec Empire
2. hard work, received little in return, were powerless

Critical Thinking
3. The Aztec thought the Spaniards were like gods, and the Spaniards had armor and horses and unknowingly brought diseases with them.
4. Colonists had developed their own way of life and didn't want to pay taxes to a distant country that was taking riches from them without giving much back in return.

Organizing What You Know
5. Cortés conquers Aztec; Spanish destroy Tenochtitlán, build Mexico City; Spanish control spreads over Mexico; Spanish colonial rulers mistreat native peoples; Mexicans revolts against Spain; Texas breaks away from Mexico; Mexican Revolution; Large farms broken up.

REVIEW, ASSESS, RETEACH

Have students complete the Section Review. Then have pairs of students re-read the section to each other aloud, pausing to discuss any difficulties. Then have students complete Daily Quiz 7.3.

Have students complete Main Idea Activity S3. Then ask each student to compile two multiple-choice questions for each Read to Discover question.

EXTEND

Have interested students conduct research on the murals of Diego Rivera or Jose Clemente Orozco and how events of Mexican history are portrayed in the two artists' work. **BLOCK SCHEDULING**

CHAPTER 7 REVIEW

Define and Identify
For definitions and identifications, see the glossary and index.

Review the Main Ideas
15. many plazas, broad marketplace, apartment buildings, residential neighborhoods, hundreds of pyramids, Pyramid of the Sun built over a natural cave
16. astronomy
17. to keep the world from falling apart and to get a new day to dawn every day
18. conquered neighboring peoples, forced them to pay taxes and provide captives for sacrifices; resentment weakened the empire
19. animals and other shapes scratched into the surface of the Peruvian desert by the Nazca people, perhaps used in ceremonies
20. from what is now southern Colombia to central Chile; 12 million people
21. Pachacutec worshipped as a god, Viracocha was supreme god, men descended from the Sun and women from the Moon, Inca emperor known as Son of the Sun, Inca queen known as Daughter of the Moon
22. irrigation systems, roads, stone construction, bridge-building
23. conquered by Pizarro
24. mainly gold and silver
25. torn down, Mexico City built on top of the ruins

Think Critically
26. cut terraces into hillsides, built irrigation systems
27. Possible answer: All were technologically advanced in some ways, built great cities, and practiced human sacrifice. They differed in their particular skills. For example, the Inca didn't

Chapter 7 Review and Practice

Define and Identify
Identify each of the following:
1. Olmec
2. glyphs
3. Pacal
4. pok-a-tok
5. obsidian
6. Nazca
7. Quechua
8. quipu
9. Atahualpa
10. Hernán Cortés
11. Moctezuma II
12. epidemic
13. Francisco Pizarro
14. Simón Bolívar

Review the Main Ideas
15. What were some features of the city of Teotihuacán?
16. In what scientific field were the Maya particularly interested?
17. Why did the Maya and Aztec perform human sacrifices?
18. What was the relationship between the Aztec and the people they conquered? What were the results of this relationship?
19. What are the Nazca lines?
20. What areas did the Inca Empire include by the early 1500s? How many people lived in the Inca Empire?
21. What were some features of Inca religion?
22. In what engineering and building skills did the Inca excel?
23. How did the Inca Empire end?
24. What were the Spaniards looking for in Middle and South America?
25. What happened to Tenochtitlán?

Think Critically
26. **Analyzing Information** What farming techniques used by the people of Middle and South America altered the environment?
27. **Comparing and Contrasting** How were the cultures of the Maya, Aztec, and Inca similar? How were they different?
28. **Drawing Inferences** Why are the development of a calendar, a counting system, and a writing system so important to civilization?
29. **Identifying Cause and Effect** How did Spanish colonialism change the lives of people living in Middle and South America?
30. **Analyzing Information** What role did religion play in the culture of the ancient civilizations in Middle and South America?

Map Activity
31. Identify the places marked on the map.
   - Mesoamerica
   - Yucatán Peninsula
   - Tenochtitlán
   - Andes
   - Cuzco
   - Lake Titicaca

have a writing system, but developed the use of quipus. (NGS 10)

28. Possible answer: A calendar allows people to plan for important events like planting crops. A counting system helps people keep records and do business. A writing system allows people to record messages, instructions, and literature for other people far away or later in time.

29. placed them under Spanish rule, had to work in mines and on plantations, had no land rights, saw their temples torn down and replaced, had to follow strict Spanish rules and customs

30. very significant role, to the extent of requiring human sacrifice

Map Activity
31. A. Tenochtitlán
    B. Mesoamerica
    C. Lake Titicaca
    D. Yucatán Peninsula
    E. Cuzco
    F. Andes

Writing Activity

Imagine that you are the archaeologist who found the three Inca mummies in 1999. Write a letter to a friend or family member describing how you feel about your discovery. Think about both positive and negative reactions you may have to finding the mummies.

internet connect

Internet Activity: go.hrw.com
KEYWORD: SJ5 GT7

Choose a topic to explore about the history of Middle and South America:
- Dive into a sacred Maya well.
- Explore Aztec ruins in the heart of Mexico City.
- Learn more about struggles for independence in South America.

CHAPTER 7 REVIEW

Writing Activity
Letters will vary but should display an effort to consider both positive and negative reactions to the discovery. Use Rubric 41, Writing to Express, to evaluate student work.

Interpreting Artifacts
1. probably for their brilliant green color, perhaps for their rarity
2. Because it is beautiful and required a great deal of skill to create, it was a suitable gift for a king.
3. metalwork, perhaps weaving
4. Depending on how common quetzal birds were, overuse of feathers may have depleted the quetzal population.

Analyzing Primary Sources
1. because they would consider it a very gracious gift worthy of important visitors
2. dislikes the taste
3. They believe that it is good for catarrh, or the common cold.
4. Answers will vary, but most students will be more familiar with chocolate desserts of various kinds.

Social Studies Skills Practice

Interpreting Artifacts

An artifact is an object left by a past civilization. Archaeologists and historians study artifacts to learn about the daily lives of the people who created the objects. Study this picture of a quetzal feather headdress that Moctezuma sent to the king of Spain. Then answer the questions.

1. Why do you think the Aztec valued quetzal feathers?
2. Why may Moctezuma have chosen this object to send to the king?
3. Besides feather working, what other craft skills are displayed in the headdress?
4. How might creation of objects like this headdress have affected the environment?

Analyzing Primary Sources

You have read that the Aztec drank chocolate. Read the following description of chocolate by Spanish missionary José de Acosta in the late 1500s. Then answer the questions.

"*Loathsome [undesirable] to such as are not acquainted with it, having a scum or froth that is very unpleasant to taste. Yet it is a drink very much esteemed [liked] among the Indians, where with they feast noble men who pass through their country. The Spaniards, both men and women, that are accustomed to the country, are very greedy of this Chocolaté. They say they make diverse [different] sorts of it, some hot, some cold, and some temperate [medium], and put therein much of that "chili"; yea, they make paste thereof, the which they say is good for the stomach and against the catarrh [common cold].*"

1. How do we know that the Aztec valued chocolate highly?
2. Does the speaker like or dislike the taste of chocolate?
3. What health benefits do the Spaniards believe chocolate provides?
4. How does the preparation of chocolate described compare to preparation methods with which you are familiar?

History of Middle and South America • 185

CHAPTER 7: REVIEW AND ASSESSMENT RESOURCES

Reproducible
- Readings in World Geography, History, and Culture 17
- Critical Thinking Activity 7
- Vocabulary Activity 7

Technology
- Chapter 7 Test Generator (on the One-Stop Planner)

- HRW Go site
- Audio CD Program, Chapter 7

Reinforcement, Review, and Assessment
- Chapter 7 Review and Practice
- Chapter Summaries and Review
- Chapter 7 Test

- Unit 3 Test
- Chapter 7 Test for English Language Learners and Special-Needs Students
- Unit 3 Test for English Language Learners and Special-Needs Students

internet connect
GO TO: go.hrw.com
KEYWORD: SJ5 Teacher
FOR: a guide to using the Internet in your classroom

Chapter 8: Mexico
Chapter Resource Manager

Objectives	Pacing Guide	Reproducible Resources
SECTION 1 **Physical Geography** (pp. 187–90) 1. Identify the main physical features of Mexico. 2. Identify the climate types, plants, and animals found in Mexico. 3. Identify Mexico's main natural resources.	**Regular** 1 day Lecture Notes, Section 1 **Block Scheduling** .5 day *Block Scheduling Handbook, Chapter 8*	RS Know It Notes S1 ELL Main Idea Activity S1
SECTION 2 **History and Culture** (pp. 191–95) 1. Identify some early cultures that developed in Mexico. 2. Describe what Mexico was like under Spanish rule and after independence. 3. Identify some important features of Mexican culture.	**Regular** 1 day Lecture Notes, Section 2 **Block Scheduling** 1 day *Block Scheduling Handbook, Chapter 8*	RS Know It Notes S2 RS Graphic Organizer 8 SM Geography for Life Activity 8 SM Map Activity 8 E Cultures of the World Activity 2 IC Interdisciplinary Activity for the Middle Grades 12 E Biography Activity: Frida Kahlo ELL Main Idea Activity S2
SECTION 3 **Mexico Today** (pp. 198–201) 1. Describe the kind of government and economy Mexico has today. 2. Identify the important features of Mexico's six culture regions.	**Regular** 1 day Lecture Notes, Section 3 **Block Scheduling** .5 day *Block Scheduling Handbook, Chapter 8*	RS Know It Notes S3 E Creative Strategies for Teaching World Geography, Lesson 9 E Environmental and Global Issues Activity 2 ELL Main Idea Activity S3

Chapter Resource Key

- **RS** Reading Support
- **IC** Interdisciplinary Connections
- **E** Enrichment
- **SM** Skills Mastery
- **A** Assessment
- **REV** Review
- **ELL** Reinforcement and English Language Learners and English for Speakers of Other Languages (ESOL)
- Transparencies
- CD–ROM
- Music
- Video
- Internet
- Holt Presentation Maker Using Microsoft® PowerPoint®

One-Stop Planner CD–ROM

See the *One-Stop Planner* for a complete list of additional resources for students and teachers.

One-Stop Planner CD–ROM

It's easy to plan lessons, select resources, and print out materials for your students when you use the *One-Stop Planner CD–ROM with Test Generator*.

internet connect

HRW ONLINE RESOURCES

GO TO: go.hrw.com
Then type in a keyword.

TEACHER HOME PAGE
KEYWORD: **SJ5 TEACHER**

CHAPTER INTERNET ACTIVITIES
KEYWORD: **SJ5 GT8**

Choose an activity to:
- travel along Mexico's coastlines.
- see the arts and crafts of Mexico.
- use ancient Maya hieroglyphs.

CHAPTER ENRICHMENT LINKS
KEYWORD: **SJ5 CH8**

CHAPTER MAPS
KEYWORD: **SJ5 MAPS8**

ONLINE ASSESSMENT
Homework Practice
KEYWORD: **SJ5 HP8**
Standardized Test Prep Online
KEYWORD: **SJ5 STP8**
Rubrics
KEYWORD: **SS Rubrics**

COUNTRY INFORMATION
KEYWORD: **SJ5 Almanac**

CONTENT UPDATES
KEYWORD: **SS Content Updates**

HOLT PRESENTATION MAKER
KEYWORD: **SJ5 PPT8**

ONLINE READING SUPPORT
KEYWORD: **SS Strategies**

CURRENT EVENTS
KEYWORD: **S5 Current Events**

Technology Resources

 One-Stop Planner CD–ROM, Lesson 8.1
 Geography and Cultures Visual Resources with Teaching Activities 18–22
 ARGWorld CD–ROM
Homework Practice Online
HRW Go site

 One-Stop Planner CD–ROM, Lesson 8.2
 ARGWorld CD–ROM
 Music of the World Audio CD Program, Selection 3
Homework Practice Online
HRW Go site

 One-Stop Planner CD–ROM, Lesson 8.3
 ARGWorld CD–ROM
 Music of the World Audio CD Program, Selection 3
 Homework Practice Online
HRW Go site

Review, Reinforcement, and Assessment Resources

ELL	Main Idea Activity S1
REV	Section 1 Review
A	Daily Quiz 8.1
REV	Chapter Summaries and Review
ELL	English Audio Summary 8.1
ELL	Spanish Audio Summary 8.1

ELL	Main Idea Activity S2
REV	Section 2 Review
A	Daily Quiz 8.2
REV	Chapter Summaries and Review
ELL	English Audio Summary 8.2
ELL	Spanish Audio Summary 8.2

ELL	Main Idea Activity S3
REV	Section 3 Review
A	Daily Quiz 8.3
REV	Chapter Summaries and Review
ELL	English Audio Summary 8.3
ELL	Spanish Audio Summary 8.3

Meeting Individual Needs

Ability Levels

Level 1 Basic-level activities designed for all students encountering new material

Level 2 Intermediate-level activities designed for average students

Level 3 Challenging activities designed for honors and gifted-and-talented students

ESOL Activities that address the needs of students with Limited English Proficiency

Chapter Review and Assessment

E	Readings in World Geography, History, and Culture 15 and 16
SM	Critical Thinking Activity 8
REV	Chapter 8 Review and Practice
REV	Chapter Summaries and Review
ELL	Vocabulary Activity 8
A	Chapter 8 Test
	Chapter 8 Test Generator (on the One-Stop Planner)
	Audio CD Program, Chapter 8
A	Chapter 8 Test for English Language Learners and Special-Needs Students
	HRW Go site

CHAPTER 8

Mexico
Previewing Chapter Resources

Holt Online Learning

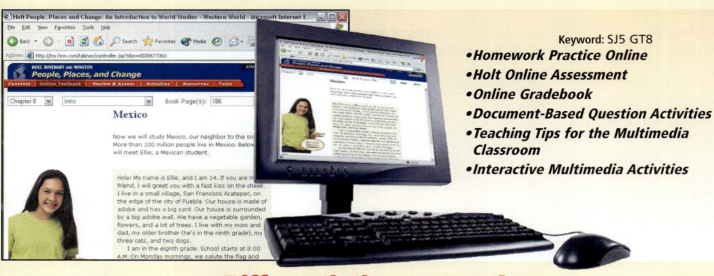

Keyword: SJ5 GT8
- Homework Practice Online
- Holt Online Assessment
- Online Gradebook
- Document-Based Question Activities
- Teaching Tips for the Multimedia Classroom
- Interactive Multimedia Activities

Differentiating Instruction

Reading and Writing Support
- Graphic Organizer Activity
- Vocabulary Activity
- Chapter Summaries and Review
- Know It Notes
- Audio CD

Active Learning
- Block Scheduling Handbook
- Cultures of the World Activity
- Interdisciplinary Activity
- Map Activity: Cortés Conquers Mexico
- Critical Thinking Activity 8
- Music of the World Audio CD Program: Mariachi Music

Primary Sources and Advanced Learners
- Geography for Life Activity: Female Pioneers
- Map Activity: Cortés Conquers Mexico
- Readings in World Geography, History and Culture:
  - 15 Mexico in Transition
  - 16 No Fair Air to Spare

Assessment Program
- Daily Quizzes S1–3
- Chapter Test
- Chapter Test for English Language Learners and Special-Needs Students

Spanish and ESOL
- Vocabulary Activity
- Main Idea Activities for English Language Learners and Special-Needs Students
- Chapter Summaries and Review
- Spanish Audio Summary
- Know It Notes S1–3
- Chapter Test for English Language Learners and Special-Needs Students

Special Education Modifications
Your I.D.E.A. Works! CD-ROM will provide modified versions of the following teaching materials:
- Know It Notes S1–3
- Vocabulary Activity
- Main Idea Activities S1–3
- Daily Quizzes S1–3
- Chapter 8 Test
- Flash cards of chapter vocabulary terms

185C

Teacher Resources

Books for Teachers

Berger, Bruce. *Almost an Island: Travels in Baja California.* University of Arizona Press, 1998.

Collier, George A. *Basta!: Land and the Zapatista Rebellion in Chiapas.* Food First Books, 1999.

Limón, Graciela. *The Day of the Moon.* Arte Público Press, 1999.

Books for Students

Franklin, Sharon. *Mexico and Central America.* Raintree/Steck-Vaughn, 1999. Geography, natural resources, economics, and the environment.

Kopinak, Kathryn. *Desert Capitalism: Maquiladoras in North America's Western Industrial Corridor.* University of Arizona Press, 1996. Examines the impact of NAFTA on Mexican border towns.

Maitland, Katherine. *Ashes for Gold: A Tale from Mexico.* Mondo, 1995. A retelling of a Mexican folktale that also includes nonfiction cultural material about Mexico. **SHELTERED ENGLISH**

O'Dell, Scott. *The Black Pearl.* Houghton Mifflin, 1967. Ramon learns respect for local traditions when he learns how to dive for pearls on the Mexican coast.

Multimedia Materials

Mexican Way of Life. (Laserdisc with Teacher's Guide) Educational Software Institute.

Mexico. (Video: 200 min.) PBS.

Mexico before Cortez. (Video, 20 min.) AIMS Media.

Videos and CDs

Videos
- CNN Presents Geography: Yesterday and Today, Segment 9 Baseball Mexican Style
- CNN Presents World Cultures: Yesterday and Today, Segments 13 and 34
- ARG World

Holt Researcher

http://researcher.hrw.com

- de la Cruz, Juana Ines
- Montezuma II
- North American Free Trade Agreement (NAFTA)
- Rivera, Diego
- Mexico

Transparency Packages

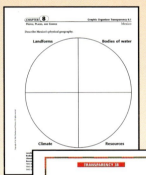

Graphic Organizer Transparencies 8.1–3

Geography and Cultures Visual Resources Transparencies

32 Middle and S. America: Physical

33 Middle and S. America: Political

34 Middle and S. America: Climate

35 Middle and S. America: Population

36 Middle and S. America: Land Use and Resources

37 Mexico: Physical-Political

38 Mosaic at the University of Mexico

Map Activities Transparency
08 Cortés Conquers Mexico

CHAPTER 8

WHY IT MATTERS

Consider using the following points to explain the importance of learning about Mexico:

- Mexico is one of only two countries that have land borders with the United States.
- More immigrants come to the United States from Mexico than from any other country.
- Students have used or consumed many products, particularly vegetables and fruits, from Mexico. In fact, most of Mexico's exports go to the United States.
- Mexico is the second largest importer of goods produced in the United States.
- Millions of Americans, whatever their background, enjoy the foods, music, festivals, and other traditions of Mexico.

CHAPTER 8

Mexico

Now we will study Mexico, our neighbor to the south. More than 100 million people live in Mexico. Below you will meet Ellie, a Mexican student.

Hola! My name is Ellie, and I am 14. If you are my friend, I will greet you with a fast kiss on the cheek. I live in a small village, San Francisco Acatepec, on the edge of the city of Puebla. Our house is made of adobe and has a big yard. Our house is surrounded by a big adobe wall. We have a vegetable garden, flowers, and a lot of trees. I live with my mom and dad, my older brother (he's in the ninth grade), my three cats, and two dogs.

I am in the eighth grade. School starts at 8:00 A.M. On Monday mornings, we salute the flag and sing the Mexican national anthem. School ends at 2:15 but on Friday I have to stay till 4:45 to take an additional drama class. I love drama since I want to be an actress someday and a marine biologist.

My favorite holiday is Dia de los Muertos (Day of the Dead). On that day, we make bread and put out offerings to honor the dead. We put out clothes, sugar cane, chocolate, sugar candy skulls, flowers, bread, pictures, incense, and candles.

¿Has estado alguna vez en México?

Translation: Have you ever been to Mexico?

CHAPTER PROJECT

Have a Mexican fiesta! Organize the class into groups to research and plan various aspects of the party—costumes, dances, decorations, games, music, refreshments—so that it is as authentic as possible. Students should write summaries of their findings and take photographs of their contributions. Place summaries and photos in portfolios.

STARTING THE CHAPTER

Display a picture, poster, or reproduction of the Mexican flag. Explain to students that the illustrations on flags often tell us what a nation's citizens value about their country. Point out the eagle holding the snake in its beak and the cactus on which it rests. Ask students what these designs may tell us about how the Mexican people feel about their country. (Possible answers: They are proud and free, like the eagle. They have survived in a sometimes harsh environment.) Tell students they will learn more about the physical and human geography of Mexico in this chapter.

Section 1 Physical Geography

CHAPTER 8, Section 1

Read to Discover
1. What are the main physical features of Mexico?
2. What climate types, plants, and animals are found in Mexico?
3. What are Mexico's main natural resources?

Vocabulary
sinkholes

Places
Gulf of Mexico
Baja California
Gulf of California
Río Bravo (Rio Grande)
Mexican Plateau
Sierra Madre Oriental
Sierra Madre Occidental
Mount Orizaba
Yucatán Peninsula

Reading Strategy
VISUALIZING INFORMATION Previewing the Physical-Political map of Mexico will help you understand what you are about to read. What physical features are shown on the map? What can you predict about Mexico's climate just by studying the map? Write your answers on a sheet of paper.

SECTION 1 RESOURCES
Reproducible
- Lecture Notes, Section 1
- Block Scheduling Handbook, Chapter 8
- Know It Notes S1

Technology
- One-Stop Planner CD–ROM, Lesson 8.1
- Homework Practice Online
- Geography and Cultures Visual Resources with Teaching Activities 32–38
- HRW Go site

Reinforcement, Review, and Assessment
- Section 1 Review
- Daily Quiz 8.1
- Main Idea Activity S1
- Chapter Summaries and Review
- English Audio Summary 8.1
- Spanish Audio Summary 8.1

Mexico • 187

Section 1

Objectives
1. Describe the main physical features of Mexico.
2. Name the climate types, plants, and animals that are found in Mexico.
3. Identify Mexico's main natural resources.

FOCUS

 Bellringer

Copy the following instructions onto the chalkboard: *Look at the map on this page. What kind of climate do you think the Mexican Plateau has? Why do you think so?* Have students explain their predictions. (Possible answers: It is fairly dry, because the mountains along Mexico's eastern and western edges seem to create a rain shadow. Or, the fact that there are few rivers may indicate that there is little surface water.) Tell students that in Section 1 they will learn more about Mexico's physical geography.

Using the Physical-Political Map
Have students examine the map. Ask them to describe the relative locations of the Mexican Plateau, Yucatán Peninsula, Isthmus of Tehuantepec, Río Bravo, Gulf of California, and Baja California. Explain that *baja* means "lower."

Building Vocabulary
Write the key term **sinkholes** on the chalkboard. Have students divide the word into its two parts and describe what each one means. Call on a volunteer to read the definition of the word in the text. You may want to ask if students know of sinkholes in your state or region.

Mexico   187

CHAPTER 8, Section 1

EYE ON EARTH

A Dangerous Neighbor

Mexico's Popocatépetl volcano is located just 45 miles (72 km) east of Mexico City. It is North America's second-highest volcano. Farmers have settled near the volcano for centuries because the area's rich soil, sunshine, and reliable rainfall ensure good crops.

The most recent significant volcanic activity at Popocatépetl dates to the 1920s. Both U.S. and Mexican scientists extensively monitor the volcano, because more than 30 million people live within view of the crater. Hundreds of thousands live close enough to be threatened by mudflows, rock showers, and clouds of hot gases and ash.

Activity: Have students locate Popocatépetl on a map and determine the relative locations of nearby major population centers.

internet connect
GO TO: go.hrw.com
KEYWORD: SJ5 CH8
FOR: Web sites about Popocatépetl

Visual Record Answer

Climate would vary according to elevation, from mild to freezing.

▶ Volcanic Mount Orizaba rises southeast of Mexico City.
Interpreting the Visual Record
Region What kinds of climates do you think people living in this area might experience?

▲ Thousands of monarch butterflies migrate south to the mountains of central Mexico for the winter.

188 • Chapter 8

Physical Features

Mexico is a large country. It has a long coast on the Pacific Ocean. It has a shorter one on the Gulf of Mexico. In far southern Mexico, the two bodies of water are just 137 miles (220 km) apart. This part of Mexico is called the Isthmus of Tehuantepec (tay-WAHN-tah-pek). The Caribbean Sea washes the country's sunny southeastern beaches. Beautiful Caribbean and Pacific coastal areas attract many tourists.

Baja (BAH-hah) California is a long, narrow peninsula. It extends south from Mexico's northwestern border with the United States. The peninsula separates the Gulf of California from the Pacific Ocean. One of Mexico's few major rivers, the Río Bravo, forms the Mexico-Texas border. In the United States this river is called the Rio Grande.

Plateaus and Mountains Much of Mexico consists of a rugged central region called the Mexican Plateau. The plateau's wide plains range from 3,700 feet (1,128 m) to 9,000 feet (2,743 m). Isolated mountain ridges rise much higher. Two mountain ranges form the edges of the Mexican Plateau. The Sierra Madre Oriental rise to the east. The Sierra Madre Occidental lie in the west.

At the southern end of the plateau lies the Valley of Mexico. Mexico City, the capital, is located there. The mountains south of Mexico City include towering, snowcapped volcanoes. Volcanic eruptions and earthquakes are a threat in this area. The highest peak, Mount Orizaba (oh-ree-SAH-buh), rises to 18,700 feet (5,700 m).

The Yucatán The Yucatán (yoo-kah-TAHN) Peninsula is generally flat. Limestone underlies much of the area, and erosion has created numerous caves and **sinkholes**. A sinkhole is a steep-sided depression formed when the roof of a cave collapses. The climate in the northern part of the peninsula is hot and dry. Scrub forest is the main vegetation. Farther south, rainfall becomes much heavier. Tropical rain forests cover much of the southern Yucatán.

✓ **READING CHECK:** *Places and Regions* What are Mexico's major physical features? coasts on the Pacific Ocean and the Gulf of Mexico; Caribbean Sea; the Rio Bravo; Mexican Plateau; Sierra Madre Oriental and Sierra Madre Occidental; Valley of Mexico; Yucatán Peninsula

TEACH

Teaching Objectives 1–3

LEVELS 1 AND 2: (Suggested time: 20 min.) Copy the following graphic organizer onto the chalkboard, omitting the blue answers. Use it to help students learn about the physical features of Mexico. Organize the class into four groups and assign each group one of the organizer topics. Have groups use their textbook to find as much information about their topic as possible. Ask students to come to the chalkboard to complete the organizer with information from their group.
ESOL, COOPERATIVE LEARNING, LS **VISUAL-SPATIAL**

The Physical Geography of Mexico

MEXICO

Landforms	Bodies of Water	Climates/Animals/Plants	Resources
Isthmus of Tehuantepec, Baja California, Mexican Plateau, Sierra Madre Occidental, Sierra Madre Oriental, Yucatán Peninsula, Valley of Mexico	Río Bravo, Gulf of Mexico, Caribbean Sea, Pacific Ocean, Gulf of California	deserts, steppe, savanna, humid tropical; cougars, coyotes, deer, anteaters, jaguars, monkeys, parrots; desert scrub, rain forests, dry grasslands	oil, gold, silver, copper, lead, zinc

188 Chapter 8

The States of Mexico

Climate, Vegetation, and Wildlife

Mexico's climate varies by region. Its mountains, deserts, and forests also support a variety of plants and animals.

A Tropical Area Mexico extends from the middle latitudes into the tropics. It has desert, steppe, savanna, and humid tropical climates. Most of northern Mexico is dry. There, Baja California's Sonoran Desert meets the Chihuahuan (chee-WAH-wahn) Desert of the plateau. Desert scrub vegetation and dry grasslands are common. Cougars, coyotes, and deer can be found in some areas of the north.

The forested plains along Mexico's southeastern coast are hot and humid much of the year. Summer is the rainy season. Forests cover about 20 percent of Mexico's land area. Tropical rain forests provide a home for anteaters, jaguars, monkeys, parrots, and other animals.

Many varieties of cactus thrive in the Sonoran Desert.

CHAPTER 8, Section 1

Across the Curriculum
SCIENCE
From Mexico to Mars Mexico is home to a wide variety of plants and animals, including a unique group of species that dwells underground. Cueva de Villa Luz, a sulfur-spring cave in the Mexican state of Tabasco, contains organisms that use sulfur compounds rather than photosynthesis to make their food.

Other microbes consume the sulfur-eating bacteria. Tiny invertebrates eat the microbes. They, in turn, are eaten by spiders, worms, and water bugs. Tiny fish feast on this food supply. Local people, descendants of the Maya, catch the fish by sprinkling a natural pesticide in the water. The fish come to the surface gasping for air.

Some scientists believe that Mars, a sulfur-rich planet, may contain similar places. They suspect that such places could provide habitats where life could exist beneath the hostile surface of that planet.

Activity: Have students draw the food chain that exists in the sulfur-spring cave.

LEVEL 3: (Suggested time: 45 min.) Have students complete the Levels 1 and 2 lesson. Then ask students to use the information from the graphic organizer to design a Web site on Mexico. The Web site should include a sample home page as well as sample pages for landforms, bodies of water, climates, animals, plants, and natural resources. Remind students to include other elements common to Web sites, such as a frequently-asked-questions page or a multimedia-map page.

TEACHER TO TEACHER
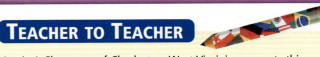

Marcia J. Clevenger, of Charleston, West Virginia, suggests this activity to help students summarize their knowledge about Mexico. Have students search the Internet, newsmagazines, and newspapers for articles about Mexico, such as material on politics, economic challenges, and social issues. They should then create summaries, using your classroom's multimedia equipment to the greatest extent available to them. For example, students might simply combine their information onto a paper collage. Other students might use a tape recorder and an overhead projector. If your school has the necessary equipment, have students scan their information into a computer and create a multimedia presentation.

Section 1 Review

Answers to Section 1 Review

Define For definition, see the glossary.

Working with Sketch Maps Maps will vary, but listed places should be labeled in their approximate locations. The Yucatán is flat and has caves and sinkholes. It is hot and dry with scrub forest in the north. Farther south are tropical rain forests and heavier rainfall.

Reading for the Main Idea

1. Baja California, Río Bravo, Mexican Plateau, Sierra Madre Oriental, Sierra Madre Occidental, Valley of Mexico, Mount Orizaba, Yucatán Peninsula **(NGS 4)**
2. desert, steppe, savanna, humid tropical **(NGS 4)**

Critical Thinking

3. possible answers: coastal areas, Valley of Mexico, along rivers
4. possible answer: Mountains and lack of rivers could limit movement and communication.

Organizing What You Know

5. landforms—mountains, plateaus, caves, sinkholes; bodies of water—Caribbean Sea, Gulf of Mexico, Río Bravo, Gulf of California, Pacific Ocean; climate—desert, steppe, savanna, humid tropical; resources—oil, metals, limited water

---

Climate Variations In some areas changes in elevation cause climates to vary widely within a short distance. Many people have settled in the mild environment of the mountain valleys. The valleys along Mexico's southern coastal areas also have pleasant climates.

The areas of high elevation on the Mexican Plateau experience surprisingly cool temperatures. Freezing temperatures sometimes reach as far south as Mexico City.

✓ **READING CHECK:** *Places and Regions* What are Mexico's climate zones? **desert, steppe, savanna, humid tropical**

So much water has been pumped from under Mexico City that the ground is sinking, or subsiding. Parts of the central city have subsided about 25 feet (7.6 m) in the last 100 years. This has damaged buildings, pipes, sewers, and subway tunnels.

Resources

Petroleum is Mexico's most important energy resource. Oil reserves lie primarily under southern and Gulf coastal plains as well as offshore in the Gulf of Mexico. In 2001 Mexico had the world's ninth-largest crude oil reserves.

Mining is also important in Mexico. Some gold and silver mines begun centuries ago are still in operation. Fresnillo has been a silver-mining center since 1569. New mines have been developed in Mexico's northern and southern mountains. Silver is the most valuable part of Mexico's mining industry. In 2001 Mexico's silver production totaled 2,800 tons (2,520,000 kg). Mexico also produces large amounts of copper, gold, lead, and zinc.

Water is a limited resource in parts of Mexico. Water scarcity, particularly in the dry north, is a serious issue.

✓ **READING CHECK:** *Environment and Society* What problems might water scarcity cause for Mexican citizens? **not enough clean water to drink, farm with, use for power**

Define and explain: sinkholes

Working with Sketch Maps On a map of Mexico that you draw or that your teacher provides, label the following: Gulf of Mexico, Baja California, Gulf of California, Río Bravo (Rio Grande), Mexican Plateau, Sierra Madre Oriental, Sierra Madre Occidental, Mount Orizaba, and Yucatán Peninsula. In a caption, describe the Yucatán.

Reading for the Main Idea
1. *Places and Regions* What are Mexico's major physical features?
2. *Places and Regions* What are the major climate zones of Mexico?

Critical Thinking
3. **Drawing Inferences and Conclusions** Based on physical features and climate, which areas of Mexico provide the best conditions for people to live?
4. **Drawing Inferences and Conclusions** How do you think Mexico's geography affects movement and communication between different parts of the country?

Organizing What You Know
5. **Summarizing** Copy the following graphic organizer. Use it to describe Mexico's physical geography.

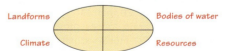

190 • Chapter 8

CLOSE

Point out on a map the major landforms and climate regions of Mexico. Have students describe how these physical features might affect the ways in which people live.

REVIEW, ASSESS, RETEACH

Have students complete the Section Review. Then distribute index cards to students. Have students develop questions and answers for a quiz game using these categories: physical features, climate types, vegetation, animals, and resources. Have students use their cards to quiz each other. Then have students complete Daily Quiz 8.1.

Have students complete Main Idea Activity S1. Display a blank wall map of Mexico and have each student create symbols for one physical feature, one resource, and one climate type. Then have students glue their symbols to the map and lead a discussion about the map. **ESOL**

EXTEND

Have students use primary and secondary sources to conduct research on a place in Mexico and create an illustrated brochure that addresses the six essential elements of geography or the five themes. Students can also research the customs of one of the ethnic groups in Mexico and present an oral presentation based on their information. **BLOCK SCHEDULING**

Section 2 — History and Culture

CHAPTER 8, Section 2

Read to Discover
1. What early cultures developed in Mexico?
2. What was Mexico like under Spanish rule and after independence?
3. What are some important features of Mexican culture?

Vocabulary
chinampas
conquistadores
epidemic
empire
mestizos
mulattoes
missions
ejidos
haciendas

People
Maya
Aztec
Hernán Cortés
Benito Juárez

Reading Strategy
FOLDNOTES: KEY-TERM FOLD Create the FoldNote titled **Key-Term Fold** described in the Appendix. Before you read, write the vocabulary terms on the tabs of the paper. As you read the section, write down the meaning of each term underneath its tab.

Section 2 Resources

Reproducible
- Lecture Notes, Section 2
- Know It Notes S2
- Graphic Organizer 8
- Geography for Life Activity 8
- Cultures of the World Activity 2
- Interdisciplinary Activity for the Middle Grades 12
- Map Activity 8
- Biography Activity: Frida Kahlo

Technology
- One-Stop Planner CD–ROM, Lesson 8.2
- Music of the World Audio CD Program, Selection 3
- Homework Practice Online
- HRW Go site

Reinforcement, Review, and Assessment
- Section 2 Review
- Daily Quiz 8.2
- Main Idea Activity S2
- Chapter Summaries and Review
- English Audio Summary 8.2
- Spanish Audio Summary 8.2

Early Cultures

Mesoamerica (*meso* means "in the middle") is the cultural area including Mexico and much of Central America. Many scientists think the first people to live in Mesoamerica arrived from the north about 12,000 years ago. By about 5,000 years ago, people in Mesoamerica were growing beans, peppers, and squash. They also domesticated an early form of corn. It eventually developed into the corn that we see today.

By about 1500 B.C. many people throughout the region were living in small farming villages. Along the humid southern coast of the Gulf of Mexico lived the Olmec people. The Olmec built temples, pyramids, and huge statues. They traded carved jade and obsidian, a volcanic stone, throughout eastern Mexico.

By about A.D. 200, other complex cultures were developing in what is now Mexico. Many of these civilizations had large city centers. Those centers had apartments, great avenues, open plazas, and pyramid-shaped temples. Some temple areas throughout Mesoamerica had stone ball courts. Players on those courts competed in a game somewhat like basketball. However, this ball game was not simply a sport. It had deep religious importance. Players who lost might be sacrificed to the gods.

Maya ruins include stone carvings and pyramid-type structures. Figures such as this Chac Mool are thought to represent the rain god.

Mexico • 191

Section 2

Objectives
1. Analyze the early cultures that developed in Mexico.
2. Describe what Mexico was like under Spanish rule and after independence.
3. Identify some important features of Mexican culture.

Focus

Bellringer

Copy the following statement and questions onto the chalkboard: *Mexico and the United States used to be European colonies. How are they different today? What might be the cause for these differences?* Discuss students' answers and tell them that in Section 2 they will learn more about Mexico's colonial period and independence.

Building Vocabulary

Write the key terms on the chalkboard. Pronounce the terms and have students repeat them aloud. Call on volunteers to find and read aloud the definitions of the terms. Ask: What English words does the word **conquistadores** resemble? (conquer, conquest) Call on students to make connections among these words. Ask: Which of the other key terms refer to groups of people? (mestizos, mulattoes) Which refer to farming or farmland? (*chinampas, ejidos,* haciendas) Call on volunteers to compose sentences using **epidemic**, **empire**, or **missions**.

Mexico 191

CHAPTER 8, Section 2

Culture and Music

Regional Foods of Mexico and Music Most Americans are familiar with "Tex-Mex" dishes of northern Mexico, with its chilies, beef, cheese, and pinto beans. The cuisine of Mexico's regions, however, is much more varied. Oaxacans prefer black beans to pintos and snack on *chapulines*—fried grasshoppers. Puebla's specialty is *mole,* a pungent sauce that combines chocolate and more than 20 other ingredients. Jalisco specializes in *pozole,* a hominy and pork stew. In Mexico City the thin French pancakes called crepes are popular. On the Gulf coast diners enjoy *huachinango* (red snapper) in a spicy sauce.

Discussion: Many Mexican restaurants hire mariachi bands to entertain customers. For a mariachi tune, play Selection 3 on the Music of the World Audio CD Program. Use the text and questions in the Teacher's Guide.

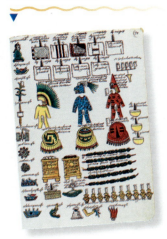

This copy of an original Aztec tax record shows items that were to be collected as tribute.

The Maya ruins of Tulum, an ancient Maya ceremonial and religious center, lie on the Caribbean coast.
Interpreting the Visual Record *Place*
What natural and human-made features would have protected Tulum?

Visual Record Answer
the stone wall and the rocky cliffs

The Maya Maya civilization developed in the tropical rain forest of southeastern Mexico, Guatemala, Belize, and Honduras. Maya city-states were at their peak between about A.D. 250 and 800. The Maya made accurate astronomical calculations and had a detailed calendar. Modern scholars can now read some Maya writing. This has helped us understand their civilization.

The Maya grew crops on terraced hillsides and on raised fields in swampy areas. They dug canals, piling the rich bottom mud onto the fields alongside the canals. This practice enriched the soil. Using this productive method of farming, the Maya supported an extremely dense population.

Sometime after A.D. 800, Maya civilization collapsed. The cities were abandoned. This decline may have been caused by famine, disease, warfare, or some combination of factors. However, the Maya did not die out. Millions of people of Maya descent still live in Mexico and Central America today.

The Aztec A people called the Aztec began moving into central Mexico from the north about A.D. 1200. They later established their capital on an island in a lake in the Valley of Mexico. Known as Tenochtitlán (tay-nawch-teet-LAHN), this capital grew into a splendid city. Its population in 1519 is estimated to have been at least 200,000. It was one of the largest cities in the world at that time. The Aztec conquered other Indian peoples around them. They forced these peoples to pay taxes and provide captives for sacrifice to Aztec gods.

The Aztec practiced a version of raised-field agriculture in the swampy lakes of central Mexico. The Aztec called these raised fields **chinampas** (chee-NAHM-pahs). There they grew the corn, beans, and peppers that most people ate. Only rich people in this society ate meat. On special occasions common people sometimes ate dog meat. The upper classes also drank chocolate.

✓ **READING CHECK:** What were the main features of Mexico's early civilizations?
Maya—lived in city-states, made astronomical calculations, kept a calendar, farmed; Aztec—built Tenochtitlán, conquered other peoples, farmed

TEACH

Teaching Objective 1

LEVEL 1: (Suggested time: 30 min.) Organize students into four groups. Have each group create a time line from 1500 B.C. to A.D. 1519 that includes information on Mexico's early cultures. Tell students to use the text to find information for the time line and to draw pictures illustrating the items. Have students present their time lines to the class.
ESOL, COOPERATIVE LEARNING, LS **VISUAL-SPATIAL**

LEVELS 2 AND 3: (Suggested time: 20 min.) Have students imagine that they are participating in an archaeological dig at a site in Mexico. At this site they are uncovering artifacts of early Mexican civilizations. Have students write a report detailing the artifacts that they have found. The reports should include information identifying the civilization and the location of the site. LS **VISUAL-SPATIAL, VERBAL-LINGUISTIC**

Connecting to History

Tenochtitlán

Tenochtitlán—now Mexico City—was founded by the Aztec in the early 1300s. According to their legends, they saw an eagle sitting atop a cactus on a swampy island in Lake Texcoco. The eagle held a snake in its mouth. A prophecy had instructed them to build a city where they saw such an eagle.

Within 200 years this village had become an imperial capital and the largest city in the Americas. It was a city of pyramids, palaces, markets, and gardens. Canals and streets ran through the city. Stone causeways connected the island to the mainland.

Bernal Díaz, a Spanish soldier, described his first view of the Aztec capital in 1519.

"When we saw so many cities and villages built in the water and other great towns on dry land and that straight and level Causeway going towards [Tenochtitlán], we were amazed and said that it was like the enchantments they tell of in the legend of Amadis, on account of the great towers and temples and buildings rising from the water, and all built of masonry. And some of our soldiers asked whether the things that we saw were not a dream."

The Spaniards went on to conquer the Aztec and destroy Tenochtitlán. On the ruins they built Mexico City. They also drained Lake Texcoco to allow the city to expand.

Understanding What You Read

1. Where and when was Tenochtitlán first built?
2. What was the Spaniards' reaction to Tenochtitlán?

A sketch map of the Aztec capital of Tenochtitlán

Colonial Mexico and Independence

Spanish Conquest Hernán Cortés, a Spanish soldier, arrived in Mexico in 1519 with about 600 men. These **conquistadores** (kahn-kees-tuh-DAWR-eez), or conquerors, had both muskets and horses. These were unknown in the Americas at that time. However, the most important factor in the conquest was disease. The native people of the Americas had no resistance to European diseases. The first **epidemic**, or widespread outbreak, of smallpox struck central Mexico in 1520. The death toll from disease greatly weakened the power of the Aztec. In 1521 Cortés completed his conquest of the Aztec and the other American Indian peoples of southern Mexico. They named the territory New Spain.

Colonial Mexico During this period, Spain ruled an **empire**. An empire is a system in which a central power controls a number of

Mexico • 193

CHAPTER 8, Section 2

Linking Past to Present
Differing Reports of a Death

When the Spanish entered Tenochtitlán, the Aztec leader Moctezuma was unsure of how to welcome the foreigners. Fearing that the Spanish were powerful Aztec gods, Moctezuma tried to buy off the Spaniards with gifts. The conquistadores refused and instead imprisoned the Aztec leader. Moctezuma's submission to the Spaniards cost him the respect of his people. Although accounts vary, the Spaniards claimed that when Moctezuma tried to speak to his people, they attacked him with stones and arrows. They claimed that it was this attack that caused the injuries that resulted in Moctezuma's death three days later. The Aztec, however, believed that the Spaniards had killed their leader, and they attacked the conquistadores.

Critical Thinking: Why might the Spanish account of Moctezuma's death differ from the Aztec account?

Answer: The Spaniards may not have wanted to seem responsible for the death of the Aztec leader.

Connecting to History Answers
1. on an island in Lake Texcoco; in the early 1300s
2. They were amazed.

CHAPTER 8, Section 2

DAILY LIFE

A Special Birthday Celebration One of the many cultural traditions and customs from Mexico is the *quinceañera* (keen-se-ahn-YE-rah). The *quinceañera* celebration marks a girl's 15th birthday. It begins with a thanksgiving mass. The girl, wearing a pastel gown and a matching tiara or headpiece, is seated at the foot of the altar during the mass. She can have up to seven maids of honor and as many male attendants. A big fiesta follows the mass. The party can rival a wedding in terms of its preparation, food, and costs.

The *quinceañera* tradition may have its roots in the Aztec practice of marking girls' transition into womanhood. The Aztec ceremony stressed the importance of following society's rules.

Critical Thinking: Why might *quinceañeras* be important in Hispanic communities?

Answer: Students might say it is a historical celebration that strengthens community, religious, and family ties.

Biography Answer ▶ may have given him a deeper understanding of the common people's problems

BIOGRAPHY

Benito Juárez
(1806–72)

Character Trait: Citizenship

Over time, control of Mexico passed from Spaniards born in Spain to the Mexicans themselves. Benito Juárez was the country's first president of Indian heritage. He is also a national hero. A passionate political leader, Juárez stood up for the rights of all Mexicans and laid the foundation for a democratic government. *How may Juárez's heritage have affected his efforts for Mexico's citizens?*

The Spanish built many beautiful churches in Mexico, including this one in Taxco.

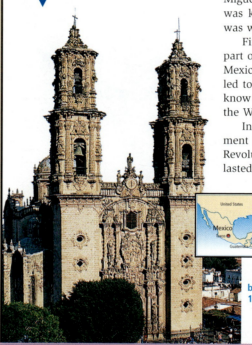

territories. New Spain was just one of Spain's colonies in the Americas. Mainland New Spain extended north from Mexico to what is now northern California and south to Panama.

After the initial conquest, Spanish and American Indian peoples and cultures mixed. This mix formed a new Mexican identity. The Spaniards called people of mixed European and Indian ancestry **mestizos** (me-STEE-zohs). When enslaved Africans were brought to Spanish America, they added to this blend of cultures. The Spaniards called people of mixed European and African ancestry **mulattoes** (muh-LA-tohs). Africans and Indians also intermarried.

Large areas of northern Mexico were left to the Roman Catholic Church to explore and to rule. Church outposts known as **missions** were scattered throughout the area. Mission priests often learned Indian languages and tried to convert the Indians to Catholicism.

Colonial Economy At first, the Spaniards were mainly interested in mining gold and silver in Mexico. Gradually, agriculture also became an important part of the colonial economy. Indians did most of the hard physical labor on farms and in mines. Many of them died from disease and overwork. Therefore, Spaniards began to bring enslaved Africans to the Americas as another source of labor.

Before the arrival of the Spaniards, Indian communities owned and worked land in groups. The lands they worked in common are called **ejidos** (e-HEE-thohs). After the conquest, the Spanish monarch granted **haciendas** (hah-see-EN-duhs), or huge expanses of farmlands, to favored people. Peasants, usually Indians, lived and worked on these haciendas. Cattle ranching operated according to a similar system.

Independence and After In 1810 a Catholic priest named Miguel Hidalgo y Costilla began a revolt against Spanish rule. Hidalgo was killed in 1811. However, fighting continued until independence was won in 1821.

Fifteen years later, Texas broke away from Mexico. Texas became part of the United States in 1845. Shortly after, the United States and Mexico argued over the location of their common border. This conflict led to a war in which Mexico lost about half its territory. Americans know this conflict as the Mexican War. Mexicans usually refer to it as the War of the North American Invasion.

In the early 1900s many Mexicans grew unhappy with the government of military leader Porfirio Díaz. As a result, in 1910 the Mexican Revolution broke out. Fighting between various leaders and groups lasted until 1920.

One of the major results of the revolution was land reform. The new government took land from the haciendas. This land was given back to peasant villages according to the old *ejido* system. Today *ejidos* make up about half of Mexico's farmland.

✓ **READING CHECK:** (Human Systems) How did Mexico gain independence from Spain? **Mexican Priest Miguel Hidalgo y Costilla began a revolt in 1810; fighting continued until independence was won in 1821.**

Teaching Objective 3

LEVEL 1: (Suggested time: 25 min.) Pair students and have them design and write a children's book on the culture and customs of Mexico. Remind students that a children's book should include a cover, be easy to read, and contain illustrations or pictures. Bind the books with string or yarn and display them around the classroom. **ESOL, COOPERATIVE LEARNING**

LEVELS 2 AND 3: (Suggested time: 25 min.) Ask students to imagine that they are traveling through Mexico. Have students prepare several journal entries about their trip. Entries should include descriptions of cultural events and customs as well as differences in languages that they might find on the trip. **LS VISUAL-SPATIAL**

▶**ASSIGNMENT:** Ask students to imagine that they are Mexican Indians who have recently returned to Mexico during the time of Spanish exploration and colonization. Tell students that they had been away from Mexico for 10 years and therefore were not there for the arrival of the Spaniards. Have students write an account of how Mexico has changed during their years away.

CLOSE

Have students take turns using one of the key terms in a sentence that describes an aspect of Mexican history or culture.

Mexicans light candles for relatives on the Day of the Dead.

Interpreting the Visual Record

Movement What celebrations in your community reflect special customs that began in other countries?

Culture and Customs

About 89 percent of Mexico's people are Roman Catholic. The Day of the Dead is an example of how cultures mix in Mexico. This holiday takes place on November 1 and 2. These are the same dates the Catholic Church celebrates All Saints' Day and All Souls' Day. The Day of the Dead honors dead ancestors. Families often place different foods on the graves of dead relatives. This recalls the Indian belief that the dead need material things just as the living do.

In Mexico ethnic identity is associated more with culture than with ancestry. One major indicator of a person's ethnic identity is language. Speaking one of the American Indian languages identifies a person as Indian. People who speak only Spanish are usually not considered Indian. This may be true even if they have Indian ancestors.

✓ **READING CHECK:** *Human Systems* What is the significance of the Day of the Dead? Honors dead ancestors—recalls both Indian belief that the dead need material things and the religious holiday of All Saints' Day and All Souls' Day

Define or identify: Maya, Aztec, *chinampas,* Hernán Cortés, conquistadores, epidemic, empire, mestizos, mulattoes, missions, *ejidos,* haciendas, Benito Juárez

Working with Sketch Maps On the map you created in Section 1, shade the areas once controlled by the Maya and Aztec. Which civilization occupied the Yucatán Peninsula?

Reading for the Main Idea

1. *Human Systems* What were some notable achievements of the Maya and Aztec civilizations?
2. *Human Systems* What were the effects of Spanish rule on Mexico?

Homework Practice Online Keyword: SJ5 HP8

Critical Thinking

3. **Analyzing Information** What advantages did Cortés have in his conquest of the Aztec?
4. **Finding the Main Idea** What is a sign of a person's ethnic identity in Mexico?

Organizing What You Know

5. **Identifying Cause and Effect** Copy the following graphic organizer. Use it to develop a cause-and-effect chart to identify events related to the Mexican War.

Section 2 Review

Answers to Section 2 Review

Define or identify For definitions and identifications, see the glossary and index.

Working with Sketch Maps Maya—southeastern Mexico; Aztec—central Mexico

Reading for the Main Idea

1. Maya—astronomical calculations, calendar, writing system, complex agricultural systems; Aztec—built Tenochtitlán, grew crops on *chinampas* (NGS 10)
2. blend of cultures, spread of Roman Catholicism, mining of gold and silver, the division of land into haciendas (NGS 13)

Critical Thinking

3. muskets, horses
4. language

Organizing What You Know

5. first box—Texas breaks away from Mexico and later becomes U.S. state; second box—Mexico and the United States dispute border; fourth box—Mexico loses territory

▲ **Visual Record Answer**

Students might mention holidays and community activities.

REVIEW, ASSESS, RETEACH

Have students complete the Section Review. Then organize students into small groups and have them create crossword puzzles using Define terms, names of groups and individuals, and customs of Mexico. Have students complete them. Then have students complete Daily Quiz 8.2.

Have students complete Main Idea Activity S2. Organize them into three groups. Have groups create posters depicting the ancient civilizations of Mexico, Spanish conquest and rule, and festivals and customs.
ESOL, COOPERATIVE LEARNING

EXTEND

Tell students that according to legend, the Aztec god Huitzilopochtli told the Aztec people to settle at the site where they saw an eagle with a snake in its beak perched on a cactus. That emblem now forms the center of the Mexican flag. Have interested students research Aztec history further and write a poem that retells the legend. **BLOCK SCHEDULING**

CHAPTER 8

HISTORICAL GEOGRAPHY

The Colonial Plantation System Although the scale and speed of global trade are unique to the modern age, far-flung trading networks have existed throughout history. The colonial plantation system of the New World is one example. First developed in the 1400s by the Portuguese, plantation agriculture was the dominant economic system in the Americas during the colonial era. Specialized crops, such as cotton, tobacco, indigo, sugarcane, and rice, were grown on large estates that relied on poorly paid workers or slave labor. After harvest, the crops were shipped mostly to European markets for sale.

Activity: Have students conduct research on the trading routes important to the colonial plantation system. Suggest that students find out which crops were raised for export, which modern countries had extensive plantation economies, and the sources of plantation labor.

▶ This Case Study feature addresses National Geography Standards 1 and 11.

Visual Record Answer ▶

Differences in tax laws and environmental laws have encouraged the growth of *maquiladoras* on Mexico's side of the border.

CASE STUDY

MAQUILADORAS ALONG THE U.S.-MEXICO BORDER

Geographers are often interested in borders. Borders are more than just lines on a map. They are places where different countries, cultures, and ways of life meet. For example, the U.S.-Mexico border separates a developing country from a very rich country. This fact has had an important influence on the location of industries in the region.

On the Mexican side of the border there are many *maquiladoras* (mah-kee-lah-DOHR-ahs)—factories that can be owned by foreign companies. The first *maquiladoras* were built in the mid-1960s. Since then, their numbers have increased dramatically. There are now more than 2,000 *maquiladoras* in Mexico. They employ hundreds of thousands of workers.

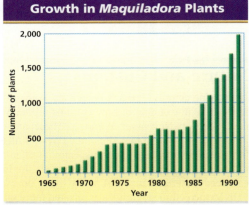

Growth in *Maquiladora* Plants

Source: Instituto Nacional de Estadistica Geografia e Informatica, Mexico

▲ The border separates Mexicali, Mexico, from Calexico, California. The big buildings are *maquiladoras*.

Interpreting the Visual Record *Location* How have each country's laws affected how land is used along the border?

Many *maquiladoras* are owned by American companies. They produce goods such as vacuum cleaners, automobile parts, and electronics. These goods are usually exported to the United States. Most *maquiladoras* are located within about 20 miles (32 km) of the U.S.-Mexico border. Cities such as Tijuana, Ciudad Juárez, and Nuevo Laredo have many *maquiladoras*.

Why have so many American companies chosen to build factories across the border in Mexico? The location allows companies to take advantage of the difference in wealth between the two countries. Mexico has a much lower standard of living than the United States. Workers there get paid less. Therefore, factories in Mexico can produce goods more cheaply. The United States has a higher standard of living. People there have more money to buy goods. They buy the products that have been

196 • Chapter 8

CASE STUDY

Setting the Scene
Globalization has given rise to complex manufacturing, shipping, and marketing networks. Companies headquartered in one country can finance, construct, and manage factories in other countries. Additionally, parts manufactured in one country can be assembled in another country into finished goods. These goods can then be shipped to and sold in a third country. *Maquiladoras* are a concrete example of this system in operation and illustrate the importance of cheap labor in locating manufacturing enterprises. The North American Free Trade Agreement (NAFTA) removed trade barriers among Canada, Mexico, and the United States. Since the agreement was implemented in 1994, Mexican trade with the United States and Canada has nearly doubled. The number of *maquiladoras* has increased.

Building a Case
Have students read "*Maquiladoras* Along the U.S.–Mexico Border." Then ask the students the following questions: What are *maquiladoras*? (factories in Mexico along the U.S.–Mexico border that can be owned by foreign companies) When were the first *maquiladoras* built? (mid-1960s) What are some of the cities where *maquiladoras* are found? (Tijuana, Ciudad Juárez, Nuevo Laredo, Monterrey) What are some of the goods manufactured in *maquiladoras*? (vacuum cleaners, automobile parts, electronics) Present students with the following facts about the lower standard of living in Mexico: High wages in Mexico are limited to a small portion of the workforce—the top 20 percent of income earners receive 55 percent of the total wages paid. In 1998, 27 percent of the population was estimated to live in poverty. These economic realities enable U.S.-based companies to pay lower wages to Mexican workers than to American workers.

U.S.-Mexico Border Region

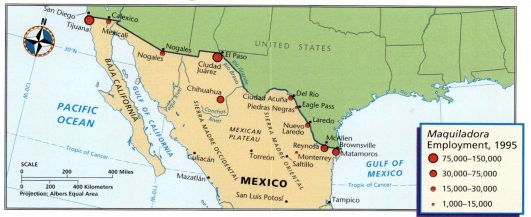

Understanding What You Read

1. Companies want to employ low-wage workers while remaining close to wealthy markets. They have therefore built *maquiladoras* close to the U.S.-Mexico border.
2. Goods produced include household appliances, like vacuum cleaners. Automobile parts and electronics are also manufactured in Mexico.

assembled in Mexico and shipped to American stores.

American companies have other reasons for building factories in Mexico. The Mexican government has given tax breaks to foreign companies that own and operate *maquiladoras*. It has encouraged the growth of *maquiladoras*. They create jobs for Mexican citizens and bring money into the country. Also, environmental laws in Mexico are not as strict as in the United States. Therefore, companies in Mexico do not have to spend as much money to control pollution.

Maquiladoras have become an important part of the border economy. They are also a good example of how borders can influence the landscape. The U.S.-Mexico border has attracted *maquiladoras* because it is more than just a line on a map. It separates two countries with different cultures, economies, and governments. Some American companies have built factories on the Mexican side of the border that export goods to the United States. These companies benefit from the different standards of living in the two countries and the border that separates them.

◀ Trucks carrying goods from Mexico to the United States are inspected by U.S. Customs officials in Laredo, Texas.

Understanding What You Read

1. Why have some American companies built factories in Mexico?
2. What are some of the goods that are produced in *maquiladoras*?

Mexico • 197

Drawing Conclusions

Lead students in a discussion of the global flow of goods and money. Discuss how the producers and consumers of goods do not always live in the same place. What criteria do manufacturers use to decide where to locate new factories? (low wages, transportation costs, tax breaks, or fewer environmental protections) Look at a road atlas of North America. Locate the Mexican cities where *maquiladoras* are concentrated. (Tijuana, Ciudad Juarez, Nuevo Laredo, Monterrey) What are the important interstate highways that might carry finished goods from these areas to consumers in the United States? (Tijuana: I 5 and I 8; Ciudad Juarez: I 25 and I 10; Nuevo Laredo and Monterrey: I 35) Have students trace a route from one of these cities to their hometown. Challenge them to look for items in their homes that were manufactured in Mexico.

Going Further: Thinking Critically

Maquiladoras are only one example of the global manufacturing network. Multinational manufacturing enterprises have also been active in Asia. China, Taiwan, South Korea, and India all have large workforces willing to work for relatively low wages. Have students discuss the following issues:
- Many of the Asian export-manufacturing areas are near port cities. Why is it important for factories to be located there?
- Some countries do not have strong regulations governing working conditions. Pollution controls, child labor restrictions, minimum-wage laws, and workweek standards are often not as strict as those in the United States and Western Europe. How might this affect where American and European companies locate their factories? Challenge students to monitor news stories about foreign working conditions.

Mexico | 197

Section 3: Mexico Today

Read to Discover
1. What kind of government and economy does Mexico have today?
2. What are the important features of Mexico's six culture regions?

Vocabulary
- inflation
- cash crops
- smog
- *maquiladoras*
- slash-and-burn agriculture

Places
- Tijuana
- Ciudad Juárez
- Acapulco
- Mazatlán
- Cancún
- Mexico City
- Guadalajara
- Tampico
- Campeche
- Monterrey

Reading Strategy

TAKING NOTES As you read this section, create an outline using the headings from the section. Beneath the heading write some important details from what you learn.

Mexico

Country	Population/Growth Rate	Life Expectancy	Literacy Rate	Per Capita GDP
Mexico	104,907,991 / 1.4%	69, male / 75, female	92%	$9,000
United States	290,342,554 / 0.9%	74, male / 80, female	97%	$37,600

Source: Central Intelligence Agency, *The World Factbook 2003*

Interpreting the Chart What does the per capita GDP in Mexico indicate about its economic development?

Government and Economy

Like that of the United States, Mexico's government includes an elected president and a congress. However, in Mexico one political party—the Partido Revolucionario Institucional (PRI)—controlled the Mexican government for 71 years. This control ended in 2000 when Vicente Fox of the National Action Party was sworn in as president.

For many years, Mexico operated more on the principles of a command economy in which the government controlled economic activity. In recent decades, however, Mexico has worked to reduce government control of the economy. Mexico's economy is growing and modernizing. However, living standards are much lower than in other nations.

Mexico began to export oil in 1911 and is a leading oil exporter today. However, problems began when the price of oil fell in the 1980s. Since then, Mexico has wrestled with debts to foreign banks, high unemployment, and **inflation**. Inflation is the rise in prices that occurs when currency loses its buying power.

The North American Free Trade Agreement (NAFTA) has helped Mexico's economy. NAFTA took effect in 1994. It made trade between Mexico, the United States, and Canada easier. Mexico's leaders hope increased trade will create more jobs in their country.

198 • Chapter 8

CHAPTER 8, Section 3

SECTION 3 RESOURCES

Reproducible
- Lecture Notes, Section 3
- Know It Notes S3
- Creative Strategies for Teaching World Geography, Lesson 9
- Environmental and Global Issues Activity 2

Technology
- One-Stop Planner CD–ROM, Lesson 8.3
- Music of the World Audio CD Program, Selection 3
- Homework Practice Online
- HRW Go site

Reinforcement, Review, and Assessment
- Section 3 Review
- Daily Quiz 8.3
- Main Idea Activity S3
- Chapter Summaries and Review
- English Audio Summary 8.3
- Spanish Audio Summary 8.3

Chart Answer
that many Mexican citizens live in poverty

Section 3

Objectives
1. Describe the government and economy of Mexico today.
2. Identify the important features of Mexico's six culture regions.

FOCUS

Bellringer
Copy the following question onto the chalkboard: *What kinds of factors distinguish one region from another?* Have students discuss their answers. (Possible answers: economic, political, and social) Tell students that in Section 3 they will learn about the six culture regions of Mexico as well as about its government and economy.

Building Vocabulary
Write the key terms on the chalkboard. Ask volunteers to find and read aloud the definitions of **cash crops**, **smog**, and **slash-and-burn agriculture**. Relate **inflation** to blowing up a balloon. Pronounce *maquiladoras* for them and have them repeat it and give its meaning. Then have students volunteer to use two of the terms in a sentence.

Agriculture Agriculture has long been an important part of the Mexican economy. In fact, farming is the traditional focus of life in the country. This is true even though just 12 percent of the land can grow crops. Rainfall supports agriculture in the southern part of the Mexican Plateau and in southern valleys. Plantations in coastal lowlands and on mountain slopes along the Gulf of Mexico also produce important crops. Those crops include coffee and sugarcane. Northern drylands are important for livestock ranching.

High demand in the United States has encouraged a shift to the growing of **cash crops**. A cash crop is produced primarily to sell, rather than for the farmer to eat. Trucks bring Mexican vegetables, fruits, and other cash crops to the United States.

Industry Many Mexicans work in primary and secondary industries. These include the oil industry, mining, and manufacturing. The country's fastest-growing industrial centers lie along the U.S. border. Tijuana (tee-HWAH-nah) and Ciudad Juárez (syoo-thahth HWAHR-es) are two of these major industrial centers.

Many U.S. and other foreign companies have built factories in Mexico. This is because wages are lower there. Mexican workers in these factories assemble products for export to other countries. (See the Case Study in this chapter.)

Tourism Tourism and other service industries are also important to Mexico's economy. Many tourists visit old colonial cities and Maya and Aztec monuments. Popular coastal cities and resorts include Acapulco, Mazatlán, and Cancún. Acapulco and Mazatlán are located on Mexico's Pacific coast. Cancún is on the Yucatán Peninsula.

✓ **READING CHECK:** *Environment and Society* How does geography affect the location of economic activities in Mexico?
Good rainfall produces land that can support agriculture; oil and mineral reserves support mining and drilling; good beaches support tourism.

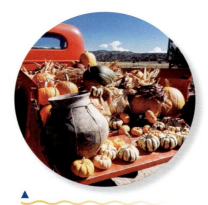
Gourds—hard-shelled ornamental fruits—are just some of Mexico's many agricultural products.

Puerto Vallarta—a popular beach resort—is on the Pacific coast.
Interpreting the Visual Record
Movement How do you think tourism has changed settlement patterns?

CHAPTER 8, Section 3

Across the Curriculum
ART
Murals and Mosaics One cultural feature of Mexico that attracts tourists is the beautiful murals. Murals decorate the walls of many public buildings in Mexico. One of the most famous mural artists was Diego Rivera, who painted frescoes and designed mosaics showing scenes from Mexican history and daily life. Architect Juan O'Gorman designed the huge mosaic mural on the library at the National Autonomous University of Mexico. These murals along with old colonial architecture combine to form a distinct style found in many Mexican cities.

Discussion: Lead a discussion on the relationship between Mexican history and murals and mosaics.

GO TO: go.hrw.com
KEYWORD: SJ5 CH8
FOR: Web sites about murals

◄ **Visual Record Answer**
New jobs generated by increased tourism would probably draw more people to live in those areas.

TEACH

Teaching Objective 1
ALL LEVELS: (Suggested time: 20 min.) Copy the following graphic organizer onto the chalkboard, omitting the blue answers. Organize the class into five groups. Assign each group one of the organizer topics and have students use their textbooks to find information. Ask volunteers from each group to write their information onto the organizer.
ESOL, COOPERATIVE LEARNING, **LS** VISUAL-SPATIAL

Government and Economy of Mexico

GOVERNMENT
elected president and a congress, Partido Revolucionario Institucional controlled government for 71 years

ECONOMY—Challenges
foreign debts, poverty, high unemployment, inflation

MEXICO

ECONOMY—Agriculture
farming, coffee, sugarcane, livestock ranching, cash crops

ECONOMY—Industry
oil, mining, manufacturing many foreign companies build factories in Mexico

ECONOMY—Tourism
visit old colonial sites, Maya and Aztec monuments, coastal resorts

Mexico 199

CHAPTER 8, Section 3

FOOD FESTIVAL

Traditional Guacamole
Have students prepare guacamole as it might have been made 2,000 years ago in Oaxaca.

To make the popular dip, boil 4 cups of water in a saucepan. Add 3 large husked, washed tomatillos. Turn off heat and allow tomatillos to soften—about five minutes. Remove from water and puree in blender. Chill. Combine the flesh of 2 large avocados and ½ minced serrano or jalapeño pepper in a bowl. Add tomatillo puree and mash until combined. Serve with baked tortilla chips.

Visual Record Answer
smoke and fog

Mexico City was 250 miles (400 km) away from the center of the 1985 earthquake on Mexico's Pacific coast. However, the city suffered heavy damage and thousands of deaths. The city sits on a former lake bed. The loose soil under the city made the damage worse.

Mexico's Culture Regions

Mexico's 31 states and one federal district can be grouped into six culture regions. These regions are highly diverse in their resources, climate, population, and other features.

Greater Mexico City Greater Mexico City is Mexico's most developed and crowded region. This area includes Mexico City and about 50 smaller cities. More than 20 million people live there. It is one of the most densely populated urban areas in the world.

Mexico City is also one of the world's most polluted cities. Thousands of factories and millions of automobiles release exhaust and other pollutants into the air. Surrounding mountains trap the resulting **smog**—a mixture of smoke, chemicals, and fog. Smog can cause health problems like eye irritation and breathing difficulties.

Wealth and poverty exist side by side in Mexico City. The city has very poor slums. It also has busy highways, modern office buildings, high-rise apartments, museums, universities, and old colonial cathedrals.

Central Interior Mexico's central interior region lies north of the capital. It extends toward both coasts. Many cities here began as mining or ranching centers during the colonial period. Small towns with a central square and a colonial-style church are common.

The region has many fertile valleys and small family farms. In recent years the central interior has attracted new industries from overcrowded Mexico City. As a result, cities like Guadalajara are growing rapidly.

Oil Coast The forested coastal plains between Tampico and Campeche (kahm-PAY-chay) were once lightly settled. However, the population has grown as oil production in this region has increased. In addition, large forest areas are being cleared for farming and ranching.

Smog covers Mexico City. The city continues to work toward solutions to challenges facing it as one of the world's largest cities.
Interpreting the Visual Record What two words do you think the word *smog* comes from?

200 • Chapter 8

Teaching Objective 2

LEVEL 1: (Suggested time: 30 min.) Organize students into six groups and assign each group a culture region. Have students design and draw on a posterboard a commemorative stamp that highlights distinctive characteristics of their assigned culture region.
ESOL, COOPERATIVE LEARNING

LEVEL 3: (Suggested time: 20 min.) Have students design their own graphic organizer to identify the characteristics of the six culture regions of Mexico. Organizers may be in a variety of formats, such as charts or idea webs. Have volunteers copy their graphic organizer onto the chalkboard. Then lead a class discussion on the culture regions.

CLOSE

Ask volunteers to give examples of the relationship between environment and society in each of the six culture regions of Mexico.

Southern Mexico Many people in southern Mexico speak Indian languages. They live in the country's poorest region. It has few cities and little industry. Subsistence farming is common. Poverty and corrupt local governments have led to unrest. In the 1990s people in the state of Chiapas staged an antigovernment uprising.

Northern Mexico Northern Mexico has become one of the country's most prosperous and modern areas. NAFTA has helped the region's economy grow. Monterrey and Tijuana are important cities here. Factories called *maquiladoras* (mah-kee-lah-DORH-ahs) are located along the northern border and are often foreign owned.

American music, television, and other forms of entertainment are popular near the border. Many Mexicans cross the border to shop, work, or live in the United States. In recent decades, the U.S. government has increased its efforts to stop illegal immigration across the border.

The Yucatán Most of the Yucatán Peninsula is sparsely populated. Mérida is this region's major city. As in other parts of Mexico, some farmers in the region practice **slash-and-burn agriculture**, in which an area of forest is burned to clear it for planting. The ashes enrich the soil. After a few years of planting crops, the soil is exhausted. The farmer then moves on to a new area of forest. Farmers can return to previously farmed areas years later.

Maya ruins and sunny beaches have made tourism a major industry in this area. The popular resort of Cancún and the island of Cozumel are located here.

✓ **READING CHECK:** *Human Systems* What are the six culture regions of Mexico? Greater Mexico City, Central Interior, Oil Coast, Southern Mexico, Northern Mexico, the Yucatán

Celebrations, such as Danza de Los Viejitos—Dance of the Old Men—are popular throughout Mexico.

Section Review 3

Keyword: SJ5 HP8

Define and explain: inflation, cash crops, smog, *maquiladoras*, slash-and-burn agriculture

Working with Sketch Maps On the map you created in Section 2, label Tijuana, Ciudad Juárez, Acapulco, Mazatlán, Cancún, Mexico City, Guadalajara, Tampico, Campeche, and Monterrey. Which city is the national capital? Which cities are located at or near sea level? Which are located at higher elevations?

Reading for the Main Idea
1. *Human Systems* What are three economic problems faced by Mexico in recent decades?
2. *Human Systems* What are Mexico's six culture regions? Describe a feature of each.

Critical Thinking
3. **Analyzing Information** How have changes in the price of oil affected Mexico?
4. **Drawing Inferences and Conclusions** Why would farmers in Mexico grow only cash crops?

Organizing What You Know
5. **Categorizing** Copy the following graphic organizer. Use it to list key facts about the population and economy of each culture region in Mexico.

	Population	Economy
Greater Mexico City		
Central interior		
Oil coast		
Southern Mexico		
Northern Mexico		
Yucatán		

Section 3 Review

Answers to Section 3 Review

Define For definitions, see the glossary.

Working with Sketch Maps Mexico City; near sea level—Acapulco, Tampico, Cancún, Tijuana, Campeche, Mazatlán; higher elevation—Guadalajara, Mexico City, Ciudad Juárez, Monterrey

Reading for the Main Idea
1. debts to foreign banks, high unemployment, inflation (NGS 12)
2. Greater Mexico City—most developed and crowded; Central Interior—fertile valleys; Oil Coast—forested plain with growing population; Southern Mexico—poorest region; Northern Mexico—prosperous and modern; Yucatán—tourism, sparsely populated (NGS 10)

Critical Thinking
3. hurt the country's economy because Mexico is a major exporter of oil
4. Farmers buy the food with the cash they earn from selling their crops.

Organizing What You Know
5. See Section 3 text for answers.

REVIEW, ASSESS, RETEACH

Have students complete the Section Review. Then organize students into six groups and assign each group a culture region. Have each group use the text and map to prepare five questions, with answers, about the economy and geography of the culture regions of Mexico for a quiz game. When questions are completed, have the class play the quiz game. Then have students complete Daily Quiz 8.3.

Have students complete Main Idea Activity S3. Organize students into two groups and have them create a wall map of Mexico. Have one group label the cultural regions of Mexico and the other group draw or glue symbols depicting the economic activities of the country. Display and discuss the maps. **ESOL, COOPERATIVE LEARNING**

EXTEND

Have interested students find out more about Mexico's tourist industry by contacting a travel agent. Ask students to plan a vacation itinerary based on their research. **BLOCK SCHEDULING**

CHAPTER 8 REVIEW

Define and Identify
For definitions and identifications, see the glossary and index.

Review the Main Ideas

15. narrow area of land connecting far southern Mexico to the rest of the country; narrow peninsula in the far northwest (NGS 3)
16. rugged plains area that extends throughout central Mexico; Sierra Madre Occidental and Sierra Madre Oriental (NGS 3)
17. cougars, coyotes, deer; anteaters, jaguars, monkeys, parrots (NGS 8)
18. oil; silver
19. built temples, pyramids, and huge statues; traded carved jade and obsidian (NGS 10)
20. between A.D. 250 and 800; after A.D. 800 (NGS 10)
21. built on an island in Lake Texcoco, at least 200,000 people, pyramids, palaces, markets, gardens, canals, stone causeways to the mainland (NGS 12)
22. killed huge numbers of them because they had no resistance to the diseases
23. Spaniards, mestizos, mulattoes (NGS 10)
24. November 1 and 2, holiday that honors dead ancestors (NGS 10)
25. NAFTA made trade among Mexico, the United States, and Canada easier. (NGS 11)
26. greater Mexico City, central interior, oil coast, southern Mexico, northern Mexico, Yucatán (NGS 5)

Think Critically
27. differences in elevation
28. terraced hillsides, dug canals and used bottom mud to enrich soil
29. from land worked in common (*ejidos*) to haciendas owned by favored people
30. volcanic eruptions, earthquakes, overcrowding, pollution that leads to health problems like eye irritation and breathing difficulties
31. exhausts the soil

Map Activity
32. **A.** Ciudad Juárez
    B. Tijuana
    C. Cancún
    D. Río Bravo
    E. Mount Orizaba
    F. Guadalajara
    G. Yucatán Peninsula
    H. Mexico City
    I. Acapulco

Review and Practice

Define and Identify

Identify each of the following:
1. sinkholes
2. Maya
3. Aztec
4. conquistadores
5. epidemic
6. empire
7. mestizos
8. Benito Juárez
9. missions
10. haciendas
11. inflation
12. cash crops
13. smog
14. *maquiladoras*

Review the Main Ideas

15. What are the Isthmus of Tehuantepec and Baja California?
16. What is the Mexican Plateau? What forms its edges?
17. What are some animals that live in Mexico's northern deserts? in its southern rain forests?
18. What is Mexico's main energy resource? mineral resource?
19. What were some features of Olmec civilization?
20. When was the Maya civilization at its peak, and when did it decline?
21. What was the city of Tenochtitlán like?
22. How did European diseases affect the Indians in Mexico?
23. What were the main ethnic divisions in New Spain?
24. What is the Day of the Dead?
25. Why did Mexico's economy improve after 1994?
26. What are Mexico's six main culture regions?

Think Critically

27. **Drawing Inferences and Conclusions** Why do climates in southern Mexico vary so widely?
28. **Finding the Main Idea** How did the Maya and Aztec modify their environment to suit their needs?
29. **Comparing** How did land ownership in Mexico change under Spanish rule?
30. **Summarizing** What problems and hazards face the people of Mexico City?
31. **Finding the Main Idea** What is the major drawback of slash-and-burn agriculture in Mexico?

Map Activity

32. On a separate sheet of paper, match the letters on the map with their correct labels.

    Río Bravo (Rio Grande)
    Mexico City
    Mount Orizaba
    Yucatán Peninsula
    Tijuana
    Ciudad Juárez
    Acapulco
    Cancún
    Guadalajara

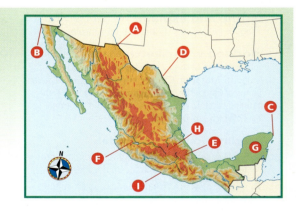

202 • Chapter 8

CHAPTER 8 REVIEW

Writing Activity

Imagine that you are a Spanish soldier reporting back to Spain on the situation in Mexico. Research and write a short report on the effects of disease on the Aztec. Include a map, chart, graph, model, or database illustrating the information in your report. Be sure to use standard grammar, spelling, sentence structure, and punctuation.

internet connect

Internet Activity: go.hrw.com
KEYWORD: SJ5 GT8

Choose a topic to explore about Mexico:
- Travel along Mexico's coastlines.
- See the arts and crafts of Mexico.
- Use ancient Maya hieroglyphs.

Writing Activity

Reports should contain information about disease and the Aztec. Use Rubric 37, Writing Assignments, to evaluate student work.

Social Studies Skills Practice

Interpreting Graphs

You have read about Mexico City's pollution problem. Most people use public transportation, but private vehicles still crowd the city's streets. Study the following graph. Then answer the questions.

Vehicles in Mexico City

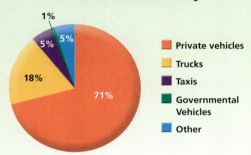

- Private vehicles — 71%
- Trucks — 18%
- Taxis — 5%
- Governmental Vehicles — 1%
- Other — 5%

1. What is the largest category on the graph? the smallest?
2. If more people used public transportation, which group or groups might get smaller?
3. Why do you think trucks are listed as a separate category?
4. What does the graph tell you about the actual number of vehicles in Mexico City? Support your answer.

Analyzing Primary Sources

In 1910, Mexican president Porfirio Díaz had his political opponent Francisco Madero thrown in prison. Madero wrote a letter from prison encouraging Mexicans to revolt against the government. Read the passage from Madero's letter. Then answer the questions.

"A force of tyranny . . . oppresses us in such a manner that it has become intolerable. In exchange for . . . tyranny we are offered peace, but peace full of shame for the Mexican nation, because its basis is not law, but force; because its object is not the . . . prosperity [wealth and happiness] of the country, but to enrich a small group who . . . have converted the public charges [responsibilities] into fountains of . . . personal benefit . . . ."

1. From the context, what do you think the word *tyranny* means?
2. How does Madero feel about Mexico's being at peace?
3. Madero uses the word *fountains* to describe the wealth that a small group of people is taking from the government. Why may Madero have chosen that word?
4. How do you think Mexicans who read this letter reacted to it?

Interpreting Graphs

1. private vehicles; governmental vehicles
2. private vehicles, taxis, other
3. Bigger, heavier trucks may produce more pollutants than private vehicles.
4. nothing; only percentages of vehicles

Analyzing Primary Sources

1. cruel or unfair rule, oppression
2. that it is a shameful peace
3. to describe the large amount or unending flow of benefits going to the small group
4. probably encouraged to rise up against the government

Mexico • 203

REVIEW AND ASSESSMENT RESOURCES

Reproducible
- Readings in World Geography, History, and Culture 15 and 16
- Critical Thinking Activity 8
- Vocabulary Activity 8

Technology
- Chapter 8 Test Generator (on the One-Stop Planner)
- Audio CD Program, Chapter 8
- HRW Go site

Reinforcement, Review, and Assessment
- Chapter 8 Review and Practice
- Chapter Summaries and Review
- Chapter 8 Test
- Chapter 8 Test for English Language Learners and Special-Needs Students

internet connect

GO TO: go.hrw.com
KEYWORD: SJ5 Teacher
FOR: a guide to using the Internet in your classroom

Mexico 203

Chapter 9: Central America and the Caribbean Islands

Chapter Resource Manager

Objectives	Pacing Guide	Reproducible Resources
SECTION 1 **Physical Geography** (pp. 205–07) 1. Identify the physical features of Central America and the Caribbean islands. 2. Identify the climates found in the region. 3. Identify the natural resources in the region.	**Regular** .5 day Lecture Notes, Section 1 **Block Scheduling** .5 day Block Scheduling Handbook, Chapter 9	**RS** Know It Notes S1 **E** Lab Activities for Geography and Earth Science, Demonstrations 5, 6, 7 **ELL** Main Idea Activity S1
SECTION 2 **Central America** (pp. 208–12) 1. Describe what Central America's early history was like. 2. Describe how the region's history is reflected in its people today. 3. Describe what the countries of Central America are like today.	**Regular** 1.5 days Lecture Notes, Section 2 **Block Scheduling** .5 day Block Scheduling Handbook, Chapter 9	**RS** Know It Notes S2 **RS** Graphic Organizer 9 **E** Cultures of the World Activity 2 **IC** Interdisciplinary Activities for the Middle Grades 9, 11, 12 **ELL** Main Idea Activity S2
SECTION 3 **The Caribbean Islands** (pp. 213–17) 1. Describe the Caribbean's history. 2. Describe how the region's history is reflected in its people today. 3. Describe what the countries of the Caribbean are like today.	**Regular** .5 day Lecture Notes, Section 3 **Block Scheduling** .5 day Block Scheduling Handbook, Chapter 9	**RS** Know It Notes S3 **SM** Geography for Life Activity 9 **SM** Map Activity 9 **E** Biography Activity: Roberto Clemente **ELL** Main Idea Activity S3

Chapter Resource Key

- **RS** Reading Support
- **IC** Interdisciplinary Connections
- **E** Enrichment
- **SM** Skills Mastery
- **A** Assessment
- **REV** Review
- **ELL** Reinforcement and English Language Learners and English for Speakers of Other Languages (ESOL)
- Transparencies
- CD–ROM
- Music
- Video
- Internet
- Holt Presentation Maker Using Microsoft® PowerPoint®

 One-Stop Planner CD–ROM

See the *One-Stop Planner* for a complete list of additional resources for students and teachers.

One-Stop Planner CD–ROM

It's easy to plan lessons, select resources, and print out materials for your students when you use the *One-Stop Planner CD–ROM with Test Generator*.

Technology Resources

 One-Stop Planner CD–ROM, Lesson 9.1

 Geography and Cultures Visual Resources with Teaching Activities 18–22

 ARGWorld CD–ROM

 Homework Practice Online
HRW Go site

 One-Stop Planner CD–ROM, Lesson 9.2

 ARGWorld CD–ROM

 Homework Practice Online
HRW Go site

 One-Stop Planner CD–ROM, Lesson 9.3

 ARGWorld CD–ROM

 Music of the World Audio CD Program, Selection 4

 Homework Practice Online
HRW Go site

Review, Reinforcement, and Assessment Resources

ELL	Main Idea Activity S1
REV	Section 1 Review
A	Daily Quiz 9.1
REV	Chapter Summaries and Review
ELL	English Audio Summary 9.1
ELL	Spanish Audio Summary 9.1

ELL	Main Idea Activity S2
REV	Section 2 Review
A	Daily Quiz 9.2
REV	Chapter Summaries and Review
ELL	English Audio Summary 9.2
ELL	Spanish Audio Summary 9.2

ELL	Main Idea Activity S3
REV	Section 3 Review
A	Daily Quiz 9.3
REV	Chapter Summaries and Review
ELL	English Audio Summary 9.3
ELL	Spanish Audio Summary 9.3

internet connect

HRW ONLINE RESOURCES

GO TO: go.hrw.com
Then type in a keyword.

TEACHER HOME PAGE
KEYWORD: SJ5 TEACHER

CHAPTER INTERNET ACTIVITIES
KEYWORD: SJ5 GT9

Choose an activity to:
- plan an ecotour of Central America.
- learn more about the Panama Canal.
- hunt for hurricanes.

CHAPTER ENRICHMENT LINKS
KEYWORD: SJ5 CH9

CHAPTER MAPS
KEYWORD: SJ5 MAPS9

ONLINE ASSESSMENT
Homework Practice
KEYWORD: SJ5 HP9
Standardized Test Prep Online
KEYWORD: SJ5 STP9
Rubrics
KEYWORD: SS Rubrics

COUNTRY INFORMATION
KEYWORD: SJ5 Almanac

CONTENT UPDATES
KEYWORD: SS Content Updates

HOLT PRESENTATION MAKER
KEYWORD: SJ5 PPT9

ONLINE READING SUPPORT
KEYWORD: SS Strategies

CURRENT EVENTS
KEYWORD: S5 Current Events

Meeting Individual Needs

Ability Levels

Level 1 Basic-level activities designed for all students encountering new material

Level 2 Intermediate-level activities designed for average students

Level 3 Challenging activities designed for honors and gifted-and-talented students

ESOL Activities that address the needs of students with Limited English Proficiency

Chapter Review and Assessment

E	Creative Strategies for Teaching World Geography, Lesson 9
E	Readings in World Geography, History, and Culture 17, 18, and 19
SM	Critical Thinking Activity 9
REV	Chapter 9 Review and Practice
REV	Chapter Summaries and Review
ELL	Vocabulary Activity 9
A	Chapter 9 Test
	Chapter 9 Test Generator (on the One-Stop Planner)
	Audio CD Program, Chapter 9
A	Chapter 9 Test for English Language Learners and Special-Needs Students
	HRW Go site

203B

CHAPTER 9
Central America and the Caribbean
Previewing Chapter Resources

Holt Online Learning

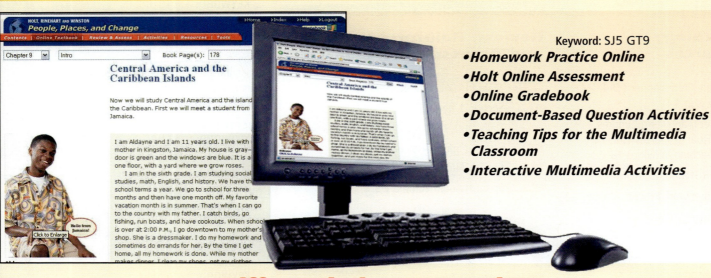

Keyword: SJ5 GT9
- Homework Practice Online
- Holt Online Assessment
- Online Gradebook
- Document-Based Question Activities
- Teaching Tips for the Multimedia Classroom
- Interactive Multimedia Activities

Differentiating Instruction

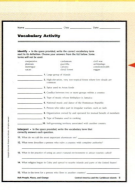

Reading and Writing Support
- Graphic Organizer Activity
- Vocabulary Activity
- Chapter Summaries and Review
- Know It Notes
- Audio CD

Active Learning
- Block Scheduling Handbook
- Cultures of the World Activity
- Interdisciplinary Activity
- Map Activity
- Critical Thinking Activity 9
- Music of the World Audio CD Program: Haitian Carnival Music

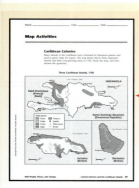

Primary Sources and Advanced Learners
- Geography for Life Activity: Planning for Tourism in Dominica
- Map Activity: Caribbean Colonies
- Readings in World Geography, History and Culture:
  - 17 Village Life in Guatemala
  - 18 Montserrat: Living Under the Volcano
  - 19 The Land and People of Nicaragua

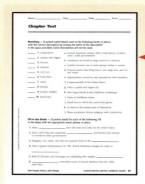

Assessment Program
- Daily Quizzes S1–3
- Chapter Test
- Chapter Test for English Language Learners and Special-Needs Students

Spanish and ESOL
- Vocabulary Activity
- Main Idea Activities for English Language Learners and Special-Needs Students
- Chapter Summaries and Review
- Spanish Audio Summary
- Know It Notes S1–3
- Chapter Test for English Language Learners and Special-Needs Students

Special Education Modifications
Your I.D.E.A. Works! CD-ROM will provide modified versions of the following teaching materials:
- Know It Notes S1–3
- Vocabulary Activity
- Main Idea Activities S1–3
- Daily Quizzes S1–3
- Chapter 9 Test
- Flash cards of chapter vocabulary terms

Islands

Teacher Resources

Books for Teachers

Coates, Anthony G., ed. *Central America: A Natural and Cultural History.* Yale University Press, 1999.

Daling, Tjabel. *Costa Rica in Focus.* Interlink Publishing Group, 1998.

Kurlansky, Mark. *A Continent of Islands: Searching for the Caribbean Destiny.* Perseus Press, 1993.

Books for Students

Gottlieb, Dale. *Where Jamaica Go?* Orchard Books, 1996. Simple rhymes about a girl named Jamaica as she explores her island home. **SHELTERED ENGLISH**

Leeper, Fran, and Fran L. Buss. *Journey of the Sparrows.* Dell, 1993. A girl and her family flee from El Salvador to the United States.

Monteyo, Victor, ed. *The Bird Who Cleans the World: And Other Mayan Fables.* Trans. Wallace Kaufman. Curbstone Press, 1992. Glimpse at Mayan fables and values.

Orozco, José-Luis, ed. and trans. *De Colores: And Other Latin-American Folk Songs for Children.* Picture Puffin, 1999. Songs from all over Middle and South America. **SHELTERED ENGLISH**

Multimedia Materials

Children of the Panamanian Rain Forest. Video, 15 min. AIMS Media.

Haitian Visions: A Diverse Cultural Legacy. Video, 30 min. Alarion Press.

People and Places: Cuba. Video, 20 min. AIMS Media.

Videos and CDs

Videos

- CNN Presents Geography: Yesterday and Today, Segment 10 Preserving Heritage
- CNN Presents World Cultures: Yesterday and Today, Segment 35 History of Haiti
- ARG World

Holt Researcher

http://researcher.hrw.com

- *Caribbean Community and Common Market (CARICOM)*
- *Organization of American States (OAS)*
- *Aristide, Jean-Bertrand*
- *Chamorro, Violeta Barrios de*
- *Cuba*

Transparency Packages

Graphic Organizer Transparencies 9.1–3

Geography and Cultures Visual Resources Transparencies 32–36

39 Central America and the Caribbean Islands: Physical-Political

Map Activities Transparency 09 Caribbean Colonies

CHAPTER 9

WHY IT MATTERS

You may want to reinforce interest in Central America and the Caribbean islands by pointing out the following facts:

- Many Central American and Caribbean immigrants have come to the United States to escape political violence and economic problems.
- The United States has a long history of military and economic involvement there.
- Some forms of music that students may enjoy, such as reggae, originated in the Caribbean region.
- Historic sites, mild weather, and sunny beaches attract tourists from around the world to Central America and the Caribbean islands.

CHAPTER 9

Central America and the Caribbean Islands

Now we will study Central America and the islands of the Caribbean. First we will meet a student from Jamaica.

I am Aldayne and I am 11 years old. I live with my mother in Kingston, Jamaica. My house is gray—the door is green and the windows are blue. It is all on one floor, with a yard where we grow roses.

I am in the sixth grade. I am studying social studies, math, English, and history. We have three school terms a year. We go to school for three months and then have one month off. My favorite vacation month is in summer. That's when I can go to the country with my father. I catch birds, go fishing, run boats, and have cookouts. When school is over at 2:00 P.M., I go downtown to my mother's shop. She is a dressmaker. I do my homework and sometimes do errands for her. By the time I get home, all my homework is done. While my mother makes dinner, I clean my shoes, get my clothes together, and get ready for the next day. My favorite dinners are rice and peas with spring chicken, or crispy fried chicken with chips (french fries).

Hello from Jamaica!

CHAPTER PROJECT

Have students conduct research on an archaeological site in Central America or the Caribbean islands. Ask them to find or draw a picture of the site. Have each student create a model of an artifact from the site, such as a pottery jar, jewelry, tool, or figurine. Ask students to share their pictures and models with the class. Photograph student work for portfolios.

STARTING THE CHAPTER

Have students look at the photographs throughout the chapter. Ask them to use the photographs to identify opportunities and challenges this region might have. Discuss responses. (Possible answers: The region's many ruins and natural beauty may offer opportunities for tourism. The varied environment and the isolation of the region's islands may cause economic challenges.) Explain that although the region has a fascinating history and widespread natural beauty, it also faces many challenges. Tell students they will learn more about the region in this chapter.

Section 1: Physical Geography

CHAPTER 9, Section 1

Section 1 Resources

Reproducible
- Lecture Notes, Section 1
- Block Scheduling Handbook, Chapter 9
- Know It Notes S1
- Lab Activities for Geography and Earth Science, Demonstrations 5, 6, 7

Technology
- One-Stop Planner CD–ROM, Lesson 9.1
- Homework Practice Online
- Geography and Cultures Visual Resources with Teaching Activities 32–36, 39
- HRW Go site

Reinforcement, Review, and Assessment
- Section 1 Review
- Daily Quiz 9.1
- Main Idea Activity S1
- Chapter Summaries and Review
- English Audio Summary 9.1
- Spanish Audio Summary 9

Read to Discover
1. What are the physical features of Central America and the Caribbean islands?
2. What climates are found in the region?
3. What natural resources does the region have?

Vocabulary
archipelago
cloud forest
bauxite

Places
Central America
Caribbean Sea
Cuba
Jamaica
Greater Antilles
Hispaniola
Puerto Rico
Lesser Antilles
Virgin Islands
Trinidad and Tobago
Bahamas

Reading Strategy

READING ORGANIZER Before you read, draw a large circle on a sheet of paper. Draw a line down the center of the circle and another line across it. Label the four parts Physical Features, Climate, Vegetation, and Resources. List the information you learn in each part.

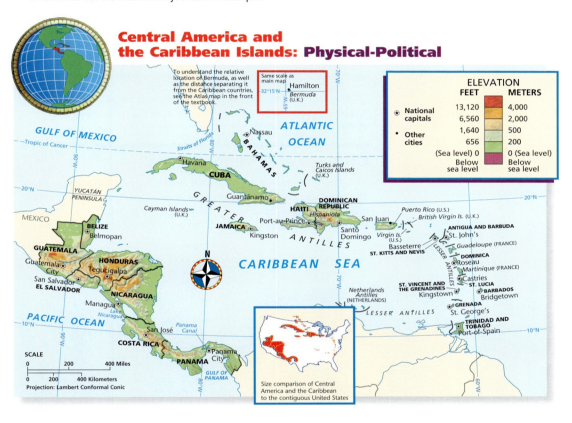

Central America and the Caribbean Islands • 205

Section 1

Objectives
1. Describe the physical features of Central America and the Caribbean islands.
2. Identify the climates found in the region.
3. Describe the region's natural resources.

Focus

Bellringer
Copy the following question and saying onto the chalkboard: *What do you think this ancient Maya saying suggests about the Maya's view of nature? "Who cuts the trees as he pleases cuts short his own life."* Allow students to write their responses. (possible answer: indicates they realized human life depends on the environment) Lead a discussion based on students' answers. You may want to compare the Maya belief to what students know about American Indians. Tell students that in Section 1 they will learn more about the region's environment.

Using the Physical-Political Map
Have students examine the map on this page. Discuss the meaning of *isthmus* (a narrow piece of land that connects two other land-masses like a bridge). Point out that Central America is an isthmus. Have students identify the region's main bodies of water and physical features. Point out that many goods pass through the Panama Canal, which plays a key economic role in the hemisphere.

Central America and the Caribbean Islands   **205**

CHAPTER 9, Section 1

PHYSICAL SYSTEMS

Big Volcano in a Small Place Montserrat, a small British territory in the Caribbean Sea, had just recovered from the devastating Hurricane Hugo of 1989 when its Soufrière Hills volcano erupted after lying dormant for hundreds of years. The eruption in 1997 set fire to the capital city. Rain mixed with volcanic ash created acid rain, damaging Montserrat's environmental systems.

Most of Montserrat is now considered a danger zone, and many residents have moved elsewhere. Decreased tourism and increased business closings have weakened its economy. On the positive side, however, farmers note that the ash has provided nutrients for its farmland.

Activity: Have students investigate the effect of volcanoes on Central America and the Caribbean islands. Ask them to prepare a line graph to show the dates of the events and the estimated costs of the damages they caused.

Visual Record Answer

humid, rainy

Physical Features

Central America and the Caribbean Sea are home to 20 countries and a number of island territories. Central America includes Guatemala, Belize, Honduras, El Salvador, Nicaragua, Costa Rica, and Panama. The Caribbean islands include Cuba, Jamaica, Haiti, and the Dominican Republic. There also are nine smaller island countries.

Central America forms a bridge between North and South America. No place on this isthmus is more than 125 miles (200 km) from the sea. Mountains separate the Caribbean and Pacific coastal plains.

The Caribbean islands form an **archipelago** (ahr-kuh-PE-luh-goh), or large group of islands. The Caribbean archipelago is arranged in a long curve. It stretches from south of Florida to South America.

There are two main island groups in the Caribbean archipelago. The four large islands of the Greater Antilles (an-TI-leez) are Cuba, Jamaica, Hispaniola, and Puerto Rico. The small islands of the Lesser Antilles stretch from the Virgin Islands to Trinidad and Tobago. Another island group, the Bahamas, lies outside the Caribbean, east of Florida. It includes nearly 700 islands and thousands of reefs.

Earthquakes and volcanic eruptions are frequent in this region. Colliding plates cause this tectonic activity. The Cocos plate collides with and dives under the Caribbean plate off Central America's western coast. Another plate boundary lies to the east. The Caribbean plate borders the North American plate there. Volcanic eruptions can cause great damage.

✓ **READING CHECK:** *Places and Regions* What are the physical features of Central America and the Caribbean islands? *Central America—land bridge, mountains, plains; Caribbean islands—archipelago*

Climate and Vegetation

Along the Caribbean coast of Central America are humid tropical plains. The area also has dense rain forests. Inland mountains rise into mild highland climates. Most of the people live there because the temperatures are more moderate. Much of the original savanna vegetation inland

Dominica, in the far southeast of the region, receives up to 250 inches (835 cm) of rain per year! In contrast, Miami, Florida, receives only about 56 inches (140 cm).

Forested mountains rise above Roseau, capital of the island country of Dominica. Dominica is in the Lesser Antilles.

Interpreting the Visual Record *Place*
What might the lush forest tell us about Dominica's climate?

TEACH

Teaching Objectives 1–3

LEVEL 1: (Suggested time: 20 min.) Copy the graphic organizer at right onto the chalkboard, omitting the blue answers. Call on students to provide words and phrases to describe the landforms, bodies of water, climates, and resources of the region. **ESOL**, **LS** VISUAL-SPATIAL

LEVELS 2 AND 3: Have students use the Level 1 activity as a basis for this activity. Ask them to write a diary entry for a Central American or a Caribbean islander who works as a volcanologist (scientist who studies volcanoes), forest ranger, hurricane tracker, or miner. Encourage students to use additional resources. **LS** VERBAL-LINGUISTIC

Physical Geography of Central America and the Caribbean Islands

Landforms	Bodies of Water
natural land bridge, archipelago, Greater Antilles, Lesser Antilles, Cocos plate, Caribbean plate	Caribbean Sea, Pacific Ocean, Lake Nicaragua, Atlantic Ocean, Gulf of Mexico
Climates	**Resources**
mild highland, humid tropical, tropical savanna	land for agriculture, timber, bauxite, copper

has been cleared. It has been replaced by plantations and ranches. The Pacific coast has a warm and sunny tropical savanna climate.

Some of Central America's mountain areas are covered by **cloud forest**. This is a high-elevation, very wet tropical forest where low clouds are common. It is home to numerous plant and animal species.

The islands of the Caribbean have pleasant humid tropical and tropical savanna climates. Winters are usually drier than summers. The islands receive 40 to 60 inches (102 to 152 cm) of rainfall each year. On some islands the bedrock is mostly limestone. Water drains quickly. As a result, drought conditions are common.

Hurricanes are a danger in the region. Hurricanes are tropical storms that bring violent winds, heavy rain, and high seas. Most occur between June and November. They can cause great destruction and loss of life.

✓ **READING CHECK:** *Environment and Society* What effect do hurricanes have on people in the region? They cause great destruction and loss of life.

Resources

Agriculture in the region can be profitable where volcanic ash has enriched the soil. Coffee, bananas, sugarcane, and cotton are major crops. Timber is exported from the rain forests of Belize and Honduras. Tourism is the most important industry, particularly in the Caribbean islands.

The region has few mineral resources. However, Jamaica has large reserves of **bauxite**, the most important aluminum ore. There are huge copper deposits in Panama. Energy resources are limited. This makes the region dependent on energy imports and limits economic development.

✓ **READING CHECK:** *Environment and Society* Why do you think tourism is the most important industry in the region? because of the region's beautiful beaches and waters

A hiker explores Costa Rica's cloud forest.

Section Review 1

Homework Practice Online Keyword: SJ5 HP9

Define and explain: archipelago, cloud forest, bauxite

Working with Sketch Maps On a map of the region that you draw or that your teacher provides, label the following: Central America, Caribbean Sea, Cuba, Jamaica, Greater Antilles, Puerto Rico, Hispaniola, Lesser Antilles, Virgin Islands, Trinidad and Tobago, and the Bahamas. Identify continents Central America links.

Reading for the Main Idea
1. *Places and Regions* What two major island groups make up the Caribbean archipelago?
2. *Places and Regions* In what climate region do most Central Americans live and why?
3. *Places and Regions* What are some of the region's crops?

Critical Thinking
4. **Making Generalizations and Predictions** What natural hazards do you think will continue to be a problem for the region? Why?

Organizing What You Know
5. **Categorizing** Copy the following graphic organizer. Use it to describe the climates, vegetation, and resources found in the region.

Climates	Vegetation	Resources

Central America and the Caribbean Islands • 207

Section 1 Review

Answers to Section 1 Review

Define For definitions, see the glossary.

Working with Sketch Maps Maps will vary, but listed places should be labeled in their approximate locations. North America and South America are linked by Central America.

Reading for the Main Idea
1. the Greater Antilles and the Lesser Antilles (NGS 4)
2. in the highland climates; because they are more moderate (NGS 4)
3. coffee, bananas, sugarcane, and cotton (NGS 4)

Critical Thinking
4. possible answers: hurricanes because of the region's climate and location; earthquakes and volcanic eruptions because of the region's continuing tectonic plate activity

Organizing What You Know
5. climates—humid tropical plains, mild highland, warm and sunny tropical savanna; vegetation—dense rain forests, plants ranging from oak trees to orchids; resources—bauxite, coffee, bananas, sugarcane, cotton, timber, and copper

---

CLOSE

Have students list as many products as they can that are made from aluminum, which comes from bauxite. (possible answers: soda cans, foil, house siding, pots, and pans)

REVIEW, ASSESS, RETEACH

Have students complete the Section Review. Then pair students. Ask each student to create a five-question crossword puzzle based on the section's main ideas. Have students exchange puzzles with their partners and solve them. Then have students complete Daily Quiz 9.1.
COOPERATIVE LEARNING, **LS** **VISUAL-SPATIAL**

Have students complete Main Idea Activity S1. Then have students create a chart with three columns labeled Physical Features, Climates, and Natural Resources. Have students write three facts in each column.
ESOL

EXTEND

Have interested students conduct research on how Panama's physical geography affected both the Panama Canal's design and the methods used to build it. Ask students to prepare diagrams of the construction process and the canal's lock system. Have students discuss any technological innovations used during construction. **BLOCK SCHEDULING**

CHAPTER 9, Section 2

SECTION 2 RESOURCES

Reproducible
- Lecture Notes, Section 2
- Know It Notes S2
- Graphic Organizer 9
- Cultures of the World Activity 2
- Interdisciplinary Activities for the Middle Grades 9, 11, 12

Technology
- One-Stop Planner CD–ROM, Lesson 9.2
- Homework Practice Online
- HRW Go site

Reinforcement, Review, and Assessment
- Section 2 Review
- Daily Quiz 9.2
- Main Idea Activity S2
- Chapter Summaries and Review
- English Audio Summary 9.2
- Spanish Audio Summary 9.2

Section 2 Central America

Read to Discover
1. What was Central America's early history like?
2. How is the region's history reflected in its people today?
3. What are the countries of Central America like today?

Vocabulary
cacao
dictators
cardamom
civil war
ecotourism

Places
Guatemala City
Lake Nicaragua
San José
Panama City
Panama Canal

Reading Strategy
MNEMONIC DEVICE Before you read, write the letters in the words **CENTRAL AMERICA** down the left side of a sheet of paper. As you read the section, write a fact you learn that begins with each letter.

▲ Maya ruins can be found here in Belize and in other parts of Central America and Mexico.

History

More than 39 million people live in the countries of Central America. These countries have a shared history.

Early History The early peoples of Central America developed different cultures and societies. The Maya, for example, built large cities with pyramids and temples. People of Maya descent still live in Guatemala and parts of Mexico. Many of their ancient customs and traditions still influence modern life.

In the early 1500s European countries began establishing colonies in the region. Most of Central America came under the control of Spain. In the 1600s the British established the colony of British Honduras, which is now Belize. The British also occupied the Caribbean coast of Nicaragua.

European colonists established large plantations. They grew crops like tobacco and sugarcane. They forced the Central American Indians to work on the plantations. Some Indians were sent to work in gold mines elsewhere in the Americas. In addition, many Africans were brought to the region as slaves.

208 • Chapter 9

Section 2

Objectives
1. Analyze the early history of Central America.
2. Describe how the region's history is reflected in its people.
3. Examine what the countries of Central America are like today.

FOCUS

 Bellringer
Copy the following instructions onto the chalkboard: *Work with a partner to write five facts about the region's physical geography.* Allow students to write their responses. Discuss students' answers. Then ask students to use their lists to predict some ways that Central America's physical geography might have affected the region's history and culture. (Possible answers: Climate and soil attracted settlers. Hurricanes contribute to poverty. Cloud forests are tourist attractions.) Tell students that in Section 2 they will learn more about Central America.

Building Vocabulary
Write the vocabulary terms cacao and cardamom on the chalkboard. Have volunteers read the definitions aloud. Ask students what the words have in common. (Both are related to food.) Explain that cacao is the tree on which cocoa beans grow and cardamom, native to India, has been used as a spice in Central America for many years. Ask students to speculate on how an Indian spice might have become widely used in Central America (through trade). Have students look up the definitions of dictators, civil war, and ecotourism.

208 Chapter 9

Independence Costa Rica, El Salvador, Guatemala, Honduras, and Nicaragua declared independence from Spain in 1821. They formed the United Provinces of Central America, but separated from each other in 1838–1839. Panama, once part of Colombia, became independent in 1903. The British left Nicaragua in the late 1800s. British Honduras gained independence as Belize in 1981.

✓ **READING CHECK:** (Human Systems) What role did Europeans play in the region's history? They colonized the region.

Culture

Central America's colonial history is reflected in its culture today. In what ways do you think this is true?

People, Languages, and Religion The region's largest ethnic group is mestizo. Mestizos are people of mixed European and Indian ancestry. People of African ancestry make up a significant minority. Various Indian peoples also live in the region.

Spanish is the official language in most countries. However, many people speak Indian languages. In the former British colony of Belize, English is the official language.

Many Central Americans practice religions brought to the region by Europeans. Most are Roman Catholics. Spanish missionaries converted many Indians to Catholicism. However, Indian religions have influenced Catholicism in the region. Protestant Christians are a large minority in some countries, particularly Belize.

Lake Nicaragua was probably once part of an ocean bay. It is a freshwater lake, but it also has some oceanic animal life. This animal life includes the Lake Nicaragua shark. It grows to a length of about 8 to 10 feet (2.4 to 3 m).

Guatemalans celebrate the Christian holiday *Semana Santa*, or Holy Week. The street is covered with colored sand and flowers.

CHAPTER 9, Section 2

National Geography Standard 13

Conflict and Cooperation in Central America The United Provinces of Central America was formed in 1823, shortly after the member countries had declared their independence from Mexico and two years since their break with Spain. Each country retained an independent government and constitution. The countries hoped that unification would give them more power to deal with larger countries and would strengthen the members' already similar cultures.

However, there was division within the union early in its history. Conservatives preferred keeping control in the hands of individual states and the Roman Catholic leadership. Liberals supported a strong central government with limited church involvement. Civil war erupted in 1826 and continued off and on through 1840, by which time the union had disbanded. As a result, Central America remained a collection of small, relatively weak countries.

TEACH

Teaching Objective 1

LEVEL 1: (Suggested time: 30 min.) In advance, prepare slips of paper—one for each student—with descriptions of different people who played a role in Central America's history. (examples: a Spanish colonist, a British colonist, a Central American Indian, or an African) Repeat roles if necessary. Ask each student to draw a slip of paper and to write a few sentences describing how the person he or she chose influenced the region's early history. To conclude, lead a discussion about important dates and events in Central America's early history. **ESOL,** **LS** INTERPERSONAL

LEVELS 2 AND 3: (Suggested time: 40 min.) Organize the class into groups. In advance, locate and duplicate brief articles—one article per group—about some aspect of the early history of Central America. Give members of each group copies of the same article. Give students time to read it. Then review the six essential elements of geography with students. Have them discuss among themselves how the information in their article illustrates one, some, or all of the elements. Then lead a class discussion about important dates and events in the region's early history. **COOPERATIVE LEARNING,** **LS** INTERPERSONAL

CHAPTER 9, Section 2

Linking Past to Present

Cacao Cacao trees are native to Central America. Chocolate is made from cacao. Spaniards brought chocolate to Europe after learning about its uses from the Aztec.

In the 1980s Costa Rica's cacao industry was destroyed by a fungus called *Monilia* pod rot. Today, scientists are reintroducing the cacao tree to Costa Rica. Instead of clear-cutting the forest to create farmland, researchers have selected specific areas to cut. Once cleared, the land is replanted with cacao trees.

This process has many benefits. Cacao is the perfect crop for small farmers. Employment has increased and insecticide use is down.

Activity: Have students conduct research on other foods known to the early peoples of Central America. Ask them to find out if or how those foods are still cultivated in the region.

Connecting to Math
Answers
1. religion, mathematics, and astronomy
2. They were partially based on religion.

Connecting to Math

Stone Maya calendar

MAYA CALENDAR

The Maya created one of the most advanced civilizations in the Americas. They built impressive cities of stone and invented a complex writing system. They also created calendars that allowed them to plan for the future.

The Maya based their calendar system on religion, mathematics, and astronomy. They believed that the days, months, and years were represented by different gods. Those gods had powers that helped determine the course of events. The Maya also understood the mathematical concepts of zero and numerical positioning. Numerical positioning is the idea that numbers can have different values depending on their position in a sequence, such as the 1 in 10 and 100. The Maya also calculated the length of the solar year. They predicted eclipses and lunar cycles.

Based on this knowledge, the Maya created two calendars. One was a religious calendar of 260 days. The other was a solar calendar of 365 days. These two calendars were used together to record historical events and to determine future actions. Using calendars, the Maya chose the best times to plant crops, hold festivals, and crown new rulers. They even believed that their calendars would help them predict the future.

Understanding What You Read
1. What were the foundations of the calendar system developed by the Maya?
2. How did the Maya's belief systems affect their use of calendars?

Food and Festivals Central America shares many traditional foods with Mexico and South America. These foods include corn and sweet potatoes. The region is also home to tomatoes, hot peppers, and **cacao** (kuh-kow). Cacao is a small tree on which cocoa beans grow.

As in other Catholic countries, each town and country celebrates special saints' feast days. Images of the saints are paraded through the streets. A community might sponsor a fair and have dancing or plays.

Government From time to time, Central American countries have been ruled by **dictators**. A dictator is a person who rules a country with complete authority. The opponents of dictators often are arrested or even killed. Such abuses are one reason for limiting the power of government. Today the region's countries have elected governments.

 READING CHECK: Human Systems Why should government powers be limited? *to prevent abuses of power*

210 • Chapter 9

Teaching Objective 2
LEVEL 1: (Suggested time: 10 min.) Copy the graphic organizer at right onto the chalkboard, omitting the blue answers. Use it to help students understand the region's culture. Ask students to copy the organizer into their notebooks and fill it in to show how the region's people, languages, religion, food, and festivals reflect its history. The first answer is filled in for them. **ESOL,** **LS** VISUAL-SPATIAL

LEVELS 2 AND 3: (Suggested time: 20 min.) Have students write a paragraph to support this thesis statement: "The European conquest of Central America has affected almost every aspect of life in the region." *(Students should include the effects on the Central American Indian population and the introduction of Roman Catholicism in their discussions.)* Call on volunteers to read their paragraphs to the class. **ESOL,** **LS** VERBAL-LINGUISTIC

Aspects of Central American Culture

Before European Conquest	After European Conquest
• Central American Indian peoples	• mestizos, people of African ancestry
• Indian languages	• Spanish and English languages
• Indian religions	• Christianity
• native food crops	• corn, sweet potatoes, hot peppers, tomatoes, and cacao
	• saints' feast days

210 Chapter 9

Central America Today

Now we will take a closer look at each of the countries of Central America today.

Guatemala Guatemala is the most populous country in Central America. More than 13 million people live there. Nearly half of the country's people are Central American Indians. Many speak Maya languages. A majority of Guatemala's population are mestizos.

Most Maya live in isolated villages in the country's highlands. Fighting between rebels and government forces has killed more than 100,000 Guatemalans since the 1960s. Guatemalans hope that recent peace agreements will end this conflict.

Coffee is Guatemala's most important crop. The country also is a major producer of **cardamom**, a spice used in Asian foods.

Belize Belize is located on the Caribbean coast of the Yucatán Peninsula. It has the smallest population in Central America. Only about 266,000 people live there. The country's Maya ruins, coral reefs, and coastal resorts attract many tourists.

Honduras Honduras is a country of rugged mountains. Most people live in mountain valleys and along the northern coast. Transportation is difficult in the rugged terrain. Only 15 percent of the land is suitable for growing crops. Fruit is an important export.

El Salvador El Salvador lies on the Pacific side of Central America. Volcanic ash has made the country's soils the most fertile in the region. Important crops include coffee and sugarcane.

Most Salvadorans live in poverty. A few powerful families own much of the best land. These conditions were a major reason behind a long **civil war** in the 1980s. A civil war is a conflict between two or more groups within a country. The war killed many Salvadorans and slowed economic progress. Salvadorans have been rebuilding their country since the war ended in 1992.

Nicaragua Nicaragua is the largest Central American country. It has coasts on both the Caribbean Sea and the Pacific Ocean. Lake Nicaragua, near the Pacific coast, is the largest lake in Central America.

Nicaragua also has been rebuilding since the end of a long civil war. Its civil war ended in 1990. Free elections that year ended the rule of the Sandinistas. The Sandinistas had overthrown a dictator in 1979. They then ruled Nicaragua without elections. Today, the country is a democracy with many political voices.

▲
A woman in the Guatemalan highlands weaves traditional fabrics.

CHAPTER 9, Section 2

EYE ON EARTH

An Underwater Wonderland Belize is a scuba diver's paradise. The clear Caribbean waters near Belize offer a splendid view of three feature called atolls. An atoll is a ring- or horseshoe-shaped formation of coral surrounded by open sea. Atolls enclose a shallow lagoon. The Belize atolls began forming some 70 million years ago. They are home to more than 60 species of stony coral and 200 species of colorful fish.

Most atolls lie in the Pacific and Indian Oceans. Only four atolls are in the Western Hemisphere. The Belize atolls, the barrier reef to their west, and the vegetation native to the atolls and reefs together constitute a rich and fragile ecosystem.

Activity: Have students conduct research on the atolls and create illustrations of the food chains of an atoll. Hold a class discussion on how these fragile environments could be protected.

Central America and the Caribbean Islands • 211

Teaching Objective 3
ALL LEVELS: (Suggested time: 30 min.) Tell students to imagine that they are tourists in Central America. Then have each student write a postcard to a family member or friend that describes pertinent features of two Central American countries. (See the Section Review answers on the following page for the correct features.) Ask volunteers to read their postcards to the class.
LS INTRAPERSONAL

▶**ASSIGNMENT:** Have each student select a Central American country. Ask students to conduct research on the chosen country's customs, such as those associated with clothing, food, celebrations, family life, or school. Encourage students to use props or other visual aids as they report on one of the customs to the class.

CLOSE

Remind students that in the 1800s several Central American countries formed the United Provinces of Central America. Ask the class to imagine that the same countries have decided to form the United States of Central America. Lead a discussion about how such a union could affect trade and political relationships with the United States of America.

Central America and the Caribbean Islands | **211**

Section 2 Review

Answers to Section 2 Review

Define For definitions, see the glossary.

Working with Sketch Maps Places should be labeled in their approximate locations.

Reading for the Main Idea
1. Spain and Great Britain (NGS 12)
2. holding parades, fairs, dances, and plays (NGS 10)

Critical Thinking
3. mix of peoples, languages, religions provides evidence of groups who settled there
4. stable democratic government and progress in reducing poverty

Organizing What You Know
5. Guatemala—largest population; Belize—smallest population; Honduras—mountainous; El Salvador—civil war ended in 1992; Nicaragua—largest; Costa Rica—democratic; Panama—Panama Canal

Chart Answer

Costa Rica, Panama; perhaps stability of Costa Rica's government and the Panama Canal

---

Central America

Country	Population/Growth Rate	Life Expectancy	Literacy Rate	Per Capita GDP
Belize	266,440 / 2.4%	65, male / 69, female	94%	$4,900
Costa Rica	3,896,092 / 1.6%	74, male / 79, female	96%	$8,500
El Salvador	6,470,379 / 1.8%	67, male / 74, female	80%	$4,700
Guatemala	13,909,384 / 2.6%	64, male / 66, female	70%	$3,700
Honduras	6,669,789 / 2.3%	65, male / 68, female	76%	$2,600
Nicaragua	5,128,517 / 2.0%	67, male / 71, female	67%	$2,500
Panama	2,960,784 / 1.3%	69, male / 74, female	92%	$6,000
United States	290,342,554 / 0.9%	74, male / 80, female	97%	$37,600

Source: Central Intelligence Agency, *The World Factbook 2003*

Interpreting the Chart Which two Central American countries have the highest per capita GDP? Why might this be?

Costa Rica Costa Rica has a long history of stable, democratic government. In the last half of the 1900s, the country remained at peace. During that time, many of its neighbors were torn by civil wars. Costa Rica has also made important progress in reducing poverty.

Costa Rica's capital, San José, is located in the central highlands. Many coffee farms are also located in the highlands. Coffee and bananas are important Costa Rican crops.

Many travelers are attracted to Costa Rica's rich tropical rain forests and national parks. **Ecotourism**—the practice of using an area's natural environment to attract tourists—is an important part of Central American and Caribbean economies.

Panama Panama lies between Costa Rica and Colombia. Most Panamanians live in areas near the Panama Canal. Canal fees and industries make the canal area the country's most prosperous region.

The Panama Canal links the Pacific Ocean to the Caribbean Sea and Atlantic Ocean. The United States finished the canal in 1914. The canal played an important role in U.S. economic and foreign policies. It also allowed the United States to control territory and extend its influence in the area. The United States controlled the canal until 1999. Then, as called for by a 1978 treaty, Panama took it over.

✓ **READING CHECK:** *The Uses of Geography* Why might Panama want control of the canal? The canal is an important corridor for trade; fees and industries near it help the surrounding area prosper.

go.hrw.com **Homework Practice Online** Keyword: SJ5 HP9

Define and explain: cacao, dictators, cardamom, civil war, ecotourism

Working with Sketch Maps On the map you created in Section 1, label the Central American countries, Guatemala City, Lake Nicaragua, San José, Panama City, and the Panama.

Reading for the Main Idea
1. (*Human Systems*) What two European powers had Central American colonies by the late 1600s?
2. (*Human Systems*) How do many Central American communities honor certain Roman Catholic saints?

Critical Thinking
3. **Finding the Main Idea** How do Central America's people, languages, and religions reflect the region's history?
4. **Contrasting** How has Costa Rica's history differed from that of its Central American neighbors?

Organizing What You Know
5. **Categorizing** Copy the following graphic organizer. Use it to write at least one important fact about each Central American country today. Add as many rows as needed to list all of the countries.

Guatemala	

212 • Chapter 9

REVIEW, ASSESS, RETEACH

Have students complete the Section Review. Then have each student make a flash card for each Central American country. Instruct students to write the country's name on one side and a descriptive statement about that country on the other. Have students use their flash cards to quiz each other. Then have students complete Daily Quiz 9.2.

Have students complete Main Idea Activity S2. Organize the class into seven groups, one for each Central American country, and give each group a large sheet of paper. Have students draw and label pictures to illustrate important facts about their assigned country. Discuss and display students' pictures. **ESOL, COOPERATIVE LEARNING,** LS **VISUAL-SPATIAL**

EXTEND

Have interested students read accounts by the early explorers, historians, and archaeologists who encountered the ancient ruins of Central America. Ask them to compare the early accounts with modern tourists' accounts of their visits and share their impressions with the class. **BLOCK SCHEDULING**

Section 3: The Caribbean Islands

Read to Discover
1. What was the Caribbean's history like?
2. How is the region's history reflected in its people today?
3. What are the countries of the Caribbean like today?

Vocabulary
Santería
calypso
reggae
merengue
guerrilla
refugees
cooperatives
plantains
commonwealth

Places
Havana
Port-au-Prince
Santo Domingo

Reading Strategy

READING ORGANIZER Before you read, draw a circle on a piece of paper. Write Caribbean Islands in the center. As you read, draw an arrow pointing toward the circle for each contribution to island culture made by people from around the world. Write these contributions on the arrows.

History

The Caribbean islands include 13 independent countries. All are former European colonies.

Early History Christopher Columbus first sailed into the Caribbean Sea for Spain in 1492. He thought he had reached the Indies, or the islands near India. He called the islands the West Indies and the people who lived there Indians. Spain established colonies there. Many Caribbean Indians died from disease or war.

In the 1600s and 1700s, the English, French, Dutch, and Danish also established Caribbean colonies. They built large plantations on the islands. Crops included sugarcane, tobacco, and cotton. Europeans brought Africans to work as slaves.

Independence A slave revolt won Haiti its independence from France in 1804. By the mid-1800s the Dominican Republic had also won independence. The United States took Cuba from Spain in the Spanish-American War in 1898. Cuba gained independence in 1902. Other Caribbean countries did not gain independence until the last half of the 1900s.

Tourists still visit Christophe's Citadel in Haiti. The fortress was built in the early 1800s after Haiti won independence from France.

✓ **READING CHECK:** *Human Systems* What was the early history of the Caribbean islands? *Christopher Columbus arrived in 1492; Spain, England, France, Holland, and Denmark established colonies there, built plantations, and brought enslaved Africans.*

CHAPTER 9, Section 3

SECTION 3 RESOURCES
Reproducible
- Lecture Notes, Section 3
- Know It Notes S3
- Map Activity 9
- Geography for Life Activity 9
- Biography Activity: Roberto Clemente

Technology
- One-Stop Planner CD–ROM, Lesson 9.3
- Music of the World Audio CD Program, Selection 4
- Homework Practice Online
- HRW Go site

Reinforcement, Review, and Assessment
- Section 3 Review
- Daily Quiz 9.3
- Main Idea Activity S3
- Chapter Summaries and Review
- English Audio Summary 9.3
- Spanish Audio Summary 9.3

Section 3

Objectives
1. Analyze the history of the Caribbean.
2. Discuss how the region's history is reflected in its people today.
3. Describe the Caribbean countries of today.

Focus

Bellringer

Copy the following instructions and questions onto the chalkboard: *Look at the photos in Section 3 of your textbook. Which of the places pictured would you like to visit? Why?* Have students write their answers. Discuss student responses. Ask students to keep what they have written at hand so they can compare their original impressions with what they learn. Tell students that in Section 3 they will learn more about the history and culture of the Caribbean islands.

Building Vocabulary

Write the vocabulary terms on the chalkboard. Invite students to suggest meanings of these words, encouraging them to use their knowledge of word parts to derive the meanings. For example, *refuge*, the base of refugees, means "a safe place." Thus, a refugee is someone who seeks a safe place. Call on students to suggest how *cooperate* and cooperatives may be connected and then to check their suggestions against the text. Tell students that guerrilla is related to the Spanish word for war, *guerra*. Have students find the remainder of the definitions in the chapter text.

CHAPTER 9, Section 3

Culture and Music
Caribbean

Traditions Calypso is a type of folk music originally sung by African slaves on the plantations of Trinidad. Forbidden to speak while they worked, the enslaved people conveyed messages to each other in song. Therefore, the words of a calypso song are at least as important as the tune. "Day-O," a calypso tune that became popular in the United States, warns banana pickers that the tarantula spider can lurk in a bunch of bananas. The worker also expresses his weariness in the song.

Discussion: For a sample of Caribbean music from a different tradition, play Selection 4 on the Music of the World Audio CD Program. Use the text and questions in the Teacher's Guide.

internet connect
GO TO: go.hrw.com
KEYWORD: SJ5 CH9
FOR: Web sites about Caribbean music

Chart Answer
Students might mention better standard of living and access to quality health care in some nations.

Caribbean Islands

Country	Population/ Growth Rate	Life Expectancy	Literacy Rate	Per Capita GDP
Antigua and Barbuda	67,897 0.6%	68, male 73, female	89%	$11,000
Bahamas	297,477 .93%	67, male 74, female	98%	$15,000
Barbados	277,264 0.5%	71, male 76, female	97%	$14,500
Cuba	11,263,429 0.4%	74, male 79, female	96%	$1,700
Dominica	69,655 -.98%	71, male 77, female	94%	$4,000
Dominican Republic	8,715,602 1.6%	71, male 76, female	82%	$5,700
Grenada	89,258 -0.06%	63, male 66, female	98%	$4,400
Haiti	7,527,817 1.4%	47, male 51, female	45%	$1,800
Jamaica	2,695,867 0.5%	74, male 78, female	85%	$3,700
St. Kitts and Nevis	38,763 0.13%	68, male 74, female	97%	$8,800
St. Lucia	162,157 1.25%	69, male 76, female	67%	$5,400
St. Vincent and the Grenadines	116,812 0.4%	71, male 74, female	96%	$2,900
Trinidad and Tobago	1,169,682 -0.51%	67, male 72, female	98%	$9,500
United States	290,342,554 0.9%	74, male 80, female	97%	$37,600

Source: Central Intelligence Agency, *The World Factbook 2003*

Interpreting the Chart Why might life expectancy be greater in some Caribbean island countries than in others?

Culture

Today, nearly every Caribbean island shows the signs of past colonialism and slavery. These signs can be seen in the region's culture.

People, Languages, and Religion

Most islanders are of African or European descent or are a mixture of the two. Much smaller numbers of Asians also live there. Chinese and other Asians came to work on the plantations after slavery ended in the region.

English, French, and mixtures of European and African languages are spoken on many islands. For example, Haitians speak French and Creole. Creole is a Haitian dialect of French. Spanish is spoken in Cuba, the Dominican Republic, Puerto Rico, and some small islands. Dutch is the main language on several territories of the Netherlands.

Another sign of the region's past are the religions practiced there. Protestant Christians are most numerous on islands that were British territories. Former French and Spanish territories have large numbers of Roman Catholics. On all the islands, some people practice a combination of Catholicism and traditional African religions. One of these religions is **Santería**. Santería began in Cuba and spread to nearby islands and parts of the United States. It has roots in West African religions and traditions.

Food, Festivals, and Music Caribbean cooking today relies on fresh fruits, vegetables, and fish or meat. Milk or preserved foods like cheese or pickled fish are seldom used. Cooking has been influenced by foods brought from Africa, Asia, and elsewhere. For example, the samosa—a spicy, deep-fried pastry—has its origins in India. Other popular foods include mangoes, rice, yams, and okra.

People on each Caribbean island celebrate a variety of holidays. One of the biggest and most widespread is Carnival. Carnival is a time of feasts and parties before the Christian season of Lent. It is celebrated with big parades and beautiful costumes.

The islands' musical styles are popular far beyond the Caribbean. Trinidad and Tobago is the home of steel-drum and **calypso** music. Jamaica is famous as the birthplace of **reggae** music. **Merengue** is the national music and dance of the Dominican Republic.

Caribbean musical styles have many fans in the United States. However, the United States has influenced Caribbean culture as well. For example, baseball has become a popular sport in the region. It is

---

TEACH

Teaching Objectives 1–2

ALL LEVELS: (Suggested time: 45 min.) Organize students into small groups. Have each group write a short poem to describe the early history of the Caribbean. Ask students to mention the various peoples, events, and dates that pertain to the region's history. (Students should mention Columbus sailing into the region in 1492; European colonization in the 1600s and 1700s; the enslavement of Africans; Haiti's independence from France in 1804; the U.S. seizure of Cuba in the Spanish-American War in 1898; Cuba's independence in 1902; other countries' independence in the late 1900s.) **COOPERATIVE LEARNING**

Teaching Objective 3

ALL LEVELS: (Suggested time: 25 min.) Organize the class into groups, one for each Caribbean island country. Give students 15 minutes to read the information about their islands. Then read aloud a fact about any of the Caribbean islands today. When group members think the fact is about their island, they are to raise their hands. Ask the class for a consensus on the correct answer, confirm the answer, and continue to the next fact. **COOPERATIVE LEARNING,** **LS KINESTHETIC**

particularly popular in the Dominican Republic and Cuba. A number of successful professional baseball players in the United States come from Caribbean countries.

✓ **READING CHECK:** *Human Systems* How do the cultures of the Caribbean islands reflect historical events?
They reflect the islands' colonial history and slavery.

The Caribbean Islands Today

Now we will look at the largest island countries. We also will examine the island territory of Puerto Rico.

Cuba Cuba is the largest and the most populous country in the Caribbean. It is about the size of Tennessee but has more than twice the population. It is located just 90 miles (145 km) south of Florida. Havana, the capital, is the country's largest and most important city.

Cuba has had a Communist government since Fidel Castro seized power in 1959. Cuba has supported Communist **guerrilla** movements trying to overthrow other governments. A guerrilla takes part in irregular warfare, such as raids.

Many Cubans who oppose Castro have become **refugees** in the United States. A refugee is someone who flees to another country, usually for economic or political reasons. Many Cuban refugees and their families have become U.S. citizens. Most live in Florida.

The U.S. government has banned trade with Cuba. It also has restricted travel by U.S. citizens to the island since the 1960s. For years Cuba received economic aid and energy supplies from the Soviet Union. The collapse of the Soviet Union in the early 1990s has hurt Cuba's economy.

Today, private businesses remain limited in Cuba. Most farmland is organized into **cooperatives** and government-owned sugarcane

▲ A girl joins the Carnival celebration in Trinidad and Tobago.

A worker cuts sugarcane in central Cuba. Sugarcane is Cuba's most important cash crop.
▼

CHAPTER 9, Section 3

DAILY LIFE

Carnival! Since the colonial era the inhabitants of the West Indies have celebrated Carnival. The holiday falls just before Lent, a holy time for Roman Catholics.

The celebration is rooted in pre-Christian European festivals that allowed general merrymaking and temporary equality for all social classes. In 1264 the pope declared it a Christian holiday. The idea of social equality during ancient festivals is echoed in Carnival. With everyone dressed in wild, colorful costumes, no one can tell rich from poor.

Carnival's blend of Catholic and pre-Christian characteristics typifies Caribbean culture's unique combination of European and pre-colonial traditions. Caribbean Carnivals include grand parades with music, floats, and parties for all.

internet connect
GO TO: go.hrw.com
KEYWORD: SJ5 CH9
FOR: Web sites about Carnival

▶**ASSIGNMENT:** Have students conduct research on a specific aspect of Caribbean culture, such as food, visual arts, literature, religion, or music. Have each student create an illustrated time line to show how the chosen cultural trait has changed through time. (example of time line title: Caribbean Music through the Ages) Have students present their time lines to the class.

Teaching Objectives 1–3

ALL LEVELS: (Suggested time: 20 min.) Copy the graphic organizer at right onto the chalkboard, omitting the blue answers. Use it to help students describe the Caribbean islands. Call on students to fill in the chart with basic facts. Then lead a discussion on the traits the island cultures have in common.

The Caribbean Islands

	History	Government and Economics	People and Culture
Cuba	• taken from Spain by the United States in 1898 • gained independence in 1902	• communist government • trade with United States restricted • farms organized into cooperatives • sugarcane, tourism	• most populous country in region • origin of Santería
Haiti	• won independence from France in 1804	• poorest country in Americas • many corrupt governments • coffee, sugarcane, plantains	• densely populated • many refugees in United States
Dominican Republic	• former Spanish colony	• more developed than Haiti • agriculture, tourism	• education, health care, and housing are improving
Puerto Rico	• former Spanish colony	• commonwealth of United States • most developed island in region	• debate over its future

Central America and the Caribbean Islands 215

CHAPTER 9, Section 3

FOOD FESTIVAL

A Mango Dessert *Postre de mangoes* is a delicious dessert from the Caribbean islands. It is easy to make.

Mangoes are available in most supermarkets. Place a pound of sliced mangoes, 15 ounces sweetened condensed milk, and the juice of a lemon in a blender and blend until smooth. Chill mixture in dessert dishes for two to three hours. Serve topped with fresh fruit and berries that have been marinated in orange juice. Sprinkle with pine nuts if desired. Note that this recipe serves six. Be prepared to increase proportions to serve your entire class.

Focus on Culture Answer
Possible answer: to remind themselves of home, or to have something familiar in an unfamiliar place.

---

plantations. A cooperative is an organization owned by its members and operated for their mutual benefit.

Sugarcane remains Cuba's most important crop and export. Tourism has also become an important part of the economy. There has been debate in the United States over ending the ban on trade and travel to Cuba.

Haiti Haiti occupies the mountainous western third of the island of Hispaniola. It is the poorest country in the Americas. It is also one of the most densely populated. Its people have suffered under many corrupt governments during the last two centuries. Many Haitian refugees have come to the United States to escape poverty and political violence.

Port-au-Prince (pohr-toh-PRINS) is the national capital and center of industry. Coffee and sugarcane are two of the country's most important crops. Most Haitians farm small plots. Many grow **plantains**. Plantains are a type of banana used in cooking.

Dominican Republic The Dominican Republic occupies the eastern part of Hispaniola. It is a former Spanish colony. The capital is Santo Domingo. Santo Domingo was the first permanent European settlement in the Western Hemisphere.

The Dominican Republic is not a rich country. However, its economy, education, health care, and housing are more developed than Haiti's. Agriculture and tourism are important parts of the Dominican Republic's economy.

FOCUS ON CULTURE

Ice Cream Houses of Curaçao

In the southeastern Caribbean is an island where the houses look like they could melt in the sun. They are painted in colors that you see in a candy store or an ice cream shop. These are the old Dutch houses of Curaçao in the Netherlands Antilles.

When Dutch settlers came to Curaçao in the 1600s they brought their architectural styles with them. They adapted the styles for the climate. For example, the settlers added porches to their plantation homes for shade from the tropical sun. Soon they were painting their houses in much brighter colors than they used in the Netherlands. This practice may have started because the local tradition of whitewashing houses produced too bright a reflection for European tastes. Today some of the old houses have been turned into hotels or shops. Others are still private homes.

Why would Dutch settlers use traditional architectural styles in a new environment?

216 • Chapter 9

TEACHER TO TEACHER

Frank Thomas of Austin, Texas, suggests this activity to introduce students to the foods and cultures of Central America and the Caribbean islands. Organize students into groups of three to five students. Provide each group with an unfamiliar fruit from the region. Examples include ugli fruit, kiwano, star fruit, plumcot, horned fruit, plantain, and mango. These fruits are available in many large supermarkets or ethnic markets, or may be ordered from suppliers. If possible, supply more than one piece of fruit per group. Do not divulge the fruits' names at this point. Ask the students to describe the exterior of the fruit in detail: texture, color, firmness, scent, and so on. Ask them to speculate what the fruits look like inside and what they taste like. Then cut open and slice the fruit. Ask students to describe the interior: texture, color, seeds or pits, juice, and taste. Ask students to create their own name for the fruit. Then reveal the fruits' names. Supply reference materials for each group. Ask them to research their fruit and report on how it is used in the region's cuisine. You may want students to create new recipes using the fruit, other ingredients from Central America and the Caribbean islands, and regional cooking techniques.

Puerto Rico Puerto Rico is the easternmost of the Greater Antilles. Once a Spanish colony, today it is a U.S. **commonwealth**. A commonwealth is a self-governing territory associated with another country. Puerto Ricans are U.S. citizens. However, they have no voting representation in the U.S. Congress.

Unemployment is higher and wages are lower in Puerto Rico than in the United States. Still, American aid and investment have helped make the economy of Puerto Rico more developed than those of other Caribbean islands. Puerto Ricans continue to debate whether their island should remain a commonwealth. Some want it to become an American state or an independent country.

Other Islands Jamaica, in the Greater Antilles, is the largest of the remaining Caribbean countries. The smallest country is St. Kitts and Nevis in the Lesser Antilles. The smallest U.S. state, Rhode Island, is nearly 12 times larger! For more about other Caribbean countries and the Bahamas, see this unit's Fast Facts chart.

A number of Caribbean and nearby islands are territories of other countries. These territories include the U.S. and British Virgin Islands. The Netherlands and France also have Caribbean territories. Bermuda, an Atlantic island northwest of the Caribbean, is a British territory.

✓ **READING CHECK:** (Human Systems) How are Puerto Rican citizens' political rights different from those of other U.S. citizens? They have no vote in Congress.

Ocho Rios, Jamaica, and other beautiful Caribbean resorts and beaches attract many tourists.

Define and explain: Santería, calypso, reggae, merengue, guerrilla, refugees, cooperatives, plantains, commonwealth

Working with Sketch Maps On the map you created in Section 2, label the Caribbean countries, Havana, Port-au-Prince, and Santo Domingo.

Reading for the Main Idea

1. (Human Systems) When did European powers establish colonies in the Caribbean islands?
2. (Human Systems) What ethnic groups make up the region's population today?

Homework Practice Online
Keyword: SJ5 HP9

3. (Human Systems) Why have Cubans and Haitians come to the United States as refugees?

Critical Thinking

4. **Comparing/Contrasting** What do the histories of Caribbean countries have in common with the history of the United States? How are they different?

Organizing What You Know

5. **Sequencing** Copy the following graphic organizer. Use it to show important events and periods in the history of the Caribbean islands since 1492.

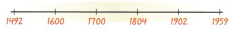

Section 3 Review

Answers to Section 3 Review

Define For definitions, see the glossary.

Working with Sketch Maps Havana, Port-au-Prince, and Santo Domingo should be located accurately.

Reading for the Main Idea

1. in 1492 and continuing into the 1600s and 1700s (NGS 12)
2. Most of the population is of African and/or European descent. (NGS 10)
3. relief from corrupt politics and unstable economies (NGS 13)

Critical Thinking

4. colonization, revolution, civil war, and eventual freedom; the remnants of colonialism still present a problem in modern-day life in many of these nations

Organizing What You Know

5. 1492—Columbus sails into Caribbean Sea; 1600–1700—Europeans establish Caribbean colonies; 1804—Haiti wins independence; 1902—Cuba gains independence; 1959—Castro seizes power in Cuba

Central America and the Caribbean Islands • 217

CLOSE

Have students read the Focus on Culture feature. Ask what elements of their own culture they would want to take with them if they moved to another country.

REVIEW, ASSESS, RETEACH

Have students complete the Section Review. Ask each student to create three multiple-choice questions, with answers, covering the information presented in this section. Have students trade and check each other's quizzes. Then have students complete Daily Quiz 9.3.

Have students complete Main Idea Activity S3. Assign each student one country in the Caribbean islands, and have students produce a brief news report about the country's history, culture, or current conditions. **ESOL**

EXTEND

Have interested students research the history of the Taino, a people who inhabited Puerto Rico before the Spanish conquest. You may want to have other students investigate Puerto Rican culture in major U.S. cities or the issue of Puerto Rican statehood. Have students present their findings to the class. **BLOCK SCHEDULING**

CHAPTER 9 REVIEW

Define and Identify
For definitions, see the glossary.

Review the Main Ideas
16. Greater Antilles and Lesser Antilles (NGS 4)
17. earthquakes, volcanoes, hurricanes (NGS 7)
18. the Maya
19. colonial control, migration, plantation-based economies, slavery, ethnic diversity, cultural blending (NGS 12)
20. Most Salvadorans live in poverty, while a few powerful families own much of the best land.
21. Guatemala; Cuba (NGS 4)
22. calypso, reggae, and merengue; won fans and spread around the world (NGS10)
23. It is communist. (NGS 13)
24. U.S. citizens, but have no voting representation in Congress

Think Critically
25. resulted in diverse mixture of European, African, and Indian peoples
26. changed from rule by dictator to elected governments
27. seeking relief from corrupt government and unstable economies
28. coffee, sugarcane, fruit; good soil, economic dependence on farming
29. earthquakes, volcanoes, and hurricanes; by moving to safer locations and/or by adjusting their lives and activities

Map Activity
30. **A.** Havana
    B. Puerto Rico
    C. Bahamas
    D. Nicaragua
    E. Haiti
    F. Jamaica
    G. Panama
    H. Guatemala
    I. Dominican Republic
    J. Cuba

218 Chapter 9

CHAPTER 9 Review and Practice

Define and Identify
Identify each of the following:
1. archipelago
2. cloud forest
3. bauxite
4. cacao
5. dictators
6. cardamom
7. civil war
8. ecotourism
9. Santería
10. calypso
11. guerrilla
12. refugees
13. cooperatives
14. plantains
15. commonwealth

Review the Main Ideas
16. What two main island groups make up the Caribbean archipelago?
17. What natural hazards often threaten Central America and the Caribbean islands?
18. Which culture dominated Central America before the Spaniards arrived?
19. How did European influence affect Central America and the Caribbean islands?
20. What was a major reason for the civil war in El Salvador during the 1980s?
21. Which is the most populous country in Central America? in the Caribbean?
22. What are some musical styles with origins in the Caribbean? What influence have they had abroad?
23. How is Cuba's government organized?
24. What is the relationship of Puerto Ricans to the United States government?

Think Critically
25. **Drawing Inferences and Conclusions** How did slavery affect the ethnic diversity of the region?
26. **Comparing** How have the governments of the Central American countries changed over time?
27. **Finding the Main Idea** Why have refugees from Cuba and Haiti come to the United States?
28. **Summarizing** What agricultural products are grown in many Central American and Caribbean countries? Why?
29. **Analyzing Information** What are some of the natural and environmental hazards in Central America and the Caribbean islands? How do you think people may have coped with these hazards?

Map Activity
30. On a separate sheet of paper, match the letters on the map with their correct labels.

   Guatemala   Haiti
   Nicaragua   Dominican Republic
   Panama   Puerto Rico
   Cuba   Bahamas
   Jamaica   Havana

CHAPTER 9 REVIEW

Writing Activity

Imagine that you have been asked to write a paragraph for a travel brochure about Central America and the Caribbean. Your paragraph should include information that tourists would want to know. This includes general information about the region's climates, vegetation, food, festivals, and other special celebrations. Be sure to use standard grammar, sentence structure, spelling, and punctuation.

internet connect

Internet Activity: go.hrw.com
KEYWORD: SJ5 GT9

Choose a topic to explore about Central America and the Caribbean islands:
- Plan an ecotour of Central America.
- Learn more about the Panama Canal.
- Hunt for hurricanes.

Social Studies Skills Practice

Interpreting Charts
Study the following chart and then answer the questions.

Population Densities of Selected Caribbean Islands

Country	Population Density (people per square mile)	Ranking among World Countries
Barbados	1,602	14
Cuba	261	92
Dominican Republic	433	60
Grenada	759	36
Haiti	644	47
Jamaica	617	50
Puerto Rico	1,106	21

1. Which country listed above has the highest population density? the lowest?
2. Which countries have densities above 1,000 people per square mile?
3. What does the chart tell you about the reasons for high population densities?
4. How do you think high population densities may affect economies? environments?

Analyzing Primary Sources

Read the quote by Henry K. Carroll, who in 1899 saw the damage caused by a hurricane in Puerto Rico. Then answer the questions.

"The gale tore up the trees, loosened the soil and the deluge of water converted the earth into a semifluid. Then followed the landslides, and thousands of acres of coffee plantations slid down into the valley . . . In such cases there is no restoration possible, for where there were smiling groves are now only bald rocks which were uncovered by the avalanche. Where the soil was not disturbed the most of the coffee trees were either uprooted, broken off, or stripped of foliage and the immature berries."

1. Based on this quote, what does the word *semifluid* mean?
2. How did the gale, or hurricane, indirectly cause the landslides?
3. Why would rebuilding many of the coffee plantations be impossible?
4. How do you think the hurricane affected Puerto Rico's economy?

Writing Activity

Answers will vary, but the information included should be consistent with text materials. Check to see that students have included accurate information about the region's climates, vegetation, food, and festivals. Use Rubric 40, Writing to Describe, to evaluate student work.

Interpreting Charts

1. Barbados; Cuba
2. Barbados, Puerto Rico
3. That information is not included on the chart.
4. may put strain on a weak economy or provide employees and consumers in a strong one; may eventually damage environments

Analyzing Primary Sources

1. like a liquid
2. loosened the soil
3. because the soil was removed completely, leaving only rock
4. probably hurt the economy, at least temporarily

CHAPTER 9 — REVIEW AND ASSESSMENT RESOURCES

Reproducible
- Readings in World Geography, History, and Culture 17, 18, and 19
- Critical Thinking Activity 9
- Vocabulary Activity 9

Technology
- Chapter 9 Test Generator (on the One-Stop Planner)
- Audio CD Program, Chapter 9
- HRW Go site

Reinforcement, Review, and Assessment
- Chapter 9 Review and Practice
- Chapter Summaries and Review
- Chapter 9 Test
- Chapter 9 Test for English Language Learners and Special-Needs Students

internet connect
GO TO: go.hrw.com
KEYWORD: SJ5 Teacher
FOR: a guide to using the Internet in your classroom

Caribbean South America
Chapter Resource Manager

Objectives	Pacing Guide	Reproducible Resources
SECTION 1 **Physical Geography** (pp. 221–23) 1. Identify the major landforms and rivers of Caribbean South America. 2. Identify the climate and vegetation types found in the region. 3. Identify the natural resources of this region.	**Regular** .5 day Lecture Notes, Section 1 **Block Scheduling** .5 day Block Scheduling Handbook, Chapter 10	**RS** Know It Notes S1 **RS** Graphic Organizer 10 **SM** Map Activity 10 **ELL** Main Idea Activity S1
SECTION 2 **Colombia** (pp. 224–27) 1. Identify the main periods of Colombia's history. 2. Describe what Colombia is like today.	**Regular** .5 day Lecture Notes, Section 2 **Block Scheduling** .5 day Block Scheduling Handbook, Chapter 10	**RS** Know It Notes S2 **E** Cultures of the World Activity 2 **E** Biography Activity: Gabriel Garcia Marquez **ELL** Main Idea Activity S2
SECTION 3 **Venezuela** (pp. 228–30) 1. Describe how the Spanish contributed to Venezuela's history. 2. Identify some characteristics of Venezuela's culture.	**Regular** .5 day Lecture Notes, Section 3 **Block Scheduling** .5 day Block Scheduling Handbook, Chapter 10	**RS** Know It Notes S3 **E** Cultures of the World Activity 2 **SM** Geography for Life Activity 10 **ELL** Main Idea Activity S3
SECTION 4 **The Guianas** (pp. 231–33) 1. Identify the countries that influenced the early history of the Guianas. 2. Describe how Guyana, Suriname, and French Guiana are similar today.	**Regular** .5 day Lecture Notes, Section 4 **Block Scheduling** .5 day Block Scheduling Handbook, Chapter 10	**RS** Know It Notes S4 **E** Cultures of the World Activity 2 **ELL** Main Idea Activity S4

Chapter Resource Key

- **RS** Reading Support
- **IC** Interdisciplinary Connections
- **E** Enrichment
- **SM** Skills Mastery
- **A** Assessment
- **REV** Review
- **ELL** Reinforcement and English Language Learners and English for Speakers of Other Languages (ESOL)
- 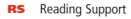 Transparencies
- CD–ROM
- Music
- Video
- Internet
- Holt Presentation Maker Using Microsoft® PowerPoint®

 One-Stop Planner CD–ROM

See the *One-Stop Planner* for a complete list of additional resources for students and teachers.

One-Stop Planner CD–ROM

It's easy to plan lessons, select resources, and print out materials for your students when you use the *One-Stop Planner CD–ROM with Test Generator*.

Technology Resources

- One-Stop Planner CD–ROM, Lesson 10.1
- Geography and Cultures Visual Resources with Teaching Activities 18–22
- Earth: Forces and Formations CD–ROM/Seek and Tell/Forces and Processes
- *ARGWorld* CD–ROM
- Homework Practice Online
- HRW Go site

- One-Stop Planner CD–ROM, Lesson 10.2
- *ARGWorld* CD–ROM
- Homework Practice Online
- HRW Go site

- One-Stop Planner CD–ROM, Lesson 10.3
- *ARGWorld* CD–ROM
- Homework Practice Online
- HRW Go site

- One-Stop Planner CD–ROM, Lesson 10.4
- *ARGWorld* CD–ROM
- Homework Practice Online
- HRW Go site

Review, Reinforcement, and Assessment Resources

ELL	Main Idea Activity S1
REV	Section 1 Review
A	Daily Quiz 10.1
REV	Chapter Summaries and Review
ELL	English Audio Summary 10.1
ELL	Spanish Audio Summary 10.1
ELL	Main Idea Activity S2
REV	Section 2 Review
A	Daily Quiz 10.2
REV	Chapter Summaries and Review
ELL	English Audio Summary 10.2
ELL	Spanish Audio Summary 10.2
ELL	Main Idea Activity S3
REV	Section 3 Review
A	Daily Quiz 10.3
REV	Chapter Summaries and Review
ELL	English Audio Summary 10.3
ELL	Spanish Audio Summary 10.3
ELL	Main Idea Activity S4
REV	Section 4 Review
A	Daily Quiz 10.4
REV	Chapter Summaries and Review
ELL	English Audio Summary 10.4
ELL	Spanish Audio Summary 10.4

internet connect

HRW ONLINE RESOURCES

GO TO: go.hrw.com
Then type in a keyword.

TEACHER HOME PAGE
KEYWORD: SJ5 TEACHER

CHAPTER INTERNET ACTIVITIES
KEYWORD: SJ5 GT10

Choose an activity to:
- trek through the Guiana Highlands.
- search for the treasures of El Dorado.
- ride with the llaneros of Venezuela.

CHAPTER ENRICHMENT LINKS
KEYWORD: SJ5 CH10

CHAPTER MAPS
KEYWORD: SJ5 MAPS10

ONLINE ASSESSMENT
Homework Practice
  KEYWORD: SJ5 HP10
Standardized Test Prep Online
  KEYWORD: SJ5 STP10
Rubrics
  KEYWORD: SS Rubrics

COUNTRY INFORMATION
KEYWORD: SJ5 Almanac

CONTENT UPDATES
KEYWORD: SS Content Updates

HOLT PRESENTATION MAKER
KEYWORD: SJ5 PPT10

ONLINE READING SUPPORT
KEYWORD: SS Strategies

CURRENT EVENTS
KEYWORD: S5 Current Events

Meeting Individual Needs

Ability Levels

Level 1 Basic-level activities designed for all students encountering new material

Level 2 Intermediate-level activities designed for average students

Level 3 Challenging activities designed for honors and gifted-and-talented students

ESOL Activities that address the needs of students with Limited English Proficiency

Chapter Review and Assessment

E	Creative Strategies for Teaching World Geography, Lesson 9
IC	Interdisciplinary Activity for the Middle Grades 12
E	Readings in World Geography, History, and Culture 20 and 21
SM	Critical Thinking Activity 10
REV	Chapter 10 Review and Practice
REV	Chapter Summaries and Review
ELL	Vocabulary Activity 10
A	Chapter 10 Test
	Chapter 10 Test Generator (on the One-Stop Planner)
	Audio CD Program, Chapter 10
A	Chapter 10 Test for English Language Learners and Special-Needs Students
	HRW Go site

CHAPTER 10
Caribbean South America
Previewing Chapter Resources

Holt Online Learning

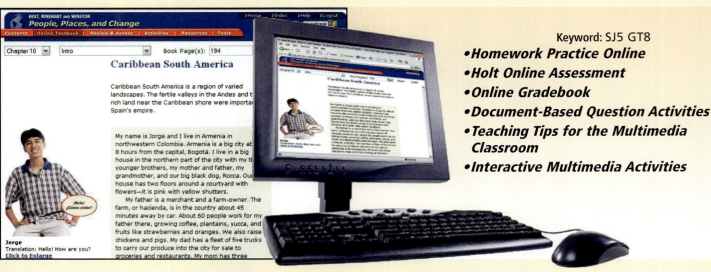

Keyword: SJ5 GT8
- *Homework Practice Online*
- *Holt Online Assessment*
- *Online Gradebook*
- *Document-Based Question Activities*
- *Teaching Tips for the Multimedia Classroom*
- *Interactive Multimedia Activities*

Differentiating Instruction

Reading and Writing Support
- ◀ Graphic Organizer Activity
- Vocabulary Activity
- Chapter Summary and Review
- Know It Notes
- Audio CD

Active Learning
- Block Scheduling Handbook
- Cultures of the World Activity
- Interdisciplinary Activity
- Map Activity
- ◀ Critical Thinking Activity: Spanish Towns in the Americas

Primary Sources and Advanced Learners
- Geography for Life Activity: Regional Images of the Venezuelan Andes
- ◀ Map Activity: Major Rivers
- Readings in World Geography, History and Culture:
  - 20 A Family in Rural Colombia
  - 21 The Fierce People of Venezuela

Assessment Program
- ◀ Daily Quizzes S1–4
- Chapter Test
- Chapter Test for English Language Learners and Special-Needs Students

Spanish and ESOL
- Vocabulary Activity
- ◀ Main Idea Activities for English Language Learners and Special-Needs Students
- Chapter Summary and Review
- Spanish Audio Summary
- Know It Notes S1–4
- Chapter Test for English Language Learners and Special-Needs Students

Special Education Modifications
Your I.D.E.A. Works! CD-ROM will provide modified versions of the following teaching materials:
- ◀ Guided Reading Strategies S1–4
- Vocabulary Activity
- Main Idea Activities S1–4
- Daily Quizzes S1–4
- Chapter 10 Test
- Flash cards of chapter vocabulary terms

Teacher Resources

Books for Teachers

Ouboter, Paul E., ed. *The Freshwater Ecosystems of Suriname.* Kluwer Academic Publishers, 1993.

Rausch, Jane M. *Colombia: Territorial Rule and the Llanos Frontier.* University Press of Florida, 1999.

Rudolph, Donna Keyse, and G. A. Rudolph. *Historical Dictionary of Venezuela.* Scarecrow Press, 1996.

Weisman, Alan. *Gaviotas: A Village to Reinvent the World.* Chelsea Green Publishing Company, 1998.

Books for Students

Collier, Simon, et al., eds. *The Cambridge Encyclopedia of Latin America and the Caribbean.* Cambridge University Press, 1992. Essays on the geography, history, politics, culture, and society of Latin America. Maps and charts included.

Horenstein, Henry. *Baseball in the Barrios.* Gulliver Books, 1997. Nine-year-old Hubaldo's photographic tour of baseball as played in Venezuela. Also available as *Béisbol en los Barrios.*
SHELTERED ENGLISH

Morrison, Marion. *Colombia.* Enchantment of the World. Children's Press, 1999. Maps, photos, charts, and fast-facts display Colombia's geography, history, and culture.

Multimedia Materials

The Andes. Video, 27 min. Films for the Humanities and Sciences.

Let's Visit South America. CD–ROM with Labpack. Educational Software Institute.

Suriname: A Country in Search of Its Identity. Video, 26 min. Lucerne Media.

Videos and CDs

Videos
- *CNN Presents Geography: Yesterday and Today,* Segment 11 The Power of Poetry
- *CNN Presents World Cultures: Yesterday and Today,* Segment 15 Worlds Meet in the Americas
- *ARG World*

Transparency Packages

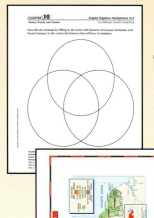

Graphic Organizer Transparencies 10.1–4

Geography and Cultures Visual Resources Transparencies 32–36
40 Caribbean South America: Physical-Political

Holt Researcher
http://researcher.hrw.com
- *Organization of American States (OAS)*
- *Colombia*
- *Venezuela*
- *Guyana*
- *Suriname*
- *Urban Population of Latin America*
- *Latin American Economic Growth*
- *Latin American Foreign Debts*
- *Latin American Governments*
- *Empires in the Americas*

Map Activities Transparency 10 Major Rivers of Caribbean South America

CHAPTER 10

Why It Matters

You might point out to the students these reasons why we should know more about Caribbean South America:

- Caribbean South America has tropical rain forests. These rain forests support many species of plants and animals as well as human inhabitants. Destruction of rain forests threatens plant, animal, and human life and could contribute to global warming.
- Gas prices in the United States are affected by the supply of foreign oil. Because Venezuela is one of the leading suppliers of oil to the United States, developments in the Venezuelan economy could affect the U.S. economy.
- Caribbean Latin America has rich and diverse cultural traditions that may interest people in the United States.

CHAPTER 10

Caribbean South America

Caribbean South America is a region of varied landscapes. The fertile valleys in the Andes and the rich land near the Caribbean shore were important to Spain's empire.

My name is Jorge and I live in Armenia in northwestern Colombia. Armenia is a big city about 8 hours from the capital, Bogotá. I live in a big house in the northern part of the city with my three younger brothers, my mother and father, my grandmother, and our big black dog, Rocca. Our house has two floors around a courtyard with flowers—it is pink with yellow shutters.

My father is a merchant and a farm-owner. The farm, or hacienda, is in the country about 45 minutes away by car. About 60 people work for my father there, growing coffee, plantains, yucca, and fruits like strawberries and oranges. We also raise chickens and pigs. My dad has a fleet of five trucks to carry our produce into the city for sale to groceries and restaurants. My mom has three people to help with the cooking at the farm.

¡Hola! ¿Cómo estás?

Translation: Hello! How are you?

Chapter Project

Have students conduct research on the flowers of Caribbean South America. Then have them re-create selected species with colored tissue paper, pipe cleaners, and markers. Attach a botanical label to the stem of each flower and decorate the classroom with them. Photograph the flowers for inclusion in student portfolios.

Starting the Chapter

Tell students that they are about to study a region with unique landforms, cultures, and animals. One of the area's odd animals is the capybara, the world's largest rodent. This creature can grow to be 4 feet long and weigh more than 100 pounds. What the turkey is to Thanksgiving in the United States the capybara is to Easter feasts in Venezuela. Some local people consider the capybara a fish because it's an excellent swimmer and spends much of its time in the water. This belief allows people in Venezuela to eat capybaras during Lent, a time when many Roman Catholics don't eat meat. Point out that this is just one of many interesting facts about Caribbean South America, the subject of this chapter.

Section 1: Physical Geography

CHAPTER 10, Section 1

Read to Discover
1. What are the major landforms and rivers of Caribbean South America?
2. What climate and vegetation types are found in the region?
3. What are the natural resources of this region?

Vocabulary
cordillera
tepuís
Llanos

Places
Andes
Guiana Highlands
Orinoco River

Reading Strategy

READING ORGANIZER As you read, create a concept map on a sheet of paper by using the headings in the section. List details you learn that support each heading.

Caribbean South America: Physical-Political

Section 1 Resources

Reproducible
- Lecture Notes, Section 1
- Block Scheduling Handbook, Chapter 10
- Know It Notes S1
- Graphic Organizer 10
- Map Activity 10

Technology
- One-Stop Planner CD-ROM, Lesson 10.1
- Homework Practice Online
- Geography and Cultures Visual Resources with Teaching Activities 32–36, 40
- Earth: Forces and Formations CD-ROM/Seek and Tell/Forces and Processes
- HRW Go site

Reinforcement, Review, and Assessment
- Section 1 Review
- Daily Quiz 10.1
- Main Idea Activity S1
- Chapter Summaries and Review
- English Audio Summary 10.1
- Spanish Audio Summary 10.1

Caribbean South America • 221

Section 1

Objectives
1. Identify and describe the major landforms and rivers of Caribbean South America.
2. Describe the climate and vegetation types found in the region.
3. List the natural resources of the region.

Focus

Bellringer

Copy the following instructions onto the chalkboard: *Study the map of Caribbean South America. Find a geographic characteristic that Caribbean South America shares with the United States.* Ask volunteers to share their answers with the class. (Students might mention that in addition to rivers and mountains, Caribbean South America stretches from the Atlantic Ocean to the Pacific Ocean.) Tell students that in Section 1 they will learn more about the physical geography of the region.

Using the Physical-Political Map

Ask students to examine the map on this page and name the landforms and rivers of Caribbean South America. Point out that the Andes in Colombia separate into three parallel ranges, or cordilleras, like the frayed end of a rope. Have students predict which parts of Caribbean South America are the most heavily populated and the most agriculturally productive.

Caribbean South America 221

Section 1 Physical Geography

CHAPTER 10, Section 1

Read to Discover
1. What are the major landforms and rivers of Caribbean South America?
2. What climate and vegetation types are found in the region?
3. What are the natural resources of this region?

Vocabulary
cordillera
tepuís
Llanos

Places
Andes
Guiana Highlands
Orinoco River

Reading Strategy
READING ORGANIZER As you read, create a concept map on a sheet of paper by using the headings in the section. List details you learn that support each heading.

SECTION 1 RESOURCES

Reproducible
- Lecture Notes, Section 1
- Block Scheduling Handbook, Chapter 10
- Know It Notes S1
- Graphic Organizer 10
- Map Activity 10

Technology
- One-Stop Planner CD–ROM, Lesson 10.1
- Homework Practice Online
- Geography and Cultures Visual Resources with Teaching Activities 32–36, 40
- Earth: Forces and Formations CD–ROM/Seek and Tell/Forces and Processes
- HRW Go site

Reinforcement, Review, and Assessment
- Section 1 Review
- Daily Quiz 10.1
- Main Idea Activity S1
- Chapter Summaries and Review
- English Audio Summary 10.1
- Spanish Audio Summary 10.1

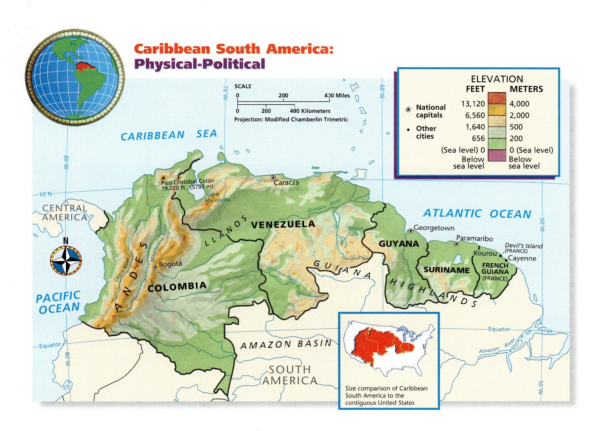

Caribbean South America • 221

Section 1

Objectives
1. Identify and describe the major landforms and rivers of Caribbean South America.
2. Describe the climate and vegetation types found in the region.
3. List the natural resources of the region.

Focus

 Bellringer
Copy the following instructions onto the chalkboard: *Study the map of Caribbean South America. Find a geographic characteristic that Caribbean South America shares with the United States.* Ask volunteers to share their answers with the class. (Students might mention that in addition to rivers and mountains, Caribbean South America stretches from the Atlantic Ocean to the Pacific Ocean.) Tell students that in Section 1 they will learn more about the physical geography of the region.

Using the Physical-Political Map
Ask students to examine the map on this page and name the landforms and rivers of Caribbean South America. Point out that the Andes in Colombia separate into three parallel ranges, or cordilleras, like the frayed end of a rope. Have students predict which parts of Caribbean South America are the most heavily populated and the most agriculturally productive.

Caribbean South America 221

CHAPTER 10, Section 1

PLACES AND REGIONS

Real Lost Worlds There are more than 100 *tepuís* in Venezuela, many of them unexplored. Years of isolation have resulted in the development of unique plant and animal life on the summits of these formations. One such plant is an orchid whose blossoms are no bigger than a pinhead.

Tepuís provide a standard by which to judge the effect that humans' activities have had on the environment. For example, of the plants found in the British Isles, 30 percent are nonnative, having been introduced accidentally or deliberately. In contrast, 100 percent of the species on the summits of the *tepuís* are native.

Critical Thinking: Why may we expect nonnative plants to be introduced to the *tepuís* at some point?

Answer: Students might suggest that as more people explore the *tepuís*, someone will accidentally introduce a nonnative species.

Visual Record Answer

tierra caliente, tierra templada, tierra fría and paramo

internet connect
GO TO: go.hrw.com
KEYWORD: SJ5 CH10
FOR: Web sites about Caribbean South America

Environments in the Andes change with elevation. Five different elevation zones are commonly recognized.

Interpreting the Visual Record
Region In which elevation zones can farmers grow crops?

Physical Features

A rugged landscape and dense forests have often separated peoples and cultures in this region. In the west, the Andes (AN-deez) rise above 18,000 feet (5,486 m). Here the mountain range forms a three-pronged **cordillera** (kawr-duhl-YER-uh). A cordillera is a mountain system made up of parallel ranges. Many active volcanoes and earthquakes shake these mountains.

In the east the Guiana Highlands have been eroding for millions of years. However, some of the steep-sided plateaus are capped by sandstone layers that have resisted erosion. These unusual formations are called **tepuís** (tay-PWEEZ). They can reach approximately 3,000 to 6,000 feet (914 to 1,829 m) above the surrounding plains.

Between these two upland areas are the vast plains of the Orinoco (OHR-ee-NOH-koh) River basin. These plains are the **Llanos** (YAH-nohs) of eastern Colombia and western Venezuela. The northeastern edge of the Guiana Highlands slopes down to a fertile coastal plain in Guyana, Suriname, and French Guiana.

Of the region's many rivers, the Orinoco is the longest. It flows for about 1,281 miles (2,061 km) through the region on its way to the Atlantic Ocean. Large oceangoing ships can travel upriver on the Orinoco for about 225 miles (362 km).

Some remarkable animals live in and around the Orinoco. They include aggressive meat-eating fish called piranhas (puh-RAH-nuhz), 200-pound (90-kg) catfish, and crocodiles as long as 20 feet (6 m). More than 1,000 bird species live in the Orinoco River basin.

✓ **READING CHECK:** *Places and Regions* What are the region's major landforms? *the Andes, the Guiana Highlands, tepuís, Orinoco River and river basin, Llanos*

Elevation Zones in the Andes

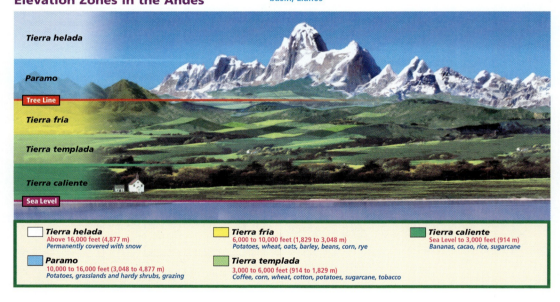

Tierra helada Above 16,000 feet (4,877 m) Permanently covered with snow

Paramo 10,000 to 16,000 feet (3,048 to 4,877 m) Potatoes, grasslands and hardy shrubs, grazing

Tierra fría 6,000 to 10,000 feet (1,829 to 3,048 m) Potatoes, wheat, oats, barley, beans, corn, rye

Tierra templada 3,000 to 6,000 feet (914 to 1,829 m) Coffee, corn, wheat, cotton, potatoes, sugarcane, tobacco

Tierra caliente Sea Level to 3,000 feet (914 m) Bananas, cacao, rice, sugarcane

222 • Chapter 10

Caribbean South America

Major Landforms and Rivers
- Andes
- Llanos
- Guiana Highlands
- Orinoco River

Climates
- tierra caliente
- tierra templada
- tierra fría
- paramo
- tierra helada

Vegetation
- sugarcane
- bananas
- mountain forests
- coffee
- potatoes
- wheat
- grasslands

Natural Resources
- good soil
- oil
- iron ore
- bauxite
- timber
- fish and shrimp

TEACH

Teaching Objectives 1–3

ALL LEVELS: (Suggested time: 25 min.) Copy the graphic organizer at left onto the chalkboard, omitting the blue answers. Use it to help students learn about the landforms, rivers, climates, vegetation, and natural resources of Caribbean South America. Pair students 0and ask each pair to complete the organizer. Ask volunteers to share their answers with the class. **ESOL, COOPERATIVE LEARNING**

Climate and Vegetation

The climates of the Andes are divided by elevation into five zones. The *tierra caliente* (tee-E-ruh kal-ee-EN-tee), or "hot country," refers to the hot and humid lower elevations near sea level. There is little difference between summer and winter temperatures in this region. Crops such as sugarcane and bananas are grown here.

Higher up the mountains the air becomes cooler. Moist climates with mountain forests are typical here. This zone of pleasant climates is called tierra templada (tem-PLAH-duh), or "temperate country." Coffee is a typical crop grown in this area. The next zone is the *tierra fría* (FREE-uh), or "cold country." The *tierra fría* has forests and grasslands. Farmers can grow potatoes and wheat. Bogotá, Colombia's capital, lies in the *tierra fría*. Above the tree line is a zone called the *paramo* (PAH-rah-moh). Grasslands and hardy shrubs are the usual vegetation. Frost may occur on any night of the year in this zone. The *tierra helada* (el-AH-dah), or "frozen country," is the zone of highest elevation. It is always covered with snow.

✓ **READING CHECK:** (Places and Regions) What are the region's climate elevation zones? *tierra caliente, tierra templada, tierra fria, paramo tierra helada*

South America's capybara is the world's largest rodent. Capybaras can weigh up to 145 pounds. Also called water hogs, capybaras live along lakes and rivers in wet tropical climates.

Resources

Good soil and moderate climates help make the region a rich agricultural area. The region has other valuable resources, including oil, iron ore, and bauxite. Lowland forests provide timber. Coastal areas yield fish and shrimp. Some rivers in the region are used to produce hydroelectric power.

✓ **READING CHECK:** (Environment and Society) How do geographic factors affect economic activities in this region? *Good soil and moderate climate—farming; minerals and petroleum; mining and drilling; forests—timber harvesting; coast—fishing*

Section Review 1

Homework Practice Online Keyword: SJ5 HP10

Define and explain: cordillera, *tepuís*, Llanos

Working with Sketch Maps On a map of Caribbean South America that you draw or that your teacher provides, label the following: Andes, Guiana Highlands, and Orinoco River.

Reading for the Main Idea
1. (Physical Systems) What effect do the Andes have on the region's climate?
2. (Environment and Society) Why is the Orinoco River important?

Critical Thinking
3. **Drawing Inferences and Conclusions** How might Colombia's location affect its trade?
4. **Analyzing Information** Which physical features make farming easier in the region? Why?

Organizing What You Know
5. **Analyzing Information** Use the graphic organizer to describe the climate and vegetation found in traveling from Bogotá to Paramaribo, Suriname.

Section 1 Review

Answers to Section 1 Review

Define For definitions, see the glossary.

Working with Sketch Maps The Andes, Guiana Highlands, and Orinoco River should be located accurately.

Reading for the Main Idea
1. create a range of climates (NGS 7)
2. It creates a corridor to the Atlantic and supports a diverse animal population. (NGS 15)

Critical Thinking
3. allows easy access to Central American trade as well as South American trade and sea trade
4. Varied elevations enable many different crops to be grown.

Organizing What You Know
5. *tierra fría*—cooler mountainous region with forests and grasslands; *tierra templada*—moist, pleasant climates with mountain forests; *tierra caliente*—hot, humid climates with tropical vegetation and crops

---

CLOSE

Tell students that volcanoes can melt snow very quickly. This happened in Colombia in November 1985. Heat from a volcano melted snow and ice on its steep peak. As the water ran down the mountain, it gathered mud and debris. By the time the mud and debris hit the town of Armero, it was a wall 130 feet (40 m) tall. About 25,000 people were killed. Ask students if volcanoes have any benefits. (They create fertile soil.)

REVIEW, ASSESS, RETEACH

Have students complete the Section Review. Then have students create eight matching quiz questions that relate a country to its landforms, climates, or natural resources. Ask students to exchange and complete their quizzes. Then have students complete Daily Quiz 10.1.

Have students complete Main Idea Activity S1. Then trace a wall map of the region. Have students create one symbol for each of the following features: landforms; wildlife and vegetation; climate types; or natural resources. Have students draw or glue the symbols onto the map. **ESOL**

EXTEND

Organize interested students into small groups. Have each group conduct research on the animals that live in and around the Orinoco River and create a short multimedia presentation. Have groups deliver their presentations to the class. **BLOCK SCHEDULING**

CHAPTER 10, Section 2

SECTION 2 RESOURCES

Reproducible
- Lecture Notes, Section 2
- Know It Notes S2
- Cultures of the World Activity 2

Technology
- One-Stop Planner CD–ROM, Lesson 10.2
- Homework Practice Online
- HRW Go site

Reinforcement, Review, and Assessment
- Section 2 Review
- Daily Quiz 10.2
- Main Idea Activity S2
- Chapter Summaries and Review
- English Audio Summary 10.2
- Spanish Audio Summary 10.2

Visual Record Answer
bird and snake

Section 2 Colombia

Read to Discover
1. What are the main periods of Colombia's history?
2. What is Colombia like today?

Vocabulary
El Dorado
cassava

Places
Colombia
Bogotá
Cauca River
Magdalena River

People
Chibcha

Reading Strategy

FOLDNOTES: TRI-FOLD Create the FoldNote titled **Tri-Fold** described in the Appendix. Your Tri-Fold will be a brochure titled Colombia. Use these themes to title panels of the brochure: Location, Place, Human-Environment Interaction, Movement, and Region. As you read, record details about Colombia that support the themes. Illustrate your brochure if time permits.

Giant stone figures near the headwaters of the Magdalena River are part of the San Agustín culture.
Interpreting the Visual Record What types of animals does the sculpture show?

Early History

Advanced cultures have lived in Colombia for centuries. Some giant mounds of earth, stone statues, and tombs found in Colombia are more than 1,500 years old.

The Chibcha In western Colombia, the Chibcha people had a well-developed civilization. The Chibcha practiced pottery making, weaving, and metalworking. Their gold objects were among the finest in ancient America.

The Chibcha had an interesting custom. New rulers were covered with gold dust and then taken to a lake to wash the gold off. Gold and emerald objects were thrown into the water as the new ruler washed. This custom inspired the legend of **El Dorado** (el duh-RAH-doh), or "the Golden One." The old legend of El Dorado describes a marvelous, rich land.

Spanish Conquest Spanish explorers arrived on the Caribbean coast of South America about 1500. They were helping to expand Spain's new empire. The Spanish conquered the Chibcha and seized much of their treasure. Spaniards and their descendants set up large estates. Powerful Spanish landlords forced South American Indians and enslaved Africans to work the land.

224 • Chapter 10

Section 2

Objectives
1. Discuss the main periods of Colombia's history.
2. Describe Colombia today.

FOCUS

Bellringer

Copy the following instruction onto the chalkboard: *Compile a list of places in the Americas that were named in honor of Christopher Columbus.* Point out that at one time many people believed that the Americas should have been named Columbia, after Columbus. Ask volunteers to share their answers with the class. (Students might mention Columbus, Ohio; the District of Columbia; the Columbia River; and the country Colombia). Tell students that in Section 2 they will learn more about the history and culture of Colombia.

Building Vocabulary

Write the terms **El Dorado** and **cassava** on the chalkboard. Ask students to guess which term has European origins and which term has American Indian origins. (Cassava has Taino Indian origins, and El Dorado has Spanish origins.) Ask volunteers to find the terms in the glossary and to read the definitions aloud. Then have them use the terms in a sentence.

Independence In the late 1700s people in Central and South America began struggling for independence from Spain. After independence was achieved, the republic of Gran Colombia was created. It included Colombia, Ecuador, Panama, and Venezuela. In 1830 the republic dissolved, and New Granada, now Colombia, was created. Present-day Panama was once part of New Granada.

After independence, debate raged in Colombia. People argued over how much power the central government and the Roman Catholic Church should have. Part of the problem had to do with the country's rugged geography. The different regions of Colombia had little contact with each other. They developed separate economies and identities. Uniting these different groups into one country was hard. Outbreaks of violence throughout the 1800s and 1900s killed thousands of people.

Colombia

Country	Population/ Growth Rate	Life Expectancy	Literacy Rate	Per Capita GDP
Colombia	41,662,073 / 1.6%	67, male / 75, female	92%	$6,500
United States	290,342,554 / 0.9%	74, male / 80, female	97%	$37,600

Source: Central Intelligence Agency, *The World Factbook 2003*

Interpreting the Chart How much larger is the U.S. population than that of Colombia?

✓ **READING CHECK:** *Environment and Society* What geographic factors influenced Colombia's ability to control its territory? **rugged geography that separated the different regions of the country**

Colombia Today

Colombia is Caribbean South America's most populous country. The national capital is Bogotá, a city located high in the eastern Andes. Most Colombians live in the fertile valleys and basins among the mountain ranges because those areas are moderate in climate and good for farming. Rivers, such as the Cauca and Magdalena, flow down from the Andes to the Caribbean. They help connect settlements between the mountains and the coast. Cattle ranches are common in the Llanos. Few people live in the tropical rain forest regions in the south.

The guard tower of an old Spanish fort stands in contrast with the modern buildings of Cartagena, Colombia.

CHAPTER 10, Section 2

Linking Past to Present

Bogotá Bogotá was a political and cultural center before Europeans began settlement in 1538. The Chibcha Indians had called the city Bacatá. The Spanish conquerors soon made the city a center of Spanish colonial power.

Present-day Bogotá is a center of commerce and industry as well as culture. Some famous Bogotá museums house artifacts from Colombia's Indian and Spanish cultures. The Gold Museum (Museo del Oro), for example, contains the world's largest collection of pre-Columbian gold objects.

Critical Thinking: How may a city's landscape and architecture be compared to a museum?

Answer: Students may mention that just as a museum houses objects from various historical periods, a city has buildings and objects that can date from the distant past.

▲ **Chart Answer**

almost seven times larger

TEACH

Teaching Objective 1

ALL LEVELS: (Suggested time: 30 min.) Organize students into groups and tell them to imagine that they are editing a book about Colombia's history. Have each group write a dust-jacket summary that briefly discusses the three historical periods prior to Colombia's modern era. (Summaries should mention the correct historical eras.) Ask volunteers to read their dust-jacket summaries to the class. **ESOL, COOPERATIVE LEARNING**

▶**ASSIGNMENT:** Tell students to imagine that it is the early 1500s and that they are Spanish explorers who are journeying through Caribbean South America for the first time. Ask each student to write journal entries that describe the landforms, rivers, climate, vegetation, natural resources, and cultures of the region. Journal entries should be descriptive, and students should feel free to invent vocabulary to name what they encounter. Ask volunteers to share their entries with the class.

CHAPTER 10, Section 2

ENVIRONMENT AND SOCIETY

Food for Millions Cassava, which originated in Central America, is now grown in areas of Africa, Asia, and the Philippines as well as the Americas. Cassava was introduced to other continents through what is known as the Columbian Exchange. This exchange began with Christopher Columbus, who took American food plants back to Europe.

Cassava is now the main food of some 500 million people. It tolerates drought and poor soil. Moreover, the cassava plant is versatile. Tapioca can be processed from the cassava root, and the leaves can be eaten as a vegetable or used as livestock feed.

Activity: Have students conduct research on the food plants involved in the Columbian Exchange.

Connecting to Science
Answers
1. Because it treated malaria, it became the subject of power struggles between nations. It remains a treatment for heart disease.
2. When the Axis Powers seized the Netherlands, they cut off the supply to the Allies, leading to the development of a black market for the drug.

Botanical print of a gray cinchona

Fighting Malaria

Malaria is a disease usually transmitted by mosquitoes. It is common in the tropics. For centuries malaria was also widespread in Europe, but Europeans had no remedy. Native peoples in the South American rain forest did have a treatment, though. They used the powdered bark of the cinchona tree, which contains the drug quinine. The history of quinine and the struggle to obtain it is a story of great adventure.

The Spanish first discovered cinchona in the 1500s, when they conquered Peru. Shipments of the bark were soon arriving in Europe, where quinine was produced. Later, some countries tried to control the supply of bark. However, the Dutch smuggled cinchona seeds out of South America. They set up their own plantations in the East Indies. Before long, the Netherlands controlled most of the world's supply of quinine.

During World War II, the Axis Powers seized the Netherlands. As a result, the Allies lost their source of quinine. A crisis was prevented when some quinine was smuggled out of Germany and sold on the black market. Since then, scientists have developed synthetic drugs for the treatment of malaria. However, quinine remains an important drug. It is used to treat heart disease and is a key ingredient in tonic water.

Understanding What You Read
1. How did native peoples' use of the cinchona tree change the world?
2. How did political decisions during World War II affect the use of quinine?

Economy Colombia's economy relies on several valuable resources. Rich soil produces world-famous Colombian coffee. Only Brazil produces more coffee. Other major export crops include bananas, corn, rice, and sugarcane. **Cassava** (kuh-SAH-vuh), a tropical plant with starchy roots, is an important food crop. Colombian farms also produce flowers that are exported around the world. In fact, only the Netherlands exports more cut flowers than Colombia.

In recent years oil has become Colombia's leading export. Oil is found mainly in eastern Colombia. Other natural resources include iron ore, gold, coal, and tin. Most of the world's emeralds also come from Colombia.

Even with these rich resources, many Colombians have low incomes. Colombia faces the same types of problems as other countries in Central and South America. For example, urban poverty and rapid population growth remain a challenge in Colombia.

226 • Chapter 10

Teaching Objective 2

LEVEL 1: (Suggested time: 15 min.). Copy the following graphic organizer onto the chalkboard, omitting the blue answers. Use it to help students learn about life in present-day Colombia. Have each student complete the organizer. Ask volunteers to share their answers with the class. **ESOL,** **LS VISUAL-SPATIAL**

LEVELS 2 AND 3: (Suggested time: 30 min.) Tell students to imagine that they are Colombian businesspeople who are trying to attract foreign investors and businesses to Colombia. Pair students and have each pair create an illustrated brochure that describes the economic resources and cultural traditions of Colombia. Ask volunteers to share their brochures with the class. **COOPERATIVE LEARNING**

Aspects of the Economy
- coffee
- bananas
- cassava
- flowers
- oil
- iron ore, gold, coal, tin, emeralds

→ Colombia Today ←

Aspects of Culture
- regional isolation
- cultural diversity
- traditional cultures
- Roman Catholicism
- soccer
- tejo

Folk dancers get ready to perform in Neiva, Colombia.
Interpreting the Visual Record
Place What aspects of culture can you see in this photograph?

Cultural Life The physical geography of Colombia has isolated its regions from one another. This is one reason why the people of Colombia are often known by the area in which they live. African traditions have influenced the songs and dances of the Caribbean coast. Traditional music can be heard in some remote areas. In addition to music, many Colombians enjoy soccer. They also play a Chibcha sport called *tejo*, a type of ringtoss game. Roman Catholicism is the country's main religion.

Conflict is a serious problem in Colombia today. Border conflicts with Venezuela have gone on for many years. Many different groups have waged war with each other and with Colombia's government. These groups have controlled large areas of the country. Many farmers have been forced off of their land, and the economy has been damaged. Because of this instability, the future of Colombia is uncertain.

✓ **READING CHECK:** **Human Systems** How have historical events affected life in Colombia today? *African traditions originating from enslaved Africans influence contemporary song and dance; border conflicts cause violence and damage the economy.*

Section Review 2

Define or identify: Chibcha, El Dorado, cassava

Working with Sketch Maps On the map you created in Section 1, label Colombia, Bogotá, and the Cauca and Magdalena Rivers.

Reading for the Main Idea
1. **Human Systems** Why did Spanish explorers come to Colombia?
2. **Human Systems** What are some characteristics of Colombia's culture?

Critical Thinking
3. **Finding the Main Idea** How have Colombia's varied landscapes affected its history?
4. **Summarizing** How have conflicts in Colombia affected its economy?

Organizing What You Know
5. **Sequencing** Copy the following graphic organizer. Use it to describe Colombia's historical periods.

Early history	Spanish period	Independence	Colombia today

Homework Practice Online
Keyword: SJ5 HP10

Caribbean South America • 227

Section 2 Review

Answers to Section 2 Review

Define or identify For definitions and identifications, see the glossary or index.

Working with Sketch Maps Places should be labeled appropriately.

Reading for the Main Idea
1. They were looking for a route to the Pacific Ocean. (NGS 9)
2. isolated regions with different cultural traditions, Spanish and South American Indian cultural influences (NGS 9)

Critical Thinking
3. hindered unity
4. damaged it

Organizing What You Know
5. early history—advanced cultures, Chibcha civilization; Spanish period—forced labor on large estates; independence—establishment of Gran Colombia and New Granada, disputes between central government and Roman Catholic Church, violence; Colombia today—reliance on oil and other primary products, diverse cultural traditions, low incomes, internal and external conflicts

◀ **Visual Record Answer**

architecture, clothing, dance, hairstyles

CLOSE

Have each student attempt to describe Colombia as completely as possible using only five adjectives or descriptive phrases. Ask volunteers to share their descriptions with the class. Conclude by supplying any adjectives or descriptions that students may have omitted.

REVIEW, ASSESS, RETEACH

Have students complete the Section Review. Then pair students and have each pair write a short essay question about Colombia. Have each pair exchange its question with another pair and complete the question it receives. **COOPERATIVE LEARNING,** LS **VISUAL-SPATIAL**

Have students complete Main Idea Activity S2. Then pair students and have each pair create a collage to depict various aspects of Colombia's history, culture, and economy. Ask volunteers to present and explain their collages to the class. **ESOL, COOPERATIVE LEARNING**

EXTEND

Have interested students conduct research on the legend of El Dorado. Then have each student write a short poem on the Chibcha custom that inspired the legend or the later search for a mythical golden city. Ask volunteers to read their poems to the class. **BLOCK SCHEDULING**

Caribbean South America **227**

CHAPTER 10, Section 3

SECTION 3 RESOURCES

Reproducible
- Lecture Notes, Section 3
- Know It Notes S3
- Geography for Life Activity 10
- Cultures of the World Activity 2

Technology
- One-Stop Planner CD–ROM, Lesson 10.3
- Homework Practice Online
- HRW Go site

Reinforcement, Review, and Assessment
- Section 3 Review
- Daily Quiz 10.3
- Main Idea Activity S3
- Chapter Summaries and Review
- English Audio Summary 10.3
- Spanish Audio Summary 10.3

Section 3 Venezuela

Read to Discover
1. How did the Spanish contribute to Venezuela's history?
2. What are some characteristics of Venezuela's culture?

Vocabulary
indigo
caudillos
llaneros
pardos

Places
Venezuela
Caracas
Lake Maracaibo

Reading Strategy

READING ORGANIZER Before you read, create a spider map. Label the map Venezuela. Create a leg for each heading in the section. As you read the section, fill in the map with details about each heading.

History of Venezuela

There were many small tribes of South American Indians living in Venezuela before the Spanish arrived. Most were led by chiefs and survived by a combination of hunting and farming.

Spanish Conquest Christopher Columbus landed on the Venezuelan coast in 1498. By the early 1500s the Spanish were exploring the area further. They forced South American Indians to dive for pearls and pan for gold. There was little gold, however. The settlers had to turn to agriculture. They grew **indigo** (IN-di-goh) and other crops. Indigo is a plant used to make a deep blue dye. South American Indians were forced to work the fields. When many of them died, plantation owners brought in enslaved Africans to take their place. Some slaves were able to escape. They settled in remote areas and governed themselves.

Margarita Island in Venezuela was the site of a Spanish fort in the 1500s.

Objectives
1. Summarize the Spanish contribution to Venezuela's history.
2. Describe some characteristics of Venezuela's culture.

FOCUS

Bellringer
Copy the following passage onto the chalkboard: *Venezuela's Angel Falls, the world's highest waterfall, was named for Jimmy Angel, a pilot from the United States whose plane crashed nearby in 1937 as he searched for gold. Why might he have thought there would be gold in Venezuela?* Discuss responses. (Students may mention the legend of El Dorado or the fact that there is gold in nearby Colombia.) Tell students that in Section 3, they will learn about Venezuela, including the country's main resource, "black gold," or oil.

Building Vocabulary
Write the terms **indigo**, **caudillos**, **llaneros**, and **pardos** on the chalkboard. Ask volunteers to find the words in the section and to read the definitions aloud. Then ask students to speculate whether each term has had an economic, political, or cultural significance.

Independence Partly because the colony was so poor, some people in Venezuela revolted against Spain. Simón Bolívar led the fight against the Spanish armies. Bolívar is considered a hero in many South American countries because he led wars of independence throughout the region. The struggle for independence finally ended in 1830, when Venezuela became an independent country.

Throughout the 1800s Venezuelans suffered from dictatorships and civil wars. The country's military leaders were called **caudillos** (kow-THEE-yohs). After oil was discovered, some caudillos kept the country's oil money for themselves. In 1958 the last dictator was forced out of power.

Oil Wealth By the 1970s Venezuela was earning huge sums of money from oil. This wealth allowed part of the population to buy luxuries. However, about 80 percent of the population still lived in poverty. Many of these people moved to the cities to find work. Some settled on the outskirts in shacks that had no running water, sewers, or electricity.

Venezuela's wealth drew many immigrants from Europe and from other South American countries. However, in the 1980s oil prices dropped sharply. Because Venezuela relied on oil for most of its income, the country suffered when prices decreased.

Venezuela is home to the anaconda—the longest snake in the world. Adult anacondas are more than 15 feet (4.6 m) long.

✓ **READING CHECK:** *Human Systems* How did the Spanish contribute to Venezuela's history? *The explored and settled there, farmed and brought enslaved Africans to work fields after many of the South American Indians died as a result of forced labor.*

Venezuela Today

Most Venezuelans live along the Caribbean coast and in the valleys of the nearby mountains. About 85 percent live in cities and towns. Caracas (kuh-RAHK-uhs), the capital, is the center of Venezuelan culture. It is a large city with a modern subway system, busy expressways, and tall office buildings. However, slums circle the city. Poverty in rural areas is also widespread. Still, Venezuela is one of South America's wealthiest countries. It is developing rapidly.

Economy Venezuela's economy is based on oil production. Lake Maracaibo (mah-rah-KY-boh) is a bay of the Caribbean Sea. The rocks under the lake are particularly rich in oil. However, the country is trying to reduce its dependence on oil income.

The Guiana Highlands in the southeast are rich in other minerals, such as iron ore for making steel. Dams on tributaries of the Orinoco River produce hydroelectricity.

Venezuela

Country	Population/ Growth Rate	Life Expectancy	Literacy Rate	Per Capita GDP
Venezuela	24,654,694 1.5%	70, male 77, female	93%	$5,500
United States	290,342,554 0.9%	74, male 80, female	97%	$37,600

Source: Central Intelligence Agency, *The World Factbook 2003*

Interpreting the Chart What is the average life expectancy for someone from Venezuela?

Environment and Society

Oil and Pollution
Venezuela's oil economy has taken a toll on the country's environment. Oil development has contributed to pollution of rivers, lakes, and groundwater.

Venezuela's state-owned oil company will have to pay heavily to clean up environmental damage caused by the oil industry. Oil spills have damaged plant life, and farmers have lost livestock in oil spills and oil pits. Oil pits collect contaminated sludge from oil wells. The sludge from these pits can seep into and contaminate water supplies.

Activity: Ask students what problems are associated with the oil industry and what steps they would take to reduce pollution from it.

GO TO: go.hrw.com
KEYWORD: SJ5 CH10
FOR: Web sites about oil spills

◀ **Chart Answer**

73 years

Llaneros herd cattle on the large ranches of the Llanos.

Interpreting the Visual Record How do these *llaneros* look similar to cowboys in the United States?

Agriculture Northern Venezuela has small family farms and large commercial farms. **Llaneros** (yah-NAY-rohs)—cowboys of the Venezuelan Llanos—herd cattle on the many ranches in this region. Few people live in the Guiana Highlands. Some small communities of South American Indians practice traditional slash-and-burn agriculture there.

Cultural Life More than two thirds of Venezuela's population are **pardos**. They are people of mixed African, European, and South American Indian ancestry. Native groups make up only about 2 percent of the population. They speak more than 25 different languages. Spanish is the official language. Most of the people are Roman Catholics. Some Venezuelan Indians follow the religious practices of their ancestors.

The *joropo*, a lively foot-stomping couples' dance, is Venezuela's national dance. *Toros coleados* is a local sport. In this rodeo event, the contestant pulls a bull down by grabbing its tail. Baseball and soccer are also popular in Venezuela.

✓ **READING CHECK:** **Human Systems** What are some aspects of Venezuela's culture? *Two thirds of population are* pardos; *native groups make up only 2 percent of population; many languages spoken; most people Roman Catholic; local sports include* toros coleados, *baseball, soccer.*

Define and explain: indigo, caudillos, llaneros, pardos

Working with Sketch Maps On the map you created in Section 2, label Venezuela, Caracas, and Lake Maracaibo. How does elevation affect the climate of Caracas?

Reading for the Main Idea
1. **Environment and Society** Why did Spanish settlers in Venezuela have to turn to agriculture?
2. **Human Systems** Who led Venezuela's revolt against Spain?

Critical Thinking
3. **Drawing Inferences and Conclusions** Why might Venezuela try to reduce its dependence on oil exports?
4. **Comparing** Compare the population densities of the Caribbean coast and the Guiana Highlands.

Organizing What You Know
5. **Analyzing Information** Copy the following graphic organizer. Use it to explain how oil is related to the history, urban poverty, and economy of Venezuela.

Oil	History	
	Urban poverty	
	Economy	

230 • Chapter 10

Section 3 Review

Answers to Section 3 Review

Define For definitions, see the glossary.

Working with Sketch Maps Venezuela, Caracas, and Lake Maracaibo should be located accurately. Its elevation creates a temperate climate.

Reading for the Main Idea
1. Settlers found little of the gold they had sought. (NGS 15)
2. Simón Bolívar (NGS 13)

Critical Thinking
3. Its economy would be less likely to suffer from hardships resulting from lower oil prices.
4. The Caribbean coast has a greater population density.

Organizing What You Know
5. history—some caudillos kept oil money; urban poverty—many poor people moved to cities, but oil wealth was not distributed evenly, and many continued to live in poverty; economy—reliant on oil production

Visual Record Answer
Answers will vary but might include the *llaneros'* clothing and equipment.

CLOSE

Tell students that there are several ways to get to Venezuela's spectacular Angel Falls. You can fly over them, but clouds may keep you from seeing them. You can hike for four or five days through the jungle. Or you can take a dugout canoe trip, travel by jeep around the rapids, and hike for an hour to the falls. Poll the class to see which methods of travel students would prefer.

REVIEW, ASSESS, RETEACH

Have students complete the Section Review. Then pair students and have each pair create a flash card for each of the vocabulary terms and places in this section. Have students within the pair quiz each other. Then have students complete Daily Quiz 10.3. **COOPERATIVE LEARNING**

Have students complete Main Idea Activity S3. Then have students design travel posters to attract tourists to Venezuela. Display posters around the classroom. **ESOL**

EXTEND

Have interested students conduct research on Simón Bolívar. Then have each student write a short eulogy for Bólivar. Ask volunteers to read their eulogies to the class. **BLOCK SCHEDULING**

The Guianas

CHAPTER 10, Section 4

Read to Discover
1. Which countries influenced the early history of the Guianas?
2. How are Guyana, Suriname, and French Guiana similar today?

Vocabulary
indentured servants
pidgin languages

Places
Guyana
Suriname
French Guiana
Georgetown
Paramaribo
Devil's Island
Kourou
Cayenne

Reading Strategy
READING ORGANIZER Before you read, create a chart with these column headings: 2 facts I have already learned about the Guianas, 2 new interesting facts I learned in this section, and 2 questions I still have about the Guianas. Fill in the chart as you read.

Section 4 Resources
Reproducible
- Lecture Notes, Section 4
- Know It Notes S4
- Cultures of the World Activity 2

Technology
- One-Stop Planner CD–ROM, Lesson 10.4
- Homework Practice Online
- HRW Go site

Reinforcement, Review, and Assessment
- Section 4 Review
- Daily Quiz 10.4
- Main Idea Activity S4
- Chapter Summaries and Review
- English Audio Summary 10.4
- Spanish Audio Summary 10.4

Early History of the Guianas

Dense tropical rain forests cover much of the region east of Venezuela. Rugged highlands lie to the south. The physical environment of this region kept it somewhat isolated from the rest of South America. Thus, the three countries known as the Guianas (gee-AH-nuhz) have a history quite different from the rest of the continent.

European Settlement Spain was the first European country to claim the Guianas. The Spanish eventually lost the region to settlers from Great Britain, France, and the Netherlands. Sometimes a war fought in Europe determined which country held this corner of South America. The Europeans established coffee, tobacco, and cotton plantations. They brought Africans to work as slaves on these plantations. Sugarcane later became the main crop.

Asian Workers European countries made slavery illegal in the mid-1800s. Colonists in the Guianas needed a new source of labor for their plantations. They brought **indentured servants** from India, China, and Southeast Asia. Indentured servants agree to work for a certain period of time, often in exchange for travel expenses. As these people worked together, they developed **pidgin languages**. Pidgin languages are simple so that people who speak different languages can understand each other.

✓ **READING CHECK:** *Human Systems* What countries influenced the early history of the Guianas?
Spain, Great Britain, France, the Netherlands

This Hindu temple is located in Cayenne, French Guiana.

Objectives
1. Identify the countries that influenced the early history of the Guianas.
2. Compare Guyana, Suriname, and French Guiana today.

FOCUS

Bellringer
Copy the following passage onto the chalkboard: *The same treaty that transferred New York City from the Dutch to the English transferred Suriname from the English to the Dutch. What if this trade had not taken place?* Discuss responses. (Possible answers: New York might still have a Dutch culture. There might be a separatist movement there, like there is in Quebec.) Tell students that in Section 4 they will learn more about the history of the Guianas, of which Suriname is a part.

Building Vocabulary
Ask a volunteer to read the definition of the term **indentured servants** from a dictionary. Point out that the root *indent* comes from the notch that was made in the copies of the contracts to make sure they matched. Indentured servants legally sold their labor for an extended period of time. Then ask a volunteer to read the definition of **pidgin languages** from the glossary.

Caribbean South America 231

CHAPTER 10, Section 4

FOOD FESTIVAL

Go Bananas! Plantains are a type of banana. Fried plantains are popular in Colombia. Specialty markets may have a thin, crisp variety similar to potato chips in the snack section or a thicker version in the frozen-food case. To make them at home, peel four large plantains and cut each into three or four pieces. Fry in hot vegetable oil until golden. Remove the plantains and pound flat. Return them to the oil and refry briefly. Remove and place on paper towels to drain. Sprinkle with salt.

Chart Answer ▶
Answers will vary, but may mention disease, people moving to new locations for economic opportunities, or fewer young people having children.

The Guianas

Country	Population/ Growth Rate	Life Expectancy	Literacy Rate	Per Capita GDP
French Guiana	186,917 / 2.7%	73, male / 80, female	83%	$6,000
Guyana	702,100 / .07%	60, male / 65, female	98%	$4,000
Suriname	433,449 / 0.3%	67, male / 72, female	93%	$3,500
United States	290,342,554 / 0.9%	74, male / 80, female	97%	$37,600

Source: Central Intelligence Agency, *The World Factbook 2003*

Interpreting the Chart *Place* Why might the populations of Guyana and Suriname be growing slowly?

Our Amazing Planet

The goliath bird-eating spider of northeastern South America is the largest spider in the world. The record holder had a leg span more than 11 inches (28 cm) across. That is as big as a dinner plate!

A woman cooks cassava cakes in Bigi Poika, Suriname.

The Guianas Today

The area formerly known as British Guiana gained its independence in 1966 and became Guyana. In 1975 Dutch Guiana broke away from the Netherlands to become Suriname. French Guiana remains a part of France.

Guyana Guyana (gy-AH-nuh) is a South American Indian word that means "land of waters." Nearly all of Guyana's agricultural lands are located along the narrow coastal plains. Guyana's most important agricultural products are rice and sugar. The country's major mineral resource is bauxite.

Guyana has a diverse population. About half of its people are of South Asian descent. Most of these people farm small plots of land or run small businesses. About one third of the population is descended from African slaves. These people control most of the large businesses and hold most of the government positions. More than one third of the country's population lives in Georgetown, the capital.

Suriname The resources and economy of Suriname (soohr-uh-NAH-muh) are similar to those of Guyana. Many farms in Suriname are found in coastal areas. Aluminum is a major export. Interior forests also supply lumber for export to other countries.

Like Guyana, Suriname has a diverse population. There are South Asians, Africans, Chinese, Indonesians, and people of mixed heritage. Muslim, Hindu, Roman Catholic, and Protestant houses of worship line the streets of the national capital, Paramaribo (pah-rah-MAH-ree-boh). Nearly half of the country's people live there.

TEACH

Teaching Objective 1
ALL LEVELS: (Suggested time: 15 min.) Copy the following graphic organizer onto the chalkboard, omitting the blue answers. Use it to help students learn about the countries that influenced the history of the Guianas. When students have completed the organizer, ask volunteers to share their answers with the class. **ESOL,** **LS VISUAL-SPATIAL**

Teaching Objective 2
ALL LEVELS: (Suggested time: 20 min.) Pair students and have each pair create a chart that depicts the similarities and differences among Guyana, Suriname, and French Guiana today. (Charts should mention government, resources, and population.) Ask volunteers to share their charts with the class. **ESOL, COOPERATIVE LEARNING**

COUNTRIES THAT INFLUENCED THE GUIANAS

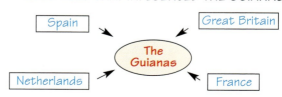

◀ Carnival is a time for celebration in Cayenne, French Guiana.

French Guiana French Guiana (gee-A-nuh) has a status in France similar to that of a state in the United States. It sends representatives to the French Parliament in Paris. France used to send some of its criminals to Devil's Island. This island was a prison colony just off French Guiana's coast. Prisoners there suffered terribly from overwork. Devil's Island was closed in the early 1950s.

Today, forestry and shrimp fishing are the most important economic activities. Agriculture is limited to the coastal areas. The people of French Guiana depend heavily on imports for their food and energy. France developed the town of Kourou (koo-ROO) into a space center. The European Space Agency launches satellites from this town.

More than 180,000 people live in French Guiana, mostly in coastal areas. About two thirds of the people are descended from Africans. Other groups include Europeans, Asians, and South American Indians. The national capital is Cayenne (keye-EN).

✓ **READING CHECK:** (Human Systems) How is French Guiana different from Guyana and Suriname? *It is not an independent country.*

Define and explain: indentured servants, pidgin languages

Working with Sketch Maps On the map you created in Section 3, label Guyana, Suriname, French Guiana, Georgetown, Paramaribo, Devil's Island, Kourou, and Cayenne.

Reading for the Main Idea
1. (Environment and Society) What crops did early settlers raise in the Guianas?
2. (Human Systems) Why did colonists in the Guianas bring indentured servants from Asia?

Critical Thinking
3. **Drawing Inferences and Conclusions** Why might the people of French Guiana prefer to remain a part of France?
4. **Drawing Inferences and Conclusions** Why do you think few people live in the interior of the Guianas?

Organizing What You Know
5. **Categorizing** Copy the following graphic organizer. Use it to describe the Guianas. Fill in the ovals with features of Guyana, Suriname, and French Guiana. In the center, list features they have in common.

Section 4 Review

Answers to Section 4 Review

Define For definitions, see the glossary.

Working with Sketch Maps Places should be labeled in their approximate locations.

Reading for the Main Idea
1. coffee, tobacco, cotton, and sugarcane (NGS 14)
2. Slavery had been outlawed by European countries, and settlers needed a new source of labor (NGS 9)

Critical Thinking
3. enjoy benefits of French citizenship
4. heavily forested

Organizing What You Know
5. Guyana—independent country, bauxite an important resource; Suriname—independent country, aluminum and forestry important to economy; French Guiana—forestry and fishing important to economy, depends on imports of food and energy, is part of France; common—diverse population, agriculture confined to coastal area

CLOSE

Tell students to read the chart on the previous page that presents statistics about the populations of the Guianas and the United States. Ask students what they can conclude from this chart. (Students may suggest that although many people in the Guianas are poor, they are relatively well-educated.)

REVIEW, ASSESS, RETEACH

Have students complete the Section Review. Then pair students. Have each pair write a quiz consisting of eight multiple-choice questions about the Guianas. Have pairs exchange and complete their quizzes. Then have students complete Daily Quiz 10.4. **COOPERATIVE LEARNING**

Have students complete Main Idea Activity S4. Then have each student write three sentences for each of the Guianas. Sentences should relate to each country's culture, history, and natural resources. **ESOL**

EXTEND

Have interested students conduct research on pidgin languages and where such languages have developed. Ask each student to present his or her research in a short written report. **BLOCK SCHEDULING**

CHAPTER 10 REVIEW

Define and Identify
For definitions and identifications, see the glossary and index.

Review the Main Ideas
13. Sandstone layers on top of formations did not erode, while highlands below them did erode to form steep-sided plateaus. (NGS 7)
14. Orinoco; piranhas, 200-pound catfish, huge crocodiles, more than 1,000 bird species (NGS 8)
15. tierra caliente, tierra templada, tierra fría, paramo, tierra helada (NGS 4)
16. to seize their gold
17. emeralds (NGS 16)
18. political and economic instability
19. gold
20. Caudillos kept it for themselves; oil wealth made some people very rich, while others remained poor. (NGS 11)
21. center of Venezuelan culture, modern subway system, busy expressways, tall office buildings, slums (NGS 4)
22. Spain, Great Britain, France, Netherlands (NGS 13)
23. It is not an independent country; its status is similar to that of a state in the U.S.A. (NGS 13)

Think Critically
24. because animals depend on different types of plants, require various weather conditions to survive, and are adapted to various conditions
25. kept people separated so that they developed different economies and identities
26. Both herd cattle on ranches.
27. to live in a more temperate climate zone rather than a hot, heavily forested zone
28. They developed as a means of communication among people who spoke different languages.

234 • Chapter 10

Chapter 10 Review and Practice

Define and Identify
Identify each of the following:
1. cordillera
2. *tepuís*
3. Llanos
4. Chibcha
5. El Dorado
6. cassava
7. indigo
8. caudillos
9. *llaneros*
10. *pardos*
11. indentured servants
12. pidgin languages

Review the Main Ideas
13. How did the *tepuís* form?
14. What is the region's longest river? What are some animals that live in and near the river?
15. What are the five elevation zones in the Andes region?
16. Why did the Spanish conquer the Chibcha?
17. Which precious jewel is an important Colombian export?
18. What kinds of conflicts have caused problems in Colombia?
19. What resource were the Spanish explorers hoping to find in Venezuela?
20. What has happened to much of Venezuela's oil wealth throughout the country's history?
21. What are some features of Caracas?
22. Which four European countries have controlled the Guianas?
23. How does French Guiana's political status differ from that of Guyana and Suriname?

Think Critically
24. **Drawing Inferences and Conclusions** Why would different animals live in the five elevation zones?
25. **Finding the Main Idea** How has geography contributed to conflict in Colombia's history?
26. **Comparing** How are Venezuelan *llaneros* like American cowboys?
27. **Drawing Inferences and Conclusions** Why do you think most Venezuelans live along the Caribbean coast and in the valleys of the nearby mountains?
28. **Analyzing Information** How are pidgin languages in the Guianas an example of cultural cooperation?

Map Activity
29. On a separate sheet of paper, match the letters on the map with their correct labels.

   Andes
   Guiana Highlands
   Orinoco River
   Magdalena River
   Lake Maracaibo
   Devil's Island
   Llanos

Map Activity
29. **A.** Orinoco River
   B. Lake Maracaibo
   C. Andes
   D. Llanos
   E. Magdalena River
   F. Devil's Island
   G. Guiana Highlands

Writing Activity

Imagine that you are a teacher living in Caracas, Venezuela. Use the information in this chapter to write a quiz, with answers, for students in your geography class. Ask questions on the history, geography, economy, and people of Venezuela. Use the chapter map and the population figures in the Venezuela chart. Be sure to use standard grammar, sentence structure, spelling, and punctuation.

internet connect

Internet Activity: go.hrw.com
KEYWORD: SJ5 GT10

Choose a topic to explore about Caribbean South America:
- Trek through the Guiana Highlands.
- Search for the treasures of El Dorado.
- Ride with the *llaneros* of Venezuela.

Social Studies Skills Practice

Interpreting Charts

Study the following chart comparing age structure of the populations of the Guianas and the United States. Then answer the questions.

Age Structure of the Guianas and the United States				
Age Range	Suriname	Guyana	French Guyana	United States
0–14 years	30.7%	27%	29.9%	20.9%
15–64 years	63.3%	67.9%	64.4%	66.7%
65 and over	6%	5.1%	5.7%	12.4%

Source: Central Intelligence Agency, *The World Factbook 2003*

1. Which country has the largest percentage of its population under the age of 14?
2. Which country has the largest percentage of people aged 65 and over?
3. Which age group is most equally represented in all of the countries?
4. Can you tell from the chart which country has the highest population growth rate? Why or why not?

Analyzing Primary Sources

The Chibcha custom of dusting their new chiefs with gold gave rise to the legend of El Dorado. Read the following account of the practice, written by Spanish historian Gonzalo Fernandez de Oviedo in 1535. Then answer the questions.

"He [the new chief] went about all covered with powdered gold, as casually as if it were powdered salt. For it seemed to him that to wear any other finery was less beautiful, and that to put on ornaments or arms made of gold worked by hammering, stamping, or by other means, was a vulgar [tacky] and common thing."

1. Why do you think Oviedo compared the gold to salt?
2. In the second sentence, what is a synonym that could be substituted for *arms*?
3. How did the chief feel about the other ornaments described?
4. Do you think Oviedo was impressed by the custom he described? Why or why not?

Caribbean South America • 235

CHAPTER 10 REVIEW

Writing Activity
Quizzes will vary, but the information included should be consistent with text material. Check to see that students have written appropriate questions using the map. Use Rubric 40, Writing to Describe, to evaluate student work.

Interpreting Charts
1. Suriname
2. United States
3. 15–64 years
4. No. Although a large percentage in the 15–64 group would indicate many people of child-bearing years, other factors, such as immigration, also affect growth rate.

Analyzing Primary Sources
1. to emphasize how common a material gold was for the Chibcha
2. armor
3. He thought they were vulgar.
4. yes, because he used words that express his amazement

REVIEW AND ASSESSMENT RESOURCES

Reproducible
- Readings in World Geography, History, and Culture 20 and 21
- Critical Thinking Activity 10
- Vocabulary Activity 10

Technology
- Chapter 10 Test Generator (on the One-Stop Planner)
- Audio CD Program, Chapter 10
- HRW Go site

Reinforcement, Review, and Assessment
- Chapter 10 Review
- Chapter Summaries and Review
- Chapter 10 Test
- Chapter 10 Test for ESOL and Special-Needs Students

internet connect

GO TO: go.hrw.com
KEYWORD: SJ5 Teacher
FOR: a guide to using the Internet in your classroom

Atlantic South America
Chapter Resource Manager

Objectives	Pacing Guide	Reproducible Resources
SECTION 1 **Physical Geography** (pp. 237–40) 1. Identify the landforms and rivers found in Atlantic South America. 2. Describe the region's climates, vegetation, and wildlife. 3. Name some of the region's important resources.	**Regular** .5 day Lecture Notes, Section 1 **Block Scheduling** .5 day Block Scheduling Handbook, Chapter 11	**RS** Know It Notes S1 **RS** Graphic Organizer 11 **E** Creative Strategies for Teaching World Geography, Lesson 8 **IC** Interdisciplinary Activity for the Middle Grades 10 **ELL** Main Idea Activity S1
SECTION 2 **Brazil** (pp. 241–44) 1. Describe the history of Brazil. 2. Identify the important characteristics of Brazil's people and culture. 3. Describe what Brazil's four major regions are like today.	**Regular** 1 day Lecture Notes, Section 2 **Block Scheduling** 1 day Block Scheduling Handbook, Chapter 11	**RS** Know It Notes S2 **E** Cultures of the World Activity 2 **SM** Geography for Life Activity 11 **SM** Map Activity 11 **ELL** Main Idea Activity S2
SECTION 3 **Argentina** (pp. 245–48) 1. Describe the history of Argentina. 2. Identify the important characteristics of Argentina's people and culture. 3. Describe what Argentina is like today.	**Regular** .5 day Lecture Notes, Section 3 **Block Scheduling** .5 day Block Scheduling Handbook, Chapter 11	**RS** Know It Notes S3 **E** Cultures of the World Activity 2 **E** Biography Activity: José de San Martín **ELL** Main Idea Activity S3
SECTION 4 **Uruguay and Paraguay** (pp. 249–51) 1. Describe what the people and economy of Uruguay are like today. 2. Describe what the people and economy of Paraguay are like today.	**Regular** 1 day Lecture Notes, Section 4 **Block Scheduling** .5 day Block Scheduling Handbook, Chapter 11	**RS** Know It Notes S4 **E** Cultures of the World Activity 2 **ELL** Main Idea Activity S4

Chapter Resource Key

- **RS** Reading Support
- **IC** Interdisciplinary Connections
- **E** Enrichment
- **SM** Skills Mastery
- **A** Assessment
- **REV** Review
- **ELL** Reinforcement and English Language Learners and English for Speakers of Other Languages (ESOL)
- Transparencies
- CD–ROM
- Music
- Video
- Internet
- Holt Presentation Maker Using Microsoft® PowerPoint®

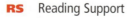 **One-Stop Planner CD–ROM**

See the *One-Stop Planner* for a complete list of additional resources for students and teachers.

One-Stop Planner CD–ROM

It's easy to plan lessons, select resources, and print out materials for your students when you use the *One-Stop Planner CD–ROM with Test Generator*.

Technology Resources

 One-Stop Planner CD–ROM, Lesson 11.1
 Geography and Cultures Visual Resources with Teaching Activities 18–22
 ARGWorld CD–ROM
 Homework Practice Online
HRW Go site

 One-Stop Planner CD–ROM, Lesson 11.2
Our Environment CD–ROM/ Seek and Tell/People Affecting Nature
ARGWorld CD–ROM
Homework Practice Online
HRW Go site

 One-Stop Planner CD–ROM, Lesson 11.3
ARGWorld CD–ROM
Homework Practice Online
HRW Go site

 One-Stop Planner CD–ROM, Lesson 11.4
ARGWorld CD–ROM
Homework Practice Online
HRW Go site

Review, Reinforcement, and Assessment Resources

ELL	Main Idea Activity S1
REV	Section 1 Review
A	Daily Quiz 11.1
REV	Chapter Summaries and Review
ELL	English Audio Summary 11.1
ELL	Spanish Audio Summary 11.1

ELL	Main Idea Activity S2
REV	Section 2 Review
A	Daily Quiz 11.2
REV	Chapter Summaries and Review
ELL	English Audio Summary 11.2
ELL	Spanish Audio Summary 11.2

ELL	Main Idea Activity S3
REV	Section 3 Review
A	Daily Quiz 11.3
REV	Chapter Summaries and Review
ELL	English Audio Summary 11.3
ELL	Spanish Audio Summary 11.3

ELL	Main Idea Activity S4
REV	Section 4 Review
A	Daily Quiz 11.4
REV	Chapter Summaries and Review
ELL	English Audio Summary 11.4
ELL	Spanish Audio Summary 11.4

internet connect

HRW ONLINE RESOURCES

GO TO: go.hrw.com
Then type in a keyword.

TEACHER HOME PAGE
KEYWORD: **SJ5 TEACHER**

CHAPTER INTERNET ACTIVITIES
KEYWORD: **SJ5 GT11**

Choose an activity to:
- journey along the Amazon River.
- compare the people of Uruguay and Paraguay.
- celebrate the Brazilian Carnival.

CHAPTER ENRICHMENT LINKS
KEYWORD: **SJ5 CH11**

CHAPTER MAPS
KEYWORD: **SJ5 MAPS11**

ONLINE ASSESSMENT
Homework Practice
KEYWORD: **SJ5 HP11**
Standardized Test Prep Online
KEYWORD: **SJ5 STP11**
Rubrics
KEYWORD: **SS Rubrics**

COUNTRY INFORMATION
KEYWORD: **SJ5 Almanac**

CONTENT UPDATES
KEYWORD: **SS Content Updates**

HOLT PRESENTATION MAKER
KEYWORD: **SJ5 PPT11**

ONLINE READING SUPPORT
KEYWORD: **SS Strategies**

CURRENT EVENTS
KEYWORD: **S5 Current Events**

Meeting Individual Needs

Ability Levels

Level 1 Basic-level activities designed for all students encountering new material

Level 2 Intermediate-level activities designed for average students

Level 3 Challenging activities designed for honors and gifted-and-talented students

ESOL Activities that address the needs of students with Limited English Proficiency

Chapter Review and Assessment

E	Creative Strategies for Teaching World Geography, Lesson 9	ELL	Vocabulary Activity 11
IC	Interdisciplinary Activity for the Middle Grades 12	A	Chapter 11 Test
			Chapter 11 Test Generator (on the One-Stop Planner)
E	Readings in World Geography, History, and Culture 22, 23, and 24		Audio CD Program, Chapter 11
SM	Critical Thinking Activity 11	A	Chapter 11 Test for English Language Learners and Special-Needs Students
REV	Chapter 11 Review and Practice		HRW Go site
REV	Chapter Summaries and Review		

CHAPTER 11

Atlantic South America

Previewing Chapter Resources

Holt Online Learning

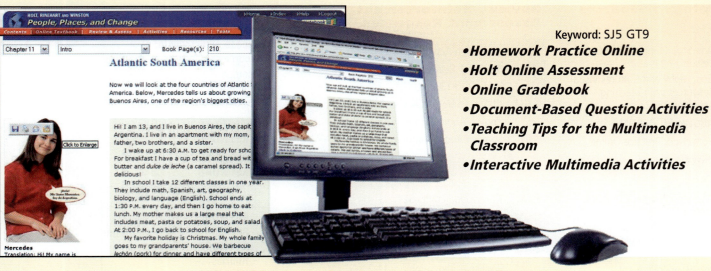

Keyword: SJ5 GT9

- Homework Practice Online
- Holt Online Assessment
- Online Gradebook
- Document-Based Question Activities
- Teaching Tips for the Multimedia Classroom
- Interactive Multimedia Activities

Differentiating Instruction

Reading and Writing Support

◀ Graphic Organizer Activity
- Vocabulary Activity
- Chapter Summary and Review
- Know It Notes
- Audio CD

Active Learning

- Block Scheduling Handbook
- Cultures of the World Activity
- Interdisciplinary Activity
◀ Map Activity
- Critical Thinking Activity 11

Primary Sources and Advanced Learners

◀ Geography for Life Activity: Mapping Wealth and Poverty in Brazil
- Map Activity: Brazil Land Use
- Readings in World Geography, History and Culture:
  - 23 Paraguay's Bumpy Ride
  - 24 Paris on La Plata

Assessment Program

- Daily Quizzes S1–4
◀ Chapter Test
- Chapter Test for English Language Learners and Special-Needs Students

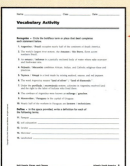

Spanish and ESOL

◀ Vocabulary Activity
- Main Idea Activities for English Language Learners and Special-Needs Students
- Chapter Summary and Review
- Spanish Audio Summary
- Know It Notes S1–4
- Chapter Test for English Language Learners and Special-Needs Students

Special Education Modifications

Your **I.D.E.A. Works! CD-ROM** will provide modified versions of the following teaching materials:

- Guided Reading Strategies S1–4
- Vocabulary Activity
◀ Main Idea Activities S1–4
- Daily Quizzes S1–4
- Chapter 11 Test
- Flash cards of chapter vocabulary terms

235C

Teacher Resources

Books for Teachers

Chatwin, Bruce. *In Patagonia.* Penguin, 1988.

Eakin, Marshall C. *Brazil: The Once and Future Country.* Griffin Trade, 1998.

Rivademar, Daniel. *Patagonia: The Last Wilderness.* Warwick Publishers, 1999.

Books for Students

Heinrichs, Ann. *Brazil.* True Books. Children's Press, 1997. Brazil's geography, history, economy, culture, and people. **SHELTERED ENGLISH**

Liebowitz, Sol. *Argentina.* Major World Nations. Chelsea House, 1998. Geography, history, economy, culture, and people of the "silver land."

Lourie, Peter. *Amazon: A Young Reader's Look at the Last Frontier.* Boyd Mills Press, 1998. Illustrated look at an endangered ecosystem.

Selby, Anna. *Argentina, Chile, Paraguay, Uruguay.* Country Fact Files. Raintree/Steck-Vaughn, 1999. Geography, natural resources, economics, and the environment.

Multimedia Materials

Central and South America: Why Do People Move? Video with Teacher's Guide, 15 min. Agency for Instructional Technology.

Rainforest Webpack. CD–ROM. Sunburst Communications, Inc.

Single Topic Videodisc: Rain Forest. Videodisc kit. National Geographic Society.

Videos and CDs

Videos
- CNN Presents Geography: Yesterday and Today, Segment 12 Destination Brazil
- ARG World

Holt Researcher
http://researcher.hrw.com

- Organization of American States (OAS)
- Brazil
- Paraguay
- Uruguay
- Argentina
- Peron, Eva
- Urban Population of Latin America
- Latin American Economic Growth
- Latin American Foreign Debts
- Latin American Governments
- Empires in the Americas

Transparency Packages

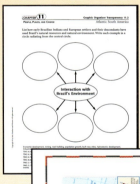

Graphic Organizer Transparencies 11.1–4

Geography and Cultures Visual Resources Transparencies 32–36
41 Atlantic South America: Physical-Political

Map Activities Transparency 11 Brazil Land Use

CHAPTER 11

Why It Matters

You may want to point out the following facts that make it important to study the countries of Atlantic South America:

- Consumers in the United States enjoy a wide range of agricultural products grown in the region.
- Brazil is so large that the health of its economy affects economies throughout Middle and South America. The U.S. economy can also be affected.
- The United States shares with the region some elements of history, such as periods of colonization and immigration, and culture, such as that of Argentina's gauchos.
- The destruction of rain forests in the region may have severe consequences for Earth's climate and environment.

CHAPTER 11

Atlantic South America

Now we will look at the four countries of Atlantic South America. Below, Mercedes tells us about growing up in Buenos Aires, one of the region's biggest cities.

Hi! I am 13, and I live in Buenos Aires, the capital of Argentina. I live in an apartment with my mom, father, two brothers, and a sister.

I wake up at 6:30 A.M. to get ready for school. For breakfast I have a cup of tea and bread with butter and *dulce de leche* (a caramel spread). It is delicious!

In school I take 12 different classes in one year. They include math, Spanish, art, geography, biology, and language (English). School ends at 1:30 P.M. every day, and then I go home to eat lunch. My mother makes us a large meal that includes meat, pasta or potatoes, soup, and salad. At 2:00 P.M., I go back to school for English.

My favorite holiday is Christmas. My whole family goes to my grandparents' house. We barbecue *lechón* (pork) for dinner and have different types of salads. We eat *turrón*, a honey and almond bar, and a special sweet bread with fruit. At midnight everyone opens their presents.

¡Hola!
Me llamo Mercedes.
Soy de Argentina.

Translation: Hi! My name is Mercedes. I am from Argentina.

Chapter Project

Have students conduct a debate between indigenous peoples who live in the rain forest and developers who want to turn it into grazing land. Following the debate, have each student write a position statement supporting one side or the other. Some students may prefer a compromise position.

Starting the Chapter

Draw two columns on the chalkboard. Label one *Rainforest Animals*, the other *Rainforest Plants*. Call on volunteers to suggest items for both categories. (Possible answers: jaguars, monkeys, sloths; mahogany trees, vines, orchids) Then tell students that the purpose of studying this chapter will be to examine the importance of the rain forest in particular and to expand their knowledge of Atlantic South America in general. Add that these countries affect the economy and security of the United States and that the destruction of rain forests may affect the entire world. Tell students they will learn more about the physical and cultural geography of Atlantic South America in this chapter.

Section 1: Physical Geography

CHAPTER 11, Section 1

Section 1 Resources

Reproducible
- Lecture Notes, Section 1
- Block Scheduling Handbook, Chapter 11
- Know It Notes S1
- Graphic Organizer 11
- Creative Strategies for Teaching World Geography, Lesson 8
- Interdisciplinary Activity for the Middle Grades 10

Technology
- One-Stop Planner CD–ROM, Lesson 11.1
- Homework Practice Online
- Geography and Cultures Visual Resources with Teaching Activities 32–36, 41
- HRW Go site

Reinforcement, Review, and Assessment
- Section 1 Review
- Daily Quiz 11.1
- Main Idea Activity S1
- Chapter Summaries and Review
- English Audio Summary 11.1
- Spanish Audio Summary 11.1

Read to Discover
1. What landforms and rivers are found in Atlantic South America?
2. What are the region's climates, vegetation, and wildlife like?
3. What are some of the region's important resources?

Vocabulary
Pampas
estuary
soil exhaustion

Places
Amazon River
Brazilian Highlands
Brazilian Plateau
Gran Chaco
Patagonia
Tierra del Fuego
Andes
Paraná River
Paraguay River
Río de la Plata

Reading Strategy

ANTICIPATING INFORMATION Before you read, predict whether you think the following statements are true or false.
- Atlantic South America has one large river system.
- The region's climate is hot and dry.
- The region's landforms vary from coastal plains to mountains.

Check your answers while reading. Then explain why each statement is true or false.

Atlantic South America • 237

Section 1

Objectives
1. Investigate the landforms and rivers of Atlantic South America.
2. Analyze the region's climates, vegetation, and wildlife.
3. Identify some of the region's important resources.

Focus

Bellringer

Copy the following instructions onto the chalkboard: *Look at the map of Atlantic South America at the beginning of the chapter. Based on what you see on the map, what recreational activities might be available or not available to the residents of the countries there?* Allow students time to write their responses. Discuss their suggestions. (Possible answers: Argentina—can go hiking in the mountains, Paraguay—cannot go sailing on the ocean) Tell students that in Section 1 they will learn more about how the physical geography affects life in Atlantic South America.

Using the Physical-Political Map

Have students examine the map on this page. Call on volunteers to point out the major physical features of the area. (Amazon River, Andes, Brazilian Highlands) Have students speculate what the climate and vegetation of each area may be. (Possible answers: warm, humid, rain forest; cold, highland, shrubs and limited vegetation; temperate, mixed forests)

Atlantic South America 237

CHAPTER 11, Section 1

ENVIRONMENT AND SOCIETY

Whiteout! Although climbers can ascend Mount Aconcagua without special equipment, its unpredictable weather threatens the unwary mountaineer. At the summit, climbers may be exposed to extremely low temperatures.

A particular danger is the *viento blanco*, or "white wind." This condition occurs when strong high-altitude winds blow from the west and create a cloud of microscopic ice crystals near the mountain's summit. Even when weather on the lower slopes is fine, a *viento blanco* can cause snow and high winds to occur farther up the mountain. Being caught inside the *viento blanco* cloud can be very dangerous.

Visual Record Answer
possible answers: farming, oil and mineral exploration

GO TO: go.hrw.com
KEYWORD: SJ5 CH11
FOR: Web sites about Atlantic South America

Ranchers herd sheep on the Pampas of Argentina.
Interpreting the Visual Record *Region*
What other economic activities are common in flat plains regions such as this?

Physical Features

The region of Atlantic South America includes four countries: Brazil (bruh-ZIL), Argentina (ahr-juhn-TEE-nuh), Uruguay (oo-roo-GWY), and Paraguay (pah-rah-GWY). This vast region covers about two thirds of South America. Brazil alone occupies nearly half of the continent.

Plains and Plateaus This region's landforms include mainly plains and plateaus. The Amazon River basin in northern Brazil is a giant, flat flood plain. To the southeast are the Brazilian Highlands, a region of old, eroded mountains. Farther west is the Brazilian Plateau, an area of upland plains.

South of the Brazilian Plateau is a lower region known as the Gran Chaco (grahn CHAH-koh). The Gran Chaco stretches across parts of Paraguay, Bolivia, and northern Argentina. It is an area of flat, low plains covered with low trees, shrubs, and savannas.

In central Argentina are the wide, grassy plains of the **Pampas**. Patagonia, a desert region of dry plains and plateaus, is in southern Argentina. A cool, windswept island called Tierra del Fuego lies at the southern tip of the continent. Tierra del Fuego and nearby small islands are divided between Argentina and Chile.

Mountains The Andes, South America's highest mountains, extend north-south along Argentina's border with Chile. Here we find the Western Hemisphere's highest peak, Mount Aconcagua (ah-kohn-KAH-gwah). It rises to 22,834 feet (6,960 m).

River Systems The world's largest river system, the Amazon, flows eastward across northern Brazil. The Amazon River is about 4,000 miles (6,436 km) long. It extends from the Andes Mountains to the Atlantic Ocean. Hundreds of tributaries flow into it. Together they drain a vast area. This area includes parts of nearly all of the countries of northern and central South America.

TEACH

Teaching Objective 1
ALL LEVELS: (Suggested time: 30 min.) Ask each student to prepare a simple schematic drawing to show how the region's landforms relate to its rivers. Provide colored markers so students can differentiate among elevations and among rivers. **ESOL**

Teaching Objective 2
ALL LEVELS: (Suggested time: 35 min.) Have each student write a paragraph that compares and contrasts the climates, vegetation, and wildlife of Atlantic South America with those of the United States. **LS INTRAPERSONAL**

Teaching Objective 3
ALL LEVELS: (Suggested time: 30 min.) Copy the graphic organizer on the next page onto the chalkboard, omitting the blue answers. Use it to help students identify the region's important resources. Have students work in pairs to fill in the blanks by using the land use and resources map in this unit's atlas and information in Section 1.
ESOL, COOPERATIVE LEARNING

As a result, the Amazon also carries more water than any other river. About 20 percent of the water that runs off Earth's surface flows down the Amazon. This freshwater lowers the salt level of Atlantic waters for more than 100 miles (161 km) out.

The Paraná (pah-rah-NAH) River system drains much of the central part of the region. The Paraná River is 3,030 miles (4,875 km) long. It forms part of Paraguay's borders with Brazil and Argentina. Water from the Paraná flows into the Paraguay River. It continues on to the Río de la Plata (REE-oh day lah PLAH-tah) and the Atlantic Ocean beyond. The Río de la Plata is an **estuary**. An estuary is a partially enclosed body of water where salty seawater and freshwater mix.

✓ **READING CHECK:** *Places and Regions* What are the region's major landforms and rivers? Amazon River and basin, Brazilian Highlands, Brazilian Plateau, Gran Chaco, Pampas, Andes, Paraná River, Rio de la Plata

Climate, Vegetation, and Wildlife

Tropical, moist climates are found in northern and coastal areas. They give way to cooler climates in southern and highland areas.

The Rain Forest The Amazon River basin's humid tropical climate supports the world's largest tropical rain forest. Rain falls almost every day in this region. The Amazon rain forest may contain the world's greatest variety of plant and animal life. Animals there include meat-eating fish called piranhas and predators such as jaguars and giant anacondas. The sloth, a mammal related to anteaters, moves slowly through the trees. It feeds on vegetation.

Plains and Plateaus Climates in the Brazilian Highlands vary widely. In the north, the coastal region is covered mostly with tropical rain forests and savannas. Inland from the coast, the highlands become drier and are covered with grasslands. The southeastern highlands have a mostly humid subtropical climate like the southeastern United States. These moist environments are major agricultural areas.

Southwest of the highlands, the Gran Chaco has a humid tropical climate. Because the Gran Chaco is flat, water drains slowly. Summer rains can turn areas of the region into marshlands. Wildlife there includes giant armadillos, pumas, red wolves, and at least 60 snake species.

The temperate grasslands of the Pampas stretch for almost 400 miles (644 km) southwest of the Río de la Plata. The rich soils and humid subtropical climate make the Pampas a major farming region. Farther south, warm summers and cold winters cause great annual temperature ranges in the Patagonia desert. The Andes block the Pacific Ocean's rain-bearing storms from reaching the area.

✓ **READING CHECK:** *Places and Regions* What are the climates of the region? humid tropical, highland, savanna, humid subtropical

Our Amazing Planet

South America's tropical rain forest blankets an area of about 2.3 million square miles (nearly 6 million sq. km). That is more than two thirds the area of the contiguous United States!

A sloth makes its way along tree branches in the Amazon rain forest.

CHAPTER 11, Section 1

EYE ON EARTH

The Biggest Boa The Amazon River basin is home to the remarkable anaconda, a large South American snake of the boa family. Anacondas are the longest snakes in the Western Hemisphere and the heaviest snakes in the world. They can weigh hundreds of pounds.

The anaconda, also called the water boa, lies in wait by the water's edge. To kill, the anaconda pulls its prey beneath the water's surface until the prey drowns. Anacondas feed on birds, fish, large rodents, and small mammals.

Activity: Have students create a food web of plants and animals in the rain forest, including anacondas. Students may need to consult other sources.

internet connect

GO TO: go.hrw.com
KEYWORD: SJ5 CH11
FOR: Web sites about anacondas

Resources of Atlantic South America

Area of Atlantic South America	Resource
Amazon River basin	rain forest—for food, wood, rubber, medicinal plants; gold, other minerals
Brazilian Highlands	oil
Brazilian Plateau	hydroelectric power, minerals
Gran Chaco	hydroelectric power
Pampas	oil, natural gas, minerals
Patagonia	oil, natural gas

Teaching Objectives 1–3

ALL LEVELS: (Suggested time: 45 min.) Have students imagine that they are going to travel from Manaus to the top of Mount Aconcagua. Organize the class into groups. Have each group plan a trip route, make a list of supplies needed, and then write a journal describing the landforms, bodies of water, vegetation, animal life, and resources they would see on their journey. Ask groups to share their travelogues with the class. The activity may require more than one class period. **COOPERATIVE LEARNING**

Section 1 Review

Answers to Section 1 Review

Define For definitions, see the glossary.

Working with Sketch Maps Maps will vary, but listed places should be labeled in their approximate locations.

Reading for the Main Idea
1. Brazilian Highlands, Brazilian Plateau, Gran Chaco, Pampas (NGS 4)
2. drains the largest area and carries more water than any other river (NGS 4)
3. The Andes prevent the Pacific Ocean's rain-bearing storms from reaching the area. (NGS 4)

Critical Thinking
4. As the soil is exhausted, people will clear new areas to plant.

Organizing What You Know
5. climates—tropical moist climates, some cooler climates; vegetation—rain forest, marshlands, grasslands; wildlife—piranhas, jaguars, sloths, armadillos, pumas, red wolves, snakes; resources—rain forest, minerals, hydroelectric power

Visual Record Answer ▶
possible answers: cheaper, easier, requires fewer tools, disposes of debris

Resources

One of the region's greatest resources is the Amazon rain forest. The rain forest provides food, wood, natural rubber, medicinal plants, and many other products. However, large areas of the rain forest are being cleared for mining, ranching, and farming.

Commercial agriculture is found throughout the region. In some areas, however, planting the same crop every year has caused **soil exhaustion**. Soil exhaustion means that the soil has lost nutrients needed by plants. Overgrazing is also a problem in some places.

The region's mineral wealth includes gold, silver, copper, and iron. There are oil deposits in the region, particularly in Brazil and Patagonia. Some of the region's large rivers provide hydroelectric power. One of the world's largest hydroelectric dams is the Itaipu Dam on the Paraná River. The dam lies between Brazil and Paraguay.

✓ **READING CHECK:** *Environment and Society* How have humans modified the region's environment? through logging, mining, ranching, farming, hydroelectric dams

◀ People are clearing large areas of the Amazon rain forest by burning and by cutting.

Interpreting the Visual Record *Human-Environment Interaction* Why do you think someone would choose to clear rain forest areas by burning rather than by cutting?

Homework Practice Online
Keyword: SJ5 HP11

Define and explain: Pampas, estuary, soil exhaustion

Working with Sketch Maps On an outline map of the region that you draw or that your teacher provides, label the following: Amazon River, Brazilian Highlands, Brazilian Plateau, Gran Chaco, Patagonia, Tierra del Fuego, Andes, Paraná River, Paraguay River, and Río de la Plata.

Reading for the Main Idea
1. *Places and Regions* What major landforms lie between the Amazon River basin and Patagonia?
2. *Places and Regions* What sets the Amazon River apart from all of the world's other rivers?
3. *Places and Regions* Why is the Patagonia desert dry?

Critical Thinking
4. **Drawing Inferences and Conclusions** How do you think soil exhaustion in Brazil could lead to more deforestation?

Organizing What You Know
5. **Categorizing** Copy the following graphic organizer. Use it to describe Atlantic South America.

Climates	Vegetation and wildlife	Resources

240 • Chapter 11

CLOSE

Tell the class about the Amazon ant, also known as a slave-making ant. They attack the nests of other ants and kidnap the helpless offspring. When the young become adults, they act as slaves to the Amazon ants. Amazon ants need the slave ants because their jaws are so long and curved that they cannot feed themselves or dig nests. The slave ants perform these tasks.

REVIEW, ASSESS, RETEACH

Have students complete the Section Review. Then have each student create a five-question crossword puzzle based on the main ideas from each section. Pair students and have them complete each other's puzzles. Then have students complete Daily Quiz 11.1. **COOPERATIVE LEARNING**

Have students complete Main Idea Activity S1. Then have students read the Read to Discover questions for each section and skim the section to find the answers. Ask volunteers to write the answers on the board. **ESOL, LS VERBAL-LINGUISTIC**

EXTEND

Have interested students conduct research on the Amazon River basin and create a diorama to show the physical features, vegetation, and animals of the area. **BLOCK SCHEDULING**

Section 2 Brazil

Read to Discover
1. What is the history of Brazil?
2. What are important characteristics of Brazil's people and culture?
3. What are Brazil's four major regions like today?

Vocabulary
favelas

Places
Rio de Janeiro
São Paulo
Manaus
Belém
Salvador
São Francisco River
Mato Grosso Plateau
Brasília

Reading Strategy

FOLDNOTES: TRI-FOLD Create a Tri-Fold FoldNote as described in the Appendix. Write what you know about Brazil in the column labeled "Know." Then write what you want to know in the column labeled "Want." As you read the section, write what you learn about Brazil in the column labeled "Learn."

CHAPTER 11, Section 2

SECTION 2 RESOURCES

Reproducible
◆ Lecture Notes, Section 2
◆ Know It Notes S2
◆ Cultures of the World Activity 2
◆ Geography for Life Activity 11
◆ Map Activity 11

Technology
◆ One-Stop Planner CD–ROM, Lesson 11.2
◆ Homework Practice Online
◆ Our Environment CD–ROM/Seek and Tell/People Affecting Nature
◆ HRW Go site

Reinforcement, Review, and Assessment
◆ Section 2 Review
◆ Daily Quiz 11.2
◆ Main Idea Activity S2
◆ Chapter Summaries and Review
◆ English Audio Summary 11.2
◆ Spanish Audio Summary 11.2

History

Most Brazilians are descended from three groups of immigrants. The first group included peoples who probably migrated to the Americas from northern Asia long ago. The second was made up of Portuguese and other Europeans who came after 1500. Africans brought as slaves made up the third group.

First Inhabitants Brazil's first human inhabitants arrived in the region thousands of years ago. They spread throughout the tropical rain forests and savannas.

These peoples developed a way of life based on hunting, fishing, and small-scale farming. They grew crops such as sweet potatoes, beans, and cassava. The root of the cassava plant is ground up and used as an ingredient in many foods in Brazil today. It also is used to make tapioca. Tapioca is a common food in grocery stores in the United States and other countries.

Europeans and Africans After 1500, Portuguese settlers began to move into Brazil. Favorable climates and soil helped make Brazil a large sugar-growing colony. Colonists brought slaves from Africa to work alongside Brazilian Indians on large sugar plantations. Sugar plantations eventually replaced forests along the Atlantic coast.

As elsewhere in the region, Brazilian Indians fought back against early European colonists. However, the Indians could not overcome powerful European forces.

Atlantic South America • 241

Section 2

Objectives
1. Examine the history of Brazil.
2. Identify important characteristics of Brazil's people and culture.
3. Describe what Brazil's four regions are like today.

Focus

Bellringer
Copy the following instructions onto the chalkboard: *What celebrations are held regularly in our area? When do they occur? What do they celebrate?* Discuss responses. Tell students that in Brazil, Carnival is a pre-Lent festival celebrated with music, dancing, parades, and colorful costumes. Explain that Lent is more widely observed in mainly Catholic countries like Brazil, but people of many religions unite for Carnival celebrations. Tell students that in Section 2 they will learn more about the diversity of Brazil.

Building Vocabulary
Write **favelas** on the chalkboard and call on a volunteer to read the term's definition. Explain that the term has Portuguese origins. Ask students to imagine what life is like for the Brazilians who live in the favelas. (Possible answers: poor housing, high crime, few opportunities for education or employment, poor health care, and so on) Then tell students they will learn more about all Brazilians in this section.

Atlantic South America 241

CHAPTER 11, Section 2

DAILY LIFE

Samba Party! The samba is a dance style popular in Brazil. Samba schools, or neighborhood social clubs, exist throughout Rio de Janeiro's favelas. Every year, the samba schools compete to have the best entry in the Carnival parade. Members select a story or theme and then spend almost a year creating music, dance, and costumes to accompany it.

Activity: Ask a volunteer to learn the basic samba steps by consulting outside sources or a dance organization in your community. Then ask that student to teach the steps to the entire class. Organize the class into groups. Have each group prepare a samba dance entry for a samba contest. Have students perform their dances and judge their classmates' entries.

Farther inland, Portuguese settlers set up cattle ranches. These ranches provided hides and dried beef for world markets. In the late 1600s and early 1700s gold and precious gems were discovered in the southeast. A mining boom drew adventurers from around the world. The coastal city of Rio de Janeiro grew during this boom. In the late 1800s southeastern Brazil became a major coffee producer. This coffee boom promoted the growth of São Paulo.

Brazil gained independence from Portugal in 1822. An emperor ruled the country until 1889. Dictators and elected governments have ruled the country at various times since then. Today, Brazil has an elected president and legislature. Like the United States, Brazil provides its citizens the opportunity to participate in the political process through voting and other political activities.

✓ **READING CHECK:** *Human Systems* How have different peoples influenced Brazilian history? **through farming, immigration, colonization**

People and Culture

Nearly 40 percent of Brazil's more than 180 million people are of mixed African and European descent. More than half of Brazilians are ethnic European. They include descendants of Portuguese, Spaniards, Germans, Italians, and Poles. Portuguese is the official language. Some Brazilians also speak Spanish, English, French, Japanese, and Indian languages.

Religion Brazil has the world's largest population of Roman Catholics. About 70 percent of Brazilians are Catholic. Some Brazilians also practice Macumba (mah-KOOM-bah). Macumba combines African, Indian, and Catholic religious ideas and practices.

▲ Brazilian fans cheer on their country's soccer team. Soccer is very popular throughout Atlantic South America. Brazilian teams often compete in international tournaments, such as the World Cup.

Carnival Other aspects of Brazilian life also reflect the country's mix of cultures. For example, Brazilians celebrate Carnival before the Christian season of Lent. However, the celebration mixes traditions from Africa, Brazil, and Europe. During Carnival, Brazilians dance the samba, which was adapted from an African dance.

Food Other examples of immigrant influences can be found in Brazilian foods. In parts of eastern Brazil, an African dish called *vatapá* (vah-tah-PAH) is popular. *Vatapá* mixes seafood, sauces, and red peppers. Many Brazilians also enjoy eating *feijoada* (fay-ZHWAH-da), a stew of black beans and meat. It is traditionally served on Saturday to large groups of people. *Feijoada* has many regional varieties.

✓ **READING CHECK:** *Human Systems* How has cultural borrowing affected Brazilian culture? **Many languages are spoken; Macumba developed; Carnival is an important holiday celebration; samba is a popular dance; a variety of influences can be seen in the food.**

242 • Chapter 11

TEACH

Teaching Objective 1
ALL LEVELS: (Suggested time: 30 min.) Pair students and have pairs create a time line listing important events in the history of Brazil. Ask them to write a brief statement by each event indicating its significance. Display and discuss the time lines. **COOPERATIVE LEARNING**

Teaching Objective 2
ALL LEVELS: (Suggested time: 20 min.) Lead a class discussion comparing and contrasting the cultures of Brazil and the United States. Include the topics of religion, diversity, language, and food. **LS INTERPERSONAL**

▶**ASSIGNMENT:** Have students consider the advantages and disadvantages that Brazil brings with it into the 2000s. Ask students to list factors that will help Brazil in its future and obstacles that Brazil must overcome if its future is to be bright. Ask students to evaluate their lists and to write a brief prediction for Brazil's future.

Day fades into night in Rio de Janeiro, Brazil's second-largest city. Sugarloaf Mountain stands near the entrance to Guanabara Bay. The Brazilian city is often referred to simply as Rio.

Brazil Today

Brazil is the largest and most populous country in South America. It ranks as the fifth-largest country in the world in both land area and population. Brazil also has the region's largest economy. Many Brazilians are poor, but the country has modern and prosperous areas. We will explore these and other areas by dividing the country into four regions. Those regions are the Amazon, the northeast, the southeast, and the interior. We will start in the Amazon and move southward.

The Amazon The Amazon region covers much of northern and western Brazil. Isolated Indian villages are scattered throughout the region's dense rain forest. Some Indians had little contact with outsiders until recently.

The major inland city in the region is Manaus. More than 1 million people live there. It is the Amazon's major river port and industrial city. South of the Atlantic port of Belém is a large mining district. New roads and mining projects are bringing more people and development to this region. However, development is destroying large areas of the rain forest. It also threatens the way of life of Brazilian Indians who live there. This development has created tensions among the Indians, new settlers, and miners.

The Northeast Northeastern Brazil includes many old colonial cities, such as Salvador. It is Brazil's poorest region. Many people there cannot read, and health care is poor. The region suffers from drought and has had trouble attracting industry. Cities in the region have huge slums called **favelas** (fah-VE-lahs).

Brazil

Country	Population/ Growth Rate	Life Expectancy	Literacy Rate	Per Capita GDP
Brazil	182,032,604 1.1%	67, male 75, female	86%	$7,600
United States	290,342,554 0.9%	74, male 80, female	97%	$37,600

Source: Central Intelligence Agency, *The World Factbook 2003*

CHAPTER 11, Section 2

Linking Past to Present

The History of Manaus Manaus is the capital of the state of Amazonas in northwestern Brazil. It has a population of more than 1 million.

Europeans built a small fort at the site in 1669. A mission and village grew up there later. A monopoly on rubber production led to an economic boom from 1890 to 1920. Magnificent buildings date from that period. Among them are the opera house, where world-famous singers and dancers performed. The boom ended when rubber plantations in other countries became profitable.

Manaus is now a thriving river port. It exports electrical equipment, oil, chemicals, rubber, Brazil nuts, and other forest products. One of these exports comes from a large South American fish called the pirarucu. Its scales are sold as nail files. In the 1970s the development of mineral wealth and agriculture and the focus on economic growth led to increased deforestation in the region surrounding the city.

Discussion: Point out that for much of its history, Manaus could be reached only by boat or air. Lead a discussion on how this may have affected the daily lives of the city's residents.

Atlantic South America • 243

Teaching Objective 3

LEVEL 1: (Suggested time: 10 min.) Copy the following graphic organizer onto the chalkboard, omitting the blue answers. Use it to help students understand the characteristics of Brazil's regions. Point out that it is shaped roughly like Brazil. Have students copy the organizer into their notebooks and complete it. **ESOL, LS VISUAL-SPATIAL**

LEVELS 2 AND 3: (Suggested time: 30 min.) Organize the class into four groups. Assign each group one of the four regions of Brazil. Have students prepare a short presentation on why a certain new industry should operate from the region. Each presentation should include the economic, social, and environmental effects of the new industry. **COOPERATIVE LEARNING**

Brazil

The Amazon: dense rain forest; isolated Brazilian Indian villages; Manaus—major city; Belém—Atlantic port; large mining district; tensions among Brazilian Indians, settlers, miners

The Interior: savannas and dry woodlands, could become agricultural area, Brasília, the national capital

The Northeast: old colonial cities like Salvador, suffers from drought, poorest region, favelas

The Southeast: coffee-growing area, Rio de Janeiro, richest region, most people, São Paulo

Atlantic South America 243

Section 2 Review

Answers to Section 2 Review

Define For definitions, see the glossary.

Working with Sketch Maps Brasília was built to help develop Brazil's interior. Although it was designed for 500,000 people, the city now has nearly 2 million residents.

Reading for the Main Idea
1. Africans, Portuguese, Spaniards, Germans, Italians, and Poles (NGS 10)
2. northeast; southeast (NGS 4)

Critical Thinking
3. possible answers: conflicts involving control of land and wealth, fear of destroying Brazilian Indians' way of life
4. possible answer: one of the world's most ethnically diverse countries, resulting in a variety of languages, cultures, religions, foods, customs

Organizing What You Know
5. economic development, mining, road building, population growth, built new cities, hydroelectric development, industrial development

Chart Answer
Brazil

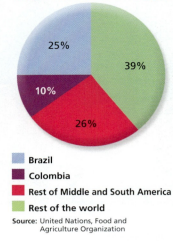

Major Producers of Coffee

- Brazil 39%
- Colombia 10%
- Rest of Middle and South America 26%
- Rest of the world 25%

Source: United Nations, Food and Agriculture Organization

Interpreting the Chart Which single South American country produces the most coffee?

The Southeast Large favelas are also found in other Brazilian cities, particularly in the southeast. Most of Brazil's people live in the southeast. However, in contrast to the northeast, the southeast is Brazil's richest region. It is rich in natural resources and has most of the country's industries and productive farms. The southeast is one of the most productive coffee-growing regions in the world.

The giant cities of São Paulo and Rio de Janeiro are located in the southeast. More than 17.9 million people live in and around São Paulo. It is the largest urban area in South America and the fourth largest in the world. The city is also Brazil's main industrial center.

Rio de Janeiro lies northeast of São Paulo. More than 10 million people live there. The city was Brazil's capital from 1822 until 1960. Today, Rio de Janeiro remains a major seaport and is popular with tourists.

The Interior The interior region is a frontier land of savannas and dry woodlands. It begins in the upper São Francisco River basin and extends to the Mato Grosso Plateau. The region's abundant land and mild climate could one day make it an important agricultural area.

Brasília, the national capital, is located in this region. Brazil's government built the city during the 1950s and 1960s. Government officials hoped the new city would help develop Brazil's interior. It has modern buildings and busy highways. Nearly 2 million people live in Brasília, although it was designed for only 500,000.

✓ **READING CHECK:** *Places and Regions* What are Brazil's four main regions? the Amazon, the Northeast, the Southeast, the Interior

Homework Practice Online
Keyword: SJ5 HP11

Section Review 2

Define and explain: favelas

Working with Sketch Maps On the map you created in Section 1, label Brazil, Rio de Janeiro, São Paulo, Manaus, Belém, Salvador, São Francisco River, Mato Grosso Plateau, and Brasília. In a margin box, write a caption explaining why Brazil's government built Brasília and how the city has grown over time.

Reading for the Main Idea
1. *Human Systems* From what major immigrant groups are many Brazilians descended?
2. *Places and Regions* What is Brazil's poorest region? What is its richest and most populated region?

Critical Thinking
3. **Drawing Inferences and Conclusions** Why do you think development in the Amazon has caused conflicts among miners, settlers, and Brazilian Indians?

4. **Finding the Main Idea** How did immigration influence Brazilian culture today?

Organizing What You Know
5. **Summarizing** Copy the following graphic organizer. Use it to list how early Brazilian Indians and European settlers and their descendants have used Brazil's natural resources and natural environment. Write each example in a circle radiating from the central circle. Create as many or as few circles as you need.

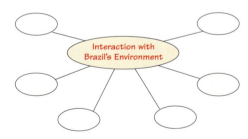

244 • Chapter 11

CLOSE

Have students pick the Brazilian region where they would most like to live. Ask students to explain why they would prefer that region and what occupation they would expect to pursue there.

REVIEW, ASSESS, RETEACH

Have students complete the Section Review. Then have students write five questions, along with the answers, using the information in the section. Collect the questions and answers. Organize the class into two teams and have the teams compete against each other. Then have students complete Daily Quiz 11.2.

Have students complete Main Idea Activity S2. Have class members imagine that they are in charge of planting a time capsule for Brazil that will be unearthed in 100 years. It should reflect Brazil's physical and human geography. Have the class decide what should be included in the time capsule. **ESOL**, **LS KINESTHETIC**

EXTEND

Ask interested students to investigate how international organizations are working to save Brazil's rain forests and to present their findings to the class. Then have the class discuss ways they could help. **BLOCK SCHEDULING**

Section 3: Argentina

Read to Discover
1. What is the history of Argentina?
2. What are important characteristics of Argentina's people and culture?
3. What is Argentina like today?

Vocabulary
- encomienda
- gauchos
- Mercosur

Places
- Buenos Aires
- Córdoba
- Rosario

People
- Eva Perón

Reading Strategy
READING ORGANIZER Before you read, create a concept map using the headings in this section. As you read, add information about the history, people, and culture of Argentina.

CHAPTER 11, Section 3

SECTION 3 RESOURCES

Reproducible
- Lecture Notes, Section 3
- Know It Notes S3
- Cultures of the World Activity 2
- Biography Activity: José de San Martin

Technology
- One-Stop Planner CD–ROM, Lesson 11.3
- Homework Practice Online
- HRW Go site

Reinforcement, Review, and Assessment
- Section 3 Review
- Daily Quiz 11.3
- Main Idea Activity S3
- Chapter Summaries and Review
- English Audio Summary 11.3
- Spanish Audio Summary 11.3

History

Like most of South America, what is now Argentina was originally home to groups of Indians. Groups living in the Pampas hunted wild game. Farther north, Indians farmed and built irrigation systems.

Early Argentina In the 1500s Spanish conquerors spread into southern South America. They moved into the region in search of riches they believed they would find there. They called the region Argentina, meaning "land of silver" or "silvery one."

The first Spanish settlement in Argentina was established in the early 1500s. Spanish settlements were organized under the **encomienda** system. Under that system, the Spanish monarch gave land to colonists. These landowners were granted the right to force Indians living there to work the land.

The Pampas became an increasingly important agricultural region during the colonial era. Argentine cowboys, called **gauchos** (GOW-chohz), herded cattle and horses on the open grasslands. Colonists eventually fenced off their lands into huge ranches. They hired gauchos to tend their herds of livestock. Today the gaucho, like the American cowboy, is vanishing. Still, the gaucho lives on in Argentine literature and popular culture.

In 1816 Argentina gained independence. However, a long period of instability and violence followed. Many Indians, particularly in the Pampas, were killed in wars with the Argentine

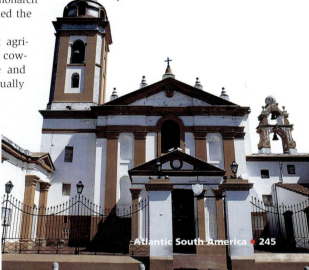

Examples of Spanish-style architecture can be seen throughout Argentina. This Roman Catholic church was built in the 1600s in Córdoba.

Atlantic South America • 245

Section 3

Objectives
1. Explore the history of Argentina.
2. Determine the important characteristics of Argentina's people and culture.
3. Explain what Argentina is like today.

Focus

Bellringer
Copy the following question onto the chalkboard: *Have you heard about Eva Perón? What do you already know about her?* Allow students time to write their answers. (Possible answer: She was the subject of a popular musical and movie.) Discuss responses. Then tell students that Eva Perón was a real person and an important figure in Argentina's history. There is a brief biography of Eva Perón in this section. Tell students that in Section 3 they will learn more about Argentina's history and culture.

Building Vocabulary
Write the key terms *encomienda* and *gauchos* on the chalkboard. Have volunteers find and read the definitions aloud. Explain that both of the terms have Spanish origins. Have students write a sentence using both terms. (Example: Gauchos and the *encomienda* system both had an effect on Argentina's agriculture.) Then write **Mercosur** on the chalkboard. Have a student read the definition. Give an example of other trade agreements or organizations, such as NAFTA.

Atlantic South America 245

CHAPTER 11, Section 3

GLOBAL PERSPECTIVES

Argentina and Great Britain fought a war for control of a small group of islands that lies about 300 miles (483 km) east of the Strait of Magellan. The Argentines call the islands the Islas Malvinas and had long claimed ownership of them. Since 1833 the British have ruled what they call the Falkland Islands.

In April 1982, Argentine troops seized the Falklands. Argentina and Britain then fought air, sea, and land battles for control of the territory. Argentina surrendered in June 1982.

Discussion: Ask students to explain the significance of the Falkland Islands. Have students find the Falklands on a map and analyze why both Britain and Argentina would claim these remote islands.

Biography Answer

by improving the living conditions and political rights of Argentines

Eva Perón
(1919–1952)

Character Trait: Kindness

Known affectionately as "Evita," Eva Perón improved the living conditions of Argentines during the late 1940s and early 1950s. As the wife of Argentina's president, Juan Perón, Evita established thousands of hospitals and schools throughout Argentina. She also helped Argentine women gain the right to vote. After years of battling cancer, Evita died at age 33. For weeks all of Argentina mourned.

How did Evita show kindness?

Couples practice the Argentine tango on a Buenos Aires sidewalk. Varieties of the tango are popular in some other Middle and South American countries and in parts of Spain.

246 • Chapter 11

government. As a result, Argentina has a small Indian population today. Most of these wars had ended by the late 1870s.

Modern Argentina New waves of European immigrants came to Argentina in the late 1800s. Immigrants included Italians, Germans, and Spaniards. Exports of meat and other farm products to Europe helped make the country richer.

However, throughout much of the 1900s, Argentina struggled under dictators and military governments. These unlimited governments abused human rights. Both the country's economy and its people suffered. In 1982 Argentina lost a brief war with the United Kingdom over the Falkland Islands. Shortly afterward, Argentina's last military government gave up power to an elected government.

✓ **READING CHECK:** *Human Systems* How was Argentina's government organized during much of the 1900s? **as a dictatorship or military government**

People and Culture

Argentina's culture has many European ties. Most of the more than 38 million Argentines are Roman Catholic. Most also are descended from Spanish, Italian, or other European settlers. Argentine Indians and mestizos make up only about 3 percent of the population. Spanish is the official language. English, Italian, German, and French are also spoken there.

Beef is an important agricultural product and a big part of the Argentine diet. A popular dish is *parrillada*. It includes sausage and steak served on a small grill. Supper generally is eaten after 9 P.M.

✓ **READING CHECK:** *Human Systems* Why are so many languages spoken in Argentina? **because of the many different cultures that make up Argentine society**

TEACH

Teaching Objective 1

LEVEL 1: (Suggested time: 15 min.) Ask students to write newspaper headlines describing events during Argentina's major historical periods. (Example: "Fences changing ways of life for gauchos.")

LEVELS 2 AND 3: (Suggested time: 45 min.) Have students use other resources to conduct research on the era that is the subject of one of the headlines they wrote for the Level 1 activity. Ask them to write the newspaper article to match the headline. **LS VERBAL-LINGUISTIC**

Teaching Objective 2

ALL LEVELS: (Suggested time: 10 min.) Copy the following graphic organizer onto the chalkboard. Use it to demonstrate the ethnic makeup of Argentina's population. Then ask students to summarize other features of Argentine culture.

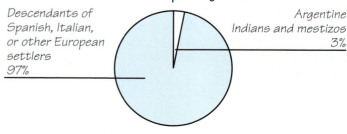

Ethnic makeup of Argentina

Descendants of Spanish, Italian, or other European settlers 97%

Argentine Indians and mestizos 3%

246 Chapter 11

Connecting to Literature

Argentine gaucho

The Gaucho Martín Fierro

José Hernández was born in 1834. A sickly boy, he was sent to regain his health on Argentina's Pampas. The gauchos lived freely on the plains there, herding cattle. As an adult, Hernández took part in his country's political struggles. He fled to Brazil after a failed revolt. In 1872 he published his epic poem, The Gaucho Martín Fierro. In this excerpt, Martín Fierro recalls his happier times as an Argentine cowboy.

Ah, those times! . . . you felt proud
to see how a man could ride.
When a gaucho really knew his job,
even if the colt went over backwards,
not one of them wouldn't land on his feet
with the halter-rein in his hand. . . .

Even the poorest gaucho
had a string of matching horses;
he could always afford some amusement,
and people were ready for
  anything. . . .
Looking out across the land
you'd see nothing but cattle
  and sky.

When the branding-time came round
that was work to warm you up!
What a crowd! lassoing the running steers
and keen to hold and throw them. . . .
What a time that was! in those days surely
there were champions to be seen. . . .

And the games that would get going
when we were all of us together!
We were always ready for them,
as at times like those
a lot of neighbors would turn up
to help out the regular hands.

Analyzing Primary Sources
1. What does Martín Fierro remember about the "old days"?
2. In what ways is a gaucho's life similar to that of an American cowboy?

Argentina Today

Argentina has rich natural resources and a well-educated population. The Pampas are the most developed agricultural region. About 12 percent of Argentina's labor force works in agriculture. Large ranches and farms produce beef, wheat, and corn for export to other countries.

Much of Argentina's industry is located in and around Buenos Aires, the national capital. Buenos Aires is the second-largest urban area in South America. Its location on the coast and near the Pampas has contributed to its economic development. It is home to nearly a

Atlantic South America • 247

Section 3 Review

Answers to Section 3 Review

Define or identify: For definitions and identifications, see the glossary or the index.

Working with Sketch Maps Places should be labeled in their approximate locations.

Reading for the Main Idea
1. killed in wars with the Argentine government; few Indians today (NGS 12)
2. Buenos Aires area; because of its beneficial position in the country (NGS 4)

Critical Thinking
3. variety of languages spoken, foods like sausage and steaks, Roman Catholic religion
4. promotes economic cooperation among Argentina, Brazil, Paraguay, Uruguay, and to a lesser extent, Chile; provides for increased imports, exports, and job opportunities; the countries are neighbors and are logical economic partners

Organizing What You Know
5. 1500s: Spanish settle Argentina; 1816: Argentina gains its independence; about 1816–80: Indian–government wars; late 1800s: new European immigrants; 1983: return of democracy to Argentina

---

Wide European-style avenues stretch through Buenos Aires. Large advertisements compete for attention in the lively city. ▶

third of all Argentines. Other large Argentine cities include the interior cities of Córdoba and Rosario.

In 1983 Argentina returned to democracy and established an elected government. In the 1900s government leaders put economic reforms in place to help businesses grow. Argentina joined **Mercosur**—a trade organization that promotes economic cooperation among its members in southern and eastern South America. By the late 1900s and early 2000s, however, government spending and heavy debt brought Argentina into an economic and political crisis. During 2001, the government changed hands four times as its leaders tried to stop the mounting problems. By 2003, the economy had stabilized somewhat. Today, Argentines are still searching for ways to improve their economy while keeping the political freedoms gained during the 1980s.

✓ **READING CHECK:** *Places and Regions* What is Argentina like today? more democratic, well-educated population, large urban areas, growing economy

Section Review 3

Define or identify: encomienda, gauchos, Eva Perón, Mercosur

Working with Sketch Maps On the map you created in Section 2, label Argentina, Buenos Aires, Córdoba, and Rosario.

Reading for the Main Idea
1. *Human Systems* What happened to Argentine Indians in the Pampas in the 1800s? How did that affect Argentine society?
2. *Places and Regions* Where is much of Argentina's industry located? Why?

Critical Thinking
3. **Finding the Main Idea** In what ways does Argentine culture reflect European influences? What are some examples of these influences?
4. **Analyzing Information** How does Mercosur help Argentina's economy grow today? How does location play a part in that process?

Organizing What You Know
5. **Sequencing** Copy the following time line. Use it to identify important dates, events, and periods in the history of Argentina.

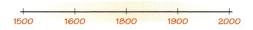

248 • Chapter 11

CLOSE

Call on volunteers to describe how the illustrations in this section reflect the history and culture of Argentina.

REVIEW, ASSESS, RETEACH

Have students complete the Section Review. Then have students work in pairs to write lyrics for a gaucho's song about Argentina's history, culture, or economy. Call on volunteers to read their lyrics aloud and explain their connection to Argentine society. Then have students complete Daily Quiz 11.3. **COOPERATIVE LEARNING,** **LS** **AUDITORY-MUSICAL**

Then assign each of three groups one of the following topics: Argentina's history, Argentina's people and culture, or Argentina today. Have each group create a radio newscast on the assigned topic. **ESOL, COOPERATIVE LEARNING** **LS** **AUDITORY-MUSICAL**

EXTEND

Buenos Aires is a very cosmopolitan city. Have students conduct research on the cultural life of Buenos Aires and create a weekend entertainment supplement for the city's newspaper. **BLOCK SCHEDULING**

Section 4: Uruguay and Paraguay

Read to Discover
1. What are the people and economy of Uruguay like today?
2. What are the people and economy of Paraguay like today?

Vocabulary
landlocked

Places
Montevideo
Asunción

Reading Strategy
READING ORGANIZER Before you read, draw two overlapping circles. As you read, write characteristics about Uruguay in one circle and characteristics about Paraguay in the other. In the space where the circles overlap, write the characteristics both countries share.

CHAPTER 11, Section 4

SECTION 4 RESOURCES
Reproducible
- Lecture Notes, Section 4
- Know It Notes S4
- Cultures of the World Activity 2

Technology
- One-Stop Planner CD–ROM, Lesson 11.4
- Homework Practice Online
- HRW Go site

Reinforcement, Review, and Assessment
- Section 4 Review
- Daily Quiz 11.4
- Main Idea Activity S4
- Chapter Summaries and Review
- English Audio Summary 11.4
- Spanish Audio Summary 11.4

Uruguay

Uruguay lies along the Río de la Plata. The Río de la Plata is the major estuary and waterway of southern South America. It stretches about 170 miles (274 km) inland from the Atlantic Ocean.

Uruguay's capital, Montevideo (mawn-tay-bee-THAY-oh), is located on the north shore of the Río de la Plata. The city is also the business center of the country.

Like its neighbors, Uruguay at times has been ruled by the military. However, in general the country has a strong democratic tradition of respect for political freedom.

Portugal claimed Uruguay during the colonial era. However, the Spanish took over the area by the 1770s. By that time, few Uruguayan Indians remained. Uruguay declared independence from Spain in 1825.

The People People of European descent make up about 88 percent of Uruguay's population. About 12 percent of the population is either mestizo, African, or Indian.

Roman Catholicism is the main religion in the country. Spanish is the official language, but many people also speak Portuguese.

More than 90 percent of Uruguayans live in urban areas. More than a third of the

Government buildings and monuments surround Independence Square in Montevideo, the capital of Uruguay.

Atlantic South America • 249

Section 4

Objectives
1. Investigate the people and economy of Uruguay.
2. Describe the people and economy of Paraguay.

FOCUS

Bellringer
Copy these instructions onto the chalkboard: *Look at the photos in this section of the chapter for clues about life in Paraguay and Uruguay. What conclusions can you draw?* Allow students time to complete their answers. (Possible answers: modern and colonial-era buildings, handmade cloth, people dressed like cowboys) Discuss responses. Have students predict what life is like in these countries based on their observations. Tell students that in Section 4 they will learn more about Uruguay and Paraguay.

Building Vocabulary
Write the key term  on the chalkboard. Call on a volunteer to find the definition in the textbook and read it aloud. Explain that Paraguay is a landlocked country. Have volunteers use a world map to locate other landlocked countries. Discuss the advantages and disadvantages a landlocked country may have.

Atlantic South America 249

FOOD FESTIVAL

Tempting Tapioca

Tapioca is a starch taken from the root of the cassava, a tropical plant native to South America. Cassava, also called manioc, has been the main starch eaten by most of the area's indigenous peoples. The roots are washed and then reduced to pulp, which is strained and dried. If cassava isn't prepared properly it's poisonous! The dried cassava forms small pellets we know as tapioca. Tapioca can be eaten plain or with flavoring. Brazilians favor sweetened tapioca with ginger and cinnamon.

Prepare tapioca according to package instructions. Serve with sugar, honey, syrup, or other flavors. Make larger quantities as needed.

Chart Answer

It is much lower.

The town of Colonia del Sacramento, Uruguay, was founded in 1680. Today it is an internationally recognized historical site.

people live in and around Montevideo. The country has a high literacy rate. In addition, many Uruguayans have good jobs and can afford a wide range of consumer goods.

Economy Uruguay's economy is tied to the economies of Brazil and Argentina. In fact, more than half of Uruguay's foreign trade is with these two Mercosur partners. In addition, many Brazilians and Argentines vacation at beach resorts in Uruguay.

Uruguay's humid subtropical climate and rich soils have helped make agriculture an important part of the economy. As in Argentina, ranchers graze livestock on inland plains. Beef is an important export.

Uruguay has few mineral resources. An important source of energy is hydroelectric power. One big challenge is developing the poor rural areas in the interior, where resources are in short supply.

✓ **READING CHECK:** *Places and Regions* What geographic factors support agriculture in Uruguay? *the humid subtropical climate and rich soils*

Uruguay and Paraguay

Country	Population/ Growth Rate	Life Expectancy	Literacy Rate	Per Capita GDP
Paraguay	6,036,900 2.5%	71, male 77, female	94%	$4,200
Uruguay	3,413,329 0.7%	72, male 79, female	98%	$7,800
United States	290,342,554 0.9%	74, male 80, female	97%	$37,600

Source: Central Intelligence Agency, *The World Factbook 2003*

Interpreting the Chart How does Paraguay's per capita GDP compare to that of Uruguay?

Paraguay

Paraguay shares borders with Bolivia, Brazil, and Argentina. It is a **landlocked** country. Landlocked means it is completely surrounded by land, with no direct access to the ocean.

The Paraguay River divides the country into two regions. East of the river is the country's most productive agricultural land. The region west of the river is part of the Gran Chaco. This region has low trees and thorny shrubs. Ranchers graze livestock in some parts of western Paraguay.

Spanish settlers claimed Paraguay in the early 1500s. The country won independence from Spain in 1811. Paraguay was ruled off and on by dictators until 1989. Today, the country has an elected government.

TEACH

Teaching Objectives 1–2

LEVEL 1: (Suggested time: 15 min.) Copy the following graphic organizer onto the chalkboard, omitting the blue answers. Have volunteers fill in the organizer. **LS VISUAL-SPATIAL**

LEVELS 2 AND 3: (Suggested time: 30 min.) Have students create an advertisement for a business magazine enticing foreign investment in either Paraguay or Uruguay.

The People and Economy of Paraguay and Uruguay

Uruguay
People
88% European; most Roman Catholic; Spanish, Portuguese; 90% urban; high literacy rate
Economy
led by Brazil and Argentina; agriculture, livestock; hydroelectric power

Paraguay
People
95% mestizo; Spanish, Guaraní; most Roman Catholic
Economy
controlled by few families and companies; surplus hydroelectricity; agriculture; not much industry

The People About 95 percent of Paraguayans are mestizos. European descendants and Paraguayan Indians make up the rest of the population. Spanish is the official language. Almost all people speak both Spanish and Guaraní (gwah-ruh-NEE), an Indian language. As in Uruguay, most people are Roman Catholic.

Asunción (ah-soon-SYOHN) is Paraguay's capital and largest city. It is located along the Paraguay River near the border with Argentina.

Economy Much of Paraguay's wealth is controlled by a few rich families and companies. These families and companies have great influence over the country's government.

Agriculture is an important part of Paraguay's economy. Much of the economy is traditional—many people are subsistence farmers. They grow just enough to feed themselves and their families. In fact, nearly half of the country's workers are farmers. They grow corn, cotton, soybeans, and sugarcane, some for profit. Paraguay also has a market economy, with thousands of small businesses but not much industry. Many Paraguayans have moved to neighboring countries to find work.

Paraguay's future may be promising as the country learns how to use its resources effectively. For example, the country has built hydroelectric dams on the Paraná River. These dams provide Paraguay with much more power than it needs. Paraguay sells the surplus electricity to Brazil and Argentina.

✓ **READING CHECK:** *Human Systems* How is Paraguay's economy organized?
Partly traditional—subsistence farming—partly market—small businesses

These Paraguayan cowboys are drinking yerba maté (yer-buh MAH-tay). The herbal tea is popular in the region. It is made from the leaves and shoots of a South American shrub called the maté.

Section Review 4

Define and explain: landlocked

Working with Sketch Maps On the map you created in Section 3, label Uruguay, Paraguay, Montevideo, and Asunción. In a box in the margin, briefly explain the significance of Montevideo and Asunción.

Reading for the Main Idea

1. *Human Systems* When and from what country did Uruguay win independence? What about Paraguay?
2. *Places and Regions* Where is Paraguay's most productive agricultural land?
3. *Environment and Society* How has Paraguay used its natural resources for economic development?

Critical Thinking

4. **Comparing** What disadvantages do you think a landlocked country might have when compared with countries that are not landlocked?

Organizing What You Know

5. **Comparing/Contrasting** Copy the following graphic organizer. Use it to compare and contrast the populations of Uruguay and Paraguay.

Uruguay	Paraguay

Atlantic South America • 251

Section 4 Review

Answers to Section 4 Review

Define For definitions, see the glossary.

Working with Sketch Maps Montevideo is the capital of Uruguay and center of government. Asunción is the capital of Paraguay.

Reading for the Main Idea
1. 1825 from Spain; 1811 from Spain (NGS 13)
2. east of Paraguay River (NGS 4)
3. erected hydroelectric projects on the Paraná River to create more power; surplus power sold to Brazil and Argentina (NGS 14)

Critical Thinking
4. no access to the ocean, restriction of trade, must maintain good relations with neighbors for imports and exports

Organizing What You Know
5. Uruguay—88 percent of population of European descent, 12 percent mestizo or of African descent, Catholic, Spanish and Portuguese spoken; Paraguay—95 percent of population mestizo, 5 percent Paraguayan Indian or of European descent, Catholic, Spanish and Guaraní spoken

---

CLOSE

Elicit student opinions about which country has a more promising future—Paraguay or Uruguay. Have students explain.

REVIEW, ASSESS, RETEACH

Have students complete the Section Review. Then write *U* and *P* on the chalkboard. Challenge the students to write a descriptive statement or phrase about each of the two countries that starts with the appropriate letter. (Example: Paraná River dams generate power for this country—Paraguay.) Then have students complete Daily Quiz 11.4.

EXTEND

Have interested students conduct research on the huge Paraná River dams and present their findings to the class. **BLOCK SCHEDULING**

CHAPTER 11 REVIEW

Define and Identify
For definitions and identifications, see the glossary and index.

Review the Main Ideas
10. Andes
11. Amazon and Paraná
12. world's largest tropical rain forest, heavy rainfall, great variety of plant and animal life, provides many resources, large areas being cleared for development (NGS 14)
13. Brazil; Spain (NGS 13)
14. Amazon, northeast, southeast, interior; southeast (NGS 11)
15. an estuary between Uruguay and Argentina (NGS 4)
16. instability, violence, dictators and military governments that abused human rights, war, economic crises, changes in government (NGS 13)
17. large cattle-raising industry, so beef is a big part of the Argentine diet (NGS 15)
18. Montevideo, north shore of the Río de la Plata
19. wealth controlled by a few rich families and companies, subsistence agriculture important (NGS 11)

Think Critically
20. All countries are primarily Roman Catholic. Primary languages are Portuguese and Spanish. Foods are a mixture of European and South American Indian influences. Political systems are modeled after European systems.
21. for economic development and for population growth
22. northern Brazil—tropical rain forest climate; southern Argentina—dry, cold climate
23. once essential to beef industry, but now live on mainly in literature and popular culture
24. Paraguay—95 percent mestizo, 5 percent of European descent or Paraguayan Indian; Uruguay—88 percent of European descent, 12 percent Uruguayan Indian, of African descent or mestizo

Chapter 11 Review and Practice

Define and Identify
Identify each of the following:
1. Pampas
2. estuary
3. soil exhaustion
4. favelas
5. *encomienda*
6. gauchos
7. Eva Perón
8. Mercosur
9. landlocked

Review the Main Ideas
10. Which mountains extend along the border between Argentina and Chile?
11. What major river systems drain much of northern and central Atlantic South America?
12. What are some features of the Amazon rain forest?
13. Which country in Atlantic South America was a Portuguese colony? What colonial power controlled the other countries before they gained independence?
14. What are the four main regions of Brazil? Of these four, which is the richest region?
15. What and where is the Río de la Plata?
16. What problems have Argentines faced throughout the 1900s and into the 2000s?
17. How does Argentina's agriculture influence what Argentines eat?
18. What is Uruguay's main city, and where is it located?
19. What is Paraguay's economy like?

Think Critically
20. **Analyzing Information** How are European influences reflected in the religions, languages, and other cultural characteristics of the countries of Atlantic South America?
21. **Finding the Main Idea** Why are large areas of Brazil's tropical rain forest being cleared?
22. **Comparing and Contrasting** How do the climates of northern Brazil and southern Argentina differ?
23. **Summarizing** How has the role of Argentina's gauchos changed?
24. **Comparing and Contrasting** How are the ethnic populations of Uruguay and Paraguay different?

Map Activity
25. On a separate sheet of paper, match the letters on the map with their correct labels.

Brazilian Highlands
Patagonia
Tierra del Fuego
Paraná River
São Paulo
Manaus
Brasília
Buenos Aires
Montevideo
Asunción

Map Activity
25. A. Tierra del Fuego
B. Buenos Aires
C. Brasília
D. Paraná River
E. Brazilian Highlands
F. Patagonia
G. São Paulo
H. Manaus
I. Asunción
J. Montevideo

Writing Activity

Imagine that you are a gaucho working on an Argentine ranch in the 1800s. Write a short song or poem that describes your daily life as a gaucho. Also describe the physical geography of the ranch. What physical features do you see? What is the climate like? Be sure to use standard grammar, sentence structure, spelling, and punctuation.

Internet Activity: go.hrw.com
KEYWORD: SJ5 GT11

Choose a topic to explore about Atlantic South America:
- Journey along the Amazon River.
- Compare Uruguayans and Paraguayans.
- Celebrate the Brazilian Carnival.

CHAPTER 11 REVIEW

Writing Activity
Answers will vary, but the information included should be consistent with text material. Use Rubric 26, Poems and Songs, to evaluate student work.

Interpreting Graphs
1. changes in Argentina's gross domestic product
2. from 1995 to 1997
3. 1997; 2002
4. After a period of economic growth in the mid-1990s, Argentina's economy suffered a sharp decline—perhaps to crisis conditions in 2002.

Analyzing Primary Sources
1. It would allow them to buy and sell as a group, increasing their economic power.
2. None of the Huni Kui knew how to read or write.
3. Indian teachers offering classes and training, members learning to read and write in two languages
4. to deal both with other Indians and with the larger business community of Brazil, which used Portuguese

Social Studies Skills Practice

Interpreting Graphs
Study the graph below and answer the questions.

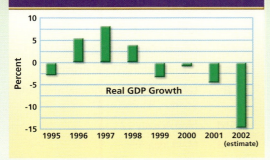

Source: Business Week Online

1. What information does this graph show?
2. During what period did the economy show positive growth?
3. During which year did the economy grow most? Decline the most?
4. What conclusions regarding the Argentine economy can you draw from this graph?

Analyzing Primary Sources
Read the quotation by Siã Kaxiniawá, a member of the Huni Kui tribe in Brazil. Then answer the questions.

"Our lands remained in the hands of those who had taken them long ago. . . . We resolved to fight for our rights. To do this, we established a cooperative that allows us to buy and sell collectively. One problem that we had to confront at the outset of our cooperative's existence is that no one knew how to read or write . . . Today we have six Indian teachers on our land, and for the last nine years they have been offering classes and training for all members of our community. We have learned to read and write, not only in Portuguese but in our own language."

1. How would forming a cooperative benefit the Huni Kui economically?
2. What problem did the Huni Kui face when they formed the cooperative?
3. In what way has life changed for the Huni Kui since forming the cooperative?
4. Why would the Huni Kui learn to write in two languages?

REVIEW AND ASSESSMENT RESOURCES

Reproducible
- Readings in World Geography, History, and Culture 22, 23, and 24
- Critical Thinking Activity 11
- Vocabulary Activity 11

Technology
- Chapter 11 Test Generator (on the One-Stop Planner)
- HRW Go site
- Audio CD Program, Chapter 11

Reinforcement, Review, and Assessment
- Chapter 11 Review
- Chapter Summaries and Review
- Chapter 11 Test
- Chapter 11 Test for English Language Learners and Special-Needs Students

GO TO: go.hrw.com
KEYWORD: SJ5 Teacher
FOR: a guide to using the Internet in your classroom

Pacific South America
Chapter Resource Manager

Objectives

SECTION 1
Physical Geography
(pp. 255–58)
1. Identify the major physical features of the region.
2. Describe the climates and vegetation that exist in the region.
3. Identify the region's major resources.

SECTION 2
History and Culture
(pp. 259–63)
1. Name some achievements of the region's early cultures.
2. Describe what the Inca Empire was like.
3. Describe the role that Spain played in the region's history.
4. Identify the governmental problems the region's people have faced.

SECTION 3
Pacific South America Today
(pp. 264–67)
1. Identify the three regions of Ecuador.
2. Describe how Bolivia might develop its economy.
3. Identify the features of Peru's regions.
4. Describe how Chile is different from its neighbors in Pacific South America.

Pacing Guide

Regular
1 day
Lecture Notes, Section 1
Block Scheduling
.5 day
Block Scheduling Handbook, Chapter 12

Regular
1.5 days
Lecture Notes, Section 2
Block Scheduling
.5 day
Block Scheduling Handbook, Chapter 12

Regular
.5 day
Lecture Notes, Section 3
Block Scheduling
.5 day
Block Scheduling Handbook, Chapter 12

Reproducible Resources

RS	Know It Notes S1
ELL	Main Idea Activity S1

RS	Know It Notes S2
RS	Graphic Organizer 12
E	Cultures of the World Activity 2
E	Lab Activity for Geography and Earth Science, Hands-On 4
SM	Map Activity 12
ELL	Main Idea Activity S2

RS	Know It Notes S3
E	Creative Strategy for Teaching World Geography, Lesson 9
E	Biography Activity: Isabel Allende
SM	Geography for Life Activity 12
ELL	Main Idea Activity S3

Chapter Resource Key

RS	Reading Support	**ELL**	Reinforcement and English Language Learners and English for Speakers of Other Languages (ESOL)		Internet
IC	Interdisciplinary Connections				Holt Presentation Maker Using Microsoft® PowerPoint®
E	Enrichment				
SM	Skills Mastery		Transparencies		
A	Assessment		CD–ROM		
REV	Review		Music		
			Video		

 One-Stop Planner CD-ROM

See the *One-Stop Planner* for a complete list of additional resources for students and teachers.

One-Stop Planner CD–ROM

It's easy to plan lessons, select resources, and print out materials for your students when you use the *One-Stop Planner CD–ROM with Test Generator*.

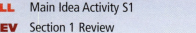

HRW ONLINE RESOURCES

GO TO: go.hrw.com
Then type in a keyword.

TEACHER HOME PAGE
KEYWORD: **SJ5 TEACHER**

CHAPTER INTERNET ACTIVITIES
KEYWORD: **SJ5 GT12**

Choose an activity to:
- analyze Chile's climate.
- hike the Inca trail and visit Machu Picchu.
- learn about the languages of the Andes.

CHAPTER ENRICHMENT LINKS
KEYWORD: **SJ5 CH12**

CHAPTER MAPS
KEYWORD: **SJ5 MAPS12**

ONLINE ASSESSMENT
Homework Practice
KEYWORD: **SJ5 HP12**
Standardized Test Prep Online
KEYWORD: **SJ5 STP12**
Rubrics
KEYWORD: **SS Rubrics**

COUNTRY INFORMATION
KEYWORD: **SJ5 Almanac**

CONTENT UPDATES
KEYWORD: **SS Content Updates**

HOLT PRESENTATION MAKER
KEYWORD: **SJ5 PPT12**

ONLINE READING SUPPORT
KEYWORD: **SS Strategies**

CURRENT EVENTS
KEYWORD: **S5 Current Events**

Technology Resources

 One-Stop Planner CD–ROM, Lesson 12.1
 Geography and Cultures Visual Resources with Teaching Activities 18–23
 ARGWorld CD–ROM
 Homework Practice Online / HRW Go site

 One-Stop Planner CD–ROM, Lesson 12.2
 ARGWorld CD–ROM
 Music of the World Audio CD Program, Selection 5
 Homework Practice Online / HRW Go site

 One-Stop Planner CD–ROM, Lesson 12.3
 ARGWorld CD–ROM
 Homework Practice Online / HRW Go site

Review, Reinforcement, and Assessment Resources

ELL	Main Idea Activity S1
REV	Section 1 Review
A	Daily Quiz 12.1
REV	Chapter Summaries and Review
ELL	English Audio Summary 12.1
ELL	Spanish Audio Summary 12.1

ELL	Main Idea Activity S2
REV	Section 2 Review
A	Daily Quiz 12.2
REV	Chapter Summaries and Review
ELL	English Audio Summary 12.2
ELL	Spanish Audio Summary 12.2

ELL	Main Idea Activity S3
REV	Section 3 Review
A	Daily Quiz 12.3
REV	Chapter Summaries and Review
ELL	English Audio Summary 12.3
ELL	Spanish Audio Summary 12.3

Meeting Individual Needs

Ability Levels

Level 1 Basic-level activities designed for all students encountering new material

Level 2 Intermediate-level activities designed for average students

Level 3 Challenging activities designed for honors and gifted-and-talented students

ESOL Activities that address the needs of students with Limited English Proficiency

Chapter Review and Assessment

IC	Interdisciplinary Activity for the Middle Grades 12	A	Unit 3 Test
E	Readings in World Geography, History, and Culture 25, 26, and 27		Chapter 12 Test Generator (on the One-Stop Planner)
SM	Critical Thinking Activity 12		Audio CD Program, Chapter 12
REV	Chapter 12 Review and Practice	A	Chapter 12 Test for English Language Learners and Special-Needs Students
REV	Chapter Summaries and Review	A	Unit 3 Test for English Language Learners and Special-Needs Students
ELL	Vocabulary Activity 12		
A	Chapter 12 Test		HRW Go site

CHAPTER 12

Pacific South America

Previewing Chapter Resources

Holt Online Learning

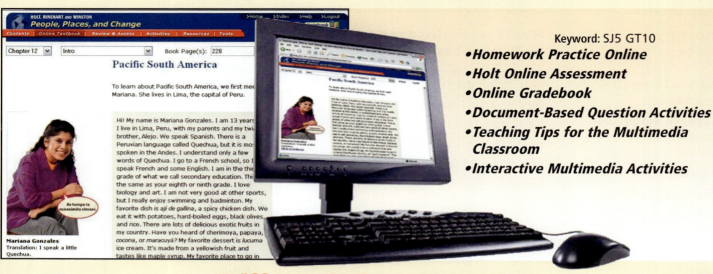

Keyword: SJ5 GT10

- Homework Practice Online
- Holt Online Assessment
- Online Gradebook
- Document-Based Question Activities
- Teaching Tips for the Multimedia Classroom
- Interactive Multimedia Activities

Differentiating Instruction

Reading and Writing Support
- ◀ Graphic Organizer Activity
- Vocabulary Activity
- Chapter Summary and Review
- Know It Notes
- Audio CD

Active Learning
- Block Scheduling Handbook
- Cultures of the World Activity
- Interdisciplinary Activity
- Map Activity
- ◀ Critical Thinking Activity 12
- Music of the World Audio CD: Music of the Peruvian Andes

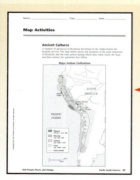

Primary Sources and Advanced Learners
- Geography for Life Activity: Agricultural Patterns
- ◀ Map Activity: Ancient Cultures
- Readings in World Geography, History and Culture:
  - 26 The Phantom Palace
  - 27 Living in the Land of Fire

Assessment Program
- ◀ Daily Quizzes S1–3
- Chapter Test
- Chapter Test for English Language Learners and Special-Needs Students

Spanish and ESOL
- Vocabulary Activity
- ◀ Main Idea Activities for English Language Learners and Special-Needs Students
- Chapter Summary and Review
- Spanish Audio Summary
- Know It Notes S1–3
- Chapter Test for English Language Learners and Special-Needs Students

Special Education Modifications
Your I.D.E.A. Works! CD-ROM will provide modified versions of the following teaching materials:
- ◀ Guided Reading Strategies S1–3
- Vocabulary Activity
- Main Idea Activities S1–3
- Daily Quizzes S1–3
- Chapter 12 Test
- Flash cards of chapter vocabulary terms

Teacher Resources

Books for Teachers

Galeano, Eduardo. *I Am Rich Potosi: The Mountain That Eats Men.* Monacelli Press, 1999.

Neruda, Pablo. *Canto General*, vol. 7 of *Latin American Literature and Culture.* Trans. Jack Schmitt. University of California Press, 1993.

Von Hagen, Adriana, and Craig Morris. *The Cities of the Ancient Andes.* Thames & Hudson, 1998.

Books for Students

Bickman, Connie. *Ecuador. Through the Eyes of Children* Abdo & Daughters, 1996. People, food, and daily life in Ecuador. **SHELTERED ENGLISH**

Galvin, Irene Flum. *Chile: Land of Poets and Patriots.* Dillon Press, 1990. History, people, politics, and other aspects of the country.

Handelsman, Michael. *Culture and Customs of Peru.* Greenwood Press, 2000. Culture and customs, past to present.

Reinhard, Johan. *Discovering the Inca Ice Maiden: My Adventures on Ampato.* National Geographic Society, 1998. A day-by-day account of the discovery of a 530-year-old mummy high in the Andes.

Multimedia Materials

Inca Ruins. CD–ROM. Softkey.

Let's Visit South America. CD–ROM with Labpack. Educational Software Institute.

Videos and CDs

Videos
- CNN *Presents Geography: Yesterday and Today,* Segment 13 Harnessing Nature
- CNN *Presents World Cultures: Yesterday and Today,* Segment 13 The Inca's Frozen Past
- ARG World

Holt Researcher
http://researcher.hrw.com

- Organization of American States (OAS)
- Bolivar and San Martin Fight for Independence
- Ecuador
- Bolivia
- Chile
- Urban Population of Latin America
- Latin American Economic Growth
- Latin American Foreign Debts
- Latin American Governments
- Empires in the Americas

Transparency Packages

Graphic Organizer Transparencies 12.1–3

Geography and Cultures Visual Resources Transparencies 32–36
42 Pacific South America: Physical-Political
43 Elevation Zones in the Andes

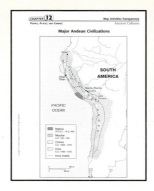

Map Activities Transparency 12 Major Andean Civilizations

CHAPTER 12

WHY IT MATTERS

You may want to share with your students the following reasons for learning about Pacific South America:
- Studying the region's past civilizations, such as the Inca, can help us understand the people who live there today.
- Chile is the world's top copper producer. Copper is used in electrical wire, consumer products, and coinage.
- Peru and Bolivia are major producers of coca leaves—the source of cocaine. Cocaine use remains a big problem in the United States.
- The weather event known as El Niño affects both Pacific South America and the United States.

CHAPTER 12

Pacific South America

To learn about Pacific South America, we first meet Mariana. She lives in Lima, the capital of Peru.

Hi! My name is Mariana Gonzales. I am 13 years old. I live in Lima, Peru, with my parents and my twin brother, Alejo. We speak Spanish. There is a Peruvian language called Quechua, but it is mostly spoken in the Andes. I understand only a few words of Quechua. I go to a French school, so I also speak French and some English. I am in the third grade of what we call secondary education. This is the same as your eighth or ninth grade. I love biology and art. I am not very good at other sports, but I really enjoy swimming and badminton. My favorite dish is *ají degallina*, a spicy chicken dish. We eat it with potatoes, hard-boiled eggs, black olives, and rice. There are lots of delicious exotic fruits in my country. Have you heard of cherimoya, papaya, *cocona*, or *maracuyá*? My favorite dessert is *lucuma* ice cream. It's made from a yellowish fruit and tastes like maple syrup. My favorite place to go in Lima is the Museo de Oro, or "gold museum". The incredible jewelry and other objects there really bring my country's ancient history to life.

As tumpa ta runasimita rimani.

Translation: I speak a little Quechua.

CHAPTER PROJECT

Inca builders created some exquisite stone architecture. Have students create a guidebook for several of the best sites for viewing Inca stonework. The guidebook should tell what structures are at the site and what the buildings were used for, if known. Students should draw or duplicate illustrations of the sites. You may also want to require a map. Some students may want to further investigate Inca stonecutting and construction methods.

STARTING THE CHAPTER

Ask students to imagine that a glorious empire has arisen in your region and they are to design its new capital city. The city is to be laid out in the shape of an animal. Ask students which animal they would choose as appropriate and to sketch a basic city plan in the shape of that animal. Call on volunteers to sketch their city plans on the chalkboard. Then tell them that, according to tradition, Cuzco, the capital of the vast Inca Empire of the Pacific South America region, was built in the shape of a cougar. Ask what this might say about what the Inca people valued. (possible answers: strength, power) Tell students that in Chapter 12 they will learn more about the ancient and recent cultures of Pacific South America.

Section 1: Physical Geography

Read to Discover
1. What are the major physical features of the region?
2. What climates and vegetation can be found in this region?
3. What are the region's major resources?

Vocabulary
- strait
- *selvas*
- Peru Current
- El Niño

Places
- Andes
- Strait of Magellan
- Tierra del Fuego
- Cape Horn
- Amazon River
- Iquitos
- Altiplano
- Lake Titicaca
- Lake Poopó
- Atacama Desert

Reading Strategy

VISUALIZING INFORMATION Look at the maps and photographs in this section. How do you think they will connect to the section's main ideas? Write down your answers.

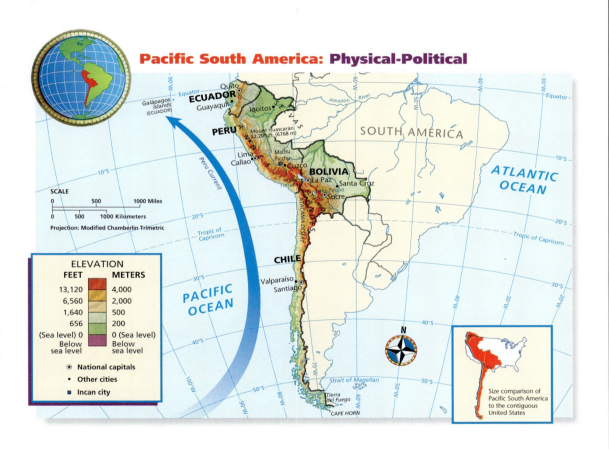

Pacific South America • 255

CHAPTER 12, Section 1

SECTION 1 RESOURCES

Reproducible
- Lecture Notes, Section 1
- Block Scheduling Handbook, Chapter 12
- Know It Notes S1

Technology
- One-Stop Planner CD–ROM, Lesson 12.1
- Homework Practice Online
- Geography and Cultures Visual Resources with Teaching Activities 32–36, 42, 43
- HRW Go site

Reinforcement, Review, and Assessment
- Section 1 Review
- Daily Quiz 12.1
- Main Idea Activity S1
- Chapter Summaries and Review
- English Audio Summary 12.1
- Spanish Audio Summary 12.1

Section 1

Objectives
1. Identify the major physical features of the region.
2. Investigate the region's climates and vegetation.
3. Describe the region's major resources.

FOCUS

 Bellringer

Copy the following instructions onto the chalkboard: *Refer to the physical-political map at the beginning of the chapter. Locate Quito, the capital of Ecuador, and estimate the city's latitude. What do you think Quito's climate is like?* Allow students to record their answers. Discuss responses. (Students should note that Quito is almost on the equator. Some students may suggest that the climate is hot.) Point out that instead of a hot tropical climate, Quito has a moderate, springlike climate. Ask students what factor besides latitude affects the climate there (elevation).

Tell students that in Section 1 they will learn more about how the region's landforms affect climate.

Using the Physical-Political Map

Have students examine the map on this page. Call on a volunteer to list the names of the countries in this region. Point out that the Andes—the world's longest mountain chain on land—extend through the region and cross the equator. Ask students to suggest how the mountains influence these countries.

Pacific South America 255

CHAPTER 12, Section 1

PLACES AND REGIONS

The Galápagos Ecuador's physical features also include a cluster of islands far from the South American mainland. The Galápagos Islands lie about 600 miles (965 km) west of Ecuador's Pacific coast. Many of the animals and plants that live there are found nowhere else on Earth. Marine iguanas and giant tortoises that can live 150 years are among the island's most unusual inhabitants. The Galápagos Islands have become a popular tourist attraction. Increased tourism has damaged the islands' fragile environment. Now there are limits on the number of tourists and the type of tours allowed.

Activity: Have students conduct research on the Galápagos Islands and identify their unique plants and animals. Ask students to suggest how tourism could hurt specific species.

GO TO: go.hrw.com
KEYWORD: SJ5 CH12
FOR: Web sites about the Galápagos Islands

Visual Record Answer
They have very thick fur.

---

internet connect
GO TO: go.hrw.com
KEYWORD: SJ5 CH12
FOR: Web sites about Pacific South America

Physical Features

Shaped like a shoestring, Chile (CHEE-lay) stretches about 2,650 miles (4,264 km) from north to south. However, at its broadest point Chile is just 221 miles (356 km) wide. As its name indicates, Ecuador (E-kwuh-dawr) lies on the equator. Peru (puh-ROO) forms a long curve along the Pacific Ocean. Bolivia (buh-LIV-ee-uh) is landlocked.

Mountains The snowcapped Andes run through all four of the region's countries. Some ridges and volcanic peaks rise more than 20,000 feet (6,096 m) above sea level. Because two tectonic plates meet at the region's edge, earthquakes and volcanoes are constant threats. Sometimes these earthquakes disturb Andean glaciers, sending ice and mud rushing down the mountain slopes.

In Chile's rugged south, the peaks are covered by an ice cap. This ice cap is about 220 miles (354 km) long. Mountains extend to the continent's southern tip. There, the Strait of Magellan links the Atlantic and Pacific Oceans. A **strait** is a narrow passageway that connects two large bodies of water. The large island south of the strait is Tierra del Fuego, or "land of fire." It is divided between Chile and Argentina. At the southernmost tip of the continent, storms swirl around Chile's Cape Horn. Many other islands lie along Chile's southern coast.

Tributaries of the Amazon River begin high in the Andes. In fact, ships can travel upriver about 2,300 miles (3,700 km) on the Amazon. This allows ships to sail from the Atlantic Ocean to Iquitos, Peru.

Altiplano In Ecuador, the Andes range splits into two ridges. The ridges separate further in southern Peru and Bolivia. A broad, high plateau called the Altiplano lies between the ridges.

Rivers on the Altiplano have no outlet to the sea. Water collects in two large lakes, Lake Titicaca and salty Lake Poopó (poh-oh-POH). Lake Titicaca lies at 12,500 feet (3,810 m) above sea level. Large ships carry freight and passengers across it. The lake covers about 3,200 square miles (8,288 sq km).

✓ **READING CHECK:** *Places and Regions* What are the major physical features of the region? *Andes, ice cap, Strait of Magellan, Tierra del Fuego, Amazon and its tributaries, Altiplano, Lake Titicaca, Lake Poopó*

▶ Llamas are used to carry loads in the Altiplano region. Llamas are related to camels and can travel long distances without water.
Interpreting the Visual Record How do llamas appear to be well-suited to the Andes environment?

256 • Chapter 12

TEACH

Teaching Objectives 1–3

LEVEL 1: (Suggested time: 20 min.) Copy the following graphic organizer onto the chalkboard, omitting the blue answers. Tell students it represents a simplified elevation profile, or cutaway view, of Pacific South America near the region's widest point. Call on students to label the profile with the region's landforms, bodies of water, climates, vegetation, and resources. Encourage them to use the Unit Atlas as a resource. **ESOL**, **LS** **VISUAL-SPATIAL**

Physical Geography of Pacific South America

Andes and Altiplano (glaciers, ice cap, Lake Titicaca, Lake Poopó, dry)

Pacific coast (Atacama Desert, fog, minerals)

eastern plains, (Amazon River rain forest, grass lands, oil, natural gas, silver, gold, other minerals)

Pacific Ocean (Peru Current, fish)

256 Chapter 12

▲ Canoes are an important form of transportation along the Napo River in eastern Ecuador.

Climate and Vegetation

Climate and vegetation vary widely in Pacific South America. Some areas, such as Chile's central valley, have a mild Mediterranean climate. Other areas have dry, wet, or cold weather conditions.

Grasslands and Forests Mountain environments change with elevation. The Altiplano region between the mountain ridges is a grassland with few trees. Eastern Ecuador, eastern Peru, and northern Bolivia are part of the Amazon River basin. These areas have a humid tropical climate. South Americans call the thick tropical rain forests in this region **selvas**. In Bolivia the rain forest changes to grasslands in the southeast. Far to the south, southern Chile is covered with dense temperate rain forests. Cool, rainy weather is typical of this area of rain forests.

Deserts Northern Chile contains the Atacama Desert. This desert is about 600 miles (965 km) long. Rain is extremely rare, but fog and low clouds are common. They form when the cold **Peru Current** chills warmer air above the ocean's surface. Cloud cover keeps air near the ground from being warmed by the Sun. The area receives almost no sunshine for about six months of the year. Yet it seldom rains. As a result, coastal Chile is one of the cloudiest—and driest— places on Earth.

In Peru, rivers cut through the dry coastal region. They bring snowmelt down from the Andes. About 50 rivers cross Peru. The rivers have made settlement possible in these dry areas.

The Atacama Desert is one of the driest places on Earth. Some spots in the desert have not received any rain for more than 400 years. Average rainfall is less than 0.004 inches (0.01 cm) per year.

CHAPTER 12, Section 1

EYE ON EARTH

Staying Current on the Peru Current While in the Americas from 1799 to 1804, German scientist Alexander von Humboldt studied the Peru Current. He discovered how the current's cold water helps create the coastal desert. The current is sometimes called the Humboldt Current.

Cold water wells up from the depths of the Pacific Ocean, bringing nutrients closer to the surface. This makes the Peru Current area one of the world's richest fishing grounds. Anchovies and big fish such as tuna that feed on the smaller fish are particularly common. Seabirds that eat the anchovies drop guano on coastal islands, where it is harvested for fertilizer.

Activity: Have students create a cutaway view of the Peru Current and the ocean's surface. Drawings should show the relationship between nutrients, fish, and birds.

◀ **Visual Record Answer**

a tropical rain forest

LEVELS 2 AND 3: (Suggested time: 30 min.) Organize the class into four groups—one for each of these four aspects of Pacific South America's physical geography—El Niño, the Peru Current, the movement of tectonic plates, and the location of resources. Have each group create a graphic organizer to show how its topic affects life in the area.
COOPERATIVE LEARNING

CLOSE

Go through Section 1 page by page, having students cover the photo captions. Ask them to speculate where the photographs were taken, based on what they learned in Section 1. Ask: *What in the photos indicates the location?* Have students read the captions to check their predictions.

REVIEW, ASSESS, RETEACH

Have students complete the Section Review. Then ask each student to use the maps in the Unit Atlas to choose a place in Pacific South America to depict. Tell students to write a sentence describing that place in terms of its physical features. Have one volunteer read a sentence and have another student try to guess the location. Continue until all the major places and points have been discussed. Then have students complete Daily Quiz 12.1.

Section 1 Review

Answers to Section 1 Review

Define For definitions, see the glossary.

Working with Sketch Maps Lake Titicaca is 12,500 feet (3,810 m) above sea level and covers about 3,200 square miles (8,288 sq km).

Reading for the Main Idea
1. the Andes (NGS 4)
2. weather pattern that causes heavy rains along the coast (NGS 7)

Critical Thinking
3. rain forest, mountains, deserts; changes in climate—warm and humid, cold and dry, cool and damp (NGS 4)
4. lack of water; possible answers: collect and condense fog, bring snow down from Andes, dig deeper wells, divert more water from rivers, remove salt from seawater

Organizing What You Know
5. western—the Andes; highland, desert; varied vegetation depending on elevation, temperate rain forest in south; rivers from the Andes; central—Altiplano; dry; grassland; Lake Titicaca and Lake Poopó; eastern—plains; humid tropical; *selvas*, grasslands; Amazon River

▲ A Bolivian miner uses a jackhammer to mine for tin.

El Niño About every two to seven years, an ocean and weather pattern affects the dry Pacific coast. This weather pattern is called **El Niño**. Cool ocean water near the coast warms. As a result, fish leave what is normally a rich fishing area. Areas along the coast often suffer flooding from heavy rains. El Niño is caused by the buildup of warm water in the Pacific Ocean. Ocean and weather events around the world can be affected. Some scientists think that greenhouse gases made a long El Niño during the 1990s even worse.

✓ **READING CHECK:** (Physical Systems) How does El Niño affect Earth? Ocean water near the Pacific coast warms, driving away the fish; coasts are hit by heavy rains; ocean and weather events around the world can be affected.

Resources

The countries of Pacific South America have many important natural resources. The coastal waters of the Pacific Ocean are rich in fish. Forests in southern Chile and east of the Andes in Peru and Ecuador provide lumber. In addition, the region has oil, natural gas, silver, gold, and other valuable mineral resources. Bolivia has large deposits of tin. It also has resources such as copper, lead, and zinc. Chile has large copper deposits. In fact, Chile is the world's leading producer and exporter of copper.

✓ **READING CHECK:** (Environment and Society) How has Chile's copper supply affected its economy? It has made Chile a leading producer and exporter of copper.

Homework Practice Online
Keyword: SJ5 HP12

Section Review 1

Define: strait, *selvas*, Peru Current, El Niño

Working with Sketch Maps On a map of South America that you draw or that your teacher provides, label the following: Andes, Strait of Magellan, Tierra del Fuego, Cape Horn, Amazon River, Iquitos, Altiplano, Lake Titicaca, Lake Poopó, and Atacama Desert. Where is Lake Titicaca, and what is it like?

Reading for the Main Idea
1. (Places and Regions) What is the main landform region of Pacific South America?
2. (Physical Systems) What is El Niño? What effect does El Niño have on coastal flooding in Peru?

Critical Thinking
3. **Finding the Main Idea** What would you encounter on a journey from Iquitos, Peru, to Tierra del Fuego?
4. **Making Generalizations and Predictions** What problem would people living on the dry coast of Chile experience, and how could they solve it?

Organizing What You Know
5. **Categorizing** Copy the following graphic organizer. Use it to describe the landforms, climate, vegetation, and sources of water of Pacific South America.

	Western	Central	Eastern
Landforms			
Climate			
Vegetation			
Water sources			

258 • Chapter 12

Have students complete Main Idea Activity S1. Then organize the class into groups. Tell each group to trace a wall map of the region. Students should choose or create symbols, colors, or shading patterns to depict landforms, bodies of water, climates, or resources. Encourage them to use the Unit Atlas for reference. Display maps around the classroom.
ESOL, COOPERATIVE LEARNING

EXTEND

Have interested students conduct research on the physical and human geography of Tierra del Fuego. Ask them to investigate how the residents have adapted to the harsh climate and isolation. Have students report their findings in a letter from a teenager in Tierra del Fuego who is trying to persuade a friend to visit. **BLOCK SCHEDULING**

History and Culture

CHAPTER 12, Section 2

Read to Discover
1. What were some achievements of the region's early cultures?
2. What was the Inca Empire like?
3. What role did Spain play in the region's history?
4. What governmental problems have the region's people faced?

Vocabulary
quinoa
quipus
viceroy
creoles
coup

Places
Cuzco
Machu Picchu

People
Atahualpa
Francisco Pizarro

Reading Strategy

TAKING NOTES As you read, use the headings in this section to create an outline. Write supporting details beneath each heading.

Section 2 Resources

Reproducible
- Lecture Notes, Section 2
- Know It Notes S2
- Graphic Organizer 12
- Cultures of the World Activity 2
- Lab Activity for Geography and Earth Science, Hands-On 4
- Map Activity 12

Technology
- One-Stop Planner CD–ROM, Lesson 12.2
- Music of the World Audio CD Program, Selection 5
- Homework Practice Online
- HRW Go site

Reinforcement, Review, and Assessment
- Section 2 Review
- Daily Quiz 12.2
- Main Idea Activity S2
- Chapter Summaries and Review
- English Audio Summary 12.2
- Spanish Audio Summary 12.2

Early Cultures

Thousands of years ago, agriculture became the basis of the region's economy. To raise crops in the steep Andes, early farmers cut terraces into the mountainsides. Peoples of the region developed crops that would be important for centuries to come. They domesticated **quinoa** (KEEN-wah), a native Andean plant that yields nutritious seeds. They also grew many varieties of potatoes. Domesticated animals included the llama (LAH-muh) and alpaca (al-PA-kuh). Both have thick wool and are related to camels. Early inhabitants raised and ate guinea pigs, which are related to mice. The people wove many fabrics from cotton and wool. These fabrics had complicated, beautiful patterns.

Peru's first advanced civilization reached its height in about 900 B.C. The main town was located in an Andean valley. This town contained large stone structures decorated with carved jaguars and other designs. Later, people in coastal areas used sophisticated irrigation systems to store water and control flooding. They also built pyramids about 100 feet (30 m) high. Huge stone carvings remain near the Bolivian shores of Lake Titicaca. They were carved by the people of the Tiahuanaco (TEE-uh-wuh-NAH-koh) culture. Another people scratched outlines of animals and other shapes into the surface of the Peruvian desert. These designs are hundreds of feet long.

This Peruvian woman is separating seeds from the quinoa plant.

 READING CHECK: **Human Systems** What were some achievements of the region's early cultures? *domesticated plants and animals, wove fabrics with complicated patterns, carved stone structures, irrigated, scratched elaborate designs into the surface of the desert*

Pacific South America • 259

Section 2

Objectives
1. Explain some achievements of the region's early cultures.
2. Describe the Inca Empire.
3. Analyze the role Spain played in the region's history.
4. Identify governmental problems the region's people have faced.

Focus

Bellringer
Copy the following question onto the chalkboard: *How might the Inca have communicated across their empire without wheeled vehicles and a written language?* Allow students to write down their answers. Summarize student responses on the chalkboard. Refer to the list as students read Section 2 and check off any suggestions that match the section's information. Tell students that in Section 2 they will learn more about the Inca and other times in the region's history.

Building Vocabulary
Write the vocabulary terms on the chalkboard. Point out that **quinoa** and **quipus** are from Quechua, a native language of the Andes region. **Viceroy** is based on a French word, *roi,* which means "king." **Creoles** is from *criollo,* a Spanish word for a person native to a certain place. French gives us **coup**, a short version of *coup d'état,* which means "stroke of state." Have students find the definitions in the textbook or glossary. Call on volunteers to relate them to the word origins.

Pacific South America 259

CHAPTER 12, Section 2

CULTURE AND MUSIC

Shopping for Textiles to Andean music People of the Andes had woven beautiful textiles long before the Spaniards arrived. The Inca prized cloth as gifts and even wrapped children to be sacrificed in the finest textiles.

Weaving traditions are still strong. For example, buyers come from around the world for textiles made in an Ecuadoran village named Otavalo. To weave the wool thread, some villagers use an ancient method—the backstrap loom. This device attaches to a pole or tree at one end and loops around the weaver's back at the other end. The backstrap loom allows workers to practice their craft almost anywhere.

Discussion: Andean musical traditions also date back many centuries. For an old tune one may hear while shopping in the Otavalo market, play Selection 5 on the Music of the World Audio CD Program. Use the text and questions in the Teacher's Guide.

Visual Record Answer
easy to defend as a fortress city

▲ The ruins of Machu Picchu, an Inca city, were discovered in 1911.
Interpreting the Visual Record Why might the Inca have chosen this site for a settlement?

Quipus were used by the Inca to keep records.
▼

The Inca

By the early 1500s, one people ruled most of the Andes region. This group, the Inca, conquered the other cultures around them. They controlled an area reaching from what is now southern Colombia to central Chile. The Inca Empire stretched from the Pacific Coast inland to the selvas of the Amazon rain forest. Perhaps as many as 12 million people from dozens of different ethnic groups were included. The Inca called their empire Tawantinsuyu (tah-WAHN-tin-soo-yoo), which means "land of the four quarters." Four highways that began in the Inca capital, Cuzco (KOO-skoh), divided the kingdom into four sections.

The Inca Empire The Inca adopted many of the skills of the people they ruled. They built structures out of large stone blocks fitted tightly together without cement. Buildings in the Andean city of Machu Picchu have survived earthquakes and the passing of centuries. Inca metalworkers created gold and silver objects, some decorated with emeralds. Artists made a garden of gold plants with silver stems. They even made gold ears for the corn plants.

Perhaps the Inca's greatest achievement was the organization of their empire. Huge irrigation projects turned deserts into rich farmland that produced food for the large population. A network of thousands of miles of stone-paved roads connected the empire. Along the highways were rest houses, temples, and storerooms. The Inca used storerooms to keep supplies of food. For example, they stored potatoes that had been freeze-dried in the cold mountain air.

To cross the steep Andean valleys, the Inca built suspension bridges of rope. The Inca had no wheeled vehicles or horses. Instead, teams of runners carried messages throughout the land. An important message could be moved up to 150 miles (241 km) in one day.

The runners did not carry letters, however, because the Inca did not have a written language. Instead, they used **quipus** (KEE-pooz). Quipus were complicated systems of knots tied on strings of various colors. Numerical information about important events, populations, animals, and grain supplies was recorded on quipus. Inca officials were trained to read the knots' meaning.

Civil War Although it was rich and efficient, the Inca Empire did not last long. When the Inca emperor died in 1525, a struggle began. Two of his sons fought over who would take his place. About seven years later, his son Atahualpa (ah-tah-WAHL-pah) won the civil war.

✓ **READING CHECK:** (Human Systems) What was the Inca's greatest achievement? *the organization of the empire through irrigation and roads*

TEACH

Teaching Objectives 1–2
LEVEL 1: (Suggested time: 20 min.) Copy the following graphic organizer onto the chalkboard, omitting the blue answers. Pair students and have the pairs record details about the cultures' history and achievements on the chart. Students may want to add more bullets than are provided. Discuss the charts. **ESOL, COOPERATIVE LEARNING**

Achievements and Characteristics of Pre-Inca and Inca Civilizations

Pre-Inca Cultures	Inca
• in area for thousands of years	• conquered other Andean peoples by early 1500s
• agriculture basis of economy	• controlled area from southern Colombia to central Chile
• cut terraces into hillsides	
• domesticated quinoa, grew potatoes	• skilled at stonework and metalwork
• raised llamas and alpacas	
• raised and ate guinea pigs	• built irrigation projects, road system, suspension bridges
	• no wheeled vehicles, horses, or writing system
	• used quipus

Connecting to Technology

Inca Roads

Inca roads had stairways to cross steep peaks.

The road system was one of the greatest achievements of Inca civilization. The roads crossed high mountains, tropical rain forests, and deserts.

The main road, Capac-nan, or "royal road," connected the capitals of Cuzco and Quito. These cities were more than 1,500 miles (2,414 km) apart. This road crossed jungles, swamps, and mountains. It was straight for most of its length. Inca roads were built from precisely cut stones. One Spanish observer described how the builders worked.

> *The Indians who worked these stones used no mortar; they had no steel for cutting and working the stones, and no machines for transporting them; yet so skilled was their work that the joints between the stones were barely noticeable.*

Another longer highway paralleled the coast and joined Capac-nan, creating a highly efficient network. Along these roads were rest houses. The Inca also built suspension bridges to span deep ravines. They built floating bridges to cross wide rivers.

When the Spanish conquered the region in the 1530s, they destroyed the road system. Today, only fragments of the Inca roads still exist.

Understanding What You Read
1. How might the road system have allowed the Inca to control their territory?
2. What were the main features of the Inca road system?

Spain in Pacific South America

While on his way to Cuzco to be crowned, Atahualpa met Spanish explorer Francisco Pizarro. Pizarro's small group of men and horses had recently landed on the continent's shore. Pizarro wanted Inca gold and silver.

Conquest and Revolt Pizarro captured Atahualpa, who ordered his people to fill a room with gold and silver. These riches were supposed to be a ransom for his freedom. However, Pizarro ordered the Inca emperor killed. The Spaniards continued to conquer Inca lands.

CHAPTER 12, Section 2

Across the Curriculum
TECHNOLOGY
Mummies and Medicine
Some of the famed Inca roads led deep into the Andes, where archaeologists have found hundreds of mummies. These mummies include the remains of children who had been buried alive as sacrifices during the Inca period. The region's dry air helped preserve the bodies.

Modern medical technology allows researchers to learn details about how these ancient people lived and died. DNA testing has proved that tuberculosis existed in the Americas 1,000 years before Europeans arrived.

Activity: Have students conduct research on Inca mummies. Then have students write short reports to present their findings.

Connecting to Technology Answers
1. They could more quickly and easily reach distant parts of the empire.
2. straight, used precisely cut stones, were connected to form a network, had rest houses, suspension bridges, and floating bridges

---

LEVELS 2 AND 3: (Suggested time: 45 min.) Organize the class into groups. Provide each group with strings or cords of different colors. Have the groups create their own quipus as devices to help them remember major events in the history of Pacific South America. Students will need to assign colors to topics and devise a knotting system. Challenge them to work without writing or taking notes. After they have recorded the events on their quipus, have the students imagine that they are officials reporting to the Inca emperor. They should use their quipus to recite their histories to the class. **COOPERATIVE LEARNING,** **LS** **KINESTHETIC**

▶**ASSIGNMENT:** Have students write a newspaper story based on an event or series of events in the history of Pacific South America. You may want to extend the activity by asking students to complete the newspaper page by adding appropriate pictures, recipes, cartoons, an advice column, advertisements, sports story, or other items ordinarily found in a newspaper.

CHAPTER 12, Section 2

National Geography Standard 17

Resources and War The location of natural resources affects history. In the late 1800s Chile wanted full use of the nitrate deposits in western Bolivia. At the time, Bolivia's territory stretched all the way to the Pacific Ocean. In 1879 Chilean forces invaded Bolivia, and the War of the Pacific began.

In 1884 Chile defeated Bolivia and Peru, which had aided Bolivia. As a result of its defeat, Bolivia had to give up Antofagasta, its Pacific port city, thus becoming landlocked. Relations between Bolivia and Chile remain strained today because Bolivia has not given up hope of regaining access to the Pacific Ocean.

▲ The stonework of an Inca temple in Cuzco now forms the foundation of this Catholic church.
Interpreting the Visual Record What does this photo suggest about how the Spanish viewed the religious practices of the Inca?

By 1535 the Inca Empire no longer existed. The last Inca rulers fled into the mountains. A tiny independent state in the foothills of the eastern Andes survived several decades more.

The new Spanish rulers often dealt harshly with the South American Indians. Many Indians had to work in gold and silver mines and on the Spaniards' plantations. Inca temples were replaced by Spanish-style Roman Catholic churches. A **viceroy**, or governor, appointed by the king of Spain enforced Spanish laws and customs.

From time to time, the people rebelled against their Spanish rulers. In 1780 and 1781 an Indian named Tupac Amarú II (too-PAHK ahm-AHR-oo) led a revolt. This revolt spread, but was put down quickly.

Independence By the early 1800s, the desire for independence had grown in South America. The people of Pacific South America began to break away from Spain. **Creoles**, American-born descendants of Europeans, were the main leaders of the revolts. Chile became an independent country in 1818. Ecuador achieved independence in 1822, and Peru became independent two years later. Bolivia became independent in 1825. In the 1880s Bolivia lost a war with Chile. As a result, Bolivia lost its strip of seacoast and became landlocked.

✓ **READING CHECK:** (**Human Systems**) What was Spain's role in the region's history? conquered Inca Empire, replaced temples with Catholic churches, ruled native population with Spanish laws; by the 1800s Spain had lost Pacific South America to independence movements

Government

Since gaining their independence, the countries of Pacific South America have had periods during which their governments were unstable. Often military leaders have taken control and limited citizens' rights. However, in recent decades the region's countries have moved toward more democratic forms of government. These governments now face the challenge of widespread poverty.

Visual Record Answer

Students may suggest that the Spanish tried to replace Inca religious practices with Catholicism.

Teaching Objectives 3–4

LEVEL 1: (Suggested time: 20 min.) Have students create a time line of events in the history of Pacific South America, beginning in 1525 and ending in the present. **ESOL,** **LS** **LOGICAL-MATHEMATICAL**

LEVELS 2 AND 3: (Suggested time: 40 min.) Have students complete the Level 1 activity and ask them try to predict which events from the distant past may have contributed to governmental problems of the recent past. Have students draw arrows that connect events from the distant past to recent governmental problems. Have them include descriptions of how the event in the distant past may have contributed to unstable governments of the recent past. If some students finish their work early, have them check their predictions in resource materials and report to the class on their findings. **LS** **VISUAL-SPATIAL**

TEACHER TO TEACHER

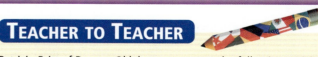

Patricia Britt of Durant, Oklahoma, suggests the following activity to help students learn about the countries of Pacific South America: Organize students into groups and assign a country to each group. Provide almanacs and other resources. Have each group create a poster with the country's flag, a map, and illustrations of important aspects of the country, such as its struggle for independence, unique cultural features, and national heroes. When the groups present their information to the class, ask some students to bring samples of the country's food, find ways to dress for the occasion, or teach the class a song from the country.

Ecuador is a democracy. Ecuador's government is working to improve housing, medical care, and literacy. Bolivia has suffered from a series of violent revolutions and military governments. It is now also a democracy. Bolivia has had one of the most stable elected governments in the region in recent years.

Peru's recent history has been particularly troubled. A terrorist group called the Sendero Luminoso, or "shining path," was active in the 1980s. The group carried out deadly guerrilla attacks. With the arrest of the group's leader in 1992, hopes for calm returned. Peru has an elected president and congress.

Chile has also recently ended a long violent period. In 1970, Chileans elected a president who had been influenced by communist ideas. A few years later he was overthrown and killed during a military **coup** (KOO). A coup is a sudden overthrow of a government by a small group of people. In the years after the coup, the military rulers tried to crush their political enemies. The military government was harsh and often violent. Thousands of people were imprisoned or killed. In the late 1980s the power of the rulers began to weaken. After more than 15 years of military rule, Chileans rejected the military dictatorship. A new, democratic government was created. Chileans now enjoy many new freedoms.

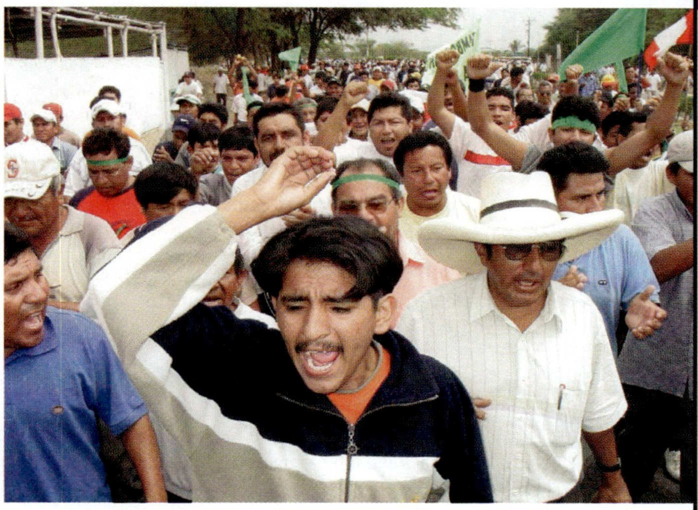

▲ Although Peru now has a more stable government, unrest continues in some areas. In this 2003 photo, farmers protest a mining project by a Canadian company. Possible pollution from the mine was one of the demonstrators' concerns.

✓ **READING CHECK:** *Human Systems* How has unlimited government been a problem for some of the nations in the region? **Military dictatorships have taken over and crushed all opposition by killing and imprisoning people.**

Section 2 Review

go.hrw.com **Homework Practice Online**
Keyword: SJ5 HP12

Define or identify: quinoa, quipus, Atahualpa, Francisco Pizarro, viceroy, creoles, coup

Working with Sketch Maps On the map you created in Section 1, label Cuzco and Machu Picchu. Then shade in the area ruled by the Inca. What may have limited Inca expansion eastward?

Reading for the Main Idea

1. *Human Systems* How did the Inca communicate across great distances?
2. *Environment and Society* What attracted the Spanish conquerors to Pacific South America?

Critical Thinking

3. **Analyzing Information** What governmental problems have many of the region's nations experienced?
4. **Drawing Inferences and Conclusions** Why do you think many leaders of the independence movement were creoles rather than Spaniards?

Organizing What You Know

5. **Sequencing** Copy the following graphic organizer. Use it to show important events in the history of Pacific South America.

	⇨		⇨		⇨		⇨	

Section 2 Review

Answers to Section 2 Review

Define or identify For definitions and identifications, see the glossary and the index.

Working with Sketch Maps Cuzco and Machu Picchu should be labeled in their approximate locations. The shaded area should extend from southern Colombia to central Chile; the Amazon rain forest may have limited eastward expansion.

Reading for the Main Idea

1. by using swift runners, a good road system, and quipus (NGS 12)
2. gold and silver (NGS 15)

Critical Thinking

3. They have had unlimited governments with military dictatorships. (NGS 13)
4. Creoles may have felt less loyalty to Spain, since they had not been born there.

Organizing What You Know

5. possible answer: early cultures, Inca Empire, conquest by Spain, independence movements, modern period of governmental instability

CLOSE

Acquire and play a selection of Andean flute music for the class. Ask students to describe its sound.

REVIEW, ASSESS, RETEACH

Have students complete the Section Review. Then call out terms, phrases, dates, names, and place names from Section 2. Ask students to identify if the word relates to the region's early history, the Spanish era, or its governments. Have another student describe the item's significance. Then have students complete Daily Quiz 12.2. **ESOL**

EXTEND

Have interested students use primary and secondary sources to research a past Andean civilization such as the Chavin, Nazca, Moche, Huari, Tiahuanaco, or Inca cultures. Others may want to conduct research on some aspect of Spanish involvement in the region. Ask students to create a written report and an illustrative poster. **BLOCK SCHEDULING**

CHAPTER 12, Section 3

SECTION 3 RESOURCES

Reproducible
- Lecture Notes, Section 3
- Know It Notes S3
- Creative Strategy for Teaching World Geography, Lesson 9
- Geography for Life Activity 12
- Biography Activity: Isabel Allende

Technology
- One-Stop Planner CD–ROM, Lesson 12.3
- Homework Practice Online
- HRW Go site

Reinforcement, Review, and Assessment
- Section 3 Review
- Daily Quiz 12.3
- Main Idea Activity S3
- Chapter Summaries and Review
- English Audio Summary 12.3
- Spanish Audio Summary 12.3

Section 3: Pacific South America Today

Read to Discover
1. What are the three regions of Ecuador?
2. How might Bolivia develop its economy?
3. What are the features of Peru's regions?
4. How is Chile different from its neighbors in Pacific South America?

Vocabulary
Quechua
junta

Places
Guayaquil
Quito
La Paz
Sucre
Santa Cruz
Callao
Lima
Santiago
Valparaíso

Reading Strategy

READING ORGANIZER Before you read, draw a large circle on a sheet of paper. Draw two intersecting lines to divide the circle into quarters. Label the quarters Ecuador, Bolivia, Peru, and Chile. As you read, fill in the quarters with information about the countries.

Ecuador Today

Many of Ecuador's people live in the coastal lowland. The country's largest city, Guayaquil (gwy-ah-KEEL), is located there. Guayaquil is Ecuador's major port and commercial center. The coastal lowland has valuable deposits of natural gas. It is also an important agricultural region. Rich fishing waters lie off the coast.

The Andean region in the heart of Ecuador is where Quito, the national capital, is located. Open-air markets and Spanish colonial buildings attract many tourists to Quito. Modern buildings surround the old city.

Large numbers of people are moving to the third region, the eastern lowlands. Here in the Amazon Basin are economically essential oil deposits.

Spanish is the official language of Ecuador. However, about 19 percent of the population speaks South American Indian languages such as **Quechua** (KE-chuh-wuh). Quechua was the language of the Inca. Ecuador's Indians are politically active and are represented in the parliament. However, many of them continue to live in terrible poverty.

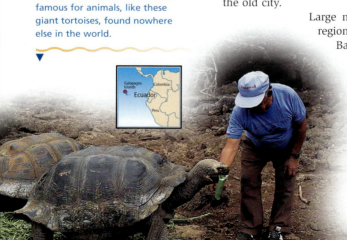
Ecuador's Galápagos Islands are famous for animals, like these giant tortoises, found nowhere else in the world.

✓ **READING CHECK:** *Human Systems* How do Ecuador's Indians participate in and influence the political process?
politically active, represented in parliament

Section 3

Objectives
1. Identify the three regions of Ecuador.
2. Suggest how Bolivia might develop its economy.
3. Describe the features of Peru's regions.
4. Explain how Chile is different from its neighbors in the region.

FOCUS

Bellringer
Copy the following question onto the chalkboard: *Is there a type of weather that you have never experienced?* Allow students to record their responses. (Students living in southern or tropical regions may answer that they never have seen snow.) Discuss responses. Ask students if they can imagine never having seen rain. Tell them that many residents of the world's driest desert, the Atacama in Chile, have never seen rain. Tell students that in Section 3 they will learn more about Chile and its neighbors.

Building Vocabulary
Write the vocabulary terms on the chalkboard and have students read the definitions in Section 3 or the glossary. Remind students that they have already learned a word from Quechua, the language spoken by the Inca. What is it? (quinoa) Tell them that millions of people in Pacific South America speak Quechua and other native languages. Ask: *How did a European language replace Quechua in much of the region?* (spread by the Spanish) The Spanish language has given us junta.

La Paz lies in a valley. Because of recent population growth, the city has spread up the valley walls.

Interpreting the Visual Record
Human-Environment Interaction
How might the growth of La Paz affect the region's environment?

CHAPTER 12, Section 3

ENVIRONMENT AND SOCIETY

Bolivia's Great Park
Ecotourism may provide more income for Bolivia. Madidi National Park, in the northwestern part of the country, will probably become a major tourist destination.

The park covers about 4.7 million acres, and it is slightly smaller than the state of New Jersey. Within its borders are glaciers, a rain forest, flat grassland, a dry forest, and a cloud forest. Because there are so many different habitats, the variety of plants and animals in the park is immense. An estimated 1,000 species of birds can be found there—about 300 more species than live in the United States and Canada combined.

Madidi's future is uncertain. The Bolivian government wants to build a dam at the park's southeastern border. Rising waters behind the dam would flood about 1,000 square miles. Bolivia does not need all the hydroelectric power the dam would generate, but it could sell the extra energy to Brazil. Construction of the dam could cost as much as $3 billion.

Bolivia Today

Bolivia has two capitals. La Paz is located in a valley of the Altiplano. At 12,001 feet (3,658 m), it is the highest capital in the world. It is also Bolivia's chief industrial city. Bolivia's congress meets in La Paz but the supreme court meets in Sucre (soo-kray), farther south. The country's fastest-growing region surrounds the city of Santa Cruz, east of the Andes.

In the plains of eastern Bolivia there are few roads and little money for investment. However, the region's fertile soil, adequate rainfall, and grazing land can help in its development. The country has other valuable resources, including natural gas and various metals, such as tin. However, coups and revolutions have slowed development. Bolivia remains a poor country.

Bolivia's population has the highest percentage of Indians of any South American country. Many Bolivian Indians follow customs and lifestyles that have existed for centuries. They often dress in traditional styles. Women wear full, sweeping skirts and derby hats. Men wear striped ponchos.

Bolivian music is bright and festive. Common instruments include flutes, drums, bronze gongs, and copper bells. The charango is a string instrument that resembles a small guitar. Its sound box is made from the shell of an armadillo.

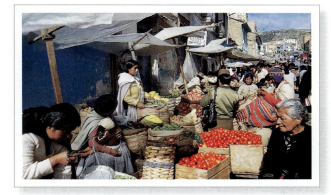

Shoppers buy food at a vegetable market in La Paz.

✓ **READING CHECK:** *Human Systems* What is Bolivia's music like?
bright and festive with lots of instruments, including a local instrument called the charango

▲ **Visual Record Answer**
erosion of slopes, pollution

TEACH

Teaching Objectives 1–3

LEVEL 1: (Suggested time: 30 min.) Copy the following graphic organizer onto the chalkboard, omitting the blue answers. Ask students to copy it into their notebooks. Pair students and have the pairs fill in the chart. Discuss any gaps in students' charts. Then lead a discussion on possible ways Bolivia could develop its economy.
ESOL, COOPERATIVE LEARNING, LS **VISUAL-SPATIAL**

Geographic and Economic Features of Ecuador, Bolivia, and Peru

	Ecuador	Bolivia	Peru
Regions	coastal lowland, Andes, eastern lowlands	coastal plain, Altiplano, eastern plains	coastal plain, Andes, eastern lowlands
Major Cities	Guayaquil, Quito	La Paz, Sucre, Santa Cruz	Lima, Callao
Economy	natural gas, farming, fishing, oil	fertile soil, natural gas, metals	forests for lumber and fruit, minerals, hydroelectric power, tourism

CHAPTER 12, Section 3

FOOD FESTIVAL

Quality Quinoa Quinoa is high in protein and low in unsaturated fats. It can be purchased at health food stores, some supermarkets, and from mail-order companies.

Before using, the quinoa grains must be washed thoroughly in five changes of fresh cold water to remove their bitter coating. The grain can then be steamed or boiled. Quinoa can be substituted for rice in many recipes. Have students experiment with substituting quinoa for rice in familiar dishes. You may also challenge them to find quinoa recipes and prepare them for the class.

Chart Answer

because until recent years it was politically unstable

Pacific South America

Country	Population/ Growth Rate	Life Expectancy	Literacy Rate	Per Capita GDP
Bolivia	8,586,443 1.6%	62, male 67, female	87%	$2,500
Chile	15,665,216 1.0%	73, male 79, female	96%	$10,000
Ecuador	13,710,234 2%	69, male 74, female	92%	$3,100
Peru	28,409,897 1.6%	68, male 73, female	90%	$4,800
United States	290,342,554 0.9%	74, male 80, female	97%	$37,600

Source: Central Intelligence Agency, *The World Factbook 2003*

Interpreting the Chart Why may Bolivia's per capita GDP be lower than those of other countries in the region?

Peru Today

Peru is making progress in its struggle against poverty and political violence. However, the government has been criticized for using harsh methods to solve political problems.

Peru, like Ecuador, has three major regions. The dense rain forests in eastern Peru provide lumber. Tropical fruit trees grow there. The Amazon River flows through this region.

The Andes highlands include the Altiplano and the heartland of what was the Inca Empire. Stone structures from the Inca period draw thousands of tourists to Machu Picchu and Cuzco. Potatoes and corn are among the crops grown in this region. Many of the people in the highlands are South American Indians. Millions of Peruvians speak Quechua.

Important mineral deposits are located near the Pacific coast. This is Peru's most modern and developed region. Hydroelectric projects on coastal rivers provide energy. The seaport city of Callao (kah-YAH-oh) serves Lima (LEE-mah), the capital, a few miles inland. Nearly one third of all Peruvians live in these two cities. Callao is Peru's leading fishing and trade center. Industry and government jobs draw many people from the countryside to Lima.

✓ **READING CHECK:** *Human Systems* What draws people to Callao and Lima? **fishing and trading, jobs in industry and government**

Tourists explore icy landscapes in southern Chile.

LEVELS 2 AND 3: (Suggested time: 45 min.) Have students imagine that they are running for election to the top office in the government of one of the region's countries. Then have students write campaign speeches that demonstrate their understanding of the country's situation. Encourage students to consult outside reference materials. Call on volunteers to deliver their speeches.

Teaching Objective 4

ALL LEVELS: (Suggested time: 30 min.) Have students use the information from the previous lesson to compare and contrast Chile with its Pacific South America neighbors. Students should note political and economic differences. Have students present their information in a graphic organizer. Ask for volunteers to present their organizers to the class. **ESOL**

CLOSE

Have students imagine that they have been hired by a rock band from Pacific South America to design the cover for the band's next CD. Tell students that the band's lyrics deal with political troubles, economic challenges, and cultural features specific to the region. You may want to have the students give the band a name, write song titles, or even lyrics for some of the songs.

Chile Today

In the late 1980s Chile ended the rule of a **junta** (HOOHN-tuh) and became a democracy. A junta is a small group of military officers who rule a country after seizing power. Chile is now also one of the most stable countries in South America. Its economy is also one of the most advanced. Chile's prospects for the future seem bright.

Chile's economy is based on mining, fishing, forestry, and farming. Copper mining is especially important. It accounts for more than one third of the country's exports. In fact, Chile has the world's largest open-pit copper mine. It is located in the Atacama Desert near the town of Chuquicamata.

About one third of all Chileans live in Central Chile. It includes the capital, Santiago, and its nearby seaport, Valparaíso (bahl-pah-rah-EE-soh). The mild Mediterranean climate allows farmers to grow a wide range of crops. Grapes grow well there, and wine is exported around the world. Cool, mountainous southern Chile has forests, oil, and farms. Few people live there, however. Northern Chile includes the Atacama Desert. Croplands along valleys there are irrigated by streams flowing down from the Andes.

Although poverty remains a problem, Chile's economy is becoming stronger. Small businesses and factories are growing quickly. More Chileans are finding work, and wages are rising. Chile hopes that the price of its main export, copper, remains high. Chile's economy would suffer if the world price of copper fell.

Chile wants to expand its trade links with the United States. Some people have suggested that Chile join the North American Free Trade Agreement (NAFTA). This free-trade group currently includes Canada, the United States, and Mexico.

✓ **READING CHECK:** *Environment and Society* How does copper affect Chile's economy? *It supports it; it could also hurt it if the price of copper fell.*

Section 3 Review

Answers to Section 3 Review

Define or identify For definitions and identifications, see the glossary and the index.

Working with Sketch Maps Dense rain forest limits settlements.

Reading for the Main Idea
1. rich oil deposits (NGS 4)
2. to find jobs in industry and government (NGS 9)

Critical Thinking
3. If demand for copper declines or prices fall, there are few other ways for the country to make money.
4. Students might suggest that foreigners may have been nervous about investing.

Organizing What You Know
5. possible answers: Bolivia—two capitals, largest number of Indians, unstable governments; Chile—one of the most stable countries, advanced economy; Ecuador—population concentrated on coast, natural gas and oil deposits, fishing, Quechua, politically active Indians; Peru—political violence, important tourist industry, Quechua

---

Section Review 3

Homework Practice Online
Keyword: SJ5 HP12

Define and explain: Quechua, junta

Working with Sketch Maps On the map you created in Section 2, label Guayaquil, Quito, La Paz, Sucre, Santa Cruz, Callao, Lima, Santiago, and Valparaíso. Why are there so few cities in the eastern part of the region?

Reading for the Main Idea
1. *Places and Regions* How did the Inca communicate across great distances?
2. *Human Systems* Why do many people move from the countryside to Lima, Peru?

Critical Thinking
3. **Drawing Inferences and Conclusions** What might be a disadvantage of Chile depending so heavily on its copper industry?
4. **Analyzing Information** Why have changes in Bolivia's government slowed development?

Organizing What You Know
5. **Summarizing** Copy the following graphic organizer. Use it to write phrases that describe each country.

Bolivia	
Chile	
Ecuador	
Peru	

REVIEW, ASSESS, RETEACH

Have students complete the Section Review. Then ask each student to write a "What Am I?" question based on the Section 3 material. (Example: "I am the language spoken by the Inca. What am I?" Answer: Quechua) Call on volunteers for their questions. Then have students complete Daily Quiz 12.3.

Have students complete Main Idea Activity S3. Then organize students into groups. Ask students to imagine that their group represents an American company interested in investing several million dollars in one country in Pacific South America. Each group should select the best country for its investment, choose business categories, and identify factors that may threaten the investment. **ESOL, COOPERATIVE LEARNING**

EXTEND

Have students conduct research on one of the nature preserves of Pacific South America, such as Manu National Park in Peru or Cayambe-Coca Ecological Reserve in Ecuador. Ask them to highlight how protecting the preserve or park fits into the country's plans for development. You may have students report their findings in the form of a proposal to the commerce or interior department of the country's government. **BLOCK SCHEDULING**

CHAPTER 12 REVIEW

Define and Identify
For definitions and identifications, see the glossary and index.

Review the Main Ideas
13. broad, high-plateau plain between Andes ridges; grassland with few trees (NGS 4)
14. cool ocean water near the coast warms, fish leave, heavy rains, flooding (NGS 7)
15. irrigation projects, road system, suspension bridges (NGS 12)
16. numerical information about important events, populations, animals, and grain supplies
17. captured and killed Atahualpa, conquered Inca lands (NGS 13)
18. unstable governments that limited citizens' rights (NGS 13)
19. Bolivia (NGS 10)
20. industry and government jobs (NGS 9)
21. northern—Atacama Desert, copper mining, irrigated farms; central—heartland, dense population, major cities, mild climate, range of crops; southern—forests, oil, farms, few people (NGS 5)

Think Critically
22. because the region was conquered by Spaniards in the 1500s
23. Because they were born in America, the creoles may have felt less connection to Spain.
24. Students might suggest that the descendants of Spanish rulers, creoles, and Indians have different interests and loyalties. Also, people in different areas within the region have different interests because they have different ways of life.
25. might make it poorer by limiting trade possibilities because all trade would have to be overland
26. They are politically active and represented in the parliament.

Chapter 12 Review and Practice

Define and Identify
Identify each of the following:
1. strait
2. *selvas*
3. El Niño
4. quinoa
5. quipus
6. Atahualpa
7. Francisco Pizarro
8. viceroy
9. creoles
10. coup
11. Quechua
12. junta

Review the Main Ideas
13. What is the Altiplano, and what kind of plants grow there?
14. How does El Niño affect the fish and weather of Pacific South America?
15. What are three types of construction projects that helped the Inca organize their empire?
16. What kinds of information did the Inca record on quipus?
17. What happened when the Spaniards arrived in Pacific South America?
18. What trend have the countries of this region experienced in their forms of government?
19. Which country's population has the highest percentage of Indians?
20. Why are many people moving to Lima, Peru from the countryside?
21. How are northern, central, and southern Chile different?

Think Critically
22. **Analyzing Information** Why is Spanish the most widely spoken language in Pacific South America?
23. **Drawing Inferences and Conclusions** Why do you think that the main leaders of revolts against Spain were creoles?
24. **Drawing Inferences and Conclusions** Why do you think the region's countries have had so many unstable governments since gaining their independence?
25. **Finding the Main Idea** How may Bolivia's landlocked position affect the country's economy?
26. **Analyzing Information** What role do Ecuador's Indians play in its political system?

Map Activity
27. On a separate sheet of paper, match the letters on the map with their correct labels.

    Peru Current Atacama Desert
    Strait of Magellan Quito
    Tierra del Fuego La Paz
    Iquitos Lima
    Lake Poopó Santiago

Map Activity
27. A. La Paz
    B. Amazon River
    C. Quito
    D. Santiago
    E. Atacama Desert
    G. Lima
    H. Lake Poopó
    I. Tierra del Fuego
    J. Peru Current

Writing Activity

Imagine that you are making a film about Ecuador, Bolivia, Peru, or Chile. Write a summary of the film you would like to make. List land features, industries, peoples, and customs that you want to cover. Explain why you think these topics would be interesting to audiences. Be sure to use standard grammar, spelling, sentence structure, and punctuation.

internet connect

Internet Activity: go.hrw.com
KEYWORD: SJ5 GT12

Choose a topic to explore Pacific South America:
- Analyze Chile's climate.
- Hike the Inca Trail and visit Machu Picchu.
- Learn about Andean languages.

Social Studies Skills Practice

Interpreting Maps

Imagine that you are a runner for the Inca Empire carrying a message from Cuzco to Machu Picchu. Study the physical map of southern Peru. Then answer the questions.

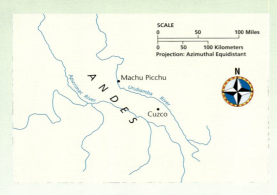

1. What kind of landforms lie along your route? In which direction do you travel?
2. At least how many miles do you have to run?
3. What physical feature may help you shorten your travel time? How?
4. Why might using this physical feature be dangerous? How can you tell from the map?

Analyzing Primary Sources

You have read about El Niño events. Read the following excerpts from the March 1999 issue of *National Geographic* in which Peruvian villagers tell about floods caused by a severe El Niño in 1998. Then answer the questions.

"'Suddenly we were surrounded from all directions,' Ipanaque Silva says. 'It took all the little animals. Then my house fell down completely.' . . . 'We thought that the water couldn't come here,' says Flora Ramirez, 'but we lost practically everything.' . . . 'They strung ropes from one house to another to rescue people,' recalls Manuel Guevara Sanchez. 'Some spent three days on the roof. Those who knew how to swim brought them food.'"

1. Did the flood happen quickly, or did the waters rise slowly?
2. What does the quote from Ipanaque Silva tell about how he made a living and what kind of house he may have had?
3. Do you think that Flora Ramirez had experienced El Niño floods before? Why or why not?
4. How did Manuel Guevara Sanchez's neighbors help each other?

Pacific South America • 269

CHAPTER 12 REVIEW

Writing Activity

Information included should be consistent with text material. Check that students discuss physical features, industries, peoples, and customs and explain why the chosen topics would be interesting to audiences. Use Rubric 43, Writing to Persuade, to evaluate student work.

Interpreting Maps

1. mountains; northwest
2. about 60 miles
3. Urubamba River; by using a boat to sail or paddle down the river
4. The river appears to be in a steep-sided valley, so getting to it and climbing away from it could be dangerous. Also, there could be rapids on the river, since it's in a mountainous area.

Analyzing Primary Sources

1. quickly
2. Silva was probably a farmer, and his house was probably not sturdy.
3. She had experienced floods before, because she had some idea of where waters could and could not come.
4. strung ropes from one house to another to rescue people, swam to bring them food

---

REVIEW AND ASSESSMENT RESOURCES

Reproducible
- Readings in World Geography, History, and Culture 25, 26, and 27
- Critical Thinking Activity 12
- Vocabulary Activity 12

Technology
- Chapter 12 Test Generator (on the One-Stop Planner)

- Audio CD Program, Chapter 12
- HRW Go site

Reinforcement, Review, and Assessment
- Chapter 12 Review and Practice
- Chapter Summaries and Review

- Chapter 12 Test
- Chapter 12 Test for English Language Learners and Special-Needs Students
- Unit 4 Test
- Unit 4 Test for English Language Learners and Special-Needs Students

internet connect

GO TO: go.hrw.com
KEYWORD: SJ5 Teacher
FOR: a guide to using the Internet in your classroom

CHAPTER 12

GEOGRAPHY SIDELIGHT

Cassava—Deadly or Delicious? A major food source for the native peoples of the Amazon rain forest can be poisonous if not prepared properly. Cassava, also known as manioc, forms a starchy root that looks much like a sweet potato. A variety of cassava contains a deadly chemical similar to cyanide.

Two basic methods make cassava edible. A cook can either boil it for a long time or grate the flesh and press out the poison. A porous basket may be used for this pressing technique.

Critical Thinking: How may people have first discovered the processes by which manioc is made edible?

Answer: Students may suggest that the discovery was accidental. For example, people may have learned quickly that the plant was poisonous, but then a piece of cassava may have fallen unseen into a cooking pot and boiled along with other foods. When someone ate it and discovered it was good, other people would have continued the boiling process.

GO TO: go.hrw.com
KEYWORD: SJ5 CH12
FOR: more information on the Amazon rain forest.

COULD YOU SURVIVE THE AMAZON?

ON-LINE EXPEDITIONS
GO TO: go.hrw.com
KEYWORD: SJ5 CH12

A Land of Danger and Beauty
Welcome to the Amazon, the biggest rain forest in the world! The forest is very beautiful. Brightly colored orchids hang from the trees. Parrots and butterflies look like flying jewels. Watch out, though. The rain forest hides some dangerous residents. Just touching some of the frogs can kill a human. The bite of a fer-de-lance, one of the world's scariest snakes, causes death by internal bleeding. Really big anacondas can swallow a teenager whole. In the forest's many streams, electric eels and piranhas lurk. Caimans, which are related to alligators, can be 15 feet long. Their teeth are just as sharp as those of their relatives.

SURVIVAL CHALLENGE
Now place yourself in an airplane flying over the Amazon rain forest. You're exploring the area to investigate business opportunities. From the air, the trees look like a sea of green. Suddenly, you're *in* the trees because the plane has crashed! You're amazed to find that you are the only survivor and that you are unhurt. However, you are lost and surrounded by danger. How will you survive long enough to find your way back to a city?

Fortunately, you know some of the local language. When you ask someone for help, she draws a map in the dirt and colors it with natural dyes. Her mental map is shown on the next page. Can you read it? How does her map differ from your own mental map of the rain forest? Why do you think two people could have different mental maps of the same region?

A jaguar snarls to warn visitors away from his territory.

270 • Unit 3

Survival Challenge Activity
Point out that mental maps show the elements of one's environment that have meaning to the individual. Then focus attention on the mental map on the opposite page.* Begin by asking what elements of her environment would be most important to the woman who drew the map. (sources of food and danger, directions to other villages, features of physical geography) Then challenge students to decipher the map by concentrating on how the symbols reflect the essential quality of what it represents. (For example, the fangs in the upper left area stand for the jaguar, because it is significant for the danger it poses.) Tell students that the Y shape that runs across the map is a river. Then discuss all reasonable suggestions before disclosing the rest of the map "key": baskets—fields where cassava is grown and processed (See the Geography Sidelight feature); fire—the mapmaker's village; upside down fire—an enemy village; orange and yellow shapes—oranges and bananas; chevrons in center—tail ridges of caimans, which rest on the riverbank; crooked parallel lines—rapids or waterfall; jagged line near the rapids—piranhas in a pool; thick crooked line in an oval—anaconda in a swamp; eye—tall tree that villagers climb to see distances; orange semicircles—the end points of the distance one can travel between two sunrises; larger dots in the river—downstream. Then discuss what would be on the visitor's mental map of the area (distances to roads, trading posts on the river, and so on). Discuss why these elements would not appear on the woman's map. (They are unknown or unimportant to her.)

*The map is fictitious.

270 Chapter 12

Seeing the Forest *and* the Trees

By carefully comparing the map to your surroundings, you unravel its secrets. What are they? You find food, avoid danger, and eventually return home. Then you see the other map below in a magazine. You also read that while many people worry about the loss of the rain forest, others see great benefits in developing it. Your experience and this new information give you plenty of food for thought. Will the way you think about the rain forest change?

CHAPTER 12

Going Further: Thinking Critically

Focus students' attention on the map on this page. Point out the large cities and Natural World Heritage sites marked on it. Organize students into groups and assign each group one of these issues:

- What role does the expansion of cities in Brazil and the surrounding countries play in threats to the rain forest?
- What roles do farming, ranching, and logging play in these threats?
- What are the Natural World Heritage sites within the Amazon rain forest? What are they like?
- Should there be more Natural World Heritage sites designated within the rain forest? Why or why not?

Have groups conduct research to answer the assigned questions. Then ask them to present their findings in the setting of an international conference titled "The Amazon Rain Forest—Where Do We Go From Here"?

➤ This Could You Survive? feature addresses National Geography Standards 2, 6, 8, 13, and 14.

Seeing the Forest *and* the Trees Activity

By comparing the map to the surroundings, the crash survivor climbs the tall tree to get his bearings, finds fruit to eat, sees how to avoid dangerous animals, and finds the river, which will eventually take him downstream to a city. Perhaps he arrives in Manaus, where he sees the map and reads about issues surrounding destruction of the Amazon rain forest. He learns that the rain forest is sometimes called the "lungs of the planet" for the oxygen it produces and that new lifesaving drugs may be found in the forest's plants. He hears also that logging, farming, and ranching have claimed large parts of the forest—at the rate of about one acre per minute. He also hears from other sources, however, that the threats to the forest have been exaggerated.

The survivor may decide to devote his energies to publicizing the destruction of the rain forest. From his experience in the forest, he knows that the forest sustains not just development but also people who depend entirely on its resources. Rare and beautiful animals—only some of which are dangerous—also live there. Or, he may decide that the most important thing to do is provide jobs to the woman who drew the map and the other villagers. Whichever path the survivor takes, he has learned an important concept about perceptions. What could it be? The survivor's perceptions, or the way he thinks about the rain forest, have been changed by his experience.

UNIT 3

PRACTICING THE SKILL

1. Students might suggest the following: push—wars, discrimination, unemployment, limited resources, natural disasters, famine, forced military service; pull—jobs or higher salary, greater political freedom, freedom from war, plentiful resources, or family members already living in the other place.

2. If possible, students should discuss their mother's and father's ancestors. Students may also research a friend's family. Students' ancestors may have come to the United States for any of the reasons listed in the answer to the previous question or for other reasons. Some students may mention that their ancestors were brought here against their will as slaves.

3. Students may suggest any place in the world and describe their emotions about migrating.

➤ This GeoSkills feature addresses National Geography Standards 6, 9, 10, 12, and 15.

Building Skills for Life: Understanding Migration Patterns

People have always moved to different places. This movement is called migration. Understanding migration patterns is very important in geography. These patterns help explain why certain places are the way they are today. In South America, for example, there are people whose ancestors came from Africa, Asia, Europe, and North America. All of these people migrated to South America sometime in the past.

Why do people migrate? There are many different reasons. Sometimes, people do not want to move, but they are forced to. This is called forced migration. Other times, people migrate because they are looking for a better life. This is an example of voluntary migration.

Geographers who study migration patterns often use the words *push* and *pull*. They identify situations that push people out of places. For example, wars often push people away. They also identify situations that pull people to new places. A better job might pull someone to a new place. Usually, people migrate for a combination of reasons. They might be pushed from a place because there is not enough farmland. They might also be pulled to a new place by good farmland.

Geographers are also interested in barriers to migration. Barriers make it harder for people to migrate. There are cultural barriers, economic barriers, physical barriers, and political barriers. For example, deserts, mountains, and oceans can make it harder for people to migrate. Unfamiliar languages and ways of life can also block migration.

Migration changes people and places. Both the places that people leave and the places where they arrive are changed. Can you think of some ways that migration has changed the world?

▲ Many people from Japan migrated to the area around São Paulo, Brazil in the 1900s.

PRACTICING THE SKILL

1. List some factors that can push people out of a place or pull them to a new place.
2. Research the migration of your ancestors or a friend's ancestors. Where did they come from? When did they migrate? Why?
3. Imagine you had to migrate to a new place. Where would you go? Why would you pick this place? Do you think you would be scared, excited, or both?

272 • Unit 3 GeoSkills

GEOSKILLS

Going Further: Thinking Critically

Prepare in advance slips of paper on which you have written the names of countries that have experienced heavy migration, either into, out of, or from one region to another within the country. Here are some possibilities: Canada, Ireland, Mauritania, Mexico, Brazil, Thailand, and Vietnam. You may want to omit the United States because the wide availability of information could put other groups at a disadvantage.

Organize the class into as many groups as you have countries and have a representative of each group draw a country name from a hat. Have the students work together to investigate their chosen country's migration patterns. Statistics are available from the *CIA World Factbook* online. Newspapers and newsmagazines can provide detail. Ask students to concentrate on the concept of push and pull—what social, environmental, or economic factors pull or push the residents into or out of the place.

When their research is complete, have students write and perform skits to illustrate some of the issues they have investigated. Their skits may take place in the country where new residents have arrived or the place they have left. After the performances, lead a class discussion on what students have learned from the activity.

272 Unit 3 GeoSkills

HANDS on GEOGRAPHY

The following passage was written by a woman from Argentina who migrated to the United States. Read the passage and then answer the Lab Report questions.

> My nephew and I came from a faraway country called Argentina. When I mention this country to others, they say, "Oh, Argentina! It is so beautiful!" However, as beautiful as Argentina is, life there is very difficult now.
>
> In Argentina, there are three social classes: rich, middle class, and poor. The middle class, of which I am a member, is the largest. We are the workers and the businesspeople. Because of bad economic decisions and corrupt government, the middle class has almost disappeared. Factories have closed, and people have no work. The big companies move to other countries. The small businesses depend on the big companies and often have to close. Argentina has a very high rate of unemployment. Many people are hungry.
>
> My husband and I had some friends who worked in Argentina. They advised us to sell everything we owned and move to Houston. They told us that life was better there and they had relatives who would help us find a house to rent. They told us a lawyer would help us put our papers in order so we could work. I had a small sewing shop with some sewing machines, which I sold so I could travel.

Poverty and unemployment are problems in some parts of Argentina.
Interpreting the Visual Record What evidence can you see of poor living conditions?

Lab Report

1. What pushed the author out of Argentina?
2. Why did she choose Houston as her destination?
3. According to the author, what do other people think Argentina is like? does she agree?

Lab Report
Answers
1. Poor economic conditions pushed the author out of Argentina.
2. The author believed life would be better in Houston. She and her husband also knew people in Houston who could help them find a house to rent.
3. Other people think Argentina is beautiful. The author believes that Argentina is physically beautiful but is a very difficult place to live.

◀ **Visual Record Answer**

possible answers: shacks, substandard housing materials, unpaved streets, garbage, puddles of dirty water

UNIT 4

Unit Objectives

1. Describe the major landforms, bodies of water, climates, and resources of Europe.
2. Explain the historical development of the European nations and the influence of European cultures on other parts of the world.
3. Identify different cultural groups in Europe and understand how they interact with one another.
4. Discuss Europe's influence in international affairs.
5. Interpret special-purpose maps to analyze relationships among climates, population patterns, and economic resources in Europe.

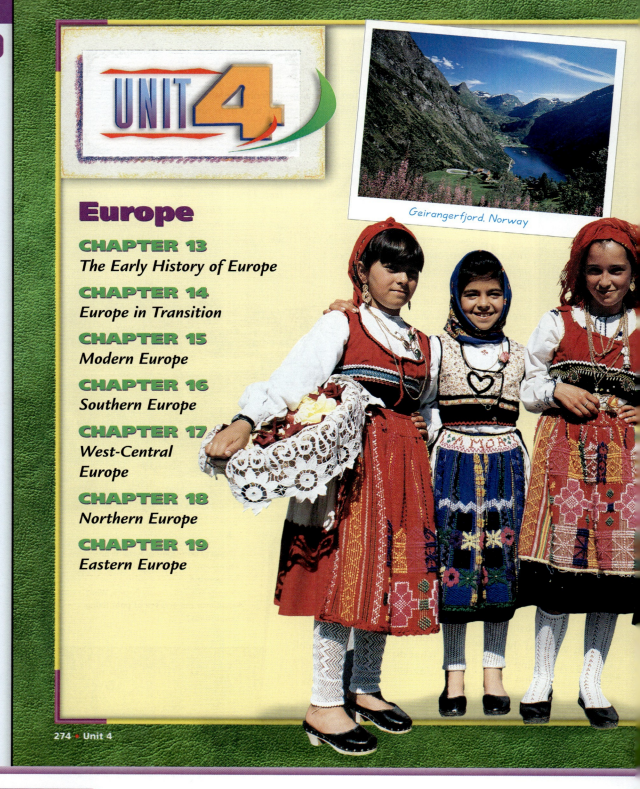

Europe

CHAPTER 13
The Early History of Europe

CHAPTER 14
Europe in Transition

CHAPTER 15
Modern Europe

CHAPTER 16
Southern Europe

CHAPTER 17
West-Central Europe

CHAPTER 18
Northern Europe

CHAPTER 19
Eastern Europe

Geirangerfjord, Norway

Using the Illustrations

Direct students' attention to the photographs on these pages. Tell them that instead of streets Venice, Italy, has canals. The city's only paved streets are narrow and for pedestrians only. Venice was built on a group of islands in a lagoon. You may want to read the sidebar feature about Venice's gondolas in the chapter on southern Europe. Ask students to speculate about all the ways their lives would be different if the major thoroughfares of their community were canals instead of streets.

Remind students that various forces of erosion shape the land. Ask how the valley in the small photo may have been created *(by a glacier)*.

Tell students that in the chapter on northern Europe they will learn more about fjords, like the one pictured on this page, and how they were formed.

Direct students' attention to the photograph of the swan. Point out that Europe is densely populated and that very few large wild animals live there except in nature preserves.

Finally, refer to the photo taken in Prague. The writer Franz Kafka lived on the street pictured. The house in the center is tiny, and visitors must stoop to enter it.

Notes from the Field

A Professor in the Czech Republic

Meredith Walker teaches English at Clemson University. She also teaches English As a Second Language courses. Here she describes a visit to Prague, the capital of the Czech Republic. **WHAT DO YOU THINK?** Does Prague sound like a city you would like to see?

The castle in Prague sits on a hill high above the Vltava River. This river divides the city. A castle has stood on that hillside for 1,000 years. Rising from the inner courtyard of the castle is a huge medieval building, St. Vitus' Cathedral. Together, the castle and cathedral look almost magical, especially at night when spotlights shine on them. The castle is the most important symbol of the city. A great Czech writer, Franz Kafka, believed that the castle influenced everything and everyone in the city.

Another important landmark in Prague is Charles Bridge, one of eight bridges that cross the Vltava River. The bridge is part of the route that kings once traveled on their way to the castle to be crowned. Today, large crowds of tourists walk there. Many stop to photograph some of the 22 statues that line the bridge. No cars are allowed on the bridge today.

The first time I walked across the bridge, heading up toward the castle, it was at night. Fireworks were lighting the sky all around me. It was a colorful welcome.

Street scene in Prague, Czech Republic

Portuguese girls in native costume

Understanding Primary Sources

1. How does the city's physical geography help make the castle a symbol of Prague?
2. How did the fireworks display affect Meredith Walker's feelings about Prague?

Whooper swan

MORE FROM THE FIELD

Events in Prague have given the world an unusual word: *defenestration*, which means "a throwing of a person or thing out of a window." The word is taken from the Latin word *fenestra*, which means "window." In 1419, religious reformers defenestrated the entire town council. A second case was part of a Protestant rebellion. Three Catholic officials were thrown from a window in Prague's Hradčany Castle. The Second Defenestration of Prague, as the episode was called, led directly to the Thirty Years' War (1618–48).

In the aftermath of the Communist takeover of 1948, Jan Masaryk, the non-Communist foreign minister, committed suicide or was assassinated in a fall from his office window. Controversy arose after poet and screenwriter Bohumil Hrabal fell to his death from the window of his fifth-floor hospital room in 1997.

Activity: Have students conduct research on how certain buildings in Eastern Europe relate to the local or regional history of the area in which they are located.

Understanding Primary Sources
Answers
1. It is on a hill.
2. It made her feel more welcome.

CHAPTERS

13 The Early History of Europe
traces European civilizations from the Greeks through the Middle Ages.

14 Europe in Transition
explores the centuries from the Renaissance to the Industrial Revolution.

15 Modern Europe
describes the events of the twentieth century.

16 Southern Europe
explores Portugal and the Mediterranean countries—Greece, Italy, and Spain.

17 West-Central Europe
focuses on France, Germany, Belgium, the Netherlands, Switzerland, and Austria.

18 Northern Europe
describes the United Kingdom, the Republic of Ireland, and the Scandinavian countries.

19 Eastern Europe
describes the political and economic changes and ethnic conflicts that have characterized Eastern Europe in recent years.

UNIT 4 ATLAS

PEOPLE IN THE PROFILE

Note that the elevation profile crosses the Great Hungarian Plain. The nation of Hungary dates back to when the nomadic Magyar people, whose ancestors came from central Russia, moved into the sparsely populated plain during the A.D. 890s.

The Magyars spent much of their time on horseback. They lived mainly on meat, mare's milk, and fish. The Magyars were organized into clans, which in turn banded together into tribes.

Until the mid-900s Magyars raided far into western Europe. They were skilled with their favorite weapon, the bow and arrow, and their horses were fast. The Magyars captured slaves and stole treasure until Otto the Great of Germany stopped them. According to tradition, they adopted Christianity on Christmas Day, 1000, when, with the pope's approval, the Magyar king, Stephen I, was crowned.

Today, most Hungarians still call themselves Magyars. There are large Magyar minorities in other countries, such as Romania. In fact, perhaps half of the world's Magyars live in countries other than Hungary.

Critical Thinking: Where did the Magyar people originate?

Answer: central Russia

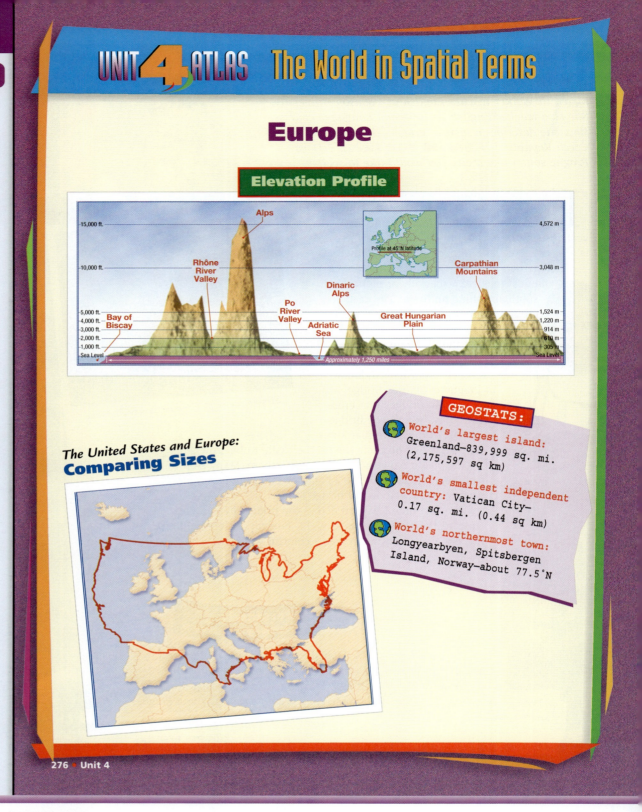

OVERVIEW

In this unit students will learn about the landscape and cultures of one of the world's most densely settled continents.

A wide range of climates, from steppe to ice-cap, has allowed Europeans to use the land in many ways. In general, the farms are so productive that the majority of the population can live in cities and towns and work in manufacturing and service jobs.

Europe's past is dynamic and turbulent. Countless leaders have gone into battle to control its resources. Explorers, conquerors, and colonists spread out from Europe and have influenced most parts of the world. The continent was at the center of two world wars. Ethnic conflicts continue to trouble postwar Europe. Recently created republics struggle to find their place among the other countries.

Over the centuries, European art, architecture, music, literature, and drama have been valued by people around the world. The region's international influence has grown since many of the countries have joined the European Union.

276 ◆ Unit 4

Europe: Physical

UNIT 4 ATLAS

internet connect

ONLINE ATLAS
GO TO: go.hrw.com
KEYWORD: SJ5 MapsU4
FOR: Web links to online maps of the region

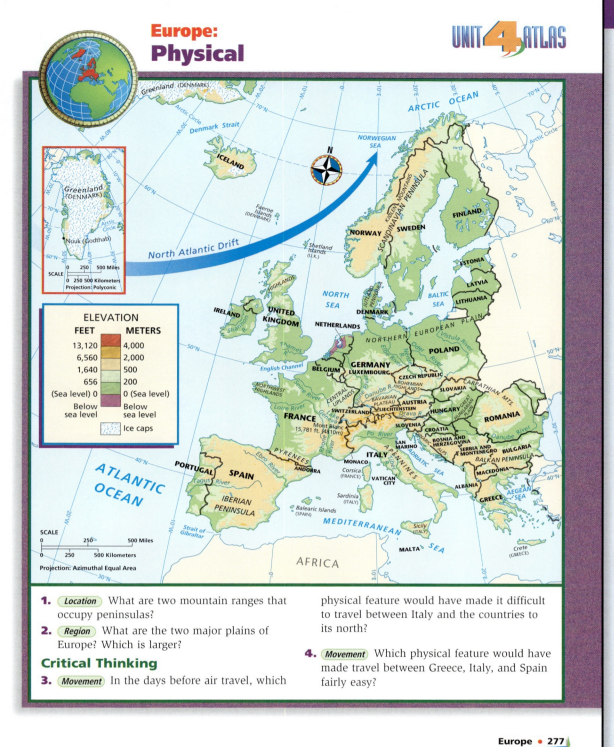

1. **Location** What are two mountain ranges that occupy peninsulas?
2. **Region** What are the two major plains of Europe? Which is larger?

Critical Thinking
3. **Movement** In the days before air travel, which physical feature would have made it difficult to travel between Italy and the countries to its north?
4. **Movement** Which physical feature would have made travel between Greece, Italy, and Spain fairly easy?

Physical Map
Answers
1. Apennines and Kjølen Mountains
2. Northern European Plain and Great Hungarian Plain; Northern European Plain

Critical Thinking
3. Alps
4. Mediterranean Sea

Europe • 277

USING THE PHYSICAL MAP

Direct students' attention to the **physical map** on this page. Ask a volunteer to name the highest physical feature on the map and its location (Mont Blanc, on France's border with Italy and Switzerland). Then ask them to identify the area that is below sea level (large area in the Netherlands). Have students compare this map to the **population map** and have them suggest a problem that people of the Netherlands had to solve before the country could support a large population (how to keep the North Sea from flooding the land).

Ask students to suggest areas where no people live (southeast Iceland, most of Greenland). Then ask how they could guess this without looking at the population map (presence of ice caps).

Europe 277

UNIT 4 ATLAS

Your Classroom Time Line

These are the major dates and time periods for this unit. Have students enter them on the time line you created earlier. You may want to watch for these dates as students progress through the unit.

- **c.* 2000 B.C.** Complex civilization exists on Crete.
- **c. 800 B.C.** City-states organize on Greek mainland.
- **c. 750 B.C.** The Latins establish Rome.
- **c. 750–450 B.C.** The Celts come to the British Isles.
- **c. 400s B.C.** Construction of the Parthenon begins.

*c. stands for *circa* and means "about."

internet connect

ONLINE ATLAS
GO TO: go.hrw.com
KEYWORD: SJ5 MapsU4
FOR: Web links to online maps of the region

Political Map
Answers
1. Spain, France
2. Pyrenees

Critical Thinking
3. Bosnia and Herzegovina, Slovenia
4. It is separated from other countries by the English Channel, the Atlantic Ocean, and the North Sea.

Europe: Political

1. **Place** Which countries border both the Atlantic and the Mediterranean?
2. **Region** Compare this map to the **physical map** of the region. Which physical feature helps form the boundary between Spain and France?

Critical Thinking

3. **Location** Which countries have the shortest coastlines on the Adriatic Sea?
4. **Location** The United Kingdom has not been invaded successfully since A.D. 1066. Why do you think this is so?

278 • Unit 4

USING THE POLITICAL MAP

Tell the class that Europe is often called a peninsula of peninsulas. On a wall map, trace the outline of Europe so that students can observe how the entire continent is a peninsula of the Eurasian land mass. Then ask them to look at the **political map** on this page and to identify countries or pairs of countries that are peninsulas. (Examples: Spain and Portugal, Italy, Denmark, Norway and Sweden, Greece)

Also ask students to identify the largest country in Europe and those that are so small that their area is not apparent on the map (France; Andorra, Liechtenstein, Malta, Monaco, San Marino, Vatican City). Then ask which country would be the largest if territory under its control were included in its area (Denmark, because it controls Greenland). Point out that most of the large islands and island groups in the Mediterranean Sea are not independent countries. Call on volunteers to identify the countries to which the islands belong (Balearic Islands, Spain; Corsica, France; Sardinia and Sicily, Italy; Crete, Greece).

278 Unit 4

Europe: Climate

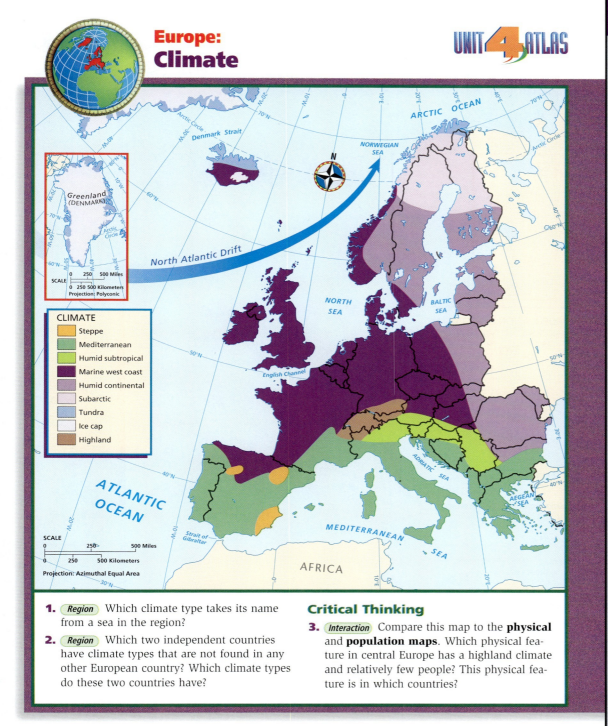

1. **Region** Which climate type takes its name from a sea in the region?
2. **Region** Which two independent countries have climate types that are not found in any other European country? Which climate types do these two countries have?

Critical Thinking

3. **Interaction** Compare this map to the **physical** and **population maps**. Which physical feature in central Europe has a highland climate and relatively few people? This physical feature is in which countries?

Europe • 279

UNIT 4 ATLAS

Your Classroom Time Line (continued)

c. 300 B.C. Euclid writes *Elements*.

A.D. 100s The Roman Empire is at its greatest extent.

early 300s Constantine adopts Christianity.

400s The Roman Empire is divided into two parts.

400s Angles and Saxons migrate to the British Isles.

476 Rome falls to invaders.

early 700s Moors conquer the Iberian Peninsula.

800 Charlemagne is crowned Emperor of the Romans.

1066 The duke of Normandy invades the British Isles.

1100s England conquers Ireland.

1200s The Mongols invade Hungary.

1300s The Renaissance begins in Italy.

1337–1453 England and France fight the Hundred Years' War.

1453 Ottoman Turks conquer Constantinople.

Climate Map
Answers
1. Mediterranean
2. Iceland and Spain; tundra, marine west coast, ice cap; marine west coast, Mediterranean, steppe

Critical Thinking
3. Alps; France, Italy, Germany, Austria, Switzerland

USING THE CLIMATE MAP

Direct students' attention to the **climate map** on this page. Ask one student to call out the names of the individual countries that make up Europe and have other students name the main climate types in each country. Have students compare this map to the **political map** to answer these questions: Which island countries have only a marine west coast climate? (Ireland, United Kingdom) Which Atlantic coast country has only a Mediterranean climate? (Portugal) Which large Eastern European country is divided about equally between marine west coast and humid continental climate regions? (Poland)

Europe 279

UNIT 4 ATLAS

Your Classroom Time Line (continued)

1492 King Ferdinand and Queen Isabella take Granada, Spain, from Moors. Christopher Columbus sails to America.

1500s Germany becomes the center of the Reformation.

1503–06 Leonardo da Vinci paints *Mona Lisa*.

1588 The English defeat the Spanish Armada.

1616 William Shakespeare dies.

1789 The French Revolution begins.

1815 Napoléon Bonaparte is defeated.

1840s The Irish potato famine occurs.

1871 Prussia unites Germany.

1914–18 World War I is fought.

---

internet connect

ONLINE ATLAS
GO TO: go.hrw.com
KEYWORD: SJ5 MapsU4
FOR: Web links to online maps of the region

Population Map
Answers
1. cold subarctic and tundra climates
2. Latvia, Lithuania

Critical Thinking
3. nuclear power; large amounts of energy required by densely populated areas and industry of central Europe

---

Europe: Population

POPULATION DENSITY

Persons per sq. mile	Persons per sq. km
520	200
260	100
130	50
25	10
3	1
0	0

● Metropolitan areas with more than 2 million inhabitants
○ Metropolitan areas with 1 million to 2 million inhabitants

1. **Region** Examine the **climate map**. Why are northern Norway, Sweden, and Finland so thinly populated?

2. **Place** Compare this map to the **political map**. Which countries have between 25 and 130 persons per square mile in all areas?

Critical Thinking

3. **Interaction** Compare this map to the **land use and resources map** of the region. What type of power generation is common in central Europe but not in the far north? Why do you think this is so?

280 • Unit 4

USING THE POPULATION MAP

 As students examine the **population map** on this page, point out that many European cities are located on or near rivers. Have students compare this map to the **physical map** to identify some of these cities and rivers. Students may need to use the chapter maps to confirm detail. (Possible answers: London—Thames, Paris—Seine, Rome—Tiber, Rotterdam—Rhine, Budapest—Danube)

Ask students to identify the countries with the largest areas of high population density (United Kingdom, Netherlands, Belgium, Germany, Italy).

Europe: Land Use and Resources

UNIT 4 ATLAS

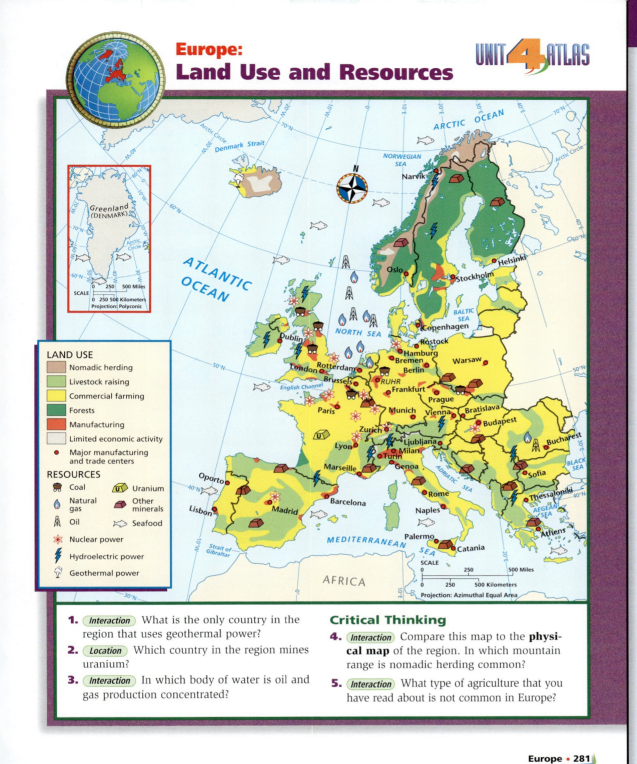

1. **Interaction** What is the only country in the region that uses geothermal power?
2. **Location** Which country in the region mines uranium?
3. **Interaction** In which body of water is oil and gas production concentrated?

Critical Thinking
4. **Interaction** Compare this map to the **physical map** of the region. In which mountain range is nomadic herding common?
5. **Interaction** What type of agriculture that you have read about is not common in Europe?

Europe • 281

UNIT 4 ATLAS

Your Classroom Time Line (continued)

- **1921** Most of Ireland becomes independent.
- **1933** The Nazi Party seizes power in Germany.
- **1936–39** The Spanish Civil War is fought.
- **1939** World War II begins.
- **1944** Allies invade Normandy.
- **1945** Germany is defeated.
- **1956** Hungary revolts against the Soviet Union.
- **1961** The Berlin Wall is built.
- **1974** Greece becomes a republic.
- **1975** Francisco Franco's rule of Spain ends.
- **1989** Soviet control of Eastern Europe ends.
- **1989** The Berlin Wall is opened.
- **1993** Czechoslovakia divides into two countries.
- **1990s** Civil war and fighting in former Yugoslavia begins.
- **2003** The United Kingdom is the main U.S. ally in the invasion of Iraq.
- **2004** Madrid, Spain, is devastated by terrorist attacks on commuter trains.

Land Use and Resources Map
Answers
1. Iceland
2. France
3. North Sea

Critical Thinking
4. Kjølen Mountains
5. subsistence farming

USING THE LAND USE AND RESOURCES MAP

Focus students' attention on the **land use and resources map** on this page. Ask students to name countries that do not have major manufacturing and trade centers (Iceland, Estonia, Latvia, Lithuania, Yugoslavia, Albania, Macedonia, Croatia, Bosnia and Herzegovina) and to identify other economic activities that are important to these countries (commercial farming, livestock raising, some mineral production). Then ask which countries appear to have the largest number of major manufacturing and trade centers. (Germany and Italy)

Europe 281

FAST FACTS

UNITED STATES OF AMERICA

CAPITAL: Washington, D.C.
AREA: 3,717,792 sq. mi. (9,629,091 sq km)
POPULATION: 290,342,554
MONEY: U.S. dollar (US$)
LANGUAGES: English, Spanish (spoken by a large minority)
CARS: 131,838,538

Fast Facts: Europe

ALBANIA
CAPITAL: Tiranë
AREA: 11,100 sq. mi. (28,748 sq km)
POPULATION: 3,582,205
MONEY: lek
LANGUAGES: Albanian, Greek
CARS: data not available

ANDORRA
CAPITAL: Andorra la Vella
AREA: 181 sq. mi. (468 sq km)
POPULATION: 69,150
MONEY: euro
LANGUAGES: Catalan (official), French Castilian
CARS: 35,358

AUSTRIA
CAPITAL: Vienna
AREA: 32,378 sq. mi. (83,858 sq km)
POPULATION: 8,188,207
MONEY: euro
LANGUAGES: German
CARS: 3,780,000

BELGIUM
CAPITAL: Brussels
AREA: 11,780 sq. mi. (30,510 sq km)
POPULATION: 10,289,088
MONEY: euro
LANGUAGES: Dutch, French, German
CARS: 4,420,000

BOSNIA AND HERZEGOVINA
CAPITAL: Sarajevo
AREA: 19,741 sq. mi. (51,129 sq km)
POPULATION: 3,989,018
MONEY: marka
LANGUAGES: Croatian, Serbian, Bosnian
CARS: data not available

BULGARIA
CAPITAL: Sofia
AREA: 42,822 sq. mi. (110,910 sq km)
POPULATION: 7,537,929
MONEY: lev
LANGUAGES: Bulgarian
CARS: 1,650,000

CROATIA
CAPITAL: Zagreb
AREA: 21,831 sq. mi. (56,542 sq km)
POPULATION: 4,422,248
MONEY: Croatian kuna
LANGUAGES: Croatian
CARS: 698,000

CZECH REPUBLIC
CAPITAL: Prague
AREA: 30,450 sq. mi. (78,866 sq km)
POPULATION: 10,249,216
MONEY: Czech koruna
LANGUAGES: Czech
CARS: 4,410,000

DENMARK
CAPITAL: Copenhagen
AREA: 16,639 sq. mi. (43,094 sq km)
POPULATION: 5,384,384
MONEY: Danish krone
LANGUAGES: Danish, Faroese, Greenlandic (an Inuit dialect), German
CARS: 1,790,000

ESTONIA
CAPITAL: Tallinn
AREA: 17,462 sq. mi. (45,226 sq km)
POPULATION: 1,408,556
MONEY: Estonian kroon
LANGUAGES: Estonian (official), Russian, Ukrainian, English, Finnish
CARS: 338,000

Countries not drawn to scale.

FAST FACTS ACTIVITIES

LEVEL 1: (Suggested time: 30 min.) Ask students to look at the population and area figures on these pages. Tell them that the United States has a population of more than 290 million people living in an area of 3,717,792 square miles. Have students work with a partner to compare the U.S. population per square mile with that of the European countries. Ask the students to decide if the population in the United States is more or less dense than the population of the European countries. **(Population density in Europe is higher than it is in the United States.)**

Then ask each pair of students to share their answer with another pair of students. Encourage the students to define the concept of population density and to demonstrate how they determined whether the United States or European countries tended to have a higher population density. **(Divide population by square miles. A larger number indicates a higher density—more people per square mile.)**

LEVEL 2: (Suggested time: 25 min.) Have students examine the figures for population and cars for the European countries. Mention that the U.S. population of approximately 290 million owns more than 130 million cars. Those figures translate roughly to one car for every two people in the United States, which is far more than in most European countries. You may want to invite students to verify this statement by making rough estimates of the European figures.

UNIT 4 ATLAS

FINLAND
CAPITAL: Helsinki
AREA: 130,127 sq. mi. (337,030 sq km)
POPULATION: 5,190,785
MONEY: euro
LANGUAGES: Finnish, Swedish
CARS: 1,940,000

FRANCE
CAPITAL: Paris
AREA: 211,208 sq. mi. (547,030 sq km)
POPULATION: 60,180,529
MONEY: euro
LANGUAGES: French
CARS: 25,500,000

GERMANY
CAPITAL: Berlin
AREA: 137,846 sq. mi. (357,021 sq km)
POPULATION: 82,398,326
MONEY: euro
LANGUAGES: German
CARS: 41,330,000

GREECE
CAPITAL: Athens
AREA: 50,942 sq. mi. (131,940 sq km)
POPULATION: 10,665,989
MONEY: euro
LANGUAGES: Greek (official), English, French
CARS: 2,340,000

HUNGARY
CAPITAL: Budapest
AREA: 35,919 sq. mi. (93,030 sq km)
POPULATION: 10,045,407
MONEY: forint
LANGUAGES: Hungarian
CARS: 2,280,000

ICELAND
CAPITAL: Reykjavik
AREA: 39,768 sq. mi. (103,000 sq km)
POPULATION: 280,798
MONEY: Icelandic krona
LANGUAGES: Icelandic
CARS: 132,468

IRELAND
CAPITAL: Dublin
AREA: 27,135 sq. mi. (70,280 sq km)
POPULATION: 3,924,140
MONEY: euro
LANGUAGES: English, Irish (Gaelic)
CARS: 1,060,000

ITALY
CAPITAL: Rome
AREA: 116,305 sq. mi. (301,230 sq km)
POPULATION: 57,998,353
MONEY: euro
LANGUAGES: Italian, German, French, Slovene
CARS: 31,000,000

LATVIA
CAPITAL: Riga
AREA: 24,938 sq. mi. (64,589 sq km)
POPULATION: 2,348,784
MONEY: Latvian lat
LANGUAGES: Lettish (official), Lithuanian, Russian
CARS: 252,000

LIECHTENSTEIN
CAPITAL: Vaduz
AREA: 62 sq. mi. (160 sq km)
POPULATION: 33,145
MONEY: Swiss franc
LANGUAGES: German
CARS: data not available

Sources: Central Intelligence Agency, *The World Factbook 2003*; *The World Almanac and Book of Facts 2003*; population figures are 2003 estimates.

FAST FACTS

UNIT 4 ASSESSMENT RESOURCES

Reproducible
- Unit 4 Test
- Unit 4 Test for English Language Learners and Special-Needs Students

internet connect
COUNTRY STATISTICS
GO TO: go.hrw.com
KEYWORD: SJ5 MapsU4

Highlights of Country Statistics
- CIA World Factbook
- Library of Congress country studies
- Flags of the world

Have the students refer to the accompanying table listing the miles of railroads in selected European countries. Point out the figure for the United States, and mention that the United States is larger than all of the European countries combined. (Students may verify this statement by totaling the areas of the European countries and comparing the result to the area of the United States.) Ask students to write a sentence or two explaining why they think Europe has fewer cars. (Possible answers: Europe's population density may indicate that many people live in apartments and do not have a place to park a car. Because Europe has an extensive rail system, people do not need to rely as much on cars.)

FAST FACTS

LITHUANIA
CAPITAL: Vilnius
AREA: 25,174 sq. mi. (65,200 sq km)
POPULATION: 3,592,561
MONEY: litas
LANGUAGES: Lithuanian (official), Polish, Russian
CARS: 653,000

MONACO
CAPITAL: Monaco
AREA: 0.75 sq. mi. (1.95 sq km)
POPULATION: 32,130
MONEY: euro
LANGUAGES: French (official), English, Italian, Monegasque
CARS: 17,000

LUXEMBOURG
CAPITAL: Luxembourg
AREA: 998 sq. mi. (2,586 sq km)
POPULATION: 454,157
MONEY: euro
LANGUAGES: Luxembourgish, German, French
CARS: 231,666

NETHERLANDS
CAPITAL: Amsterdam
AREA: 16,033 sq. mi. (41,526 sq km)
POPULATION: 16,150,511
MONEY: euro
LANGUAGES: Dutch
CARS: 5,810,000

MACEDONIA
CAPITAL: Skopje
AREA: 9,781 sq. mi. (25,333 sq km)
POPULATION: 2,063,122
MONEY: Macedonian denar
LANGUAGES: Macedonian, Albanian, Turkish, Serbo-Croatian
CARS: 263,000

NORWAY
CAPITAL: Oslo
AREA: 125,181 sq. mi. (324,220 sq km)
POPULATION: 4,546,123
MONEY: Norwegian krone
LANGUAGES: Norwegian
CARS: 1,760,000

MALTA
CAPITAL: Valletta
AREA: 122 sq. mi. (316 sq km)
POPULATION: 400,420
MONEY: Maltese lira
LANGUAGES: Maltese (official), English (official)
CARS: 122,100

POLAND
CAPITAL: Warsaw
AREA: 120,728 sq. mi. (312,685 sq km)
POPULATION: 38,622,660
MONEY: zloty
LANGUAGES: Polish
CARS: 7,520,000

MOLDOVA
CAPITAL: Chișinău
AREA: 13,067 sq. mi. (33,843 sq km)
POPULATION: 4,439,502
MONEY: Moldovan leu
LANGUAGES: Moldovan (official), Russian, Gagauz
CARS: 169,000

PORTUGAL
CAPITAL: Lisbon
AREA: 35,672 sq. mi. (92,391 sq km)
POPULATION: 10,102,022
MONEY: euro
LANGUAGES: Portuguese
CARS: 2,950,000

Countries not drawn to scale.

MILES OF RAILROAD IN SELECTED EUROPEAN COUNTRIES AND THE UNITED STATES

Country	Miles	Country	Miles
Austria	3,524	Norway	2,485
Belgium	2,093	Poland	14,904
Denmark	1,780	Romania	7,062
Finland	3,641	Slovakia	2,277
France	19,847	Spain	8,252
Germany	54,994	Sweden	6,756
Greece	1,537	Switzerland	3,132
Hungary	8,190	United Kingdom	23,518
Italy	9,944	United States	137,900
Netherlands	1,702		

Source: *The World Almanac and Book of Facts 2003*

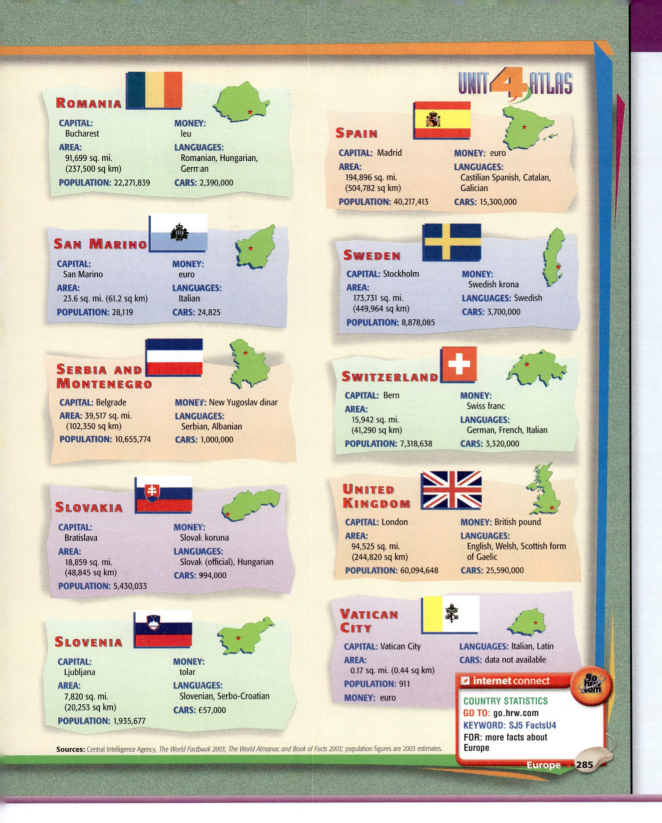

LEVEL 3: (Suggested time: 30 min.) Tell students that Europe has an economic organization called the European Union (EU). It was formed to strengthen the economies of European nations. In 1991, countries of the EU began to discuss adopting a common currency, to be called the euro. By May of 1998, nearly every interested EU country had met the requirements for membership, which include maintaining a low inflation rate, low budget deficit, and low interest rate. Soon after, the European National Bank was formed. Then, on January 1, 2002, the countries adopted the euro as their standard currency.

Ask students to consider the effect that changing to a common currency may have on a nation's culture, economy, and relationships with neighboring countries. Have them imagine that they live in Europe in 1991 and are weighing the pros and cons of changing to the euro. In one paragraph, students should give reasons why they support their country's adoption of a common currency. In another paragraph, they should defend a position against adopting the euro. Invite them to refer back to their arguments as they learn more about the culture, economies, and relationships among European countries.

Europe 285

CHAPTER 13: Early History of Europe
Chapter Resource Manager

Objectives	Pacing Guide	Reproducible Resources
SECTION 1		
Early Greek Civilizations (pp. 287–291) 1. Identify some of the achievements of early Greek civilizations. 2. Explore the Greek city-states. 3. Explain how Greek government changed over time. 4. Analyze the features of democracy in Athens.	**Regular** 2 days *Lecture Notes, Section 1* **Block Scheduling** 1 day *Block Scheduling Handbook, Chapter 13*	**RS** Know It Notes S1 **RS** Graphic Organizer 13 **ELL** Main Idea Activity S1
SECTION 2		
The Glory of Greece (pp. 292–296) 1. Trace how the Persian Wars affected Greek power. 2. Understand why Greek power weakened and what took its place. 3. Evaluate some accomplishments of the Greeks.	**Regular** 3 days *Lecture Notes, Section 2* **Block Scheduling** 1.5 days *Block Scheduling Handbook, Chapter 13*	**RS** Know It Notes S2 **E** Biography Activity: Hippocrates **ELL** Main Idea Activity S2
SECTION 3		
The Roman Republic (pp. 297–301) 1. Identify the early peoples of Italy. 2. Explain how government and society were organized in the early Roman Republic? 3. Trace the key events in Rome's expansion. 4. Investigate the issues that caused problems for the late Roman Republic.	**Regular** 2 days *Lecture Notes, Section 3* **Block Scheduling** 1.5 days *Block Scheduling Handbook, Chapter 13*	**RS** Know It Notes S3 **E** Readings in World Geography, History, and Culture: Reading 29 **ELL** Main Idea Activity S3
SECTION 4		
The Roman Empire (pp. 302–307) 1. Describe the Pax Romana. 2. Explain how Christianity began and spread. 3. Analyze why the Roman Empire declined. 4. Explore the contributions that Rome made to other cultures.	**Regular** 2 days *Lecture Notes, Section 4* **Block Scheduling** 1 day *Block Scheduling Handbook, Chapter 13*	**RS** Know It Notes S4 **E** Readings in World Geography, History, and Culture: Reading 29 **SM** Critical Thinking Activity 13 **SM** Map Activity 13 **ELL** Main Idea Activity S4
SECTION 5		
The Middle Ages (pp. 308–313) 1. Trace some key events of the Early Middle Ages. 2. Analyze how society was organized during the Middle Ages. 3. Summarize what life was like during the High Middle Ages.	**Regular** 2 days *Lecture Notes, Section 5* **Block Scheduling** 1 day *Block Scheduling Handbook, Chapter 13*	**RS** Know It Notes S5 **E** Biography Activity: Geoffrey Chaucer **ELL** Main Idea Activity S5

Chapter Resource Key

- **RS** Reading Support
- **IC** Interdisciplinary Connections
- **E** Enrichment
- **SM** Skills Mastery
- **A** Assessment
- **REV** Review
- **ELL** Reinforcement and English Language Learners and English for Speakers of Other Languages (ESOL)
- Transparencies
- CD-ROM
- Music
- Video
- Internet
- Holt Presentation Maker Using Microsoft® PowerPoint®

One-Stop Planner CD-ROM

See the *One-Stop Planner* for a complete list of additional resources for students and teachers.

One-Stop Planner CD–ROM

It's easy to plan lessons, select resources, and print out materials for your students when you use the *One-Stop Planner CD–ROM with Test Generator*.

Technology Resources	Review, Reinforcement, and Assessment Resources
One-Stop Planner CD–ROM, Lesson 13.1 Geography and Cultures Visual Resource 49 *ARGWorld* CD–ROM Homework Practice Online HRW Go site	**ELL** Main Idea Activity S1 **REV** Section 1 Review **A** Daily Quiz 13.1 **REV** Chapter Summaries and Review **ELL** English Audio Summary 13.1 **ELL** Spanish Audio Summary 13.1
One-Stop Planner CD–ROM, Lesson 13.2 Geography and Cultures Visual Resource 49 *ARGWorld* CD–ROM Homework Practice Online HRW Go site	**ELL** Main Idea Activity S2 **REV** Section 2 Review **A** Daily Quiz 13.2 **REV** Chapter Summaries and Review **ELL** English Audio Summary 13.2 **ELL** Spanish Audio Summary 13.2
One-Stop Planner CD–ROM, Lesson 13.3 Geography and Cultures Visual Resources 49, 50 *ARGWorld* CD–ROM Homework Practice Online HRW Go site	**ELL** Main Idea Activity S3 **REV** Section 3 Review **A** Daily Quiz 13.3 **REV** Chapter Summaries and Review **ELL** English Audio Summary 13.3 **ELL** Spanish Audio Summary 13.3
One-Stop Planner CD–ROM, Lesson 13.4 Geography and Cultures Visual Resource 49 *ARGWorld* CD–ROM Homework Practice Online HRW Go site	**ELL** Main Idea Activity S4 **REV** Section 4 Review **A** Daily Quiz 13.4 **REV** Chapter Summaries and Review **ELL** English Audio Summary 13.4 **ELL** Spanish Audio Summary 13.4
One-Stop Planner CD–ROM, Lesson 13.5 Geography and Cultures Visual Resources 49, 51, 54, 55 *ARGWorld* CD–ROM Homework Practice Online HRW Go site	**ELL** Main Idea Activity S5 **REV** Section 5 Review **A** Daily Quiz 13.5 **REV** Chapter Summaries and Review **ELL** English Audio Summary 13.5 **ELL** Spanish Audio Summary 13.5

internet connect

HRW ONLINE RESOURCES

GO TO: go.hrw.com
Then type in a keyword.

TEACHER HOME PAGE
KEYWORD: SJ5 TEACHER

CHAPTER INTERNET ACTIVITIES
KEYWORD: SJ5 GT13

Choose an activity to:
- report on Minoan civilization.
- create a newspaper article about ancient Athens.
- write a report on daily life in the Middle Ages.

CHAPTER ENRICHMENT LINKS
KEYWORD: SJ5 CH13

CHAPTER MAPS
KEYWORD: SJ5 MAPS13

ONLINE ASSESSMENT
Homework Practice
KEYWORD: SJ5 HP13
Standardized Test Prep Online
KEYWORD: SJ5 STP13
Rubrics
KEYWORD: SS Rubrics

COUNTRY INFORMATION
KEYWORD: SJ5 Almanac

CONTENT UPDATES
KEYWORD: SS Content Updates

HOLT PRESENTATION MAKER
KEYWORD: SJ5 PPT13

ONLINE READING SUPPORT
KEYWORD: SS Strategies

CURRENT EVENTS
KEYWORD: S5 Current Events

Meeting Individual Needs

Ability Levels

Level 1 Basic-level activities designed for all students encountering new material

Level 2 Intermediate-level activities designed for average students

Level 3 Challenging activities designed for honors and gifted-and-talented students

ESOL Activities that address the needs of students with Limited English Proficiency

Chapter Review and Assessment

E	Readings in World Geography, History, and Culture 29		Chapter 13 Test Generator (on the One-Stop Planner)
SM	Critical Thinking Activity 13		Audio CD Program, Chapter 13
REV	Chapter 13 Review and Practice	**A**	Chapter 13 Test for English Language Learners and Special-Needs Students
REV	Chapter Summaries and Review		
ELL	Vocabulary Activity 13		HRW Go site
A	Chapter 13 Test		

Chapter 13

Early History of Europe
Previewing Chapter Resources

Holt Online Learning

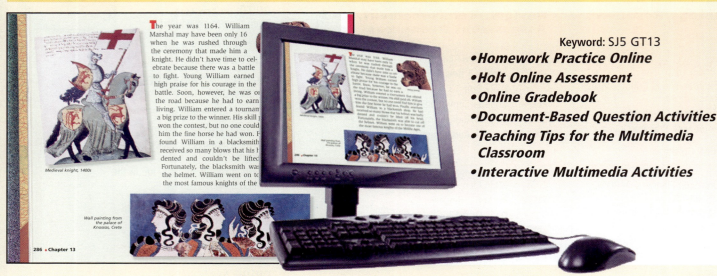

Keyword: SJ5 GT13
- Homework Practice Online
- Holt Online Assessment
- Online Gradebook
- Document-Based Question Activities
- Teaching Tips for the Multimedia Classroom
- Interactive Multimedia Activities

Differentiating Instruction

Reading and Writing Support
◄ Graphic Organizer Activity
- Vocabulary Activity
- Chapter Summaries and Review
- Know-It Notes S1–5
- Audio CD

Active Learning
◄ Block Scheduling Handbook
- Cultures of the World Activity
- Interdisciplinary Activity: Biographical Profiles of Greek Scientists and Mathematicians
- Map Activity

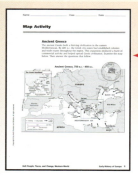

Primary Sources and Advanced Learners
◄ Map Activity: Ancient Greece
- Readings in World Geography, History and Culture:
  - 29 The Geography of Ancient Rome

Assessment Program
◄ Daily Quizzes S1–5
- Chapter Test
- Chapter Test for English Language Learners and Special-Needs Students

Spanish and ESOL
- Vocabulary Activity
- Main Idea Activities for English Language Learners and Special-Needs Students
- Chapter Summaries and Review
- Spanish Audio Summary
◄ Know-It Notes S1–5
- Chapter Test for English Language Learners and Special-Needs Students

Special Education Modifications
Your **I.D.E.A. Works! CD-ROM** will provide modified versions of the following teaching materials:
- Know It Notes S1–5
- Vocabulary Activity
- Main Idea Activities S1–5
- Daily Quizzes S1–5
◄ Chapter 13 Test
- Flash cards of chapter vocabulary terms

Teacher Resources

Books for Teachers

Sheehan, Sean. *Illustrated Encyclopedia of Ancient Greece.* Getty Trust, 2002.

Connolly, Peter and Hazel Dodge. *The Ancient City: Life in Classical Athens and Rome.* Oxford Press, 2000.

Adkins, Lesley, and Roy A. Adkins. *Handbook to Life in Ancient Rome.* Oxford University Press, 1998.

Kohne, Eckart. *Gladiators and Caesars: The Power of Spectacle in Ancient Rome.* University of California Press, 2000.

Cantor, Norman F. *The Encyclopedia of the Middle Ages.* Viking, 1999.

Singman, Jeffery L. *Daily Life in Medieval Europe.* Greenwood Publishing, 1999.

Books for Students

Carlson, Laurie. *Classical Kids: An Activity Guide to Life in Ancient Greece and Rome.* Chicago Review Press, 1998. Provides brief background information on Greece and Rome with hands-on activities.

Connolly, Peter. *Ancient Greece.* Oxford University Press Children's Books, 2001. Covers daily life, religion, government, theater, and food.

James, Simon. *Ancient Rome.* DK Publishing, 2000. Includes information on how the Romans built roads, why the baths were so popular, and how Roman physicians healed the sick.

Eastwood, Kay. *Women and Girls in the Middle Ages.* Crabtree Publishing, 2003. Shows the similarities and differences between the lives of noblewomen and peasants with an emphasis on raising a family, education, learning a trade, and medieval dress.

Multimedia Materials

The Greeks: Crucible of Civilization. Video, PBS.

The Roman Empire in the First Century. Video, PBS.

In the Footsteps of Alexander the Great. Video, PBS.

NOVA: Secrets of the Lost Empires II: Medieval Siege. Video, WGBH

Videos and CDs

Videos
- CNN Presents World Cultures: Yesterday and Today, Segment 6 The Ancient Theaters of Epidaurus

CDs
- ARG World
- I.D.E.A. Works! CD–ROM

Transparency Packages

Geography and Cultures Visual Resources Transparencies

49 Southern Europe: Physical-Political

50 Etruscan Musicians\

51 West-Central Europe: Physical-Political

54 Northern Europe: Physical-Political

55 Eastern Europe: Physical-Political

Map Activities Transparency Ancient Greece

Holt Researcher

http://researcher.hrw.com

- The Roman World
- Europe
- Greece's Golden and Hellenistic Ages
- Petrarch
- The Rise of the Middle Ages

CHAPTER 13

WHY IT MATTERS

Share with your students these reasons for learning about the early history of Europe:

- European civilizations of today share some characteristics with the continent's first civilizations.
- Ideas about democracy and representative government can be traced to early cultures of Europe.
- Members of some European ethnic groups are proud to trace their heritage back to ancient times.
- Europe's early history is full of fascinating stories and magnificent works of art.

CHAPTER 13

Early History of Europe

To understand modern Europe, we need to explore the continent's history. It is a remarkable story, full of both glory and grief.

The year was 1164. William Marshal may have been only 16 when he was rushed through the ceremony that made him a knight. He didn't have time to celebrate because there was a battle to fight. Young William earned high praise for his courage in the battle. Soon, however, he was on the road because he had to earn a living. William entered a tournament that offered a big prize to the winner. His skill paid off. William won the contest, but no one could find him to give him the fine horse he had won. Finally, searchers found William in a blacksmith shop. He had received so many blows that his helmet was badly dented and couldn't be lifted off his head. Fortunately, the blacksmith was able to cut off the helmet. William went on to become one of the most famous knights of the Middle Ages.

Medieval knight, 1400s

Viking carving

Wall painting from the palace of Knossos, Crete

CHAPTER PROJECT

Have students conduct research on sports of the eras covered by this chapter. Included may be bull-leaping in Crete, the Olympic Games of Greece, Roman chariot racing, and sports of medieval Europe. Ask students to examine the role of religious ritual in some of the sporting events. Students may also try to make comparisons between practices of the early times with amateur and professional sports practices of today. You may want to have students create dioramas to display their work.

STARTING THE CHAPTER

After students have read the introduction on this page, focus their attention on the illustrations—two showing people and the other a snarling imaginary beast. What may these pictures tell us about the cultures that created them? (Possible answers: The Viking carving was made to frighten the people who saw it, perhaps indicating that the Vikings were fierce. The knight shows armor and elaborate horse trappings, perhaps indicating that warfare played a big role in the society. The women have fancy hairdos decorated with jewels, perhaps indicating that some people of Crete were quite wealthy.) Tell students they will learn in this chapter if those or other predictions are correct.

Section 1: Early Greek Civilizations

CHAPTER 13, Section 1

Read to Discover
1. What were some of the achievements of early Greek civilizations?
2. What were the Greek city-states?
3. How did Greek government change over time?
4. What were some features of democracy in Athens?

Vocabulary
city-states
polis
acropolis
agora
aristocrats
oligarchy
tyrants
democracy
citizenship

Places
Aegean Sea
Balkan Peninsula
Crete
Troy
Athens

People
Minoans
Mycenaeans
Cleisthenes
Pericles

Section 1 Resources
Reproducibles
- Lecture Notes, Section 1
- Block Scheduling Handbook, Chapter 13
- Know It Notes S1

Technology
- One-Stop Planner CD-ROM, Lesson 13.1
- Homework Practice Online
- Geography and Cultures Visual Resources 49
- Homework Practice Online
- HRW Go Site

Review, Reinforcement, and Assessment Resources
- Section 1 Review
- Daily Quiz 13.1
- Main Idea Activity S1
- Chapter Summaries and Review
- English Audio Summary 13.1
- Spanish Audio Summary 13.1

Reading Strategy
USING SIGNAL WORDS Before you read, look at the list of vocabulary words. Skim the section to find their meanings. What do you think the main ideas of this section will be? Write down your predictions. Read the section. Revise your predictions based on what you learned.

Early Greece

Greece has a long, uneven coastline.
Interpreting the Map What other physical features may have encouraged the Greeks to become sailors and traders?

◀ **Map Answer**
mountainous interior, many islands, natural harbors

The Early Greeks

By 2000 B.C., civilizations had developed in the Nile valley and the Fertile Crescent. At the same time, another was forming near the Aegean Sea. The people who settled this area became known as the Greeks. From the Greeks came many ideas that helped create Western civilization.

Geography has much to do with the history of Greece. Located on the southwestern part of the Balkan Peninsula, Greece is surrounded by water on three sides. Smaller peninsulas jut from the main peninsula into the sea. Most of Greece is mountainous, with little vegetation. As a result, early Greeks lived in small, independent coastal communities. They became skilled sailors and traded with people who lived on islands of the Mediterranean and Aegean Seas. In fact, on one of these islands—Crete—the earliest Greek civilization developed. We call the people who lived there Minoans. The name comes from Minos, a legendary king of Crete.

Early History of Europe • 287

Objectives
1. Identify some of the achievements of early Greek civilizations.
2. Explore the Greek city-states.
3. Explain how Greek government changed over time.
4. Analyze the features of democracy in Athens.

Focus

 Bellringer

Write the following instruction and question on the chalkboard: *Examine the top photo on the next page and read the caption. What would it be like to take part in this event?* Discuss responses. (Students may say that it would be scary but exciting.) Point out that bull-leaping wasn't just a sport; it was a religious ritual. Bull-leaping was a unique feature of Minoan civilization, one of the civilizations introduced in this section.

Building Vocabulary

Write the vocabulary terms on the chalkboard and have students find their definitions. Point out that **aristocrats, oligarchy, tyrants,** and **democracy** all have ancient roots in the Greek language, but they are also sometimes used to describe modern governments or the people who run those governments.

Early History of Europe **287**

CHAPTER 13, Section 1

DAILY LIFE

Living It Up with the Minoans Although little is known about the earliest palaces of the Minoans, their later palaces are distinctive for the quality of their workmanship and the sophistication of their designs. The carefully planned palaces had wide staircases, multiple stories, and storage rooms for supplies and food. Windows opened onto broad vistas. Artisans painted the interior walls with scenes of everyday life. Built-in bathtubs with running water could be found inside the palaces.

Critical Thinking: What may the remains of the palaces show about the society that built them?

Answer: The palaces show that the societies were concerned with not just practical matters, but also with beauty.

This fresco shows bull-leaping, a Minoan sport and ritual. An athlete would grasp the bull by the horns, somersault over its back, and be caught by another athlete.

This gold wreath was made by Mycenaeans.

The Minoans By 2000 B.C., the Minoans had developed a great civilization. Traders from Crete sailed to ports as far away as Egypt and Palestine. They traded goods like wood and olive oil for precious metals and stones. Trade made the Minoans wealthy. With their wealth, they built huge palaces for their rulers, with advanced features like running water. Colorful paintings decorated the walls.

Historians are not sure what caused the decline of the Minoan civilization in about 1500 B.C. Many think that a volcanic eruption on a nearby island caused terrible flooding on Crete. The Minoans never recovered from the disaster. In about 1450 B.C., the Mycenaeans, a warlike people from the Greek mainland, took over Crete.

The Mycenaeans The Mycenaeans controlled the Greek mainland from about 1600 B.C. to 1200 B.C. The Mycenaeans raided and traded across the eastern Mediterranean. Historians think that sometime between 1250 and 1150 B.C. the Mycenaeans attacked the rival city of Troy in what is now Turkey. After many years the Mycenaeans defeated the Trojan army and destroyed the city. The story of the Trojan War is one of the most famous Greek legends.

However, Mycenaean civilization didn't last long past the Trojan War. With its decline, trade across the Aegean stopped. Slowly, the region slipped into disorder. Historians call this period Greece's Dark Age.

✓ **READING CHECK:** (Human Systems) What were some features of the Minoan and Mycenaean civilizations?
Minoan—trade, wealth, huge palaces; Mycenaeans—warlike, controlled Greek mainland, raiders and traders, attacked Troy and destroyed it, declined

---

TEACH

Teaching Objective 1

ALL LEVELS: (Suggested time: 15 min.) Copy the following graphic organizer onto the chalkboard, omitting the blue answers. Have students complete it to distinguish between the Minoan and Mycenaean civilizations. **ESOL,** **LS** **VISUAL-SPATIAL**

LEVEL 3: (Suggested time: 30 min.) Have each student imagine that he or she is a merchant of either the Minoan or Mycenaean civilizations. Ask students to write an entry in the merchant's ship's log in which the merchant reflects on the connections between the Greek world's physical geography and success in trade. **LS** **INTRAPERSONAL**

	Minoans	Mycenaeans
Where?	Crete	Greek mainland
When?	about 2000 B.C. to 1450 B.C.	about 1600 B.C. to 1200 B.C.
What?	made wealthy by trade to distant ports, built huge palaces with advanced features	took over Crete, raided and traded across the Mediterranean, probably attacked and defeated Troy
Then what?	perhaps weakened by volcanic eruption and flooding	declined, trade across Aegean stopped, Greece's Dark Age

The Greek City-States

Because we have no written records from the Dark Age, historians know little about Greek life during this time. By about 700 B.C., however, Greek society had changed. People began to band together in small groups for protection. Over time, these groups developed into independent **city-states**.

The Greek word for a city-state is **polis** (PAH-luhs). For defense purposes, the typical Greek polis was built around a fort on a high hill, called the **acropolis** (uh-KRAH-puh-luhs). As the polis grew, it included not just the original fort and city but also the nearby fields and farming villages. The polis quickly became the heart of Greek civilization. People thought of themselves as citizens of their polis, not as Greeks.

A city's marketplace, or **agora** (A-guh-ruh), was the focus of Greek life. It served as a place for buying and selling, for religious activities, and for trials. Political assemblies also met in the agora.

✓ **READING CHECK:** (Human Systems) What was at the center of the early Greek city-state? *acropolis*

FOCUS ON CULTURE

Greek Myths

People of all cultures enjoy a good story. The Greeks were no different. Some of their tales, also called myths, tried to explain human nature or how the natural world works. The myth of Demeter and Persephone, for example, explains why the seasons change. Others focused on the adventures of heroes or gods. These stories have become part of our daily lives. For example, the chubby little guy who shoots arrows through hearts on Valentine's Day is based on a Greek god. We know him by the name the Romans gave him—Cupid.

The Greeks' gods had very human qualities. Just like people, they could be cruel, jealous, kind, or helpful. According to the myths, they lived not in some far-away heaven, but on an actual mountain in northern Greece—Mount Olympus. High at the mountain's top, Zeus ruled over the other gods.

One myth about Zeus explains the presence of evil in the world. Although Zeus was the most powerful god, he was jealous of the gifts another god, Prometheus, had given humans. For revenge, Zeus introduced evil into the world. He and the other gods created the first woman, Pandora. Each god gave her a gift. One gift was a box that she was warned never to open. Eventually, curiosity got the better of her. She opened the box, releasing hunger, disease, war, greed, anger, jealousy, and all the other misfortunes that plague humans.

Other myths teach cultural or moral values. The story of King Midas, who was granted his wish to turn whatever he touched into gold, shows the dangers of greed. Because these myths deal with basic human emotions, people today still find them meaningful.

What evidence of Greek myths can you find in movies, television programs, advertisements, and other aspects of modern life?

According to Greek myth, Prometheus stole fire from Zeus and gave it to humans. This statue of Prometheus is in New York City.

CHAPTER 13, Section 1

Linking Past to Present

Government for All The ideal Greek polis was small enough that citizens could participate meaningfully in the government. Many were the size of modern cities along with their suburbs. Most people had to walk to the agora if they wanted to take part in decisions.

Critical Thinking: Ask students how the size of the United States affects citizen participation in government.

Answer: Some students may answer that U.S. citizens can participate freely in government at all levels and are not hindered by the country's size, partly because electronic media link us. Other students may say that the country is so big that meaningful participation by individuals is hindered.

◄ **Focus on Culture Answer**

Answers will vary according to community and interests of students and the most recent elements of popular culture.

Teaching Objectives 2–3

ALL LEVELS: (Suggested time: 20 min.) Pair students and have pairs create flow charts to display the establishment of the Greek city-states and the changes that occurred in Greek government.
ESOL, COOPERATIVE LEARNING, LS **VISUAL-SPATIAL**

LEVEL 3: Provide extra resources for this activity. Have students write paragraphs or brief essays about the changes that Greek government underwent from the organization of the city-states to the beginnings of the idea of self-rule. LS **VERBAL-LINGUISTIC**

CHAPTER 13, Section 1

Across the Curriculum
ART

Black and Red and Read All Over Although the Greeks left extensive written records of their civilization, we have also learned a great deal from another source—their clay vases. There were many types. Each one had a specific purpose and name. For examples, the *hydria* was a water jar with three handles, the *lekythos* was a narrow-necked flask for oil, and the *amphora* was a tall jar used for storage.

Starting in about 700 B.C., there were two basic types of vase decoration. An early style featured human figures and other details painted in black against the reddish color of the clay. In a later style, the background was covered in black and the figures were left red. The artist then added details in paint. By using this so-called red-figure style, vase artists were able to portray faces and emotions vividly.

Scholars now "read" the illustrations on Greek vases to learn about religious practices, myths, daily life, and other aspects of the Greek world.

Visual Record Answers

spear, shield, and helmet

selecting fabric

▲ Soldiers similar to this one helped the rulers of early Greece to take and keep power.
Interpreting the Visual Record What equipment and armor does the soldier have?

▶ Ladies of the early Greek aristocracy had few rights but enjoyed great wealth.
Interpreting the Visual Record What do the women shown on this vase appear to be doing?

Early Greek Government

The city-states of Greece began as small kingdoms ruled by warriors. These rulers relied on wealthy landowners to support them and provide armies. Over time, the small group of landowners, called **aristocrats**, or "best men" in Greek, became the noble class. Gradually, the nobles gained more land and power. By about 700 B.C., nobles in many of the Greek city-states had overthrown the kings and taken power.

Greek city-states ruled by these nobles were called aristocracies. *Aristocracy* in Greek meant "rule by the best." As time went on, however, the term came to mean "control by a class of people made up of mostly wealthy landowners." The aristocrats controlled almost every part of Greek life. The Greek aristocracy formed an **oligarchy** (AH-luh-gahr-kee)—a government in which power lies in the hands of just a few people. The name comes from the Greek for "rule by a few."

In time, the common people became unhappy with the aristocracies. They hoped other leaders would provide a better life. **Tyrants** began to take control of city-state governments. A tyrant was someone who illegally took power but had the people's support. Between 650 B.C. and 500 B.C., tyrants ruled many city-states. At first, many people were happy with the tyrants' rule because they ended the nobles' hold on power and promoted trade. In time, however, many of these powerful rulers became unjust. The word tyrant came to mean "someone who uses power with absolute force."

Eventually, the tyrants lost power. In some places, such as Athens, the idea developed that people can and should rule themselves.

✓ **READING CHECK:** *Human Systems* Through what stages did early Greek government progress? small kingdoms ruled by warriors, aristocracies, tyrants, idea of ruling themselves

Teaching Objective 4

ALL LEVELS: (Suggested time: 45 min.) Read the side wrap feature about Greek vases on this page to students. Then pair students and have each pair create an illustration for a vase in which students display key features of democracy in Athens. Be sure to provide red and black crayons, map pencils, or pens so that the illustrations can resemble black-figure or red-figure vase paintings as closely as possible.
COOPERATIVE LEARNING, LS **VISUAL-SPATIAL**

ALL LEVELS: (Suggested time: 30 min.) Pair students and have each pair create a recruitment poster encouraging Athenian citizens to participate in the city-state's government or to run for election to the assembly. To add realism, you may want to locate and display the Greek alphabet and encourage students to "translate" text in their posters from our Latin alphabet to the Greek alphabet. **ESOL, COOPERATIVE LEARNING**

Democracy in Athens

In about 508 B.C., Cleisthenes (KLYS-thuh-neez) came to power in Athens. Under his leadership, the Athenians developed the world's first **democracy**. A democracy is a type of government in which people rule themselves. For this reason, Cleisthenes is sometimes called the "father of democracy."

Cleisthenes built on reforms that had been made earlier. All free adult men—but not women or slaves—had received **citizenship**. Citizenship granted the right to participate in government. Cleisthenes encouraged the citizens to do so. Because all free men were citizens, no small group could take control of Athens.

Citizens became part of an assembly. This assembly met outdoors on a hillside to write the city-state's laws. During meetings, people stood before the crowd to express their views. When all the speakers had finished, the assembly voted on the issues.

Athens remained a democracy for about 200 years. It reached its height under the statesman Pericles (PER-uh-kleez). He led the government from about 460 B.C. until his death in 429 B.C. Pericles believed that all citizens should vote and serve in the assembly. These tasks were as important as defending Athens in times of war. Centuries later, modern government leaders still looked to Athens for inspiration.

✓ **READING CHECK:** *Human Systems* How were citizens involved in the government of Athens? take part in an assembly, vote on issues

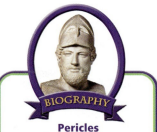

BIOGRAPHY

Pericles
(c. 495–429 B.C.)

Character Trait: Citizenship

Pericles helped Athens reach the height of its glory. He carried out reforms that made Athens's government more democratic. For example, he paid all government officials a salary so that citizens who weren't rich could still hold office. *How did Pericles support good citizenship?*

Section Review 1

Define or identify: Minoans, Mycenaeans, city-states, polis, acropolis, agora, aristocrats, oligarchy, tyrants, Cleisthenes, democracy, citizenship, Pericles

Reading for the Main Idea

1. *Environment and Society* How did geography affect early Greek civilizations?
2. *Human Systems* What were some accomplishments of the Minoans? How may their civilization have ended?
3. *Human Systems* How did the concept of tyrants change?

Critical Thinking

4. **Drawing Inferences and Conclusions** In what way was Athenian democracy limited?

Organizing What You Know

5. **Summarizing** Copy the graphic organizer below. Use it to identify the elements of an early Greek city-state. Label the acropolis, the main city, the agora, and the surrounding farms and villages.

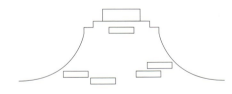

Homework Practice Online
Keyword: SJ5 HP13

Section 1 Review

Answers to Section 1 Review

Define or identify For definitions and identifications, see the glossary and index.

Reading for the Main Idea

1. The interior is mountainous and has little vegetation, limiting settlement and trade there. Because Greek civilizations lived on a peninsula surrounded by the sea, they became sailors and traders.
2. traded within a large area, wealthy, built huge palaces with advanced features; perhaps caused by floods brought on by a volcanic eruption on a nearby island
3. changed from someone who illegally took power but had the people's support to someone who uses power with absolute force (NGS 13)

Critical Thinking

4. It didn't include slaves or women.

Organizing What You Know

5. top rectangle—acropolis; area just below the acropolis—the main city; rectangle within the main city—agora; rectangles at the bottom of the hill—surrounding villages and farms (NGS 12)

◀**Biography Answer**

by ensuring that not just wealthy people could participate in government

---

CLOSE

Refer to the Focus on Culture feature in this section and the myth about Pandora. Ask students why cultures may create myths like this to explain various phenomena. *(Possible answer: Without extensive scientific knowledge about disease and other misfortunes, people look for ways to explain what goes on around them, especially the problems that Pandora released upon the world.)*

REVIEW, ASSESS, RETEACH

Have students complete the Section Review. Then have half the class work in pairs to create Venn diagrams comparing the Minoan and Mycenaean civilizations. Have the other half create sequential step diagrams of the development of Athenian democracy. Then have students complete Daily Quiz 13.1. **COOPERATIVE LEARNING**

Have students complete Main Idea Activity S1. Then ask them to outline the section. **ESOL**

EXTEND

Have interested students explore the connections among the legend of Atlantis, a volcanic eruption of the Mediterranean island of Thera, and the decline of Minoan civilization. **BLOCK SCHEDULING**

CHAPTER 13, Section 2

SECTION 2 RESOURCES

Reproducibles
- Lecture Notes, Section 2
- Block Scheduling Handbook, Chapter 13
- Know It Notes S2
- Biography Activity: Hippocrates

Technology
- One-Stop Planner CD-ROM, Lesson 13.2
- Homework Practice Online
- Geography and Cultures Visual Resources 49
- Homework Practice Online
- HRW Go Site

Review, Reinforcement, and Assessment Resources
- Section 2 Review
- Daily Quiz 13.2
- Main Idea Activity S2
- Chapter Summaries and Review
- English Audio Summary 13.2
- Spanish Audio Summary 13.2

Section 2 The Glory of Greece

Read to Discover
1. How did the Persian Wars affect Greek power?
2. How did Greek power weaken? What took its place?
3. What were some accomplishments of the Greeks?

Vocabulary
league
Hellenistic

Places
Athens
Sparta
Peloponnese
Macedon

People
Xerxes I
Alexander the Great
Homer
Socrates
Aristotle

Reading Strategy
TAKING NOTES As you read, create an outline of this section. Use the headings for the titles in your outline. Write supporting details beneath each heading.

This memorial in Thermopylae, Greece, honors the brave Spartan soldiers who died there in a battle against the Persians.

The Rise of Greek Power

For many years, the Greek city-states developed without interference. Eventually, however, they were threatened by the Persian Empire, centered in what is now Iran.

The Persian Wars In 546 B.C., Persia conquered the Greek colonies on the west coast of Asia Minor, but the colonies later rebelled. Athens and other Greek city-states sent soldiers to help them fight the Persians. In 494 B.C., the mighty Persian army crushed the revolt. To punish the Greeks, the Persians invaded the Greek mainland. To everyone's surprise, the Athenians and their allies pushed the Persians back to the sea.

In 480 B.C., the Persian king Xerxes I (ZUHRK-seez) again invaded Greece with a huge show of force. After some ferocious battles, the Greeks again defeated the Persians. To make up for their smaller numbers the Greeks had used strategy. For example, the Greeks won a sea battle by luring the Persian navy into a narrow waterway where the enemy ships couldn't maneuver. Beating the Persians was an incredible feat. As a result, the Greeks gained new confidence in themselves and in their way of life. That confidence, however, would soon be shaken.

Section 2

Objectives
1. Trace how the Persian Wars affected Greek power.
2. Understand why Greek power weakened and what took its place.
3. Evaluate some accomplishments of the Greeks.

FOCUS

Bellringer

Write the following questions on the chalkboard: *Have you ever run a marathon? From where do you think this type of race got its name?* (Marathons are named after a legend that in 490 B.C., a Greek soldier ran about 26 miles from the town of Marathon to Athens, carrying news of a victory over the Persians. Some versions of the story tell that he dropped dead after delivering his news.) Tell students they will learn more about the Persian Wars and related topics in Section 2.

Building Vocabulary

Write the vocabulary words on the board and have students look up the definitions. Point out that adding *–istic* to a word means that it is like whatever is in the root word. Here Hellenistic means "Greek-like" because the Greeks called themselves *Hellenes* and their land *Hellas*.

The Parthenon in Athens was built in the mid-400s B.C. to honor the goddess Athena. The temple is made of white marble, but was once painted with bright colors. Inside the Parthenon was a tall gold and ivory statue of Athena.
Interpreting the Visual Record What buildings have you seen that have architectural features similar to the Parthenon's?

Athens and Sparta Two of the largest Greek city-states, Athens and Sparta, had fought the Persians together. The two developed quite differently. These differences would contribute to conflict.

In Sparta, the army was the most important group in society. All male citizens had to join the army at the age of seven. Boys' education focused on physical activities, such as running, jumping, and hunting, rather than on reading or writing. Men stayed in the army until age 30 and lived in army barracks instead of with their families. As a result, women served as the heads of households. Like Spartan men, women were trained in physical activities. They raised their children according to Sparta's military ideals.

Although the Athenians also believed a strong army was important, the military didn't govern their society. Athenian boys learned to run and fight, but also to read and write. They even studied music and dance. The Athenians believed that this kind of education produced better citizens. Because women in Athens had few rights, though, Athenian girls received almost no education. A few learned how to read and write at home, but most girls learned only household tasks like sewing.

✓ **READING CHECK:** (Human Systems) How did life in Athens differ from life in Sparta? army not so important in Athens, more education in a range of subjects to create better citizens

Shifts in Power

After the Greeks defeated the Persians, many city-states joined together in 478 B.C. in a **league**, or alliance, for protection. It was called the Delian League, after the island of Delos, where the group's treasury was kept. As the most powerful member of the Delian League, Athens became its leader. Soon the Athenians began to dominate the other members. For example, Athens forced the other members to use Athenian coins. Athenian leaders also began taking money from the league's treasury to pay for new buildings in Athens. In effect, the Delian League had been turned into an Athenian empire.

CHAPTER 13, Section 2

Linking Past to Present
Greek and English The standardized form of the Athenian dialect was known as *Koine*, which means "common Greek." For centuries *Koine* was the language of commerce throughout the Eastern Mediterranean world.

Today, the English language has countless words that come from Greek. Most of these words were introduced to English during the Renaissance, an era that began in the mid-1300s. We are still adding words based on Greek roots to English. Greek roots are especially common in science and technology.

◀ **Visual Record Answer**
Answers will vary according to location, but students may mention the columns or other features.

TEACH

Teach Objectives 1–2
LEVEL 1: (Suggested time: 15 min.) Copy the following graphic organizer onto the chalkboard. Have students fill in details in each box to help them understand the rise and shifts in Greek power. Although he was Macedonian, include Alexander the Great's history in the graphic organizer also. **ESOL**, LS **VISUAL-SPATIAL**

LEVELS 2 AND 3: Provide extra time for this activity. After students have completed the Level 1 activity, have them work in pairs to outline a play about the rise and decline of Greek power. Ask whether the play should be in the form of a tragedy. Why or why not? In addition, have students designate the "playwright" as an Athenian, Spartan, or a soldier in Alexander's army. Discuss why the playwright's background is a factor in what is included in the play and how the events are depicted.
COOPERATIVE LEARNING, LS **VERBAL-LINGUISTIC**

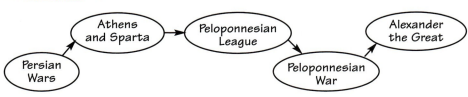

CHAPTER 13, Section 2

Across the Curriculum
LITERATURE

Thucydides Many accounts of historic events were written down decades, even centuries, after they happened. It isn't surprising that some of those accounts contain errors, exaggerations, and unexplained gaps.

Thucydides, however, wrote about the Peloponnesian War as it happened. He was probably born no later than 460 B.C., so he was about 30 years old when the war began. Thucydides held public office and served as a naval commander. A military blunder cost Thucydides his freedom. He was sent into exile but turned the punishment into opportunity. In exile, he could gather information about the war from Sparta and its allies. Thucydides may have died violently, since his *History* stops abruptly.

Connecting to Literature Answers

1. It is not a rival, and it doesn't copy its neighbors. Instead, it is an example to them.
2. Like the Athenians, our government is in the hands of the many, not the few; our laws apply to all Americans; we encourage able people to run for office; and all Americans—rich and poor alike—can serve their country.

History of the Peloponnesian War
translated by Benjamin Jowett

History is among the many types of literature at which Greek writers excelled. Thucydides (thoo-SID-uh-deez), an Athenian, was one of the greatest historians of the ancient world. His History of the Peloponnesian War *still provides insights about conflict. Here he reports a speech that Pericles gave at a funeral for Athenian soldiers.*

Our form of government does not enter into rivalry with the institutions of others. We do not copy our neighbors, but are an example to them. It is true that we are called a democracy, for the administration is in the hands of the many and not of the few. But while the law secures equal justice to all alike in their private disputes, the claim of excellence is also recognized; and when a citizen is in any way distinguished, he is preferred [urged] to the public service, not as a matter of privilege, but as the reward of merit. Neither is poverty a bar, but a man may benefit his country whatever be the obscurity of his condition.

Analyzing Primary Sources
1. How did Athens relate to its neighbors?
2. How are Athenian ideals similar to those of American democracy?

The Peloponnesian War Many city-states, including Sparta, feared the growth of Athenian power. Eventually Sparta and its allies, called the Peloponnesian League, declared war on Athens. (The name comes from the Peloponnese, the peninsula where the city-states were located.) Thus the Peloponnesian War began in 431 B.C.

The war dragged on for 28 years, with periods of peace and hard fighting. In the end, the Athenians were defeated in 404 B.C. Athens was ruined. Sparta became the most powerful Greek city-state. Others came to resent Sparta's control, though, and another period of fighting among the city-states began. It continued until the 330s B.C., when invaders from the north conquered not just Greece, but a vast part of the known world.

Alexander's Conquests While the Greek city-states wore themselves out with warfare, Macedon (MA-suhd-uhn), a small kingdom to the north, grew stronger. Macedon's king, Philip II, invaded Greece and united it under his rule. When the Greeks revolted against Macedonian rule, Philip's 20-year-old son, Alexander, put down the rebellion. He then went on to expand his control. He soon ruled all of Greece.

Alexander had a bigger ambition. He wanted to conquer the world. In 334 B.C., he led his army into battle. Alexander was a brilliant general, and his soldiers were fiercely loyal. Persia, Egypt, kingdoms of Central

Teaching Objective 3
ALL LEVELS: You will need to provide resource material and extra time for this activity. Organize the class into pairs and assign each pair one of these topics: Greek sculpture, vases, temples, tragedies, comedies, the *Iliad*, the *Odyssey*, Socrates, Plato, Aristotle, Euclid, Eratosthenes, Hippocrates, or Archimedes. Ask each pair to find additional information on its topic and present a one- or two-minute oral report to the class on the topic. Have all students take notes on the reports.
COOPERATIVE LEARNING, LS AUDITORY-MUSICAL

▶**ASSIGNMENT:** Have each student choose an illustration from this section or the previous one and write a response to it in the style of an art critic.

Asia—all fell to Alexander and his mighty army. These conquests would give Alexander his place in history—as Alexander the Great.

At the time, it must have seemed that nothing could stop him. The success could not last forever, though. In 327 B.C., Alexander reached the Indus River, in what is now Pakistan. There his exhausted armies rebelled. Some 3,000 miles from home, they refused to continue into India. Disappointed, Alexander led his army back toward Greece.

He never made it. In 323 B.C., Alexander died of a fever in Babylon. Left without a leader, Alexander's generals fought and divided the conquered lands among themselves.

At left is a marble portrait of Alexander. At right is a detail from a mural. It shows the Persian king Darius III at the Battle of Issus, which he lost to Alexander. In fact, Alexander never lost a battle.

The Legacy of Alexander the Great It wasn't just Alexander's military conquests that earned him the name "the Great." Alexander's empire was the largest the world had ever seen. It reached from Greece east to the Indus River and south to Egypt. Alexander had also created a new culture. He adopted Greek customs as well as some customs of Persia—one of the places he had conquered. Alexander encouraged his soldiers to follow his lead in combining cultures. He founded more than 70 new cities, where Greeks and Macedonians settled. In this way, Greek culture spread thousands of miles from where it began. As a result, historians call this era the **Hellenistic** Age. *Hellenistic* means "Greek-like."

✓ READING CHECK: **Human Systems** How did Alexander change the culture of the places he conquered? *combined Greek culture with Persian culture*

Accomplishments of the Greeks

The Greeks made immense contributions to the arts, philosophy, and science. They have influenced culture for centuries after Greece faded.

Art and Architecture Greek artists admired the human form. In fact, some of their statues of people look like they could come to life at any moment. Most of what we know about Greek painting is from vases. Artists decorated the vases with all kinds of scenes, from banquets to Olympic games. Architects built great marble temples to their gods. Some of the temples still stand. The Parthenon, in Athens, is probably the most famous. Today, you can see modern buildings that feature Greek columns and other design elements of Greek temples.

Section 2 Review

Answers to Section 2 Review

Define or identify For definition and identification, see the glossary and index.

Reading for the Main Idea

1. It was a surprise because the Persians outnumbered the Greeks; Greeks gained confidence in themselves and their way of life.
2. Athenian—society not governed by military, boys learned wide range of subjects, little education for girls; Spartan—army most important, all boys joined army at seven and then lived in barracks, education focused on physical activity, women trained in physical activities

Critical Thinking

3. Although Athens prided itself on being a democracy—in which all participants were supposed to be equal—it treated the other members of the Delian League as if they were subjects, not equals.
4. Students may say that his conquests and legacy earned him the name or that he was too violent to be called "the Great."

Organizing What You Know

5. Use the content under Accomplishments of the Greeks for answers.

Literature and Philosophy The Greeks were the first known people to write drama, or plays. Some are tragedies, while others are comedies. Actors performed the plays in big outdoor theaters. Greek writers also wrote poetry. According to tradition, a blind poet named Homer wrote the *Iliad* and the *Odyssey*, two long poems about the Trojan War. Thinkers called philosophers discussed important ideas about reality and human existence. Socrates made people think by asking them questions until they figured out a problem for themselves. Among the many subjects Plato wrote about were what government should be like and the nature of right and wrong. Aristotle wrote about philosophy and science. He taught Alexander the Great when the future conqueror was a teenage Macedonian prince.

Math and Science Greeks developed new mathematical and scientific concepts. For example, Euclid figured out the basic laws of geometry. Aristarchus realized that the Earth went around the Sun. Eratosthenes calculated how big around the Earth is with incredible accuracy. The physician Hippocrates is called the father of medical science. Archimedes invented machines, including a system for lifting a ship out of the water.

All these Greeks and many more would affect civilizations for centuries. Greece would lose its power to a new conqueror—Rome. The Romans, however, would help preserve Greek culture for later generations.

The Greek sculptor Myron created this statue called the *Discus Thrower* in about 450 B.C. Myron studied athletes in motion.

✓ **READING CHECK:** **Human Systems** In what fields did Greek thinkers excel? *literature, philosophy, mathematics, science*

Homework Practice Online
Keyword: SJ5 HP13

Define or identify: Xerxes I, league, Alexander the Great, Hellenistic, Homer, Socrates, Aristotle

Reading for the Main Idea

1. **Human Systems** Why was the outcome of the Persian Wars a surprise? What was an important result of the wars?
2. **Human Systems** How were Athenian and Spartan societies different?

Critical Thinking

3. **Comparing and Contrasting** How did Athens's treatment of the Delian League conflict with its democratic ideals?
4. **Defending a Point of View** Do you think Alexander deserved to be called "the Great"? Why or why not?

Organizing What You Know

5. **Categorizing** Copy the graphic organizer below. Use it to identify some of the achievements of the Greeks.

Area of Accomplishment	Example(s)
Art	
Architecture	
Literature	
Philosophy	
Math and Science	

REVIEW, ASSESS, RETEACH

Have students complete the Section Review. Then have each student compile four multiple-choice questions about the section content, exchange their questions with another student, and answer that student's question. Then have students complete Daily Quiz 13.2.

Have students complete Main Idea Activity S2. Then ask students to work in pairs to re-read the section to each other, pausing to discuss any concepts that are unclear. **ESOL, COOPERATIVE LEARNING,** **LS AUDITORY-MUSICAL**

EXTEND

Have interested students conduct research on the Parthenon, including its original plan, the optical tricks the architect incorporated into its construction, and the gigantic statue of Athena that once occupied its interior. Students should present an illustrated report to the class. **BLOCK SCHEDULING**

Section 3: The Roman Republic

Read to Discover
1. Who were the early peoples of Italy?
2. How were government and society organized in the early Roman Republic?
3. What were some key events in Rome's expansion?
4. What issues caused problems for the late Roman Republic?

Vocabulary
republic
patricians
plebeians
consuls
forum
dictator

People
Hannibal
The Gracchi
Marius
Sulla
Julius Caesar
Octavian

Reading Strategy

PAIRED SUMMARIZING   Read this section silently. In pairs, take turns summarizing the material. Stop to discuss any ideas that seem confusing.

Early Peoples of Italy

Italy's geography helped a great civilization to develop there. The Alps protect Italy to the north. The Mediterranean Sea to the west and south and the Adriatic Sea to the east of this boot-shaped peninsula made trade and travel easy. Much of the peninsula has rich soil and a mild climate. In the 700s B.C., a people called the Latins took advantage of these benefits. They settled in villages along the Tiber River.

The city of Rome grew up from several of these small villages. Rome was first ruled by Latin kings. During the late 600s B.C., the Romans were conquered by a people called the Etruscans. The Etruscans brought written language to Rome. Skilled and clever craftspeople, they built paved roads and sewers. Rome grew into a large and successful city. In time, Greeks also settled in Italy. Their ideas and culture strongly influenced the Romans. Even the Roman religion was partly based on Greek beliefs.

In 510 B.C., the Romans revolted against Etruscan rule and threw out the last Etruscan king. The Roman aristocrats, or noble class, then established a **republic**—a government in which voters elect their leaders.

In this detail from an Etruscan tomb painting, men are carrying food and playing music.

Interpreting the Visual Record Why might the Etruscans have placed a picture such as this in a tomb?

✓ **READING CHECK:**
Human-Environment Interaction   Why did the Latins settle in Italy? to take advantage of the peninsula's location, rich soil, and mild climate

Early History of Europe • 297

Section 3

Objectives
1. Identify the early peoples of Italy.
2. Explain how government and society were organized in the early Roman Republic.
3. Trace the key events in Rome's expansion.
4. Investigate the issues that caused problems for the late Roman Republic.

Focus

Bellringer
Write this question on the chalkboard: *What do you know about chariots?* Discuss responses. Tell students that the Etruscans, a people of ancient Italy, contributed an interesting custom related to chariots to Roman custom. When a Roman general rode his chariot through the streets in a great victory parade, a slave rode in the general's chariot with him. The slave held a gold wreath over the general's head, but over and over told him to remember that he would die like any other man. Students will learn more about the Etruscans and the Romans in Section 3.

Building Vocabulary
Write the vocabulary terms on the chalkboard and call on volunteers to find their definitions. Point out that **dictator** was once an office to which Roman leaders could be appointed in emergencies. When the emergency had passed they gave up the office. Compare this meaning to what it means to modern global politics.

CHAPTER 13, Section 3

SECTION 3 RESOURCES
Reproducibles
◆Lecture Notes, Section 3
◆Block Scheduling Handbook, Chapter 13
◆Know It Notes S3
◆Readings in World Geography, History, and Culture, Reading 29

Technology
◆One-Stop Planner CD-ROM, Lesson 13.3
◆Geography and Cultures Visual Resources 49, 50
◆Homework Practice Online
◆HRW Go Site

Review, Reinforcement, and Assessment Resources
◆Section 3 Review
◆Daily Quiz 13.3
◆Main Idea Activity S3
◆Chapter Summaries and Review
◆English Audio Summary 13.3
◆Spanish Audio Summary 13.3

◀ **Visual Record Answer**

perhaps to entertain the person who is buried in the tomb in the afterlife

Early History of Europe 297

CHAPTER 13, Section 3

GLOBAL PERSPECTIVES

Hannibal's Travels Hannibal successfully regained several territories for Carthage in the Second Punic War, including much of what is now Spain. Following those victories, however, his army was weakened by the brutal trip through the Alps. In Italy, Hannibal's position was further weakened when his plans to ally with free Italians, Macedonians, Spaniards, and Gauls failed.

Hannibal never received reinforcements from Carthage, leaving him too weak to mount a powerful attack against Rome. His allies lost interest as the chance for victory faded and as the Romans became more aggressive. Although Hannibal's tactics and skills surpassed those of most Roman generals, Rome ultimately claimed victory in the Second Punic war.

Government and Society

In the early days of the Roman Republic, the heads of a small number of aristocratic families, known as **patricians**, elected officials from among themselves to rule. Eventually, the common people, known as **plebeians**, also took part in the government. The government consisted of three main bodies—the Senate, elected rulers called magistrates, and citizens' assemblies. The Senate controlled the republic's funds and relations with other governments. Two magistrates, called **consuls**, ran the government and commanded the army. The consuls governed with the advice of the Senate. The assemblies performed a variety of functions, including making laws and electing officials.

The center of life for all of Roman society was the **forum**. Public meetings, trials, sporting events, and political activities all took place there. Markets and shops lined the sides of the complex. In one end of the forum was the Senate house, called the curia.

Another important focus of Roman life was the army. The Romans believed that only those citizens who had property to protect would fight bravely. Therefore, all Roman citizens between the ages of 17 and 46 who owned property were required to serve in the military.

Roman Expansion

As the Roman population grew, so did its need for more land. Soon Rome began conquering its neighbors and settling its people on the conquered lands. By 275 B.C., Rome controlled all of Italy.

South of the Italian mainland, Rome came into conflict with Carthage (KAHR-thij), a powerful Phoenician trading city. From its position on the North African coast, Carthage controlled trade in the western Mediterranean.

In 264 B.C., Rome attacked the Carthaginians, starting the First Punic (the Latin word for "Phoenician") War. The war dragged on until the Carthaginians asked for peace. Then Carthaginian general Hannibal invaded Italy in 218 B.C., starting the Second Punic War. This war is best known for Hannibal's incredible feat of crossing the Alps with a huge army, including 6,000 men on horseback. He had even brought 37 elephants from Africa, but only one survived the trip into Italy. The Carthaginians won several important battles and for a time controlled parts of Italy. However, Hannibal had to return to defend Carthage. In 202 B.C., he was defeated.

Roman armies completely destroyed Carthage. They then went on to conquer Greece. By 133 B.C., Rome ruled land from the Atlantic Ocean to the Aegean Sea. However, the people who lived in the areas far from the city of Rome were not given Roman citizenship.

✓ **READING CHECK:** (Human Systems) What was the outcome of the Punic Wars? Rome ruled land from the Atlantic to the Aegean.

298 • Chapter 13

TEACH

Teach Objective 1

ALL LEVELS: (Suggested time: 15 min.) Copy the following graphic organizer onto the chalkboard, omitting the blue answers. Have students complete it to learn the progression of events leading up to the establishment of the Roman Republic. **ESOL,** **LS** VISUAL-SPATIAL

LEVELS 2 AND 3: (Suggested time: 15 min.) Have students suggest slogans or statements that Romans may have used to encourage each other to revolt against the Etruscans and found a republic. **LS** VERBAL-LINGUISTIC

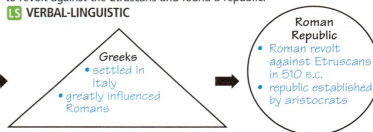

Latins
- took advantage of Italy's geography
- settled in villages along Tiber River
- Rome ruled by Latin kings

→ **Etruscans**
- conquered Romans late 600s B.C.
- brought written language to Rome
- paved roads and sewers

→ **Greeks**
- settled in Italy
- greatly influenced Romans

→ **Roman Republic**
- Roman revolt against Etruscans in 510 B.C.
- republic established by aristocrats

298 Chapter 13

History Close-Up

The Roman Forum This Illustration shows how part of the Roman Forum may have looked. To the left is the curia, where the Roman Senate met. In the background is the Basilica Aemilia, a large hall where politicians, moneylenders, moneychangers, and other people would gather. It was built in 179 B.C. and was slightly longer than a football field. Today, visitors to the site of the basilica can see small round greenish spots on the pavement. Some people say these are the remains of copper coins that melted when the building burned in A.D. 410. **Why would the Roman Forum be a logical place for moneychangers to set up their businesses?**

CHAPTER 13, Section 3

Using Illustrations

Life in the Forum Lead a discussion about what activities are going on in this illustration of the Roman Forum. Then have students conduct further research on daily life during the Roman Republic. Each student should choose a specific topic, such as toys, food, slavery, clothing, and so on. Challenge students to write a brief report on the chosen topic and to propose how they would fit an illustration related to the topic into the forum picture. (Example: Children may have played with their toys on the forum's pavement while the adults bought food in the market.)

◀ **History Close-Up Answer**

Many different peoples, some with their own currencies, came to be included under Rome's control. Eventually, Rome's trading relationships included even the Chinese. In order for merchants from different areas to do business with each other, they may have needed to exchange their money for a common currency. Because the forum was the center of Rome, it was a logical place for this activity.

Teaching Objective 2
ALL LEVELS: (Suggested time: 15 min.) Have students work in pairs to create an organizational chart of the Roman Republic's government. Instruct them to include all the governing bodies (Senate, magistrates, citizens' assemblies) and officials (consuls). Then lead a discussion about how patricians, plebeians, and the army contributed to society during the republic. **COOPERATIVE LEARNING**

Teaching Objective 3
ALL LEVELS: Organize the class into groups. Have each group choose an event in Rome's expansion and create a storyboard about that event for a video game. **COOPERATIVE LEARNING, LS VISUAL-SPATIAL**

CHAPTER 13, Section 3

USING ILLUSTRATIONS

SPQR Focus students' attention on the battle standards shown in the illustration. Roman battle standards bore the images of eagles and the letters SPQR. The letters stand for *Senatus Populusque Romanus*—"the Senate and the people of Rome." These same letters were carved on public buildings, showing the world that an alliance of upper and lower classes stood together in defense of Rome.

Today, SPQR is still part of Rome's public image. Visitors to the city of Rome may notice the four famous letters on water mains, manhole covers, busses, and signs asking strollers to stay off the grass.

Visual Record Answer

probably is successful, because the Romans appear unprepared to defend themselves

Trouble for the Republic

Controlling such a vast area was difficult. The republic was frequently at war with its neighbors. Political problems began to develop within the republic itself.

The Gracchi In 133 B.C., government officials named Tiberius and Gaius Gracchus (GRAK-uhs) wanted to help the poor people who had no land. The Gracchus brothers, or the Gracchi, said that land won through conquest should be given to these poor workers. The public supported the idea. The Roman Senate, however, opposed it. Because Tiberius had bypassed Senate rules to get his way, some Senate members wanted to stop him. The senators caused a riot, during which mobs killed Tiberius. Gaius died soon after. The deaths of the Gracchi marked a turning point in Roman history. From then on, violence became a major political tool.

Internal Conflicts Three more conflicts changed other features of the Roman Republic. The first involved the role of the army. In 107 B.C., a general named Gaius Marius was elected consul. Marius got rid of the property requirements for the army, and poor men began to join in large numbers. The army became devoted to Marius, who treated the troops as his private force. Other generals followed Marius's example. As time went on, troops were often more loyal to their generals than to the Roman Republic. This change would cause big problems in later years.

Meanwhile, trouble was brewing in Italy. The conquered peoples there had asked for Roman citizenship, but the Senate had refused. In 90 B.C., the Italians rebelled. This conflict, known as the Social War, was one of the bloodiest in Roman history. Eventually, the revolt was put down, but the Senate did agree to grant the Italians citizenship. With this decision, the Roman state grew beyond the city of Rome to include all of Italy.

Then in 88 B.C. a general named Lucius Cornelius Sulla was elected consul. Marius, who was still a consul also, wanted to limit

In this modern artist's drawing, Sulla is shown invading Rome in 88 B.C.
Interpreting the Visual Record From this picture, could you conclude if Sulla was successful? Support your answer.

300 • Chapter 13

Teaching Objective 4
LEVEL 3: (Suggested time: 30 min.) Ask students to imagine that a Roman fell asleep in 200 B.C. and, through some mysterious process, woke up 170 years later. Have students work in pairs to write a dialog between this well-rested person and a resident of Rome in 30 B.C. The dialogs should highlight the hopes the sleeper had for the Roman Republic and what has changed to dim those hopes.

▶**ASSIGNMENT:** Have students write a summary of the changes that ended the Roman Republic. Students should also consider whether those changes could have been halted and the republic restored.

Sulla's influence. Sulla responded by marching on Rome with his army, starting a civil war. In the end, Sulla defeated Marius and became **dictator**. The Senate could give someone this title—and along with it temporary absolute power—in an emergency. Sulla used illegal means to punish his enemies cruelly. By breaking the rules and taking all power into his hands, Sulla put the whole idea of representative government in danger.

Julius Caesar In 60 B.C. Gnaeus Pompey, Julius Caesar, and Marcus Licinius Crassus formed an alliance to govern Rome. The alliance was called the First Triumvirate, or "rule of three."

Caesar knew that he needed a loyal army to hold on to power. He went to Gaul, where he proved his brilliance as a military leader. Caesar was also very successful at organizing areas that he conquered. By writing reports and sending them back to Rome, Caesar kept the people at home informed. His fame grew. Caesar returned to Rome a hero.

Crassus died, and Caesar defeated Pompey in a civil war. The way was clear for Caesar to take power. The Senate declared Caesar dictator for life. However, some Roman leaders feared Caesar's popularity. On March 15, 44 B.C., senators assassinated Julius Caesar in the Senate house.

Octavian In 43 B.C., a Second Triumvirate formed. Its members were Caesar's heir, Octavian, an officer named Marc Antony, and a consul named Lepidus. Soon Lepidus was pushed aside. Antony and Octavian agreed that each would control half of the republic, but civil war broke out between them. Octavian finally defeated Antony and his ally, Queen Cleopatra of Egypt, in a naval battle in 31 B.C. The suicides of Antony and Cleopatra the following year marked the end of an era. Octavian alone now ruled Rome. The republic was gone, and a new period in Roman history was beginning.

✓ **READING CHECK:** (Human Systems) How did Julius Caesar rise to power? member of the First Triumvirate, went to Gaul, proved to be brilliant military leader, wrote reports, returned to Rome a hero, defeated Pompey in civil war, declared dictator for life

Julius Caesar
(100 B.C.–44 B.C.)

During his lifetime Julius Caesar was hated, loved, feared, and admired. Historians still debate whether Caesar was a hero or a villain.

Julius Caesar was ambitious and ruthless. He was also a brilliant general, politician, writer, and public speaker. The people of Rome adored him because he stood up for their rights. They also praised his conquests of faraway lands. Caesar's enemies in the Roman Senate, however, saw him as a threat to their own power. Even former friends and men he had helped resented Caesar's popularity. They were among the men who stabbed him to death. **Who are some other historical figures who were loved by some people and hated by others?**

Section Review 3

Define or identify: republic, patricians, plebeians, consuls, forum, Hannibal, the Gracchi, Marius, Sulla, dictator, Julius Caesar, Octavian

Reading for the Main Idea
1. (Human Systems) Who were the early peoples of Italy, and what did they accomplish?
2. (Human Systems) How were Roman society and government organized during the early Republic?

Critical Thinking
3. **Analyzing Information** How did the Punic Wars affect Rome's expansion?
4. **Drawing Inferences and Conclusions** How did the changing role of the army contribute to the Roman Republic's end?

Organizing What You Know
5. **Sequencing** Copy the following graphic organizer. Use it to identify key events leading to the end of the Roman Republic.

Homework Practice Online
Keyword: SJ5 HP13

Section 3 Review

Answers to Section 3 Review

Define or identify For definitions and identifications, see the glossary and index.

Reading for the Main Idea
1. Latins; Etruscans—brought written language to Rome, roads and sewers
2. society divided between patricians and plebeians; government included the Senate, elected rulers called magistrates, and citizens' assemblies—all under the leadership of two consuls, who ran the government and the army

Critical Thinking
3. allowed Rome to expand its influence into the western Mediterranean and throughout the Mediterranean
4. As armies became more loyal to generals than to the Roman Republic, having an army became essential to getting and keeping power.

Organizing What You Know
5. After the Punic Wars, not all people given citizenship; deaths of the Gracchi began use of violence as political tool; Marius changed role of the army; the Social War; Sulla became dictator; Julius Caesar became dictator.

◀ **Biography Answer**
Students may mention Gandhi, Martin Luther King Jr. or others.

CLOSE

Read to the class one or both of the eulogies, spoken by Brutus and Mark Antony, for Julius Caesar in William Shakespeare's *Julius Caesar*. Challenge students to decipher the speakers' messages.

REVIEW, ASSESS, RETEACH

Have students complete the Section Review. Then display a map of the Mediterranean and have students take turns pointing out stages in Rome's expansion on the map. Then have students complete Daily Quiz 13.3. **ESOL**, LS **VISUAL-SPATIAL**

Have students complete Main Idea Activity S3. Then have students write a sentence to summarize each paragraph in the section.
LS **VERBAL-LINGUISTIC**

EXTEND

Point out that, although the Latin alphabet developed from the Etruscan alphabet, the Etruscan language itself has never been deciphered. Have interested students conduct research on the Etruscan language and efforts by scholars to understand it. **BLOCK SCHEDULING**

CHAPTER 13, Section 4

Section 4 Resources

Reproducibles
- Lecture Notes, Section 4
- Block Scheduling Handbook, Chapter 13
- Know It Notes S4
- Readings in World Geography, History, and Culture, Reading 29
- Map Activity 13
- Critical Thinking Activity 13

Technology
- One-Stop Planner CD-ROM, Lesson 13.4
- Geography and Cultures Visual Resources 49
- Homework Practice Online
- HRW Go Site

Review, Reinforcement, and Assessment Resources
- Section 4 Review
- Daily Quiz 13.4
- Main Idea Activity S4
- Chapter Summaries and Review
- English Audio Summary 13.4
- Spanish Audio Summary 13.4

Section 4 The Roman Empire

Read to Discover
1. What was the Pax Romana?
2. How did Christianity begin and spread?
3. Why did the Roman Empire decline?
4. What did the Romans contribute to other cultures?

Vocabulary
empire
Pax Romana
disciples
gladiators
aqueduct

People
Augustus Caesar
Claudius
Trajan
Hadrian
Marcus Aurelius
Jesus
Constantine
Diocletian

Reading Strategy

READING ORGANIZER Before you read, create a time line from 27 B.C. to A.D. 476 down the center of a sheet of paper. On the left side of the line, write down key events in the history of the Roman Empire as you read. On the right side of the line write supporting details about the events.

This statue of Augustus shows the emperor as strong and healthy, although he was ill much of the time. The tiny figure of Cupid was supposed to show that Augustus was descended from the goddess Venus, Cupid's mother.

The Pax Romana

With the end of the Roman Republic, a new era in Roman history began. In 27 B.C. the Senate gave Octavian the title Augustus, which meant "the honored one." He became known as Augustus Caesar. Historians refer to him as the first emperor of Rome.

Augustus Caesar Under Augustus, the republic became an **empire**. An empire is a form of government that unites different places and peoples under one ruler. Augustus sent his armies out to conquer new lands. Soon the empire reached from Spain to Syria.

The reign of Augustus began a period known as the **Pax Romana**, or "Roman Peace." This period would last for more than 200 years. During the Pax Romana, Rome was relatively stable and peaceful. Laws became more fair. Widespread trade created a strong economy. Roman engineers built roads and bridges that promoted trade and helped unite the large empire. The Roman army kept the peace by defending Rome's borders against invaders.

Romans paid a price for peace, however. Augustus limited the powers of the Senate and gave himself full control of the government. He took the title *princeps*, or "first citizen," and ruled much like a king. Later emperors would abuse this structure of unlimited power.

The Julio-Claudian Emperors Augustus died in A.D. 14. For the next 54 years, adopted relatives of Julius Caesar, called the Julio-Claudian emperors, ruled the empire. Some of them were effective

302 • Chapter 13

Section 4

Objectives
1. Describe the Pax Romana.
2. Explain how Christianity began and spread.
3. Analyze why the Roman Empire declined.
4. Explore the contributions that Rome made to other cultures.

Focus

Bellringer

Write the following question on the chalkboard: *Which of these dishes would you want to eat—jellyfish and eggs, boiled ostrich, roasted parrot, flamingo boiled with dates, or stewed roses?* Point out that these are among the foods served at banquets for the upper classes during the time of the Roman Empire. Students will learn more about the Roman Empire in this section.

Building Vocabulary

Have students find the definitions for the vocabulary terms and read them aloud. Point out that all the terms have Latin roots. **Gladiator** comes for *gladiaus*, the Latin word for "sword." The first letters of **aqueduct** indicate that the word has something to do with water. What other English words related to water start with *aqu-*? (Examples: aqua, aquarium, aquatic, and so on.)

leaders, while others were not. Tiberius was generally a good leader, but the people didn't like him. His successor, Caligula, routinely tortured or murdered his enemies. A palace guard murdered him.

The emperor Claudius came next. He improved the government structure and gave Roman citizenship to many people in the empire's distant lands. He extended the empire all the way to Britain. Like many emperors, however, Claudius met a violent death. His wife, Agrippina, probably killed him with poisonous mushrooms. Nero, the last of the Julio-Claudian emperors, was mentally unstable. He spent far too much money, neglected government, and shocked the Romans by behaving foolishly. Finally, some people decided to get rid Nero. Hearing of their plans, Nero killed himself.

The Good Emperors Later, a series of rulers came to power who became known as the Five Good Emperors for their wise rule. Of the five, Trajan, Hadrian, and Marcus Aurelius stand out.

Trajan conquered new lands for Rome, and the empire became the largest it would ever be. Hadrian realized that Rome should protect what it had, instead of conquering still more land. So, Hadrian built walls at the empire's boundaries. The most famous, called Hadrian's Wall, still stands in northern England. Marcus Aurelius began his reign in A.D. 161. He wrote philosophy and improved Roman law. However, Marcus Aurelius spent much of his time defending the empire against invaders. These invaders would later play key roles in Rome's future.

✓ **READING CHECK:** Human Systems How did the Julio-Claudian emperors compare to the Five Good Emperors? *as a group, more unstable and cruel, not as capable*

CHAPTER 13, Section 4

National Geography Standard 12

Economic Networks to Feed an Empire The Roman Empire depended on a huge and expertly constructed road system to move armies, send messages, and ship supplies across the vast expanse within its borders.

In spite of the excellent roads, however, overland travel over long distances wasn't easy. Supplies were hauled in two- or four-wheeled carts drawn by horses or oxen. Traffic in each direction may have kept to one side of the road, although historians aren't sure which side that was. Overland trade was much more expensive than trade by sea. For example, in A.D. 301, bulk shipments of grain could be carried by sea from Spain to Syria at less than the cost of moving the same cargo overland a distance of 75 miles.

The Roman Empire stretched from the Atlantic Ocean to the Persian Gulf and from the North Sea to the Red Sea.

Interpreting the Map About how many miles by sea was Carthago Nova from Antioch? What are some modern European countries that were partially conquered by Rome? Why was the Mediterranean Sea sometimes called a Roman lake?

The Roman Empire

◄ **Map Answer**

more than 2,000 miles; Germany, Romania, Austria, Hungary, United Kingdom; because it was completely enclosed by the Roman Empire

TEACH

Teaching Objective 1

LEVEL 2: (Suggested time: 30 min.) Ask students to work with a partner to create an outline for a television special to be titled "Glories of the Pax Romana." Encourage students to consider what they would include, given the program's title, and what they would leave out.
COOPERATIVE LEARNING

LEVEL 3: (Suggested time: 30 min.) Point out that when the President of the United States gives the State of the Union address in January, the opposition party always gets a chance to air its version of the same topics covered in the speech. Have students propose what they would include in a segment called "The Other Side of the Pax Romana" to be broadcast immediately after the program described in the Level 2 activity. *(Students should note the loss of personal freedoms, the dreadful reigns by Caligula and Nero, the murder of Claudius, and so on.)*

Early History of Europe 303

CHAPTER 13, Section 4

Cultural Kaleidoscope

An Egyptian Cult in Rome Christianity wasn't the only religion that drew people away from the old Roman gods. A cult from Egypt gained many followers. The cult of the Egyptian goddess Isis was extremely popular, particularly among Roman women.

According to Egyptian tradition, Isis was the daughter of the sky. The cow was Isis's sacred symbol. Legend held that Isis had discovered wheat and barley and showed humans how to cultivate the grains. She eventually came to be regarded as queen of the whole universe. Her followers believed that she would watch over them in their earthly lives as well as give them blessed eternal life.

Critical Thinking: Why may the cult of Isis have appealed particularly to Roman women?

Answer: Students may reply that the cult gave Roman women a feeling of power, which they largely lacked otherwise. It also promised a happy afterlife, which would have appealed to women who worked hard but received few rewards.

▲ This sixth-century mosaic from Italy shows Jesus performing a miracle. According to the Gospels, Jesus turned five loaves of bread and two fishes into enough food to feed the huge crowd of people who had come to hear him preach.

The Rise of Christianity

In 63 B.C. the land called Judaea came under Roman control. Judaea was the birthplace of Christianity. It was there that a man named Jesus began to teach in about A.D. 27. Most of what we know about Jesus comes to us from the Gospels, the first four books of the Christian New Testament.

Jesus' teachings were grounded in Jewish tradition. He taught his followers to believe in only one God and to love others as they loved themselves. According to the Gospels, Jesus performed miracles and defended the poor. People came from all over to hear Jesus speak. Many of these people believed that Jesus was the Messiah, or the savior of the Jews.

Some religious leaders thought that Jesus was putting himself above religious law. Other officials didn't like the fact that Jesus was so popular. Finally, the authorities decided that Jesus was a serious problem.

Jesus was arrested in Jerusalem. He was sentenced to death by hanging on a cross, called crucifixion. His followers, or **disciples**, believed that Jesus rose from the dead, walked among them for 40 days, and then rose into heaven. Soon, the disciples began to spread this message to other people. A new faith, Christianity, had been born.

At first, the Romans ignored Christianity. As it grew in popularity, they outlawed it and persecuted Christians. Still the new faith spread throughout the Mediterranean world over the next 300 years. In A.D. 312, the Roman emperor Constantine converted to Christianity. By the end of the 300s, Christianity had become the official religion of the Roman Empire.

✓ **READING CHECK:** (Human Systems) What events led to the death of Jesus? *rising popularity, accusations of putting himself above religious law, arrest*

The Decline of the Empire

In the early A.D. 200s, Rome was facing problems. Ambitious generals assassinated emperors and became emperors themselves. Wealthy people could buy the army's loyalty. Dishonest leaders neglected defense, allowing invaders to threaten the borders. Fighting these invaders drained the empire's resources. Too much money went to keeping Romans entertained. Among their entertainments were fights to the death between trained slaves called **gladiators**. Crime increased. Taxes rose as the government spent more money to protect Roman citizens.

A Split in the Empire By A.D. 286, the Roman Empire could no longer be ruled well by one person. Emperor Diocletian selected a co-emperor to help him rule. Diocletian ruled in the east, while his co-emperor ruled in the west. Under Diocletian, the government con-

304 • Chapter 13

Teaching Objective 2

ALL LEVELS: You will need to provide extra time and art supplies for this activity. Draw students' attention to the mosaic on this page. Have students work in groups to create mosaics about the beginnings of Christianity. **COOPERATIVE LEARNING,** LS **VISUAL-SPATIAL**

LEVEL 3: Have all students complete the All Levels activity. Then provide research materials. Have students conduct research on Roman persecution of early Christians and the role of martyrdom in the spread of the faith. (The Romans calculated that the Christians' deaths would persuade other Christians to abandon their faith. However, the courage that many of the martyrs exhibited in the face of death may have convinced some people to convert to the new religion.)

trolled almost every part of life. Defense and security of the empire came first. Individual freedom was second. Diocletian enforced the laws of the empire and drove out the invading barbarian tribes. He also tried to improve the economy.

About 20 years later, the emperor Constantine took over the eastern part of the empire. Constantine was a strong ruler. The Eastern Empire fared much better than the weakened Western Empire. Constantine is remembered for supporting Christianity. He also established his capital city in the east. Then called Constantinople, it is now known as Istanbul.

Constantine died in A.D. 337. Although the empire remained stable for about 50 years, it was becoming permanently divided. The Western Empire grew weaker and weaker, while the Eastern Empire became the center of power and wealth.

The End of the Empire As the years passed, the empire was increasingly plagued by invasions. Tribes such as the Vandals, Visigoths, and Huns pushed west and south from their homelands, looking for wealth and new land. Roman armies fought the invaders, but with limited success.

In 410, Visigoths attacked the city of Rome itself. In 476, invaders overthrew the last Roman emperor in the west. Invading tribes set up their own kingdoms, destroying the empire's unity. People began to leave the cities, hoping to find safety in the countryside. Schools and libraries crumbled. Little by little, the Western Empire fell apart. The Eastern Empire had more success in fighting off invaders. It became known as the Byzantine Empire. For hundreds of years it would survive—until 1453, when the Byzantine Empire fell to the Ottoman Turks.

Although its power faded, Rome had changed much of the world forever. Its people had made immense contributions to human society. Many of these contributions are part of our daily lives.

✓ **READING CHECK:** *Human Systems* What led to the fall of the empire in the west? generals assassinating emperors, army disloyalty, neglected defense, invasions, too much money spent on entertainment, increased crime, higher taxes, overthrow of the last emperor

This statue shows Diocletian and his co-emperor, each with a vice-ruler.
Interpreting the Visual Record How may this sculpture show growing concerns about the Roman Empire's future?

These marble pieces are fragments of a seated statue of Constantine.
Interpreting the Visual Record How tall do you think the original statue may have been?

CHAPTER 13, Section 4

Across the Curriculum
SCIENCE
Lead and the Roman Empire Over the centuries, scholars have blamed many factors for the decline of the Roman Empire. One possible factor is lead poisoning. Consuming lead can cause confusion, lethargy, shaking, digestion problems, deafness, blindness, and brain damage—among other ailments. Eventually, it can kill.

Although they knew the metal could be harmful, upper-class Romans consumed a large amount of lead. They seasoned their food and preserved wine with it. Nero is said to have worn a breastplate made of lead. The emperor believed the metal would improve his singing. The most widespread use of lead was as lining for the pipes of the vast plumbing network that provided water to Roman cities. In fact, the word *plumbing* comes from *plumbum,* the Latin word for "lead."

Discussion: How could lead poisoning eventually contribute to the decline of the Roman Empire?

▲ **Visual Record Answer**

by showing the rulers with worried faces and their arms protecting each other

possible answer: probably at least 22 feet tall

Teaching Objective 3
LEVEL 1: Locate and display a photo of Trajan's Column, which stands in the ruins of Trajan's Forum in Rome. It is a stone column 125 feet high on which is carved a long band that spirals around the column. This band—4 feet high and 800 feet long—is made up of carvings that tell the story of Trajan's campaigns in Dacia, now Romania. Provide butcher paper and art supplies. Have students construct a similar band that could be twisted around a column to tell the story of the Roman Empire's decline.
LS KINESTHETIC

LEVELS 2 AND 3: (Suggested time: 20 min.) Organize the class into two groups. Have students of one half write epitaphs for the Roman Empire in which they describe the factors that contributed to the empire's fall. Have students in the other half write a response to this statement: "That the Roman Empire fell is not remarkable; what is remarkable is that it survived for so long." Call on volunteers to read their epitaphs and their responses.
LS VERBAL-LINGUISTIC

CHAPTER 13, Section 4

DAILY LIFE

A Day at the Baths The use by Roman engineers of round arches, vaults, and crossed vaults made possible buildings that could accommodate huge crowds. One such building was the public bath completed by the emperor Caracalla in A.D. 216. Some 1,600 people could enjoy the facility at a time.

The baths contained three main rooms: the *calidarium,* a room with a hot-water pool; the *frigidarium,* which had cold water; and the *tepidarium,* with lukewarm water. The *natatio* was an outdoor swimming pool. An immense hall with a vaulted ceiling connected the *calidarium* and the *frigidarium.* Marble sculptures, mosaics, and wall paintings decorated the interior. Patrons could enjoy a full day at the baths, listening to lectures, discussing politics, buying food and drink from vendors, exercising, and just relaxing in the pools.

Connecting to Technology
Answer
Examples will vary by community, but students may note arches supporting bridges or sports facilities, or as design elements on buildings.

Rome's Contributions

Just as ancient Greece affected later cultures, so did Rome. Because the empire was so huge, Rome's influence spread to many lands.

Engineering and Architecture The Romans applied what they had learned from other peoples, especially the Greeks, to useful purposes. The Romans planned cities, built water and sewer systems, paved roads, and improved livestock breeding. To supply water to the empire's cities, they built aqueducts. An **aqueduct** is a sloped bridge-like structure that carries water from one place to another. Arches and concrete, a Roman invention, made construction of big public buildings possible. Roman engineers also built immense structures for outdoor events. The Circus Maximus could seat a quarter of a million people for the chariot races held there.

Language and Literature The language you speak and the alphabet you write owe much to the Romans. They learned the Greek alphabet from the Etruscans. With a few changes, it's the alphabet we use today.

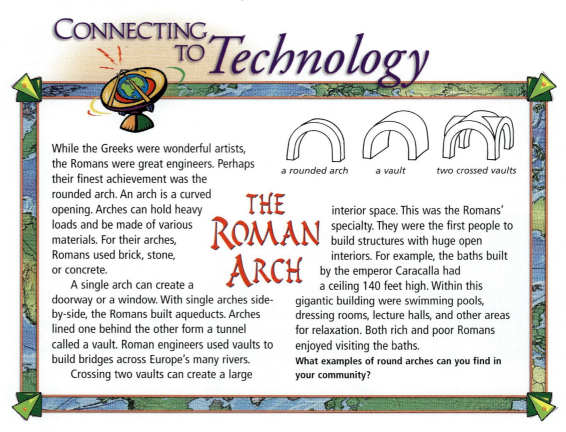

Connecting to Technology

THE ROMAN ARCH

While the Greeks were wonderful artists, the Romans were great engineers. Perhaps their finest achievement was the rounded arch. An arch is a curved opening. Arches can hold heavy loads and be made of various materials. For their arches, Romans used brick, stone, or concrete.

A single arch can create a doorway or a window. With single arches side-by-side, the Romans built aqueducts. Arches lined one behind the other form a tunnel called a vault. Roman engineers used vaults to build bridges across Europe's many rivers.

Crossing two vaults can create a large interior space. This was the Romans' specialty. They were the first people to build structures with huge open interiors. For example, the baths built by the emperor Caracalla had a ceiling 140 feet high. Within this gigantic building were swimming pools, dressing rooms, lecture halls, and other areas for relaxation. Both rich and poor Romans enjoyed visiting the baths.

What examples of round arches can you find in your community?

a rounded arch   a vault   two crossed vaults

306 • Chapter 13

Teaching Objective 4

LEVEL 1: You will need to provide resource materials and perhaps extra time for this activity. Depending on the size of your class, have students work in pairs or as individuals to conduct research on these topics: Roman city planning, water systems (including aqueducts), sewers, roads, livestock breeding, arches, concrete, the Colosseum, the Circus Maximus, the Roman alphabet, Latin roots in English, medieval Latin, Romance languages, Cicero, Virgil, Ovid, Tacitus, Plutarch, Suetonius, Roman law, and European law codes based on Roman law. Ask each student or each pair to present a brief oral report on the assigned topic. Instruct students to take notes while their classmates present their reports.

LEVEL 2: (Suggested time: 10 min.) Have students complete the Level 1 activity. Then ask students to write a few sentences about which of the contributions that the Romans made to other cultures is the most important and to support their choices. **LS VERBAL-LINGUISTIC**

Latin, the language of the Romans, is still the official language of the Roman Catholic Church. During the Middle Ages, European universities used Latin in their classes. Latin combined with local languages to become French, Italian, Spanish, Portuguese, and Romanian. We call these the Romance languages, after Rome. Although English isn't a Romance language, more than a third of all English words come from Latin.

Rome had its share of talented writers. Cicero wrote letters and speeches in which he argued for the values of the old republic. Virgil wrote the *Aeneid*, which tells a legend about the founding of Rome by a Trojan prince named Aeneas. Ovid wrote love poems and *Metamorphoses*, a collection of myths. Tacitus, one of Rome's greatest historians, scolded wealthy Romans for their wasteful lifestyle. Plutarch wrote biographies of famous Greeks and Romans. Suetonius wrote *Lives of the Caesars*, about the first 12 emperors. Personal details make it lively reading today.

Government and Law At its height, the Roman Empire included 100 million people. A clear system of laws made governing this population possible. Laws were written down and placed in public view so that everyone could see them. Judges interpreted the laws to fit changing times and local customs. Roman judges also established another idea we believe in today—that an accused person is innocent until proven guilty. Eventually, all the European countries that had been part of the Roman Empire based their law codes on Roman law.

Rome is often called the Eternal City. The nickname reflects the fact that Rome's influence will continue to last for a long, long time.

✓ **READING CHECK:** (Human Systems) What were some accomplishments of the Romans? *various accomplishments in engineering, architecture, language, literature, government, and law*

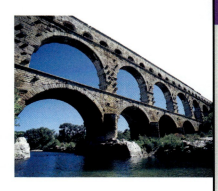

▲ Aqueducts brought water to Rome from as far away as 57 miles. Other cities throughout the empire also got their water by means of aqueducts. This one is in France. The water flowed through a channel on top of the highest level of arches.

Homework Practice Online
Keyword: SJ5 HP13

Define or identify: empire, Augustus Caesar, Pax Romana, Claudius, Trajan, Hadrian, Marcus Aurelius, Jesus, disciples, gladiators, Constantine, Diocletian, aqueduct

Reading for the Main Idea

1. (Human Systems) What were some features of life during the Pax Romana?
2. (Human Systems) How did the Romans' attitude toward Christianity change?

Critical Thinking

3. **Comparing and Contrasting** Why might Caligula and Nero be called the Bad Emperors?

4. **Analyzing Information** What led to the split in the Roman Empire?

Organizing What You Know

5. **Categorizing** Copy the graphic organizer below. Use it to identify some of the contributions of the Romans.

Area of Contribution	Example(s)
Engineering and Architecture	
Language and Literature	
Government and Law	

Section 4 Review

Answers to Section 4 Review

Define or identify For definitions and identifications, see the glossary and index.

Reading for the Main Idea

1. relative peace and stability, fairer laws, widespread trade, strong economy, good roads and bridges that promoted trade and unified the empire, protection from invaders by the army
2. ignored it at first, then outlawed it as it became more popular, finally made it the official religion of the empire

Critical Thinking

3. Caligula—routinely tortured or murdered his enemies; Nero—spent too much money, neglected government, shocked the Romans by behaving foolishly
4. Internal problems had weakened the empire so that it could no longer be ruled well by one person.

Organizing What You Know

5. See text under Rome's Contributions for answers.

CLOSE

Focus students' attention on the aqueduct photo on this page. Ask students to propose how the arches were constructed. (Workers first built wooden forms on which the arches were constructed. When the mortar was dry, the forms were removed, and the arches stood because the elements of which they were made pressed against each other.)

REVIEW, ASSESS, RETEACH

Have each student write a question about the content under each subhead. Call on students to read their questions and on other to provide answers. Then have students complete Daily Quiz 13.4.

Have students complete Main Idea Activity S4. Then organize students into four groups—one for each Read to Discover question. Have group members write three true-false statements that relate to their question. Quiz the class with the statements. **ESOL, COOPERATIVE LEARNING**

EXTEND

Have interested students create maps of the city of Rome during the period of the Roman Empire. They should mark buildings that still stand or the ruins of which still stand. **BLOCK SCHEDULING**

CHAPTER 13, Section 5

SECTION 5 RESOURCES

Reproducibles
- Lecture Notes, Section 5
- Block Scheduling Handbook, Chapter 13
- Know It Notes S5
- Biography Activity: Geoffrey Chaucer

Technology
- One-Stop Planner CD-ROM, Lesson 13.5
- Geography and Cultures Visual Resources 49, 51, 54, 55
- Homework Practice Online
- HRW Go Site

Review, Reinforcement, and Assessment Resources
- Section 5 Review
- Daily Quiz 13.5
- Main Idea Activity S5
- Chapter Summaries and Review
- English Audio Summary 13.5
- Spanish Audio Summary 13.5

Section 5 The Middle Ages

Read to Discover
1. What were some key events of the Early Middle Ages?
2. How was society organized during the Middle Ages?
3. What was life like during the High Middle Ages?

Vocabulary
medieval
feudalism
nobles
fief
vassals
knight
chivalry
manors
serfs
clergy
cathedrals
Crusades
middle class
vernacular

People
Franks
Charlemagne
Vikings
Geoffrey Chaucer

Reading Strategy

FOLD-NOTES: TRI-FOLD Create the FoldNote titled **Tri-Fold** in the Appendix. Label the columns Know, Want, and Learn. Write down some facts that you already know about the Middle Ages. Then write down what you want to know. After you study the section, write down what you learned.

▲ This purse cover was found in the grave of an Anglo-Saxon king. The design includes men, ducks, and eagles worked in gold and enamel.

308 • Chapter 13

The Early Middle Ages

Tribes that defeated the last of the western Roman emperors in the A.D. 400s brought new ideas with them. These ideas developed into new ways of life for Europeans. Historians see the years between the fall of the Roman Empire and the beginnings of the modern world in about 1500 as a period of change. Because it falls between the ancient and modern worlds, this time is called the Middle Ages or the **medieval** period. Medieval comes from the Latin for "middle age."

The time from the 400s to about 1000 is known as the Early Middle Ages. As this period began, the Roman system of laws and government had broken down. Western Europe was in disorder, divided into many kingdoms. For example, Britain was largely controlled by two tribes from Germany, the Angles and the Saxons.

The Franks The Franks were among the Germanic tribes that moved into western Europe. In the 490s, Clovis, the king of the Franks, became a Christian. He won control of Gaul. Today this area is called France, after the Franks. In 732 a Frankish army under Charles Martel held off a Muslim army that invaded from Muslim Spain. The defeat created a border between the Christian and Muslim worlds.

Section 5

Objectives
1. Trace some key events of the Early Middle Ages.
2. Analyze how society was organized during the Middle Ages.
3. Summarize what life was like during the High Middle Ages.

FOCUS

 Bellringer

Write these questions on the chalkboard: *What movies, TV shows, or video games have been set in the Middle Ages? What impressions of the time do they provide?* (Answers to the first question will vary with the latest releases. Students may include dragons, filth, disease, knights, swords, or many other items in their answers to the second question.) Lead a brief discussion about which of these elements are historically accurate and which are not. Tell students they will learn more about the facts and fictions of the Middle Ages in this section.

Building Vocabulary

Call on volunteers to find and read aloud the definitions of the vocabulary terms. Point out that **medieval** is one of the most misspelled words in the English language. Students often spell it incorrectly as *midevil*. Some students misspell **knight** or confuse it with the word *night*. During the Middle Ages, all the letters in *knight* were pronounced; there were no silent letters. At the time, it may have been pronounced something like "kunyckt."

308 Chapter 13

The greatest Frankish king, Charlemagne (SHAHR-luh-mayn), ruled from 768 to 814. A strong, smart leader, Charlemagne established schools and encouraged people to learn to read and write. His biggest accomplishment was to unite most of western Europe under him. Charlemagne's empire included parts of Europe that had been under Roman rule. On Christmas Day, in the year 800, the pope declared Charlemagne "Emperor of the Romans."

After Charlemagne died, his grandsons divided the empire among themselves, weakening it. Threats came from other directions also. Some tribes invaded from the east. From the north came the dreaded Vikings.

The Vikings During the 800s and 900s, the Vikings caused terror throughout Europe. They came from what are now the countries of Denmark, Norway, and Sweden looking for loot. The Vikings were not only skilled sailors and fierce warriors who raided towns along the coasts, but also farmers and traders. Eventually the Vikings settled in England, Ireland, and other parts of Europe. A large Viking settlement in northwestern France gave that region its name. It is called Normandy, from the French word for "Northmen." The Vikings there came to be known as Normans.

✓ READING CHECK: (Human Systems) What groups of people invaded western Europe during the Early Middle Ages? Angles, Saxons, Franks, Muslims, Vikings

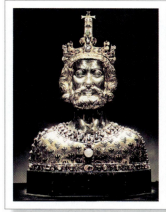

▲ Charlemagne built libraries and supported the collection and copying of Roman literature. This gold statue of him dates from more than 500 years after his death.

Life in the Middle Ages

Within 100 years of Charlemagne's death, the central government he had put in place was gone. In the absence of a strong central government, European society organized under a system based on relationships.

Feudalism By the 900s, most of Europe was governed by local leaders under a system known as **feudalism**. It was a way of organizing and governing people based on land and service. In most feudal societies, the king, who owned all the land in his kingdom, granted some lands to **nobles**—people who were born into wealthy, powerful families. The grant of land was called a **fief**. Nobles had complete power over their land—power to collect taxes, enforce laws, and maintain armies. In return for land, they became **vassals** of the king. This means that they promised to serve the king, especially in battle. A noble could, in turn, grant fiefs to lesser nobles. In so doing, that noble would become a lord, and the lesser nobles would become his vassals. A vassal owed service—especially military service—to his lord.

This stained glass window shows a lord, on the left, and his vassals. ▼

CHAPTER 13, Section 5

DAILY LIFE

Inheriting a Fief The most important nobles received large fiefs directly from the king. These nobles in turn divided their land and granted fiefs to lesser nobles. This division continued down to the level of the lowest noble, who held a single manor. Originally, the granting of fiefs was repeated whenever a lord or vassal died. Eventually, however, control of the fief became hereditary.

Critical Thinking: How may hereditary control have affected the running of the fief?

Answer: Possible answer: Hereditary control may have given nobles further incentives to take care of their lands so their children could inherit profitable lands, accrue wealth, and build the family's power.

Early History of Europe • 309

TEACH

Teaching Objectives 1–3
ALL LEVELS: (Suggested time: 45 min.) Organize the class into groups—one for each subhead in the section. Tell students to imagine that they are location managers of a movie that will have these topics as background material to a sweeping epic about the adventures, loves, and losses of one family—say, the Bernards of northern France—throughout the Middle Ages. Instruct each group to describe the scene that would be related to its assigned material, including where the scene would be filmed. (For example, the group assigned to the Vikings may describe a raid on a coastal Irish village in which a Bernard hero fights the invaders.) Call on one student from each group to present the group's scene.
ESOL, COOPERATIVE LEARNING, LS **VISUAL-SPATIAL**

Teaching Objective 1
ALL LEVELS: (Suggested time: 45 min.) Use the same basic concept as the Teaching Objectives 1–3 activity, but limit the number of groups and the scope to the Early Middle Ages.
ESOL, COOPERATIVE LEARNING, LS **VISUAL-SPATIAL**

CHAPTER 13, Section 5

USING ILLUSTRATIONS

Medieval "Logos" Draw students' attention to the illustration on this page. Point out the designs on the shields and ask students the questions in the caption.

As early as the 1000s, knights carried personal symbols mounted on banners or shields into battle. In the 1100s it became customary for sons to inherit their father's banners and shields. Later, three-dimensional crests, mostly of animals, were added to the helmets. In time these crests became badges of nobility. By the 1200s, the crest, helmet, and shield had been incorporated into family coats of arms.

Visual Record Answer

swords; helmets, chain mail under tunics; by the colors and designs on their shields

---

Feudalism was a complex system. Its rules varied from kingdom to kingdom. Feudal relationships in France, for example, were not the same as those in Germany or England. In addition, the nature of feudal relationships was constantly changing. Laws that governed a king's or a vassal's behavior one year might not apply just a few years later. It was sometimes very difficult for people to keep track of their feudal obligations.

Nevertheless, powerful lords were the ruling class in Europe for more than 400 years. Some lords were so powerful that the king remained on the throne only with their support. Over time, it became the custom that the owner of a fief would pass his land on to his son. By about 1100, the custom was that the oldest son inherited his father's land. Women had few rights when it came to owning property. If a woman who owned land married, her husband got control of her land.

Knights The most common type of nobleman was the **knight**, or warrior, who received land from a lord in return for military service. Knights lived by a code of behavior called **chivalry**. This code said that a knight had to be brave, fight fairly, be loyal, and keep his word. He had to treat defeated enemies with respect and be polite to women.

Medieval knights usually fought on horseback.
Interpreting the Visual Record What weapons are the knights using? What are they wearing into battle? Since their faces are hidden, how do you think these knights recognized each other?

In battle, a knight wore heavy metal armor and a metal helmet. He carried a sword, a shield, a lance, and other weapons. Knights had plenty of opportunities to fight. In addition to large-scale wars that occurred during the Middle Ages, frequent smaller battles took place between lords who tried to take each other's lands.

The Manorial System As the Roman Empire declined, so did trade. People had to raise more of their own food and supply more of their needs for themselves. Some nobles developed large estates called **manors**. Such manors included large houses, planted fields, woodlands, pastures, and villages. The lord of a manor ruled over peasants called **serfs** who lived on the manor. Serfs had few rights. They had to work the lord's land and give him part of their crops. They couldn't leave the manor without the lord's permission. A manor was usually self-sufficient. Almost everything people needed, including food and clothing, was produced on the manor.

310 • Chapter 13

Teaching Objective 2
LEVEL 1: (Suggested time: 15 min.) Copy the following graphic organizer onto the board, omitting the blue answers. Call on volunteers to fill in the organizer with information about life in the Middle Ages.
ESOL, **LS** **VISUAL-SPATIAL**

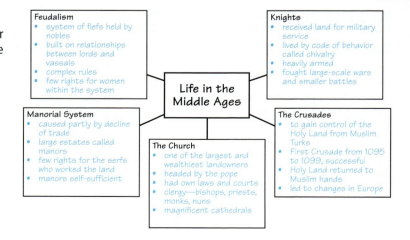

310 Chapter 13

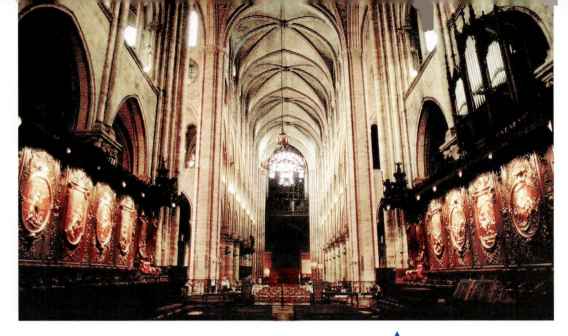

Notre Dame in Paris is one of the most famous of the medieval cathedrals. Its pointed arches are visible along the sides and at the ceiling. The church's ceiling rises 110 feet above the floor. Tall ceilings, pointed arches, and stained glass windows are all features of the architectural style called Gothic.

The Church One of the largest and wealthiest landowners during the Middle Ages was the Christian Church. Headed by the pope, the church was enormously powerful, with its own laws and courts.

Officials of the church were known as the **clergy**. Beneath the pope were bishops and priests. Other members of the clergy were monks, who lived in monasteries, and nuns, who lived in convents. While most ordinary people could not read or write, many members of the clergy were educated. In monasteries, monks prayed, studied, and copied ancient books.

Eventually, Europeans built huge churches, called **cathedrals**. Many of these magnificent buildings still stand. They feature tall ceilings, pointed arches, and glorious stained glass windows.

The Crusades In the late 1000s, the pope asked the lords of Europe to join in a great war against the Muslim Turks, who had gained control of Palestine. Christians called Palestine the Holy Land because it was where Jesus had lived and preached and where Christianity began.

This war turned into a series of battles called the **Crusades**. The First Crusade lasted from 1095 to 1099. Crusaders captured Jerusalem and killed many of the Muslims and Jews who lived there. However, over the next 100 years, the Turks won back the land they had lost. Three more major Crusades claimed countless lives on both sides. Although the Holy Land stayed in Muslim control, the Crusades led to big changes in Europe.

✓ **READING CHECK:** (Human Systems) How did feudalism require that nobles and their vassals depend on each other? **Each received something important from the other.**

CHAPTER 13, Section 5

National Geography Standard 9

The Crusades and Cultural Diffusion The Crusades brought Europeans and their customs to the Holy Land. After the capture of Jerusalem, the crusaders set up four small states. They introduced feudalism and subdivided their newly won land among feudal lords.

The European occupiers were affected as well. Christians and Muslims lived alongside each other. Often this nearness led to mutual respect. Some Europeans adopted Eastern customs and wore Eastern clothes and ate Eastern foods.

Activity: Ask students to imagine they are Europeans living in one of the crusader states. Have them write letters to family members back home comparing and contrasting life in the Holy Land with life in Europe.

Teaching Objectives 2–3

LEVEL 2: (Suggested time: 45 min.) Organize the class into groups. Ask each group to write a skit in which group members play the parts of figures in medieval society, such as kings, nobles, knights, and serfs. Tell students that their skits should demonstrate the ways in which various members of society interacted with one another. Call on volunteers to perform their skits for the class. **COOPERATIVE LEARNING**

LEVEL 3: (Suggested time: 10 min.) Lead a discussion about whether students would like to have lived during the Middle Ages. Ask students to support their statements with facts from the section. **LS INTERPERSONAL**

CHAPTER 13, Section 5

FOOD FESTIVAL

Beautiful, Bountiful Barley
Barley is one of the world's oldest grain crops. It was grown in ancient times and was a staple in both Roman and Greek diets. Much of Europe depended through the 1500s on barley for making bread. Today, pearl barley, which has had its hull and outer bran removed, is an ingredient in soups and porridges. It is also ground into flour for flat breads.

Have students find recipes for barley soup or barley bread. Ask students to bring their dishes to class to sample. To create a complete but humble Roman meal, you may want to provide figs, dates, or raisins.

Visual Record Answer
stocking, shoes, shirts, among other items

The High Middle Ages

The Crusades brought about major economic and political changes in Europe. The period following the Crusades to about 1500 is known as the High Middle Ages.

Stronger Nations Many lords sold their lands to raise money so they could join the Crusades. Without land, they had no power. In addition, many lords died in the Crusades. With fewer powerful lords, kings grew stronger. By the end of the Middle Ages, England, France, and Spain had become powerful nations. Strong central governments and the decline of the nobility's power helped to bring about the end of feudalism in Europe.

In 1066 William, Duke of Normandy, claimed the English throne. He landed in England, defeated the Anglo-Saxon army, and was crowned King William I of England. He became known as William the Conqueror. William built a strong central government in England. When William's descendant John took the throne, however, he pushed the nobles too far by raising taxes.

In 1215, a group of nobles forced King John to sign Magna Carta, one of the most important documents in English history. Magna Carta stated that the king could not collect new taxes without the consent of the Great Council, a body of nobles and church leaders. In addition, the king couldn't take property without paying for it. Any noble accused of a crime had the right to a trial by jury. The most important provision of Magna Carta was that the law, not the king, is the supreme power in England. The king had to obey the law. The Great Council was the forerunner of Parliament, which governs Great Britain today.

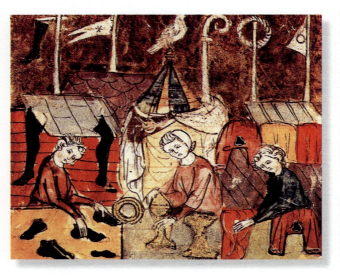

As trade revived, merchants sold their goods at fairs.
Interpreting the Visual Record What are these merchants selling?

The Growth of Trade and Cities The Crusades increased Europeans' demand for Asian dyes, medicines, silks, and spices. They also wanted lemons, apricots, melons, rice, and sugar from Asia. In exchange, Europeans traded timber, leather, wine, glassware, and wool. Increased trade led to the growth of manufacturing and banking. A **middle class** of merchants and craftsmen arose between the nobility and the peasants. The late medieval economy formed the basis for our modern economic system.

As Europe's economy got stronger, cities grew. Centers for trade and industry, cities attracted merchants and craftsmen as well as peasants, who hoped to have better lives and more freedom. Both the manorial system and the feudal system began to fall apart.

312 • Chapter 13

Teaching Objective 3

ALL LEVELS: Have students create a time line of the High Middle Ages along the bottom of a strip of butcher paper and, above the time line, to create a mural illustrating the era's events, important people, and concepts. You could also expand this activity to include the entire section.
ESOL, **LS** VISUAL-SPATIAL

▶**ASSIGNMENT:** Have students write paragraphs in which they summarize the elements of modern life that were evident during the Middle Ages.

During the Middle Ages, cities were crowded and dirty. When disease struck, it spread rapidly. In 1347, a horrible disease called the Black Death swept through Europe. Estimates of the death toll vary, but some historians say that up to a third of Europe's people died. Even this disaster, however, had some positive results. With the decrease in population came a labor shortage. As a result, people could demand higher wages for their work.

Education and Literature Most people could not read or write. As cities grew and trade increased, so did the demand and need for education. Between the late 1000s and the late 1200s, several major universities developed in England, France, and Italy. By the end of the 1400s, many more universities had opened throughout Europe.

Most people during the Middle Ages didn't speak, read, or write Latin, the language of the Roman Catholic Church. They spoke **vernacular** languages—everyday speech that varied from place to place. Writers such as Dante Alighieri in Italy and Geoffrey Chaucer in England wrote literature in vernacular languages. Dante is best known for *The Divine Comedy*. Chaucer's most famous work is *The Canterbury Tales*. Because these works were so popular, the languages in which they were written became the standard forms of Italian and English.

The End of the Middle Ages The decline of feudalism and the manorial system, the growth of stronger central governments, the growth of cities, and a renewed interest in education brought an end to the Middle Ages. In addition, stronger kings challenged the power of the Church. By the end of the 1400s, a new age had begun.

✓ **READING CHECK:** (Human Systems) How did the Black Death affect Europe? *killed up to a third of the population, allowed workers to demand higher wages*

This illustration decorates a page from "The Cook's Tale," one of Chaucer's stories about pilgrims on their way to Canterbury Cathedral.

Section Review 5

Define or identify: medieval, Franks, Charlemagne, Vikings, feudalism, nobles, fief, vassals, knight, chivalry, manors, serfs, clergy, cathedrals, Crusades, Magna Carta, middle class, vernacular, Geoffrey Chaucer

Reading for the Main Idea

1. (Human Systems) Why is the time between the A.D. 400s and about 1500 called the Middle Ages?
2. (Human Systems) How did feudalism work? How did the manorial system work?
3. (Human Systems) What role did the Christian Church play in medieval European society?

Critical Thinking

4. **Evaluating** Why is Magna Carta considered one of the most important documents in English history?

Organizing What You Know

5. **Understanding Cause and Effect** Copy the following graphic organizer. Use it to describe the results of the Crusades.

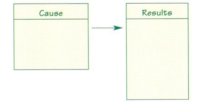

Homework Practice Online
Keyword: SJ5 HP13

Early History of Europe • 313

Section 5 Review

Answers to Section 5 Review

Define or identify For definitions and identifications, see the glossary and index.

Reading for the Main Idea

1. because it falls between the ancient and modern worlds
2. feudalism—King granted land (fief) to nobles, nobles had power over their land, nobles were vassals of the king and owed him service, nobles could grant fiefs to lesser nobles. manorial system—Manors included houses, fields, woodlands, pastures, villages; lord ruled over serfs, who worked land; manors were self-sufficient. (NGS 13)
3. one of the largest and wealthiest landowners, very powerful

Critical Thinking

4. because it established the idea that the law, not the king, is the supreme power in England

Organizing What You Know

5. cause—Muslim Turks had gained control of the Holy Land; results—Crusades fought, Jerusalem captured, Holy Land lost again to Muslims, stronger central governments, increased demand for Asian products

---

CLOSE

Ask students if they know the nursery rhyme "Ring around the Rosy." Point out that some historians think that it refers to the Black Death and reddish rings that sometimes appeared on a plague victim's skin.

REVIEW, ASSESS, RETEACH

Have students complete the Section Review. Then have students review the section material by writing phrases describing the significance of key terms, people, and events. Then have students complete Daily Quiz 13.5.

Have students complete Main Idea Activity S5. Then organize the class into groups. Tell each group to create a two-column chart with the headings "Early Middle Ages" and "High Middle Ages." Have students fill in the space beneath each heading with information about the period. **ESOL, COOPERATIVE LEARNING**

EXTEND

Have interested students conduct research on the art, music, or literature of the Middle Ages. Encourage students to choose a specific topic to research, such as stained glass windows or medieval music. **BLOCK SCHEDULING**

CHAPTER 13 REVIEW

Chapter 13 Review and Practice

Define and Identify
For definitions and identifications, see the glossary and index.

Identify each of the following:

1. polis
2. democracy
3. league
4. Alexander the Great
5. Socrates
6. republic
7. patricians
8. dictator
9. Julius Caesar
10. Pax Romana
11. medieval
12. Charlemagne
13. feudalism
14. chivalry
15. middle class

Review the Main Ideas

16. What were some features of the Minoan and Mycenaean civilizations?
17. How has Athens influenced modern government leaders?
18. What was the most important group in Spartan society?
19. What was life like for women in Athens?
20. What was the Delian League?
21. In what way were the Gracchi's deaths a turning point in Roman history?
22. How did the government of the Roman Empire differ from the government of the Roman Republic?
23. How did the Romans respond to the teachings of Jesus?
24. What were some of Rome's contributions to other cultures?
25. What was the life of serfs like?
26. Why did the nobles demand that King John sign Magna Carta?
27. How did the Black Death affect workers?

Think Critically

28. **Summarizing** How did the governments of Greek city-states change over time?
29. **Making Predictions** How may history have been different if Athens had dealt more fairly with the members of the Delian League?
30. **Summarizing** What led to the decline of the Roman Empire?
31. **Analyzing Information** How did Roman engineering contribute to the daily lives of both rich and poor Romans?
32. **Evaluating** How did the Crusades change life in Europe?

Map Activity

33. Identify the places marked on the map.
    - Aegean Sea
    - Crete
    - Troy
    - Athens
    - Sparta
    - Peloponnese
    - Macedon

Answers

Review the Main Ideas

16. Minoan—traded with ports as far away as Egypt and Palestine, traded wood and olive oil, built huge palaces with advanced features, created colorful paintings, practiced bull-leaping, may have declined about 1500 B.C. because of volcanic eruption and floods; Mycenaeans—warlike, controlled mainland 1600 B.C. to 1200 B.C., raided and traded across the Mediterranean, attacked rival city of Troy, declined after Trojan War.
17. by being the first civilization to practice democracy
18. the army
19. had few rights, received almost no education besides what they got at home, learned mostly household tasks like sewing
20. an alliance for protection of Greek city-states that was eventually dominated by Athens
21. From that time on, violence became a major political tool.
22. Roman Empire—all power in emperor's hands; Roman Republic—allowed participation by aristocrats and common people (NGS 13)
23. arrested Jesus and crucified him
24. advances in city planning, water and sewer systems, paved roads, livestock breeding, aqueducts, arches, concrete, Latin alphabet and language, literature, government, law
25. very hard work, had few rights, couldn't leave the manor without the lord's permission, had to give the lord part of their crops
26. They wanted to limit the king's power by requiring that he not raise taxes without the Great Council's consent, take property without paying for it, or deny the right to trial by jury. Magna Carta placed the king under the law.
27. Because there was a labor shortage, people could demand higher wages for their work.

Think Critically

28. small city-states ruled by warriors, city-states became aristocracies, tyrants took over, democracy developed in some places
29. The Peloponnesian War may not have happened, and Athenian civilization—including democracy—may have spread widely. (NGS 13)
30. rapid and often violent turnover of emperors, army's loyalty for sale, dishonest leaders, defense neglected, invaders crossing the borders, drain on empire's resources, too much money going toward entertainment, increased crime, high taxes
31. They built huge structures that housed activities that everyone could participate in, such as public baths, and improved water supplies, sewer systems, and roads—facilities that could help rich and poor Romans.
32. Central governments under kings grew stronger, feudalism declined, and Europeans' demand for Asian dyes, medicines, silks, spices, and foods increased. As a result, trade increased and towns grew.

Writing Activity

The *Iliad*, a long poem written by the Greek poet Homer, tells the story of a terrible war—the Trojan War. Write a short poem that tells the story of another event from ancient or medieval history. Your poem doesn't have to rhyme. Use adjectives and verbs that help paint a vivid picture of the events.

internet connect

Internet Activity: go.hrw.com
KEYWORD: SJ5 GT13

Choose a topic to explore about the early history of Europe:
- Report on Minoan civilization.
- Create a newspaper article about ancient Athens.
- Write a report on daily life in the Middle Ages.

Social Studies Skills Practice

Interpreting Maps

You have read how the Black Death spread rapidly throughout Europe. Study the map below. Use it and this unit's atlas to answer the questions.

1. Where and when did the Black Death enter Europe?
2. How many years did it take the disease to spread to the rest of Europe?
3. What area of Europe was last to fall victim to the Black Death?
4. What geographical features on the map seem to have allowed the rapid spread of the disease?

Analyzing Primary Sources

Read the following quote from *The Dialogue between Master & Disciple: On Laborers, c. 1000*. The dialogue was written by an anonymous medieval author. Then answer the questions.

"O my lord, I work very hard: I go out at dawn, driving the cattle to the field, and I yoke them to the plow. Nor is the weather so bad in winter that I dare to stay at home, for fear of my lord: but when the oxen are yoked . . . to the plow, I must plow one whole field a day, or more."

1. Based on your knowledge of the Middle Ages, who is probably speaking?
2. What are the speaker's responsibilities?
3. How does the speaker see his life?
4. Whom does the speaker fear?

Early History of Europe • 315

CHAPTER 13 REVIEW

Map Activity
33. **A.** Crete
    B. Athens
    C. Aegean Sea
    D. Sparta
    E. Peloponnese
    F. Macedon
    G. Troy

Writing Activity
Poems will vary widely, but the information they contain should be consistent with text or outside resource material. Students' adjectives, verbs, and other language should be appropriate for the topic. Use Rubric 26, Poems and Songs, to evaluate student work.

Interpreting Maps
1. Sicily, 1347
2. five years
3. far northeast
4. Black Sea, Mediterranean Sea

Analyzing Primary Sources
1. a serf
2. drive cattle to the field, yoke them to the plow, plow the fields
3. as a life of hard work, drudgery, and fear
4. his lord; he can't stay home even in the worst winter weather because of fear of his lord

---

REVIEW AND ASSESSMENT RESOURCES

Reproducible
- Readings in World Geography, History, and Culture, Reading 29
- Critical Thinking Activity 13
- Vocabulary Activity 13

Technology
- Chapter 13 Test Generator (on the One-Stop Planner)
- HRW Go site
- Audio CD Program, Chapter 13

Reinforcement, Review, and Assessment
- Chapter 13 Review and Practice
- Chapter Summaries and Review
- Chapter 13 Test
- Unit 4 Test
- Chapter 13 Test for English Language Learners and Special-Needs Students
- Unit 4 Test for English Language Learners and Special-Needs Students

internet connect

GO TO: go.hrw.com
KEYWORD: SJ5 Teacher
FOR: a guide to using the Internet in your classroom

CHAPTER 14
Europe in Transition
Chapter Resource Manager

Objectives	Pacing Guide	Reproducible Resources
SECTION 1 **The Renaissance and Reformation** (pp. 317–322) 1. Identify the main interests of Renaissance scholars. 2. Clarify how the arts changed during the Renaissance. 3. Explain how people's lives changed during the Renaissance. 4. Describe changes that occurred during the Reformation and Counter-Reformation.	**Regular** 2 days *Lecture Notes, Section 1* **Block Scheduling** 1 day *Block Scheduling Handbook, Chapter 14*	**RS** Know It Notes S1 **RS** Graphic Organizer 14 **SM** Map Activity 14 **ELL** Main Idea Activity S1
SECTION 2 **Exploration and Conquest** (pp. 323–329) 1. Provide details about the Scientific Revolution. 2. Explain what happened during the Age of Exploration. 3. Analyze how the English monarchy was different from others in Europe. 4. Examine the relationship between England and its colonies.	**Regular** 1 day *Lecture Notes, Section 2* **Block Scheduling** .5 day *Block Scheduling Handbook, Chapter 14*	**RS** Know It Notes S2 **ELL** Main Idea Activity S2
SECTION 3 **Enlightenment and Revolution** (pp. 330–336) 1. Describe the new ideas that the Enlightenment introduced. 2. Analyze how the French Revolution changed France. 3. Explain how Napoleón changed Europe.	**Regular** 2 days *Lecture Notes, Section 3* **Block Scheduling** 1 day *Block Scheduling Handbook, Chapter 14*	**RS** Know It Notes S3 **E** Biography Activity: John Locke **ELL** Main Idea Activity S3
SECTION 4 **Industrial Revolution and Reform** (pp. 337–343) 1. Trace how the Industrial Revolution began. 2. Explain which developments and inventions helped industry grow. 3. Analyze how the Industrial Revolution spread. 4. Examine how the Industrial Revolution affected daily life in Europe.	**Regular** 2 days *Lecture Notes, Section 4* **Block Scheduling** 1.5 days *Block Scheduling Handbook, Chapter 14*	**RS** Know It Notes S4 **E** Biography Activity: Emmeline Pankhurst **E** Readings in World Geography, History, and Culture: Reading 35 **SM** Map Activity 14 **ELL** Main Idea Activity S4

Chapter Resource Key

- **RS** Reading Support
- **IC** Interdisciplinary Connections
- **E** Enrichment
- **SM** Skills Mastery
- **A** Assessment
- **REV** Review
- **ELL** Reinforcement and English Language Learners and English for Speakers of Other Languages (ESOL)
- Transparencies
- CD–ROM
- Music
- Video
- Internet
- Holt Presentation Maker Using Microsoft® PowerPoint®

One-Stop Planner CD–ROM

See the *One-Stop Planner* for a complete list of additional resources for students and teachers.

One-Stop Planner CD–ROM

It's easy to plan lessons, select resources, and print out materials for your students when you use the *One-Stop Planner CD–ROM with Test Generator.*

Technology Resources

- One-Stop Planner CD-ROM, Lesson 14.1
- *ARGWorld* CD–ROM
- Homework Practice Online
- HRW Go Site

- One-Stop Planner CD-ROM, Lesson 14.2
- *ARGWorld* CD–ROM
- Homework Practice Online
- HRW Go site

- One-Stop Planner CD-ROM, Lesson 14.3
- Geography and Cultures Visual Resource 49, 51, 54, 55
- *ARGWorld* CD–ROM
- Homework Practice Online
- HRW Go site

- One-Stop Planner CD-ROM, Lesson 14.4
- Geography and Cultures Visual Resources 49, 51, 52, 54, 55
- *ARGWorld* CD–ROM
- Homework Practice Online
- HRW Go site

Review, Reinforcement, and Assessment Resources

ELL	Main Idea Activity S1
REV	Section 1 Review
A	Daily Quiz 14.1
REV	Chapter Summaries and Review
ELL	English Audio Summary 14.1
ELL	Spanish Audio Summary 14.1

ELL	Main Idea Activity S2
REV	Section 2 Review
A	Daily Quiz 14.2
REV	Chapter Summaries and Review
ELL	English Audio Summary 14.2
ELL	Spanish Audio Summary 14.2

ELL	Main Idea Activity S3
REV	Section 3 Review
A	Daily Quiz 14.3
REV	Chapter Summaries and Review
ELL	English Audio Summary 14.3
ELL	Spanish Audio Summary 14.3

ELL	Main Idea Activity S4
REV	Section 4 Review
A	Daily Quiz 14.4
REV	Chapter Summaries and Review
ELL	English Audio Summary 14.4
ELL	Spanish Audio Summary 14.4

internet connect

HRW ONLINE RESOURCES

GO TO: go.hrw.com
Then type in a keyword.

TEACHER HOMEPAGE
KEYWORD: **SJ5 TEACHER**

CHAPTER INTERNET ACTIVITIES
KEYWORD: **SJ5 GT14**

Choose an activity to:
- create a biography of a Renaissance artist or writer.
- learn more about an explorer described in this chapter.
- write a report on the Reign of Terror.

CHAPTER ENRICHMENT LINKS
KEYWORD: **SJ5 CH14**

CHAPTER MAPS
KEYWORDS: **SJ5 MAPS14**

ONLINE ASSESSMENT
Homework Practice
  KEYWORD: **SJ5 HP14**
Standardized Test Prep Online
  KEYWORD: **SJ5 STP14**
Rubrics
  KEYWORD: **SS Rubrics**

COUNTRY INFORMATION
KEYWORD: **SJ5 Almanac**

CONTENT UPDATES
KEYWORD: **SS Contents Updates**

HOLT PRESENTATION MAKER
KEYWORD: **SJ5 PPT14**

ONLINE READING SUPPORT
KEYWORD: **SS Strategies**

CURRENT EVENTS
KEYWORD: **SS Current Events**

Meeting Individual Needs

Ability Levels

Level 1 Basic-level activities designed for all students encountering new material

Level 2 Intermediate-level activities designed for average students

Level 3 Challenging activities designed for honors and gifted-and-talented students

ESOL Activities that address the needs of students with Limited English Proficiency

Chapter Review and Assessment

E	Readings in World Geography, History, and Culture 35
SM	Critical Thinking Activity 14
REV	Chapter 14 Review and Practice
REV	Chapter Summaries and Review
ELL	Vocabulary Activity 14
A	Chapter 14 Test
A	Chapter 14 Test Generator (on the One-Stop Planner)
	Audio CD Program, Chapter 14
A	Chapter 14 Test for English Language Learners and Special-Needs Students
	HRW Go site

315B

Chapter 14

Europe in Transition
Previewing Chapter Resources

Holt Online Learning

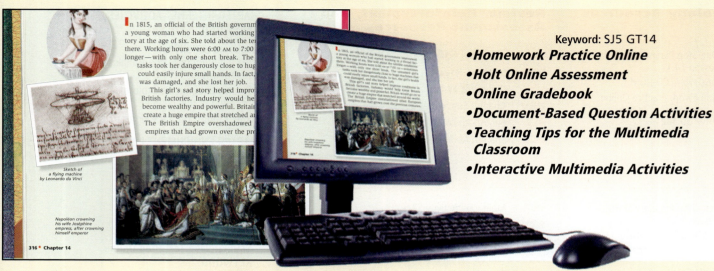

Keyword: SJ5 GT14

- Homework Practice Online
- Holt Online Assessment
- Online Gradebook
- Document-Based Question Activities
- Teaching Tips for the Multimedia Classroom
- Interactive Multimedia Activities

Differentiating Instruction

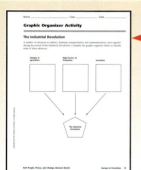

Reading and Writing Support
- Graphic Organizer Activity
- Vocabulary Activity
- Chapter Summaries and Review
- Know-It Notes S1–4
- Audio CD

Active Learning
- Block Scheduling Handbook
- Cultures of the World Activity
- Interdisciplinary Activity: Visual Time Line of the Arts
- Map Activity

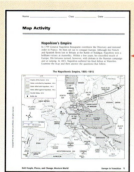

Primary Sources and Advanced Learners
- Map Activity: Napoleon's Empire

Assessment Program
- Daily Quizzes S1–4
- Chapter Test
- Chapter Test for English Language Learners and Special-Needs Students

Spanish and ESOL
- Vocabulary Activity
- Main Idea Activities for English Language Learners and Special-Needs Students
- Chapter Summaries and Review
- Spanish Audio Summary
- Know-It Notes S1–4
- Chapter Test for English Language Learners and Special-Needs Students

Special Education Modifications
Your I.D.E.A. Works! CD-ROM will provide modified versions of the following teaching materials:
- Know It Notes S1–4
- Vocabulary Activity
- Main Idea Activities S1–4
- Daily Quizzes S1–4
- Chapter 14 Test
- Flash cards of chapter vocabulary terms

315C

Teacher Resources

Books for Teachers

Hartt, Frederick. *History of Italian Renaissance Art: Painting, Sculpture, Architecture.* Prentice Hall Press, 2002.

MacCulloch, Diarmaid. *The Reformation: A History.* Viking Press, 2004.

Doyle, William. *The French Revolution: A Very Short Introduction.* Oxford Press, 2001.

Worth, Martin. *Sweat and Inspiration: Pioneers of the Industrial Age.* Sutton Publishing, 2001.

Books for Students

Grant, Neil. *Atlas of the Renaissance World.* Peter Bedrick Books, 2001. Provides a historical overview of Renaissance daily life, trade, art, music, and literature in different regions of Europe.

Romei, Francesca. *Leonardo da Vinci: Artist, Inventor, and Scientist of the Renaissance.* Peter Bedrick Books, 2001. Illustrations and text explain how da Vinci created inventions and works of art.

McGowen, Tom. *Robespierre and the French Revolution in World History.* Enslow Publishers, 2000. Covers the storming of the Bastille through the rise of Napoleon.

Smith, Nigel. *The Industrial Revolution.* Raintree/Steck-Vaughn, 2003.

Multimedia Materials

The Medici, Godfathers of the Renaissance. Video, PBS.

Biography: Michelangelo. Video, A & E Entertainment.

Christopher Columbus: The Discovery of the New World. Video, Robin Williams.

Napoleon. Video, PBS.

Videos and CDs

Videos
- CNN Presents World Cultures: Yesterday and Today, Segment 17 *The New Globe Theater;* Segment 18 *A Key to the Bastille*

CDs
- ARG World
- I.D.E.A. Works! CD–ROM

Holt Researcher
http://researcher.hrw.com
- *Exploration and Expansion*
- *The Renaissance and Reformation*
- *Europe on the Eve of the French Revolution*
- *European Industrialization*
- *Life in the Industrial Age*

Transparency Packages

Geography and Cultures Visual Resources Transparencies
49 *Southern Europe: Physical-Political*
51 *West-Central Europe: Physical-Political*
52 *The Gare Saint-Lazare, Paris*
54 *Northern Europe: Physical-Political*
55 *Eastern Europe: Physical-Political*

Map Activities Transparency Napoleon's Empire

CHAPTER 14

WHY IT MATTERS

You may want to share with your students the following reasons for learning about these periods of change:

- Some challenges facing governments today are similar to those faced in the Renaissance and Reformation.
- Certain patterns of change that began in this period, such as the shift of population from rural areas to urban, have continued to the present.
- Works of art and literature from these periods are still enjoyed today.
- These times represent important eras in our own country's history as well.

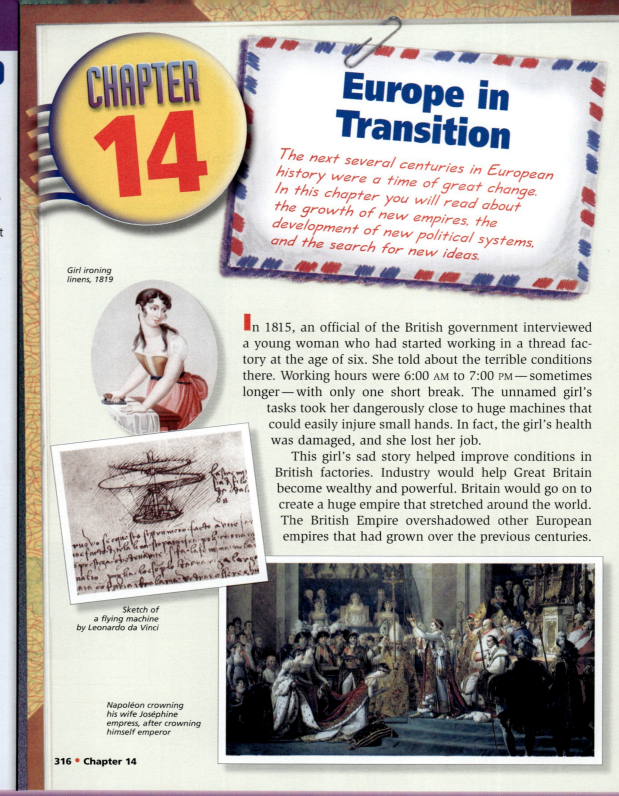

CHAPTER 14

Europe in Transition

The next several centuries in European history were a time of great change. In this chapter you will read about the growth of new empires, the development of new political systems, and the search for new ideas.

Girl ironing linens, 1819

In 1815, an official of the British government interviewed a young woman who had started working in a thread factory at the age of six. She told about the terrible conditions there. Working hours were 6:00 AM to 7:00 PM—sometimes longer—with only one short break. The unnamed girl's tasks took her dangerously close to huge machines that could easily injure small hands. In fact, the girl's health was damaged, and she lost her job.

This girl's sad story helped improve conditions in British factories. Industry would help Great Britain become wealthy and powerful. Britain would go on to create a huge empire that stretched around the world. The British Empire overshadowed other European empires that had grown over the previous centuries.

Sketch of a flying machine by Leonardo da Vinci

Napoléon crowning his wife Joséphine empress, after crowning himself emperor

316 • Chapter 14

CHAPTER PROJECT

Have students build dioramas that show memorable events from the Renaissance, Reformation, Scientific Revolution, Age of Exploration, French Revolution, or Industrial Revolution. Ask each student to write a short description of the scene he or she has depicted. Place these descriptions and photos of the dioramas in student portfolios.

STARTING THE CHAPTER

Ask students to suggest reasons why people travel today. (Possible answers: for pleasure, business, religious purposes, or to explore a new place) Tell students that throughout history people have had similar reasons for travel—for trade, on government business, or to explore new lands in order to gain political and economic power. Point out that while all of these people were moving about, changes were happening at home. Students will learn more about how some of these changes affected Europe.

316 Chapter 14

Section 1: The Renaissance and Reformation

Read to Discover
1. What were the main interests of Renaissance scholars?
2. How did the arts change during the Renaissance?
3. How did people's lives change during the Renaissance?
4. What changes took place during the Reformation and Counter-Reformation?

Vocabulary
Renaissance
humanists
Reformation
Protestants
Counter-Reformation

Places
Rome
Florence

People
Leonardo da Vinci
Michelangelo
William Shakespeare
Martin Luther
John Calvin
Henry VIII

Reading Strategy
FOLDNOTES: TWO-PANEL FLIP CHART Create the FoldNote titled **Two-Panel Flip Chart** in the Appendix. On one flap write Renaissance. Write Reformation on the other flap. As you read this section, write beneath the flaps details you learn about each topic.

New Interests and New Ideas

The Crusades and trade in distant lands caused great changes in Europe. During their travels, traders and Crusaders discovered scholars who had studied and preserved Greek and Roman learning. While trading in Southwest Asia and Africa, people learned about achievements in science and medicine. Such discoveries encouraged more curiosity. During the 1300s, this new creative spirit developed and sparked a movement known as the **Renaissance** (re-nuh-SAHNS). This term comes from the French word for "rebirth." The Renaissance brought fresh interest in exploring the achievements of the ancient world, its ideas, and its art.

Beginning of the Renaissance The Renaissance started in Italy. Italian cities such as Florence and Venice had become rich through industry and trade. Among the population was a powerful middle class. Many members of this class were wealthy and well-educated. They had many interests beside their work. Many studied ancient history, the arts, and education. They used their fortunes to support painters, sculptors, and architects, and to encourage learning. Scholars revived the learning of ancient Greece and Rome. Enthusiasm for art and literature increased. Over time the ideas of the Renaissance spread from Italy into other parts of Europe.

The Humanities As a result of increased interest in ancient Greece and Rome, scholars encouraged the study of subjects that had been taught in ancient Greek and Roman schools. These subjects, including history, poetry, and grammar, are called the humanities.

▲ The powerful Medici family ruled Florence for most of the Renaissance. Banker Cosimo de' Medici, seen here, was a great supporter of the arts.

Europe in Transition • 317

Section 1

Objectives
1. Identify the main interests of Renaissance scholars.
2. Clarify how the arts changed during the Renaissance.
3. Explain how people's lives changed during the Renaissance.
4. Describe changes that occurred during the Reformation and Counter-Reformation.

Focus

Bellringer
Copy the following instructions onto the chalkboard: *Look at the artwork from the Middle Ages in the previous chapter. Then look at the artwork from the Renaissance in this section. How are the styles different?* Discuss responses. Explain that art in the Renaissance became more realistic. Students will learn more about the Renaissance and the period that followed it, the Reformation, in this section.

Building Vocabulary
Write the vocabulary terms on the chalkboard. Underline *human* in **humanists**. Point out that humanist thinkers in the Renaissance stressed the importance of human reason. Then underline *protest* and *reform* in **Protestant** and **Reformation**. Explain that the Protestants of the Reformation protested against certain teachings and wanted to reform the Catholic Church. Point out that the *counter-* in **Counter-Reformation** means "against." Tell students that this movement was staged against the effects of the Reformation.

Europe in Transition **317**

CHAPTER 14, Section 1

USING ILLUSTRATIONS

Breughel and Renaissance Ideas Have students examine the painting by Peter Breughel on this page. Ask them why the subject matter of the painting may be considered unusual. (Possible answer: It was unusual at the time for a painter to focus on children at play.) Also ask how the painting reflects Renaissance ideas. (It shows normal people in their daily lives; it is realistic, it shows people enjoying themselves.)

Activity: Have students find other examples of paintings by Breughel or other Renaissance artists. Ask them to write short descriptions of the works and how they reflect Renaissance ideas. Have students display the paintings and read their descriptions to the class.

Visual Record Answer ▶

somersaults, tag, tug-of-war, hanging from a crossbar, leap-frog

---

▲ Isabella d'Este, a very intelligent and powerful member of a wealthy Italian noble family, was a leading figure of the Renaissance. She was educated in languages and poetry. She supported the arts and hired noted architects to design parts of her palace.

Humanists, the people who studied these subjects, were practical. They wanted to learn more about the world and how things worked. Reading ancient texts helped them recover knowledge that had been forgotten or even lost. They believed that people should support the arts. They also thought that education was the only way to become a well-rounded person. People were urged to focus on what they could achieve in this life.

✓ **READING CHECK:** (Cause and Effect) How did the Renaissance begin? Through trade people became curious about the world; wealthy and well-educated middle class supported painters, sculptors, education.

The Creative Spirit

During the Renaissance, interest in painting, sculpture, architecture, and writing was renewed. Inspired by Greek and Roman works, artists produced some of the world's greatest masterpieces for private buyers as well as for churches and other public places.

Art Leonardo da Vinci and Michelangelo truly represented the Renaissance. Leonardo achieved the Renaissance ideal of excelling in many things. He was not only a painter but also an architect, engineer, sculptor, and scientist. He sketched plants and animals. He made detailed drawings of a flying machine and a submarine. He used mathematics to organize space in his paintings and knowledge about the human body to make figures more realistic. Michelangelo was not only a brilliant sculptor, but also an accomplished painter, musician, poet, and architect.

Northern European merchants carried Italian paintings home, and painters went from northern Europe to study with Italian masters. In time, Renaissance ideas spread into northern and western Europe.

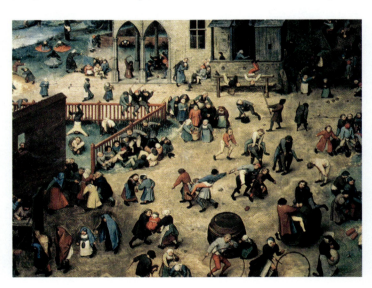

▶ Pieter Brueghel was a Renaissance artist of northern Europe. This painting by Brueghel shows children's games in the 1500s. Many Renaissance painters chose to focus their attention on daily life.

Interpreting the Visual Record What activities do you see that children still do today?

318 • Chapter 14

TEACH

Teaching Objective 1

LEVEL 1: (Suggested time: 10 min.) Copy the following graphic organizer onto the chalkboard. Use it to lead a discussion about Renaissance attitudes. Point out that during the Middle Ages, in general, people were very much focused on life after death. In contrast, during the Renaissance, people became more focused on life on Earth. **ESOL,** LS **VISUAL-SPATIAL**

```
        Middle Ages
       life after death

         Renaissance
         life on Earth
```

ALL LEVELS: (Suggested time: 15 min.) Write the following questions on the chalkboard: *What events and discoveries sparked the Renaissance? What subjects were scholars interested in during this period?* Tell students to write down their responses. Then call on volunteers to share their answers and discuss them in class. **ESOL,** LS **INTERPERSONAL**

318 Chapter 14

Connecting to Technology

The Printing Press

During the Middle Ages books were written and copied by hand. It took a long time and great expense to produce a book. A German inventor, Johannes Gutenberg, developed a printing press in the 1400s. It could print much faster than a human could write. Gutenberg used his printing press to print copies of the Bible. This began the era of the printed book, which had a huge impact on the world of learning. Books printed on the printing press helped to spread the ideas of the Renaissance, and later of the Reformation.

Understanding What You Read
1. How was the printing press an improvement over the old ways of making books?
2. Why do you think the printing press helped to spread ideas?

CHAPTER 14, Section 1

Across the Curriculum
LITERATURE
Thomas More's *Utopia* One important Renaissance figure was the English writer Thomas More. In 1516 More published *Utopia*, a book that became very popular throughout Europe. In the book, More criticized corrupt and harsh governments in Europe and inequality in European society. He imagined a world in which all male citizens were equal and everyone worked to support society. As a result of More's book, the word *Utopia* has come to mean "an ideal place or society."

Activity: Have students conduct research on great writers or thinkers of the Renaissance. Have each student create a collector's card (much like a baseball card) with a picture, short biography, and list of the person's achievements.

Writing Writers of the time expressed the attitudes of the Renaissance. Popular literature was written in the vernacular, the people's language, instead of in Latin. Dutch writer Desiderius Erasmus criticized ignorance and superstition is his work *In Praise of Folly*. In *Gargantua*, French writer François Rabelais promoted the study of the arts and sciences. Spanish writer Miguel de Cervantes wrote *Don Quixote* in which he mocked the ideals of the Middle Ages. Italian writers such as Machiavelli and Baldassare Castiglione wrote handbooks of behavior for rulers and nobles.

Of all Renaissance writers, William Shakespeare is probably the most widely known. He was talented at turning popular stories into great drama. His plays and poetry show a deep understanding of human nature. He used the popular English language of his time to skillfully express the thoughts and human feelings of his characters. Shakespeare's subjects and ideas are still valued today.

✓ **READING CHECK:** (Summarizing) What was the Renaissance attitude?
curiosity about world, focus on achievement in this world, involvement in the arts, education important

William Shakespeare wrote such famous plays as *Romeo and Juliet*, *Hamlet*, and *Macbeth*.

Connecting to Technology
Answers
1. Copying by hand took a long time and made books expensive. Printing was much quicker and reduced the costs of books.
2. Printed material can be passed around a wider area and more quickly than word of mouth.

Teaching Objective 2

ALL LEVELS: (Suggested time: 15 min.) Use the Objective 1 graphic organizer to lead a discussion about differences in medieval and Renaissance art. Point out that although the subjects of Renaissance art were often religious, this is partly because churches and church officials were major sponsors of art. That is, they hired artists to create paintings and sculptures to place in churches. So, although the subjects may be religious, still Renaissance art usually looks much more realistic than medieval art. Focus students' attention on the Cosimo de' Medici portrait and that the portrait is probably an accurate depiction of the man's face. You may want to provide more examples from both periods for comparisons.

 ➤**ASSIGNMENT:** Have students use library or Internet resources to find works of art from the Renaissance and to describe how the paintings or sculptures expresses the ideas of the Renaissance.

CHAPTER 14, Section 1

ENVIRONMENT AND SOCIETY

Reforestation during the Renaissance The depopulation caused by the Black Death had major consequences for both the economy and environment of Europe. A shortage of farm workers caused many landowners to stop cultivating some of their land. This resulted in fewer farm products and reduced trade. It also meant that forests that had been cut down to clear fields could grow back again. Across Europe, many fields returned to their natural forested condition.

Discussion: Ask students how reforestation might have been beneficial to Europeans (provided wood for building and heating, created healthier environment). Then lead a discussion about other environmental effects that may result from a shrinking or growing population.

Visual Record Answer

More women were becoming educated and could take over more of the work once reserved for men.

During the Renaissance, more people learned to read and write. This painting shows a couple working in their banking business.
Interpreting the Visual Record What does this painting suggest about the changing role of women during the Renaissance?

The Renaissance and Daily Life

The Renaissance was not only a time of learning, art, and invention. It was also a time of change in people's daily lives. As the manorial system of the Middle Ages fell apart, many peasants left the manors on which they had lived. Because there were fewer people to work the land, many of these peasants could now demand wages for their labor. For the first time, they had money to spend. As Europe's population began to increase again after the Black Death, however, prices rose very quickly. Only wealthy people could afford some goods.

Although they now had more money, most peasants were still poor. Some moved to cities in search of work. Instead of raising their food, they bought it in shops. In the 1500s traders brought to Europe new fruits and vegetables such as beans, lettuce, melons, spinach, and tomatoes. Traders also brought new luxury items such as coffee and tea. As the printing press caught on in Europe, books became more common. More and more people learned how to read. Gradually a new way of life developed, and the quality of life slowly began to change.

✓ **READING CHECK:** *Comparing and Contrasting* In what ways did life in Europe change during the Renaissance? migration to cities; less dependence on farming as a means of support; work for wages; new foods, more varied diets

The city of Florence was the center of the early Renaissance. The large domed building is the Duomo, the cathedral of Florence.

Teaching Objective 3

LEVEL 2: (Suggested time: 45 min.) Organize the class into pairs. One student in each pair should pretend to be a very old person in the year 1500. The other student in the pair should pretend to be a descendant of the old person. Have the "younger" persons conduct an interview of the "older" persons, as if they were doing an oral history project for their Renaissance-era class. Have students concentrate on what has changed since the old person's distant childhood in the Middle Ages. Call on volunteers to present their interviews to the class.
COOPERATIVE LEARNING, LS **AUDITORY-MUSICAL**

LEVEL 3: (Suggested time: 15 min.) Organize the class into pairs. Have each pair write down a dialogue between the man-and-wife merchants in the painting on this page. Have them concentrate also on how changes of the Renaissance have changed the business world. Call on some pairs to present their dialogues.
COOPERATIVE LEARNING, LS **VERBAL-LINGUISTIC**

The Reformation

As humanism spread, some people began to question religious beliefs. Northern humanists thought the Roman Catholic Church had become too powerful and too worldly. They thought that it was too rich and owned too much land and that it had lost the true message of Jesus. Some people began to question the pope's authority. The humanists' claims sparked a movement that split the church in western Europe during the 1500s. This movement is called the **Reformation**.

Martin Luther A German monk named Martin Luther disagreed with the Catholic Church about how people should act. The Church taught that the way to heaven lay in attending church, giving money to the church, and doing good deeds. Luther said that the way to heaven was simply to have faith in God. He argued that the Bible was the only authority for Christians. The printing press helped Luther's ideas spread. He gained followers who became known as **Protestants** because they protested against the Catholic Church's teachings and practices. Luther eventually broke with the church. His teachings formed the basis of the Lutheran Church.

▲ Martin Luther believed that God viewed all people of faith equally.

John Calvin Another important thinker of the Reformation was John Calvin. Many of his ideas were similar to those of Martin Luther. Like Luther, Calvin taught that the Bible was the most important element of Christianity. Priests and other clergy were not necessary. Unlike Luther, however, Calvin believed that God had already decided who was going to go to heaven, even before those people were born. He encouraged his followers to dedicate themselves completely to God and to live lives of self-restraint.

Calvin's teachings were very popular, particularly in Switzerland. In 1536 he and his followers took over the city of Geneva. There they passed laws requiring that everyone live according to Calvinist teachings.

Henry VIII of England Henry brought major religious change to England. At first he was a defender of the Roman Catholic Church, but this changed after a conflict with the pope. Henry wanted a son to inherit his throne, but his wife could not have more children after their daughter was born. Henry asked the pope for permission to divorce her so he could marry a woman who might bear a son. The pope refused. Henry then claimed that the pope did not have authority over the powerful English monarchy. He broke away from the Roman Catholic Church and had laws passed that created the Church of England. The new Church granted Henry VIII a divorce.

▲ Renaissance painter Hans Holbein the Younger created this famous portrait of King Henry VIII.

CHAPTER 14, Section 1

Linking Past to Present
Soup, Watches, and Protestant Geneva In the mid-1500s John Calvin established a religious government in Geneva, Switzerland. The city became a Protestant stronghold. Legend has it that Geneva Protestant leaders owe their success to a pot of soup.

In 1602 the Catholic Duke of Savoy sent an army to drive the Protestants out of Geneva. The attackers tried to slip quietly over the city walls, but an alert cook heard them and emptied a cauldron of hot soup onto their heads. She then inspired fellow townspeople to fight while the Genevese army readied itself for battle. The city was saved and the Protestant leaders remained in power. These same leaders urged the city's goldsmiths to stop making jewelry, because wearing jewelry had been forbidden. The jewelers then focused their talents on what is now one of Switzerland's most famous industries—watchmaking.

Critical Thinking: How did the religious government of Geneva affect its economy?

Answer: By forbidding the wearing of jewelry the government encouraged the growth of watchmaking.

Europe in Transition • 321

Teach Objective 4

ALL LEVELS: (Suggested time: 15 min.) Copy the following graphic organizer onto the chalkboard, omitting the blue answers. Use it to help students understand the key changes brought on by the Reformation and Counter-Reformation.

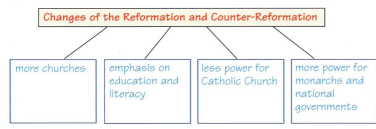

LEVEL 3: (Suggested time: 45 min.) Organize the class into four groups, for Martin Luther, John Calvin, Henry VIII, and Roman Catholic Church leaders. Ask each group to prepare for debates by reviewing their basic ideas in the text and in other sources. First, have the three Protestants elect spokespersons and debate each other about basic concepts of their faith. Then, as a class decide which one had the clearest arguments. Ask that person to debate the representative of the Roman Catholic Church.
COOPERATIVE LEARNING, LS LOGICAL-MATHEMATICAL

Section 1 Review

Answers to Section 1 Review

Define or identify For definitions and identifications, see the glossary and index.

Reading for the Main Idea
1. Travel brought people into contact with ideas; curiosity about the world awakened. (NGS 6)
2. developing cities; new foods; new sources of income; more freedom; work for hire (NGS 15)
3. Many different churches; more emphasis on education; increased power of national governments and monarchs. (NGS 12)

Critical Thinking
4. The Pope and the Church during the Middle Ages had tremendous power over nations and monarch. The less powerful the church became, the more powerful nations and governments became.

Organizing What You Know
5. Leonardo—great artist and inventor; Michelangelo—sculptor, painter, musician, poet, and architect; Shakespeare—popular plays and poems; Luther—started Protestantism; Gutenberg—developed a printing press

Visual Record Answer
education, literacy

The Counter-Reformation In response to the rise of Protestantism, the Catholic Church attempted to reform itself. This movement is called the **Counter-Reformation**. Church leaders began to focus more on spiritual matters and on making Church teachings easier for people to understand. They also attempted to stop the spread of Protestantism. Since about 1478, Spanish leaders had put on trial and severely punished people who questioned Catholic teachings. Leaders of what was called the Spanish Inquisition saw their fierce methods as a way to protect the Catholic Church from its enemies. During the Counter-Reformation, the pope brought the Spanish Inquisition to Rome.

Results of Religious Struggle Terrible religious wars broke out in France, Germany, the Netherlands, and Switzerland after the Reformation. By the time these wars ended, important social and political changes had occurred in Europe. For example, many different churches began in Europe.

A stronger interest in education arose. Catholics saw education as a tool to strengthen people's belief in the teachings of the Church. Protestants believed that people could find their own way to Christian faith by studying the Bible. Although both Catholics and Protestants placed importance on literacy, the ability to read, education did not make people more tolerant. Both Catholic and Protestant leaders opposed views that differed from their own.

As Protestantism became more popular, the Catholic Church lost some of its power. It was no longer the only church in Europe. As a result, it lost some of the tremendous political power it had held there. As the power of the Church and the pope decreased, the power of monarchs and national governments increased.

Many schools, including the Dutch University of Leiden shown here, were established during the Reformation.
Interpreting the Visual Record What goal of the Renaissance humanists did Catholics and Protestants share?

✓ **READING CHECK:** *Identifying Cause and Effect* How did the religious conflicts of the 1500s change life in Europe? many different churches, education more important, more power for national governments

Section Review 1

Define or identify: Renaissance, humanists, Leonardo da Vinci, Michelangelo, William Shakespeare, Reformation, Martin Luther, Protestants, John Calvin, Henry VIII, Counter-Reformation

Reading for the Main Idea
1. *Human Systems* What brought about the Renaissance?
2. *Human Systems* What were some important changes in daily life during the Renaissance?
3. *Human Systems* After the Reformation and Counter-Reformation, how was life in Europe different?

Critical Thinking
4. **Drawing Inferences** Why did national governments gain strength as the power of the Catholic Church declined?

Organizing What You Know
5. **Categorizing** Copy and complete the following graphic organizer with the achievements of some key people of the Renaissance and the Reformation.

Person	Achievement

322 • Chapter 14

CLOSE

Tell students that during the Renaissance it became more common for very rich people to show off their wealth. One of Rome's richest men, Agostino Chigi, had such beautiful dishes that his dinner guests would steal them. He got so tired of replacing plates that after one dinner he amazed his guests by suddenly throwing the plates out the window into the Tiber River. Unbeknownst to his guests, however, Chigi had strung a net under the water before his guests arrived. After they left, the servants went swimming and retrieved all the plates!

REVIEW, ASSESS, RETEACH

Hand out index cards and have students write questions for a quiz game about the Renaissance, the Reformation, and the Counter-Reformation. Have students quiz each other. Then have students work in pairs to create charts with three column headings—"Renaissance," "Reformation," and "Counter-Reformation"—and two row labels, "Origins" and "Features."
ESOL, COOPERATIVE LEARNING

EXTEND

Have interested students conduct research on the Renaissance in northern Europe. Encourage students to select one work from the Northern Renaissance and compare it to the art of southern Europe of the same time period.
BLOCK SCHEDULING

Exploration and Conquest

Read to Discover
1. What was the Scientific Revolution?
2. What happened during the Age of Exploration?
3. How was the English monarchy different from others in Europe?
4. What was the relationship between England and its colonies?

Vocabulary
Scientific Revolution
Age of Exploration
colony
mercantilism
absolute authority
limited monarchy
Parliament
Puritan
constitution
Restoration

People
Sir Isaac Newton
Christopher Columbus
Louis XIV
Oliver Cromwell

CHAPTER 14, Section 2

SECTION 2 RESOURCES
Reproducibles
- Lecture Notes, Section 2
- Block Scheduling Handbook, Chapter 14
- Know It Notes S2
- Biography Activity: Elizabeth I

Technology
- One-Stop Planner CD-ROM, Lesson 14.2
- Homework Practice Online
- HRW Go Site

Review, Reinforcement, and Assessment Resources
- Section 3 Review
- Daily Quiz 14.2
- Main Idea Activity S2
- Chapter Summaries and Review
- English Audio Summary 14.2
- Spanish Audio Summary 14.2

Reading Strategy

VISUALIZING INFORMATION Look at the map, photographs, and chart in this section. How may they connect to the section's main ideas? Write down your answer. As you read this section, add more information that supports what you stated in your answer.

The Scientific Revolution

You have read that Renaissance humanists encouraged learning, curiosity, and discovery. The spirit of the Renaissance paved the way for a development during the 1500s and 1600s known as the **Scientific Revolution**. During this period, Europeans began looking at the world in a different way. Using new instruments such as the microscope and the telescope, they made more accurate observations than were possible before. They set up scientific experiments and used mathematics to learn about the natural world.

This scientific approach produced new knowledge in the fields of astronomy, physics, and biology. For example, in 1609 Galileo Galilei built a telescope and observed the sky. He eventually proved that an earlier scientist, Copernicus, had been correct in saying that the planets circle the sun. Earlier, people had believed that the planets moved around the Earth. In 1687 Sir Isaac Newton explained the law of gravity. In the 1620s William Harvey discovered the circulation of blood.

Other discoveries and advances such as better ships, improved maps, and compasses allowed explorers to venture farther over the seas than before. These discoveries paved the way for the Age of Exploration.

✓ **READING CHECK:** *Identifying Cause and Effect* What brought about the Scientific Revolution? Renaissance attitude of curiosity, a desire to learn and discover

Although Galileo didn't invent the telescope, he was the first person to publish what he saw through the instrument when he used it to look at the sky. Below is a picture of one of his telescopes.

Europe in Transition • 323

Objectives
1. Provide details about the Scientific Revolution.
2. Explain what happened during the Age of Exploration.
3. Analyze how the English monarchy was different from others in Europe.
4. Examine the relationship between England and its colonies.

FOCUS

Bellringer

Copy the following question onto the chalkboard: *How has science changed the world? Write down your ideas.* Discuss student responses. Point out that many of the scientific advances of the modern age have their roots in the Scientific Revolution. Tell students that they will learn about scientific advances and other developments in the 1500s and 1600s in this section.

Building Vocabulary

Write the vocabulary terms on the board. Ask students to read the definitions from the glossary aloud. Have students discuss what kind of government comes to mind when they hear **monarchy**. Point out that in addition to a monarchy, the United Kingdom has a **Parliament** that is responsible for making laws. This makes their government a **limited monarchy**. Have students read the definitions for the other vocabulary terms from the glossary.

Europe in Transition 323

CHAPTER 14, Section 2

Linking Past to Present

Port and Starboard The use of *port* and *starboard* to designate the sides of a ship originates from the placement of the rudder on early vessels. The long oar that served as the rudder was always on the helmsman's right side as he faced forward. Because the rudder steered the vessel, the right side became known as the "steer-board"—now starboard—side of the ship. The rudder's location also kept the right side of the ship from being brought against the dock. Thus, the left side was always the one to be tied up when the ship was in port, making it the "port" side of the vessel.

Map Answer

sailed around the tip of South America through what is now called the Strait of Magellan

This map shows the routes taken by Portuguese, Spanish, French, English, and Dutch explorers.

Interpreting the Map Find Magellan's course on the map. Describe the route he found from the Atlantic Ocean to the Pacific Ocean.

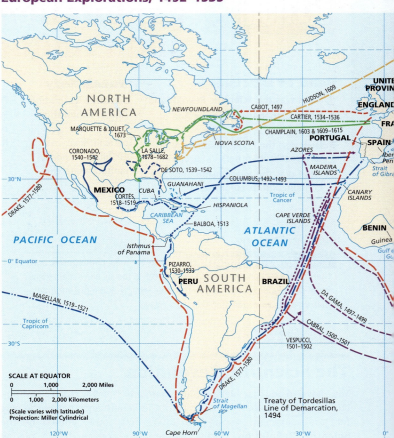

European Explorations, 1492–1535

▲ Sailors of the 1500s had many new tools such as this astrolabe to hold a course and measure their progress. A sailor would sight a star along the bar of the astrolabe. By lining the bar with markings on the disk, he could figure out the latitude of the ship's position.

324 • Chapter 14

The Age of Exploration

Europeans were eager to find new and shorter sea routes so that they could trade with distant lands such as India and China for spices, silks, and jewels. The combination of curiosity, technology, and the demand for new and highly valued products launched a remarkable period known as the **Age of Exploration**.

A member of the Portuguese royal family named Prince Henry encouraged Portugal to become a leader in exploration. He wanted to find a route to the rich spice trade of India. Portuguese explorers did eventually succeed in finding a way. They reached India by sailing around Africa.

Hoping to find another route to India, Spain sponsored the voyage of the Italian navigator Christopher Columbus. He hoped to find a direct route to India by sailing westward across the Atlantic Ocean. In

---

Teaching Objective 1

LEVEL 1: (Suggested time, 20 min.) Ask the students to name some of the defining characteristics of the Scientific Revolution. Then have each student write a paragraph summarizing those aspects. Tell them that their paragraphs should describe the Scientific Revolution by answering the 5 "W" questions—Who? What? Where? When? Why? **ESOL**

LEVELS 2 AND 3: (Suggested time: 45 min.) Provide students with encyclopedias or other reference books and have them conduct research about key figures of the Scientific Revolution. Then have each student prepare a brief report about his or her chosen person's life and achievements. Challenge students to evaluate the historic significance of the scientist's work and its influence on the modern world. **LS VERBAL-LINGUISTIC**

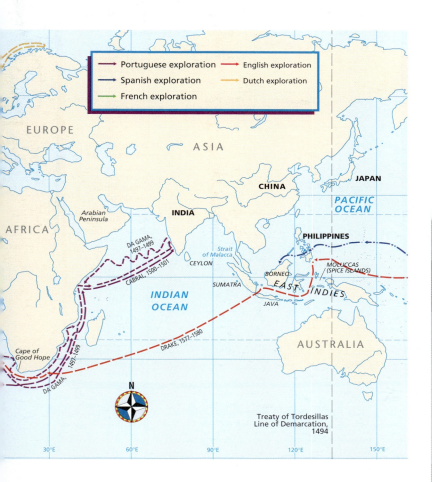

1492 Columbus reached an island in what is now called the Bahamas. Because he had no idea that the Americas lay between Europe and Asia, Columbus believed he had reached the east coast of India.

Later Spanish explorers who knew of the Americas were motivated more by the promise of conquest and riches than by curiosity and the opening of trade routes. The chart on the following page provides an overview of the major explorers from the late 1400s through the 1500s, their voyages, and their accomplishments.

Conquest and Colonization Over time the Spanish, French, English, Dutch, and others established American colonies. A **colony** is a territory controlled by people from a foreign land. As they expanded overseas, Europeans developed an economic theory called **mercantilism**. This theory said that a government should do everything it could to increase its wealth. One way it could do so was by

Christopher Columbus
(1451–1506)

Character Trait: Pursuit of Excellence

Christopher Columbus became an expert sailor as a young man, but his travels kept him close to Europe. Some of his fellow sailors, however, told rumors of islands farther west. Columbus dreamed of finding them. For years, he tried to raise money for a voyage west—into unknown waters. First the king of Portugal turned him down. Columbus didn't give up. Next, he applied to King Ferdinand and Queen Isabella of Spain. They finally gave in eight years later.

The voyages of Columbus opened the Americas to European exploration. Some of the results, such as the slave trade, were tragic. Others were grand. No one can deny, however, the courage and determination shown by the Italian sailor. *How might history be different today if Columbus had not pursued his goal?*

CHAPTER 14, Section 2

GLOBAL PERSPECTIVES

Free Trade One way that the colonial powers kept economic control over their enemies was to erect trade barriers, such as tariffs. These barriers helped prevent colonies from trading with other countries. Similar barriers still exist in varying degrees in modern nations, mainly as a way to protect local industries from foreign competition.

Today, however, many countries support free trade policies that lower barriers to foreign trade. Free trade agreements like the North American Free Trade Agreement (NAFTA) between the United States, Canada, and Mexico have reduced tariffs and stimulated foreign trade. Many economists believe that free trade benefits all nations in the long run. However, critics of free trade note that it can also cause job losses and result in movement of factories from high-wage countries to low-wage countries.

Discussion: Lead a class discussion about the benefits and drawbacks of free trade. Ask students to evaluate the arguments, pro and con, and decide whether free trade is a good idea or not.

◀ **Biography Answer**

The European discovery of the Americas may have been delayed for many years, which would have dramatically affected their history and development in unpredictable ways.

Teaching Objective 2

LEVELS 1 AND 2: (Suggested time 30 min.) Copy the following graphic organizer onto the board, omitting the blue answers. Ask the students to copy it into their notebooks. Then pair students and have each pair fill in the chart with factors that led to the beginning of the Age of Exploration. Call on the volunteers to share their answers with the class. Discuss the information in the students' charts. **ESOL, COOPERATIVE LEARNING**

Scientific Factors	Economic Factors	Early events
• curiosity about the world • better ships, maps, and equipment	• desire for trade with Asia • search for shorter trade routes by sea	• Portuguese discovered sea route around Africa. • Columbus landed in Americas.

HUMAN SYSTEMS

The Columbian Exchange

The conquest and colonization of the Americas brought a diffusion of culture and products between the Old and New Worlds. One result was the transfer of foods and animals known as the Columbian Exchange.

The effects of this exchange are still felt today. For example, diets on both sides of the Atlantic changed. Potatoes from the Andes now feed millions of people in Europe. Corn, first grown by native Americans, is a staple around the world. Wheat was not grown in the Americas until the Europeans arrived. The tomato first grew not in Italy, but in the Americas. Horses, cattle, goats, sheep, and other animals came from Europe, while North America contributed turkeys, gray squirrels, and muskrats.

Interpreting the Chart Which explorer do you think made the most important discovery? Give reasons for your answer.

European Explorers

Name	Sponsoring Country	Date	Accomplishment
Christopher Columbus	Spain	1492–1504	Discovered islands in the Americas, claimed them for Spain
Amerigo Vespucci	Spain, Portugal	1497–1504	Reached America, realized it was not part of Asia
Vasco Núñez de Balboa	Spain	1513	Reached Pacific Ocean, proved that the Americas were not part of Asia
Ferdinand Magellan	Spain	1519	Made the first round-the-world voyage, first to reach Asia by water
Hernán Cortés	Spain	1519	Conquered Aztec civilization, brought smallpox to Central America
Francisco Pizarro	Spain	1530	Conquered Inca Empire, claimed the land from present-day Ecuador to Chile for Spain
Jacques Cartier	France	1535	Claimed the Quebec region for France
Sir Francis Drake	England	1577–1580	Sailed around the World, claimed the California coast for England

The model pictured is of an English explorer's ship. The *Golden Hind*, Sir Francis Drake's ship, was 90 feet long at the waterline and only 18 feet wide. Sometimes more than 80 sailors lived and worked in these cramped quarters.

selling more than it bought from other countries. A country that could get natural resources from colonies would not have to import resources from competing countries. The desire to win overseas sources of materials helped fuel the race for colonies. The Age of Exploration changed both Europe and the lands it colonized. Colonized lands did benefit from these changes. However, in general, Europe gained the most. During this time, goods, plants, animals, and even diseases crossed the ocean between Europe and the Americas.

The Slave Trade A tragic result of exploration and colonization was the spread of slavery. During the 1500s Europeans began to use enslaved Africans to work in their colonies overseas. In exchange for slaves, European merchants shipped cotton goods, weapons, and liquor to Africa. These slaves were sent across the Atlantic to the Americas, where they were traded for goods such as sugar and cotton. These goods were then sent to Europe in exchange for manufactured products to be sold in the Americas. Conditions aboard the slave ships were horrific, and slaves were treated brutally. Many died crossing the Atlantic.

✓ **READING CHECK:** (Identifying Cause and Effect) What were two results of European exploration? *increased trade and slave trade*

Activity: Have students conduct research on the Columbian Exchange and create charts or posters detailing its features and effects.

Chart Answer
Answers will vary, but students should support their answers.

LEVEL 3: (Suggested time: 50 min.) Write the following statement on the board. *Without the scientific discoveries of the 1400s and 1500s, the Age of Exploration would not have been possible.* Challenge students to write essays that either support or dispute this statement. Encourage students to conduct additional research on the Age of Exploration. Call on volunteers to read and discuss their essays in class. **LS VERBAL-LINGUISTIC**

Teaching Objective 3

LEVEL 1: (Suggested time 15 min.) Copy the graphic on the next page onto the board, omitting the blue answers. Have students copy it into their notebooks and fill it in with descriptions of the continental European monarchies and the British monarchy. Tell students that the space where the circles overlap should be filled with features common to both types of monarchies. When students have finished, ask them how the English monarchy was different from others in Europe. *(Its power was limited by laws.)* **ESOL, LS VISUAL-SPATIAL**

Monarchies in Europe

Wealth flowed into European nations from their colonies. At the same time the Church's power over rulers and governments lost strength. The power of monarchs increased. In France, Russia, and Central Europe, monarchs ruled with **absolute authority**, meaning they alone had the power to make all the decisions about governing their nation. This situation would not change much until the 1700s.

France was ruled by a royal family called the Bourbons. Its most powerful member was Louis XIV, who ruled France from 1643 to 1715. Like many European monarchs, Louis believed that he had been chosen by God to rule. He had absolute control of the government and made all important decisions himself. Under Louis, France became a very powerful nation. In Russia, the Romanov dynasty came to power in the early 1600s. The most powerful of the Romanov czars was Peter the Great, who took the throne in 1682. He wanted to make Russia more like countries in Western Europe. Like Louis XIV, Peter the Great was an absolute monarch who strengthened his country. In Central Europe, two great families competed for power. The Habsburgs ruled the Austrian Empire, while the Hohenzollerns controlled Prussia to the north.

England's situation was different. When King John signed Magna Carta during the Middle Ages, he set a change in motion for England's government. England became a **limited monarchy**. This meant that the powers of the king were limited by law. By the 1500s, **Parliament**, an assembly made up of nobles, clergy, and common people, had gained the power to pass laws and make sure they were upheld.

English Civil War English monarchs such as Henry VIII and Elizabeth I had to work with or around Parliament to achieve their political goals. Later English monarchs fought with Parliament for power. Some even went to war over this issue. The struggle between king and Parliament reached its peak in the mid-1600s. Armies of Parliament supporters under Oliver Cromwell defeated King Charles I, ended the monarchy, and proclaimed England a commonwealth, a nation in which the people held most of the authority.

A special court tried Charles I for crimes against the people. Oliver Cromwell, a **Puritan**, took control of England. Puritans were a group of Protestants who thought that the Church of England was too much like the Catholic Church. The Puritans were a powerful group in Parliament at the time, and Cromwell was their leader.

Empress Maria Theresa of Austria was a member of the Habsburg family.

Oliver Cromwell led the Puritan forces that overthrew the English monarchy. He ruled England from 1653 to 1658.

Europe in Transition • 327

CHAPTER 14, Section 2

Cultural Kaleidoscope
African Culture in Latin America The slave trade brought Africans and African culture to many parts of the Americas. Large populations of African ancestry live in Brazil, on the Caribbean islands and Caribbean coast of South and Central America, and along the Pacific coast of South America as far south as Lima, Peru.

African influences are a key feature of the cultural mosaic that characterizes Middle and South America today. Music is one notable example. Reggae, calypso, samba, salsa, cumbia and merengue are just a few of the musical styles that bear the strong imprint of African rhythms. Music is not the only area of influence. African cultural influences affect everything from dance, art, and literature to food, language, and religion.

Activity: Have students research a cultural feature of the Americas that reflects African influence. They might choose a style of music, a type of cooking, an art form or dance, or a particular writer or musician. Ask students to present brief oral reports based on their research.

Features of European Monarchies

European Monarchies
Most Monarchies—absolute authority; monarchs' authority grew during period

Shared features—headed by a king or queen

British Monarchy
England—power limited by law; Parliament makes laws

LEVELS 2 AND 3: (Suggested time: 30 min.) Organize students into groups and have each group create a chart showing how Parliament exercised power over English rulers in the 1500s and 1600s. Charts should describe Parliament and its functions and trace its influence through events like the English Civil War, the Restoration, and the Glorious Revolution. Have students discuss their charts in class. **COOPERATIVE LEARNING**

CHAPTER 14, Section 2

USING ILLUSTRATIONS

A Princely Suit of Clothes
Focus students' attention on the painting of Charles II as a boy. Point out that his clothing, made of satin and lace, was common for royalty at the time. No one wearing such fine materials, of course, was expected to do any manual labor. People who did have to work in workshops or the fields could not afford such rich clothing. They may have tried to copy the general cut of upper-class styles. They had to use rougher, cheaper materials, however—usually wool.

Visual Record Answer

to make a public example and public statement; a warning to any monarch who might try to gain power

The death warrant of Charles I was signed and sealed by members of Parliament. Parliament chose to behead King Charles I in public.
Interpreting the Visual Record Why might Parliament have decided to have Charles beheaded where everyone could see?

Charles II, shown here as a boy, became king following the fall of Cromwell's commonwealth in 1660.

Cromwell's Commonwealth Cromwell controlled England for about five years. He used harsh methods to create a government that represented the people. Twice he tried to establish a **constitution**, a document that outlined the country's basic laws, but his policies were unpopular. Discontent became widespread. In 1660, two years after Cromwell died, Parliament invited the son of Charles I to rule England. Thus the English monarchy was restored under Charles II. This period of English history was called the **Restoration**.

Last Change in Government Cheering crowds greeted Charles II when he reached London. One observer recalled that great celebrations were held in the streets, which were decorated with flowers and tapestries. People hoped that the Restoration would bring peace and progress to England.

Although England had a king again, the Civil War and Cromwell's commonwealth had made lasting changes in the government. Parliament strictly limited the king's power.

The Glorious Revolution When Charles II died, his brother became King James II. James's belief in absolute rule angered Parliament. They demanded that he give up the throne and invited his daughter, Mary, and her Dutch husband, William of Orange, to replace him. This transfer of power, which was accomplished without bloodshed, was called the Glorious Revolution. The day before William and Mary took the throne in 1689, they had to agree to a document called the Declaration of Rights. It stated that Parliament would choose who ruled the country. It also said that the ruler could not make laws, impose taxes, or maintain an army without Parliament's approval. By 1700 Parliament had replaced the monarchy as the major source of political power in England.

✓ **READING CHECK:** *Drawing Inferences* How did the English Civil War and events that followed affect the English government? **Parliament strictly limited monarch's power.**

328 • Chapter 14

Teaching Objective 4

ALL LEVELS: (Suggested time: 15 min.) First, review the issues that separated the British government from the British colonies. Then have students create bumper stickers that colonists might have placed on their carriages and carts to protest British treatment of the colonies.
ESOL, LS **VERBAL-LINGUISTIC**

 ▶**ASSIGNMENT:** Have each student design a movie poster for a film set in or about the Scientific Revolution, the Age of Exploration, or another aspect of the 1500s and 1600s. Direct students to create names for their movies and a few characters who may appear in the film. Display the posters in the classroom.
LS **VISUAL-SPATIAL**

328 Chapter 14

English Colonial Expansion

During the 1600s, English explorers began claiming and conquering lands overseas. In 1607 the British established Jamestown in what is now the state of Virginia. Jamestown was the first permanent English settlement in North America. In 1620, settlers founded Plymouth in what is now Massachusetts.

Mercantilism and the British Colonies The British government, with its policy of mercantilism, thought that the colonies should exist only for the benefit of England. Parliament passed laws that required colonists to sell certain products only to Britain, even if another country would pay a higher price. Other trade laws imposed taxes on sugar and other goods that the colonies bought from non-British colonies.

The settlers at Jamestown settled close by the James River.
Interpreting the Visual Record
Human-Environment Interaction Why do you think the colonists built their settlement in the manner shown here?

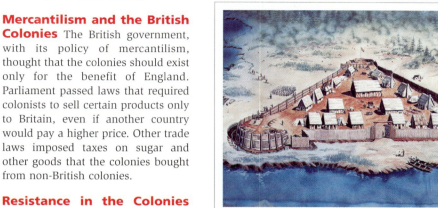
Colonial Williamsburg Foundation

Resistance in the Colonies
The American colonists saw these trade laws as a threat to their liberties. They found many ways to break the laws. For example, they avoided paying taxes whenever and however they could. Parliament, however, continued to impose new taxes. With each new tax, colonial resistance increased. Relations between England and the colonies grew steadily worse. The stage was set for revolution.

✓ **READING CHECK:** *Finding the Main Idea* How did England regard the American colonies? *as existing only for the benefit of England*

Define or identify: Scientific Revolution, Sir Isaac Newton, Age of Exploration, Christopher Columbus, colony, mercantilism, absolute authority, Louis XIV, limited monarchy, Parliament, Oliver Cromwell, Puritan, constitution, Restoration

Reading for the Main Idea
1. *Human Systems* How did the Scientific Revolution aid European exploration?
2. *Places and Regions* What prompted Europeans to explore and colonize land overseas?
3. *Human Systems* How was England different from other monarchies in Europe?

Homework Practice Online
Keyword: SJ5 HP14

Critical Thinking
4. *Drawing Inferences* How did England's treatment of the American colonies set the stage for revolution?

Organizing What You Know
5. *Summarizing* Copy the following graphic organizer. Use it to show how the slave trade worked between Europe, Africa, and the Americas. Alongside each arrow, list the items that were traded along that route.

Americas ⇄ Europe
Africa

Europe in Transition • 329

Section 2 Review

Answers to Section 2 Review

Define or identify: For definitions and identifications, see the glossary and index.

Reading for the Main Idea
1. Improvements in science and technology allowed sailors to explore distant lands. (NGS 12)
2. curiosity, a desire for new products, and a desire for wealth (NGS12)
3. others absolute; England became limited monarchy (NGS 13)

Critical Thinking
4. Policy of mercantilism antagonized the colonists by disregarding their rights.

Organizing What You Know
5. Europe to Africa—cotton, goods, weapons, liquor; Americas to Europe—sugar and cotton; Europe to Americas—manufactured goods; Africa to the Americas—slaves

◀ **Visual Record Answer**
for defense against attack

CLOSE

Focus students' attention on the portrait of Oliver Cromwell in this section. Tell them that when Cromwell was having his portrait painted by a famous French artist, he told the painter not to flatter him, but to show the "warts and all." Ask students if they think the portrait is realistic, and if it follows Cromwell's instructions. Ask also what Cromwell's instructions to the painter may reveal about the Puritan leader.

REVIEW, ASSESS, RETEACH

Have students complete the Section Review. Then have them write a question about each person or event covered in the section. Have students ask each other their questions and complete Daily Quiz 14.2.

Have students complete Main Idea Activity S2. Then organize the class into groups to create and perform skits based on the section's main topics.
COOPERATIVE LEARNING, LS **AUDITORY-MUSICAL**

EXTEND

Have interested students conduct research on one of the explorers named on the chart in this section and report on their findings to the class.
BLOCK SCHEDULING

Europe in Transition 329

Enlightenment Thinking The Enlightenment is also called the Age of Reason. This is because scientists began to use **reason**, or logical thinking, to discover the laws of nature. They thought that the laws of nature governed the universe and all its creatures. Some also thought there was a natural law that governed society and human behavior. They tried to use their powers of reasoning to discover this natural law. By following natural law, they hoped to solve society's problems.

Religion was important to some thinkers. Others played down its importance. Playing down the importance of religion became known as **secularism**. The ideas of secularism and **individualism**—a belief in the political and economic independence of individuals—were important steps in the separation of church and state in government.

The Enlightenment in England The English philosopher John Locke believed that natural law gave individuals the right to govern themselves. Locke wrote that freedom was people's natural state. He thought individuals had natural rights to life, liberty, and property. Locke also claimed everyone should have equality under the law.

Much of Locke's writing focused on government. Locke argued that government should be based on an agreement between the people and their leaders. According to Locke, people give their rulers the power to rule. If the ruler does not work for the public good, the people have the right to change the government. Locke's writings greatly influenced other Enlightenment thinkers. They also influenced the Americans who wrote the Declaration of Independence and the Constitution.

Enlightenment thinking developed along with advances in science. Both philosophers and scientists used logic to reach their conclusions. This English painting from the 1760s is titled *The Orrery*. An orrery was a clockwork-driven model of the sun, planets, and moons. English philosophers believed that human actions followed laws similar to the scientific laws that explained the planets' movements.

CHAPTER 14, Section 3

DAILY LIFE

Enlightenment and Education The revolutionary ideas of Enlightenment thinkers did not spread rapidly to the general populations of England and France. During the 1700s, most people in those countries could not read well, if they could read at all. Few common people had money or time to buy and read a book. So in general, only privileged members of society met to discuss Enlightenment ideas. The daily lives of these wealthy and cultured people had little in common with daily lives of most people. Nevertheless, the writings and conversations of Enlightenment thinkers gradually spread the new ideas far and wide.

Critical Thinking: How does requiring everyone to go to school and providing free education affect society?

Answer: If everyone can read, everyone has access to new ideas about government, and new ideas often lead to positive changes.

Teaching Objective 1
ALL LEVELS: (Suggested time: 10 min.) Have students list some of the Enlightenment's beliefs about human beings and nature. (Possible answers: The laws of nature govern all creatures; people can discover natural laws through reason; following natural law improves people's lives.) Ask students what bigger idea these beliefs led to during the Enlightenment. (Possible responses: They all led to the idea that people should have a part in governing themselves; people should have freedom.)

ALL LEVELS: (Suggested time: 15 min.) Pair students and tell each pair to create flash cards for the terms *reason, secularism,* and *individualism.* Students should write each term on one side of a flash card and its definition and details about how it affected the Enlightenment on the other. **ESOL, COOPERATIVE LEARNING, LS KINESTHETIC**

CHAPTER 14, Section 3

USING ILLUSTRATIONS

Art as History Have students examine the painting of the Bastille on this page. Ask students why freeing prisoners was a major accomplishment for the mob of angry citizens. (Possible answer: The prison was a symbol of the King's power). Ask students to note other details about this historic event based on the painting. (Possible answer: The mob seems to have set fire to part of the prison, the mob was armed with at least one cannon; some soldiers in uniform seem to have taken part in the attack.) Invite students to draw conclusions about how the storming of the Bastille might have affected the revolutionaries. (Possible answer: They would have been emboldened by this success to take further steps against the king and nobility).

You may also want to have students conduct further research on the storming of the Bastille. Compare these facts with what you see in the illustration.

Visual Record Answer ▶

The civilian appears to be talking to the soldiers. Perhaps he is trying to convince them to join in the rebellion.

The Enlightenment and Society As time passed, Enlightenment ideas about freedom, equality, and government spread far and wide. Eventually, they inspired the American Revolution. As you know, Britain's American colonies united against Britain and won their independence. The American Revolution was a major world event because it put Enlightenment ideas into practice. It also gave hope to French people who wanted to change their government.

✓ **READING CHECK:** (Human Systems) What about the social and political order of European nations caused many people to want change? monarchs' desire for absolute control over their governments and their subjects; people suffering from inequality and injustice in daily life

The French Revolution

French discontent with the king and the nobility was widespread by the 1770s. Food shortages and rising prices led to widespread hunger. To make matter worse, the nobles, who owned most of the land, raised rents. Taxes were also raised on the peasants and middle classes while the nobles and the clergy paid no taxes. Some French people took to the streets, rioting against high prices and taxes.

At the same time, the French monarchy was losing authority and respect. Due to the king's expensive habits and spending on foreign

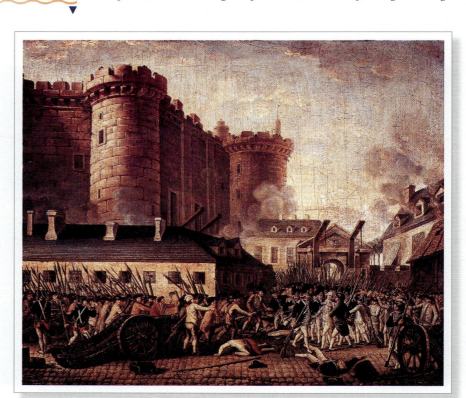

On July 14, 1789, a crowd destroyed the Bastille, freeing its prisoners. Bastille Day marked the spread of the Revolution and is celebrated in France every July 14.

Interpreting the Visual Record What do you think the men in the foreground are doing?

332 • Chapter 14

LEVEL 1: (Suggested time: 10 min.) Copy the following graphic organizer onto the chalkboard, omitting the blue answers. Call on students to fill it in with the ideas of John Locke. Then ask how John Locke's ideas affected Americans. (They helped inspire the writers of the Declaration of Independence and the U.S. Constitution.)

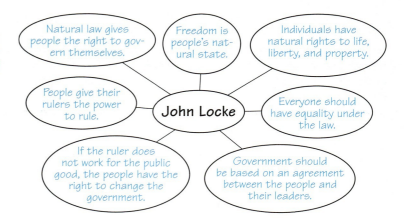

wars, France was deep in debt. To pay the debts, King Louis XVI tried to tax the nobles and the clergy. When they refused to pay, France faced financial collapse.

The French peasants and middle classes had different complaints against the king. They did, however, share certain Enlightenment ideas. For example, they spoke of liberty and equality as their natural rights. These ideas united them against the king and nobles.

The Outbreak of Revolution In 1789, a group representing the majority of the people declared itself to be the National Assembly. It was determined to change the existing government. This action marked the beginning of the French Revolution. Within months, the king lost all power.

When Louis XVI moved troops into Paris and Versailles, there was fear that the soldiers would drive out the National Assembly by force. In Paris, the people took action. Angry city dwellers stormed the Bastille prison, a symbol of royal oppression, and released its prisoners. The violence spread as peasants attacked manor houses and monasteries throughout France.

The National Assembly quickly took away the privileges of the clergy and nobles. Feudalism was ended and peasants were freed from their old duties. The National Assembly also adopted the *Declaration of the Rights of Man and Citizen*. This document stated that men are born equal and remain equal under the law. It guaranteed basic rights and defined the principles of the French Revolution—liberty, equality, and fraternity, or brotherhood.

The End of the Monarchy In 1791 the National Assembly completed a constitution for France. This constitution allowed for the king to be the head of the government, but limited his authority. The constitution divided the government into three branches—executive, legislative, and judicial. Louis XVI pretended to agree to this new government. In secret, he tried to overthrow it. When he and his family tried to escape France in 1791, they were arrested and sent back to Paris.

The French Republic In 1792, a new governing body, the National Convention, gathered and declared France a republic. The National Convention put Louis XVI on trial as an enemy of the state. Urged on by a lawyer named Maximilien Robespierre (ROHBZ-pyehr), the members found the king guilty. In 1793, the king was sent to the **guillotine** (GI-luh-teen), a machine that drops a huge blade to cut off a person's head.

This poster summarizes the main goals of the French Revolution: liberty, equality, and fraternity. Fraternity means "brotherhood."

The painting shows a French prisoner being beheaded by means of the guillotine. It was a more humane execution method than those used before. As the French Revolution continued, the guillotine would claim many victims.

CHAPTER 14, Section 3

Linking Past to Present

A Palace as Big as a Town Louis XVI's lavish lifestyle contributed to his unpopularity. Maintaining his immense palace at Versailles was a drain on the treasury. The palace was also a striking example of extravagance at the taxpayer's expense. While Louis XVI ruled, 10,000 people lived or worked in his household. There were special rooms for a clock, the king's throne, and the royal billiard table. The grounds at Versailles covered 2,000 acres and included miles of wide pathways and thousands of exotic plants. Versailles was sacked during the Revolution. Only a portion of its grandeur has been restored.

Activity: In 1999 a powerful storm swept through France and downed some 10,000 of the trees at Versailles. Have some students conduct research on the restoration of the palace's garden. Ask a second group to investigate ongoing restoration of Versailles' interior. Have a third group research Versailles' role as a major tourist attraction.

Teaching Objective 2

LEVEL 1: (Suggested time: 10 min.) Copy the following graphic organizer onto the chalkboard, omitting the blue answers. Have students list the causes of the French Revolution on the organizer. Lead a discussion based on the organizer. Point out that, although the French Revolution went through a very troubled time, its accomplishments can be seen to outweigh the problems. **ESOL**

The French Revolution

Causes	Results
• Enlightenment ideas about government	• creation of National Assembly
• food shortages, rising prices, widespread hunger	• storming of the Bastille
• higher rents, higher taxes	• Declaration of Rights of Man and Citizen
• resentment against nobles and clergy	• creation of National Convention
• French monarchy's loss of authority and respect	• execution of Louis XVI
• threat of financial collapse	• Reign of Terror

CHAPTER 14, Section 3

Across the Curriculum
MUSIC

National Anthems Play a recording of the French national anthem, *La Marseillaise,* for the class. Ask students to share their reactions to the music. Tell students that the anthem was written in 1792 by a captain in the French Army, Rouget de Lisle. Originally a marching song, the words were sung by soldiers from Marseilles, a city in southern France, who were going to defend their homeland against invaders from Austria. Play the music again and ask students why a marching song is appropriate for a national anthem. *(Possible answer: The stirring rhythm inspires patriotism and feelings of pride among citizens.)*

Activity: Have students research the history of the American national anthem. Then have students compare and contrast the *Star-Spangled Banner* and the *Marseillaise.*

Visual Record Answer

probably so, because the artist makes enlisting appear to be the patriotic thing to do and the soldiers look quite glamorous

A group called the Jacobins controlled the National Convention. Robespierre was a powerful leader of the Jacobins.

Robespierre was the leader of a political group known as the Jacobins. Many of the Jacobins wanted to bring about sweeping reforms that would benefit all classes of French society. As the French Revolution went on, the Jacobins gained more and more power. By the time Louis XVI was executed, Robespierre was probably the most powerful man in France. He and his allies controlled the National Convention.

Under Robespierre, the National Convention looked for other enemies. Anyone who had supported the king or criticized the revolution was a suspect. Thousands of people—nobles and peasants alike—died at the guillotine. This period, called the **Reign of Terror**, ended in 1794 when Robespierre himself was put to death.

Despite the terror, the revolutionaries did achieve some goals. They replaced the monarchy with a republic and gave peasants and workers new political rights. They opened schools and supported elementary education for all. To end inflation, they set up wage and price controls. They ended slavery in France's colonies and encouraged religious tolerance.

Between 1795 and 1799, a government called the Directory tried to govern France. A new two-house legislature was created to make laws. This legislature also elected five officials called directors to run the government. The directors, however, could not agree on many issues. They were corrupt and quarreled. They quickly became unpopular with the French people. In addition, by 1799, enemy armies were again threatening France. Food shortages were causing panic in the cities. Many people concluded their country needed one strong leader to restore law and order.

✓ **READING CHECK:** Why did many French peasants and poor workers support the Revolution? believed in liberty and equality, tired of being oppressed

In the 1790s France began building up its military. This painting shows French citizens enlisting in the new army.

Interpreting the Visual Record Do you think the artist wanted men to join the army? Why or why not?

334 • Chapter 14

LEVELS 2 AND 3: (Suggested time: 30 min.) Organize the class into groups. Ask students to imagine that the year is 1789 and they are French peasants or laborers attending a neighborhood meeting. Each group should write a petition spelling out the group's complaints about the monarchy and other ills of society and recommending specific actions that the monarchy should take. The petition is to be a document that group members want their neighbors to sign. Call on volunteers from the groups to read their petitions to the class.
COOPERATIVE LEARNING, **LS** **VERBAL-LINGUISTIC**

Teaching Objective 3
LEVEL 1: Copy the following graphic organizer onto the chalkboard, omitting the blue answers. Have students complete it to summarize Napoléon's effect on France. **ESOL,** **LS** **VISUAL-SPATIAL**

NAPOLÉON'S FRANCE	
Before Napoléon	After Napoléon
• enemy armies threatening France	• France had reorganized and dominated Europe.
• law and order breaking down	• French law organized into the Napoléonic Code
• food shortages in cities	• France's finances run by the Bank of France
• feudalism and serfdom common in countries around France	• Feudalism and serfdom abolished by Napoléon

334 Chapter 14

The Napoléonic Era

In 1799, a young general named Napoléon Bonaparte overthrew the Directory and took control of the French government. Most of the French people accepted Napoléon because he seemed to support the ideas of the Revolution. In 1804, France was declared an empire and Napoléon crowned himself emperor.

Napoléon as Emperor

In France, Napoléon used his unlimited power to restore order. He organized French law into one system—the Napoléonic Code. He set up the Bank of France to run the country's finances. Influenced by the Enlightenment, he built schools and universities.

A brilliant general, Napoléon won many land battles in Europe. By 1809, he ruled the Netherlands and Spain. He forced Austria and Prussia to be France's allies. He abolished the Holy Roman Empire. He also unified the northern Italian states into the Kingdom of Italy, under his control. Within five years of becoming emperor, Napoléon had reorganized and dominated Europe. Because of the important role that he played, the wars that France fought from 1796 until 1815 are called the Napoléonic Wars.

Napoléon also made changes in the conquered lands. He put the Napoléonic Code into effect, ended feudalism and serfdom, and introduced new military techniques. However, feelings of patriotism for their native lands were increasing among the people that Napoléon controlled. Opposition to French rule grew, and Napoléon's enemies grew stronger.

In 1812, Napoléon invaded Russia with some 500,000 soldiers. The invasion was a disaster. Battles, the cold Russian winter, hunger, and disease claimed the lives of most of the French soldiers. In fact, only about 10,000 men were able to stagger back to Europe.

Napoléon's Defeat

The monarchs of Europe took advantage of Napoléon's weakened state. Prussia, Austria, and Great Britain joined together to invade France. These allies captured Paris in 1814. Napoléon gave up the throne and went into exile. Louis XVIII, the brother of the executed king, was made the new king of France.

The following year, Napoléon made a short-lived attempt to retake his empire. In 1815, Napoléon regained control of France. Soon, however, Napoléon's enemies sent armies against him. The other European countries defeated him at Waterloo in Belgium. Napoléon was sent to St. Helena, a small island in the South Atlantic. He lived there under guard and died in 1821.

This painting captures the glory of Napoléon as a military leader.
Interpreting the Visual Record How might an artist who did not support Napoléon have shown the emperor?

Across the Curriculum
ART
Art and Politics

The portrait of Napoléon on this page was painted by Jacques-Louis David, who lived from 1748 to 1825. David was the leading French painter during the French Revolution and the Napoléonic era. His popular paintings helped build support for the Revolution. In fact, as a member of the Jacobin political party, David himself voted to send King Louis XVI to the guillotine. Later, the artist recorded the big events of Napoléon's life. Have students study David's portrait of Napoleon. Ask the students to note the techniques the artist used to display Napoleon in a positive light.

◀ **Visual Record Answer**

Possible answer: standing still on the ground, dirty or wounded, looking foolish or evil instead of heroic, and so on

---

LEVEL 2: (Suggested time: 15 min.) Have students design recruiting posters for Napoléon's army. Posters may review the problems that had been troubling France before Napoléon's rise to power and express the hopes that the French people placed in the general. **LS VISUAL-SPATIAL**

LEVEL 3: Challenge students to find passages in Leo Tolstoy's *War and Peace* that describe the miseries of Napoléon's retreat from Moscow. Internet sources may be able to help students locate appropriate segments of this very long novel. Students should read the passages to the class. You may want to have other students illustrate the scenes.
LS VERBAL-LINGUISTIC

Section 3 Review

Answers to Section 3 Review

Define or identify For definitions and identifications, see the glossary and index.

Reading for the Main Idea

1. Government should be based on agreement between people and leaders, people give leaders the right to rule, people have the right to change their government.
2. causes—rising costs of food and taxes, resentment toward the nobility and clergy; effects—new ruling bodies, end of the monarchy, improvements in some areas of life and new political rights, rise to power of Napoléon

Critical Thinking

3. Their ideas helped inspire the American and French Revolutions, the Declaration of Independence, and the U.S. Constitution

Organizing What You Know

4. See section content for events of 1789, 1791, 1792, 1793, 1794, 1795–99, 1799, 1809, 1812, 1814, 1815, and 1821.

▲ Many of Europe's royal families came to Vienna during the winter of 1814–15. They attended balls while diplomats and rulers discussed the situation of Europe after Napoléon.

Europe After Napoléon Napoléon had not always upheld the ideals of the French Revolution. However, he did extend their influence throughout Europe. As a result, other governments feared that rebellions against the monarchy might spread. After Napoléon's defeat, delegates from all over Europe met at the Congress of Vienna. The major European powers wanted to restore order, keep the peace, and put down the ideas of the revolution. They also wanted to bring back the **balance of power** in Europe. Having a balance of power is a way to keep peace by making sure no one country or group of countries becomes too powerful.

Many delegates to the Congress of Vienna were **reactionaries**. Reactionaries not only oppose change. They actually would like to undo certain changes. In this case, the reactionaries wanted their countries to remain monarchies. These delegates were not comfortable with the ideas of liberty and equality.

The Congress of Vienna redrew the map of Europe. Lands that Napoléon had conquered were taken away from France. In the end, France's boundaries were returned to where they had been in 1790. Small countries around France were combined into bigger, stronger ones. This was done to prevent France from ever again threatening Europe's peace. France also had to pay other countries for the damage it had caused.

✓ **READING CHECK:** *Drawing Conclusions* Why did the other countries of Europe want to defeat Napoléon? restore order, keep the peace, put down the ideas of revolution, and bring back the balance of power in Europe

Section Review 3

Define or identify: Enlightenment, reason, secularism, individualism, John Locke, King Louis XVI, Robespierre, guillotine, Reign of Terror, Napoléon Bonaparte, balance of power, reactionaries

Reading for the Main Idea

1. *Human Systems* What important ideas about government came from Enlightenment thinkers?
2. *Human Systems* What were the causes and effects of the French Revolution?

Critical Thinking

3. **Analyzing** In what ways did John Locke and other philosophers of the Enlightenment help pave the way for democracy in other countries?

Organizing What You Know

4. **Identifying Time Order** Copy the following time line. Use it to list some important events of the French Revolution and the Napoléonic era.

336 • Chapter 14

CLOSE

Play the *1812 Overture*, by Pyotr Ilich Tchaikovsky, for the class. This famous symphony commemorates Napoléon's defeat by the brutal Russian winter. Challenge students to listen for the Russian church music and folk music that the composer worked into the score. Tchaikovsky also incorporated the French national anthem and the czar's anthem into the music.

REVIEW, ASSESS, RETEACH

Have students complete the Section Review. Then call on volunteers to read aloud terms, phrases, dates, and names from the section. Ask other students to explain the words' significance. Have students complete Daily Quiz 14.3.

Have students complete Main Idea Activity S3. Then have students work in pairs to create news reports on important events covered in the section.
COOPERATIVE LEARNING, **AUDITORY-MUSICAL**

EXTEND

Have interested students conduct research on outlandish fashions of the French Revolution and Napoléonic era. For example, during the Reign of Terror, some fashionable ladies wore thin red ribbons around their necks—a reference to the guillotine's deadly work.

Section 4: Industrial Revolution and Reform

Read to Discover
1. How did the Industrial Revolution begin?
2. Which developments and inventions helped industry grow?
3. How did the Industrial Revolution spread?
4. How did the Industrial Revolution affect daily life in Europe?

Vocabulary
Industrial Revolution
factors of production
capital
factory system
capitalism
mass production
suffragettes

People
Jethro Tull
Richard Arkwright
James Watt
Samuel F.B. Morse
Emmeline Pankhurst

READING ORGANIZER Before you read this section, create a spider graph. First draw a circle in the center of your paper and label it Industrial Revolution and Reform. Create a leg for each of these topics: Agriculture, Industry, Transportation and Communication, Capitalism, Political Reform, and Social Reform. As you read the section, fill in the map with details about each type of change.

The Industrial Revolution

In the early 1700s, inventors began putting the ideas of the Scientific Revolution to work by creating new machines. Advances in industry, business, transportation, and communications changed people's lives in almost every way. This period, which lasted through the 1700s and 1800s, was called the **Industrial Revolution**.

New Needs in Agriculture The first stages of the Industrial Revolution took place in agricultural communities in Great Britain. Ways of dividing, managing, and using the land had changed greatly since the Middle Ages. People had begun to think about land in new ways. Wealthy farmers began to buy more land to create bigger farms. These big farms were more efficient. Small farmers, unable to compete with these large operations, sometimes lost their land. At the same time, Europe's population continued to grow, which meant that the demand for food grew as well. Farmers saw that they had to improve farming methods and increase production.

One such farmer was Jethro Tull. He invented a new farm machine, called a seed drill, for planting seeds in straight rows. More inventors soon followed with other new farm machines. The machinery made farms more productive. That is, farmers could grow more food with fewer workers. As a result, many farm workers lost their jobs. Many of these people moved to cities to look for other kinds of work.

▲ This painting shows the original McCormick reaper, used to cut grain. It was invented by Cyrus H. McCormick in 1831.

Europe in Transition • 337

CHAPTER 14, Section 4

SECTION 4 RESOURCES
Reproducibles
- Lecture Notes, Section 4
- Block Scheduling Handbook, Chapter 14
- Know It Notes S4
- Readings in World Geography, History, and Culture, Reading 35
- Biography Activity: Emmeline Pankhurst

Technology
- One-Stop Planner CD-ROM, Lesson 14.4
- Geography and Cultures Visual Resources 49, 51, 52, 54, 55
- Homework Practice Online
- HRW Go Site

Review, Reinforcement, and Assessment Resources
- Daily Quiz 14.4
- Main Idea Activity S4
- Chapter Summaries and Review
- English Audio Summary 14.4
- Spanish Audio Summary 14.4

Section 4

Objectives
1. Trace how the Industrial Revolution began.
2. Explain which developments and inventions helped industry grow.
3. Analyze how the Industrial Revolution spread.
4. Examine how the Industrial Revolution affected daily life in Europe.

Focus

Bellringer
Write the word *revolution* on the chalkboard and ask the students about its various meanings. Remind students that the previous section described political revolutions brought about by military means. Point out that a second meaning of revolution is "a complete change". Have students name some major changes in society that have been or might be called revolutions. Tell students that they will learn about one of these, the Industrial Revolution, in this section.

Building Vocabulary
Write the vocabulary terms on the chalkboard. Circle the word *production* in **factors of production** and **mass production**. Ask students to provide a definition for *production* (the act of making things). Based on this definition, have students infer what the vocabulary terms may mean. (Mass production—making large numbers of things; factors of production—items needed to produce many things). Then have students locate and read the definitions of other terms.

Europe in Transition 337

CHAPTER 14, Section 4

Across the Curriculum
TECHNOLOGY

Telford's Canals Among the factors of production that made Great Britain the birthplace of the Industrial Revolution was its system of canals. One of the great canal-builders was Thomas Telford. He built the Ellesmere Canal in Wales, which included two great aqueducts. The canal and aqueducts have survived in their original form for about 200 years. Telford also built the Caledonian Canal, a waterway that connects the east and west coasts of Scotland.

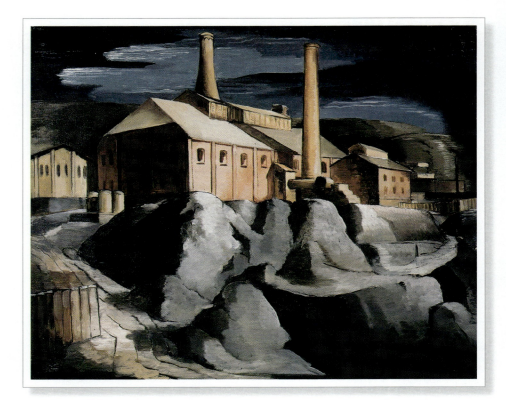

▲ This painting shows one artist's view of a factory. By 1800, textiles made in English factories were shipped all over the world.

One early water-powered machine in an English mill was said to spin more than 300 million yards of silk thread every day!

Factors of Production The Industrial Revolution began in Great Britain because the country had the right **factors of production**. These are items necessary for industry to grow. They include land, natural resources, workers, and **capital**. Capital refers to the money and tools needed to make a product.

Great Britain had rich deposits of coal and iron ore. Coal would eventually be a fuel for steam engines. Together, coal and iron were essential for making steel, the basic material for making big new machines. Steel would also go into the bridges, railways, and other elements of transportation that would be so important to the Industrial Revolution. Britain also had many rivers to provide waterpower for factories. Rivers and canals provided transportation within Britain. The country's many ports allowed for trade across the seas. Raw materials could come in by sea, too. Money, or capital, was available, since many people had grown wealthy during the 1700s. They were willing to invest their money in new businesses. The British government allowed people to start businesses and protected their property. Parliament passed laws supporting business. Labor was available since many ex-farmworkers needed jobs.

✓ **READING CHECK:** (Cause and Effect) What factors of production helped Great Britain to develop early industries? land; natural resources including coal, iron ore, and many rivers; investment capital; many available workers; and political stability

---

TEACH

Teaching Objective 1

ALL LEVELS: (Suggested time: 10 min.) Lead a discussion about the changes in agricultures that led to changes in industry. You may want to compare the agricultural changes to a snowball effect. You may also want to discuss how some of the agricultural changes had immediate benefits (being able to grow more food) but also caused problems (put many laborers out of work). **LS** **INTERPERSONAL**

LEVEL 1: (Suggested time: 15 min.) Copy the following graphic organizer onto the chalkboard, omitting the blue answers. Ask students to complete it with descriptions of how Great Britain was able to begin to industrialize. When students have completed the organizer ask what might have happened if one of the factors had been missing. **ESOL**

The Growth of Industry

As mentioned earlier, agricultural needs led to new machines and methods for farming. People in other industries began to wonder how machines could help them as well. For example, before the early 1700s, the people had spun thread and woven their own cloth at home on simple spinning wheels and looms. It was a slow process, and the demand for cloth was always greater than the supply.

The Textile Industry To speed up cloth-making in the early 1700s, English inventors built new types of spinning machines and looms. In 1769, Richard Arkwright invented a water-powered spinning machine. He eventually set up his spinning machines in mills and hired workers to run them. Workers earned a fixed rate of pay for a set number of hours of work. Arkwright brought his workers and machinery together in a large building called a factory. Arkwright's arrangement with his workers was the beginning of the **factory system**.

In 1785, Edmund Cartwright built a water-powered loom. It could weave cloth much faster than could a hand loom. In fact, one worker with a powered loom could produce as much cloth as several people with traditional ones. Each new invention that improved the spinning and weaving process led to more inventions and improvements.

The factory system soon spread to other industries. People invented machines for making shoes, clothing, furniture, and other goods. Machines were also used in printing, papermaking, lumber and food processing, and for making other machines. More and more of the British people went to work in factories and mills.

Steam-Powered Factories Early machines in factories were driven by water power. This system, however, had drawbacks. It meant that a factory had to be located on a stream or river, preferably next to a waterfall or dam. In many cases these waterways were far from raw materials and overland transportation routes. The water flow in rivers can change from season to season, and sometimes rivers run dry. People recognized that a lighter, movable, and more dependable power source was needed. Many inventors thought that using steam power to run machines was the answer.

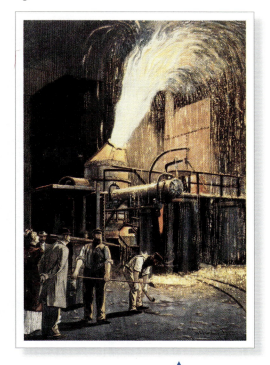

▲ New industries needed much steel for machinery. The Bessemer converter, invented in the 1850s, was a cheaper, better way to make steel.

CHAPTER 14, Section 4

Linking Past to Present

The Textile Industry Changes in the factors of production, especially labor, have played an important role in the American textile industry over the last 200 years. In the early 1800s most textile mills were in New England near fast-moving rivers that provided power. Displaced farm workers and immigrants provided much of the labor.

By the early 1900s the old textile mills of New England were shutting down as capitalists moved their operations to the South to take advantage of lower labor costs. Then, in the late 1900s many southern mills were closed as textile companies again looked for cheaper labor in foreign countries.

Activity: Have students conduct research to create time lines illustrating key events in the history of the American textile industry.

The Beginnings of the Industrial Revolution

Factor of Production	How It Was Supplied in Britain
Natural resources	iron ore, coal, rivers for water power, canals, ports
Labor	people put out of work by changes in agriculture
Capital	money from people who had become wealthy, willing to invest

Teaching Objectives 2–3

LEVEL 1: (Suggested time: 25 min.) Provide students with blank index cards. Have each student make a flash card for each of the following items: *water-powered spinning machines and looms, factories, steam engine, canals, paved road, locomotive, telegraph.* On the back of each card, have students write a sentence or two that describes how each item helped industry develop and spread. **ESOL**

CHAPTER 14, Section 4

DAILY LIFE

The Luddites Although the textile factories of Great Britain put many people to work, they also eliminated jobs. During the early 1800s, some weavers who had made cloth by hand organized into secret bands called Luddites. They called their leader, who may have been imaginary, King Ludd.

The Luddites put on masks and, under cover of darkness, damaged factory machinery. They didn't try to injure people, however. The authorities punished Luddites when they could catch them, but local people sometimes helped members of the secret society.

Discussion: Point out that some people who try to avoid modern technology are called—or call themselves—Luddites. Lead a discussion about how use of the term has changed.

Steam engines boil water and use the steam to do work. Early steam engines were not efficient, though. In 1769 James Watt, a Scottish inventor, built a modern steam engine that worked well. With Watt's invention, steam power largely replaced water power. This meant that factories could be built anywhere.

The Factory System For centuries, workers lived where they practiced their crafts. In addition, workers had taken years to learn a trade. With the Industrial Revolution, the factory system changed workers' lives. Workers had to leave home, often walking several miles, to work in a factory. Unlike on the farm, where tasks changed in tune with the weather and the seasons, factories operated six days a week year round. Factory workers had to obey new rules. If they broke the rules they were sometimes punished severely, even beaten. For many factory jobs, the tasks employees performed were simple. A worker could learn to run a machine in just a day or two. As a result, factory owners hired unskilled laborers. They found that women and children could operate the machines as well as men but demanded lower wages. So children as young as five years old worked in the factories. Meanwhile, older skilled workers were often unemployed.

Conditions in many of the factories were terrible. Employees worked long hours and had few breaks. Working more than 12 hours a day was not unusual. Factory work could ruin employees' health. In the summer the factories were hot and steamy. In the winter they were cold. Year round, the factory air was thick with dust. Big machines caused many injuries, and some child workers never recovered from injuries or illnesses caused by factory conditions. At home, workers' problems continued. So many people had come to the cities for jobs that housing was in short supply. People crowded together wherever they could find room, which further endangered health and safety.

✓ **READING CHECK:** *Summarizing* How did the factory system affect peoples' lives? had to leave home to work in factories; obey rules; health problems and injuries; crowded housing

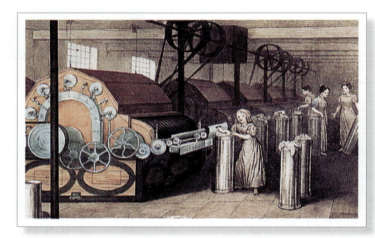

Girls and young women worked hard for low wages. Factory workers, however, could make more money than maids.
Interpreting the Visual Record What task does this girl appear to be performing?

340 • Chapter 14

LEVEL 2: (Suggested time: 45 min.) Tell students to imagine they are the inventors of one of the machines described in this section. Ask each student to write a short speech in which he or she describes his invention and how it helped the Industrial Revolution to begin or spread. Encourage students to conduct additional research to find more information for their speeches. Call on volunteers to deliver their speeches. **LS AUDITORY-MUSICAL**

▶**ASSIGNMENT:** Have students look around their rooms at home and write down a list of from 5 to 10 objects. For each object, the student should describe how the Industrial Revolution affected its development.

The Spread of the Industrial Revolution

Great Britain quickly became the world's leading industrial power. British laws encouraged people to use capital to set up factories. Great Britain's stable government was good for industry, too.

The rest of Europe did not develop industry as quickly. For one thing, the French Revolution and Napoléon's wars had disrupted Europe's economies. That made it difficult to put the factors of production to work. Many countries also lacked the resources needed to industrialize.

The Industrial Revolution did spread quickly to the United States, though. The United States had a stable government, rich natural resources, and a growing labor force. Americans were quick to adapt British inventions and methods to their own industries.

Transportation Since the Middle Ages, horse-drawn wagons had been the main form of transportation in Europe. Factory owners needed better transportation to get raw materials and send goods to market. To move goods faster, stone-topped roads were built in Europe and the United States. Canals were dug to link rivers. The steam engine was also put to work in transportation. In 1808, American inventor Robert Fulton built the first steamboat. Within a few decades, steamships were crossing the Atlantic.

These steamboats from the 1850s carried people and goods on the Mississippi River.

Steam also powered the first railroads. An English engineer, George Stephenson, perfected a steam locomotive that ran on rails. By the 1830s, railways were being built across Great Britain, mainland Europe, and the United States.

Communication Even before 1800, scientists had known that electricity and magnetism were related. American inventor Samuel F. B. Morse put this knowledge to practical use. Morse sent an electrical current through a wire. The current made a machine at the other end click. Morse also invented a code of clicking dots and dashes to send messages this way.

Morse's inventions—the telegraph and Morse code—brought about a major change in communications. Telegraph wires soon stretched across continents and under oceans. Suddenly, information and ideas could travel at the speed of electricity.

The telegraph revolutionized communications in the 1850s. This device is a telegraph receiver.

✓ **READING CHECK:** *Environment and Society* In what two nations did industrialization spread fastest? Why? **Great Britain and the United States; laws encouraging people to use capital to set up factories; stable government; rich natural resources; growing labor force**

Across the Curriculum
TECHNOLOGY

The Telegraph Samuel Morse's early telegraph worked much like a doorbell. The sending device was a switch, or key, that acted like a doorbell button. When pressed, the key completed the telegraph circuit, allowing current to flow to a receiving sounder. When the key was released, the circuit was broken and no current flowed.

Activity: Invite interested students to research the scientific principles on which the telegraph was based.

CHAPTER 14, Section 4

FOOD FESTIVAL

Banquets and Crumbs In the periods covered by this section, there were often big gaps between the rich and the poor. These gaps affected what the two classes ate. The very rich consumed mountains of intricately designed rich food, while the poor scraped together whatever they could find. Sometimes they couldn't find enough to keep them from starving.

Organize the class into groups to conduct research on eating habits of the upper and lower classes during the Renaissance, under the great European and Russian ruling families of the 1600s and 1700s, of France under Louis XVI, and of the British industrial leaders of the 1800s. It would be difficult to prepare the dishes that kings and queens enjoyed, but students may want to prepare murals comparing the eras' eating habits.

Visual Record Answer
perhaps made their work easier, but also more tedious and repetitious

Life in the Industrial Age

The 1800s are sometimes called the Industrial Age. This was an age of new inventions. It was also a time when businesses found new ways to produce and distribute goods. The owners of factories in the Industrial Age often became very wealthy. Low factory wages, however, meant many workers faced poverty.

The Rise of Capitalism In the late 1800s, European and American individuals owned and operated factories. This economic system is called **capitalism**. In a capitalist system, individuals or companies, not the government, control the factors of production.

The early capitalists wanted to make as much profit as possible from their factories. Factory owners used machines to make the parts for their products. These parts were identical and interchangeable. Thus if a part broke, a new one did not have to be custom-made to fit. In another move to increase profits, they divided each manufacturing process into a series of steps. Each worker performed just one step, over and over again. This division of labor meant workers could produce more goods in less time.

To speed up production even more, the parts were brought to the workers in the factory. Each worker added one part, and the product moved on to the next worker. This method of production is called an assembly line.

In the early 1900s, Henry Ford used an assembly line to build cars.
Interpreting the Visual Record How do you think development of the assembly line affected the daily lives of these workers?

342 • Chapter 14

LEVELS 2 AND 3: (Suggested time: 20 min.) Ask students to imagine they have just gotten jobs in one of the large new factories of the late 1800s. In a letter to a relative or friend, have each student describe the factory in which he or she works and describe how his or her work is organized. Direct students to note in their letters which aspects of their jobs they like and which they dislike. Remind students that their letters should mention what type of product is made in the factory. **LS INTRAPERSONAL**

TEACHER TO TEACHER

Susan Walker of Beaufort, South Carolina, suggests this activity to review the impact that the Industrial Revolution has had on our society. Have students select a pre-industrial society, such as Australian Aborigines that live in the outback or one of the Amazon rain forest peoples. Ask students to write essays about the differences in these peoples' ways of life and ours, and how the Industrial Revolution has caused those differences.

Mass Production The division of labor, interchangeable parts, and the assembly line made mass production possible. **Mass production** is a system of producing large numbers of identical items. Mass production lowered the cost of clothing, furniture, and other goods. It allowed more people to buy manufactured products and to enjoy a higher standard of living.

Political and Social Reform In addition to great advances in technology and communications, science and medicine also progressed. In addition, the mid-1800s and early 1900s saw many political and social reforms. To reform something is to remove its faults. Around the world, citizens tried to improve their governments and societies.

In Great Britain, reformers passed laws that allowed male factory workers to vote although they didn't own property. Laws were also passed to improve factory conditions. Slavery was abolished. New laws established health insurance, unemployment insurance, and money for the elderly. In France, free speech was guaranteed and all men got the right to vote.

Beginning in the late 1800s, many women in Great Britain became **suffragettes**. These women campaigned for their right to vote. They were led by outspoken women like Emmeline Pankhurst. British women won the vote in 1928.

Education for women was changing during the late 1800s, also. The young women in this classroom are studying subjects such as geography and science.

✓ **READING CHECK:** *Identifying Cause and Effect* How did women in Great Britain win the right to vote? *campaigned and were led by outspoken leaders*

Section Review 4

Define or identify: Industrial Revolution, Jethro Tull, factors of production, capital, Richard Arkwright, factory system, James Watt, Samuel F.B. Morse, capitalism, mass production, suffragettes, Emmeline Pankhurst

Reading for the Main Idea
1. *Environment and Society* Where did the Industrial Revolution begin and why?
2. *Human Systems* What advances in transportation and communications helped spread the Industrial Revolution?
3. *Human Systems* Why did many people's lives improve during the last half of the 1800s?

Critical Thinking
4. *Drawing Conclusions* Why do you think the steam engine was such an important invention of the Industrial Revolution?

Organizing What You Know
5. *Categorizing* Copy the following graphic organizer. Use it to describe some important inventions of the Industrial Revolution.

Invention	Inventor	Importance
seed drill		
spinning machine		
water-powered loom		
steam engine		
steam locomotive		
telegraph		

Europe in Transition • 343

Section 4 Review

Answers to Section 4 Review

Define or identify For definitions and identifications, see the glossary and index.

Reading for the Main Idea
1. in Great Britain, because it had the factors of production: land, natural resources, labor, and capital
2. stone-topped roads, canals, steamships, railroads, telegraph and Morse code
3. lowered the cost of goods, which improved standard of living

Critical Thinking
4. It allowed the development of mechanized industries and transportation systems

Organizing What You Know
5. seed drill—Jethro Tull, mechanized farming; spinning machine—Richard Arkwright, made thread easier to spin; water-powered loom—Edmund Cartwright, produced cloth faster; steam engine—James Watt, new source of power; steam locomotive—George Stephenson, transport people and goods quickly; telegraphy—Samuel F. B. Morse, allowed long-distance communication

CLOSE

Locate and read to the class excerpts from the writings of suffragette Emmeline Pankhurst. Discuss the readings.

REVIEW, ASSESS, RETEACH

Have students complete the Section Review. Then call on students to choose one of the vocabulary terms from this section and explain its significance with regard to the Industrial Revolution. Then have students complete Daily Quiz 14.3. **ESOL**

Have students complete Main Idea Activity S4. Then have students imagine that they are American capitalists from the late 1800s trying to decide what type of factory to build and where to build it. Have students discuss how the factors of production, transportation, and communication technologies may affect their decisions.

EXTEND

Have interested students conduct research on the latest innovations in factory design and present illustrated reports to the class.
BLOCK SCHEDULING

CHAPTER 14 REVIEW

Define and Identify
For definitions and identifications, see the glossary and index.

Review the Main Ideas

14. philosophy that focused on life here and now rather than life after death, placed importance on individual achievement

15. Desiderius Erasmus, François Rabelais, Miguel de Cervantes, Machiavelli, Baldassare Castiglione, William Shakespeare

16. Luther believed that attending church, giving money to the church, and doing good deeds didn't matter—only faith in God mattered.

17. religious wars, new churches, interest in education, reforms in Catholic Church, governments gained power, church's power diminished

18. by fostering curiosity and through scientific and technological improvements

19. See the chart in Section 2 for major explorers and their accomplishments.

20. France—Bourbons; Russia—Romanovs; Austrian Empire—Habsburgs; Prussia—Hohenzollerns

21. Conflict between Parliament and the monarchy led to a revolution, and the monarchy was ended. In 1660, the English monarchy was restored under Charles II.

22. widespread hunger, high taxes, high prices, resentment against nobility and clergy, extravagant lifestyle of the monarchy, debt (NGS 13)

23. land, natural resources, labor, capital

24. mass production

Chapter 14 Review and Practice

Define and Identify
Identify each of the following:
1. Renaissance
2. Reformation
3. Leonardo da Vinci
4. Martin Luther
5. Scientific Revolution
6. Parliament
7. Sir Isaac Newton
8. Enlightenment
9. Reign of Terror
10. Napoléon Bonaparte
11. Industrial Revolution
12. suffragettes
13. James Watt

Review the Main Ideas
14. What was humanism?
15. Who were some of the great writers of the Renaissance?
16. How did Luther's teachings conflict with those of the Roman Catholic Church?
17. What were the results of the Reformation and Counter-Reformation?
18. How did the Scientific Revolution pave the way for European exploration?
19. Who were the major explorers, and what did they accomplish?
20. Who were the main ruling families in Europe in the 1600s?
21. What happened to the English monarchy in the mid-1600s? What happened in 1660?
22. Why did the French people revolt against the monarchy?
23. What are the factors of production?
24. What did the division of labor, interchangeable parts, and the assembly line make possible?

Think Critically
25. **Comparing and Contrasting** How did the goals of King Henry VIII compare with those of John Calvin?
26. **Analyzing Information** How did mercantilism both help and hurt Great Britain?
27. **Finding the Main Idea** What were some of the basic ideas of the Enlightenment?
28. **Drawing Inferences and Conclusions** Why do you think historians might have widely differing opinions about Napoléon Bonaparte?
29. **Understanding Cause and Effect** How did changes in agriculture lead to the Industrial Revolution?

Map Activity
30. Identify the places marked on the map.
    - Spain
    - Portugal
    - North America
    - Mexico
    - South America
    - Europe

344 • Chapter 14

Think Critically
25. Calvin wanted to live lives of self-restraint, while Henry VIII was more interested in being able to get a divorce and remarry.
26. made it wealthy, but created resentment in the colonies
27. use of reason to discover laws of nature, secularism, individualism, responsibility of rulers to work for the public good, the right of people to change their government and govern themselves
28. because he accomplished a great deal for France and other conquered lands, but also used ruthless methods and caused terrible wars to be fought
29. New farming methods created more efficient farms, throwing many people out of work. These people were then available as labor for the factories.

Map Activity
30. A. Spain
    B. Portugal
    C. North America
    D. Mexico
    E. South America
    F. Europe

CHAPTER 14 REVIEW

Writing Activity

Imagine that you are a child working in a textile factory in the early 1800s. Write a brief dialog in which you tell another person about your day. Explain how your family's situation required that you go to work. Describe the factory's working conditions and your reactions to those conditions. Assume also that the other person has asked if you can say anything positive about your work. Be sure to use standard grammar, spelling, sentence structure, and punctuation.

internet connect

Internet Activity: go.hrw.com
KEYWORD: SJ5 GT14

Choose a topic to explore about the world in transition:
- Create a biography of a Renaissance artist or writer.
- Learn more about an explorer described in this chapter.
- Write a report on the Reign of Terror.

Writing Activity (Teacher's notes)
Dialogues will vary, but should give an accurate picture of factory conditions of the early 1800s. Students should express both positive and negative views of their situations. Use Rubric 40, Writing to Describe, to evaluate student work.

Interpreting Maps (Answers)
1. Madeira Islands, Canary Islands, Cape Verde Islands
2. Brazil
3. almost 5,000 miles
4. southwest; southeast

Analyzing Primary Sources (Answers)
1. Possible answer: to emphasize that what he is saying should be obvious to the listener
2. an unnamed Spanish explorer
3. Possible answer: no, because they would sound ridiculous, even to the speaker
4. Possible answer: no, because he notes that they had been living in peace before and that the Spaniards would cut them to pieces if they didn't follow orders

Social Studies Skills Practice

Interpreting Maps

Pedro Alvares Cabral was a Portuguese explorer. In 1500 he set off for India. Study the map of Cabral's voyage. Then answer the questions.

1. In which island groups may Cabral have stopped for rest, food, and water?
2. Where did Cabral land before he proceeded to India?
3. About how far did Cabral sail in the first part of his voyage?
4. In which direction did Cabral first sail? To which direction did he turn?

Analyzing Primary Sources

Bartolomé de Las Casas was a Spanish priest who traveled to the Americas and wrote about Spain's conquests there. For years Las Casas lived and worked among the native peoples. Read the following quote by Las Casas. Then answer the questions.

"Any reasonable person who knows something . . . of rights and of civil law can imagine for himself what the likely reaction would be of any people living peaceably within their own frontiers, unaware that they owe allegiance to anyone save their natural lords, were a stranger suddenly to issue a demand along the following lines: 'You shall henceforth obey a foreign king, whom you have never seen nor ever heard of and, if you do not, we will cut you to pieces'—Especially when they discover that these strangers are indeed quite prepared to carry out this threat to the letter."

1. Why does Las Casas begin by using the phrase *any reasonable person*?
2. Who is speaking in the quote that begins "You shall . . ."?
3. Do you think anyone ever used those exact words? Why or why not?
4. Did Las Casas approve of how Spain treated the native peoples? Support your answer.

Europe in Transition • 345

CHAPTER 14 — REVIEW AND ASSESSMENT RESOURCES

Reproducible
- Readings in World Geography, History, and Culture 35
- Critical Thinking Activity 14
- Vocabulary Activity 14

Technology
- Chapter 14 Test Generator (on the One-Stop Planner)

- HRW Go site
- Audio CD Program, Chapter 14

Reinforcement, Review, and Assessment
- Chapter 14 Review and Practice
- Chapter Summaries and Review
- Chapter 14 Test

- Chapter 14 Test for English Language Learners and Special-Needs Students

internet connect
GO TO: go.hrw.com
KEYWORD: SJ5 Teacher
FOR: a guide to using the Internet in your classroom

CHAPTER 15: Modern Europe
Chapter Resource Manager

Objectives	Pacing Guide	Reproducible Resources
SECTION 1		
World War I (pp. 347–351) 1. Identify the three main causes of World War I. 2. Examine how technology made this war different from earlier wars. 3. Investigate how Europe changed because of World War I.	**Regular** 2 days Lecture Notes, Section 1 **Block Scheduling** 1 day Block Scheduling Handbook, Chapter 15	**RS** Know It Notes S1 **RS** Graphic Organizer 15 **ELL** Main Idea Activity S1
SECTION 2		
The Great Depression and the Rise of Dictators (pp. 352–355) 1. Identify the causes of the Great Depression. 2. Describe a dictatorship. 3. Analyze how the Great Depression helped dictators come to power in Europe.	**Regular** 3 days Lecture Notes, Section 2 **Block Scheduling** 1.5 days Block Scheduling Handbook, Chapter 15	**RS** Know It Notes S2 **ELL** Main Idea Activity S2
SECTION 3		
World War II (pp. 356–360) 1. Identify the causes of World War II. 2. Describe the Holocaust. 3. Analyze how World War II came to an end.	**Regular** 3 days Lecture Notes, Section 3 **Block Scheduling** 1.5 days Block Scheduling Handbook, Chapter 15	**RS** Know It Notes S3 **E** Biography Activity: Winston Churchill **ELL** Main Idea Activity S3
SECTION 4		
Europe Since 1945 (pp. 361–365) 1. Describe how the Cold War affected Europe. 2. Identify the new alliances that countries formed in response to the Cold War. 3. Investigate some other conflicts that troubled Europe after World War II.	**Regular** 3 days Lecture Notes, Section 4 **Block Scheduling** 1.5 days Block Scheduling Handbook, Chapter 15	**RS** Know It Notes S4 **E** Biography Activity: Margaret Thatcher **E** Creative Strategies for Teaching World Geography, Lesson 10 **E** Readings in World Geography, History, and Culture: Readings 30–33, 37, 38 **SM** Critical Thinking Activity 15 **ELL** Main Idea Activity S4

Chapter Resource Key

- **RS** Reading Support
- **IC** Interdisciplinary Connections
- **E** Enrichment
- **SM** Skills Mastery
- **A** Assessment
- **REV** Review
- **ELL** Reinforcement and English Language Learners and English for Speakers of Other Languages (ESOL)
- Transparencies
- CD–ROM
- Music
- Video
- Internet (go.hrw.com)
- Holt Presentation Maker Using Microsoft® PowerPoint®

One-Stop Planner CD–ROM

See the *One-Stop Planner* for a complete list of additional resources for students and teachers.

One-Stop Planner CD–ROM

It's easy to plan lessons, select resources, and print out materials for your students when you use the *One-Stop Planner CD–ROM with Test Generator*.

HRW ONLINE RESOURCES

GO TO: go.hrw.com
Then type in a keyword.

TEACHER HOMEPAGE
KEYWORD: SJ5 TEACHER

CHAPTER INTERNET ACTIVITIES
KEYWORD: SJ5 GT15

Choose an activity to:
- learn about the effects of the Treaty of Versailles.
- write a report about Anne Frank.
- create a poster about D-Day.

CHAPTER ENRICHMENT LINKS
KEYWORD: SJ5 CH15

CHAPTER MAPS
KEYWORDS: SJ5 MAPS15

ONLINE ASSESSMENT
Homework Practice
  KEYWORD: SJ5 HP15
Standardized Test Prep Online
  KEYWORD: SJ5 STP15
Rubrics
  KEYWORD: SS Rubrics

COUNTRY INFORMATION
KEYWORD: SJ5 Almanac

CONTENT UPDATES
KEYWORD: SS Contents Updates

HOLT PRESENTATION MAKER
KEYWORD: SJ5 PPT15

ONLINE READING SUPPORT
KEYWORD: SS Strategies

CURRENT EVENTS
KEYWORD: SS Current Events

Technology Resources	Review, Reinforcement, and Assessment Resources	
One-Stop Planner CD-ROM, Lesson 15.1 Geography and Cultures Visual Resources 44, 45 *ARGWorld* CD-ROM Homework Practice Online HRW Go Site	ELL	Main Idea Activity S1
	REV	Section 1 Review
	A	Daily Quiz 15.1
	REV	Chapter Summaries and Review
	ELL	English Audio Summary 15.1
	ELL	Spanish Audio Summary 15.1
One-Stop Planner CD-ROM, Lesson 15.2 *ARGWorld* CD-ROM Homework Practice Online HRW Go site	ELL	Main Idea Activity S2
	REV	Section 2 Review
	A	Daily Quiz 15.2
	REV	Chapter Summaries and Review
	ELL	English Audio Summary 15.2
	ELL	Spanish Audio Summary 15.2
One-Stop Planner CD-ROM, Lesson 15.3 Geography and Cultures Visual Resources 44, 45 *ARGWorld* CD–ROM Homework Practice Online HRW Go site	ELL	Main Idea Activity S3
	REV	Section 3 Review
	A	Daily Quiz 15.3
	REV	Chapter Summaries and Review
	ELL	English Audio Summary 15.3
	ELL	Spanish Audio Summary 15.3
One-Stop Planner CD-ROM, Lesson 15.4 Geography and Cultures Visual Resources 44, 45 *ARGWorld* CD–ROM CNN Presents World Cultures: Yesterday and Today Segment 30: NATO at 50 Homework Practice Online HRW Go site	ELL	Main Idea Activity S4
	REV	Section 4 Review
	A	Daily Quiz 15.4
	REV	Chapter Summaries and Review
	ELL	English Audio Summary 15.4
	ELL	Spanish Audio Summary 15.4

Meeting Individual Needs

Ability Levels

Level 1 Basic-level activities designed for all students encountering new material

Level 2 Intermediate-level activities designed for average students

Level 3 Challenging activities designed for honors and gifted-and-talented students

ESOL Activities that address the needs of students with Limited English Proficiency

Chapter Review and Assessment

E	Readings in World Geography, History, and Culture 30–33, 37, 38
SM	Critical Thinking Activity 15
REV	Chapter 15 Review and Practice
REV	Chapter Summaries and Review
ELL	Vocabulary Activity 15
	Holt PuzzlePro
A	Chapter 15 Test
A	Chapter 15 Test Generator (on the One-Stop Planner)
	Audio CD Program, Chapter 15
A	Chapter 15 Test for English Language Learners and Special-Needs Students
	HRW Go site

CHAPTER 15

Modern Europe
Previewing Chapter Resources

Holt Online Learning

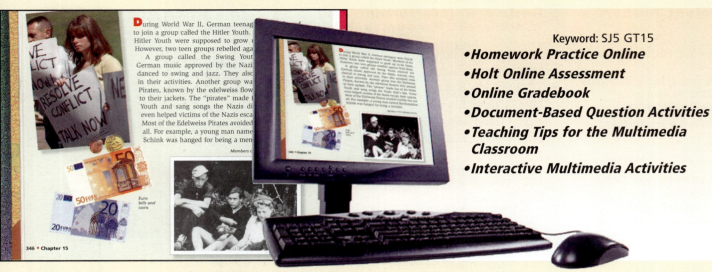

Keyword: SJ5 GT15

- **Homework Practice Online**
- **Holt Online Assessment**
- **Online Gradebook**
- **Document-Based Question Activities**
- **Teaching Tips for the Multimedia Classroom**
- **Interactive Multimedia Activities**

Differentiating Instruction

Reading and Writing Support
- ◄ *Graphic Organizer Activity*
- *Vocabulary Activity*
- *Chapter Summaries and Review*
- *Know-It Notes S1–4*
- *Audio CD*

Active Learning
- ◄ *Block Scheduling Handbook*
- *Cultures of the World Activity*
- *Interdisciplinary Activity: Reader's Theater*
- *Map Activity*

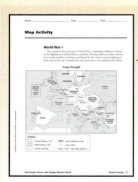

Primary Sources and Advanced Learners
- ◄ *Map Activity: World War I*
- *Readings in World Geography, History and Culture:*
  - *32 Living Behind the Wall*
  - *34 Surviving in Wartime London*

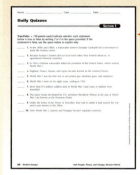

Assessment Program
- ◄ *Daily Quizzes S1–4*
- *Chapter Test*
- *Chapter Test for English Language Learners and Special-Needs Students*

Spanish and ESOL
- *Vocabulary Activity*
- *Main Idea Activities for English Language Learners and Special-Needs Students*
- *Chapter Summaries and Review*
- *Spanish Audio Summary*
- ◄ *Know-It Notes S1–4*
- *Chapter Test for English Language Learners and Special-Needs Students*

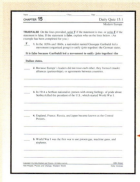

Special Education Modifications
Your **I.D.E.A. Works! CD-ROM** will provide modified versions of the following teaching materials:
- *Know It Notes S1–4*
- *Vocabulary Activity*
- *Main Idea Activities S1–4*
- ◄ *Daily Quizzes S1–4*
- *Chapter 15 Test*
- *Flash cards of chapter vocabulary terms*

Teacher Resources

Books for Teachers

Howard, Michael. *The First World War.* Oxford University Press, 2003.

Keegan, John. *An Illustrated History of the First World War.* Knopf, 2001.

World War II Day by Day. DK Publishing, 2001.

Kagan, Neil ed., *Great Photographs of World War II.* Oxmoor House, 2004.

Gaddis, John Lewis. *We Now Know: Rethinking Cold War History.* Oxford Press, 1998.

Books for Students

Perrin, Pat. *World War I: Researching American History.* Discovery, 2001.

Adams, Simon. *Eyewitness: World War II.* DK Publishing, 2000.

Panchyk, Richard. *World War II for Kids: A History with 21 Activities.* Chicago Review Press, 2002. Presents a personal perspective with wartime letters, interviews with former soldiers, ordinary citizens, and Holocaust survivors.

Fox, Anne L. *Ten Thousand Children: True Stories Told By Children Who Escaped the Holocaust on the Kindertransport.* Behrman House, 1998.

Levy, Patricia. *The Fall of the Berlin Wall.* Raintree/Steck-Vaughn, 2002.

Multimedia Materials

World War I. Video, A & E Entertainment, 2001.

World War II: The Lost Color Archives. Video, A & E Entertainment, 2000.

Untold Stories of World War II. Video, National Geographic, 2001.

Fall of the Berlin Wall. Video, Warner Home Video, 2000.

Videos and CDs

Videos
- CNN Presents World Cultures: Yesterday and Today, Segment 15 Europe's Immigration Challenge

CDs
- ARG World
- I.D.E.A. Works! CD–ROM

Transparency Packages

Geography and Cultures Visual Resources Transparencies
44 Europe: Physical
45 Europe: Political

Holt Researcher

http://researcher.hrw.com

- World War II
- Unemployment in Europe
- European Democracies
- Communist Europe
- World War I and the Russian Revolution

CHAPTER 15

WHY IT MATTERS

Share with your students the following reasons for learning about Europe in the 1900s:

- World War I and World War II led to the redrawing of Europe's boundaries. Some of the boundaries created after these wars created conflict long after their creation.
- Countries that underwent great changes in the 1900s are still affected by these changes.
- Organizations like the United Nations and NATO founded after World War II remain active in political affairs today.

CHAPTER 15

Modern Europe

Europe went through tremendous changes during the 1900s. Horrible wars, economic depression, cruel injustices, and positive advances all took place. You'll find out more in this chapter.

Irish youth peace demonstration

During World War II, German teenagers were forced to join a group called the Hitler Youth. Members of the Hitler Youth were supposed to grow up to be Nazis. However, two teen groups rebelled against Nazi ideas.

A group called the Swing Youth rejected the German music approved by the Nazis. Instead, they danced to swing and jazz. They also accepted Jews in their activities. Another group was the Edelweiss Pirates, known by the edelweiss flowers they pinned to their jackets. The "pirates" made fun of the Hitler Youth and sang songs the Nazis didn't like. Some even helped victims of the Nazis escape their captors. Most of the Edelweiss Pirates avoided trouble, but not all. For example, a young man named Bartholomäus Schink was hanged for being a member.

Euro bills and coins

Members of the Edelweiss Pirates

CHAPTER PROJECT

Organize the class into groups and have each group create a short play that depicts a major event from Chapter 9. Have each group present its play to the class. Remind students that they should create programs to accompany their plays, listing the cast, describing the event depicted, and explaining the plot of the play. Place these programs in student portfolios.

STARTING THE CHAPTER

Ask students to think about some things that have been invented or improved during their lifetimes. Then ask if any students have heard stories about their parents' lives when they were in school. Ask if any students know how their grandparents or great-grandparents lived when they were young. If no students have any family accounts, ask if they have seen pictures or read stories about life in the early to mid-1900s. Tell students that they will learn what life was like in Europe in the 1900s in this chapter.

Section 1 World War I

Read to Discover
1. What were three main causes of World War I?
2. How did technology make this war different from earlier wars?
3. How did World War I change Europe?

Vocabulary
nationalism
militarism
alliances
U-boats
armistice
Treaty of Versailles

People
Giuseppe Garibaldi
Otto von Bismarck

Reading Strategy
READING ORGANIZER Before you read this section, create a three-column chart. Title the columns Causes of War, War Events, and After-War Changes. As you read, write information about each topic on your chart. Then use your chart to outline the section.

Beginning of World War I

By 1900, many European countries were competing for power. They built up strong armies to protect themselves and their interests. The stage was set for a war. It would claim millions of lives. At the time it was called The Great War. Later, we would call it World War I. What caused this terrible war? For the answer, we must go back to the 1800s.

Causes of the War During the 1800s, nationalism was sweeping Europe. Nationalism is the love of one's country more than the love of one's native region or state. The idea would help create new countries and destroy old ones.

In the early 1800s, Italy was divided into several states. In the 1850s and 1860s, a nationalist named Giuseppe Garibaldi led a movement to unify these states. Largely because of his efforts, most of present-day Italy had been unified by 1861.

Meanwhile, Germany in the mid-1800s was a patchwork of small separate states. The largest was Prussia, ruled by William I. He appointed Otto von Bismarck to be his chief adviser. Like Garibaldi had done in Italy, Bismarck led efforts to unify the German states. Eventually, they joined to become the German Empire. William I became its first kaiser, or emperor.

These two new countries—Italy and Germany—began to build up their industries and armies. With these armies, both countries would play big roles in the coming war.

Otto von Bismarck was known for his strong will and determination. These qualities helped earn him the nickname "the Iron Chancellor." Bismarck worked hard to unite Germany, but opposed any form of democracy.

Modern Europe • 347

CHAPTER 15, Section 1

SECTION 1 RESOURCES

Reproducibles
- Lecture Notes, Section 1
- Block Scheduling Handbook, Chapter 15
- Know It Notes S1

Technology
- One-Stop Planner CD-ROM, Lesson 15.1
- Geography and Cultures Visual Resources 44, 45
- Homework Practice Online
- HRW Go Site

Review, Reinforcement, and Assessment Resources
- Section 1 Review
- Daily Quiz 15.1
- Main Idea Activity S1
- Chapter Summaries and Review
- English Audio Summary 15.1
- Spanish Audio Summary 15.1

Section 1

Objectives
1. Identify the three main causes of World War I.
2. Examine how technology made this war different from earlier wars.
3. Investigate how Europe changed because of World War I.

Focus

Bellringer
Copy this passage onto the chalkboard: *What do you think the expression "world war" means?* Discuss student responses. (Possible answer: a war involving many countries or a large area) Call on students to suggest some reasons a small or local conflict between two countries might turn into a world war. (Students might say that a country could have many enemies or that other countries could take sides in an existing conflict.) Tell students that in Section 1 they will learn about the First World War.

Building Vocabulary
Write the vocabulary terms on the chalkboard. Call on volunteers to find the definitions and read them to the class. Point out the words **nationalism** and **militarism**, and circle the suffix *-ism*. Explain that this suffix indicates an idea, concept, or behavior. Ask students to use the suffix to explain the meaning of these two words. (Possible answer: Nationalism is the idea that one should honor one's nation; militarists act in a way that glorifies the military.)

Modern Europe 347

CHAPTER 15, Section 1

DAILY LIFE

Women and the War
Although the United States didn't enter the war immediately, American women helped war efforts early by saving food. At the time of World War I, most homemakers were women. Some 20 million homemakers signed pledges promising not to serve meat on Mondays or bread on Wednesdays and to grow their own vegetables in "Victory Gardens."

In return, they received stickers to display in the windows of their homes, showing that they were helping with the war effort. Their voluntary rationing efforts helped the United States double its shipments of food to the Allies in Europe, who badly needed it.

Eventually, women would serve in the armed forces.

Discussion: During times of crisis, why are people willing to make sacrifices that they might ordinarily complain about?

Answer: They feel patriotic; they want to help others; they want to join in with what others are doing.

Map Answer
Triple Entente

Europe at the Beginning of World War I

The alliance of Great Britain, France, and Russia was called the Triple Entente. The word *entente* means "intent" or "understanding."
Interpreting the Map Which alliance was split by the territory of the other?

The assassination of Francis Ferdinand was the event that touched off the war.

Many other European countries also sought more power and more land. To get what they wanted, they followed a policy of **militarism**. Militarism is the use of strong armies and the threat of force to gain power.

With the major European countries heavily armed, Europe's leaders didn't trust each other. To protect their countries against threats to their security, they formed **alliances**. An alliance is an agreement between countries. If one country is attacked, its allies—the members of the alliance—help it fight. By 1907, Europe was divided into two opposing sides. Germany, Austria-Hungary, and Italy formed one alliance. Great Britain, France, and Russia formed another.

Nationalism, militarism, and alliances formed a dangerous mix. Europeans were nervous—with good reason. An event in the Balkans, in southeastern Europe, would show just how dangerous the situation was.

The War Starts In 1878 Serbia, on the Balkan Peninsula, had become an independent country. Serbians influenced by nationalism wanted control of Bosnia and Herzogovina, which was controlled by Austria-Hungary. On June 28, 1914, a Serb shot and killed the heir to the Austro-Hungarian throne, Archduke Francis Ferdinand. As a result, Austria-Hungary declared war on Serbia. Russia supported Serbia, while Germany supported Austria-Hungary. With Russia and its allies on one side and Germany and its allies on the other, conflict quickly spread.

In August 1914 Germany declared war on Russia. Russia was allied with France, so Germany declared war on France too. Britain declared war on Germany. Japan also declared war on Germany. Britain, France, Russia, and Japan became known as the Allied Powers. The alliance of Germany, Austria-Hungary, the Ottoman Empire, and Bulgaria was called the Central Powers. In 1915, Italy joined the Allied side. Eventually, the Allied Powers included about 30 countries.

✓ **READING CHECK:** *Identifying Cause and Effect* How did the system of alliances help set the stage for war? *divided Europe into two opposing sides of countries that had to defend each other*

348 • Chapter 15

TEACH

Teaching Objective 1
ALL LEVELS: (Suggested time: 20 min.) Copy the following graphic organizer onto the board, omitting the blue answers. Have students fill in the chart with descriptions and examples of the factors that led to World War I. After students have completed their charts, lead a class discussion about how each of the listed factors contributed to the outbreak of war.
ESOL, **LS** **VISUAL-SPATIAL**

THE CAUSES OF WORLD WAR I		
Nationalism	Militarism	Alliances
People began to feel fierce pride in their countries. Countries wanted more land.	Countries built strong armies. Strong countries used the threat of force to gain power.	Europe was organized into alliances. Allied countries would have to help each other fight.

348 Chapter 15

A New Kind of War

New weapons played a major role in World War I. Germany introduced submarines, which were called **U-boats**. The name is short for a German phrase that means "underwater boats." Germany also introduced poison gas, which was later used by both sides and caused many deaths. Other new weapons included large, long-range cannons and machine guns.

World War I was also the first war to use airplanes. At first airplanes were used mainly to observe enemy troops. Later, soldiers placed machine guns on airplanes, so they could shoot at troops and at each other's planes from the air. The British introduced the tank, equipped with machine guns.

The Early Years of the War Major fighting began when Germany attacked France. The German army almost reached Paris, the French capital. However, Russia attacked Germany and Austria-Hungary, forcing Germany's attention east. At sea, England used its powerful navy to stop supplies from reaching Germany by ship. Germany used its deadly U-boats to sink ships carrying supplies to Britain.

At first, both sides thought they would win a quick victory. They were wrong. In France and Belgium, the opposing armies dug trenches facing each other. In the trenches, soldiers suffered from cold, thirst, hunger, and disease, along with the constant noise of bombs falling around them. Month after month, trench warfare continued. Sometimes soldiers would "go over the top" of their trenches and fight for a few hours, only to retreat to the same position without making any progress. In this way, World War I went on for four years.

This modern painting gives some idea of the horrors of trench warfare.
Interpreting the Visual Record
What elements of modern technology do you see in the picture? How did technology seem to affect the battlefields?

CHAPTER 15, Section 1

USING ILLUSTRATIONS

Trench Warfare Focus students' attention on the illustration on this page. Challenge them to image what it would have been like for a young soldier who, for example, had recently been a farmer in the peaceful English countryside, to be immersed in this battle. Discuss responses.

Trench warfare has been vividly portrayed in several movies. The most famous may be *All Quiet on the Western Front*, made in 1930. Although the film follows the progress of the war through the eyes of a group of German boys, it portrays the experiences of both sides as they are mired in the horrors of trench warfare. Some students may want to watch *All Quiet on the Western Front* and report on it to the class.

◀**Visual Record Answer**

airplanes, tanks, artillery fire; devastated the battlefields and turned them into cratered, muddy landscape

---

Teaching Objective 2

ALL LEVELS: (Suggested time: 30 min.) Organize the class into four groups. Have each group prepare a chart, diagram, or report that shows how new weapons and technologies affected the way World War I was fought. Tell students that their projects should clearly demonstrate the differences between World War I and early wars in which the European countries were involved. Encourage interested students to note developments from World War I that are still employed in wars today.
ESOL, COOPERATIVE LEARNING

Teaching Objective 3

LEVELS 1 AND 2: (Suggested time: 10 min.) Ask students to find examples in the text of ways in which Europe changed after World War I. As students name changes, write them on the chalkboard. Then have students compare the political changes made after the war to the boundaries on a modern map of Europe.

LEVEL 3: Obtain samples of art and music from the era immediately following World War I. Play or show these materials to the class. Lead a discussion of how this music and art represent changes brought about by the war. Paint out that the new styles refleted a feeling that nothing made sense to people after the war.

CHAPTER 15, Section 1

GLOBAL CONNECTIONS

The Zimmerman Telegram
A 1917 incident shows how a single small event can have a huge effect on world affairs. In January of that year, German foreign secretary Arthur Zimmermann sent a telegram to Count Johann von Bernstorff, Germany's ambassador to the United States. In the telegram, Zimmermann said that Mexico should be persuaded to enter the war on Germany's side. The lure would be a promise that Mexico would receive the territories in Texas, New Mexico, and Arizona that it had lost to the United States decades before.

British intelligence personnel intercepted the telegram and broke the news to the U.S. government. When President Woodrow Wilson released the telegram's contents, the American public was outraged. The United States declared war on Germany shortly thereafter.

Graph Answer
Russia; about 1.75 million

The United States and the War At first, the United States stayed out of the war. However, German U-boats were attacking American ships carrying supplies to the Allies. As a result, the United States lost many ships and people. Then in 1917, Germany secretly tried to persuade Mexico to join the Central Powers. When British intelligence broke the news, many Americans were very angry.

Changes in Russia also affected feelings in the United States. In 1917, a revolution forced the Russian czar to give up power. Americans felt better about fighting for Russia's new government, which offered the hope of being more democratic, than they had about fighting for the czar. On April 2, 1917, President Woodrow Wilson asked the U.S. Congress to declare war on Germany. It did so four days later.

✓ **READING CHECK:** (Identifying Cause and Effect) How Why did the United States enter World War I? German U-boats attacked U.S. ships; Central Powers tried to get Mexico to join them; revolution in Russia offered hope of democracy.

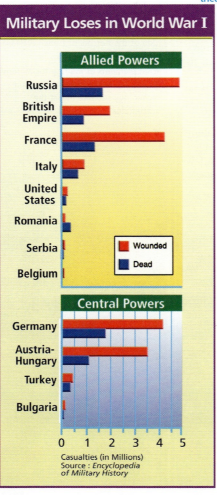

Interpreting the Graph Which of the Allied Powers had the highest number of total casualties? About how many German soldiers died during the war?

The War Ends

In March 1918 Russia made a separate peace treaty with Germany and pulled out of the war. With Russia no longer fighting on the eastern front the tide began to turn in favor of Germany. The German army made steady progress. However, when the United States entered the war, the German army was pushed back to its own border. Germany's allies began to surrender. At last, Germany itself surrendered. Both sides signed an **armistice**. An armistice is an agreement to stop fighting.

The fighting stopped on November 11, 1918. More than 8.5 million soldiers had been killed, and 21 million more wounded. Millions of civilians were killed as well—many from starvation or disease.

Making Peace In January 1919 representatives of the Allied nations met near Paris to decide what would be done now that the war was over. This meeting is known as the Paris Peace Conference.

President Wilson wanted fair peace terms after the war. He felt that harsh terms might lead to future wars. His ideas were called the Fourteen Points. These ideas called for freedom of the seas for everyone, prohibiting secret treaties, and the establishment of an association of nations to promote peace and international cooperation. That association, the League of Nations, was formed in 1919 but the United States refused to join.

Other Allied leaders wanted to punish Germany. They felt that Germany had started the war and should pay for it. They believed that the way to prevent future wars was to make sure that Germany could never become powerful again.

CLOSE

Point out to students that the term *World War I* was not actually used during the war itself. People who lived through the war often referred to it as the "war to end all wars." Ask students what they think people meant by this name. (Possible answer: The war was so long and destructive that people thought it would discourage countries from ever going to war again.) Then ask students why we no longer use this name. (World War I did not, obviously, end warfare. World War II was fought later.)

REVIEW, ASSESS, RETEACH

Have students complete the Section Review. Then organize students into teams. Give each team an index card. Have the members of each team choose an event or person discussed in the section and write a question about that event or person on their cards. Pass the cards from team to team. Ask each team to copy each question into their notebooks and to answer them. Continue until all each team has seen every question. Then have students complete Daily Quiz 15.1. **COOPERATIVE LEARNING**

The agreement these leaders finally reached became known as the **Treaty of Versailles** (ver-SY). Germany had to admit it had started the war and to pay money to the Allies. Germany also lost territory. The treaty stated that Germany could not rebuild its military. The United States never agreed to the Treaty of Versailles. It eventually signed a separate peace treaty with Germany.

A New Europe World War I changed the map of Europe. France and Belgium gained territory that had belonged to Germany. Austria and Hungary became separate countries. Poland and Czechoslovakia gained their independence. Bosnia and Herzegovina, Croatia, Montenegro, Serbia, and Slovenia were combined as Yugoslavia. Finland, Estonia, Latvia, and Lithuania, all of which had been part of Russia, also became independent countries. Bulgaria and the Ottoman Empire likewise lost territory.

Across Europe, millions of people were dead. Trench warfare had destroyed huge areas of land. Economies had been wrecked. For many Europeans, life no longer made sense. After two decades, they would find that World War I was just the beginning of a troubled century. You will read more about these problems in the next sections.

Allied leaders met at Paris to decide what would happen in Europe after the war. President Woodrow Wilson is at the far right.

✓ **READING CHECK:** *Summarizing* What new countries were created at the end of World War I? Austria, Hungary, Poland, Czechoslovakia, Yugoslavia, Finland, Estonia, Latvia, and Lithuania

Section Review 1

Define or identify: nationalism, militarism, alliances, U-boats, armistice, Treaty of Versailles, Giuseppe Garibaldi, Otto von Bismarck

Reading for the Main Idea
1. *Human Systems* What tensions made Europeans nervous before World War I?
2. *Human Systems* What new weapons were used in the World War I?
3. *Human Systems* What issues divided the Allies after the war?

Critical Thinking
4. **Drawing Inferences and Conclusions** Do you think World War I would have happened if Europe had not been divided into two major alliances? Why or why not?

Organizing What You Know
5. **Categorizing** Copy the following chart. Use it to list the members of each alliance.

Allied Powers	Central Powers

Section 1 Review

Answers to Section 1 Review

Define For definitions, see the glossary and index.

Reading for the Main Idea
1. Militarism encouraged nations to build strong armies; nations did not trust one another; alliances meant countries had to go to war to help their allies. (NGS 13)
2. U-boats, poison gas, long-range cannons, machine guns, airplanes, tanks. (NGS 14)
3. terms of the peace treaty, how to treat Germany. (NGS 13)

Critical Thinking
4. The war would not have been as widespread; it might have been a war between only Serbia and Austria-Hungary.

Organizing What You Know
5. Allied Powers—England, France, Russia, Japan, Italy, United States; Central Powers—Germany, Austria-Hungary, Ottoman Empire, Bulgaria

Section 2: The Great Depression and the Rise of Dictators

Read to Discover
1. What led to the Great Depression?
2. What is a dictatorship?
3. How did the Great Depression help dictators come to power in Europe?

Vocabulary
stock market
bankrupt
Great Depression
New Deal
dictator
fascism
communism
police state

People
Benito Mussolini
Adolf Hitler
Joseph Stalin

Reading Strategy

TAKING NOTES Use the headings of this section to create an outline. As you read, use the section headings in your outline and write details you learn about the Great Depression and the rise of dictators in Europe.

After World War I, German currency was so useless that it was cheaper to burn it as fuel than to buy wood. Here a Berlin woman burns millions of marks, the German currency, in her stove.

352 • Chapter 15

The Great Depression

During the 1920s industrialized Allied countries such as Great Britain experienced a surge of economic growth. However, less than 10 years later, both the winners and losers of World War I struggled with unemployment and poverty.

Causes of the Depression During World War I, much farmland in Europe was destroyed. Farmers all over the world planted more crops to sell food to European countries. In the United States many farmers borrowed money to buy farm machinery and more land. When the war ended, Europe required less food. Prices went down. Farmers could not pay back the money they had borrowed. Many lost their land.

During the 1920s, the American **stock market** did very well. The stock market is an organization through which shares of stock in companies are bought and sold. People who buy stock are buying shares in a company. If people sell their stock when the price per share has risen above the original price, they make a profit.

In the 1920s, as stock prices rose, more and more people invested their money in the stock market. People thought stock prices would keep rising, so they borrowed money to buy more stocks. Unfortunately, stock prices fell. Falling stock prices made people rush to sell their shares before they lost any more money. When many people all sold their stock at once, prices were driven down even further. Finally the stock market crashed, or hit bottom, on October 29, 1929. Because the U.S. economy was connected to Europe's, the crash affected Europeans and European banks.

CHAPTER 15, Section 2

SECTION 2 RESOURCES

Reproducibles
- Lecture Notes, Section 2
- Block Scheduling Handbook, Chapter 15
- Know It Notes S2

Technology
- One-Stop Planner CD-ROM, Lesson 15.2
- Homework Practice Online
- HRW Go Site

Review, Reinforcement, and Assessment Resources
- Section 2 Review
- Daily Quiz 15.2
- Main Idea Activity S2
- Chapter Summaries and Review
- English Audio Summary 15.2
- Spanish Audio Summary 15.2

Objectives
1. Identify the causes of the Great Depression.
2. Analyze how the Great Depression helped dictators come to power in Europe.

FOCUS

Bellringer
Copy the following question onto the board: *What do you think would happen if, suddenly, most people had no money?* Discuss student responses. (Possible answers: People might go hungry; businesses might close as people stopped spending; many might panic or come to depend on government assistance.) Point out that these things happened in the 1930s during the Great Depression. Tell students that in Section 2 they will learn more about the Great Depression and how it affected Europe and the world.

Building Vocabulary
Write the key terms on the board. Call on volunteers to find the definitions of the terms in the textbook, and read them to the class. Point out the suffix *–or* in the word **dictator**, meaning "one who." Ask students if they are familiar with the word *dictate*. Call on a volunteer to explain how its meaning is reflected in the definition of *dictator*. (A dictator's rules dictate the actions of a country's people.)

352 Chapter 15

During the 1930s, people marched from communities across the United Kingdom to London. They hoped to draw attention to the need for jobs and food. In this photo, women take part in a demonstration called the National Hunger March in 1932.

People who had borrowed to buy stocks suddenly had to pay back the money. They rushed to the banks to take money out. But the banks did not have enough funds to give everyone their savings all at once. In a very short time, many banks, factories, farms, and people went **bankrupt**. This meant they had no more money.

This was the beginning of the **Great Depression**. All over the world, wages fell, banks closed, business slowed or stopped, and people could not find jobs. Many people were poor. Many did not even have enough money to buy food. Some people sold apples on street corners to make a little money.

Governments and the Depression Governments around the world tried to lessen the effects of the Depression. Some limited the number of imports they allowed into their countries. They thought this would encourage citizens to buy products made by businesses in their own countries. This plan did not work. In fact, the loss of foreign markets for their products drove many countries even further into debt.

The United States took a different approach. In 1933 Franklin D. Roosevelt became president of the United States. He created programs to help end the Depression. These programs together were called the **New Deal**. The federal government gave money to each state to help people. The government also created jobs. It hired people to construct buildings and roads and work on other public projects.

These government programs helped the U.S. economy grow somewhat, but they were not enough to solve the economic crisis completely. The Great Depression would not end in the United States until the early 1940s.

✓ **READING CHECK:** *Identifying Cause and Effect* How did the Depression start? **Stock prices dropped; then rush to sell before the loss was great; selling panic drove stock values down more; many people lost all their money.**

The Great Depression affected the entire world. By 1932, more than 30 million people throughout the world could not find jobs.

CHAPTER 15, Section 2

National Geography Standard 11
Economic Interdependence and Financial Disaster

A common practice during the 1920s was called speculating on the margin. This meant that investors borrowed money from their stock brokers. As late as September 1929 even Winston Churchill, Britain's Chancellor of the Exchequer, speculated on the margin. Churchill seemed to have made a small fortune on only a few thousand pounds. Like many others, however, Churchill's fortune quickly dwindled to nothing.

Critical Thinking: What may Churchill's story illustrate about stock market investment in 1929?

Answer: Students may suggest that Churchill's experience showed how easy it was to make and lose money in the market. (It also shows that even financial experts could make decisions that had unforeseen and unfortunate results.)

Modern Europe • 353

TEACH

Teaching Objective 1
ALL LEVELS: (Suggested time: 20 min.) Copy the following graphic organizer onto the board, omitting the blue answers. Have each student complete the organizer with factors that led to the Great Depression. Ask volunteers to share their answers with the class. Use their completed organizers to lead a discussion about the beginnings of the Great Depression.
ESOL, LS VISUAL-SPATIAL

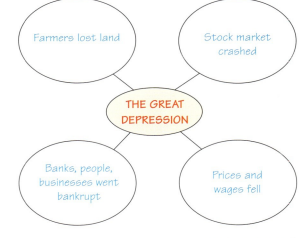

Modern Europe 353

CHAPTER 15, Section 2

HUMAN SYSTEMS

Fascist Violence When Mussolini's Fascist party first tried to gain power, it failed. The Fascists then turned to violence. They fought with communists in the streets of Italy's cities. They beat up people who tried to organize unions.

Discussion: Ask students how they would feel if a political party in the United States tried to gain power by using the same methods the Fascists used in Italy. Lead a discussion on how political groups in the United States today gain support for their ideas.

▲
When he became dictator of Italy, Benito Mussolini took the title *il Duce* (il DOO-chay), Italian for "the leader."

▲
Hitler was a very powerful speaker. He often twisted the truth in his speeches. He claimed that the bigger a lie was, the more likely people would be to believe it.

354 • Chapter 15

The Rise of Dictators in Europe

As the Great Depression continued in Europe, life got harder. Many people became unhappy with their governments, which were not able to help them. In some countries, people were willing to give up democracy to have strong leaders who promised them more money and better lives. It was easy for dictators to take control of these governments. A **dictator** is an absolute, or total, ruler. A government ruled by a dictator is called a dictatorship. Powerful dictators seized control of Italy and Germany.

Italy Becomes a Dictatorship Benito Mussolini told the Italians that he had the answers to their problems. Mussolini called his ideas **fascism** and started the Fascist Party. Fascism was a political movement that put the needs of the nation above the needs of the individual. The nation's leader was supposed to represent the will of the nation. The leader had total control over the people and the economy.

Fascist nations became strong through militarism. Their leaders feared communism for a good reason. **Communism** promised a society in which property would be shared by everyone. Mussolini promised that he would not let communists take over Italy. He also promised he would bring Italy out of the Great Depression and return Italy to the glory of the Roman Empire.

In 1924, the Fascist Party won Italy's national election. Mussolini took control of the government and became a dictator. He turned Italy into a police state. A **police state** is a country in which the government has total control over people and uses secret police to find and punish people who rebel or protest.

Germany After World War I many Germans felt that their government had betrayed them by signing the Treaty of Versailles. Many also blamed the German government for the unemployment and inflation brought by the Great Depression. Several groups attempted to overthrow and replace the old government. Eventually a new party called the Nazi Party gained power. It too was a fascist party. Adolf Hitler was its leader.

Hitler promised to break the Treaty of Versailles. He said he would restore Germany's economy, rebuild Germany's military power, and take back territory that Germany had lost after the war. Hitler told the Germans that they were superior to other people. Many Germans eagerly listened to Hitler's message. They thought he would restore Germany to its former power.

The Nazis quickly gained power in Germany. In 1933 Hitler took control of the German government. He made himself dictator and used the title *der Führer* (FYOOHR-uhr), which is German for "the leader." He

---

▶**ASSIGNMENT:** Have each student write a short story that describes what they think daily life might have been like in Europe during the Great Depression. Tell students that their stories should note some of the hardships that people faced in the 1930s. Encourage them also to note the success or failure of government programs passed to alleviate some of this hardship. Call on volunteers to share their stories with the class.

Teaching Objective 2–3
ALL LEVELS: (Suggested time: 30 min.) Ask students to name some rights that people have in a democracy. (Freedom of speech; freedom of the press; freedom of religion; right to a fair trial; free elections; different political parties) List each response on the board and ask students why this freedom is important to them. Explain that people who live in dictatorships seldom enjoy these freedoms. Ask students to find examples in the text of what life was like in Italy and Germany under Mussolini and Hitler. Then lead a discussion about factors that led to the rise of each of these dictators. **ESOL, LS INTERPERSONAL**

turned Germany into a police state. Newspapers and political parties that opposed the Nazis were outlawed. Groups of people that Hitler claimed were inferior, especially Jews, lost their civil liberties.

Hitler began secretly to rebuild Germany's army and navy. He was going to make Germany a mighty nation again. He called his rule the Third Reich. *Reich* is the German word for "empire." In 1936 Hitler formed a partnership with Mussolini called the Rome-Berlin Axis.

The Soviet Union Russia had suffered terribly during World War I. The Communist government had promised an ideal society in which people would share wealth and live well. However, most Russians remained poor.

In the 1920s, Russia's name changed. Joseph Stalin gained control of the Soviet Union's Communist Party. Stalin's government took land from farmers and forced them to work on large collective farms owned and controlled by the central government. Stalin also tried to industrialize the Soviet Union. However, for ordinary Russians food and manufactured goods remained scarce.

Religious worship was forbidden. Artists were even told what kind of pictures to paint. Secret police spied on people. Those who did not obey Stalin's policies were arrested and put in jail or killed. Scholars think that by 1939 more than 5 million people had been arrested, deported, sent to forced labor camps, or killed.

▲ At a political rally, Nazis parade with flags displaying swastikas, the Nazi symbol.

✓ **READING CHECK:** *Analyzing* How did Hitler take advantage of the Treaty of Versailles to gain power in Germany? **Germans' problems blamed on Treaty of Versailles; Hitler promised to ignore the treaty and rebuild Germany's economy and military power.**

Section Review 2

Homework Practice Online
Keyword: SJ5 HP15

Define or identify: stock market, bankrupt, Great Depression, New Deal, dictator, fascism, communism, police state, Benito Mussolini, Adolf Hitler, Joseph Stalin

Reading for the Main Idea
1. *Human Systems* What happened during the Great Depression?
2. *Human Systems* What is life like in a dictatorship?
3. *Human Systems* How did European dictators take advantage of the Great Depression to gain power?

Critical Thinking
4. **Drawing Inferences** Refer back to Section 1. How were Woodrow Wilson's concerns about harsh peace terms for Germany proven correct by the rise of Adolf Hitler?

Organizing What You Know
5. **Identifying Cause and Effect** Copy the following graphic organizer. Fill it in to summarize events that led to the Great Depression.

Cause	Effect
Europe needs food during World War I.	
The war ends and crop prices fall.	
Stock prices rise very high.	
People rush to sell their stocks.	
People rush to take money out of the banks.	

Modern Europe • 355

CHAPTER 15, Section 3

SECTION 3 RESOURCES

Reproducibles
- Lecture Notes, Section 3
- Block Scheduling Handbook, Chapter 15
- Know It Notes S3
- Biography Activity: Winston Churchill

Technology
- One-Stop Planner CD-ROM, Lesson 15.3
- Geography and Cultures Visual Resources 44, 45
- Homework Practice Online
- HRW Go Site

Review, Reinforcement, and Assessment Resources
- Section 3 Review
- Daily Quiz 15.3
- Main Idea Activity S3
- Chapter Summaries and Review
- English Audio Summary 15.3
- Spanish Audio Summary 15.3

Visual Record Answer ▶

fear, suffering, horror, despair

Section 3 World War II

Read to Discover
1. What were the causes of World War II?
2. What was the Holocaust?
3. How did World War II end?

Vocabulary
aggression
anti-Semitism
genocide
Holocaust

People
Francisco Franco
Winston Churchill
Anne Frank

Reading Strategy

USING PRIOR KNOWLEDGE Before you read this section, write down some of the facts that you already know about Europe in World War II. Then write down what you want to know. After you study the section, write down new information that you learned.

Threats to World Peace

During the 1930s, Japan, Italy, and Germany committed acts of aggression against other countries. **Aggression** is warlike action, such as an invasion or an attack. At first, little was done to stop them. Eventually, their actions led to a full-scale war that involved much of the world.

In 1931, Japanese forces took control of Manchuria, a part of China. The League of Nations protested, but took no military action to stop Japan. Continuing its aggressive actions, Japan succeeded in controlling about one fourth of China by 1939. In 1935, Italy invaded Ethiopia, a country in East Africa. Many countries protested, but they did not want another war. Like Japan, Italy saw that the rest of the world would not try hard to stop its aggression.

Pablo Picasso's painting *Guernica* is named for a town bombed during the Spanish Civil War.
Interpreting the Visual Record What human feelings about war does Picasso express?

356 • Chapter 15

Section 3

Objectives
1. Identify the causes of World War II.
2. Describe the Holocaust.
3. Analyze how World War II came to an end.

FOCUS

Bellringer

Copy these instructions onto the board: *Think about television programs, movies, and books with which you are familiar. What images do you associate with World War II?* Discuss student responses. (Students might mention Nazis, tanks, fighter planes, aircraft carriers, the Holocaust, or similar images.) Tell students that they will learn more about the history of World War II in this section.

Building Vocabulary

Write the vocabulary terms on the chalkboard. Call on volunteers to locate and read the definitions in the glossary or text. Point out the prefix *anti-* in **anti-Semitism** means "against." *Semitism* comes from *Semite*, a word that refers to several peoples from Southwest Asia, including the Hebrews. **Genocide** is derived from the Latin words *gens*, which means "race" or "people," and *caedere*, meaning "to kill." Have students write a sentence using the word *aggression*.

356 Chapter 15

Spanish Civil War In 1936, civil war broke out in Spain. On one side were fascists led by General Francisco Franco. Supporting Franco were wealthy landowners, the Roman Catholic Church, and the military. Both Italy and Germany sent troops and supplies to help Franco's forces. On the other side were Loyalists, people loyal to the elected Spanish government. The Soviet Union sent aid to the Loyalists. Volunteers from France, Great Britain, and the United States also fought on their side, but their help was not enough. In 1939, the fascists defeated the Loyalists. Franco set up a dictatorship. He ended free elections and most civil rights. With Franco's victory, it was clear that fascism was growing in Europe.

Hitler's Aggressions In the 1930s many Germans lived in Austria, Czechoslovakia, and Poland. Hitler wanted to unite these countries to bring all Germans together. In 1938 German soldiers marched into Austria, and Hitler declared Austria to be part of the Third Reich. Britain and France protested but did not attack Germany. Later that year Hitler took over the Sudetenland (soo-DAYT-uhn-land), a region of western Czechoslovakia. Other European countries were worried, but they still did not want a war. Hitler soon conquered the rest of Czechoslovakia.

Eventually Britain and France realized they could not ignore Hitler. They asked the Soviet Union to be their ally in a war against Germany. However, Soviet leader Joseph Stalin had made a secret agreement with Hitler. They decided that their countries would never attack each other. This deal was called the German-Soviet nonaggression pact. However, many historians believe that neither the Germans nor the Soviets thought that the treaty would last.

On September 1, 1939, Hitler invaded Poland. Two days later, Great Britain and France declared war on Germany. World War II had begun. On one side were Germany, Italy, and Japan. They are called the Axis Powers, or the Axis. Britain, France, and other countries that fought against the Axis are known as the Allies.

✓ **READING CHECK:** *Drawing Inferences* How might British and French leaders have prevented World War II? **stopped aggression of Japan, Italy, and Germany; stopped Hitler before he became too powerful**

Women cry as they give the Nazi salute to German troops in Sudetenland.

Joseph Stalin (second from right) made an agreement that the Soviet Union and Germany would not attack each other.

CHAPTER 15, Section 3

DAILY LIFE

Bombs over Britain Even before World War II began, the leaders of Great Britain began making plans to protect its people from German air attacks. The British government sent thousands of children away from London to the countryside, where German bombers were less likely to attack. Moving children separated families, but it saved many lives.

When the war began, London was bombed night and day by German planes. People took shelter in subways and the basements of buildings. These bombing raids became known as the Blitz, after *blitzkrieg*, a German word for "lightning war." The British people were famous for bravely carrying on with their normal lives as much as possible.

Discussion: Lead a discussion about what life was like during the Blitz. Call on students to share their ideas and impressions.

Modern Europe • 357

TEACH

Teaching Objective 1
ALL LEVELS: (Suggested time: 20 min.) Copy the following graphic organizer onto the board, omitting the blue answers. Call on students to fill in the boxes on the chart with actions taken by each country that led to the outbreak of World War II. Then lead a discussion about the underlying causes that led to these actions. **ESOL**

ACTIONS AND EVENTS THAT LED TO WORLD WAR II	
Japan	1. took control of Manchuria
	2. conquered more of China
Italy	1. invaded Ethiopia
Germany	1. made Austria part of Germany
	2. took over the Sudetenland
	3. conquered Czechoslovakia
	4. invaded Poland

CHAPTER 15, Section 3

National Geography Standard 9

The Ghettos In many occupied cities, the Nazis crowded Jews into small areas called *ghettos*. The ghetto in Warsaw, Poland, was surrounded by a wall topped with barbed wire and held 500,000 people in a small, cramped area. As the Germans began to deport Jews from the Warsaw ghetto to the death camps, German troops tried to enter the ghetto, only to be driven out by Jewish resistance forces. Starting in April 1943, about 600 to 1,000 Jews armed with little more than pistols battled 2,000 to 3,000 German soldiers and tanks for 27 days.

Discussion: Lead a class discussion about the meaning of the word *ghetto* today. Ask students how this meaning is related to the historical one.

Biography Answer ▶

by not letting setbacks keep him from his goal of serving his country

▶ Carrying whatever belongings they can, people in northern France try to escape from attacks.

BIOGRAPHY
Sir Winston Churchill
(1874–1965)

Character Trait: Pursuit of Excellence

During the Battle of Britain, Winston Churchill led the British people to resist the Nazis. Churchill had been in the military and was later a member of the British Parliament. Even though he faced setbacks in both positions, Churchill never lost sight of his goal—to serve his country. Churchill became prime minister in 1940. While Germany was bombing Britain night after night, the British people gathered around their radios to hear the prime minister's speeches. Churchill challenged them never to give up, never to surrender. *How did Winston Churchill show the pursuit of excellence?*

358 • Chapter 15

War

At the beginning of the war, the Germans won many victories. Poland fell in one month. In 1940 Germany conquered Denmark, Norway, the Netherlands, Belgium, and Luxembourg. In June 1940 Germany invaded and quickly defeated France. In less than one year, Hitler had gained control of almost all of western Europe. Next he sent German planes to bomb Great Britain. The British fought back with their own air force. This struggle became known as the Battle of Britain.

In June 1941, Hitler turned on his ally and invaded the Soviet Union. As winter set in, however, the Germans found themselves vulnerable to Soviet attacks. Without enough supplies, Hitler's troops were defeated by a combination of the freezing Russian winter and the Soviet Red Army. For the first time in the war, German soldiers were forced to retreat.

The United States Many people in the United States did not want their country to go to war. The United States sent supplies, food, and weapons to the Allies but did not actually enter the war until late 1941. In that year Japan was taking control of Southeast Asia and the Pacific. Seeing the United States as a possible enemy, Japanese military leaders attempted to destroy the U.S. naval fleet in the Pacific. On December 7, 1941, Japan launched a surprise air attack on the naval base at Pearl Harbor, Hawaii. The attack sank or damaged U.S. battleships and killed more than 2,300 American soldiers. The next day President Franklin D. Roosevelt announced that the United States was at war with Japan. Great Britain also declared war on Japan. Three days later, Germany and Italy—both allies of Japan—declared war on the United States. In response, Congress declared war on both countries.

✓ **READING CHECK:** (Evaluating) How were Hitler's invasion of the Soviet Union and Japan's attack on Pearl Harbor turning points in the war? **Invasion of Soviet Union led to Germany's retreat; attack on Pearl Harbor brought U.S. into the war.**

The Holocaust

Hitler believed that Germans were a superior people, and planned to destroy or enslave people whom he believed were inferior. Hitler hated many peoples, but he particularly hated the Jews. Hatred of Jews is

---

Teaching Objective 2
ALL LEVELS: (Suggested time: 40 min.) Organize the class into groups and have each group design a museum exhibit about the Holocaust. Tell students that their designs should list the causes of the Holocaust and describe events associated with it. Call on students to share their ideas with the class. **ESOL, COOPERATIVE LEARNING,** **LS** **VISUAL-SPATIAL**

Teaching Objective 3
ALL LEVELS: (Suggested time: 30 min.) Have students work in pairs to create time lines of the last years of World War II. Direct students to fill their time lines with events from the text. Next to each entry on their time lines, have students note how each event contributed to ending the war. Display the completed time lines around the classroom.
ESOL, COOPERATIVE LEARNING

called **anti-Semitism**. The Nazis rounded up Europe's Jews and imprisoned them in concentration camps.

Death Camps In 1942, Hitler ordered the destruction of Europe's entire Jewish population. The Nazi **genocide**, the planned killing of a race of people, is called the **Holocaust**.

The Nazis built death camps in Poland and elsewhere to carry out this terrible plan. People who could work were forced into slave labor. Those who could not work were sent to gas chambers where they were killed. Some Jews were shot in large groups. Thousands of other people died from conditions in the camps. The dead were buried in mass graves or burned in large ovens. By the time the Nazi government was defeated, its leaders and followers had murdered an estimated 6 million European Jews. Millions of non-Jews were also killed.

Resisting the Nazis Some Jews tried to fight back. Others hid. Most, however, were unable to escape. Many Europeans ignored what was happening to the Jews, but some tried to save people from the Holocaust. The Danes helped about 7,000 Jews escape to Sweden. In Poland and Czechoslovakia, the German businessman Oskar Schindler saved many Jews by employing them in his factories.

✓ READING CHECK: Summarizing What were Nazi concentration camps like?
slave labor, death in the gas chambers, by being shot, or through starvation and disease

The End of the War

In 1942 the Germans tried to capture the Soviet city of Stalingrad. The battle lasted six months, but the Soviet defenders held out. The Germans were never able to take the city. This was a major blow to the Germans, who now were weakened on the eastern front. At the same time, American and British forces defeated the Germans in North Africa. The war began to turn in favor of the Allies. That same year in the Pacific Japan lost several important battles. Led by the United States, Allied forces—including troops from Australia and New Zealand—began a campaign to regain some of the Pacific islands Japan had taken. Island by island, the Allies slowly pushed the Japanese forces back across the Pacific Ocean.

In the summer of 1943 the Allies captured the Italian island of Sicily. Italians forced Mussolini to resign, and Italy's new leader dissolved the Fascist Party. In September, Italy agreed to stop fighting the Allies.

Victory in Europe On June 6, 1944, Allied forces landed on the beaches of Normandy in northwestern France. This was the D-Day invasion. The invasion was a success. In August, Allied troops entered Paris. By September they were at Germany's western border. With the Soviets attacking Germany from the east, the Nazis' defenses fell apart. On April 30 Hitler killed himself, and a week later, Germany surrendered.

Anne Frank
(1929-1944)

Character Trait: Respect

One of the Holocaust's victims was a young Jewish girl named Anne Frank. While she and her family hid from the Nazis in an attic, Anne kept a diary. Although Anne was captured and died in a concentration camp, her diary survived. In it, she expressed her belief in the basic goodness of people. She held this belief in spite of her tragic situation. Anne also gave the world insight into the horrors of the Holocaust. The publication of her diary made Anne one of the world's best-known teenage authors. *How did Anne Frank show respect for other people?*

CHAPTER 15, Section 3

National Geography Standard 17

Geography of the Pacific and the War The war against Japan stretched across the Pacific Ocean. Therefore ships played a very important role in this part of World War II. U.S. submarines attacked Japanese shipping in an effort to cut off Japan's oil supply. Aircraft carriers transported planes to scenes of battle.

Early in the war, Japan advanced eastward across the Pacific Ocean by capturing many Pacific islands. To take back this territory, Allied forces used a strategy called "island hopping." They attacked only certain Japanese-held islands, skipping others but leaving them without supplies. The plan was successful in stopping Japan and pushing its forces back across the Pacific.

Discussion: Lead a class discussion on this topic: How was the war in the Pacific different from the war in Europe?

▲ **Biography Answer**

by believing in their basic goodness in spite of her tragic situation

---

➤**ASSIGNMENT:** Tell students to imagine that they are American newspaper editors in 1941 immediately following the bombing of Pearl Harbor. Have each student write an editorial for his or her newspaper arguing whether or not the United States should enter the war.

TEACHER TO TEACHER

Alfred J. Hamel, of Worcester, Massachusetts, suggests the following activity to help students understand the war in the Pacific. The American-led strategy called island hopping was eventually successful in defeating the Japanese. Have students conduct research on the Pacific war and draw maps that show which Pacific islands were taken by the Allies. Ask students to explain how the taking of these islands helped lead to the defeat of the Japanese.

Section 3 Review

Answers to Section 3 Review

Define or identify For definitions and identifications, see the glossary and index.

Reading for the Main Idea
1. acts of aggression by Japan, Italy, and Germany (NGS 13)
2. Jews were put in concentration camps where millions were murdered; millions of others who the Nazis thought were not pure were murdered.
3. Axis defeated; millions of soldiers and civilians killed; enormous destruction; atomic age began (NGS 13)

Critical Thinking
4. Fascist nations became strong through militarism; Mussolini and Hitler set out to restore their nations' glory and power by invading other countries.

Organizing What You Know
5. World War II begins; Germany begins bombing England; Germans retreat for first time in war; United States enters war; Allies begin to retake Europe; Japan surrenders, war ends.

Graph Answer ▶
Soviet Union, China, Germany; locations of much of the fighting

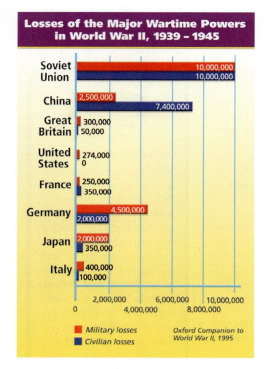

Interpreting the Graph What three countries had the highest civilian losses? What factors may have contributed to these losses?

Victory over Japan Fighting continued in the Pacific. The Allies bombed Japan, but the Japanese would not surrender. Finally President Harry Truman decided to use the new atomic bomb against Japan. On August 6, 1945, the most powerful weapon the world had ever seen was dropped on the Japanese city of Hiroshima. The blast reduced the city to ashes and destroyed the surrounding area. On August 9 another atomic bomb was dropped on the Japanese city of Nagasaki. About 200,000 people were killed in the attacks and many more were hurt. Countless more people died of injuries. Five days later Japan surrendered.

The War's Cost World War II resulted in more destruction than any other war in history. More than 50 million people died, and millions more were wounded. Unlike in most earlier wars, many of the people killed were civilians. A civilian is anyone who is not in the military. Millions were killed in the Holocaust. Thousands were killed by bombs dropped on cities in Europe and Asia. Thousands more died in prison camps in Japan and the Soviet Union. In time, people began to question how such cruel acts against human life and human rights were allowed to happen and how they could be prevented in the future.

The American use of the atomic bomb began the atomic age. With it came many questions and fears. How would this new weapon be used? What effect would it have on future wars? After World War II, world leaders would struggle with these questions.

✓ **READING CHECK:** Analyzing How was World War II unlike any war that came before it? most destructive war in history; large number of civilian deaths; human rights ignored in new ways; atomic bomb introduced

Define or identify: aggression, anti-Semitism, genocide, Holocaust, Francisco Franco, Winston Churchill, Anne Frank

Reading for the Main Idea
1. *Human Systems* What events led to World War II?
2. *Human Systems* What happened during the Holocaust?
3. *Human Systems* What were the results of World War II?

Critical Thinking
4. **Cause and Effect** How did the rise of fascism in Europe lead to World War II?

Organizing What You Know
5. **Drawing Inferences and Conclusions** Copy the following graphic organizer. Fill it in, telling why each event was important in the war.

Event	Why Important?
Hitler invades Poland.	
Hitler gains control of western Europe.	
Germany invades the Soviet Union.	
Japan attacks Pearl Harbor.	
The Allies invade Europe on D-Day.	
The United States drops the atomic bomb on Japan.	

Homework Practice Online
Keyword: SJ5 HP15

CLOSE
Call on students to name individuals who played major roles in World War II. As people are named, call on other students to describe the actions for which they are known.

Have students complete Main Idea Activity S3. Then copy onto the chalkboard each of the major topics discussed in this section. Call on students to provide facts that apply to each topic. **ESOL**

REVIEW, ASSESS, RETEACH
Have students complete the Section Review. Then ask students to write one sentence about the role each of the following countries played in World War II: Italy, Japan, Germany, England, Soviet Union, United States. Then have students complete Daily Quiz 15.3. **ESOL, VERBAL-LINGUISTIC**

EXTEND
Have interested students conduct research on the British home front during World War II. Direct students to pay particular attention to the roles of women during the war. Call on volunteers to share their findings with the class. **BLOCK SCHEDULING**

Section 4: Europe Since 1945

Read to Discover
1. How did the Cold War affect Europe?
2. What new alliances did countries form in response to the Cold War?
3. What are some other conflicts that troubled Europe after World War II?

Vocabulary
communism
capitalism
bloc
Iron Curtain
NATO
arms race

People
Mikhail Gorbachev

Reading Strategy
READING ORGANIZER Before you read, draw a line across a large piece of paper. Write 1945 at the left end of the line. Write Today at the right end. As you read this section, create a time line of events that occurred in Europe since 1945. You may want to add recent events from a newspaper to your time line.

The Cold War

Although Europeans were relieved when World War II ended, new problems arose. A major issue involved the Soviet Union. The Soviet Union clashed with its former allies over ideas about freedom, government, and economics. Because this struggle did not turn into a shooting or "hot" war, it is known as the Cold War.

A Struggle of Ideas The struggle that started the Cold War was between two ideas—**communism** and **capitalism**. Communism is an economic system in which a central authority controls the government and the economy. Capitalism is a system in which businesses are privately owned. During the Cold War, the Soviet government was a dictatorship that controlled the economy. In contrast, Great Britain, France, the United States, and other democratic countries practiced some form of capitalism.

Police officers arrest a Communist during a London demonstration.

CHAPTER 15, Section 4

SECTION 4 RESOURCES

Reproducibles
- Lecture Notes, Section 4
- Block Scheduling Handbook, Chapter 15
- Know It Notes S4
- Readings in World Geography, History, and Culture, Readings 30–33, 37, 38
- Critical Thinking Activities 15, 16
- Creative Strategies for Teaching World Geography, Lesson 10
- Biography Activity: Margaret Thatcher

Technology
- One-Stop Planner CD-ROM, Lesson 15.4
- Geography and Cultures Visual Resources 44, 45

Review, Reinforcement, and Assessment Resources
- Daily Quiz 15.4
- Main Idea Activity S4
- Chapter Summaries
- English Audio Summary 15.4
- Spanish Audio Summary 15.4

Section 4

Objectives
1. Describe how the Cold War affected Europe.
2. Identify the new alliances that countries formed in response to the Cold War.
3. Investigate some other conflicts that troubled Europe after World War II.

FOCUS

Bellringer
Copy the following instructions onto the board: *What are some recent events that have affected Europe? Write down a few of these events.* Discuss the responses and list them on the board. Point out that our world is constantly changing. Tell students that in Section 4 they will learn some changes that have happened since 1945 and how they have shaped Europe.

Building Vocabulary
Write the vocabulary terms on the chalkboard. Then point out that the word *arms* in **arms race** refers to weapons. Call on a volunteer to suggest a definition for the phrase. Then have a student locate and read the definitions for all the key terms. Point out that in the world of international politics we use the French spelling of *block* for a group of nations united for a common purpose—**bloc**.

CHAPTER 15, Section 4

HUMAN SYSTEMS

Checkpoint Charlie When the Berlin Wall was built in 1961, only a few border crossings were left open. The most famous of these was named Checkpoint C, but it was generally referred to as Checkpoint Charlie. Over time, it became the main crossing point between the two parts of the city. By the time the wall came down, thousands of East Germans had tried to enter West Berlin, often through Checkpoint Charlie. Some tried simply to elude the checkpoint guards, but others sought more unusual passage. Many amazing stories of daring escapes are told at the Checkpoint Charlie Museum in Berlin.

Europe Divided After World War II, Joseph Stalin, leader of the Soviet Union, took most countries in Eastern Europe under communist control. The Soviet Union and those communist-controlled countries were known as the Eastern, or Soviet, bloc. A **bloc** is a group of nations united under a common idea or for a common purpose. The line dividing the Eastern bloc from the Western countries came to be known as the **Iron Curtain**.

While Western countries experienced periods of great economic growth, industries in most communist countries did not develop. People there suffered from shortages of goods, food, and money.

Germany and Eastern Europe After World War II the Allies divided Germany into four zones to keep it from becoming powerful again. Britain, France, the United States, and the Soviet Union each controlled a zone. By 1948, the Western Allies were ready to unite their zones, but the Soviets did not want Germany united as a democratic country. The next year the American, British, and French zones became the Federal Republic of Germany, or West Germany. The Soviets established the German Democratic Republic, or East Germany. The city of Berlin, although located deep within East Germany, was divided into East and West Berlin. West Berlin remained under Allied control. However, the Soviets tried to block off West Berlin completely, hoping that the Allies would abandon the city. Instead, Allied airplanes flew some 277,000 flights over West Berlin, dropping food and supplies to the people below. This event was called the Berlin airlift. Later, in 1961, communist leaders of East Germany built the Berlin Wall, separating the two parts of the city.

During the 1950s and 1960s some of the other Eastern bloc countries tried to break free of communism. In Czechoslovakia and Hungary, for example, people rebelled against Soviet control. The Soviets brutally crushed these revolts.

Soviet tanks and troops block a street in Prague, Czechoslovakia, in 1968. The Soviet invasion ended a period of democratic reforms known as the "Prague Spring."

362 • Chapter 15

✓ **READING CHECK:**
Analyzing Information How did the Cold War affect political divisions in Europe? **the Soviet Union took most of Eastern Europe under communist control; Germany was divided into East Germany and West Germany.**

TEACH

Teaching Objectives 1–2
ALL LEVELS: (Suggested time: 20 min.) Copy the following graphic organizer onto the board, omitting the blue answers. Ask students to reread the discussion of the Cold War in their textbooks and to provide a definition for the term. Remind students that the Cold War was largely a conflict between the United States and its allies and the Soviet Union and its allies. Have students complete the graphic organizer with descriptions of these two sides. Lead a discussion about how the facts reflected in the completed organizer affected Europe. **ESOL, LS VISUAL-SPATIAL**

362 Chapter 15

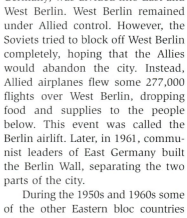

THE COLD WAR

Western Bloc
- Strongest Country
  United States
- Economic System
  capitalism
- Political System
  democracy
- Alliances
  NATO
- Economy
  rapid economic growth

Eastern Bloc
- Strongest Country
  Soviet Union
- Economic System
  communism
- Political System
  not democratic
- Alliances
  Warsaw Pact
- Economy
  shortages of goods, food, money

New Alliances and the Cold War

As the Cold War became more dangerous, European countries again looked to alliances to provide security. Two of them survive to this day and play important roles in world events.

The United Nations Although the League of Nations had failed to prevent World War II, people still wanted an international organization that could settle problems peacefully. In April 1945 the United Nations (UN) was created. Its purpose is to solve economic and social problems as well as to promote international cooperation and maintain peace. In 2004, there were 191 member nations. The six official languages of the United Nations are Arabic, Chinese, English, French, Russian, and Spanish. The headquarters of the United Nations is in New York City. The UN also has offices in Geneva, Switzerland, and Vienna, Austria.

NATO and the Warsaw Pact So that they could protect themselves, countries formed new alliances. In 1949, 12 Western nations created the North Atlantic Treaty Organization (NATO). Among the founding members were Canada, France, Great Britain, Italy, the Netherlands, and the United States.

The Eastern bloc formed its own alliance. Most of the Eastern European countries and the Soviet Union signed the Warsaw Pact in 1955. The Warsaw Pact countries had more total troops than the NATO members. This difference in the number of troops was one reason why Western powers came to rely on nuclear weapons to establish a balance of power.

European Alliances in Europe after World War II

After World War II, Eastern Europe was dominated by communism.
Interpreting the Map Which communist nation was not a member of the Warsaw Pact?

GLOBAL PERSPECTIVES

Organization of the UN The United Nations is composed of six main bodies. The General Assembly investigates disputes and recommends action to resolve them. The Security Council reviews these actions and approves all military actions. The International Court of Justice decides questions of international law. The Economic and Social Council sponsors trade and human rights organizations. The Trusteeship Council controls territories that are under UN supervision. Finally, the Secretariat runs the UN itself.

Critical Thinking: What are some things the UN can do to settle disputes?

Answer: encourage international communication, take military action, sponsor economic actions

◀ **Map Answer**

Yugoslavia

Teaching Objective 3

ALL LEVELS: (Suggested time: 20 min.) Organize the class into pairs. Have one student of a pair concentrate on Northern Ireland and the other student concentrate on Yugoslavia. Each student should explain to his or her partner the main points about the conflict in the assigned country. Encourage students to answer "who, what, when, where, and why" questions about the conflict. When pairs have completed their work, lead a class discussion to summarize the conflicts if any questions remain unanswered.
ESOL, COOPERATIVE LEARNING, LS INTERPERSONAL

▶**ASSIGNMENT:** Have each student consult newspapers, television news programs, Internet news sites, or other sources to find information about a conflict affecting Europe today. Have each student write a brief paragraph that tells something about this conflict. Students might note the cause of their chosen conflicts or efforts that have been undertaken to resolve them.

In October 1990 young people in Berlin wave German flags to celebrate the reunification of Germany.

The End of the Cold War Throughout the Cold War, the opposing sides had waged an arms race. The United States and the Soviet Union competed to create more advanced weapons and to have more nuclear missiles. The arms race was hugely expensive and eventually took its toll on the already shaky Soviet economy.

In 1985, Mikhail Gorbachev became head of the Soviet Union. He reduced government control of the economy and increased individual liberties, such as freedom of speech and the press. He also improved relations with the United States. These reforms in the Soviet Union encouraged democratic movements in Eastern bloc countries. In 1989, Poland and Czechoslovakia threw off communist rule. In November, the Berlin Wall came down. People around the world celebrated as Germans tore down the hated wall. In October 1990, East and West Germany became one democratic nation. Soviet republics also began to seek freedom and independence. The Cold War was over. The arms race could finally stop. By the end of 1991, the Soviet Union no longer existed.

The breakup of the Soviet Union created more than a dozen independent countries. Russia was the largest of these new nations. Its new leader was Boris Yeltsin. Under Yeltsin, Russia moved toward democracy. Yeltsin also improved Russia's relations with the West. In 2000, Vladimir Putin became leader of Russia. Under Putin, relations with the United States continued to improve.

✓ **READING CHECK:** (Evaluating) How did the fall of communism affect Europe? encouraged democratic movements in Eastern bloc countries; Berlin Wall came down; East and West Germany united; end of Soviet Union; arms race ended

Other Conflicts in Europe

Although the end of the Cold War eased tensions in Europe, other conflicts continued. Religious or ethnic differences caused many problems. Two of the most severe were in Northern Ireland and Yugoslavia.

Northern Ireland When the Republic of Ireland gained independence from Great Britain in 1922, the territory of Northern Ireland remained part of Britain. The Protestant majority in Northern Ireland controlled both the government and the economy. This caused resentment among Northern Ireland's Catholics. During the late 1960s some Catholic protests turned violent. The British have tried to resolve the conflict both through political means and military force. While the situation has improved, a permanent peaceful solution has not yet been found.

The Breakup of Yugoslavia Yugoslavia was created after World War I by uniting several countries. These included Bosnia, Croatia, Slovenia, and Serbia. Some had been independent in the past. After the fall of communism in Eastern Europe, Serbs, who were mainly Eastern Orthodox, tried to dominate parts of Yugoslavia where people were mainly Roman Catholic or Muslim. Fighting broke out between Serbia and Croatia, which was mainly Roman Catholic. Yugoslavia was once again divided into several countries in the early 1990s, but this did not end the violence. In 1992 Bosnian Serbs began a campaign of terror and murder intended to drive the Muslims out of Bosnia. Finally, NATO bombed Serbian targets in 1995, and the fighting stopped. Several Serb leaders were tried as war criminals.

Mostar, the unofficial capital of Bosnia and Herzegovina, was bombed heavily in the 1990s.

✓ **READING CHECK:** *Summarizing* Why did Catholics resent Protestants in Northern Ireland? **Protestants controlled both the government and the economy.**

Section Review 4

Homework Practice Online
Keyword: SJ5 HP15

Define or identify: communism, capitalism, bloc, NATO, arms race, Mikhail Gorbachev

Reading for the Main Idea
1. *Human Systems* What happened in Europe during the Cold War?
2. *Human Systems* What are some reasons why different groups have opposed each other in both Northern Ireland and Yugoslavia?

Critical Thinking
3. **Supporting a Point of View** Do you think most countries believe it is in their best interest to keep peace? Why or why not?
4. **Comparing and Contrasting** Did the formation of alliances after World War II have the same effect as the formation of alliances after World War I? Why or why not?

Organizing What You Know
5. **Sequencing** Copy the following time line. Use it to identify important dates and events in Europe after 1945.

1945 ———————————————————— 2005

CHAPTER 15 REVIEW

Define and Identify
For definitions, see the glossary and index.

Review the Main Ideas

13. Countries competed for power and feared each other; nationalism and militarism were strong; alliances were formed and Europe was divided into two sides.

14. Allied—Britain, France, Russia, and Japan (later—Italy); Central—Germany, Austria-Hungary, the Ottoman Empire, and Bulgaria **(NGS 5)**

15. noisy, dirty, frightening, dangerous, frustrating from "going over the top" but not making progress

16. United States—wanted fair terms for Germany; other Allies—wanted to punish Germany and make sure it could never be powerful again

17. Stock prices fell, people rushed to sell shares, and the market crashed. Banks did not have enough money. Banks, farms, factories, business, and individuals went bankrupt. Prices and wages around the world fell.

18. police state, with the government in complete control over people and using secret police to find and punish people who protested

19. Japanese takeover of Manchuria and most of China, Italy's invasion of Ethiopia, Spanish Civil War, Hitler's takeover of Austria and the Sudetenland

20. Answers may vary but might include: the Germans failed to capture Stalingrad; American and British forces defeated the Germans in North Africa, the Japanese were pushed back across the Pacific, the Allies captured Sicily, and the D-Day invasion was a success.

Chapter 15 Review and Practice

Define and Identify
Identify each of the following:

1. nationalism
2. militarism
3. armistice
4. Treaty of Versailles
5. Great Depression
6. dictator
7. fascism
8. Benito Mussolini
9. Adolf Hitler
10. Holocaust
11. Winston Churchill
12. Iron Curtain

Review the Main Ideas

13. How did European countries react to the growing power of their neighbors?
14. Which countries made up the Allied Powers and the Central Powers?
15. What was trench warfare like?
16. How did the United States and its allies differ over the treatment of Germany at the end of World War I?
17. What events led to the Great Depression?
18. What was life like for Italians under Mussolini's rule and Germans under Hitler's control?
19. What acts of aggression happened before September 1, 1939?
20. What events caused World War II to turn in favor of the Allies?
21. How was Europe divided during the Cold War?
22. What is the purpose of the United Nations?
23. What are two places in Europe where ethnic and religious conflicts became violent?

Think Critically

24. **Summarizing** What ideas, actions, and incidents were the major causes of World War I?
25. **Understanding Cause and Effect** How did the Treaty of Versailles lead to the rise of the Nazi Party?
26. **Analyzing Information** How did Hitler's beliefs affect millions of Europe's Jews?
27. **Evaluating** Do you agree with the historians who say that the twentieth century was the worst that humanity ever experienced? Why or why not?
28. **Comparing and Contrasting** How do communism and capitalism differ?

Map Activity

29. On a separate sheet of paper, match the letters on the map with their correct labels.

   Austria Italy
   France Poland
   Germany Russia
   Great Britain

366 • Chapter 15

21. between free countries in western Europe, and communist countries under Soviet domination in eastern
22. solve social and economic problems as well as to promote international cooperation and maintain peace **(NGS 13)**
23. Northern Ireland, Yugoslavia **(NGS 13)**

Think Critically

24. nationalism, militarism, alliances SS.A.2.3.6
25. Germans were angry about the Treaty of Versailles; Hitler used this anger to gain support and power. **(NGS 13)**
26. created the Holocaust, during which millions of Jews were killed
27. Possible answers: agree—more than 60 million people dead in world wars, many other deadly conflicts, Holocaust, rise of fascism and communism **(NGS 17)**
28. communism—central authority controls economy; capitalism—businesses privately owned

366 Chapter 15

Writing Activity

Imagine that you are making a film about a Jewish family in Germany trying to escape the Nazis in the late 1930s, before World War II started. Write a summary of the film you would like to make. List characters who will appear in the film, events that will occur, problems that will arise, and how the characters will face them.

Internet Activity: go.hrw.com
KEYWORD: SJ5 GT4

Choose a topic about modern Europe.
- Learn about the effects of the Treaty of Versailles.
- Write a report about Anne Frank.
- Create a poster about D-Day.

CHAPTER 15 REVIEW

Map Activity
29. A. Great Britain
    B. France
    C. Germany
    D. Russia
    E. Austria
    F. Italy
    G. Poland

Writing Activity
Students' film summaries should contain accurate information. Characters, events, problems, and potential solutions should be logical for the time and place. Use Rubric 40, Writing to Describe, to evaluate student work.

Interpreting Political Cartoons
1. hat—Nazi rule; candle—German civilization
2. The Nazi regime was snuffing out or suffocating German civilization.
3. the meaning of the swastika and that the title refers to Goethe's dying words
4. strongly against it

Analyzing Primary Sources
1. cold, wet, scary, uncomfortable, dangerous
2. It was the worst.
3. patience, endurance, camaraderie with others, courage, strength
4. The morale was strong and the soldiers accepted their difficult situation without complaint.

Social Studies Skills Practice

Interpreting Political Cartoons

This cartoon's title was taken from the dying words of a great German writer of the 1800s, Johann Wolfgang von Goethe. The cartoonist, an American, was known as Herblock. Study the cartoon, which was published in 1933. Then answer the questions.

"Light! More light!" —Goethe's Last Words
—from *Herblock: A Cartoonist's Life* (Time Books, 1998)

1. What do the hat and the candle stand for?
2. What does the cartoon mean?
3. The cartoonist assumes that the reader already knows two things. What are they?
4. How do you think the cartoonist feels about the Nazi regime?

Analyzing Primary Sources

Bruce Bairnsfather, a lieutenant in the British Army, fought in the trenches during World War I. He wrote two books about his experiences. Read the following excerpt from *Bullets and Billets* by Bairnsfather. Then answer the questions.

"It was quite the worst trench I have ever seen. A number of men were in it, standing and leaning, silently enduring the following conditions. It was quite dark. The enemy were about two hundred yards away, or rather less. It was raining, and the trench contained over three feet of water. The men, therefore, were standing up to the waist in water. The front parapet [earthen wall] was nothing but a rough earth mound which, owing to the water about, was practically non-existent. They were all wet through and through, with a great deal of their equipment below the water at the bottom of the trench. There they were, taking it all as a necessary part of a great game; not a grumble nor a comment."

1. What were conditions like for soldiers in the trench?
2. How did this trench compare to others Bairnsfather had seen?
3. What are some character traits that the soldiers described seem to have?
4. Based on Bairnsfather's description, what was the morale of the soldiers?

REVIEW AND ASSESSMENT RESOURCES

Reproducible
- Readings in World Geography, History, and Culture 15, 23, 32, 34, 38, 74
- Critical Thinking Activity 9
- Vocabulary Activity 9

Technology
- Chapter 15 Test Generator (on the One-Stop Planner)

- HRW Go site
- Audio CD Program, Chapter 15

Reinforcement, Review, and Assessment
- Chapter 15 Review and Practice
- Chapter Summaries and Review Students, Parents, Mentors, and Peers

- Chapter 15 Test
- Chapter 15 Test for English Language Learners and Special-Needs Students
- Unit 4 Test
- Unit 4 Test for English Language Learners and Special-Needs Students

GO TO: go.hrw.com
KEYWORD: SJ5 Teacher
FOR: a guide to using the Internet in your classroom

CHAPTER 16: Southern Europe
Chapter Resource Manager

Objectives	Pacing Guide	Reproducible Resources
SECTION 1		
Physical Geography (pp. 369–71) 1. Identify the major landforms and rivers of southern Europe. 2. Identify the major climate types and resources of this region.	**Regular** .5 day Lecture Notes, Section 1 **Block Scheduling** .5 day Block Scheduling Handbook, Chapter 16	**RS** Know It Notes S1 **RS** Graphic Organizer 16 **E** Creative Strategies for Teaching World Geography, Lessons 10 and 11 **SM** Geography for Life Activity **IC** Interdisciplinary Activity for Middle Grades 4 **ELL** Main Idea Activity S1
SECTION 2		
Greece (pp. 372–75) 1. Identify some achievements of the ancient Greeks. 2. Identify two features of Greek culture. 3. Describe what Greece is like today.	**Regular** 1 day Lecture Notes, Section 2 **Block Scheduling** .5 day Block Scheduling Handbook, Chapter 16	**RS** Know It Notes S2 **IC** Interdisciplinary Activity for Middle Grades 16 **E** Cultures of the World Activity 3 **E** Biography Activity: Plato **ELL** Main Idea Activity S2
SECTION 3		
Italy (pp. 376–79) 1. Describe the early history of Italy. 2. Describe how Italy has added to world culture. 3. Describe what Italy is like today.	**Regular** 1 day Lecture Notes, Section 3 **Block Scheduling** .5 day Block Scheduling Handbook, Chapter 16	**RS** Know It Notes S3 **SM** Map Activity 16 **E** Cultures of the World Activity 3 **E** Biography Activity: Leonardo da Vinci **ELL** Main Idea Activity S3
SECTION 4		
Spain and Portugal (pp. 380–83) 1. Identify some major events in the history of Spain and Portugal. 2. Describe the cultures of Spain and Portugal. 3. Describe what Spain and Portugal are like today.	**Regular** 1 day Lecture Notes, Section 4 **Block Scheduling** .5 day Block Scheduling Handbook, Chapter 16	**RS** Know It Notes S4 **E** Cultures of the World Activity 3 **ELL** Main Idea Activity S4

Chapter Resource Key

- **RS** Reading Support
- **IC** Interdisciplinary Connections
- **E** Enrichment
- **SM** Skills Mastery
- **A** Assessment
- **REV** Review
- **ELL** Reinforcement and English Language Learners and English for Speakers of Other Languages (ESOL)
- Transparencies
- CD–ROM
- Music
- Video
- Internet
- Holt Presentation Maker Using Microsoft® PowerPoint®

One-Stop Planner CD–ROM

See the *One-Stop Planner* for a complete list of additional resources for students and teachers.

One-Stop Planner CD–ROM

It's easy to plan lessons, select resources, and print out materials for your students when you use the *One-Stop Planner CD–ROM with Test Generator.*

Technology Resources	Review, Reinforcement, and Assessment Resources	
One-Stop Planner CD–ROM, Lesson 16.1 Geography and Cultures Visual Resources with Teaching Activities 24–29 *ARGWorld* CD–ROM Homework Practice Online HRW Go site	ELL REV A REV ELL ELL	Main Idea Activity S1 Section 1 Review Daily Quiz 16.1 Chapter Summaries and Review English Audio Summary 16.1 Spanish Audio Summary 16.1
One-Stop Planner CD–ROM, Lesson 16.2 *ARGWorld* CD–ROM Homework Practice Online HRW Go site	ELL REV A REV ELL ELL	Main Idea Activity S2 Section 2 Review Daily Quiz 16.2 Chapter Summaries and Review English Audio Summary 16.2 Spanish Audio Summary 16.2
One-Stop Planner CD–ROM, Lesson 16.3 *ARGWorld* CD–ROM Homework Practice Online HRW Go site	ELL REV A REV ELL ELL	Main Idea Activity S3 Section 3 Review Daily Quiz 16.3 Chapter Summaries and Review English Audio Summary 16.3 Spanish Audio Summary 16.3
One-Stop Planner CD–ROM, Lesson 16.4 *ARGWorld* CD–ROM Music of the World Audio CD Program, Selection 8 Homework Practice Online HRW Go site	ELL REV A REV ELL ELL	Main Idea Activity S4 Section 4 Review Daily Quiz 16.4 Chapter Summaries and Review English Audio Summary 16.4 Spanish Audio Summary 16.4

internet connect

HRW ONLINE RESOURCES

GO TO: go.hrw.com
Then type in a keyword.

TEACHER HOME PAGE
KEYWORD: **SJ5 TEACHER**

CHAPTER INTERNET ACTIVITIES
KEYWORD: **SJ5 GT16**

Choose an activity to:
- explore the islands and peninsulas on the Mediterranean coast.
- take an online tour of ancient Greece.
- learn the story of pizza.

CHAPTER ENRICHMENT LINKS
KEYWORD: **SJ5 CH16**

CHAPTER MAPS
KEYWORD: **SJ5 MAPS16**

ONLINE ASSESSMENT
Homework Practice
KEYWORD: **SJ5 HP16**
Standardized Test Prep Online
KEYWORD: **SJ5 STP16**
Rubrics
KEYWORD: **SS Rubrics**

COUNTRY INFORMATION
KEYWORD: **SJ5 Almanac**

CONTENT UPDATES
KEYWORD: **SS Content Updates**

HOLT PRESENTATION MAKER
KEYWORD: **SJ5 PPT16**

ONLINE READING SUPPORT
KEYWORD: **SS Strategies**

CURRENT EVENTS
KEYWORD: **S5 Current Events**

Meeting Individual Needs

Ability Levels

Level 1 Basic-level activities designed for all students encountering new material

Level 2 Intermediate-level activities designed for average students

Level 3 Challenging activities designed for honors and gifted-and-talented students

ESOL Activities that address the needs of students with Limited English Proficiency

Chapter Review and Assessment

IC	Interdisciplinary Activity for the Middle Grades 13, 14, 15
E	Readings in World Geography, History, and Culture 28, 29, and 30
SM	Critical Thinking Activity 16
REV	Chapter 16 Review and Practice
REV	Chapter Summaries and Review
ELL	Vocabulary Activity 16
A	Chapter 16 Test
	Chapter 16 Test Generator (on the One-Stop Planner)
	Audio CD Program, Chapter 16
A	Chapter 16 Test for English Language Learners and Special-Needs Students
	HRW Go site

367B

CHAPTER 16

Southern Europe
Previewing Chapter Resources

Holt Online Learning

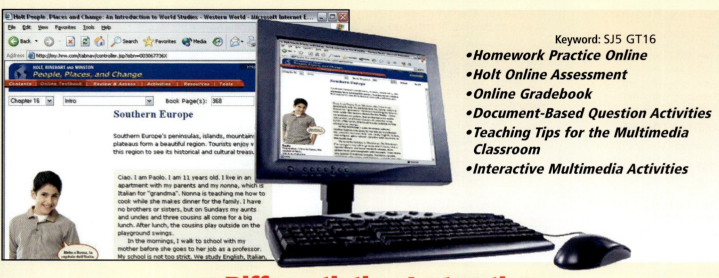

Keyword: SJ5 GT16
- Homework Practice Online
- Holt Online Assessment
- Online Gradebook
- Document-Based Question Activities
- Teaching Tips for the Multimedia Classroom
- Interactive Multimedia Activities

Differentiating Instruction

Reading and Writing Support
- Graphic Organizer Activity
- ◄ Vocabulary Activity
- Chapter Summaries and Review
- Know It Notes
- Audio CD

Active Learning
- ◄ Block Scheduling Handbook
- Cultures of the World Activity
- Interdisciplinary Activity
- Map Activity
- Critical Thinking Activity
- Music of the World Audio CD Program: Flamenco Music of Spain

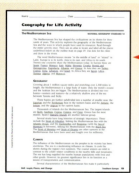

Primary Sources and Advanced Learners
- ◄ Geography for Life Activity: The Mediterranean Sea
- Map Activity: The Roman Empire
- Readings in World Geography, History and Culture:
  - 28 Community of Greeks
  - 29 Geography of Ancient Rome
  - 30 A Farmer's Life in Spain

Assessment Program
- ◄ Daily Quizzes S1–4
- Chapter Test
- Chapter Test for English Language Learners and Special-Needs Students

Spanish and ESOL
- Vocabulary Activity
- Main Idea Activities for English Language Learners and Special-Needs Students
- Chapter Summaries and Review
- Spanish Audio Summary
- Know It Notes S1–4
- ◄ Chapter Test for English Language Learners and Special-Needs Students

Special Education Modifications
Your **I.D.E.A. Works! CD-ROM** will provide modified versions of the following teaching materials:
- Know It Notes S1–4
- Vocabulary Activity
- ◄ Main Idea Activities S1–4
- Daily Quizzes S1–4
- Chapter 16 Test
- Flash cards of chapter vocabulary terms

Teacher Resources

Books for Teachers

Clark, Robert P. *The Basque Insurgents: ETA, 1952–1980.* University of Wisconsin Press, 1984.

Freeman, Charles. *The Greek Achievement: The Foundation of the Western World.* Viking, 1999.

Noble, Judith, and Jaime Lacasa. *The Hispanic Way.* NTC/Contemporary Publishing, 1990.

Allard, Denise. *Greece (Postcards From).* Raintree/Steck-Vaughn, 1997. Places and people within Greece. **ESOL**

Books for Students

Angilillo, Barbara W. *Italy.* Steck-Vaughn, 1990. Social life, customs, industries, culture, and other aspects of Italy.

Lyle, Keith. *Passport to Spain.* Franklin Watts, 1997. Surveys the geography, people, industry, natural resources, and culture of Spain.

Woff, Richard. *Bright-Eyed Athena: Stories from Ancient Greece.* Getty Trust, 1999. Stories about the goddess Athena, as told by a group of women.

Multimedia Materials

Italian Renaissance Art and Architecture. Video, 101 min. Alarion Press.

Eternal Greece, vol. 12 of Traveloguer Video Collection. Video, 60 min. Glencoe.

Portugal and the Azores. Video vol. 18 of Traveloguer Video Collection. 60 min. Glencoe.

Videos and CDs

Videos
- CNN. *Presents Geography: Yesterday and Today,* Segment 16 The Mountain People of Yo
- CNN. *Presents World Cultures: Yesterday and Today,* Segments 5, 6, 7 and 14

CDs
- ARG World
- I.D.E.A. Works! CD–ROM
- Music of the World Audio CD Program

Holt Researcher
http://researcher.hrw.com

- Solon
- Themistocles
- Thucydides
- Treaty of Tordesillas
- Prince Henry
- Spain
- Picasso, Pablo
- Dali, Salvador
- Italy
- Mussolini, Benito
- Vatican City
- Greece
- European Religions

Transparency Packages

Graphic Organizer Transparencies 16.1–4

Geography and Cultures Visual Resources Transparencies
44 Europe: Physical
45 Europe: Political
46 Europe: Climate
47 Europe: Population
49 Southern Europe: Physical-Political
50 Etruscan Musicians

Map Activities Transparency 16 The Roman Empire

CHAPTER 16

Why It Matters

These are reasons why studying southern Europe may interest students:

- Many ideas that are basic to the Western world's way of life originated with the ancient Greeks and Romans.
- Spanish and Portuguese sailors opened the New World to European exploration.
- Artists, musicians, writers, scientists, and scholars from southern Europe have made significant contributions to the world's cultural heritage.
- The U.S. economy is closely linked with the economies of these countries.

CHAPTER 16

Southern Europe

Southern Europe's peninsulas, islands, mountains, and plateaus form a beautiful region. Tourists enjoy visiting this region to see its historical and cultural treasures.

Ciao. I am Paolo. I am 11 years old. I live in an apartment with my parents and my *nonna*, which is Italian for "grandma." Nonna is teaching me how to cook while she makes dinner for the family. I have no brothers or sisters, but on Sundays my aunts and uncles and three cousins all come for a big lunch. After lunch, the cousins play outside on the playground swings.

In the mornings, I walk to school with my mother before she goes to her job as a professor. My school is not too strict. We study English, Italian, and religion. After school I practice with my team at the swim club.

My favorite holiday is Christmas. On Christmas Eve we go to my other grandmother's house for a special dinner. We have smoked salmon, then grilled trout and spaghetti with mussels. Then there are special Christmas sweets: Pandoro—a cake sprinkled with sugar, and Torrone—a candy log with chocolate and nuts.

Abito a Roma, la capitale dell'Italia.

▲ Translation: I live in Rome, the capital of Italy.

Chapter Project

Not all citizens of modern Spain consider themselves Spaniards. Many people living in the country's northeastern Basque region want an independent Basque nation. Have students conduct research on the Basque conflict and debate whether the region should be allowed to break away from Spain. Place research notes and debate outlines in student portfolios.

Starting the Chapter

In a democracy such as the United States, people participate in the government in a variety of ways. Citizens vote, hold office, write letters, and demonstrate peacefully. Ask students where they think Americans got these ideas. Have them locate Greece and Italy on the map on the following page. Tell students that in the 400s B.C. citizens of the Greek city-state of Athens voted on their government's decisions. Romans began to elect people to represent them in their government at about the same time. Tell students they will learn more about these cultures, what came after them, and the nearby countries of Spain and Portugal in this chapter.

Section 1: Physical Geography

Read to Discover
1. What are the major landforms and rivers of southern Europe?
2. What are the major climate types and resources of this region?

Vocabulary
mainland
sirocco

Places
Mediterranean Sea
Strait of Gibraltar
Iberian Peninsula
Cantabrian Mountains
Pyrenees Mountains
Alps
Apennines
Aegean Sea
Peloponnesus
Ebro River
Douro River
Tagus River
Guadalquivir River
Po River
Tiber River

Reading Strategy

READING ORGANIZER Before you read, create a two-column chart. Title one column Advantages and the other column Challenges. As you read this section, list features of Southern Europe's physical geography that make life in the region easier for the people who live there. Under the other column, list those that create challenges for them.

CHAPTER 16, Section 1

SECTION 1 RESOURCES

Reproducible
- Lecture Notes, Section 1
- Graphic Organizer 16
- Know It Notes S1
- Geography for Life Activity
- Interdisciplinary Activity for the Middle Grades 4
- Creative Strategies for Teaching World Geography, Lessons 10 and 11

Technology
- One-Stop Planner CD–ROM, Lesson 16.1
- Homework Practice Online
- Geography and Cultures Visual Resources with Teaching Activities 44–50
- HRW Go site

Reinforcement, Review, and Assessment
- Section 1 Review
- Daily Quiz 16.1
- Main Idea Activity S1
- Chapter Summaries and Review
- English Audio Summary 16.1
- Spanish Audio Summary 16.1

Southern Europe: Physical-Political

Section 1

Objectives
1. Identify the major landforms and rivers of southern Europe.
2. Examine the major climate types and resources of this region.

Focus

 Bellringer

Copy the following instructions onto the chalkboard: *Look through Section 1 and find a picture you think is interesting. What do you want to know about that picture? Write down a question.* Ask volunteers to share their questions with the class. Discuss some of the questions. Invite students to suggest answers to each other's questions. Tell students that in Section 1 they will learn more about the physical geography of southern Europe.

Using the Physical-Political Map

Have students examine the map on this page. Remind students that Europe is often called a peninsula of peninsulas. Point out the Iberian, Italian, and Greek peninsulas and call on students to name the bodies of water around them. Ask students how the countries' locations may have influenced the region's history and economy. (Access to the sea would help trade and travel.)

CHAPTER 16, Section 1

EYE ON EARTH

Mount Etna Sicily's Mount Etna is the tallest and most active volcano in Europe. Its name comes from a Greek word meaning "I burn." The mountain has three ecological zones, each with its own vegetation. The lowest zone is fertile and rich in citrus fields, olive groves, and vineyards. Catania, a city of about 330,000 residents, is located on the mountain's lowest slopes. Forests are found farther up the mountain in the second ecological zone. Ash, sand, and lava fragments cover the mountain at heights more than 6,500 feet (1,980 m) in the final zone.

The mountain has had more than 100 serious eruptions in the past 2,500 years. The resulting lava flows have repeatedly destroyed villages, fields, and vineyards.

Discussion: Point out Catania and Mount Etna on a map of Italy. Ask students what advantages may counterbalance the city's dangerous location. (possible answers: seaport, fertile fields from lava flows)

Graph Answer
Greece

Visual Record Answer
because the hilltop location was easily defended but was close to the sea

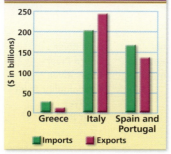

Imports and Exports of Southern Europe

Source: Central Intelligence Agency, *The World Factbook, 2003*

Interpreting the Graph Which country has the fewest imports and exports?

Greece, a land of mountains and sea, is home to the ancient city of Lindos on the island of Rhodes.
Interpreting the Visual Record *Place* Why do you think the people who founded Lindos chose this site?

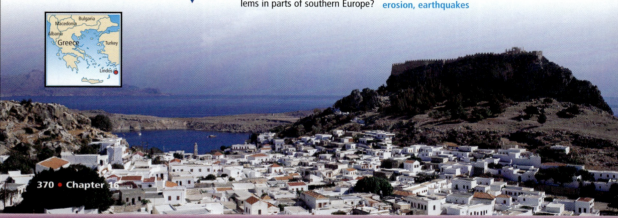

Physical Features

Southern Europe is also known as Mediterranean Europe because most of its countries are on the sea's shores. The Mediterranean Sea stretches some 2,300 miles (3,700 km) from east to west. *Mediterranean* means "middle of the land" in Latin. In ancient times, the Mediterranean was considered the center of the Western world, since it is surrounded by Europe, Africa, and Asia. The narrow Strait of Gibraltar (juh-BRAWL-tuhr) links the Mediterranean to the Atlantic Ocean.

The Land Southern Europe is made up of three peninsulas. Portugal and Spain occupy one, Italy occupies another, and Greece is located on a third peninsula. Portugal and Spain are on the Iberian (eye-BRI-ee-uhn) Peninsula. Much of the peninsula is a high, rocky plateau. The Cantabrian (kan-TAY-bree-uhn) and the Pyrenees (PIR-uh-neez) Mountains form the plateau's northern edge. Italy's peninsula includes the southern Alps. A lower mountain range, the Apennines (A-puh-nynz), runs like a spine down the country's back. Islands in the central and western Mediterranean include Italy's Sicily and Sardinia (sahr-DI-nee-uh), as well as Spain's Balearic (ba-lee-AR-ik) Islands.

Greece's **mainland**, or the country's main landmass, extends into the Aegean (ee-JEE-uhn) Sea in many jagged little peninsulas. The largest one is the Peloponnesus (pe-luh-puh-NEE-suhs). Greece is mountainous and includes more than 2,000 islands. The largest island is Crete (KREET).

On all three peninsulas, coastal lowlands and river valleys provide excellent areas for growing crops and building cities. Soils on the region's uplands are thin and stony. They are also easily eroded. In this area of young mountains, earthquakes are common. They are particularly common in Greece and Italy.

The Rivers Several east-west rivers cut through the Iberian Peninsula. The Ebro River drains into the Mediterranean. The Douro, Tagus, and Guadalquivir (gwah-thahl-kee-VEER) Rivers, however, flow to the Atlantic Ocean. The Po (POH) is Italy's largest river. It creates a fertile agricultural region in northern Italy. Farther south, along the banks of the much smaller Tiber River, is the city of Rome.

✓ **READING CHECK:** *Physical Systems* What physical processes cause problems in parts of southern Europe? erosion, earthquakes

370 • Chapter 16

TEACH

Teaching Objectives 1–2

ALL LEVELS: (Suggested time: 30 min.) Copy the following graphic organizer onto the chalkboard, omitting the blue answers. Use it to help students understand the physical geography of southern Europe. Have students complete the organizer. **ESOL, LS VISUAL-SPATIAL**

The Physical Geography of SOUTHERN EUROPE
Shared Characteristics:
1. peninsulas 2. mountains 3. rivers 4. climate 5. resources

Spain and Portugal	Italy	Greece
1. Iberian Peninsula	1. shaped like a boot	1. largest peninsula is Peloponnesus
2. Cantabrian and Pyrenees	2. southern Alps, Apennines	2. very mountainous
3. several east-west	3. Po and Tiber	3. most rivers are short
4. some semiarid climates; northern Spain is cool and humid	4. sirocco	4. warm and sunny
5. trade, fishing, iron ore, beaches	5. trade, marble	5. bauxite, chromium, lead, marble, and zinc

370 Chapter 16

Climate and Resources

Much of southern Europe enjoys a warm, sunny climate. Most of the rain falls during the mild winter. Rainfall sometimes causes floods and mudslides due to erosion from overgrazing and deforestation. A hot, dry wind from North Africa called a **sirocco** (suh-RAH-koh) picks up some moisture over the Mediterranean Sea. It blows over Italy during spring and summer. The Po Valley is humid. Northern Italy's Alps have a highland climate. In Spain, semiarid climates are found in pockets. Northern Spain is cool and humid.

Southern Europeans have often looked to the sea for trade. Important Mediterranean ports include Barcelona, Genoa, Naples, Piraeus (py-REE-uhs)—the port of Athens—and Valencia. Lisbon, the capital of Portugal, is an important Atlantic port. The Atlantic Ocean supports Portugal's fishing industry. Although the Mediterranean suffers from pollution, it has a wealth of seafood.

The region's resources vary. Northern Spain has iron ore mines. Greece mines bauxite, chromium, lead, and zinc. Italy and Greece quarry marble. Falling water generates hydroelectricity throughout the region's uplands. Otherwise, resources are scarce.

The region's sunny climate and natural beauty have long attracted visitors. Millions of people explore castles, museums, ruins, and other cultural sites each year. Spain's beaches help make that country one of Europe's top tourist destinations.

✓ **READING CHECK:** *Places and Regions* What climate types and natural resources are found in the region?
mostly warm, sunny; also highland, semiarid, cool, humid; seafood; iron ore, bauxite, chromium, lead, zinc, marble

▲ Workers prepare to separate a giant block of marble from a wall in a quarry in Carrara, Italy.

Section Review 1

Define and explain: mainland, sirocco

Working with Sketch Maps On a map of southern Europe that you draw or that your teacher provides, label Greece, Italy, Spain, and Portugal. Also label the Mediterranean Sea and the Strait of Gibraltar.

Reading for the Main Idea
1. *Places and Regions* Why is southern Europe known as Mediterranean Europe?
2. *Places and Regions* What countries occupy the region's three main peninsulas?
3. *Environment and Society* Why might people settle in river valleys and in coastal Southern Europe?

Critical Thinking
4. **Drawing Inferences and Conclusions** In what ways could the region's physical geography aid the development of trade?

Organizing What You Know
5. **Summarizing** Copy the following graphic organizer. Use it to list the region's physical features, climate, and resources.

	Physical Features	Climate	Resources
Spain and Portugal			
Italy			
Greece			

Homework Practice Online
Keyword: SJ5 HP16

Section 1 Review

Answers to Section 1 Review

Define For definitions, see the glossary.

Working with Sketch Maps Maps will vary, but listed places should be in their approximate locations.

Reading for the Main Idea
1. because most of its countries are on the sea's shores (NGS 4)
2. Portugal, Spain, Italy, and Greece (NGS 4)
3. access to water transportation, trade, natural resources like fertile soil, moderate climate (NGS 15)

Critical Thinking
4. access to the sea, many good harbors

Organizing What You Know
5. Spain and Portugal—on the Iberian Peninsula rocky plateau, Cantabrian and Pyrenees Mountains, Balearic Islands; east-west rivers; warm, sunny; seafood, iron ore, beaches; Italy—southern Alps, Apennines, islands of Sicily and Sardinia; Po and Tiber Rivers; warm, sunny, sirocco; seafood, marble; Greece—large and small peninsulas, mountains, Crete; warm, sunny; seafood, bauxite, chromium, lead, zinc, marble

---

CLOSE

Have students review the questions they wrote for the Bellringer Activity. Ask students if they can answer more of them now. What else do they need to learn to find the answers?

Have students complete Main Idea Activity S1. Then have volunteers come to the chalkboard and write explanations of the main physical features discussed in Section 1. **ESOL**, **LS** VERBAL-LINGUISTIC

REVIEW, ASSESS, RETEACH

Organize students into teams. Give each team an index card with a vocabulary term or place in Southern Europe on one side. Have teams create a question about its term on the card. Pass the cards from team to team. Ask each team to read the question aloud and to answer it. Continue until all the questions have been answered. Then have students complete Daily Quiz 16.1. **COOPERATIVE LEARNING**

EXTEND

Have interested students conduct research on the connections between the physical geography of southern Europe and economic activities relating to agriculture. Have students consider climate, soil, and vegetation in their study. Ask them to report their findings in the form of a graph or a map. **BLOCK SCHEDULING**

CHAPTER 16, Section 2

SECTION 2 RESOURCES

Reproducible
- Lecture Notes, Section 2
- Know It Notes S2
- Cultures of the World Activity 3
- Interdisciplinary Activity for the Middle Grades 16
- Biography Activity: Plato

Technology
- One-Stop Planner CD–ROM, Lesson 16.2
- Homework Practice Online
- HRW Go site

Reinforcement, Review, and Assessment
- Section 2 Review
- Daily Quiz 16.2
- Main Idea Activity S2
- Chapter Summaries and Review
- English Audio Summary 16.2
- Spanish Audio Summary 16.2

Section 2 Greece

Read to Discover
1. What were some of the achievements of the ancient Greeks?
2. What are two features of Greek culture?
3. What is Greece like today?

Vocabulary
city-states
mosaics

Places
Athens
Thessaloníki

People
Philip of Macedonia
Alexander the Great
Melina Mercouri

Reading Strategy
FOLDNOTES: THREE-PANEL FLIP CHART Create the FoldNote titled **Three-Panel Flip Chart** described in the Appendix. Title the flaps Greek History, Greek Culture, and Greece Today. As you read, write the information you learn about each topic beneath its flap.

History

The Greek islands took an early lead in the development of trade and shipping between Asia, Africa, and Europe. By about 2000 B.C. large towns and a complex civilization existed on Crete.

Ancient Greece About 800 B.C. Greek civilization arose on the mainland. The mountainous landscape there favored small, independent **city-states**. Each Greek city-state, or *polis*, was made up of a city and the land around it. Each had its own gods, laws, and form of government. The government of the city-state of Athens was the first known democracy. Democracy is the form of government in which all citizens take part. Greek philosophers, artists, architects, and writers made important contributions to Western civilization. For example, the Greeks are credited with inventing theater. Students still study ancient Greek literature and plays.

Eventually, Greece was conquered by King Philip. Philip ruled Macedonia, an area north of Greece. About 330 B.C. Philip's son, Alexander the Great, conquered Asia Minor, Egypt, Persia, and part of India. His empire combined Greek culture with influences from Asia and Africa. In the 140s B.C. Greece and Macedonia were conquered by the Roman Empire.

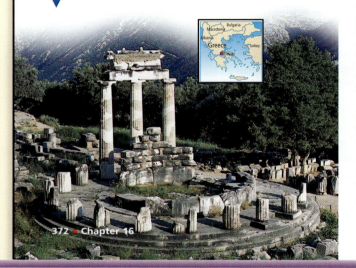

The Greeks believed that the Temple of Delphi—shown below—was the center of the world.

Section 2 Objectives
1. Describe some of the achievements of the ancient Greeks.
2. Identify two features of Greek culture.
3. Examine what Greece is like today.

FOCUS

Bellringer
Copy the following questions onto the chalkboard: *What is one way your life would be different if U.S. citizens had no say in the government? What if you did not know about atoms or the true size of Earth?* Ask students to respond to the questions in writing. Ask volunteers to read their answers. Tell students that our form of government, physics, and geography are part of what we have learned from the ancient Greeks. Tell students that they will learn more about Greece in Section 2.

Building Vocabulary
Write the vocabulary terms on the chalkboard. Have students suggest a meaning for **city-states**, based on the component words, and check their definitions against the text. Have students find the definition of **mosaic**. Tell them that the word comes from *muse*. The muses were nine Greek goddesses of the arts. Ask students how *mosaic* may relate to goddesses of the arts.

372 Chapter 16

The Byzantine Empire About A.D. 400 the Roman Empire was divided into two parts. The western half was ruled from Rome. It soon fell to Germanic peoples the Romans called barbarians. Barbarian means both *illiterate* and *wanderer*. The eastern half of the Roman Empire was known as the Byzantine Empire. It was ruled from Constantinople. Constantinople was located on the shore of the Bosporus in what is now Turkey. This city—today known as Istanbul—served as a gathering place for people from Europe and Asia. The Byzantine Empire carried on the traditions of the Roman Empire for another 1,000 years. Gradually, an eastern form of Christianity developed. It was influenced by Greek language and culture. It became known as Eastern Orthodox Christianity. It is the leading form of Christianity in Greece, parts of eastern Europe, and Russia.

Turkish Rule In 1453 Constantinople was conquered by the Ottoman Turks, a people from Central Asia. Greece and most of the rest of the region came under the rule of the Ottoman Empire. It remained part of this empire for nearly 400 years. In 1821 the Greeks revolted against the Turks, and in the early 1830s Greece became independent.

Government In World War II Greece was occupied by Germany. After the war Greek communists and those who wanted a king and constitution fought a civil war. When the communists lost, the military took control. Finally, in the 1970s the Greek people voted to make their country a republic. They adopted a new constitution that created a government with a president and a prime minister.

✓ **READING CHECK:** **Human Systems** What were some of the achievements of ancient Greece? democracy, contributions of Greek philosophers, artists, architects and writers

Culture

Turkish influences on Greek art, food, and music can still be seen. However, Turkey and Greece disagree over control of the islands and shipping lanes of the Aegean Sea.

Religion Some 98 percent of Greeks are Eastern Orthodox Christians, commonly known as Greek Orthodox. Easter is a major holiday and cause for much celebration. The traditional Easter meal is eaten on Sunday—roasted lamb, various vegetables, Easter bread, and many desserts. Because the Greek Orthodox Church has its own calendar, Christmas and Easter are usually celebrated one to two weeks later than in the West.

▲ The Acropolis in Athens was built in the 400s B.C. The word *acropolis* is Greek for "city at the top."
Interpreting the Visual Record
Human-Environment Interaction Why would it be important to build a city on a hill?

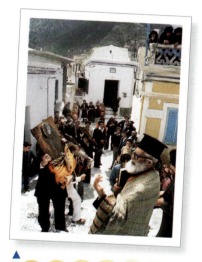

▲ The people of Karpathos and their religious leaders are participating in an Easter celebration.

CHAPTER 16, Section 2

Linking Past to Present

The Seafaring Greeks Greece has long been linked to the sea. Many Greek cities were established where ships could drop anchor. Naval power allowed Athens to dominate the Aegean in the 400s B.C.

Modern Greece also depends on the sea. Shipping and tourism are its major sources of income. The Greek merchant fleet—more than 2,000 ships—is one of the world's largest.

Critical Thinking: Point out that ancient Romans developed their navy more slowly than did the Greeks. Have students consult the physical-political map in this chapter and then ask them why may this be so.

Answer: Italy has fewer harbors, and therefore travel by sea was more difficult there. Also, because Romans could easily cross the Apennines and trade inland, they did not depend as heavily on the sea.

▲ **Visual Record Answer**
Students might suggest that a city on a hill is easier to defend against attack.

TEACH

Teaching Objective 1
ALL LEVELS: (Suggested time: 20 min.) Copy the following graphic organizer onto the chalkboard, omitting the blue answers. Use it to help students understand the achievements of the ancient Greeks.
ESOL, **LS VISUAL-SPATIAL**

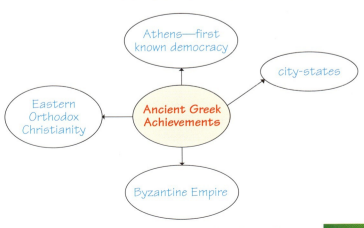

Ancient Greek Achievements

CHAPTER 16, Section 2

ENVIRONMENT AND SOCIETY

Ancient Land, Modern Problem Greece became an industrial nation in the 1970s. Since then heavy air and water pollution have made some people ill and eroded the marble of many ancient monuments and statues. Recent efforts have reduced some air pollution, but heavy traffic still dirties the air. In some places untreated sewage and industrial wastes have polluted the Mediterranean Sea.

Connecting to Math Answers

1. using deduction in mathematical proofs, developing the Pythagorean Theorem, stating the basic principles of geometry, and calculating the value of pi
2. the creation of a model of the solar system, the estimation of the circumference of Earth, the treatment of medicine as a science, the gathering of information on plants and animals, and an understanding of the importance of observation and classification

Connecting to Math

Greek postage stamp of the Pythagorean Theorem

Greek Math and Science

Greek civilization made many contributions to world culture. We still admire Greek art and literature. Greek scholars also paved the way for modern mathematics and science.

More than 2,000 years ago Thales (THAY-leez), a philosopher, began the use of deduction in mathematical proofs. Pythagoras (puh-THAG-uh-ruhs) worked out an equation to calculate the dimensions of a right triangle. The equation became known as the Pythagorean Theorem. By 300 B.C. Euclid (YOO-kluhd) had stated the basic principles of geometry in his book *Elements*. Soon after, Archimedes (ahr-kuh-MEED-eez) calculated the value of *pi*. This value is used to measure circles and spheres. He also explained how and why the lever, a basic tool, works.

Aristarchus (ar-uh-STAHR-kuhs), an astronomer, worked out a model of the solar system. His model placed the Sun at the center of the universe. Eratosthenes (er-uh-TAHS-thuh-neez) estimated the circumference of Earth with great accuracy.

Two important figures in the life sciences were Hippocrates (hip-AHK-ruh-teez) and Aristotle (AR-uh-staht-uhl). Hippocrates was a doctor who treated medicine as a science. He understood that diseases have natural causes. Aristotle gathered information on a wide variety of plants and animals. He helped establish the importance of observation and classification in the study of nature. In many ways, the Greeks began the process of separating scientific fact from superstition.

Understanding What You Read
1. How did Greeks further the study of mathematics?
2. What were some of the Greeks' scientific achievements?

▶ This Greek vase shows a warrior holding a shield. Kleophrades is thought to have made this vase, which dates to 500 B.C.

▶ This mosaic of a dog bears the inscription "Good Hunting."

The Arts The ancient Greeks produced beautiful buildings, sculpture, poetry, plays, pottery, and gold jewelry. They also made **mosaics** (moh-ZAY-iks)—pictures created from tiny pieces of colored stone—that were copied throughout Europe. The folk music of Greece shares many features with the music of Turkey and Southwest Asia. In 1963 the Greek writer George Seferis won the Nobel Prize in literature.

✓ **READING CHECK:** (Human Systems) Why is there a Turkish influence in Greek culture? because the Ottoman Turks conquered Greece and controlled it for nearly 400 years

---

Teaching Objective 2
ALL LEVELS: (Suggested time: 20 min.) Pair students and have one student in each pair write a few sentences about religion in Greece. Have the other student write about the arts. Then have pairs explain their topics to each other. **ESOL, COOPERATIVE LEARNING,** LS **INTERPERSONAL**

Teaching Objective 3
ALL LEVELS: (Suggested time: 30 min.) Pair students and give each pair two sheets of heavy white paper, several pieces of colored paper, scissors, and glue. Have students cut the colored paper into small squares and then arrange the squares to create mosaics depicting some of the agricultural products of Greece. **ESOL, COOPERATIVE LEARNING,** LS **KINESTHETIC**

▶**ASSIGNMENT:** Have students write about some of the objects in their everyday lives that are related to ideas from ancient Greece. (examples: Newspapers reflect freedom of speech, which is important to our democracy. Televisions broadcast dramas, which the Greeks developed.)

CLOSE
Tell students that the first Olympic Games were held in Greece in 776 B.C. Stage a Class Olympics based on what students have learned about Greece. Events may be organized around physical features, history, or culture. Organize team or individual events.

Greece Today

When people think of Greece now, they often recall the past. For example, many have seen pictures of the Parthenon, a temple built in the 400s B.C. in Athens. It is one of the world's most photographed buildings.

Economy Greece today lags behind other European nations in economic growth. More people work in agriculture than in any other industry. However, only about 19 percent of the land can be farmed because of the mountains. For this reason old methods of farming are used rather than modern equipment. Farmers raise cotton, tobacco, vegetables, wheat, lemons, olives, and raisins.

Service and manufacturing industries are growing in Greece. However, the lack of natural resources limits industry. Tourism and shipping are key to the Greek economy.

Cities About 40 percent of Greeks live in rural areas. In the past few years, people have begun to move to the cities to find better jobs. More people now work in services than in agriculture.

Athens, in central Greece, is the capital and by far the largest city. About one third of Greece's population lives in the area in and around Athens. Athens and its seaport, Piraeus, have attracted both people and industries. Most of the country's economic growth is centered there. However, the city suffers from air pollution, which causes health problems. Air pollution also damages historical sites, such as the Parthenon. Greece's second-largest city is Thessaloníki. It is the major seaport for northern Greece.

✓ **READING CHECK:** *Environment and Society* How does scarcity of natural resources affect Greece's economy? **It limits industry and forces Greece to rely on tourism and shipping.**

BIOGRAPHY
Melina Mercouri
(1925–1994)

Character Trait: Integrity

Melina Mercouri was among the Greek citizens who fought for personal rights. Mercouri was an international movie star. In the late 1960s, she entered politics to fight the army colonels who had taken over Greece's government. To punish her, the government took away Mercouri's citizenship. When the government later changed, Mercouri became Greece's minister of culture. Greece honored Mercouri in 1995 by putting her face on a postage stamp.

How did Melina Mercouri show her integrity?

Define or identify: city-states, Philip of Macedonia, Alexander the Great, mosaics, Melina Mercouri

Working with Sketch Maps On the map you created in Section 1, label Athens and Thessaloníki. What physical features do these cities have in common? What economic activities might they share?

Reading for the Main Idea
1. *Human Systems* What groups influenced Greek culture?
2. *Human Systems* For what art forms is Greece famous?

Critical Thinking
3. **Drawing Inferences and Conclusions** How did the physical geography of this region influence the growth of major cities?
4. **Finding the Main Idea** On what does Greece rely to keep its economy strong?

Organizing What You Know
5. **Sequencing** Create a time line that documents the history of ancient Greece from 2000 B.C. to A.D. 1453.

2000 B.C. ————————————— A.D. 1453

Homework Practice Online
Keyword: SJ5 HP16

Section 2 Review

Answers to Section 2 Review

Define or identify For definitions and identifications, see the glossary and index.

Working with Sketch Maps Maps will vary, but places should be labeled in their approximate locations. Athens and Thessaloníki are both near the sea; shipping, fishing

Reading for the Main Idea
1. Macedonians, Romans, and Turks (NGS 10)
2. buildings, sculpture, poetry, plays, pottery, gold jewelry, mosaics, and folk music (NGS 10)

Critical Thinking
3. The mountainous landscape favored the creation of small city-states.
4. tourism and shipping

Organizing What You Know
5. Answers will vary but might include: 2000 B.C.—civilization on Crete; 800 B.C.—civilization on mainland; about 330 B.C.—Alexander the Great creates empire; 140s B.C.—conquered by Rome; A.D. 400s—Byzantine Empire begins; 1453—Ottoman Turks conquer Constantinople.

▲ **Biography Answer**
by risking punishment to fight for Greece

REVIEW, ASSESS, RETEACH

Have students reread the subsection on Greek history in Section 2. Pair students and tell one student to close the textbook and to summarize the main points. The other student should keep the book open and ask questions. Have students reverse the roles for the next subsection. Continue until the entire section is completed. **COOPERATIVE LEARNING**

Have students complete Main Idea Activity S2. Then tell students about the battle in 490 B.C. at Marathon, where Greek soldiers defeated the Persians. According to legend, a messenger ran more than 26 miles to report the news. Modern marathons commemorate the event. Hold a marathon in class. Organize students into teams, mark off 26 spaces on the floor, and allow "runners" to advance one "mile" for each fact from Section 2 that the team can report to the class. **ESOL, KINESTHETIC**

EXTEND

Have interested students conduct research on Greek mythology and how it explained natural phenomena. Each student should focus on one myth. Then have students compare the Greek explanation with their culture's explanation. Ask volunteers to present their findings to the class. **BLOCK SCHEDULING**

Section 3: Italy

Read to Discover
1. What was the early history of Italy like?
2. How has Italy added to world culture?
3. What is Italy like today?

Vocabulary
pope
Renaissance
coalition governments

Places
Rome
Genoa
Naples
Milan
Turin
Florence

People
Leonardo da Vinci
Galileo Galilei

Reading Strategy

USING PRIOR KNOWLEDGE: ABC BRAINSTORM List the letters of the alphabet on a sheet of notebook paper. Try to think of a word or phrase about Italy for each of the letters. Then share your information with a partner. As you read this section, put a check beside the information you listed and add information for the letters that are still blank.

The Appian Way was a road from Rome to Brindisi. It was started in 312 B.C. by the emperor Claudius.
Interpreting the Visual Record
Human-Environment Interaction How do you think this road has withstood more than 2,000 years of use?

History

About 750 B.C. a tribe known as the Latins established the city of Rome on the Tiber River. Over time, these Romans conquered the rest of Italy. They then began to expand their rule to lands outside Italy.

Roman Empire At its height about A.D. 100, the Roman Empire stretched westward to what is now Spain and Portugal and northward to England and Germany. The Balkans, Turkey, parts of Southwest Asia, and coastal North Africa were all part of the empire. Roman laws, roads, engineering, and the Latin language could be found throughout this huge area. The Roman army kept order, and people could travel safely throughout the empire. Trade prospered. The Romans made advances in engineering, including roads and aqueducts—canals that transported water. They also learned how to build domes and arches. Romans also produced great works of art and literature.

About A.D. 200, however, the Roman Empire began to weaken. The western part, with its capital in Rome, fell in A.D. 476. The eastern part, the Byzantine Empire, lasted until 1453.

Roman influences in the world can still be seen today. Latin developed into the modern languages of French, Italian, Portuguese, Romanian, and Spanish. Many English words have Latin origins as well. Roman laws and political ideas have influenced the governments and legal systems of many modern countries.

376 • Chapter 16

Section 3

Objectives
1. Explore the early history of Italy.
2. Describe how Italy has added to world culture.
3. Explain what Italy is like today.

Focus

Bellringer

Copy the following question onto the chalkboard: *What do you already know about Rome or the Roman Empire?* Discuss responses. (Possible answers: chariot races, gladiators, the persecution of Christians) Tell students that although Rome spread and maintained its power by force, it also made lasting contributions to literature, language, law, city planning, architecture, engineering, and other fields. Tell students that in Section 3 they will learn more about ancient Rome and modern Italy.

Building Vocabulary

Write the vocabulary terms on the chalkboard. Explain that **pope** comes from the Latin word *papa*, meaning "father," and that the pope is considered the father of the Catholic Church. Tell students that the word **Renaissance** combines *re-*, which means "again," with a Latin word, *nasci*, which means "to be born." Renaissance means "to be born again" or "rebirth." Point out that the Renaissance was a rebirth of learning. Call on a volunteer to find and read the definition of **coalition governments**.

CHAPTER 16, Section 3

SECTION 3 RESOURCES

Reproducible
◆ Lecture Notes, Section 3
◆ Know It Notes S3
◆ Cultures of the World Activity 3
◆ Map Activity
◆ Biography Activity: Leonardo da Vinci

Technology
◆ One-Stop Planner CD–ROM, Lesson 16.3
◆ Homework Practice Online
◆ HRW Go site

Reinforcement, Review, and Assessment
◆ Section 3 Review
◆ Daily Quiz 16.3
◆ Main Idea Activity S3
◆ Chapter Summaries and Review
◆ English Audio Summary 16.3
◆ Spanish Audio Summary 16.3

Visual Record Answer

high-quality construction

The Colosseum is a giant amphitheater. It was built in Rome between A.D. 70 and 80 and could seat 50,000 people.

Interpreting the Visual Record
For what events do you think the Colosseum was used? What type of modern buildings look like this?

CHAPTER 16, Section 3

Across the Curriculum
TECHNOLOGY

Roman Engineering The Romans were the best civil engineers of the ancient world. They used arches, concrete, and tunnel-like vaults to create bridges and buildings.

The Romans also built more than 50,000 miles of roads across an area that now includes 30 countries. The roads were built in layers of stone, gravel, and sand. Smooth stones covered the surface, which was higher in the center so that water would drain to the sides.

The Romans were also famous for their aqueducts, or covered stone water channels. Aqueducts supplied the city of Rome with more than 200 million gallons of water each day.

Activity: Organize students into groups to research, build, and label models of aqueducts, baths, or arenas.

Christianity began in the Roman province of Judaea (modern Israel and the West Bank). It then spread through the Roman Empire. Some early Christians were persecuted for refusing to worship the traditional Roman gods. However, in the early A.D. 300s the Roman emperor, Constantine, adopted Christianity. It quickly became the main religion of the empire. The **pope**—the bishop of Rome—is the head of the Roman Catholic Church.

The Renaissance Beginning in the 1300s a new era of learning began in Italy. It was known as the **Renaissance** (re-nuh-SAHNS). In French this word means "rebirth." During the Renaissance, Italians rediscovered the work of ancient Roman and Greek writers. Scholars applied reason and experimented to advance the sciences. Artists pioneered new techniques. Leonardo da Vinci, painter of the *Mona Lisa*, was also a sculptor, engineer, architect, and scientist. Another Italian, Galileo Galilei, perfected the telescope and experimented with gravity.

Christopher Columbus opened up the Americas to European colonization. Although Spain paid for his voyages, Columbus was an Italian from the city of Genoa. The name *America* comes from another Italian explorer, Amerigo Vespucci.

Government Italy was divided into many small states until the late 1800s. Today Italy's central government is a democracy with an elected parliament. Italy has had many changes in leadership in recent years. This has happened because no political party has won a majority of votes in Italian elections. As a result, political parties must form **coalition governments**. A coalition government is one in which several parties join together to run the country. Unfortunately, these coalitions usually do not last long.

✓ **READING CHECK:** *Human Systems* How is the Italian government different from that of the United States? **Many changes in leadership, coalition governments**

Leonardo da Vinci painted the *Mona Lisa* about 1503–06.
Interpreting the Visual Record Why do you think Leonardo's painting became famous?

GO TO: go.hrw.com
KEYWORD: SJ5 CH16
For: Web sites about Rome

▲ **Visual Record Answers**

sporting events and public displays; stadiums

probably the mysterious smile

TEACH

Teaching Objectives 1–2
ALL LEVELS: (Suggested time: 40 min.) Copy the following graphic organizer onto the chalkboard, omitting the blue answers. Use it to help students explore the early history of Italy and how it has added to world culture. Complete the organizer as a class. Then pair students and have each pair write one sentence about each entry.
ESOL, COOPERATIVE LEARNING

The History and Culture of ITALY

History	Culture
• 750 B.C. Rome established	• Latin
• Roman Empire	• Roman Catholic Church
• Christianity	• Mediterranean diet
• Renaissance	• glassware
• coalition governments	• jewelry
	• painting
	• sculpture

Southern Europe • 377

CHAPTER 16, Section 3

USING ILLUSTRATIONS

A World-Famous Smile
Focus students' attention on the *Mona Lisa* on the previous page. Remind students that Italian artist Leonardo da Vinci painted the *Mona Lisa* about 500 years ago. Ask them to identify other places they may have seen the image. **(possible answers: T-shirts, cartoons, and advertisements)** Point out that images of the *Mona Lisa* have been popular for many years and that the painting is recognized around the world. How have modern media helped spread the image to people around the world? You may want to challenge students to search the media for more images that began as part of one country's culture but are now encountered worldwide.

Culture

People from other places have influenced Italian culture. During the Renaissance, many Jews who had been expelled from Spain moved to Italian cities. Jews often had to live in segregated areas called ghettoes. Today immigrants have arrived from former Italian colonies in Africa. Others have come from the eastern Mediterranean and the Balkans.

Religion and Food Most Italians are Roman Catholics, but the number of practicing Catholics is declining. The leadership of the church is still based in the Vatican in Rome. Christmas and Easter are major holidays in Italy. Italians also celebrate All Souls' Day on November 2 by cleaning and decorating their relatives' graves.

Italians enjoy a range of regional foods. Recipes are influenced by the history and crops of each area. In the south, Italians eat a Mediterranean diet of olives, bread, and fish. Dishes are flavored with lemons from Greece and spices from Africa. Tomatoes, originally from the Americas, have become an important part of the diet. Some Italian foods, such as pizza, are popular in the United States. Modern pizza originated in Naples. Northern Italians eat more rice, butter, cheeses, and mushrooms than southern Italians.

The Arts The ancient Romans created beautiful glassware and jewelry as well as marble and bronze sculptures. During the Renaissance, Italy again became a center for art, particularly painting and sculpture. Italian artists discovered ways to make their paintings more lifelike. They did this by creating the illusion of three dimensions. Italian writers like Francesco Petrarch and Giovanni Boccaccio wrote some of the most important literature of the Renaissance. More recently, Italian composers have written great operas. Today, Italian designers, actors, and filmmakers are celebrated worldwide.

✓ **READING CHECK:** *Human Systems* What are some examples of Italian culture? **Italian food, such as pizza; glassware, jewelry, painting, sculpture, literature, opera, film**

In Rome people attend mass in St. Peter's Square, Vatican City. Vatican City is an independent state within Rome.

Teaching Objective 3

ALL LEVELS: (Suggested time: 20 min.) Organize students into triads. Have each triad write a brief magazine article titled "Italy Today." Articles should focus on Italy's economy, its cities, and the differences between northern and southern Italy. **ESOL, COOPERATIVE LEARNING**

CLOSE

Have volunteers write on the chalkboard one fact about Roman and Italian contributions to culture. To prompt students, you might first write categories such as architecture, politics, religion, art, food, and fashion on the chalkboard.

REVIEW, ASSESS, RETEACH

Organize the class into groups of four, to represent the four horses of a Roman chariot team. Then stage a chariot race by clearing a space in the classroom, asking questions from Section 3 of each group, and allowing the groups to take one step forward with each correct answer.

Have students complete Main Idea Activity S3. Then create sets of index cards with the names of major historical periods and famous Italians written on them. Organize the class into groups. Give each group a set of cards. Have students place the cards in correct chronological order as quickly as possible. Discuss results. **ESOL, COOPERATIVE LEARNING**

Italy Today

Italy is slightly smaller than Florida and Georgia combined, with a population of about 58 million. A shared language, the Roman Catholic Church, and strong family ties continue to bind Italians together.

Economy After its defeat in World War II, Italy rebuilt its industries in the north. Rich soil and plenty of water make the north Italy's "breadbasket," or wheat growing area. Italy's most valuable crop is grapes. Although grapes are grown throughout the country, northern Italy produces the best crops. These grapes help make Italy the world's largest producer of wine. Tourists are also important to Italy's economy. They visit northern and central Italy to see ancient ruins and Renaissance art. Southern Italy remains poorer with lower crop yields. Industrialization there also lags behind the north. Tourist resorts, however, are growing in the south and promise to help the economy.

Cities The northern cities of Milan, Turin, and Genoa are important industrial centers. Their location near the center of Europe helps companies sell products to foreign customers. Also in the north are two popular tourist sites. One is Venice, which is famous for its romantic canals and beautiful buildings. The other is Florence, a center of art and culture. Rome, the capital, is located in central Italy. Naples, the largest city in southern Italy, is a major manufacturing center and port.

✓ **READING CHECK:** *Environment and Society* What geographic factors influence Italy's economy? Rich soil and plenty of water are good for growing crops, particularly grapes.

Italy

Country	Population/ Growth Rate	Life Expectancy	Literacy Rate	Per Capita GDP
Italy	57,998,353 .1%	76, male 83, female	98%	$25,000
United States	290,342,554 0.9%	74, male 80, female	97%	$37,600

Source: Central Intelligence Agency, *The World Factbook 2003*

Interpreting the Chart What is the difference in the growth rate of Italy and the United States?

Define or identify: pope, Renaissance, Leonardo da Vinci, Galileo Galilei, coalition governments

Working with Sketch Maps On the map you created in Section 2, label Florence, Genoa, Milan, Naples, Rome, and Turin. Why are they important?

Reading for the Main Idea
1. *Human Systems* What were some of the important contributions of the Romans?
2. *Human Systems* What are some art forms for which Italy is well known?

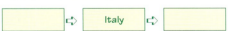

Critical Thinking
3. **Finding the Main Idea** Which of Italy's physical features encourage trade? Which geographical features make trading difficult?
4. **Analyzing Information** Why is the northern part of Italy known as the country's "breadbasket"?

Organizing What You Know
5. **Finding the Main Idea** Copy the following graphic organizer. Use it to describe the movement of goods and ideas to and from Italy during the early days of trade and exploration.

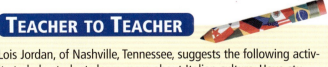

Section 3 Review

Answers to Section 3 Review

Define or identify For definitions and identifications, see the glossary and index.

Working with Sketch Maps Maps will vary, but places should be labeled correctly. These cities serve as centers of culture, industry, and government.

Reading for the Main Idea
1. Latin, art, literature, roads, aqueducts, domes, arches, laws (NGS 10)
2. architecture, glassware, jewelry, sculpture, painting, literature, opera, drama, and film (NGS 10)

Critical Thinking
3. access to the sea and its location at the center of the Mediterranean; few major rivers or harbors and its central mountains
4. its plentiful wheat harvests

Organizing What You Know
5. to—Jews expelled from Spain, African and Balkan immigrants; from—laws, roads, engineering, language, art, literature, architecture, Christianity, Renaissance ideas

▲ **Chart Answer**
Italy's growth is declining, while that of the United States is increasing.

EXTEND

Have interested students conduct research on the major languages derived from Latin—French, Italian, Portuguese, and Spanish. Challenge them to find and compare common words in those languages. Students might create web diagrams to share their findings with the class. **BLOCK SCHEDULING**

TEACHER TO TEACHER

Lois Jordan, of Nashville, Tennessee, suggests the following activity to help students learn more about Italian culture. Have students conduct research on what typical Italians eat. Then have students compare the Italian diet with the diet in a region or country with different physical and climatic characteristics, such as northern Canada. Students may investigate how climate and natural resources affect diet, how much of the average person's income is spent on food, and whether most people eat their meals at home or elsewhere.

CHAPTER 16, Section 4

SECTION 4 RESOURCES

Reproducible
- Lecture Notes, Section 4
- Know It Notes S4
- Cultures of the World Activity 3

Technology
- One-Stop Planner CD–ROM, Lesson 16.4
- Music of the World Audio CD Program, Selection 8
- Homework Practice Online
- HRW Go site

Reinforcement, Review, and Assessment
- Section 4 Review
- Daily Quiz 16.4
- Main Idea Activity S4
- Chapter Summaries and Review
- English Audio Summary 16.4
- Spanish Audio Summary 16.4

Visual Record Answer
Blades catch the wind and drive a mechanical system to draw water from the ground.

Section 4: Spain and Portugal

Read to Discover
1. What were some major events in the history of Spain and Portugal?
2. What are the cultures of Spain and Portugal like?
3. What are Spain and Portugal like today?

Vocabulary
Moors
dialect
cork

Places
Lisbon
Madrid
Barcelona

People
Philip II
General Francisco Franco
Pablo Picasso

Reading Strategy

VENN DIAGRAM Before you read, create a Venn diagram for Spain and Portugal. Draw two overlapping circles. Label one circle Spain and the other Portugal. As you read, fill in the circles with unique details about each country. Where the circles overlap, write down information about what the countries have in common.

History

Beautiful paintings of bison and other animals are found in caves in northern Spain. Some of the best known are at Altamira and were created as early as 16,000 B.C. Some cave paintings are much older. These paintings give us exciting clues about the early people who lived here.

Ancient Times Spain has been important to Mediterranean trade for several thousand years. First, the Greeks and then the Phoenicians, or Carthaginians, built towns on Spain's southern and eastern coasts. Then, about 200 B.C. Iberia became a part of the Roman Empire and adopted the Latin language.

These windmills in Consuegra, Spain, provided water for the people of the region.
Interpreting the Visual Record
Human-Environment Interaction How do you think windmills pump water?

380 • Chapter 16

Section 4 Objectives

1. Identify some major events in the history of Spain and Portugal.
2. Describe the cultures of Spain and Portugal.
3. Investigate what Spain and Portugal are like today.

Focus

Bellringer

Copy the following instructions onto the chalkboard: *Use the Fast Facts features in your textbook to find countries other than Spain or Portugal where Spanish or Portuguese is spoken. How many can you list?* Discuss students' lists. Ask students how they think these languages spread so far. Tell them that in Section 4 they will learn more about the history and culture of Spain and Portugal.

Building Vocabulary

Write the vocabulary terms on the chalkboard. Explain that **Moors** refers to Muslims from North Africa who conquered much of Spain in the A.D. 700s. Point out that **dialect** comes from Greek, Latin, and French roots that mean "between" or "over" (dia-) and "to speak" (-lect). Have students relate the roots to the term. Conclude by having a volunteer find and read aloud the definition of the term **cork**.

380 Chapter 16

The Muslim North Africans, or **Moors**, conquered most of the Iberian Peninsula in the A.D. 700s. Graceful Moorish buildings, with their lacy patterns and archways, are still found in Spanish and Portuguese cities. This is particularly true in the old Moorish city of Granada in southern Spain.

Great Empires From the early 900s to the 1400s Christian rulers fought to take back the peninsula. In 1492 King Ferdinand and Queen Isabella conquered the kingdom of Granada, the last Moorish outpost in Spain. That same year, they sponsored the voyage of Christopher Columbus to the Americas. Spain soon established a large empire in the Americas.

The Portuguese also sent out explorers. Some of them sailed around Africa to India. Others crossed the Atlantic and claimed Brazil. In the 1490s the Roman Catholic pope drew a line to divide the world between Spain and Portugal. Western lands, except for Brazil, were given to Spain, and eastern lands to Portugal.

With gold and agricultural products from their American colonies, and spices and silks from Asia, Spain and Portugal grew rich. In 1588 Philip II, king of Spain and Portugal, sent a huge armada, or fleet, to invade England. The Spanish were defeated, and Spain's power began to decline. However, most Spanish colonies in the Americas did not win independence until the early 1800s.

Government In the 1930s the king of Spain lost power. Spain became a workers' republic. The new government tried to reduce the role of the church and to give the nobles' lands to farmers. However, conservative military leaders under General Francisco Franco resisted. A civil war was fought from 1936 to 1939 between those who supported Franco and those who wanted a democratic form of government. Franco's forces won the war and ruled Spain until 1975. Today Spain is a democracy, with a national assembly and prime minister. The king also plays a modest role as head of state.

Portugal, like Spain, was long ruled by a monarch. In the early 1900s the monarchy was overthrown. Portugal became a democracy. However, the army later overthrew the government, and a dictator took control. A revolution in the 1970s overthrew the dictatorship. For a few years disagreements between the new political parties brought violence. Portugal is now a democracy with a president and prime minister.

✓ **READING CHECK:** (Human Systems) How did Spain and Portugal move from unlimited to limited governments? **both were ruled by monarchs and military governments, and now both have democratic governments.**

The interior of the Great Mosque in Córdoba, Spain, shows the lasting beauty of Moorish architecture. A cathedral was built within the mosque after Christians took back the city.
Interpreting the Visual Record Why do you think arches are important in certain building designs?

CHAPTER 16, Section 4

Culture and Music
Flamenco The musical and dance performance known as flamenco developd in southern Spain hundreds of years ago. Flamenco reflects Gypsy, Andalusian, and Arabic influences, among others. Early flamenco combined *cante* (song) and *baile* (dance), accompanied by rhythmic handclapping.

The golden age of flamenco lasted from 1869 to 1910. It became popular in cafés, and many performers added *guitarra*, or guitar playing. In the 1900s jazz, salsa, and bossa nova influenced flamenco. Flamenco has gained popularity recently, and some of its spontaneity has been replaced by rehearsed routines.

Discussion: To hear a flamenco song, listen to Selection 8 on the Music of the World Audio CD Program. Use the text and questions in the Teacher's Guide.

GO TO: go.hrw.com
KEYWORD: SJ5 CH16
FOR: Web sites about flamenco

▲ **Visual Record Answer**
They create large, open interior spaces.

TEACH

Teaching Objective 1
ALL LEVELS: (Suggested time: 30 min.) Tell students to imagine that they are tour guides in charge of a trip to Spain and Portugal. Before they leave on the trip they must present a brief history of Spain and Portugal to their clients. Pair students and have each pair write a presentation. Ask volueters to present their histories to the class. **ESOL, COOPERATIVE LEARNING,** LS **VERBAL-LINGUISTIC**

Teaching Objectives 2–3
ALL LEVELS: (Suggested time: 20 min.) Copy the graphic organizer on the following page onto the chalkboard, omitting the blue answers. Use it to help students compare the cultures of Spain and Portugal and what the countries are like today. Have each student complete it.
ESOL, LS **VISUAL-SPATIAL**

CHAPTER 16, Section 4

FOOD FESTIVAL

Mediterranean Munching
This is the perfect opportunity for a pizza party. You may want to have students bring different toppings for purchased crusts. Or, have students conduct research on the history of pizza and make one as historically accurate as possible. For example, in Italy, pizza is sometimes made without tomato sauce.

To celebrate Spain, enjoy tapas. These appetizers can range from olives, cubes of cheese, or ham to fancier cold omelets, stuffed peppers, or small sandwiches.

Focus on Culture Answer ▶
Answers will vary, depending on the community.

Chart Answer ▶
They are almost the same.

Spain and Portugal

Country	Population/ Growth Rate	Life Expectancy	Literacy Rate	Per Capita GDP
Portugal	10,102,022 0.2%	73, male 80, female	93%	$18,000
Spain	40,217,413 0.2%	76, male 83, female	98%	$20,700
United States	290,342,554 0.9%	74, male 80, female	97%	$37,600

Source: Central Intelligence Agency, *The World Factbook 2003*

Interpreting the Chart How do the growth rates of these countries compare?

Some Basque people want to be separate from Spain and are using violence to achieve this goal.

FOCUS ON CULTURE

Party Time!
One of Seville's major events, La Feria de Abril, or "The April Festival," features two of Spain's favorite things—horses and flamenco. Thousands of tents decorated with paper lanterns draw dancers and partygoers. Each day a parade of horses and horse-drawn carriages winds through the fairgrounds.

382 • Chapter 16

Culture

The most widely understood Spanish **dialect** (DY-uh-lekt), or variation of a language, is Castilian. This is the form spoken in central Spain. Spanish and Portuguese are not the only languages spoken on the Iberian Peninsula, however. Catalan is spoken in northeastern Spain (Catalonia). Basque is spoken by an ethnic group living in the Pyrenees.

Spain faces a problem of unrest among the Basque people. The government has given the Basque area limited self-rule. However, a small group of Basque separatists continue to use violence to protest Spanish control.

Food and Festivals Spanish and Portuguese foods are typical of the Mediterranean region. Many recipes use olives and olive oil, lemons, wheat, wine, and fish. Foods the explorers brought back from the Americas—such as tomatoes and peppers—are also important.

Both Spain and Portugal remain strongly Roman Catholic. The two countries celebrate major Christian holidays like Christmas and Easter. As in Italy, each village has a patron saint whose special day is the occasion for a fiesta, or festival. A bull fight, or *corrida*, may take place during the festival.

The Arts Spanish and Portuguese art reflects the many peoples who have lived in the region. The decoration of Spanish porcelain recalls Islamic art from North Africa. The sad melodies of the Portuguese fado singers and the intense beat of Spanish flamenco dancing also show African influences. In the 1900s the Spanish painter Pablo Picasso boldly experimented with shape and perspective. He became one of the most famous artists of modern times.

✓ **READING CHECK:** Human Systems How has the mixture of different ethnic groups created some conflict in Spanish society?

What role do dance or other arts play in your community's festivals?

The Culture of SPAIN and PORTUGAL

Food and Festivals	The Arts	Today
• olives and olive oil • limes • wine • fish • wheat • foods from the Americas • Roman Catholic holidays • bullfights	• porcelain • fado singers • flamenco dancers • Picasso	• European Union • agricultural products: wine, fruit, olive oil, olives, and cork • clothing • timber products • cars and trucks • tourism

CLOSE

Tell students about *castell* building—a sport popular in the Spanish region of Catalonia. *Castellers* build castles out of people. Dressed in traditional clothing, a group pushes together tightly to form the foundation of the castle. Other people press in against them. Lighter, barefoot participants then scramble over their backs to stand on their shoulders. Finally a child climbs to the top. In this way, Catalonians build human towers about 35 feet (10.6 m) tall. Ask students to speculate on how this custom began.

Porto, Portugal, combines modern industry with the historical sea trade.

Spain and Portugal Today

Both Spain and Portugal belong to the European Union (EU). The EU allows free trade, travel, and exchange of workers among its members. The economies of Spain and Portugal have been growing rapidly. However, they remain poorer than the leading EU countries.

Agricultural products of Spain and Portugal include wine, fruit, olives, olive oil, and **cork**. Cork is the bark stripped from a certain type of oak tree. Spain exports oranges from the east, beef from the north, and lamb from ranches on the Meseta. Portugal also makes and exports clothing and timber products. Spain makes cars and trucks, and most of its industry is located in the north. Tourism is also an important part of the Spanish economy. This is particularly true along Spain's coasts and on the Balearic Islands.

Portugal's capital and largest city is Lisbon. It is located on the Atlantic coast at the mouth of the Tagus River. Madrid, Spain's capital and largest city, is located inland on the Meseta. Spain's second-largest city is the Mediterranean port of Barcelona.

✓ **READING CHECK:** *Places and Regions* What are Spain and Portugal like today? *rapidly growing economies with agricultural exports and industry*

Homework Practice Online
Keyword: SJ5 HP16

Section Review 4

Define or identify: Moors, Philip II, General Francisco Franco, dialect, Pablo Picasso, cork

Working with Sketch Maps On the map that you created in Section 3, label Lisbon, Madrid, and Barcelona. How are Lisbon and Barcelona different from Madrid?

Reading for the Main Idea

1. *Human Systems* How do the performing arts of this region reflect different cultures?
2. *Human Systems* How have Spain and Portugal worked to improve their economies?

Critical Thinking

3. **Analyzing Information** Which groups influenced the culture of Spain and Portugal?
4. **Summarizing** How was the government of Spain organized during the 1900s?

Organizing What You Know

5. **Sequencing** Copy the following graphic organizer. Use it to list important events in the history of Spain and Portugal from the 700s to the 1600s.

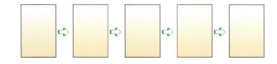

Section 4 Review

Answers to Section 4 Review

Define or identify For definitions and identifications, see the glossary and index.

Working with Sketch Maps Maps will vary, but should correctly depict the locations of the three cities. Lisbon and Barcelona are seaports while Madrid is located inland.

Reading for the Main Idea

1. Portuguese fado music and Spanish flamenco dancing reflect African influence. (NGS 10)
2. by joining the European Union, which provides free trade, travel, exchange of workers, and rapid growth (NGS 11)

Critical Thinking

3. Greeks, Phoenicians, Romans, and Moors
4. 1930s—king lost power and Spain became a workers' republic; 1936–1939—civil war, which led to conservative military rule under Francisco Franco until 1975; since 1975—democracy

Organizing What You Know

5. A.D. 700s—Moorish advance on area; 1492—kingdom of Granada conquered and Columbus sails to the Americas; 1588—defeat of Spanish Armada.

REVIEW, ASSESS, RETEACH

Have students complete the Section Review. Then organize the class into triads. Have each triad work together to create an outline of Section 4. Call on volunteers to write their outlines on the chalkboard. Compare the outlines and fill in any blanks. To conclude have students complete Daily Quiz 16.4. **COOPERATIVE LEARNING**

Have students complete Main Idea Activity S4. Then have them suggest words that describe Spain or Portugal. Have the class decide whether the word relates to the physical or the cultural geography of the region.
ESOL, **LS VERBAL-LINGUISTIC**

EXTEND

Have interested students conduct research on a Spanish artist, such as El Greco, Goya, Murillo, or Velázquez. Ask students to prepare posters illustrating works by their chosen artists. Have students include a statement about how the artist's work reflects Spanish cultural traditions.
BLOCK SCHEDULING

CHAPTER 16 REVIEW

Chapter 16 Review and Practice

Define and Identify
For definitions and identifications, see the glossary and index.

Review the Main Ideas
14. Iberian, Italian, Greek (NGS 4)
15. volcanoes and earthquakes; soil that is stony, thin, and easily eroded; hot, dry wind; scarcity of resources in some areas (NGS 15)
16. Barcelona, Genoa, Naples, Piraeus, Valencia, Lisbon (NGS 4)
17. early form of democracy; great works by philosophers, artists, architects, and writers, especially for the theater
18. Eastern Orthodox, also known as Greek Orthodox (NGS 10)
19. in architecture, language, law, political ideas
20. northern—good farmland, industrial cities, major tourist attractions; southern—poorer, lower crop yields, less industrialized (NGS 12)
21. glassware, jewelry, marble and bronze sculpture, painting, opera, film among others
22. rich, because of the gold and agricultural products from the American colonies; 1588 (NGS 13)
23. Castilian, other forms of Spanish, Portuguese, Catalan, Basque (NGS 10)
24. Basque (NGS 13)

Think Critically
25. Answers will vary but should refer to the region's access to the Mediterranean Sea and the Atlantic Ocean.
26. art, food, and music; the proximity of the two countries and former Turkish rule of Greece
27. its location in the center of the Mediterranean world
28. Olives are used to make olive oil; grapes are used to make wine; and other staple crops such as lemons, mushrooms, tomatoes, and wheat are used in many dishes.
29. the region's cultural events, historical sites, and pleasant climate

Define and Identify
Identify each of the following:
1. mainland
2. sirocco
3. city-states
4. Alexander the Great
5. mosaics
6. pope
7. Renaissance
8. Leonardo da Vinci
9. coalition governments
10. Moors
11. dialect
12. Pablo Picasso
13. cork

Review the Main Ideas
14. What peninsulas do the countries of southern Europe occupy?
15. What features of southern Europe's physical geography have caused problems for the people who live there?
16. What are some of southern Europe's major port cities?
17. What are some of the accomplishments of the ancient Greeks?
18. What is the major religion of Greece?
19. How can Roman influence still be seen today?
20. What are the major economic differences between northern and southern Italy?
21. In what arts have many Italians excelled?
22. What was Spain's empire like? When did Spain's power begin to decline?
23. What languages are spoken in Spain and Portugal?
24. What ethnic group has used violence to protest Spanish control?

Think Critically
25. **Drawing Inferences and Conclusions** In what ways do you think the geography of southern Europe made trade and exploration possible?
26. **Summarizing** What parts of Greek culture have been most strongly influenced by Turkish customs? Why is this the case?
27. **Drawing Inferences and Conclusions** Recall what you have learned about the Roman Empire. What about the Italian peninsula made it a good location for a Mediterranean empire?
28. **Drawing Inferences and Conclusions** How are agricultural products of southern Europe used in food?
29. **Finding the Main Idea** Why do many tourists continue to visit historical cities in southern Europe?

Map Activity
30. On a separate sheet of paper, match the letters on the map with their correct labels.

Alps
Apennines
Aegean Sea
Peloponnesus
Ebro River
Po River
Tiber River
Naples
Sicily
Meseta

Map Activity
30. A. Sicily
B. Po River
C. Tiber River
D. Apennines
E. Aegean Sea
F. Peloponnesus
G. Meseta
H. Naples
I. Ebro River
J. Alps

Writing Activity

Find a recording of Portuguese fado music. Then write a review that explains what the lyrics of the songs reveal about Portuguese culture. Be sure to use standard grammar, spelling, sentence structure, and punctuation in your review.

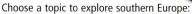

Internet Activity: go.hrw.com
KEYWORD: SJ5 GT16

Choose a topic to explore southern Europe:
- Explore the islands and peninsulas on the Mediterranean coast.
- Take an online tour of ancient Greece.
- Learn the story of pizza.

CHAPTER 16 REVIEW

Writing Activity

Reviews will vary but should include information about Portuguese culture. Use Rubric 37, Writing Assignments, to evaluate student work.

Interpreting Maps

1. north; south
2. 1150
3. 1150–1212
4. that they were very close

Analyzing Primary Sources

1. the south
2. It was the music of poor people.
3. People have moved from the countryside to the cities, bringing their music with them.
4. It has helped the Spanish people recover important cultural roots.

Social Studies Skills Practice

Interpreting Maps

You have read that starting in the 900s, Christian rulers began taking back the Iberian Peninsula from the Moors. Study the map of this re-conquest. Then answer the questions.

The Re-conquest of Spain

1. In what part of the Iberian Peninsula did the re-conquest begin? In what direction did it move?
2. By what year was Madrid again in Christian hands?
3. During what time period was the smallest amount of land taken from the Moors?
4. From the map, what can you assume about the political connections between Spain and Portugal during these centuries?

Analyzing Primary Sources

Read the following quote from a popular flamenco singer named Schwarma. Then answer the questions.

"For many years flamenco was seen as very bad in Spain. It came from the south, the poor region, and nobody was interested. It came from a sector of people who were poor, who lived outside the cities. Now it's just the opposite. Flamenco's very important. The Spanish people have recovered important cultural roots."

1. In what part of Spain did flamenco originate?
2. Why did many Spaniards ignore flamenco?
3. How may changes in Spain's settlement patterns affect flamenco's popularity?
4. Why does Schwarma think that flamenco is important?

CHAPTER 16 — REVIEW AND ASSESSMENT RESOURCES

Reproducible
- Readings in World Geography, History, and Culture 28, 29, and 30
- Critical Thinking Activity 16
- Vocabulary Activity 16

Technology
- Chapter 16 Test Generator (on the One-Stop Planner)
- HRW Go site
- Audio CD Program, Chapter 16

Reinforcement, Review, and Assessment
- Chapter 16 Review and Practice
- Chapter Summaries and Review
- Chapter 16 Test
- Chapter 16 Test for English Language Learners and Special-Needs Students

GO TO: go.hrw.com
KEYWORD: SJ5 Teacher
FOR: a guide to using the Internet in your classroom

Chapter 17: West–Central Europe
Chapter Resource Manager

Objectives	Pacing Guide	Reproducible Resources
SECTION 1		
Physical Geography (pp. 387–89) 1. Identify the area's major landform regions. 2. Describe the role rivers, canals, and harbors play in the region. 3. Identify west-central Europe's major resources.	**Regular** .5 day Lecture Notes, Section 1 **Block Scheduling** .5 day Block Scheduling Handbook, Chapter 17	**RS** Know It Notes S1 **RS** Graphic Organizer 17 **ELL** Main Idea Activity S1
SECTION 2		
France (pp. 390–93) 1. Identify which foreign groups affected the historical development of France. 2. Identify the main features of French culture. 3. Identify the products France exports.	**Regular** 1 day Lecture Notes, Section 2 **Block Scheduling** .5 day Block Scheduling Handbook, Chapter 17	**RS** Know It Notes S2 **E** Cultures of the World Activity 3 **E** Creative Strategies for Teaching World Geography, Lessons 10 and 11 **SM** Geography for Life Activity **E** Biography Activity: Charlemagne **ELL** Main Idea Activity S2
SECTION 3		
Germany (pp. 394–97) 1. Describe the effects wars have had on Germany. 2. Identify Germany's major contributions to world culture. 3. Describe how the division of Germany affected its economy.	**Regular** 1 day Lecture Notes, Section 3 **Block Scheduling** .5 day Block Scheduling Handbook, Chapter 17	**RS** Know It Notes S3 **E** Creative Strategies for Teaching World Geography, Lessons 10 and 11 **SM** Map Activity 17 **E** Biography Activity: Ludwig van Beethoven **ELL** Main Idea Activity S3
SECTION 4		
The Benelux Countries (pp. 398–400) 1. Describe how larger countries influenced the Benelux countries. 2. Describe what this region's culture is like. 3. Describe what the Benelux countries are like today.	**Regular** 1 day Lecture Notes, Section 4 **Block Scheduling** .5 day Block Scheduling Handbook, Chapter 17	**RS** Know It Notes S4 **E** Creative Strategies for Teaching World Geography, Lessons 10 and 11 **ELL** Main Idea Activity S4
SECTION 5		
The Alpine Countries (pp. 401–03) 1. Identify some of the major events in the history of the Alpine countries. 2. Identify some of the cultural features of the region. 3. Describe how the economies of Switzerland and Austria are similar.	**Regular** 1 day Lecture Notes, Section 5 **Block Scheduling** .5 day Block Scheduling Handbook, Chapter 17	**RS** Know It Notes S5 **E** Creative Strategies for Teaching World Geography, Lessons 10 and 11 **ELL** Main Idea Activity S5

Chapter Resource Key

- **RS** Reading Support
- **IC** Interdisciplinary Connections
- **E** Enrichment
- **SM** Skills Mastery
- **A** Assessment
- **REV** Review
- **ELL** Reinforcement and English Language Learners and English for Speakers of Other Languages (ESOL)
- Transparencies
- CD–ROM
- Music
- Video
- Internet
- Holt Presentation Maker Using Microsoft® PowerPoint®

One-Stop Planner CD-ROM

See the *One-Stop Planner* for a complete list of additional resources for students and teachers.

One-Stop Planner CD–ROM

It's easy to plan lessons, select resources, and print out materials for your students when you use the *One-Stop Planner CD–ROM with Test Generator.*

Technology Resources

- One-Stop Planner CD–ROM, Lesson 17.1
- Geography and Cultures Visual Resources with Teaching Activities 24–30
- *ARGWorld* CD–ROM
- Homework Practice Online
- HRW Go site

- One-Stop Planner CD–ROM, Lesson 17.2
- *ARGWorld* CD–ROM
- Homework Practice Online
- HRW Go site

- One-Stop Planner CD–ROM, Lesson 17.3
- *ARGWorld* CD–ROM
- Homework Practice Online
- HRW Go site

- One-Stop Planner CD–ROM, Lesson 17.4
- *ARGWorld* CD–ROM
- Homework Practice Online
- HRW Go site

- One-Stop Planner CD–ROM, Lesson 17.5
- *ARGWorld* CD–ROM
- Homework Practice Online
- HRW Go site

Review, Reinforcement, and Assessment Resources

- **ELL** Main Idea Activity S1
- **REV** Section 1 Review
- **A** Daily Quiz 17.1
- **REV** Chapter Summaries and Review
- **ELL** English Audio Summary 17.1
- **ELL** Spanish Audio Summary 17.1

- **ELL** Main Idea Activity S2
- **REV** Section 2 Review
- **A** Daily Quiz 17.2
- **REV** Chapter Summaries and Review
- **ELL** English Audio Summary 17.2
- **ELL** Spanish Audio Summary 17.2

- **ELL** Main Idea Activity S3
- **REV** Section 3 Review
- **A** Daily Quiz 17.3
- **REV** Chapter Summaries and Review
- **ELL** English Audio Summary 17.3
- **ELL** Spanish Audio Summary 17.3

- **ELL** Main Idea Activity S4
- **REV** Section 4 Review
- **A** Daily Quiz 17.4
- **REV** Chapter Summaries and Review
- **ELL** English Audio Summary 17.4
- **ELL** Spanish Audio Summary 17.4

- **ELL** Main Idea Activity S5
- **REV** Section 5 Review
- **A** Daily Quiz 17.5
- **REV** Chapter Summaries and Review
- **ELL** English Audio Summary 17.5
- **ELL** Spanish Audio Summary 17.5

internet connect

HRW ONLINE RESOURCES

GO TO: go.hrw.com
Then type in a keyword.

TEACHER HOME PAGE
KEYWORD: **SJ5 TEACHER**

CHAPTER INTERNET ACTIVITIES
KEYWORD: **SJ5 GT17**

Choose an activity to:
- tour the land and rivers of Europe.
- travel back in time to the Middle Ages.
- visit schools in Belgium and the Netherlands.

CHAPTER ENRICHMENT LINKS
KEYWORD: **SJ5 CH17**

CHAPTER MAPS
KEYWORD: **SJ5 MAPS17**

ONLINE ASSESSMENT
Homework Practice
KEYWORD: **SJ5 HP17**
Standardized Test Prep Online
KEYWORD: **SJ5 STP17**
Rubrics
KEYWORD: **SS Rubrics**

COUNTRY INFORMATION
KEYWORD: **SJ5 Almanac**

CONTENT UPDATES
KEYWORD: **SS Content Updates**

HOLT PRESENTATION MAKER
KEYWORD: **SJ5 PPT17**

ONLINE READING SUPPORT
KEYWORD: **SS Strategies**

CURRENT EVENTS
KEYWORD: **S5 Current Events**

Meeting Individual Needs

Ability Levels

Level 1 Basic-level activities designed for all students encountering new material

Level 2 Intermediate-level activities designed for average students

Level 3 Challenging activities designed for honors and gifted-and-talented students

ESOL Activities that address the needs of students with Limited English Proficiency

Chapter Review and Assessment

- **IC** Interdisciplinary Activities for the Middle Grades 13, 14, 15
- **E** Readings in World Geography, History, and Culture 31–33
- **SM** Critical Thinking Activity 17
- **REV** Chapter 17 Review and Practice
- **REV** Chapter Summaries and Review
- **ELL** Vocabulary Activity 17

- **A** Chapter 17 Test
- Chapter 17 Test Generator (on the One-Stop Planner)
- Audio CD Program, Chapter 17
- **A** Chapter 17 Test for English Language Learners and Special-Needs Students
- HRW Go site

CHAPTER 17

West-Central Europe
Previewing Chapter Resources

Holt Online Learning

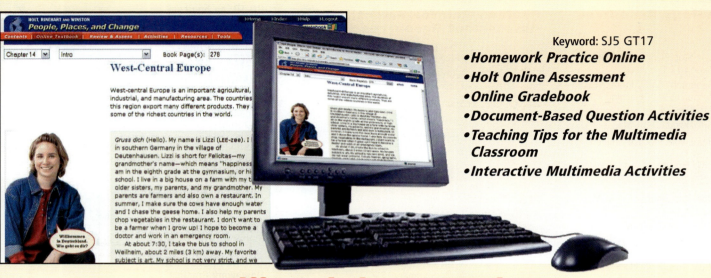

Keyword: SJ5 GT17

- Homework Practice Online
- Holt Online Assessment
- Online Gradebook
- Document-Based Question Activities
- Teaching Tips for the Multimedia Classroom
- Interactive Multimedia Activities

Differentiating Instruction

Reading and Writing Support
- ◀ Graphic Organizer Activity
- Vocabulary Activity
- Chapter Summaries and Review
- Know It Notes
- Audio CD

Active Learning
- Block Scheduling Handbook
- Cultures of the World Activity
- Interdisciplinary Activity
- ◀ Map Activity
- Critical Thinking Activity

Primary Sources and Advanced Learners
- ◀ Geography for Life Activity: The EU and NATO
- Map Activity: Population
- Readings in World Geography, History and Culture:
  - 31 France's Unsettled Immigrants
  - 32 Living Behind the Wall
  - 33 Peril in the Alps

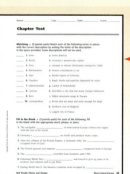

Assessment Program
- Daily Quizzes S1–5
- ◀ Chapter Test
- Chapter Test for English Language Learners and Special-Needs Students

Spanish and ESOL
- Vocabulary Activity
- ◀ Main Idea Activities for English Language Learners and Special-Needs Students
- Chapter Summaries and Review
- Spanish Audio Summary
- Know It Notes S1–5
- Chapter Test for English Language Learners and Special-Needs Students

Special Education Modifications

Your **I.D.E.A. Works!** CD-ROM will provide modified versions of the following teaching materials:
- ◀ Know It Notes S1–5
- Vocabulary Activity
- Main Idea Activities S1–5
- Daily Quizzes S1–5
- Chapter 17 Test
- Flash cards of chapter vocabulary terms

Teacher Resources

Books for Teachers

Berman, Russell A. *Cultural Studies of Modern Germany: History, Representation, and Nationhood.* University of Wisconsin Press, 1994.

Raifsnyder, William E., and Marylou Raifsnyder. *Adventuring in the Alps: France, Switzerland, Germany, Austria, Liechtenstein, Italy, Slovenia.* Sierra Club Books, 1999.

Robitaille, Louis-Bernard, and Donald Winkler (translator). *And God Created the French.* Robert Davies Publishing, 1998.

Books for Students

Austria in Pictures. Lerner Publications Company, 1998. Topography, history, society, economy, and government. **SHELTERED ENGLISH**

Bussolin, Veronique. *France (Country Fact Files).* Raintree/Steck-Vaughn, 1995. Geography, natural resources, economy, and the environment.

Degens, T. *Freya on the Wall.* Browndeer Press, 1997. East German 14-year-old Freya offers view of the complex events leading to the fall of the Berlin Wall.

Multimedia Materials

Let's Visit France. CD–ROM with Labpack. Educational Software Institute.

Making of the German Nation. CD–ROM with Labpack. Educational Software Institute.

The Netherlands. Video, 29 min. Films for the Humanities and Sciences.

Videos and CDs

Videos
- CNN *Presents Geography: Yesterday and Today,* Segment 15 Europe's Immigration Challenge
- CNN *Presents World Cultures: Yesterday and Today,* Segments 30 and 36
- ARG World

Holt Researcher
http://researcher.hrw.com

- European Union (EU)
- France
- European Religions
- Revolutionary France Expands
- Joan of Arc
- England and France on the Eve of the Hundred Years' War
- Netherlands
- Belgium
- Germany
- Austria
- Switzerland

Transparency Packages

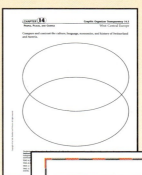

Graphic Organizer Transparencies 17.1–5

Geography and Cultures Visual Resources Transparencies
51 West-Central Europe: Physical-Political
52 The Gare Saint-Lazare
53 Creating a Polder

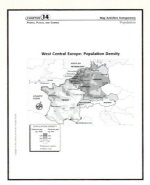

Map Activities Transparency 17 Population

CHAPTER 17

WHY IT MATTERS

There are many reasons why American students should know more about the countries of west-central Europe. Here are a few of them:

- All of the countries of west-central Europe are friendly to the United States.
- Although Germany was once our enemy, it is now an ally. The United States has military bases in Germany.
- A large percentage of Americans trace their ancestry to the region.
- The region has produced some of the world's greatest composers, writers, and artists.

CHAPTER 17

West-Central Europe

West-central Europe is an important agricultural, industrial, and manufacturing area. The countries of this region export many different products. They are some of the richest countries in the world.

Gruss dich (Hello). My name is Lizzi (LEE-zee). I live in southern Germany in the village of Deutenhausen. Lizzi is short for Felicitas—my grandmother's name—which means "happiness." I am in the eighth grade at the gymnasium, or high school. I live in a big house on a farm with my three older sisters, my parents, and my grandmother. My parents are farmers and also own a restaurant. In summer, I make sure the cows have enough water and I chase the geese home. I also help my parents chop vegetables in the restaurant. I don't want to be a farmer when I grow up! I hope to become a doctor and work in an emergency room.

At about 7:30, I take the bus to school in Weilheim, about 2 miles (3 km) away. My favorite subject is art. My school is not very strict, and we do not wear uniforms. I study German, geography, English, and Latin. Next year I will start classical Greek.

After school is over at 12:30, I go home to have lunch with my grandmother. Then, I play with my friends outdoors, even when it rains.

Willkommen in Deutschland. Wie geht es dir?

Translation: Welcome to Germany! How are you?

CHAPTER PROJECT

Avalanches are a constant threat in the Austrian and Swiss Alps. Have students conduct research on Alpine avalanche control measures. They might build scale models to demonstrate the most common methods. Cotton batting can substitute for snow. Place photos of the models and written descriptions of the project in portfolios.

STARTING THE CHAPTER

Write the names of the countries of west-central Europe on the chalkboard. Then ask students leading questions about the countries. (Examples: What is the Eiffel Tower, and where is it located? What country used to be two separate countries but has been reunited? What kind of cheese is full of holes? What country do you associate with tulips and windmills?) Students will probably know the answers to some of these questions. Encourage them to ask other questions based on yours. (Examples: What do windmills actually do? Why are they important?) Create a web of student responses and questions on the chalkboard. Have a volunteer copy the web into his or her notes to allow class members to compare their initial questions to what they learn in this chapter.

Section 1 Physical Geography

CHAPTER 17, Section 1

Read to Discover
1. Where are the area's major landform regions?
2. What role do rivers, canals, and harbors play in the region?
3. What are west-central Europe's major resources?

Vocabulary
navigable
loess

Places
Northern European Plain
Pyrenees
Alps
Seine River
Rhine River
Danube River
North Sea
Mediterranean Sea
English Channel
Bay of Biscay

Reading Strategy
READING ORGANIZER Before you read, create a three-column chart. Title the columns Physical Features, Climate, and Resources. As you read this section, write down what you learn about those characteristics of West-Central Europe.

SECTION 1 RESOURCES

Reproducible
- Lecture Notes, Section 1
- Block Scheduling Handbook, Chapter 17
- Graphic Organizer 17
- Know It Notes S1

Technology
- One-Stop Planner CD–ROM, Lesson 17.1
- Homework Practice Online
- Geography and Cultures Visual Resources with Teaching Activities 44–48, 51–53
- HRW Go site

Reinforcement, Review, and Assessment
- Section 1 Review
- Daily Quiz 17.1
- Main Idea Activity S1
- Chapter Summaries and Review
- English Audio Summary 17.1
- Spanish Audio Summary 17.1

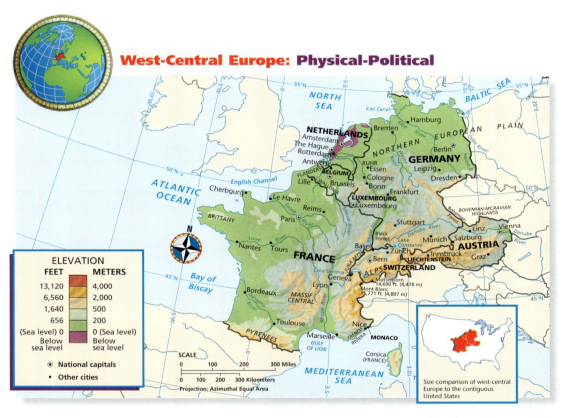

West-Central Europe • 387

Section 1

Objectives
1. Describe the area's major landform regions.
2. Analyze the role that rivers, canals, and harbors play in the region.
3. Identify west-central Europe's major resources.

FOCUS

 Bellringer

Copy the following question onto the chalkboard: *What are some of the sports at which European athletes have excelled?* Discuss responses. (Possible answers: bicycling, skiing, ice skating, sailing, or mountain climbing) Then ask students to suggest what these sports may indicate about the landforms of west-central Europe. (The region includes mountains, water, plains, cold and warm climates.) Tell students that they will learn about the physical geography of west-central Europe in Section 1.

Using the Physical-Political Map
Have students examine the map on this page. Then have them name countries that fit these categories: countries on the North Sea (Germany, Netherlands, Belgium, France), countries with elevations over 6,560 feet (1,999 m) (France, Germany, Switzerland, Austria, Liechtenstein), landlocked countries (Switzerland, Austria, Liechtenstein, Luxembourg), country on the Bay of Biscay and the English Channel (France). Have students list the countries through which the Loire, Rhine, and Danube Rivers flow.

West-Central Europe **387**

CHAPTER 17, Section 1

EYE ON EARTH

The Rhine Reborn During the 1880s commercial fishers would take about 250,000 Atlantic salmon each year from the Rhine River. However, in 1958 the last known salmon was pulled from the river. What had happened?

For decades, the mighty Rhine had been dredged and straightened. This process altered the water's flow, clarity, and temperature. Overfishing and dumping of toxic chemicals from factories depleted the salmon and other species. Then, in 1986, following a fire at a chemical plant, over 30 tons (27 metric tons) of dyes, herbicides, pesticides, fungicides, and mercury poured into the river. The Rhine seemed to be poisoned forever.

European governments and citizens responded by banding together to clean up the river. Finally, in 1990, an Atlantic salmon was pulled from the Sieg, a tributary of the Rhine. The "king of fish" had returned to live and breed.

Visual Record Answer

Many industries might locate near the Rhine to facilitate the transportation of goods.

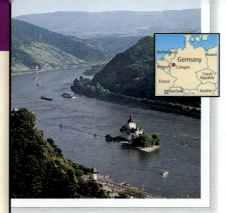

The Rhine River has been an important transportation route for many centuries.

Interpreting the Visual Record

Movement How might the Rhine influence the location of German industry?

The Alps have many large glaciers, lakes, and valleys.

Physical Features

West-central Europe includes France, Germany, Belgium, the Netherlands, Luxembourg, Switzerland, and Austria. Belgium, the Netherlands, and Luxembourg are called the Benelux countries. The word Benelux is a combination of the first letters of each country's name. They are also sometimes called the Low Countries. Large areas of Switzerland and Austria lie in the Alps mountain range. For this reason, they are called the Alpine countries.

Lowlands The main landform regions of west-central Europe are arranged like a fan. The outer edge of the fan is the Northern European Plain. Brittany, a peninsula jutting from northern France, rises slightly above the plain. In Belgium and the Netherlands, the Northern European Plain dips below sea level.

Uplands Toward the middle of the fan a wide band of uplands begins at the Pyrenees (PIR-uh-neez) Mountains. Another important uplands region is the Massif Central (ma-SEEF sahn-TRAHL) in France. Most of the southern two thirds of Germany is hilly. The Schwarzwald (SHFAHRTS-vahlt), or Black Forest, occupies the southwestern corner of Germany's uplands region.

Mountains At the center of the fan are the Alps, Europe's highest mountain range. Many peaks in the Alps reach heights of more than 14,000 feet (4,267 m). The highest peak, France's Mont Blanc (mawn BLAHN), reaches to 15,771 feet (4,807 m). Because of their high elevations, the Alps have large glaciers and frequent avalanches. During the Ice Age, glaciers scooped great chunks of rock out of the mountains, carving peaks such as the Matterhorn.

✓ **READING CHECK:** Places and Regions What are the area's major landforms? Northern European Plain; uplands—Pyrenees Mountains and Massif Central, Black Forest; Alps

Climate and Waterways

West-central Europe's marine west coast climate makes the region a pleasant place to live. Winters can be cold and rainy, but summers are mild. However, areas that lie farther from the warming influence of the North Atlantic are colder. For example, central Germany receives more snow than western France. The Alps have a highland climate.

Snowmelt from the Alps feeds west-central Europe's many **navigable** rivers. Navigable rivers are deep enough and wide enough to be used by ships. France has four major rivers: the Seine (SEN), the Loire

---

TEACH

Teaching Objectives 1–3

ALL LEVELS: (Suggested time: 20 min.) Copy the following graphic organizer onto the chalkboard, omitting the blue answers. Have each student complete the organizer by filling in west-central Europe's major landform regions; the role of canals, rivers, and harbors in the region; and the region's major resources. Ask volunteers to share their answers with the class.

ESOL, **LS** **VISUAL-SPATIAL**

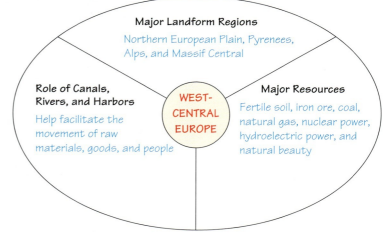

388 ◆ Chapter 17

(LWAHR), the Garonne (gah-RAWN), and the Rhone (ROHN). Germany has five major rivers: the Rhine (RYN), the Danube (DAN-yoob), the Elbe (EL-buh), the Oder (OH-duhr), and the Weser (VAY-zuhr). These rivers and the region's many canals are important for trade and travel. Many large harbor cities are located where rivers flow into the North Sea, Mediterranean Sea, English Channel, or Bay of Biscay. The region's heavily indented coastline has hundreds of excellent harbors.

✓ **READING CHECK:** *Environment and Society* What economic role do rivers, canals, and harbors play in west-central Europe? They are important for trade and travel.

The Grindelwald Valley in Switzerland has excellent pastures.

Resources

Most of the forests that once covered west-central Europe were cut down centuries ago. The fields that remained are now some of the most productive in the world. Germany's plains are rich in **loess** (LES)—fine, wind-blown soil deposits. Germany and France produce grapes for some of the world's finest wines. Switzerland's Alpine pastures support dairy cattle.

The distribution of west-central Europe's mineral resources is uneven. Germany and France have deposits of iron ore but must import oil. Energy resources are generally in short supply in the region. However, there are deposits of coal in Germany and natural gas in the Netherlands. Nuclear power helps fill the need for energy, particularly in France and Belgium. Alpine rivers provide hydroelectric power in Switzerland and Austria. Natural beauty is perhaps the Alpine countries' most valuable natural resource, attracting millions of tourists every year.

✓ **READING CHECK:** *Places and Regions* What geographic factors contribute to the economy of the region? Rich soils are good for farming; Alpine pastures support dairy cattle; lack of energy resources leads to energy imports; natural beauty supports tourism.

Section Review 1

Define and explain: navigable, loess

Working with Sketch Maps On a map of west-central Europe that you draw or that your teacher provides, label the following: the Northern European Plain, Alps, North Sea, Mediterranean Sea, English Channel, and Bay of Biscay.

Reading for the Main Idea
1. *Places and Regions* What are the landform regions of west-central Europe?
2. *Places and Regions* What type of climate dominates this region?

Critical Thinking
3. **Making Generalizations and Predictions** What might be the advantages of having many good harbors and navigable rivers?
4. **Drawing Inferences and Conclusions** How do you think an uneven distribution of resources has affected this region?

Organizing What You Know
5. **Categorizing** Copy the following graphic organizer. Use it to describe the major rivers of west-central Europe. Add rows as needed.

River	Country/Countries	Flows into...

Homework Practice Online
Keyword: SJ5 HP17

Section 1 Review

Answers to Section 1 Review

Define For definitions, see the glossary.

Working with Sketch Maps Maps will vary, but listed places should be labeled in their approximate locations.

Reading for the Main Idea
1. the Northern European Plain, the Pyrenees, the Alps, and the Massif Central (NGS 4)
2. marine west coast (NGS 4)

Critical Thinking
3. They would help move materials, goods, and people.
4. influenced types of goods and energy the region produces, what resources it must import

Organizing What You Know
5. Seine—France, English Channel; Loire—France, Bay of Biscay; Garonne—France, Bay of Biscay; Rhone—France, Mediterranean; Rhine—Switzerland, Germany, the Netherlands, North Sea; Danube—Germany and Austria; Elbe—Germany, North Sea; Oder—Germany, the Baltic; and Weser—Germany, North Sea

CLOSE

Call on volunteers to use the physical-political map to name the landforms and rivers they would encounter if they were to travel eastward from Cherbourg to Berlin or southward from Hamburg to Marseille.

REVIEW, ASSESS, RETEACH

Have students complete the Section Review. Then call on a student to choose a place on the physical-political map of west-central Europe and on another student to describe its physical geography. Continue until all major features have been covered. Then have students complete Daily Quiz 17.1.

Have students complete Main Idea Activity S1. Then pair students and have each pair create a jumble puzzle of 10 words from the key terms or places on the physical-political map. Students should scramble the letters of each term and write a clue describing it. **ESOL, COOPERATIVE LEARNING**

EXTEND

Have interested students conduct research on the mistral—a dry, cold northerly wind that blows from the Alps through the Rhone Valley, or the foehn—a warm, dry wind that blows down from the Alps into Switzerland. Ask students to use their research to create a poster illustrating what creates these winds and how they affect daily life.

CHAPTER 17, Section 2

SECTION 2 RESOURCES

Reproducible
- Lecture Notes, Section 2
- Know It Notes S2
- Cultures of the World Activity 3
- Geography for Life Activity 17
- Creative Strategies for Teaching World Geography, Lessons 10 and 11
- Biography Activity: Charlemagne

Technology
- One-Stop Planner CD–ROM, Lesson 17.2
- Homework Practice Online
- HRW Go site

Reinforcement, Review, and Assessment
- Section 2 Review
- Daily Quiz 17.2
- Main Idea Activity S2
- Chapter Summaries and Review
- English Audio Summary 17.2
- Spanish Audio Summary 17.2

Section 2 France

Read to Discover
1. Which foreign groups affected the historical development of France?
2. What are the main features of French culture?
3. What products does France export?

Vocabulary
medieval
NATO
impressionism

Places
Brittany
Normandy
Paris
Marseille
Nice

People
Franks
Charlemagne
Napoléon Bonaparte

Reading Strategy

READING ORGANIZER Before you read, create a spider map. Label the map France. Create a leg for each heading in the section. As you read the section, fill in the map with details about each heading.

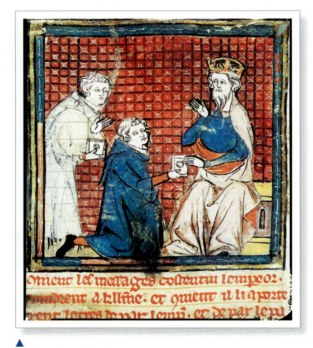

In this illustration messengers inform Charlemagne of a recent military victory.

History

France has been occupied by people from many other parts of Europe. In ancient times, France was part of a region known as Gaul. Thousands of years ago, people moved from eastern Europe into Gaul. These people spoke Celtic languages related to modern Welsh and Gaelic. Breton is a Celtic language still spoken in the region of Brittany.

Early History About 600 B.C. the Greeks set up colonies on Gaul's southern coast. Several centuries later, the Romans conquered Gaul. They introduced Roman law and government to the area. The Romans also established a Latin-based language that developed into French.

Roman rule lasted until the A.D. 400s. A group of Germanic people known as the Franks then conquered much of Gaul. It is from these people that France takes its name. Charlemagne was the Franks' greatest ruler. He dreamed of building a Christian empire that would be as great as the old Roman Empire. In honor of this, the pope crowned Charlemagne Emperor of the Romans in

---

Section 2

Objectives
1. Discuss which foreign groups have affected France's history.
2. Describe the main features of French culture.
3. Identify the products that France exports.

Focus

Bellringer
Copy the following question onto the chalkboard: *What are three things that come to mind when you think of France?* Discuss responses. (Possible answers: fashion, food, Eiffel Tower) Then ask students where they might have received their impressions of France. (movies, television commercials, news broadcasts) You may want to ask what important aspects of the country are missing from the list. (Possible answers: history, daily life, economy) Tell students that in Section 2 they will learn more about France.

Building Vocabulary
Copy the vocabulary terms **medieval**, **NATO**, and **impressionism** onto the chalkboard. Tell students that *medieval* is one of the most frequently misspelled words in the English language. Have a volunteer read aloud the word's definition and history from the text. For **NATO**, introduce the concept of acronyms. Finally, tell students that **impressionism** comes from a painting by Claude Monet titled *Impression—Sunrise*. Ask students why Monet may have given his painting this title. (It was his impression of the sunrise, not a faithful reproduction of every detail.)

390 • Chapter 17

A.D. 800. During his rule, Charlemagne did much to strengthen government and improve education and the arts in Europe.

The Franks divided Charlemagne's empire after his death. Invading groups attacked from many directions. The Norsemen, or Normans, were one of these groups. They came from northern Europe. The area of western France where the Normans settled is known today as Normandy.

The period from the collapse of the Roman Empire to about 1500 is called the Middle Ages, or **medieval** period. The word medieval comes from the Latin words *medium*, meaning "middle," and *aevum*, meaning "age." During much of this period kings in Europe were not very powerful. They depended on cooperation from nobles, some of whom were almost as powerful as kings.

In 1066 a noble, the duke of Normandy, conquered England, becoming its king. As a result, the kings of England also ruled part of France. In the 1300s the king of England tried to claim the throne of France. This led to the Hundred Years' War, which lasted from 1337 to 1453. Eventually, French armies drove the English out of France. The French kings then slowly increased their power over the French nobles.

During the Middle Ages the Roman Catholic Church created a sense of unity among many Europeans. Many tall, impressive cathedrals were built during this time. Perhaps the most famous is the Cathedral of Notre Dame in Paris. It took almost 200 years to build.

Revolution and Napoléon's Empire From the 1500s to the 1700s France built a global empire. The French established colonies in the Americas, Asia, and Africa. During this period most French people lived in poverty and had few rights. In 1789 the French Revolution began. The French overthrew their king and established an elected government. About 10 years later a brilliant general named Napoléon Bonaparte took power. As he gained control, he took the title of emperor. Eventually, Napoléon conquered most of Europe. Napoléon built new roads throughout France, reformed the French educational system, and established the metric system of measurement. In 1815 an alliance including Austria, Great Britain, Prussia, and Russia finally defeated Napoléon. The French king regained the throne.

World Wars During World War I (1914–18) the German army controlled parts of northern and eastern France. In the early years of World War II, Germany defeated France and occupied the northern and western parts of the country. In 1944, Allied armies including U.S., British, and Canadian soldiers landed in Normandy and drove the Germans out. However, after two wars in 30 years France was devastated. Cities, factories, bridges, railroad lines, and train stations had been destroyed. The North Atlantic Treaty Organization, or **NATO**, was formed in 1949 with France as a founding member. This military alliance was created to defend Western Europe against future attacks.

▲ French and English knights clash in this depiction of the Hundred Years' War.

▲ Napoléon Bonaparte became the ruler of France and conquered most of Europe.

CHAPTER 17, Section 2

Linking Past to Present

Links between England and France During part of the Middle Ages, England and France were closely linked politically. In 1066 William, duke of Normandy, conquered England. Later, King Henry II of England also ruled Normandy and western France because his wife had inherited a huge piece of France. Only after its defeat in the Hundred Years' War did England lose most of its French territory. For the next several centuries, England and France were often in conflict.

In 1994 a new era in British-French cooperation dawned with the completion of the "Chunnel." It consists of two railroad tunnels and one service tunnel that link France and England under the English Channel.

Critical Thinking: How did the two countries' resources affect the building of the Chunnel?

Answer: A project like the Chunnel would be very expensive and could only be completed by wealthy countries.

GO TO: go.hrw.com
KEYWORD: SJ5 CH17
FOR: Web sites about the Chunnel

TEACH

Teaching Objective 1

ALL LEVELS: (Suggested time: 15 min.) Copy the following graphic organizer onto the chalkboard, omitting the blue answers. Have each student complete the organizer by describing how Celts, Romans, Franks, and Normans affected France's historical development. Ask volunteers to share their answers with the class. **ESOL,** **LS** VISUAL-SPATIAL

INFLUENCES ON FRANCE'S EARLY HISTORY

Celts	Romans	Franks	Normans
• migrated from eastern Europe to Gaul	• conquered Gaul	• conquered Gaul	• migrated from Normandy and conquered England
• introduced Celtic languages, including Breton	• introduced Roman law and government and established Latin-based language that developed into French	• Frankish emperor Charlemagne strengthened government and improved education	• Norman kings of England claimed throne of France, which led to Hundred Years' War

CHAPTER 17, Section 2

DAILY LIFE

No Multiple-Choice for French Teens! Have the class look up the word *baccalaureate* in a dictionary. (The word refers to the bachelor's degree bestowed by a college or university, or to a religious service for graduates.)

Explain that in France *baccalaureate* refers to a difficult examination students take when they have completed high school. Students who want to go to a university or find a good job must do well on *"le bac."* The emphasis placed on the baccalaureate exam reflects the high value the French place on education.

Activity: Have students acquire information about various placement examinations from a high school counselor. Then lead a discussion comparing the French examination system to systems found in the United States.

Visual Record Answer

no need to convert currencies, eased trade

modern vehicle, otherwise still traditional

The euro replaced the currencies of most of the individual EU countries.
Interpreting the Visual Record *Region*
What are the advantages of a shared currency?

Workers harvest grapes at a vineyard in the Rhone Valley near Lyon.
Interpreting the Visual Record
Human-Environment Interaction Has modern technology changed the grape-growing process?

392 • Chapter 17

Government In the 1950s and 1960s most French colonies in Asia and Africa achieved independence. However, France still controls several small territories around the world. Today, France is a republic with a parliament and an elected president. France is also a founding member of the European Union (EU). France is gradually replacing its currency, the franc, with the EU currency, the euro.

✓ **READING CHECK:** *Human Systems* Which foreign groups have affected France's historical development? **Greeks, Romans, Franks, Normans, English**

Culture

About 85 percent of French people are Roman Catholic, and 5 to 10 percent are Muslims. Almost all French citizens speak French. However, small populations of Bretons in the northwest and Basques in the southwest speak other languages. In Provence-Alpes-Côte d'Azur and Languedoc-Roussillon in the south and on the island of Corsica, some people speak regional dialects along with French. Immigrants from former colonies in Africa, the Caribbean, and Southeast Asia also influence French culture through their own styles of food, clothing, music, and art.

Customs In southern France people eat Mediterranean foods like wheat, olives and olive oil, cheeses, and garlic. In the north food is more likely to be prepared with butter, herbs, and mushrooms. Wine is produced in many French regions, and France produces more than 400 different cheeses. French people celebrate many festivals, including Bastille Day on July 14. On this date in 1789 a mob stormed the Bastille, a royal prison in Paris. The French recognize this event as the beginning of the French Revolution.

Teaching Objectives 2–3

ALL LEVELS: (Suggested time: 30 min.) Pair students and have each pair create a collage depicting some of the main features of French culture as well as products that France exports. (The collages' images and symbols may pertain to Roman Catholicism; predominance of the French language; traditions of wine and cheese making; various immigrant cultures; French literary, artistic, and philosophical traditions; and exports such as wheat, olives, cars, airplanes, shoes, clothing, machinery, and chemicals.) Display collages around the classroom.
ESOL, COOPERATIVE LEARNING, **LS** **VISUAL-SPATIAL**

TEACHER TO TEACHER

Rebecca Minnear of Las Vegas, Nevada, suggests the following activity to help students learn more about France: Have each student create two postcards to illustrate and describe aspects of France's economy, history, and culture. Students should create an illustration for one side of the postcard. On the reverse side of the card, students should write a note to a friend or family member describing the significance of the illustration. Have volunteers present and explain their postcards to the class.

The Arts and Literature France has a respected tradition of poetry, philosophy, music, and the visual arts. In the late 1800s and early 1900s France was the center of an artistic movement called **impressionism**. Impressionist artists tried to capture the rippling of light rather than an exact, realistic image. Famous impressionists include Monet, Renoir, and Degas. French painters, like Cézanne and Matisse, influenced styles of modern painting. Today, France is a world leader in the arts and film industry.

READING CHECK: *Human Systems* How French painters are respected around the world and influenced modern painting.

France

Country	Population/ Growth Rate	Life Expectancy	Literacy Rate	Per Capita GDP
France	60,180,529 0.4%	75, male 83, female	99%	$26,000
United States	290,342,554 0.9%	74, male 80, female	97%	$37,600

Sources: Central Intelligence Agency, *The World Factbook 2003*

Interpreting the Chart How do France's life expectancy and literacy rate compare to those of the United States?

France Today

France is a major agricultural and industrial country. Its resources, labor force, and location in the heart of Europe have helped spur economic growth. France exports wheat, olives, wine, and cheeses as well as other dairy products. French factories produce cars, airplanes, shoes, clothing, machinery, and chemicals. France's largest city is Paris, which has nearly 10 million people in its metropolitan area. Other major cities include Marseille, Nice, Lyon, and Lille. France's major cities are linked by high-speed trains and excellent highways.

READING CHECK: *Human Systems* What are some products that France wheat, olives, wine, cheeses, cars, airplanes, shoes, clothing, machinery, chemicals

Section Review 2

Define or identify: Franks, Charlemagne, medieval, Napoléon Bonaparte, NATO, impressionism

Working with Sketch Maps On the map you created in Section 1, label Brittany, Normandy, Paris, Marseille, and Nice.

Reading for the Main Idea
1. (*Human Systems*) What were the main periods of French history?
2. (*Human Systems*) What are the main features of French culture?

Critical Thinking
3. **Finding the Main Idea** What were some long-lasting achievements of Charlemagne and Napoléon
4. **Summarizing** What is the French economy like?

Organizing What You Know
5. **Identifying Cause and Effect** Copy the following graphic organizer. Use it to list the causes and effects of the Hundred Years' War.

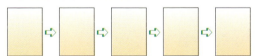

Section 2 Review

Answers to Section 2 Review

Define or identify: For definitions and identifications, see the glossary and the index.

Working with Sketch Maps Maps will vary, but listed places should be labeled in their approximate locations.

Reading for the Main Idea
1. Greek colonization, Romans, Franks, medieval period, colonial empire, French Revolution, Napoleonic era, world wars (NGS 13)
2. mostly Roman Catholic; French language; immigrant cultures; popularity of wine and cheese; respected cultural traditions (NGS 10)

Critical Thinking
3. Charlemagne—strengthened government, helped to improve education and arts in Europe; Napoléon—built new roads, reformed French educational system, instituted metric system in France
4. major agricultural and industrial producer and exporter; resources, location

Organizing What You Know
5. duke of Normandy conquers England; Norman kings of England continue to rule part of France; English king tries to claim French throne; Hundred Years' War; French drive English out

▲ **Chart Answer**

They are higher.

CLOSE

Display impressionist paintings for students and lead a discussion about how they depict the effects of light.

REVIEW, ASSESS, RETEACH

Have students complete the Section Review. Then teach the class the phrase "*Je sais*" (ZHUH SAY)—meaning "I know" in French. Call on volunteers to say *Je sais* and follow it with an important fact pertaining to Section 2. Then have students complete Daily Quiz 17.2.

Have students complete Main Idea Activity S2. Then organize students into small groups and have each group prepare an outline of Section 2.
ESOL, COOPERATIVE LEARNING, LS **VERBAL-LINGUISTIC**

EXTEND

Have interested students compile a "Who's Who" of famous French musicians, writers, political leaders, and other historical figures. Examples include Joan of Arc, Napoléon, Debussy, and Hugo, among others. Have each student choose two or three figures and write a short description of his or her chosen figures' significance. Arrange the descriptions in alphabetical order. Compile the biographies into a scrapbook and use it as a classroom reference.

CHAPTER 17, Section 3

SECTION 3 RESOURCES

Reproducible
- Lecture Notes, Section 3
- Know It Notes S3
- Map Activity 17
- Creative Strategies for Teaching World Geography, Lessons 10 and 11
- Biography Activity: Ludwig van Beethoven

Technology
- One-Stop Planner CD–ROM, Lesson 17.3
- Homework Practice Online
- HRW Go site

Reinforcement, Review, and Assessment
- Section 3 Review
- Daily Quiz 17.3
- Main Idea Activity S3
- Chapter Summaries and Review
- English Audio Summary 17.3
- Spanish Audio Summary 17.3

Visual Record Answer ▶
on a hill overlooking a river

Section 3 Germany

Read to Discover
1. What effects have wars had on Germany?
2. What are Germany's major contributions to world culture?
3. How did the division of Germany affect its economy?

Vocabulary
Reformation
Holocaust
chancellor

Places
Berlin
Bonn
Essen
Frankfurt
Munich
Hamburg
Cologne

People
Adolf Hitler
Johannes Gutenberg
Ludwig van Beethoven
Richard Wagner

Reading Strategy
FOLDNOTES: TRI-FOLD Create the FoldNote titled **Tri-Fold** as described in the Appendix. Label the columns Know, Want, and Learn. In the "Know" column, write down some facts that you already know about Germany. Then write down what you want to know. After you read the section, summarize what you have learned in the "Learn" column.

This medieval castle overlooks a German town.
Interpreting the Visual Record *Place*
What geographic features made this a good place to build a fortress?
▼

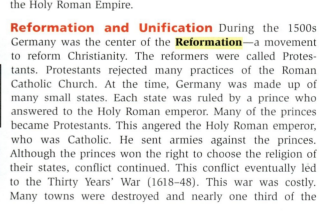

History

Many Germans are descendants of tribes that migrated from northern Europe in ancient times. The Romans conquered the western and southern fringes of the region. They called this land Germania, from the name of one of the tribes that lived there.

The Holy Roman Empire When the Roman Empire collapsed, the Franks became the most important tribe in Germany. The lands ruled by the Frankish king Charlemagne in the early 800s included most of what is now Germany. Charlemagne's empire was known as the Holy Roman Empire.

Reformation and Unification During the 1500s Germany was the center of the **Reformation**—a movement to reform Christianity. The reformers were called Protestants. Protestants rejected many practices of the Roman Catholic Church. At the time, Germany was made up of many small states. Each state was ruled by a prince who answered to the Holy Roman emperor. Many of the princes became Protestants. This angered the Holy Roman emperor, who was Catholic. He sent armies against the princes. Although the princes won the right to choose the religion of their states, conflict continued. This conflict eventually led to the Thirty Years' War (1618–48). This war was costly. Many towns were destroyed and nearly one third of the

---

Section 3

Objectives
1. Examine the effects that wars have had on Germany.
2. Describe Germany's major contributions to world culture.
3. Analyze how the division of Germany affected its economy.

FOCUS

🔔 Bellringer
Copy the following passage onto the chalkboard: *Imagine that the American Civil War had resulted in the creation of two separate countries. Imagine that the two "Americas" were separated for 40 years before they were reunified. What is one problem that the country might face after reunification?* Discuss responses. Explain that after World War II Germany was divided into two countries that have since been reunited. Tell students that in Section 3 they will learn more about Germany.

Building Vocabulary

Locate a newspaper headline that includes the word *reform*. Discuss with students how the word is used in the headline and article. Compare modern political reform with the **Reformation** of the 1500s. Then tell students that the word **Holocaust** comes from the Greek *holokauston*, which means "that which is completely burnt." Tell students that the Holocaust refers to the mass killing, or genocide, of millions of Jews and other people by the Nazis during World War II. Finally, have a volunteer read aloud the definition of the word **chancellor** from the glossary.

394 Chapter 17

population died. Germany remained divided for more than 200 years. In the late 1800s Prussia, the strongest state, united Germany.

World Wars In 1914 national rivalries and a conflict in the Balkans led to World War I. Austria, Germany, and the Ottoman Empire, later joined by Bulgaria, fought against Britain, France, and Russia, later joined by Italy and the United States. By 1918 Germany and its allies were defeated.

During the 1920s Austrian war veteran Adolf Hitler led a new political party in Germany called the Nazis. The Nazis took power in 1933. In the late 1930s Germany invaded Austria, Czechoslovakia, and finally Poland, beginning World War II. By 1942 Germany and Italy had conquered most of Europe. The Nazis forced many people from the occupied countries into concentration camps to be enslaved or killed. About 6 million Jews and millions of other people were murdered in a mass killing called the **Holocaust**.

To defeat Germany, several countries formed an alliance. These Allies included Britain, the Soviet Union, the United States, and many others. The Allies defeated Germany in 1945. Germany and its capital, Berlin, were divided into Soviet, French, British, and U.S. occupation zones. Britain, France, and the United States later combined their zones to create a democratic West Germany with its capital at Bonn. In its zone, the Soviet Union set up the Communist country of East Germany with an unlimited totalitarian government. Its capital became East Berlin; however, West Berlin became part of West Germany. In 1961 the East German government built the Berlin Wall across the city to stop East Germans from escaping to the West.

Reunification and Modern Government West Germany's roads, cities, railroads, and industries were rebuilt after the war with U.S. financial aid. East Germany was also rebuilt, but it was not as prosperous as West Germany. Unlike the West German government, the East German government allowed people very little freedom. Also, its command economy—managed by the government—was less productive than the free enterprise, market system of West Germany. In the late 1980s East Germans and people throughout Eastern Europe demanded democratic reform. In 1989 the Berlin Wall was torn down. In 1990 East and West Germany reunited. Germany's capital again became Berlin. Today, all Germans enjoy democratic rights. A parliament elects the president and prime minister, or **chancellor**. Germany is a member of the EU and NATO.

✓ **READING CHECK:** (Human Systems) How were the economies of East and West Germany organized following World War II? *East Germany—command economy controlled by a communist government; West Germany—free enterprise, market-based economy*

▲ German youth salute Adolf Hitler in Nürnberg in 1938.

▲ For nearly 30 years the Berlin Wall separated East and West Berlin. Many people in West Berlin protested by painting graffiti on the wall. **Interpreting the Visual Record** Why would the government make the wall solid instead of a barrier that would allow people visual access?

West-Central Europe • 395

CHAPTER 17, Section 3

Cultural Kaleidoscope
The Jews of Berlin When Adolf Hitler came to power in 1933, more than 170,000 Jews lived in Berlin. By 1945 Berlin's Jewish population stood at some 5,000. The vast majority of Berlin's Jews had fled or been killed.

Now Berlin's Jewish community is growing again. Many of the city's new Jewish residents are emigrants from Russia. New Jewish shops, restaurants, schools, and even a chess team have been established. A new Jewish museum has opened. A synagogue that had been damaged by the Nazis and almost destroyed by Allied bombs has been restored.

Activity: Have each student conduct research on the history of Jews in Germany and create a time line to depict major events. volunteers to deliver their speeches to the class.

◀**Visual Record Answer**

Possible answer: The government did not want people to communicate through the wall or see that conditions were better on the other side.

TEACH

Teaching Objective 1

ALL LEVELS: (Suggested time: 10 min.) Copy the following graphic organizer onto the chalkboard, omitting the blue answers. Ask each student to complete the organizer by describing the effects of the Thirty Years' War and World Wars I and II on Germany. Ask volunteers to share their answers with the class. **ESOL,** LS **VISUAL-SPATIAL**

EFFECTS OF WARS ON GERMANY

Thirty Years' War	World War I	World War II
• many towns destroyed • nearly one third of the population died	• lost territory and overseas colonies • paid heavy fines after the war	• Jewish population was nearly wiped out • divided into two countries

Teaching Objective 1

LEVELS 2 AND 3: (Suggested time: 30 min.) Tell students to imagine that they are Germans who oppose their country's involvement in any military actions. Then ask each student to write an antiwar speech. Students' speeches should reference the effects of previous wars on Germany. Ask volunteers to deliver their speeches. LS **VERBAL-LINGUISTIC**

West-Central Europe 395

CHAPTER 17, Section 3

Across the Curriculum
ART
Landscape Painting Some of the world's greatest landscape artists have been from west-central Europe. Among these are the Dutch painter Vincent van Gogh (1853–90), French artist Antoine Watteau (1684–1721), and German painter Caspar David Friedrich (1774–1840).

Activity: Have students choose a landscape artist of the 1700s or 1800s from west-central Europe. Ask them to compare how the artist portrayed the region's landscape with photographs they find in the text and other sources. Are the physical features painted realistically? Was the painting meant to be realistic?

internet connect
GO TO: go.hrw.com
KEYWORD: SJ5 CH17
FOR: Web sites about landscapes

BIOGRAPHY
Ludwig van Beethoven (1770–1827)

Character Trait: Pursuit of Excellence

Perhaps the greatest composer who ever lived, Beethoven (BAYT-hoh-vuhn) didn't let a physical handicap keep him from writing glorious music. In his many songs and symphonies, Beethoven added powerful, intense emotion to established musical styles. Gradually Beethoven lost his hearing, but continued to compose. Beethoven's last works, which he could never hear performed, are often described as the most beautiful of his long career.

How did Beethoven pursue excellence?

Culture

About 34 percent of Germans are Roman Catholic, and 38 percent are Protestant. Most other Germans have no religious association. Many of these people are from eastern Germany, where the communist government suppressed religion from 1945 to 1990.

Diversity About 90 percent of Germany's inhabitants are ethnic Germans. However, significant numbers of Turks, Poles, and Italians have come to Germany to live and work. These "guest workers" do not have German citizenship. Germany has also taken in thousands of refugees from Eastern Europe during the last 50 years.

Customs Traditional German food emphasizes the products of the forests, farms, and seacoasts. Each region produces its own varieties of sausage, cheese, wine, and beer. German celebrations include Oktoberfest; *Sangerfast*, a singing festival; and *Fastnacht*, a religious celebration. The major German festival season is Christmas. The Germans began the custom of bringing an evergreen tree indoors at Christmas and decorating it with candles.

The Arts and Literature Germany has a great tradition of literature, music, and the arts. The first European to print books using movable metal type was a German, Johannes Gutenberg. In the 1700s and 1800s, Germany led Europe in the development of classical music. World-famous German composers include Johann Sebastian Bach and Ludwig van Beethoven. The operas of Richard Wagner revived the folktales of ancient Germany.

✓ **READING CHECK:** **Human Systems** What technology and other contributions have Germans made to world culture? *movable type, classical music*

Crowds gather in a German town for a Christmas market. Christmas markets have been popular in Germany for more than 400 years. From the beginning of Advent until Christmas, booths are set up on the market place in most cities. Here people can buy trees, decorations, and gifts.

396 • Chapter 17

Teaching Objective 2
ALL LEVELS: (Suggested time: 30 min.) Tell students to imagine that they have been hired to design a Web page that highlights Germany's major contributions to world culture. Then have each student design a Web page that includes headlines and links. (Web pages should mention the invention of movable metal type, the development of classical music, including the work of Bach and Beethoven as well as the operas of Wagner, and German traditions in literature and the arts.) Ask volunteers to present their Web pages to the class. **ESOL**

Teaching Objective 3
LEVEL 1: (Suggested time: 15 min.) Tell students to imagine that they are journalists who are writing about how the division of Germany affected the country's economy. Then pair students and have pairs write three headlines that describe the effects of the country's division on the economy. Have volunteers read their headlines to the class.
ESOL, COOPERATIVE LEARNING, **LS** VERBAL-LINGUISTIC

LEVELS 2 AND 3: (Suggested time: 30 min.) Have each student create an editorial cartoon that might accompany an article printed below one of the headlines from the Level 1 activity. **LS** VISUAL-SPATIAL

396 Chapter 17

Germany Today

Germany has a population of 82 million, more people than any other European country. Germany also has Europe's largest economy. Nearly one fourth of all goods and services produced by the EU come from Germany.

Economy Ample resources, labor, and capital have made Germany one of the world's leading industrial countries. The nation exports a wide variety of products. You may be familiar with German automakers like Volkswagen, Mercedes-Benz, and BMW. The German government provides education, medical care, and pensions for its citizens, but Germans pay high taxes. Unemployment is high. Many immigrants work at low-wage jobs. These "guest workers" are not German citizens and cannot receive many government benefits. Since reunification, Germany has struggled to modernize the industries, housing, and other facilities of the former East Germany.

Cities Germany's capital city, Berlin, is a large city with wide boulevards and many parks. Berlin was isolated and economically restricted during the decades after World War II. However, Germans are now rebuilding their new capital to its former splendor.

Near the Rhine River and the coal fields of Western Germany is a huge cluster of cities, including Essen and Düsseldorf. They form Germany's largest industrial district, the Ruhr. Frankfurt is a city known for banking and finance. Munich is a manufacturing center. Other important cities include Hamburg, Bremen, Cologne, and Stuttgart.

✓ **READING CHECK:** *Human Systems* How did the division of Germany affect its economy? *It delayed the modernization of East German industry, housing, and other facilities.*

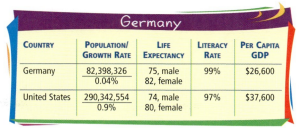

Germany

Country	Population/ Growth Rate	Life Expectancy	Literacy Rate	Per Capita GDP
Germany	82,398,326 0.04%	75, male 82, female	99%	$26,600
United States	290,342,554 0.9%	74, male 80, female	97%	$37,600

Source: Central Intelligence Agency, *The World Factbook 2003*

Interpreting the Chart What might the literacy rate of Germany suggest about its culture?

Section Review 3

Define or identify: Reformation, Adolf Hitler, Holocaust, chancellor, Ludwig van Beethoven, Johannes Gutenberg, Richard Wagner

Working with Sketch Maps On the map you created in Section 2, label Berlin, Bonn, Essen, Frankfurt, Munich, Hamburg, and Cologne.

Reading for the Main Idea
1. *Human Systems* How did wars affect the development of Germany in the 1900s?
2. *Human Systems* What are some notable features of the German economy?

Critical Thinking
3. **Drawing Inferences and Conclusions** How has Germany's history influenced the religious makeup of the population?
4. **Summarizing** What have been some results of the unification of Germany in 1990?

Organizing What You Know
5. **Sequencing** Create a time line listing key events in the history of Germany from 1000 B.C. to 1990.

1000 B.C. ———————————— A.D. 1990

Section 4: The Benelux Countries

CHAPTER 17, Section 4

Section 4 Resources

Reproducible
- Lecture Notes, Section 4
- Know It Notes S4
- Creative Strategies for Teaching World Geography, Lessons 10 and 11

Technology
- One-Stop Planner CD–ROM, Lesson 17.4
- Homework Practice Online
- HRW Go site

Reinforcement, Review, and Assessment
- Section 4 Review
- Daily Quiz 17.4
- Main Idea Activity S4
- Chapter Summaries and Review
- English Audio Summary 17.4
- Spanish Audio Summary 17.4

Visual Record Answer

It is located at the mouth of a major river and is on the North Sea.

Read to Discover
1. How were the Benelux countries influenced by larger countries?
2. What is this region's culture like?
3. What are the Benelux countries like today?

Vocabulary
cosmopolitan

Places
Flanders
Wallonia
Amsterdam
Antwerp
Brussels

People
Flemish
Walloons
Vincent van Gogh

Reading Strategy
TAKING NOTES Use the headings in this section to create an outline. As you read about the Benelux countries, write what you learn below each heading.

The Dutch city of Rotterdam is one of the world's busiest ports.
Interpreting the Visual Record
Movement Why might this city be an important transportation center?

History

Celtic and Germanic tribes once lived in this region, as in most of west-central Europe. They were conquered by the Romans. After the fall of the Roman Empire and the conquests of Charlemagne, the region was ruled alternately by French rulers and by the Holy Roman emperor.

In 1555 the Holy Roman emperor presented the Low Countries to his son, King Philip II of Spain. In the 1570s the Protestants of the Netherlands won their freedom from Spanish rule. Soon after, the Netherlands became a great naval and colonial power. Belgium had been ruled at times by France and the Netherlands. However, by 1830 Belgium had broken away to become an independent kingdom.

Both world wars scarred this region. Many of the major battles of World War I were fought in Belgium. Then in World War II Germany occupied the Low Countries. In 1949 Belgium, the Netherlands, and Luxembourg were founding members of NATO. Later they joined the EU. Today, each of the three countries is ruled by a parliament and a monarch. The monarchs' duties are mostly ceremonial. The Netherlands controls several Caribbean islands. However, its former colonies in Asia and South America are now independent.

✓ **READING CHECK:** *Human Systems* How are the governments of the Benelux countries organized? Each is ruled by a parliament and a monarch, who has mostly ceremonial duties.

398 • Chapter 17

Objectives
1. Investigate how the Benelux countries were influenced by larger countries.
2. Describe what the region's culture is like.
3. Discuss what the Benelux countries are like today.

Focus

Bellringer

Copy the following question onto the chalkboard: *If you lived at the seashore and wanted to recover some of the land under the water, how might you do it?* Ask volunteers to explain their ideas or draw them on the chalkboard. Tell students that the people of the Netherlands have succeeded in reclaiming land from the sea by building earthen walls to keep out the seawater and then pumping water from reclaimed lands. Tell students that in Section 4 they will learn more about the Netherlands and the other Benelux countries.

Building Vocabulary

Write the word **cosmopolitan** on the chalkboard. Remind students that the Greek word *polis* referred to city-states. *Cosmos* means universe. Ask students to infer the term's meaning. Then read the definition aloud.

Connecting to Technology

Dutch Polders

A polder in the Netherlands

Much of the Netherlands lies below sea level and was once covered with water. For at least 2,000 years, the Dutch have been holding back the sea. First they lived on raised earthen mounds. Later they built walls or dikes to keep the water out. After building dikes, the Dutch installed windmills to pump the water out of reclaimed areas, called polders.

Using this system, the Dutch have reclaimed large amounts of land. Cities like Amsterdam and Rotterdam sit on reclaimed land. The dike and polder system has become highly sophisticated. Electric pumps have largely replaced windmills, and dikes now extend along much of the country's coastline. However, this system is difficult to maintain. It requires frequent and expensive repairs. Creating polders has also produced sinking lowlands and other environmental damage. As a result, the Dutch are considering changes to the system. These changes might include restoring some of the polders to wetlands and lakes.

Understanding What You Read
1. What are polders?
2. How did the Dutch use technology to live on land previously under water?

Culture

The people of Luxembourg and Belgium are mostly Roman Catholic. The Netherlands is more evenly divided among Catholic, Protestant, and those who have no religious ties.

Dutch is the language of the Netherlands. Flemish is a language related to Dutch that is spoken in Flanders, the northern part of Belgium. Belgium's coast and southern interior are called Wallonia. People in Wallonia speak mostly French and are called Walloons. In the past, cultural differences between Flemish and Walloons have produced conflict in Belgium. Today street signs and other notices are often printed in both Flemish and French. The Benelux countries are also home to immigrants from Asia and Africa.

West-Central Europe • 399

CHAPTER 17, Section 4

PLACES AND REGIONS

A Sparkling City
Antwerp, Belgium, is one of the world's four leading diamond-cutting centers. (The others are New York, Tel Aviv, and Mumbai.) According to legend, the first diamond was cut in Antwerp in 1476. Since the 1500s establishments that cut and deal in diamonds have flourished in a neighborhood near the central train station.

At Antwerp's Diamond Museum, employees demonstrate the art of cutting and polishing diamonds. Priceless jewelry sparkles in the museum's treasure chamber.

Activity: Have students conduct research on the diamond industry. Tell students to create a map showing sources, processing centers, and major markets.

Connecting to Technology
Answers
1. areas reclaimed from the sea
2. They have used dikes, windmills, and electric pumps to reclaim land.

TEACH

Teaching Objectives 1–3
ALL LEVELS: (Suggested time: 40 min.) Copy the graphic organizer at the right onto the chalkboard, omitting the blue answers. Have each student complete it by filling in information about the influence of larger countries on the Benelux countries and the region's culture. Then lead a discussion based on how students might spend their day if they lived in the Netherlands, Belgium, or Luxembourg. **ESOL**

ASSIGNMENT: Have each student write a paragraph that analyzes the economies of the Benelux region and proposes a reason why the Benelux countries may have become cosmopolitan.

Benelux Countries

Influences from Larger Countries
- Ruled by France and the Holy Roman Empire
- Netherlands ruled by Spain
- Belgium ruled by France and the Netherlands
- WWI battles fought in Belgium
- Low Countries occupied by Germany during WWII

→

Culture of the Benelux Countries
- Belgians and Luxembourgers predominantly Roman Catholic
- Dutch evenly divided between Catholics, Protestants, and nonreligious persons
- Dutch spoken in Netherlands
- Flemish and French spoken in Belgium

West-Central Europe   399

Section 4 Review

Answers to Section 4 Review

Define For definition, see the glossary.

Working with Sketch Maps Listed places should be labeled accurately.

Reading for the Main Idea
1. Belgium and Luxembourg are predominantly Roman Catholic; Netherlands has more equal proportion of Catholics, Protestants, and nonreligious people; Dutch spoken in Netherlands; Flemish and French spoken in Belgium; Belgium and Netherlands have famous artistic traditions. (NGS 10)
2. They speak different languages and have different religious traditions and different economies. (NGS 10)

Critical Thinking
3. The Benelux countries are small and rely on international trade for their income and to obtain resources such as oil. (NGS 11)
4. because of cultural differences

Organizing What You Know
5. Belgium—cheese, chocolates, cocoa, and diamond cutting; Luxembourg—service industries such as banking; Netherlands—flowers, cheese, chocolates, cocoa, diamond cutting, and oil refining

Chart Answer

Belgium's

Benelux Countries

Country	Population/ Growth Rate	Life Expectancy	Literacy Rate	Per Capita GDP
Belgium	10,289,088 / 0.1%	75, male 81, female	98%	$29,200
Luxembourg	454,157 / 1.2%	74, male 81, female	100%	$48,900
Netherlands	16,150,511 / 0.5%	76, male 82, female	99%	$27,200
United States	290,342,554 / 0.9%	74, male 80, female	97%	$37,600

Source: Central Intelligence Agency, *The World Factbook 2003*

Interpreting the Chart Which country's per capita GDP is closest to that of the United States?

The region's foods include dairy products, fish, and sausage. The Dutch spice trade led to dishes flavored with spices from Southeast Asia. The Belgians claim they invented french fries, which they eat with mayonnaise.

The Netherlands and Belgium have been world leaders in fine art. In the 1400s and 1500s, Flemish artists painted realistic portraits and landscapes. Dutch painters like Rembrandt and Jan Vermeer experimented with different qualities of light. In the 1800s Dutch painter Vincent van Gogh portrayed southern France with bold brush strokes and bright colors.

✓ **READING CHECK:**  What is the relationship between cultures in Belgium? Many different cultures; in the past, Walloons and Flemish have had conflict but now cooperate

The Benelux Countries Today

The Netherlands is famous for its flowers, particularly tulips. Belgium and the Netherlands export cheeses, chocolate, and cocoa. Amsterdam and Antwerp, Belgium, are major diamond-cutting centers. The Netherlands also imports and refines oil. Luxembourg earns much of its income from services such as banking. The region also produces steel, chemicals, and machines. Its **cosmopolitan** cities are centers of international business and government. A cosmopolitan city is one that has many foreign influences. Brussels, Belgium, is the headquarters for many international organizations such as the EU and NATO.

✓ **READING CHECK:**  What are the Benelux countries like today? They are major exporters and are very cosmopolitan.

Section Review 4

Define or identify: Flemish, Walloons, Vincent van Gogh, cosmopolitan

Working with Sketch Maps On the map you created in Section 3, label Flanders, Wallonia, Amsterdam, Antwerp, and Brussels.

Reading for the Main Idea
1. (Human Systems) What are the main cultural features of the Benelux countries?
2. (Human Systems) In what ways do the people of the Benelux countries differ?

Critical Thinking
3. **Drawing Inferences and Conclusions** Why might the economies of the Benelux countries be dependent on international trade?
4. **Analyzing Information** Why have groups in Belgium been in conflict?

Organizing What You Know
5. **Comparing** Copy the following graphic organizer. Use it to compare the Benelux countries' industries.

Belgium	Luxembourg	Netherlands

Homework Practice Online Keyword: SJ5 HP17

400 • Chapter 17

CLOSE

Tell students about the "Tulip Mania" of the 1600s. Tulips were brought to the Netherlands from Turkey in the 1550s and soon became very popular. People speculated on tulip prices—they bought bulbs planning to resell them at higher prices. At the height of the craze, a single bulb of a prized variety could cost 4,000 guilders—as valuable as a ship loaded with cargo! When the tulip market crashed in 1637, many people went bankrupt.

REVIEW, ASSESS, RETEACH

Have students complete the Section Review. Then pair students and have each pair write two or three verses for a new national anthem for one of the Benelux countries. Verses should incorporate information from Section 4. Ask volunteers to share their work with the class. Have students complete Daily Quiz 17.4. **COOPERATIVE LEARNING, LS AUDITORY-MUSICAL**

EXTEND

Have interested students conduct research on the mix of cultures in Belgium or another Benelux country. Then have students write short stories based on their research. **BLOCK SCHEDULING**

Section 5: The Alpine Countries

CHAPTER 17, Section 5

Read to Discover
1. What are some of the major events in the history of the Alpine countries?
2. What are some cultural features of this region?
3. How are the economies of Switzerland and Austria similar?

Vocabulary
cantons
nationalism

Places
Geneva
Salzburg
Vienna
Zurich
Basel
Bern

People
Habsburgs
Wolfgang Amadeus Mozart

Reading Strategy
FOLDNOTES: TWO-PANEL FLIP CHART Create the FoldNote titled **Two-Panel Flip Chart** described in the Appendix. Write Switzerland on one of the flaps and Austria on the other. As you read, write what you learn about each country beneath its flap.

Section 5 Resources

Reproducible
- Lecture Notes, Section 5
- Know It Notes S5
- Creative Strategies for Teaching World Geography, Lessons 10 and 11

Technology
- One-Stop Planner CD–ROM, Lesson 17.5
- Homework Practice Online
- HRW Go site

Reinforcement, Review, and Assessment
- Section 5 Review
- Daily Quiz 17.5
- Main Idea Activity S5
- Chapter Summaries and Review
- English Audio Summary 17.5
- Spanish Audio Summary 17.5

History

Austria and Switzerland share a history of Celtic occupation, Roman and Germanic invasions, and rule by the Holy Roman Empire.

Switzerland Swiss **cantons**, or districts, gradually broke away from the Holy Roman Empire, and in the 1600s Switzerland became independent. Today Switzerland is a confederation of 26 cantons. Each controls its own internal affairs, and the national government handles defense and international relations. Switzerland's location in the high Alps has allowed it to remain somewhat separate from the rest of Europe. It has remained neutral in the European wars of the last two centuries. Switzerland is not a member of the EU or NATO. In 2002, however, it joined the United Nations. Committed to its neutrality, Switzerland remains active in many international organizations.

Austria During the Middle Ages, Austria was a border region of Germany. This region was the home of the Habsburgs, a powerful family of German nobles. From the 1400s onward the Holy Roman emperor was always a Habsburg. At the height of their power the Habsburgs ruled Spain and the Netherlands, as well as large areas of Germany, eastern Europe, and Italy. This empire included different ethnic

The International Red Cross helps people around the world. This is the Red Cross headquarters in Geneva, Switzerland.

West-Central Europe • 401

Section 5

Objectives
1. Identify some of the major events in the history of the Alpine countries.
2. Describe some of the cultural features of the region.
3. Compare the economies of Switzerland and Austria.

Focus

Bellringer
Copy the following passage onto the chalkboard: *Look up cacao in the textbook's index. What is it? Where is it grown? Why might we think of Switzerland when we think of chocolate?* Discuss responses. Tell students that in 1876 a Swiss man added concentrated milk to chocolate for the first time, forming milk chocolate. Today Switzerland imports the raw materials for making chocolate and exports the finished product. Tell students that in Section 5 they will learn more about Switzerland and Austria.

Building Vocabulary
Copy the terms **cantons** and **nationalism** onto the chalkboard and call on volunteers to read the definitions aloud from the glossary. Ask students what other names they know that refer to political divisions of territory. (Examples: state, province, territory, county) *Canton* comes from a Latin word meaning "corner." So, students might think of a canton as a corner of Switzerland. Nationalism contains the word *nation*. People who want to form their own country or nation are nationalists.

West-Central Europe 401

The Danube River passes through Vienna, the capital of Austria.
Interpreting the Visual Record
Movement How does this river influence movement and trade?

groups, each with its own language, government, and system of laws. The empire was united only in its allegiance to the emperor and in its defense of the Roman Catholic religion.

With the conquests of Napoléon after 1800, the Holy Roman Empire was formally eliminated. It was replaced with the Austrian Empire, which was also under Habsburg control. When Napoléon was defeated, the Austrian Empire became the dominant power in central Europe.

Through the 1800s the diverse peoples of the empire began to develop **nationalism**, or a demand for self-rule. In 1867 the Austrians agreed to share political power with the Hungarians. The Austrian Empire became the Austro-Hungarian Empire. After World War I the empire was dissolved. Austria and Hungary became separate countries. Shortly before World War II the Germans took over Austria and made it part of Germany. After the war, the Allies occupied Austria. Today Austria is an independent member of the EU.

✓ **READING CHECK:** *Human Systems* What were the major events in the history of the Alpine countries? *Switzerland—breaking away from Holy Roman Empire; end of that empire, beginning of Austrian Empire, shared power with Hungarians, World Wars I and II*

Culture

About 46 percent of the population in Switzerland is Roman Catholic, and 40 percent is Protestant. Austria's population is mainly Roman Catholic. Only about 5 percent of its people are Protestant, while 17 percent follow Islam or other religions.

Languages and Diversity About 64 percent of Swiss speak German, 18 percent speak French, and 10 percent speak Italian. Small groups in the southeast speak a language called Romansh. Other European languages are also spoken in Switzerland. Austria is almost entirely German-speaking, but contains small minorities of Slovenes and Croatians.

Customs Christmas is a major festival in both countries. People make special cakes and cookies at this time. In rural parts of Switzerland people take cattle up to the high mountains in late spring

▲ Austrians wearing carved wooden masks celebrate the return of spring and milder weather.

CHAPTER 17, Section 5

FOOD FESTIVAL

Say Cheese The countries of west-central Europe are famous for their cheese. Point out that cheese comes in hundreds of varieties, based on these factors and others: the type of milk used to make the cheese (cow, goat, or sheep); fresh or ripened; soft, hard, semisoft, or semifirm; and the herbs, spices, mold spores, or bacteria that have been added to the cheese.

Students could search the supermarket for different types of cheese from west-central Europe, and the class could hold a cheese-tasting party. Serve French or German breads and a beverage with the cheese.

Visual Record Answer
It flows through many countries, giving millions of people who live far inland access to the sea.

TEACH

Teaching Objectives 1–3
ALL LEVELS: (Suggested time: 30 min.) Copy the following graphic organizer onto the chalkboard, omitting the blue answers. Pair students and have each pair complete the organizer with major events in the history of the Alpine countries, cultural features of each country, and economic features of each country. Ask volunteers to share their answers with the class.
ESOL, COOPERATIVE LEARNING

COMPARING AUSTRIA AND SWITZERLAND

	Austria	Switzerland
History	Invasion by Celts, Romans, and Germanic tribes; ruled by the Holy Roman Empire; part of Habsburg, Austrian, and Austro-Hungarian Empires; became republic; annexed by Germany; became republic	Invasion by Celts, Romans, and Germanic tribes; ruled by the Holy Roman Empire; gained independence in the 1600s
Culture	Predominantly Roman Catholic and German-speaking with small minority of Slovenes and Croatians; known for classical music	Majority of Swiss are Roman Catholic or Protestant.
Economy	Dairy products, including cheese; Vienna is Austria's commercial and industrial center.	Dairy products, including cheese; manufacturer of watches, optical instruments, and other machinery; Zurich is the center of Swiss banking.

and return in the fall. Their return is celebrated by decorating homes and cows' horns with flowers. A special feast is also prepared.

The Alpine region is well known for its music. In the 1700s Wolfgang Amadeus Mozart wrote symphonies and operas in the Austrian city of Salzburg. Every year a music festival is held there in his honor. Austria's capital, Vienna, is also a center for music and fine art.

✓ **READING CHECK:** Human Systems What role have the arts played in this region? **The region is well known for its music.**

The Alpine Countries

Country	Population/ Growth Rate	Life Expectancy	Literacy Rate	Per Capita GDP
Austria	8,188,207 0.2%	75, male 81, female	98%	$27,700
Switzerland	7,318,638 0.3%	77, male 83, female	99%	$31,700
United States	290,342,554 0.9%	74, male 80, female	97%	$37,600

Source: Central Intelligence Agency, *The World Factbook 2003*

Interpreting the Chart How do the populations of the Alpine countries compare with that of the United States?

The Alpine Countries Today

Switzerland and Austria both produce dairy products, including many kinds of cheese. Switzerland is also famous for the manufacturing of watches, optical instruments, and other machinery. Swiss chemists discovered how to make chocolate bars. Switzerland is a major producer of chocolate, although it must import the cocoa beans.

Switzerland and Austria are linked to the rest of Europe by excellent highways, trains, and airports. Several long tunnels allow trains and cars to pass through mountains in the Swiss Alps. Both countries attract many tourists with their mountain scenery, lakes, and ski slopes.

Located on the Danube, Vienna is Austria's commercial and industrial center. Switzerland's two largest cities are both in the German-speaking north. Zurich is a banking center, while Basel is the starting point for travel down the Rhine to the North Sea. Switzerland's capital is Bern, and Geneva is located in the west.

✓ **READING CHECK:** Places and Regions How are the economies of Switzerland and Austria similar? **They both produce dairy products and attract tourists.**

Homework Practice Online
Keyword: SJ5 HP17

Define or identify: cantons, Habsburgs, nationalism, Wolfgang Amadeus Mozart

Working with Sketch Maps On the map you created in Section 4, label Geneva, Salzburg, Vienna, Zurich, Basel, and Bern.

Reading for the Main Idea

1. Human Systems What were the main events in the history of the Alpine countries?
2. Human Systems What are some notable aspects of Swiss and Austrian culture?

Critical Thinking

3. **Drawing Inferences and Conclusions** How might geography have been a factor in Switzerland's historical neutrality?
4. **Drawing Inferences and Conclusions** How have foreign invasions of Austria shaped its history?

Organizing What You Know

5. **Comparing/Contrasting** Use this graphic organizer to compare and contrast the culture, language, economies, and history of Switzerland and Austria.

West-Central Europe • 403

Section 5 Review

Answers to Section 5 Review

Define or identify For definitions and identifications, see the glossary and index.

Working with Sketch Maps Maps will vary, but listed places should be labeled in their approximate locations.

Reading for the Main Idea

1. Switzerland—independence in 1600s, neutral; Austria—part of larger empires, republic, annexed by Germany, and republic (NGS 13)

2. Swiss—three languages; Austrian—mainly Roman Catholic, German-speaking, Slovene and Croatian minorities, known for music (NGS 10)

Critical Thinking

3. Switzerland's mountains helped the country remain neutral.

4. Napoléon's conquest led to end of Holy Roman Empire; Germany drew Austria into World War II.

Organizing What You Know

5. Students should mention the elements of culture, language, economics, and history in the section. (NGS 10)

▲ **Chart Answer**

They are much smaller.

CLOSE

Refer students to the comments in the chapter introduction. Have each student write a similar self-introduction for a boy or girl from Switzerland or Austria, using information from Section 5. Ask volunteers to share their introductions with the class.

REVIEW, ASSESS, RETEACH

Have students complete the Section Review questions. Then have students work in pairs to create flash cards of vocabulary words and key concepts from the section. Ask them to quiz each other using the flash cards. Then have students complete Daily Quiz 17.5.
ESOL, COOPERATIVE LEARNING

EXTEND

Have interested students conduct research on how Switzerland has been able to maintain neutrality since the 1500s. Students may focus on the relationship of the country's physical geography to its neutrality.

West-Central Europe **403**

CHAPTER 17 REVIEW

Define and Identify
For definitions and identifications, see the glossary and index.

Review the Main Ideas

12. Northern European Plain, uplands, Alps (NGS 4)
13. many harbor cities located where rivers enter the sea
14. introduced Roman law and government, plus language that would develop into French
15. During both wars, German forces invaded and occupied parts of France.
16. East Germany—command economy; West Germany—market economy
17. Oktoberfest, *Sangerfast*, *Fastnacht*, Christmas (NGS 10)
18. Spain; after revolt, became a great naval and colonial power
19. flowers, cheeses, chocolate, cocoa, diamonds; also oil, steel, chemical, machines
20. dissolved; taken over by Germans and made part of Germany
21. has remained neutral through two world wars, continues policy of neutrality (NGS 13)

Think Critically

22. Rivers have facilitated trade; the Alps have somewhat hindered travel and trade.
23. by building tunnels through the Alps
24. the Rhine River, Jura Mountains, Pyrenees, and Brittany; borders with Belgium, Luxembourg, and part of the border with Germany
25. The EU has its headquarters in Brussels.
26. low population growth, long life expectancy, high literacy rate, and high incomes; each of the nations is economically developed (NGS 9)

404 Chapter 17

Chapter 17 Review and Practice

Define and Identify
Identify each of the following:

1. navigable
2. loess
3. Charlemagne
4. medieval
5. impressionism
6. Reformation
7. Holocaust
8. Ludwig van Beethoven
9. cosmopolitan
10. cantons
11. nationalism

Review the Main Ideas

12. What are the three main landform regions of west-central Europe?
13. How have the region's rivers affected the location of harbor cities?
14. How did Roman rule affect the history of France?
15. How did the world wars affect France?
16. How did the economies of East Germany and West Germany differ?
17. What are some of Germany's holidays?
18. What country controlled the Low Countries after 1555? What happened to the Netherlands soon after?
19. For what products are the Benelux countries famous?
20. What happened to the Austro-Hungarian Empire after World War I? What happened to Austria during World War II?
21. How is Switzerland's position in world affairs unique?

Think Critically

22. **Drawing Inferences and Conclusions** What geographic features have encouraged travel and trade in west-central Europe? What geographic features have hindered travel and trade?
23. **Finding the Main Idea** How have the people of Switzerland altered their environment?
24. **Analyzing Information** What landform regions give France natural borders? Which French borders do not coincide with physical features?
25. **Drawing Inferences and Conclusions** Why might Brussels, Belgium, be called the capital of Europe?
26. **Comparing** What demographic factors are shared by all countries of west-central Europe today? How do they reflect levels of economic development?

Map Activity

27. On a separate sheet of paper, match the letters on the map with their correct labels.

Northern European Plain
Pyrenees
Alps
Seine River
Rhine River
Danube River
North Sea
Mediterranean Sea
Paris
Berlin

404 • Chapter 17

Map Activity

27. **A.** Mediterranean Sea
    B. Seine River
    C. Pyrenees
    D. Rhine River
    E. Berlin
    F. Danube River
    G. North Sea
    H. Alps
    I. Northern European Plain
    J. Paris

Writing Activity

Imagine you are taking a boat tour down the Rhine River. You will travel from Basel, Switzerland, to Rotterdam, the Netherlands. Keep a journal describing the places you see and the stops you make. Be sure to use standard grammar, spelling, sentence structure, and punctuation.

internet connect

Internet Activity: go.hrw.com
KEYWORD: SJ5 GT17

Choose a topic to explore about west-central Europe:
- Tour the land and rivers of Europe.
- Travel back in time to the Middle Ages.
- Visit Belgian and Dutch schools.

Social Studies Skills Practice

Interpreting Maps

Study this map of Germany after World War II. Then answer the questions.

1. Which countries occupied zones of West Germany?
2. Which country occupied East Germany?
3. Which country may have had the most difficulty re-supplying its troops? Why?
4. How did Berlin's location increase the difficulty of re-supplying troops and civilians in West Berlin?

Analyzing Primary Sources

France is a leader in the fashion industry. Read the following quote from TIME Magazine about Coco Chanel, a French designer. Then answer the questions.

"Coco Chanel wasn't just ahead of her time. She was ahead of herself. If one looks at the work of contemporary [today's] fashion designers . . . one sees that many of their strategies echo what Chanel once did. The way, 75 years ago, she mixed up the vocabulary of male and female clothes and created fashion that offered the wearer a feeling of hidden luxury rather than ostentation [fancy show] are just two examples of how her taste and sense of style overlap with today's fashion."

1. What impact has Coco Chanel's work had on other designers?
2. In the first sentence, what does it mean that Chanel was "ahead of her time?"
3. In the fourth sentence, what does the word vocabulary mean?
4. What about Chanel's designs was highly unusual for the time?

CHAPTER 17 REVIEW

Writing Activity

Journals will vary, but the place descriptions should be consistent with text material. Use Rubric 15, Journals, to evaluate student work.

Interpreting Maps

1. United States, Great Britain, France
2. Soviet Union
3. United States; no direct access to the sea, farthest from home country
4. It was located deep within the Soviet zone.

Analyzing Primary Sources

1. significant impact on today's designers
2. She designed clothes that would be more like clothes from years in her future.
3. design elements or ideas
4. mixed up male and female clothes, emphasized hidden luxury over ostentation

REVIEW AND ASSESSMENT RESOURCES

Reproducible
- Readings in World Geography, History, and Culture 31, 32, and 33
- Critical Thinking Activity 17
- Vocabulary Activity 17

Technology
- Chapter 17 Test Generator (on the One-Stop Planner)
- HRW Go site
- Audio CD Program, Chapter 17

Reinforcement, Review, and Assessment
- Chapter 17 Review
- Chapter Summaries and Review
- Chapter 17 Test
- Chapter 17 Test for English Language Learners and Special-Needs Students

internet connect

GO TO: go.hrw.com
KEYWORD: SJ5 Teacher
FOR: a guide to using the Internet in your classroom

Chapter 18: Northern Europe
Chapter Resource Manager

Objectives	Pacing Guide	Reproducible Resources
SECTION 1		
Physical Geography (pp. 402–11) 1. Describe the region's major physical features. 2. Identify the region's most important natural resources. 3. Identify the climates that are found in northern Europe.	**Regular** .5 day Lecture Notes, Section 1 **Block Scheduling** .5 day Block Scheduling Handbook, Chapter 18	**RS** Know It Notes S1 **RS** Graphic Organizer 18 **E** Creative Strategies for Teaching World Geography, Lessons 10 and 11 **E** Lab Activity for Geography and Earth Science, Demonstration 4 **ELL** Main Idea Activity S1
SECTION 2		
The United Kingdom (pp. 412–15) 1. Identify some important events in the history of the United Kingdom. 2. Describe what the people and culture of the country are like. 3. Describe the United Kingdom of today.	**Regular** 1 day Lecture Notes, Section 2 **Block Scheduling** .5 day Block Scheduling Handbook, Chapter 18	**RS** Know It Notes S2 **SM** Map Activity 18 **E** Cultures of the World Activity 3 **E** Biography Activities: Geoffrey Chaucer, William Shakespeare, Elizabeth I **ELL** Main Idea Activity S2
SECTION 3		
The Republic of Ireland (pp. 416–18) 1. Identify the key events in Ireland's history. 2. Describe the people and culture of Ireland. 3. Identify the kinds of economic changes Ireland has experienced in recent years.	**Regular** 1 day Lecture Notes, Section 3 **Block Scheduling** .5 day Block Scheduling Handbook, Chapter 18	**RS** Know It Notes S3 **E** Cultures of the World Activity 3 **ELL** Main Idea Activity S3
SECTION 4		
Scandinavia (pp. 419–23) 1. Describe the people and culture of Scandinavia. 2. Identify some important features of each of the region's countries, plus Greenland and Lapland.	**Regular** 1.5 days Lecture Notes, Section 4 **Block Scheduling** .5 day Block Scheduling Handbook, Chapter 18	**RS** Know It Notes S4 **E** Cultures of the World Activity 3 **SM** Geography for Life Activity **ELL** Main Idea Activity S4

Chapter Resource Key

- **RS** Reading Support
- **IC** Interdisciplinary Connections
- **E** Enrichment
- **SM** Skills Mastery
- **A** Assessment
- **REV** Review
- **ELL** Reinforcement and English Language Learners and English for Speakers of Other Languages (ESOL)
- Internet
- Holt Presentation Maker Using Microsoft® PowerPoint®
- Transparencies
- CD–ROM
- Music
- Video

One-Stop Planner CD–ROM

See the *One-Stop Planner* for a complete list of additional resources for students and teachers.

One-Stop Planner CD–ROM

It's easy to plan lessons, select resources, and print out materials for your students when you use the *One-Stop Planner CD–ROM with Test Generator.*

Technology Resources

- One-Stop Planner CD–ROM, Lesson 18.1
- Geography and Cultures Visual Resources with Teaching Activities 24–29
- *ARGWorld* CD–ROM
- Homework Practice Online
- HRW Go site

- One-Stop Planner CD–ROM, Lesson 18.2
- *ARGWorld* CD–ROM
- Music of the World Audio CD Program, Selection 6
- Homework Practice Online
- HRW Go site

- One-Stop Planner CD–ROM, Lesson 18.3
- *ARGWorld* CD–ROM
- Homework Practice Online
- HRW Go site

- One-Stop Planner CD–ROM, Lesson 18.4
- *ARGWorld* CD–ROM
- Homework Practice Online
- HRW Go site

Review, Reinforcement, and Assessment Resources

ELL	Main Idea Activity S1
REV	Section 1 Review
A	Daily Quiz 18.1
REV	Chapter Summaries and Review
ELL	English Audio Summary 18.1
ELL	Spanish Audio Summary 18.1

ELL	Main Idea Activity S2
REV	Section 2 Review
A	Daily Quiz 18.2
REV	Chapter Summaries and Review
ELL	English Audio Summary 18.2
ELL	Spanish Audio Summary 18.2

ELL	Main Idea Activity S3
REV	Section 3 Review
A	Daily Quiz 18.3
REV	Chapter Summaries and Review
ELL	English Audio Summary 18.3
ELL	Spanish Audio Summary 18.3

ELL	Main Idea Activity S4
REV	Section 4 Review
A	Daily Quiz 18.4
REV	Chapter Summaries and Review
ELL	English Audio Summary 18.4
ELL	Spanish Audio Summary 18.4

internet connect

HRW ONLINE RESOURCES

GO TO: go.hrw.com
Then type in a keyword.

TEACHER HOME PAGE
KEYWORD: SJ5 TEACHER

CHAPTER INTERNET ACTIVITIES
KEYWORD: SJ5 GT18

Choose an activity to:
- explore the island and fjords on the Scandinavian coast.
- visit historic palaces in the United Kingdom.
- investigate the history of skiing.

CHAPTER ENRICHMENT LINKS
KEYWORD: SJ5 CH18

CHAPTER MAPS
KEYWORD: SJ5 MAPS18

ONLINE ASSESSMENT
Homework Practice
KEYWORD: SJ5 HP18
Standardized Test Prep Online
KEYWORD: SJ5 STP18
Rubrics
KEYWORD: SS Rubrics

COUNTRY INFORMATION
KEYWORD: SJ5 Almanac

CONTENT UPDATES
KEYWORD: SS Content Updates

HOLT PRESENTATION MAKER
KEYWORD: SJ5 PPT18

ONLINE READING SUPPORT
KEYWORD: SS Strategies

CURRENT EVENTS
KEYWORD: S5 Current Events

Meeting Individual Needs

Ability Levels

Level 1 Basic-level activities designed for all students encountering new material

Level 2 Intermediate-level activities designed for average students

Level 3 Challenging activities designed for honors and gifted-and-talented students

ESOL Activities that address the needs of students with Limited English Proficiency

Chapter Review and Assessment

IC	Interdisciplinary Activities for the Middle Grades 13, 14, 15
E	Readings in World Geography, History, and Culture 34, 35, 36
SM	Critical Thinking Activity 18
REV	Chapter 18 Review and Practice
REV	Chapter Summaries and Review
ELL	Vocabulary Activity 18
A	Chapter 18 Test
	Chapter 18 Test Generator (on the One-Stop Planner)
	Audio CD Program, Chapter 18
A	Chapter 18 Test for English Language Learners and Special-Needs Students
	HRW Go site

CHAPTER 18

Northern Europe
Previewing Chapter Resources

Holt Online Learning

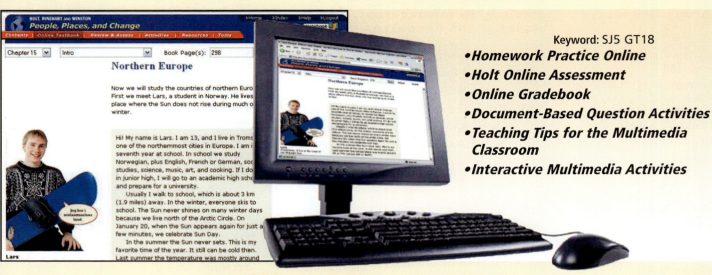

Keyword: SJ5 GT18

- Homework Practice Online
- Holt Online Assessment
- Online Gradebook
- Document-Based Question Activities
- Teaching Tips for the Multimedia Classroom
- Interactive Multimedia Activities

Differentiating Instruction

Reading and Writing Support
◀ Graphic Organizer Activity
- Vocabulary Activity
- Chapter Summaries and Review
- Know It Notes
- Audio CD

Active Learning
- Block Scheduling Handbook
- Cultures of the World Activity
- Interdisciplinary Activity
- Map Activity
◀ Critical Thinking Activity: Connecting Europe by Chunnel
- Music of the World Audio CD Program: Songs of Ireland

Primary Sources and Advanced Learners
- Geography for Life Activity: The Vikings Abroad
◀ Map Activity: The British Empire
- Readings in World Geography, History and Culture:
  - 34 Wartime London
  - 35 A Dublin Adventure
  - 36 The Sami

Assessment Program
- Daily Quizzes S1–4
- Chapter Test
◀ Chapter Test for English Language Learners and Special-Needs Students

Spanish and ESOL
◀ Vocabulary Activity
- Main Idea Activities for English Language Learners and Special-Needs Students
- Chapter Summaries and Review
- Spanish Audio Summary
- Know It Notes S1–4
- Chapter Test for English Language Learners and Special-Needs Students

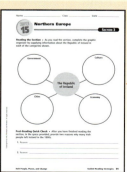

Special Education Modifications
Your I.D.E.A. Works! CD-ROM will provide modified versions of the following teaching materials:
◀ Know It Notes S1–4
- Vocabulary Activity
- Main Idea Activities S1–4
- Daily Quizzes S1–4
- Chapter 18 Test
- Flash cards of chapter vocabulary terms

Teacher Resources

Books for Teachers

Bryson, Bill. *Notes from a Small Island.* Avon Books, 1997.

Kazantzakis, Nikos. *England: A Travel Journal.* Simon and Schuster, 1965.

Lacy, Terry G. *Ring of Seasons: Iceland—Its Culture and History.* University of Michigan Press, 1998.

Books for Students

Black, Eric. *Northern Ireland: Troubled Land,* (World in Conflict). Lerner Publications Company, 1998. History of the ethnic conflict, including current issues.

Kage Carlson, Bo. *Sweden,* (Country Fact Files). Raintree/Steck Vaughn, 1999. The country's geography, natural resources, economics, and environment.

McMillan, Bruce. *Nights of the Pufflings.* Houghton Mifflin, 1995. The story of stranded baby puffins saved by Icelandic children. **SHELTERED ENGLISH**

Morley, Jacqueline. *First Facts About the Vikings (First Facts).* Peter Bedrick Books, 1996. Information about the daily lives of these warriors and traders.

Multimedia Materials

Discovering Denmark, Video vol. 6 of Traveloguer Video Collection. 60 min. Glencoe.

The Spirit of Sweden, vol. 13 of Traveloguer Video Collection. Video, 60 min. Glencoe.

The Wonders of Norway, vol. 14 of Traveloguer Video Collection. Video, 60 min. Glencoe.

Videos and CDs

Videos
- CNN *Presents Geography: Yesterday and Today,* Segment 14 *The Fishing Life*
- CNN *Presents World Cultures: Yesterday and Today,* Segment 17 *The New Globe Theater*
- *ARG World*

Holt Researcher
http://researcher.hrw.com
- European Union (EU)
- European Religions
- Iceland
- Ireland
- Irish Nationalism
- United Kingdom
- Monarchs of Europe
- Denmark
- Norway
- Sweden
- Finland

Transparency Packages

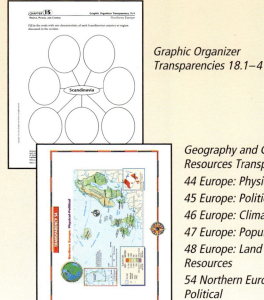

Graphic Organizer Transparencies 18.1–4

Geography and Cultures Visual Resources Transparencies
44 Europe: Physical
45 Europe: Political
46 Europe: Climate
47 Europe: Population
48 Europe: Land Use and Resources
54 Northern Europe: Physical-Political

Map Activities Transparency 18 The British Empire

CHAPTER 18

Why It Matters

You may wish to point out the following reasons why we should study northern Europe:

- The United States has strong historical and economic ties to the countries of northern Europe.
- Denmark, Iceland, Norway, and the United Kingdom are members of the North Atlantic Treaty Organization (NATO) and our political allies.
- Millions of Americans have northern European ancestry.
- American culture has been influenced by northern Europe. Our language, law, commerce, government, literature, art, holidays, and food—all bear the imprint of northern Europe.

CHAPTER 18

Northern Europe

Now we will study the countries of northern Europe. First we meet Lars, a student in Norway. He lives in a place where the Sun does not rise during much of the winter.

Hi! My name is Lars. I am 13, and I live in Tromsø, one of the northernmost cities in Europe. I am in my seventh year at school. In school we study Norwegian, plus English, French or German, social studies, science, music, art, and cooking. If I do well in junior high, I will go to an academic high school and prepare for a university.

Usually I walk to school, which is about 3 km (1.9 miles) away. In the winter, everyone skis to school. The Sun never shines on many winter days because we live north of the Arctic Circle. On January 20, when the Sun appears again for just a few minutes, we celebrate Sun Day.

In the summer the Sun never sets. This is my favorite time of the year. It still can be cold then. Last summer the temperature was mostly around 6° or 7°C (about 43° or 44°F).

Jeg bor i midnattssolens land.

Translation: I live in the Land of the Midnight Sun.

Chapter Project

For almost 100 years, Northern Ireland has had a tradition of political murals. Have students conduct research on the conflicts in Northern Ireland and draw murals advocating lasting peace on butcher paper. Photograph the murals and place the photograph in students' portfolios.

Starting the Chapter

Select a brief folktale from one of the countries of northern Europe. Two possibilities are "Three Billy Goats Gruff" from Norway or one of the King Arthur stories from Great Britain. Read the story aloud to the class. You may want to invite students to sketch illustrations for the story as you read. When you have finished the story, ask students if they have heard it before. Discuss responses. Explain that Americans have inherited many cultural elements from northern Europe, such as the stories that were told around the fire on long winter nights. Tell students they will learn more about the countries of northern Europe and the connections the United States has with those countries in Chapter 18.

Section 1: Physical Geography

CHAPTER 18, Section 1

Read to Discover
1. What are the region's major physical features?
2. What are the region's most important natural resources?
3. What climates are found in northern Europe?

Vocabulary
fjords
lochs
North Atlantic Drift

Places
British Isles
English Channel
North Sea
Great Britain
Ireland
Iceland
Greenland
Scandinavian Peninsula
Jutland Peninsula
Kjølen Mountains
Northwest Highlands
Shannon River
Baltic Sea

Reading Strategy
USING PRIOR KNOWLEDGE Look at the Physical-Political map of Northern Europe. Where are the cities located? Why do you think people settled there? Write down your answers. As you read this section, compare your answers to what you learn.

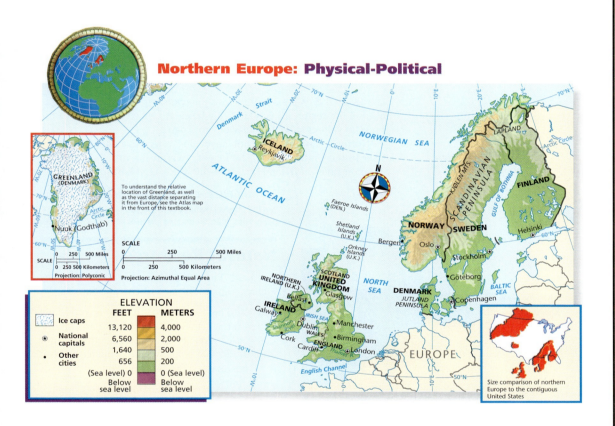

Northern Europe: Physical-Political

SECTION 1 RESOURCES

Reproducible
- Lecture Notes, Section 1
- Block Scheduling Handbook, Chapter 18
- Know It Notes S1
- Graphic Organizer 18
- Creative Strategies for Teaching World Geography, Lessons 10 and 11
- Lab Activity for Geography and Earth Science, Demonstration 4

Technology
- One-Stop Planner CD–ROM, Lesson 18.1
- Homework Practice Online
- Geography and Cultures Visual Resources with Teaching Activities 44–48, 54
- HRW Go site

Reinforcement, Review, and Assessment
- Section 1 Review
- Daily Quiz 18.1
- Main Idea Activity S1
- Chapter Summaries and Review
- English Audio Summary 18.1
- Spanish Audio Summary 18.1

Section 1

Objectives
1. Describe the major physical features of northern Europe.
2. Identify the region's most important natural resources.
3. Examine the climates found in northern Europe.

Focus

Bellringer
Copy the following instructions onto the chalkboard: *Look at the physical-political map of northern Europe. What outdoor sports might you enjoy if you lived in the lake region of Finland, in central Norway, in southern England, or on the western coast of Ireland?* (Possible answers: Finland—ice skating, Norway—skiing, England—soccer, Ireland—sailing) Give students time to write down their answers. Discuss responses. Point out that it is possible to participate in many sports in northern Europe because the region has a mix of landforms and climates. Tell students that in Section 1 they will learn more about the physical geography of northern Europe.

Using the Physical-Political Map
Have students examine the map on this page. Call on a volunteer to name the countries in the region. Have students classify the countries as islands or peninsulas. Ask students to name the seas that surround the region's countries and to speculate on the influence the sea has had on the economic activities of the people of northern Europe.

CHAPTER 18, Section 1

National Geography Standard 14

Acid Rain, Acid Lakes

Northern Europe has many lakes, rivers, and streams. Some of these waterways are polluted.

During the 1960s increased industrial production in Europe caused airborne pollutants to drift far over the continent. These pollutants combined with water vapor in the air and fell as acid rain. Forests in Scandinavia show the damaging effects. Acid rain has also corroded buildings.

In winter, snow carries pollutants to the land. When the snow melts, the acid makes its way into lakes and streams. Fish have been killed off in many lakes of Norway and Sweden.

Activity: Have students conduct research on efforts by northern European governments and organizations to solve pollution problems. Allow them to summarize their findings in a written report or in an oral presentation to the class.

internet connect
GO TO: go.hrw.com
KEYWORD: SJ5 CH8
FOR: Web sites about pollution

Visual Record Answer
carved by glaciers

Our Amazing Planet

Scotland's Loch Ness contains more fresh water than all the lakes in England and Wales combined. It is deeper, on average, than the nearby North Sea.

Fjords like this one shelter many harbors in Norway.
Interpreting the Visual Record
How are fjords created?

Physical Features

Northern Europe includes several large islands and peninsulas. The British Isles lie across the English Channel and North Sea from the rest of Europe. They include the islands of Great Britain and Ireland and are divided between the United Kingdom and the Republic of Ireland. This region also includes the islands of Iceland and Greenland. Greenland is the world's largest island.

To the east are the Scandinavian and Jutland Peninsulas. Denmark occupies the Jutland Peninsula and nearby islands. The Scandinavian Peninsula is divided between Norway and Sweden. Finland lies farther east. These countries plus Iceland make up Scandinavia.

Landforms The rolling hills of Ireland, the highlands of Great Britain, and the Kjølen (CHUH-luhn) Mountains of Scandinavia are part of Europe's Northwest Highlands region. This is a region of very old, eroded hills and low mountains.

Southeastern Great Britain and southern Scandinavia are lowland regions. Much of Iceland is mountainous and volcanic. More than 10 percent of it is covered by glaciers. Greenland is mostly covered by a thick ice cap.

Coasts Northern Europe has long, jagged coastlines. The coastline of Norway includes many **fjords** (fee-AWRDS). Fjords are narrow, deep inlets of the sea set between high, rocky cliffs. Ice-age glaciers carved the fjords out of coastal mountains.

Lakes and Rivers Melting ice-age glaciers left behind thousands of lakes in the region. In Scotland, the lakes are called **lochs**. Lochs are found in valleys carved by glaciers long ago.

Northern Europe does not have long rivers like the Mississippi River in the United States. The longest river in the British Isles is the Shannon River in Ireland. It is just 240 miles (390 km) long.

✓ **READING CHECK:** *Places and Regions* What are the physical features of the region? large islands, peninsulas, hills, mountains, glaciers, ice cap, fjords, lakes

Natural Resources

Northern Europe has many resources. They include water, forests, and energy sources.

Water The ice-free North Sea is especially important for trade and fishing. Parts of the Baltic Sea freeze over during the winter months. Special ships break up the ice to keep sea lanes open to Sweden and Finland.

Forests and Soil Most of Europe's original forests were cleared centuries ago. However,

408 ● Chapter 18

TEACH

Teaching Objectives 1–3

ALL LEVELS: (Suggested time: 20 min.) Copy the graphic organizer at right onto the chalkboard, omitting the blue answers. Use it to help students classify the landforms, lakes and rivers, natural resources, and climates of northern Europe. Call on volunteers to point out the listed physical features on a wall map. Then have students brainstorm occupations in northern Europe that depend on the listed physical features and resources. (Example: oil—oil-rig worker) **ESOL**, **LS VISUAL-SPATIAL**

Physical Geography of Northern Europe

Landforms			Climates
	hills of Ireland highlands of Great Britain Kjølen Mountains lowlands of southeastern Great Britain and southern Scandinavia glaciers fjords	marine west coast caused by North Atlantic Drift humid continental subarctic tundra	
Lakes and rivers resources	lochs of Scotland Shannon River — longest in region	North Sea, Baltic Sea fish, forests, soil oil and natural gas geothermal and hydroelectric power	Natural

408 Chapter 18

Sweden and Finland still have large, coniferous forests that produce timber. The region's farmers grow many kinds of cool-climate crops.

Energy Beneath the North Sea are rich oil and natural gas reserves. Nearly all of the oil reserves are controlled by the nearby United Kingdom and Norway. However, these reserves cannot satisfy all of the region's needs. Most countries import oil and natural gas from southwest Asia, Africa, and Russia. Some, such as Iceland, use geothermal and hydroelectric power.

✓ **READING CHECK:** *Environment and Society* In what way has technology allowed people in the region to keep the North Sea open during the winter? Special ships break up the ice.

Climate

Despite its northern location, much of the region has a marine west coast climate. Westerly winds blow over a warm ocean current called the **North Atlantic Drift**. These winds bring mild temperatures and rain to the British Isles and coastal areas. Atlantic storms often bring even more rain. Snow and frosts may occur in winter.

Central Sweden and southern Finland have a humid continental climate. This area has four true seasons. Far to the north are subarctic and tundra climates. In the forested subarctic regions, winters are long and cold with short days. Long days fill the short summers. In the tundra region it is cold all year. Only small plants such as grass and moss grow there.

✓ **READING CHECK:** *Places and Regions* What are the region's climates? marine west coast, humid continental, subarctic, tundra

Define and explain: fjords, lochs, North Atlantic Drift

Working with Sketch Maps On an outline map that you draw or that your teacher provides, label the following: British Isles, English Channel, North Sea, Great Britain, Ireland, Iceland, Greenland, Scandinavian Peninsula, Jutland Peninsula, Kjølen Mountains, Northwest Highlands, Shannon River, and Baltic Sea. In the margin, write a short caption explaining how the North Atlantic Drift affects the region's climates.

Reading for the Main Idea

1. *Places and Regions* Which parts of northern Europe are highland regions? Which parts are lowland regions?

2. *Places and Regions* What major climate types are found in northern Europe?

Critical Thinking

3. **Finding the Main Idea** How has ice shaped the region's physical geography?

4. **Making Generalizations and Predictions** Think about what you have learned about global warming. How might warmer temperatures affect the climates and people of northern Europe?

Organizing What You Know

5. **Summarizing** Copy the following graphic organizer. Use it to describe the region's important natural resources.

Water	Forests and soil	Energy

Section 1 Review

Answers to Section 1 Review

Define For definitions, see the glossary.

Working with Sketch Maps Places should be labeled in their approximate locations. The North Atlantic Drift brings mild temperatures and rain to the British Isles and coastal areas.

Reading for the Main Idea

1. hills of Ireland, highlands of Great Britain, Kjølen Mountains, much of Iceland; southeastern Great Britain, southern Scandinavia (NGS 4)

2. marine west coast, humid continental, subarctic, tundra (NGS 4)

Critical Thinking

3. carved fjords, left lakes behind

4. Possible answers: melt Iceland's glaciers and Greenland's ice cap, fill fjords, flood lowlands

Organizing What You Know

5. water—North Sea, Baltic Sea; forests and soil—coniferous forests in Sweden and Finland, soil for cool-climate crops; energy—oil, natural gas, geothermal and hydroelectric power

Northern Europe • 409

CLOSE

Challenge students to suggest ways that northern Europe's physical geography may have shaped its history. (Examples: Long coastlines and ice-free ports make long-distance trade and conquest possible. The isolation of the British Isles may have discouraged some invaders.)

REVIEW, ASSESS, RETEACH

Have students complete the Section Review. Then have students write a description of a country or region in northern Europe without naming it. Call on volunteers to read their descriptions and on others to determine the place described. Then have students complete Daily Quiz 18.1.

Have students complete Main Idea Activity S1. Then organize them into groups to create a database of facts on the region. Each database should include physical features, resources, and climate types for each area. **ESOL, COOPERATIVE LEARNING**

EXTEND

Have interested students conduct research on Surtsey, a volcanic island that emerged off the coast of Iceland in 1963. Ask students to include information on how the island was formed, the plants that now grow there, and the animals that either live on or visit the island. Have students write reports of these findings. **BLOCK SCHEDULING**

Northern Europe **409**

CHAPTER 18

GEOGRAPHY SIDELIGHT

A History of Hazards

Vestmannaeyjar (VEST-mahn-nah-AY-yahr), the town pictured in the photo, lies on Heimaey (HAY-my), an island off Iceland's southwest coast. The people there have faced many dangers over the centuries.

During the 1400s, English sailors often stole supplies from the town. In 1627, Algerian pirates carried off many inhabitants and sold them into slavery. In 1963, a nearby volcano named Surtsey erupted from the ocean floor. Ash covered Vestmannaeyjar. Just 10 years later, the eruption pictured buried houses and streets.

Activity: Have students conduct research on Heimaey's history and create items that its citizens may have placed in a time capsule throughout the years.

internet connect
GO TO: go.hrw.com
KEYWORD: SJ5 CH18
FOR: more information on and videos of Iceland's volcanoes.

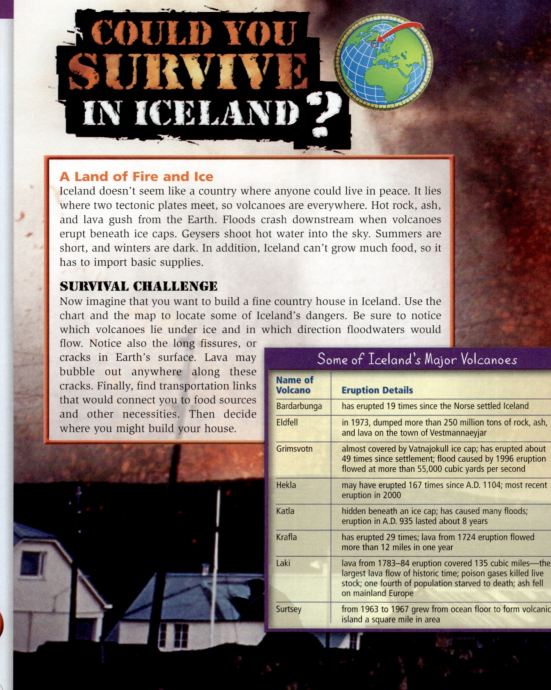

COULD YOU SURVIVE IN ICELAND?

A Land of Fire and Ice

Iceland doesn't seem like a country where anyone could live in peace. It lies where two tectonic plates meet, so volcanoes are everywhere. Hot rock, ash, and lava gush from the Earth. Floods crash downstream when volcanoes erupt beneath ice caps. Geysers shoot hot water into the sky. Summers are short, and winters are dark. In addition, Iceland can't grow much food, so it has to import basic supplies.

SURVIVAL CHALLENGE

Now imagine that you want to build a fine country house in Iceland. Use the chart and the map to locate some of Iceland's dangers. Be sure to notice which volcanoes lie under ice and in which direction floodwaters would flow. Notice also the long fissures, or cracks in Earth's surface. Lava may bubble out anywhere along these cracks. Finally, find transportation links that would connect you to food sources and other necessities. Then decide where you might build your house.

Some of Iceland's Major Volcanoes

Name of Volcano	Eruption Details
Bardarbunga	has erupted 19 times since the Norse settled Iceland
Eldfell	in 1973, dumped more than 250 million tons of rock, ash, and lava on the town of Vestmannaeyjar
Grimsvotn	almost covered by Vatnajokull ice cap; has erupted about 49 times since settlement; flood caused by 1996 eruption flowed at more than 55,000 cubic yards per second
Hekla	may have erupted 167 times since A.D. 1104; most recent eruption in 2000
Katla	hidden beneath an ice cap; has caused many floods; eruption in A.D. 935 lasted about 8 years
Krafla	has erupted 29 times; lava from 1724 eruption flowed more than 12 miles in one year
Laki	lava from 1783–84 eruption covered 135 cubic miles—the largest lava flow of historic time; poison gases killed live stock; one fourth of population starved to death; ash fell on mainland Europe
Surtsey	from 1963 to 1967 grew from ocean floor to form volcanic island a square mile in area

410 • Chapter 18

Survival Challenge Activity

Have students examine the text and the chart to answer these questions: What different dangers do the volcanoes pose? (tons of rock falling from the sky, lava flowing over land and buildings, poison gases, floods) Which dangers are fairly local, and which may affect a wider area? (Falling rock and lava would be local; flowing lava, poison gases, and floods could spread over a wide area.) How would these effects spread? (The weight of lava and floodwaters would draw them downhill; wind could spread poison gases.) How would these factors affect the decision about where to build the house? (One would not want to live downhill or downwind from an active volcano.) What kind of maps would provide more information on how to avoid these dangers? (detailed topographic maps and wind current maps to determine in which direction lava and gases may flow)

In addition, point out the highway on the map and emphasize that it is Iceland's *only* highway. How may this fact affect transportation within the country and the house-building decision? (The highway is probably crucial for transportation and trade, so settlers would want to be near it.) Where does the highway lie? (near the coast only, not in the interior) Why may this be so? (would soon be broken by the fissures that cross the interior or buried by lava from the volcanoes there) What do these facts indicate about settlement in the interior? (There is practically none.) Have students verify this fact with the population map in the unit atlas.

410 Chapter 18

Living with the Lava

With so much danger nearby, you may be surprised to know that some of Iceland's towns were first settled more than a thousand years ago. How have they endured for so long? Look at the map again for clues to how the towns marked on it survived. For example, find Akureyri (AH-koor-AYE-ree) on the north coast. It lies in the tundra climate region. Yet local gardeners grow plants that came from Africa, and Akureyri is Iceland's second-largest city. It even has a booming tourist industry. How may Akureyri's location have affected its economy, climate, and safety? What advantages may Akureyri share with some of the other towns? Should you build your new house near one of these towns?

In the photo, lava buries the town of Vestmannaeyjar (VEST-mahn-nah-AY-yahr). When the volcano Eldfell began erupting at 2:00 AM, January 23, 1973, workers started evacuating the townspeople. All were safe within a few hours. The flowing lava threatened to close off the harbor, however, which would have ruined the town's fishing industry. For weeks, workers sprayed seawater on the lava to harden it and stop its spread. They were successful. The town, the harbor, and the fishing industry all survived.

CHAPTER 18

Going Further: Thinking Critically

Provide these facts to students:
- Icelanders read more books per person than people of any other country.
- Some 88 percent of Icelanders own cell phones.
- About 78 percent of Icelanders use the Internet.

Then lead a discussion about how these figures may be related to Iceland's location and its environment. (Iceland is isolated from the rest of Europe and from North America. Yet its highly educated people, who have a high standard of living, want to stay in touch with the rest of the world. They can do so through books and the Internet. Also, the country's geography may make travel difficult. Volcanoes and floods may damage land telephone lines. Cell phones, however, help connect Icelanders.)

➤ This Could You Survive? feature addresses National Geography Standards 4, 7, and 12.

Living with the Lava Activity

Have students find Iceland's major towns and cities on the map. Base a class discussion on these questions: How do the towns' locations compare? (all located near or on the coast) What does this fact indicate about their economies? (dependent on the sea) On what economic activities may they depend? (fishing, trade) In fact, almost all the towns on the map do have long histories of fishing or sea-borne trade. In addition, since Iceland cannot grow much food and doesn't have much industry, these towns are still essential centers for processing and distributing imported goods.

Then focus students' attention on Akureyri (AH-koor-AYE-ree). How may its location at the head of a fjord affect its climate? (somewhat protected from wind and weather) How may the North Atlantic Drift affect the town? (keeps its climate relatively mild) Ask students how Akureyri's physical geography may have stimulated its tourist industry. (It has become a major whale-watching center, thanks to its coastal location. Its relatively mild climate allows trees and other plants, making it more attractive to tourists than it would be if it were very cold and bare.)

Conclude the discussion by asking if students would build their houses near one of the established towns. (Doing so would make getting supplies easier. Since these towns have survived for centuries, they will probably prosper in the future.)

Could You Survive? • **411**

CHAPTER 18, Section 2

SECTION 2 RESOURCES

Reproducible
- Lecture Notes, Section 2
- Know It Notes S2
- Map Activity 18
- Cultures of the World Activity 3
- Biography Activities: Geoffrey Chaucer, Elizabeth I, William Shakespeare

Technology
- One-Stop Planner CD–ROM, Lesson 18.2
- Homework Practice Online
- HRW Go site

Reinforcement, Review, and Assessment
- Section 2 Review
- Daily Quiz 18.2
- Main Idea Activity S2
- Chapter Summaries and Review
- English Audio Summary 18.2
- Spanish Audio Summary 18.2

Section 2 The United Kingdom

Read to Discover
1. What are some important events in the history of the United Kingdom?
2. What are the people and culture of the country like?
3. What is the United Kingdom like today?

Vocabulary
textiles
constitutional monarchy
glen

Places
England
Scotland
Wales
London
Birmingham
Manchester
Northern Ireland
Glasgow
Cardiff
Belfast

People
Normans
William Shakespeare

Reading Strategy

TAKING NOTES Use the headings in this section to create an outline. As you read about the United Kingdom, write details you learn beneath each heading.

▲ Early peoples of the British Isles built Stonehenge in stages from about 3100 B.C. to about 1800 B.C.

▶ This beautiful Anglo-Saxon shoulder clasp from about A.D. 630 held together pieces of clothing.

History

Most of the British are descended from people who came to the British Isles long ago. The Celts (KELTS) are thought by some scholars to have come to the islands around 450 B.C. Mountain areas of Wales, Scotland, and Ireland have remained mostly Celtic.

Later, from the A.D. 400s to 1000s, new groups of people came. The Angles and Saxons came from northern Germany and Denmark. The Vikings came from Scandinavia. Last to arrive in Britain were the Normans from northern France. They conquered England in 1066. English as spoken today reflects these migrations. It combines elements from the Anglo-Saxon and Norman French languages.

A Global Power England became a world power in the late 1500s. Surrounded by water, the country developed a powerful navy that protected trade routes. In the 1600s the English began establishing colonies around the world. By the early 1800s they had also united England, Scotland, Wales, and Ireland into one kingdom. From London the United Kingdom built a vast British Empire. By 1900 the empire covered nearly one fourth of the world's land area.

412 • Chapter 18

Section 2

Objectives
1. Identify some important events in the history of the United Kingdom.
2. Describe the people and culture of the country.
3. Explain what the United Kingdom is like today.

FOCUS

Bellringer

Copy the following "formula" and question onto the chalkboard: *Celts + Romans + Angles + Saxons + Jutes + Vikings + Normans + Indians + Pakistanis + others = British people. What does this formula mean?* (It refers to some of the groups of people who have come to live in what is now the United Kingdom.) Have students write their answers. Discuss responses. Explain that the British Isles have been a "melting pot" for centuries and that its population continues to become more diverse. Tell students they will learn more about the United Kingdom in Section 2.

Building Vocabulary

Write the vocabulary terms on the chalkboard. Ask volunteers to read the definitions aloud and use each one in a sentence. Point out that the word **textile** is often used as an adjective, such as in "textile mill" or "textile market." Explain that in the United Kingdom Parliament passes laws. The United Kingdom also has a reigning king or queen; he or she is called the monarch. The combination of these two parts of the government creates a **contitutional monarchy**. Ask students if they know any place names or streets that include **glen**. The word has become common in the English language.

412 Chapter 18

The United Kingdom also became an economic power in the 1700s and 1800s. It was the cradle of the Industrial Revolution, which began in the last half of the 1700s. Large supplies of coal and iron and a large labor force helped industries grow. The country also developed a good transportation network of rivers, canals, and railroads. Three of the early industries were **textiles**, or cloth products, shipbuilding, iron, and later steel. Coal powered these industries. Birmingham, Manchester, and other cities grew up near Britain's coal fields.

Decline of Empire World wars and economic competition from other countries weakened the United Kingdom in the 1900s. All but parts of northern Ireland became independent in 1921. By the 1970s most British colonies also had gained independence. Most now make up the British Commonwealth of Nations. Members of the Commonwealth meet to discuss economic, scientific, and business matters.

The United Kingdom still plays an important role in world affairs. It is a leading member of the United Nations (UN), the European Union (EU), and the North Atlantic Treaty Organization (NATO).

The Government The United Kingdom's form of government is called a **constitutional monarchy**. That is, it has a monarch—a king or queen—but a parliament makes the country's laws. The monarch is the head of state but has largely ceremonial duties. Parliament chooses a prime minister to lead the national government.

In recent years the national government has given people in Scotland and Wales more control over local affairs. Some people think Scotland might one day seek independence.

✓ **READING CHECK:** Human Systems How are former British colonies linked today? Most of them make up the British Commonwealth of Nations.

▲
Queen Elizabeth I (1533–1603) ruled England as it became a world power in the late 1500s.

The British government is seated in London, the capital. The Tower Bridge over the River Thames [TEMZ] is one of the city's many famous historical sites.
Interpreting the Visual Record
Why do you think London became a large city?
▼

CHAPTER 18, Section 2

USING ILLUSTRATIONS

A Queen and Her City
Direct students' attention to the image of Queen Elizabeth I on this page. Have them describe her clothing and jewelry. Have students contrast Elizabeth's clothing to today's styles. Point out that the queen set fashion trends of the day. Ask students who establishes today's fads and fashions.

Then focus students' attention on the photograph of London. Lead a discussion about how the London cityscape compares to cities with which the students are familiar. Your questions may include: Do U.S. cities have more or fewer skyscrapers than London? Do U.S. cities have more or less open space in their downtown areas?

internet connect
GO TO: go.hrw.com
KEYWORD: SJ5 CH8
FOR: Web sites about England

◀ **Visual Record Answer**
its location on a major river and near the sea

TEACH

Teaching Objective 1
LEVEL 1: (Suggested time: 45 min.) Organize students into groups. Ask each group to make an illustrated time line of a particular 100-year period in the history of England. Be sure all major eras are covered and that years and events are spaced accurately. Ask students to include on their time lines significant historical events and achievements that have helped make the United Kingdom the country it is today. Encourage students to consult library resources for information.
ESOL, COOPERATIVE LEARNING, LS **LOGICAL-MATHEMATICAL**

LEVELS 2 AND 3: (Suggested time: 45 min.) Have students complete the time line in the Level 1 activity. Then ask them to choose a historical figure who lived during their 100-year period. The person chosen may be famous, such as Queen Elizabeth I or William Shakespeare, or may be a representative of now anonymous citizens, such as a worker in a textile mill of the early Industrial Revolution. Have students write monologues in which their chosen figures reflect on how they fit into or played a role in British history.
LS **INTRAPERSONAL**

Northern Europe **413**

CHAPTER 18, Section 2

Cultural Kaleidoscope

Pakistanis in Britain The population of Great Britain has become increasingly diverse over the years. People from around the world, particularly from countries that were once part of the British Empire, have immigrated to Great Britain. During the 1950s and 1960s many people came to Britain from Pakistan. Today Britain's Pakistanis number more than 500,000. Most live in large cities, where some have established restaurants and other businesses.

Pakistanis living in Britain face many challenges, including discrimination. The unemployment rate among them is high partly because some recent immigrants speak little English. In addition, many Pakistani children in Britain receive a poor education. However, British-born Pakistanis have better job prospects. This segment of the population has grown up speaking English.

Activity: Have students research immigrant education in Britain and the United States and compare them.

Visual Record Answer

Students might suggest that television exposes people around the world to each other's cultures.

Chart Answer

It is higher.

Millions of Americans watched the Beatles, a British rock band, perform on television in 1964. The Beatles and other British bands became popular around the world.

Interpreting the Visual Record
Movement How do you think television helps shape world cultures today?

Culture

More than 60 million people live in the United Kingdom today. English is the official language. Some people in Wales and Scotland also speak the Celtic languages of Welsh and Gaelic [GAY-lik]. The Church of England is the country's official church. However, many Britons belong to other Protestant churches or are Roman Catholic.

Food and Festivals Living close to the sea, the British often eat fish. One popular meal is fish and chips—fried fish and potatoes. However, British food also includes different meats, oat porridge and cakes, and potatoes in many forms.

The British celebrate many religious holidays, such as Christmas. Other holidays include the Queen's official birthday celebration in June. In July many Protestants in Northern Ireland celebrate a battle in 1690 in which Protestants defeated Catholic forces. In recent years the day's parades have sometimes sparked protests and violence between Protestants and Catholics.

Art and Literature British literature, art, and music have been popular around the world. Perhaps the most famous British writer is William Shakespeare. He died in 1616, but his poetry and plays, such as *Romeo and Juliet*, remain popular. In the 1960s the Beatles helped make Britain a major center for modern popular music. Ever since then, British performers have attracted fans around the world.

✓ **READING CHECK:** *Human Systems* What aspects of British culture have spread around the world? British literature, art, and music have been popular around the world.

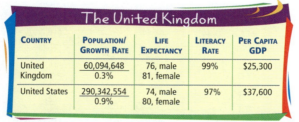

The United Kingdom

Country	Population/Growth Rate	Life Expectancy	Literacy Rate	Per Capita GDP
United Kingdom	60,094,648 / 0.3%	76, male / 81, female	99%	$25,300
United States	290,342,554 / 0.9%	74, male / 80, female	97%	$37,600

Source: Central Intelligence Agency, *The World Factbook 2003*

Interpreting the Chart How does the literacy rate in the United Kingdom compare with that of the United States?

The United Kingdom Today

Nearly 90 percent of Britons today live in urban areas. London, the capital of England, is the largest city. It is located in southeastern England. London is also the capital of the whole United Kingdom.

More than 7 million people live in London. The city is a world center for trade, industry, and services, particularly banking and insurance. London also has one of the world's busiest airports. Many tourists visit London to see its famous historical sites, theaters, and shops. Other important cities include Glasgow, Scotland; Cardiff, Wales; and Belfast, Northern Ireland.

Teaching Objectives 2–3

ALL LEVELS: (Suggested time: 10 min.) Copy the following graphic organizer onto the chalkboard, omitting the blue answers. Call on volunteers to complete it. Add more boxes as needed. Then lead a discussion of how the United Kingdom's role in world affairs has changed over the years. Have students identify historical events and factors that have led to these changes. **ESOL**, **LS VISUAL-SPATIAL**

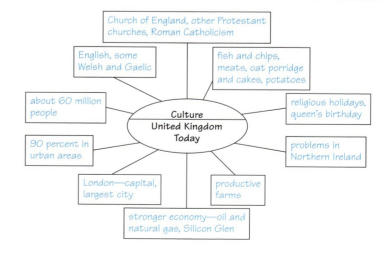

The Economy Old British industries like mining and manufacturing declined after World War II. Today, however, the economy is stronger. North Sea reserves have made the country a major producer of oil and natural gas. Birmingham, Glasgow, and other cities are attracting new industries. One area of Scotland is called Silicon Glen. This is because it has many computer and electronics businesses. **Glen** is a Scottish term for a valley. Today many British work in service industries, including banking, insurance, education, and tourism.

Agriculture Britain's modern farms produce about 60 percent of the country's food. Still, only about 1 percent of the labor force works in agriculture. Important products include grains, potatoes, vegetables, and meat.

Northern Ireland One of the toughest problems facing the country has been violence in Northern Ireland. Sometimes Northern Ireland is called Ulster. The Protestant majority and the Roman Catholic minority there have bitterly fought each other. Violence on both sides has resulted in many deaths.

Many Catholics in Northern Ireland believe they have not been treated fairly by the Protestant majority. Therefore, many want Northern Ireland to join the mostly Roman Catholic Republic of Ireland. Protestants fear becoming a minority on the island. They want to remain part of the United Kingdom. Many people hoped that agreements made in 1999 by Protestant and Roman Catholic political leaders would lead to lasting peace. However, the new government's assembly stopped meeting in 2002. Today, peace talks continue between the two sides.

✓ **READING CHECK:** *Human Systems* What has been the cause of conflict in Northern Ireland? *Historical differences between the Protestant majority and the Roman Catholic minority*

Religion: A Divided Island

Region	Roman Catholic	Protestant/other
Northern Ireland	38%	62%
Republic of Ireland	92%	8%

Source: *The Statesman's Year Book*, 1998–99.

Interpreting the Graph *Place* How does the number of Roman Catholics in the Republic of Ireland differ from that of Northern Ireland?

Section Review 2

Define or identify: Normans, textiles, constitutional monarchy, William Shakespeare, glen

Working with Sketch Maps On the map you created in Section 1, label the United Kingdom, England, Scotland, Wales, London, Birmingham, Manchester, Northern Ireland, Glasgow, Cardiff, and Belfast.

Reading for the Main Idea
1. *Human Systems* What peoples came to the British Isles after the Celts? When did they come?
2. *Places and Regions* What was the British Empire?

Critical Thinking
3. **Contrasting** How is the British government different from the U.S. government?
4. **Drawing Inferences and Conclusions** Why do you think Protestants in Northern Ireland want to remain part of the United Kingdom?

Organizing What You Know
5. **Sequencing** Create a timeline that lists important events in the period.

800 B.C. ———————————————— A.D. 2003

Section 2 Review

Answers to Section 2 Review

Define or identify For definitions and identifications, see the glossary and index.

Working with Sketch Maps Places should be labeled accurately.

Reading for the Main Idea
1. Angles, Saxons, Vikings—A.D. 400s to 1000s; Normans—1066 (NGS 9)
2. colonies around the world established by England (NGS 4)

Critical Thinking
3. Britain—constitutional monarchy; U.S.—constitutional democracy
4. fear of losing influence or of change, desire to stay in majority

Organizing What You Know
5. around 450 B.C.—Celts arrive; A.D. 400s–1000s—Angles, Saxons, Vikings, Normans arrive; late 1500s—England a world power; 1600s—colonies established; 1700s–1800s—Industrial Revolution; 1900—empire at its height; by 1921—United Kingdom weakened; 1970s—most colonies independent

▲ **Graph Answer**
Roman Catholics make up most of the population.

CLOSE
Ask students to name rock bands, television programs, fashions, cars, and fads from the United Kingdom. Ask why these influences travel to the United States so easily. (Possible answer: A common language and many cultural ties link the countries.)

REVIEW, ASSESS, RETEACH
Have students complete the Section Review. Then pair students. Ask each student to write three questions and answers related to the content of Section 2. Have students take turns reading an answer and challenging their partners to guess the corresponding question. Then have students complete Daily Quiz 18.2. **COOPERATIVE LEARNING**

EXTEND
Have interested students conduct research on differences between British and American word usage. Have students create a chart to present notable differences in usage. **BLOCK SCHEDULING**

CHAPTER 18, Section 3

SECTION 3 RESOURCES

Reproducible
- Lecture Notes, Section 3
- Know It Notes S3
- Cultures of the World Activity 3

Technology
- One-Stop Planner CD–ROM, Lesson 18.3
- Homework Practice Online
- Music of the World Audio CD Program, Selection 6
- HRW Go site

Reinforcement, Review, and Assessment
- Section 3 Review
- Daily Quiz 18.3
- Main Idea Activity S3
- Chapter Summaries and Review
- English Audio Summary 18.3
- Spanish Audio Summary 18.3

Visual Record Answer

rainy and temperate

Section 3 The Republic of Ireland

Read to Discover
1. What are the key events in Ireland's history?
2. What are the people and culture of Ireland like?
3. What kinds of economic changes has Ireland experienced in recent years?

Vocabulary
famine
bog
peat

Places
Dublin
Cork
Galway

People
Celts
Mary Robinson

Reading Strategy

READING ORGANIZER Before you read, draw a line down the center of a sheet of notebook paper. Write A.D. 400 at the bottom and A.D. 2000 near the top. As you read, fill in your time line with information about events in Irish history.

Stone fences divide the green fields of western Ireland, the Emerald Isle.
Interpreting the Visual Record *Place*
What kind of climate would you expect to find in a country with rich, green fields such as these?

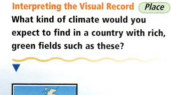

History

The Irish are descendants of the Celts. Irish Gaelic, a Celtic language, and English are the official languages. Most people in Ireland speak English. Gaelic is spoken mostly in rural western areas.

English Conquest England conquered Ireland in the A.D. 1100s. By the late 1600s most of the Irish had become farmers on land owned by the British. This created problems between the two peoples. Religious differences added to these problems. Most British were Protestant, while most Irish were Roman Catholic. Then, in the 1840s, millions of Irish left for the United States and other countries because of a poor economy and a potato famine. A **famine** is a severe shortage of food.

Independence The Irish rebelled against British rule. In 1916, for example, Irish rebels attacked British troops in the Easter Rising.

Objectives
1. Identify key events in Ireland's history.
2. Describe the people and culture of Ireland.
3. Explain the economic changes Ireland has experienced in recent years.

FOCUS

Bellringer
Copy the following questions onto the chalkboard: *Which Irish holiday is celebrated by many Americans? How is it celebrated?* (Saint Patrick's Day, wearing green, parades) Have students write their answers. Explain that Irish immigrants have contributed much to our culture. Point out that although it is now a fairly prosperous country, Ireland has had difficult times in its past. Because of those difficulties, many people left Ireland for the United States. Tell students that in Section 3 they will learn more about the Republic of Ireland.

Building Vocabulary
Write the vocabulary terms on the chalkboard and ask students to locate their definitions in the section text. Call on volunteers to read the definitions aloud. Ask students if they recall news about **famine** in other countries. You may want to ask if they have heard of the Irish potato famine. Explain that from 1845 to 1849, a disease killed so many potato plants in Ireland that hundreds of thousands of people starved. Potatoes had been a major food source, particularly among the poor. Explain that **bog** comes from the ancient language of Ireland, Gaelic. **Peat** is found in bogs.

At the end of 1921, most of Ireland gained independence. Some counties in northern Ireland remained part of the United Kingdom. Ties between the Republic of Ireland and the British Empire were cut in 1949.

Government Ireland has an elected president and parliament. The president has mostly ceremonial duties. In 1990, Irish voters elected Mary Robinson as Ireland's first woman president. Mary McAleese succeeded Robinson as president in 1997.

The parliament makes the country's laws. The Irish parliament chooses a prime minister to lead the government.

✓ **READING CHECK:** (Human Systems) What are some important events in Ireland's history? *English conquest, Easter Rising, independence for most of Ireland, end of ties between Republic of Ireland and British Empire*

Culture

Centuries of English rule have left their mark on Irish culture. For example, today nearly everyone in Ireland speaks English. Irish writers, such as George Bernard Shaw and James Joyce, have been among the world's great English-language writers.

A number of groups promote traditional Irish culture in the country today. The Gaelic League, for example, encourages the use of Irish Gaelic. Gaelic and English are taught in schools and used in official documents. Another group promotes Irish sports, such as hurling. Hurling is an outdoor game similar to field hockey and lacrosse.

Elements of Irish culture have also become popular outside the country. For example, traditional Irish folk dancing and music have attracted many fans. Music has long been important in Ireland. In fact, the Irish harp is a national symbol. Many musicians popular today are from Ireland, including members of the rock band U2.

More than 90 percent of the Irish today are Roman Catholic. St. Patrick's Day on March 17 is a national holiday. St. Patrick is believed to have brought Christianity to Ireland in the 400s.

✓ **READING CHECK:** (Human Systems) What is Irish culture like today? *English is almost universal; groups promote Irish traditions, such as the use of Gaelic and Irish sports; music is important; 90 present of Irish are Roman Catholic.*

Ireland Today

Ireland used to be one of Europe's poorest countries. Today it is a modern, thriving country with a strong economy and growing cities.

BIOGRAPHY
Mary Robinson
(1944–)
Character Trait: Kindness

Elected as Ireland's first woman president in 1990, Mary Robinson is best known for her efforts in providing humanitarian aid around the world. As Irish president, she was also a strong supporter of women's rights. After she left office, Robinson served for six years as United Nations High Commissioner for Human Rights. In this position, she worked to improve the rights and living conditions of people in more than 60 countries.

What other character traits may have helped Mary Robinson in her work for the UN?

CHAPTER 18, Section 3

Linking Past to Present
St. Patrick The young man who would later be called Saint Patrick was living in western England when he was captured by raiders and sold into slavery in Ireland. He is credited with converting the Irish people to Christianity in the A.D. 400s. He also introduced the Roman alphabet and Latin literature to Ireland.

According to legend, Patrick drove all the snakes in Ireland into the sea. However, evidence shows that any snakes that may have been living in Ireland would have died off during the Ice Age. Also, because land snakes cannot migrate across water, there are no snakes living in Ireland today. The legend may refer to Patrick's eliminating ancient non-Christian beliefs from Ireland. Snakes were among many pre-Christian symbols.

Activity: Have students work in groups to conduct research on the historical background of the holidays celebrated in their communities. You may want to have them concentrate on their community's celebration of St. Patrick's Day.

◀ **Biography Answer**

Possible answers: determination, fairness, courage, and so on

Northern Europe • 417

TEACH

Teaching Objectives 1–3

LEVEL 1: (Suggested time: 20 min.) Copy the following graphic organizer onto the chalkboard, omitting the blue answers. Have students fill in important eras in Ireland's history. Then lead a discussion about how Ireland's history has influenced its culture and the recent economic changes in the country. **ESOL,** LS **VISUAL-SPATIAL**

LEVELS 2 AND 3: (Suggested time: 45 min.) Ask students to imagine that they are the prime minister of Ireland and that they are running for re-election. Have them write campaign slogans in which they display their knowledge of Ireland's past and take credit for the country's economic progress. LS **VERBAL-LINGUISTIC**

Celtic Ireland → English conquest → Immigration to United States → Easter Rising → Independence

Northern Europe 417

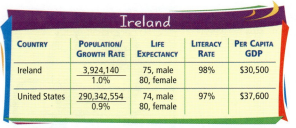

Source: Central Intelligence Agency, *The World Factbook 2003*

Country	Population/ Growth Rate	Life Expectancy	Literacy Rate	Per Capita GDP
Ireland	3,924,140 1.0%	75, male 80, female	98%	$30,500
United States	290,342,554 0.9%	74, male 80, female	97%	$37,600

Interpreting the Chart How does life expectancy in Ireland compare with that of the United States?

Economy Until recently, Ireland was mostly an agricultural country. This was true even though much of the country is either rocky or boggy. A **bog** is soft ground that is soaked with water. For centuries, **peat** dug from bogs has been used for fuel. Peat is made up of dead plants, usually mosses.

Today Ireland is an industrial country. Irish workers produce processed foods, textiles, chemicals, machinery, crystal, and computers. Finance, tourism, and other service industries are also important.

How did this change come about? Ireland's low taxes, well-educated workers, and membership in the European Union have attracted many foreign companies. Those foreign companies include many from the United States. These companies see Ireland as a door to millions of customers throughout the EU. In fact, goods from their Irish factories are exported to markets in the rest of Europe and countries in other regions.

Cities Many factories have been built around Dublin. Dublin is Ireland's capital and largest city. It is a center for education, banking, and shipping. Nearly 1 million people live there. Housing prices rapidly increased in the 1990s as people moved there for work.

Other cities lie mainly along the coast. These cities include the seaports of Cork and Galway. They have old castles, churches, and other historical sites that are popular among tourists.

✓ **READING CHECK:** *Human Systems* What important economic changes have occurred in Ireland and why? *industrial country; low taxes, well-educated workers, and EU membership have attracted foreign companies*

Define or identify: Celts, famine, Mary Robinson, bog, peat

Working with Sketch Maps On the map you created in Section 2, label Ireland, Dublin, Cork, and Galway. In the margin explain the importance of Dublin to the Republic of Ireland.

Reading for the Main Idea
1. *Human Systems* What were two of the reasons many Irish moved to the United States and other countries in the 1800s?
2. *Human Systems* What are some important reasons why the economy in Ireland has grown so much in recent years?

Critical Thinking
3. **Drawing Inferences and Conclusions** Why do you think the Irish fought against British rule?
4. **Drawing Inferences and Conclusions** Why do you suppose housing prices rapidly increased in Dublin in the 1990s?

Organizing What You Know
5. **Comparing/Contrasting** Copy the following graphic organizer. Use it to compare and contrast the history, culture, and governments of the Republic of Ireland and the United Kingdom.

Ireland	United Kingdom
Conquered by England in the 1100s	Created vast world empire

418 • Chapter 18

Section 4: Scandinavia

Read to Discover
1. What are the people and culture of Scandinavia like?
2. What are some important features of each of the region's countries, plus Greenland, and Lapland?

Vocabulary
neutral
uninhabitable
geysers

Places
Oslo
Bergen
Stockholm
Göteborg
Copenhagen
Nuuk (Godthab)
Reykjavik
Gulf of Bothnia
Gulf of Finland
Helsinki
Lapland

People
Vikings

Reading Strategy

READING ORGANIZER Before you read, create a spider map. Label the center Scandinavia. Create a leg for each Scandinavian country. As you read the section, fill in the map with details about each country.

People and Culture

Scandinavia once was home to fierce, warlike Vikings. Today the countries of Norway, Sweden, Denmark, Iceland, and Finland are peaceful and prosperous.

The people of the region enjoy high standards of living. They have good health care and long life spans. Each government provides expensive social programs and services. These programs are paid for by high taxes.

The people and cultures in the countries of Scandinavia are similar in many ways. For example, the region's national languages, except for Finnish, are closely related. In addition, most people in Scandinavia are Lutheran Protestant. All of the Scandinavian countries have democratic governments.

✓ **READING CHECK:**
Human Systems How are the people and cultures of Scandinavia similar?
Most languages closely related, most are Lutheran Protestant, all governments are democratic.

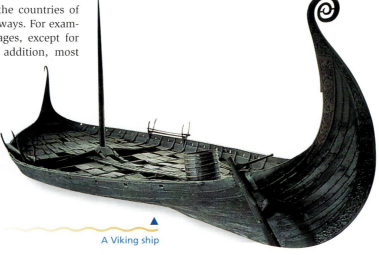

▲ A Viking ship

Northern Europe • 419

CHAPTER 18, Section 4

SECTION 4 RESOURCES

Reproducible
◆ Lecture Notes, Section 4
◆ Know It Notes S4
◆ Geography for Life Activity 18
◆ Cultures of the World Activity 3

Technology
◆ One-Stop Planner CD–ROM, Lesson 18.4
◆ Homework Practice Online
◆ HRW Go site

Reinforcement, Review, and Assessment
◆ Section 4 Review
◆ Daily Quiz 18.4
◆ Main Idea Activity S4
◆ Chapter Summaries and Review
◆ English Audio Summary 18.4
◆ Spanish Audio Summary 18.4

Objectives
1. Describe the people and culture of Scandinavia.
2. Identify important features of the region's countries, Greenland, and Lapland.

FOCUS

Bellringer
Copy the following instructions onto the chalkboard: *What do you already know about the Vikings?* (Possible answers: fierce fighters, tall, blonde, wore metal helmets) Allow students to respond and discuss responses. Explain that the Viking raiders do not represent all early Scandinavians. Many Scandinavians were farmers and merchants. Point out that most modern Scandinavians are descended from the Vikings. Tell students that in Section 4 they will learn more about ancient and modern Scandinavia.

Building Vocabulary
Write the vocabulary terms on the board and have students read the definitions. Ask a volunteer to use **neutral** in a sentence about politics or current events. For **uninhabitable**, explain that the prefix *un-* means "not." The root word *inhabit* means "to live in." The suffix *-able* means "capable of being." So, the term describes a place where no one can live. Ask students to look at a map of the region and suggest which areas may be uninhabitable. Tell students that the word **geysers** comes from the Icelandic language. It originally referred to a particular hot spring in Iceland.

Northern Europe **419**

CHAPTER 18, Section 4

ENVIRONMENT AND SOCIETY

Norwegian Transportation Norway's long shape, severe winter climate, and sparsely populated countryside make it difficult and expensive to provide transportation services throughout the country. Winter weather limits car travel—the main road between Oslo and Bergen is closed for four to six months.

The Norwegian government provides or helps to pay for some forms of transportation. The government-owned railway loses money each year. There are simply too few train riders outside the large cities to make the service profitable.

Critical Thinking: Why may the Norwegian government continue to provide rail service even though it loses money?

Answer: Students may suggest that a reliable transportation system is vital for commerce, national defense, or to minimize pollution.

Chart Answer

They are higher than those of the United States, Denmark, and Finland.

Visual Record Answer

thwart land-based attacks; create increased access to waterways for trade

Scandinavia

Country	Population/ Growth Rate	Life Expectancy	Literacy Rate	Per Capita GDP
Denmark	5,384,384 0.3%	74, male 80, female	100%	$28,900
Finland	5,190,785 0.2%	74, male 81, female	100%	$25,800
Iceland	280,798 0.5%	77, male 82, female	100%	$30,200
Norway	4,546,123 0.5%	76, male 82, female	100%	$33,000
Sweden	8,878,085 .02%	77, male 83, female	99%	$26,000
United States	290,342,554 0.9%	74, male 80, female	97%	$37,600

Source: Central Intelligence Agency, *The World Factbook 2003*

Interpreting the Chart What is noteworthy about life expectancy in Iceland, Norway, and Sweden?

Riddarholmen—Knight's Island—is one of several islands on which the original city of Stockholm was built.

Interpreting the Visual Record

Human-Environment Interaction Why might a group of islands be a good place to build a city?

Norway

Norway is a long, narrow, and rugged country along the western coast of the Scandinavian Peninsula. Norway once was united with Denmark and then Sweden. In 1905 Norway became independent. Today Norway is a constitutional monarchy with an elected parliament.

About 75 percent of the people live in urban areas. The largest cities are the capital, Oslo, and Bergen on the Atlantic coast. Oslo is a modern city. It lies at the end of a wide fjord on the southern coast. The city is Norway's leading seaport, as well as its industrial and cultural center.

Norway has valuable resources, especially oil and natural gas. However, Norway's North Sea oil fields are expected to run dry over the next century. A long coastline and location on the North Sea have helped make Norway a major fishing and shipping country. Fjords shelter Norway's harbors and its fishing and shipping fleets.

Sweden

Sweden is Scandinavia's largest and most populous country. It is located between Norway and Finland. Most Swedes live in cities and towns. The largest cities are Stockholm, which is Sweden's capital, and Göteborg. Stockholm is located on the Baltic Sea coast. It is a beautiful city of islands and forests. Göteborg is a major seaport.

Like Norway, Sweden is a constitutional monarchy. The country has been at peace since the early 1800s. Sweden remained **neutral** during World Wars I and II. A neutral country is one that chooses not to take sides in an international conflict.

Sweden's main sources of wealth are forestry, farming, mining, and manufacturing. Wood, iron ore, automobiles, and wireless telephones are exports. Hydroelectricity is important.

TEACH

Teaching Objective 1

ALL LEVELS: (Suggested time: 10 min.) Copy the following graphic organizer onto the chalkboard, omitting the blue answers. Call on students to fill in the lines with characteristics the Scandinavian countries share. **ESOL, VISUAL-SPATIAL**

Scandinavia
- peaceful and prosperous
- high standards of living
- good health care, long life spans
- social programs and services government-sponsored
- high taxes
- languages closely related (except Finnish)
- Lutheran Protestants
- democratic governments

Connecting to Art

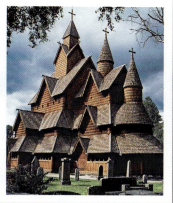

A stave church in Norway

Stave Churches

In Norway you will find some beautiful wooden churches built during the Middle Ages. They are known as stave churches because of their corner posts, or staves. The staves provide the building's basic structure. Today stave churches are a reminder of the days when Viking and Christian beliefs began to merge in Norway.

As many as 800 stave churches were built in Norway during the 1000s and 1100s. Christianity was then beginning to spread throughout the country. It was replacing the old religious beliefs of the Viking people. Still, Viking culture is clearly seen in stave buildings.

Except for a thick stone foundation, stave churches are made entirely of wood. Workers used methods that had been developed by Viking boat builders. For example, wood on Viking boats was coated with tar to keep it from rotting. Church builders did the same with the wood for their churches. They also decorated the churches with carvings of dragons and other fanciful creatures. The stave church at Urnes even has a small Viking ship decorated with nine candles.

When the plague, or Black Death, arrived in Norway about 1350, many communities were abandoned. Many stave churches fell apart. Others were replaced by larger stone buildings. Today only 28 of the original buildings remain. They have been preserved for their beauty and as reminders of an earlier culture.

Understanding What You Read
1. What are staves?
2. How did stave churches reflect new belief systems in Norway?

Denmark

Denmark is the smallest and most densely populated of the region's countries. Most of Denmark lies on the Jutland Peninsula. About 500 islands make up the rest of the country.

Denmark is also a constitutional monarchy. The capital and largest city is Copenhagen. It lies on an island between the Jutland Peninsula and Sweden. Some 1.4 million people—about 25 percent of Denmark's population—live there.

About 60 percent of Denmark's land is used for farming. Farm products, especially meat and dairy products, are important exports. Denmark also has a modern industrial economy. Industries include food processing, machinery, furniture, and electronics.

CHAPTER 18, Section 4

Across the Curriculum
LITERATURE
Hans Christian Andersen
Among the many contributions made to the arts by Scandinavians, some of the most popular are the stories written by Danish author Hans Christian Andersen. Andersen also wrote plays and novels.

The author published his first book of stories, *Tales, Told for Children,* in 1835. It included the classic "Princess and the Pea," which was the inspiration for the Broadway musical *Once upon a Mattress*. Andersen's story "The Little Mermaid" was the basis for a popular animated movie of the same name. A bronze statue of a mermaid was placed in Copenhagen's harbor to commemorate Andersen's heroine.

Critical Thinking: In what ways have Andersen's tales spread beyond Scandinavia?

Answer: They have become popular around the world and have been used for a musical and a movie.

Connecting to Art Answers
1. corner posts of wooden churches
2. They were built as Christianity was replacing Viking religious beliefs.

Teaching Objective 2

LEVEL 1: (Suggested time: 30 min.) Organize the class into five groups. Assign one of the region's countries to each group. Have the groups design a new flag for their assigned country using colors and symbols that refer to the text material. Tell students that the flags should represent the important features of the region's countries as well as Lapland and Greenland. Ask each group to choose a spokesperson to explain its meaning to the class. Then have the spokespeople make their presentations. Finally, display students' flags around the classroom. **ESOL, COOPERATIVE LEARNING, LS VISUAL-SPATIAL**

LEVELS 2 AND 3: (Suggested time: 45 min.) Have students create brochures to encourage people from other countries to invest in Scandinavian countries. Brochures should provide an introduction to the country's physical and human geography and summarize each country's economic and political characteristics as well as other important features. Instruct students to make a clear connection in their brochures between their assigned country's characteristics and its economic future. Ask students to add a catchy slogan for the country. (example: "Iceland—Cold Name, Warm Welcome") You may want to have students add drawings or pictures from magazines to add interest. Additional research may be necessary.

CHAPTER 18, Section 4

FOOD FESTIVAL

A Northern Feast In Swedish, the word *smorgasbord* means "bread and butter table," but a smorgasbord is not just a table loaded with buttered bread. It is a complete buffet-style meal, with a variety of open-faced sandwiches, sliced meats, marinated or pickled fish, cheeses, hot or cold cooked vegetables, salads, and desserts. To create your own Swedish smorgasbord, have students bring as many of the listed food items as they can. Set the food on a large table and let students help themselves.

Visual Record Answer

The interior is icy and uninhabitable.

Greenland's capital lies on the island's southwestern shore.
Interpreting the Visual Record
Place Why do most people in Greenland live along the coast?

Our Amazing Planet

The Great Geysir in southwestern Iceland can spout water nearly 200 feet (61 m) into the air. Some geysers shoot steam and boiling water to a height of more than 1,600 feet (nearly 500 m)!

Greenland

The huge island of Greenland is part of North America, but it is a territory of Denmark. Greenland's 56,000 people have their own government. They call their island Kalaallit Nunaat. The capital is Nuuk, also called Godthab. Most of the island's people are Inuit (Eskimo). Fishing is the main economic activity. Some Inuit still hunt seals and small whales.

The island's icy interior is **uninhabitable**. An uninhabitable area is one that cannot support human settlement. Greenland's people live mostly along the southwestern coast in the tundra climate regions.

Iceland

Between Greenland and Scandinavia is the country of Iceland. This Atlantic island belonged to Denmark until 1944. Today it is an independent country. It has an elected president and parliament.

Unlike Greenland, Iceland is populated mostly by northern Europeans. The capital and largest city is Reykjavik (RAYK-yuh-veek). More than 60 percent of the country's people live there.

Icelanders make good use of their country's natural resources. For example, about 70 percent of the country's exports are fish. These fish come from the rich waters around the island. In addition, hot water from Iceland's **geysers** heats homes and greenhouses. The word geyser is an Icelandic term for hot springs that shoot hot water and steam into the air. Volcanic activity forces heated underground water to rise from the geyser.

Finland

Finland is the easternmost of the region's countries. It lies mostly between two arms of the Baltic Sea: the Gulf of Bothnia and the Gulf of Finland. The capital and largest city is Helsinki, which is located on the southern coast.

TEACHER TO TEACHER

Kay A. Knowles of Montross, Virginia, suggests the following activity to show how cultures can differ within the same region. First, have students conduct research on these topics as they relate to the British Isles and Scandinavia: origins, religions, languages, ethnic groups, conflicts, and customs. Then have students create charts to organize and present their findings.

Lead a class discussion comparing what students have learned from the activity to other countries or regions they have studied. Challenge them to draw conclusions.

CLOSE

Lead a discussion on how a Viking might react if he or she visited Scandinavia today. Ask: Which aspects of the region would be familiar? Which would be unfamiliar?

The original Finnish settlers probably came from northern Asia. Finnish belongs to a language family that includes Estonian and Hungarian. About 6 percent of Finns speak Swedish. Finland was part of Sweden from the 1100s to 1809. It then became part of Russia. Finland gained independence at the end of World War I.

As in the other countries of the region, trade is important to Finland. The country is a major producer of paper and other forest products as well as wireless telephones. Metal products, shipbuilding, and electronics are also important industries. Finland imports energy and many of the raw materials needed in manufacturing.

Lapland

Across northern Finland, Sweden, and Norway is a culture region known as Lapland. This region is populated by the Lapps, or Sami, as they call themselves.

The Sami are probably descended from hunters who moved to the region from northern Asia. The languages they speak are related to Finnish. The Sami have tried to keep their culture and traditions, such as reindeer herding. Many now earn a living from tourism.

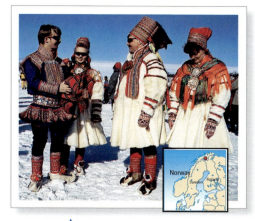

▲ Young Sami couples here are dressed in traditional clothes for an Easter celebration in northern Norway.

✓ **READING CHECK:** *Human Systems* Around what activities are the economies of the countries and territories discussed in this section organized? *Some are modern industrial economies, while others are organized around fishing, farming, or tourism.*

Section Review 4

Define or identify: Vikings, neutral, uninhabitable, geysers

Working with Sketch Maps On the map you created in Section 3, label Scandinavia, Oslo, Bergen, Stockholm, Göteborg, Copenhagen, Nuuk (Godthab), Reykjavik, Gulf of Bothnia, Gulf of Finland, Helsinki, and Lapland. In the margin describe the people of the Lapland region.

Reading for the Main Idea

1. *Human Systems* What are two of the cultural similarities among the peoples of Scandinavia?
2. *Environment and Society* In what ways have Icelanders adapted to their natural environment?
3. *Human Systems* How have the history and culture of Finland been different from that of other countries in Scandinavia?

Critical Thinking

4. **Making Generalizations and Predictions** How do you think the location of Greenland and the culture of its people will affect the island's future relationship with Denmark?

Organizing What You Know

5. **Summarizing** Copy the following graphic organizer. Label the center of the organizer "Scandinavia." In the ovals, write one characteristic of each country and region discussed in this section. Then do the same for the other countries, as well as for Greenland and Lapland.

Homework Practice Online Keyword: SJ5 HP18

Section 4 Review

Answers to Section 4 Review

Define or identify For definitions and identifications, see the glossary and index.

Working with Sketch Maps They are descendants of hunters from northern Asia, speak languages related to Finnish, earn money from reindeer herding or tourism.

Reading for the Main Idea

1. closely related languages (except for Finnish), Lutheran Protestant religion, democratic governments (NGS 10)
2. by catching fish, using hot water from geysers for heat (NGS 15)
3. country's original settlers not Vikings; Finnish not related to other Scandinavian languages (NGS 10)

Critical Thinking

4. possible answer: They may cause the cultures to become more separate and lead to independence for Greenland.

Organizing What You Know

5. Answers will vary but should be consistent with text.

REVIEW, ASSESS, RETEACH

Have students complete the Section Review. Then have students outline the main points of Section 4. Ask them to choose one topic from their outlines and create a simple graphic organizer to illustrate it. Call on volunteers to draw their organizers on the chalkboard and explain their use. Then have students complete Daily Quiz 18.4.

Have students complete Main Idea Activity S4. Then organize students into groups and assign each group one of the Scandinavian countries. Have each group become "experts" on their country. Give them chalk for writing on the board or materials for using the overhead projector, allow time for collaboration, and have them present a lesson on their country to the class.

ESOL, COOPERATIVE LEARNING

EXTEND

Have interested students conduct research on the important role Finnish ski troops played during the Soviet invasion of their country in 1939–40. Have students act out their findings in a "news broadcast" from the "front."

BLOCK SCHEDULING

CHAPTER 18 REVIEW

Define and Identify
For definitions and identifications, see the glossary and index.

Review the Main Ideas

12. Sweden and Finland (NGS 4)
13. keeps it relatively warm (NGS 7)
14. because world wars and economic competition from other countries weakened the empire
15. computer and electronics businesses, banking, insurance, education, tourism
16. conflict between Protestants and Roman Catholics (NGS 13)
17. influenced millions of Irish to leave for the United States and other countries
18. English and Gaelic (NGS 10)
19. Norway
20. uses the hot water to heat homes and greenhouses
21. Sami (NGS 10)

Think Critically

22. Answers will vary, but students should mention the themes in some of these art forms, such as Shakespearean literature or Beatles music, make them universally appealing.
23. saved transportation costs because coal, which fueled factories, was available nearby
24. history of English control; English is language of commerce, government, education (NGS 10)
25. Possible: adapted building and clothing styles; used skis, snowshoes, sleds for travel; learned to make a living from what environment makes possible, such as reindeer herding; developed diverse energy sources
26. original settlers from northern Asia, Finnish language not related to other Scandinavian languages

CHAPTER 18 Review and Practice

Define and Identify

Identify each of the following:

1. fjords
2. North Atlantic Drift
3. Normans
4. constitutional monarchy
5. famine
6. peat
7. Celts
8. neutral
9. uninhabitable
10. geysers
11. Vikings

Review the Main Ideas

12. Which countries in Northern Europe still have large forests?
13. How does the North Atlantic Drift affect the climate of Northern Europe?
14. Why did the British Empire go into decline?
15. What service industries employ many British workers?
16. What problems still trouble Northern Ireland?
17. How did the potato famine affect Ireland?
18. What are the official languages of Ireland?
19. Which Scandinavian country benefits from North Sea oil?
20. How does Iceland use the island's geysers?
21. What do the Lapps call themselves?

Think Critically

22. **Drawing Inferences and Conclusions** Why do you think British literature, art, and music have been popular around the world?
23. **Drawing Inferences and Conclusions** Why do you think industrial cities like Birmingham and Manchester in Great Britain grew up near coal deposits?
24. **Drawing Inferences and Conclusions** Why do you think most Irish speak English rather than Gaelic?
25. **Making Generalizations and Predictions** How do you think Scandinavians have adapted to life in these very cold environments?
26. **Comparing and Contrasting** What are some ways in which Finland is different from its Scandinavian neighbors?

Map Activity

27. On a separate sheet of paper, match the letters on the map with their correct labels.

   London   Oslo
   Manchester   Stockholm
   Belfast   Copenhagen
   Dublin   Reykjavik
   Cork   Helsinki

Map Activity

27. **A.** Dublin
    B. London
    C. Oslo
    D. Copenhagen
    E. Manchester
    F. Reykjavik
    G. Belfast
    H. Helsinki
    I. Cork
    J. Stockholm

CHAPTER 18 REVIEW

Writing Activity
Use print resources to find out more about the Vikings and how they lived in their cold climate. Write a short story set in a Viking village or on a Viking voyage. Describe daily life in the village or on the voyage. Include a bibliography showing references you used. Be sure to use standard grammar, spelling, sentence structure, and punctuation.

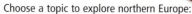

Internet Activity: go.hrw.com
KEYWORD: SJ5 GT18

Choose a topic to explore northern Europe:
- Explore the islands and fjords on the Scandinavian coast.
- Visit historic palaces in the United Kingdom.
- Investigate the history of skiing.

Writing Activity
Check stories to see that students have introduced several aspects of the Vikings' environment. Use Rubric 39, Writing to Create, to evaluate student work.

Interpreting Charts
1. Sweden; Denmark
2. Iceland and Norway
3. that they spend more on health per person than many or most of the world's other countries
4. nothing, since the chart only reports on how much money is spent on health

Analyzing Primary Sources
1. the loss of the Irish language
2. don't care if the language dies, resent having to learn it
3. because they don't speak Irish themselves
4. foolish talk that accomplishes nothing

Social Studies Skills Practice

Interpreting Charts
Study the chart below and answer the questions.

Health Spending Per Person in Scandinavia

Country	Health spending per person (in U.S. dollars)	Ranking among world countries
Denmark	1,588	11
Finland	2,046	4
Iceland	1,884	6
Norway	1,835	8
Sweden	2,343	3

Source: *The Illustrated Book of World Rankings,* Fifth Edition

1. Which Scandinavian country spends the most per person on health? the least?
2. Which two countries spend roughly the same amount per capita on health?
3. What conclusions can you draw about Scandinavian spending on health when compared to the rest of the world?
4. What can you learn from the chart about the actual health of Scandinavians?

Analyzing Primary Sources
Read the following passage from a newspaper editorial in the *Irish Independent*. Then answer the questions.

"If the Irish people, or a big majority of them, do not love their language, do not treasure it, do not care two hoots if it is allowed to die, there must be good reasons for their attitude. . . . In spite of all the blather, Irish is rarely spoken in the Irish Parliament. . . . Boys and girls exclaim: 'I hate having to waste time doing the old Irish language.' We hold that those boys and girls . . . are basically wrong in their outlook towards their native language. But they have . . . lost respect for it; even worse, they often despise it."

1. What issue does the newspaper article address?
2. According to the writer, how do most young people regard this issue?
3. Why does the writer criticize government officials in Parliament?
4. In the second sentence, what do you think the word *blather* means?

Northern Europe • 425

REVIEW AND ASSESSMENT RESOURCES

Reproducible
- Readings in World Geography, History, and Culture 34, 35, and 36
- Vocabulary Activity 18

Technology
- Chapter 18 Test Generator (on the One-Stop Planner)
- Audio CD Program, Chapter 18 (English and Spanish)
- HRW Go site

Reinforcement, Review, and Assessment
- Chapter Review and Practice
- Chapter Summaries and Review
- Chapter 18 Test
- Chapter 18 Test for English Language Learners and Special-Needs Students

GO TO: go.hrw.com
KEYWORD: SJ5 Teacher
FOR: a guide to using the Internet in your classroom

Northern Europe 425

CHAPTER 19

Eastern Europe
Chapter Resource Manager

Objectives	Pacing Guide	Reproducible Resources
SECTION 1 **Physical Geography** (pp. 427–29) 1. Identify the major physical features of Eastern Europe. 2. Identify the climates and natural resources of the region.	**Regular** .5 day Lecture Notes, Section 1 **Block Scheduling** .5 day Block Scheduling Handbook, Chapter 19	**RS** Know It Notes S1 **ELL** Main Idea Activity S1
SECTION 2 **The Countries of Northeastern Europe** (pp. 430–35) 1. Identify the peoples who contributed to the early history of northeastern Europe. 2. Describe how northeastern Europe's culture was influenced by other cultures. 3. Describe how the political organization of the region has changed since World War II.	**Regular** 2 days Lecture Notes, Section 2 **Block Scheduling** 1 day Block Scheduling Handbook, Chapter 19	**RS** Know It Notes S2 **RS** Graphic Organizer 19 **E** Cultures of the World Activity 3 **E** Creative Strategies for Teaching World Geography, Lesson 11 **SM** Geography for Life Activity **SM** Map Activity 19 **E** Biography Activities: Marie Curie, Franz Kafka **ELL** Main Idea Activity S2
SECTION 3 **The Countries of Southeastern Europe** (pp. 436–47) 1. Describe how southeastern Europe's early history helped to shape its modern societies. 2. Describe how culture affects the region. 3. Describe how the region's past has contributed to current conflicts.	**Regular** 2 days Lecture Notes, Section 3 **Block Scheduling** .5 day Block Scheduling Handbook, Chapter 19	**RS** Know It Notes S3 **E** Cultures of the World Activity 3 **E** Creative Strategies for Teaching World Geography, Lesson 11 **SM** Geography for Life Activity 19 **ELL** Main Idea Activity S3

Chapter Resource Key

- **RS** Reading Support
- **IC** Interdisciplinary Connections
- **E** Enrichment
- **SM** Skills Mastery
- **A** Assessment
- **REV** Review
- **ELL** Reinforcement and English Language Learners and English for Speakers of Other Languages (ESOL)
- Transparencies
- CD–ROM
- Music
- Video
- Internet
- Holt Presentation Maker Using Microsoft® PowerPoint®

  One-Stop Planner CD-ROM

See the *One-Stop Planner* for a complete list of additional resources for students and teachers.

One-Stop Planner CD–ROM

It's easy to plan lessons, select resources, and print out materials for your students when you use the *One-Stop Planner CD–ROM with Test Generator.*

Technology Resources

 One-Stop Planner CD–ROM, Lesson 19.1

 Geography and Cultures Visual Resources with Teaching Activities 24–29

 ARGWorld CD–ROM

Homework Practice Online

HRW Go site

 One-Stop Planner CD–ROM, Lesson 19.2

 ARGWorld CD–ROM

 Music of the World Audio CD Program, Selection 7

Homework Practice Online

HRW Go site

 One-Stop Planner CD–ROM, Lesson 19.3

 ARGWorld CD–ROM

Homework Practice Online

HRW Go site

Review, Reinforcement, and Assessment Resources

ELL	Main Idea Activity S1
REV	Section 1 Review
A	Daily Quiz 19.1
REV	Chapter Summaries and Review
ELL	English Audio Summary 19.1
ELL	Spanish Audio Summary 19.1

ELL	Main Idea Activity S2
REV	Section 2 Review
A	Daily Quiz 19.2
REV	Chapter Summaries and Review
ELL	English Audio Summary 19.2
ELL	Spanish Audio Summary 19.2

ELL	Main Idea Activity S3
REV	Section 3 Review
A	Daily Quiz 19.3
REV	Chapter Summaries and Review
ELL	English Audio Summary 19.3
ELL	Spanish Audio Summary 19.3

internet connect

HRW ONLINE RESOURCES

GO TO: go.hrw.com
Then type in a keyword.

TEACHER HOME PAGE
KEYWORD: **SJ5 TEACHER**

CHAPTER INTERNET ACTIVITIES
KEYWORD: **SJ5 GT19**

Choose an activity to:
- investigate the conflicts in the Balkans.
- take a virtual tour of Eastern Europe.
- learn about Baltic amber.

CHAPTER ENRICHMENT LINKS
KEYWORD: **SJ5 CH19**

CHAPTER MAPS
KEYWORD: **SJ5 MAPS19**

ONLINE ASSESSMENT
Homework Practice
KEYWORD: **SJ5 HP19**
Standardized Test Prep Online
KEYWORD: **SJ5 STP19**
Rubrics
KEYWORD: **SS Rubrics**

COUNTRY INFORMATION
KEYWORD: **SJ5 Almanac**

CONTENT UPDATES
KEYWORD: **SS Content Updates**

HOLT PRESENTATION MAKER
KEYWORD: **SJ5 PPT19**

ONLINE READING SUPPORT
KEYWORD: **SS Strategies**

CURRENT EVENTS
KEYWORD: **S5 Current Events**

Meeting Individual Needs

Ability Levels

Level 1 Basic-level activities designed for all students encountering new material

Level 2 Intermediate-level activities designed for average students

Level 3 Challenging activities designed for honors and gifted-and-talented students

ESOL Activities that address the needs of students with Limited English Proficiency

Chapter Review and Assessment

IC	Interdisciplinary Activities for the Middle Grades 13, 14, 15	A	Unit 4 Test
E	Readings in World Geography, History, and Culture 37, 38, and 39	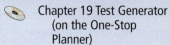	Chapter 19 Test Generator (on the One-Stop Planner)
SM	Critical Thinking Activity 19		Audio CD Program, Chapter 19
REV	Chapter 19 Review and Practice	A	Chapter 19 Test for English Language Learners and Special-Needs Students
REV	Chapter Summaries and Review	A	Unit 4 Test for English Language Learners and Special-Needs Students
ELL	Vocabulary Activity 19		HRW Go site
A	Chapter 19 Test		

CHAPTER 19

Eastern Europe
Previewing Chapter Resources

Holt Online Learning

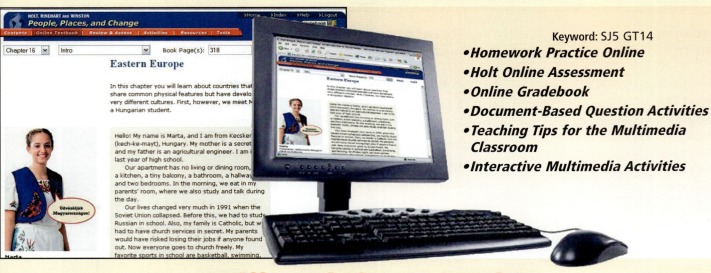

Keyword: SJ5 GT14

- *Homework Practice Online*
- *Holt Online Assessment*
- *Online Gradebook*
- *Document-Based Question Activities*
- *Teaching Tips for the Multimedia Classroom*
- *Interactive Multimedia Activities*

Differentiating Instruction

Reading and Writing Support
◀ *Graphic Organizer Activity*
- *Vocabulary Activity*
- *Chapter Summary and Review*
- *Know It Notes*
- *Audio CD*

Active Learning
◀ *Block Scheduling Handbook*
- *Cultures of the World Activity*
- *Interdisciplinary Activity*
- *Map Activity*
- *Critical Thinking Activity: Ethnic Cleansing in Bosnia*

Primary Sources and Advanced Learners
- *Geography for Life Activity: Cities and Rivers*
◀ *Map Activity: Budapest*
- *Readings in World Geography, History and Culture:*
  - *37 The Estonian Way*
  - *38 Czechoslovakia*
  - *39 The Shepherds of Transylvania*

Assessment Program
◀ *Daily Quizzes S1–3*
- *Chapter Test*
- *Chapter Test for English Language Learners and Special-Needs Students*

Spanish and ESOL
- *Vocabulary Activity*
◀ *Main Idea Activities for English Language Learners and Special-Needs Students*
- *Chapter Summary and Review*
- *Spanish Audio Summary*
- *Know It Notes S1–3*
- *Chapter Test for English Language Learners and Special-Needs Students*

Special Education Modifications
Your I.D.E.A. Works! CD-ROM will provide modified versions of the following teaching materials:
- *Guided Reading Strategies S1–3*
- *Vocabulary Activity*
◀ *Main Idea Activities S1–3*
- *Daily Quizzes S1–3*
- *Chapter 19 Test*
- *Flash cards of chapter vocabulary terms*

425C

Teacher Resources

Books for Teachers
Campbell, Greg. *The Road to Kosovo: A Balkan Diary.* Westview Press, 1999.

Havel, Václav. *Summer Meditations.* Knopf, 1992.

Swartz, Richard. *Room Service: Reports from Eastern Europe.* The New Press, 1998.

Books for Students
Hintz, Martin. *Poland.* Children's Press, 1998. Geography, history, economy, language, religion, and other topics.

Popescu, Julian. *Bulgaria.* Chelsea House, 1999. Geography, history, economy, culture and people of Bulgaria.

Symynkywicz, Jeffrey B. *1989: The Year the World Changed.* Dillion Press, 1996. The fall of communism in Romania, Bulgaria, and Hungary, accompanied by news photos.

Waterlow, Julia. *A Family from Bosnia.* Raintree/Steck-Vaughn, 1998. Daily life for a Sarajevo family in the midst of war.
SHELTERED ENGLISH

Multimedia Materials
The Road to Nowhere: Yugoslavia. (Video, 50 min.) Films for the Humanities and Sciences.

Yugoslavia: Before the Fall. (Video, 29 min.) Films for the Humanities and Sciences.

Destination Poland. (Video, 16 min.) Peace Corps, Office of World Wise Schools.

Videos and CDs

Videos
- CNN Presents Geography: Yesterday and Today, Segment 17 Castles for Sale
- ARG World

Holt Researcher
http://researcher.hrw.com
- *Breakup of the Soviet Sphere*
- *European Religions*
- *Estonia*
- *Latvia*
- *Lithuania*
- *Poland*
- *German Concentration Camps*
- *Curie, Marie*
- *Copernicus, Nicolaus*
- *Communist Europe*
- *Czech Republic*
- *Slovakia*
- *Hungary*
- *Slovenia*
- *Croatia*
- *Romania*
- *Moldova*
- *Bulgaria*
- *Macedonia*
- *Albania*
- *Yugoslavia*
- *Bosnia & Herzegovina*

Transparency Packages

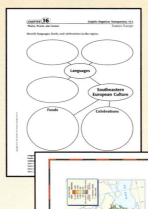

Graphic Organizer Transparencies 19.1–3

Geography and Cultures Visual Resources Transparencies
44 Europe: Physical
45 Europe: Political
46 Europe: Climate
47 Europe: Population
48 Europe: Land Use and Resources
55 Eastern Europe: Physical-Political

Map Activities Transparency 19 Budapest

425D

CHAPTER 19

Why It Matters

You may wish to point out these reasons for knowing more about Eastern Europe:

- Ethnic conflicts in the region have resulted in military involvement by the United States, NATO, and the UN.
- Many countries in the region are establishing democratic governments after decades of communism.
- Eastern Europe is a cultural and economic crossroads between Western Europe and Asia.
- The region's foods, festivals, literature, music, and other traditions can be enjoyed by all.

Chapter 19

Eastern Europe

In this chapter you will learn about countries that share common physical features but have developed very different cultures. First, however, we meet Marta, a Hungarian student.

Hello! My name is Marta, and I am from Kecskemét (KECH-ke-mayt), Hungary. My mother is a secretary, and my father is an agricultural engineer. I am in my last year of high school.

Our apartment has no living or dining room, just a kitchen, a tiny balcony, a bathroom, a hallway, and two bedrooms. In the morning, we eat in my parents' room, where we also study and talk during the day.

Our lives changed very much in 1991 when the Soviet Union collapsed. Before this, we had to study Russian in school. Also, my family is Catholic, but we had to have church services in secret. My parents would have risked losing their jobs if anyone found out. Now everyone goes to church freely. My favorite sports in school are basketball, swimming, and fencing. On Friday night we have parties organized by the school. Sometimes we go to the movies. In the summer, I used to work picking cherries. Now I work in a factory processing chickens.

Üdvözöljük Magyarországon!

▲ Translation: Welcome to Hungary!

Chapter Project

Although cultural conflict is part of Eastern Europe's history, so is cooperation. Have students work in groups to write constitutions for "Cromavania"—an imaginary Eastern European country where people live together peacefully. When the groups have completed their constitutions, lead a discussion on the strong points of each. Have students place their constitutions and a summary of what they learned in their portfolios.

Starting the Chapter

Focus students' attention on the map on the following page. Call on volunteers to locate several familiar place-names on the map and tell where they have heard the names before. (Possible answers: Transylvanian Alps—Dracula movies, Bosnia or Kosovo—television programs, Poland—history lessons on World War II) Discuss what these associations indicate about the region's history. (Possible answers: complex history, involved in wars) Tell students that cultural conflicts are part, but not all, of the region's complex history. Tell students that they will learn more about the history and cultures of Eastern Europe in this chapter.

Section 1: Physical Geography

Read to Discover
1. What are the major physical features of Eastern Europe?
2. What climates and natural resources does this region have?

Vocabulary
oil shale
lignite
amber

Places
Baltic Sea
Adriatic Sea
Black Sea
Danube River
Dinaric Alps
Balkan Mountains
Carpathian Mountains

Reading Strategy

FOLDNOTES: LAYERED BOOK Create the FoldNote titled **Layered Book** described in the Appendix. Label the pages Location and Place, Human-Environment Interaction, Movement, and Region. As you read, write details that support these Five Themes of Geography. Illustrate your layered book if time permits.

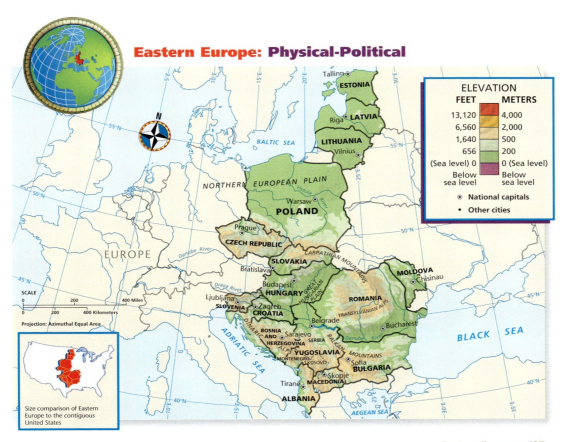

Eastern Europe: Physical-Political

CHAPTER 19, Section 1

SECTION 1 RESOURCES

Reproducible
- Lecture Notes, Section 1
- Block Scheduling Handbook, Chapter 19
- Know It Notes S1

Technology
- One-Stop Planner CD–ROM, Lesson 19.1
- Homework Practice Online
- Geography and Cultures Visual Resources with Teaching Activities 44–48, 55
- HRW Go site

Reinforcement, Review, and Assessment
- Section 1 Review
- Daily Quiz 19.1
- Main Idea Activity S1
- Chapter Summaries and Review
- English Audio Summary 19.1
- Spanish Audio Summary 19.1

Objectives
1. Identify the major physical features of Eastern Europe.
2. Describe the climates and natural resources of the region.

FOCUS

Bellringer
Copy the following instructions onto the chalkboard: *Look at the map and aerial photo in Section 1. Imagine that they illustrate magazine articles about Eastern Europe's physical geography. What might be the titles for the articles? Write down your ideas for one of the illustrations.* (Example: for the photo of the Danube River—"Danube: The Lifeblood Flowing through Romania's Heart") Discuss student responses. Tell students that in Section 1 they will learn more about the physical geography of Eastern Europe.

Using the Physical-Political Map
Tell the class that Eastern Europe has been invaded from different directions many times over the centuries. Have students examine the map on this page. Ask them to speculate how Eastern Europe's physical geography may have contributed to the region being a crossroads. (center of the continent, many rivers for navigation, few barriers to invasion)

Eastern Europe 427

CHAPTER 19, Section 1

EYE ON EARTH

A Salty Tradition Refer to the section titled Climate and Resources on the opposite page. Notice that salt mines have operated in Poland since the 1200s.

Poland's Wieliczka salt mine contains more than 124 miles (200 km) of passages that connect more than 2,000 rooms. The lowest room is 1,073 feet (327 m) below the surface.

There is a tradition among the Wieliczka miners to carve the salt into churches, altars, and large statues. In recent years, increased humidity started to dissolve the carvings. An international team of scientists has made great progress in stopping the deterioration.

Amber is golden, fossilized tree sap. The beaches along the eastern coast of the Baltic Sea are the world's largest and most famous source of amber. Baltic amber is approximately 40 million years old.

Physical Features

Eastern Europe stretches southward from the often cold, stormy shores of the Baltic Sea. In the south are the warmer and sunnier beaches along the Adriatic and Black Seas. We can divide the countries of this region into three groups. Poland, the Czech Republic, Slovakia, and Hungary are in the geographical heart of Europe. The Baltic countries are Estonia, Latvia, and Lithuania. Serbia and Montenegro, Bosnia and Herzegovina, Croatia, Slovenia, Macedonia, Romania, Moldova, Bulgaria, and Albania are the Balkan countries.

Landforms Eastern Europe is a region of mountains and plains. The plains of Poland and the Baltic countries are part of the huge Northern European Plain. The Danube River flows through the Great Hungarian Plain, also called the Great Alföld.

The Alps extend from central Europe southeastward into the Balkan Peninsula. Where they run parallel to the Adriatic coast, the mountains are called the Dinaric (duh-NAR-ik) Alps. As the range continues eastward across the peninsula its name changes to the Balkan Mountains. The Carpathian (kahr-PAY-thee-uhn) Mountains stretch from the Czech Republic across southern Poland and Slovakia and into Ukraine. There they curve south and west into Romania. In Romania they are known as the Transylvanian Alps.

Rivers Eastern Europe's most important river for trade and transportation is the Danube. The Danube stretches for 1,771 miles (2,850 km) across nine countries. It begins in Germany's Alps and flows eastward to the Black Sea. Some 300 tributaries flow into the Danube. The river carries and then drops so much silt that its Black Sea delta grows by 80 to 100 feet (24 to 30 m) every year. The river also carries a heavy load of industrial pollution.

✓ **READING CHECK:** *Places and Regions* What are the main physical features in Eastern Europe? areas—Baltics, heartland, Balkans; landforms—mountains, plains; rivers—Danube, tributaries

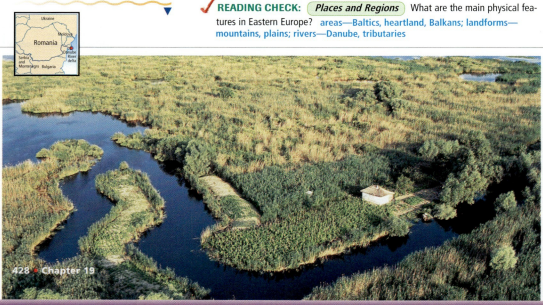

This aerial view of the Danube Delta shows Romania's rich farmland.

internet connect
GO TO: go.hrw.com
KEYWORD: SJ5 CH19
FOR: Web sites about Poland

TEACH

Teaching Objectives 1–2

ALL LEVELS: (Suggested time: 20 min.) Copy the following graphic organizer onto the chalkboard, omitting the blue answers. Point out that it shows the general location of Eastern Europe's main regions. Call on students to provide words and phrases to summarize the physical features, climates, and resources of each region. Encourage students to use the unit's atlas as an additional resource. Then have students speculate how the location and availability of resources might affect economic development.
LS VISUAL-SPATIAL

LEVELS 2 AND 3: (Suggested time: 20 min.) Have students complete the All Levels lesson. Then have each student select an Eastern European country and write a paragraph that describes its landforms, climates, rivers, and resources. Again, encourage students to use the unit's atlas as a resource. Call on volunteers to read their paragraphs to the class. Then have students speculate what effect pollution might have on the country they selected.
LS VERBAL-LINGUISTIC

The Physical Geography of Eastern Europe

Baltic Countries	Heartland	Balkan Countries
• plains	• plains, mountains	• mountains
• cold winters	• cold winters in east, warmer in west	• cold winters in east, warmer in south and west
• amber, oil shale	• bauxite, lignite, salt	• bauxite, oil, lignite

Climate and Resources

The eastern half of the region has long, snowy winters and short, rainy summers. Farther south and west, winters are milder and summers become drier. A warm, sunny climate has drawn visitors to the Adriatic coast for centuries.

Eastern Europe's mineral and energy resources include coal, natural gas, oil, iron, lead, silver, sulfur, and zinc. The region's varied resources support many industries. Some areas of the Balkan region and Hungary are major producers of bauxite. Romania has oil. Estonia has deposits of **oil shale**, or layered rock that yields oil when heated. Estonia uses this oil to generate electricity, which is exported to other Baltic countries and Russia. Slovakia and Slovenia mine a soft form of coal called **lignite**. Nevertheless, many countries must import their energy because demand is greater than supply.

For thousands of years, people have traded **amber**, or fossilized tree sap. Amber is found along the Baltic seacoast. Salt mining, which began in Poland in the 1200s, continues in central Poland today.

During the years of Communist rule industrial production was considered more important than the environment. The region suffered serious environmental damage. Air, soil, and water pollution, deforestation, and the destruction of natural resources were widespread. Many Eastern European countries have begun the long and expensive task of cleaning up their environment.

✓ **READING CHECK:** *Environment and Society* What factors affect the location of economic activities in the region? **climate, location of resources**

Section Review 1

Homework Practice Online
Keyword: SJ5 HP19

Define and explain: oil shale, lignite, amber

Working with Sketch Maps On a map of Eastern Europe that you draw or that your teacher provides, label the following: Baltic Sea, Adriatic Sea, Black Sea, Danube River, Dinaric Alps, Balkan Mountains, and Carpathian Mountains.

Reading for the Main Idea
1. *Places and Regions* On which three major seas do the countries of Eastern Europe have coasts?
2. *Environment and Society* What types of mineral and energy resources are available in this region? How does this influence individual economies?

Critical Thinking
3. **Making Generalizations and Predictions** Would this region be suitable for agriculture? Why?
4. **Identifying Cause and Effect** How did Communist rule contribute to the pollution problems of this region?

Organizing What You Know
5. **Summarizing** Copy the following graphic organizer. Use it to summarize the physical features, climate, and resources of the heartland, the Baltics, and the Balkans. Then write and answer one question about the region's geography based on the chart.

Region	Physical features	Climate	Resources

Section 1 Review

Answers to Section 1 Review

Define For definitions, see the glossary.

Working with Sketch Maps Maps will vary, but listed places should be labeled in their approximate locations.

Reading for the Main Idea
1. Adriatic, Baltic, and Black Seas (NGS 4)
2. coal, iron, lead, natural gas, silver, sulfur, zinc, bauxite, oil shale, lignite, amber, salt; wide range of industries, energy shortages, need to import (NGS 4)

Critical Thinking
3. yes; wide plains, plenty of rain
4. increased production and ignored pollution

Organizing What You Know
5. heartland—Northern European Plain, Great Hungarian Plain, Carpathian Mountains; cold winters in east, milder in west; bauxite, lignite, salt; Baltics—Northern European Plain; cold winters; amber, oil shale; Balkans—Dinaric Alps, Balkan Mountains, Transylvanian Alps; cold winters in east, warm in south and west; bauxite, oil, lignite; questions will vary but should focus on geographic distributions

CLOSE

Ask a student to describe one of the region's countries just by naming the bodies of water or countries that border it, plus one fact about its physical geography. Then have that student call on another student to name the country. Continue until all of the countries have been covered.

REVIEW, ASSESS, RETEACH

Have students complete the Section Review. Then pair students. Have one student name a country in Eastern Europe and the other name a physical feature or resource found in or bordering that country. Then have students complete Daily Quiz 19.1. **COOPERATIVE LEARNING**

Have students complete Main Idea Activity S1. Then organize the class into triads and give each student an outline map of the region. Assign each group member the task of labeling either the plains, mountains, or rivers. Instruct members to exchange maps until all maps are complete. **ESOL, COOPERATIVE LEARNING**

EXTEND

Invite interested students to conduct research on ways that the physical geography of the Northern European Plain has affected history. They may want to create an illustrated map that shows the invasions and influences that have swept across this broad, lowland area. **BLOCK SCHEDULING**

CHAPTER 19, Section 2

SECTION 2 RESOURCES

Reproducible
- Lecture Notes, Section 2
- Know It Notes S2
- Graphic Organizer
- Geography for Life Activity
- Map Activity
- Cultures of the World Activity 3
- Creative Strategies for Teaching World Geography, Lesson 11
- Biography Activity: Franz Kafka

Technology
- One-Stop Planner CD–ROM, Lesson 19.2
- Music of the World Audio CD Program, Selection 7
- Homework Practice Online
- HRW Go site

Reinforcement, Review, and Assessment
- Section 2 Review
- Daily Quiz 19.2
- Main Idea Activity S2
- Chapter Summaries and Review
- English Audio Summary 19.2
- Spanish Audio Summary 19.2

Section 2: The Countries of Northeastern Europe

Read to Discover
1. What peoples contributed to the early history of northeastern Europe?
2. How was northeastern Europe's culture influenced by other cultures?
3. How has the political organization of this region changed since World War II?

Vocabulary
Indo-European

Places
Estonia
Poland
Czech Republic
Slovakia
Hungary
Lithuania
Latvia
Prague
Tallinn
Riga
Warsaw
Vistula River
Bratislava
Budapest

People
Vaclav Havel

Reading Strategy

READING ORGANIZER Before you read, draw a circle in the center of a sheet of paper. Draw seven surrounding circles connected by lines to the center circle. Label the center circle Northeastern Europe. As you read, write information about each of the seven countries in the outer circles.

The Teutonic knights, a German order of soldier monks, brought Christianity and feudalism to northeastern Europe. They built this castle at Malbork, Poland, in the 1200s.

History

Migrants and warring armies have swept across Eastern Europe over the centuries. Each group of people brought its own language, religion, and customs. Together these groups contributed to the mosaic of cultures we see in Eastern Europe today.

Early History Among the region's early peoples were the Balts. The Balts lived on the eastern coast of the Baltic Sea. They spoke **Indo-European** languages. The Indo-European language family includes many languages spoken in Europe. These include Germanic, Baltic, and Slavic languages. More than 3,500 years ago, hunters from the Ural Mountains moved into what is now Estonia. They spoke a very different, non-Indo-European language. The language they spoke provided the early roots of today's Estonian and Finnish languages. Beginning around A.D. 400, a warrior people called the Huns invaded the region from Asia. Later, the Slavs came to the region from the plains north of the Black Sea.

Section 2

Objectives
1. Identify what peoples contributed to the early history of northeastern Europe.
2. Analyze how northeastern Europe's culture was influenced by other cultures.
3. Describe how the political organization of the region has changed since World War II.

FOCUS

Bellringer

Copy the following question onto the chalkboard: *What does a country need to do or have to attract tourists?* (Possible answers: good hotels and restaurants, historical sites, beautiful scenery, entertainment, reliable transportation) Tell students that many of the countries of northeastern Europe became popular tourist destinations during the 1990s. Before that time, few people traveled to the region because the governments were communist and tourist facilities were undeveloped.

Building Vocabulary

Write **Indo-European** on the chalkboard and call on a volunteer to read the text's definition aloud. Point out that the definition only tells about the languages the Indo-European peoples spoke—not what they looked like or what their customs were. Ask what two large regions are represented in the term. (India and Europe) Many languages of India are related to European languages.

430 Chapter 19

In the 800s the Magyars moved into the Great Hungarian Plain. They spoke a language related to Turkish. In the 1200s the Mongols rode out of Central Asia into Hungary. At the same time German settlers pushed eastward, colonizing Poland and Bohemia—the western region of the present-day Czech Republic.

Emerging Nations Since the Middle Ages, Austria, Russia, Sweden, and the German state of Prussia have all ruled parts of Eastern Europe. After World War I ended in 1918, a new map of Eastern Europe was drawn. The peace treaty created two new countries: Yugoslavia and Czechoslovakia. Czechoslovakia included the old regions of Bohemia, Moravia, and Slovakia. At about the same time, Poland, Lithuania, Latvia, and Estonia also became independent countries.

✓ READING CHECK: *Places and Regions* What peoples contributed to the region's early history? Balts, hunters from Ural Mountains, Huns, Slavs, Magyars, Mongols, Germans

Hungarian dancers perform in traditional dress.
Interpreting the Visual Record
Region How does this Hungarian costume compare to those you have seen from other countries?

Culture

The culture and festivals of this region show the influence of the many peoples who contributed to its history. As in Scandinavia, Latvians celebrate a midsummer festival. The festival marks the summer solstice, the year's longest day. Poles celebrate major Roman Catholic festivals. Many of these have become symbols of the Polish nation. The annual pilgrimage, or journey, to the shrine of the Black Madonna of Częstochowa (chen-stuh-KOH-vuh) is an example.

Traditional Foods The food of the region reflects German, Russian, and Scandinavian influences. As in northern Europe, potatoes and sausages are important in the diets of Poland and the Baltic countries. Although the region has only limited access to the sea, the fish of lakes and rivers are often the center of a meal. These fish often include trout and carp. Many foods are preserved to last through the long winter. These include pickles, fruits in syrup, dried or smoked hams and sausages, and cured fish.

The Arts, Literature, and Science
Northeastern Europe has made major contributions to the arts, literature, and sciences. For example, Frédéric Chopin (1810–1849) was a famous Polish pianist and composer. Marie Curie (1867–1934), one of the first female physicists, was also born in Poland. The writer Franz Kafka (1883–1924) was born to Jewish parents in Prague (PRAHG), the

CHAPTER 19, Section 2

Cultural Kaleidoscope
Czech Texans

During the 1850s affordable land attracted Czech settlers to the fertile low hills of southeastern Texas. The newcomers missed the great cathedrals of their homeland. As soon as they could afford to do so, the immigrants built churches with high vaulted ceilings, stained glass windows, and religious statuary. Interior walls were elaborately painted with angels, clouds, trailing ivy, flowers, and symbols. One surviving ceiling features 66 types of flowers, vines, and shrubs.

Today, services and festivals held at the painted churches of Fayette County draw thousands of visitors, Czech and non-Czech alike. At its Veterans Day ceremony, airplanes drop flower petals on one of the churchyards to honor church members who died in World War II.

Critical Thinking: How did Czech architecture in Texas reflect architectural traditions from the homeland?

Answer: The Czechs built churches in Texas that reflected the great cathedrals of their homeland.

◄ **Visual Record Answer**
Answers will vary according to students' experiences.

Eastern Europe • 431

TEACH

Teaching Objective 1

ALL LEVELS: (Suggested time: 10 min.) Copy the following graphic organizer onto the chalkboard, omitting the blue answers. Call on students to fill in the outer circles with the names of peoples who contributed to northeastern Europe's early history. Then call on others to supply details about each group to fill in the circles. **LS VISUAL-SPATIAL**

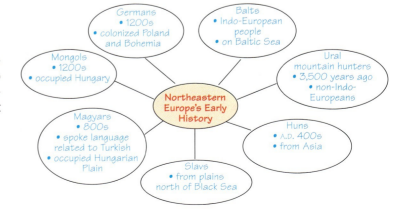

Northeastern Europe's Early History
- Germans: 1200s; colonized Poland and Bohemia
- Balts: Indo-European people; on Baltic Sea
- Mongols: 1200s; occupied Hungary
- Ural mountain hunters: 3,500 years ago; non-Indo-Europeans
- Magyars: 800s; spoke language related to Turkish; occupied Hungarian Plain
- Huns: A.D. 400s; from Asia
- Slavs: from plains north of Black Sea

Eastern Europe 431

CHAPTER 19, Section 2

DAILY LIFE

Baltic Music Folk music is an important part of Baltic cultures. Many folk artists from the region now record for the world market.

The *kokle* is a native Latvian instrument. It is played flat on the musician's lap. The strings are plucked. Because the *kokle* can be adapted to a wide range of musical styles, musicians often include non-Latvian songs in their performances.

Modern *kokles* have 30 strings and can be several feet long. Earlier versions had between 5 and 13 strings and were hollowed from a single block of wood. A soundboard was then attached. No two instruments were exactly alike.

Activity: Challenge students to find examples of *kokle* music and bring recordings to class.

GO TO: go.hrw.com
KEYWORD: SJ5 CH19
FOR: Web sites about Baltic culture

Chart Answer

Latvia, Lithuania

Northeastern Europe

Country	Population/Growth Rate	Life Expectancy	Literacy Rate	Per Capita GDP
Czech Republic	10,249,216 −0.1%	72, male 79, female	100%	$15,300
Estonia	1,408,566 −0.5%	64, male 77, female	100%	$10,900
Hungary	10,045,407 −0.3%	68, male 77, female	99%	$13,300
Latvia	2,348,784 −0.7%	63, male 75, female	100%	$8,300
Lithuania	3,592,561 −0.2%	64, male 76, female	100%	$8,400
Poland	38,622,660 0%	70, male 78, female	99%	$9,500
Slovakia	5,430,033 0.1%	70, male 79, female	not available	$10,200
United States	290,342,554 0.9%	74, male 80, female	97%	$37,600

Source: Central Intelligence Agency, *The World Factbook 2003*

Interpreting the Chart *Place* Which two countries have the lowest levels of economic development?

This suspension bridge spans the Western Dvina River in Riga, the capital of Latvia.

present-day capital of the Czech Republic. Astronomer Nicolaus Copernicus (1473–1543) was born in Toruń (TAWR-oon), a city in north-central Poland. He set forth the theory that the Sun—not Earth—is the center of the universe.

✓ **READING CHECK:** *Human Systems* How is the region's culture a reflection of its past and location? **includes festivals and foods introduced by invaders, migrants, and neighbors**

Northeastern Europe Today

Estonia, Latvia, and Lithuania lie on the flat plain by the eastern Baltic Sea. Once part of the Russian Empire, the Baltic countries gained their independence after World War I ended in 1918. However, they were taken over by the Soviet Union in 1940 and placed under Communist rule. The Soviet Union collapsed in 1991. Since then, the countries of northeastern Europe have been moving from communism to capitalism and democracy.

Estonia A long history of Russian control is reflected in Estonia today. Nearly 30 percent of Estonia's population is ethnic Russian. Russia remains one of Estonia's most important trading partners. However, Estonia is also building economic ties to other countries, particularly Finland. Ethnic Estonians have close cultural ties to Finland. In fact, the Estonian language is related to Finnish. Also, most people in both countries are Lutherans. Ferries link the Estonian capital of Tallinn (TA-luhn) with Helsinki, Finland's capital.

Teaching Objective 2

ALL LEVELS: (Suggested time: 30 min.) Organize the class into small groups. Provide each group with colored markers and a sheet of butcher paper. Instruct the students to create a mural showing the cultural traits of the region. Ask them also to label their pictures, explaining the origins of the various contributions. Display the murals around the classroom.
ESOL, COOPERATIVE LEARNING, **LS** **VISUAL-SPATIAL**

TEACHER TO TEACHER

Jean Eldredge of Altamonte Springs, Florida, suggests the following activity to teach students about northeastern Europe: Have students choose a country in the region and write five complete sentences about it, using the material in Section 2, the unit's atlas, and any other resources available in your classroom. Collect the papers. Call on a volunteer to read one student's statements. Have the other students guess which country is being described. Limit the number of guesses. You may want to offer extra-credit points for correct identifications. Repeat the process until all the countries have been covered. This activity can be used as an initial teaching activity, to check on student progress, or to review for a test.

Connecting to Literature

Toy robot

While he wrote many books, Czech writer Karel Capek is probably best known for his play *R.U.R.* This play added the word *robot* to the English language. The Czech word *robota* means "drudgery" or forced labor. The term is given to the artificial workers that Rossum's Universal Robots factory make to free humans from drudgery. Eventually, the Robots develop feelings and revolt. The play is science fiction. Here, Harry Domin, the factory's manager, explains the origin of the Robots to visitor Helena Glory.

Domin: "Well, any one who has looked into human anatomy will have seen at once that man is too complicated, and that a good engineer could make him more simply. So young Rossum began to overhaul anatomy and tried to see what could be left out or simplified.... [He] said to himself: 'A man is something that feels happy, plays the piano, likes going for a walk, and in fact, wants to do a whole lot of things that are really unnecessary....

ROBOT ROBOTA

But a working machine must not play the piano, must not feel happy, must not do a whole lot of other things. A gasoline motor must not have tassels or ornaments, Miss Glory. And to manufacture artificial workers is the same thing as to manufacture gasoline motors. The process must be of the simplest, and the product of the best from a practical point of view....

Young Rossum ... rejected everything that did not contribute directly to the progress of work—everything that makes man more expensive. In fact, he rejected man and made the Robot. My dear Miss Glory, the Robots are not people. Mechanically they are more perfect than we are, they have an enormously developed intelligence, but they have no soul."

Analyzing Primary Sources
1. Why does Rossum design the Robots without human qualities?
2. How has Karel Capel's play influenced other cultures?

Latvia Latvia is the second largest of the Baltic countries. Its population has the highest percentage of ethnic minorities. Some 57 percent of the population is Latvian. About 30 percent of the people are Russian. The capital, Riga (REE-guh), has more than 1 million people. It is the largest urban area in the three Baltic countries. Like Estonia, Latvia also has experienced strong Scandinavian and Russian influences. As well as having been part of the Russian Empire, part of the country once was ruled by Sweden. Another tie between Latvia, Estonia, and the Scandinavian countries is religion. Traditionally most people in these countries are Lutheran. In addition, Sweden and Finland are important trading partners of Latvia today.

Eastern Europe • 433

CHAPTER 19, Section 2

DAILY LIFE

What's on TV in Tallinn? As countries in northeastern Europe have gained freedom from communism, television and radio have been released from government control.

However, there are few comedies or dramas on television stations in the Baltic countries. Private groups have little experience creating television programs. Broadcasting is still dominated by political discussions and news programs.

Activity: Organize students into small groups and have them create a premise for a television comedy or drama set in any of the Baltic countries.

Connecting to Literature Answers
1. because he wished to create a machine that was simple, inexpensive, and that only contributed to the progress of work
2. by contributing the word *robot* to the English language

Teaching Objective 3

LEVEL 1: (Suggested time: 30 min.) Have students create covers for a special edition of a magazine titled *News from the Northeast*. In advance, duplicate a sheet of paper with the magazine title and date printed on it. (You may want to use the magazine cover template available on the go.hrw.com Web site at Keyword: SK5 Teacher.) Tell students that the special edition highlights the many changes that have occurred in northeastern Europe in the last 100 years or so. Have students think about what images and selected article titles would best represent the concept and re-create them for their own magazine covers.

LEVELS 2 AND 3: (Suggested time: 45 min.) Have students write an article for the *News from the Northeast* magazine.
LS VERBAL-LINGUISTIC

 ➤**ASSIGNMENT:** Collect the articles from the Levels 2 and 3 lesson. Duplicate several, removing students' names, and distribute them to the class. Then instruct students to write a letter to the magazine's editor commenting on or disputing a point or fact in one of the articles.

Eastern Europe 433

CHAPTER 19, Section 2

COOPERATIVE LEARNING

Auschwitz The Polish city of Auschwitz was the site of the largest Nazi concentration camp during World War II. More than 4 million people died in the camp complex. Most of the Auschwitz victims were Jews, but thousands of Roma (Gypsies), Poles, and Soviet prisoners of war were killed also.

Organize the class into groups to research the history of Auschwitz during and since World War II. Encourage students to note the effects of the war on the city's culture.

Biography Answer

He stood up for what he believed was right, even though he faced imprisonment.

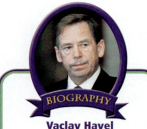

BIOGRAPHY

Vaclav Havel
(1936–)

Character Trait: Integrity

Communism ended peacefully in Czechoslovakia thanks in part to writer Vaclav Havel. For years Havel had criticized the communist government in his plays and poems. The government put him in jail. Havel and a pro-democracy group he led finally forced the Communist Party to share power. He was elected president of Czechoslovakia in 1989 and of the Czech Republic in 1993.

How did integrity affect Vaclav Havel's actions?

Prague's Charles Bridge is lined with historical statues. ▼

Lithuania Lithuania is the largest and southernmost Baltic country. Its capital is Vilnius (VIL-nee-uhs). Lithuania's population has the smallest percentage of ethnic minorities. More than 80 percent of the population is Lithuanian. Nearly 9 percent is Russian, while 7 percent is Polish. Lithuania has ancient ties to Poland. For more than 200 years, until 1795, they were one country. Roman Catholicism is the main religion in both Lithuania and Poland today. As in the other Baltic countries, agriculture and production of basic consumer goods are important parts of Lithuania's economy.

Poland Poland is northeastern Europe's largest and most populous country. The total population of Poland is about the same as that of Spain. The country was divided among its neighbors in the 1700s. Poland regained its independence shortly after World War I. After World War II the Soviet Union established a Communist government to rule the country.

In 1989 the Communists finally allowed free elections. Many businesses now are owned by people in the private sector rather than by the government. The country has also strengthened its ties with Western countries. In 1999 Poland, the Czech Republic, and Hungary joined the North Atlantic Treaty Organization (NATO).

Warsaw, the capital, has long been the cultural, political, and historical center of Polish life. More than 2 million people live in the urban area. The city lies on the Vistula River in central Poland. This location has made Warsaw the center of the national transportation and communications networks as well.

The Former Czechoslovakia Czechoslovakia became an independent country after World War I. Until that time, its lands had been part of the Austro-Hungarian Empire. Then shortly before World War II, it fell under German rule. After the war the Communists, with the support of the Soviet Union, gained control of the government. As in Poland, the Communists lost power in 1989. In 1993 Czechoslovakia peacefully split into two countries. The western part became the Czech Republic. The eastern part became Slovakia. This peaceful split helped the Czechs and Slovaks avoid the ethnic problems that have troubled other countries in the region.

The Czech Republic The Czech Republic's economy is growing and attracting foreign investment. Most of the country's businesses are completely or in part privately owned. However, some Czechs worry that the government remains too involved in the economy. As in Poland, a variety of political parties compete in free elections. Czech lands have coal and other

---

Teaching Objectives 1–3

LEVEL 1: (Suggested time: 45 min.) Pair students and assign each pair one of the region's countries. Using the text and other sources, have each pair summarize the major ethnic groups, cultural traits, and important facts about its country. Then have students organize their information into a brief oral report. You may want to require a visual aid as part of the presentation. **COOPERATIVE LEARNING**

LEVELS 2 AND 3: (Suggested time: 45 min.) Have students use the information they compiled for the Level 1 lesson to prepare a lesson about the selected country for an elementary classroom. Encourage them to use comparisons with familiar concepts so the younger children can understand the material.

important mineral resources that are used in industry. Much of the country's industry is located in and around Prague, the capital. The city is located on the Vltava River. More than 1.2 million people live there. Prague has beautiful medieval buildings. It also has one of Europe's oldest universities.

Slovakia Slovakia is more rugged and rural, with incomes lower than in the Czech Republic. The move toward a freer political system has been slow. However, progress has been made. Bratislava (BRAH-tyee-slah-vah), the capital, is located on the Danube River. The city is the country's most important industrial area and cultural center. Many rural Slovaks move to Bratislava looking for better-paying jobs. Most of the country's population is Slovak. However, ethnic Hungarians account for more than 10 percent of Slovakia's population.

Hungary Hungary separated from the Austro-Hungarian Empire at the end of World War I. Following World War II, a Communist government came to power. A revolt against the government was put down by the Soviet Union in 1956. The Communists ruled until 1989.

Today the country has close ties with the rest of Europe. In fact, most of Hungary's trade is with members of the European Union. During the Communist era, the government experimented with giving some businesses the freedom to act on their own. For example, it allowed local farm managers to make key business decisions. These managers kept farming methods modern, chose their crops, and marketed their products. Today, farm products from Hungary's fertile plains are important exports. Much of the country's manufacturing is located in and around the capital, Budapest (BOO-duh-pest). Budapest is Hungary's largest city. Nearly 20 percent of the population lives there.

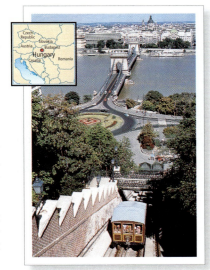

▲ The Danube River flows through Budapest, Hungary.

Interpreting the Visual Record
Human-Environment Interaction
Why might Hungary's capital have grown up along a river?

✓ **READING CHECK:** *Human Systems* How have the governments and economies of the region been affected by recent history? moved from communism to democracy and private ownership following collapse of Soviet Union

Section Review 2

Define or identify: Indo-European, Vaclav Havel

Working with Sketch Maps On the map you drew in Section 1, label the countries of the region, Prague, Tallinn, Riga, Warsaw, Vistula River, Bratislava, and Budapest.

Reading for the Main Idea
1. *Human Systems* How did invasions and migrations help shape the region?
2. *Places and Regions* What has the region contributed to the arts?

Critical Thinking
3. **Drawing Inferences and Conclusions** How did the Soviet Union influence the region?
4. **Summarizing** What social changes have taken place here since the early 1990s?

Organizing What You Know
5. **Sequencing** Copy the following graphic organizer. Use it to show the history of the Baltics since 1900.

Eastern Europe • 435

CHAPTER 19, Section 3

SECTION 3 RESOURCES

Reproducible
- Lecture Notes, Section 3
- Know It Notes S3
- Geography for Life Activity
- Cultures of the World Activity 3
- Creative Strategies for Teaching World Geography, Lesson 11

Technology
- One-Stop Planner CD–ROM, Lesson 19.3
- Homework Practice Online
- HRW Go site

Reinforcement, Review, and Assessment
- Section 3 Review
- Daily Quiz 19.3
- Main Idea Activity S3
- Chapter Summaries and Review
- English Audio Summary 19.3
- Spanish Audio Summary 19.3

Visual Record Answer ▶
Greek or Roman

Section 3: The Countries of Southeastern Europe

Read to Discover
1. How did Southeastern Europe's early history help shape its modern societies?
2. How does culture both link and divide the region?
3. How has the region's past contributed to current conflicts?

Vocabulary
Roma

Places
Bulgaria
Romania
Croatia
Slovenia
Serbia
Bosnia and Herzegovina
Albania
Kosovo
Serbia and Montenegro
Macedonia
Belgrade
Podgorica
Sarajevo
Zagreb
Ljubljana
Skopje
Bucharest
Moldova
Chișinău
Sofia
Tiranë

Reading Strategy
ANTICIPATING INFORMATION This region is sometimes called the Powder Keg of Europe. What do you think that means? Write down your answer. As you read this section, write down information that explains why the Balkan countries were given this nickname.

These ancient ruins in southern Albania date to the 500s B.C.
Interpreting the Visual Record
Place What cultural influence does this building show?

History

Along with neighboring Greece, this was the first region of Europe to adopt agriculture. From here farming moved up the Danube River valley into central and western Europe. Early farmers and metalworkers in the south may have spoken languages related to Albanian. Albanian is an Indo-European language.

Early History Around 750–600 B.C. the ancient Greeks founded colonies on the Black Sea coast. The area they settled is now Bulgaria and Romania. Later, the Romans conquered most of the area from the Adriatic Sea to the Danube River and across into Romania. When the Roman Empire divided into west and east, much of the Balkans and Greece became part of the Eastern Roman Empire. This eastern region eventually became known as the Byzantine Empire. Under Byzantine rule, many people of the Balkans became Orthodox Christians.

436 • Chapter 19

Section 3

Objectives
1. Describe the early history of southeastern Europe.
2. Explain how culture links and divides the region.
3. Identify how the region's past contributed to current conflicts.

FOCUS

Bellringer
Copy the following question onto the chalkboard: *How do you identify yourself in terms of your country, state, region, or ethnic group? Write down more than one term.* (Examples: American, Texan, Puerto Rican, African American) Then ask how students would feel if suddenly they had to define themselves as Canadians or as of a different ethnic group. Explain that some people in southeastern Europe have had to make similar changes. Tell students that in Section 3 they will learn more about the countries of southeastern Europe.

Building Vocabulary
Write the vocabulary term on the chalkboard. Point out that the people who call themselves **Roma** were once known as Gypsies, when their origins were thought to be in Egypt. If your class has studied Canada, ask students if they recall another group of people who are referred to now by the name they call themselves. (Inuit) If they have not covered Canada, lead a discussion about the terms *Hispanic, Chicano, African American*, or others.

436 Chapter 19

Kingdoms and Empires Many of today's southeastern European countries first appear as kingdoms between A.D. 800 and 1400. The Ottoman Turks conquered the region and ruled until the 1800s. The Ottomans, who were Muslims, tolerated other religious faiths. However, many peoples, such as the Bosnians and Albanians, converted to Islam. As the Ottoman Empire began to weaken in the late 1800s, the Austro-Hungarians took control of Croatia and Slovenia. They imposed Roman Catholicism.

Slav Nationalism The Russians, meanwhile, were fighting the Turks for control of the Black Sea. The Russians encouraged Slavs in the Balkans to revolt against the Turks. The Russians appealed to Slavic nationalism—to the Slav's sense of loyalty to their country. The Serbs did revolt in 1815 and became self-governing in 1817. By 1878 Bulgaria and Romania were also self-governing.

The Austro-Hungarians responded to Slavic nationalism by occupying additional territories. Those territories included the regions of Bosnia and Herzegovina. To stop the Serbs from expanding to the Adriatic coast, European powers made Albania an independent kingdom.

In August 1914 a Serb nationalist shot and killed the heir to the Austro-Hungarian throne. Austria declared war on Serbia. Russia came to Serbia's defense. These actions sparked World War I. All of Europe's great powers became involved. The United States entered the war in 1917.

Creation of Yugoslavia At the end of World War I Austria-Hungary was broken apart. Austria was reduced to a small territory. Hungary became a separate country but lost its eastern province to Romania. Romania also gained additional lands from Russia. Albania remained independent. The peace settlement created Yugoslavia. Yugoslavia means "land of the southern Slavs." Yugoslavia brought the region's Serbs, Bosnians, Croatians, Macedonians, Montenegrins, and Slovenes together into one country. Each ethnic group had its own republic within Yugoslavia. Some Bosnians and other people in Serbia were Muslims. Most Serbs were Orthodox Christians, and the Slovenes and Croats were Roman Catholics. These ethnic and religious differences created problems that eventually led to civil war in the 1990s.

✓ **READING CHECK:** (Human Systems) How is southeastern Europe's religious and ethnic makeup a reflection of its past? Colonizers and conquerors introduced different religions.

This bridge at Mostar, Bosnia, was built during the 1600s. This photograph was taken in 1982.

This photograph shows Mostar after civil war in the 1990s.
Interpreting the Visual Record Place
What differences can you find in the two photos?

CHAPTER 19, Section 3

Linking Past to Present

The Slavs The Slavs are the largest ethnic and language group of the European peoples. Long ago, the Slavs' ancestors migrated out of Asia into what is now Eastern Europe. During the A.D. 400s and 500s they moved into the Balkan Peninsula. Little unity developed among the Slavic groups, however, as they adopted ideas from their new neighbors.

In the 1800s some Slavic intellectuals and poets founded the Pan-Slav movement. (*Pan* means "all.") Its supporters hoped to unite the Slavic peoples politically and culturally. The movement did not succeed, partly because the various Slavic peoples remained separated by their own rivalries.

Ideas about Slavic unity continue to affect world events. Russia's support for Serbian interests during the conflicts of the 1990s is due partly to their shared Slavic heritage.

◀ **Visual Record Answer**

The lower photo shows that the bridge and wall have been destroyed. The buildings have also been damaged.

Eastern Europe • 437

TEACH

Teaching Objective 1

LEVEL 1: (Suggested time: 20 min.) Pair students and have each pair create a flowchart to show how the ancient Greeks, the Roman Empire, the Ottoman Empire, the Austro-Hungarian Empire, and World War I affected the boundaries and religions of the countries of southeastern Europe.
ESOL, COOPERATIVE LEARNING, LS **LOGICAL-MATHEMATICAL**

LEVELS 2 AND 3: (Suggested time: 30 min.) Focus students' attention on the photographs of buildings and other structures in Section 3. Ask if they have heard the phrase "if these walls could talk." Discuss the meaning of the phrase. Then have students use the information from the Level 1 lesson to write what the walls of one of those structures would say about southeastern Europe's history if they could indeed talk. You may want to invite some students to dramatize their "wall soliloquies." LS **INTRAPERSONAL**

Eastern Europe **437**

CHAPTER 19, Section 3

HUMAN SYSTEMS

Conflict and Cyberspace
During the conflict in Kosovo in the late 1990s, American teenagers used e-mail to keep in touch with teens in the war-torn region. The Kosovar youths shared their concerns and fears. The American teens distributed those messages to the news media and to charity groups in order to spread the word about the war's effects.

Critical Thinking: How has access to e-mail affected the world?

Answer: It has improved communication around the world and has allowed people to communicate almost instantaneously.

Ethnic Albanians worship at a mosque in Pristina, Serbia.

The Danube Delta, on the Romanian coast of the Black Sea, is part of a unique ecosystem. Most of the Romanian caviar-producing sturgeon are caught in these waters. Caviar is made from the salted eggs from three types of sturgeon fish. Caviar is considered a delicacy and can cost as much as $50 per ounce.

Culture

The Balkans are the most diverse region of Europe in terms of language, ethnicity, and religion. It is the largest European region to have once been ruled by a Muslim power. It has also been a zone of conflict between eastern and western Christianity. The three main Indo-European language branches—Romance (from Latin), Germanic, and Slavic—are all found here, as well as other branches such as Albanian. Non-Indo-European languages like Hungarian and Turkish are also spoken here.

Balkan diets combine the foods of the Hungarians and the Slavs with those of the Mediterranean Greeks, Turks, and Italians. In Greek and Turkish cuisines, yogurt and soft cheeses are an important part of most meals, as are fresh fruits, nuts, and vegetables. Roast goat or lamb are the favorite meats for a celebration.

In the Balkans Bosnian and ethnic Albanian Muslims celebrate the feasts of Islam. Christian holidays—Christmas and Easter—are celebrated on one day by Catholics and on another by Orthodox Christians. Holidays in memory of ancient battles and modern liberation days are sources of conflict between ethnic groups.

✓ **READING CHECK:** *Places and Regions* Why is religion an important issue in southeastern Europe? source of conflict within and between countries

Southeastern Europe Today

Like other southeastern European countries, Yugoslavia was occupied by Germany in World War II. A Communist government under Josip Broz Tito took over after the war. Tito's strong central government prevented ethnic conflict. After Tito died in 1980, Yugoslavia's Communist government held the republics together. Then in 1991 the republics of Slovenia, Croatia, Bosnia and Herzegovina, and Macedonia began to break away. Years of bloody civil war followed. Today the region struggles with the violence and with rebuilding economies left weak by years of Communist-government control.

The Former Yugoslavia Located on the Danube River, Belgrade is the capital of Serbia and Montenegro. The Serbian government supported ethnic Serbs fighting in civil wars in Croatia and in Bosnia and Herzegovina in the early 1990s. Tensions between ethnic groups also have been a problem within Serbia. About 65 percent of the people in Serbia and Montenegro are Orthodox Christians. In the southern Serbian province of Kosovo, the majority of people are ethnic Albanian

438 • Chapter 19

Teaching Objective 2
ALL LEVELS: (Suggested time: 45 min.) Organize the class into small groups. Ask each group to plan a feast for a major Roman Catholic, Orthodox Christian, or Muslim holiday. They should include the history of the religion in southeastern Europe as background. Have students use the information in the text as a starting point for creating their menus and conduct additional research as necessary. Then have the groups present their work to the class. **COOPERATIVE LEARNING**

Teaching Objective 3
ALL LEVELS: Copy the following graphic organizer onto the chalkboard, omitting the blue answers. Call on volunteers to fill in the charts. Then lead a discussion on how the various groups have caused changes in the region's governments during the 1980s and 1990s. **ESOL**

Ethnic and Religious Groups of Southeastern Europe

	Major ethnic or religious group	Important minority group
Yugoslavia	Orthodox Christians	Albanian Muslims
Bosnia and Herzegovina	Muslims	Catholic Croats, Orthodox Serbs
Croatia	Roman Catholics	Orthodox Christian Serbs
Slovenia	Roman Catholics	
Macedonia	Orthodox Christians	Albanian Muslims
Romania	Romanian	Roma, Hungarians
Moldova	(diverse)	
Bulgaria	Bulgarians	Turks, Macedonians
Albania	Muslims	

438 Chapter 19

and Muslim. Many of the Albanians want independence. Conflict between Serbs and Albanians led to civil war in the late 1990s. In 1999 the United States, other Western countries, and Russia sent troops to keep the peace. In Feburary, 2003, Serbia and Montenegro unified as one country. Today, 2,500 troops remain in the region.

Bosnia and Herzegovina Bosnia and Herzegovina generally are referred to as Bosnia. Some 40 percent of Bosnians are Muslims, but large numbers of Roman Catholic Croats and Orthodox Christian Serbs also live there. Following independence, a bloody civil war broke out between these groups as they struggled for control of territory. During the fighting the once beautiful capital of Sarajevo (sar-uh-YAY-voh) was heavily damaged.

Croatia Croatia's capital is Zagreb (ZAH-greb). Most of the people of Croatia are Roman Catholic. In the early 1990s, Serbs made up about 12 percent of the population. In 1991 the ethnic Serbs living in Croatia claimed part of the country for Serbia. This resulted in heavy fighting. By the end of 1995 an agreement was reached and a sense of stability returned to the country. Many Serbs left the country.

Slovenia Slovenia is a former Austrian territory. It looks to Western European countries for much of its trade. Most people in Slovenia are Roman Catholic, and few ethnic minorities live there. Partly because of the small number of ethnic minorities, little fighting occurred after Slovenia declared independence from Yugoslavia. The major center of industry is Ljubljana (lee-oo-blee-AH-nuh), the country's capital.

These Muslim refugees are walking to Travnik, Bosnia, with the assistance of UN troops.
Interpreting the Visual Record
Movement What effect might the movement of refugees have on a region?

Slovenia's capital, Ljubljana, lies on the Sava River.

CHAPTER 19, Section 3

National Geography Standard 10

Bosnians ands Islam In the 1380s, Muslim Turkish armies began raiding the region that is now Bosnia and Herzegovina. The Turks had gained complete control of the area within about 100 years.

Unlike most other Europeans conquered by the Ottoman Empire, a large percentage of Bosnians converted to Islam. There were several reasons for this. First, Muslims had a higher legal status than Christians. Second, Sarajevo and Mostar were mainly Muslim, and those who wanted to participate fully in city life had to convert. Also, the Bosnian Catholic Church was relatively weak.

Discussion: Lead a discussion about the goals, needs, and ideas that people of different religions might have in common.

▲ **Visual Record Answer**

possible answer: ethnic conflict, overcrowding, political ramifications, new cultural traditions introduced in new countries

---

➤**ASSIGNMENT:** Copy the following sentence onto the chalkboard: *Times are always changing in southeastern Europe.* Have students copy the sentence into their notebooks. Ask students to write a paragraph supporting or disputing this statement. (To agree with the statement, students might cite the many changes in governmental control over the countries in the region. Those who dispute the statement might state that constant change and ethnic or religious conflict are so common in southeastern Europe that times do not really change.)

Teaching Objectives 1–3

LEVEL 1: (Suggested time: 40 min.) Give each student two or three index cards. Assign or have each student select a country of southeastern Europe. Be sure that each country is selected by at least one student. Instruct students to provide basic information about the country (relative location, history, culture, economy, and government) on one side of the card and to draw a simple map of the country on the other side. Have students exchange cards to evaluate them. **LS INTERPERSONAL**

CHAPTER 19, Section 3

FOOD FESTIVAL

A Sweet Treat *Kolaches* are popular Czech or Polish pastries. For a shortcut version, use frozen bread dough. Or, make a sweetened yeast dough from scratch.

After the dough has risen, roll it out, cut it into circles 2–3 inches across, and indent the center of each. Add a filling of fruit preserves, cottage cheese with egg and sugar, or a sweetened poppyseed paste. Let rise again. Sprinkle with a streusel topping of sugar, cinnamon, butter, and a little flour. Bake at 375° for 15–20 minutes. There are many *kolache* recipes on the Internet. *Kolacky* and *kolachke* are alternate spellings.

Focus on Culture Answer ▲

to go to school, pursue careers, be independent

Macedonia When Macedonia declared its independence from Yugoslavia, Greece immediately objected to the country's new name. Macedonia is also the name of a province in northern Greece that has historical ties to the republic. Greece feared that Macedonia might try to take over the province.

Greece responded by refusing to trade with Macedonia until the mid-1990s. This slowed Macedonia's movement from the command— or government-controlled—economy it had under Communist rule to a market economy in which consumers help to determine what is to be produced by buying or not buying certain goods and services. Despite its rocky start, in recent years Macedonia has made progress in establishing free markets.

Romania A Communist government took power in Romania at the end of World War II. Then in 1989 the Communist government was overthrown during bloody fighting. Change, however, has been slow. Bucharest, the capital, is the biggest industrial center. Today more people work in agriculture than in any other part of the economy. Nearly 90 percent of the country's population is ethnic Romanian. Roma, or Gypsies as they were once known, make up more than 2 percent of the population. They are descended from people who may have lived in northern India and began migrating centuries ago. Most of the rest of Romania's population are ethnic Hungarian.

Moldova Throughout history control of Moldova has shifted many times. It has been dominated by Turks, Polish princes, Austria, Hungary, Russia, and Romania. Not surprisingly, the country's popu-

FOCUS ON CULTURE

Roma Women in a Changing World

The Roma nomadic way of life has changed. Now some Roma live in cities, go to school, and enter professions. Many Roma, however, are poor and have no jobs. They also experience discrimination. Part of the problem is that some Roma customs conflict with non-Roma customs. Some of these customs relate to women.

In traditional Roma communities, girls quit school early and marry when very young. Parents arrange many marriages. A ceremony seals the arrangement. The groom's father places a necklace of gold coins around the bride's neck to show that she is promised to his son. During their marriage, the young couple will probably have many children. Families celebrate the birth of a boy more than the birth of a girl.

Now, some Roma women are organizing for better social services and more respect in their communities. **What are some opportunities that Roma girls lose if they marry when very young?**

440 • Chapter 19

LEVELS 2 AND 3: (Suggested time: 45 min.) Have students use the cards they created for the Level 1 lesson to design a card-trading game. The game should have a goal, rules, and a point system. For example, the goal might be to acquire wealth by collecting the countries with the strongest economies. As an example of the point system, countries with coastlines along the Mediterranean might be worth more points than landlocked countries. Have students play the game and summarize what they learned about the countries for which they did not create a card.

LS LOGICAL-MATHEMATICAL

lation reflects this diverse past. Moldova declared its independence in 1991 from the Soviet Union. However, the country suffers from difficult economic and political problems. About 40 percent of the country's labor force works in agriculture. Chișinău (kee-shee-NOW), the major industrial center of the country, is also Moldova's capital.

Bulgaria Mountainous Bulgaria has progressed slowly since the fall of communism. However, a market economy is growing gradually, and the people have more freedoms. Most industries are located near Sofia (SOH-fee-uh), the capital and largest city. About 9 percent of Bulgaria's people are ethnic Turks.

Albania Albania is one of Europe's poorest countries. The capital, Tiranë (ti-RAH-nuh), has a population of about 270,000. About 70 percent of Albanians are Muslim. Albania's Communist government feuded with the Communist governments in the Soviet Union and, later, in China. As a result, Albania became isolated. Since the fall of its harsh Communist government in the 1990s, the country has tried to move toward both democracy and a free market system.

✓ **READING CHECK:** *Human Systems* What problems does the region face, and how are they reflections of its Communist past? ethnic violence—Communist government prevented conflict; economic conditions—years of government control left economies weak; democratic reforms—Communist government limited freedoms

Southeastern Europe

Country	Population/Growth Rate	Life Expectancy	Literacy Rate	Per Capita GDP
Albania	3,582,205 1.0%	70, male 75, female	87%	$4,500
Bosnia and Herzegovina	3,989,018 0.5%	70, male 75, female	not available	$1,900
Bulgaria	7,537,929 –1.1%	68, male 76, female	99%	$6,600
Croatia	4,422,248 .3%	71, male 78, female	99%	$8,800
Macedonia	2,063,122 0.4%	72, male 77, female	not available	$5,000
Moldova	4,439,502 0.1%	61, male 69, female	99%	$2,500
Romania	22,271,839 –0.2%	67, male 75, female	98%	$7,400
Serbia and Montenegro	10,655,774 –0.1%	71, male 77, female	93%	$2,370
United States	290,342,554 0.9%	74, male 80, female	97%	$37,600

Source: Central Intelligence Agency, *The World Factbook 2003*

Interpreting the Chart *Place* Which southeastern European country has the highest level of economic development?

Section Review 3

Define and explain: Roma

Working with Sketch Maps On the map you drew in Section 2, label the region's countries and their capitals. They are listed at the beginning of the section. In a box in the margin, identify the countries that once made up Yugoslavia.

Reading for the Main Idea
1. *Human Systems* How has the region's history influenced its religious and ethnic makeup?
2. *Human Systems* What events and factors have contributed to problems in Bosnia and other countries in the region since independence?

Critical Thinking
3. *Summarizing* How was Yugoslavia created?
4. *Analyzing Information* How are the region's governments and economies changing?

Organizing What You Know
5. *Categorizing* Copy the following graphic organizer. Use it to identify languages, foods, and celebrations in the region.

Section 3 Review

Answers to Section 3 Review

Define For definition, see the glossary.

Working with Sketch Maps Slovenia, Croatia, Bosnia and Herzegovina, Macedonia, Serbia, and Montenegro made up Yugoslavia.

Reading for the Main Idea
1. Invasions and foreign control have led to multiple religious and ethnic groups living in the region.
2. conflict among ethnic, religious groups

Critical Thinking
3. created after World War I in response to Slav nationalism
4. independent countries without Communist governments; political and economic troubles; developing market economies

Organizing What You Know
5. languages—Romance, Germanic, Slavic, and non-Indo-European languages; foods—yogurt, soft cheeses, fresh fruits, nuts, vegetables, goat, lamb; celebrations—Catholic and Orthodox Christian holidays, Islamic feasts, national holidays

▲ **Chart Answer**

Croatia

CLOSE

Read the Why It Matters feature at the beginning of the chapter to the class. Call on volunteers to add a detail or to explain each point further. Then ask students to propose a single sentence to answer the question "Why should we study Eastern Europe?" (Possible answer: Events in Eastern Europe can affect people everywhere.)

REVIEW, ASSESS, RETEACH

Have students complete the Section Review. Then put the names of all the countries on slips of paper in a hat and have each student draw a name. (You will need to repeat country names.) Ask students to write a sentence that begins "If I lived in this country, I would . . . " and complete it with a detail from Section 3 about the country they have drawn. Have other students guess which country is being discussed. Then have students complete Daily Quiz 19.3.

Have students complete Main Idea Activity S3. Then, pair students and provide each pair with an outline map of the region. Have students take turns finding two facts about each country on the map. **ESOL, COOPERATIVE LEARNING**

EXTEND

Have interested students create maps of southeastern Europe to show how boundaries have changed, areas where different ethnic and religious groups have settled, and areas where conflicts have been most severe. Let the students who created the maps lead a discussion on conclusions that may be drawn from the maps. **BLOCK SCHEDULING**

CHAPTER 19 REVIEW

Define and Identify
For definitions and identifications, see the glossary and index.

Review the Main Ideas
7. Northern European Plain, Great Hungarian Plain, Dinaric Alps, Balkan Mountains, Carpathian Mountains, Transylvanian Alps (NGS 4)
8. Danube (NGS 4)
9. coal, natural gas, oil, iron, lead, silver, sulfur, zinc, bauxite, oil shale, lignite, amber, salt
10. Balts, hunting people from the Ural Mountains, Huns, Slavs, Magyars, Mongols, Turks, Germans; language, customs, religions (NGS 9)
11. Yugoslavia and Czechoslovakia were created; Poland, Lithuania, Latvia, and Estonia gained independence. (NGS 13)
12. Frédéric Chopin, Marie Curie, Franz Kafka, Nicolaus Copernicus
13. Since the 1990s, the countries of Eastern Europe have been moving away from communism and toward capitalism and democracy. (NGS 11)
14. Prague, Tallinn, Riga, Vilnius, Warsaw, Bratislava, Budapest; Belgrade, Podgorica, Sarajevo, Zagreb, Ljubljana, Skopje, Bucharest, Chisinau, Sofia, Tiranë
15. A long series of invasions has created great diversity in language, religion, and ethnicity in the Balkans. (NGS 10)
16. Slovenia, Croatia, Bosnia and Herzegovina, and Macedonia; Serbia and Montenegro unified as one country.

Think Critically
17. Possible answer: Balkan diets combine the foods of the Hungarians and the Slavs with those of the Mediterranean Greeks, Turks, and Italians.

CHAPTER 19 Review and Practice

Define and Identify
Identify each of the following:
1. oil shale
2. lignite
3. amber
4. Indo-European
5. Vaclav Havel
6. Roma

Review the Main Ideas
7. What are the major landforms of Eastern Europe?
8. What is Eastern Europe's major river?
9. What are some of Eastern Europe's resources?
10. What groups influenced the culture of Eastern Europe? How can these influences be seen today?
11. How did the close of World War I change the countries of Eastern Europe?
12. Who are some important contributors to art, literature, and sciences that came from Northeastern Europe?
13. How did changes of the 1990s affect the politics and economics of Eastern Europe?
14. What are the main cities of Northeastern Europe? of Southeastern Europe?
15. What makes the Balkans the most diverse region in Europe?
16. What countries broke away from Yugoslavia in the early 1990s? What happened in the region in 2003?

Think Critically
17. **Drawing Inferences and Conclusions** How has Eastern Europe's location influenced the diets of the region's people?
18. **Analyzing Information** How did Communist economic policies affect the region's environment? its major river?
19. **Identifying Cause and Effect** What geographic factors help make Warsaw the transportation and communication center of Poland? If Warsaw were located along the Baltic coast of Poland or near the German border instead, how may the city have developed differently?
20. **Comparing and Contrasting** Compare and contrast the breakups of Yugoslavia and Czechoslovakia.
21. **Summarizing** How has political change affected the economies of Eastern European countries?

Map Activity
22. On a separate sheet of paper, match the letters on the map with their correct labels.
   Baltic Sea
   Adriatic Sea
   Black Sea
   Danube River
   Dinaric Alps
   Balkan Mountains
   Carpathian Mountains

18. Because industrial production was considered more important than the environment, the region suffered severe environmental damage. The Danube River carries a heavy load of industrial pollution.
19. its location on the Vistula River in central Poland; perhaps less connected to the rest of Poland, more open to attack or Western influence
20. Yugoslavia—violent; Czechoslovakia—peaceful
21. Change to capitalism and market economies is happening at the same time as the change from communism to democracy.

Map Activity
22. A. Dinaric Alps
    B. Black Sea
    C. Balkan Mountains
    D. Carpathian Mountains
    E. Baltic Sea
    F. Adriatic Sea
    G. Danube River

Writing Activity

Imagine that you are a teenager living in Romania and want to write a family memoir of life in Romania. Include accounts of life for your grandparents under strict Soviet rule and life for your parents during the Soviet Union's breakup. Also describe your life in free Romania. Be sure to use standard grammar, sentence structure, and punctuation.

Internet Activity: go.hrw.com
KEYWORD: SJ5 GT19

Choose a topic to explore Eastern Europe:
- Investigate the conflicts in the Balkans.
- Take a virtual tour of Eastern Europe.
- Learn about Baltic amber.

CHAPTER 19 REVIEW

Writing Activity
Answers will vary, but students should discuss all three generations. Details should be consistent with text information. Use Rubric 40, Writing to Describe, to evaluate student work.

Interpreting Graphs
1. Muslim; Protestant
2. Muslim and Orthodox
3. that many different peoples have invaded or settled in the region
4. that each of the "other" religions has a small number of followers; otherwise, they would have their own listing in the graph

Analyzing Primary Sources
1. enjoyed it; didn't laugh, remained impassive
2. the different peoples represented by the entertainers, some familiarity with languages of Italians, Huns, and Goths
3. stand-up comedy
4. Possible answer: The fun and pleasant atmosphere contrasts sharply with Attila's image as a terrifying conqueror.

Social Studies Skills Practice

Interpreting Graphs
You have learned about the cultural diversity of the Balkan region. Study the following graph about Bosnia and Herzegovina. Then answer the questions below.

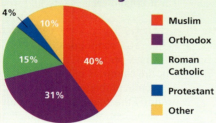

Religious Practice in Bosnia and Herzegovina
- Muslim: 40%
- Orthodox: 31%
- Roman Catholic: 15%
- Protestant: 4%
- Other: 10%

Source: Central Intelligence Agency, *The World Fact Book*, 2003.

1. Which religion claims the largest percentage of followers? the smallest?
2. Which two religions, when combined, total almost three-fourths of the country's people?
3. Based on this information, what is one thing that you may conclude about the country's history?
4. What can you assume about how many people follow any one of the "other" religions? Why?

Analyzing Primary Sources
Attila the Hun was a fierce warrior who invaded Eastern Europe in the A.D. 400s. Attila spread terror among the peoples he conquered. In this passage, a Roman historian named Priscus reports on having dinner in Attila's tent and on the entertainment that followed the meal. Read the passage. Then answer the questions.

"After the songs a Scythian entered, a crazy fellow who told a lot of strange and completely false stories, not a word of truth in them, which made everyone laugh. Following him came the Moor, Zerkon, totally disorganized in appearance, clothes, voice and words. By mixing up the languages of the Italians with those of the Huns and Goths, he fascinated everyone and made them break out into uncontrollable laughter, all that is except Attila. He remained impassive, without any change of expression . . ."

1. How do the guests react to the entertainment? How does Attila react?
2. What indicates that Attila had contacts with many different peoples?
3. If the Scythian and Zerkon were living and entertaining today, what would we call their profession?
4. How does the image of Attila's court in this report compare to Attila's reputation among the peoples he conquered?

REVIEW AND ASSESSMENT RESOURCES

Reproducible
- Readings in World Geography, History, and Culture 37, 38, and 39
- Critical Thinking Activity 21
- Vocabulary Activity 21

Technology
- Chapter 19 Test Generator (on the One-Stop Planner)

- HRW Go site
- Audio CD Program, Chapter 19

Reinforcement, Review, and Assessment
- Chapter 19 Review
- Chapter Summaries and Review
- Chapter 19 Test

- Chapter 19 Test for English Language Learners and Special-Needs Students
- Unit 5 Test
- Unit 5 Test for English Language Learners and Special-Needs Students

GO TO: go.hrw.com
KEYWORD: SJ5 Teacher
FOR: a guide to using the Internet in your classroom

UNIT 4

GEOGRAPHY SIDELIGHT

As it is working to unite the economic and political aspects of the member countries, the EU is also supporting the preservation of particular ethnic cultures. For example, almost 50 million Europeans speak minority languages such as Wendish, Frisian, or Basque. The European Union supports several organizations that try to ensure the survival of these languages.

The EU has an ambitious range of goals. If successful, it will have eased intercountry commerce among its member countries and strengthened the region's political and social systems while maintaining the unique culture of each member country.

Critical Thinking: How is the EU working to link its member countries?

Answer: by easing intercountry commerce, strengthening the region's political and social systems

➤ This Focus On Government feature addresses National Geography Standards 6, 11, and 13.

Focus on ECONOMICS

The European Union

What if . . . ? Imagine you are traveling from Florida to Pennsylvania. You have to go through a border checkpoint in Georgia to prove your Florida identity. The guard charges a tax on the cookies you are bringing to a friend in Pennsylvania. Buying gas presents more problems. You try to pay with Florida dollars, but the attendant just looks at you. You discover that they speak "Virginian" in Virginia and use Virginia coins. All this would make traveling from one place to another much more difficult.

The European Union Fortunately, that was just an imaginary situation. However, it is similar to what might happen while traveling across Europe. European countries have different languages, currencies, laws, and cultures. For example, someone from France has different customs than someone from Ireland.

However, many Europeans also share common interests. For example, they are interested in peace in the region. They also have a common interest in Europe's economic success.

A shared belief in economic and political cooperation has resulted in the creation of the European Union (EU). The EU has eliminated boundaries to job opportunities. For example, it is estimated that as many as 40,000 people from member countries in Eastern Europe may migrate to the United Kingdom (Great Britain) each year to find work.

The Beginnings of a Unified Europe

Proposals for an economically integrated Europe first came about in the 1950s. After World War II, the countries of Europe had many economic problems. A plan was made to unify the coal and steel production of some countries. In 1957 France, Germany, Italy, Belgium, the Netherlands, and Luxembourg formed the European Economic Community (EEC). The name was shortened in 1992 to simply the European Community (EC). The goal of the EC was to combine each country's economy into a single market. Having one market would make trading among them easier. Eventually, more countries became interested in joining the EC. In 1973 the United Kingdom, Denmark, and Ireland joined. In the 1980s Greece, Portugal, and Spain

The Eurostar train carries passengers from London to Paris. These two cities are only about 200 miles (322 km) apart. However, they have different cultures and ways of life.

Focus On Government

Analyzing an Economic System

Ask students to list the 15 current member countries of the European Union (Austria, Belgium, Denmark, Finland, France, Germany, Greece, Ireland, Italy, Luxembourg, the Netherlands, Portugal, Spain, Sweden, and the United Kingdom). Point out that each country had to meet specific requirements before it was admitted into the union. Organize the class into pairs. Assign one EU country to each pair or call on some pairs to volunteer for more than one country. Have students conduct research on the requirements their assigned country had to meet to become a member of the EU and what changes the country had to make. Ask the pairs to compile lists of the requirements and changes.

The 25 EU countries produce a wide range of exports and are one of the world's richest markets.

The flag of the EU features 12 gold stars on a blue background. The EU's currency, the euro, replaced the currencies of most EU countries.

joined. Austria, Finland, and Sweden were added in the 1990s.

In 2004 countries from Eastern Europe and the Mediterranean joined the EU. (See the map to locate these countries.) Bulgaria, Romania, and Turkey are candidates to join in the next several years.

The Future Some people believe the EU is laying the foundation for a greater sense of European identity. A European Court of Justice has been set up to enforce EU rules. According to some experts, this is helping to build common European beliefs, responsibilities, and rights.

On January 1, 2002, the euro became the common currency for most EU countries. The symbol of the euro is €. With the exception of Denmark, Sweden, and the United Kingdom, the euro replaced the currencies of all other member countries. The 12 countries that currently use the euro are commonly referred to as the "euro zone."

The EU has resulted in many important changes in Europe. Cooperation between member countries has increased. Trade has also increased. EU members have adopted a common currency and common economic laws. The EU is creating a more unified Europe. Some people even believe that the EU might someday lead to a "United States of Europe."

Understanding What You Read

1. What was the first step toward European economic unity?
2. What is the euro? How do you think the euro helps unify Europe?

Understanding What You Read

Answers
1. The first step toward European economic unity was a proposal that came about in 1950, following World War II.
2. The euro is the common currency of most of the European Union. It replaced the currencies of most of the EU countries.

Going Further: Thinking Critically

Have students identify the issues and benefits awaiting the member countries of the European Union during the early phase of unification. Then have students conduct research on the economic issues that faced the United States as the country was evolving from a group of colonies into a unified country. As a class, compare and contrast the U.S. experience with those arising now for the European countries. Have students prepare a report that warns European member countries of potential pitfalls, recommends how to overcome them, and lists likely benefits.

UNIT 4

PRACTICING THE SKILL

1. Students should compare their definitions with dictionary definitions. They should note that the differences among the three types of settlements is primarily size; a city is larger than a town, which is larger than a village. Students should note how their definitions are different from the dictionary's.

2. Students should note the apparent age of their settlement and about how many people live there. Students should describe some jobs in their settlement and how their settlement is connected to others, such as by highway or rail. Students might note unique features, such as buildings, parks, and cultural attractions.

3. Students might suggest capital cities, mountain cities, river cities, port cities, colonial cities, modern cities, tourist cities, or other types.

▶ This GeoSkills feature addresses National Geography Standards 4, 6, 12, and 17.

GeoSKILLS

Building Skills for Life: Analyzing Settlement Patterns

There are many different kinds of human settlements. Some people live in villages where they farm and raise animals. Others live in small towns or cities and work in factories or offices. Geographers analyze these settlement patterns. They are interested in how settlements affect people's lives.

All settlements are unique. Even neighboring villages are different. One village might have better soil than its neighbors. Another village might be closer to a main road or highway. Geographers are interested in the unique qualities of human settlements.

Geographers also study different types of settlements. For example, many European settlements could be considered medieval cities. Medieval cities are about 500–1,500 years old. They usually have walls around them and buildings made of stone and wood. Medieval cities also have tall churches and narrow, winding streets.

This illustration shows a German medieval city in the 1400s.

Analyzing settlement patterns is important. It helps us learn about people and environments. For example, the architecture of a city might give us clues about the culture, history, and technology of the people who live there. You can ask questions about individual villages, towns, and cities to learn about settlement patterns. What kinds of activities are going on? How are the streets arranged? What kinds of transportation do people use? You can also ask questions about groups of settlements. How are they connected? Do they trade with each other? Are some settlements bigger or older than others? Why is this so?

THE SKILL

1. How do you think a city, a town, and a village are different from each other? Write down your own definition of each word on a piece of paper. Then look them up in a dictionary and write down the dictionary's definition. Were your definitions different?

2. Analyze the settlement where you live. How old is it? How many people live there? What kinds of jobs do people have? How is it connected to other settlements? How is it unique?

3. Besides medieval cities, what other types of cities can you think of? Make a list of three other possible types.

446 • Unit 4 GeoSkills

GEOSKILLS

Going Further: Thinking Critically

Edge cities are defined as "nodal concentrations of retail and office space that are situated on the outer fringes of metropolitan areas, typically near major highway intersections." Essentially, edge cities are major commercial centers that grow up near major cities. They differ from residential suburbs in that they contain much more office, retail, and hotel space than the communities made up mainly of houses and apartments. Tysons Corner, outside Washington, D.C., in Fairfax County, Virginia, is a typical example. Edge cities are particularly common near the rapidly growing cities of the Sunbelt.

Have students research the development of an edge city in your state or region. Organize the class into groups and have them pursue specific aspects of the topic. Here are some suggestions for the different groups' investigations:

- Contact the administration of the nearby large city for information on how the edge city has affected it.
- Acquire old and recent maps of the area.
- Find old and new photos of the development.
- Find information on how the edge city has affected utility services.
- Ask highway department officials how traffic patterns have changed.
- Investigate changes in property values and taxes in the tax assessor's office.
- Search newspaper files for news stories about the development.
- Research the effect on employment and unemployment patterns.

When the research is complete, have the groups compile their information in a large flowchart.

HANDS on GEOGRAPHY

One type of settlement is called a planned city. A planned city is carefully designed before it is built. Each part fits into an overall plan. For example, the size and arrangement of streets and buildings might be planned.

There are many planned cities in the world. Some examples are Brasília, Brazil; Chandigarh, India; and Washington, D.C. Many other cities have certain parts that are planned, such as individual neighborhoods. These neighborhoods are sometimes called planned communities.

Suppose you were asked to plan a city. How would you do it? On a separate sheet of paper, create your own planned city. These guidelines will help you get started.

1. First, decide what the physical environment will be like. Is the city on the coast, on a river, or somewhere else? Are there hills, lakes, or other physical features in the area?

2. Decide what to include in your city. Most cities have a downtown, different neighborhoods, and roads or highways that connect areas together. Many cities also have parks, museums, and an airport.

3. Plan the arrangement of your city. Where will the roads and highways go? Will the airport be close to downtown? Try to arrange the different parts of your city so that they fit together logically.

4. Draw a map of your planned city. Be sure to include a title, scale, and orientation.

▲ Some people think the city plan for Brasília looks like a bird, a bow and arrow, or an airplane.
Interpreting the Visual Record What do you notice about the arrangement of Brasília's streets?

Lab Report

1. How was your plan influenced by the physical environment you chose?
2. How do you think planned cities are different from cities that are not planned?
3. What problems might people have when they try to plan an entire city?

Lab Report

Answers

1. Students might note that streets would have to fit around physical features such as rivers or mountains. They may also note that the environment affected the businesses in their cities. For example, a port city might have docks and businesses related to fishing, travel, or recreation located near the waterfront.

2. Students might suggest that planned cities are more efficient, have stronger economies, or have a higher standard of living. They might also argue that planned cities have less character or "atmosphere."

3. Students might suggest the difficulty of accommodating different populations, such as locating the airport near downtown for easy business travel or on the outskirts so that noise pollution bothers fewer people. Students may mention other problems, such as the difficulty of predicting growth.

◀ **Visual Record Answer**

possible answers: wide, symmetrical arrangement; attractive pattern

Unit 4 Hands On • 447

UNIT 5

UNIT OBJECTIVES

1. Describe the physical features of Russia and its western neighbors and link the region's natural environment with its economic development.
2. Examine the progression of the region's history, from early periods through communism to the breakup of the Soviet Union.
3. Analyze the relationships among the region's ethnic and culture groups.
4. Use special-purpose maps to analyze relationships among climate, population patterns, and economic activities in Russia and its western neighbors.
5. Identify the challenges that lie ahead for the governments and peoples of Russia and its western neighbors.

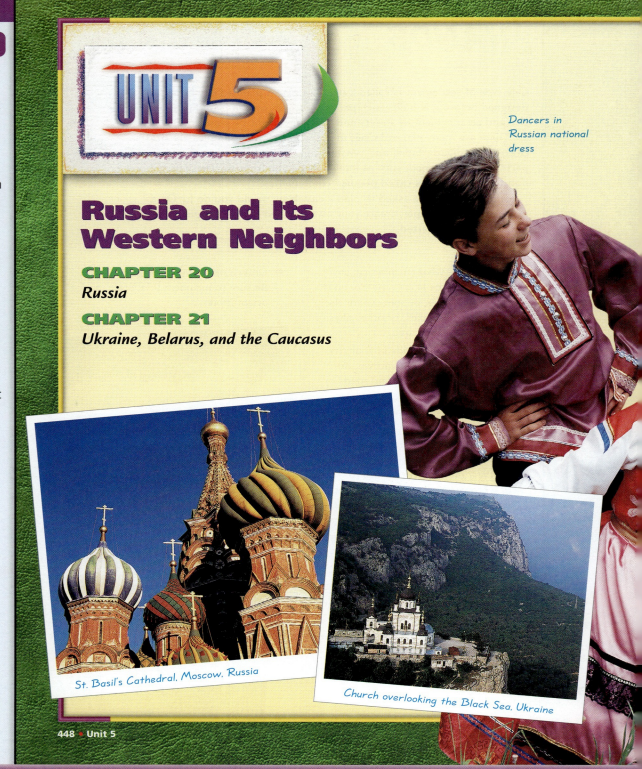

UNIT 5

Russia and Its Western Neighbors

CHAPTER 20
Russia

CHAPTER 21
Ukraine, Belarus, and the Caucasus

Dancers in Russian national dress

St. Basil's Cathedral, Moscow, Russia

Church overlooking the Black Sea, Ukraine

448 ◆ Unit 5

USING THE ILLUSTRATIONS

Direct students' attention to the photographs on these pages. Point out that the bear is a symbol of Russia. Ask what other animal symbols students have seen and for which countries they stand. **(Possible answers: bald eagle—United States; kangaroo, koala—Australia; panda, dragon, tiger—China)** Ask why animal symbols seem to be popular. **(Possible answers: portray strength and power, not associated with any one ethnic group or political party, refer to the country's natural heritage)**

Refer to the photo of the Buryat people. Ask how they compare to the Russian citizens and politicians that are typically seen on news broadcasts. **(Possible answers: more colorful clothing, facial features similar to those of Chinese people)** Point out that the Buryat and some other ethnic groups in Russia have more in common with the peoples of Mongolia and China than they do with Russians who live in cities thousands of miles to the west.

Point out the domes on St. Basil's Cathedral in Moscow. Ask students to suggest why they are shaped like onions. **(so snow does not accumulate)** The cathedral was built in the 1550s to commemorate a major military victory.

448 Unit 5

Notes from the Field

Journalists in Russia

Journalists Gary Matoso and Lisa Dickey traveled more than 5,000 miles across Russia. They wrote this account of their visit with Buyanto Tsydypov. He is a Buryat farmer who lives in the Lake Baikal area. The Buryats are one of Russia's many minority ethnic groups. **WHAT DO YOU THINK?** If you visited a Buryat family, what would you like to see or ask?

"You came to us like thunder out of the clear blue sky," said our host. The surprise of our visit did not, however, keep him from greeting us warmly.

Buyanto brought us to a special place of prayer. High on a hillside, a yellow wooden frame holds a row of tall, narrow sticks. On the end of each stick, Buddhist prayer cloths flutter in the biting autumn wind.

In times of trouble and thanks, Buryats come to tie their prayer cloths—called *khimorin*—to the sticks and make their offerings to the gods. Buyanto builds a small fire. He unfolds an aqua-blue *khimorin* to show the drawings.

"All around are the Buddhist gods," he says, "and at the bottom we have written our names and the names of others we are praying for."

He fans the flames slowly with the cloth, purifying it with sacred smoke. After a time he moves to the top of the hill where he ties the *khimorin* to one of the sticks.

Buryat people, Lake Baikal area, Russia

Understanding Primary Sources

1. How do you know that Buyanto Tsydypov was surprised to meet the two American journalists?
2. What is a *khimorin*?

Brown bear

UNIT 5

MORE FROM THE FIELD

In the early 1930s the Soviets began enforcing a policy of state ownership of farmland. Harsh measures were used—land confiscations, arrests, and deportations to prison camps. Soviet farm policies resulted in a famine during 1932–33 in which millions of people died.

Since the fall of the Soviet Union, the Russian government has given land grants and tax breaks to private farmers. They decide for themselves what crops to plant and are not required to sell to state agencies. Buyanto Tsydypov, the Buryat farmer described on this page, is one such private farmer. Many people in his village admire his independence and determination.

Critical Thinking: What type of economic system did the Soviet Union have?

Answer: command

Understanding Primary Sources Answers

1. He compares their arrival to thunder out of a clear blue sky.
2. prayer cloth

CHAPTERS

20 Russia introduces the physical geography of the world's largest country along with the historical, economic, and political issues that face its people.

21 Ukraine, Belarus, and the Caucasus examines ways of life in the newly independent countries along Russia's western edge.

UNIT 5 ATLAS

PEOPLE IN THE PROFILE

Note that the elevation profile crosses the West Siberian Plain. The Khanty are one of the many indigenous groups that live in this region of subarctic forest and bogs. They have adapted to the harsh environment. Winters are very cold, and the summer skies are filled with mosquitoes.

The Khanty, who settle in extended family groups, live mainly by fishing, hunting, and reindeer herding. They make almost everything they use, including their shelters, fishing boats, winter clothing, and containers. Arts and crafts include colorful birchbark baskets.

Russia's oil wealth poses problems for the Khanty and other Siberian peoples. Oil spills and pollution threaten the wetlands. Raised roads trap water, causing floods and ruining the land's ability to function as pasture for reindeer. Fires caused by worker carelessness and oil-soaked debris are common. Acid rain has damaged huge areas of land. The Khanty have responded to these threats by organizing to protect their land and way of life from further decline.

Critical Thinking: To what harsh conditions have the Khanty adapted?

Answer: very cold winters, summer skies filled with mosquitoes

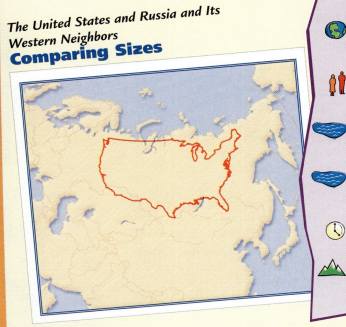

UNIT 5 ATLAS: The World in Spatial Terms

Russia and Its Western Neighbors

Elevation Profile

The United States and Russia and Its Western Neighbors Comparing Sizes

GEOSTATS: Russia

- **World's largest country in area:** 6,659,328 sq. mi. (17,075,200 sq km)
- **World's seventh-largest population:** 144,526,278 (July 2003 estimate)
- **World's largest lake:** Caspian Sea—143,244 sq. mi. (371,002 sq km)
- **World's deepest lake:** Lake Baikal—5,715 ft. (1,742 m)
- **Largest number of time zones:** 11
- **Highest mountain in Europe:** Mount Elbrus—18,510 ft. (5,642 m)

OVERVIEW

In this unit, students will learn about the land and people of Russia and its western neighbors—a vast region that is undergoing many political and economic changes.

Huge open plains and deep evergreen forests dominate Russia's landscape. The population is concentrated in the western plains, where the best farmland and the largest cities are located. Harsh climates keep Siberia and Russia's Far East thinly populated. Development of the region's rich resources may increase settlement there.

For most of the country's history, Russia's leaders have limited citizens' personal freedoms. During the more-than-70 years of communist rule, the Soviet Union became a superpower. Since the collapse of the Soviet Union, Russia has struggled with rising crime, corruption, and unemployment.

The other countries of the region were also part of the Soviet Union. They are now independent republics. Their economies are emerging, with varying degrees of success. Distinctive religious and ethnic groups live in the area.

Russia and Its Western Neighbors: Physical

UNIT 5 ATLAS

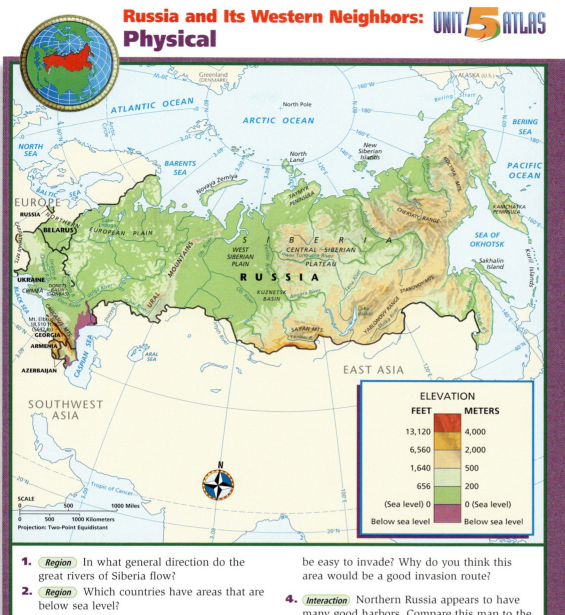

1. **Region** In what general direction do the great rivers of Siberia flow?
2. **Region** Which countries have areas that are below sea level?

Critical Thinking

3. **Movement** Russia has often been invaded by other countries. Which part of Russia might be easy to invade? Why do you think this area would be a good invasion route?
4. **Interaction** Northern Russia appears to have many good harbors. Compare this map to the **climate map** of the region. Why have few harbors been developed on Russia's north coast?

internet connect

ONLINE ATLAS
GO TO: go.hrw.com
KEYWORD: SJ5 MapsU5
FOR: Web links to online maps of the region

Physical Map
Answers
1. north
2. Azerbaijan and Russia

Critical Thinking
3. western Russia; because it is an open plain
4. because the water there is frozen much of the year

USING THE PHYSICAL MAP

Focus students' attention on the **physical map** of Russia and its western neighbors on this page. What is the first thing that students notice about Russia? (Many students will note its large size.) Challenge students to estimate the distance between Russia's eastern and western borders. (about 6,000 miles or 9,650 km) Note that the Northern European Plain is a physical feature of western Russia and that the eastern portion of the country is called Siberia. Ask students what physical feature appears to separate European Russia from Siberia. (Ural Mountains)

UNIT 5 ATLAS

Your Classroom Time Line

These are the major dates and time periods for this unit. Have students enter them on the time line you created earlier. You may want to watch for these dates as students progress through the unit.

600s B.C. Greeks establish trading colonies along the Black Sea.

500s B.C. The Persian Empire controls the Caucasus.

A.D. 400 The Georgian language has its own alphabet by this date.

800s The Rus establish Kiev as their capital.

1200s Tatars sweep across the steppes.

ONLINE ATLAS
GO TO: go.hrw.com
KEYWORD: SJ5 MapsU5
FOR: Web links to online maps of the region

Political Map
Answers
1. Ural Mountains
2. Vladivostok

Critical Thinking
3. less than 100 mi. (161 km); about 780 mi. (1,255 km)
4. yes, because the lines are irregular, not straight

Russia and Its Western Neighbors: Political

UNIT 5 ATLAS

1. **Region** Compare this map to the **physical map** of the region. What physical feature seems to define a border between Russia and the countries of Europe?

2. **Location** What is the southernmost Russian city shown on the map?

Critical Thinking

3. **Location** About how far apart are Russia and the Alaskan mainland? the Russian mainland and the North Pole?

4. **Region** Do Russia's western and southern borders appear to follow natural boundaries? Why or why not?

452 • Unit 5

USING THE POLITICAL MAP

Refer students to the **political map** of Russia and its western neighbors on this page. Tell the class that all the countries represented in color on the map used to be part of the Soviet Union, but that the Soviet Union broke up in 1991. New independent countries emerged. Ask students to use the **physical** and **land use** and **resources maps** to predict how the breakup of the Soviet Union may have affected Russia's economy and transportation links. (lost access to valuable mineral and energy resources, reduced access to the Caspian and Black Seas)

Russia and Its Western Neighbors: Climate

UNIT 5 ATLAS

1. **Region** Which climate types stretch across Russia from Europe to the Pacific?
2. **Region** Compare this map to the **political map**. Which country has only a humid continental climate?
3. **Region** Which climate region in Russia is the smallest?

Critical Thinking
4. **Region** Compare this map to the **physical map**. Why do you think Siberia has so few climate types?
5. **Interaction** Compare this map to the **land use and resources map**. What is one reason why most commercial farming is in Russia's western region?

Your Classroom Time Line, (continued)

late 1400s Muscovy wins control over parts of Russia from the Mongols.

late 1400s The Kremlin's red brick walls and towers are built.

1547 Ivan IV crowns himself czar of all Russia.

early 1700s Peter the Great expands the Russian Empire.

1700s Russian fur traders establish settlements along North America's Pacific coast.

late 1800s The Russian Empire begins to decline.

1867 Russia sells Alaska to the United States.

1891 Construction of the Trans-Siberian Railroad begins.

1893 Composer Peter Tchaikovsky dies.

Climate Map
Answers
1. tundra and subarctic
2. Belarus
3. Mediterranean

Critical Thinking
4. northern latitude, lack of mountains, large land mass, and distance from the sea
5. ample rains in the humid continental climate region

USING THE CLIMATE MAP

Have students examine the **climate map** of Russia and its western neighbors on this page. Ask them to name the climates of the largest areas of Russia. (subarctic, tundra) Have them compare the climate map to the **population map** on the next page. Ask students to answer the following questions: In which climate region is the population density highest? (humid continental) In what three types of climate is the population density lowest? (tundra, subarctic, desert)

UNIT 5 ATLAS

Your Classroom Time Line, (continued)

1917 Czar Nicholas II abdicates his throne.

1917 The Russian Revolution begins.

1918 Writer Aleksandr Solzhenitsyn is born.

1922 The Soviet Union is established.

1922 Georgia, Armenia, and Azerbaijan unite to oppose Soviet rule.

1939–45 World War II is fought.

late 1940s The Cold War begins.

1957 The Soviets launch Sputnik.

internet connect

ONLINE ATLAS
GO TO: go.hrw.com
KEYWORD: SJ5 MapsU5
FOR: Web links to online maps of the region

Population Map
Answers
1. Russia, Ukraine
2. Russia

Critical Thinking
3. that the land is fairly flat and that farming is common in western Russia
4. presence of the Caucasus Mountains

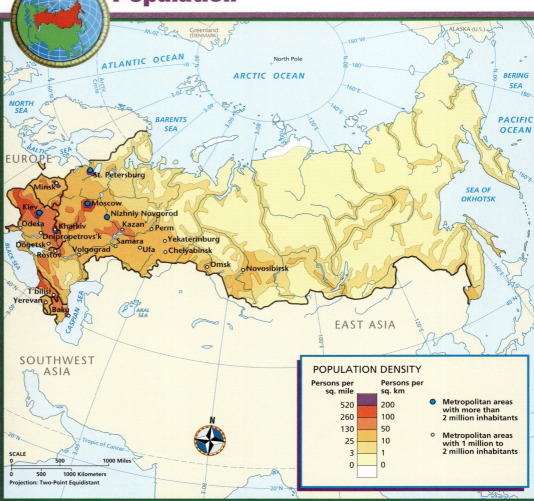

Russia and Its Western Neighbors: Population

1. **Region** Which countries have a large area with more than 260 people per square mile and cities of more than 2 million people?

2. **Region** Which country has areas in the north where no one lives?

Critical Thinking

3. **Interaction** What can you assume about landforms and farming in western Russia, Ukraine, and Belarus just by looking at the **population map**? Check the **physical** and **land use and resources maps** to be sure.

4. **Interaction** Compare this map to the **physical map**. What is one reason why the area between the Black Sea and Caspian Sea has few big cities?

454 • Unit 5

USING THE POPULATION MAP

Direct your students' attention to the **population map** on this page. Ask them to write a question, with answer, about the population patterns they see on the map. (Possible answer: Most people live in the western part of the region; the eastern part is sparsely populated.) Have students exchange their questions with another student and then answer the exchanged questions. Then ask students to suggest reasons for the patterns of population density. They may consult the **climate map** for assistance.

454 Unit 5

Russia and Its Western Neighbors: Land Use and Resources

UNIT 5 ATLAS

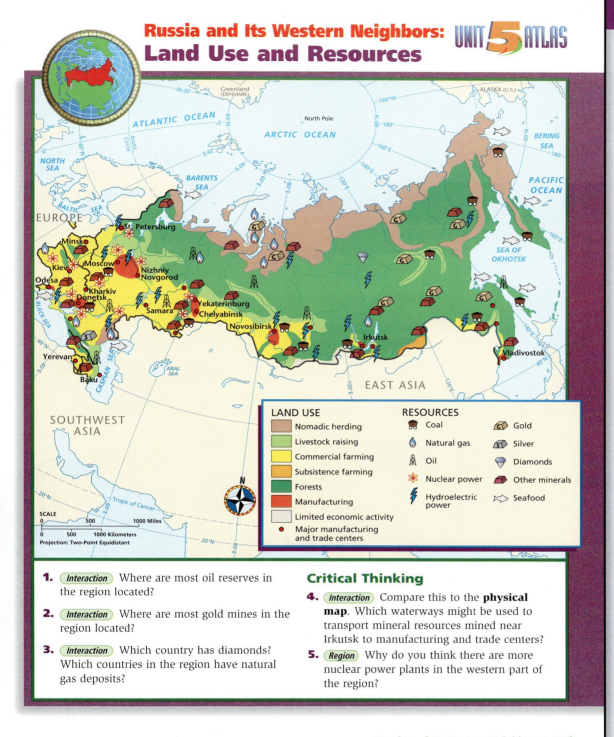

LAND USE
- Nomadic herding
- Livestock raising
- Commercial farming
- Subsistence farming
- Forests
- Manufacturing
- Limited economic activity
- ● Major manufacturing and trade centers

RESOURCES
- Coal
- Natural gas
- Oil
- Nuclear power
- Hydroelectric power
- Gold
- Silver
- Diamonds
- Other minerals
- Seafood

1. **Interaction** Where are most oil reserves in the region located?
2. **Interaction** Where are most gold mines in the region located?
3. **Interaction** Which country has diamonds? Which countries in the region have natural gas deposits?

Critical Thinking
4. **Interaction** Compare this to the **physical map**. Which waterways might be used to transport mineral resources mined near Irkutsk to manufacturing and trade centers?
5. **Region** Why do you think there are more nuclear power plants in the western part of the region?

Russia and Its Western Neighbors • 455

UNIT 5 ATLAS

Your Classroom Time Line, (continued)

1986 The Chernobyl nuclear reactor disaster occurs.

1989 The Baikal–Amur Mainline (BAM) railway is completed.

1991 The Soviet Union collapses.

1990s Many civil wars erupt in the former Soviet republics.

1995 In the Russian Far East, an earthquake causes severe damage on Sakhalin Island.

2002 Chechen rebels hold some 800 hostages in a Moscow theater, and more than 100 hostages die during rescue attempt.

2004 Republic of Georgia stages peaceful revolution.

Land Use and Resources Map
Answers
1. in the Caspian Sea area and in Siberia
2. eastern Siberia
3. Russia; Russia and Ukraine

Critical Thinking
4. Angara River and Lake Baikal
5. Large population and manufacturing centers there require large amounts of power.

USING THE LAND USE AND RESOURCES MAP

Direct students' attention to the **land use and resources map** on this page. Then have them compare it to the **population map**. Ask: What area is rich in natural resources but sparsely populated? (Siberia) Challenge students to use information from this and the other maps to suggest why Russia may have trouble making use of Siberia's resources. (Possible answers: vast distance from population centers, difficulties in transporting goods across the region)

Russia and Its Western Neighbors 455

FAST FACTS

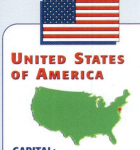

UNITED STATES OF AMERICA

CAPITAL:
Washington, D.C.
AREA:
3,717,792 sq. mi. (9,629,091 sq km)
POPULATION:
290,342,554
MONEY:
U.S. dollar
LANGUAGES:
English, Spanish (spoken by a large minority)
UNEMPLOYMENT:
5.8 percent

Fast Facts: Russia and Its Western Neighbors

ARMENIA
CAPITAL: Yerevan
AREA: 11,506 sq. mi. (29,800 sq km)
POPULATION: 3,326,448
MONEY: dram
LANGUAGES: Armenian, Russian
UNEMPLOYMENT: 20 percent

BELARUS
CAPITAL: Minsk
AREA: 80,154 sq. mi. (207,600 sq km)
POPULATION: 10,322,151
MONEY: Belarusian rubel
LANGUAGES: Byelorussian, Russian
UNEMPLOYMENT: 2.1 percent (and many underemployed workers)

AZERBAIJAN
CAPITAL: Baku
AREA: 33,436 sq. mi. (86,600 sq km)
POPULATION: 7,830,764
MONEY: manat
LANGUAGES: Azeri, Russian, Armenian
UNEMPLOYMENT: 16 percent

GEORGIA
CAPITAL: T'bilisi
AREA: 26,911 sq. mi. (69,700 sq km)
POPULATION: 4,934,413
MONEY: lari
LANGUAGES: Georgian (official), Russian, Armenian, Azeri
UNEMPLOYMENT: 17 percent

Family eating breakfast in Georgia

Geese flock to this pasture in Ukraine

Countries not drawn to scale.

FAST FACTS ACTIVITIES

LEVEL 1: (Suggested time: 25 min.) Explain that the unemployment rate shows the percentage of people who could work but cannot find a job. The U.S. unemployment rate of 5.8 percent meant that 5.8 percent of the people who were of age to work—that is, older than 16 and younger than 64—and could work did not have jobs when the data was collected.

Have students create a two-column chart with these headings: Less than 10 percent unemployment and More than 10 percent unemployment. Ask students to place each of the unit's countries in the correct column.

LEVEL 2: (Suggested time: 30 min.) After the collapse of the Soviet Union, many of its former member countries were left with unstable economies and high unemployment and underemployment rates. To demonstrate a 20 percent unemployment rate, have students compute 20 percent of the class. (Multiply the total number of students by 0.2.) Have 20 percent of the class stand on one side of the room while the remaining students stand on the other.

Define the term "underemployment." (Underemployed workers can only find jobs that require less skill than they have, or pay less money than their skills are generally worth, or both.) Separate out another 20 percent from the employed group of students to represent the underemployed.

UNIT 5 ATLAS

RUSSIA
CAPITAL: Moscow
AREA: 6,592,735 sq. mi. (17,075,200 sq km)
POPULATION: 144,526,278
MONEY: Russian ruble
LANGUAGES: Russian
UNEMPLOYMENT: 7.9 percent (and many underemployed workers)

UKRAINE
CAPITAL: Kiev
AREA: 233,089 sq. mi. (603,700 sq km)
POPULATION: 48,055,439
MONEY: hryvna
LANGUAGES: Ukranian, Russian, Romanian, Polish, Hungarian
UNEMPLOYMENT: 3.8 percent officially registered (and many unregistered or underemployed)

Church of the Transfiguration, Kizhi Island, Russia

Russian ballet dancers

Sources: Central Intelligence Agency, *The World Factbook 2003*; *The World Almanac and Book of Facts 2003*; pop. figures are 2003 estimates.

internet connect
COUNTRY STATISTICS
GO TO: go.hrw.com
KEYWORD: SJ5 FactsU5
FOR: more facts about Russia and its western neighbors

FAST FACTS

UNIT 5 ASSESSMENT RESOURCES

Reproducible
- Unit 5 Test
- Unit 5 Test for English Language Learners and Special-Needs Students

internet connect
COUNTRY STATISTICS
GO TO: go.hrw.com
KEYWORD: SJ5 MapsU5

Highlights of Country Statistics
- *CIA World Factbook*
- Library of Congress country studies
- Flags of the world

Ask: Why might a country have a high rate of underemployment? (Workers are likely to accept any job available, whether or not it meets their skill level or salary needs.) When students have sat down, have them summarize their observations.

LEVEL 3: (Suggested time: 45 min.) Explain to students that during the Soviet era, the economies of the areas under Soviet control were closely interconnected. When the Soviet Union broke up, many countries did not have enough resources to sustain their populations independently. Have students use the **land use and resources map** to make connections between resources and unemployment rates.

Organize the class into small groups. Have each group brainstorm and create a list of possible solutions to the problems of unemployment and underemployment in the independent republics. Then have each group present its list of solutions to the class.

CHAPTER 20: Russia
Chapter Resource Manager

Objectives	Pacing Guide	Reproducible Resources
SECTION 1		
Physical Geography (pp. 459–62) 1. Identify the physical features of Russia. 2. Identify the climates and vegetation found in Russia. 3. Describe the natural resources of Russia.	**Regular** .5 day Lecture Notes, Section 1 **Block Scheduling** .5 day Block Scheduling Handbook, Chapter 20	**RS** Know It Notes S1 **E** Creative Strategies for Teaching World Geography, Lessons 12 and 13 **ELL** Main Idea Activity S1
SECTION 2		
History and Culture (pp. 463–68) 1. Describe Russia's early history. 2. Describe how the Russian empire grew and then fell. 3. Describe the former Soviet Union. 4. Describe what Russia is like today.	**Regular** 2 days Lecture Notes, Section 2 **Block Scheduling** .5 day Block Scheduling Handbook, Chapter 20	**RS** Know It Notes S2 **RS** Graphic Organizer 20 **E** Cultures of the World Activity 4 **SM** Geography for Life Activity **IC** Interdisciplinary Activities for Middle Grades 17, 18, 20 **SM** Map Activity 20 **E** Biography Activity: Vladimir Lenin, Leo Tolstoy **ELL** Main Idea Activity S2
SECTION 3		
The Russian Heartland (pp. 469–71) 1. Describe why European Russia is considered the country's heartland. 2. Identify the characteristics of the four major regions of European Russia.	**Regular** 1 day Lecture Notes, Section 3 **Block Scheduling** .5 day Block Scheduling Handbook, Chapter 20	**RS** Know It Notes S3 **ELL** Main Idea Activity S3
SECTION 4		
Siberia (pp. 472–74) 1. Describe the human geography of Siberia. 2. Identify the economic features of the region. 3. Describe how Lake Baikal has been threatened by pollution.	**Regular** 1 day Lecture Notes, Section 4 **Block Scheduling** .5 day Block Scheduling Handbook, Chapter 20	**RS** Know It Notes S4 **ELL** Main Idea Activity S4
SECTION 5		
The Russian Far East (pp. 475–77) 1. Describe how the Russian Far East's climate affects agriculture in the region. 2. Identify the major resources and cities of the region. 3. Identify the island regions that are part of the Russian Far East.	**Regular** 1 day Lecture Notes, Section 5 **Block Scheduling** .5 day Block Scheduling Handbook, Chapter 20	**RS** Know It Notes S5 **ELL** Main Idea Activity S5

Chapter Resource Key

- **RS** Reading Support
- **IC** Interdisciplinary Connections
- **E** Enrichment
- **SM** Skills Mastery
- **A** Assessment
- **REV** Review
- **ELL** Reinforcement and English Language Learners and English for Speakers of Other Languages (ESOL)
- Transparencies
- CD–ROM
- Music
- Video
- Internet
- Holt Presentation Maker Using Microsoft® PowerPoint®

One-Stop Planner CD–ROM

See the *One-Stop Planner* for a complete list of additional resources for students and teachers.

One-Stop Planner CD–ROM

It's easy to plan lessons, select resources, and print out materials for your students when you use the *One-Stop Planner CD–ROM with Test Generator*.

Technology Resources

- One-Stop Planner CD–ROM, Lesson 20.1
- Geography and Cultures Visual Resources with Teaching Activities 31–36
- *ARGWorld* CD–ROM
- Homework Practice Online
- HRW Go site

- One-Stop Planner CD–ROM, Lesson 20.2
- *ARGWorld* CD–ROM
- Homework Practice Online
- HRW Go site

- One-Stop Planner CD–ROM, Lesson 20.3
- *ARGWorld* CD–ROM
- Homework Practice Online
- HRW Go site

- One-Stop Planner CD–ROM, Lesson 20.4
- *ARGWorld* CD–ROM
- Homework Practice Online
- HRW Go site

- One-Stop Planner CD–ROM, Lesson 20.5
- Geography and Cultures Visual Resources with Teaching Activities 24–29
- *ARGWorld* CD–ROM
- Homework Practice Online
- HRW Go site

Review, Reinforcement, and Assessment Resources

ELL	Main Idea Activity S1
REV	Section 1 Review
A	Daily Quiz 20.1
REV	Chapter Summaries and Review
ELL	English Audio Summary 20.1
ELL	Spanish Audio Summary 20.1

ELL	Main Idea Activity S2
REV	Section 2 Review
A	Daily Quiz 20.2
REV	Chapter Summaries and Review
ELL	English Audio Summary 20.2
ELL	Spanish Audio Summary 20.2

ELL	Main Idea Activity S3
REV	Section 3 Review
A	Daily Quiz 20.3
REV	Chapter Summaries and Review
ELL	English Audio Summary 20.3
ELL	Spanish Audio Summary 20.3

ELL	Main Idea Activity S4
REV	Section 4 Review
A	Daily Quiz 20.4
REV	Chapter Summaries and Review
ELL	English Audio Summary 20.4
ELL	Spanish Audio Summary 20.4

ELL	Main Idea Activity S5
REV	Section 5 Review
A	Daily Quiz 20.5
REV	Chapter Summaries and Review
ELL	English Audio Summary 20.5
ELL	Spanish Audio Summary 20.5

internet connect

HRW ONLINE RESOURCES

GO TO: go.hrw.com
Then type in a keyword.

TEACHER HOME PAGE
KEYWORD: SJ5 TEACHER

CHAPTER INTERNET ACTIVITIES
KEYWORD: SJ5 GT20

Choose an activity to:
- take a trip on the Trans-Siberian Railroad.
- examine the breakup of the Soviet Union.
- view the cultural treasures of Russia.

CHAPTER ENRICHMENT LINKS
KEYWORD: SJ5 CH20

CHAPTER MAPS
KEYWORD: SJ5 MAPS20

ONLINE ASSESSMENT
Homework Practice
KEYWORD: SJ5 HP20
Standardized Test Prep Online
KEYWORD: SJ5 STP20
Rubrics
KEYWORD: SS Rubrics

COUNTRY INFORMATION
KEYWORD: SJ5 Almanac

CONTENT UPDATES
KEYWORD: SS Content Updates

HOLT PRESENTATION MAKER
KEYWORD: SJ5 PPT20

ONLINE READING SUPPORT
KEYWORD: SS Strategies

CURRENT EVENTS
KEYWORD: S5 Current Events

Meeting Individual Needs

Ability Levels

Level 1 Basic-level activities designed for all students encountering new material

Level 2 Intermediate-level activities designed for average students

Level 3 Challenging activities designed for honors and gifted-and-talented students

ESOL Activities that address the needs of students with Limited English Proficiency

Chapter Review and Assessment

E	Readings in World Geography, History, and Culture 40, 41, 42		Chapter 20 Test Generator (on the One-Stop Planner)
SM	Critical Thinking Activity 20		Audio CD Program, Chapter 20
REV	Chapter 20 Review and Practice	A	Chapter 20 Test for English Language Learners and Special-Needs Students
REV	Chapter Summaries and Review		
ELL	Vocabulary Activity 20		HRW Go site
A	Chapter 20 Test		

CHAPTER 20

Russia
Previewing Chapter Resources

Holt Online Learning

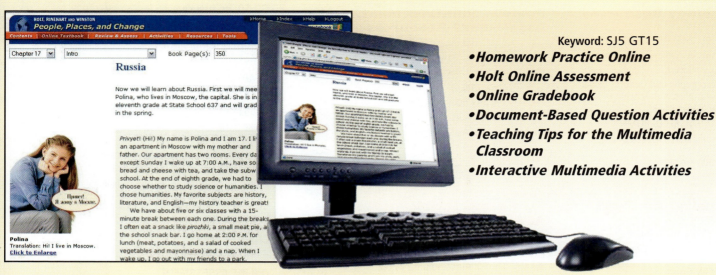

Keyword: SJ5 GT15

- Homework Practice Online
- Holt Online Assessment
- Online Gradebook
- Document-Based Question Activities
- Teaching Tips for the Multimedia Classroom
- Interactive Multimedia Activities

Differentiating Instruction

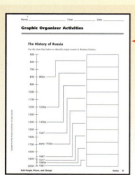

Reading and Writing Support
- ◀ Graphic Organizer Activity
- Vocabulary Activity
- Chapter Summary and Review
- Know It Notes
- Audio CD

Active Learning
- Block Scheduling Handbook
- Cultures of the World Activity
- Interdisciplinary Activity
- Map Activity
- ◀ Critical Thinking Activity: A Russian Space Mystery

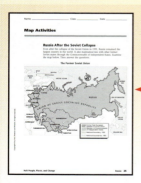

Primary Sources and Advanced Learners
- Geography for Life Activity: The Soviet "Game of the Name"
- ◀ Map Activity: Russia After the Soviet Collapse
- Readings in World Geography, History and Culture:
  - 40 A Russian Student
  - 41 Moscow
  - 42 Russia in Transition

Assessment Program
- ◀ Daily Quizzes S1–5
- Chapter Test
- Chapter Test for English Language Learners and Special-Needs Students

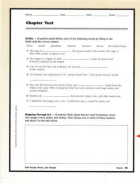

Spanish and ESOL
- Vocabulary Activity
- Main Idea Activities for English Language Learners and Special-Needs Students
- Chapter Summary and Review
- Spanish Audio Summary
- Know It Notes S1–5
- ◀ Chapter Test for English Language Learners and Special-Needs Students

Special Education Modifications
Your **I.D.E.A. Works! CD-ROM** will provide modified versions of the following teaching materials:
- ◀ Guided Reading Strategies S1–5
- Vocabulary Activity
- Main Idea Activities S1–5
- Daily Quizzes S1–5
- Chapter 20 Test
- Flash cards of chapter vocabulary terms

Teacher Resources

Books for Teachers

Barker, Hazel. *Russia and Central Asia by Road: 4WD, Motorbike, Bicycle.* Globe Pequot, 1997.

Montaigne, Fen. *Reeling in Russia.* St. Martin's Press, 1998.

Tayler, Jeffrey. *Siberian Dawn: A Journey across the New Russia.* Hungry Mind Press, 1999.

Books for Students

Sallnow, John. *Russia,* Country Fact Files. Raintree/Steck-Vaughn, 1997. Wide range of basic facts.

Haskins, Jim. *Count Your Way through Russia.* Carolrhoda Books, 1987. Uses Russian numbers to introduce concepts about culture. **SHELTERED ENGLISH**

Otfinoski, Steven. *Boris Yeltsin and the Rebirth of Russia.* Millbrook Press, 1995. Biography of Yeltsin interwoven with recent Russian history.

Stanley, Diane. *Peter the Great.* Morrow Junior Books. 1999. Focuses on the czar's efforts to modernize Russia.

Multimedia Materials

A Journey across Russia. Video, 25 min. Educational Video Network.

A Week in the Life of a Russian Student. Video, 20 min. AIMS Media.

Trans-Siberian Railroad. CD–ROM. Softkey.

Videos and CDs

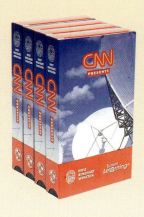

Videos
- CNN *Presents Geography: Yesterday and Today,* Segment 18 Lake Baykal
- CNN *Presents Geography: Yesterday and Today,* Segments 16, 23, and 25
- ARG World

Holt Researcher
http://researcher.hrw.com

- *Gorbachev, Mikhail*
- *Khrushchev, Nikita Sergeyevich*
- *Lenin, Vladimir I.*
- *Russian Expansion*
- *Russia*
- *Russian Expansion*

Transparency Packages

Graphic Organizer Transparencies 20.1–5

Geography and Cultures Visual Resources Transparencies 56–60
61 Russia: Physical-Political
62 History of Russian Expansion
63 Peter I at the Founding of St. Petersburg

Map Activities Transparency 20 Russia After the Soviet Collapse

457D

CHAPTER 20

Why It Matters

You may wish to highlight to students these reasons why we should know more about Russia:

- Russia occupies more land area than any other country on Earth. It also has one of the largest populations.
- For many years, the Soviet Union and the United States were enemies. Now connections between the countries are increasing.
- As one of the few countries with nuclear weapons, Russia could pose a threat to U.S. national security.
- Russia continues to struggle with economic, environmental, and political problems that can affect people everywhere.

CHAPTER 20

Russia

Now we will learn about Russia. First we will meet Polina, who lives in Moscow, the capital. She is in the eleventh grade at State School 637 and will graduate in the spring.

Privyet! (Hi!) My name is Polina and I am 17. I live in an apartment in Moscow with my mother and father. Our apartment has two rooms. Every day except Sunday I wake up at 7:00 A.M., have some bread and cheese with tea, and take the subway to school. At the end of eighth grade, we had to choose whether to study science or humanities. I chose humanities. My favorite subjects are history, literature, and English—my history teacher is great!

We have about five or six classes with a 15-minute break between each one. During the breaks, I often eat a snack like *pirozhki*, a small meat pie, at the school snack bar. I go home at 2:00 P.M. for lunch (meat, potatoes, and a salad of cooked vegetables and mayonnaise) and a nap. When I wake up, I go out with my friends to a park. Sometimes my parents and I join my uncle, aunt, and grandmother for Sunday dinner. My uncle makes my favorite dishes, like meat salad with mayonnaise. I love ice cream, too!

Привет! Я живу в Москве.

Translation: Hi! I live in Moscow.

Chapter Project

Have students create a "family tree" of important rulers and leaders of Russia and the Soviet Union. Some of the most significant are Rurik, Ivan I, Peter the Great, Catherine the Great, Nicholas II, Vladimir Lenin, Joseph Stalin, Nikita Khrushchev, Mikhail Gorbachev, and Boris Yeltsin. Students should use biographies to research each person then summarize how he or she affected Russian or Soviet history and culture.

Starting the Chapter

Tell students that Russia occupies more land area than any other country in the world. Then ask them to consider the advantages and disadvantages of such enormous size. (Students may mention as advantages the possibility of many natural resources and access to trade with many other countries. Disadvantages may include difficulties in communication, defense, distribution of goods and services, and maintaining a sense of unity.)

Section 1: Physical Geography

CHAPTER 20, Section 1

Read to Discover
1. What are the physical features of Russia?
2. What climates and vegetation are found in Russia?
3. What natural resources does Russia have?

Vocabulary
taiga
steppe

Places
Arctic Ocean
Caucasus Mountains
Caspian Sea
Ural Mountains
West Siberian Plain
Central Siberian Plateau
Kamchatka Peninsula
Kuril Islands
Volga River
Baltic Sea

Reading Strategy

USING VISUAL INFORMATION Look at the map below. Why do you think the Trans-Siberian Railroad is shown on the map? Why do you think it was built? Would it have been difficult to build? Write down your answers. As you read, write down facts that support or disprove your statements.

Russia: Physical-Political

Section 1 Resources

Reproducible
- Lecture Notes, Section 1
- Block Scheduling Handbook, Chapter 20
- Know It Notes S1
- Creative Strategies for Teaching World Geography, Lessons 12 and 13

Technology
- One-Stop Planner CD–ROM, Lesson 20.1
- Homework Practice Online
- Geography and Cultures Visual Resources with Teaching Activities 56–63
- HRW Go site

Reinforcement, Review, and Assessment
- Section 1 Review
- Daily Quiz 20.1
- Main Idea Activity S1
- Chapter Summaries and Review
- English Audio Summary 20.1
- Spanish Audio Summary 20.1

Section 1

Objectives
1. Identify the physical features of Russia.
2. Name the climates and vegetation that are found in Russia.
3. List Russia's natural resources.

Focus

Bellringer

Copy the following instructions onto the chalkboard: *Look at the physical-political map of Russia in your textbook. Choose a place on the map and write a sentence describing what you think that place might look like.* Discuss student responses in terms of the landscapes found across Russia. Tell students that in Section 1 they will learn more about the physical geography of Russia.

Using the Physical-Political Map

Have students examine the map on this page. Call on students to describe the general physical characteristics of Russia. **(more mountains in eastern half, flat lowlands, long rivers, one large lake)** Ask if they are already familiar with any of the features on the map. **(Possible answers: Moscow, Siberia, Arctic Circle, Arctic Ocean)** Ask students to predict the general climate of Russia. **(cold)**

Russia • 459

CHAPTER 20, Section 1

EYE ON EARTH

The Caspian Sea, Long Ago
The Caspian Sea is the world's largest lake. Stretching 746 miles (1,200 km) long and 270 miles (434 km) wide, the Caspian Sea covers an area of about 143,550 square miles (371,795 sq km). Scientific studies have shown that until recent times, geologically speaking, the Caspian Sea was linked to the Atlantic Ocean through the Sea of Azov, the Black Sea, and the Mediterranean Sea.

Activity: Have students use the physical-political map to find which bodies of water once connected the Caspian Sea to the Atlantic Ocean.

GO TO: go.hrw.com
KEYWORD: SJ5 CH20
FOR: Web sites about the Caspian Sea

Visual Record Answer
that Siberia has a cold climate and rugged mountains

Physical Features

Russia was by far the largest republic of what was called the Union of Soviet Socialist Republics, or the Soviet Union. Russia is the largest country in the world. It stretches 6,000 miles (9,654 km), from Eastern Europe to the Bering Sea and Pacific Ocean.

The Land Much of western, or European, Russia is part of the Northern European Plain. This is the country's heartland, where most Russians live. To the north are the Barents Sea and the Arctic Ocean. Far to the south are the Caucasus (KAW-kuh-suhs) Mountains. There Europe's highest peak, Mount Elbrus, rises to 18,510 feet (5,642 m). The Caucasus Mountains stretch from the Black Sea to the Caspian (KAS-pee-uhn) Sea. The Caspian is the largest inland body of water in the world.

East of the Northern European Plain is a long range of eroded low mountains and hills. These are called the Ural (YOOHR-uhl) Mountains. The Urals divide Europe from Asia. They stretch from the Arctic coast in the north to Kazakhstan in the south. The highest peak in the Urals rises to just 6,214 feet (1,894 m).

East of the Urals lies a vast region known as Siberia. Much of Siberia is divided between the West Siberian Plain and the Central Siberian Plateau. The West Siberian Plain is a large, flat area with many marshes. The Central Siberian Plateau lies to the east. It is a land of elevated plains and valleys.

A series of high mountain ranges runs through southern and eastern Siberia. The Kamchatka (kuhm-CHAHT-kuh) Peninsula, Sakhalin (sah-kah-LEEN) Island, and the Kuril (KYOOHR-eel) Islands surround the Sea of Okhotsk (uh-KAWTSK). These are in the Russian Far East. The rugged Kamchatka Peninsula and the Kurils have active volcanoes. Earthquakes and volcanic eruptions are common. The Kurils separate the Sea of Okhotsk from the Pacific Ocean.

Rivers Some of the world's longest rivers flow through Russia. These include the Volga (VAHL-guh) and Don Rivers in European Russia. The Ob (AWB), Yenisey (yi-ni-SAY), Lena (LEE-nuh), and Amur (ah-MOOHR) Rivers are located in Siberia and the Russian Far East. The Amur forms part of Russia's border with China.

The Volga is Europe's longest river. Its course and length make it an important transportation route. It flows southward for 2,293 miles (3,689 km) across the Northern European Plain to the Caspian Sea. Barges can travel by canal from the Volga to the Don River. The Don empties into the Black Sea. Canals also connect the Volga to rivers that drain into the Baltic Sea far to the northwest.

In Siberia, the Ob, Yenisey, and Lena Rivers all flow thousands of miles northward. Eventually, they reach Russia's Arctic coast. These and other Siberian rivers that drain into the Arctic Ocean freeze in winter. In spring, these rivers thaw first in the south. Downstream in

▲ A train chugs through the cold Siberian countryside.

Interpreting the Visual Record (Place)
What does this photograph tell you about the physical features and climate of Siberia?

The coldest temperature ever recorded outside of Antarctica in the last 100 years was noted on February 6, 1933, in eastern Siberia: –90° F (–68°C).

460 • Chapter 20

TEACH

Teaching Objectives 1–3
LEVEL 1: (Suggested time: 15 min.) Copy the following graphic organizer onto the chalkboard, omitting the blue answers. Call on volunteers to fill in the circle's quarters with Russia's major landforms, rivers, climate and vegetation types, and natural resources. ESOL, **LS** VISUAL-SPATIAL

460 Chapter 20

the north, however, the rivers remain frozen much longer. As a result, ice jams there block water from the melting ice and snow. This causes annual floods in areas along the rivers.

✓ **READING CHECK:** *Places and Regions* What are the major physical features of Russia? *Northern European Plain, Caucasus Mountains, Caspian Sea, Ural Mountains, Siberia, Kamchatka Peninsula, Sakhalin Island, Kuril Islands, several long rivers, including the Volga*

Climate and Vegetation

Nearly all of Russia is located at high northern latitudes. The country has tundra, subarctic, humid continental, and steppe climates. Because there are no high mountain barriers, cold Arctic winds sweep across much of the country in winter. Winters are long and cold. Ice blocks most seaports until spring. However, the winters are surprisingly dry in much of Russia. This is because the interior is far from ocean moisture.

Winters are particularly severe throughout Siberia. Temperatures often drop below –40°F (–40°C). Although they are short, Siberian summers can be hot. Temperatures can rise to 100°F (38°C).

Vegetation varies with climates from north to south. Very cold temperatures and permafrost in the far north keep trees from taking root. Mosses, wildflowers, and other tundra vegetation grow there.

The vast **taiga** (TY-guh), a forest of mostly evergreen trees, grows south of the tundra. The trees there include spruce, fir, and pine. In European Russia and in the Far East are deciduous forests. Many temperate forests in European Russia have been cleared for farms and cities.

Wide grasslands known as the **steppe** (STEP) stretch from Ukraine across southern Russia to Kazakhstan. Much of the steppe is used for growing crops and grazing livestock.

✓ **READING CHECK:** *Physical Systems* How does Russia's location affect its climate?
Arctic winds blow, creating winters that are very cold.

FOCUS ON CULTURE

A Wooden World

One of Russia's main resources, its huge forests, have affected many aspects of daily life. For centuries, the people of northern Russia have made things they needed from wood—from roads to houses to toys.

Snow and mud make travel difficult. Long ago, Russians learned to "pave" roads by laying logs side by side on the ground. These are called corduroy roads, after the ribbed fabric.

Most early houses of Siberia were made of whole logs fitted together without nails. They were similar to the log cabins of the American frontier. Finely cut carvings decorated the houses' windows. Inside, the furni-

ture, shelves, kitchen utensils, and toys were all handmade from wood. Today, several outdoor museums preserve Russia's heritage of wooden architecture.

Human-Environment Interaction How have local resources shaped your community's architecture?

CHAPTER 20, Section 1

National Geography Standard 8

The Tundra Ecosystem

Tundra plants are well adapted to Russia's harsh climate. Vegetation in Russia's tundra climate is limited to lichens and mosses, small shrubs, and grasses. Most plants grow low to the ground to reduce the effects of cold and wind, but may have massive root systems to store nutrients. Other plants have waxy or hairy surfaces that protect them from freezing winds.

Critical Thinking: What adaptations may humans make to survive cold environments like the tundra? How would the adaptations made by humans compare to those made by plants?

Answer: Students may mention that like plants, humans cover themselves with insulating materials, try to keep abundant supplies of food, and try to minimize exposure to wind and cold.

◀ **Focus on Culture Answer**
Answers will vary, depending on communities and resources.

LEVEL 2: (Suggested time: 20 min.) Ask students to imagine that they are taking part in a summer camp exchange program in Russia. First, students should choose a rural area where their camp is located. Then tell students to write a letter home to their families. They should describe the land, weather conditions, vegetation, and the outdoor recreational activities they are enjoying. Students should also mention some of the natural resources that are located near their camp. **LS INTRAPERSONAL**

LEVEL 3: (Suggested time: 20 min.) Have students write an outline for a documentary film script about the physical geography of Russia. Outlines should indicate the various physical features, climates, vegetation types, and resources found in Russia. Ask students to write descriptions of the scenes that the film would include. **LS VISUAL-SPATIAL**

Section 1 Review

Answers to Section 1 Review

Define For definitions, see the glossary.

Working with Sketch Maps Maps will vary, but listed places should be labeled accurately.

Reading for the Main Idea
1. the Ural Mountains (NGS 4)
2. by canals to the Don and other rivers that empty into Baltic and Black Seas (NGS 4)
3. severe, with temperatures as low as −40°F (−40°C), and surprisingly dry; answers will vary, but students might mention various human adaptations to the cold, such as more indoor activities. (NGS 15)

Critical Thinking
4. by providing Russia with materials to export as well as limiting its need for imported goods

Organizing What You Know
5. climates—tundra, subarctic, humid continental, and steppe; vegetation—mosses, wildflowers, tundra vegetation, evergreen trees, deciduous forests, and grasslands; resources—oil, coal, iron ore, copper, manganese, gold, platinum, nickel, diamonds, forests

A blast furnace is used to process nickel in Siberia. Nickel is just one of Russia's many natural resources.

Resources

Russia has enormous energy, mineral, and forest resources. However, those resources have been poorly managed. For example, much of the forest west of the Urals has been cut down. Now wood products must be brought long distances from Siberia. Still, the taiga provides a vast supply of trees for wood and paper pulp.

Russia has long been a major oil producer. However, many of its oil deposits are far from cities, markets, and ports. Coal is also plentiful. More than a dozen metals are available in large quantities. Russia also is a major diamond producer. Many valuable mineral deposits in remote Siberia have not yet been mined.

✓ **READING CHECK:** *Places and Regions* How might the location of its oil deposits prevent Russia from taking full advantage of this resource?
It makes transporting to other markets difficult.

Homework Practice Online
Keyword: SJ5 HP20

Section Review 1

Define and explain: taiga, steppe

Working with Sketch Maps On a map of Russia that you sketch or that your teacher provides, label the following: Arctic Ocean, Caucasus Mountains, Caspian Sea, Ural Mountains, West Siberian Plain, Central Siberian Plateau, Kamchatka Peninsula, Kuril Islands, Volga River, and Baltic Sea.

Reading for the Main Idea
1. *Places and Regions* What low mountain range in central Russia divides Europe from Asia?
2. *Places and Regions* How is the Volga River linked to the Baltic and Black Seas?
3. *Environment and Society* What are winters like in much of Russia? How might they affect people?

Critical Thinking
4. **Making Generalizations and Predictions** How might Russia's natural resources make the country more prosperous?

Organizing What You Know
5. **Categorizing** Copy the following graphic organizer. Use it to list the climates, vegetation, and resources of Russia.

Climates	Vegetation	Resources

462 • Chapter 20

CLOSE

Refer students to the chapter map and the time zone map in the textbook's Skills Handbook. Call out physical features and ask students what time it is where that feature is located when it is 3 P.M. in Moscow. (Examples: western Siberian lowlands: 5 P.M.; White Sea: 3 P.M.; mouth of the Lena River: 9 P.M.)

REVIEW, ASSESS, RETEACH

Have students complete the Section Review. Then pair students. Tell each student to create five fill-in-the-blank questions based on the material in Section 1. Then have students take turns asking their questions. Students should copy the questions and answers into their notes. Then have students complete Daily Quiz 20.1. **COOPERATIVE LEARNING**

Have students complete Main Idea Activity S1. Then have students work in groups to create large sketch maps of Russia. Students should take turns labeling physical features, climates, or locations of natural resources on their maps. **ESOL, COOPERATIVE LEARNING**

EXTEND

Have interested students conduct research on the Tunguska Event of 1908, when a huge explosion of mysterious origin leveled about 1,200 square miles of the Siberian wilderness. Ask students to identify when plant and animal life returned. **BLOCK SCHEDULING**

Section 2: History and Culture

Read to Discover
1. What was Russia's early history like?
2. How did the Russian Empire grow and then fall?
3. What was the Soviet Union?
4. What is Russia like today?

Vocabulary
czar
abdicated
allies
superpowers
Cold War
consumer goods

Places
Moscow

People
Ivan the Terrible
Peter the Great
Vladimir Lenin
Joseph Stalin
Mikhail Gorbachev

Reading Strategy

READING ORGANIZER As you read this section, create a time line that begins in A.D. 800 and goes to 2000. Write down important events in the history of Russia on your time line.

CHAPTER 20, Section 2

SECTION 2 RESOURCES
Reproducible
- Lecture Notes, Section 2
- Know It Notes S2
- Graphic Organizer 20
- Geography for Life Activity
- Interdisciplinary Activities for the Middle Grades 17, 18, 20
- Map Activity 20
- Cultures of the World Activity 4
- Biography Activities: Count Leo Tolstoy, Vladimir Lenin

Technology
- One-Stop Planner CD–ROM, Lesson 20.2
- Homework Practice Online
- HRW Go site

Reinforcement, Review, and Assessment
- Section 2 Review
- Daily Quiz 20.2
- Main Idea Activity S2
- Chapter Summaries and Review
- English Audio Summary 20.2
- Spanish Audio Summary 20.2

Early Russia

The roots of the Russian nation lie deep in the grassy plains of the steppe. For thousands of years, people moved across the steppe bringing new languages, religions, and ways of life.

Early Migrations Slavic peoples have lived in Russia for thousands of years. In the A.D. 800s, Viking traders from Scandinavia helped shape the first Russian state among the Slavs. These Vikings called themselves Rus (ROOS). The word *Russia* comes from their name. The state they created was centered on Kiev. Today Kiev is the capital of Ukraine.

In the following centuries, missionaries from southeastern Europe brought Orthodox Christianity and a form of the Greek alphabet to Russia. Today the Russian language is written in this Cyrillic alphabet.

Mongols After about 200 years, Kiev's power began to decline. In the 1200s, Mongol invaders called Tatars swept out of Central Asia across the steppe. The Mongols conquered Kiev and added much of the region to their vast empire.

The Mongols demanded taxes but ruled the region through local leaders. Over time, these local leaders established various states. The strongest of these was Muscovy, north of Kiev. Its chief city was Moscow.

✓ **READING CHECK:** *Human Systems* What was the effect of Viking traders on Russia? They helped shape the first Russian state, centered on Kiev, now the capital of Ukraine.

▲ This painting from the mid-1400s shows a battle between soldiers of two early Russian states.

Russia • 463

Objectives
1. Outline the major events in Russia's early history.
2. Describe the growth and decline of the Russian Empire.
3. Report on the Soviet Union.
4. Identify characteristics of present-day Russia.

FOCUS

Bellringer

Arrange the classroom so that the desks are in two large groups with one aisle down the middle. Ask a volunteer to walk from one corner of the room to the opposite corner by the easiest route. (Most students will use the aisle.) Then, explain to the class that the great Russian steppe, or plain, was like a flat aisle or hallway that created easy access to the Russian interior for both invaders and immigrants. Tell students that in Section 2 they will learn more about those groups as they study the history and culture of Russia.

Building Vocabulary

Write the vocabulary terms on the board. Tell students that **czar** comes from a Latin word, *caesar*, which means "emperor." Point out that **abdicate** comes from two Latin word parts: *ab-* ("away") and *dicare* ("to proclaim"). Have students suggest other words related to **allies**. Call on volunteers to define **superpowers** and **consumer goods** based on the terms' component words. Ask students to contrast the **Cold War** with other wars they have studied. Check all suggestions against definitions.

Russia **463**

CHAPTER 20, Section 2

Linking Past to Present
Invasions of Russia Russia has been invaded several times during its long history. Each invasion eventually failed. In (1707–09) Sweden's king Charles XII invaded Russia, only to be defeated by brutal winter weather, burned land and crops, and the czar's army. In 1812, Napoléon I of France invaded Russia with about 400,000 men. Only 30,000 or so survived the battles, cold, disease, hunger, and attacks by Russian soldiers and citizens. In 1941 Nazi Germany invaded the Soviet Union. Again, cold was a major factor in the Nazis' defeat.

Critical Thinking: What roles might Russia's size and landforms have played in these defeats?

Answer: Students may reply that the size made supply lines extremely long and thus difficult to maintain. Armies had to cover such great distances that severe weather could trap unprepared troops before they could return home. The featureless steppe offered little shelter.

Map Answer

between 1533 and 1689

History of Russian Expansion

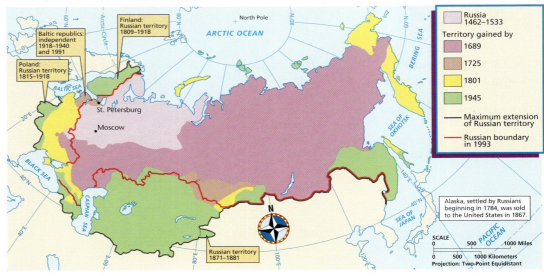

The colors in this map show land taken by the Russian Empire and the Soviet Union over time.
Interpreting the Map When was the period of Russia's greatest expansion?

Ivan the Terrible became grand prince of Moscow in 1533. He was just three years old. He ruled Russia from 1547 to his death in 1584.

The Russian Empire

In the 1400s Muscovy won control over parts of Russia from the Mongols. In 1547 Muscovy's ruler, Ivan IV—known as Ivan the Terrible—crowned himself **czar** (ZAHR) of all Russia. The word *czar* comes from the Latin word *Caesar* and means "emperor."

Expansion Over more than 300 years, czars like Peter the Great (1672–1725) expanded the Russian empire. By the early 1700s the empire stretched from the Baltic to the Pacific.

Russian fur traders crossed the Bering Strait in the 1700s and 1800s. They established colonies along the North American west coast. Those colonies stretched from coastal Alaska to California. Russia sold Alaska to the United States in 1867. Around the same time, Russia expanded into Central Asia.

Decline The Russian Empire's power began to decline in the late 1800s. Industry grew slowly, so Russia remained largely agricultural. Most people were poor farmers. Far fewer were the rich, factory workers, or craftspeople. Food shortages, economic problems, and defeat in war further weakened the empire in the early 1900s.

In 1917, during World War I, the czar **abdicated**, or gave up his throne. Later in 1917 the Bolshevik Party, led by Vladimir Lenin, overthrew the government. This event is known as the Russian Revolution.

✓ **READING CHECK:** *Human Systems* What conflict brought a change of government to Russia?
the Russian Revolution in which the Bolshevik Party overthrew the government

464 • Chapter 20

TEACH

Teaching Objective 1
ALL LEVELS: (Suggested time: 20 min.) Have students draw a time line of the major events in Russian history up to the Russian Revolution in 1917. You may want to have students color-code the entries based on the ethnic or religious group involved. Display the time lines around the classroom.
ESOL, COOPERATIVE LEARNING, LS **VISUAL-SPATIAL**

Teaching Objective 2
ALL LEVELS: (Suggested time: 20 min.) Copy the following graphic organizer onto the chalkboard, omitting the blue answers. Use it to help students understand the rise and fall of the Russian Empire. Call on volunteers to fill in details to connect the events. **ESOL,** LS **INTERPERSONAL**

464 Chapter 20

The Soviet Union

The Bolsheviks, or Communists, established the Soviet Union in 1922. Most of the various territories of the Russian Empire became republics within the Soviet Union.

Under Lenin and his successor, Joseph Stalin, the Communists took over all industries and farms. Religious practices were discouraged. The Communists outlawed all other political parties. Many opponents were imprisoned, forced to leave the country, or even killed.

The Soviet leaders established a command economy, in which industries were controlled by the government. At first these industries grew dramatically. However, over time the lack of competition made them inefficient and wasteful. The quality of many products was poor. Government-run farms failed to produce enough food to feed the population. By the late 1950s the Soviet Union had to import large amounts of grain.

Cold War The Soviet Union in the 1950s was still recovering from World War II. The country had been a major battleground in the war. The United States and the Soviet Union had been **allies**, or friends, in the fight against Germany. After the war the two **superpowers**, or powerful countries, became rivals. This bitter rivalry became known as the **Cold War**. The Cold War lasted from the 1940s to the early 1990s. The Soviet Union and the United States built huge military forces, including nuclear weapons. The two countries never formally went to war with each other. However, they supported allies in small wars around the world.

Collapse of the Soviet Union The costs of the Cold War eventually became too much for the Soviet Union. The Soviet government spent more and more money on military goods. **Consumer goods** became expensive and in short supply. Consumer goods are products used at home and in everyday life. The last Soviet leader, Mikhail Gorbachev, tried to bring about changes to help the economy. He also promoted a policy allowing more open discussion of the country's problems. However, the various Soviet republics pushed for independence. Finally, in 1991 the Soviet Union collapsed. The huge country split into 15 republics.

In late 1991 Russia and most of the other former Soviet republics formed the Commonwealth of Independent States, or CIS. Minsk, Belarus, serves as the CIS administrative capital. The CIS does not have a strong central government. Instead, it provides a way for the former Soviet republics to address shared problems. For example, CIS representatives meet to discuss foreign relations, defense, economics, law enforcement, immigration policies, and environmental issues.

✓ **READING CHECK:** *Human Systems* What was the Cold War, and how did it eventually cause the Soviet Union's collapse?
rivalry between Soviet Union, U.S.; military costs eventually ruined Soviet economy

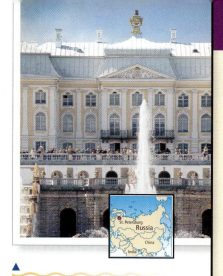

▲ Tourists can visit the czar's Summer Palace in St. Petersburg.

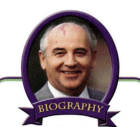

Mikhail Gorbachev
(1931–)

Character Trait: Citizenship

Mikhail Gorbachev saw problems in his country and set out to solve them. Although he was a member of the Communist party, Gorbachev supported two new ideas that led to the party's decline. One was *glasnost*, or "openness" in Russian. It meant that Russians could finally talk openly about their country's problems. The other was *perestroika*, or "restructuring" of the Soviet Union's crumbling economy. These policies helped end communist rule of the Soviet Union.

How did Gorbachev's actions show good citizenship?

CHAPTER 20, Section 2

ENVIRONMENT AND SOCIETY

Russia's Environmental Quandary Russia is faced with many environmental problems that it inherited from the era of Soviet rule. During the 1900s, the Soviet government expanded settlement into Siberia with little concern for environmental impacts. The size and richness of the land made it seem that there was no limit to the resources or to the land on which to dump wastes.

Now Russia is left with large areas that have polluted air, soil, or water. The Russian economy is troubled, and Russia has limited resources to devote to leftover environmental damage.

Discussion: Where should environmental issues, such as cleaning up pollution and toxic waste, rank in national priorities? Have students discuss the issue from different points of view. (Students may suggest that such issues are important but that they decline in priority in the face of an economic crisis. Others may feel environmental issues should take first priority because life itself depends on a healthy environment.)

◀ **Biography Answer**

He worked for what he thought was best for his country's citizens, rather than for his political party.

Teaching Objective 3

LEVEL 1: (Suggested time: 20 min.) Pair students and have each pair design a political poster for the Soviet Union. Posters should include references to the Russian Revolution, past leaders, and Cold War elements concerning competition between the Soviet Union and the United States. **ESOL, COOPERATIVE LEARNING,** LS **VISUAL-SPATIAL**

LEVEL 2: (Suggested time: 30 min.) Have students create editorial cartoons referring to the Soviet Union during the Cold War from an American viewpoint. Ask them to explain how their cartoons show Americans' frame of reference regarding the Cold War.

LEVEL 3: (Suggested time: 30 min.) Have students play the role of an American journalist living in the Soviet Union just after its collapse in 1991. Tell them to write newspaper articles describing the conditions and factors leading up to the collapse of the Soviet Union, doing additional research as needed. Have each student write an appropriate headline for his or her article and share it with the class. LS **VERBAL-LINGUISTIC**

CHAPTER 20, Section 2

HUMAN SYSTEMS

Crimean Tatars The Tatars, also known as the Tartars, are an ethnic group living in various parts of Russia. One branch of this group is the Crimean Tatars. They have a unique history. The Crimean Tatars formed their own Soviet republic in 1921, but this republic was dissolved in 1945 when they were accused of helping the Germans in World War II. Most of the Crimean Tatars were deported to other parts of the Soviet Union and forbidden to speak their native language. In 1956 they regained their civil rights but were still refused the right to move back to the Crimea region. It was not until the breakup of the Soviet Union in 1991 that Crimean Tatars were allowed back into that region. Today there are about 270,000 Tatars in the Crimea.

Critical Thinking: Why might a government outlaw a specific language?

Answer: to reduce association with a specific ethnic group

Connecting to Literature
Answers
1. She is living in a Soviet republic where there is little information about the United States.
2. a wonderful place with many consumer goods

Connecting to Literature

The former Soviet Union was composed of many republics, which are now independent countries. Nina Gabrielyan's The Lilac Dressing Gown *is told from the point of view of an Armenian girl living in Moscow before the Soviet breakup.*

Aunt Rimma. . . came to visit and gave me a pink caramel which I, naturally, popped straight in my mouth. "Don't swallow it," Aunt Rimma says in an odd sort of voice. "You're not supposed to swallow it, only chew it." "Why," I ask, puzzled by her solemn tone. "It's chewing gum," she says with pride in her eyes. "Chewing gum?" I don't know what she means. "American chewing gum," Aunt Rimma explains. "Mentor's sister sent it to us from America." "Oh, from America? Is that where the capitalists are? What is she doing there?" "She's living there," says Aunt Rimma, condescending to my foolishness.

But I am not as foolish as I used to be. I know that Armenians live in Armenia. Our country is very big and includes many republics: Armenia, Georgia, Azerbaijan, Tajikistan, Uzbekistan, Ukraine, Belorussia [Belarus], the Caucasus and Transcaucasia. All this together is the Soviet Union. Americans . . . live in America. Clearly, Mentor's sister cannot possibly be American. . . . Rimma goes on boasting: "Oh! the underwear they have there! . . . And the children's clothes!" I begin to feel a bit envious. . . . Nobody in our house has anyone living in America, but Aunt Rimma does. My envy becomes unbearable. So I decide to slay our boastful neighbor on the spot: "Well we have cockroaches! This big! Lots and lots of them!"

Analyzing Primary Sources
1. How does the Armenian girl's frame of reference affect her view of the United States?
2. What does Aunt Rimma seem to think the United States is like?

Russia Today

Russia has been making a transition from communism to democracy and a free market economy since 1991. Change has been slow, and the country faces difficult challenges.

People and Religion More than 144 million people live in Russia today. More than 80 percent are ethnic Russians. The largest of Russia's many minority groups are Ukrainians and Tatars. These Tatars are the descendants of the early Mongol invaders of Russia.

466 • Chapter 20

ASSIGNMENT: Have students design a tombstone or write an obituary for the Soviet Union. You may want to provide students with examples of obituaries from the daily newspaper to use as models for their work. Display tombstones or obituaries around the classroom. **LS VISUAL-SPATIAL**

Teaching Objective 4
LEVELS 1 AND 2: (Suggested time: 20 min.) Have students use their textbooks to create a chart on modern-day Russia. The chart should include information on the country's ethnic makeup, religions, foods and festivals, arts and sciences, and government. When all students have completed their charts, ask volunteers to share their charts with the class. **ESOL**

LEVEL 3: (Suggested time: 30 min.) Pair students and instruct them to create a chart with two columns, one labeled "Russia Today" and the other "United States." Using their textbooks, students should select a fact about life in Russia and write it in the first column. Then they should compare or contrast that fact with life in the United States in the second column. Tell them to be sure to include government, economy, and culture in their charts. **COOPERATIVE LEARNING**

In the past, the government encouraged ethnic Russians to settle in areas of Russia far from Moscow. They were encouraged to move to places where other ethnic groups were in the majority. Today, many non-Russian peoples in those areas resent the domination of ethnic Russians. Some non-Russians want independence from Moscow. At times this has led to violence and even war, as in Chechnya in southern Russia.

Since 1991 a greater degree of religious expression has been allowed in Russia. Russian Orthodox Christianity is becoming popular again. Cathedrals have been repaired, and their onion-shaped domes have been covered in gold leaf and brilliant colors. Muslims around the Caspian Sea and the southern Urals have revived Islamic practices.

Food and Festivals Bread is an important part of the Russian diet. It is eaten with every meal. It may be a rich, dark bread made from rye and wheat flour or a firm white bread. As in other northern countries, the growing season is short and winter is long. Therefore, the diet includes many canned and preserved foods, such as sausages, smoked fish, cheese, and vegetable and fruit preserves.

Black caviar, one of the world's most expensive delicacies, comes from Russia. The fish eggs that make up black caviar come from sturgeon. Sturgeon are fish found in the Caspian Sea.

The anniversary of the 1917 Russian Revolution was an important holiday during the Soviet era. Today the Orthodox Christian holidays of Christmas and Easter are again becoming popular in Russia. Special holiday foods include milk puddings and cheesecakes.

The Arts and Sciences Russia has given the world great works of art, literature, and music. For example, you might know *The Nutcracker*, a ballet danced to music composed by Peter Tchaikovsky (1840–93). It is a popular production in many countries.

Russia

Country	Population/Growth Rate	Life Expectancy	Literacy Rate	Per Capita GDP
Russia	144,526,278 / –0.3%	62, male / 73, female	99%	$9,300
United States	290,342,554 / 0.9%	74, male / 80, female	97%	$37,600

Source: Central Intelligence Agency, *The World Factbook 2003*

Interpreting the Chart How many times greater is the U.S. population than the Russian population?

Ballet dancers perform Peter Tchaikovsky's *Swan Lake* at the Mariinsky Theater in St. Petersburg.

Section 2 Review

Answers to Section 2 Review

Define or identify For definitions and identifications, see the glossary and index.

Working with Sketch Maps Moscow should be labeled in its approximate location. Kiev was the first Russian state among the Slavs.

Reading for the Main Idea
1. traders, who called themselves Rus and organized the first Russian state **(NGS 4)**
2. Its leaders overthrew the Russian government in 1917. **(NGS 13)**
3. struggling economy, corruption, competing political groups **(NGS 4)**

Critical Thinking
4. Russian Empire—food shortages, economic problems, and defeat in war; Soviet Union—lack of consumer goods, too much money spent on military goods

Organizing What You Know
5. Answers will vary but should include information from the section.

Many Russian writers are known for how they capture the emotions of characters in their works. Some writers, such as Aleksandr Solzhenitsyn (1918–), have written about Russia under communism.

Russian scientists also have made important contributions to their professions. For example, in 1957 the Soviet Union launched *Sputnik*. It was the first artificial satellite in space. Today U.S. and Russian engineers are working together on space projects. These include building a large space station and planning for a mission to Mars.

Government Like the U.S. government, the Russian Federation is governed by an elected president and a legislature called the Federal Assembly. The Federal Assembly includes representatives of regions and republics within the Federation. Non-Russians are numerous or in the majority in many of those regions and republics.

The government faces tough challenges. One is improving the country's struggling economy. Many government-owned companies have been sold to the private sector. However, financial problems have limited investment. In addition, many Russians criticized the government in the 2000s for limiting freedom of the press.

Corruption is a serious problem. A few people have used their connections with government officials to get rich. Also, many Russians avoid paying taxes. This means the government has less money for salaries and services. Agreement on solutions to these problems has been hard.

Republics of the Russian Federation

Adygea	Karachay-Cherkessia
Alania	Karelia
Bashkortostan	Khakassia
Buryatia	Komi
Chechnya	Mari El
Chuvashia	Mordvinia
Dagestan	Sakha
Gorno-Altay	Tatarstan
Ingushetia	Tuva
Kabardino-Balkaria	Udmurtia
Kalmykia	

✓ **READING CHECK:** Human Systems
What are the people and culture of Russia like today? 80 percent ethnic Russian; free practice of religion; bread and preserved foods important; many great works of art, literature, and ballet, and scientific contributions.

Homework Practice Online
Keyword: SJ5 HP20

Section Review 2

Define or identify: Ivan the Terrible, czar, Peter the Great, abdicated, Vladimir Lenin, Joseph Stalin, allies, superpowers, Cold War, consumer goods, Mikhail Gorbachev

Working with Sketch Maps On the map you created in Section 1, label Moscow. In the margin, explain the role Kiev played in Russia's early history.

Reading for the Main Idea
1. *Places and Regions* How did Russia get its name?
2. *Human Systems* What was the Bolshevik Party?
3. *Places and Regions* What are some of the challenges that Russia faces today?

Critical Thinking
4. **Comparing** Compare the factors that led to the decline of the Russian Empire and the Soviet Union. List the factors for each.

Organizing What You Know
5. **Summarizing** Copy the following graphic organizer. Use it to identify important features of Russia's ethnic population, religion, food, and arts and sciences.

(Graphic organizer: Russian people and culture)

468 • Chapter 20

CLOSE

Remind students that the United States and the Soviet Union were bitter enemies for many years. Ask students to suggest reasons why the Cold War never exploded into World War III. (Students might mention the threat of mutual destruction by nuclear weapons.)

REVIEW, ASSESS, RETEACH

Have students complete the Section Review. Then pair students and have each student write five major events in Russian history, in random order. Students should exchange lists with their partners and place the events in chronological order. Then have students complete Daily Quiz 20.2. **COOPERATIVE LEARNING**

Have students complete Main Idea Activity S2. Then have students work in groups to create time lines of major events in Russian history. Caution students that their time lines should show the years spaced accurately. **ESOL, COOPERATIVE LEARNING, LS LOGICAL-MATHEMATICAL**

EXTEND

Have interested students conduct research on the current Russian government and another government of their choice. Ask them to create a chart comparing the two governments. **BLOCK SCHEDULING**

Section 3: The Russian Heartland

Read to Discover
1. Why is European Russia considered the country's heartland?
2. What are the characteristics of the four regions of European Russia?

Vocabulary
light industry
heavy industry
smelters

Places
St. Petersburg
Nizhniy Novgorod
Astrakhan
Yekaterinburg
Chelyabinsk
Magnitogorsk

Reading Strategy

READING ORGANIZER Draw a circle on a sheet of paper and label it Russian Heartland. Add four circles around the central one and connect them to it by spokes. Label the outer circles as the four regions discussed in the section and write down what you learn in each circle.

The Heartland

The European section of Russia is the country's heartland. The Russian nation expanded outward from there. It is home to the bulk of the Russian population. The national capital and large industrial cities are also located there.

The plains of European Russia make up the country's most productive farming region. Farmers focus mainly on growing grains and raising livestock. Small gardens near cities provide fresh fruits and vegetables for summer markets.

The Russian heartland can be divided into four major regions. These four are the Moscow region, the St. Petersburg region, the Volga region, and the Urals region.

✓ **READING CHECK:** *Places and Regions* Why is European Russia the country's heartland? The bulk of the population, the national capital, and large industrial cities are there.

The Moscow Region

Moscow is Russia's capital and largest city. More than 9 million people live there. In addition to being Russia's political center, Moscow is the country's center for transportation and communication. Roads, railroads, and air routes link the capital to all points in Russia.

At Moscow's heart is the Kremlin. The Kremlin's red brick walls and towers were built in the late 1400s. The government offices, beautiful palaces, and gold-domed churches within its walls are popular tourist attractions.

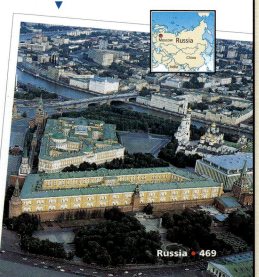

Twenty towers, like the one in the lower left, are spaced along the Kremlin's walls.

Interpreting the Visual Record Why would leaders place government buildings and palaces within the walls of one central location?

◀ **Visual Record Answer**
for defense purposes, so that government can function if parts of the city are under attack

---

CHAPTER 20, Section 3

SECTION 3 RESOURCES

Reproducible
- Lecture Notes, Section 3
- Know It Notes S3

Technology
- One-Stop Planner CD–ROM, Lesson 20.3
- Homework Practice Online
- HRW Go site

Reinforcement, Review, and Assessment
- Section 3 Review
- Daily Quiz 20.3
- Main Idea Activity S3
- Chapter Summaries and Review
- English Audio Summary 20.3
- Spanish Audio Summary 20.3

Objectives
1. Explain why European Russia is considered the heartland of the country.
2. Describe the four major regions of European Russia.

Focus

Bellringer

Copy the following "equation" and question onto the chalkboard: *St. Petersburg → Petrograd → Leningrad → St. Petersburg. What do you think this means?* Tell students that "-burg" and "-grad" mean "city" and that the city now called St. Petersburg has changed names several times. Ask students to speculate what may have prompted the name changes. (changes in government or rulers) Tell students that in Section 3 they will learn more about St. Petersburg and other cities of Russia's heartland.

Building Vocabulary

Write the terms **light industry** and **heavy industry** on the chalkboard. Based on what students know about industry, ask them to speculate what the adjective before each of these terms does to the meaning of the term. (Light and heavy generally reflect the weight of the product created by the industry.) Have a student locate and read aloud a definition of **smelters**. Call on a volunteer to describe the relationship between smelters and heavy industry. (Smelters process metal ores that are primarily used in heavy industry.)

Russia 469

CHAPTER 20, Section 3

Across the Curriculum
SCIENCE

The Pulkovo Observatory Among the many learning institutions of the St. Petersburg region is the Pulkovo Observatory. The observatory's 15-inch (38 cm) refracting telescope was the world's largest when it was built in 1839. Known for its quality of observations, the observatory doubled the size of its refracting telescope to 30 inches (76 cm) in 1878. Although it was destroyed during World War II, the Pulkovo Observatory was rebuilt in 1951.

Critical Thinking: Why might an observatory be destroyed during a war?

Answer: The enemy might have targeted all scientific sites in an effort to destroy technological advancements and to reduce potential surveillance.

Vendors sell religious art and other crafts at a sidewalk market in Moscow.
Interpreting the Visual Record What do the items in this market suggest about the status of religion in Russia since the communist era?

Visual Record Answer
It is practiced freely.

Moscow is part of a huge industrial area. This area also includes the city of Nizhniy Novgorod, called Gorky during the communist era. About one third of Russia's population lives in this region.

The Soviet government encouraged the development of **light industry**, rather than **heavy industry**, around Moscow. Light industry focuses on the production of lightweight goods, such as clothing. Heavy industry usually involves manufacturing based on metals. It causes more pollution than light industry. The region also has advanced-technology and electronics industries.

The St. Petersburg Region

Northwest of Moscow is St. Petersburg, Russia's second-largest city and a major Baltic seaport. More than 5 million people live there. St. Petersburg was Russia's capital and home to the czars for more than 200 years. This changed in 1918. Palaces and other grand buildings constructed under the czars are tourist attractions today. St. Petersburg was known as Leningrad during the communist era. Much of the city was heavily damaged during World War II.

The surrounding area has few natural resources. Still, St. Petersburg's harbor, canals, and rail connections make the city a major center for trade. Important universities and research institutions are located there. The region also has important industries.

The Mariinsky Theater of Opera and Ballet is one of St. Petersburg's most beautiful buildings. It was called the Kirov during the communist era.

✓ **READING CHECK:** *Human Systems* Why are Moscow and St. Petersburg such large cities? *centers of politics, transportation, communication, industry, trade, education*

TEACH

Teaching Objectives 1–2
ALL LEVELS: (Suggested time: 15 min.) Copy the following graphic organizer onto the chalkboard, omitting the blue answers. Call on students to fill in the chart with descriptive characteristics that make this region Russia's heartland. **ESOL, VISUAL-SPATIAL**

REGIONS OF THE RUSSIAN HEARTLAND

Moscow	St. Petersburg	Volga	Ural
• capital and largest city • huge industrial area	• second-largest city • major seaport • important centers of learning	• major shipping route • many factories and industries	• many mineral resources

Teaching Objective 2
ALL LEVELS: (Suggested time: 30 min.) Organize the class into four groups, assigning each group a region of the Russian heartland. Have students create a "Welcome to ___" billboard to be placed at the region's border. Students should emphasize positive aspects of their region. Display the billboards around the classroom. **ESOL, COOPERATIVE LEARNING**

The Volga Region

The Volga region stretches along the middle part of the Volga River. The Volga is often more like a chain of lakes. It is a major shipping route for goods produced in the region. Hydroelectric power plants and nearby deposits of coal and oil are important sources of energy.

During World War II, many factories were moved to the Volga region. This was done to keep them safe from German invaders. Today the region is famous for its factories that produce goods such as motor vehicles, chemicals, and food products. Russian caviar comes from a fishery based at the old city of Astrakhan on the Caspian Sea.

The Urals Region

Mining has long been important in the Ural Mountains region. Nearly every important mineral except oil has been discovered there. Copper and iron **smelters** are still important. Smelters are factories that process copper, iron, and other metal ores.

Many large cities in the Urals started as commercial centers for mining districts. The Soviet government also moved factories to the region during World War II. Important cities include Yekaterinburg (yi-kah-ti-reem-BOOHRK) (formerly Sverdlovsk), Chelyabinsk (chel-YAH-buhnsk), and Magnitogorsk (muhg-nee-tuh-GAWRSKY). Now these cities manufacture machinery and metal goods.

✓ **READING CHECK:** *Places and Regions* What industries are important in the Volga and Urals regions?
automobile, chemical, food, mining, machinery, metal goods

A fisher gathers sturgeon in a small shipboard pool in the Volga region.

Section Review 3

Define and explain: light industry, heavy industry, smelters

Working with Sketch Maps On the map you created in Section 2, label St. Petersburg, Nizhniy Novgorod, Astrakhan, Yekaterinburg, Chelyabinsk, and Magnitogorsk. In the margin of your map, write a short caption explaining the significance of Moscow and St. Petersburg.

Reading for the Main Idea
1. *Places and Regions* Why might so many people settle in Russia's heartland?
2. *Places and Regions* Where did the Soviet government move factories during World War II?

Critical Thinking
3. **Drawing Inferences and Conclusions** Why do you think the Soviet government encouraged the development of light industry around Moscow?
4. **Finding the Main Idea** What role has the region's physical geography played in the development of European Russia's economy?

Organizing What You Know
5. **Contrasting** Use this graphic organizer to identify European Russia's four regions. Write one feature that makes each region different from the other three.

Homework Practice Online
Keyword: SJ5 HP20

Russia • 471

CHAPTER 20, Section 4

SECTION 4 RESOURCES

Reproducible
- Lecture Notes, Section 4
- Know It Notes S4

Technology
- One-Stop Planner CD–ROM, Lesson 20.4
- Homework Practice Online
- HRW Go site

Reinforcement, Review, and Assessment
- Section 4 Review
- Daily Quiz 20.4
- Main Idea Activity S4
- Chapter Summaries and Review
- English Audio Summary 20.4
- Spanish Audio Summary 20.4

Section 4 Siberia

Read to Discover
1. What is the human geography of Siberia like?
2. What are the economic features of the region?
3. How has Lake Baikal been threatened by pollution?

Vocabulary
habitation fog

Places
Siberia
Trans-Siberian Railroad
Baikal-Amur Mainline
Kuznetsk Basin
Ob River
Yenisey River
Novosibirsk
Lake Baikal

Reading Strategy

READING ORGANIZER Draw a line down the center of a sheet of paper. Title one column "What I know about Siberia." Title the other column "What I learned about Siberia." Write down what you already know about Siberia in the first column. As you read, add what you learn in the other column.

A Sleeping Land

East of European Russia, across the Ural Mountains, is Siberia. Siberia is enormous. It covers more than 5 million square miles (12.95 million sq. km) of northern Asia. It extends all the way to the Pacific Ocean. That is nearly 1.5 times the area of the United States! To the north of Siberia is the Arctic Ocean. To the south are the Central Asian countries, Mongolia, and China.

Many people think of Siberia as simply a vast, frozen wasteland. In fact, in the Tatar language, *Siberia* means "Sleeping Land." In many ways, this image is accurate. Siberian winters are long, dark, and severe. Often there is little snow, but the land is frozen for months. During winter, **habitation fog** hangs over cities. A habitation fog is a fog caused by fumes and smoke from cities. During the cold Siberian winter, this fog is trapped over cities.

Siberia has lured Russian adventurers for more than 400 years. It continues to do so today. This vast region has a great wealth of natural resources. Developing those resources may be a key to transforming Russia into an economic success.

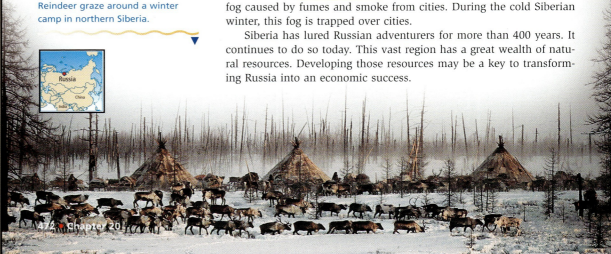

Reindeer graze around a winter camp in northern Siberia.

Section 4

Objectives
1. Describe the human geography of Siberia.
2. Identify the economic features of the region.
3. Analyze how Lake Baikal has been threatened by pollution.

Focus

Bellringer
Copy the following question onto the chalkboard: *Where are the coldest places in the world?* If students do not name Siberia, refer them to the "Our Amazing Planet" feature in Section 1. You may want to point out Verkhoyansk, in Siberia, where the temperature was recorded, on a more detailed wall map of Russia. Tell students that in Section 4 they will learn more about Siberia.

Building Vocabulary
Write **habitation fog** on the chalkboard. Ask students to infer the meaning of the term based on what they know about the words "habitat" or "inhabit" and "fog." (Habitation fogs occur over cities—places people inhabit.) To confirm the meaning, call on a volunteer to find and read the term's definition aloud.

472 Chapter 20

People Siberia is sparsely populated. In fact, large areas have no human population at all. Most of the people live in cities in western and southern parts of the region.

Ethnic Russians make up most of the population. However, minority groups have lived there since long before Russians began to expand into Siberia.

Settlements Russian settlement in Siberia generally follows the route of the Trans-Siberian Railroad. Construction of this railway started in 1891. When it was completed, it linked Moscow and Vladivostok, a port on the Sea of Japan.

Russia's Trans-Siberian Railroad is the longest single rail line in the world. It is more than 5,700 miles (9,171 km) long. For many Siberian towns, the railroad provides the only transportation link to the outside world. Another important railway is the Baikal-Amur Mainline (BAM), which crosses many mountain ranges and rivers in eastern Siberia.

The Omsk (AWMSK) Cathedral in Omsk, Siberia, provides an example of Russian architecture. Omsk was founded in the early 1700s.

✓ **READING CHECK:** Places and Regions Where is Russian settlement located in Siberia, and why do you think this is the case?
along the trans-Siberian Railroad; because it provides a means of transportation and communication in this vast land

Siberia's Economy

The Soviet government built the Baikal-Amur Mainline so that raw materials from Siberia could be easily transported to other places. Abundant natural resources form the foundation of Siberia's economy. They are also important to the development of Russia's struggling economy. Siberia's natural resources include timber, mineral ores, diamonds, and coal, oil, and natural gas deposits.

Although Siberia has rich natural resources, it contains a small percentage of Russia's industry. The harsh climate and difficult terrain have discouraged settlement. Many people would rather live in European Russia, even though wages may be higher in Siberia.

Lumbering and mining are the most important Siberian industries. Large coal deposits are mined in the Kuznetsk Basin, or the Kuzbas. The Kuzbas is located in southwestern Siberia between the Ob and Yenisey Rivers. It is one of Siberia's most important industrial regions.

Siberia's largest city, Novosibirsk, is located near the Kuznetsk Basin. The city's name means "New Siberia." Almost 1.5 million people live there. It is located about halfway between Moscow and Vladivostok on the Trans-Siberian Railroad. Novosibirsk is Siberia's manufacturing and transportation center.

✓ **READING CHECK:** Environment and Society How do Siberia's natural resources influence the economies of Siberia and Russia?
They are the foundation of Siberia's economy and could help develop Russia's economy.

CHAPTER 20, Section 4

HUMAN SYSTEMS

All Aboard for Siberia
The *Rossiya* train takes 153 hours and 49 minutes to travel from Moscow to Vladivostok on the Trans-Siberian Railroad. The famous railroad required 12 years and more than 70,000 workers to complete. It opened Siberia to settlement and provided access to the region's vast natural resources for development.

The number of Russians using the Trans-Siberian Railroad declined about 50 percent between 1991 and 1997. Even so, trains carry half of all passenger traffic in Russia, compared to less than 1 percent in the United States.

internet connect
GO TO: go.hrw.com
KEYWORD: SJ5 CH20
FOR: Web sites about the Trans-Siberian Railroad

Russia • 473

TEACH

Teaching Objectives 1–2
ALL LEVELS: (Suggested time: 20 min.) Copy the following graphic organizer onto the chalkboard, omitting the blue answers. Have students list human geographic and economic reasons for or against living in Siberia.
ESOL, LS **VISUAL-SPATIAL**

Living in Siberia	
Reasons for:	Reasons against:
great wealth and natural resources, Trans-Siberian Railroad and the BAM, higher wages	severe climate, sparsely populated, little industry

Teaching Objective 3
ALL LEVELS: (Suggested time: 30 min.) Pair students and have them write contracts for new commercial development at or near Lake Baikal. Contracts should start with a review of Lake Baikal's special qualities, include a review of past problems, and conclude with requirements for operating a business that will not harm the lake or its plants and animals.
ESOL, COOPERATIVE LEARNING, LS **VERBAL-LINGUISTIC**

Section 4 Review

Answers to Section 4 Review

Define For definition, see the glossary.

Working with Sketch Maps Maps will vary, but listed places should be labeled accurately.

Reading for the Main Idea
1. west—Ural Mountains; east—Pacific Ocean; south—Central Asian republics, Mongolia, and China; north—Arctic Ocean (NGS 4)
2. in cities in the western and southern parts along the Trans-Siberian Railroad; because it is a means of transportation and communication (NGS 9)
3. The harsh climate and difficult terrain have discouraged settlement there. (NGS 9)

Critical Thinking
4. Answers will vary, but students should include reasons to justify their responses.

Organizing What You Know
5. natural resources—timber, mineral ores, diamonds, coal, oil, and natural gas; major industries—lumbering and mining

Visual Record Answer
cause health problems for the plants and animals

Lake Baikal is seven times as deep as the Grand Canyon.
Interpreting the Visual Record
Human-Environment Interaction How would pollution affect this lake and the plants and animals that live there?

Lake Baikal covers less area than do three of the Great Lakes: Superior, Huron, and Michigan. Still, Baikal is so deep that it contains about one fifth of all the world's freshwater!

Lake Baikal

Some people have worried that economic development in Siberia threatens the region's natural environment. One focus of concern has been Lake Baikal (by-KAHL), the "Jewel of Siberia."

Baikal is located north of Mongolia. It is the world's deepest lake. In fact, it holds as much water as all of North America's Great Lakes. The scenic lake and its surrounding area are home to many kinds of plants and animals. Some, such as the world's only freshwater seal, are endangered.

For decades people have worried about pollution from a nearby paper factory and other development. They feared that pollution threatened the species that live in and around the lake. In recent years scientists and others have proposed plans that allow some economic development while protecting the environment.

✓ **READING CHECK:** *Environment and Society* How has human activity affected Lake Baikal?
The paper factory and other developments have posed an environmental threat.

Homework Practice Online
Keyword: SJ5 HP20

Define and explain: habitation fog

Working with Sketch Maps On the map you created in Section 3, label Siberia, Trans-Siberian Railroad, Baikal-Amur Mainline, Kuznetsk Basin, Ob River, Yenisey River, Novosibirsk, and Lake Baikal.

Reading for the Main Idea
1. *Places and Regions* What are the boundaries of Siberia?
2. *Human Systems* Where do most people in Siberia live? Why?
3. *Places and Regions* Why does this huge region with many natural resources have little industry?

Critical Thinking
4. **Making Generalizations and Predictions** Do you think Russians should be more concerned about rapid economic development or protecting the environment? Why?

Organizing What You Know
5. **Categorizing** Use this organizer to list the region's resources and industries that use them.

| Natural Resources | | Major Industries |

474 • Chapter 20

CLOSE

Remind students that Siberia alone is 1.5 times the size of the United States. Lead a discussion on the various problems Russia faces governing such a large area.

REVIEW, ASSESS, RETEACH

Have students complete the Section Review. Then have each student create a web diagram with "Siberia" in the center that shows Siberia's important features. When they have finished, call on volunteers to reproduce their webs on the chalkboard. Then have students complete Daily Quiz 20.4.

Have students complete Main Idea Activity S4. Then organize the class into small groups and have groups create a script for an educational television special on Siberia. The script should cover the physical, human, economic, and environmental geography of the region. Have students add pictures and other visual aids if possible. **ESOL, COOPERATIVE LEARNING**

EXTEND

Have interested students conduct research on the rivers of Siberia, the problems caused by their freezing and thawing, and what life is like on board the rivers' freight barges. They may want to compile their findings into a job description and résumé for a barge worker. **BLOCK SCHEDULING**

The Russian Far East

CHAPTER 20, Section 5

Read to Discover
1. How does the Russian Far East's climate affect land use in the region?
2. What are the major resources and cities of the region?
3. What island regions are part of the Russian Far East?

Vocabulary
icebreakers

Places
Sea of Okhotsk
Sea of Japan
Khabarovsk
Vladivostok
Amur River
Sakhalin Island

Reading Strategy
TAKING NOTES Use the headings in this section to create an outline. As you read, write down what you learn under each heading.

Land Use

Off the eastern coast of Siberia are the Sea of Okhotsk and the Sea of Japan. Their coastal areas and islands make up a region known as the Russian Far East.

The Russian Far East has a less severe climate than the rest of Siberia. Summer weather is mild enough for some successful farming. Farms produce many goods, including wheat, sugar beets, sunflowers, meat, and dairy products. However, the region cannot produce enough food for itself. As a result, food must also be imported.

Fishing and hunting are important in the region. There are many kinds of animals, including deer, seals, rare Siberian tigers, and sables. Sable fur is used to make expensive clothing.

✓ **READING CHECK:** **Environment and Society** How does scarcity of food affect the Russian Far East?
It forces people in the region to import food.

◀ The Siberian tiger is endangered. The few remaining of these large cats roam parts of the Russian Far East. They are also found in northern China and on the Korean Peninsula.

SECTION 5 RESOURCES

Reproducible
◆ Lecture Notes, Section 5
◆ Know It Notes S5

Technology
◆ One-Stop Planner CD–ROM, Lesson 20.5
◆ Homework Practice Online
◆ Geography and Cultures Visual Resources with Teaching Activities 56–62
◆ HRW Go site

Reinforcement, Review, and Assessment
◆ Section 5 Review
◆ Daily Quiz 20.5
◆ Main Idea Activity S5
◆ Chapter Summaries and Review
◆ English Audio Summary 20.5
◆ Spanish Audio Summary 20.5

Russia • 475

Objectives
1. Explain the relationship between climate and agriculture in the Russian Far East.
2. List the major resources and cities of the Russian Far East.
3. Identify the islands of the Russian Far East.

Focus

Bellringer
Ask students to predict what the economy of the Russian Far East might be like based solely on its location. (Students might suggest that shipping, fishing, and lumbering are important there.) Tell students that in Section 5 they will learn more about the economy of the Russian Far East.

Building Vocabulary
Write **icebreakers** on the chalkboard. Tell students that when a group of people gets together for the first time, such as in a classroom or at a club meeting, the leader of the group often starts with an activity called an icebreaker. Ask students if they have ever been part of such an activity and to describe its purpose. (Possible answer: to break up the cold atmosphere so that people can better communicate and work together) Ask students to relate that description to the ships called icebreakers.

Russia **475**

CHAPTER 20, Section 5

FOOD FESTIVAL

Beautiful Borscht Here is a basic recipe for borscht, a traditional Russian soup.

In a large pot, sauté a chopped onion in 2 tbsp. butter. Stir in 1½ lb. sliced raw red beets, ¼ c. red wine vinegar, 1 tsp. sugar, 2 chopped fresh tomatoes, 1 tsp. salt, and some black pepper. Pour in ½ c. beef stock, cover, and simmer one hour. Pour in 5 c. more of beef stock and ½ lb. shredded cabbage. Bring to a boil. Add ¼ lb. cubed ham, 1 lb. cooked sliced beef, ½ c. chopped parsley, and a bay leaf. Simmer for 30 minutes. Garnish with sour cream.

Economy

Like the rest of Siberia, the Russian Far East has a wealth of natural resources. These resources have supported the growth of industrial cities and ports in the region.

Resources Much of the Russian Far East remains forested. The region's minerals are only beginning to be developed. Lumbering, machine manufacturing, woodworking, and metalworking are the major industries there.

The region also has important energy resources, including coal and oil. Another resource is geothermal energy. This resource is available because of the region's tectonic activity. Two active volcanic mountain ranges run the length of the Kamchatka Peninsula. Russia's first geothermal electric-power station was built on this peninsula.

Cities Industry and the Trans-Siberian Railroad aided the growth of cities in the Russian Far East. Two of those cities are Khabarovsk (kuh-BAHR-uhfsk) and Vladivostok (vla-duh-vuh-STAHK).

Some 700,000 people live in Khabarovsk, which was founded in 1858. It is located where the Trans-Siberian Railroad crosses the Amur River. This location makes Khabarovsk ideal for processing forest and mineral resources from the region.

Vladivostok is slightly larger than Khabarovsk. *Vladivostok* means "Lord of the East" in Russian. The city was established in 1860 on the coast of the Sea of Japan. Today it lies at the eastern end of the Trans-Siberian Railroad.

Vladivostok is a major naval base and the home port for a large fishing fleet. **Icebreakers** must keep the city's harbor open in winter. An icebreaker is a ship that can break up the ice of frozen waterways. This allows other ships to pass through them.

Historical monuments and old architecture compete for attention in Vladivostok.

TEACH

Teaching Objective 1
ALL LEVELS: (Suggested time: 30 min.) Have students draw picture postcards detailing the relationship between land use and climate in the Russian Far East. **ESOL**, **LS VISUAL-SPATIAL**

Teaching Objectives 2–3
ALL LEVELS: (Suggested time: 15 min.) Copy the following graphic organizer onto the chalkboard, omitting the blue answers. Call on volunteers to come fill in the diagram. **ESOL**

The Soviet Union considered Vladivostok very important for defense. The city was therefore closed to foreign contacts until the early 1990s. Today it is an important link with China, Japan, the United States, and the rest of the Pacific region.

✓ **READING CHECK:** *Environment and Society* How do the resources of the Russian Far East affect its economy? They have supported mining and timber industries, as well as the growth of industrial cities and ports.

Islands

The Russian Far East includes two island areas. Sakhalin is a large island that lies off the eastern coast of Siberia. The Kuril Islands are much smaller. They stretch in an arc from Hokkaido to the Kamchatka Peninsula.

Sakhalin has oil and mineral resources. The waters around the Kurils are important for commercial fishing. Russia and Japan have argued over who owns these islands since the 1850s. At times they have been divided between Japan and Russia or the Soviet Union. The Soviet Union took control of the islands after World War II. Japan still claims rights to the southernmost islands. By the 2000s, however, increased tourism had helped ease tensions.

Like other Pacific regions, Sakhalin and the Kurils sometimes experience earthquakes and volcanic eruptions. An earthquake in 1995 caused severe damage on Sakhalin Island, killing nearly 2,000 people.

✓ **READING CHECK:** *Environment and Society* How does the environment of the Kuril Islands and Sakhalin affect people? Earthquakes, such as the one in 1995, and volcanoes pose a constant threat to lives and property.

▲ An old volcano created Crater Bay in the Kuril Islands. The islands' beauty is matched by the terrible power of earthquakes and volcanic eruptions in the area.

Interpreting the Visual Record What do you think happened to the volcano that formed Crater Bay?

Section Review 5

Define and explain: icebreakers

Working with Sketch Maps On the map you created in Section 4, label the Sea of Okhotsk, the Sea of Japan, Khabarovsk, Vladivostok, the Amur River, and Sakhalin Island. In the margin, explain which countries dispute possession of Sakhalin Island and the Kuril Islands.

Reading for the Main Idea

1. *Places and Regions* How does the climate of the Russian Far East compare to the climate throughout the rest of Siberia?
2. *Places and Regions* What are the region's major crops and energy resources?

Critical Thinking

3. **Drawing Inferences and Conclusions** In what ways do you think Vladivostok is "Lord of the East" in Russia today?
4. **Drawing Inferences and Conclusions** Why do you think Sakhalin and the Kuril Islands have been the subject of dispute between Russia and Japan?

Organizing What You Know

5. **Finding the Main Idea** Copy the following graphic organizer. Use it to explain how the location of each city has played a role in its development.

Khabarovsk	Vladivostok

Homework Practice Online
Keyword: SJ5 HP20

Section 5 Review

Answers to Section 5 Review

Define For definition, see the glossary.

Working with Sketch Maps Russia and Japan dispute possession of Sakhalin Island and the Kuril Islands.

Reading for the Main Idea

1. far less severe (NGS 4)
2. wheat, sugar beets, sunflowers, meat, dairy products; coal, oil, and geothermal energy (NGS 4)

Critical Thinking

3. It remains a major naval base and home port for a large fishing fleet.
4. The natural resources around these islands make them attractive to both countries.

Organizing What You Know

5. Answers will vary but could include the following: Khabarovsk—its location where the Trans-Siberian Railroad crosses the Amur River made it ideal for processing forest and mineral resources; Vladivostok—its location on the Sea of Japan made it ideal as a naval base and fishing port.

▲ **Visual Record Answer**

It became extinct and was filled with water.

CLOSE

Ask students why residents of the Russian Far East might feel closer to Japan and other Pacific nations than to European Russia. (Possible answers: physically closer to Japan, trade relationships with Pacific countries, isolation created by Siberia) Ask students to predict if this isolation will increase or decrease. (Students may predict that new communication technology will help decrease isolation.)

REVIEW, ASSESS, RETEACH

Have students complete the Section Review. Then have each student write two true-false questions about land use, resources, cities, and islands in the Russian Far East. Pair students and have them quiz each other. Then have students complete Daily Quiz 20.5. **COOPERATIVE LEARNING**

Have students complete Main Idea Activity S5. Then, organize the class into small groups, assigning resources, cities, land use, and islands to different groups. Ask each group to create a visual aid to illustrate the important facts about its topic. **ESOL, COOPERATIVE LEARNING**

EXTEND

Have interested students conduct research on one of the non-Russian ethnic groups of the Russian Far East. Have them include information on the group's common occupations, history, language, and customs. **BLOCK SCHEDULING**

CHAPTER 20 REVIEW

Review and Practice

Define and Identify
For definitions and identifications, see the glossary and index.

Review the Main Ideas

14. Caucasus, Urals, and ranges that run through southern and eastern Siberia; Urals (NGS 4)
15. Volga, Don, Ob, Yenisey, Lena, and Amur rivers (NGS 4)
16. The czar gave up his throne, and the Bolsheviks took over the government.
17. weakened by high costs of the Cold War (NGS 13)
18. great works of art, literature, and music; major scientific accomplishments
19. Moscow—center for government, transportation, communication, and industry; St. Petersburg—Baltic seaport, major center for tourism, trade, education, and industry; Volga—shipping route, hydroelectric power plants, coal and oil deposits; Urals—mining, copper and iron smelters, important cities (NGS 4)
20. long severe winters; mosses and wildflowers in the tundra, evergreen forests south of the tundra (NGS 4)
21. timber, mineral ores, diamonds, coal, oil, natural gas
22. once was closed to foreign contacts, but no longer; now an important link with countries of the Pacific and the United States
23. earthquakes and volcanic eruptions (NGS 4)

Think Critically

24. by development of its natural resources
25. command; government-, not individual-, owned industries
26. because the size of the country and movement of goods and resources; built two transcontinental railroads
27. resentment of domination by ethnic Russians, desire for independence among some ethnic groups, violence
28. food shortages, economic problems, defeat in war, and lack of consumer goods; collapse of the Russian Empire and the Soviet Union (NGS 17)

Define and Identify

Identify each of the following:

1. taiga
2. steppe
3. czar
4. Peter the Great
5. Vladimir Lenin
6. Joseph Stalin
7. superpowers
8. Cold War
9. consumer goods
10. Mikhail Gorbachev
11. heavy industry
12. smelters
13. habitation fog

Review the Main Ideas

14. What are Russia's major mountain ranges? Which range separates Europe from Asia?
15. What are Russia's major rivers?
16. How did Russia's government change in 1917?
17. Why did the Soviet Union collapse?
18. How has Russia contributed to world culture?
19. What four major regions make up the Russian Heartland, and what are their main features?
20. What are Siberia's climate and vegetation like?
21. What resources can be found in Siberia?
22. How has Vladivostok changed? Why is it still an important city?
23. What natural hazards threaten Sakhalin and the Kuril Islands?

Think Critically

24. **Finding the Main Idea** How might Siberia help make Russia an economic success?
25. **Contrasting** What kind of economic system did the Soviet Union have, and how did it differ from that of the United States?
26. **Drawing Inferences and Conclusions** Why is transportation an issue for Russia? What have Russians done to ease transportation between European Russia and the Russian Far East?
27. **Summarizing** What issues trouble some of Russia's ethnic groups?
28. **Identifying Cause and Effect** What problems existed in the Russian Empire and the Soviet Union in the 1900s, and what was their effect?

Map Activity

29. On a separate sheet of paper, match the letters on the map with their correct labels.

    Arctic Ocean
    Caucasus Mountains
    Caspian Sea
    West Siberian Plain
    Central Siberian Plateau
    Kamchatka Peninsula
    Volga River
    Moscow
    St. Petersburg
    Vladivostok

478 • Chapter 20

Map Activity

29. A. Vladivostok
    B. Kamchatka Peninsula
    C. Moscow
    D. Arctic Ocean
    E. West Siberian Plain
    F. Volga River
    G. Caucasus Mountains
    H. Central Siberian Plateau
    I. Caspian Sea
    J. St. Petersburg

Writing Activity

Imagine that you are a tour guide on a trip by train from St. Petersburg to Vladivostok. Use the chapter map or a classroom globe to write a one-page description of some of the places people would see along the train's route. How far would you travel? Be sure to use standard grammar, spelling, sentence structure, and punctuation.

internet connect

Internet Activity: go.hrw.com
KEYWORD: SJ5 GT20

Choose a topic to explore about Russia:
- Take a trip on the Trans-Siberian Railroad.
- Examine the breakup of the Soviet Union.
- View the cultural treasures of Russia.

CHAPTER 20 REVIEW

Writing Activity
Students' descriptions should include the various physical features along the route and an accurate estimation of the distance of the trip. Use Rubric 40, Writing to Describe, to evaluate student work.

Interpreting Political Cartoons
1. the period after the breakup of the Soviet Union
2. The hammer and sickle is a symbol of the Soviet Union.
3. Prices for goods are rising faster than wages.
4. They may not have the money needed to buy consumer goods.

Analyzing Primary Sources
1. steel production
2. trouble breathing, increased risk of heart attacks
3. When there is no wind, the pollution hangs over the city, causing problems.
4. watery eyes, a bad smell

Social Studies Skills Practice

Interpreting Political Cartoons
Study the political cartoon below. Then answer the questions.

Harvell/The Greenville Piedmont, S.C. Reprinted with permission.

1. To what period in Russian history do you think this cartoon refers?
2. How does the cartoonist show that it is about Russia?
3. What economic problem does the cartoonist show?
4. How might the situation shown in the cartoon affect the Russian people?

Analyzing Primary Sources
Read the following passage by B. Frederick Kempe, who visited the Siberian city of Novokuznetsk. Then answer the questions.

"The doctors at Novokuznetsk's Hospital Number 7 know by the way the wind is blowing whether they will have a busy day. If the air is calm and humid, the poisons from the two of the largest steel smelters in the world hang in the air. The hospital's waiting room will then fill . . . parents will rush in with children who can't breathe. Hospital emergency rooms across town will register more heart attacks than usual. . . . My eyes watered as we drove through Novokuznetsk . . . The city produced more steel than any other place in the Soviet Union. And it smelled it. The moist air reeked of rotten egg . . ."

1. What kind of economic activity takes place in Novokuznetsk?
2. What health problems has pollution caused the city's residents?
3. How do weather patterns affect the pollution levels in the city?
4. What problems did Kempe experience when he visited Novokuznetsk?

Russia • 479

CHAPTER 20 REVIEW AND ASSESSMENT RESOURCES

Reproducible
- Readings in World Geography, History, and Culture 40, 41, and 42
- Critical Thinking Activity 20
- Vocabulary Activity 20

Technology
- Chapter 20 Test Generator (on the One-Stop Planner)
- Audio CD Program, Chapter 20
- HRW Go site

Reinforcement, Review, and Assessment
- Chapter 20 Review and Practice
- Chapter Summaries and Review
- Chapter 20 Test
- Chapter 20 Test for English Language Learners and Special-Needs Students

internet connect

GO TO: go.hrw.com
KEYWORD: SJ5 Teacher
FOR: a guide to using the Internet in your classroom

Russia 479

One-Stop Planner CD–ROM

It's easy to plan lessons, select resources, and print out materials for your students when you use the *One-Stop Planner CD–ROM with Test Generator*.

Technology Resources

- One-Stop Planner CD–ROM, Lesson 21.1
- Geography and Cultures Visual Resources with Teaching Activities 31–35
- *ARGWorld* CD–ROM
- Homework Practice Online
- HRW Go site

- One-Stop Planner CD–ROM, Lesson 21.2
- *ARGWorld* CD–ROM
- Homework Practice Online
- HRW Go site

- One-Stop Planner CD–ROM, Lesson 21.3
- *ARGWorld* CD–ROM
- Music of the World Audio CD Program, Selection 9
- Homework Practice Online
- HRW Go site

Review, Reinforcement, and Assessment Resources

ELL	Main Idea Activity S1
REV	Section 1 Review
A	Daily Quiz 21.1
REV	Chapter Summaries and Review
ELL	English Audio Summary 21.1
ELL	Spanish Audio Summary 21.1

ELL	Main Idea Activity S2
REV	Section 2 Review
A	Daily Quiz 21.2
REV	Chapter Summaries and Review
ELL	English Audio Summary 21.2
ELL	Spanish Audio Summary 21.2

ELL	Main Idea Activity S3
REV	Section 3 Review
A	Daily Quiz 21.3
REV	Chapter Summaries and Review
ELL	English Audio Summary 21.3
ELL	Spanish Audio Summary 21.3

internet connect

HRW ONLINE RESOURCES

GO TO: go.hrw.com
Then type in a keyword.

TEACHER HOME PAGE
KEYWORD: **SJ5 TEACHER**

CHAPTER INTERNET ACTIVITIES
KEYWORD: **SJ5 GT21**

Choose an activity to:
- trek through the Caucasus Mountains.
- design Ukrainian Easter eggs.
- investigate the Chernobyl disaster.

CHAPTER ENRICHMENT LINKS
KEYWORD: **SJ5 CH21**

CHAPTER MAPS
KEYWORD: **SJ5 MAPS21**

ONLINE ASSESSMENT
Homework Practice
KEYWORD: **SJ5 HP21**
Standardized Test Prep Online
KEYWORD: **SJ5 STP21**
Rubrics
KEYWORD: **SS Rubrics**

COUNTRY INFORMATION
KEYWORD: **SJ5 Almanac**

CONTENT UPDATES
KEYWORD: **SS Content Updates**

HOLT PRESENTATION MAKER
KEYWORD: **SJ5 PPT21**

ONLINE READING SUPPORT
KEYWORD: **SS Strategies**

CURRENT EVENTS
KEYWORD: **S5 Current Events**

Meeting Individual Needs

Ability Levels

Level 1 Basic-level activities designed for all students encountering new material

Level 2 Intermediate-level activities designed for average students

Level 3 Challenging activities designed for honors and gifted-and-talented students

ESOL Activities that address the needs of students with Limited English Proficiency

Chapter Review and Assessment

E	Readings in World Geography, History, and Culture 43 and 44		Audio CD Program, Chapter 21
SM	Critical Thinking Activity 21	A	Chapter 21 Test for English Language Learners and Special-Needs Students
REV	Chapter 21 Review and Practice	A	Unit 5 Test for English Language Learners and Special-Needs Students
REV	Chapter Summaries and Review		HRW Go site
ELL	Vocabulary Activity 21		
A	Chapter 21 Test		
A	Unit 5 Test		
	Chapter 21 Test Generator (on the One-Stop Planner)		

479B

CHAPTER 21
Ukraine, Belarus, and the Caucasus
Previewing Chapter Resources

Holt Online Learning

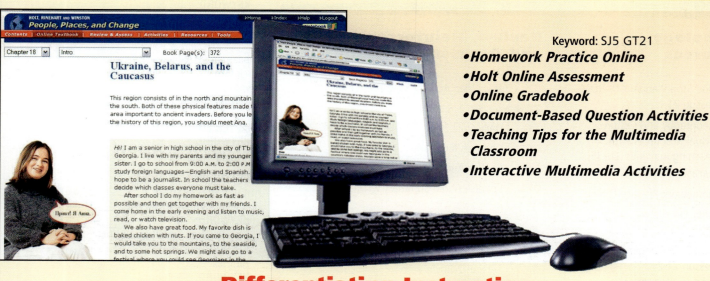

Keyword: SJ5 GT21

- Homework Practice Online
- Holt Online Assessment
- Online Gradebook
- Document-Based Question Activities
- Teaching Tips for the Multimedia Classroom
- Interactive Multimedia Activities

Differentiating Instruction

Reading and Writing Support
- Graphic Organizer Activity
- ◄ Vocabulary Activity
- Chapter Summaries and Review
- Know It Notes
- Audio CD

Active Learning
- Block Scheduling Handbook
- Cultures of the World Activity
- Interdisciplinary Activity
- Map Activity
- ◄ Critical Thinking Activity
- Music of the World Audio CD Program: Choral Music from Georgia

Primary Sources and Advanced Learners
- ◄ Geography for Life Activity: Agriculture and Environment in the Caucasus
- Map Activity: Conflict in the Caucasus
- Readings in World Geography, History and Culture:
  - 43 The Hutsuls of Ukraine
  - 44 The Fractured Caucasus

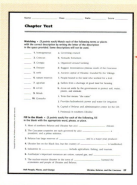

Assessment Program
- Daily Quizzes S1–3
- ◄ Chapter Test
- Chapter Test for English Language Learners and Special-Needs Students

Spanish and ESOL
- Vocabulary Activity
- ◄ Main Idea Activities for English Language Learners and Special-Needs Students
- Chapter Summaries and Review
- Spanish Audio Summary
- Know It Notes S1–3
- Chapter Test for English Language Learners and Special-Needs Students

Special Education Modifications
Your **I.D.E.A. Works!** CD-ROM will provide modified versions of the following teaching materials:
- ◄ Know It Notes S1–3
- Vocabulary Activity
- Main Idea Activities S1–3
- Daily Quizzes S1–3
- Chapter 21 Test
- Flash cards of chapter vocabulary terms

CHAPTER 21
Ukraine, Belarus, and the Caucasus
Previewing Chapter Resources

Holt Online Learning

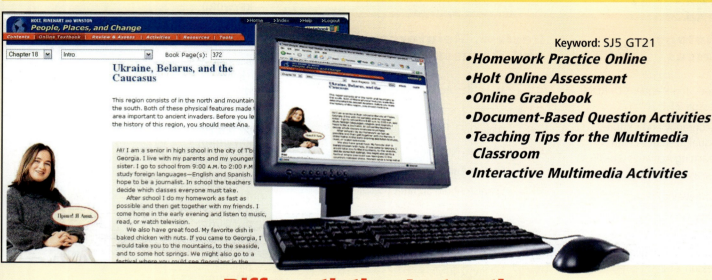

Keyword: SJ5 GT21

- Homework Practice Online
- Holt Online Assessment
- Online Gradebook
- Document-Based Question Activities
- Teaching Tips for the Multimedia Classroom
- Interactive Multimedia Activities

Differentiating Instruction

Reading and Writing Support
- Graphic Organizer Activity
- ◀ Vocabulary Activity
- Chapter Summaries and Review
- Know It Notes
- Audio CD

Active Learning
- Block Scheduling Handbook
- Cultures of the World Activity
- Interdisciplinary Activity
- Map Activity
- ◀ Critical Thinking Activity
- Music of the World Audio CD Program: Choral Music from Georgia

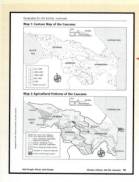

Primary Sources and Advanced Learners
- ◀ Geography for Life Activity: Agriculture and Environment in the Caucasus
- Map Activity: Conflict in the Caucasus
- Readings in World Geography, History and Culture:
  - 43 The Hutsuls of Ukraine
  - 44 The Fractured Caucasus

Assessment Program
- Daily Quizzes S1–3
- ◀ Chapter Test
- Chapter Test for English Language Learners and Special-Needs Students

Spanish and ESOL
- Vocabulary Activity
- ◀ Main Idea Activities for English Language Learners and Special-Needs Students
- Chapter Summaries and Review
- Spanish Audio Summary
- Know It Notes S1–3
- Chapter Test for English Language Learners and Special-Needs Students

Special Education Modifications
Your **I.D.E.A. Works! CD-ROM** will provide modified versions of the following teaching materials:
- ◀ Know It Notes S1–3
- Vocabulary Activity
- Main Idea Activities S1–3
- Daily Quizzes S1–3
- Chapter 21 Test
- Flash cards of chapter vocabulary terms

479C

Teacher Resources

Books for Teachers

Allworth, Edward A., ed. *The Tatars of the Crimea: Return to the Homeland (Central Asia Book Series)* Duke University Press, 1998.

Garnett, Sherman W., and Robert Legvold, eds. *Belarus at the Crossroads.* Carnegie Endowment for International Peace, 1999.

Golz, Thomas. *Azerbaijan Diary: A Rogue Reporter's Adventures in an Oil-rich, War-torn Post-Soviet Republic.* M.E. Sharpe, 1999.

Reid, Anna. *Borderland: A Journey through the History of Ukraine.* Westview Press, 1999.

Books for Students

Caucasus. Hammond, 1999. Maps and information on the former Soviet states.

Kort, Michael. *Russia (Nations in Transition).* Facts on File, 1998. Culture, history, and geography of Russia, emphasizing its transition, since 1991, from a communist to a free nation. **SHELTERED ENGLISH**

Lerner Geography Dept. *Ukraine (Then and Now).* Lerner Publications Company, 1993. Range of topics, with emphasis on the unique ethnicity of the country.

Roberts, Elizabeth, and Sharon Akiner (illustrator). *Georgia, Armenia, and Azerbaijan (Former Soviet States).* Millbrook Press, 1992. History, development, current status, and possible future of the former Soviet countries. **SHELTERED ENGLISH**

Multimedia Materials

Lifting the Yoke: Ukraine. Video, 50 min. Films for the Humanities and Sciences.

The Steppes of Northern Caucasus. Video, 20 min. Films for the Humanities and Sciences.

Videos and CDs

Videos
- CNN Presents Geography: Yesterday and Today, Segment 19 Cossacks Return to Power
- ARG World

Holt Researcher
http://researcher.hrw.com
- *Commonwealth of Independent States (CIS)*
- *Breakup of the Soviet Sphere*
- *Ukraine*
- *Belarus*
- *Georgia Republic*
- *Armenia*
- *Azerbaijan*

Transparency Packages

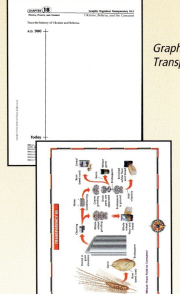

Graphic Organizer Transparencies 21.1–3

Geography and Cultures Visual Resources Transparencies 56–60
64 Ukraine, Belarus, and the Caucasus: Physical-Political
65 Wheat: From Field to Consumer

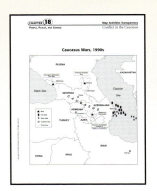

Map Activities Transparency 21 Conflict in the Caucasus

CHAPTER 21

Why It Matters

You may point out these reasons why we should know more about Ukraine, Belarus, and the three nations of the Caucasus:

- The countries in this region are struggling to adopt freer economic and political practices. Americans are now free to travel to these countries and to invest in them.
- These countries possess many natural resources, including deposits of oil, natural gas, metals, and minerals.
- Ukraine's government has the task of ensuring that the damaged Chernobyl nuclear reactor is adequately contained.

CHAPTER 21

Ukraine, Belarus, and the Caucasus

This region consists of plains in the north and mountains in the south. Both of these physical features made this area important to ancient invaders. Before you learn the history of this region, you should meet Ana.

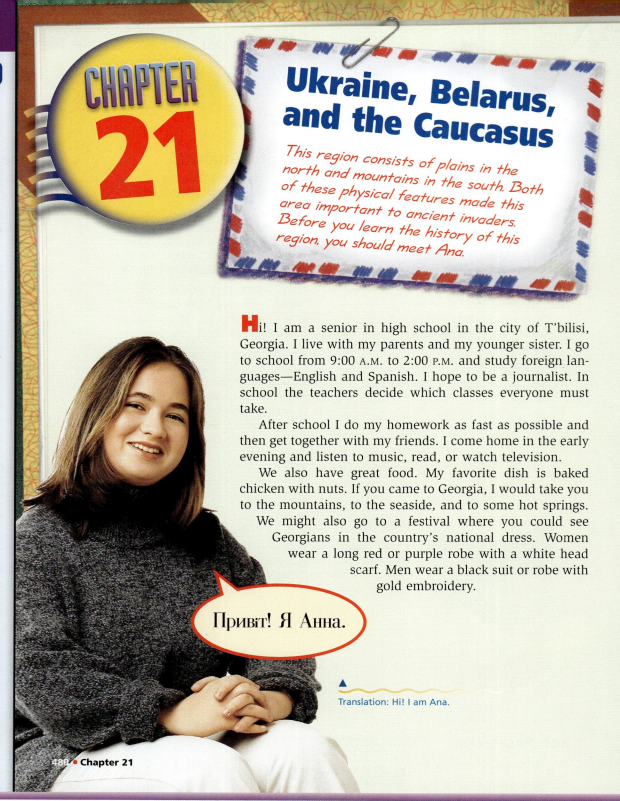

Hi! I am a senior in high school in the city of T'bilisi, Georgia. I live with my parents and my younger sister. I go to school from 9:00 A.M. to 2:00 P.M. and study foreign languages—English and Spanish. I hope to be a journalist. In school the teachers decide which classes everyone must take.

After school I do my homework as fast as possible and then get together with my friends. I come home in the early evening and listen to music, read, or watch television.

We also have great food. My favorite dish is baked chicken with nuts. If you came to Georgia, I would take you to the mountains, to the seaside, and to some hot springs. We might also go to a festival where you could see Georgians in the country's national dress. Women wear a long red or purple robe with a white head scarf. Men wear a black suit or robe with gold embroidery.

Привіт! Я Анна.

Translation: Hi! I am Ana.

Chapter Project

Tell students to imagine that they work for the tourist bureau of one of the Caucasus countries. Organize students into small groups and have each group choose a country. Then have each group prepare a three-minute radio commercial that advertises its chosen country's cultural and geographical features to tourists. Have groups perform their radio commercials for the class. Have students place their commercials in their portfolios.

Starting the Chapter

Read the following quotation from Russian writer Nikolay Gogol's *Taras Bulba*: "The farther they penetrated the steppe, the more beautiful it became.... Nothing in nature could be finer. The whole surface resembled a golden-green ocean, upon which were sprinkled millions of different flowers.... Oh, steppes, how beautiful you are!" Ask what resources the region described might have. (arable land) Tell students that in this chapter they will learn more about the fertile area described, which extends into the countries of Belarus and Ukraine. The countries of the Caucasus Mountains, which have a very different landscape, are also covered in this chapter.

Section 1: Physical Geography

CHAPTER 21, Section 1

Read to Discover
1. What are the region's major physical features?
2. What climate types and natural resources are found in the region?

Vocabulary
nature reserves

Places
Black Sea
Caucasus Mountains
Caspian Sea
Pripyat Marshes
Carpathian Mountains
Crimean Peninsula
Sea of Azov
Mount Elbrus
Dnieper River
Donets Basin

Reading Strategy

USING VISUAL INFORMATION Draw a line down the center of a sheet of paper. Title one column Similarities. Title the other column Differences. Look at the two colored regions on the Physical-Political map. What geographical characteristics do they share? How may they be different? Write your answers in the proper column. As you read, add more details.

SECTION 1 RESOURCES

Reproducible
- Lecture Notes, Section 1
- Block Scheduling Handbook, Chapter 21
- Know It Notes S1
- Creative Strategies for Teaching World Geography, Lesson 13

Technology
- One-Stop Planner CD–ROM, Lesson 21.1
- Homework Practice Online
- Geography and Cultures Visual Resources with Teaching Activities 56–60, 64, 65
- HRW Go site

Reinforcement, Review, and Assessment
- Section 1 Review
- Daily Quiz 21.1
- Main Idea Activity S1
- Chapter Summaries and Review
- English Audio Summary 21.1
- Spanish Audio Summary 21.1

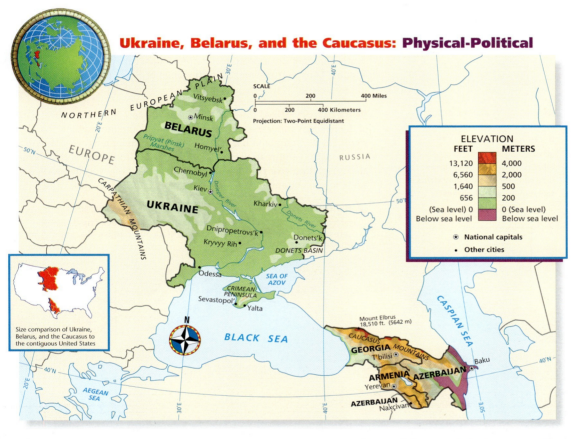

Ukraine, Belarus, and the Caucasus • 481

Section 1

Objectives
1. Identify the region's major physical features.
2. Describe the climate types and natural resources found in the region.

FOCUS

 **Bellringer**

Copy the following passage and instructions onto the chalkboard: *Ukraine was considered the breadbasket of the Soviet Union, while Georgia was a popular vacation spot. Name a pair of states in the United States that could fit the same description.* Discuss student responses. (Possible answers: Nebraska/Florida; Iowa/California; Kansas/Hawaii) Tell students that in Section 1 they will learn more about the physical geography of Ukraine, Belarus, and the Caucasus nations.

Using the Physical-Political Map
Have students examine the map on this page. Call on individual students to locate the Dnieper River, the Donets River, and the Black Sea. Point out why navigable waterways are important in agricultural and industrial regions such as Ukraine (for shipping agricultural products, manufactured goods, and mineral resources to markets or processing plants).

Ukraine, Belarus, and the Caucasus 481

CHAPTER 21, Section 1

Linking Past to Present

Coal Mining in the Donets Basin Note in the section on resources that the Donets Basin is an important coal-mining area. Coal was first discovered there in 1721. However, coal mining became a significant industry only after 1869, when the first railway reached the region. Donets Basin coal mining reached its peak importance by 1913, when the region produced 87 percent of Russian coal. The main part of the coal field covers nearly 9,000 square miles (23,300 sq km) in Ukraine and southwestern Russia, an area slightly smaller than the state of Vermont.

Activity: Have students conduct further research on how the coal mines of the Donets Basin have affected the political and economic history of the region. Ask them to create a time line showing major developments.

Visual Record Answer

volcanic action

GO TO: go.hrw.com
KEYWORD: SJ5 CH21
FOR: Web sites about Ukraine, Belarus, and the Caucasus

Snow-capped Mount Elbrus is located along the border between Georgia and Russia.

Interpreting the Visual Record *Place*
What physical processes do you think may have formed the mountains in this region of earthquakes?

Physical Features

The countries of Ukraine (yoo-KRAYN) and Belarus (byay-luh-ROOS) border western Russia. Belarus is landlocked. Ukraine lies on the Black Sea. Georgia, Armenia (ahr-MEE-nee-uh), and Azerbaijan (a-zuhr-by-JAHN) lie in a rugged region called the Caucasus (KAW-kuh-suhs). It is named for the area's Caucasus Mountains. The Caucasus region is located between the Black Sea and the Caspian Sea.

Landforms Most of Ukraine and Belarus lie in a region of plains. The Northern European Plain sweeps across northern Belarus. The Pripyat (PRI-pyuht) Marshes, also called the Pinsk Marshes, are found in the south. The Carpathian Mountains run through part of western Ukraine. The Crimean (kry-MEE-uhn) Peninsula lies in southern Ukraine. The southern Crimean is very rugged and has high mountains. It separates the Black Sea from the Sea of Azov (uh-ZAWF).

In the north along the Caucasus's border with Russia is a wide mountain range. The region's and Europe's highest peak, Mount Elbrus (el-BROOS), is located here. As you can see on the chapter map, the land drops below sea level along the shore of the Caspian Sea. South of the Caucasus is a rugged, mountainous plateau. Earthquakes often occur in this region.

Rivers One of Europe's major rivers, the Dnieper (NEE-puhr), flows south through Belarus and Ukraine. Ships can travel much of its length. Dams and reservoirs on the Dnieper River provide hydroelectric power and water for irrigation.

Vegetation Mixed forests were once widespread in the central part of the region. Farther south, the forests opened onto the grasslands of the steppe. Today, farmland has replaced much of the original vegetation.

Ukraine is trying to preserve its natural environments and has created several **nature reserves**. These are areas the government has set aside to protect animals, plants, soil, and water.

✓ **READING CHECK:** *Places and Regions* What are the region's major physical features? **Caucasus Mountains, Northern European Plain, Pripyat Marshes, Carpathian Mountains, Crimean Peninsula, Black Sea, Caspian Sea, Sea of Azov, Dnieper River**

482 • Chapter 21

TEACH

Teaching Objective 1

ALL LEVELS: (Suggested time: 30 min.) Tell students to imagine that they are tourists visiting Ukraine, Belarus, and the Caucasus countries. Then have students write a postcard or letter that describes the region's physical features to a friend back home. Ask volunteers to read their postcards or letters to the class. **ESOL**

Teaching Objective 2

ALL LEVELS: (Suggested time: 20 min.) Copy the following graphic organizer onto the chalkboard, omitting the blue answers. Have students complete the organizer, placing the resource that all three have in common in the center. Then pair students and have each pair draw a map that depicts the region's various climates. Have students create keys for their maps.
ESOL, COOPERATIVE LEARNING, **LS** **VISUAL-SPATIAL**

NATURAL RESOURCES

- Ukraine: coal, iron
- Belarus: (no specific resources listed)
- Caucasus Countries: oil, gas, copper, manganese, iron, other metals
- Center: farmland

482 Chapter 21

Climate

Like much of western Russia, the northern two thirds of Ukraine and Belarus have a humid continental climate. Winters are cold. Summers are warm but short. Southern Ukraine has a steppe climate. Unlike the rest of the country, the Crimean Peninsula has a Mediterranean climate. There are several different climates in the Caucasus. Georgia's coast has a mild climate similar to the Carolinas in the United States. Azerbaijan contains mainly a steppe climate. Because it is so mountainous, Armenia's climate changes with elevation.

✓ **READING CHECK:** *Places and Regions* What climate types are found in this area? humid continental, steppe, Mediterranean

Resources

Rich farmlands are Ukraine's greatest natural resource. Farming is also important in Belarus. Lowland areas of the Caucasus have rich soil and good conditions for farming.

The Donets (duh-NYETS) Basin in southeastern Ukraine is a rich coal-mining area. Kryvyy Rih (kri-VI RIK) is the site of a huge open-pit iron-ore mine. The region's most important mineral resources are Azerbaijan's large and valuable oil and gas deposits. These are found under the shallow Caspian Sea. Copper, manganese, iron, and other metals are also present in the Caucasus.

✓ **READING CHECK:** *Environment and Society* How have this region's natural resources affected economic development? Rich farmlands, minerals, metals and oil and gas support the economy.

Section Review 1

Define and explain: nature reserves

Working with Sketch Maps On a map of Europe that you draw or that your teacher provides, label the following: Black Sea, Caucasus Mountains, Caspian Sea, Pripyat Marshes, Carpathian Mountains, Crimean Peninsula, Sea of Azov, Mount Elbrus, Dnieper River, and Donets Basin. Where in the region is a major coal-mining area?

Reading for the Main Idea

1. *Places and Regions* What three seas are found in this region?
2. *Places and Regions* What creates variation in Armenia's climate?

Critical Thinking

3. **Drawing Inferences and Conclusions** Why has so much farming developed in Ukraine, Belarus, and the Caucasus?
4. **Drawing Inferences and Conclusions** How do you think heavy mining in this region could create pollution?

Organizing What You Know

5. **Categorizing** Copy the following graphic organizer. Use it to describe the region's physical features, climates, and resources.

	Physical features	Climate	Resources
Belarus			
Caucasus			
Ukraine			

Section 1 Review

Answers to Section 1 Review

Define For definition, see the glossary.

Working with Sketch Maps Maps will vary, but listed places should be labeled in their approximate locations. The Donets Basin is a major coal-mining area.

Reading for the Main Idea
1. Black Sea, Sea of Azov, Caspian Sea (NGS 4)
2. elevation (NGS 4)

Critical Thinking
3. because of the areas' rich soil and good weather conditions
4. metals being washed into water supply

Organizing What You Know
5. Belarus—Northern European Plain, Pinsk Marshes, Dnieper River; humid continental; farmland; Caucasus region—Black Sea, Caspian Sea, Caucasus Mountains, Mount Elbrus; steppe climate, mild coastal climate; rich soil, copper, manganese, iron, oil, and gas; Ukraine—plains, steppe, Carpathian Mountains, Crimea, Black Sea, Sea of Azov, Dnieper River; humid continental, steppe, Mediterranean; farmland, coal, iron

---

CLOSE

Ask students to describe some things they might do for fun if they visited this region.

REVIEW, ASSESS, RETEACH

Have students complete the Section Review. Then organize the class into triads and have each triad write eight quiz questions that match a country to its landforms, climate, or natural features. Have groups exchange their quizzes and then solve them. Then have students complete Daily Quiz 21.1.

Have students complete Main Idea Activity S1. Then have students illustrate the postcards or letters they created earlier with appropriate physical features, climate type(s), and natural resources. **ESOL**

EXTEND

Have interested students conduct further research on the plants and animals of the Pripyat Marshes of Belarus. Then have students create a publicity campaign to raise awareness of the region's unique characteristics and the forces that endanger it. **BLOCK SCHEDULING**

Section 2: Ukraine and Belarus

Read to Discover
1. Which groups have influenced the history of Ukraine and Belarus?
2. What are some important economic features and environmental concerns of Ukraine?
3. How has the economy of Belarus developed?

Vocabulary
serfs
soviet

Places
Ukraine
Belarus
Kiev
Chernobyl
Minsk

People
Mongols
Cossacks

Reading Strategy

TAKING NOTES Use the headings in this section to create an outline. As you read, write down details about Ukraine and Belarus beneath each heading.

гео·гра·фия

These are the syllables for the Russian word for geography, written in the Cyrillic alphabet.

History and Government

About 600 B.C. the Greeks established trading colonies along the coast of the Black Sea. Much later—during the A.D. 400s—the Slavs began to move into what is now Ukraine and Belarus. Today, most people in this region speak closely related Slavic languages.

Vikings and Christians In the 800s Vikings took the city of Kiev. Located on the Dnieper River, it became the capital of the Vikings' trading empire. Today, this old city is Ukraine's capital. In the 900s the Byzantine, or Greek Orthodox, Church sent missionaries to teach the Ukrainians and Belorussians about Christianity. These missionaries introduced the Cyrillic alphabet.

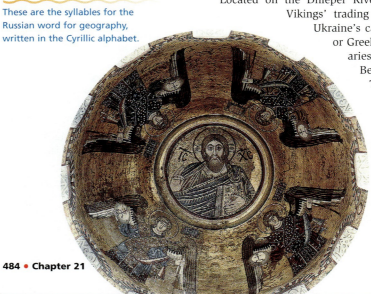

St. Sophia Cathedral in Kiev was built in the 1000s. It was one of the earliest Orthodox cathedrals in this area. Religious images decorate the dome's interior.

484 • Chapter 21

Focus

Bellringer

Copy the following instructions onto the chalkboard: *Compile a list of countries that formerly ruled different parts of what is now the United States.* Ask volunteers to share their lists with the class. (Students may mention England, France, Spain, Mexico, and Russia.) Tell students that in Section 2 they will learn more about the various groups that have influenced the culture and history of Ukraine and Belarus.

Building Vocabulary

Write the words **serfs, Cossacks,** and **soviet** on the chalkboard. Ask volunteers to look up the definitions and origins of the vocabulary terms in the dictionary and to read the definitions and origins aloud. (The word *Serf* is from the Latin *servus,* which means "slave"; *Cossack,* which has Polish, Ukrainian, and Turkish origins, means "pirate"; and *soviet* is a Russian word for a council.) Tell students that the origins of these words indicate some of the historical influences on Ukraine and Belarus.

CHAPTER 21, Section 2

SECTION 2 RESOURCES

Reproducible
- Lecture Notes, Section 2
- Know It Notes S2
- Graphic Organizer 21
- Cultures of the World Activity 4

Technology
- One-Stop Planner CD–ROM, Lesson 21.2
- Homework Practice Online
- HRW Go site

Reinforcement, Review, and Assessment
- Section 2 Review
- Daily Quiz 21.2
- Main Idea Activity S2
- Chapter Summaries and Review
- English Audio Summary 21.2
- Spanish Audio Summary 21.2

Section 2

Objectives
1. Identify the groups that influenced the history of Ukraine and Belarus.
2. Discuss some important economic features and environmental concerns of Ukraine.
3. Trace the development of Belarus's economy.

Mongols and Cossacks A grandson of Genghis Khan led the Mongol horsemen who conquered Ukraine in the 1200s. They destroyed most of the towns and cities there, including Kiev.

Later, northern Ukraine and Belarus came under the control of Lithuanians and Poles. Under foreign rule, Ukrainian and Belorussian **serfs** suffered. Serfs were people who were bound to the land and worked for a lord. In return, the lords provided the serfs with military protection and other services. Some Russian and Ukrainian serfs left the farms and formed bands of nomadic horsemen. Known as Cossacks, they lived on the Ukrainian frontier.

The Russian Empire North and east of Belarus, a new state arose around Moscow. This Russian kingdom of Muscovy won independence from the Mongols in the late 1400s. The new state set out to expand its borders. By the 1800s all of modern Belarus and Ukraine were under Moscow's rule. Now the Cossacks served the armies of the Russian czar. However, conditions did not improve for the Ukrainian and Belorussian serfs and peasants.

Soviet Republics The Russian Revolution ended the rule of the czars in 1917. Ukraine and Belarus became republics of the Soviet Union in 1922. Although each had its own governing **soviet**, or council, Communist leaders in Moscow made all major decisions.

Ukraine was especially important as the Soviet Union's richest farming region. On the other hand, Belarus became a major industrial center. It produced heavy machinery for the Soviet Union. While Ukraine and Belarus were part of the Soviet Union, the Ukrainian and Belorussian languages were discouraged. Practicing a religion was also discouraged.

After World War II economic development continued in Ukraine and Belarus. Factories and power plants were built with little concern for the safety of nearby residents.

This watercolor on rice paper depicts Kublai Khan. He was the founder of the vast Mongol empire in the 1200s. The Mongols conquered large areas of Asia and Europe, including Ukraine.

Kiev remained an important cultural and industrial center during the Soviet era. Parts of the city were destroyed during World War II and had to be rebuilt. Today tree-lined streets greet shoppers in the central city.

Environment and Society

Onagers and Ostriches, Oh My! Although the Soviet era left parts of Ukraine badly polluted, there are also large natural areas that are protected from industry.

Ukrainians have long supported conservation. Ukraine's first nature reserve began as a private wildlife refuge in 1875. This reserve covers about 27,400 acres (11,000 hectares) and protects a portion of virgin steppe. A successful breeding program for endangered species has been established there. Two of the species are onagers, or wild donkeys, and ostriches.

The Black Sea Nature Reserve, established in 1927, includes protected areas of the sea. The Danube Water Meadows was established for the scientific study and protection of the Danube River's tidewater plant life. The Ukrainian Steppe Reserve, consisting of three separate sections, preserves three special kinds of steppe: meadow steppe, black-earth steppe, and stony steppe. Other reserves protect forest-steppe woodlands, marshes, forests, and mountains.

Activity: Have students conduct additional research and create a collage of pictures of animals found in Ukraine's nature reserves.

CHAPTER 21, Section 2

Daily Life

A Ukrainian Birthday The Ukrainian custom of the first haircutting, *postryzhyny*, marks a child's first birthday. The child's whole family gathers to participate in the event and to share a feast.

Guests contribute coins that are collected and placed in a soup bowl. Each of the child's godparents then takes a turn cutting the child's hair as the guests observe. First a lock is cut from the front of the child's head, then from the back, and then from each side. These cuttings are taken from four areas on the head, which represent the four directions of the compass.

After the haircutting, liquor is poured into the bowl to cover the coins. The baby's feet are then dipped into the bowl. This ritual symbolizes that the child will never be controlled by alcohol or money in years to come. The coins are then dried and saved for the child.

Activity: Have students recall rites of passage in their lives such as religious confirmations or graduations and explain the relationship between these rituals and their culture.

Near the end of World War II, Soviet, American, and British leaders met at Livadia Palace in Yalta, Ukraine. There they planned the defeat and occupation of Germany.

End of Soviet Rule When the Soviet Union collapsed in 1991, Belarus and Ukraine declared independence. Each now has a president and a prime minister. Both countries still have economic problems. Ukraine has also had disagreements with Russia over control of the Crimean Peninsula and the Black Sea naval fleet.

✓ **READING CHECK:** Human Systems Which groups have influenced the history of Ukraine and Belarus? Greeks, Slavs, Vikings, Christians, Mongols, Lithuanians, Poles

Ukraine

Ethnic Ukrainians make up almost 78 percent of Ukraine's population. The largest minority group in the country is Russian. There are other ties between Ukraine and Russia. For example, the Ukrainian and Russian languages are closely related. In addition, both countries use the Cyrillic alphabet.

Economy Ukraine has a good climate for growing crops and some of the world's richest soil. As a result, agriculture is important to its economy. Ukraine is the world's largest producer of sugar beets. Ukraine's food-processing industry makes sugar from the sugar beets. Farmers also grow fruits, potatoes, vegetables, and wheat. Grain is made into flour for baked goods and pasta. Livestock is also raised. Ukraine is one of the world's top steel producers. Ukrainian factories make automobiles, railroad cars, ships, and trucks.

486 • Chapter 21

Teaching Objective 2

LEVEL 1: (Suggested time: 30 min.) Tell students to imagine that they are compiling an almanac about contemporary Ukraine. Pair students and have each pair compile a list of important economic features and environmental concerns of Ukraine. (Lists should mention Ukraine's rich soil and the importance of agriculture; it is the world's largest producer of sugar beets; it is a top steel producer; Ukraine experienced rapid industrial growth under the Soviets; the world's worst nuclear disaster occurred at Chernobyl in 1986.) Ask volunteers to present their lists to the class.
ESOL, COOPERATIVE LEARNING

LEVELS 2 AND 3: (Suggested time: 30 min.) Have students use the lists they created for the Level 1 activity as the basis for recommendations to Ukraine's government for developing the country's economy and protecting its environment.

Teacher to Teacher

Joanne Sadler of Buffalo, New York, suggests this activity to teach about the geography and culture of Ukraine and Belarus. Organize students into groups, and have groups study either Ukraine or Belarus. Have students write and illustrate another section for this textbook, to be titled "Ukraine (or Belarus), Close-Up and in Detail."

Connecting to Science

A combine used during July harvest

Wheat: From Field to Consumer

Wheat is one of Ukraine's most important farm products. The illustration below shows how wheat is processed for use by consumers.

- The head of the wheat plant contains the wheat kernels, wrapped in husks. The kernel includes the bran or seed coat, the endosperm, and the germ from which new wheat plants grow.

- Whole wheat flour contains all the parts of the kernel. White flour is produced by grinding only the endosperm. Vitamins are added to some white flour to replace vitamins found in the bran and germ.

- People use wheat to make breads, pastas, and breakfast foods. Wheat by-products are used in many other foods.

GLOBAL PERSPECTIVES

Chernobyl's Lasting Legacy Some effects of the Chernobyl nuclear explosion only became apparent years after the accident. The resulting radioactive contamination of the region's food supply and environment has hurt human and animal health and the region's economies.

Some 10 years after the accident, children's cancer rates in parts of Belarus, Russia, and Ukraine were as much as 30 times higher than before the accident. Also, scientists have noted that genetic damage in humans and animals has been passed on to the next generation.

The contaminated part of Ukraine and Belarus was about the size of England, Wales, and Northern Ireland. Moreover, Belarus has spent up to 20 percent of its annual budget to cope with Chernobyl's aftermath.

GO TO: go.hrw.com
KEYWORD: SJ5 CH21
FOR: Web sites about Chernobyl

Environment During the Soviet period, Ukraine experienced rapid industrial growth. There were few pollution controls, however. In 1986 at the town of Chernobyl, the world's worst nuclear-reactor disaster occurred. Radiation spread across Ukraine and parts of northern Europe. People near the accident died. Others are still suffering from cancer. Many Ukrainians now want to reduce their country's dependence on nuclear power. This has been hard because the country has not developed enough alternative sources of power.

✓ **READING CHECK: Environment and Society** How has the scarcity of alternative sources of power affected Ukraine? *It has forced a reliance upon nuclear power.*

Teaching Objective 3

ALL LEVELS: (Suggested time: 15 min.) Copy the graphic organizer onto the chalkboard, omitting the blue answers. Use it to help students understand the development of Belarus's economy. Have each student complete the organizer. Ask volunteers to share their answers with the class. Conclude by leading a discussion about Belarus's culture, natural resources, and products. **ESOL**

▶**ASSIGNMENT:** Distribute outline maps of Belarus to students. Have each student fill in the map with symbols that represent the various natural resources and products of Belarus. Have students create keys for their maps.

Economic Development in Belarus

- WWII destroyed most of Belarus's agriculture and industry.
- Belarus received the worst of the radiation fallout from Chernobyl.
- The country has resisted economic reforms.
- Belarus has limited mineral resources.

⇒ ⇒ ⇒ *slow economic growth*

Section 2 Review

Answers to Section 2 Review

Define or identify For definitions and identifications, see the glossary and index.

Working with Sketch Maps Listed places should be labeled accurately.

Reading for the Main Idea
1. trading colonies, Slavic languages, city of Kiev, Christianity, Cyrillic alphabet (NGS 9)
2. Ukrainian, Belorussian, Russian (NGS 9)

Critical Thinking
3. Ukraine and Belarus declared independence but have economic problems. Ukraine and Russia have had disagreements about political and military issues.
4. contaminated region, killed people, led to cancer

Organizing What You Know
5. 900s—Christianity, Cyrillic alphabet brought in; 1200s—Mongols invade; late 1400s—Muscovy wins independence; 1800s—region ruled by Moscow; 1917—Russian Revolution, beginning of Soviet rule; 1991—Soviet Union collapses

Chart Answer
lower; nuclear fallout, poverty, diet, or other causes

Belarus and Ukraine

Country	Population/ Growth Rate	Life Expectancy	Literacy Rate	Per Capita GDP
Belarus	10,322,151 −0.1%	63, male 75, female	99%	$8,200
Ukraine	48,055,439 −0.7%	61, male 72, female	99%	$4,500
United States	290,342,554 0.9%	74, male 80, female	97%	$37,600

Source: Central Intelligence Agency, *The World Factbook 2003*

Interpreting the Chart *Place* How does life expectancy in the region compare to that of the United States? Why do you think this is the case?

Belarus

The people of Belarus are known as Belorussians, which means "white Russians." Ethnically they are closely related to Russians. Their language is also very similar to Russian.

Culture Ethnic Belorussians make up about 80 percent of the country's population. Russians are the second-largest ethnic group. Both Belorussian and Russian are official languages. Belorussian also uses the Cyrillic alphabet. Minsk, the capital of Belarus, is the administrative center of the Commonwealth of Independent States.

Economy Belarus has faced many difficulties. Fighting in World War II destroyed most of the agriculture and industry in the country. Belarus also received the worst of the radiation fallout from the Chernobyl nuclear disaster, which contaminated the country's farm products and water. Many people developed health problems as a result. Another problem has been slow economic progress since the collapse of the Soviet Union. Belarus has resisted economic changes made by other former Soviet republics.

There are various resources in Belarus, however. The country has a large reserve of potash, which is used for fertilizer. Belarus leads the world in the production of peat, a source of fuel found in the damp marshes. Mining and manufacturing are important to the economy. Flax, one of the country's main crops, is grown for fiber and seed. Cattle and pigs are also raised. Nearly one third of Belarus is covered by forests that produce wood and paper products.

✓ **READING CHECK:** *Human Systems* How has the economy of Belarus developed? **slowly, because of the collapse of the Soviet Union and resistance to economic change**

Section Review 2

Define or identify: Mongols, serfs, Cossacks, soviet

Working with Sketch Maps On your map from Section 1, label Ukraine, Belarus, Kiev, Chernobyl, and Minsk.

Reading for the Main Idea
1. *Human Systems* What contributions were made by early groups that settled in this region?
2. *Human Systems* What ethnic groups and languages are found in this region today?

Critical Thinking
3. **Finding the Main Idea** How did the end of Soviet rule affect Ukraine and Belarus?
4. **Summarizing** How has the nuclear disaster at Chernobyl affected the region?

Organizing What You Know
5. **Sequencing** Copy the time line below. Use it to trace the region's history from the A.D. 900s to today.

A.D. 900 ——————————————— Today

Homework Practice Online Keyword: SJ5 HP21

488 • Chapter 21

CLOSE

Ask students to name some cultural and historical similarities between Ukraine and Belarus. (Students should mention similarities in languages, use of a Cyrillic alphabet, and Soviet rule.)

REVIEW, ASSESS, RETEACH

After students complete the Section Review, have them write four quiz questions related to the history and culture of Ukraine and Belarus. Collect the questions and use them to quiz the class before students complete Daily Quiz 21.2.

Have students complete Main Idea Activity S2. Then organize the class into small groups; have each group use the vocabulary and places lists and a few other terms from this section to create a crossword puzzle with clues. Have groups exchange their puzzles and then solve them. **ESOL, COOPERATIVE LEARNING**

EXTEND

Have students research the Mongol conquest of the Ukraine or the role of the Cossacks in Russian and Ukrainian history. Ask students to prepare a five-minute oral report based on their research. **BLOCK SCHEDULING**

Section 3: The Caucasus

CHAPTER 21, Section 3

Read to Discover
1. What groups influenced the early history and culture of the Caucasus?
2. What is the economy of Georgia like?
3. What is Armenia like today?
4. What is Azerbaijan like today?

Vocabulary
homogeneous
agrarian

Places
Georgia
Armenia
Azerbaijan

Reading Strategy
READING ORGANIZER Before you read, create a spider map. Label the center of the map The Caucasus. Create a leg for Georgia, Armenia, and Azerbaijan. As you read the section, fill in the map with details about each country.

Section 3 Resources
Reproducible
- Lecture Notes, Section 3
- Know It Notes S3
- Cultures of the World Activity 4
- Geography for Life Activity 21
- Map Activity 21
- Biography Activity: Aram Khachaturian

Technology
- One-Stop Planner CD–ROM, Lesson 21.3
- Music of the World Audio CD, Program, Selection 9
- Homework Practice Online
- HRW Go site

Reinforcement, Review, and Assessment
- Section 3 Review
- Daily Quiz 21.3
- Main Idea Activity S3
- Chapter Summaries and Review
- English Audio Summary 21.3
- Spanish Audio Summary 21.3

History

In the 500s B.C. the Caucasus region was controlled by the Persian Empire. Later it was brought under the influence of the Byzantine Empire and was introduced to Christianity. About A.D. 650, Muslim invaders cut the region off from Christian Europe. By the late 1400s other Muslims, the Ottoman Turks, ruled a vast empire to the south and west. Much of Armenia eventually came under the rule of that empire.

Modern Era During the 1800s Russia took over eastern Armenia, much of Azerbaijan, and Georgia. The Ottoman Turks continued to rule western Armenia. Many Armenians spread throughout the Ottoman Empire. However, they were not treated well. Their desire for more independence led to the massacre of thousands of Armenians. Hundreds of thousands died while being forced to leave Turkey during World War I. Some fled to Russian Armenia.

After the war Armenia, Azerbaijan, and Georgia were briefly independent. By 1922 they had become part of the Soviet Union. They again became independent when the Soviet Union collapsed in 1991.

This wall painting is one of many at the ancient Erebuni Citadel in Yerevan, Armenia's capital. The fortress was probably built in the 800s B.C. by one of Armenia's earliest peoples, the Urartians.

Objectives
1. List the groups that influenced the early history and culture of the Caucasus.
2. Discuss Georgia's economy.
3. Describe today's Armenia.
4. Discuss what Azerbaijan is like today.

Focus

Bellringer
Copy the following scenario onto the chalkboard: *Imagine that you live in a small country that has recently gained independence from a large country. Your country is struggling to change in ways that bring more freedom to your citizens. Independence has been difficult, however. Many people have concluded life was better under the large country's rule. Do you agree? Write down your response.* Discuss responses. Tell students that in Section 3 they will learn about three countries—Georgia, Armenia, and Azerbaijan—where this scenario is a reality.

Building Vocabulary
Have volunteers read aloud the definitions of **homogeneous** and **agrarian** from the glossary. Then ask students to apply these terms to describe various societies or economies they have already studied.

CHAPTER 21, Section 3

FOOD FESTIVAL

Yummy Over Ice Cream!
Compote is a popular dessert in Ukraine. It is sweetened stewed fruit, cooked carefully to keep the fruit as whole as possible.

To make the compote, wash and drain 1 pound of fresh strawberries or raspberries. Combine ¾ cup of sugar and 1 cup of water and bring it to a boil. Pour the boiling syrup over the fruit and let it stand for several hours before eating.

▲ This Georgian family's breakfast includes local specialties such as *khachapuri*—bread made with goat cheese.

Interpreting the Visual Record
What other agricultural products do you see on the table?

Visual Record Answers
cucumbers and other vegetables

Government Each country has an elected parliament, president, and prime minister. In the early 1990s there was civil war in Georgia. Armenia and Azerbaijan were also involved in a war during this time. Ethnic minorities in each country want independence. Disagreements about oil and gas rights may cause more regional conflicts in the future.

✓ **READING CHECK:** (Human Systems) How has conflict among cultures been a problem in this region? **Ethnic minorities want independence; disagreements about oil and gas rights may cause problems.**

Georgia

Georgia is a small country located between the high Caucasus Mountains and the Black Sea. About 70 percent of the people are ethnic Georgians. The official language, Georgian, has its own alphabet. This alphabet was used as early as A.D. 400.

When the Soviet Union fell, Georgia lost a valuable trading partner and a source of cheap fuel. Since then, poverty, corruption, and civil war have troubled the country. In 2003, the Georgians forced the government to resign in a bloodless revolution.

Georgia has little good farmland. Tea and citrus fruits are the major crops. Vineyards are an important part of Georgian agriculture. Fish, livestock, and poultry contribute to the economy. Tourism on the Black Sea has also helped the economy. Because its only energy resource is hydropower, Georgia imports most of its energy supplies.

✓ **READING CHECK:** (Human Systems) In what way has scarcity of energy resources affected Georgia's economy? **It has made Georgia dependent on other nations for energy imports.**

Armenia

Armenia is a little smaller than Maryland. It lies just east of Turkey. It has fewer than 4 million people and is not as diverse as other countries

The Orthodox Christian Haghartsin Monastery was built in Armenia in the 1100s.

490 • Chapter 21

TEACH

Teaching Objectives 1–4
ALL LEVELS: (Suggested time: 30 min.) Copy the following graphic organizer onto the chalkboard, omitting the blue answers. Use it to help students understand the shared history and culture of the Caucasus countries and the economic and cultural differences between these countries. Have students work in pairs to complete the organizer.
ESOL, COOPERATIVE LEARNING, LS **VISUAL-SPATIAL**

SHARED HISTORY AND CULTURE
- ruled by ancient Persian Empire
- under Byzantine influence
- Caucasus isolated from Christian groups in Europe
- mostly taken over by Russia

CURRENT CULTURAL AND ECONOMIC SITUATION

GEORGIA	ARMENIA	AZERBAIJAN
• Georgian language	• Armenian language predominant	• Turkic language predominant
• shortage of good farmland	• varied industry includes mining, carpets, clothes, and footwear	• agrarian society
• tea, citrus fruits, vineyards, and tourism important to economy	• agriculture important	• oil, natural gas, cotton, and fishing important to economy
• imports most of its energy		

490 Chapter 21

in the Caucasus. Almost all the people are Armenian, belong to the Armenian Orthodox Church, and speak Armenian.

Armenia's progress toward economic reform has not been easy. In 1988 a massive earthquake destroyed nearly one third of its industry. Armenia's industry today is varied. It includes mining and the production of carpets, clothing, and footwear.

Agriculture accounts for about 40 percent of Armenia's gross domestic product. High-quality grapes and fruits are important. Beef and dairy cattle and sheep are raised on mountain pastures.

✓ **READING CHECK:** **Environment and Society** How did the 1998 earthquake affect the people of Armenia? *Destroyed nearly one third of Armenian industry*

Azerbaijan

Azerbaijan has nearly 8 million people. Its population is becoming ethnically more **homogeneous**, or the same. The Azeri, who speak a Turkic language, make up about 90 percent of the population.

Azerbaijan has few industries except for oil production. It is mostly an **agrarian** society. An agrarian society is organized around farming. The country's main resources are cotton, natural gas, and oil. Baku, the national capital, is the center of a large oil-refining industry. Oil is the most important part of Azerbaijan's economy. Fishing is also important because of the sturgeon of the Caspian Sea.

✓ **READING CHECK:** **Human Systems** What are some cultural traits of the people of Azerbaijan? *They are mostly ethnically homogeneous and speak a Turkic language.*

A troupe performs traditional folk dances of Azerbaijan.

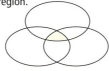

Define and explain: homogeneous, agrarian

Working with Sketch Maps On the map you created for Section 2, label Georgia, Armenia, and Azerbaijan. How has the location of this region helped and hindered its growth?

Reading for the Main Idea

1. **Human Systems** Which groups influenced the early history of the Caucasus?
2. **Human Systems** Which country controlled the Caucasus during most of the 1900s?

Critical Thinking

3. **Analyzing Information** Why has economic reform been difficult in Armenia?
4. **Finding the Main Idea** How is Azerbaijan's economy organized?

Organizing What You Know

5. **Comparing/Contrasting** Copy the following graphic organizer. Use it to show the similarities and differences among the countries of the Caucasus region.

Section 3 Review

Answers to Section 3 Review

Define For definitions, see the glossary.

Working with Sketch Maps Maps will vary, but listed places should be labeled in their approximate locations. Proximity to Asia has led to Turkish, Persian, and Muslim influences. Geographic and cultural isolation from the rest of Europe is a result of the Caucasus Mountains.

Reading for the Main Idea

1. Persians, Byzantine Empire, Muslims, Ottoman Turks (NGS 9)
2. the Soviet Union (NGS 13)

Critical Thinking

3. The massive 1988 earthquake destroyed much of the country's industry. (NGS 15)
4. around farming, oil

Organizing What You Know

5. Students should discuss physical, historical, and cultural differences. They might mention that the countries share a history of Soviet domination and reliance on agriculture.

CLOSE

Have students use the information in the graphic organizer to compose a few lines of rhyming verse about one of the countries.

REVIEW, ASSESS, RETEACH

Have students complete the Section Review. Then organize students into groups. Have each group create eight flash cards using information in the section and exchange these flash cards with another group. Have students within each group use the flash cards to quiz each other. Then have students complete Daily Quiz 21.3. **COOPERATIVE LEARNING**

Have students complete Main Idea Activity S3. Then ask students to outline the section. **ESOL**

EXTEND

Have interested students conduct research on the cultural history of a resource or product of one of the Caucasus countries. Examples may include carpets in Armenia, vineyards in Georgia, or caviar in Azerbaijan. Then have each student deliver a short oral report to the class about his or her chosen subject. **BLOCK SCHEDULING**

CHAPTER 21 REVIEW

Define and Identify
For definitions and identifications, see the glossary and index.

Review the Main Ideas
8. highest—Mount Elbrus; lowest—along western shore of the Caspian Sea
9. the Crimean Peninsula (NGS 4)
10. rich farmland
11. Vikings—invaded and founded Kiev as the capital of their trading empire; Byzantine missionaries—taught Christianity and introduced the Cyrillic alphabet
12. because Ukraine was the Soviet Union's richest farming area and Belarus was a major industrial center (NGS 11)
13. Ukrainian and Belorussian languages discouraged, religious practice discouraged, pollution caused by industrialization
14. world's worst nuclear-reactor disaster; received worst of the radiation fall-out from the disaster
15. Persians, Byzantines, Muslims, Ottoman Turks, Russians
16. Hundreds of thousands died while being forced to leave Turkey.
17. Georgians forced the government to resign in a bloodless revolution.
18. massive earthquake
19. homogeneous
20. oil production

Think Critically
21. Students might suggest that ethnic rivalries can intensify conflicts. (NGS 13)
22. They suffered under the rule of Lithuanians and Poles.
23. Answers will vary. Students should use information from the chapter to justify their opinions.

CHAPTER 21 Review and Practice

Define and Identify
Identify each of the following:
1. nature reserves
2. Mongols
3. serfs
4. Cossacks
5. soviet
6. homogeneous
7. agrarian

Review the Main Ideas
8. Where are this region's highest and lowest points?
9. What part of Ukraine has a Mediterranean climate?
10. What is Ukraine's greatest natural resource?
11. How did Vikings and Byzantine missionaries affect Ukraine?
12. Why were Ukraine and Belarus so valuable to the Soviet Union?
13. How did Soviet rule affect Ukraine and Belarus?
14. What happened at Chernobyl in 1986? How did this event affect Belarus?
15. What groups of people have ruled the Caucasus region?
16. What happened to the Armenians during World War I?
17. What happened in Georgia in 2003?
18. What natural disaster occured in Armenia in 1988?
19. What kind of society does Azerbaijan have?
20. What is Azerbaijan's main industry?

Think Critically
21. **Drawing Inferences and Conclusions** How might ethnic diversity affect relations among the countries in this chapter?
22. **Summarizing** What is the history of the serfs in Ukraine and Belarus?
23. **Analyzing Information** Of the countries covered in this chapter, which do you think was the most important to the former Soviet Union? Why do you think this was so?
24. **Summarizing** Why did the countries of the Caucasus develop so differently from Russia, Ukraine, and Belarus?
25. **Finding the Main Idea** Why are the economies of each of the Caucasus countries so different from one another?

Map Activity
26. On a separate sheet of paper, match the letters on the map with their correct labels.

   Caucasus Mountains
   Pripyat Marshes
   Carpathian Mountains
   Crimean Peninsula
   Mount Elbrus
   Donets Basin
   Chernobyl

492 • Chapter 21

---

24. Possible answer: They are physically isolated, have different physical features, and different ethnic groups.
25. Possible answer: Their climates and resources differ, therefore their economies differ.

Map Activity
26. A. Donets Basin
    B. Chernobyl
    C. Caucasus Mountains
    D. Pripyat Marshes
    E. Mount Elbrus
    F. Crimean Peninsula
    G. Carpathian Mountains

Writing Activity

Choose one of the countries covered in this chapter to research. Write a report about your chosen country's struggle to establish stability since 1991. Include information about the country's government and economic reforms. Describe the social, political, and economic problems the country has faced. Be sure to use standard grammar, sentence structure, spelling, and punctuation.

Internet Activity: go.hrw.com
KEYWORD: SJ5 G21

Choose a topic to explore about Ukraine, Belarus, and the Caucasus.
- Trek through the Caucasus Mountains.
- Design Ukrainian Easter eggs.
- Investigate the Chernobyl disaster.

CHAPTER 21 REVIEW

Writing Activity
Answers will vary but should consider the social, political, and economic problems faced by the country. Use Rubric 30, Research, to evaluate student work.

Interpreting Maps
1. placed it in a good location for trade across the Caspian Sea
2. by a line hooked on each end
3. Because it is completely separated from the rest of the country, its residents may feel isolated or neglected, or the culture may have developed differently. The people there may eventually demand either connection to the rest of Azerbaijan or independence from it.
4. It is below sea level.

Analyzing Primary Sources
1. that the world community was not ready to face global disasters
2. People are better prepared to combat possible catastrophes.
3. Possible answer: yes, because people can protect Earth's future better now that they know the risks of not doing so
4. delicate, easily damaged

Social Studies Skills Practice

Interpreting Maps
Study the following map of Azerbaijan. Then answer the questions.

Source: Central Intelligence Agency, *The World Factbook 2003*

1. How may Baku's location have affected the city's economic development?
2. Note the part of Azerbaijan named Naxçivan. How is its connection to the rest of the country indicated?
3. How may the location of Naxçivan lead to political problems?
4. Compare this map to the physical-political map at the beginning of the chapter. What is unusual about the area labeled Kur-Araz Ovaligi?

Analyzing Primary Sources
Read the following passage from *Chernobyl Legacy*, by Paul Fusco. Then answer the questions.

"The Chernobyl disaster revealed that the world community was not ready to face global disasters. Today, due to the grievous [painful] experience gained from Chernobyl, people are better prepared to combat possible catastrophes protecting life and health of themselves and those of their children. Chernobyl resulted in a worldwide realization of the fact that the Earth is our common home . . . having become so fragile in the hands of man who harnessed atomic power."

1. According to the passage, what truth did the disaster reveal?
2. What does the author think has been gained from the Chernobyl disaster?
3. Do you think the author is hopeful about the future? Why or why not?
4. In the last sentence, what does the word *fragile* mean?

Ukraine, Belarus, and the Caucasus • 493

CHAPTER 21 — REVIEW AND ASSESSMENT RESOURCES

Reproducible
- Readings in World Geography, History, and Culture 43 and 44
- Critical Thinking Activity 23
- Vocabulary Activity 21

Technology
- Chapter 21 Test Generator (on the One-Stop Planner)
- HRW Go site
- Audio CD Program, Chapter 21

Reinforcement, Review, and Assessment
- Chapter 21 Review and Practice
- Chapter Summaries and Review
- Chapter 21 Test
- Chapter 21 Test for English Language Learners and Special-Needs Students

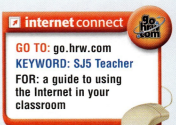

GO TO: go.hrw.com
KEYWORD: SJ5 Teacher
FOR: a guide to using the Internet in your classroom

UNIT 5

GEOGRAPHY SIDELIGHT

Islam and Political Movements Many Central Asians have been working to restore the practice of Islam in their region. These efforts have been met with a certain amount of governmental resistance. In order to limit the power of Islamic political movements, some governments in the region have imposed restrictions on Muslims. For example, some Islamic-based political groups have been banned. Even the wearing of long beards, which can symbolize adherence to fundamentalist Islamic beliefs, has been outlawed in some areas.

Kazakhstan, Kyrgyzstan, and Turkmenistan are viewed as less politically vulnerable to Islamic fundamentalist movements. Russian cultural influences are more widespread in these three countries than in Uzbekistan and Tajikistan. In addition to being geographically close to Iran and Afghanistan—countries where Islamic political movements have been very powerful—Uzbekistan and Tajikistan have well-established Islamic institutions.

Critical Thinking: What is the relationship of Islam to Central Asian countries?

Answer: Many people have tried to increase its influence, while governments have tried to limit it.

➤ This Focus On Culture feature addresses National Geography Standards 3, 5, 10, and 13.

Focus on Culture

Changing Perceptions of Russia's Southern Neighbors

Connections between countries can change quickly. For example, trade relationships change as new industries or new sources for products develop. Changes in government also affect relationships between countries. A country that becomes more democratic may gain allies among other democratic countries. Shifts in government have had a big effect on one area in particular. That area is Central Asia. The countries that make up the region are Kazakhstan, Kyrgyzstan, Tajikistan, Turkmenistan, and Uzbekistan. These are Russia's southern neighbors.

Central Asia Since the breakup of the Soviet Union, many changes have taken place in Central Asia. In the past, Central Asia had strong ties to the Soviet Union. For example, the economies of the two regions were linked. Central Asia exported cotton and oil to Russia and to countries in Eastern Europe. In exchange, Central Asia received manufactured goods. The Soviet Union also influenced Central Asian culture. Many Central Asians learned to speak Russian.

Looking South Today, Central Asia's links to the former Soviet Union have weakened. At the same time, it has strengthened ancient ties to Southwest Asia—sometimes called the Middle East. The Silk Road once linked Central Asian cities to Southwest Asian ports on the Mediterranean. Now the peoples of Central Asia are again looking southward. New links are forming between Central Asia and Turkey. Many people in Central Asia are traditionally Turkic in culture and language. Turkey's business leaders are expanding their industries in Central Asia. Also, regular air travel from Turkey to cities in Central Asia is now possible.

Religion also links Central and Southwest Asia. Islam was introduced into Central Asia in the A.D. 700s and became the region's main religion. However, Islam declined during the Soviet era. Missionaries from Arab countries and Iran are now strengthening this connection. Iran is also building roads and rail lines to Central Asia.

◀ **Region** These children are learning about Islam in Dushanbe, Tajikistan. Although the former Communist government discouraged the practice of religion, today Islam flourishes in the independent Central Asian republics.

494 • Unit 5

FOCUS ON CULTURE

Recalling Concepts

Review with students what they learned in the preceding unit about the political and economic relationships between the countries of Central Asia and the former Soviet Union. (Students should mention that these countries were Soviet republics, that the economies of these countries were part of the Soviet economy, and that the Soviet Union set up schools and hospitals and made Russian the language of government and business.) Point out that these countries were part of the Soviet Union for approximately 70 years.

Remind students that the cultural and ethnic differences between the people of these countries and of Russia contributed to the drive by Central Asians to gain independence from the Soviet Union. On a wall map show students the relative location of Kazakhstan, Uzbekistan, Turkmenistan, Azerbaijan, Kyrgyzstan, and Tajikistan between Russia and the countries of Southwest Asia.

494 Unit 5

Language Groups of Southwest and Central Asia

This map shows the major language groups that link peoples throughout Southwest and Central Asia. Very often, however, the links between peoples are overshadowed by differences in culture and history.

DOMINANT LANGUAGES
- Turkic
- Iranic
- Semitic
- Greek
- Other
- Sparsely populated

Place Many people in Central and Southwest Asia grow cotton, such as here in Uzbekistan.

Central Asia and Southwest Asia share a similar climate, environment, and way of life. Both regions are dry, and water conservation and irrigation are necessary. Many people in both regions herd animals. In addition, both Central Asia and Southwest Asia are dealing with changes caused by the growing influence of Western culture. Some people are worried that Western technology and entertainment threaten traditional beliefs and ways of life. Shared fears of cultural loss may bring Central Asia and Southwest Asia even closer together.

Changing Perceptions As the world changes, geographers reexamine this and other regions. Some geographers are now including the countries of Central Asia with those of Southwest Asia. Just as geographers are altering their perceptions of Russia's southern neighbors, our perceptions are changing as well.

Understanding What You Read

1. What ties did Central Asia have to the Soviet Union in the past?
2. Why are ties between Central Asia and Southwest Asia growing today?

Focus on Culture • 495

UNIT 5

Understanding What You Read

Answers
1. economic—Central Asia exported cotton and oil to Soviet territories and imported Soviet manufactured goods; cultural—Soviet Union strongly influenced culture of Central Asia, and many Central Asians learned how to speak Russian
2. because Turkey's business leaders are trying to expand their industries into Central Asia; because of expanded air travel, roads, and rail lines; because of the resurgence of Islam; and because of common reaction against Western culture

---

Going Further: Thinking Critically

Direct students' attention to the map on this page. Have them name the countries that share each language group. Then ask the following questions: What language is common in a very small area of Southwest Asia and Central Asia? **(Greek)** What is the main language group of Central Asia? **(Turkic)** What language groups are most common in Southwest Asia? **(Iranic and Semitic)** Then organize the class into three groups and assign each group one of the three dominant language groups. Have each group conduct research on the history of the language group in Central Asia or Southwest Asia.

Focus On Culture 495

UNIT 5

PRACTICING THE SKILL

1. Students should describe a local environmental problem fully. They should relate the environmental problem to their community.
2. Students should present options for solving the problem.
3. Students should list advantages and disadvantages of options.
4. Students should choose an option, create a plan with the option, explain their plan, and present it.

Visual Record Answer

Possible answer: by containing the oil within a flexible barrier and removing it manually from the surface

➤ This GeoSkills feature addresses National Geography Standards 4 and 14.

Building Skills for Life: Addressing Environmental Problems

The natural environment is the world around us. It includes the air, animals, land, plants, and water. Many people today are concerned about the environment. They are called environmentalists. Environmentalists are worried that human activities are damaging the environment. Environmental problems include air, land, and water pollution, global warming, deforestation, plant and animal extinction, and soil erosion.

People all over the world are working to solve these environmental problems. The governments of many countries are trying to work together to protect the environment. International organizations like the United Nations are also addressing environmental issues.

▲
An oil spill in northwestern Russia caused serious environmental damage in 1995.
Interpreting the Visual Record
Can you see how these people are cleaning up the oil spill?

THE SKILL

1. **Gather Information.** Create a plan to present to the city council for solving a local environmental problem. Select a problem and research it using databases or other reference materials. How does it affect people's lives and your community's culture or economy?
2. **List and Consider Options.** After reviewing the information, list and consider options for solving this environmental problem.
3. **Consider Advantages and Disadvantages.** Now consider the advantages and disadvantages of taking each option. Ask yourself questions like, "How will solving this environmental problem affect business in the area?" Record your answers.
4. **Choose, Implement, and Evaluate a Solution.** After considering the advantages and disadvantages, you should create your plan. Be sure to make your proposal clear. You will need to explain the reasoning behind the choices you made in your plan.

496 • Unit 5 GeoSkills

GEOSKILLS

Going Further: Thinking Critically

Have students investigate ways in which their peers are involved in environmental movements. Organize students into groups. Have each group find an example of young people's activism in environmental issues. Students may select an individual or an organization to profile. If a group has selected an individual, ask its members to prepare a résumé for that person. If a group selected an organization, ask its members to prepare a brochure about the organization. Have students include answers to as many of the following questions as possible:
• What is the individual's or organization's main goal?

• Did a certain specific incident or issue inspire the activist(s) to get involved?
• How might other students become involved in this effort?
• Are there aspects of the work done by the organization or individual that might appeal especially to young people?
• How is work done by the organization or individual publicized?
• What is the most important accomplishment achieved so far by the individual or organization?

Have each group present its work to the class.

HANDS on GEOGRAPHY

The countries of the former Soviet Union face some of the worst environmental problems in the world. For more than 50 years, the region's environment was polluted with nuclear waste and toxic chemicals. Today, environmental problems in this region include air, land, and water pollution.

One place that was seriously polluted was the Russian city of Chelyabinsk. Some people have called Chelyabinsk the most polluted place on Earth. The passage below describes some of the environmental problems in Chelyabinsk. Read the passage and then answer the Lab Report questions.

Chelyabinsk was one of the former Soviet Union's main military production centers. A factory near Chelyabinsk produced nuclear weapons. Over the years, nuclear waste from this factory polluted a very large area. A huge amount of nuclear waste was dumped into the Techa River. Many people in the region used this river as their main source of water. They also ate fish from the river.

In the 1950s many deaths and health problems resulted from pollution in the Techa River. Because it was so polluted, the Soviet government evacuated 22 villages along the river. In 1957 a nuclear accident in the region released twice as much radiation as the Chernobyl accident in 1986. However, the accident near Chelyabinsk was kept secret. About 10,000 people were evacuated. The severe environmental problems in the Chelyabinsk region led to dramatic increases in birth defects and cancer rates.

▲ The village of Mitlino was evacuated after a nuclear accident in 1957.

Lab Report

1. How did environmental problems near Chelyabinsk affect people who lived in the region?
2. What might be done to address environmental problems in the Chelyabinsk region?
3. How can a geographical perspective help to solve these problems?

Lab Report
Answers

1. The environmental problems in Chelyabinsk caused many deaths and health problems, including birth defects and cancer.
2. Students might suggest cleaning up the nuclear waste in Chelyabinsk and the Techa River. Students may also suggest further evacuating the area until it is safe for people to live there.
3. Physical geographic studies can help locate sources of pollution and demonstrate the effects of pollution on air, land, soil, and water. Cultural geographic studies can show the effects of pollution on people. These studies can propose ways to prevent similar problems in the future.

internet connect

GO TO: go.hrw.com
KEYWORD: SJ5 CH21
FOR: Web sites about children and pollution

FOLDNOTES APPENDIX

FoldNote Instructions

Have you ever tried to study for a test or quiz but didn't know where to start? Or have you read a chapter and found that you can remember only a few ideas? Well, FoldNotes are a fun and exciting way to help you learn and remember the ideas you encounter as you read!

FoldNotes are tools that you can use to organize concepts. By focusing on a few main concepts, FoldNotes help you learn and remember how the concepts fit together. They can help you see the "big picture." Below you will find instructions for building 10 different FoldNotes.

Pyramid

1. Place a sheet of paper in front of you. Fold the lower left-hand corner of the paper diagonally to the opposite edge of the paper.
2. Cut off the tab of paper created by the fold (at the top).
3. Open the paper so that it is a square. Fold the lower right-hand corner of the paper diagonally to the opposite corner to form a triangle.
4. Open the paper. The creases of the two folds will have created an X.
5. Using scissors, cut along one of the creases. Start from any corner, and stop at the center point to create two flaps. Use tape or glue to attach one of the flaps on top of the other flap.

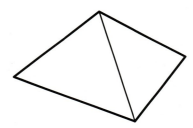

Double Door

1. Fold a sheet of paper in half from the top to the bottom. Then, unfold the paper.
2. Fold the top and bottom edges of the paper to the crease.

Booklet

1. Fold a sheet of paper in half from left to right. Then, unfold the paper.
2. Fold the sheet of paper in half again from the top to the bottom. Then, unfold the paper.
3. Refold the sheet of paper in half from left to right.
4. Fold the top and bottom edges to the center crease.
5. Completely unfold the paper.
6. Refold the paper from top to bottom.
7. Using scissors, cut a slit along the center crease of the sheet from the folded edge to the creases made in step 4. Do not cut the entire sheet in half.
8. Fold the sheet of paper in half from left to right. While holding the bottom and top edges of the paper, push the bottom and top edges together so that the center collapses at the center slit. Fold the four flaps to form a four-page book.

Layered Book

1. Lay one sheet of paper on top of another sheet. Slide the top sheet up so that 2 cm of the bottom sheet is showing.
2. Hold the two sheets together, fold down the top of the two sheets so that you see four 2 cm tabs along the bottom.
3. Using a stapler, staple the top of the FoldNote.

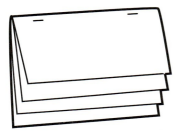

FOLDNOTES

Key-Term Fold

1. Fold a sheet of lined notebook paper in half from left to right.
2. Using scissors, cut along every third line from the right edge of the paper to the center fold to make tabs.

Four-Corner Fold

1. Fold a sheet of paper in half from left to right. Then, unfold the paper.
2. Fold each side of the paper to the crease in the center of the paper.
3. Fold the paper in half from the top to the bottom. Then, unfold the paper.
4. Using scissors, cut the top flap creases made in step 3 to form four flaps.

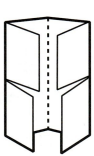

Three-Panel Flip Chart

1. Fold a piece of paper in half from the top to the bottom.
2. Fold the paper in thirds from side to side. Then, unfold the paper so that you can see the three sections.
3. From the top of the paper, cut along each of the vertical fold lines to the fold in the middle of the paper. You will now have three flaps.

Table Fold

1. Fold a piece of paper in half from the top to the bottom. Then, fold the paper in half again.
2. Fold the paper in thirds from side to side.
3. Unfold the paper completely. Carefully trace the fold lines by using a pen or pencil.

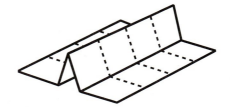

Two-Panel Flip Chart

1. Fold a piece of paper in half from the top to the bottom.
2. Fold the paper in half from side to side. Then, unfold the paper so that you can see the two sections.
3. From the top of the paper, cut along the vertical fold line to the fold in the middle of the paper. You will now have two flaps.

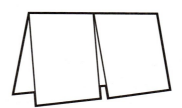

Tri-Fold

1. Fold a piece a paper in thirds from the top to the bottom.
2. Unfold the paper so that you can see the three sections. Then, turn the paper sideways so that the three sections form vertical columns.
3. Trace the fold lines by using a pen or pencil. Label the columns "Know," "Want," and "Learn."

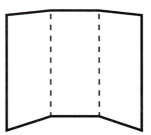

GAZETTEER

Phonetic Respelling and Pronunciation Guide

Many of the key terms in this textbook have been respelled to help you pronounce them. The letter combinations used in the respelling throughout the narrative are explained in this phonetic respelling and pronunciation guide. The guide is adapted from *Merriam-Webster's Collegiate Dictionary, Tenth Edition*; *Merriam-Webster's Geographical Dictionary*; and *Merriam-Webster's Biographical Dictionary*.

MARK	AS IN	RESPELLING	EXAMPLE
a	alphabet	a	*AL-fuh-bet
ā	Asia	ay	AY-zhuh
ä	cart, top	ah	KAHRT, TAHP
e	let, ten	e	LET, TEN
ē	even, leaf	ee	EE-vuhn, LEEF
i	it, tip, British	i	IT, TIP, BRIT-ish
ī	site, buy, Ohio	y	SYT, BY, oh-HY-oh
	iris	eye	EYE-ris
k	card	k	KAHRD
ō	over, rainbow	oh	OH-vuhr, RAYN-boh
u̇	book, wood	ooh	BOOHK, WOOHD
ȯ	all, orchid	aw	AWL, AWR-kid
ȯi	foil, coin	oy	FOYL, KOYN
au̇	out	ow	OWT
ə	cup, butter	uh	KUHP, BUHT-uhr
ü	rule, food	oo	ROOL, FOOD
yü	few	yoo	FYOO
zh	vision	zh	VIZH-uhn

*A syllable printed in small capital letters receives heavier emphasis than the other syllable(s) in a word.

Acapulco (17°N 100°W) city on the southwestern coast of Mexico, 187
Adriatic Sea sea between Italy and the Balkan Peninsula, 287, 427
Aegean (ee-JEE-uhn) **Sea** sea between Greece and Turkey, 369
Albania country in Eastern Europe on the Adriatic Sea, 427
Alberta province in Canada, 135
Aleutian Islands volcanic islands extending from Alaska into the Pacific Ocean, 81
Alps major mountain system in south-central Europe, 267
Altiplano broad, high plateau in Peru and Bolivia, 255
Amazon River major river in South America, 237
Amsterdam (52°N 5°E) capital of the Netherlands, 387
Amur (ah-MOOHR) **River** river in northeast Asia forming part of the border between Russia and China, 459
Andes (AN-deez) great mountain range in South America, 174, 237
Andorra European microstate in the Pyrenees mountains, A15
Andorra la Vella (43°N 2°E) capital of Andorra, A15
Antarctic Circle line of latitude located at 66.5° south of the equator; parallel beyond which no sunlight shines on the June solstice (first day of winter in the Southern Hemisphere), A4–A5, A22
Antarctica continent around the South Pole, A22
Antigua and Barbuda island country in the Caribbean, 205
Antwerp (51°N 4°E) major port city in Belgium, 387
Apennines (A-puh-nynz) mountain range in Italy, 369
Appalachian Mountains mountain system in eastern North America, 81, 109
Arctic Circle line of latitude located at 66.5° north of the equator; the parallel beyond which no sunlight shines on the December solstice (first day of winter in the Northern Hemisphere), A4–A5, A22
Arctic Ocean ocean north of the Arctic Circle; world's fourth-largest ocean, A2–A3
Argentina second-largest country in South America, 237
Armenia country in the Caucasus region of Asia; former Soviet republic, 481
Astrakhan (46°N 48°E) old port city on the Volga River in Russia, 459
Asunción (25°S 58°W) capital of Paraguay, 237
Atacama Desert desert in northern Chile, 255
Athens (38°N 24°E) capital and largest city in Greece, 291
Atlanta (34°N 84°W) capital and largest city in the U.S. state of Georgia, 81, 114
Atlantic Ocean ocean between the continents of North and South America and the continents of Europe and Africa; world's second-largest ocean, A2
Australia only country occupying an entire continent, located between the Indian Ocean and the Pacific Ocean, A3

Austria country in west-central Europe south of Germany, 387

Azerbaijan country in the Caucasus region of Asia; former Soviet republic, 481

B

Bahamas island country in the Atlantic Ocean southwest of Florida, 205

Baja California peninsula in northwestern Mexico, 187

Baku (40°N 50°E) capital of Azerbaijan, 481

Balkan Mountains mountain range that rises in Bulgaria, 427

Baltic Sea body of water east of the North Sea and Scandinavia, 407

Baltimore (39°N 77°W) city in Maryland on the western shore of Chesapeake Bay, 81, 109

Barbados island country in the Caribbean, 205

Barcelona (41°N 2°E) Mediterranean port city and Spain's second-largest city, 369

Basel (48°N 8°E) city in northern Switzerland on the Rhine River, 387

Basseterre (17°N 63°W) capital of St. Kitts and Nevis, 205

Bay of Biscay body of water off the western coast of France and the northern coast of Spain, 387

Belarus country located north of Ukraine; former Soviet republic, 481

Belém (1°S 48°W) port city in northern Brazil, 237

Belfast (55°N 6°W) capital and largest city of Northern Ireland, 407

Belgium country between France and Germany in west-central Europe, 387

Belgrade (45°N 21°E) capital of Serbia and Montenegro on the Danube River, 427

Belize country in Central America bordering Mexico and Guatemala, 205

Belmopan (17°N 89°W) capital of Belize, 205

Bergen (60°N 5°E) seaport city in southwestern Norway, 407

Berkshire Hills hilly region of western Massachusetts, 109

Berlin (53°N 13°E) capital of Germany, 387

Bern (47°N 7°E) capital of Switzerland, 387

Birmingham (52°N 2°W) major manufacturing center of south-central Great Britain, 407

Black Sea sea between Europe and Asia, A14

Blue Ridge Mountains southern region of the Appalachians, 114

Bogotá (5°N 74°W) capital and largest city of Colombia, 221

Bolivia landlocked South American country, 255

Bonn (51°N 7°E) city in western Germany; replaced by Berlin as the capital of reunified Germany, 387

Bosnia and Herzegovina country in Eastern Europe between Serbia and Montenegro and Croatia, 427

Boston (42°N 71°W) capital and largest city of Massachusetts, 81

Brasília (16°S 48°W) capital of Brazil, 237

Bratislava (48°N 17°E) capital of Slovakia, 427

Brazil largest country in South America, 237

Brazilian Highlands regions of old, eroded mountains in southeastern Brazil, 237

Brazilian Plateau area of upland plains in southern Brazil, 237

Bridgetown (13°N 60°W) capital of Barbados, 205

British Columbia province on the Pacific coast of Canada, 135

British Isles island group consisting of Great Britain and Ireland, A15

Brittany region in northwestern France, 387

Brussels (51°N 4°E) capital of Belgium, 387

Bucharest (44°N 26°E) capital of Romania, 427

Budapest (48°N 19°E) capital of Hungary, 427

Buenos Aires (34°S 59°W) capital of Argentina, 237

Bulgaria country on the Balkan Peninsula in Eastern Europe, 427

C

Calgary (51°N 114°W) city in the western Canadian province of Alberta, 135

Callao (kah-YAH-oh) (12°S 77°W) port city in Peru, 255

Campeche (20°N 91°W) city in Mexico on the west coast of the Yucatán Peninsula, 187

Canada country occupying most of northern North America, 135

Canadian Shield major landform region in central Canada along Hudson Bay, 135

Cancún (21°N 87°W) resort city in Mexico on the Yucatán Peninsula, 187

Cantabrian (kan-TAY-bree-uhn) **Mountains** mountains in northwestern Spain, 369

Cape Cod peninsula off the coast of southern New England, 109

Cape Horn (56°S 67°W) cape in southern Chile; southernmost point of South America, 255

Caracas (kuh-RAHK-uhs) (11°N 67°W) capital of Venezuela, 221

Cardiff (52°N 3°W) capital and largest city of Wales, 407

Caribbean Sea arm of the Atlantic Ocean between North and South America, A10, 205

Carpathian Mountains mountain system in Eastern Europe, 427

Cascade Range mountain range in the Northwestern United States, 81, 127

Caspian Sea large inland salt lake between Europe and Asia, A16, 459

Castries (14°N 61°W) capital of St. Lucia, 205

Cauca River river in western Colombia, 221

Caucasus Mountains mountain range between the Black Sea and the Caspian Sea, 459

Cayenne (5°N 52°W) capital of French Guiana, 221

Central America narrow southern portion of the North American continent, 205

Central Siberian Plateau upland plains and valleys between the Yenisey and Lena Rivers in Russia, 459

Central Valley narrow plain between the Sierra Nevada and Coast Ranges, 127
Chelyabinsk (chel-YAH-buhnsk) (55°N 61°E) manufacturing city in the Urals region of Russia, 459
Chernobyl (51°N 30°E) city in north-central Ukraine; site of a major nuclear accident in 1986, 481
Chesapeake Bay largest estuary on the Atlantic Coast, 109
Chicago (42°N 88°W) major city on Lake Michigan in northern Illinois, 81, 118
Chile country in South America, 255
Chissinau (formerly Kishinev) (47°N 29°E) capital of Moldova, 427
Ciudad Juárez (syoo-thahth HWAHR-es) (32°N 106°W) city in northern Mexico near El Paso, 187
Coast Ranges rugged coastline along the Pacific, 127
Coastal Plain North American landform region stretching along the Atlantic Ocean and Gulf of Mexico, 81
Cologne (51°N 7°E) manufacturing and commercial city along the Rhine River in Germany, 387
Colombia country in northern South America, 221
Colorado Plateau uplifted area of horizontal rock layers in the western United States, 81
Columbia Basin region of dry basins and mountains east of the Cascades, 127
Columbia River river that drains the Columbia Basin in the northwestern United States, 81
Copenhagen (56°N 12°E) seaport and capital of Denmark, 407
Córdoba (30°S 64°W) large city in Argentina northwest of Buenos Aires, 237
Cork (52°N 8°W) seaport city in southern Ireland, 407
Costa Rica country in Central America, 205
Crater Lake lake in Oregon; deepest in the United States, 127
Crete largest of the islands of Greece, *m*235
Crimean Peninsula peninsula in Ukraine that juts southward into the Black Sea, 481
Croatia Eastern European country and former Yugoslav republic, 427
Cuba country and largest island in Caribbean, 205
Cumberland Plateau landform in the Coastal Plain area of the South, 114
Cuzco (14°S 72°W) city southwest of Lima, Peru; former capital of the Inca Empire, 178, 255
Czech Republic Eastern European country and the western part of the former country in Czechoslovakia, 427

Dallas (33°N 97°W) city in northern Texas, 114
Danube River major river in Europe that flows into the Black Sea in Romania, 387
Death Valley east of the Sierra Nevada; the lowest point in all of North America, 127
Denmark country in northern Europe, 407
Detroit (42°N 83°W) major industrial city in Michigan, 81, 121

Devil's Island (5°N 53°W) French island off the coast of French Guiana in South America, 221
Dinaric Alps mountains extending inland from the Adriatic coast to the Balkan Peninsula, 427
Dnieper River major river in Ukraine, 481
Dominica Caribbean island country, 205
Dominican Republic country occupying the eastern part of Hispaniola in the Caribbean, 205
Donets Basin industrial region in eastern Ukraine, 481
Douro River river on the Iberian Peninsula that flows into the Atlantic Ocean in Portugal, 369
Dublin (53°N 6°W) capital of the republic of Ireland, 407

Ebro River river in Spain that flows into the Mediterranean Sea, 369
Ecuador country in western South America, 255
Edmonton (54°N 113°W) provincial capital of Alberta, Canada, 135
El Salvador country on the Pacific side of Central America, 205
England southern part of Great Britain and part of the United Kingdom in northern Europe, 407
English Channel channel separating Great Britain from the European continent, 387
equator the imaginary line of latitude that lies halfway between the North and South Poles and circles the globe, A4–A5
Essen (51°N 7°E) industrial city in western Germany, 387
Estonia country located on the Baltic Sea; former Soviet republic, 427
Europe continent between the Ural Mountains and the Atlantic Ocean, A3
Everglades large wetland area in Florida, 114

Finland country in northern Europe located between Sweden, Norway, and Russia, 407
Flanders northern coastal part of Belgium where Dutch is the dominant language, 387
Florence (44°N 11°E) city on the Arno River in central Italy, 369
France country in west-central Europe, 387
Frankfurt (50°N 9°E) main city of Germany's Rhineland region, 387
French Guiana French territory in northern South America, 221

Galway (53°N 9°W) city in western Ireland, 407
Geneva (46°N 6°E) city in southwestern Switzerland, 387
Genoa (44°N 10°E) seaport city in northwestern Italy, 369
Georgetown (8°N 58°W) capital of Guyana, 221

R6 • Gazetteer

Georgia (Eurasia) country in the Caucasus region; former Soviet republic, 481

Germany country in west-central Europe located between Poland and the Benelux countries, 387

Glasgow (56°N 4°W) city in Scotland, United Kingdom, 407

Göteberg (58°N 12°E) seaport city in southwestern Sweden, 407

Gran Chaco (grahn CHAH-koh) dry plains region in Paraguay, Bolivia, and northern Argentina, 237

Great Basin dry region in the western United States, 81

Great Bear Lake lake in the Northwest Territories of Canada, 135

Great Britain major island of the United Kingdom, 407

Great Lakes largest freshwater lake system in the world; located in North America, 81

Great Plains grassland region in the central United States, 81, 122

Great Slave Lake lake in the Northwest Territories of Canada, 135

Great Smoky Mountains southern mountain range in the Appalachians, 114

Greater Antilles larger islands of the West Indies in the Caribbean Sea, 205

Greece country in southern Europe located at the southern end of the Balkan Peninsula, 287

Green Mountains major range of the Appalachian Mountains in Vermont, 109

Greenland self-governing province of Denmark between the North Atlantic and Arctic Oceans, 407

Grenada Caribbean island country, 205

Guadalajara (21°N 103°W) industrial city in west-central Mexico, 187

Guadalquivir (gwah-thahl-kee-VEER) **River** important river in southern Spain, 369

Guatemala City (15°N 91°W) capital of Guatemala, 205

Guatemala most populous country in Central America, 205

Guayaquil (gwy-ah-KEEL) (2°S 80°W) port city in Ecuador, 255

Guiana Highlands elevated region in northeastern South America, 221

Gulf of Bothnia part of the Baltic Sea west of Finland, 407

Gulf of California part of the Pacific Ocean east of Baja California, Mexico, 187

Gulf of Mexico gulf of the Atlantic Ocean between Florida, Texas, and Mexico, 187

Gulf of St. Lawrence gulf between New Brunswick and Newfoundland Island in North America, 135

Guyana (gy-AH-nuh) country in South America, 221

Haiti country occupying the western third of the Caribbean island of Hispaniola, 205

Halifax (45°N 64°W) provincial capital of Nova Scotia, Canada, 135

Hamburg (54°N 10°E) seaport on the Elbe River in northwestern Germany, 387

Havana (23°N 82°W) capital of Cuba, 205

Hawaii U.S. Pacific state consisting of a chain of eight large islands and more than 100 smaller islands, 127

Helsinki (60°N 25°E) capital of Finland, 407

Hispaniola large Caribbean island divided into the countries of Haiti and the Dominican Republic, 205

Honduras country in Central America, 205

Houston (30°N 95°W) major port and largest city in Texas, 81, 114

Hudson Bay large bay in Canada, 135

Hungary country in Eastern Europe between Romania and Austria, 427

Iberian Peninsula peninsula in southwestern Europe occupied by Spain and Portugal, 369

Iceland island country between the North Atlantic and Arctic Oceans, 407

Indian Ocean world's third-largest ocean; located east of Africa, south of Asia, west of Australia, and north of Antarctica, A3

Interior Plains vast area between the Appalachians and the Rocky Mountains in North America, 81, 83, 118

Iquitos (4°S 73°W) city in northeastern Peru on the Amazon River, 255

Ireland country west of Great Britain in the British Isles, 407

Irish Sea sea between Great Britain and Ireland, 407

Italy country in southern Europe, 369

Jamaica island country in the Caribbean Sea, 205

Jutland Peninsula peninsula in northern Europe made up of Denmark and part of northern Germany, 407

Kamchatka Peninsula peninsula along Russia's northeastern coast, 459

Khabarovsk (kuh-BAHR-uhfsk) (49°N 135°E) city in southeastern Russia on the Amur River, 459

Kiev (50°N 31°E) capital of Ukraine, 481

Kingston (18°N 77°W) capital of Jamaica, 205

Kingstown (13°N 61°W) capital of St. Vincent and the Grenadines, 205

Kjölen (CHUHL-uhn) **Mountains** mountain range in the Scandinavian Peninsula, 407

Kosovo province in southern Serbia and Montenegro, 427

Kourou (5°N 53°W) city in French Guiana, 221

Kuril (KYOOHR-eel) **Islands** Russian islands northeast of the island of Hokkaido, Japan, 459

Kuznetsk Basin (Kuzbas) industrial region in central Russia, 459

La Paz (17°S 68°W) administrative capital and principal industrial city of Bolivia with an elevation of 12,001 feet (3,658 m); highest capital in the world, 255

Labrador region in the province of Newfoundland and Labrador, Canada, 135

Lake Baikal (by-KAHL) world's deepest freshwater lake; located north of the Gobi in Russia, 459

Lake Maracaibo (mah-rah-KY-buh) extension of the Gulf of Venezuela in South America, 221

Lake Nicaragua lake in southwestern Nicaragua, 205

Lake Poopó (poh-oh-POH) lake in western Bolivia, 255

Lake Titicaca lake between Bolivia and Peru at an elevation of 12,500 feet (3,810 m), 175, 255

Lapland region extending across northern Finland, Sweden, and Norway, 407

Las Vegas (36°N 115°W) city in southern Nevada, 81, 122

Latvia country on the Baltic Sea; former Soviet republic, 427

Lesser Antilles chain of volcanic islands in the eastern Caribbean Sea, 205

Liechtenstein microstate in west-central Europe located between Switzerland and Austria, 387

Lima (12°S 77°W) capital of Peru, 255

Lisbon (39°N 9°W) capital and largest city of Portugal, 369

Lithuania European country on the Baltic Sea; former Soviet republic, 427

Ljubljana (lee-oo-blee-AH-nuh) (46°N 14°E) capital of Slovenia, 427

London (52°N 0°) capital of the United Kingdom, 407

Longfellow Mountains major range of the Appalachian Mountains in Maine, 109

Los Angeles, California (34°N 118°W) major city in California, 127

Luxembourg (50°N 7°E) capital of Luxembourg, 387

Luxembourg small European country bordered by France, Germany, and Belgium, 387

Macedonia Balkan country; former Yugoslav republic, 427

Machu Picchu (13°S 73°W) ancient Inca city in the Andes of Peru, 255

Madrid (40°N 4°W) capital of Spain, 369

Magdalena River river in Colombia that flows into the Caribbean Sea, 221

Magnitogorsk (53°N 59°E) manufacturing city of the Urals region of Russia, 459

Malta island country in southern Europe located in the Mediterranean Sea between Sicily and North Africa, 278

Managua (12°N 86°W) capital of Nicaragua, 205

Manaus (3°S 60°W) city in Brazil on the Amazon River, 237

Manchester (53°N 2°W) major commercial city in west-central Great Britain, 407

Manitoba prairie province in central Canada, 135

Marseille (43°N 5°E) seaport in France on the Mediterranean Sea, 387

Martha's Vineyard island off the coast of southern New England, 109

Mato Grosso Plateau highland region in southwestern Brazil, 237

Mazatlán (23°N 106°W) seaport city in western Mexico, 187

Mediterranean Sea sea surrounded by Europe, Asia, and Africa, m235

Mexican Plateau large, high plateau in central Mexico, 187

Mexico City (19°N 99°W) capital of Mexico, 187

Mexico country in North America, 187

Miami (26°N 80°W) city in southern Florida, 81, 114

Milan (45°N 9°E) city in northern Italy, 369

Minsk (54°N 28°E) capital of Belarus, 481

Mississippi Delta low swampy area of the Mississippi formed by a buildup of sediment, 114

Mississippi River major river in the central United States, 81

Moldova Eastern European country located between Romania and Ukraine; former Soviet republic, 427

Monaco (44°N 8°E) European microstate bordered by France, 387

Monterrey (26°N 100°W) major industrial center in northeastern Mexico, 187

Montevideo (mawn-tay-bee-THAY-oh) (35°S 56°W) capital of Uruguay, 237

Montreal (46°N 74°W) financial and industrial city in Quebec, Canada, 135

Moscow (56°N 38°E) capital of Russia, 459

Mount Elbrus (43°N 42°E) highest European peak (18,510 ft.; 5,642 m); located in the Caucasus Mountains, 481

Mount Orizaba (19°N 97°W) volcanic mountain (18,700 ft.; 5,700 m) southeast of Mexico City; highest point in Mexico, 187

Mount Whitney highest peak in the 48 contiguous United States, 127

Munich (MYOO-nik) (48°N 12°E) major city and manufacturing center in southern Germany, 387

Nantucket island off the coast of southern New England, 109

Naples (41°N 14°E) major seaport in southern Italy, 369

Nassau (25°N 77°W) capital of the Bahamas, 205

Netherlands country in west-central Europe, 387

New Brunswick province in eastern Canada, 135

New Orleans (30°N 90°W) major Gulf port city in Louisiana located on the Mississippi River, 81, 114

New York Middle Atlantic state in the northeastern United States, 81, 109

R8 • Gazetteer

Newfoundland and Labrador eastern province in Canada including Labrador and the island of Newfoundland, 135

Nicaragua country in Central America, 205

Nice (44°N 7°E) city in the southeastern coast in France, 387

Nizhniy Novgorod (Gorky), Russia (56°N 44°E) city on the Volga River east of Moscow, 459

North America continent including Canada, the United States, Mexico, Central America, and the Caribbean Islands, A2

North Pole the northern point of Earth's axis, A22

North Sea major sea between Great Britain, Denmark, and the Scandinavian Peninsula, 387

Northern European Plain broad coastal plain from the Atlantic coast of France into Russia, 387

Northern Ireland the six northern counties of Ireland that remain part of the United Kingdom; also called Ulster, 365, 407

Northwest Highlands region of rugged hills and low mountains in Europe, including parts of the British Isles, northwestern France, the Iberian Peninsula, and the Scandinavian Peninsula, 275

Northwest Territories division of a northern region of Canada, 135

Norway European country located on the Scandinavian Peninsula, 407

Nova Scotia province in eastern Canada, 135

Novosibirsk (55°N 83°E) industrial center in Siberia, Russia, 459

Nunavut Native American territory of northern Canada, 135

Nuuk (Godthab) (64°N 52°W) capital of Greenland, 407

Ob River large river system that drains Russia and Siberia, 459

Okefenokee Swamp large wetland area in Florida, 114

Ontario province in central Canada, 135

Orinoco River major river system in South America, 221

Oslo (60°N 11°E) capital of Norway, 407

Ottawa (45°N 76°W) capital of Canada; located in Ontario, 135

Ozark Plateau rugged, hilly region located mainly in Arkansas, 114

Pacific Ocean Earth's largest ocean; located between China and the Americas, A2–A3

Panama Canal canal allowing shipping between the Pacific Ocean and the Caribbean Sea; located in central Panama, 205

Panama City (9°N 80°W) capital of Panama, 205

Panama country in Central America, 205

Paraguay country in South America, 237

Paraguay River river that divides Paraguay into two separate regions, 237

Paramaribo (6°N 55°W) capital of Suriname in South America, 221

Paraná River major river system in southeastern South America, 237

Paris (49°N 2°E) capital of France, 387

Patagonia arid region of dry plains and windswept plateaus in southern Argentina, 237

Pearl Harbor U.S. naval base in Hawaii; attacked by Japan in 1941, 127

Peloponnesus (pe-luh-puh-NEE-suhs) peninsula forming the southern part of the mainland of Greece, 369

Peru country in South America, 255

Philadelphia (40°N 75°W) important port and industrial center in Pennsylvania in the northeastern United States, 81, 109

Phoenix (34°N 112°W) capital of Arizona, 81, 122

Po River river in northern Italy, 369

Podgorica (PAWD-gawr-ett-sah) capital of Serbia and Montenegro, 438

Poland country in Eastern Europe located east of Germany, 427

Port-au-Prince (pohr-toh-PRINS) (19°N 72°W) capital of Haiti, 205

Portland (46°N 123°W) seaport and largest city in Oregon, 81, 127

Port-of-Spain (11°N 61°W) capital of Trinidad and Tobago, 205

Portugal country in southern Europe located on the Iberian Peninsula, 369

Prague (50°N 14°E) capital of the Czech Republic, 427

Prince Edward Island province in eastern Canada, 135

Pripyat (Pinsk) Marshes (PRI-pyuht) marshlands in southern Belarus and northwest Ukraine, 481

Puerto Rico U.S. commonwealth in the Greater Antilles in the Caribbean Sea, 205

Puget Sound lowland area of Washington state, 127

Pyrenees (PIR-uh-neez) mountain range along the border of France and Spain, 387

Quebec (47°N 71°W) provincial capital of Quebec, Canada, 135

Quebec province in eastern Canada, 135

Quito (0° 79°W) capital of Ecuador, 178, 255

Reykjavik (RAYK-yuh-veek) (64°N 22°W) capital of Iceland, 407

Rhine River major river in Western Europe, 387

Riga (57°N 24°E) capital of Latvia, 427

Río Bravo Mexican name for the river between Texas and Mexico, 187

Rio de Janeiro (23°S 43°W) major port in southeastern Brazil, 237

Río de la Plata estuary between Argentina and Uruguay in South America, 237

Rocky Mountains major mountain range in western North America, 81
Romania country in Eastern Europe, 427
Rome (42°N 13°E) capital of Italy, 369
Rosario (roh-SAHR-ee-oh) (33°S 61°W) city in eastern Argentina, 237
Roseau (15°N 61°W) capital of Dominica in the Caribbean, 205
Russia world's largest country, stretching from Europe and the Baltic Sea to eastern Asia and the coast of the Bering Sea, 459

Sakhalin Island Russian island north of Japan, 459
Salvador (13°S 38°W) seaport city of eastern Brazil, 237
Salzburg state of central Austria, 387
San Andreas Fault point in California where the Pacific and North American Plates meet, 127
San Diego (33°N 117°W) California's third largest urban area, 81
San Francisco (38°N 122°W) California's second largest urban area, 81
San José (10°N 84°W) capital of Costa Rica, 205
San Juan (19°N 66°W) capital of Puerto Rico, 205
San Marino microstate in southern Europe surrounded by Italy, 369
San Salvador (14°N 89°W) capital of El Salvador, 205
Santa Cruz (18°S 63°W) city in south central Bolivia, 255
Santiago (33°S 71°W) capital of Chile, 255
Santo Domingo (19°N 70°W) capital of the Dominican Republic, 205
São Francisco River river in eastern Brazil, 237
São Paulo (24°S 47°W) Brazil's largest city, 237
Sarajevo (sar-uh-YAY-voh) (44°N 18°E) capital of Bosnia and Herzegovina, 427
Saskatchewan province in central Canada, 135
Scandinavian Peninsula peninsula of northern Europe occupied by Norway and Sweden, 407
Scotland northern part of the island of Great Britain, 407
Sea of Azov sea in Ukraine connected to and north of the Black Sea, 481
Sea of Okhotsk inlet of the Pacific Ocean on the eastern coast of Russia, 459
Seattle (48°N 122°W) largest city in the U.S. Pacific Northwest located in Washington, 81, 127
Seine River river that flows through Paris in northern France, 387
Serbia and Montenegro country in Eastern Europe; former Yugoslav republics, 427
Shannon River river in Ireland; longest river in the British Isles, 407
Siberia vast region of Russia extending from the Ural Mountains to the Pacific Ocean, 459
Sicily island region of Italy, 369
Sierra Madre Occidental mountain range in western Mexico, 187
Sierra Madre Oriental mountain range in eastern Mexico, 187

Sierra Nevada located in eastern California; one of the longest and highest mountain ranges in the United States, 81, 127
Skopje (SKAW-pye) (42°N 21°E) capital of Macedonia, 427
Slovakia country in Eastern Europe; formerly the eastern part of Czechoslovakia, 427
Slovenia country in Eastern Europe; former Yugoslav republic, 427
Sofia (43°N 23°E) capital of Bulgaria, 427
South Pole the southern point of Earth's axis, A22
Spain country in southern Europe occupying most of the Iberian Peninsula, 369
St. George's (12°N 62°W) capital of Grenada in the Caribbean Sea, 205
St. John's (17°N 62°W) capital of Antigua and Barbuda in the Caribbean Sea, 205
St. Kitts and Nevis Caribbean country in the Lesser Antilles, 205
St. Lawrence River major river linking the Great Lakes with the Gulf of St. Lawrence and the Atlantic Ocean in southeastern Canada, 135
St. Lucia Caribbean country in the Lesser Antilles, 205
St. Petersburg (formerly Leningrad; called Petrograd 1914 to 1924) (60°N 30°E) Russia's second largest city and former capital, 459
St. Vincent and the Grenadines Caribbean country in the Lesser Antilles, 205
Stockholm (59°N 18°E) capital of Sweden, 407
Strait of Gibraltar (juh-BRAWL-tuhr) strait between the Iberian Peninsula and North Africa that links the Mediterranean Sea to the Atlantic Ocean, 369
Strait of Magellan strait in South America connecting the South Atlantic with the South Pacific, 255
Sucre (19°S 65°W) constitutional capital of Bolivia, 255
Suriname (soohr-uh-NAH-muh) country in northern South America, 221
Susquehanna River one of several major rivers that cut through the Appalachians, 109
Sweden country in northern Europe, 407
Switzerland country in west-central Europe located between Germany, France, Austria, and Italy, 387

T'bilisi (42°N 45°E) capital of Georgia in the Caucasus region, 481
Tagus River longest river on the Iberian Peninsula in southern Europe, 369
Tampico (22°N 98°W) Gulf of Mexico seaport in central-eastern Mexico, 187
Tegucigalpa (14°N 87°W) capital of Honduras, 205
Thessaloníki (41°N 23°E) city in Greece, 369
Tiber River river that flows through Rome in central Italy, 369
Tierra del Fuego group of islands at the southern tip of South America, 237
Tijuana (33°N 117°W) city in northwestern Mexico, 187

Tiranë (ti-RAH-nuh) (42°N 20°E) capital of Albania, 427

Toronto (44°N 79°W) capital of the province of Ontario, Canada, 135

Trinidad and Tobago Caribbean country in the Lesser Antilles, 205

Tropic of Cancer parallel 23.5° north of the equator; parallel on the globe at which the Sun's most direct rays strike the earth during the June solstice (first day of summer in the Northern Hemisphere), A4–A5

Tropic of Capricorn parallel 23.5° south of the equator; parallel on the globe at which the Sun's most direct rays strike the earth during the December solstice (first day of summer in the Southern Hemisphere), A4–A5

Turin (45°N 8°E) city in northern Italy, 369

Ukraine country located between Russia and Eastern Europe; former Soviet republic, 481

United Kingdom country in northern Europe occupying most of the British Isles; Great Britain and Northern Ireland, 407

United States North American country located between Canada and Mexico, 81

Ural Mountains mountain range in west central Russia that divides Asia from Europe, 459

Uruguay country on the northern side of the Río de la Plata between Brazil and Argentina in South America, 237

Vaduz (47°N 10°E) capital of Liechtenstein, A15

Valletta (36°N 14°E) capital of Malta, 278

Valparaíso (33°S 72°W) Pacific port for the national capital of Santiago, Chile, 255

Vancouver (49°N 123°W) Pacific port in Canada, 135

Vatican City (42°N 12°E) European microstate surrounded by Rome, Italy, 369

Venezuela country in northern South America, 221

Vienna (48°N 16°E) capital of Austria, 387

Vilnius (55°N 25°E) capital of Lithuania, 427

Virgin Islands island chain lying just east of Puerto Rico in the Caribbean Sea, 205

Vistula River river flowing through Warsaw, Poland, to the Baltic Sea, 427

Vladivostok (43°N 132°E) chief seaport of the Russian Far East, 459

Volga River Europe's longest river; located in west central Russia, 459

Wales part of the United Kingdom occupying a western portion of Great Britain, 407

Wallonia region in southern Belgium, 387

Warsaw (52°N 21°E) capital of Poland, 427

Washington, D.C. (39°N 77°W) U.S. capital; located between Virginia and Maryland on the Potomac River, 81, 109

West Siberian Plain region with many marshes east of the Urals in Russia, 459

White Mountains major range of the Appalachian Mountains in New Hampshire, 109

Willamette Valley lowland area of Oregon, 127

Windsor (42°N 83°W) industrial city across from Detroit, Michigan, in the Canadian province of Ontario, 135

Winnipeg (50°N 97°W) provincial capital of Manitoba in central Canada, 135

Yekaterinburg (formerly Sverdlovsk) (57°N 61°E) city in the Urals region in Russia, 459

Yenisey (yi-ni-SAY) major river in central Russia, 459

Yerevan (40°N 45°E) capital of Armenia, 481

Yucatán Peninsula peninsula in southeastern Mexico, 167, 169, 187

Yukon Territory Canadian territory bordering Alaska, 135

Zagreb (46°N 16°E) capital of Croatia, 427

Zurich (47°N 9°E) Switzerland's largest city, 387

GLOSSARY

Phonetic Respelling and Pronunciation Guide

Many of the key terms in this textbook have been respelled to help you pronounce them. The letter combinations used in the respelling throughout the narrative are explained in this phonetic respelling and pronunciation guide. The guide is adapted from *Merriam-Webster's Collegiate Dictionary, Tenth Edition; Merriam-Webster's Geographical Dictionary;* and *Merriam-Webster's Biographical Dictionary.*

MARK	AS IN	RESPELLING	EXAMPLE
a	alphabet	a	*AL-fuh-bet
ā	Asia	ay	AY-zhuh
ä	cart, top	ah	KAHRT, TAHP
e	let, ten	e	LET, TEN
ē	even, leaf	ee	EE-vuhn, LEEF
i	it, tip, British	i	IT, TIP, BRIT-ish
ī	site, buy, Ohio	y	SYT, BY, oh-HY-oh
	iris	eye	EYE-ris
k	card	k	KAHRD
ō	over, rainbow	oh	OH-vuhr, RAYN-boh
ú	book, wood	ooh	BOOHK, WOOHD
ȯ	all, orchid	aw	AWL, AWR-kid
ȯi	foil, coin	oy	FOYL, KOYN
aú	out	ow	OWT
ə	cup, butter	uh	KUHP, BUHT-uhr
ü	rule, food	oo	ROOL, FOOD
yü	few	yoo	FYOO
zh	vision	zh	VIZH-uhn

*A syllable printed in small capital letters receives heavier emphasis than the other syllable(s) in a word.

abdicated Gave up the throne, 464
absolute authority Monarch's power to make all the governing decisions, 327
absolute location The exact spot on Earth where something is found, often stated in latitude and longitude, 7
acculturation The process of cultural changes that result from long-term contact with another society, 49
acid rain A type of polluted rain, produced when pollution combines with water vapor, 30
acropolis Greek polis built around a fort on a high hill, 289
adobe Sun-dried bricks made from clay and straw, 88
Age of Exploration A period when Europeans were eager to find new and shorter sea routes so that they could trade with India and China, 324
aggression Warlike action, such as an invasion or an attack, 356
agora Marketplace of a Greek city that was used for economic, religious, and political activities, 289
agrarian A society organized around farming, 491
alliance A formal agreement or treaty among nations formed to advance common interests or causes, 94, 348
Allied Powers Nations that united during World War II against Nazi Germany, 101
allies Friendly countries that support one another against enemies, 465
alluvial fan A fan-shaped landform created by deposits of sediment at the base of a mountain, 21
amber Fossilized tree sap, 429
Anasazi American Indians who lived in the southwestern part of North America, 88
anti-Semitism Hatred of Jews, 359
aqueducts Artificial channels for carrying water, 306
aquifers Underground, water-bearing layers of rock, sand, or gravel, 26
archipelago (ahr-kuh-PE-luh-goh) A large group of islands, 206
aristocrats Small group of wealthy landowners, 290
armistice An agreement to stop fighting, 350
atmosphere The layer of gases that surrounds Earth, 31

badlands Rugged areas of soft rock that have been eroded by wind and water into small gullies and have little vegetation or soil, 123
balance of power A way of keeping peace when no one nation or group of nations is more powerful than the others, 336
bankrupt Having no money, 353
barrier islands Long, narrow, sandy islands separated from the mainland, 115
basins Regions surrounded by mountains or other higher land, 83
bauxite The most important aluminum ore, 207

R12 • Glossary

birthrate Number of births per 1,000 people in a year, **59**

bloc A group of nations united under a common idea or for a common purpose, **362**

bog Soft ground that is soaked with water, **418**

cacao (kuh-KOW) A small tree on which cocoa beans grow, **210**

caldera A large depression formed after a major eruption and collapse of a volcanic mountain, **129**

calypso A type of music with origins in Trinidad and Tobago, **214**

cantons Political and administrative districts in Switzerland, **401**

capital The money and tools needed to make a product, **338**

capitalism Economic system in which private individuals control the factors of production, **342, 361**

cardamom A spice used in Asian foods, **211**

cartography The art and science of mapmaking, **13**

cash crops Crops produced primarily to sell rather than for the farmer to eat, **199**

cassava (kuh-SAH-vuh) A tropical plant with starchy roots, **226**

cathedrals Huge churches sometimes decorated with elaborate stained-glass windows, **311**

caudillos (kow-THEE-yohs) Military leaders who ruled Venezuela in the 1800s and 1900s, **229**

center-pivot irrigation A method of irrigation that uses long sprinkler systems mounted on huge wheels that rotate slowly, irrigating the area within a circle, **125**

chancellor Germany's head of government, or prime minister, **395**

chinampas (chee-NAHM-pahs) The name the Aztecs gave to raised fields on which they grew crops, **171, 192**

chinooks Strong, dry winds that blow from the Rocky Mountains onto the Great Plains in the United States during drought periods, **124**

chivalry A code of behavior including bravery, fairness, loyalty, and integrity, **310**

citizenship The right to participate in government, **291**

city-states Self-governing cities, such as those of ancient Greece, **289, 372**

civilization A highly complex culture with growing cities and economic activity, **52**

civil war A conflict between two or more groups within a country, **211**

clergy Officials of the church, including the priests, bishops, and pope, **311**

climate The weather conditions in an area over a long period of time, **32**

climatology The field of tracking Earth's larger atmospheric systems, **13**

cloud forest A high-elevation, very wet tropical forest where low clouds are common, **207**

coalition governments Governments in which several political parties join together to run a country, **377**

Cold War Rivalry between the United States and the Soviet Union that lasted from the 1940s to the early 1990s, **102, 465**

colony Territory controlled by people from a foreign land, **90, 325**

command economy An economy in which the government owns most of the industries and makes most of the economic decisions, **56**

commercial agriculture A type of farming in which farmers produce food for sale, **52**

commonwealth A self-governing territory associated with another country, **217**

communism An economic and political system in which the government owns or controls almost all of the means of production, industries, wages, and prices, **354, 361**

condensation The process by which water changes from a gas into tiny liquid droplets, **27**

conquistadores (kahn-kees-tuh-DAWR-ez) Spanish conquerors during the era of colonization in the Americas, **180, 193**

constitution A document that outlines basic laws that govern a nation, **328**

constitutional monarchy A government with a monarch as head of state and a parliament or other legislature that makes the laws, **413**

consuls Roman magistrates who ran the government and commanded the army, **298**

consumer goods Products used at home and in everyday life, **465**

contiguous Units, such as states, that connect to or border each other, **82**

Continental Divide The crest of the Rocky Mountains that divides North America's rivers into those that flow eastward and those that flow westward, **83**

cooperatives Organizations owned by their members and operated for their mutual benefit, **215**

cordillera Mountain system made up of parallel ranges, **222**

cork The bark stripped from a certain type of oak tree and often used as stoppers and insulation, **383**

Corn Belt The corn-growing region in the Midwest from central Ohio to central Nebraska, **119**

cosmopolitan Having many foreign influences, **400**

Cossacks Nomadic horsemen who once lived on the Ukrainian frontier, **485**

Counter-Reformation Attempt by the Catholic Church, following the Reformation, to return the Church to an emphasis on spiritual matters, **322**

coup (KOO) A sudden overthrow of a government by a small group of people, **263**

creoles American-born descendents of Europeans in Spanish South America, **262**

Crusades A long series of battles starting in 1095 between the Christians of Europe and the Muslims to gain control of Palestine, **311**

culture A learned system of shared beliefs and ways of doing things that guide a person's daily behavior, **47**

culture region Area of the world in which people share certain culture traits, **47**

culture traits Elements of culture such as dress, food, or religious beliefs, **47**

Glossary • R13

currents Giant streams of ocean water, **34**
czar (ZAHR) Emperor of the Russian Empire, **464**

D

Dairy Belt Area including Wisconsin and most of Minnesota and Michigan which produces milk, cheese, and dairy products, **119**
death rate Number of people per thousand who die in a year, **59**
deforestation The destruction or loss of forest area, **39**
delta Landform created by the deposits of sediment at the mouths of rivers, **21**
democracy A political system in which a country's people elect their leaders and rule by majority, **291**
developing countries Nations in different stages of moving toward development, **55**
dialect A variation of a language, **382**
dictator One who rules a country with complete authority, **210, 301, 354**
diffusion The movement of ideas or behaviors from one cultural region to another, **9**
disciples Small group of followers, **304**
diversify To produce a variety of things, **116**
domestication Changing form and behavior of a species so that it depends on people to survive, **51**
dominion A territory or area of influence, **140**
droughts Periods when little rain falls and crops are damaged, **63, 119**

E

earthquakes Sudden, violent movement along a fracture in the Earth's crust, **20**
ecotourism The practice of using an area's natural environment to attract tourists, **212**
ejidos (e-HEE-thohs) Lands owned and worked by groups of Mexican Indians, **194**
El Dorado (el duh-RAH-doh) "The Golden One," a legend of the early Chibcha people of Colombia, **224**
El Niño An ocean and weather pattern in the Pacific Ocean in which ocean waters become warmer, **258**
Emancipation Proclamation Lincoln's document that freed the slaves, **98**
emigrant One who leaves one's own country to move to another, **59**
empire A system in which a central power controls a number of territories, **193, 302**
encomienda A system in which Spanish monarchs gave land to Spanish colonists in the Americas; landowners could force Indians living there to work the land, **245**
Enlightenment An era of new ideas from the mid-1600s through the 1700s, **330**
epidemic Widespread outbreak, often referring to a disease, **180, 193**
erosion Movement by water, ice, or wind of rocky materials to another location, **21**
estuary A partially enclosed body of water where salty seawater and freshwater mix, **112, 239**
ethnic groups Cultural groups of people who share learned beliefs and practices, **47**
ethnocentrism Seeing differences in other cultures as inferior to one's own, **49**
evaporation The process by which heated water becomes water vapor and rises into the air, **27**
exports A country's products sold to other countries, **57**

F

factors of production The natural resources, money, labor, and capital needed for business operation, **338**
factory system Bringing workers and machinery together into a factory and paying workers a fixed rate of pay for a set number of hours of work, **339**
famine A great shortage of food, **63, 416**
fascism A political movement that puts the needs of the nation above the needs of the individual, **354**
fault A fractured surface in Earth's crust where a mass of rock is in motion, **20**
favelas (fah-VE-lahs) Huge slums that surround some Brazilian cities, **243**
federal System in which power is divided between a central government and individual states, **95**
feudalism A system after the 900s under which most of Europe was organized and governed by local leaders based on land and service, **309**
fief A grant of land, **309**
fjords (fee-AWRDS) Narrow, deep inlets of the sea set between high, rocky cliffs, **408**
floodplain A landform of level ground built by sediment deposited by a river or stream, **21**
fossil fuels Nonrenewable resources formed from the remains of ancient plants and animals, **40**
forum Public gathering place in Roman society, **298**
free enterprise An economic system in which people, not government, decide what to make, sell, or buy, **56**
frontier Unsettled land, **91**

G

gauchos (GOW-chohz) Argentine cowboys, **245**
genocide The planned killing of a race of people, **359**
geography The study of Earth's physical and cultural features, **3**
geothermal energy A renewable energy resource produced from the heat of Earth's interior, **41**
geysers Hot springs that shoot hot water and steam into the air, **422**
glaciers Large, slow-moving sheets or rivers of ice, **22**
gladiators Slaves in the Roman Empire who fought to the death as entertainment, **304**
glen A Scottish term for a valley, **415**
global warming A slow increase in Earth's average temperature, **30**
globalization Process in which connections around the world increase and cultures around the world share similar practices, **60**
glyphs Written characters representing objects and sounds, **169**

Great Depression Period after the Stock Market crashed in 1929 when worldwide business slowed down, banks closed, prices and wages dropped, and many people were out of work, **100, 353**

greenhouse effect The process by which Earth's atmosphere traps heat, **30**

gross domestic product The value of all goods and services produced within a country, **53**

gross national product The value of all goods and services that a country produces in one year within or outside the country, **53**

groundwater The water from rainfall, rivers, lakes, and melting snow that seeps into the ground, **26**

guerrilla An armed person who takes part in irregular warfare, such as raids, **215**

guillotine A machine that uses a huge blade to cut off a person's head, **333**

habitation fog A fog caused by fumes and smoke trapped over Siberian cities by very cold weather, **472**

haciendas (hah-see-EN-duhs) Huge farmlands granted by the Spanish monarch to favored people in Spain's colonies, **194**

heavy industry Industry that usually involves manufacturing based on metals, **470**

Hellenistic Greek-like, **295**

Hohokam American Indians who lived in the southwestern part of North America, **88**

Holocaust The mass murder of millions of Jews and other people by the Nazis in World War II, **359, 395**

homogeneous Sharing the same characteristics, such as ethnicity, **491**

human geography The study of people, past or present, **11**

human-environment interaction Relationship between people and the environment, **9**

humanists Scholars of the Renaissance who studied history, poetry, grammar, and other subjects taught in ancient Greece and Rome, **318**

humanitarian aid Medicine and food provided to distressed peoples from international relief agencies, **63**

hurricanes Tropical storms that bring violent winds, heavy rain, and high seas, **14**

hydroelectric power A renewable energy resource produced from dams that harness the energy of falling water to power generators, **41**

icebreakers Ships that can break up the ice of frozen waterways, allowing other ships to pass through them, **476**

immigrant Person who arrives in a place from another country, **59**

imports Products a country buys from other countries, **57**

impressionism A form of art that developed in France in the late 1800s and early 1900s, **393**

indentured servants People who agree to work for a certain period of time, often in exchange for travel expenses, **231**

indigo (IN-di-goh) A plant used to make a deep blue dye, **228**

individualism A belief in the political and economic independence of individuals, **331**

Indo-European A language family that includes many languages of Europe, such as Germanic, Baltic, and Slavic languages, **430**

Industrial Revolution Period that lasted through the 1700s and 1800s when advances in industry, business, transportation, and communications changed people's lives in almost every way, **337**

industrialized countries Countries that rely more on industry than agriculture, **54**

inflation The rise in prices that occurs when currency loses its buying power, **198**

interdependence Depending on another country for resources or goods and services, **57**

Inuit North American Eskimos, **147**

Iron Curtain Line that divided Eastern and Western bloc nations, **362**

Iroquois League Agreement made by the Iroquois to keep the peace among themselves, **89**

junta (HOOHN-tuh) A small group of military officers who rule a country after seizing power, **267**

kiva A special room used by the Anasazi for sacred ceremonies, **88**

knight A nobleman who serves as a professional warrior, **310**

landforms The shapes of land on Earth's surface, **19**

landlocked Completely surrounded by land, with no direct access to the ocean, **250**

lava Magma that has broken through the crust to Earth's surface, **20**

league An alliance of states joined together for protection, **293**

light industry Industry that focuses on the production of lightweight goods, such as clothing, **470**

lignite A soft form of coal, **429**

limited monarchy Monarchy in which the powers of the king were limited by law, **327**

Glossary • R15

literacy rate Percent of people who can read and write, **54**

llaneros (yah-NAY-rohs) Cowboys of the Venezuelan Llanos, **230**

Llanos (YAH-nohs) A plains region in eastern Colombia and western Venezuela, **222**

lochs Scottish lakes located in valleys carved by glaciers, **408**

loess (LES) Fine, windblown soil that is good for farming, **389**

mainland A region or country's main landmass, **370**

manors Large farm estates developed by nobles, **310**

maquiladoras (mah-kee-lah-DORH-ahs) Foreign-owned factories located along Mexico's northern border with the United States, **201**

maritime On or near the sea, such as Canada's Maritime Provinces, **144**

market economy An economy in which consumers help determine what is to be produced by buying or not buying certain goods and services, **56**

mass production System of producing large numbers of identical items, **343**

medieval Refers to the period from the collapse of the Roman Empire to about 1500, **308, 391**

megalopolis A string of cities that have grown together, **110**

mercantilism Economic theory using colonies to increase a nation's wealth by gaining access to labor and natural resources, **325**

Mercosur A trade organization that includes Argentina, Brazil, Paraguay, Uruguay, and two associate members (Bolivia and Chile), **248**

merengue The national music and dance of the Dominican Republic, **214**

mestizos (me-STEE-zohs) People of mixed European and American Indian ancestry, **194**

meteorology The field of forecasting and reporting rainfall, temperatures, and other atmospheric conditions, **13**

Métis (may-TEES) People of mixed European and Canadian Indian ancestry in Canada, **141**

middle class Class of skilled workers between the upper class and poor and unskilled workers, **312**

migrate To move from place to place, **86**

migration Movement from one region or climate to another, **59**

militarism Use of strong armies and the threat of force to gain power, **348**

missions Spanish church outposts established during the colonial era, particularly in the Americas, **194**

mixed economy A goods and services exchange system based on at least two other types of systems, **57**

monarchy A territory ruled by a king who has total power to govern, **327**

Moors Muslim North Africans, **381**

moraine A ridge of rocks, gravel, and sand piled up by a glacier, **111**

mosaics (moh-ZAY-iks) Pictures created from tiny pieces of colored stone, **374**

movement People and ideas moving from place to place, **9**

mulattoes (muh-LA-tohs) People of mixed European and African ancestry, **194**

multicultural A mixture of different cultures within the same country or community, **47**

Nahuatl Native Aztec language, **173**

nationalism The demand for self-rule and a strong feeling of loyalty to one's nation, **347, 402**

nationalist Person or movement seeking self-rule or independence, **182**

national parks Large scenic areas of natural beauty preserved by the United States government for public use, **126**

NATO North Atlantic Treaty Organization, a military alliance of various European countries, the United States, and Canada, **363, 391**

nature reserves Areas a government has set aside to protect animals, plants, soil, and water, **482**

navigable Water routes that are deep enough and wide enough to be used by ships, **388**

neutral Not taking a side in a dispute or conflict, **420**

New Deal Franklin D. Roosevelt's program to help end the Great Depression, **100, 353**

newsprint Cheap paper used mainly for newspapers, **137**

nobles People who were born into wealthy, powerful families, **309**

nonrenewable resources Materials useful and valued by people, such as coal and oil, that cannot be replaced by Earth's natural processes, **38**

North Atlantic Drift A warm ocean current that brings mild temperatures and rain to parts of northern Europe, **409**

obsidian Natural glass that forms when volcanic lava cools quickly, **171**

oil shale Layered rock that yields oil when heated, **429**

oligarchy Government in which power lies in the hands of a few people, **290**

one-crop economy Economy based on a single crop, such as bananas, sugarcane, or cacao, **57**

overpopulation More people than a country can support without outside help, **58**

ozone layer A shell of a form of oxygen in the atmosphere that helps protect Earth from harmful solar radiation, **30**

Pampas A wide, grassy plains region in central Argentina, **238**

pardos Venezuelans of mixed African, European, and South American Indian ancestry, **230**

Parliament An English assembly made up of nobles, clergy, and common people who had the power to pass and enforce laws, **327**

patricians The heads of a small number of Roman aristocratic families, **298**

Patriots Colonists who wanted independence from British rule, **93**

Pax Romana Peaceful time in Roman history that lasted more than 200 years, **302**

peat Matter made from dead plants, usually mosses, **418**

perspective Point of view based on a person's experience and personal understanding, **3**

Peru Current A cold ocean current off the coast of western South America, **257**

petroleum An oily liquid that can be refined into gasoline and other fuels and oils, **40**

physical geography The study of Earth's natural landscape and physical systems, including the atmosphere, **11**

pidgin languages Simple languages that help people who speak different languages understand each other, **231**

pioneers Settlers who lead the way into new areas, **96**

place Physical and human features of a specific location, **7**

plain A nearly flat area on Earth's surface, **21**

plantains A type of banana used in cooking, **216**

plantations Large farms that grow mainly one crop to sell, **91**

plate tectonics The theory that Earth's surface is divided into several major, slowly moving plates or pieces, **19**

plebeians Common people who took part in Roman government, **298**

pok-a-tok Maya ball game, **170**

police state A country in which the government has total control over the people using the police, **354**

polis Greek city-state, **289**

pope The bishop of Rome and the head of the Roman Catholic Church, **377**

popular culture Widely shared beliefs and ways of doing things, **60**

popular sovereignty Governmental principle based on just laws and on a government created by and subject to the will of the people, **93**

population density The average number of people living within a set area, **58**

potash A mineral used to make fertilizer, **137**

precipitation Process by which water falls back to Earth, **27**

prevailing winds Breezes that consistently blow in the same direction over large areas of Earth, **33**

Protestants Christians who broke away from the Catholic Church during the Reformation, **321**

provinces Administrative divisions of a country, **140**

pulp Softened wood fibers used to make paper, **137**

Puritan Member of a group of Protestants who rebelled against the Church of England, **327**

Quechua (KE-chuh-wuh) The language of South America's Inca; still spoken in the region, **175, 264**

quinoa (KEEN-wah) A native plant of South America's Andean region that yields nutritious seeds, **259**

quipu (KEE-poo) Complicated system of knots tied on strings of various colors, used by the Inca of South America to record information, **179, 260**

race A group of people who share inherited physical or biological traits, **48**

rain shadow Dry area on the side of a mountain opposite the wind, **35**

reactionaries People who want to return to an earlier political system, **336**

reason Logical thinking, **331**

reforestation The planting of trees in places where forests have been cut down, **39**

Reformation A movement in Europe to reform Christianity in the 1500s, **321, 394**

refugees People who flee to another country, usually for economic or political reasons, **63, 215**

reggae A type of music with origins in Jamaica, **214**

region Area of Earth's surface with one or more shared characteristics, **8**

regionalism The stronger connection to one's region than to one's country, **143**

Reign of Terror Period from 1789 to 1794 when thousands of people died at the guillotine in France, **334**

relative location The position of a place in relation to another place, **7**

Renaissance (re-nuh-SAHNS) French word meaning "rebirth" and referring to a new era of learning that began in Europe in the 1300s, **317, 377**

renewable resources Resources, such as soils and forests, that can be replaced by Earth's natural processes, **38**

republic Government in which voters elect leaders to run the state, **297**

Restoration The reign of Charles II in English history in which the monarchy was restored to power, **328**

Roaring Twenties Period of wealth and good times in the United States during the 1920s, **100**

Roma An ethnic group also known as Gypsies who are descended from people who may have migrated from India to Europe long ago, **440**

rural An area of open land that is often used for farming, **4**

Santería A religion, with origins in Cuba, that mixes West African religions and traditions with those of Roman Catholicism, **214**

Scientific Revolution The period during the 1500s and 1600s when mathematics and scientific instruments were used to learn more about the natural world, **323**

secede To separate from, **98**

second-growth forests The trees that cover an area after the original forest has been cut, **112**

Glossary • R17

secularism Playing down the importance of religion, **331**

sediment Small bits of mud, sand, or gravel which collect at the river's mouth, **115**

selvas The thick tropical rain forests of eastern Ecuador, eastern Peru, and northern Bolivia, **257**

serfs Peasants who worked on manors, **310, 485**

sinkholes A steep-sided depression formed when the roof of a cave collapses, **188**

sirocco (suh-RAH-koh) A hot, dry wind from North Africa that blows across the Mediterranean to Europe, **371**

slash-and-burn agriculture A type of agriculture in which forests are cut and burned to clear land for planting, **201**

smelters Factories that process metal ores, **471**

smog A mixture of smoke, chemicals, and fog, **200**

soil exhaustion The loss of soil nutrients needed by plants, **240**

solar power Heat and light from the Sun, **41**

soviet A council of Communists who governed republics and other places in the Soviet Union, **485**

spatial perspective Point of view based on looking at where something is and why it is there, **3**

steppe (STEP) A wide, flat grasslands region that stretches from Ukraine across southern Russia to Kazakhstan, **461**

steppe climate A dry climate type generally found between desert and wet climate regions, **36**

stock market An organization through which shares of stock in companies are bought and sold, **352**

strait A narrow passageway that connects two large bodies of water, **256**

strip mining A kind of coal mining in parts of the Great Plains which strips away soil and rock, **126**

subduction The movement of one of Earth's heavier tectonic plates underneath a lighter tectonic plate, **20**

subsistence agriculture A type of farming in which farmers grow just enough food to provide for themselves and their own families, **52**

suffragettes Women who fought for all women's right to vote, **343**

superpowers Powerful countries, **465**

symbol Sign, such as a word, shape, color, or flag, that stands for something else, **49**

taiga (TY-guh) A forest of evergreen trees growing south of the tundra of Russia, **461**

tenements Crowded apartment houses where some immigrants to U.S. cities lived in the 1800s, **99**

tepees Cone-shaped tents that are usually made of animal skins, **88**

tepuís (tay-PWEEZ) Layers of sandstone that have resisted erosion atop plateaus in the Guiana Highlands, **222**

terraces Horizontal ridges built into the slopes of steep hillsides to prevent soil loss and aid farming, **22**

textiles Cloth products, **413**

third-world countries Developing countries that lack industrial economic opportunities, **55**

topography Shape, height, and arrangement of landforms in a certain place, **19**

tradition-based economy Exchange of goods or services based on custom and tradition, **56**

Treaty of Versailles Peace agreement that was signed at the end of World War I, **351**

triangular trade Network of trade between Britain, West Africa, and British colonies in the Americas, **91**

tributary Any smaller stream or river that flows into a larger stream or river, **26**

tundra climate A cold region with low rainfall, lying generally between subarctic and polar climate regions, **36**

tyrants People who illegally took power but had the people's support, **290**

U-boats German submarines from World War I, **349**

uninhabitable Not capable of supporting human settlement, **422**

United Nations International organization formed after World War II to prevent future wars, **101**

urban An area that contains a city, **4**

vassals People who held land from a feudal lord and received protection in return for service to the lord, usually in battle, **309**

vernacular Everyday speech which varies from place to place, **313**

viceroy The governor of a colony, **262**

water cycle The circulation of water from Earth's surface to the atmosphere and back, **27**

water vapor Gaseous form of water, **27**

weather The condition of the atmosphere at a given place and time, **32**

weathering Process of breaking rocks into smaller pieces through heat, water, or other means, **21**

wetlands Land areas that are flooded for at least part of the year, **115**

Wheat Belt The wheat-growing area in the United States which stretches across the Dakotas, Montana, Nebraska, Kansas, Oklahoma, Colorado, and Texas, **125**

SPANISH GLOSSARY

Phonetic Respelling and Pronunciation Guide

Many of the key terms in this textbook have been respelled to help you pronounce them. The letter combinations used in the respelling throughout the narrative are explained in this phonetic respelling and pronunciation guide. The guide is adapted from *Merriam-Webster's Collegiate Dictionary, Tenth Edition; Merriam-Webster's Geographical Dictionary;* and *Merriam-Webster's Biographical Dictionary.*

MARK	AS IN	RESPELLING	EXAMPLE
a	alphabet	a	*AL-fuh-bet
ā	Asia	ay	AY-zhuh
ä	cart, top	ah	KAHRT, TAHP
e	let, ten	e	LET, TEN
ē	even, leaf	ee	EE-vuhn, LEEF
i	it, tip, British	i	IT, TIP, BRIT-ish
ī	site, buy, Ohio	y	SYT, BY, oh-HY-oh
	iris	eye	EYE-ris
k	card	k	KAHRD
ō	over, rainbow	oh	OH-vuhr, RAYN-boh
ù	book, wood	ooh	BOOHK, WOOHD
ò	all, orchid	aw	AWL, AWR-kid
òi	foil, coin	oy	FOYL, KOYN
aù	out	ow	OWT
ə	cup, butter	uh	KUHP, BUHT-uhr
ü	rule, food	oo	ROOL, FOOD
yü	few	yoo	FYOO
zh	vision	zh	VIZH-uhn

*A syllable printed in small capital letters receives heavier emphasis than the other syllable(s) in a word.

abdicated/abdicar Renunciar al trono, **464**
absolute authority/autoridad absoluta Poder de un rey o reina para tomar todas las decisiones de gobierno, **327**
absolute location/posición exacta Lugar exacto de la tierra donde se localiza un punto, por lo general definido en términos de latitud y longitud, **7**
acculturation/aculturación Proceso de asimilación de una cultura a largo plazo por el contacto con otra sociedad, **49**
acid rain/lluvia ácida Tipo de lluvia contaminada que se produce cuando partículas de contaminación del aire se combinan con el vapor de agua de la atmósfera, **30**
acropolis/acrópolis ciudad-estado griega construida alrededor de una fortaleza encima de una cumber de un cerro, **289**
adobe/adobe ladrillos secados al sol y hecho de barro y paja, **88**
Age of Exploration/Edad de la exploración Periodo en que los europeos estaban ansiosos por hallar rutas nuevas y más cortas para comerciar con la India y China, **324**
aggression/agresión Acción militar, **356**
agora/ágora plaza pública en la Grecia Antigua, **289**
agrarian/agrario Sociedad basada en la agricultura, **491**
alliance/alianza Acuerdo entre diferentes países para respaldarse los temas de interès y las causas, **94, 348**
Allied Powers/potencias aliadas naciones que se unieron durante la Segunda Guerra Mundial contra Alemania nazi, **101**
allies/aliados Países que se apoyan entre sí para defenderse de sus enemigos, **465**

alluvial fan/abanico aluvial Accidente geográfico en forma de abanico que se origina por la acumulación de sedimentos en la base de una montaña, **21**
amber/ámbar Savia de árbol fosilizada, **429**
Anasazi/Anasazi Tribu de indígenas americanos que habitaron la parte suroeste de América del norte, **88**
anti-Semitism/antisemitismo Sentimiento de rechazo hacia los judíos, **359**
aqueducts/acueductos Canales artificiales usados para transportar agua, **306**
aquifers/acuíferos Capas subterráneas de roca, arena y grava en las que se almacena el agua, **26**
archipelago/archipiélago Grupo grande de islas, **206**
aristocrats/aristócratas clase noble de terratenientes, **290**
atmosphere/atmósfera Capa de gases que rodea a la tierra, **31**

badlands/tierras de baldío Terrenos irregulares de roca blanda y escasa vegetación o poco suelo, **123**
balance of power/equilibrio de poder Condición que surge cuando varios países o alianzas mantienen niveles tan similares de poder evitar guerras, **336**
bankrupt/bancarrota Sin dinero, **353**
barrier islands/islas de barrera Islas costeras formadas por depósitos de arema arrastrada por las mareas y las corrientes de aguas poco profundas, **115**
basins/cuencas Regiones rodeadas por montañas u otras tierras altas, **83**
bauxite/bauxita El mineral con contenido de aluminio más importante, **207**

Spanish Glossary • R19

birthrate/índice de natalidad número de nacimientos por 1,000 personas en un año, **59**

bloc/bloque Grupo de naciones unidas por una idea o un propósito común, **362**

bog/ciénaga Tierra suave, humedecida por el agua, **418**

cacao/cacas Árbol pequeño que produce los granos de cacao, **210**

caldera/caldera Depresión grande formada por la erupción y explosión de un volcán, **129**

calypso/calipso Tipo de música originado en Trinidad y Tobago, **214**

cantons/cantones Distritos políticos y administrativos de Suiza, **401**

capital/capital Dinero ganado, ahorrado e invertido para conseguir ganancias, **338**

capitalism/capitalismo Sistema económico en el que los negocios, las industrias y los recursos son de propiedad privada, **342, 361**

cardamom/cardamomo Especia que se usa en Asia para condimentar alimentos, **211**

cartography/cartografía Arte y ciencia de la elaboración de mapas, **13**

cash crops/cultivos para la venta Cultivos producidos para su venta y no para consumo del agricultor, **199**

cassava/mandioca Planta tropical de raíces almidonadas, **226**

cathedrals/catedrales Iglesias grandes, **311**

caudillos/caudillos Líderes militares que gobernaron Venezuela en los siglos XIX y XX, **229**

center-pivot irrigation/irrigación de pivote central Tipo de riego que usa aspersores montadios en grandes ruedas giratorias regando un area dentro de un círculo, **125**

chancellor/canciller jefe de gobierno o primer ministro alemán, **395**

chinampas/**chinampas** Nombre dado por los aztecas a los campos elevados que usaban como tierras de cultivo, **171, 192**

chinooks/chinooks Vientos cálidos y fuertes que soplan de las montañas Rocosas hacia las Grandes Planicies, **124**

chivalry/caballerosidad Código o sistema medieval de cavellería, **310**

citizenship/ciudadanía El derecho a participar en el gobierno, **291**

city-states/ciudades estado Ciudades con un sistema de autogobierno, como en la antigua Grecia, **289, 372**

civil war/guerra civil conflicto entre dos o más grupos dentro de un país, **211**

civilization/civilización Cultura altamente complexa con grandes ciudades y abundante actividad económica, **52**

clergy/clérigo Oficiante de la Iglesia, **311**

climate/clima condiciones meteorológicas registradas en un periodo largo, **32**

climatology/climatología Registro de los sistemas atmosféricos de la Tierra, **13**

cloud forest/bosque nuboso Bosque tropical de gran elevación y humedad donde los bancos de nubes son muy comunes, **207**

coalition governments/gobiernos de coalición Gobiernos en los que la administración del país es regida por varios partidos políticos a la vez, **377**

Cold War/guerra fría Rivalidad entre Estados Unidos y la Unión Soviética que se extendió de la década de 1940 a la década de 1990, **102, 465**

colony/colonia Territorio controlado por personas de otro país, **90, 325**

command economy/economía autoritaria Economía en la que el gobierno es propietario de la mayor parte de las industrias y toma la mayoría de las decisiones en materia de economía, **56**

commercial agriculture/agricultura comercial Tipo de agricultura cuya producción es exclusiva para la venta, **52**

commonwealth/mancomunidad Territorio autogobernado que mantiene una sociedad con otro país, **217**

communism/comunismo Sistema politica y económico en el cual los gobiernos poseen los medios de producción y controlan el planeamiento de la economía, **354, 361**

condensation/condensación Proceso mediante el cual el agua cambia de estado gaseoso y forma pequeñas gotas, **27**

conquistadores/conquistadores Españoles que participaron en la colonización de América, **180, 193**

constitution/constitución Documento que contiene las leyes y principios básicos que gobiernan una nación, **328**

constitutional monarchy/monarquía constitucional Gobierno que cuenta con un monarca como jefe de estado y un parlamento o grupo legislador similar para la aprobación de leyes, **413**

consuls/cónsules Magistrados romanos que dirigían el gobierno y mandaban el ejército, **298**

consumer goods/bienes de consumo Productos usados en la vida cotidiana, **465**

contiguous/contiguo Unidades de territorio (como los estados) que colindan entre sí, **82**

Continental Divide/divisoria continental Cordillera que divide los ríos de Estados Unidos en dos partes: los que fluyen al este y los que fluyen al oeste, **83**

cooperatives/cooperativas Organizaciones creadas por los propietarios de una empresa y operados para beneficio propio, **215**

cordillera/cordillera Sistema montañoso de cadenas paralelas, **222**

cork/corcho Corteza extraída de cierto tipo de roble, usada principalmente como material de bloqueo y aislante, **383**

Corn Belt/región maicera Región del medio oeste de Estados Unidos, de Ohio a Iowa, cuya actividad agrícola se basa en el cultivo del maíz, **119**

cosmopolitan/cosmopolita Que tiene influencia de muchas culturas, **400**

Cossacks/cosacos Arrieros nómadas que habitaban en la región fronteriza de Ucrania, **485**

Counter-Reformation/Contrareforma Intento de la Iglesia Católica, luego de la Reforma, por devolver a la Iglesia a un énfasis en asuntos espirituales, **322**

coup/golpe de estado Ataque repentino de un grupo reducido de personas para derrocar a un gobierno, **263**

creoles/criollos Personas de descendencia europea nacidas en la América colonial, **262**

Crusades/Cruzadas Expediciones hecas por los cristianos para recuperar la Tierra Santa de los musulmanes, **311**

culture/cultura Sistema de creencias y costumbres comunes que guía la conducta cotidiana de las personas, **47**

culture region/región cultural Región del mundo en la que se comparten ciertos rasgos culturales, **47**

culture traits/rasgos culturales Características de una cultura, como la ropa, la comida o las creencias religiosas, **47**

currents/corrientes Enormes corrientes del océano que transportan agua tibia a las regiones frías y viceversa, **34**

czar/zar Emperador ruso, **464**

Dairy Belt/región lechera Región del medio oeste de Estados Unidos, al norte de la franja del maíz, donde la elaboración de productos lácteos es una importante actividad económica, **119**

death rate/índice de mortalidad número de muertes por 1,000 personas en un año, **59**

deforestation/deforestación Destrucción o pérdida de un área boscosa, **39**

deltas/deltas Formaciones creadas por la acumulación de sedimentos en las desembocadura de los ríos, **21**

democracy/democracia Sistema político en el que l a población elige a sus líderes mediante el voto de mayoría, **291**

developing countries/países en vaís de desarrollo países que se encuentran en alguna etapa de su proceso de desarrollo, **55**

dialect/dialecto Variación de un idioma, **382**

dictator/dictadore Persona que ejercen total autoridad sobre un gobierno, **210, 301, 354**

diffusion/difusión Extensión de ideas o conducta de una región cultura a otra, **9**

disciples/discípulos grupo pequeño de partidarios, **304**

diversify/diversificar En la agirculturra, se refiere a la siembra de varios productos y uno solo, **116**

domestication/domesticación Cuidado de una planta o animal para uso personal, **51**

dominion/dominio Territorio en el que se ejerce una influencia, **140**

droughts/sequías Periodos en los que los cultivos sufren daños debido a la escasez de lluvia, **63, 119**

earthquakes/terremotos Movimientos repentinos y fuertes que se producen en las fisuras de la superficie de la tierra, **20**

ecotourism/ecoturismo Uso de regiones naturales para atraer visitantes, **212**

ejidos/**ejidos** Territorios de cultivo propiedad de los indígenas de México, **194**

El Dorado/El Dorado leyenda que habla de los chibchas, antiguos habitantes de Colombia, **224**

El Niño/El Niño Patrón oceánico y climatológico del océano Pacífico que elevó la temperatura del agua en dicho océano, **258**

Emancipation Proclamation/Proclama de Emancipación Decreto emitido por el presidente Abraham Lincoln en 1863 que acabó efectivamente con la esclavitud, a final de la Guerra Civil, **98**

emigrant/emigrante persona que sale de un lugar para otro, **59**

empire/imperio Sistema cuyo gobierno central controla diversos territorios, **193, 302**

encomienda/**encomienda** Sistema mediante el cual los monarcas españoles cedían territorios de América a los colonizadores de su país, quienes obligaban a los indígenas de esas dichas tierras a trabajar para ganarse el susteno, **245**

Enlightenment/Ilustración Período en los años 1700, cuando los filósofos creían que podían aplicar el método cientifico y el uso de la razón para explicar de manera lógica la naturaleza humana, **330**

epidemic/epidemia Expansión vasta, por general de una enfermedad, **180, 193**

erosion/erosión Desplazamiento de aua, hielo, viento o minerals a otro lugar, **21**

estuary/estuario Cuerpo de agua parcialmente cerrado en el que el agua de mar se combina con ague dulce, **112, 239**

ethnic groups/grupos étnicos Grupos culturales que comparten creencias y prácticas comunes, **47**

ethnocentrism/etnocentrismo ver diferencias en otra cultura como inferior, **49**

evaporation/evaporación Proceso mediante el cual el agua se convierte en vapor y se eleva en el aire, **27**

exports/exportaciones productos que un país vende a otros paises, **57**

factors of production/factores de producción Los recursos naturales, el dinero, el trabajo y los empresarios que se necesitan para las operaciones de negocios, **338**

factory system/fabricación en serie Sistema en el que los trabajadores en una fábrica grande ganan un sueldo fijo por cierto número de horas, **339**

famine/hambruna Gran escasez de alimento, **63, 416**

fascism/fascismo Teoría politica que demanda la creación de un gobierno fuerte encabezado por un solo individuo donde el estado sea más importante que el individuo, **354**

fault/falla Fractura de la superficie de la tierra que causa el movimiento de grandes masas de rocas, **20**

favelas/favelas Grandes poblaciones localizadas en los alrededores de algunas ciudades brasileñas, **243**

federal/federal Sistema en el que el poder está dividido entre un gobierno central y estados individuales, **95**

feudalism/feudalismo Sistema de gobierno local basado en la concesión de tierras como pago por lealtad, ayuda militar y otros servicios, **309**

fief/feudo Concesión de tierras de un amo a su vasayo, **309**

fjords/fiordos Grietas estrechas y profundas localizadas entre altos acantilados donde se acumula el agua de mar, **408**

floodplain/llanura aluvial Especie de plataforma a nivel de la tierra, formada por la acumulación de los sedimentos de una corriente de agua, **21**

forum/foro Lugar de asamblea pública en la sociedad romana, **298**

fossil fuels/combustibles fósiles Recursos no renovables formados por restos muy antiguos de plantas y animales, **40**

free enterprise/libre empresa Sistema económico en el que las personas, y no el gobierno, deciden qué productos fabrican, venden y compran, **56**

frontier/región fronteriza Terreno despoblado, **91**

gauchos/gauchos Arrieros argentinos, **245**

genocide/genocidio Aniquilamiento intencional de un pueblo, **359**

geography/geografía Estudio de las características físicas y culturales de la Tierra, **3**

geothermal energy/energía geotérmica Fuente energética no removable producida por el calor del interior de la tierra, **41**

geysers/géiseres Manantiales que lanzan chorros de agua caliente y vapor a gran altura, **422**

Spanish Glossary • R21

glaciers/glaciares Grandes bloques de hielo que se desplazan con lenitud sobre el agua, **22**

gladiators/gladiadores Esclavos en el imperio romano que luchaban hasta la muerte como diversión para el público, **304**

glen/glen Término de origen escocés que se sinónimo de valle, **415**

global warming/calentamiento global Aumento lento y constante de la temperatura de la Tierra, **30**

globalization/globalización Proceso mediante el que as comunicaciones alrededor del mundo se han incrementado haciendo a las culturas más parecidas, **60**

glyphs/glifos Símbolos escritos que representan objetos y sonidos, **169**

Great Depression/Gran Depresión Depresión mundial a principios de los años 1930, cuando los salarios cayeron, la actividad comercial bajó y hubo mucho desempleo, **100, 353**

greenhouse effect/efecto invernadero Proceso mediante el cual la atmósfera terrestre atrapa el calor de su superficie, **30**

gross domestic product/producto interno bruto Valor de todos los bienes y servicios producidos en un país, **53**

gross national product/producto nacional bruto Valor de todos los bienes y servicios producidos en un año por un país, dentro o fuera de sus límites, **53**

groundwater/agua subterránea Agua de lluvia, ríos, lagos y nieve derretida que se filtra al subsuelo, **26**

guerrilla/guerrillero Persona armada que participa en una lucha armada irregular (los ataques sorpresa, por ejemplo), **215**

guillotine/guillotina Máquina que usa una navaja para cortarle la cabeza a una persona, **333**

habitation fog/humo residente Especie de niebla producida por el humo atrapado en la atmósfera de las cuidades siberianas debido al intenso frío, **472**

haciendas/haciendas Granjas de gran tamaño cedidas por los monarcas españoles a los colonizadores de América, **194**

heavy industry/industra pesada Industria basada en la manufactura de metales, **470**

Hellenistic/helenístico Parecido a los griegos clásicos, **295**

Hohokam/Hohokam Tribu de indígenas americanos que habitaron la parte suroeste de América del norte, **88**

Holocaust/haulocausto Asesinato masivo de millones de judíos y personas de otros grupos a manos. de los nazis durante la Segunda Guerra Mundial, **359, 395**

homogeneous/homogéneo Agrupamiento que comparte ciertas características, como el origin étnico, **491**

human geography/geografía humana estudio del pasado y presente de la humanidad, **11**

human-environment interaction/interacción humano-ambiente relación entre personas y el medio ambiente, **9**

humanists/humanistas Filósofos del Renacimiento que hacían énfasis en la individualidad, los logros personales y la razón, **318**

humanitarian aid/ayuda humanitaria medicina, comida, y cobertizo que las agencias de ayuda internacional dan a las personas con necesidades, **63**

hurricanes/huracanes Tormentas tropicales con intensos vientos, fuertes lluvias y altas mareas, **14**

hydroelectric power/energía hidroeléctrica Fuente energética renovable producida en generadores impulsados por caídas de agua, **41**

icebreakers/rompehielos Barcos que rompen la capa de hielo que se forma en la superficie de algunos cuerpos de agua para permitir el paso de otras embarcaciones, **476**

immigrant/inmigrante persona que llega de otro país, **59**

imports/importaciones productos que un país compra de otros paises, **57**

impressionism/impresionismo Forma de arte desarrollada en Francia a finales del siglo XIX y principios del siglo XX, **393**

indentured servants/trabajadores por contrato Personas que trabajan por un tiempo determinado, en la mayoría de los casos a cambio de gastos de viaje, **231**

indigo/índigo Planta que se usa para fabricar un tinte de color azul oscuro, **228**

individualism/individualismo Creencia en la independencia económica y política de los individuos, **331**

Indo-European/Indoeuropeo Familia que incluye muchos idiomas europeos como el germánico, el báltico y los dialectos eslavos, **430**

industrialized countries/paises industrializados paises que depende más en la industria que en la agricultura, **54**

Industrial Revolution/Revolución Industrial Cambios producidos a principios de los años 1700, cuando las maquinarias empezaban a hacer mucho del trabajo que las personas tenían que hacer antes, **337**

inflation/inflación Aumento de los precios que ocurre cuando la moneda de un país pierde poder adquisitivo, **198**

interdependence/interdependencia depender en otro país para recursos o productos y servicios, **57**

Inuit/inuit Tribu esquimal de América del norte, **147**

Iron Curtain/Cortina de hierro Línea que separó las naciones del bloque oriental de las naciones del bloque occidental, **362**

Iroquois League/Liga iroquois Acuerdo hecho por la tribu iroquois para mantener la paz entre sí, **89**

junta/junta Grupo de oficiales militares que asumen el control de un país al derrocar al poder anterior, **267**

kiva/kiva Tipo de habitación especial usada por la tribu anazasi para sus ritos sagrados, **88**

knight/caballero Guerrero profesional noble, **310**

landforms/accidentes geográficos Forma de la tierra en diferentes partes de la superficie, **19**

landlocked/sin salida al mar Zona rodeada de agua por completo y sin acceso directo al océano, **250**

lava/lava Magma que emerge del interior de la tierra por un orificio de la corteza, **20**

league/liga Alianza de estados unidos por razones de protección, **293**

light industry/industria ligera Industria que se enfoca en la manufactura de objetos ligeros como la ropa, **470**

lignite/lignita Tipo de carbón suave, **429**

limited monarchy/monarquía limitada Sistema de gobierno dirigido por una reina o un rey que no tiene el control absoluto de un país, **327**

literacy rate/índice de alfabetismo porcentaje de personas que pueden leer y escribir, **54**

llaneros/**llaneros** Vaqueros de los llanos de Venezuela, **230**

Llanos/llanos Planicies localizadas al este de Colombia y al oeste de Venezuela, **222**

lochs/lagos Lagos escoceses enclavados en valles labrados por los glaciales, **408**

loess/limo Suelo fino de arenisca, excelente para la agricultura, **389**

mainland/región continental Región donde se localiza la mayor porción de terreno de un país, **370**

manors/feudos Estados de mayor tamaño gobernados por nobles, **310**

maquiladoras/**maquiladoras** Fábricas extranjeras establecidas en la frontera de México con Estados Unidos, **201**

maritime/marítimo En o cerca del mar, como las provincias marítimas de Canada, **144**

market economy/economía de mercado Tipo de economía en la qué los consumidores ayudan a determinar qué productos se fabrican al comprar o rechazar ciertos bienes y servicios, **56**

mass production/producción en serie Sistema de producción de grandes cantidades de productos idénticos, **343**

medieval/medieval Periodo de colapso del imperio romano, aproximadamente en el año 1,500 de nuestra era, **308, 391**

megalopolis/megalópolis Enorme zona urbana que abarca una serie de ciudades que se han desarrollado juntas, **110**

mercantilism/mercantilismo Creación y conservación de riquezas mediante un control minucioso de intercambios comerciales, **325**

Mercosur/Mercosur Organización comercial en la que participan Argentina, Brasil, Paraguay, Uruguay y dos países asociados (Bolivia y Chile), **248**

merengue/merengue Tipo de música y baile nacional en la República Dominicana, **214**

mestizos/mestizos Personas cuyo origen combina las razas europeas y las razas indígenas de América, **194**

meteorology/meteorología Predicción y registro de lluvias, temperaturas y otras condiciones atmosféricas, **13**

Métis/Métis Personas cuyo origin combina las razas europeas y las razas indígenas de Canadá, **141**

middle class/clase media Clase formada por comerciantes, patronos de pequeña y mediana industria y profesiones liberales. Está entre la clase noble y la clase campesina en la Edad Media, **312**

migrate/emigrar Mudarse de lugar en lugar, **86**

migration/migración movimiento de personas, **59**

militarism/militarismo Uso de armamento pesado y amenazas para obtener poder, **348**

missions/misiones Puestos españoles de evangelización establecidos en la época colonial, especialmente en América, **194**

mixed economy/economía mixta Intercambio de bienes y servicios basado en al menos dos otros sistemas, **57**

monarchy/monarquía Sistema de gobierno dirigido por un rey o una reina, **327**

Moors/moros Musulmanes del norte de África, **381**

moraine/morena Cresta de rocas, grava y arena levantada por un glaciar, **111**

mosaics/mosaicos Imágenes creadas con pequeños fragmentos de piedras coloreadas, **374**

movement/movimiento El ir y venir de gente e ideas, **9**

mulattoes/mulatos Personas cuyo origen combina las razas europeas y las razas indígenas de África, **194**

multicultural/multicultural Mezcla de culturas en un mismo país o comunidad, **47**

Nahuatl/nahuatl Idioma azteca indígena, **173**

nationalism/nacionalismo Demanda de autogo-bierno y fuerte sentimiento de lealtad hacia una nación, **347, 402**

nationalist/nacionalista Persona o movimiento que busca el autogobierno o la independencia, **182**

national parks/parques nacionales Terreno escénico grande preservado por un gobierno para uso público, **126**

NATO/OTAN (Organización del Tratado del Atlántico Norte); alianza militar formada por varios países europeos, Estados Unidos y Canadá, **363, 391**

nature reserves/reservas naturales Zonas asignadas por el gobierno para la protección de animales, plantas, suelo y agua, **482**

navigable/navegable Rutas acuáticas de profundidad suficiente para la navegación de barcos, **388**

neutral/neutral Que no toma ningún partido en una disputa o conflicto, **420**

New Deal/New Deal Pragrama del presidente Franklin D. Roosevelt en el que el gobierno federal estableció un amplio programa de obras públicas para crear empleo y conceder dinero a cada estado para sus necesidades, **100, 353**

newsprint/papel periódico Papel económico usado para imprimir publicaciones periódicas, **137**

nobles/nobles Personas que nacen entre familias ricas y poderosas, **309**

nonrenewable resources/recursos no renova-bles Recursos, como el carbón mineral y petróleo, que no pueden reemplazarse a corto plazo por medios naturales, **38**

North Atlantic Drift/Corriente del Atlántico Norte corriente de aguas tibias que aumenta la temperatura y genera lluvias en el norte de Europa, **409**

obsidian/obsidiana Vidrio natural que se forma cuando la lava volcánica se enfría, **171**

oil shale/pizarra petrolífera Capa de roca que al calentarse produce petróleo, **429**

oligarchy/oligarquía Gobierno en el que el poder está en manos de unas pocas personas, **290**

one-crop economy/economía de un cultivo Economía basada en un solo cultivo, como las bananas, la caña de azúcar o el cacao, **57**

overpopulation/superpoblación más personas que una región o un país puede mantener por sus propios medios, **58**

ozone layer/ozonosfera Forma del oxígeno en la atmósfera que ayuda a proteger a la Tierra de los daños que produce la radiación solar, **30**

Pampas/pampas Región extensa cubierta de hierba en la zona central de Argentina, **238**

pardos/**pardos** Venezolanos descendientes de la unión entre africanos, europeos e indígenas sudamericanos, **230**

Parliament/Parlamento Órgano británico de legislación, **327**

Spanish Glossary • **R23**

patricians/patricios las cabezas de unas pocas familias aristócratas romanas, **298**

Patriots/Patriotas Colonistas americanos que favorecieron con la independencia de Inglaterra, **93**

Pax Romana/Pax Romana epoca de paz en la historia romana que duró más de 200 años, **302**

peat/turba Sustancia formada por plantas muertas, por lo general musgos, **418**

perspective/perspectiva Punto de vista basado en la experiencia y la comprensión de una persona, **3**

Peru Current/corriente de Perú Corriente oceánica fría del litoral oeste de América del Sur, **257**

petroleum/petróleo Líquido graso que al refinarse produce gasolina y otros combustibles y aceites, **40**

physical geography/geografía física Estudio del paisaje natural y los sistemas físicos de la Tierra, entre ellos la atmósfera, **11**

pidgin languages/lenguas francas Lenguajes sencillos que ayuden a entenderse a personas que hablan idiomas diferentes, **231**

pioneers/pioneros Primeras personas que llegan a poblar una región, **96**

place/lugar Rasgos físicos y humanos de una ubicación específica, **7**

plain/planicie Área casi plana de la superficie terrestre, **21**

plantains/banano Tipo de plátano que se usa para cocinar, **216**

plantations/plantaciones Granjas muy grandes en las que se produce un solo tipo de cultivo para vender, **91**

plate tectonics/tectónica de placas Teoría de que la superficie terrestre está dividida en varias placas enormes que se mueven lentamente, **19**

plebeians/plebeyos Personas ordinarias que participaban en el gobierno romano, **298**

pok-a-tok/pok-a-tok Juego de pelota maya, **170**

police state/estado totalitario País en que el gobierno tiene un control total sobre la vida de las personas, **354**

polis/polis Ciudad estado griega, **289**

pope/papa Obisco de Roma y líder de la Iglesia católica romana, **377**

popular culture/cultura popular Creencias, gustos, metas y practicas generalmente compartidos, **60**

popular sovereignty/soberanía popular Principio gubernamental basado en leyes justas, y en un gobierno creado y sujeto a la voluntad del pueblo, **93**

population density/densidad de población Número promedio de personas que viven en una milla cuadrada o un kilómetro cuadrado, **58**

potash/potasa Mineral que se usa para hacer fertilizantes, **137**

precipitation/precipitación Proceso por el que el agua vuelve de regreso a la Tierra, **27**

prevailing winds/vientos predominantes brisas que sopla consistentemente en la misma dirección sobre grandes regiones de la Tierra, **33**

primary industries/industrias primarias Actividades económicas que involucran directamente recursos naturales o materia prima, tales como la agricultura y la minería, **54**

Protestants/protestantes Reformistas que protestaban por la realización de ciertas prácticas de la Iglesia Católica, **321**

provinces/provincias Divisiones administrativas de un país, **140**

pulp/pulpa Fibras reblandecidas de madera para hacer papel, **137**

Puritan/Puritano Persona que aspiraban a una doctrina más pura que la propuesta por la Iglesia Católica Inglesa, **327**

Quechua/quechua Idioma de los incas de América del Sur; todavía se habla en esta región, **175, 264**

quinoa/quinua Planta nativa de la región sudamericana de los Andes que da semillas muy nutritivas, **259**

quipu/quipu Complicado sistema de cuerdas de varios colores con nudos, que usaron los incas de América del Sur para registrar información, **179, 260**

race/raza Grupo de personas que comparten características físicas o biológicas heredades, **48**

rain shadow/barrera montañosa Área seca en el sotavento de una montaña o de una cordillera, **35**

reactionaries/reaccionarios Extremistas que se oponen al cambio, y desean deshacer ciertos cambios, **336**

reason/razón Razonamiento lógico, **331**

reforestation/reforestación Plantación de árboles donde los bosques han sido talados, **39**

Reformation/Reforma Movimiento europeo del siglo XVI para reformar el cristianismo, **321, 394**

refugees/refugiados Personas que han escapado a otro país, generalmente por razones económicas o políticas, **63, 215**

reggae/reggae Tipo de música que tiene sus orígenes en Jamaica, **214**

region/región Área de la superficie de la Tierra con una o más características compartidas, **8**

regionalism/regionalismo Conexión más fuerte con la región a la que se pertenece que con el propio país, **143**

Reign of Terror/Régimen de Terror Período durante la Revolución Francesca cuando la Convención Nacional trabajó para suprimir toda oposición, **334**

relative location/ubicación relativa Posición de un lugar en relación con otro, **7**

Renaissance/Renaissance Palabra francesa que significa "renacimiento" y se refiere a una nueva era de conocimiento que empieza en Europa en el 1300s, **317, 377**

renewable resources/recursos renovables Recursos, como el suelo y los bosques, que pueden reemplazarse por medio de procesos naturales de la Tierra, **38**

republic/república Forma de gobierno representativo en que la soberania reside en el pueblo, **297**

Restoration/Restauración Período en que reinó Carlos II de Inglaterra, cuando la monarquía fué restablecida, **328**

Roaring Twenties/años rugientes veinte Periodo de riqueza y grandes diversiones en Estados Unidos en la década de 1920, **100**

Roma/Roma Grupo étnico, también conocido como gitanos, que pudo haber migrado de la India a Europa hace mucho tiempo, **440**

rural/rural Área de terreno abierto que se usa para la agricultura, **4**

Santería/santería Religión originaria de Cuba que mezcla religiones del oesta de África y otras tradiciones, entre otras del catolicismo romano, **214**

Scientific Revolution/Revolución Cientifica Transformación de pensaminto ocurrido durante 1500 y 1600, causada por la observación científica, la experimentación, y el cuestionamiento de las opiniones tradicionales, **323**

R24 • Spanish Glossary

secede/separar Dividir un país para formar otro, **98**
second-growth forests/bosques reforestados Árboles que cubren una región después de que el bosque original ha sido talado, **112**
secularism/secularismo Énfasis en asuntos no religiosos, **331**
sediment/sedimento Pequeñas partículas de rocas fragmentadas, **115**
selvas/selvas Bosques tropicales exuberantes del oeste de Ecuador y Perú, y del norte de Bolivia, **257**
serfs/siervos Personas que estaban atados a una tierra y trabajaban para un señor, **310, 485**
sinkholes/sumideros Agujero profundo de pendiente empinada que se forma cuando el techo de una cueva se hunde, **188**
sirocco/siroco Viento seco y caliente del norte de África que viaja por el mar Mediterráneo hacia Europa, **371**
slash-and-burn agriculture/agricultura de corte y quema Tipo de agricultura en que los bosques se talan y se queman para limpiar el terreno y plantarlo, **201**
smelters/fundidoras Fábricas que procesan menas de metal, **471**
smog/smog Mezcla de humo, sustancias químicas y niebla, **200**
soil exhaustion/agotamiento del suelo Pérdida de los nutrientes del suelo que necesitan las plantas, **240**
solar power/energía solar calor y luz del sol, **41**
soviet/soviet supremo Consejo comunista que gobernó la república y otras regiones de la Unión Soviética, **485**
spatial perspective/perspectiva espacial Punto de vista basado o visto en relación con el lugar en que se encuentra un objeto, así como la razón por la que está ahí, **3**
steppe/estepa Gran llanura de pastos altos que se extiende desde Ucrania, pasa por el sur de Rusia y llega hasta Kazajistán, **461**
steppe climate/clima estepario Tipo de clima, generalmente seco, que se encuentra entre las regiones de climas desértico y húmedo, **36**
stock market/mercado de valores Organización mediante la cual se venden y se compran partes de compañías, **352**
strait/estrecho Paso angosto que une dos grandes cuerpos de agua, **256**
strip mining/minería a cielo abierto Tipo de minería en que se retiran la tierra y las rocas para extraer carbón y otros recursos que están bajo la superficie terrestre, **126**
subduction/subducción Movimiento en el que una placa tectónica terrestre más gruesa se sumerge debajo de una más delgada, **20**
subsistence agriculture/agricultura de subsistencia Tipo de agricultura en que los campesinos siembran sólo lo necesario para mantenerse a ellos mismos y a sus familias, **52**
suffragettes/sufragistas Mujeres que lucharon por el derecho de las mujeres de votar, **343**
superpowers/superpotencias Países poderosos, **465**
symbol/símbolo Palabra, forma, color, estandarte o cualquier otra cosa que se use en representación de algo, **49**

taiga/taiga Bosque de árboles siempre verdes que existen en el sur de la tundra en Rusia, **461**
tenements/casas de vecindad Casas de apartamentos donde vivían algunos inmigrantes a las ciudades grandes de Estados Unidos en el siglo diecinueve, **99**

tepees/tepees Tiendas de forma cónica, hechas de piel de búfalo, **88**
tepuís/tepuís Capas de roca arenisca resistentes a la erosión en las mesetas de los altiplanos de las Guyanas, **222**
terraces/terrazas Crestas horizontales que se construyen sobre las laderas de las colinas para prevenir la pérdida de suelo y favorecer la agricultura, **22**
textiles/textiles Productos para fabricar ropa, **413**
third-world countries/países del tercer mundo países en desarrollo que faltan oportunidades económicas, **55**
topography/topografía forma, altura y arreglo de la tierra en un cierto lugar, **19**
tradition-based economy/economía tradicional Economía basada en las costumbres y las tradiciones, **56**
Treaty of Versailles/Tratado de Versalles Acuerdo de paz firmado al final de la Primera Guerra Mundial, **351**
triangular trade/comercio triangular Red comercial entre Gran Bretaña, África occidental y las colonias británicas en las Américas, **91**
tributary/tributario Cualquier corriente pequeña o río que fluye hacia un río o una corriente más grande, **26**
tundra climate/clima de la tundra Región fría de lluvias escasas, que por lo genera se encuentra entre los climas de las regiones subártica y polar, **36**
tyrants/tiranos personas que tomaron el poder fuera de la ley pero tenía el apoyo de la gente, **290**

U-boats/U-boats Submarinos alemanes usados en la Primer Guerra Mundial, **349**
uninhabitable/inhabitable Que no es propicio para el establecimiento de seres humanos, **422**
United Nations/Naciones Unidas Organización internacional formada después de la Segunda Guerra Mundial para impedir guerras futuras, **101**
urban/urbano Área en que se encuentra una ciudad, **4**

vassals/vassalos Personas a las que un amo les concedía tierras, como pago por sus servicios, **309**
vernacular/vernácular Lenguaje doméstico, natino, propio de un país, **313**
viceroy/virrey Gobernador de una colonia, **262**

water cycle/ciclo del agua Circulación del agua del la superficie de la Tierra a la atmósfera y su regreso, **27**
water vapor/vapor de agua Estado gaseoso del agua, **27**
weather/tiempo Condiciones de la atmósfera en un tiempo y un lugar determinados, **32**
weathering/desgaste Proceso de desintegración de las rocas en pedazos pequeños por la acción del calor, el agua y otros medios, **21**
wetlands/terreno pantanoso Paisaje cubierto de agua al menos una parte del año, **115**
Wheat Belt/región triguera Zona de la región de las Grandes Planicies en Estados Unidos en la que la actividad principal es el cultivo del trigo, **125**

INDEX

S *indicates Skills Handbook*   g *indicates graphic*   m *indicates map*   p *indicates photograph*

abdicated, 464
absolute authority, 327
absolute location, 7, *g7*
Acapulco, Mexico, *m187*, 199
acid rain, 30
acropolis, 289
Acropolis, Athens, Greece, *p373*
adobe, 88
Adriatic Sea, *m427*, 428
Aegean civilization, 287, *m287*, *m369*
Aegean Sea, 287
Aeneid (Virgil), 307
Age of Exploration, 324–26, *m324–25*, *p324*, *p325*, *g326*
Age of Reason, 331
age structure diagrams, S11, *gS11*
aggression, 356
agora, Greek, 289
agrarian, 491
agriculture: Aztec method, 192; cash crops, 199; civilization and, 52; commercial, 52; corn, 119, 226; development of, 51–52; domestication and, 51; environment and, 52; plantations, 91; slash-and-burn, 201; subsistence, 52; types of, 52
air: as natural resource, 30–31
Aix-en-Provence, France, *p38*
Alabama, *m81*; climate, 84–85, 116; economy, 117; natural resources, 85; physical features, 82–83, *m83*, 115–16; statistics, 78
Alaska, *m127*, *p129*; climate, 129; economy, 131; natural resources, 85; physical features, 128; statistics, 78; tundra, *p32*
Albania, *m427*, 436–38, 441, *g441*, statistics, 282
Alberta, Canada, 79, *m135*, 141, 147
Aleutian Islands, *m81*, 84
Alexander the Great, 294–95, *p295*, 372
Alighieri, Dante, 313
alliance, 94, 348
Allied Powers, 101
allies, 357, 465
alluvial fan, 21
alpaca, 174
Alpine countries, *m387*, 388, 403, *g403*. See also Austria; Switzerland
Alps, 370, 388, *p388*
Altiplano, *m237*, 256
Amazon River, 238, 256, 270–71, *m271*
amber, 428, 429

American Indians, 86, *p86*, *m87*. See also specific peoples
American Revolution, 140, 332
Amsterdam, the Netherlands, *m387*, 400
Amur River, *m459*, 475
Anasazi, 88
Andes, 174–79, 222, *g222*, *m237*, 238, 256
Andorra, 282
Angles, 410
Anne of Green Gables (Montgomery), 145
annexed, 356
Antigua and Barbuda, 162, *m205*, *g214*, 216
anti-Semitism, 356, 358, 359
Antwerp, Belgium, *m387*, 400
Apennines, *m369*, 370
Appalachian Mountains, *m81*, 82, *p82*, *m83*, 96, 136
Appian Way, Italy, *p376*
aqueducts, 306, *p306*, 376
aquifers, 26
arch, Roman, 306
archipelago, 206
architecture, in early Greece, 295
Arctic Ocean, 460
Argentina, *m237*; climate, 239; economy, *g253*; history, 245–46, *p245*, *p246*; in modern times, 247–48; people and culture, 246, *p246*; physical features, 238–39; resources, 240; statistics, 162, *g246*; vegetation and wildlife, 239
aristocrats, 290, *p290*
Aristotle, 296
Arizona, *m122*; climate, 124; economy, 125–26; landforms, 123; natural resources, 85; physical features, 82–83, *m83*, 123–24; statistics, 78
Arkansas, *m114*; climate, 84–85, 116; economy, 117; natural resources, 85; physical features, 82–83, 115; statistics, 78
Arkwright, Richard, 339
Armenia, 456, *m481*, 489–91
armistice, 350
arms race, 364
art: early Greek, 295; French impressionists, 393; Norwegian stave churches, 421; Renaissance, 318
Articles of Confederation, 94
assembly line, 342
Astrakhan, Russia, *m459*, 471
astrolabe, *p324*
Asunción, Paraguay, *m237*, 251
Atacama Desert, *m255*, 257
Atahualpa, 179, 181
Athens, Greece, 291, 293, 373, *p373*, 375

Atlanta, Georgia, *m81*, *m114*, 117
Atlantic South America, *m237*; Argentina, 245–47; Brazil, 241–43; climate, 239; culture, 236; Paraguay, 250–51; physical features 238–39; resources, 240; student profile, 236, *p236*; Uruguay, 249–50; vegetation, 239; wildlife, 239. See also specific countries
atmosphere, 31
atomic bombs, 101, 360
Attila the Hun, 443
Aurelius, Marcus, 303
Austria, *m387*; culture, 402–03; economy, 403; history, 357, 401–02; resources, 389; statistics, 282, *g403*
Austrian Empire, 402. See also Austria
Austro-Hungarian Empire, 348, *m348*, 402, 435. See also Austria
avalanche, *p13*
Axis Powers, 357
Azerbaijan, 456, *m481*, 489–90, 491, *p491*, *m493*
Aztec, 171–73; agriculture, 171; art and language, 173, *p171*; daily life, 172; history and culture, 192, *p192*; law and society, 171; Spanish conquest, 180–81

badlands, 123
Bahamas, 162, *m205*, 206, 325
Baikal-Amur Mainline (BAM), 473
Baja California, *m187*, 188
balance of power, 336
Balkan countries, *m427*, 428, 437, 438
Balkan Mountains, 428
Balkan Peninsula, *m427*, 428
Baltic countries, 428
Baltic Sea, *m407*, 408, 428, 460
Baltimore, Maryland, *m81*, *m109*, 110
bananas, *g211*, 223, 226
Banff National Park, Alberta, *p136*, 141
bankrupt, 352, 353
bar graphs, S10, *gS10*
Barbados, 162, *m205*, *g214*, 216
Barcelona, Spain, *m369*, 383
barrier islands, 114, 115
Basel, Switzerland, *m387*, 403
basins, 83
Bastille (Paris), *p332*, 333
bauxite, 207, 223, 232, 371
Bay of Biscay, *m387*, 389
Bay of Fundy, 144
Beatles, *p414*

INDEX

Belarus, *m481*, 482–83; culture, 488; economy, 488; history and government, 484–86; statistics, 456, *g488*. See also Russia
Belém, Brazil, *m237*, 243
Belfast, Northern Ireland, *m407*, 412
Belgium, *m387*; culture, 399–400; history, 351, 398; statistics, 282, *g400*
Belgrade, Serbia and Montenegro, *m427*, 438
Belize, *m205*; climate and vegetation, 206–07; culture, 209–10; history, 208–09; physical features, 206; resources, 207; statistics, 162, *g212*
Benelux countries, *m387*, 388, 400, *g400*. See also Belgium; Luxembourg; Netherlands
Bergen, Norway, *m407*, 420
Berkshires (Massachusetts), *m109*, 111
Berlin, Germany, *m387*, 395, 397
Berlin Wall, 362, 364
Bermuda, *m205*, 217
Bern, Switzerland, *m387*, 403
Bessemer converter, *p339*
Big Bend National Park, Texas, *p83*
Bill of Rights, 95
Birmingham, England, *m407*, 411, 415
birthrate, 59
Bismarck, Otto von, 347, *p347*
Black Death, *m315*, 320
Black Forest, 388
Black Sea, 428, 458, 482, 486
bloc, 362
Blue Ridge Mountains, 115
bog, 418
Bogotá, Colombia, 225
Bohemia, 431. See also Czech Republic
Bolívar, Simón, 182, *p182*, *p262*, *p355*
Bolivia, *m255*, 263, 265; climate and vegetation, 257–58; early cultures, 259; government, 262–63; Inca, 260, 261, 262; landforms and water, 256; resources, 258; Spanish conquest, 261–62; statistics, 162, *g266*
Bonaparte, Napoléon. See Napoléon
Bonn, Germany, 395
Bosnia and Herzegovina, 282, 351, *m427*, 436–38, *p437*, 439, *g441*, *g443*
Boston, Massachusetts, 110
Boston Massacre, *p92*
Bourbons, 327
Brasília, Brazil, 244
Bratislava, Slovakia, 435
Brazil, Amazon region, *p43*, 243; climate, 239; coffee producers, *g244*; history, 241–42; interior region, 244; as major coffee producer, *g244*; Northeast region, 243; people and culture, 242, *p242*; physical features, 238–39; resources, 240; Southeast region, 244; statistics, 162, *g243*; vegetation and wildlife, 239
Brazilian Highlands, 238
Brazilian Plateau, 238
breadbasket, 379
Breton language, 390

Britain, Battle of, 358
British colonies, *m92*
British Columbia, Canada, 79, *m135*, *p137*, *p140*, 141, 147
British Empire, 410–11
British Isles, *m407*, 408
Brittany, *m387*, 388, 390
Brueghel, Pieter (the Younger), *p318*
Brussels, Belgium, *m387*, 400
Bucharest, Romania, *m427*, 440
Budapest, Hungary, *m427*, 435
Buenos Aires, Argentina, *m237*, *p246*, 247, *p248*
Bulgaria, 282, *m427*, 436–38, 441, *g441*; World War I, 348, 351
Byzantine Empire, 373, 376, 436, 489
Byzantium See Constantinople

Cabral, Pedro Alvares, *m345*
cacao, 210
cacti, *p124*
Caesar, Augustus, 302, *p302*
Caesar, Julius, 301, *p301*
Cahokia, 89
caldera, 129
Calgary, Alberta, *m135*, 147
California, *p35*, *p84*, *m127*; climate, 84–85, 129; economy, 131; natural resources, 85; physical features, 82–83; statistics, 78
Callao, Peru, *m255*, 266
Calvin, John, 321
calypso, 214
Cameroon, *p39*
Campeche, Mexico, *m187*, 200
Canada, *m135*, *p136*, *p137*, *p140*, *p141*, *p142*, 144, 146; Canadian arctic, 150–51; capitals of provinces, 79; climate, *m75*, 136; creation of, 140–41; culture, 134, 141–42; eastern provinces, 144; elevation profile, *g72*; English and French Canada, 143; ethnic groups, *p140*, 141–42; geostats, *g72*; government, 141; heartland provinces, 144; history, 138–39; immigration, 142–43; land use, *m77*; languages, *m149*; ; northern Canada, 147; Northwest Territories, 147; Nunavut, 147; physical geography, *m73*, 135–37, *m135*; physical regions, *m83*; political geography, *m74*; population, *m76*; resources, *m77*; statistics, 79, *g141*; western provinces, 146–47; Yukon Territory, 147
Canadian Shield, *m135*, 136
canal, *g120*, 212
Cancún, Mexico, *m187*, 199, 201
Cantabrian Mountains, *m369*, 370
Canterbury Tales, The (Chaucer), 313
cantons, 401
Cape Cod, 111, *m111*
Cape Horn, 255, 256
Capek, Karel, 433
capital, 338

capitalism, 342, 361
Caracas, Venezuela, *m221*, 229
cardamom, 211
Cardiff, Wales, *m407*, 412
Caribbean islands, *m205*; climate and vegetation, 206–07; Cuba, 215–16; culture, 204, 214–15; history, 213; physical features, 206; resources, 207; statistics, *g214 g219*. See also specific islands
Caribbean Sea, *m205*, 206
Caribbean South America, *m221*; climate and vegetation, 223; Colombia, 224–25; culture, 220; the Guianas, 231–32; physical features, 222; resources, 223; statistics, *g225*, *g229*, *g232*; student profile, 220, *p220*; Venezuela, 228–29. See also specific countries
Carpathian Mountains, *m427*, 428, 482
Cartagena, Colombia, *p225*
Cartier, Jacques, 138
cartography, *p12*, 13
Cartwright, Edmund, 339
Cascade Range, *m81*, *m127*, 128
case studies: hurricanes, 14–15; *maquiladoras*, 196–97
cash crops, 199
Caspian Sea, *m245*, 460, 482, 491
cassava, 176, 226
Castiglione, Baldassare, 319
Castro, Fidel, 215
cathedrals, 311, *p311*
Cauca River, *m221*, 225
Caucasus Mountains, *m459*, 460, 482
Caucasus region, *m481*, 482–83; Armenia, 490–91; Azerbaijan, 481; Georgia, 490; government, 490; history, 489; statistics, 456. See also Russia
caudillos, 229
caviar, 438
Cayenne, French Guiana, *m221*, *p231*, 233, *p233*
Celtic languages, 390
Celts, 410
Central America, *m205*; banana exports, *g211*; Belize, 211; climate and vegetation, 206–07; Costa Rica, 212; early cultures, 204, 209–10; El Salvador, 211; Guatemala, 211, *p211*; history, 208–09; Honduras, 211; Nicaragua, 211–12; Panama, 212; physical features, 206; resources, 207; statistics, *g212*; student profile, 204, *p204*. See also specific countries
Central Siberian Plateau, *m459*, 460
Central Valley (California), *m127*
Cervantes, Miguel de, 319
Champlain, Samuel de, 139, *p139*
chancellor, 395
Chanel, Coco, 405
Charlemagne, 309, *p309*, 390–91, *p390*, 394, 398
Charles I (King), 327; death warrant, *p328*
Charles II (King), 328, *p328*
charts, S12–S13

Index • R27

Chaucer, Geoffrey, 313
Chavín, 174
Chelyabinsk, Russia, *m459*, 471, 497
Chernobyl, Ukraine, *m481*, 487
Chesapeake Bay, 109, 112, *p113*
Chibcha, 224
Chicago, Illinois, *m81*, *m118*, 121, *p121*
Chihuahuan Desert, 189
Chile, *m255*, 263, 266–67, *g266*, *p266*; climate and vegetation, 257–58; early cultures, 259; government, 262–63; Inca, 260, 261, 262; landforms and water, 256; resources, 258; Spanish conquest, 261–62; statistics, 162, *g267*
chinampas, 171, 192
chinooks, 122, 124
Chișinău, Moldova, *m427*, 441
chivalry, 310
Chopin, Frédéric, 411
Christianity, 321–22, 373, 377, 489
chromium, 371
Churchill, Winston, 358, *p358*
Cicero, 307
citizenship, in early Greece, 291
city planning, 447
city-states, Greek, 289–91
Ciudad Juárez, Mexico, 187, 199
Civil War (U.S.), 97–98
civil war, 211, 438, 490
civilization, 52
Claudius, 303
Cleisthenes, 291
clergy, 311
cliff dwelling, *p88*
climate, 32, *g36*, *m37*. See also specific continents, countries, and regions; weather
climate maps, *m37*
climatology, 13
cloud forest, 207
Clovis (King of the Franks), 308
coal, 40, *p40*
coalition governments, 377
Coast Ranges, *m127*
Coastal Plain (U.S.), *m81*, 82, *m83*
coffee: major producers of, 207, 223, 226, 231, 242, 244, *g244*
Cold War, 102, 361–64, *m363*, 465
collective farms, 355
Cologne, Germany, *m387*, 397
Colombia, *m221*, *p224*, *p227*; climate and vegetation, 223; coffee producers, *g244*; culture, 227; economy, 226; history, 224–25; physical features, 222; resources, 223; statistics, 163, *g225*
Colonia del Sacramento, Uruguay, *p250*
colonization, 90–92, 325–26, 329, *p329*
colony, 90, 325
Colorado, *p84*, *m122*; climate, 84–85, 124; economy, 125–26; natural resources, 85; physical features, 82–83, *m83*, 123–24; statistics, 78
Colorado Plateau, 84
Colorado River, *p124*
Colosseum (Rome), *p377*
Columbia Basin, *m127*, 129

Columbia River, *m81*, 83
Columbus, Christopher, 213, 324–25, *p325*, 377
command economy, 56
commercial agriculture, 52
commonwealth, 217
Commonwealth of Independent States (CIS), 465, 486, 488
communication, 9
communism, 215, 354, 361, 396, 432, 434, 438, 440, 441, 465
Communists, *p361*, 373, 434, 438, 440, 465, 488–90
community, 4
condensation, 27, *g27*
Confederate States of America (Confederacy), 98
Congress of Vienna, 336
conic projections, S5, *g5*
Connecticut, *m109*; climate, 84–85, 111; economy, 112; natural resources, 85; physical features, 82–83; statistics, 78
conquistadores, 180, 193
Constantine, 305
Constantinople, Turkey, 373. See also Istanbul, Turkey
constitution, 328
Constitution, U.S., 94–95, 331
constitutional monarchy, 413
consuls, 298
consumer goods, 465
contiguous, 81, 82, 127
Continental Congress, 93, *p93*
Continental Divide, *m81*, 83
Cook's Tale, The, *p313*
cooperatives, 215
Copenhagen, Denmark, *m407*, 421
Copernicus, Nicolaus, 323, 432
cordillera (mountains), 222
Córdoba, Argentina, *m237*, 248
cork, 383, *p383*
Cork, Ireland, *m407*, 418
corn, *g119*, *p119*, 226; global producers of, 119
Corn Belt (U.S.), 119
Cortés, Hernán, 180, 193
cosmopolitan, 400
Cossacks, 485
Costa Rica, *m205*, 212, climate and vegetation, 207; culture, 209–10; history, 208–09; physical features, 206; resources, 207; statistics, 163, *g212*
cotton, 91, 97, 231
Counter-Reformation, 322
coup, 263
Crassus, Licinius, 301
Crater Lake, *m127*, 128, *p128*
creoles, 262
Crete, 287–88
Crimean Peninsula, *m481*, 482
Croatia, 282, 351, 365, *m427*, 436–38, 439, *g441*
Cromwell, Oliver, 327–28, *p327*
Crusades, 311, 312
Cuba, *m205*, 215–16; climate and vegetation, 207; culture, 214–15;

history, 213; physical features, 206; resources, 207; statistics, 163, *g214*
cultural geography See human geography
culture: 47; agriculture and, 51–52; aspects of, 47–49; cultural difference, 49; definition, 47; development of, 50. See also specific continents, countries, and regions
culture areas, North American, *m87*
culture region, 47
culture traits, 47
Cumberland Plateau, *m114*, 115
Curaçao, Netherlands Antilles, 216, *p216*
Curie, Marie, 431
currents, 34
Cuzco, Peru, 177, 178, *m255*, 260
cylindrical projections, S4, *gS4*
Cyrillic alphabet, 484, 486, 488
czar, 464
Czech Republic, 275, 282, *m427*, *g432*, 434–35
Czechoslovakia, 351, 357, 362. See also Czech Republic; Slovakia

da Vinci, Leonardo, 318, 377
Dairy Belt (U.S.), 118, 119
Dallas, Texas, *m114*, 117
Danube River, *m387*, 389, *p402*, 428
Danville, California, *p39*
Darius III, *p295*
Dark Age, of Greece, 288–89
Davenport, Iowa, *p28*
Day of the Dead, 195
death camps, 359
death rate, 59
Death Valley, *m122*, 129
Declaration of Independence, 93, 331
Declaration of the Rights of Man and Citizen, 333
deforestation, 39, 429
degrees, S2
Delaware, *m109*; climate, 84–85, 111; economy, 112; natural resources, 85; physical features, 82–83, 111; statistics, 78
Delian League, 293
delta, 21, *p21*
democracy, 95, 377, 381; Athens, first known democracy, 291
Denmark, 282, 358, *m407*, 408, 420–21, *g420*. See also Scandinavia
deserts: as dry climates, *g36*, *m37*
Detroit, Michigan, *m117*, 121, *m121*
developing countries, 55, *g55*
Devil's Island, French Guiana, *m221*, 233
diagrams, S10–S11
dialect, 382
Díaz, Porfirio, 183
dictator, 210, 301, 354–55
diffusion, 9

Dinaric Alps, *m427,* 428
Diocletian, 305
Directory (French), 334–35
disciples, 304
Discus Thrower (Myron), *p296*
diversify, 115, 116, 117
Dnieper River, *m481,* 482
doctors, patients per, *g486*
domestication, 51
Dominica, 163, *m205, p206, g214,* 226
Dominican Republic, 163, *m205,* 206, *g214*
dominion, 140
Don Quixote (Cervantes), 319
Don River, 460
Donets Basin, *m481,* 483
Douro River, *m369,* 370
droughts, 63, 119
dry climates, *g36, m37*
Dublin, Ireland, *m407,* 418
Duomo, *p320*
Düsseldorf, Germany, 397
Dutch language, 399

E

Earth: climate and vegetation, 32–37, *g36, m37;* energy resources, 40–41; landforms, 19; minerals, 42; forests, 39; plate tectonics, 19, *m19*
earthquakes, 20, 256, 370, 477
East Germany, 395. *See also* Germany
Easter Rising, 416
Eastern bloc, 362
Eastern Europe, 426, *m427;* climate and resources, 429; northeastern countries, 430–35; physical features, 428; student profile, 426, *p426;* southeastern countries, 436–41. *See also* individual countries and regions
Eastern Hemisphere, S3, *gS3*
Eastern Woodlands culture, 89
Ebro River, 370
economic geography *See* human geography
economy: command economy, 56; definition of, 53; economic activities, *g54;* global population and, 54–55; gross domestic product, 53; gross national product, 53; one-crop economy, 57
ecotourism, 212
Ecuador, *m255,* 263, 264; climate and vegetation, 257–58; early cultures, 259; government, 262–63; Inca, 260, 261, 262; landforms and water, 256; resources, 258; Spanish conquest, 261–62; statistics, 163, *g266*
Edelweiss Pirates, 346, *p346*
Edmonton, Alberta, *m135,* 147
ejidos, 194
El Dorado, 224
El Niño, 258

El Salvador, *m205,* 211; climate and vegetation, 206–07; culture, 209–10; history, 208–09; physical features, 206; resources, 207; statistics, 163, *g212*
Elbe River, 389
elevation, zones, *g222*
Elizabeth I (Queen), 327, *p411*
Emancipation Proclamation, 98
emigrant, 59
empire, 193, 302
encomienda, 245
energy consumption, U. S., *g45*
energy resources: coal, 40; fossil fuels, 40; geothermal energy, 41; hydroelectric power, 41, *p40;* natural gas, 40; nonrenewable resources, 38; nuclear energy, 41, *p41;* petroleum, 40; renewable resources, 38; solar energy, 41; wind, *p40,* 41
England, civil war, 327–28; colonial expansion, 329; during Enlightenment, 331–32; exploration, 325; Glorious Revolution, 328; Puritans, 327; Reformation, 321 Restoration, 328. *See also* Great Britain; United Kingdom
English Channel, *m387,* 389, 408
Enlightenment, the, 92, 330, *p330*
environment: forests, 39; soil, 38
environmental issues, 103
epidemic, 180, 193
equator, S2, *gS2*
Erasmus, Desiderius, 319
erosion, 21–22, *p21*
Essen, Germany, *m387,* 397
essential elements of geography, 6
Este, Isabella d', *p318*
Estonia, 282, 351, *m387, m427,* 432, *g432*
estuary, 109, 112, 239
ethnic groups, 47, *g140,* 194, 195, 264–65, 396, 399, *g440*
ethnocentrism, 49
Etruscans, 297, *p297*
euro, 392, *p392, p346,* 445
Europe: before World War I, *m348;* climate, *m279;* eastern region, *m427,* 428–41; elevation profile, *g274;* explorations, *m324, g326;* European Union, 444–45, *g445;* geostats, *g274;* land use, *m281;* northern region, *m407,* 408–23; physical geography, *m275;* political geography, *m278;* population, *m280;* resources, *m281;* southern region, *m369,* 370–383; statistics, 282–83; west central region, *m387,* 388–403. *See also* specific countries and regions
European Space Agency, 233
European Union (EU), 383, 392, 395, 398, 400, 402, 418, 435, 444–45, *m445*
evaporation, 27, *g27*
Everglades (Florida), *m114,* 115, *p115*
exports, 57, *g370*

factors of production, 338
factory system, 339–40, *p340*
falaj, p28
famine, 63, 416
fascism, 352, 354, 357
Fascist Party, 354
fault, 20
favelas, 243
federal, 95
feudalism, 309
fief, 309
Finland, 283, 351, *m407,* 408, 409, *g420,* 422–23. *See also* Scandinavia
fjords, 408, 420
Flanders, *m387,* 399
flat-plane projections, S5, *gS5*
Flemish language, 399
floodplain, 21
floods, 28, *p28*
Florence, Italy, *p320,* 379
Florida, *p21, p84, m114, m133;* climate, 84–85, 116; economy, 117; natural resources, 85; physical features, 82–83, *m83,* 115–16; statistics, 78
flowcharts, S13, *gS13*
Ford, Henry, 342
forests: cloud forest, 207; deforestation, 39; as natural resource, 39; reforestation, 39; rain forests, 239, *p239,* 240, *p240*
Forum, Roman, 298, 299, *g299*
fossil fuels, 40, 68
Fourteen Points, 350
France, *m387;* culture, 392–93; history, 390–91; statistics, 283, *g393;* World War I, 348–51; World War II, 357–59
Francis Ferdinand (Archduke), 348, *p348*
Franco, Francisco, 357, 381
Frank, Anne, 359, *p359*
Frankfurt, Germany, *m387,* 397
Franks, 308–09, 390–91
free enterprise, 56
French and Indian War, 92
French Guiana, *m221,* 233, *p233;* climate and vegetation, 223; physical features, 222; resources, 223; statistics, 163, *g232*
French Revolution, 332–34; guillotine, 333–34, *p333;* National Assembly, 333; National Convention, 333–34; Reign of Terror, 334
frontier, 91
Fulton, Robert, 341

Gabrielyan, Nina, 466
Galápagos Islands, *p264*
Galileo, 323; telescope, *p323*
Galway, Ireland, *m407,* 418

Index • R29

Gargantua (Rabelais), 319
Garibaldi, Giuseppe, 347
Garonne River, 388
gas, natural, 142, 483
Gateway Arch (St. Louis, Missouri), *p118*
Gaucho Martín Fierro, The (Hernández), 247
gauchos, 245, 247, *p247*
Gaul, 390
Geneva, Switzerland, 321, 363, *m387*, 401, 403
Genoa, Italy, *m369*, 379
genocide, 359
geography: 3; branches of, 11–13; cartography and, 13; climatology and, 13; geographic issues, 4; global studies, 5; human geography, 11; local studies, 4; meteorology and, 13; perspectives, 3; physical geography, 11–12; as profession, 11–13; regional studies, 5; themes of, 6–10
Georgetown, Guyana, *m221*, 232
Georgia (Eurasia), 456, *m481*, 489–90
Georgia (U.S.), *m114*; climate, 84–85, 116; economy, 117; natural resources, 85; physical features, 82–83, 115; statistics, 78
geothermal energy, 41
Germania, 394
Germany, *m387*; culture, 396; economy, 397; history, 394–95, *m405*; Holocaust, 358–59, 395; population, *gS11*, *g397*; Reformation, 394; reunification, *p364*, 395; statistics, 283, *g397*; World War I, 100, 347–51; World War II, 101, 354–55, 395
geysers, 422
GIS (geographic information system), 12
glaciers, 22, *p25*
gladiators, 304
Glasgow, Scotland, *m407*, 412, 415
glen, 415
global climates, 30–31, *g36*, *m37*
global issues, 5
global village, 102
global warming, 30, 31
globalization, 60
globe, S2, *gS2*
Glorious Revolution, 328
glyphs, 169
Godthab, Greenland *See* Nuuk, Greenland
gold, 226; discovered in California, 96
Gorbachev, Mikhail, 364, 465, *p465*
Gorky *See* Nizhniy Novgorod, Russia
Göteberg, Sweden, *m407*, 420
government: communism, 361; democracy, 95, 291, 377, 381
Gracchi (Gracchus brothers), the, 300
Gracchus, Tiberius, *p300*
Gran Chaco, 237, 238–39
Grand Canyon, *p5*
Great Alföld *See* Great Hungarian Plain
Great American Desert, 96
Great Basin, *m81*, 83
Great Bear Lake, *m135*, 136

Great Britain, *m407*, 408; Industrial Revolution, 338; World War I, 348–51, *m348*; World War II, 357–59. *See also* England; United Kingdom
Great Depression, 100, *p100*, 352, *p352*, 353–54, *p353*
Great Hungarian Plain, 428
Great Lakes, *m81*, 82, 120, 136
Great Plains, *m81*, 83, 96, *m122*
Great Slave Lake, *m135*, 136
Great Smoky Mountains (Tennessee), *p82*, *m114*, 115
Great War, the *See* World War I
Greater Antilles, *m205*, 206
Greece, *p370*, *p372*, *m369*; Aegean civilization, *m369*; agora, 289; aristocracies in early, 290; art and architecture in early, 295; Athens, 291, 293; Byzantine Empire, 373; citizenship in early, 291; city-states, 289–91; climate and resources, 371; Crete, 287–88; Dark Age, 288–89; Delian League, 293; democracy in early, 291; economy, 375; geography, 287, 370–71; government in early, 290; history, *m287*, 372–73; Hellenistic Age, 295; literature and philosophy in early, 296; Macedon's conquest of, 294; math and science in early, 296; Minoan civilization, 287–88; modern culture, 373–74; Mycenaean civilization, 288; myths of, 289, *p289*; oligarchy in early, 290; Ottoman Empire, 373; Parthenon, *p293*, 295; Peloponnesian War, 294; Persian invasion of, Persian wars, 292–93; physical features, 370; Roman conquest of, 298; Sparta, 283; statistics, 283, *g375*; Thermopylae, *p292*; Trojan War, 288; tyrants in early, 290
Greek myths, 289
Green Mountains (Vermont), *m109*, 111
greenhouse effect, 30, 31, *g31*
Greenland, *m407*, 408, 422, *p422*
Greenwich mean time (GMT), S14–15, *mS14–S15*
Grenada, 163, *m205*, *g214*, 216
grid, S2
Grindelwald Valley, Switzerland, *p389*
gross domestic product, 53
gross national product, 53
groundwater, 26, *p27*
Guadalajara, Mexico, *m83*, 200
Guadalquivir River, *m369*, 370
Guatemala, *m205*, 211; climate and vegetation, 207; culture, 209–10; history, 208–09; physical features, 206; resources, 207; statistics, *g212*
Guayaquil, Ecuador, *m255*, 264
Guernica (Picasso), *p356*
guerrilla, 215
Guiana Highlands, *m221*, 222
guillotine, 333–34, *p333*
Gulf of Bothnia, *m407*, 422
Gulf of California, *m187*, 188
Gulf of Finland, 422

Gulf of Mexico, *m187*, 188
Gulf of St. Lawrence, *m135*, 144
Gulf Stream, *p34*
Gutenberg, Johannes, 319, 396
Guyana, *m221*, 232; climate and vegetation, 223; physical features, 222; resources, 223; statistics, *g232*

habitation fog, 472
Habsburgs, 327, 401–02
haciendas, 194
Hadrian, 303
Haiti, *m205*, 206, *p213*, 214, *g214*, 216
Halifax, Nova Scotia, *m135*, 144
Hamburg, Germany, *m387*, 397
Hannibal, 299
Harvey, William, 323
Havana, Cuba, *m205*, 215
Havel, Vaclav, 434, *p434*
Hawaii, *m127*, *p128*, *p129*; climate, 85–86, 129; economy, 131; natural resources, 85; physical features, 84; statistics, 78
heavy industry, 470
Hellenistic Age, 295
Helsinki, Finland, *m407*, 422, 432
hemispheres, S3, *gS3*
Henry (Prince), 324
Henry VIII (King), 321, *p321*
Hernández, José, 247
highland climates, *g36*, *m37*
Hiroshima, Japan, 360
Hispaniola, *m205*, 206
history *See* specific continents, countries, and regions
Hitler, Adolf, 101, 354–55, *p354*, *p356*, 357–59, 395, *p395*
Hitler Youth, 346
Hohenzollerns, 327
Hohokam, 88
Holland *See* Netherlands
Holocaust, 358–59, 395
Holy Roman Empire, 394–95, 401–02
Homer, 296
homogeneous, 491
Honduras, *m205*, 211; climate and vegetation, 206–07; culture, 209–10; history, 208–09; physical features, 206; resources, 207; statistics, *g212*
Hopewell culture, 89
hoplite, *p290*
Houplines, France, *p350*
Houston, Texas, *m81*, *m114*, 117
Huáscar, 179
Huayna Capac, 179
Hudson Bay, *m135*, 136
human geography, 11
human-environment interaction, 9
humanists, 318, 321
humanitarian aid, 63
humid continental climate, *g36*, *m37*

humid subtropical climate, *g36, m37*
humid tropical climate, *g36, m37*
Hungary, 283, *m427, g432,* 435
hunger march, *p353*
Huns, 305
hurricanes, 14–15, *m14, g14, g15,* 207
Hussein, Saddam, 103
hydroelectric power, *p40,* 41, 196, 229, 371

Iberian Peninsula, *m369,* 370, 380, 381
icebreakers, 476
ice-cap climate, *g36, m37*
Iceland, 283, *m407,* 408, 409, 410–11; *g410; m411, g420,* 422. *See also* Scandinavia
Idaho, *m122;* climate, 84–85, 124; economy, 125–26; natural resources, 85; physical features, 82–83, 123; statistics, 78
Illiad, The (Homer), 296
Illinois, *m118;* climate, 84–85, 119; economy, 119–20; landforms, 119; natural resources, 85; physical features, 82–83, 123; statistics, 78
immigrants, 59, 141, 142, 201, 229, 241, 246, 378, 392, 396, 399
imports, 57, *g370*
Impressionism, 393
In Praise of Folly (Erasmus), 319
Inca, *m175,* 260, *p260,* 262, *p262;* lands, *m269;* roads, 261
indentured servants, 231
Indiana, *m118;* climate, 84–85, 119; economy, 119–21; natural resources, 85; physical features, 82–83, 119; statistics, 78
indigo, 228
individualism, 331
Indo-European, 430, 438
Industrial Age, 342–43
Industrial Revolution, 337–41, 411; agriculture, 337; factors of production, 338; factory system, 339–40; technology and communication, 341; textiles, 339
industrialized countries, 54
industries, primary, secondary, tertiary, quaternary, *g54. See also* specific countries and regions
inflation, 198
inset maps, *S7, mS7*
interdependence, 57
Interior Plains (U.S.), 82–83, *m83,* 116
Interior West (U.S.), *m118,* 123–24; agriculture, 125; climate, 124; economy, 125–26; landforms, 123; mining industry, 126; Wheat Belt, 125. *See also* specific states
international date line, *mS14, S15*
Internet, 102

Inuit, 147
Iowa, *m118;* climate, 84–85, 119; economy, 119–21; natural resources, 85; physical features, 82–83; statistics, 78
Iquitos, Peru, *m255,* 256
Iraq, 103
Ireland, 283, *p346, m407,* 408, *g415,* language, 425. *See also* Northern Ireland; Republic of Ireland
Iron Curtain, 362, *m363*
iron ore, *p42,* 223, 226, 229, 371
Iroquois League, 89
irrigation, *p26,* 122, 125
islands, S3
Issus, Battle of, *p295*
Istanbul, Turkey, 373. *See also* Constantinople, Turkey
Italy, *m369;* climate and resources, 371; culture, 378; economy, 379; history, 297–306, 376–77; physical features, 370; Renaissance, 377; statistics, *g379,* 283; world wars, 347–48, 354–58. *See also* Roman Republic; Roman Empire
Ivan the Terrible, 464, *p464*

Jacobins, 334
Jamaica, 164, *m205,* 206, *g214,* 216, 217, *p217*
James II (King), 328
Jamestown, Virginia, 90, *p329*
Jefferson, Thomas, 93
Jesus, 304, *p304*
Juárez, Benito, 194, *p194*
junta, 267
Jutland Peninsula, *m407,* 408, 420–21

Kamchatka Peninsula, *m459,* 460
Kansas, *p26, m122;* climate, 84–85, 124; economy, 125–26; landforms, 123; natural resources, 85, 126; physical features, 82–83, *m82,* 123–24; statistics, 78
Kazakhstan, 494–95, *m495*
Kentucky, *m114;* climate, 84–85, 116; economy, 117; landforms, 115; natural resources, 85, 116; physical features, 82–83, statistics, 78
Khabarovsk, Russia, *m459,* 476
khacapuri, p490
Kiev, Ukraine, *m481,* 484, *p485*
King, Martin Luther, Jr. , *p80,* 102
kivas, 88
Kjølen Mountains, 408
knight, 310, *p310*
Kosovo, Serbia and Montenegro, *m427,* 439
Kourou, French Guiana, 233

Kremlin, The (Moscow), 469, *p469*
Kublai Khan, *p485*
Kuril Islands, *m459,* 460, 477, *p477*
Kuznetsk Basin, *m459,* 473
Kyrgystan, 494–95, *m495*

La Paz, Bolivia, *m255,* 265, *p265*
Labrador, *m135,* 144
Lake Baikal, *m459,* 474, *p474*
Lake Maracaibo, *m221,* 229
Lake Nicaragua, *m205,* 209, 211
Lake Poopó, *m255,* 256
Lake Texcoco, 171
Lake Titicaca, 175, *m255,* 256
land bridge, 86
land use and resource maps, *S9, mS9*
landforms, 19; and precipitation, *g35. See also* specific continents, countries, and regions
landlocked, 250
language, 49. *See also* specific countries
Lapland, *m407,* 423, *p423*
Las Casas, Bartolomé, 345
Las Vegas, Nevada, *m81, m122,* 126, 153
Latins, 297
latitude, *S2, gS2*
Latvia, 283, 351, *m427, g432,* 433
lava, 20
lead, 371
league, 293
League of Nations, 350
legend, *S6–S7, gS7*
Leiden, University of, *p322*
Lenin, Vladimir, 464, 465
Leningrad *See* St. Petersburg, Russia
Lesser Antilles, *m205,* 206, 217
levees, 10
Liechtenstein, 283, *m387*
light industry, 470
lightning, *p44*
lignite, 429
Lilac Dressing Gown, The (Gabrielyan), 466
Lima, Peru, *m255,* 266
limited monarchy, 327
Lincoln, Abraham, 98, *p98*
line graphs, *S10, gS10*
Lisbon, Portugal, *m369,* 383
literacy rate, 54
literature: Argentina, 247; Canada, 145; Czech, 433; Greece, 294, 296; Russia, 466
Lithuania, 284, 351, *m427, g432,* 434
Livadia Palace (Yalta), *p486*
Lives of the Caesars (Seutonius), 307
Ljubljana, Slovenia, *m427,* 439, *p439*
llamas, 174
llaneros, 230, *p230*
Llanos, 222, 225, *p230*
local studies, 4
lochs, 408

Index • R31

INDEX

Locke, John, 331
loess, 389
Loire River, 388
London, England, *m407,* 410, *p411,* 412
Longfellow Mountains (Maine), *m109,* 111
longitude, S2, *gS2*
Los Angeles, California, *p30*
Louis XIV (King), 327
Louis XVI (King), 332
Louis XVIII (King), 335
Louisiana, *m114;* climate, 84–85, 116; economy, 116, *p117;* natural resources, 85; physical features, 82–83, 115; statistics, 78
Loyalists: British, 93; Spanish, 357
Ludington, Sybil, 80
Luther, Martin, 321, *p321*
Luxembourg, *m387;* culture, 399–400; history, 358, 398; statistics, 284, *g400*

Maastricht Treaty, 445
Macedon, conquest of Greece, 294
Macedonia, 284, *m427,* 436–38, 440, *g440, g441*
Machiavelli, 319
Machu Picchu, Peru, *m255,* 260, *p260*
Madrid, Spain, *m369,* 383
Magdalena River, *m221,* 225
Magna Carta, 327
Magnitogorsk, Russia, *m459,* 471
Maine, *m109;* climate, 84–85, 111; economy, 112; landforms, 111; natural resources, 85; physical features, 82–83; statistics, 78
mainland, 370
malaria, 226
Malta, *m277, m278,* 284
mammoth, *p86*
Manaus, Brazil, *m237,* 243
Manchester, England, *m407,* 411
Manitoba (Canada), 79, *m135,* 141
manorial system, 310
map projections, S4–S5, *gS4, gS5*
maps: cartography, 13; definition, S4; elements of maps, S6–S7; mapmaking, S4–S5; mapping the earth, S2–S3; map projections, S4; mental, 69; time-zone maps, S14–S15; types of maps, S8–S9
maquiladoras, 196–97, *g196, p196,* 201
Maria Theresa, *p327*
marine west coast climate, *g36, m37*
maritime, 144
Marius, Gaius, 300
market economy, 56
Marseille, France, *m387,* 393
Martel, Charles, 308
Martha's Vineyard, Massachusetts, 111
Maryland, *m109;* climate, 84–85, 113; economy, 113; natural resources, 85; physical features, 82–83; statistics, 78
mass production, 343

Massachusetts, *p84, m109;* climate, 84–85, 111; economy, 112; natural resources, 85; physical features, 82–83; statistics, 78
Massif Central, 388
mathematics: Greek math and science, 296, 374; Maya calendar, 210
Matisse, Henri, 393
Mato Grosso Plateau, 244
Matterhorn, 388
Maya, 169–71, *m170;* calendar and math, 210; games, 170; glyphs, 169, *g169;* history and culture, *p169, p191,* 192, *p192;* sacrifices, 170; trade, 171
Mazatlán, Mexico, 199
McCormick reaper, *p337*
Medici, Cosimo de, *p317*
medieval, 308, *p312,* 391
Mediterranean climate, *g36, m37*
Mediterranean Sea, 370, 389
megalopolis, 109, 110
mental maps, 68
mercantilism, 325–26, 329
Mercosur, 248
Mercouri, Melina, 375, *p375*
merengue, 214
meridians, S2, *gS2*
Meseta, Spain, 383
Mesoamerica, 167–73, *m170,* 191
mestizos, 209
Metamorphoses (Ovid), 307
meteorology, 13
Métis, 141
Mexican Plateau, *m187,* 188
Mexico, 167, *m187;* agriculture, 199; central interior region, 200; climate, 189–90; colonial Mexico and independence, 193–94; culture regions of, 200–01; early cultures, *p191, p192;* government and economy, 198–99; history and culture, 191–92; industry, 199; *maquiladoras,* 196–97, *g196;* Mexico City region, 200, *p200;* NAFTA and, 198, 201; northern region, 201; oil coast region, 200; physical features, 188; resources, 190; southern region, 201; states of, *m189;* statistics, 164, *g198;* student profile, 186, *p186;* tourism, 199; vegetation, 189; wildlife, 189; Yucatán Peninsula, 188, 201
Mexico City, Mexico, *m187,* 200, *p200, g203*
Miami, Florida, *p61, m81, m114,* 117
Michelangelo, 318
Michigan, *m118;* climate, 84–85, 119; economy, 119–21; natural resources, 85; physical features, 82–83, 119; statistics, 78
Middle Ages, 308–13; church and clergy, 311; cities and trade growth, 312, *p312;* Crusades, 311; early Middle Ages, 309–11; education and literature, 313; feudalism, 309; fiefs, nobles, and vassals, 309; high Middle Ages, 312–13; knights and chivalry, 310, *p310;* manorial system, 310; middle class, 312; nations' growth, 312; serfs, 310; vernacular languages, 313; Viking raids, 309

Middle America: climate, *m159;* elevation profile, *g156* geostats, *g156;* land use, *m161;* physical geography, *m157;* political geography, *m158;* population, *m160;* resources, *m161;* statistics, 162–65. *See also* Caribbean Islands; Central America; specific countries
Middle Atlantic States (U.S.), 112–13
middle class, 312
Midwest (U.S.), 118–21, *m118;* agriculture, 119; climate, 119; Corn Belt, 119; Dairy Belt, 119; economy, 119, 121; industry, 121; landforms, 119. *See also* specific states
migration, 9, 59, 86, 273
Milan, Italy, *m369,* 379
militarism, 348
minerals, as natural resources, 42
mining, Interior West, U.S., 125; Pennsylvania, *m112*
Minnesota, *m118;* climate, 84–85, 119; economy, 119, 121; natural resources, 85; physical features, 82–83, 119; statistics, 78
Minoan civilization, 287–88
Minsk, Belarus, *m481,* 488
minutes, S2
missions, 194
Mississippi, *m114;* climate, 84–85, 116; economy, 117; natural resources, 85; physical features, 82–83, 115; statistics, 78
Mississippi Delta, 114, 115
Mississippi River, *p21, m81,* 83
Mississippian culture, 89
Missouri, *m81, m118;* climate, 84–85, 119; economy, 119, 121; natural resources, 85; physical features, 82–83, 119; statistics, 78
Missouri Compromise, 97
Mitlino, Russia, *p497*
mixed economy, 57
Moche, 174
Moctezuma II, 180
Moldova, 284, *m427,* 436–38, 440–41, *g441*
Mona Lisa (da Vinci), 377, *p377*
Monaco, 284, *m387*
monarchy, 327, *p327*
Mont Blanc, 388
Montana, *m122;* climate, 84–85, 124; economy, 125–26; natural resources, 85; physical features, 82–83, 123; statistics, 78
Monterrey, Mexico, *m187,* 201
Montevideo, Uruguay, *m237,* 249, *p249*
Montgomery, Lucy Maud, 145
Montreal, Quebec, *m135,* 146
Moors, 381
moraine, 109, 111
Morse, Samuel F. B., Morse code, 341

mosaics, 374
Moscow, Russia, *m464,* 469, *p469, p470*
Mostar, Bosnia and Herzegovina, *p365*
Mount Elbrus, *m481,* 482, *p483*
Mount Olympus, 289
Mount Orizaba, *m187,* 188, *p188*
Mount Whitney, *m127*
mountain effects, *p35*
movement, 9
mulattoes, 194
multicultural, 47
mummies, 177, *p177*
Munich, Germany, *m387,* 397
Mussolini, Benito, 354, *p354,* 359
Mycenaean civilization, 288

Nagasaki, Japan, 360
Nahuatl, 173
Nantucket, Rhode Island, *m109,* 111
Naples, Italy, *m369,* 379
Napoléon Bonaparte, *p316,* 335, *p335,* 391, *p391,* 392
Napoléonic Code, 335
Napoléonic Era, 335
Nashville, Tennessee, 117
National Assembly (French), 333
National Convention (French), 333
national parks, 122, 126
nationalism, 348, 402; in Europe, 347; in Latin America, 182; Slav, 437
NATO *See* North Atlantic Treaty Organization
natural resources, 85; economy and people, 42–43; energy resources, 40–41; forests, 39; minerals, 42–43; nonrenewable, 38; rain forests, 240; renewable, 38; soil, 38–39. *See also* specific continents; countries; regions
nature reserves, 482
navigable, 388
Nazca, 175
Nazis, 101, 354–55, 359, 395
Nebraska, *m122;* climate, 84–85, 124; economy, 125–26; natural resources, 85, 126; physical features, 82–83, 124; statistics, 78
Netherlands, *m387, p398;* culture, *p322,* 399–400; history, 358, 398; statistics, *g400*
neutral, 420
Nevada, *m122;* climate, 84–85, 124; economy, 125–26; natural resources, 85; physical features, 82–83, 124; statistics, 78
New Brunswick, Canada, 79, *m135,* 140, 141, 144
New Deal, 100, 352, 353
New England (U.S.), 111–12. *See also* specific states
New France, 139
New Granada, 225

New Hampshire, *m109;* climate, 84–85, 111; economy, 112; natural resources, 85; physical features, 82–83, 111; statistics, 78
New Jersey, *m109;* climate, 84–85, 113; economy, 113; natural resources, 85; physical features, 82–83, 112; statistics, 78
New Mexico, *m122;* climate, 84–85, 124; economy, 112; natural resources, 85; physical features, 82–83, 124; statistics, 78
New Orleans, Louisiana, *m81, m114,* 117
New York City, New York, 110, *p110*
New York, *m109;* climate, 84–85; economy, 113; natural resources, 85; physical features, 82–83, 111; statistics, 78
Newfoundland and Labrador, Canada, 79, *m135,* 144
Newfoundland, 140, 144
newsprint, 137
Newton, Sir Isaac, 323
Nicaragua, *m205,* 211–12; climate and vegetation, 206–07; culture, 209–10; history, 208–09; physical features, 206; resources, 207; statistics, 164, *g212*
Nice, France, *m387,* 393
Nicholas II (Russian czar), 465
nickel, *p462*
Nizhniy Novgorod, Russia, *m459,* 470
nobles, 309
nonrenewable resources, 38
Normandy, France, 391
Normans, 391, 410
Norsemen, 391
North American Free Trade Agreement (NAFTA), 198, 200
North American Indians, 86–89
North Atlantic Drift, 409
North Atlantic Treaty Organization (NATO), 363, *m363,* 391, 395, 400, 411, 434
North Carolina, *m114;* climate, 84–85, 116; economy, 116; natural resources, 116; physical features, 82–83, 115; statistics, 79
North Dakota, *m122;* climate, 84–85, 124; economy, 125–26; natural resources, 85, 126; physical features, 82–83, 123–24; statistics, 79
North Pole, A22, S2–S3
North Sea, *m387,* 389, 408, 409, 415, 420
Northeast (U.S.), *m109,* 110–37, *g110;* economy, 112, 113; megalopolis, 110; Middle Atlantic States, 112–13; New England, 111–12. *See also* specific states
Northeastern Europe, *m427,* 428–29, 430–32, *g432;* culture, 431–32; Czech Republic, 434–35; Estonia, 432; history, 430–31; Hungary, 435; Latvia, 433; Lithuania, 434; Poland, *g434;* Slovakia, 435; statistics *g432.* *See also* specific countries

Northern Eurasia, *m481;* Caucasus region, 489; climate, *m453,* 483; elevation profile, *g450;* geostats, *g450;* land use, *m455;* physical features, 482; physical geography, *m451;* political geography, *m452;* population, *g454;* resources, *g455,* 483; statistics, 456–58; Ukraine and Belarus, 484–88. *See also* Central Asia; Russia; specific countries
Northern Europe, 406, *m407;* climate, 409; natural resources, 408–09; physical features, 408; Republic of Ireland, 416–18; Scandinavia, 419–25; student profile, 406, *p406;* United Kingdom, 410–15. *See also* specific countries and regions
Northern European Plain, *m387,* 388, 428
Northern Hemisphere, S3, *gS3*
Northern Ireland, 365, *m407,* 415, *g415*
Northwest Highlands, *m275,* 408
Northwest Territories, Canada, 79, *m135,* 147
Norway, 284, 358, *m407,* 408, *g419,* 420. *See also* Scandinavia
Notre Dame Cathedral (Paris), *p311*
Nova Scotia, Canada, 79, *m135,* 140, 141, 144
Novosibirsk, Russia, *m459,* 473
nuclear power, 41, *p41*
nuclear weapons, 363
Nunavut, Canada, 79, *m135,* 147
Nuuk, Greenland, *m407,* 422

Ob River, *m459,* 473
obsidian, 171
ocean currents, 34
Octavian (Caesar Augustus), 301, 302
Oder River, 389
Odyssey, The (Homer), 296
Ohio, *m118;* climate, 84–85, 119; economy, 119, 121; natural resources, 85, 119; physical features, 82–83, 119; statistics, 79
oil: deposits and production, 40, 190, 198, 258, 264; pipeline, *p42*
oil shale, 429
Okefenokee Swamp (Georgia), *m114,* 115
Oklahoma, *m122;* climate, 84–85, 124; economy, 125–26; natural resources, 85, 126; physical features, 82–83, 123–24; statistics, 79
oligarchy, in early Greece, 290
Olmec, 167
Olympic National Forest, Washington, *p131*
Ontario, Canada, 79, *m135,* 140, 141, 144, 146
Oporto, Portugal, *p383*

Oregon, *m127*; climate, 84–85, 129; economy, 131; natural resources, 85, 131; physical features, 82–83; statistics, 79
Orinoco River, *m221*, 222
Orrery, The, p331
Oslo, Norway, *m407*, 420
Ottawa, Ontario, *m135*, 146
Ottoman Empire, 437, 489; in Greece, 373; World War I, 348, 351
Ottoman Turks, 437, 489
overpopulation, 58
Ovid, 307
Ozark Plateau, *m114*, 116
ozone layer, 30

Pacal, 170
Pachacutec, 175–76
Pacific South America, 254, *m255*; Bolivia, 263, 265; Chile, 263, 267; climate and vegetation, 257–58; early cultures, 259; Ecuador, 263, 264; government, 262–63; the Inca, 260, 261, 262; landforms and water, 256; Peru, 263, 266; resources, 258; Spanish conquest of, 261–62; statistics *g266*, *g267*; student profile, 254, *p254*. See also specific countries
Pacific States (U.S.), *m127*; climate, 129; economy, 131. See also specific states
Palenque, 170
Pampas, 238, *p238*
Panama, *m205*, 212; climate and vegetation, 206–07; culture, 209–10; history, 208–09; physical features, 206; resources, 207; statistics, 164, *g212*, 284
Panama Canal, *p24*, *m205*, 212
Panama City, Panama, *m205*, 212
Pankhurst, Emmeline, 343
Paraguay, *m237*, 250–51, *p251*; climate, 239; physical features, 238–39; resources, 240; statistics, 164, 132, *g250*; vegetation and wildlife, 239
Paraguay River, *m237*, 239, 250
parallels, S2
Paramaribo, Suriname, *m221*, 232
Paraná River, *m237*, 239
pardos, 230
Paris Peace Conference, 350, *p351*
Paris, France, *m387*, 393
Parliament, 327
Parthenon, Athens, *p293*, 375
Patagonia, *m237*, 238. See also Argentina
patricians, 298
Patriots, 93
Pax Romana, 302
Pearl Harbor, 101, *p101*, *m127*, 358
peat, 418
Peloponnesian League, 294
Peloponnesian War, 294
Peloponnesus, *m369*, 370

Pennsylvania, *m109*; climate, 84–85, 111; economy, 113; natural resources, 85; physical features, 82–83, 112; statistics, 79
Pericles, 291, *p291*
Perón, Eva, 246, *p246*
Persia, 372
Persian Wars, in Greece, 292–93
perspective, 3
Peru, 174, *m255*, 263, 266; climate and vegetation, 257–58; early cultures, 259; government, 262–63; Inca, 260, 261, 262; landforms and water, 256; resources, 258; Spanish conquest, 261–62; statistics, 164, 132, *g266*
Peru Current, 257
Peter the Great, 327, 464
petroleum, See oil
Philadelphia, Pennsylvania, *m81*, *m109*, 110
Philip II (King), 294
philosophy, in early Greece, 296
Phoenix, Arizona, *m81*, *m122*, 126
physical geographer, 1
physical geography, 11. See also specific continents; countries; regions
physical maps, *gS6*, S7–S8
physical-political maps, S8
Picasso, Pablo, 382
pidgin languages, 231
pie graph, S10, *gS10*
Piedmont, 115; Fall Line, *m114*
Pinsk Marshes See Pripyat Marshes
pioneers, 96, *p96*
Pizarro, Francisco, 181, 261–62
place, 7
plain, 21
plantains, 216
plantations, 91, *p91*
plate tectonics, 19, *m19*, 206
plebeians, 298
Plymouth, Massachusetts, 90
Po River, *m369*, 370
pok-a-tok, 170
Poland, *m277*; history, 351, 357; modern, 434; physical features, 429; statistics, 284, *g432*
polders, Dutch, 399, *p399*
police state, 352, 354
polis, 289
political cartoons, 479
political geography See human geography
pollution, *g29*, 428, 429
Pompey, Gnaeus, 301
pope, 377
popular culture, 60
popular sovereignty, 93
population See specific continents, countries, regions
population density, 58
population geography See human geography
population maps, S9, *mS9*
population pyramid See age structure diagrams

Port-au-Prince, Haiti, *m205*, 216
Portugal, *m369*; climate and resources, 371; culture, 382; government, 381; history, 380–81; physical features, 370; statistics, 284, *g382*
potash, 137, 142, 488
potatoes, 176
Prague, Czech Republic, *m427*, 431, *p362*, *p434*, 435
precipitation, 27, *g27*; and landforms, *g35*
prevailing winds, 33
prime meridian, S2
Prince Edward Island, Canada, 79, 140, 141, 144
printing press, 319, *p319*, 320
Pripyat Marshes, *m481*, 482
Priscus, 443
Prometheus, 289, *p289*
Protestants, 321
provinces, 140
Prussia, 395. See also Germany
Puerto Rico, 165, *m205*, 206, 217
Puget Sound Lowland, *m127*, 128
pulp, 137
Puritan, 327
pyramids, 168, 174, 193
Pyrenees Mountains, 370, *m387*, 388

Quebec, Canada, 79, *m135*, 140, 141, 142, 143, 144, 146
Quebec City, Quebec, *m135*, 139, 146
Quechua, 175, 264
quinoa, 259
quipu, 179, 260
Quito, Ecuador, 178, *m255*, 264

R.U.R. (Capek), 433
Rabelais, François, 319
race, 48
railroads, first, 341
rain forests, 239, *p239*, 240, *p240*, *p155*
rain shadow, 35
reactionaries, 336
reason, 331
reforestation, 39
reform, political and social, 343
Reformation, 321, 394
refugees, 63, *p63*, 215
reggae, 214
region, 8, 10, 66
regional studies, 5
regionalism, 143
Reign of Terror, 334
relative location, 7, *m17*
religions, *m48*; See also culture, specific religions

Renaissance, 317–20, *p318*, *p320*; humanists, 318; in Italy, 377
renewable resources, 38
republic, 297
Republic of Ireland, *m407*, 408–09; culture, 417; economy, 417–18; history, 416–17; statistics, 283, *g415*, *g418*
resources *See* natural resources
Restoration, 328
Revere, Paul, 80
Revolutionary War, 94, *p94*
Reykjavik, Iceland, 422
Rhine River, *m387*, *p388*, 389
Rhode Island, *m109*; climate, 84–85, 111; economy, 112; natural resources, 85; physical features, 82–83, 112; statistics, 79
Rhone River, 389
rice paddy, *g22*
Riga, Latvia, *m427*, 433
Río Bravo (Rio Grande), *m187*, 188
Rio de Janeiro, Brazil, *m237*, *p243*, 244
Río de la Plata, *m237*, 239
Rio Grande, *p83*
Roaring Twenties, 100
Robespierre, Maximilien, 333–34, *p334*
Robinson, Mary, 417, *p417*
Robinson projection, S5
robot, 433
Rocky Mountains, *m81*, 82, *m83*, *p123*, 136
Roma, 440, *p440*
Roman Empire, 302–07, *m303*; Christianity's rise, 304; decline and fall, 304–05; engineering and architecture, 306; Five Good Emperors, 303; gladiators, 304; government and law, 307; Julio-Claudian emperors, 302–03; language and literature, 306–07; Pax Romana, 302
Roman Republic, 297–301; conquest of Carthage and Greece, 298; curia, 298; Etruscans, 297; early Rome, 297; expansion, 298; Forum, 298, 299, *g299*; founding, 297; governing consuls and magistrates, 298; Hannibal's invasion, 298; Latins, 297; patricians and plebians, 298; Punic Wars, 298; Senate, 298; Social War, 300; Triumvirates, 301
Romania, 285, *m427*, 436–38, 440, *g441*
Romanov czars, 327
Romans, 376, 390–91, 436
Rome, Italy, 297, *m369*, 379
Roosevelt, Franklin D., 100, 353, 358
Rosario, Argentina, *m237*, 248
Rotterdam, Netherlands, *p398*
Rouseau, Dominica, *p206*
rural, 4
Russia (Russian Federation), 449, *m459*; climate, *m453*, 461; culture, 458, 466–67; elevation profile, *g450*; environment, 497; geostats, *g450*; government, 468, *p468*; heartland of, 469–71; history, 463–65, *m464*, *p464*, *p465*; Lake Baikal, 474; land use, *m455*; Moscow region, 469–71, *p469*, *p470*; physical features, 460–61, *p460*; physical geography, *m451*, physical–political, *m459*; political geography, *m452*; population, *g454*; republics of, *g468*; resources, *g455*, 462, *p462*; Russian Empire, 464, *m464*; Russian Far East, 475–77; St. Petersburg region, 470, *p470*; Siberia, 472–74; Soviet Union, 465; statistics, 456–57, *g467*; student profile, 458, *p458*; Urals region, 471; vegetation, 461, *p461*; Volga region, 471, *p471*
Russian Federation *See* Russia

sacrifices, 170, 177
Saffir-Simpson Scale, 14
Sakhalin Island, *m459*, 460, 477
Salvador, Brazil, *m237*, 243
Salzburg, Austria, *m387*, 403
San Andreas Fault, *m127*
San Antonio, Texas, 117
San José, Costa Rica, *m205*, 212
San Marino, 285
Santa Cruz, Bolivia, *m255*, 265
Santería, 214
Santiago, Chile, *m255*, 267
Santo Domingo, Dominican Republic, *m205*, 216
São Francisco River, *m237*, 244
São Paulo, Brazil, *m237*, 244
Sarajevo, Bosnia and Herzegovina, *m427*, 439
Sardinia, *m369*, 370
Saskatchewan, Canada, 79, *m135*, 141
Saxons, 410
scale, S6, *mS6*
Scandinavia, *m407*, 408–09; Denmark, 421; Finland, 422–23; Greenland, 422; Iceland, 422; Lapland, 423; Norway, 420; people and culture, 419; statistics, *g420*, *g425*; Sweden, 420. *See also* specific countries
Scandinavian Peninsula, *m407*, 408
Schwarzwald *See* Black Forest
science, in early Greece, 296
Scientific Revolution, 323
Scotland, *m407*, 408, 410, 411, 412, 415
Sea of Azov, *m481*, 482
Sea of Okhotsk, *m459*, 475
seasons, *g33*
Seattle, Washington, *m81*, *m126*, 131
seceded, 98
second-growth forests, 109, 112
secularism, 331
sediment, 115
Seine River, *m387*, 388
selvas, 257
Serbia and Montenegro, 351, 365, *m427*, 437, 438–39. *See also* Eastern Europe
Serbs, 365

serfs, 310, 485
serpent mound, *p89*
Shakespeare, William, 319, *p319*
Shannon River, *m407*, 408
Siberia, Russia, *m459*, 472–74, *p472*, *p473*, *p474*
Sicily, *m369*, 370
Sierra Madre Occidental, *m187*, 188
Sierra Madre Oriental, *m187*, 188
Sierra Nevada, *p35*, *m81*, 84, *m127*
sinkholes, 188
sirocco, 371
skills and geography: addressing environmental problems, 496; analyzing changing landscapes, 152; analyzing settlement patterns, 446; drawing mental maps, 68; understanding migration patterns, 272
Skills Handbook: charts, S12–13; diagrams, S10–S11; elements of maps, S6–S7; globe, S2–S3; graphs, S10–S11; mapmaking, S4–S5; mapping Earth, S2–S3; tables, S12–S13; time-zone maps, S14–S15; types of maps, S8–S9
Skopje, Macedonia, *m427*, 440
slash-and-burn agriculture, 201, 230
Slav nationalism, 437
slave trade, 326
slavery, 91, 97
Slavs, 430
Slovakia, 285, *m427*, *g432*, 435. *See also* Eastern Europe
Slovenia, 285, 351, *m427*, 436–38, 439. *See also* Eastern Europe
smelters, 471
smog, *p30*, 200
Socrates, 296
Sofia, Bulgaria, *m427*, 441
soil exhaustion, 240
solar power, 41
solstice, *g33*, 431
Sonoran Desert, 189, *p189*
South (U.S.), 114–15, *m114*; agriculture, 117; climate, 116; economy, 116–17, *p116*; industry, 117; landforms, 115. *See also* specific states
South America: banana exports, *g211*; Caribbean region, 221–33, *m221*; climate, *m159*; elevation profile, *g156*; geostats, *g156*; history, 166–83; land use, *m161*; Pacific region, 255–67, *m255*; physical geography, *m157*; political geography, *m158*; population, *m160*; resources, *m161*; statistics, 162–63. *See also* specific countries and regions
South Carolina, *m114*; climate, 84–85, 116; economy, 116; natural resources, 85, 116–17; physical features, 82–83, 115; statistics, 79
South Dakota, *m122*; climate, 84–85, 124; economy, 125–26; natural resources, 85, 126; physical features, 82–83, 123; statistics, 79
South Pole, A22, S2–S3

Southeastern Europe, *m427*, 428–29, 436–38, *g441*; Albania, 441; Bosnia and Herzegovina, 439; Bulgaria, 441; Croatia, 439; culture, 438; history, 436–37; Macedonia, 440, *g440*; Moldova, 440–41; Romania, 440; Slovenia, 439; Yugoslavia, 437, 438–39. *See also* specific countries
Southern Europe, *m369*; climate and resources, 371; culture, 368; imports and exports, *g370*; Greece, 372–75; Italy, 376–79; physical features, 370; Portugal, 380–83; Spain, 380–83; student profile, 368, *p368*. *See also* specific countries
Southern Hemisphere, S3, *gS3*
Southwest Asia, 494–95, *m495*
Soviet Union, 485, 486, 489; Cold War, 361–64; rise and fall, 465; World War II, 355, 357–60. *See also* Russia
Spain, *m369*; climate and resources, 371; culture, 382; government, 381; history, 380–81, *m385*; physical features, 370; Spanish Civil War, 357; statistics, 285, *g382*
Spanish Civil War, 357
Spanish conquest, 224, 228
Sparta, ancient Greece, 293
spatial perspective, 3
Sputnik, 468
St. Kitts and Nevis, 165, *m205*, *g216*, 217
St. Lawrence River, 136
St. Lawrence Seaway, 120, *g120*
St. Lucia, 165, *m205*, *g214*, 216
St. Peter's Square (Vatican City), *p378*
St. Petersburg, *m459*, Russia, 470
St. Vincent and the Grenadines, 165, *m205*, *g214*, 216
Stalin, Joseph, 355, 357, *p357*, 465
Statue of Liberty (New York), *p109*
stave churches, 421, *p421*
steam engine, 340
steamboats, *p341*
steam-powered factories, 339–40
Stephenson, George, 341
steppe, 461
steppe climate, *g36*, *m37*
stock market, 352
Stockholm, Sweden, *m407*, 420
Stonehenge, *p412*
strait, 256
Strait of Gibraltar, *m369*, 370
Strait of Magellan, *m255*, 256
strip mining, 122, 126
subarctic climate, *g36*, *m37*
subduction, 20
subsistence agriculture, 52
Sucre, Bolivia, 255
Sudetenland, 357, *p357*
Suetonius, 307
suffragettes, 343
sugarcane, 215, *p215*, 223, 226, 231
Sulla, Lucius Cornelius, 300, *p300*

Sun: solstice, 431; tilt of the Earth's axis and, 32–33, *g33*; time zones, S14–S15, *mS14–S15*
superpowers, 465
surface water, 26
Suriname, 221, *m221*, 232, *p232*; climate and vegetation, 223; physical features, 222; resources, 223; statistics, *g232*, 285
Susquehanna River, *m109*, 112
Swan Lake (Tchaikovsky), 467, *p467*
Sweden, 285, *m407*, 408, 420, *g420*. *See also* Scandinavia
Switzerland, *m387*; culture, 402–03; economy, 403; history, 401; physical features, 388; resources, 389, *p389*; statistics, 285, *g403*
symbols, 49

tables, S12–S13, *gS12*, 488–89, *g488*
Tacitus, 307
Tagus River, *m369*, 370
taiga, 461
Tajikistan, 494–95, *p494*, *m495*
Tallinn, Estonia, 432
Tamil Nadu, India, *p27*
Tampico, Mexico, *m187*, 200
tango, 246, *p246*
Tchaikovsky, Peter, 467, *p467*
technology: computer mapping, 12; Dutch polders, 399, *p399*; printing press, 319; Inca roads, 261; St. Lawrence Seaway, 120, *g120*; U-boats, 349
tectonic plates *See* plate tectonics
Temple of Delphi (Greece), *p372*
tenements, 99
Tennessee, *m114*; climate, 84–85, 116; economy, 117; natural resources, 85; physical features, 82–83, 115; statistics, 79
Tenochtitlán, 168, 192, 193
tepees, 88
tepuís, 222
terraces, 22
Texas, *m114*; climate, 84–85, 116; economy, 117; natural resources, 85; physical features, 82–83, 115; statistics, 79
textile industry, 339
textiles, 413
Thermopylae, Greece, *p292*
Thessaloníki, Greece, *m369*, 375
Third Reich, 355, 357
third-world countries, 55
Thucydides, 294
Tiber River, *m369*, 370, 376
Tierra del Fuego, *m237*, 238, 256. *See also* Argentina
tigers, 475, *p475*
Tijuana, Mexico, *m187*, 199, 201
time lines, S12, *gS12*

time-zone map, S14–S15, *mS14–S15*
Tiranë, Albania, *m427*, 441
Tito, Josip Broz, 438
tobacco, 91, 97
topographic map, reading a, 23, *m23*
topography, 19
tornado, 4
Toronto, Ontario, *m135*, 142, 146, *p146*
tourism, from natural resources, 85; in southern U.S., 117
tradition-based economy, 56
Trajan, 303
Trans-Alaska Pipeline, *p131*
transcontinental railroad, 99
Trans-Siberian Railroad, 473, 476
Transylvanian Alps, 428
Treaty of Paris (1783), 94
Treaty of Versailles, 351, 354
trench warfare, 349, *p349*, 351
triangular trade, 91, *m107*
tributary, 26
Trinidad and Tobago, 165, *m205*, 206, 214, *g214*, *p215*, 216
Trojan War, 288
tropical savanna climate, *g36*, *m37*
Troy, 288
Tull, Jethro, 337
tundra climate, *p32*, *g36*, *m37*
Tupac Amarú II, 182
Turin, Italy, *m369*, 379
Turkmenistan, 494–95, *m495*
tyrants, in early Greece, 290

U-boats, 349
Ukraine, *m481*, 482–83; economy, 486; environment, 487; history and government, 484–86; statistics, 457; student profile, 480, *p480*. *See also* Russia
Ulster *See* Northern Ireland
uninhabitable, 422
United Kingdom, *m407*, 408–09; culture, 412; economy, 412–13; history, 410–13; Northern Ireland, 415; statistics, 285, *g414*. *See also* specific countries
United Nations (UN), 101, 363
United States, 80, *m81*; American Indians, 86, *p86*, *m87*; Civil War, 97–99, *p98*; climate, *m75*, 84–85; Cold War, 361–64; colonial era, 90–92; elevation profile, *g72*; energy consumption, *g45*; geostats, *g72*; government, 93–95; history, 86–103; land use, *m77*; natural resources, 85; physical geography, *m73*; physical-political, *m81*; physical regions, 82–83, *m83*; political geography, *m74*; population, *m76*; resources, *m77*; state capitals, 78–79; state nicknames, 78–79, World War I, 100, 350–51;

World War II, 101, 358. *See also* specific regions and states
Ural Mountains, *m459*, 460, 471
urban, 4
urban geography *See* human geography
Uruguay, *m237*, 249–50, *p249*, *p250*; climate, 239; physical features, 238–39; resources, 240; statistics, 165, *g250*; vegetation and wildlife, 239
Utah, *m122*; climate, 84–85, 124; economy, 125–26; natural resources, 85; physical features, 82–83, 123; statistics, 79, 165
Uzbekistan, 494–95, *m495*, *p495*

Valparaíso, Chile, *m255*, 267
Vancouver, British Columbia, *m135*, *p137*, 147
Vandals, 305
vassals, 309
Vatican City, 285, *m369*, *p378*
Venezuela, *m221*; agriculture, 230; climate and vegetation, 223; culture, 230; economy, 229; history, 228–29; physical features, 222; resources, 223; statistics, 165, *g229*
Venice, Italy, 379
Vermont, *m109*; climate, 84–85, 111; economy, 112; natural resources, 85; physical features, 82–83, 111; statistics, 79
vernacular, 313
Vespucci, Amerigo, 377
Vesuvius, 370
viceroy, 262
Vienna, Austria, *p336*, *m387*, *p402*, 403
Vikings, 138, 309, 410, 484
Vilnius, Lithuania, *m427*, 434
Virgil, 307
Virgin Islands, *m205*, 206, 217
Virginia, *m109*; climate, 84–85, 113; economy, 117; natural resources, 85; physical features, 82–83, 112; statistics, 79
Visigoths, 305
Vistula River, *m427*, 434
Vladivostok, Russia, *m459*, 476, *p476*
Vltava River, 435
volcanoes, 408, *m411*, 477
Volga River, *m459*, 460

Wagner, Richard, 396
Wales, *m407*, 410, 411, 412
Wallonia, *m387*, 399
Warsaw, Poland, *p358*, *m427*, 434
Warsaw Pact, 363, *m363*
Washington, George, 94, *p94*
Washington (state), *m127*; climate, 84–85, 129; economy, 131; natural resources, 85; physical features, 82–83; statistics, 79
Washington, D. C., *m81*, *m109*, 110
water: characteristics of, 25; Dutch polders, 399, *p399*; geographic distribution of, 25–26; groundwater, 26; hydroelectric power, 40; oceans, 25; surface water, 26; water cycle, 27, *g27*; water vapor, 27
Waterloo, Belgium, 335
Watt, James, 340
weather, 32; global warming, 30, 31; greenhouse effect, 30, 31, *g31*; weather maps, *m34*
weathering, 21, *p21*
Weser River, 389
West Germany, 395. *See also* Germany
West Siberian Plain, *m459*, 460
West Virginia, *m109*; climate, 84–85, 113; economy, 113; natural resources, 85; physical features, 82–83, 112; statistics, 79
West-central Europe, *m387*; Alpine countries, 401–02; Austria, 401–03; Belgium, 398–99; Benelux countries, 398–99; climate and waterways, 388–89; culture, 386; France, 390–93; Germany, 394–97; Luxembourg, 398–99; Netherlands, 398–400; physical features, 388; resources, 389; student profile, 386, *p386*; Switzerland, 401–03. *See also* specific countries
Western bloc, 362
Western Hemisphere, S3, *gS3*
wetlands, 115
wheat, 125, *p125*, 223, 487, *g487*, *p487*
Wheat Belt (U.S.), 125
White Mountains, (New Hampshire), *m109*, 111
Willamette Valley, *m127*, 128
William of Orange, 328
Wilson, Woodrow, 350–51, *p351*
wind: as energy resource, *p40*, 41; sirocco, 371
Windsor, Ontario, *m135*, 144
Winnipeg, Manitoba, *m135*, 147
Wisconsin, *m118*; climate, 84–85, 119; economy, 119–20; natural resources, 85, 119; physical features, 82–83, 119; statistics, 79
wooden culture, 461
world population growth, *gS10*; issues, 58–59
world regions, *m67*
World War I, 347–51, *m348*; airplanes, 349; African American soldiers, *p100*; alliances before, 348; Allied leaders, *p351*; armistice ends, 350; assassination begins, 348; Central Powers, 348; Italy and Germany before, 347; militarism, 348; military losses, *g350*; nationalism before, 347; Treaty of Versailles, 351, 354; trench warfare, 349, *p349*; U-boats, 349; United States enters, 100; weapons, 349
World War II, 101, 356–60, 391, 395, *p395*, 402, 432, 434, 437; Allied Powers, 101; atomic bombs, 101; fascism, 354; Germany invades Poland, 101, 357; human losses, *g360*; Japan, 102, 357,–60; Nazi party, 101, 354–55, 359, 395; Pearl Harbor, 101, *p101*; United States after, 102
Wright, Joseph, 331
Wyoming, *m122*; climate, 84–85, 124; economy, 125; natural resources, 85, 126; physical features, 82–83, 123; statistics, 79

Xerxes I (King), 292

Yalta, Ukraine, *p486*
Yekaterinburg, Russia, *m459*, 471
Yellowstone National Park (Wyoming, Montana, and Idaho), 126, *p126*
Yeltsin, Boris, 364
Yenisey River, *m459*, 473
Yucatán Peninsula, 167, 169, *m187*, 188, 201
Yugoslavia, history, 351, 365, 437
Yukon Territory, Canada, 79, *m135*, 147

Zagreb, Croatia, *m427*, 439
Zurich, Switzerland, *m387*, 403

ACKNOWLEDGMENTS

For permission to reproduce copyrighted material, grateful acknowledgment is made to the following sources:

Business Week: "Argentina's Shrinking Economy" (table) from *BusinessWeek* online, accessed October 27, 2003, at http://www.businessweek.com/magazine/content/02_17...

Duke University Press: From "The History of the Huni Kui People" by Sia Kaxinawá from *The Brazil Reader*, edited by Robert M. Levine and John J. Crocitti. Copyright © 1999 by Duke University Press.

FocalPoint f/8: From "October 5—Galtai" from "Daily Chronicles" and from "Buddhist Prayer Ceremony" from "Road Stories" by Gary Matoso and Lisa Dickey from *The Russian Chronicles* from FocalPoint f/8, accessed October 14, 1999, at http://www.f8.com/FP/Russia.

National Geographic Society: From "El Niño/La Niña" by Curt Suplee from *National Geographic*, vol. 195, no. 3, March 1999. Copyright © 1999 by National Geographic Society.

National Public Radio: Quote by Schwarma from *National Public Radio*, August 31, 2003. Copyright © 2003 by National Public Radio.

Sierra Club: From "Letter Regarding Jordan Creek Parkway Old Growth Forests, May 9, 2003" by Al Wurth, Ph.D. from *Sierra Club* Web site, accessed December 9, 2003, at http://pennsylvania.sierraclub.org/lv/Issues/jordanoldgrowth.htm.

Time, Inc.: From "Coco Chanel" by Ingrid Sischy from *Time*, June 8, 1998. Copyright © 1998 by Time, Inc.

Sources Cited:

From "Dinner with Attila the Hun, c. AD 450" by Priscus from *Historici Graeci Minores*, translated by B. K. Workman. Published in *They Saw It Happen in Classical Times* by Blackwell, Oxford, UK, 1964.

From "Where We Stand Today: Overview of Nunavut" by Stephen Vail and Graeme Clinton from *Nunavut Economic Outlook*, May 2001. Published by The Conference Board of Canada, 2001.

Quote by Bartolomé Las Casas from *The Conquest of America: The Question of the Other* by Tzvetan Todorov, translated by Richard Howard. Published by HarperCollins Publishers, Inc., New York, NY, 1984.

From "Industrial Wasteland" from *Siberian Odyssey: A Voyage into the Russian Soul* by Frederick Kempe. Published by G. P. Putnam's Sons, New York, NY, 1992.

From "The Wild Irish West" from *The Irish: Portrait of a People* by Richard O'Connor. Published by G. P. Putnam's Sons, New York, NY, 1971.

From "The Aztecs in 1519" from *The Discovery and Conquest of Mexico* by Bernal Díaz. Published by Routledge and Kegan Paul, London, 1938.

Quote by Sergei Ling from *Chernobyl Legacy* by Paul Fusco and Magdalena Caris. Published by de.MO, Millbrook, NY, 2001.

Quote by José de Acosta from "The History of Chocolate" from *Wikipedia* web site, accessed on January 27, 2004, at http://en.wikipedia.org/wiki/Chocolate.

ART CREDITS

Abbreviated as follows: (t) top, (b) bottom, (l) left, (r) right, (c) center.

Unit flags of United States created by One Mile Up, Inc. Unit flags of Canadian provinces created by EyeWire, Inc. Other flags, country silhouettes, feature maps and atlas maps created by MapQuest.com., Inc. All other illustrations, unless otherwise noted, contributed by Holt, Rinehart and Winston.

Table of Contents: Page vii, Uldis Klavins; xvi, Dave Henderson.

Atlas: Page A2, MapQuest.com, Inc.; A4, MapQuest.com, Inc.; A6, MapQuest.com, Inc.; A8, MapQuest.com, Inc.; A10, MapQuest.com, Inc.; A11, MapQuest.com, Inc.; A12, MapQuest.com, Inc.; A13, MapQuest.com, Inc.; A14, MapQuest.com, Inc.; A15, MapQuest.com, Inc.; A16, MapQuest.com, Inc.; A17, MapQuest.com, Inc.; A18, MapQuest.com, Inc.; A19, MapQuest.com, Inc.; A20, MapQuest.com, Inc.; A21, MapQuest.com, Inc.; A22, MapQuest.com, Inc.

Geography and Map Skills Handbook: Page S2, MapQuest.com, Inc.; S3, MapQuest.com, Inc.; S4 (cl, bl), MapQuest.com, Inc.; S5, MapQuest.com, Inc.; S6, MapQuest.com, Inc.; S7, MapQuest.com, Inc.; S8, MapQuest.com, Inc.; S9, MapQuest.com, Inc.; S10 (t, br), Leslie Kell; S11 (t), Leslie Kell; S11 (b), Ortelius Design; S12 (b), Leslie Kell; S13, Uhl Studios, Inc.; S14, MapQuest.com, Inc.; S16, Robert Hynes.

Chapter 1: Page 5, MapQuest.com, Inc.; 6 (bl), MapQuest.com, Inc.; 8 (l, bc), MapQuest.com, Inc.; 9 (tr), MapQuest.com, Inc.; 11 (bc), MapQuest.com, Inc.; 14 (b), MapQuest.com, Inc.; 16 (b), MapQuest.com, Inc.; 17, MapQuest.com, Inc.

Chapter 2: Page 19, MapQuest.com, Inc.; 26, Uhl Studios, Inc.; 27, Uhl Studios, Inc.; 28, MapQuest.com, Inc.; 29, HRW art; 31, Uhl Studios, Inc.; 32, MapQuest.com, Inc.; 33, Uhl Studios, Inc.; 34, MapQuest.com, Inc.; 35 (tl) Uhl Studios, Inc.; 37, MapQuest.com, Inc.; 38, MapQuest.com, Inc.; 41, MapQuest.com, Inc.; 42 (t), MapQuest.com, Inc.; 42 (b, t), MapQuest.com, Inc.; 44, MapQuest.com, Inc.; 45, Leslie Kell.

Chapter 3: Page 48 (t), MapQuest.com, Inc.; 48 (b), MapQuest.com, Inc.; 49 (tr), MapQuest.com, Inc.; 50 (bl), MapQuest.com, Inc.; 53 (t), MapQuest.com, Inc.; 54, MapQuest.com, Inc.; 55 (t), MapQuest.com, Inc.; 58, MapQuest.com, Inc.; 64, MapQuest.com, Inc.; 67, MapQuest.com, Inc.

Unit 2: Page 72 (t, bl), Ortelius Design; 73, MapQuest.com, Inc.; 74, MapQuest.com, Inc.; 75, MapQuest.com, Inc.; 76, MapQuest.com, Inc.; 77, MapQuest.com, Inc.; 78–79, MapQuest.com, Inc.

Chapter 4: Page 81, MapQuest.com, Inc.; 82 (bl), MapQuest.com, Inc.; 83 (t, br), MapQuest.com, Inc.; 87, MapQuest.com, Inc.; 92, MapQuest.com, Inc.; 106, MapQuest.com, Inc.; 107, MapQuest.com, Inc.

Chapter 5: Page 109 (b), MapQuest.com, Inc.; 110, MapQuest.com, Inc.; 111, MapQuest.com, Inc.; 112, MapQuest.com, Inc.; 114, MapQuest.com, Inc.; 117, MapQuest.com, Inc.; 118, MapQuest.com, Inc.; 119, Uhl Studios, Inc.; 120, MapQuest.com, Inc.; 121, MapQuest.com, Inc.; 122, MapQuest.com, Inc.; 123 (t,b), MapQuest.com, Inc.; 124 (t,b), MapQuest.com, Inc.; 125, MapQuest.com, Inc.; 127, MapQuest.com, Inc.; 128, MapQuest.com, Inc.; 129, MapQuest.com, Inc.; 130 (t,b), MapQuest.com, Inc.; 131, MapQuest.com, Inc.; 133, MapQuest.com, Inc.

Chapter 6: Page 135, MapQuest.com, Inc.; 136, MapQuest.com, Inc.; 137, MapQuest.com, Inc.; 139, MapQuest.com, Inc.; 140, MapQuest.com, Inc.; 141, MapQuest.com, Inc.; 142, MapQuest.com, Inc.; 144, MapQuest.com, Inc.; 148, MapQuest.com, Inc.; 149, MapQuest.com, Inc.; 150 (t), MapQuest.com, Inc.; 150 (b), Russ Charpentier; 151 (t, b), Jack Scott/line art; 151 (t, b), Joe LeMonnier/paper graphic.

Unit 3: Page 156 (t,bl), Ortelius Design; 157, MapQuest.com, Inc.; 158, MapQuest.com, Inc.; 159, MapQuest.com, Inc.; 160, MapQuest.com, Inc.; 161, MapQuest.com, Inc.; 162–165, MapQuest.com, Inc.

Chapter 7: Page 169, Stephen Brayfield; 170, MapQuest.com, Inc.; 172, Uldis Klavins; 175, MapQuest.com, Inc.; 184, MapQuest.com, Inc.

Chapter 8: Page 187, MapQuest.com, Inc.; 188, MapQuest.com, Inc.; 189 (t, br), MapQuest.com, Inc.; 192, MapQuest.com, Inc.; 194, MapQuest.com, Inc.; 196, Leslie Kell; 197, MapQuest.com, Inc.; 199, MapQuest.com, Inc.; 200, MapQuest.com, Inc.; 202, MapQuest.com, Inc.; 203, Leslie Kell.

Chapter 9: Page 205, MapQuest.com, Inc.; 206, MapQuest.com, Inc.; 208, MapQuest.com, Inc.; 209, MapQuest.com, Inc.; 213, MapQuest.com, Inc.; 215 (t, b), MapQuest.com, Inc.; 217, MapQuest.com, Inc.; 218, MapQuest.com, Inc.; 219, MapQuest.com, Inc.

Chapter 10: Page 221 (b), MapQuest.com, Inc.; 222, Uhl Studios, Inc.; 224, MapQuest.com, Inc.; 225 (br), MapQuest.com, Inc.; 227 (tr), MapQuest.com, Inc.; 228 (bl) MapQuest.com, Inc.; 231 (br) MapQuest.com, Inc.; 232 (bl) MapQuest.com, Inc.; 233, MapQuest.com, Inc.; 234 MapQuest.com, Inc.

Chapter 11: Page 237 MapQuest.com, Inc.; 238, MapQuest.com, Inc.; 243 MapQuest.com, Inc.; 244, Leslie Kell; 248 (b), MapQuest.com, Inc.; 249, MapQuest.com, Inc.; 250, MapQuest.com, Inc.; 252, MapQuest.com, Inc.; 253, Leslie Kell.

Chapter 12: Page 255, MapQuest.com, Inc.; 257, MapQuest.com, Inc.; 260, MapQuest.com, Inc.; 262, MapQuest.com, Inc.; 264, MapQuest.com, Inc.; 265, MapQuest.com, Inc.; 268, MapQuest.com, Inc.; 269, MapQuest.com, Inc.; 270; MapQuest.com, Inc.; 271 (b), Elizabeth Wolf.

Unit 4: Page 276 (t, bl), Ortelius Design; 277, MapQuest.com, Inc.; 278, MapQuest.com, Inc.; 279, MapQuest.com, Inc.; 280, MapQuest.com, Inc.; 281, MapQuest.com, Inc.; 282–285, MapQuest.com, Inc.

Chapter 13: Page 287 (b), MapQuest.com, Inc.; 299, Uldis Klavins; 303, MapQuest.com, Inc.; 306, Stephen Brayfield; 314, MapQuest.com, Inc.; 315, MapQuest.com, Inc.

Chapter 14: Page 324, MapQuest.com, Inc.; 325, MapQuest.com, Inc.; 344, MapQuest.com, Inc.; 345, MapQuest.com, Inc.

Chapter 15: Page 348, MapQuest.com, Inc.; 350, HRW Art; 360, Leslie Kell; 363, MapQuest.com, Inc.; 366, MapQuest.com, Inc.

Chapter 16: Page 369 (b), MapQuest.com, Inc.; 370 (t), Leslie Kell; 370 (b), MapQuest.com, Inc.; 371, MapQuest.com, Inc.; 372, MapQuest.com, Inc.; 373, MapQuest.com, Inc.; 376, MapQuest.com, Inc.; 377, MapQuest.com, Inc.; 378, MapQuest.com, Inc.; 380, MapQuest.com, Inc.; 381, MapQuest.com, Inc.; 383, MapQuest.com, Inc.; 384, MapQuest.com, Inc.; 385, MapQuest.com, Inc.

Chapter 17: 387, MapQuest.com, Inc.; 388 (t, b), MapQuest.com, Inc.; 389, MapQuest.com, Inc.; 392, MapQuest.com, Inc.; 394, MapQuest.com, Inc.; 395, MapQuest.com, Inc.; 396, MapQuest.com, Inc.; 398, MapQuest.com, Inc.; 402, MapQuest.com, Inc.; 404, MapQuest.com, Inc.; 405, MapQuest.com, Inc.

Chapter 18: Page 407 (b), MapQuest.com, Inc.; 408 (bl), MapQuest.com, Inc.; 412 (bl), MapQuest.com, Inc.; 413 (br), MapQuest.com, Inc.; 415, Leslie Kell; 416, MapQuest.com, Inc.; 420, MapQuest.com, Inc.; 422 (tl), MapQuest.com, Inc.; 423 (tr), MapQuest.com, Inc.; 424, MapQuest.com, Inc.

Chapter 19: Page 427 (b), MapQuest.com, Inc.; 428, MapQuest.com, Inc.; 432, MapQuest.com, Inc.; 434, MapQuest.com, Inc.; 435, MapQuest.com, Inc.; 436, MapQuest.com, Inc.; 437, MapQuest.com, Inc.; 438, MapQuest.com, Inc.; 439 (t,b), MapQuest.com, Inc.; 442, MapQuest.com, Inc.; 443, Leslie Kell; 445, MapQuest.com, Inc.

Unit 5: Page 450 (t, bl), Ortelius Design; 451, MapQuest.com, Inc.; 452, MapQuest.com, Inc.; 453, MapQuest.com, Inc.; 454, MapQuest.com, Inc.; 455, MapQuest.com, Inc.; 456–457, MapQuest.com, Inc.

Chapter 20: Page 459 (b), MapQuest.com, Inc.; 464 (t), MapQuest.com, Inc.; 465, MapQuest.com, Inc.; 467, MapQuest.com, Inc.; 469, MapQuest.com, Inc.; 470 (t,b), MapQuest.com, Inc.; 471, MapQuest.com, Inc.; 472, MapQuest.com, Inc.; 473, MapQuest.com, Inc.; 474, MapQuest.com, Inc.; 476, MapQuest.com, Inc.; 477, MapQuest.com, Inc.; 478, MapQuest.com, Inc.

Chapter 21: Page 481, MapQuest.com, Inc.; 482, MapQuest.com, Inc.; 485, MapQuest.com, Inc.; 486, MapQuest.com, Inc.; 487, Uhl Studios, Inc.; 490, MapQuest.com, Inc.; 492, MapQuest.com, Inc.; 493, MapQuest.com, Inc.; 495, MapQuest.com, Inc.

PHOTO CREDITS

Cover and Title Page: (child image) AlaskaStock Images; (bkgd) Image Copyright © 2003 PhotoDisc, Inc./HRW

Table of Contents: Page iv, SuperStock; v (t), S. Sherbell/Corbis SABA; v (b), © Richard Paisley/Viesti Collection; vi (t), © STONE/Robert Frerck/Getty Images; vii (t), © STONE/William J. Hebert/Getty Images; vi (b), © Robert Frerck/Odyssey/Chicago; vii (b), Rosenback/ZEFA/Index Stock Imagery; viii (t), © Travelpix/FPG International/Getty Images; viii (b), © The State Russian Museum/CORBIS; ix (t), Steve Raymer/National Geographic Society Image Collection; ix (b), © Marc Riboud/Magnum; x (t), Ed Kashi © 1995; x (b), © Alex Wasinski/FPG International/Getty Images; xi (b), Daniel J. Cox/Natural Exposures; xi (tl), Giraudon/Art Resource, NY; xii (bl), © C. Rennie/Art Directors & TRIP Photo Library; xii (t), Richard Bickel/CORBIS; xiii (b), Ric Ergenbright; xiii (c), CORBIS; xiv (b), Digital Stock Corp.; xiv (t), © Frans Lanting/Minden Pictures; **Geography and Map Skills:** Page S1 (tr), HRW photo by Sam Dudgeon; S1 (br), HRW photo by Sam Dudgeon; S4 (tr), Andy Christiansen/HRW Photo; **Unit 1:** Page 0 (c), © Joe Viesti/The Viesti Collection; 0 (t), © Norbert Wu/www.norbertwu.com; 0-1 (b), Photo © Transdia/Panoramic Images, Chicago 1998; 1 (tr), Francois Gohier/Photo Researchers, Inc.; 1 (br), Steven David Miller/Animals Animals/Earth Scenes; **Chapter 1:** Page 2 (cl), © Stone/Philip & Karen Smith/Getty Images; 2 (bl), Sam Dudgeon/HRW Photo; 2 (tr), CORBIS Images/HRW; 2 (c), © Joseph Sohm; ChromoSohm Inc./CORBIS; 3 (bl), © Stone/Ken McVey/Getty Images; 4 (tr), Luca Turi/AP/Wide World Photos; 5 (cl), Jose Fuste Raga/Corbis Stock Market; 5 (cr), NASA; 6 (cl), Robert Caputo/Aurora; 7 (br), © Bob Daemmrich; 8, © Bob Daemmrich; 8 (b), K.D. Frankel/Bilderberg/Aurora; 9 (t), Wolfgang Kaehler Photography; 9 (b), Wolfgang Kaehler Photography; 10, © Nik Wheeler/CORBIS; 11 (b), © Ilene Perlman/Stock, Boston; 12, Corbis/Roger Ressmeyer; 13 (cr), © Chris Rainier/CORBIS; 15 (cr), NASA; **Chapter 2:** Page 18 (bc), © Stone/Glenn Christianson/Getty Images; 18 (tr), © Stone/A. Witte/C. Mahaney/Getty Images; 18 (tl), Image Copyright © 2002 PhotoDisc, Inc.; 18 (cl), Image © copyright Digital Stock Inc.; 20, © Galen Rowell/CORBIS; 21 (b), 1996 CORBIS; Original image courtesy of NASA/CORBIS; 21 (tr); Wendell Metzen/Bruce Coleman, Inc.; 22 (b), Nenad Jakesevic/HRW Art & Stone/Denis Waugh; 23, HRW; 24, The Granger Collection, New York; 25, Carr Clifton/Minden Pictures; 26 (t), Grant Heilman/Grant Heilman Photography; 27 (br), © Stone/Martin Puddy/Getty Images; 28 (t), Boll/Liaison Agency/Getty Images; 28 (br), Wolfgang Kaehler Photography; 30 (bl), Steven Burr Williams/Liaison International/Getty Images; 31 (t), Uhl Studios, Inc.; 32 (b), © Darrell Gulin/CORBIS; 34 (t), Rosentiel School of Marine and Atmospheric Science, University of Miami; 35 (c), David Madison/Bruce Coleman, Inc.; 35 (b), © John Elk III; 38, © Michael Busselle/CORBIS; 39 (t), © Kevin Schafer; 39 (b), L. Linkhart/Visuals Unlimited; 40 (t), © Stone/Mike Abrahams/Getty Images; 40 (b), © Telegraph Colour Library/Taxi/Getty Images; 41 (b), David R. Frazier Photolibrary; 41 (t), B. Brander/Photo Researchers, Inc.; 42 (b), © Ernest Manewal/Taxi/Getty Images; 42 (t), CORBIS/AFP Photo/Vanderlei Almeida; 43, David Hiser/Photographers/Aspen; **Chapter 3:** Page 46 (t), © Gerald Brimacombe/International Stock Photography/ImageState; 46 (br), © Bob Firth/International Stock Photography; 46 (c), © Wally McNamee/CORBIS; 46-47 (b), © Ahu Tongariki/Bruce Coleman, Inc.; 47 (b), © Bob Daemmrich/Stock, Boston; 48 (b), © Bohdam Hrynewch/Stock, Boston/PNI; 49 (b), © Stone/Ron Sherman/Getty Images; 49 (t), © Stone/Rich La Salle/Getty Images; 50 (b), Bruno Barbey/Magnum Photos; 50 (t), S. Sherbell/Corbis SABA Press Photos, Inc.; 51 (c), © Werner Forman/CORBIS; 52 (c), © Eric and David Hosking/CORBIS; 53 (b), © Rich Iwasaki/AllStock/STONE/Getty Images; 54 (t), © Michelle Gabel/The Image Works; 54 (tc), © Richard Hamilton Smith/CORBIS; 54 (bc), Henry Friedman; 54 (cr), © Stephen Frisch/Stock, Boston/PNI; 54 (bl), © Glen Allison/Getty Images/Stone; 54, John Elk III/Bruce Coleman, Inc.; 56 (b), Carolyn Schaefer/SCHAE/Bruce Coleman, Inc.; 57 (t), Martin Rogers/CORBIS; 58, © Sally Mayman/Getty Images/Stone; 58, MapQuest.com,Inc./HRW Art; 59, Alon Reininger/Woodfin Camp & Associates; 60 (b), Richard T. Nowitz/CORBIS; 61 (b), Dave G. Houser/CORBIS; 61 (t), © Ulrike Welsch; 62 (b), Reuters/CORBIS; 63 (t), Peter Turnley/Black Star; 65, Martin Guhl;

Unit 2: Page 70 (bl), © Walter Bibikow/Taxi/Getty Images; 70 (t), SuperStock; 70 (bc), Lawrence Migdale; 71 (cr), © Stone/Zigy Kaluzny/Getty Images; 71 (br), Alan Nelson/Animals Animals/Earth Scenes; **Chapter 4:** Page 80, AP/Wide World Photos; 80 (bl), dbox for the Lower Manhattan Development Corporation/Corbis; 80, Detroit Publishing Company Photograph Collection, Library of Congress; 86, Tom McHugh/Photo Researchers; 88 (b), Wild Country/Corbis; 89, Richard A. Cooke/Corbis; 90, The Granger Collection, New York; 91 (t), Bettmann/CORBIS; 91 (b), The Metropolitan Museum of Art, Gift of Edgar William and Bernice Chrysler Garbish, 1963.; 92 (b), Stock Montage; 93, Hulton Archive/Getty Images; 94 (t), Christie's Images/SuperStock; 94 (b), The Granger Collection, New York; 95, CORBIS/Joseph Sohm/Chromosohm Inc.; 96 (b), Albert Bierstadt, "Emigrants Crossing the Plains," 1867, Oil on Canvas, A.011.1T: National Cowboy Hall of Fame, Oklahoma City, OK.; 97, Courtesy of the California History Room, California State Library, Sacramento, California; 97, Corbis-Bettmann; 98 (b), Francis G. Mayer/CORBIS; 98 (t), Collection of the Mercer Museum of The Bucks County Historical Society; 99 (t), Bettmann/Corbis; 99 (b), Andrew Russell/Culver Pictures; 99, Corbis-Bettmann; 100 (t), Archive Photos; 100 (bl), © Bettmann/CORBIS; 100 (br), Library of Congress; 101, The Granger Collection, New York; 102 (t), © 1971 Time, Inc. Reprinted by Permission; 102 (c), Charles Moore/LIFE Magazine © Time, Inc.; 102 (b), Sanford Kossin/LIFE Magazine © Time, Inc.; 103 (r), Matthew McDermott/Corbis Sygma; 104 (l), Catherine Karnow/CORBIS; 105 (tl), Jeff Albertson/CORBIS ; 105 (tr), Catherine Karnow/CORBIS; **Chapter 5:** Page 108, Steve Ewert Photography; 110 (b), STONE/Getty Images/Jake Rajs; 111, Ace Photo Agency; 112 Michael Sullivan/TexaStock; 113, John Ficara/Woodfin Camp & Associates; 115, Jeff Greenberg/Photo Researchers; 116, AP Photo/The Beaufort Gazette; 117, D. Donne Bryant/DDB Stock; 121, Donald Johnson/Corbis Stock Market; 123 (b), James Randkley/Tony Stone Images; 123 (t), Dan Abernathy/ProFiles West, Inc./Index Stock Photo; 124 (b), Tom Bean/Stone/Getty Images; 124 (t), Larry Ulrich/DRK Photo; 125 (tr), Cotton Coulson/Woodfin Camp & Associates, Inc.; 125 (bl), Charles R. Belinky/Photo Researchers, Inc.; 125 (tl), Larry Ulrich/DRK Photo; 128 Kevin Schaefer/Stone/Getty Images; 129 (t), SuperStock; 129 (b), Greg Vaughn/Pacific Stock; 130 (b), Tom & Pat Leeson/DRK Photo; 130 (t), © 2003 Galen Rowell/Mountain Light Photography; 131, Charles A. Mauzy/Stone/Getty Images; **Chapter 6:** Page 134 (b), Catherine Karnow/CORBIS; 136, © Carr Clifton/Minden Pictures; 137 (c), © Stone/Gordon Fisher/Getty Images; 137 (t), © Walter Bibikow/Viesti Collection; 138 (c), Henry E. Huntington Library and Art Gallery; 139 (t), © Bill Terry/Viesti Collection, Inc.; 139 (r), Hulton Archive/Getty Images; 140, © Stone/Bob Herger/Getty Images; 141, © Robert Winslow/Viesti Collection; 142, © Mark E. Gibson; 143 (b), © Nazima Kowall/CORBIS; 144, © Nik Wheeler/CORBIS; 145, Sam Dudgeon/HRW Photo; 146 (b), © Stone/George Hunter/Getty Images; 146 (t), © Stone/Cosmo Condine/Getty Images; 150-151, Kennan Ward/CORBIS; 152, © Planet Art; 153, © Landiscor Aerial Information; 153, © Landiscor Aerial Information; **Unit 3:** Page 154 (b), Francois Gohier/Photo Researchers, Inc.; 154 (t), George Holton/Photo Researchers, Inc.; 154-155 (c), Cliff Hollenbeck/International Stock Photography; 155 (cr), Stephen J. Krasemann/Nature Conservancy/Photo Researchers, Inc.; 155 (b), C.K. Lorenz/Photo Researchers, Inc.; **Chapter 7:** Page 166 (br), Archivo Iconografico, S.A./CORBIS; 166 (bl), CORBIS; 166 (t), Art Resource, NY; 167, Danny Lehman/CORBIS; 168 (b), Randy Faris/CORBIS; 169 (t), Charles & Josette Lenars/CORBIS; 170 Merle Greene Robertson; 171, Werner Forman Archive/National Museum of Anthropology, Mexico City/Art Resource, NY; 174, © Robert Frerck/Odyssey/Chicago; 175, Yann Arthus-Bertrand/CORBIS; 176, Hubert Stadler/CORBIS; 177, Stephen L. Alvarez/NGS Image Collection; 178, J.C.KANNY/LORPRESSE/CORBIS SYGMA; 178, Loren McIntyre/Woodfin Camp & Associates; 180, Historical Picture Archive/CORBIS; 181 (b), Sergio Dorantes/CORBIS; 181 (t), INDEX/BRIDGEMAN ART LIBRARY; 182, © Robert Frerck/Odyssey/Chicago; 182, Bob Krist/CORBIS; 183, Schalkwijk/Art Resources; 185, Museum fur Volkerkunde, Vienna, Austria,/BRIDGEMAN ART LIBRARY; **Chapter 8:** Page 186, Steve Ewert Photography; 188 (t), © Robert Frerck/Odyssey/Chicago; 188 (cl), © Stone/George Lepp/Getty Images;

188 (b), Image copyright © 2001 PhotoDisc, Inc.; 189 (b), © Robert Frerck/Odyssey/Chicago; 191 (b), Dallas and John Heaton/Corbis; 192 (b), © Stone/Richard A. Cooke III/Getty Images; 192 (t), The Bodleian Library, Oxford, MS Arch. Selden A. 1, fol 37R; 193 (c), Library of Congress; 194 (bl), © Robert Frerck/Odyssey/Chicago; 194 (tl), CORBIS; 195 (t), © Danny Lehman/CORBIS; 196 (b), Alex S. MacLean/Landslides; 197, © Bob Daemmrich Photo, Inc.; 199 (b), © Danny Lehman/CORBIS; 199 (t), © Jan Butchofsky-Houser/CORBIS; 200 (b), John Neubauer; 201 (t), © Stone/David Hiser/Getty Images; **Chapter 9:** Page 204, Steve Ewert Photography; 206, Bruce Dale/National Geographic Society Image Collection; 207 (tr); K.M. Westermann/CORBIS; 208 (c), © Frank Staub/Index Stock Imagery, Inc.; 208 (b), © 1995 Kevin Schafer; 209, © Robert Frerck/Odyssey/Chicago; 210, Ancient Art and Architecture Collection Ltd.; 211, © Robert Frerck/Odyssey/Chicago; 213 (b), © Carol Lee/Index Stock Imagery; 215 (t), © Stone/Doug Armand/Getty Images; 215 (b), © Jose Azel/Aurora; 215, Terry Eggers 1998/Corbis Stock Market; 216 (bc), Nik Wheeler/CORBIS; **Chapter 10:** Page 220, Steve Ewert Photography; 223, © Kevin Schafer; 224 (b), Patrick Rouillard/Latin Stock/Corbis Stock Market; 225, © Dave G. Houser/CORBIS; 226, © Gianni Dagli Orti/CORBIS; 227 (t), © Jeremy Horner/CORBIS; 228 (b), James Marshall/Corbis Stock Market; 230, © Kevin Schafer/CORBIS; 231 (b), Chip and Rosa Maria Peterson; 232, © Nicole Duplaix/CORBIS; 233 (t), © B.Barbey/Magnum Photos; **Chapter 11:** Page 236, Steve Ewert Photography; 238, © Stone/Robert Van Der Hilst/Getty Images; 239, © Gail Shumway/Taxi/Getty Images; 240, © Carlos Humberto T.D.C./Contact Press Images/PNI; 241 (b), © Archivo Iconografico, S.A./CORBIS; 242, David Leah/Allsport/Getty Images; 243, © Stone/Chad Ehlers/Getty Images; 245 (b), Sepp Seitz/Woodfin Camp & Associates; 246 (br), © Stone/Robert Frerck/Getty Images; 246 (tl), CORBIS; 247, © Yann Arthus-Bertrand/CORBIS; 248, © Johnny Stockshooter/International Stock Photography; 249 (b), RAGA/Corbis Stock Market; 250 (t), © Daniel Rivademar/Odyssey/Chicago; 251, © Alex Webb/Magnum Photos; **Chapter 12:** Page 254, Steve Ewert Photography; 256, © Stone/William J. Hebert/Getty Images; 257, © Robert Frerck/Odyssey/Chicago; 258, Mirielle Vautier/Woodfin/PNI; 259 (br), Don Mason 1986/Corbis Stock Market; 259 (bl), Don Mason 1989/Corbis Stock Market; 260 (b), © Robert Frerck/Odyssey/Chicago; 260 (t), © Robert Frerck/Odyssey/Chicago; 261, © Robert Frerck/Odyssey/Chicago; 262 (t), © Robert Frerck/Odyssey/Chicago; 263, EPA/Diario El Tiempo de Piura PERU; 264 (b); © Kevin Schafer; 265 (t), © Robert Frerck/Odyssey/Chicago; 265 (b), © Index Stock Imagery, Inc.; 266, Daniel Rivadamar/Odyssey/Chicago; 270-271, Kennan Ward/CORBIS; 272 (t), Nair Benedicto/f4/DDB Stock Photo; 272 (b), Nair Benedicto/f4/DDB Stock Photo; 273, Bruce Coleman Inc.; **Unit 4:** Page 274 (t), © E. Nagele/Taxi/Getty Images; 274 (bl), Alfredo Venturi/Masterfile; 274-275 (c), SuperStock; 275 (t), Taxi/Getty Images; 275 (br), Robert Maier/Animals Animals/Earth Scenes; **Chapter 13:** Page 286 (t), Archivo Iconografico, S.A./CORBIS; 286 (b), Kevin Schafer/CORBIS; 286, Eirik Irgens Johnsen/University Museum of National Antiquities, Oslo, Norway; 288, National Archaeological Museum, Athens, Greece/Bridgeman Art Library; 288, National Archaeological Museum, Athens, Greece/Bridgeman Art Library; 289, Lee Snider; Lee Snider/CORBIS; 290, Photo credit: Erich Lessing; 290, Gianni Dagli Orti/Corbis; 291, Scala/Art Resource, NY; 292, Wolfgang Kaehler/CORBIS; 293 (b), George Grigoriou/Stone/Getty Images; 295, Staatliche Glypothek, Munich, Germany/ET Archive, London/SuperStock; 295, Araldo de Luca/CORBIS; 296, Scala/Art Resource, NY; 297, Scala; 300, Bettmann/CORBIS; 301 (t), Christie's Images/SuperStock; 302, Robert Emmett Bright/Photo Researchers; 304, Giraudon/Bridgeman Art Library; 305 (t), Paul Almasy/CORBIS; 305 (b), Carmen Redondo/CORBIS; 307 (t), Jose Fuste Raga/Corbis Stock Market; 308, ANCIENT ART AND ARCHITECTURE COLLECTION LTD; 309, AKG London; 309 (t), Bettmann/CORBIS; 310 (b), The Pierpont Morgan Library/Art Resource, NY; 311, Craig Aurness/CORBIS; 312 (b), Giraudon/Art Resource, NY; 313, Huntington Library and Art Gallery, San Marino, CA, USA/Bridgeman Art Library; **Chapter 14:** Page 316 (t), Bettmann/Corbis; 316 (c), Historical Picture Archive/CORBIS; 316, Giraudon/Art Resource, NY; 317 (b), Dagli Orti/Galleria degli Uffizi Florence/The Art Archive;

ACKNOWLEDGEMENTS

318 (t), Ali Meyer/Bridgeman Art Library; 318 (b), Kunsthistorisches Museum, Vienna, Austria/Bridgeman Art Library; 319 (t), Erich Lessing/Art Resource, NY; 319 (b), Art Resource, NY; 319 (c), The Pierpont Morgan Library/Art Resource, NY; 320 (tl), Giraudon/Art Resource, NY; 320 (b), Gary Yeowell/Stone/Getty Images; 321 (t), Scala/Art Resource, NY; 321 (b), Belvoir Castle, Leicestershire/Bridgeman Art Library; 322, Bridgeman Art Library; 323 (bl), Scala/Art Resource, NY; 324, David Parker/Science Photo Library/Photo Researchers; 325, The Metropolitan Museum of Art; 326 (b), New-York Historical Society, New York, USA/Bridgeman Art Library; 327 (t), Palace of Versailles, France/Lauros-Giraudon, Paris/SuperStock; 327 (b), National Portrait Gallery, London/SuperStock; 328 (t), Bridgeman Art Library; 328 (b), Dreweatt Neate Fine Art Auctioneers, Newbury/Bridgeman Art Library; 329, Colonial Williamsburg Foundation; 330 (b), Erich Lessing/Art Resource, NY; 331, Jeseph Wright of Derby/Bridgeman Art Library; 332, AKG, Berlin/SuperStock; 333 (t), Dagli Orti/Musée de l'Affiche, Paris/The Art Archive; 333 (b), Dagli Orti/Musée Carnavalet, Paris/The Art Archive; 334 (t), Dagli Orti/Musée Carnavalet, Paris/The Art Archive; 334, Giraudon/Art Resource, NY; 335, Erich Lessing/Art Resource, NY; 336, Bettmann/CORBIS; 337 (b), Stock Montage; 338, Steidle Collection, College of Earth and Mineral Sciences, Pennsylvania State University/Steidle Art Collection/SuperStock; 339, AKG London; 340, Slater Mill Historic Site/PRC Archive; 341 (b), Science Museum London/The Art Archive; 341 (t), Palubniak Studios; 342, From the Collections of Henry Ford Museum and Greenfield Village; 343 (t), Culver Pictures; **Chapter 14:** Page 316 (t), Bettmann/Corbis; 316 (c), Historical Picture Archive/CORBIS; 316, Giraudon/Art Resource, NY; 317 (b), Dagli Orti/Galleria degli Uffizi Florence/The Art Archive; 318 (t), Ali Meyer/Bridgeman Art Library; 318 (b), Kunsthistorisches Museum, Vienna, Austria/Bridgeman Art Library; 319 (t), Erich Lessing/Art Resource, NY; 319 (b), Art Resource, NY; 319 (c), The Pierpont Morgan Library/Art Resource, NY; 320 (tl), Giraudon/Art Resource, NY; 320 (b), Gary Yeowell/Stone/Getty Images; 321 (t), Scala/Art Resource, NY; 321 (b), Belvoir Castle, Leicestershire/Bridgeman Art Library; 322, Bridgeman Art Library; 323 (bl), Scala/Art Resource, NY; 324, David Parker/Science Photo Library/Photo Researchers; 325, The Metropolitan Museum of Art; 326 (b), New-York Historical Society, New York, USA/Bridgeman Art Library; 327 (t), Palace of Versailles, France/Lauros-Giraudon, Paris/SuperStock; 327 (b), National Portrait Gallery, London/SuperStock; 328 (t), Bridgeman Art Library; 328 (b), Dreweatt Neate Fine Art Auctioneers, Newbury/Bridgeman Art Library; 329, Colonial Williamsburg Foundation; 330 (b), Erich Lessing/Art Resource, NY; 331, Jeseph Wright of Derby/Bridgeman Art Library; 332, AKG, Berlin/SuperStock; 333 (t), Dagli Orti/Musée de l'Affiche, Paris/The Art Archive; 333 (b), Dagli Orti/Musée Carnavalet, Paris/The Art Archive; 334 (t), Dagli Orti/Musée Carnavalet, Paris/The Art Archive; 334, Giraudon/Art Resource, NY; 335, Erich Lessing/Art Resource, NY; 336, Bettmann/CORBIS; 337 (b), Stock Montage; 338, Steidle Collection, College of Earth and Mineral Sciences, Pennsylvania State University/Steidle Art Collection/SuperStock; 339, AKG London; 340, Slater Mill Historic Site/PRC Archive; 341 (b), Science Museum London/The Art Archive; 341 (t), Palubniak Studios; 342, From the Collections of Henry Ford Museum and Greenfield Village; 343 (t), Culver Pictures; **Chapter 15:** Page 346, © European Communities; 346 (b), Courtesy of Palladio Film, Cologne and the Edelweiss Pirates film.; 346 (t), Mathew POLAK/corbis; 347, AKG Berlin/SuperStock; 348 (b), Leonard de Selva/CORBIS; 349, HRW; 351, Bettmann/CORBIS; 352, bettmann/corbis; 353, Hulton-Deutsch Collection/CORBIS; 354 (t), AKG London; 354 (b), Bettmann/Corbis; 355, Getty Images; 356 (b), Giraudon/Art Resource, NY; 357 (t), UPI/Bettmann/CORBIS; 357 (b), AP/Wide World Photos; 358, AKG London; 358, Carl Mydans/TimePix; 359 (t), Loomis Dean/TimePix; 361, Getty Images; 362, Lancaster/Corbis; 364 (t), Bruno Barbey/Magnum/PictureQuest; 365, Mario Corvetto/Evergreen Photo Alliance; 367, Herblock: A Cartoonist's Life (Times Books, 1998); **Chapter 16:** Page 368, Steve Ewert Photography; 370, Photo © Earl Bronsteen 1/Panoramic Images, Chicago 1998; 371, © Gary Braasch/CORBIS; 372 (b), © Travelpix/Taxi/Getty Images; 373 (b), © Joe Viesti/The Viesti Collection; 373 (t), Steve Vidler/Leo de Wys; 374 (tr), University at Buffalo Science & Engineering Library; 374 (br), © Araldo de Luca/CORBIS; 374 (bl), Museo di Cipro/Art Resource, NY; 375, Bettmann/CORBIS; 376 (l), © Archivo Iconographico, S.A./CORBIS; 377 (t), © Louis Goldman/Taxi/Getty Images; 377 (b), © Gianni Dagli Orti/CORBIS; 378 (b), Siegfried Tauqueur/Leo de Wys; 380 (b), Rosenback/ZEFA/Index Stock Imagery, Inc.; 381, © Jean Kugler/Taxi/Getty Images; 382, Patrick Ward/CORBIS; 383 (t), © Sitki Tarlan/Panoramic Images; **Chapter 17:** Page 386, Steve Ewert Photography; 388 (t), J. Messerschmidt/Leo de Wys; 388 (b), John Miller/Leo de Wys; 389, H.P. Merton/Corbis Stock Market; 390 (l), Castres, Musee Goya/Art Resource, NY; 391 (t), The Art Archive; 391 (b), Scala/Art Resource; 392 (l), Pierre Witt/Rapho Agence Photographique; 392 (r), Mike Busselle/Leo de Wys; 394 (b), Wolfgang Kaehler Photography; 395 (t), CORBIS/Bettmann; 395, inset Archive Photos/Getty Images; 396, Fridmar Damm/Leo de Wys; 396 (tl), Archivo Iconografico, S.A./CORBIS ; 398 (l), Sigfried Tuaqueur/Leo de Wys; 400 (t), Wolfgang Kaehler Photography; 400 (cl), Tiziana and Gianni Baldizzone/CORBIS; 401 (b), © Ken Ross/Taxi/Getty Images; 402 (l), © G. Wagner/Viesti Collection; 402 (t), © Stone/Siegfried Layda/Getty Images; **Chapter 18:** Page 406, Steve Ewert Photography; 408, © Walter Bibikow/Viesti Collection; 410-411, Bettman/CORBIS; 412 (b), British Museum, London, UK/Bridgeman Art Library, London/New York; 412 (c), © Yann Arthus-Bertrand/CORBIS; 413 (t), Private Collection/Bridgeman Art Library, London/New York; 413, © Stone/Ed Pritchard/Getty Images; 414 (t), Popperfoto/Archive Photos/Getty Images; 416-417 (b), © Joe Englander/Viesti Collection; 417 (tr), AP Photo/Donald Stampfli; 419 (b), Index Stock Imagery, Inc.; 421 (b), © Walter Bibikow/Taxi/Getty Images; 422, Tom Stewart/Corbis Stock Market; 423, © Bryan & Cherry Alexander; **Chapter 19:** Page 426, Steve Ewert Photography; 429 (tr), Robert Harding Picture Library Ltd/Alamy; 431, Aldo Pavan/Liaison International/Getty Images; 432, © David Bartruff/Taxi/Getty Images; 433 (t), Image Copyright © 2001 PhotoDisc, Inc.; 434 (b), © Fergus O'Brien/Taxi/Getty Images; 434 (tl), Getty News Services; 435, © Garbor Feher/Sygma; 436 (l), © Francois de Mulder/CORBIS; 437 (t), © Michael S. Yamashita/CORBIS; 437 (b), Krpan Jasmin/Liaison International/Getty Images; 438, Daniels Marleen/Liaison International/Getty Images; 439 (b), Francis Li/Liaison International/Getty Images; 439 (t), Patrick Chauvel/Corbis Sygma; 440 (b), Bogdan Cristel/Corbis; 444, Bill Ross/CORBIS; 445 (tr), © European Communities; 446 (t), AKG Photo, London; 447, © Stone/Getty Images; **Unit 5:** Page 448 (bl), SuperStock; 448 (br), Ed Kashi; 448-449 (c), Mark Wadlow/Russia and Eastern Images; 449 (t), Bruce Coleman Inc.; 449 (br), Gerard Lacz/Peter Arnold, Inc.; 456 Robert S. Semeniuk/Black Star; 456 (t); CORBIS/Stephanie Maze; 457, © Steve Raymer/CORBIS; 457 (b), Enzo & Paolo Ragazzini/CORBIS; **Chapter 20:** Page 458, Steve Ewert Photography; 460, Tass/Sovfoto/Eastfoto; 461 (b), Enzo & Paolo Ragazzini/CORBIS; 462, © Hans J. Burkard/AURORA; 463 (b), Battle of the Novgorodians with the Suzdalians, Novgorod School, mid 15th century (tempera and gold on panel)/Tretyakov Gallery, Moscow, Russia/Bridgeman Art Library, London/New York; 464, Bettmann/CORBIS; 465 (t), © Steve Raymer/CORBIS; 465 (br), Peter Turnley/CORBIS; 466 (t), © Wally McNamee/CORBIS; 467, © Steve Raymer/CORBIS; 469 (b), © Vladamir Pcholkin/Taxi/Getty Images; 470 (t), © Steve McCurry/Magnum Photos; 470 (b), Steve Raymer/CORBIS; 471, Claus Meyer/Black Star/PNI; 472 (b), © Bryan & Cherry Alexander; 473, Sovfoto/Eastfoto; 474, © Dean Conger/CORBIS; 475 (b), © Planet Earth Pictures 1998/Taxi/Getty Images; 476, © Wolfgang Kaehler/CORBIS; 477, © Michael S. Yamashita/CORBIS; 479, Roger Harvell/The Greenville News; **Chapter 21:** Page 480, Steve Ewert Photography; 482, © Dean Conger/CORBIS; 484 (b), AKG Photo, London; 485 (b), Steve Raymer/National Geographic Society Image Collection; 485 (t), AKG Photo, London; 486, Steve Raymer/National Geographic Society Image Collection; 487, Randall Hyman; 489 (b), © Charles Lenars/CORBIS; 490 (b), Sovfoto/Eastfoto; 490 (t), CORBIS/Stephanie Maze; 494, © 1990 Abbas/Magnum Photos; 495 (c), Marc Garanger/CORBIS; 496 (t), BIOS/M. Gunther/Peter Arnold, Inc.; 497, Sovfoto/Eastfoto.

R40 • Credits